Collins

CANADIAN

THESAURUS

HarperCollins Publishers
2 Bloor Street East,
20th floor,
Toronto,
Ontario,
Canada M4W 1A8

Second edition 2016

10 9 8 7 6 5

© HarperCollins Publishers 2011

ISBN 978-0-00-818458-2

Collins ® is a registered
trademark of HarperCollins
Publishers Limited

www.harpercollins.ca

A catalogue record for this book is
available from the British Library

Typeset by Market House Books
Ltd, Aylesbury, Great Britain

Printed in USA by Quad/Graphics

Acknowledgements
We would like to thank those
authors and publishers who
kindly gave permission for
copyright material to be used
in the Collins Corpus. We
would also like to thank Times
Newspapers Ltd for providing
valuable data.

CONTENTS

List of Contributors iv

Using This Thesaurus v – vii

Abbreviations Used in This Thesaurus viii

Collins Canadian Thesaurus **1 – 631**

LIST OF CONTRIBUTORS

Senior Editor
Robert Pontisso

Editors
Lorna Gilmour
Robert Groves
Mary O'Neill

For the Publisher
Gerry Breslin
Michelle Fullerton

USING THIS THESAURUS

Main entry words are printed in large, bold type, eg

abate

Variant spellings are shown in full, eg

amid, amidst

Parts of speech are shown in italics. When a word can be used as more than one part of speech, the change of part of speech is shown after an arrow, eg

academic *adjective* **1 = scholarly**,
literary, bookish...
▶ *noun* **3 = scholar**, professor,
fellow, master, don

Parts of speech may be combined for words, eg

astray *adjective, adverb*

Meanings of the word are separated by bold numbers, eg

acid *adjective* **1 = sour**, tart,
acerbic, pungent, acrid, vinegary
2 = sharp, bitter, harsh, cutting,
vitriolic, caustic, biting

Synonyms are shown in order of appropriateness to the meaning of the main entry word. Synonyms are separated by commas, with the best, or 'key', synonym for that particular meaning listed first in bold type, eg

abate *verb* **= decrease**, diminish,
wane, lessen, subside, ebb

Examples illustrate certain meanings of the main entry words, and are shown in italics, preceded by a bullet point, following the meaning to which they apply, eg

> **ability** *noun* = **skill**, talent, capability, expertise, competence • *the ability to get along with others*

Antonyms are words which have the opposite meaning to a certain meaning of the main entry word. These are preceded by 'OPPOSITE' in small capital letters, following the meaning to which they apply, eg

> **abrupt** *adjective* ...
> **2** = **curt**, short, rude, terse ...
> OPPOSITE: polite

Cross references refer the user to another entry, and are shown in bold, preceded by explanatory text in italics, eg

> **accommodation** *noun*
> = **housing**, house, digs ...
> *See also*: **space**

Related words follow the heading 'RELATED WORD' or 'RELATED WORDS', and are preceded by a word in italics explaining their relation to the main entry word, eg

> **alcohol** *noun* = **drink**, liquor, booze (*informal*), spirits...
> RELATED WORD
> *like*: dipsomania

Phrases, idioms, and derived forms are included within the main entry, following the meanings of the part of speech to which they apply, eg

> **abreast** *adverb* = **alongside**,
> beside, side by side
> ▷ **abreast of** = **informed about**,
> acquainted with

> **apology** *noun* = **defence**, plea,
> excuse ... acknowledgment
> ▷ **apology for** = **mockery of**,
> caricature of, excuse for

If a phrase, idiom, or derived form has more than one meaning, the meanings are separated by a semi-colon, eg

> **aware** *adjective*
> ▷ **aware of** = **conscious of**,
> acquainted with, familiar with,
> mindful of • *She was acutely aware*
> *of the noise of the city*; = **informed**,
> knowledgeable, in the picture

Context labels indicate when the main entry word or a synonym is commonly used with another word or phrase (a 'collocate'). The main entry word or synonym is indicated by a tilde (~), and the collocate appears in italics, within round brackets, eg

> **break** *verb*
> **6** (~ *a record, etc.*) = **beat**, top,
> surpass, exceed, better

ABBREVIATIONS USED IN THIS THESAURUS

Austral	Australia(n)
Brit	British
Canad	Canadian
Esp.	especially
etc.	et cetera
fem.	feminine
Nfld	Newfoundland
NZ	New Zealand
Queb	Quebec
Scot	Scottish
US	United States
Zool	Zoology

Aa

abandon *verb* **1 = leave**, desert, maroon, forsake, jilt, leave behind, leave in the lurch, bail on (*slang*) • *He abandoned the car and walked home.*
2 = give up, surrender, yield, relinquish
▶ *noun* **3 = wildness**, recklessness • *He began to laugh with abandon.*
OPPOSITE: control
See also: **cancel**

abandoned *See* **derelict**

abandonment *noun* **= leaving**, dereliction, desertion, forsaking

abashed *adjective* **= embarrassed**, ashamed, dismayed, chagrined, disconcerted, humiliated, mortified, shamefaced, taken aback

abate *verb* **= decrease**, diminish, wane, lessen, subside, ebb • *The four-day flood at last abated.*
See also: **ease**, **moderate**

abbey *noun* **= monastery**, convent, friary, nunnery, priory

abbreviate *verb* **= shorten**, cut, contract, reduce, compress, summarize, condense, abridge

abbreviation *noun* **= shortening**, reduction, summary, contraction, synopsis, abridgment

abdicate *verb* **= give up**, resign, quit, abandon, renounce, relinquish, step down (*informal*)

abdication *noun* **= giving up**, retirement, surrender, resignation, abandonment, renunciation, quitting

abduct *verb* **= kidnap**, seize, snatch (*slang*), carry off

abduction *noun* **= kidnaping**, seizure, carrying off

aberration *noun* **= oddity**, defect, irregularity, lapse, abnormality, quirk, anomaly, peculiarity

abet *verb* **= help**, support, assist, aid, connive at

abeyance *noun*
▷ **in abeyance = shelved**, suspended, hanging fire, on ice (*informal*), pending

abhor *verb* **= hate**, loathe, detest, abominate, shrink from, shudder at

abhorrence *See* **horror**

abhorrent *adjective* **= hateful**, offensive, horrid, distasteful, abominable, repulsive, disgusting, hated, loathsome, scuzzy (*slang*)

abide *verb* **= tolerate**, stand, bear, suffer, accept, endure, put up with

abide by *verb* **= obey**, follow, observe, agree to, comply with, conform to, submit to

abiding *adjective* **= everlasting**, permanent, persistent, lasting, enduring, unchanging, continuing

ability *noun* **= skill**, talent, capability, expertise, competence • *the ability to get along with others*
OPPOSITE: inability
See also: **capacity**, **gift**, **potential**, **qualification**

abject *adjective* **1 = miserable**, deplorable, hopeless, wretched, forlorn, pitiable
2 = servile, submissive, cringing, degraded, fawning, grovelling

ablaze *adjective* **= on fire**, burning, fiery, flaming, aflame, lighted, alight, blazing, ignited

able *adjective* **= capable**, expert, efficient, skilled, talented, accomplished, first-rate • *She*

a

proved herself to be an able politician.
See also: **proficient, skilful**

able-bodied *adjective* = **strong**, healthy, sound, fit, robust, sturdy

ably *See* **well**

abnormal *adjective* = **unusual**, odd, extraordinary, strange, exceptional, irregular, uncommon, atypical, peculiar

abnormality *noun* = **oddity**, exception, irregularity, deformity, peculiarity, singularity, strangeness

abode *noun* = **home**, house, pad (*slang, dated*), residence, habitat, lodging, dwelling, habitation, domicile, quarters

abolish *verb* = **do away with**, overturn, annul, put an end to • *Their objective was to abolish the new tax.*

abolition *noun* = **ending**, end, destruction, cancellation, elimination, termination, extermination, wiping out

abominable *adjective* = **terrible**, horrible, despicable, lousy (*slang*), hateful, vile, horrid, repulsive, disgusting, detestable, revolting, scuzzy (*slang*)

abort *verb* **1** = **terminate** (a pregnancy), miscarry
2 = **stop**, end, arrest, fail, check, halt, axe (*informal*), terminate, call off

abortion *noun* = **termination**, miscarriage, deliberate miscarriage

abortive *adjective* = **failed**, unsuccessful, useless, vain, futile, fruitless, ineffectual, miscarried

abound *verb* = **be plentiful**, swell, thrive, flourish, swarm, teem, proliferate

abounding *adjective* = **plentiful**, full, rich, prolific, abundant, bountiful, copious, profuse

about *preposition* **1** = **regarding**, on, concerning, relating to • *anxiety about his sick son*
2 = **near**, nearby, beside, circa (of a date), adjacent to, close to

▷ *adverb* **3** = **nearly**, around, almost, roughly, approximately • *The procedure takes about 30 minutes.*

above *preposition* **1** = **over**, higher than • *above the clouds*
OPPOSITE: below
RELATED WORDS
prefixes: super-, supra-, sur-
2 = **greater than**, beyond, exceeding • *The temperature is above 30°.*

above board *adjective* = **honest**, straight, fair, square, legitimate, genuine

abrasion *noun* (*Medical*) = **graze**, scratch, scrape, chafe, scuff, surface injury

abrasive *adjective*
1 = **unpleasant**, sharp, rough, cutting, caustic, galling, grating, irritating
2 = **rough**, scratchy, grating, chafing, scraping

abreast *adverb* = **alongside**, beside, side by side
▷ **abreast of** = **informed about**, acquainted with, *au courant* with (*French*), *au fait* with (*French*), conversant with, familiar with, in the picture about, in touch with, keeping one's finger on the pulse of, knowledgeable about, up to date with, up to speed with

abridge *verb* = **shorten**, cut, reduce, decrease, summarize, abbreviate, condense

abroad *adverb* = **overseas**, in foreign lands, out of the country

abrupt *adjective* **1** = **sudden**, unexpected, unforeseen • *the abrupt resignation of the prime minister*
2 = **curt**, short, rude, terse • *He was taken aback by her abrupt manner.*
OPPOSITE: polite
See also: **sharp**

abscond *verb* = **flee**, escape, disappear, clear out, make off, run off, steal away

absence *noun*
1 = **nonattendance**, absenteeism, truancy

2 = lack, want, need, deficiency, omission, unavailability

absent *adjective* **1 = missing**, away, elsewhere, gone • *absent from work*
OPPOSITE: present
2 = absent-minded, blank, vacant, vague, oblivious, distracted, inattentive, preoccupied
▶ *verb*
▷ **absent oneself = stay away**, withdraw, keep away, play truant

absent-minded *adjective*
= **vague**, distracted, forgetful
• *Her absent-minded stepfather left the camera in the taxi.*

absolute *adjective* **1 = complete**, total, pure, utter, thorough, sheer, downright • *He is talking absolute nonsense.*
2 = supreme, dictatorial, tyrannical • *an absolute ruler*
See also: **final, perfect, rank**

absolutely *adverb* = **totally**, completely, fully, entirely, perfectly, wholly, utterly, one hundred per cent

absolutely not *See* **no**

absolution *noun* = **forgiveness**, release, pardon, mercy, exoneration, deliverance, exculpation

absolve *verb* = **forgive**, release, deliver, excuse, pardon, exculpate, let off, set free

absorb *verb* **1 = soak up**, digest, take in • *Plants absorb carbon dioxide.*
2 = preoccupy, engage, fascinate, captivate, rivet, engross
See also: **busy, grasp**

absorbed *adjective*
1 = preoccupied, lost, involved, captivated, engrossed, fascinated, immersed, rapt, riveted, wrapped up
2 = digested, incorporated, assimilated, received, soaked up

absorbent *adjective* = **permeable**, receptive, porous, spongy

absorbing *adjective*
= **fascinating**, interesting, captivating, engrossing, gripping, intriguing, riveting, spellbinding

absorption *noun* **1 = soaking up**, consumption, digestion, assimilation, incorporation, sucking up
2 = concentration, involvement, fascination, preoccupation, immersion, intentness

abstain *verb* = **refrain**, avoid, forgo, deny oneself, give up • *The patient had to abstain from food for several hours.*
See also: **decline, refuse**

abstemious *adjective* = **self-denying**, moderate, sober, austere, frugal, temperate, ascetic

abstention *noun* = **refusal**, abstinence, avoidance, self-control, self-restraint, abstaining, forbearance, refraining, self-denial

abstinence *noun* = **self-denial**, moderation, avoidance, self-restraint, abstemiousness, forbearance, soberness, teetotalism, temperance

abstinent *adjective* = **self-denying**, moderate, sober, temperate, abstaining, abstemious, forbearing, self-controlled

abstract *adjective* **1 = theoretical**, general, indefinite, hypothetical, abstruse, notional, recondite
▶ *noun* **2 = summary**, outline, digest, synopsis, epitome, abridgment, précis, résumé
▶ *verb* **3 = summarize**, outline, shorten, digest, epitomize, abbreviate, condense, abridge, précis
4 = remove, separate, withdraw, isolate, extract, detach, take away, take out

abstraction *noun* **1 = idea**, thought, theory, formula, concept, notion, hypothesis, generalization, theorem
2 = absent-mindedness, absence, preoccupation, inattention, remoteness,

dreaminess, pensiveness, woolgathering

abstruse adjective = **obscure**, deep, complex, vague, enigmatic, arcane, unfathomable, esoteric, recondite

absurd adjective = **ridiculous**, crazy (informal), ludicrous, illogical, nonsensical • an absurd waste of money
See also: **impossible, incredible, irrational, silly, stupid**

absurdity noun = **ridiculousness**, joke, nonsense, stupidity, farce, folly, foolishness, silliness, incongruity

abundance noun = **plenty**, bounty, affluence • an abundance of wildlife
OPPOSITE: shortage
See also: **lot, lots, wealth**

abundant adjective = **plentiful**, full, ample, copious • an abundant supply of fuel
OPPOSITE: scarce
See also: **generous, rich**

abuse noun 1 = **ill-treatment**, hurt, harm, exploitation, oppression • the prevention of animal abuse
2 = **insults**, censure, derision, invective • I was left shouting abuse as the car sped off.
3 = **misuse**, misapplication
▶ verb 4 = **insult**, curse, scold • The baseball umpire was verbally abused by the hometown fans.
5 = **ill-treat**, damage, injure, hurt, harm, exploit, misuse, maltreat, take advantage of
See also: **impose on, mistreat, wrong**

abused See **oppressed**

abusive adjective 1 = **insulting**, offensive, scathing, rude, disparaging • abusive language
2 = **harmful**, rough, brutal, cruel, destructive, hurtful, injurious

abysmal adjective = **terrible**, bad, dire, awful, appalling, dreadful

abyss noun = **pit**, void, fissure, gorge, chasm • He crawled forward to peer over the edge of the abyss.
See also: **hell**

academic adjective 1 = **scholarly**, literary, bookish, erudite, highbrow, learned, studious
2 = **hypothetical**, abstract, speculative, theoretical, impractical, conjectural, notional
▶ noun 3 = **scholar**, professor, fellow, master, don, lecturer, tutor, academician

accede verb 1 = **agree**, endorse, accept, admit, grant, comply, concede, consent, concur, assent, acquiesce
2 = **inherit**, assume, succeed, attain, come to, enter upon, succeed to (of an heir)

accelerate verb = **speed up**, hurry, quicken, step up (informal) • She accelerated away from the curb.

accelerated See **fast**

acceleration noun = **speeding up**, hastening, hurrying, quickening, stepping up (informal)

accent noun 1 = **pronunciation**, tone, inflection, articulation, brogue, enunciation, intonation, modulation
2 = **emphasis**, force, beat, pitch, stress, rhythm, cadence, timbre
▶ verb 3 = **emphasize**, stress, underscore, underline, accentuate

accentuate verb = **emphasize**, stress, highlight, underscore, underline, accent, foreground, draw attention to

accept verb 1 = **receive**, take • She accepted the award on his behalf.
OPPOSITE: refuse
2 = **agree to**, acknowledge, concur with, consent to • All those invited to next week's conference have accepted.
See also: **admit, assume, believe, grant, resign oneself, tolerate**

acceptable adjective = **satisfactory**, fair, adequate, tolerable, passable, all right, good enough • an acceptable standard of living

See also: **correct, okay, right, suitable**

acceptance noun 1 = **accepting**, receipt, taking, acquiring, gaining, getting, obtaining, securing
2 = **agreement**, approval, recognition, admission, consent, adoption, cooperation, acknowledgment, assent, acquiescence, concurrence

accepted adjective = **agreed**, common, traditional, normal, conventional, established, customary, acknowledged, approved, recognized

access noun = **entrance**, road, approach, entry, path, passage, admission, admittance

accessibility noun
1 = **handiness**, possibility, availability, readiness, nearness
2 = **approachability**, friendliness, informality, affability, cordiality
3 = **openness**, susceptibility

accessible adjective 1 = **handy**, near, available, nearby, achievable, attainable, reachable, at hand, obtainable
2 = **approachable**, available, friendly, informal, cordial, affable
3 = **open**, vulnerable, liable, susceptible, wide-open, exposed

accessory noun 1 = **addition**, extra, supplement, decoration, attachment, adjunct, trimming, accompaniment, appendage, adornment
2 = **accomplice**, partner, associate, colleague, assistant, helper, abettor, confederate

accident noun 1 = **misfortune**, disaster, mishap, misadventure, calamity
2 = **collision**, crash, wreck, hit-and-run
3 = **chance**, fate, hazard, luck, fortune, fluke, fortuity

accidental adjective
= **unintentional**, chance, random, casual, inadvertent
• *The fire was accidental.*
OPPOSITE: deliberate

accidentally adverb
= **unintentionally**, randomly, inadvertently, unwittingly, incidentally, haphazardly, by accident, by chance, fortuitously

acclaim verb 1 = **praise**, approve, celebrate, cheer, hail, applaud, salute, honour, commend, clap, exalt
▶ noun 2 = **praise**, approval, celebration, applause, honour, kudos, commendation, acclamation

acclamation noun = **praise**, approval, tribute, ovation, acclaim, plaudit, adulation

acclimatization noun
= **adaptation**, adjustment, habituation, inurement, naturalization

acclimatize verb = **adapt**, adjust, accommodate, accustom, naturalize, inure, get used to, habituate

accolade noun = **praise**, approval, tribute, recognition, ovation, applause, acclaim, compliment, commendation, props (*informal*)

accommodate verb 1 = **house**, shelter, put up • *a hotel built to accommodate many guests*
2 = **help**, serve, assist, aid, oblige
3 = **adapt**, settle, fit, adjust, comply, modify, reconcile, conform, harmonize

accommodating adjective
= **helpful**, kind, considerate, hospitable, obliging • *his polite, accommodating manner*

accommodation noun
= **housing**, house, digs (*informal*), lodgings, quarters • *Travel and overnight accommodation are included in the price.*
See also: **space**

accompaniment noun
1 = **supplement**, accessory, companion, complement
2 = **backing music**, backing

accompany verb 1 = **go with**, conduct (*formal*), escort, usher
• *Children must be accompanied by an adult.*
2 = **occur with**, come with, go together with • *severe pain*

accompanied by fever
See also: **guide**

accompanying *adjective*
= **additional**, related, attendant, complementary, supplementary, associated, attached

accomplice *noun* = **helper**, partner, associate, colleague, assistant, ally, accessory, collaborator, henchman, abettor

accomplish *verb* = **do**, complete, manage, achieve, fulfill, bring about • *We could accomplish a lot by working together.*
See also: **carry out**

accomplished *adjective* = **skilled**, expert, talented, gifted, polished, proficient, masterly, practiced

accomplishment *noun*
1 = **completion**, performance, execution, conclusion, finishing, fulfillment, bringing about, carrying out
2 = **achievement**, act, stroke, triumph, coup, exploit, feat, deed

accord *noun* 1 = **agreement**, sympathy, correspondence, harmony, unison, rapport, conformity
▶ *verb* 2 = **fit**, agree, match, suit, tally, correspond, conform, harmonize
▶ *adverb*
▷ **according to** = **as stated by**, as believed by, as maintained by, in the light of, on the authority of, on the report of; = **in keeping with**, after, after the manner of, consistent with, in accordance with, in compliance with, in line with, in the manner of

accordingly *adverb*
1 = **appropriately**, properly, suitably, correspondingly, fitly
2 = **consequently**, so, therefore, thus, hence, as a result, ergo, in consequence

accost *verb* = **approach**, hail, greet, confront, buttonhole

account *noun* 1 = **description**, report, statement, story, version, tale, explanation, narrative
2 (*Commerce*) = **statement**,

charge, score, bill, register, balance, tally, invoice, reckoning, books
3 = **importance**, note, value, worth, standing, consequence, significance, honour
▶ *verb* 4 = **consider**, think, rate, judge, value, estimate, count, regard, reckon
▷ **account for** = **explain**, justify, clarify, illuminate, rationalize, answer for, clear up, elucidate

accountability *noun*
= **responsibility**, liability, culpability, answerability, chargeability

accountable *adjective*
= **responsible**, liable, amenable, answerable, charged with, obligated, obliged

accountant *noun* = **auditor**, bean counter (*informal*), book-keeper

accredited *adjective*
= **authorized**, official, licensed, certified, appointed, empowered, endorsed, guaranteed, recognized

accrue *verb* = **increase**, follow, grow, collect, flow, arise, accumulate, amass, enlarge, be added, build up

accumulate *verb* = **collect**, increase, store, gather, amass, hoard, accrue, build up, pile up

accumulation *noun* = **collection**, increase, stock, store, mass, gathering, pile, stockpile, stack, hoard, heap, build-up

accuracy *noun* = **exactness**, precision, authenticity, correctness, closeness, veracity, fidelity, truthfulness, accurateness, carefulness, strictness

accurate *adjective* = **exact**, right, true, correct, strict, faithful, precise • *Quartz watches are very accurate.*
OPPOSITE: inaccurate

accurately *adverb* = **exactly**, strictly, closely, truly, correctly, precisely, faithfully, authentically, scrupulously, to the letter, unerringly

accursed *adjective* **1** = **cursed**, unfortunate, doomed, ill-fated, damned, unlucky, hopeless, wretched, bewitched, condemned, ill-omened, jinxed **2** = **hateful**, horrible, despicable, lousy (*slang*), abominable, detestable, hellish, execrable, scuzzy (*slang*)

accusation *noun* = **charge**, allegation, complaint, indictment, denunciation, recrimination, incrimination

accuse *verb* = **charge**, blame, cite, denounce, censure • *He accused me of cheating.*

accustom *verb* = **adapt**, train, exercise, discipline, acquaint, acclimatize, familiarize

accustomed *adjective* **1** = **used**, adapted, familiar • *I've become accustomed to his poor performance.* OPPOSITE: unaccustomed **2** = **usual**, common, regular, traditional, normal, conventional, ordinary, everyday, established, customary, habitual, expected

ace *noun* **1** (*Cards, dice, etc.*) = **one**, single point **2** (*Informal*) = **expert**, champion, star, master, wizard (*informal*), virtuoso

ache *verb* **1** = **hurt**, suffer, pain, pound, smart, throb, twinge ▶ *noun* **2** = **pain**, hurt, suffering, soreness, pang, pounding, throbbing

achieve *verb* = **accomplish**, do, complete, perform, nail (*sports*), fulfill, carry out • *She has achieved her best tournament result yet.* *See also:* **gain, win**

achievement *noun* = **accomplishment**, exploit, feat, deed • *His presence here is an achievement in itself.* *See also:* **act, action, qualification**

aching *See* **painful, tender**

acid *adjective* **1** = **sour**, tart, acerbic, pungent, acrid, vinegary **2** = **sharp**, bitter, harsh, cutting, vitriolic, caustic, biting, trenchant

acidity *noun* **1** = **sourness**, acerbity, pungency, tartness **2** = **sharpness**, bitterness, harshness

acknowledge *verb* **1** = **accept**, allow, own, admit, declare, recognize, grant, concede, yield, confess, profess **2** = **greet**, address, recognize, notice, hail, salute **3** = **reply to**, return, answer, recognize, notice, react to, respond to

acknowledged *adjective* = **accepted**, approved, accredited, confessed, declared, professed, recognized, returned

acknowledgment *noun* **1** = **acceptance**, declaration, confession, admission, profession, realization, allowing, yielding **2** = **greeting**, notice, hail, recognition, salute, salutation, addressing, hailing **3** = **appreciation**, return, credit, response, answer, reaction, reply, recognition, gratitude, kudos, thanks, props (*informal*)

acquaint *verb* = **tell**, reveal, disclose, inform, notify, divulge, enlighten, familiarize, let (someone) know

acquaintance *noun* **1** = **associate**, contact, colleague **2** = **knowledge**, experience, relationship, understanding, awareness, familiarity, fellowship

acquainted with *adjective* = **familiar with**, alive to, apprised of, *au fait* with (*French*), aware of, conscious of, experienced in, informed of, knowledgeable about, versed in

acquiesce *verb* = **agree**, allow, approve, accept, submit, comply, yield, consent, conform, concur, assent, accede, give in, go along with

acquiescence *noun* = **agreement**, approval, consent, submission, compliance, acceptance, assent, obedience, conformity, giving in, yielding

acquire *verb* = **get**, gain, secure, obtain, attain, procure, pick up • *I have recently acquired a digital camera*.
See also: **buy, earn, possess**

acquisition *noun* **1** = **possession**, buy, gain, purchase, property, prize
2 = **acquiring**, procurement, attainment, gaining

acquisitive *adjective* = **greedy**, avid, predatory, avaricious, covetous, grabbing, grasping, rapacious

acquit *verb* **1** = **clear**, release, free, discharge, liberate, vindicate
2 = **behave**, bear, perform, conduct, comport

acquittal *noun* = **clearance**, release, relief, discharge, liberation, vindication, exoneration, absolution, deliverance

acrid *adjective* = **pungent**, sharp, bitter, harsh, vitriolic, caustic

acrimonious *adjective* = **bitter**, testy, caustic, irascible, rancorous, petulant, spiteful, splenetic

acrimony *noun* = **bitterness**, virulence, harshness, ill will, irascibility, rancour

act *verb* **1** = **do**, work, operate, perform, function • *The bank acted properly in the best interests of the depositors*.
2 = **perform**, play, portray, act out, play the part of, characterize, personify • *He acted at the Stratford Festival in Ontario*.
▷ **act against** See **counteract**
▷ **act for** = **stand in for**, represent, replace, cover for, deputize for, fill in for, substitute for, take the place of
▷ **act on** See **affect**
▷ **act out** See **act**
▷ **act toward** See **treat**
▷ **act up** (*Informal*) = **make a fuss**, misbehave, have a fit, horse around, raise Cain, raise hell
▶ *noun* **3** = **deed**, achievement, accomplishment, feat,

undertaking • *an act of disloyalty to the king*
4 = **law**, bill, measure, resolution, decree, statute, ordinance, edict, enactment
5 = **performance**, show, turn, routine, sketch
6 = **pretense**, show, front, performance, pose, attitude, posture, affectation
See also: **appear, behave, conduct yourself**

> **INFORMALLY SPEAKING**
> **act up**: behave badly; be troublesome
> **get your act together**: get organized

acting *noun* **1** = **performance**, portrayal, theatre, characterization, impersonation, performing, playing, stagecraft
▶ *adjective* **2** = **temporary**, interim, substitute, provisional, surrogate, pro tem

action *noun* **1** = **activity**, operation, process • *He had to take evasive action to avoid being hit*.
2 = **deed**, achievement, exploit, accomplishment, feat • *He did not like his actions questioned*.
3 = **lawsuit**, case, suit, prosecution, proceeding, litigation
4 = **energy**, force, activity, spirit, vitality, vigour, liveliness, vim
5 = **battle**, fight, contest, conflict, clash, combat, encounter, engagement, skirmish, sortie

activate *verb* = **start**, move, stir, initiate, energize, mobilize, arouse, galvanize, rouse, set in motion

active *adjective* **1** = **energetic**, lively, restless, vivacious, sprightly • *Having an active child around the house can be exhausting*.
2 = **busy**, enthusiastic, involved, hard-working, occupied, industrious, engaged • *people who are active in local politics*
3 = **in operation**, working,

operative, acting, at work, effectual, in action, in force
See also: **alive, healthy, vital**

activist noun = **militant**, organizer, partisan

activity noun 1 = **action**, energy, bustle, liveliness • There is an extraordinary level of activity in the office.
2 = **hobby**, interest, pursuit, pastime • sports and other leisure activities
See also: **excitement, exercise**

actor noun = **performer**, actress, player, Thespian

actress noun = **performer**, player, actor, starlet, leading lady, Thespian

actual adjective = **real**, true, realistic, genuine, authentic, verified • That is the estimated figure. The actual figure is much higher.
See also: **precise**

actually adverb = **really**, truly, indeed, literally, as a matter of fact, in fact, in point of fact, in reality, in truth

acumen noun = **judgment**, intelligence, insight, ingenuity, astuteness, cleverness, perspicacity, shrewdness

acute adjective 1 = **serious**, great, critical, severe, intense, extreme, grave • an acute shortage of supplies
2 = **perceptive**, quick, alert, sharp, bright, keen, shrewd, astute • an acute mind
3 = **sharp**, powerful, violent, severe, intense, shooting, fierce, piercing, excruciating
See also: **brilliant, intelligent, uncommon**

acuteness noun 1 = **seriousness**, importance, severity, gravity, urgency
2 = **perceptiveness**, discrimination, insight, sharpness, astuteness, cleverness, perspicacity

ad See **advertisement**

adage See **saying**

adamant adjective = **determined**, firm, stubborn, resolute,
uncompromising, fixed, obdurate, unbending

adapt verb = **adjust**, change, convert, modify, alter • The TV series was adapted from a movie.
See also: **fit**

adaptability noun = **flexibility**, resilience, versatility, changeability

adaptable adjective = **flexible**, plastic, versatile, resilient, easy-going, compliant, adjustable, changeable, pliant

adaptation noun
1 = **acclimatization**, familiarization, naturalization
2 = **conversion**, change, version, variation, adjustment, transformation, modification, alteration

adapted See **accustomed**

add verb 1 = **include**, supplement, attach, augment, affix, append, adjoin • Add the grated cheese to the sauce.
2 = **count up**, total, add up
• Banks add all the interest and other charges together.
OPPOSITE: subtract
▷ **add to** = **increase**, raise, boost, advance, extend, spread, expand, supplement, strengthen, escalate, intensify, enhance, heighten, inflate, multiply, magnify, augment, amplify, enlarge, proliferate, step up (informal)
▷ **add up** = **count up**, add, total, count, compute, reckon, tot up
▷ **add up to** See **total**

| INFORMALLY SPEAKING
| **add up**: make sense
| **add up to**: amount to

added See **extra, more**

addendum noun = **addition**, extra, extension, supplement, attachment, appendage, appendix, postscript

addict noun 1 = **junkie** (informal), freak (informal), fiend (informal)
2 = **fan**, enthusiast, follower, nut (slang), buff (informal), devotee, adherent

addicted adjective = **hooked** (slang), dependent, dedicated, devoted, absorbed, accustomed, habituated

addiction noun = **dependence**, habit, obsession, craving, enslavement

addition noun 1 = **increase**, supplement, addendum, adjunct, appendage • recent additions to their CD collection
2 = **inclusion**, extension, attachment, enlargement, augmentation, amplification, adding, increasing
3 = **counting up**, computation, adding up, totalling, totting up
▷ **in addition**, **in addition to** = **as well** or **as well as**, also, too, besides, moreover, additionally, into the bargain, over and above, to boot
See also: **extra**

additional adjective = **extra**, new, other, further, fresh, spare, added, supplementary

address noun 1 = **location**, home, house, situation, residence, whereabouts, dwelling, abode
2 = **speech**, talk, lecture, sermon, discourse, dissertation, oration
▶ verb 3 = **speak to**, approach, hail, greet, talk to
▷ **address (oneself) to** = **concentrate on**, apply (oneself) to, attend to, devote (oneself) to, engage in, focus on, take care of

adept adjective 1 = **skilful**, expert, able, skilled, accomplished, proficient, adroit, practiced, versed
▶ noun 2 = **expert**, master, genius, hotshot (informal)

adequacy noun = **sufficiency**, capability, fairness, competence, suitability, tolerability

adequate adjective = **enough**, acceptable, sufficient, ample, satisfactory • an adequate diet
OPPOSITE: insufficient
See also: **all right**, **decent**, **tolerable**

adequately See **well**

adhere verb = **stick**, fix, attach, paste, cling, glue, fasten, cleave, hold fast

▷ **adhere to** See **obey**

adherent noun = **supporter**, fan, follower, admirer, devotee, disciple, upholder

adhesive adjective 1 = **sticky**, tenacious, cohesive, gluey, clinging, glutinous
▶ noun 2 = **glue**, gum, paste, cement

adieu noun = **good-bye**, farewell, parting, leave-taking, valediction

adjacent adjective = **next**, close, near, beside, touching, adjoining, bordering, cheek by jowl, neighbouring, next door
▷ **adjacent to** See **beside**, **near**

adjoin verb = **connect**, link, border, join, touch

adjoining adjective = **connecting**, adjacent, touching, abutting, bordering, neighbouring, next door

adjourn verb = **postpone**, delay, suspend, interrupt, defer, discontinue, put off

adjournment noun = **postponement**, delay, suspension, recess, interruption, discontinuation, putting off

adjudicate verb = **judge**, decide, determine, settle, referee, mediate, umpire, arbitrate, adjudge

adjudication noun = **judgment**, decision, ruling, settlement, finding, verdict, conclusion, arbitration, pronouncement

adjust verb = **alter**, modify, adapt, accustom, make conform

adjustable adjective = **alterable**, flexible, adaptable, movable, malleable, modifiable

adjustment noun 1 = **alteration**, regulation, adaptation, modification, redress, tuning
2 = **acclimatization**, orientation, settling in

ad-lib verb = **improvise**, busk, extemporize, make up, speak off the cuff, wing it (informal)

administer verb 1 = **manage**, run, control, direct, command, supervise, be in charge of • people who administer large companies

2 = **carry out**, deal, perform, impose, execute, inflict, dispense • *He administered most of the punishment.*
See also: **handle, rule**

administration noun = **management**, government, control, conduct, application, direction, supervision, running

administrative adjective = **managerial**, executive, regulatory, directorial, governmental, organizational, supervisory

administrator noun = **manager**, official, executive, organizer, bureaucrat, supervisor

admirable adjective = **excellent**, fine, wonderful, worthy, exquisite, commendable, laudable, praiseworthy

admirably See **well**

admiration noun = **regard**, respect, approval, appreciation, esteem • *I have always had the greatest admiration for him.*
See also: **worship**

admire verb 1 = **respect**, value, appreciate, look up to • *All those who knew him admired his work.*
OPPOSITE: scorn
2 = **marvel at**, appreciate, delight in, take pleasure in, wonder at
See also: **approve, praise**

admirer noun 1 = **suitor**, lover, boyfriend, sweetheart, beau, wooer
2 = **fan**, supporter, enthusiast, follower, partisan, devotee, disciple

admissible adjective = **permissible**, acceptable, allowable, tolerable, passable

admission noun 1 = **entrance**, access, entry, introduction, acceptance, initiation, admittance, entrée
2 = **confession**, disclosure, declaration, revelation, allowance, acknowledgment, divulgence

admit verb 1 = **accept**, grant, acknowledge • *I admit that your actions were justified.*

OPPOSITE: deny
2 = **let in**, receive, accept, take in • *He was admitted to university.*
OPPOSITE: exclude
3 = **confess**, own, reveal, declare, acknowledge, disclose, divulge, fess up (*informal*)

admonish verb = **reprimand**, rebuke, scold, berate, chide, slap on the wrist, tell off (*informal*)

adolescence noun 1 = **youth**, minority, boyhood, girlhood, teens
2 = **youthfulness**, immaturity, childishness

adolescent adjective 1 = **young**, teenage, youthful, juvenile, immature, boyish, girlish, puerile
▶ noun 2 = **youth**, teenager, minor, youngster, juvenile

adopt verb 1 = **foster**, take in
2 = **choose**, follow, accept, maintain, assume, espouse, take up

adoption noun 1 = **fostering**, adopting, taking in
2 = **choice**, selection, endorsement, assumption, appropriation, embracing, espousal, taking up

adorable adjective = **lovable**, attractive, cute, dear, charming, appealing, pleasing, delightful, fetching

adoration See **love, worship**

adore verb = **love**, admire, honour, revere, worship, glorify, cherish, esteem, idolize, exalt, dote on, put on a pedestal (*informal*)

adored See **beloved**

adoring adjective = **loving**, fond, devoted, affectionate, admiring, doting

adorn verb = **decorate**, array, embellish, festoon

adornment noun = **decoration**, supplement, accessory, ornament, trimming, embellishment, festoon, frill, frippery

adrift adjective 1 = **drifting**, afloat, unanchored, unmoored
2 = **aimless**, goalless, directionless, purposeless

▶ *adverb* **3 = wrong**, astray, amiss, off course

adroit *adjective* **= skilful**, expert, skilled, clever, neat, adept, masterful, deft, proficient, dexterous

adulation *noun* **= worship**, fawning, fulsome praise, servile flattery, sycophancy

adult *noun* **1 = grown-up**, man, woman • *I'd like tickets for three children and two adults.*
OPPOSITE: child
▶ *adjective* **2 = fully grown**, mature, ripe, grown-up, full grown, fully developed, of age

adulterous *See* **unfaithful**

advance *verb* **1 = progress**, proceed, make inroads, press on • *Rebel forces are advancing on the capital.*
2 = benefit, improve, further, prosper
3 = suggest, offer, present, submit, proffer, put forward
4 = lend, pay beforehand, supply on credit
▶ *noun* **5 = progress**, step, gain, development, breakthrough • *a scientific advance*
6 = forward movement, development, progress, advancement, headway, inroads, onward movement
7 = loan, credit, deposit, retainer, prepayment, down payment
▷ **advances = overtures**, approach, proposition, approaches, moves, proposals
▶ *adjective* **8 = prior**, early, forward, beforehand, in front
▷ **advance warning** *See* **notice**
▷ **in advance = beforehand**, ahead, previously, earlier
See also: **develop, go, improvement, payment, produce, raise**

advanced *adjective* **= foremost**, forward, ahead, higher, progressive, cutting-edge, avant-garde, precocious, leading

advancement *noun*
= promotion, rise, gain, progress, improvement, betterment, preferment

advantage *noun* **= benefit**, dominance, superiority, ascendancy • *We have a competitive advantage.*
OPPOSITE: disadvantage
See also: **beauty, merit, value, virtue**

advantageous *adjective*
1 = beneficial, valuable, useful, profitable, helpful, convenient, worthwhile, expedient, of service
2 = superior, dominant, win-win (*informal*), favourable, dominating

advent *See* **appearance**

adventure *noun* **= escapade**, experience, incident, venture, exploit, enterprise, occurrence, undertaking

adventurer *noun* **1 = mercenary**, gambler, rogue, speculator, opportunist, charlatan, fortune-hunter
2 = hero, daredevil, heroine, traveller, knight-errant, voyager

adventurous *adjective* **= daring**, bold, reckless, daredevil, intrepid, enterprising

adversary *noun* **= opponent**, rival, competitor, enemy, contestant, foe, antagonist

adverse *adjective* **= unfavourable**, negative, contrary, hostile, detrimental, inopportune, opposing

adversity *noun* **= hardship**, trouble, disaster, reverse, distress, misfortune, affliction, bad luck, hard times

advertise *verb* **= publicize**, push, promote, plug (*informal*) • *They advertise their products on television.*
See also: **announce**

advertisement *noun* **= notice**, ad (*informal*), commercial, plug (*informal*) • *She recently placed an advertisement in the local newspaper.*
See also: **announcement**

advertising *See* **publicity**

advice *noun* **= guidance**, opinion, counsel (*formal*), suggestion • *Take my advice and stay away from him!*
See also: **help, hint**

advisability noun = **wisdom**, fitness, prudence, suitability, expediency, appropriateness, desirability, aptness, propriety

advisable adjective = **wise**, appropriate, recommended, fitting, prudent, desirable, sensible, politic, expedient, seemly

advise verb 1 = **recommend**, caution, suggest, urge, counsel • They advised him to leave as soon as possible.
2 = **inform**, notify, make known • I think it best that I advise you of my decision to quit.
See also: **brief**

| CONFUSABLES
| Advice is the noun.
| Advise is the verb.

adviser noun = **consultant**, aide, guru, mentor, counsellor, tutor, consigliere • The premier and her advisers spent the day in meetings.

advisory adjective = **advising**, consultative, counselling, helping, recommending

advocate verb 1 = **support**, back, endorse, champion, promote, recommend, favour, uphold • She advocates better conditions for prisoners.
▶ noun 2 = **supporter**, spokesman, champion, defender, promoter, proponent, campaigner, counsellor, upholder
3 (Law) = **lawyer**, attorney, counsel, barrister
See also: **suggest**

afar See **far**

affable adjective = **friendly**, pleasant, cordial, amicable, courteous, sociable, amiable, genial, approachable, congenial, urbane

affair noun 1 = **event**, issue, business, question, matter, situation, subject • The funeral was a sad affair.
2 = **relationship**, romance, fling, liaison • He had an affair with someone he met on vacation.
See also: **concern, experience, occasion, undertaking**

affect¹ verb 1 = **influence**, change, alter, act on, impinge on • More than 7 million people have been affected by the drought.
2 = **move**, touch, upset, overcome, stir, disturb, perturb
See also: **concern, infect**

| CONFUSABLES
| Affect means influence, and is a verb.
| Effect means result, and is usually a noun.

affect² verb = **put on**, adopt, assume, pretend, simulate, imitate, feign, aspire to, contrive

affectation noun = **pretense**, show, act, pose, artificiality, assumed manners, façade, insincerity, pretentiousness

affected adjective = **pretended**, artificial, phony (informal), contrived, unnatural, feigned, insincere, mannered, put-on

affecting adjective = **moving**, sad, pathetic, poignant, touching, pitiful

affection noun = **fondness**, love, attachment, warmth, liking • She thought of him with affection.
OPPOSITE: dislike
See also: **friendship**

affectionate adjective = **fond**, tender, loving, caring • She gave me a long and affectionate hug.
OPPOSITE: cold
See also: **friendly, warm**

affiliate verb = **join**, link, associate, combine, ally, unite, incorporate, amalgamate, band together

affiliation noun = **association**, link, tie, union, league, connection, relationship, coalition, combination, alliance, amalgamation, confederation, incorporation, banding together, joining, merging

affinity noun 1 = **attraction**, sympathy, fondness, inclination, leaning, liking, rapport, partiality
2 = **similarity**, connection, relationship, correspondence, likeness, resemblance, closeness, analogy, kinship

affirm verb = **declare**, state, confirm, maintain, testify, swear, pronounce, assert, certify

affirmation noun = **declaration**, statement, testimony, certification, confirmation, assertion, oath, pronouncement

affirmative adjective = **agreeing**, positive, favourable, approving, assenting, concurring, confirming, consenting, corroborative

affix See **attach, connect**

afflict verb = **torment**, hurt, pain, trouble, plague, grieve, distress, harass, oppress

affliction noun = **suffering**, disease, trial, trouble, plague, woe, ordeal, curse, hardship, scourge, adversity, misfortune, torment

affluence noun = **wealth**, plenty, fortune, prosperity, abundance, riches, opulence

affluent adjective = **wealthy**, rich, prosperous, loaded (slang), well-heeled (informal), opulent, well-off, well-to-do, moneyed

afford verb 1 = **have the money for**, stand, bear, manage, sustain, spare
2 = **give**, offer, provide, produce, supply, yield, render

affordable adjective = **inexpensive**, cheap, moderate, modest, reasonable, low-cost, economical

affront noun 1 = **insult**, slight, outrage, slur, offence, provocation, slap in the face (informal)
▶ verb 2 = **offend**, anger, insult, provoke, slight, outrage, annoy, displease

aflame adjective = **burning**, fiery, ablaze, flaming, alight, blazing, lit, on fire

afoot adverb = **going on**, up (informal), current, abroad, brewing, happening, in preparation, in progress, on the go (informal)

afraid adjective 1 = **scared**, nervous, fearful, frightened, apprehensive • I was afraid

of the large dog.
OPPOSITE: unafraid
2 = **sorry**, unhappy, regretful

afresh adverb = **again**, newly, anew, once again, once more, over again

after adverb = **later**, following, afterwards, subsequently
• Shortly after, police arrested five suspects.
OPPOSITE: before
RELATED WORD
prefix: post-

aftermath noun = **effects**, wake, outcome, sequel, upshot, aftereffects, consequences, end result, results

afterwards See **after, next**

again adverb 1 = **once more**, anew, afresh • He told the story again.
2 = **also**, besides, moreover, furthermore, in addition

against preposition 1 = **in opposition to**, versus, averse to, hostile to • I am against animal cruelty.
RELATED WORDS
prefixes: anti-, contra-, counter-
2 = **in preparation for**, in anticipation of, in expectation of • precautions against fire
3 = **beside**, on, upon, touching, facing, abutting, in contact with, opposite to

age noun 1 = **time**, day or days, period, date, generation, era, lifetime, span, duration, epoch
2 = **old age**, decline, majority, maturity, seniority, advancing years, senescence, senility
▶ verb 3 = **grow old**, decline, mature, deteriorate, mellow, ripen

aged adjective = **old**, elderly, ancient, antique, grey, antiquated, getting on

agency noun 1 = **business**, office, organization, department, bureau
2 (Old-fashioned) = **medium**, activity, means, mechanism

agenda noun = **list**, plan, program, schedule, timetable, calendar, diary

agent noun 1 = **representative**, envoy, negotiator, rep (informal), surrogate, go-between
2 = **worker**, author, operator, performer, doer, mover
3 = **force**, cause, power, agency, vehicle, instrument, means

aggravate verb 1 = **make worse**, increase, worsen, intensify, exacerbate, inflame, exaggerate, magnify
2 (Informal) = **annoy**, provoke, bother, irritate, get on one's nerves (informal), nettle

aggravation noun
1 = **worsening**, increase, exaggeration, intensification, exacerbation, heightening, inflaming, magnification
2 (Informal) = **annoyance**, grief (informal), provocation, hassle (informal), irritation, gall, exasperation

aggregate noun 1 = **total**, body, amount, whole, mass, collection, combination, pile, bulk, sum, accumulation
▶ adjective 2 = **total**, mixed, combined, composite, cumulative, accumulated, collected
▶ verb 3 = **combine**, collect, mix, pile, assemble, accumulate, amass, heap

aggression noun 1 = **hostility**, antagonism, belligerence, destructiveness, pugnacity
2 = **attack**, injury, assault, offensive, raid, invasion, onslaught

aggressive adjective 1 = **hostile**, quarrelsome • These fish are very aggressive.
OPPOSITE: peaceful
2 = **forceful**, militant, bold, energetic, dynamic, vigorous, assertive, enterprising, pushy (informal)
See also: **fierce**

aggressor noun = **attacker**, assailant, invader, assaulter

aggrieved adjective = **hurt**, injured, unhappy, distressed, disturbed, afflicted, harmed, wronged

aghast adjective = **horrified**, shocked, amazed, awestruck, appalled, astonished, astounded, confounded, startled, stunned

agile adjective 1 = **nimble**, supple, lithe, sprightly • as agile as a cat
OPPOSITE: clumsy
2 = **acute**, alert, sharp, bright (informal), clever, lively, quick-witted

agility noun = **nimbleness**, quickness, litheness, liveliness, suppleness, swiftness

agitate verb 1 = **campaign**, push, protest, demonstrate • They began to agitate for better conditions.
2 = **upset**, bother, distress, worry, trouble, disturb, faze (informal), perturb • Everything she said was beginning to agitate me.
3 = **stir**, beat, shake, toss, disturb, rouse, convulse
See also: **excite**
▷ **agitate for** See **incite**

agitated adjective = **upset**, troubled, nervous, anxious, excited, distressed, worried, uneasy, edgy, shaken, disturbed, alarmed, rattled (informal), unsettled, unnerved, antsy (informal), angsty, disconcerted, worked up, ruffled, perturbed, on edge, in a flap (informal), ill at ease, hot under the collar (informal), hot and bothered (informal), flustered, fazed, distracted, disquieted, discomposed, all of a flutter (informal)
OPPOSITE: calm

agitation noun 1 = **turmoil**, trouble, confusion, excitement, disturbance, upheaval, clamour, commotion, ferment
2 = **turbulence**, disturbance, convulsion, shaking, stirring, tossing

agitator noun = **troublemaker**, revolutionary, instigator, firebrand, agent provocateur, rabble-rouser, stirrer (informal)

agog adjective = **eager**, curious, enthusiastic, excited, avid, impatient, expectant, enthralled, in suspense, wired (*slang*)

agonize *verb* = **suffer**, struggle, worry, strain, labour, be distressed, be in agony, be in anguish, go through the mill

agony *noun* = **suffering**, pain, torture, distress, misery, anguish, torment, throes

agree *verb* **1** = **concur**, assent, be of the same opinion, see eye to eye • *So we both agree there's a problem?*
OPPOSITE: disagree
2 = **match**, accord, square, tally, conform, jibe (*informal*) • *Her second statement agrees with facts as stated by the other witnesses.*
▷ **agree to** *See* **accept**
▷ **agree with** *See* **side with**
See also: **correspond**, **settle**, **submit**, **suit**

agreeable *adjective* **1** = **pleasant**, nice, lovely, enjoyable, delightful, pleasurable • *I found it a most agreeable experience.*
OPPOSITE: disagreeable
2 = **willing**, game, ready, happy, prepared • *She said she was agreeable to this plan.*

agreement *noun*
1 = **arrangement**, deal (*informal*), contract, pledge, settlement, treaty, pact, covenant • *The two countries have signed agreements on fishing and oil rights.*
2 = **assent**, union, consent, compliance, harmony, unison, agreeing, concord, concurrence
3 = **correspondence**, similarity, compatibility, consistency, conformity, congruity
See also: **approval**, **bond**, **understanding**

agricultural *adjective* = **farming**, country, rural, rustic, agrarian

agriculture *noun* = **farming**, culture, cultivation, husbandry, tillage

aground *adverb* = **beached**, ashore, stuck, foundered, grounded, high and dry, on the rocks, stranded

ahead *adverb* = **in front**, before, winning, cutting-edge, at an advantage, at the head, in advance, in the lead, leading, to the fore

ahead of time *See* **early**

aid *noun* **1** = **help**, service, support, benefit, relief, assistance, promotion, favour, encouragement
▶ *verb* **2** = **help**, support, serve, assist, promote, encourage, sustain, subsidize, favour

aide *noun* = **assistant**, second, supporter, attendant, helper, right-hand man, consigliere

ailing *adjective* = **ill**, weak, sick, poorly, unwell, infirm, indisposed, under the weather (*informal*)

ailment *noun* = **illness**, disease, complaint, disorder, sickness, malady, affliction, infirmity

aim *verb* **1** = **intend**, plan, attempt, propose, strive, aspire • *The company aims to sign up a million customers within the next five years.*
▶ *noun* **2** = **intention**, plan, goal, target, objective, ambition • *Our main aim is to offer a superior product.*
See also: **cause**, **focus**, **mean**, **object**, **point**, **purpose**, **seek**

aimed *See* **calculated**

aimless *adjective* = **purposeless**, random, stray, pointless, directionless

aimlessly *See* **at random**

air *noun* **1** = **atmosphere**, sky, heavens
2 = **wind**, draft, breeze, zephyr
3 = **manner**, look, appearance, atmosphere, mood, impression, aura, demeanour
4 = **tune**, song, lay, melody, aria
▶ *verb* **5** = **publicize**, reveal, express, display, voice, exhibit, circulate, give vent to, make known, make public
6 = **ventilate**, expose, freshen, aerate

airborne *adjective* = **flying**, floating, gliding, hovering, in flight, in the air, on the wing

airing *noun* **1** = **ventilation**,

aeration, drying, freshening
2 = exposure, display,
expression, circulation,
publicity, vent, dissemination,
utterance

airless *adjective* = **stuffy**, close,
heavy, oppressive, sultry, muggy,
stifling, suffocating

airs *plural noun* = **affectation**,
arrogance, haughtiness,
hauteur, pomposity,
pretensions, superciliousness

airy *adjective* **1** = **well-ventilated**,
open, light, fresh, spacious,
uncluttered
2 = **light-hearted**, lively,
cheerful, jaunty, blithe, high-
spirited, sprightly

aisle *noun* = **passageway**, path,
passage, lane, alley, corridor,
gangway

ajar *See* **open**

akin *See* **like**

alacrity *noun* = **eagerness**, speed,
enthusiasm, willingness,
readiness, zeal, quickness,
alertness, promptness

alarm *noun* **1** = **fear**, scare,
panic, anxiety, apprehension,
nervousness, fright • *The cat
sprang back in alarm.*
OPPOSITE: calm
2 = **danger signal**, distress
signal, warning, siren • *a burglar
alarm*
▶ *verb* **3** = **frighten**, scare, panic,
distress, startle, unnerve • *We
could not see what had alarmed him.*
OPPOSITE: calm
See also: **horror**

alarmed *See* **frightened**

alarming *adjective* = **frightening**,
shocking, daunting, startling,
distressing, disturbing, scaring,
unnerving

alcohol *noun* = **drink**, liquor,
booze (*informal*), spirits • *There
wasn't any alcohol at the party.*
RELATED WORD
like: dipsomania

alcoholic *noun* **1** = **drunkard**,
drunk, drinker, wino (*informal*),
inebriate, dipsomaniac, tippler,
toper
▶ *adjective* **2** = **intoxicating**,

strong, hard, distilled, brewed,
fermented

alcove *noun* = **recess**, corner, bay,
niche, compartment, cubicle,
nook, cubbyhole

alert *adjective* **1** = **watchful**, wary,
vigilant, attentive, observant,
on guard • *apprehended by alert
security staff*
OPPOSITE: unaware
▶ *verb* **2** = **warn**, inform, notify,
forewarn • *I was hoping she'd alert
the police.*
▶ *noun* **3** = **warning**, signal,
alarm, siren
See also: **acute, alive, astute,
scare, sharp**

alertness *noun* = **watchfulness**,
vigilance, attentiveness,
heedfulness, liveliness

alias *adverb* **1** = **also known as**,
otherwise, also called, otherwise
known as
▶ *noun* **2** = **pseudonym**, assumed
name, nom de guerre, nom de
plume, pen name, stage name

alibi *noun* = **excuse**, reason,
plea, explanation, defence,
justification, pretext

alien *adjective* **1** = **foreign**,
strange, exotic, unfamiliar,
incongruous
▶ *noun* **2** = **foreigner**, stranger,
newcomer, outsider

alienate *verb* = **set against**,
estrange, disaffect, make
unfriendly, shut out, turn away

alienation *noun* = **setting
against**, separation,
remoteness, estrangement,
disaffection, turning away

alight¹ *verb* **1** = **get off**, descend,
disembark, dismount, get down
2 = **land**, light (*archaic*), settle,
descend, perch, come down,
come to rest, touch down

alight² *adjective* **1** = **on fire**,
burning, fiery, ablaze, flaming,
aflame, lighted, blazing, lit
2 = **lit up**, bright, brilliant,
illuminated, shining

align *verb* **1** = **ally**, agree, join,
side, associate, affiliate,
cooperate, sympathize
2 = **line up**, order, range,

a

regulate, straighten, even up
alignment noun **1** = **alliance**,
agreement, union, association,
sympathy, affiliation,
cooperation
2 = **lining up**, order,
arrangement, adjustment,
evening up, straightening up
alike adjective **1** = **similar**, close,
identical, analogous, the same
• You and your father are so alike.
OPPOSITE: different
▶ adverb **2** = **similarly**, equally,
uniformly, in the same way • I
punish all players alike who break the
rules.
See also: **like, same**
alive adjective **1** = **living**,
breathing, animate • The lost skier
was found alive.
OPPOSITE: dead
2 = **lively**, alert, active,
animated, energetic, vivacious,
full of life • I never expected to feel
so alive in my life again.
OPPOSITE: dull
3 = **in existence**, active,
operative, existing, extant,
functioning, in force
See also: **live**
all pronoun **1** = **the whole of**, each,
everything, every one, the whole
amount, the (whole) lot (informal)
• Why did you have to say all that?
RELATED WORDS
prefixes: pan-, panto-
▶ adjective **2** = **the whole of**, every
bit of, the complete, the entire,
the sum of, the totality of, the
total of, the whole schmear
(informal), the whole enchilada
(slang)
3 = **every**, each, each and every,
every one of, every single
4 = **complete**, full, total, perfect,
entire, utter, greatest
▷ **all right** = **acceptable**,
average, fair, OK (informal),
adequate • It was all right, but
nothing special; = **O.K.** or **okay**
(informal), well, safe, healthy,
sound, whole, unharmed,
uninjured
See also: **okay, satisfactory**
▷ **all-out** = **total**, complete,

full, maximum, full-scale,
exhaustive, undivided,
unrestrained, thoroughgoing,
unremitting
▶ adverb **5** = **completely**, fully,
totally, entirely, altogether,
wholly, utterly
▶ noun **6** = **whole amount**, total,
everything, aggregate, utmost,
entirety, totality, sum total
See also: **whole**

| INFORMALLY SPEAKING
| **all but**: almost; nearly
| **all in**: very tired
| **go all out**: use all your
| resources

allegation noun = **claim**,
charge, statement, accusation,
declaration, assertion,
affirmation
allege verb = **claim**, charge,
state, declare, maintain, assert,
affirm
alleged adjective **1** = **stated**,
affirmed, asserted, declared,
described, designated
2 = **supposed**, so-called,
purported, doubtful, dubious,
ostensible, professed,
unproved
allegiance noun = **loyalty**,
devotion, fidelity, obedience,
constancy, faithfulness
allegorical adjective = **symbolic**,
emblematic, figurative,
symbolizing
allegory noun = **symbol**, story,
tale, myth, symbolism, fable,
parable
allergic adjective = **sensitive**,
susceptible, affected by,
hypersensitive
allergy noun = **sensitivity**,
susceptibility, antipathy,
hypersensitivity
alleviate verb = **ease**, reduce,
moderate, relieve, lessen, allay,
lighten, soothe
alley noun = **passage**, walk, lane,
pathway, alleyway, passageway,
backstreet
alliance noun = **union**,
agreement, league, connection,
marriage, coalition, association,
combination, partnership,

treaty, pact, federation, affiliation, confederation

allied *adjective* = **united**, combined, related, connected, affiliated, associated, in league, linked

allocate *verb* = **assign**, allow, budget, designate, earmark, allot, mete, apportion, set aside, share out

allocation *noun* = **assignment**, share, lot, portion, quota, allowance, ration, allotment

allot *verb* = **assign**, budget, designate, allocate, earmark, mete, apportion, set aside, share out

allotment *noun* 1 = **plot**, patch, tract, kitchen garden
2 = **assignment**, share, grant, portion, quota, stint, allowance, ration, allocation

allow *verb* 1 = **permit**, let, approve, authorize, tolerate, stand for • *Talking will not be allowed during the exam.*
OPPOSITE: forbid
2 = **set aside**, grant, assign, allocate, allot • *Allow four hours for the paint to dry.*
3 = **acknowledge**, own, admit, grant, concede, confess
See also: **sanction**
▷ **allow for** = **take into account**, consider, make allowances for, make concessions for, make provision for, plan for, provide for, take into consideration

allowable *adjective* = **permissible**, appropriate, acceptable, suitable, admissible, tolerable, all right

allowance *noun* 1 = **portion**, share, lot, amount, grant, quota, stint, ration, allocation
2 = **concession**, reduction, discount, rebate, deduction

alloy *noun* 1 = **mixture**, combination, compound, composite, hybrid, blend, amalgam, admixture
▶ *verb* 2 = **mix**, combine, compound, blend, fuse, amalgamate

allude *verb* = **refer**, suggest, mention, hint, intimate, imply, touch upon

allure *noun* 1 = **attractiveness**, appeal, lure, charm, attraction, temptation, glamour, persuasion, enchantment, enticement, seductiveness
▶ *verb* 2 = **attract**, lure, persuade, charm, entice, tempt, captivate, seduce, enchant, win over

alluring *adjective* = **attractive**, glamorous, tempting, seductive, beguiling, captivating, come-hither, fetching

allusion *noun* = **reference**, mention, hint, suggestion, implication, innuendo, insinuation, casual remark, intimation

ally *noun* 1 = **partner**, friend, associate, colleague, accomplice, collaborator, helper, homeboy (*slang*), homegirl (*slang*)
▶ *verb* 2 = **unite**, join, associate, combine, collaborate, unify, join forces

almighty *adjective* 1 = **all-powerful**, absolute, unlimited, supreme, invincible, omnipotent
2 (*Informal*) = **great**, severe, intense, terrible, loud, enormous, excessive

almost *adverb* = **nearly**, about, approximately, practically, close to, not quite • *Over the past decade their salaries have almost doubled.*
See also: **barely**

alone *adjective* = **by oneself**, single, separate, isolated, detached • *He was all alone in the middle of the hall.*
See also: **lonely, on your own**

alongside See **beside, near**

aloof *adjective* = **distant**, remote, unfriendly, detached, haughty, standoffish, supercilious, unapproachable

aloud *adverb* = **out loud**, audibly • *Our father reads aloud to us.*

already *adverb* = **before now**, before, previously, at present, by now, by then, even now,

heretofore, just now
also *adverb* = **as well**, besides, furthermore, too, moreover, into the bargain • *The artist is also a well-known writer.*
alter *verb* = **change**, turn, reform, convert, adjust, modify, revise, vary, adapt, transform, amend
alteration *noun* = **change**, difference, amendment, conversion, variation, adjustment, adaptation, revision, transformation, modification, reformation
altercation *noun* = **argument**, dispute, row, clash, controversy, contention, disagreement, squabble, wrangle, quarrel, bickering, discord, dissension
alternate *verb* **1** = **change**, substitute, rotate, fluctuate, interchange, act reciprocally, oscillate, take turns
▶ *adjective* **2** = **every other**, alternating, every second, interchanging, rotating
alternative *noun* **1** = **choice**, other, option, selection, substitute, preference, recourse
▶ *adjective* **2** = **different**, other, second, another, alternate, substitute
alternatively *adverb* = **or**, instead, otherwise, as an alternative, if not, on the other hand
although *conjunction* = **though**, while, albeit, notwithstanding, despite the fact that, even if, even though
altogether *adverb*
1 = **completely**, quite, fully, absolutely, totally, perfectly, thoroughly, wholly, utterly
2 = **on the whole**, generally, collectively, all in all, all things considered, as a whole, in general
3 = **in total**, all told, everything included, in all, in sum, taken together
altruistic *adjective* = **selfless**, humanitarian, charitable, generous, philanthropic, unselfish, benevolent, public-

spirited, self-sacrificing
always *adverb* = **continually**, forever, invariably, perpetually, every time • *You're always moaning*.
amalgamate *verb* = **combine**, ally, unite, merge, incorporate, blend, integrate, fuse, mingle
amalgamation *noun* = **combination**, union, coalition, merger, compound, blend, mixture, fusion, joining
amass *verb* = **collect**, gather, compile, assemble, accumulate, hoard, pile up
amateur *noun* = **nonprofessional**, layman, dabbler, dilettante
amateurish *adjective* = **unprofessional**, crude, amateur, clumsy, bungling, inexpert, unaccomplished
amaze *verb* = **astonish**, surprise, shock, stun, stagger, astound • *He amazed us by his knowledge of sports history.*
amazement *noun* = **astonishment**, surprise, shock, wonder • *Much to my amazement, he arrived on time.*
amazing *adjective* = **astonishing**, startling, astounding, staggering, stunning, surprising • *some of the most amazing stunts you're ever likely to see*
See also: **extraordinary, incredible, wonderful**
ambassador *noun* = **representative**, minister, agent, deputy, diplomat, envoy, consul, legate
ambiguity *noun* = **vagueness**, doubt, uncertainty, obscurity, equivocation, dubiousness
ambiguous *adjective* = **unclear**, vague, obscure, indefinite, dubious, inconclusive, enigmatic, indeterminate, equivocal
ambition *noun* **1** = **enterprise**, drive, desire, aspiration, longing, zeal, yearning, eagerness, striving
2 = **goal**, hope, aim, dream, wish, purpose, desire, intent, objective, aspiration

ambitious *adjective*
= **enterprising**, hopeful, intent, eager, avid, zealous, purposeful, aspiring, striving

ambivalent *adjective*
= **undecided**, uncertain, doubtful, contradictory, equivocal, in two minds, wavering

amble *verb* = **stroll**, walk, wander, ramble, dawdle, meander, saunter, mosey (*informal*)

ambush *noun* 1 = **trap**, lying in wait, waylaying
▶ *verb* 2 = **trap**, attack, surprise, ensnare, bushwhack (US), waylay

amenable *adjective* = **receptive**, open, susceptible, responsive, agreeable, able to be influenced, acquiescent, persuadable

amend *verb* = **change**, improve, fix, repair, reform, correct, modify, revise, alter, remedy, mend

amendment *noun* 1 = **change**, repair, reform, improvement, correction, remedy, revision, modification, alteration, emendation
2 = **alteration**, addition, attachment, clarification, addendum

amends *plural noun*
= **compensation**, satisfaction, redress, restitution, reparation, atonement, recompense

amenity *noun* = **facility**, service, advantage, comfort, convenience

amiable *adjective* = **pleasant**, friendly, charming, engaging, lovable, likable *or* likeable, affable, agreeable, genial, congenial

amicable *adjective* = **friendly**, civil, peaceful, cordial, courteous, sociable, amiable, harmonious, neighbourly

amid, amidst *preposition* = **in the middle of**, among, amongst, in the midst of, in the thick of, surrounded by

amiss *adverb* 1 = **wrongly**, mistakenly, improperly, incorrectly, inappropriately, erroneously, unsuitably
▶ *adjective* 2 = **wrong**, faulty, incorrect, mistaken, awry, untoward
▷ **take (something) amiss** = **take as an insult**, take as offensive, take out of turn, take wrongly

ammunition *noun* = **munitions**, shot, powder, armaments, explosives, rounds, shells

amnesty *noun* = **general pardon**, immunity, reprieve, forgiveness, remission, absolution, dispensation

amok, amuck *adverb*
▷ **run amok** = **go mad**, go berserk, go into a frenzy, go insane, lose control, turn violent, go wild

among, amongst *preposition*
1 = **in the middle of**, amid, amidst, in the thick of, surrounded by • *The bike lay among piles of chains and pedals.*
2 = **to each of** • *The money will be divided among seven charities.*
3 = **in the group of**, in the class of, in the company of, in the number of, out of

amorous *adjective* = **loving**, tender, passionate, erotic, impassioned, in love, lustful

amount *noun* = **quantity**, volume, expanse • *I still do a certain amount of work for them.*
See also: **figure, measure, price**

amount to *verb* = **add up to**, become, mean, total, equal, come to, develop into

ample *adjective* = **plenty of**, enough, sufficient, abundant • *There is ample space for a good-sized kitchen.*
See also: **adequate, generous, handsome, plentiful, spacious**

amplify *verb* 1 = **explain**, develop, expand, elaborate, enlarge, flesh out, go into detail
2 = **increase**, extend, expand, strengthen, widen, intensify, heighten, magnify, enlarge

amply *adverb* = **fully**, completely, generously, richly, abundantly, profusely, copiously

a

amputate *verb* = **cut off**, remove, separate, sever, curtail, lop, truncate

amuck see **amok**

amuse *verb* = **entertain**, interest, please, cheer, charm, delight, tickle
▷ **amuse oneself** *See* **play**

amusement *noun*
1 = **entertainment**, fun, cheer, pleasure, enjoyment, merriment, mirth
2 = **entertainment**, game, sport, joke, diversion, recreation, hobby, pastime

amusing *adjective* = **funny**, enjoyable, humorous, witty, comical, interesting, droll, entertaining

analogous *adjective* = **comparable**, like, similar, equivalent, related, parallel, alike, akin, corresponding, homologous, resembling
OPPOSITE: different

analogy *noun* = **similarity**, relation, comparison, parallel, correspondence, likeness, correlation, resemblance

analysis *noun* = **examination**, test, investigation, inquiry, scrutiny, breakdown, dissection, perusal, sifting

analytic, analytical *adjective* = **rational**, organized, investigative, logical, systematic, inquiring, inquisitive, problem-solving

analyze *verb* 1 = **examine**, test, research, investigate, evaluate, work over
2 = **break down**, separate, resolve, divide, dissect, think through

anarchic *adjective* = **lawless**, chaotic, rebellious, disorganized, riotous, ungoverned

anarchist *noun* = **revolutionary**, terrorist, rebel, insurgent, nihilist

anarchy *noun* = **lawlessness**, disorder, riot, chaos, confusion, revolution, disorganization

anatomy *noun* 1 = **examination**, study, investigation, inquiry, division, analysis, dissection
2 = **structure**, build, frame, framework, composition, make-up

ancestor *noun* = **forefather**, parent, predecessor, forebear
• *He could trace his ancestors back 700 years.*

ancestry *See* **origin**, **stock**

ancient *adjective* = **old**, antique, old-fashioned, archaic, primordial, aged, primeval, timeworn

ancillary *adjective* = **supplementary**, extra, additional, subsidiary, secondary, subordinate, auxiliary, supporting

and *conjunction* = **also**, plus, moreover, furthermore, along with, as well as, in addition to, including, together with

anecdote *noun* = **story**, tale, sketch, yarn, reminiscence, short story, urban legend

anemic *adjective* = **pale**, weak, feeble, sickly, pallid, wan, ashen, colourless

anesthetic *noun* 1 = **painkiller**, narcotic, sedative, opiate, analgesic, anodyne, soporific
▶ *adjective* 2 = **pain-killing**, sedative, analgesic, anodyne, deadening, dulling, numbing, soporific

anew *See* **again**

angel *noun* 1 = **divine messenger**, cherub, archangel, seraph
2 (*Informal*) = **dear**, beauty, treasure, jewel, gem, saint, darling, paragon

angelic *adjective* 1 = **pure**, beautiful, lovely, adorable, virtuous, entrancing, saintly
2 = **heavenly**, celestial, ethereal, cherubic, seraphic

anger *noun* 1 = **rage**, outrage, wrath, fury • *We vented our anger at the umpire.*
▶ *verb* 2 = **enrage**, outrage, infuriate • *remarks that will anger his critics*

OPPOSITE: calm
See also: **irritate, provoke, resentment**

angle[1] *noun* **1 = intersection**, point, edge, corner, elbow, bend, crook, nook

2 = point of view, side, position, approach, outlook, perspective, aspect, viewpoint, standpoint, slant

angle[2] *verb* **= fish**, cast

angry *adjective* **= furious**, cross, mad (*informal*), enraged • *She gets angry with me if I'm late.*
See also: **resentful**

angst *noun* **= anxiety**, worry, apprehension, unease

anguish *noun* **= suffering**, pain, woe, grief, distress, misery, sorrow, agony, torment, heartache

animal *noun* **= creature**, beast • *attacked by wild animals*
RELATED WORD
prefix: zoo-

animate *verb* **1 = enliven**, move, fire, inspire, excite, stimulate, energize, invigorate, kindle
▶ *adjective* **2 = living**, live, alive, breathing, moving, alive and kicking

animated *adjective* **= lively**, passionate, energetic, enthusiastic, excited, spirited, ebullient, vivacious, wired (*slang*)

animation *noun* **= liveliness**, energy, spirit, passion, excitement, enthusiasm, zest, verve, ebullience, fervour, vivacity

animosity *noun* **= hostility**, hatred, dislike, resentment, antagonism, malice, antipathy, ill will • *There is no animosity between these two players.*
See also: **hate**

annals *plural noun* **= records**, history, archives, accounts, chronicles

annex *verb* **1 = seize**, acquire, appropriate, occupy, conquer, take over

2 = join, add, connect, attach, fasten, adjoin

annihilate *verb* **= destroy**, eradicate, abolish, decimate, extinguish, obliterate, exterminate, wipe out

annihilation See **destruction**

anniversary See **festival**

announce *verb* **= make known**, tell, reveal, advertise, proclaim • *He will announce tonight that he is resigning from office.*
See also: **declare**

announcement *noun* **= statement**, report, broadcast, declaration, advertisement, bulletin, post • *There has been no formal announcement by either government.*
See also: **word**

announcer *noun* **= anchor** or **anchorperson**, reporter, broadcaster, commentator, newscaster, newsreader, master of ceremonies

annoy *verb* **= irritate**, bother, displease, plague, hassle (*informal*), vex, get on someone's nerves (*informal*), tee off (*slang*), piss off (*taboo slang*) • *Try making a note of the things that annoy you.*
See also: **pester, provoke**

annoyance *noun* **1 = irritation**, displeasure • *He made no secret of his annoyance.*
2 = nuisance, pain (*informal*), drag (*informal*), bore, pest, pain in the neck (*informal*) • *Snoring can be more than an annoyance.*
See also: **bother**

annoyed See **cross**

annoying *adjective* **= irritating**, troublesome, maddening, disturbing, exasperating

annual *adjective* **= yearly**, yearlong, once a year

annually *adverb* **= yearly**, by the year, once a year, per annum, per year

annul *verb* **= invalidate**, cancel, retract, abolish, repeal, negate, nullify, declare null and void or render null and void

anoint *verb* **= consecrate**, bless, hallow, sanctify

anomalous *adjective* **= unusual**, odd, exceptional, abnormal, inconsistent, irregular,

a

eccentric, peculiar, incongruous

anomaly noun = **irregularity**, exception, oddity, abnormality, inconsistency, eccentricity, incongruity, peculiarity

anonymous adjective = **unnamed**, unknown, unidentified, unsigned, nameless, incognito, unacknowledged, uncredited

another See **different**

answer verb 1 = **reply**, respond, retort • *I knew he was lying when he answered me.*
OPPOSITE: ask
▷ **answer for** = **be responsible for**, be accountable for, be answerable for, be chargeable for, be liable for, be to blame for
▶ noun 2 = **reply**, response, retort • *Without waiting for an answer, he left the room.*
OPPOSITE: question
See also: **meet, reaction**
| INFORMALLY SPEAKING
| **answer back**: reply
| disrespectfully
| **answer for**: bear the
| consequences of

answerable adjective (usually with *for* or *to*) = **responsible**, subject, accountable, liable, amenable, chargeable, to blame

antagonism noun = **hostility**, opposition, conflict, rivalry, friction, discord, dissension, antipathy

antagonist noun = **opponent**, rival, competitor, enemy, contender, foe, adversary

antagonistic adjective = **hostile**, incompatible, conflicting, unfriendly, at odds, at variance, in dispute, opposed

antagonize verb = **annoy**, anger, offend, irritate, hassle (*informal*), get on one's nerves (*informal*)

anthem noun 1 = **hymn**, chant, carol, psalm, canticle, chorale
2 = **song of praise**, paean

anthology noun = **collection**, selection, treasury, compilation, compendium, miscellany

anticipate verb = **expect**, predict, await, foresee, foretell, hope for, look forward to, prepare for

anticipated See **likely**

anticipation noun = **expectation**, expectancy, foresight, forethought, premonition, prescience

anticlimax noun = **disappointment**, letdown, bathos, comedown (*informal*)

antics plural noun = **clowning**, mischief, escapades, horseplay, playfulness, pranks, tomfoolery, tricks

antidote noun = **cure**, remedy, countermeasure

antipathy noun = **hostility**, hatred, dislike, aversion, enmity, bad blood, ill will

antiquated adjective = **obsolete**, antique, old-fashioned, archaic, dated, out-of-date, passé

antique noun 1 = **period piece**, relic, bygone, heirloom
▶ adjective 2 = **vintage**, classic, antiquarian, olden
3 = **old-fashioned**, outdated, obsolete, archaic

antiquity noun 1 = **old age**, age, ancientness, elderliness, oldness
2 = **distant past**, ancient times, olden days, time immemorial

antiseptic adjective 1 = **hygienic**, clean, pure, sterile, sanitary, uncontaminated, germ-free
▶ noun 2 = **disinfectant**, purifier, germicide

antisocial adjective
1 = **unsociable**, reserved, unfriendly, alienated, misanthropic, retiring, uncommunicative, withdrawn
2 = **disruptive**, hostile, disorderly, rebellious, belligerent, antagonistic, menacing, uncooperative

antithesis noun = **opposite**, reverse, contrast, contrary, converse, inverse

anxiety noun = **worry**, concern, fear, apprehension, nervousness, unease, misgiving • *our growing anxiety about their safety*

See also: **alarm, burden, care, strain, stress**

anxious adjective **1 = worried**, troubled, nervous, concerned, fearful, uneasy, apprehensive, bothered • *He admitted he was still anxious about the situation.*
2 = eager, intent, impatient, desirous, keen, yearning
See also: **tense**

any minute now See **soon**

apart adverb **1 = to pieces**, asunder, in bits, in pieces, to bits
2 = separate, away, alone, aside, isolated, by oneself, to one side
▷ **apart from** = **except for**, but, save, besides, aside from, excluding, not counting, other than

apartment noun = **rooms**, flat, pad (*slang*), accommodation, lodging, penthouse, living quarters, bachelor pad (*slang*), bachelorette (*Canad*), bachelor apartment, studio apartment • *a two-bedroom apartment*

apathetic adjective
= **uninterested**, cool, indifferent, passive • *apathetic about politics*
OPPOSITE: enthusiastic

apathy noun = **lack of interest**, indifference, inertia, passivity, coolness, nonchalance, torpor, unconcern

ape See **copy, imitate**

apex noun = **highest point**, point, top, summit, crown, peak, crest, culmination, pinnacle

apiece adverb = **each**, respectively, separately, individually, for each, from each, to each

aplomb noun = **self-possession**, confidence, poise, composure, self-confidence, calmness, level-headedness, sang-froid, self-assurance

apocryphal adjective
= **dubious**, legendary, questionable, doubtful, mythical, unsubstantiated, unauthenticated

apologetic adjective = **regretful**, sorry, remorseful, contrite, penitent, rueful

apologize verb = **say sorry**, ask forgiveness, beg someone's pardon, express regret • *I apologize for being late.*

apology noun = **defence**, plea, excuse, confession, explanation, justification, acknowledgment
▷ **apology for** = **mockery of**, caricature of, excuse for, imitation of, travesty of

apostle noun **1 = evangelist**, herald, missionary, preacher, messenger
2 = supporter, champion, advocate, pioneer, proponent, propagandist

apotheosis noun = **deification**, elevation, glorification, exaltation, idealization, idolization

appall verb = **horrify**, shock, alarm, outrage, frighten, dismay, dishearten, unnerve, daunt

appalling adjective = **horrifying**, horrible, shocking, awful, fearful, daunting, dreadful, frightful, alarming, terrifying

apparatus noun **1 = equipment**, device, tackle, gear, mechanism, appliance, machinery, contraption (*informal*), tools
2 = organization, system, network, structure, setup (*informal*), bureaucracy, hierarchy, chain of command

apparent adjective **1 = obvious**, visible, evident, distinct, marked, manifest, unmistakable, discernible
2 = seeming, superficial, outward, ostensible

apparently adverb = **it appears that**, seemingly, ostensibly, it seems that, on the face of it, outwardly, superficially

apparition noun = **ghost**, spirit, phantom, chimera, spectre, wraith

appeal verb **1 = plead**, request, pray, beg, implore, call upon, entreat • *The police appealed for witnesses to come forward.*
2 = attract, interest, please, fascinate • *The idea appealed to him.*

▷ **appeal to** See **attract**
▶ noun **3** = **plea**, request, petition
• *an appeal for peace*
4 = **attraction**, beauty, charm, allure, fascination
See also: **ask**
appealing adjective = **attractive**, charming, desirable, engaging, alluring, winsome
appear verb **1** = **come into view**, emerge, surface, crop up (informal), show up (informal), turn up • *A woman appeared at the far end of the street.*
OPPOSITE: disappear
2 = **come into existence**, become available, be invented, come into being, come out • *small white flowers that appear in the spring*
3 = **perform**, play, act, play a part • *He is soon to appear in two more episodes.*
4 = **look**, **look like**, *or* **look as if**, seem, occur, strike one as
See also: **come**
appearance noun **1** = **arrival**, debut, introduction, dawn, emergence, advent, coming • *the appearance of modern technology*
2 = **look**, image, bearing, looks • *I used to be so fussy about my appearance.*
3 = **impression**, front, image, illusion, guise, pretense, semblance, outward show
See also: **entrance**, **entry**
appease verb **1** = **pacify**, quiet, calm, satisfy, soothe, placate, mollify, conciliate, de-stress
2 = **ease**, calm, relieve, alleviate, allay, soothe
appeasement noun
1 = **pacification**, compromise, concession, accommodation, conciliation, mollification, placation
2 = **easing**, soothing, alleviation, lessening, relieving
appendage noun = **attachment**, addition, supplement, accessory
appendix noun = **supplement**, addition, adjunct, addendum, appendage, postscript
appetite noun = **desire**, demand,

taste, passion, stomach, hunger, relish, longing, craving, liking, yearning
appetizing adjective = **delicious**, tasty, appealing, tempting, palatable, yummy (informal), succulent, inviting, mouthwatering
applaud verb = **clap**, approve, encourage, praise, cheer, acclaim, compliment, commend, extol
applause noun = **ovation**, hand, approval, praise, accolade, big hand, cheers, clapping
appliance noun = **device**, tool, machine, implement, gadget, instrument, mechanism, apparatus
applicable adjective
= **appropriate**, useful, relevant, suitable, fitting, apt, pertinent
applicant noun = **candidate**, claimant, inquirer
application noun **1** = **request**, claim, appeal, inquiry, petition, requisition
2 = **effort**, industry, commitment, dedication, diligence, perseverance, hard work
applied See **practical**
apply verb **1** = **request**, claim, appeal, petition, inquire, put in, requisition
2 = **use**, practise, exercise, implement, employ, exert, utilize, bring to bear, carry out
3 = **put on**, place, paint, smear, cover with, lay on, spread on
4 = **be relevant**, relate, refer, fit, pertain, be applicable, be appropriate, bear upon, be fitting
▷ **apply oneself** = **try**, concentrate, persevere, be diligent, buckle down (informal), commit oneself, dedicate oneself, devote oneself, work hard
appoint verb **1** = **assign**, name, choose, commission, elect, select, nominate, delegate
2 = **decide**, set, choose, fix,

establish, designate, arrange, assign, allot
3 = equip, provide, supply, furnish, fit out
appointed *adjective* **1 = assigned**, selected, elected, chosen, delegated, named, nominated
2 = decided, set, established, assigned, allotted, arranged, chosen, designated, fixed
3 = equipped, fitted out, furnished, provided, supplied
appointment *noun* **1 = meeting**, interview, date, rendezvous • *She has an appointment with her accountant.*
2 = selection, election, nomination, naming • *his appointment as manager*
3 = job, post, place, position, assignment • *He applied for a diplomatic appointment.*
▷ **appointments = fittings**, gear, outfit, paraphernalia, fixtures, furnishings, trappings
apportion *verb* = **divide**, share, distribute, assign, allocate, dispense, allot, dole out, ration out
apportionment *noun* = **division**, distribution, assignment, allocation, allotment, dispensing, doling out, rationing out, sharing
apposite *adjective* = **appropriate**, relevant, suitable, fitting, applicable, apt, pertinent, to the point
appraisal *noun* = **assessment**, estimate, opinion, judgment, evaluation, estimation
appraise *verb* = **assess**, rate, review, judge, value, estimate, evaluate, gauge
appreciable *adjective* = **significant**, substantial, obvious, considerable, evident, marked, pronounced, definite, noticeable, discernible
appreciate *verb* **1 = value**, respect, treasure, admire, prize, rate highly • *I appreciate fine food.*
OPPOSITE: scorn
2 = understand, recognize, realize, perceive, be aware of • *I*

didn't appreciate the seriousness of it at the time.
3 = be grateful for, be appreciative, be indebted, be obliged, be thankful for, give thanks for
4 = increase, rise, grow, gain, improve, enhance
See also: **comprehend, enjoy, grasp, like, love, see, take in**
appreciation *noun* **1 = gratitude**, obligation, acknowledgment, indebtedness, gratefulness, thankfulness, thanks
2 = awareness, understanding, recognition, perception, sympathy, sensitivity, admiration, realization, enjoyment, comprehension
3 = increase, rise, gain, growth, improvement, enhancement
appreciative *adjective*
1 = grateful, thankful, indebted, beholden, obliged
2 = aware, sensitive, understanding, enthusiastic, sympathetic, respectful, responsive, admiring
apprehend *verb* **1 = arrest**, catch, capture, seize, take prisoner
2 = understand, recognize, realize, perceive, conceive, grasp, comprehend, get the picture
apprehension *noun* **1 = anxiety**, concern, fear, worry, alarm, suspicion, dread, trepidation, foreboding
2 = arrest, capture, seizure, taking, catching
3 = awareness, understanding, perception, grasp, comprehension
apprehensive *adjective*
= **anxious**, nervous, concerned, worried, uneasy, foreboding, wired (*slang*)
apprentice *noun* = **trainee**, student, pupil, novice, beginner, learner, probationer
approach *verb* **1 = move towards**, reach, near, come close, come near, draw near
2 = make a proposal to, appeal to, apply to, make overtures to, sound out

3 = **set about**, undertake, commence, begin work on, embark on, enter upon, make a start
▶ noun **4** = **coming**, advance, arrival, drawing near, nearing
5 (often plural) = **proposal**, offer, appeal, advance, application, invitation, proposition, overture
6 = **access**, way, road, passage, entrance, avenue
7 = **way**, style, method, technique, manner, means
8 = **likeness**, semblance, approximation

approachable adjective
1 = **friendly**, open, cordial, affable, sociable, congenial
2 = **accessible**, attainable, reachable

approaching See **future, near**

appropriate adjective
1 = **suitable**, correct, proper, fitting, apt • Jeans are not appropriate clothing for some jobs.
OPPOSITE: inappropriate
▶ verb **2** = **seize**, confiscate, commandeer, usurp, impound, take possession of
3 = **steal**, pocket, misappropriate, pilfer, embezzle, filch
4 = **set aside**, devote, assign, allocate, earmark, allot, apportion
See also: **relevant, right**

approval noun **1** = **consent**, agreement, sanction, mandate, permission, blessing, endorsement, authorization, ratification, assent, green light (informal), imprimatur, endorsation (Canad) • The plan will require approval from those in charge.
2 = **favour**, praise, admiration, esteem, respect • He wanted to gain his parents' approval.
OPPOSITE: disapproval

approve verb **1** = **favour**, respect, praise, admire, think highly of • Not everyone approves of his idea.
OPPOSITE: disapprove
2 = **consent to**, endorse, sanction, permit, authorize • The court approved the compensation plan.

OPPOSITE: veto
See also: **allow**

approved See **formal**

approving See **favourable**

approximate adjective **1** = **rough**, estimated, loose, inexact • We believe that an approximate figure of 20 per cent is more accurate.
OPPOSITE: exact
2 = **close**, near
▶ verb **3** = **come close**, reach, approach, touch, resemble, border on, come near, verge on
See also: **broad**

approximately adverb = **almost**, about, around, nearly, roughly, circa (of a date), close to, in the region of, just about, more or less

approximation noun = **guess**, estimate, estimation, conjecture, guesswork, rough calculation, rough idea

apron noun = **pinafore**

apt adjective **1** = **inclined**, likely, ready, prone, liable, given, disposed, of a mind
2 = **appropriate**, relevant, suitable, fitting, pertinent, to the point
3 = **gifted**, quick, sharp, smart, talented, clever

aptitude noun **1** = **tendency**, inclination, leaning, propensity, predilection, proclivity
2 = **gift**, ability, intelligence, talent, capability, faculty, proficiency

arable adjective = **productive**, fertile, fruitful, farmable

arbiter noun **1** = **judge**, referee, arbitrator, umpire, adjudicator
2 = **authority**, expert, governor, master, dictator, controller, ruler, pundit, lord

arbitrarily See **at random**

arbitrary adjective = **random**, chance, personal, inconsistent, erratic, subjective, whimsical, capricious

arbitrate verb = **settle**, judge, decide, determine, referee, mediate, umpire, adjudicate, pass judgment

arbitration noun = **settlement**,

decision, judgment,
determination, adjudication

arbitrator noun = **judge**, referee,
umpire, adjudicator, arbiter

arc noun = **curve**, bow, bend, arch,
crescent, half-moon

arcade noun = **gallery**, cloister,
colonnade, portico

arcane adjective = **mysterious**,
secret, hidden, occult, esoteric,
recondite

arch[1] noun 1 = **curve**, span, vault,
dome, archway
2 = **curve**, bow, bend, arc, hump,
semicircle
▶ verb 3 = **curve**, bridge, bow,
span, bend, arc

arch[2] adjective = **playful**,
mischievous, sly, saucy,
frolicsome, pert, roguish,
waggish

archaic adjective 1 = **old**, ancient,
antique, primitive, bygone,
olden (archaic)
2 = **old-fashioned**, obsolete,
antiquated, outmoded,
behind the times, out of date,
passé

archetypal adjective 1 = **typical**,
standard, model, classic, ideal
2 = **original**, prototypic or
prototypical

archetype noun 1 = **standard**,
model, pattern, paradigm, prime
example
2 = **original**, prototype

architect noun = **designer**,
planner, master builder

architecture noun 1 = **design**,
building, construction,
planning
2 = **structure**, design,
construction, style, framework,
make-up

archive noun = **record office**,
museum, registry, repository
▷ **archives** = **records**, annals,
chronicles, documents, papers,
rolls

arctic adjective (Informal)
= **freezing**, cold, icy, frigid,
chilly, glacial, frozen

Arctic adjective = **polar**, far-
northern, hyperborean

ardent adjective 1 = **enthusiastic**,
intense, keen, passionate, avid,
devoted, fervent • an ardent
supporter of animal rights
2 = **passionate**, intense,
impassioned, hot-blooded,
amorous, lusty
See also: **eager**

ardour noun 1 = **passion**, spirit,
intensity, warmth, fervour,
vehemence
2 = **enthusiasm**, zeal, eagerness,
avidity, keenness

arduous adjective = **difficult**,
rigorous, strenuous, onerous,
gruelling, exhausting,
fatiguing, laborious, punishing,
taxing, tiring

area noun 1 = **region**, zone,
neighbourhood, district, locality
• a built-up area of the city
2 = **size**, range, extent, footprint,
expanse • The islands cover a total
area of 625 square kilometres.
3 = **part**, sector, section, portion
4 = **field**, province, department,
territory, domain, realm, sphere
See also: **place, stretch**

arena noun 1 = **ring**, field,
ground, stadium, bowl,
enclosure, amphitheatre
2 = **sphere**, province, area, field,
sector, territory, domain, realm

argue verb 1 = **quarrel**, fight,
disagree, feud, squabble,
wrangle, bicker, fall out (informal)
• They argued over the cost of the taxi
fare.
2 = **claim**, reason, debate,
maintain, assert • She argued that
her client had been wrongly accused.

argument noun 1 = **quarrel**,
fight, dispute, row, clash, feud,
squabble • She got into an argument
with the referee.
2 = **reasoning**, case, logic,
grounds • There's a strong argument
for lowering the price.
3 = **discussion**, claim, debate,
dispute, plea, assertion,
questioning, remonstration
See also: **defence, disagreement**

argumentative adjective
= **quarrelsome**, contrary,
contentious, combative,
belligerent, opinionated,

disputatious, litigious

arid *adjective* **1 = dry**, desert, torrid, sterile, barren, parched, waterless
2 = boring, dry, dull, dreary, tedious, tiresome, uninspired, uninteresting

arise *verb* **1 = happen**, start, begin, follow, result, occur, emerge, stem, ensue
2 = get up, rise, get to one's feet, go up, stand up, wake up

aristocracy *noun* **= upper class**, elite, nobility, gentry, patricians, peerage, ruling class

aristocrat *noun* **= noble**, lady, peer, lord, grandee, patrician, peeress

aristocratic *adjective* **= upper-class**, genteel • *He loves talking about his aristocratic family.*

arm¹ *noun* **= upper limb**, limb, appendage

arm² *verb* (Especially with weapons) **= equip**, provide, supply, array, furnish, accoutre, deck out, issue with

armada *noun* **= fleet**, navy, squadron, flotilla

armaments *plural noun* **= weapons**, ammunition, ordnance, weaponry, munitions, materiel, arms, guns

armed *adjective* **= carrying weapons**, protected, equipped, fitted out, primed

armistice *noun* **= truce**, peace, ceasefire, suspension of hostilities

armour *noun* **= protection**, shield, covering, armour plate, sheathing

armoured *adjective* **= protected**, bulletproof, ironclad, armour-plated, bombproof, mailed, steel-plated

arms *plural noun* **1 = weapons**, ordnance, weaponry, armaments, firearms, guns, instruments of war
2 = heraldry, crest, insignia, blazonry, escutcheon

army *noun* **1 = soldiers**, military, armed force, legions, military force, soldiery, troops

2 = vast number, host, pack, array, swarm, throng, multitude, horde

aroma *noun* **= scent**, smell, perfume, fragrance, bouquet, odour, redolence, savour

aromatic *adjective* **= fragrant**, balmy, spicy, pungent, perfumed, redolent, savoury, sweet-scented, sweet-smelling

around *preposition*
1 = surrounding, about, encircling, enclosing, encompassing, on all sides of, on every side of
2 = approximately, about, roughly, circa (of a date)
▶ *adverb* **3 = everywhere**, about, throughout, all over, here and there, in all directions, on all sides, to and fro
4 = near, close, nearby, nigh (*archaic or dialect*), at hand, close at hand

arouse *verb* **1 = stimulate**, spur, provoke, excite, incite, instigate, stir up, summon up, whip up
2 = awaken, rouse, waken, wake up

arrange *verb* **1 = plan**, schedule, organize • *Why don't you arrange to meet him later?*
2 = put in order, group, order, sort, organize, classify, fix up • *He started to arrange the CDs in alphabetical order.*
3 = agree, determine, settle, adjust, compromise, come to terms
4 = adapt, score, instrument, orchestrate
See also: **fit, lay, position, set up, stage**

arranged *See* **set**

arrangement *noun* **1** (*often plural*) **= plan**, schedule, organization, preparation, provision, planning
2 = agreement, deal, settlement, compromise, adjustment, compact, terms
3 = order, system, form, organization, structure, classification, alignment
4 = adaptation, score, version,

interpretation, orchestration, instrumentation

array noun 1 = **arrangement**, show, supply, display, collection, exhibition, parade, formation, line-up
2 (*Poetic*) = **clothing**, dress, clothes, apparel, attire, regalia, finery, garments
▶ verb 3 = **arrange**, show, group, range, display, exhibit, parade
4 = **dress**, clothe, deck, decorate, adorn, attire, festoon

arrest verb 1 = **capture**, seize, apprehend, take prisoner • *Police arrested five men in connection with the attack.*
2 = **stop**, end, delay, slow, block, interrupt, suppress, obstruct, inhibit
3 = **grip**, hold, engage, occupy, absorb, intrigue, fascinate, engross
▶ noun 4 = **capture**, seizure, apprehension • *The police made two arrests.*
5 = **stopping**, end, delay, obstruction, interruption, blockage, suppression, hindrance
See also: **catch**

arresting adjective = **striking**, cool (*informal*), impressive, remarkable, outstanding, engaging, noticeable, phat (*slang*), stunning, surprising

arrival noun 1 = **coming**, appearance, entrance, occurrence, happening, advent, arriving, taking place
2 = **newcomer**, visitor, caller, entrant, incomer

arrive verb 1 = **come**, reach, appear, enter, get to, show up (*informal*), turn up
2 (*Informal*) = **succeed**, become famous, make good, make it (*informal*), make the grade (*informal*)

arrive at See **reach**

arrogance noun = **conceit**, pride, swagger, disdainfulness, haughtiness, high-handedness, insolence, superciliousness

arrogant adjective = **conceited**, proud, high-handed, disdainful, haughty, overbearing, scornful, supercilious

arrow noun 1 = **dart**, flight, bolt, shaft (*archaic*), quarrel
2 = **pointer**, indicator

arsenal noun = **armoury**, store, supply, stockpile, storehouse, ammunition dump, arms depot, ordnance depot

art noun = **skill**, craft, expertise, mastery, ingenuity, virtuosity

artful adjective = **cunning**, smart, clever, wily, crafty, shrewd, sly

article noun 1 = **piece**, story, feature, item • *There's an article about it in today's paper.*
2 = **thing**, item, object • *household articles*
3 = **clause**, point, part, item, section, portion, passage, paragraph

articulate adjective
1 = **expressive**, clear, fluent, coherent, lucid, eloquent, well-spoken
▶ verb 2 = **express**, say, talk, state, speak, voice, pronounce, utter, enunciate

artifice noun 1 = **trick**, device, tactic, machination, manoeuvre, subterfuge, contrivance, stratagem
2 = **cleverness**, skill, ingenuity, inventiveness

artificial adjective 1 = **synthetic**, plastic, man-made, manufactured, non-natural
2 = **fake**, counterfeit, mock, bogus, sham, simulated, imitation
3 = **insincere**, false, affected, phony (*informal*), forced, contrived, unnatural, feigned

artillery noun = **big guns**, battery, cannon, ordnance, cannonry, gunnery

artisan noun = **craftsman**, mechanic, technician, journeyman, skilled workman

artistic adjective = **creative**, beautiful, sophisticated, elegant, stylish, refined, aesthetic, tasteful, cultured

artistry noun = **skill**, creativity,

mastery, brilliance, finesse, proficiency, craftsmanship, virtuosity

artless adjective
1 = **straightforward**, open, plain, frank, guileless
2 = **natural**, simple, pure, plain, unaffected, unpretentious, homey, unadorned

as conjunction **1** = **when**, while, at the time that, during the time that, just as
2 = **in the way that**, like, in the manner that
3 = **what**, that which
4 = **since**, because, considering that, seeing that
5 = **for instance**, like, such as
▶ preposition **6** = **being**, in the character of, in the role of, under the name of
▷ **as a result** See **therefore**
▷ **as a result of** See **by virtue of**
▷ **as a rule** See **on average**
▷ **as good as** See **nearly**
▷ **as one** See **together**
▷ **as well** See **also, too**

ascend verb = **move up**, climb, scale, mount, go up

ascendancy See **advantage, power**

ascent noun **1** = **rise**, climb, rising, ascension, mounting, ascending, scaling, upward movement
2 = **upward slope**, rise, grade, ramp, incline, gradient, rising ground

ascertain verb = **find out**, confirm, learn, discover, determine, establish

ascetic noun **1** = **monk**, nun, recluse, hermit, abstainer
▶ adjective **2** = **self-denying**, austere, frugal, celibate, puritanical, abstinent, self-disciplined

ascribe verb = **attribute**, charge, credit, refer, assign, impute, put down, set down

ashamed adjective
= **embarrassed**, guilty, sorry, sheepish, humiliated • He was not even ashamed of what he had done.

OPPOSITE: proud

ashen adjective = **pale**, white, grey, pallid, wan, colourless, leaden, like death warmed up (informal)

ashore adverb = **on land**, aground, landwards, on dry land, on the beach, on the shore, shorewards, to the shore

aside adverb **1** = **to one side**, apart, privately, beside, separately, on one side, out of the way, to the side
▶ noun **2** = **interpolation**, parenthesis

asinine adjective = **stupid**, foolish, senseless, idiotic, moronic, fatuous, imbecilic

ask verb **1** = **inquire**, question, quiz, interrogate, query • She asked me if I'd enjoyed my dinner.
OPPOSITE: answer
2 = **request**, seek, demand, appeal, plead, beg, implore, beseech, entreat • We had to ask him to leave.
3 = **invite**, bid (literary) • Not everybody had been asked to the wedding.
▷ **ask (for)** See **charge**
▷ **ask for advice** See **consult**
▷ **ask forgiveness** See **apologize**
▷ **ask oneself** See **wonder**
See also: **pose**

askew adverb **1** = **crookedly**, awry, obliquely, aslant, off-centre, to one side
▶ adjective **2** = **crooked**, lopsided, oblique, awry, cockeyed (informal), off-centre

asleep adjective = **sleeping**, dormant, dozing, fast asleep, napping, slumbering, snoozing (informal), sound asleep

aspect noun **1** = **feature**, point, part, side, factor, element, consideration • Test results are only one aspect of a school's success.
2 = **position**, view, situation, scene, prospect, outlook, point of view
3 = **appearance**, look, air, condition, attitude, manner, expression, bearing, demeanour
See also: **detail, face, quality**

asphyxiate verb = **suffocate**,

choke, stifle, smother, strangle,
throttle, strangulate
aspiration noun = **aim**, goal,
hope, dream, wish, desire,
objective, ambition
aspire verb = **aim**, long, hope,
seek, dream, wish, desire, set
one's heart on
aspiring adjective = **hopeful**,
would-be, eager, ambitious,
longing, wannabe (informal)
ass noun 1 = **donkey**
2 = **fool**, idiot, blockhead, dork
(slang), halfwit, jackass, oaf,
schmuck (slang)
assail verb = **attack**, assault, fall
upon, set upon
assailant noun = **attacker**,
invader, aggressor, assailer,
assaulter
assassin noun = **murderer**, killer,
executioner, hatchet man (slang),
hit man (slang), liquidator, slayer
assassinate verb = **murder**, kill,
hit (slang), eliminate (slang), slay,
liquidate, take out (slang)
assassination See **murder**
assault noun 1 = **attack**, charge,
offensive, invasion, onslaught
▷ verb 2 = **attack**, beset, fall
upon, set about, set upon, strike
at
assemble verb 1 = **gather**,
mass, collect, convene, muster,
congregate, come together • a
convenient place for students to
assemble between classes
2 = **put together**, make, build,
construct, erect • Workers were
assembling planes.
See also: **form, manufacture,
meet, piece together**
assembly noun 1 = **gathering**,
company, group, conference,
meeting, crowd, mass,
collection, council, muster,
congress
2 = **putting together**,
construction, connecting,
building up, piecing together,
setting up
assent noun 1 = **agreement**,
approval, sanction, permission,
consent, compliance,
acceptance, concurrence

▷ verb 2 = **agree**, allow, approve,
grant, permit, consent
assert verb 1 = **state**, declare,
maintain, swear, pronounce,
affirm, profess
2 = **insist upon**, claim, defend,
press, stress, uphold, put
forward, stand up for
▷ **assert oneself** = **be forceful**,
exert one's influence, make
one's presence felt, put oneself
forward, put one's foot down
(informal)
assertion noun 1 = **statement**,
claim, declaration,
pronouncement
2 = **insistence**, maintenance,
stressing
assertive adjective = **confident**,
positive, aggressive, feisty
(informal), forceful, emphatic,
insistent, strong-willed,
domineering, pushy (informal)
assess verb 1 = **judge**, rate, value,
estimate, weigh, evaluate,
appraise, size up (informal)
2 = **evaluate**, rate, tax, value, fix,
impose, levy
assessment noun 1 = **judgment**,
estimate, rating, evaluation,
valuation, appraisal
2 = **evaluation**, charge, fee, toll,
rating, levy, valuation
asset noun = **benefit**, help,
service, aid, advantage, resource,
blessing, boon, feather in one's
cap
▷ **assets** = **property**, money,
capital, estate, wealth,
funds, goods, possessions,
resources
assiduous adjective = **diligent**,
persistent, hard-working,
industrious, indefatigable,
persevering, unflagging
assign verb 1 = **select**, name,
choose, appoint, nominate,
delegate, designate
2 = **give**, grant, distribute,
allocate, allot, consign,
apportion, give out
3 = **attribute**, accredit, ascribe,
put down
assignation noun 1 = **secret
meeting**, rendezvous, tryst,

clandestine meeting, illicit meeting

2 = selection, choice, nomination, appointment, delegation, assignment, designation

assignment noun = **task**, post, job, mission, position, commission, duty, responsibility, appointment

assimilate verb **1 = learn**, absorb, incorporate, digest, take in
2 = adjust, adapt, mingle, blend in

assist verb = **help**, support, serve, aid, cooperate, abet, lend a helping hand

assistance noun = **help**, support, aid, backing, cooperation, helping hand

assistant noun = **helper**, colleague, deputy, ally, aide, right-hand person • *His assistant took over while he was out of town.*

associate verb **1 = connect**, link, couple, identify • *Poverty is sometimes associated with old age.*
2 = socialize, mix, mingle, hang out (*informal*), run around (*informal*) • *I began associating with different crowds of people.*
▶ noun **3 = colleague**, co-worker • *the restaurant owner's business associates*
4 = friend, ally, comrade, companion, homeboy (*slang*), homegirl (*slang*)

associate with See **identify with**

association noun **1 = group**, company, body, club, league, society, institution, syndicate, confederation • *a research association*
2 = connection, tie, relationship, bond, affiliation, attachment • *his association with an animal rights group*
See also: **fellowship, link, organization, union**

assorted adjective = **various**, different, mixed, diverse, varied, miscellaneous, motley, sundry

assortment noun = **variety**, choice, collection, selection, array, mixture, medley, jumble

assume verb **1 = suppose**, think, believe, guess (*informal*), imagine • *I assumed that he would turn up.*
2 = take on, accept, shoulder, undertake • *She will assume the position of chief executive officer.*
3 = put on, affect, adopt, mimic, simulate, imitate, impersonate, feign, pretend to
See also: **expect, gather, reckon**

assumed adjective **1 = false**, fake, counterfeit, bogus, fictitious, made-up, make-believe
2 = taken for granted, hypothetical, presumed, accepted, supposed, expected, presupposed, surmised

assumption noun
1 = presumption, guess, belief, hypothesis, inference, conjecture, surmise, supposition
2 = taking on, takeover, acquisition, adoption, acceptance, entering upon, putting on, shouldering, taking up
3 = taking, takeover, acquisition, seizure, appropriation

assurance noun **1 = assertion**, statement, promise, word, pledge, vow, guarantee, declaration, oath
2 = confidence, conviction, poise, faith, nerve, certainty, self-confidence, boldness

assure verb **1 = promise**, confirm, pledge, vow, guarantee, swear, certify, declare confidently, give one's word to
2 = convince, encourage, persuade, comfort, reassure, embolden, hearten
3 = make certain, confirm, complete, ensure, secure, guarantee, seal, clinch, make sure

assured adjective **1 = confident**, positive, certain, self-assured, poised, self-confident, sure of oneself
2 = certain, sure, secure, beyond doubt, confirmed, ensured, fixed, guaranteed, in the bag (*slang*), settled

astonish verb = **amaze**, surprise, stun, stagger, astound, daze, bewilder, confound, dumbfound

astonishing adjective = **amazing**, brilliant, sensational (informal), breathtaking, astounding, bewildering, staggering, stunning, surprising

astonishment noun = **amazement**, surprise, wonder, confusion, awe, consternation, bewilderment, wonderment

astound See **amaze, surprise**

astounding adjective = **amazing**, cool (informal), impressive, brilliant, sensational (informal), breathtaking, astonishing, bewildering, phat (slang), staggering, stunning, surprising

astray adjective, adverb = **off the right track**, off, lost, adrift, amiss, off course, off the mark, off the subject

astringent See **bitter**

astute adjective = **intelligent**, quick, alert, sharp, smart, keen, clever, shrewd, perceptive • an astute judge of character
See also: **acute**

asylum noun 1 = **refuge**, safety, preserve, retreat, shelter, haven, sanctuary, harbour
2 (Old-fashioned) = **psychiatric hospital**, hospital, institution, funny farm (slang), madhouse (informal), mental hospital, psychiatric ward

asymmetrical See **irregular**

at an end See **over**

at ease See **comfortable, relaxed**

at fault See **responsible**

at hand, on hand adjective = **nearby**, close, near, available, handy, within reach, at the ready, at one's fingertips

atheism noun = **nonbelief**, skepticism, disbelief, infidelity, godlessness, heathenism, irreligion, paganism, unbelief

atheist noun = **nonbeliever**, infidel, skeptic, pagan, heathen, disbeliever, unbeliever

athlete noun = **sportsperson**, player, competitor, runner, contestant, gymnast, sportsman, sportswoman

athletic adjective = **fit**, strong, powerful, active, energetic, muscular, sturdy, strapping

athletics plural noun = **sports**, gymnastics, track and field events, contests, races, exercises

at home See **comfortable**

at large See **free**

at last See **finally**

at liberty See **free**

atmosphere noun 1 = **air**, sky, aerosphere, heavens
2 = **feeling**, climate, environment, character, spirit, tone, mood, surroundings, ambience

at no time See **never**

atom noun = **particle**, spot, bit, trace, dot, molecule, speck

at once adverb 1 = **immediately**, now or right now, directly, instantly, forthwith, right away, straight away, this minute or this very minute
2 = **simultaneously**, together, at the same time

atone verb (usually with for) = **make amends**, compensate, redress, do penance, make redress, make reparation, make up for, pay for, recompense

atonement noun = **amends**, compensation, redress, restitution, reparation, penance, recompense

atrocious adjective 1 = **cruel**, brutal, vicious, wicked, savage, barbaric, monstrous, fiendish, infernal
2 (Informal) = **shocking**, terrible, horrible, appalling, grievous, detestable, horrifying

atrocity noun 1 = **cruelty**, horror, brutality, savagery, viciousness, barbarity, fiendishness, wickedness
2 = **act of cruelty**, crime, outrage, evil, horror, abomination

at someone's disposal See **available**

attach verb 1 = **connect**, link, join, couple, tie, fasten, affix

• The gadget can be attached to any surface.
OPPOSITE: separate
2 = put, associate, connect, attribute, assign, ascribe
See also: **add**, **fix**, **hang**, **secure**, **stick**

attached adjective **= spoken for**, married, engaged, accompanied, partnered
▷ **attached to = fond of**, affectionate towards, devoted to, full of regard for

attachment noun **1 = fondness**, love, bond, affection, liking • The puppies formed a close attachment to each other.
2 = accessory, part, unit, component, fitting, fixture
• The drill comes with a wide range of attachments.
See also: **association**, **friendship**, **link**

attack verb **1 = assault**, charge, storm, raid, invade, set upon • I thought the dog was going to attack me.
2 = criticize, blast, censure, berate, lambaste, vilify (formal), put down (informal), revile • She attacked the government's economic policies.
▷ noun **3 = assault**, charge, offensive, raid, invasion, onslaught • a vicious attack on an unarmed person
4 = criticism, blame, abuse, stick (slang), censure, denigration, vilification
5 = bout, stroke, fit, seizure, spasm, convulsion, paroxysm
See also: **bomb**, **savage**

attacker noun **= assailant**, intruder, raider, invader, aggressor, assaulter

attain verb **= achieve**, get, reach, gain, complete, acquire, obtain, accomplish, fulfill

attainable See **possible**

attainment noun
= achievement, accomplishment, completion, feat

attempt verb **1 = try**, seek, strive, endeavour, try your hand at

• They attempted to escape.
▷ noun **2 = try**, go (informal), shot (informal), bid, crack (informal), stab (informal) • one of his rare attempts at humour
See also: **aim**, **effort**

attend verb **1 = be present**, visit, appear, frequent, haunt, go to, put in an appearance, show oneself, turn up
2 = take care of, nurse, tend, care for, look after, minister to
3 = pay attention, note, hear, mark, listen, observe, heed, pay heed
▷ **attend to = apply oneself to**, concentrate on, deal with, devote oneself to, get to work on, look after, occupy oneself with, see to, take care of

attendance noun **1 = presence**, appearance, attending, being there
2 = turnout, house, crowd, audience, gate, number present

attendant noun **1 = assistant**, guard, aide, escort, servant, companion, follower, helper
▷ adjective **2 = accompanying**, related, accessory, associated, consequent, concomitant

attention noun
1 = concentration, deliberation, heed, intentness, thought, scrutiny, thinking
2 = notice, regard, recognition, consideration, awareness, observation, consciousness
3 = care, concern, treatment, looking after, ministration

attentive adjective **1 = intent**, alert, careful, awake, watchful, mindful, observant, concentrating, heedful, studious
2 = considerate, kind, helpful, polite, respectful, thoughtful, courteous, obliging

at the last moment See **finally**

attic noun **= loft**, garret

at times See **sometimes**

attire noun **= clothes**, wear, dress, costume, outfit, apparel, garb, garments, robes

attitude noun **1 = outlook**, position, perspective, stance,

point of view • *negative attitudes to work*
2 = position, pose, stance, posture
See also: **conduct, view, viewpoint**
attorney See **lawyer**
attract *verb* = **appeal to**, pull (*informal*), draw, lure, entice, tempt • *The championship has attracted many leading skaters.*
OPPOSITE: repel
See also: **appeal**
attraction *noun* = **appeal**, pull (*informal*), lure, charm, temptation, allure, fascination, magnetism, enticement
attractive *adjective* = **appealing**, pretty, lovely, charming, handsome, fetching • *an attractive woman*
OPPOSITE: unattractive
See also: **beautiful, cute**
attractiveness See **beauty**
attribute *noun* **1 = quality**, feature, property, characteristic, trait • *a normal attribute of human behaviour*
▶ *verb* **2 = ascribe**, charge, credit, refer, assign, put down to, set down to, trace to
See also: **point, virtue**
attune *verb* = **accustom**, regulate, adjust, adapt, harmonize, familiarize
at your fingertips See **handy**
audacious *adjective* **1 = daring**, brave, bold, reckless, rash, courageous, fearless, intrepid
2 = cheeky, defiant, brazen, shameless, presumptuous, impertinent, impudent, insolent
audacity *noun* **1 = daring**, nerve, courage, bravery, recklessness, boldness, fearlessness, rashness
2 = cheek, nerve, chutzpah (*informal*), effrontery, impertinence, impudence, insolence
audible *adjective* = **clear**, distinct, detectable, discernible, hearable, perceptible
audibly See **aloud**
audience *noun* **1 = spectators**,

crowd, gallery, assembly, gathering, turnout, listeners, onlookers, viewers
2 = interview, meeting, hearing, reception, consultation
augment *verb* = **increase**, add to, boost, supplement, reinforce, complement, top up • *a good way to augment your income*
See also: **add**
aura *noun* = **air**, quality, feeling, atmosphere, tone, mood, ambience
auspicious *adjective* = **favourable**, bright, hopeful, promising, encouraging, felicitous
austere *adjective* **1 = stern**, serious, severe, formal, strict, solemn, forbidding
2 = ascetic, strict, solemn, sober, puritanical, abstemious, self-disciplined, strait-laced
3 = plain, simple, harsh, spare, bleak, stark, Spartan, homey
austerity *noun* **1 = sternness**, severity, seriousness, stiffness, formality, rigour, inflexibility, solemnity, strictness
2 = asceticism, sobriety, puritanism, self-denial, self-discipline
3 = plainness, simplicity, starkness
authentic *adjective* = **real**, true, genuine, bona fide • *an authentic French recipe*
OPPOSITE: fake
See also: **actual, exact, realistic**
authenticity *noun* = **genuineness**, certainty, legitimacy, accuracy, validity, purity, truthfulness, faithfulness
author *noun* **1 = writer**, creator, composer
2 = creator, producer, father, founder, designer, architect, inventor, originator
authoritarian *adjective* **1 = strict**, severe, autocratic, dictatorial, tyrannical, dogmatic, doctrinaire
▶ *noun* **2 = disciplinarian**,

dictator, tyrant, despot, absolutist, autocrat

authoritative *adjective*
1 = **reliable**, accurate, valid, definitive, authentic, dependable, trustworthy
2 = **commanding**, assertive, imposing, imperious, self-assured, masterly

authority *noun* 1 = **power**, control, weight, influence, direction, command, sway, supremacy
2 (*usually plural*) = **powers that be**, government, police, management, administration, officialdom, the Establishment
3 = **expert**, judge, professional, specialist, master, connoisseur

authorization *noun*
= **permission**, leave, approval, warrant, permit, licence, a blank check

authorize *verb* 1 = **empower**, commission, enable, entitle, accredit, give authority
2 = **permit**, allow, approve, warrant, sanction, license, give authority for

authorized *See* **legal, official**

autocracy *noun* = **dictatorship**, tyranny, absolutism, despotism

autocrat *noun* = **dictator**, tyrant, despot, absolutist

autocratic *adjective* = **dictatorial**, absolute, despotic, tyrannical, imperious, all-powerful, domineering

automated *See* **automatic**

automatic *adjective*
1 = **mechanical**, robotic, automated, self-propelled • *An ATM is an automatic teller machine.*
2 = **involuntary**, natural, reflex, instinctive • *automatic body functions*

automobile *noun* = **car**, vehicle • *the Japanese automobile manufacturer*

autonomous *adjective* = **self-ruling**, free, independent, sovereign, self-determining, self-governing

autonomy *noun*
= **independence**, freedom,

sovereignty, self-government, self-determination, self-rule, home rule

auxiliary *adjective*
1 = **supplementary**, reserve, emergency, subsidiary, secondary, substitute, back-up, fall-back
2 = **supporting**, accessory, ancillary, aiding, assisting, helping
▶ *noun* 3 = **backup**, reserve
4 = **helper**, supporter, associate, assistant, companion, subordinate

avail *verb* 1 = **benefit**, help, profit, assist, aid, be of advantage, be useful
▶ *noun* 2 = **benefit**, help, good, use, profit, aid, advantage

availability *noun* = **accessibility**, readiness, attainability, handiness

available *adjective* = **accessible**, free, handy, at someone's disposal, on hand • *There are three campsites still available for the long weekend.*
OPPOSITE: unavailable
See also: **ready**

avalanche *noun* 1 = **snow-slide**, landslide, landslip
2 = **flood**, barrage, deluge, torrent, inundation

avant-garde *adjective*
= **progressive**, experimental, innovative, unconventional, ground-breaking, pioneering

avarice *noun* = **greed**, covetousness, meanness, miserliness, niggardliness, parsimony, stinginess

avaricious *adjective* = **greedy**, cheap, stingy, miserly, parsimonious, covetous, niggardly, grasping

avenge *verb* = **get revenge for**, get even for (*informal*), punish, repay, retaliate, hit back

avenue *noun* = **street**, way, drive, road, course, approach, route, path, passage, boulevard

average *adjective* 1 = **usual**, standard, regular, normal, typical • *the average Canadian teenager*

2 = mean, medium, middle, median, intermediate

▶ *noun* **3 = usual**, mean, medium, standard, normal, par, norm, midpoint

▷ **on average = usually**, generally, normally, as a rule, typically • *Men are, on average, taller than women*.

▶ *verb* **4 = make on average**, balance out to, be on average, do on average, even out to

See also: **all right, common, moderate**

averse *adjective* **= opposed**, reluctant, hostile, unwilling, loath, disinclined, ill-disposed

aversion *noun* **= hatred**, hostility, dislike, unwillingness, animosity, revulsion, antipathy, disinclination

avert *verb* **1 = turn away**, turn aside

2 = ward off, prevent, avoid, frustrate, forestall, preclude, fend off, stave off

aviator *noun* **= pilot**, flyer, airman, aeronaut

avid *adjective* **1 = enthusiastic**, intense, eager, keen, passionate, devoted, zealous, ardent, fanatical

2 = insatiable, hungry, thirsty, greedy, voracious, ravenous, grasping, rapacious

avoid *verb* **1 = refrain from**, dodge, shirk, duck out of (*informal*) • *He avoids talking about unpleasant things.*

2 = keep away from, shun, elude, evade, dodge, sidestep, eschew (*formal*), steer clear of • *She thought he was trying to avoid her.*

3 = prevent, avert

See also: **abstain, escape**

avoidance *noun* **= evasion**, escape, dodging, eluding, keeping away, shunning, steering clear

avowed *adjective* **1 = declared**, open, self-proclaimed, professed, sworn

2 = confessed, acknowledged, admitted

await *verb* **1 = wait for**, expect, anticipate, abide, look for, look forward to, stay for

2 = be in store for, attend, be in readiness for, be prepared for, be ready for, wait for

awake *adjective* **1 = not sleeping**, aware, conscious, aroused, awakened, wakeful, wide-awake

2 = alert, alive, aware, vigilant, watchful, attentive, observant, heedful, on the lookout

▶ *verb* **3 = wake up**, wake, awaken, rouse

4 = alert, revive, provoke, stimulate, arouse, kindle, stir up

awaken *verb* **1 = awake**, wake, revive, arouse, rouse

2 = alert, provoke, stimulate, kindle, stir up

awakening *noun* **= waking up**, revival, stimulation, rousing, arousal, stirring up

award *verb* **1 = give**, present, grant, bestow, confer, endow, hand out

▶ *noun* **2 = prize**, grant, gift, trophy, decoration

▷ **award-winning** See **prize**

aware *adjective*

▷ **aware of = conscious of**, acquainted with, familiar with, mindful of • *She was acutely aware of the noise of the city*; **= informed**, knowledgeable, in the picture • *Keep me aware of any developments.*

OPPOSITE: unaware

See also: **perceptive**

awareness *noun* **= knowledge**, understanding, recognition, perception, consciousness, realization, familiarity

away *adverb* **1 = off**, elsewhere, abroad, hence, from here, from home

2 = at a distance, far, apart, remote

3 = aside, out of the way, to one side

4 = continuously, repeatedly, relentlessly, incessantly, interminably, uninterruptedly, unremittingly

▶ *adjective* **5** = **not present**, out, elsewhere, abroad, absent, gone, not at home, not here

awe *noun* **1** = **wonder**, fear, respect, terror, horror, dread, admiration, amazement, astonishment, reverence

▶ *verb* **2** = **impress**, stun, intimidate, terrify, frighten, astonish, amaze, horrify

awesome *adjective* **1** = **awe-inspiring**, cool (*informal*), amazing, impressive, formidable, breathtaking, astonishing, intimidating, phat (*slang*), stunning

2 (*Informal*) = **first-class**, choice, excellent, elite, superior, world-class, hand-picked, first-rate

awful *adjective* = **terrible**, horrendous, appalling, dreadful, ghastly, frightful • *the same awful jokes*

See also: **horrible**

awfully *adverb* **1** = **badly**, woefully, disgracefully, dreadfully, reprehensibly, unforgivably, unpleasantly, wretchedly

2 (*Informal*) = **very**, extremely, greatly, terribly, exceptionally, immensely, exceedingly, dreadfully

awkward *adjective* **1** = **clumsy**, lumbering, ungainly, gauche, gawky, inelegant, uncoordinated

2 = **unmanageable**, difficult, inconvenient, troublesome, cumbersome, clunky (*informal*), unwieldy

3 = **embarrassing**, difficult, delicate, uncomfortable, inconvenient, ill at ease

awkwardness *noun*

1 = **clumsiness**, gawkiness, inelegance, ungainliness

2 = **unwieldiness**, difficulty, inconvenience

3 = **embarrassment**, difficulty, inconvenience, delicacy

axe *noun* **1** = **hatchet**, chopper, adze

▷ **the axe** (*Informal*) = **dismissal**, termination, the boot (*slang*), the chop (*slang*)

▶ *verb* **2** (*Informal*) = **cut back**, fire (*informal*), remove, cancel, eliminate, dismiss, sack (*informal*), dispense with, get rid of

axiom *noun* = **principle**, adage, maxim, truism, dictum, aphorism, precept

axiomatic *adjective* = **self-evident**, certain, manifest, granted, accepted, given, assumed, understood

axis *noun* = **pivot**, shaft, spindle, axle, centre line

axle *noun* = **shaft**, pin, pivot, rod, axis, spindle

aye *See* **yes**

Bb

babble verb 1 = **blabber**, chatter, gurgle, burble, gabble, jabber, prattle, gibber • *He babbled on and on.*
2 *See* **gurgle**
▶ noun 3 = **gabble**, drivel, burble, gibberish
See also: **ramble, rave**

babies *See* **young**

baby noun 1 = **infant**, child, newborn *or* newborn child, tot, babe, suckling, little one, babe in arms, neonate, rug rat (*informal*), ankle biter (*informal*) • *I've had a dimple since I was a baby.*
2 = **sissy**, suck (*chiefly Canad*), coward, wimp, pansy (*offensive slang*), weakling, pussy (*taboo slang*), wuss (*slang*), milquetoast, pantywaist (*informal*)
▶ adjective 3 = **small**, minute, little, tiny, mini, miniature, wee, teeny-weeny

babyish adjective = **childish**, juvenile, foolish, immature, infantile, puerile, sissy, spoiled

back noun 1 = **rear**, end, reverse, stern • *the back of a postcard*
OPPOSITE: front
▷ **behind one's back** = **secretly**, surreptitiously, covertly, deceitfully, sneakily
▶ verb 2 = **support**, second, endorse, champion, promote, favour, encourage, advocate, espouse • *His friends are backing him.*
OPPOSITE: oppose
3 = **move back**, retire, withdraw, retreat, reverse, backtrack, back off, go back, turn tail
▷ **back away** *See* **retreat**
▷ **back down** = **give in**, withdraw, submit, surrender, concede, yield, cave *or* cave in, accede, admit defeat, back-pedal

▷ **back off** *See* **retreat**
▷ **back out** (often with *of*) = **withdraw**, cancel, resign, quit, abandon, retreat, excuse oneself, give up, go back on, wimp out (*slang*)
▷ **back up** = **support**, second, confirm, assist, aid, bolster, reinforce, substantiate, corroborate, stand by
▶ adjective 4 = **rear**, end, tail, hind, posterior, hindmost
5 = **previous**, former, past, earlier, delayed, overdue, elapsed
See also: **finance, gamble, sanction**

backbiting noun = **slander**, gossip, defamation, malice, bitchiness (*slang*), cattiness (*informal*), disparagement, scandalmongering, spitefulness

backbone noun 1 (*Medical*) = **spinal column**, spine, vertebrae, vertebral column
2 = **strength of character**, character, resolution, nerve, determination, courage, pluck, grit, fortitude

backbreaking adjective = **exhausting**, hard, arduous, strenuous, gruelling, crushing, laborious, punishing

backer noun = **supporter**, second, advocate, sponsor, subscriber, patron, promoter, angel (*informal*), benefactor

backfire verb = **fail**, rebound, disappoint, flop (*informal*), miscarry, recoil, boomerang

background noun = **social circumstances**, history, environment, culture, upbringing • *What is your family's background?*
See also: **foil, record, surroundings**

backing noun = **support**, aid, sponsorship, assistance, endorsement, encouragement, patronage, moral support

backlash noun = **reaction**, response, resistance, retaliation, repercussion, recoil, counteraction

backlog noun = **build-up**, stock, reserve, supply, excess, hoard, accumulation

backside See **buttocks**

backslide verb = **relapse**, slip, weaken, lapse, stray, revert, go astray, go wrong

backslider noun = **relapser**, deserter, renegade, apostate, turncoat, recidivist, recreant

backward adjective = **slow**, behind, undeveloped, underdeveloped

backwards, backward adverb = **towards the rear**, behind, in reverse, rearward

bacteria plural noun = **microorganisms**, bacilli, bugs (slang), germs, microbes, pathogens, viruses

bad adjective 1 = **inferior**, poor, faulty, inadequate, defective, lousy (slang), substandard, unsatisfactory, imperfect • bad roads
OPPOSITE: satisfactory
2 See **harmful**
3 = **evil**, mean, criminal, wrong, corrupt, wicked, immoral, sinful, villainous • a bad person
OPPOSITE: good
4 = **naughty**, unruly, mischievous, disobedient
5 = **rotten**, decayed, mouldy, sour, rancid, putrid, spoiled
6 = **unfavourable**, troubled, unfortunate, adverse, grim, gloomy, unpleasant, distressing
See also: **serious**

badge noun = **mark**, sign, device, brand, stamp, identification, token, emblem, insignia

badger verb = **pester**, plague, bully, harass, hound, nag, torment, goad, importune

badinage noun = **banter**, mockery, wordplay, teasing, repartee, pleasantry

badly adverb 1 = **poorly**, wrongly, incorrectly, inadequately, carelessly, imperfectly, ineptly • This essay is badly written.
OPPOSITE: well
2 = **unfavourably**, unfortunately, unsuccessfully
OPPOSITE: well
3 = **severely**, seriously, extremely, deeply, greatly, desperately, intensely, exceedingly

bad-mouth verb (Slang) = **criticize**, abuse, insult, mock, deride, malign, slander

badness See **evil**

baffle verb = **puzzle**, confuse, stump, mystify, bewilder, perplex, confound, flummox, nonplus

baffled See **confused**

baffling adjective = **puzzling**, unclear, mysterious, strange, weird, confusing, elusive, enigmatic, incomprehensible, inexplicable, unfathomable, unaccountable, perplexing, bewildering, mystifying
OPPOSITE: understandable

bag noun 1 = **container**, sack, pouch, receptacle
2 = **handbag**, clutch or clutch bag, purse, shoulder bag, evening bag
3 = **luggage**, chest, baggage, backpack, trunk, suitcase, knapsack, crate, overnighter
▶ verb 4 = **catch**, kill, shoot, land, capture, acquire, trap

baggage noun = **luggage**, equipment, gear, paraphernalia, accoutrements, bags, belongings, suitcases, things

baggy adjective = **loose**, slack, floppy, ill-fitting, oversize, droopy, roomy, bulging, sagging

bail noun (Law) = **security**, pledge, bond, guarantee, warranty, surety
▶ verb
▷ **bail out** = **help**, aid, rescue, relieve, save (someone's) bacon (informal); = **escape**, quit,

withdraw, retreat, flee, recede, slip away

bait noun **1** = **lure**, incentive, attraction, bribe, temptation, snare, inducement, decoy, allurement, enticement • *He isn't taking the bait.*
▶ verb **2** = **tease**, bother, harass, annoy, hound, irritate, hassle (*informal*), persecute, torment
See also: **pick on**

bake See **cook, harden**

baked adjective = **dry**, torrid, arid, parched, sun-baked, desiccated, scorched, seared

balance verb **1** = **stabilize**, level, steady • *Balancing on one leg is difficult.*
2 = **compare**, consider, estimate, weigh, assess, evaluate, deliberate
3 (*Accounting*) = **calculate**, total, settle, square, tally, compute
▶ noun **4** = **equilibrium**, parity, equity • *the chemical balance of the brain*
5 = **stability**, poise, composure, self-control, equanimity, self-possession, steadiness
6 = **remainder**, rest, difference, surplus, residue
See also: **compensate**

balcony noun **1** = **terrace**, veranda
2 = **upper circle**, gallery, gods, peanut gallery (*informal*)

bald adjective **1** = **hairless**, baldheaded, depilated
2 = **plain**, direct, blunt, straightforward, forthright, unadorned, unvarnished

baldness noun **1** = **hairlessness**, alopecia (*pathology*), baldheadedness
2 = **plainness**, severity, simplicity, austerity, bluntness

balk verb **1** = **recoil**, refuse, resist, evade, hesitate, shirk, flinch, jib, shrink from
2 = **foil**, defeat, prevent, check, frustrate, thwart, hinder, obstruct, counteract

ball noun = **sphere**, drop, globe, pellet, orb, globule,
spheroid • *a soccer ball*
See also: **lump**

ballast noun = **counterbalance**, weight, balance, stability, sandbag, equilibrium, counterweight, stabilizer

balloon verb = **swell**, expand, inflate, billow, dilate, blow up, distend, grow rapidly, puff out

ballot noun = **vote**, election, poll, polling, voting

ballyhoo noun = **fuss**, noise, racket, commotion, to-do, babble, hubbub, hue and cry, hullabaloo

balm noun **1** = **ointment**, cream, lotion, balsam, embrocation, emollient, salve, unguent
2 = **comfort**, solace, consolation, palliative, restorative, curative, anodyne

balmy adjective = **mild**, pleasant, temperate, clement, summery

baloney noun (*Informal*) = **nonsense**, garbage, crap (*slang*), drivel, hogwash, claptrap (*informal*), poppycock (*informal*), trash, tripe (*informal*), balderdash, hot air (*informal*)

bamboozle verb (*Informal*)
1 = **cheat**, trick, fool, con (*informal*), dupe, deceive, swindle, hoodwink
2 = **puzzle**, confuse, baffle, stump, mystify, perplex, confound, befuddle

ban verb **1** = **prohibit**, bar, exclude, forbid, banish, outlaw, suppress, disqualify, proscribe • *The coach was banned from the game.*
OPPOSITE: permit
▶ noun **2** = **prohibition**, embargo, suppression, disqualification • *a ban on smoking*
OPPOSITE: permit
See also: **sanctions, veto**

banal adjective = **unoriginal**, pedestrian, stale, mundane, trite, unimaginative, hackneyed, humdrum, stereotyped

band[1] noun **1** = **group**, orchestra • *a singer in a rock band*

2 = gang, company, party, crowd, bunch, troupe • *a band of thugs*
See also: **body, ring, team**

band² noun = **strip**, bond, chain, belt, cord, strap, ribbon

bandage noun **1 = dressing**, compress, Band-Aid (*trademark*), gauze
▶ *verb* **2 = dress**, cover, bind, swathe

bandit noun = **robber**, thief, knock, outlaw, desperado, highwayman, marauder

bane noun = **plague**, ruin, curse, pest, scourge, nuisance, torment, bête noire

bang verb **1 = hit**, beat, pound, slam, knock, hammer, thump • *a toddler banging a saucepan with a wooden spoon*
2 = explode, boom, thump, thunder, resound, clang
▶ *noun* **3 = explosion**, boom, crack, thump, detonation • *The balloon exploded with a bang.*
4 = blow, knock, thump, whack • *a nasty bang on the elbow*
▶ *adverb* **5 = hard**, abruptly, suddenly, noisily
6 = straight, slap, smack, precisely
See also: **bump, crash**

| INFORMALLY SPEAKING
| **bang for your buck**: value for your money
| **bang into**: hit
| **with a bang**: with great success

banish verb **1 = exile**, deport, expel, eject, evict • *banished to a distant island*
2 = dispel, remove, eliminate, dismiss, eradicate, discard • *to banish illness*

banishment noun = **expulsion**, deportation, exile, transportation, expatriation

banisters plural noun = **railing**, rail, handrail, balusters, balustrade

bank¹ noun **1 = store**, fund, stock, reserve, hoard • *a blood bank*
2 = storehouse, repository, depository
▶ *verb* **3 = save**, keep, deposit

bank² noun **1 = side**, edge, shore, brink • *He sat fishing on the bank.*
2 = mound, mass, banking, pile, heap, ridge, embankment
▶ *verb* **3 = pile**, mass, mound, amass, stack, heap
4 = tilt, pitch, tip, heel, slope, incline, cant, slant, camber
▷ **bank on** See **depend**

bank³ noun = **row**, group, file, series, line, rank, array, sequence, succession

banking See **finance**

bankrupt adjective = **insolvent**, impoverished, broke (*informal*), destitute, in the red, ruined, wiped out (*informal*)

bankruptcy noun = **insolvency**, failure, ruin, liquidation

banned See **illegal**

banner noun = **flag**, standard, pennant, placard, streamer, colours, ensign

banquet noun = **feast**, treat, dinner, meal, revel, repast

banter verb **1 = joke**, kid (*informal*), rib (*informal*), taunt, tease, jest
▶ *noun* **2 = joking**, wordplay, badinage, jesting, kidding (*informal*), repartee, teasing

baptism noun (*Christianity*) = **christening**, purification, immersion, sprinkling

baptize verb (*Christianity*) = **christen**, cleanse, purify, immerse

bar noun **1 = rail**, pole, shaft, rod • *bars across the windows*
2 = obstacle, stop, block, barrier, obstruction, barricade, deterrent, impediment, hindrance
3 = pub, tavern, canteen, saloon, counter, parlour (*Canad*), inn, brasserie (*Quebec*), watering hole (*facetious slang*), booze can (*Canad*), beer parlour (*Canad*), beverage room (*Canad*)
▶ *verb* **4 = obstruct**, prevent • *His bodyguards barred the way.*
5 = fasten, secure, lock, bolt, barricade, latch
6 = exclude, ban, prohibit, forbid, blackball, keep out
See also: **close**

barb noun 1 = **dig**, cut, insult, scoff, affront, sarcasm, sneer, gibe

2 = **point**, spur, spike, bristle, thorn, prickle, prong, quill

barbarian noun 1 = **savage**, yahoo, brute

2 = **lout**, bigot, boor, philistine

barbaric adjective 1 = **uncivilized**, wild, rude, primitive

2 = **brutal**, crude, fierce, cruel, savage, inhuman, coarse, barbarous

barbarism noun = **savagery**, coarseness, crudity

barbarity See **cruelty**

barbarous adjective

1 = **uncivilized**, wild, rough, rude, savage, primitive, barbarian, brutish, uncouth

2 = **brutal**, vicious, cruel, ferocious, inhuman, barbaric, ruthless, monstrous, heartless

barbecue See **cook**

barbed adjective 1 = **cutting**, critical, nasty, hostile, scathing, pointed, hurtful, unkind

2 = **spiked**, thorny, hooked, jagged, prickly, spiny

bare adjective 1 = **naked**, nude, exposed, uncovered, undressed • bare legs

OPPOSITE: covered

2 = **empty**, open, vacant, spartan • a small bare office

3 = **plain**, simple, basic, stark, sheer, bald, unembellished

See also: **blank**

barefaced adjective 1 = **obvious**, open, transparent, blatant, flagrant, unconcealed

2 = **shameless**, bold, brazen, audacious, brash, impudent, insolent

barely adverb = **hardly**, just, almost, scarcely • She is barely sixteen.

barf (Slang) verb 1 = **vomit**, spew, heave, puke (slang), retch, throw up (informal), toss one's cookies (slang)

▶ noun 2 = **vomit**, puke

bargain noun 1 = **agreement**, contract, promise, pledge, pact, arrangement

2 = **good buy**, purchase or cheap purchase, reduction, discount, giveaway, good deal, steal (informal), bargoon (Canad slang)

▶ verb 3 = **negotiate**, agree, contract, promise, stipulate, covenant, transact

4 = **haggle**, deal, trade, sell, traffic, barter

barge noun = **canal boat**, lighter, flatboat, narrow boat

bark¹ noun, verb = **yap**, bay, howl, snarl, growl, yelp, woof

bark² noun = **covering**, skin, crust, casing, cortex (anatomy, botany), rind, husk

barracks plural noun = **camp**, garrison, encampment, billet, quarters

barrage noun 1 = **torrent**, mass, hail, stream, burst, deluge, onslaught, plethora

2 (Military) = **bombardment**, battery, gunfire, salvo, volley, cannonade, fusillade, shelling

barren adjective 1 waste, dry, empty, desert, arid, unproductive, desolate • a barren desert

OPPOSITE: fertile

2 = **infertile**, sterile, childless

barricade noun 1 = **barrier**, blockade, fence, obstruction, rampart, bulwark, palisade, stockade

▶ verb 2 = **bar**, protect, defend, block, blockade, fortify, obstruct, shut in

barrier noun 1 = **barricade**, wall, fence, obstacle, obstruction • The eager fans broke through the barriers.

2 = **obstacle**, hurdle, impediment, handicap, hindrance • trade barriers between Canada and the United States

See also: **disadvantage**, **protection**, **safeguard**

barter verb = **trade**, sell, traffic, exchange, bargain, swap, haggle, drive a hard bargain

base¹ noun 1 = **bottom**, stand, foot, bed, foundation, pedestal • the base of the cliffs

OPPOSITE: top

2 = **centre**, post, station, camp,

headquarters • *a military base*

3 = **basis**, heart, key, source, core, root, origin, essence

▶ *verb* **4** = **ground**, build, found, derive, hinge • *The movie is based on a true story.*

5 = **place**, post, station, locate

CONFUSABLES

A *base* supports something physical, like a statue.
A *basis* supports a belief or opinion.

base² *adjective* **1** = **dishonourable**, evil, despicable, shameful, wicked, immoral, lousy (*informal*), sordid, contemptible, disreputable, scuzzy (*slang*)

2 = **counterfeit**, fake, fraudulent, alloyed, debased, forged, impure

baseless *adjective* = **unfounded**, unjustified, unconfirmed, unsupported, unsubstantiated, groundless, uncorroborated, ungrounded

bash *verb* (*Informal*) = **hit**, strike, smash, belt (*informal*), wallop (*informal*), sock (*slang*)

bashful *adjective* = **shy**, timid, reserved, coy, reticent, blushing, diffident, retiring

bashfulness *See* **embarrassment**

basic *adjective* = **fundamental**, key, central, necessary, primary, essential, vital, elementary, indispensable • *the basic requirements for the job*
See also: **straightforward**

basically *adverb* = **essentially**, mostly, primarily, fundamentally, inherently, intrinsically, at heart, in substance

basics *plural noun* = **essentials**, ABCs, brass tacks (*informal*), fundamentals, nitty-gritty (*informal*), nuts and bolts (*informal*), principles, rudiments

basis *noun* = **foundation**, heart, core, principle, fundamental, premise • *The same theme is the basis of several poems.*
See also: **cause, grounds**

bask *verb* = **lie in**, relax, lounge, sunbathe, laze, loll, swim in

bass *adjective* = **deep**, low, deep-toned, low-pitched, resonant, sonorous

bastard *noun* **1** (*Informal, offensive*) = **rogue**, villain, miscreant, reprobate, scoundrel, wretch

2 = **illegitimate child**, love child, natural child

bastion *noun* = **stronghold**, support, rock, prop, defence, mainstay, fortress, citadel, bulwark, tower of strength

bat *noun*, *verb* = **hit**, strike, bang, thump, smack, wallop (*informal*), whack, swat

batch *noun* = **group**, set, lot, amount, crowd, collection, pack, bunch, quantity, assemblage

bath *noun* **1** = **wash**, shower, soak, cleansing, scrubbing, douche

2 = **bathtub**, tub

bathe *verb* **1** = **wash**, soak, cleanse, rinse

2 = **cover**, flood, steep, immerse, suffuse

bathroom *noun* = **washroom**, lavatory, loo, latrine, toilet, convenience *or* public convenience, restroom, outhouse, powder room, water closet, W.C., commode

baton *noun* **1** = **stick**, staff, rod, crook, wand, sceptre

2 = **club**, truncheon, mace, nightstick, billy club

batten *verb* (usually with *down*) = **fasten**, fix, secure, tighten, board up, clamp down, cover up, nail down

batter *verb* = **beat**, pound, pummel, wallop (*informal*), clobber (*slang*), pelt, buffet, thrash

battery *noun* = **artillery**, cannon, cannonry, gun emplacements, guns

battle *noun* **1** = **fight**, attack, action, combat, encounter, engagement, skirmish, hostilities

2 = **conflict**, campaign, struggle, dispute, contest, crusade

▶ *verb* **3** = **struggle**, fight, war, dispute, argue, strive, clamour, lock horns

battlefield noun = **battleground**, field, front, combat zone, field of battle

battleship noun = **warship**, gunboat, man-of-war

batty adjective = **crazy**, absentminded, bonkers (informal), daft (informal), mad, odd, eccentric, peculiar

bauble noun = **trinket**, toy, plaything, trifle, bagatelle, gewgaw, gimcrack, knick-knack

baulk See **balk**

bawdy adjective = **rude**, dirty, indecent, lewd, coarse, salacious, lascivious, lecherous, ribald, smutty

bawl verb 1 = **cry**, weep, sob, wail, blubber
2 = **shout**, call, roar, yell, howl, clamour, bellow

bay[1] noun = **cove**, sound, inlet, gulf • the Bay of Fundy

bay[2] noun = **recess**, opening, niche, compartment, nook, alcove

bay[3] verb = **howl**, cry, bark, yelp • wolves baying in the moonlight

bazaar noun 1 = **market**, exchange, marketplace
2 = **rummage sale**, fair, carnival, garage sale, flea market

be verb = **exist**, live, breathe, inhabit, be alive

beach noun = **seaside**, coast, shore, sands, seashore • building sandcastles on the beach

beached adjective = **stranded**, ashore, abandoned, aground, deserted, grounded, high and dry, marooned, wrecked

beacon noun = **signal**, sign, flare, beam, bonfire, lighthouse, watchtower

bead noun 1 = **ball**, pill, globe, pellet, pearl, sphere, orb, spherule
2 = **drop**, pill, bubble, dot, pellet, droplet, blob, globule

beady adjective = **bright**, sharp, gleaming, glinting, glittering, shining

beak noun = **bill**, mandible, nib

beam noun 1 = **ray**, streak, stream, glow, shaft, gleam, glimmer, glint
2 = **rafter**, support, plank, spar, timber, girder, joist
3 = **smile**, grin
▶ verb 4 = **radiate**, shine, glow, glitter, glare, gleam
5 = **send out**, broadcast, transmit, emit, stream
6 = **smile**, grin

bear verb 1 = **carry**, take, support, shoulder, convey • The ice wasn't thick enough to bear their weight.
2 = **display**, have, exhibit, harbour • The room bore the signs of a party.
3 = **suffer**, endure, stomach, tolerate, abide • He can't bear to talk about it.
4 = **produce**, generate, yield, breed, engender, beget, bring forth, give birth to
▷ **bear a resemblance to** See **resemble**
▷ **bear in mind** See **consider**
▷ **bear out** = **support**, confirm, endorse, prove, uphold, justify, vindicate, substantiate, corroborate
See also: **bring, put up with**

bearable adjective = **tolerable**, sustainable, manageable, admissible, passable, endurable, sufferable, supportable

bearer noun = **carrier**, agent, runner, servant, orderly, messenger, conveyor, porter, doorman

bearing noun 1 (usually with on or upon) = **relevance**, connection, import, relation, application, reference, significance, pertinence
2 = **manner**, air, attitude, aspect, behaviour, posture, demeanour, deportment

bearings plural noun = **position**, way, track, aim, situation, course, location, direction, orientation, whereabouts

beast noun 1 = **animal**, creature, brute
2 = **brute**, monster, savage, swine, barbarian, ogre, fiend, sadist

b

b

beastly adjective = **unpleasant**, mean, nasty, awful, rotten, horrid, disagreeable

beat verb 1 = **hit**, strike, pound, batter, buffet, thrash • He started to beat the poor dog.
2 = **defeat**, overcome, overwhelm, outstrip, outdo, vanquish, surpass, master, conquer • She was easily beaten in the race.
3 = **throb**, pound, quake, thump, vibrate, pulsate, palpitate
▷ **beat up** (Informal) = **assault**, attack, pound, batter, thrash, pulverize, beat the living daylights out of (informal), knock around
▶ noun 4 = **rhythm**, time, stress, metre, cadence, groove (informal), pace, swing (old-fashioned, informal) • the thumping beat of the music
5 = **throb**, pulse, palpitation, pulsation
6 = **route**, way, course, path, circuit, rounds
▶ adjective 7 See **exhausted**
See also: **bang, club, top**

beaten adjective 1 = **stirred**, mixed, frothy, blended, foamy, whipped, whisked
2 = **defeated**, overcome, overwhelmed, cowed, thwarted, vanquished

beau noun 1 (Old-fashioned) = **boyfriend**, lover, suitor, sweetheart, admirer, fiancé
2 = **dandy**, gallant, coxcomb, fop, ladies' man

beautiful adjective = **attractive**, fine, lovely, gorgeous, exquisite, pleasing, delightful • beautiful music
OPPOSITE: ugly
See also: **pretty**

beautify verb = **make beautiful**, decorate, adorn, ornament, garnish, embellish, festoon, glamorize

beauty noun 1 = **attractiveness**, charm, grace, glamour, elegance, loveliness, comeliness, exquisiteness, handsomeness • a scene of outstanding beauty

OPPOSITE: ugliness
2 = **belle**, lovely (slang), stunner (informal), good-looker • a dark-haired beauty with a great smile
3 = **advantage**, benefit, asset, attraction • The beauty of the deal is that everyone makes money.

becalmed adjective = **still**, motionless, stuck, settled, stranded

because conjunction = **since**, as, due to, owing to, in that, on account of, owing to • I went home because I was tired.
▷ **because of** See **by virtue of**

beckon verb = **gesture**, bid, motion, signal, nod, summon, gesticulate, wave at

become verb 1 = **come to be**, be transformed into, change into, develop into, grow into, mature into, ripen into
2 = **suit**, fit, enhance, flatter, embellish, set off

becoming adjective
1 = **appropriate**, proper, worthy, suitable, fitting, compatible, in keeping, seemly
2 = **flattering**, pretty, attractive, neat, graceful, tasteful, comely, enhancing

bed noun 1 = **cot**, berth, crib, couch, cradle, bunk, divan, bedstead
2 = **plot**, area, border, row, strip, patch, garden
3 = **bottom**, base, foundation, groundwork

bedevil verb 1 = **torment**, worry, trouble, plague, distress, harass, afflict, vex
2 = **confuse**, confound

bedlam noun = **pandemonium**, chaos, confusion, turmoil, uproar, furor, commotion, tumult

bedraggled adjective = **messy**, dirty, dishevelled, disordered, muddied, scuzzy (slang), unkempt, untidy

bedridden adjective = **confined to bed**, confined, flat on one's back, incapacitated, laid up (informal)

bedrock noun 1 = **bottom**, bed, foundation, rock bottom,

substratum, substructure
2 = basics, basis, core, essentials, fundamentals, nuts and bolts (*informal*), roots

beefy *adjective* (*Informal*) = **brawny**, muscular, bulky, sturdy, stocky, hulking, strapping, thickset

befall *verb* = **happen**, fall, chance, occur, transpire (*informal*), come to pass, take place

befitting *adjective* = **appropriate**, right, fit, proper, suitable, fitting, apposite, becoming, seemly

before *adverb* **1 = previously**, earlier, formerly, sooner, in advance • *Have you been to Greece before?*
OPPOSITE: after
2 = in front, ahead
▶ *preposition* **3 = ahead of**, in advance of, in front of
4 = earlier than, in advance of, prior to
RELATED WORDS
prefixes: ante-, fore-, pre-
5 = in the presence of, in front of
▷ **before long** See **soon**

beforehand *adverb* = **in advance**, before, already, previously, earlier, sooner, ahead of time, in anticipation

befriend *verb* = **help**, back, support, assist, aid, welcome, encourage, side with, stand by

beg *verb* **1 = plead**, petition, implore, beseech (*formal*) • *I begged him to come to the party.*
2 = scrounge, mooch, seek charity, solicit charity, sponge on, panhandle (*informal*)
▷ **beg someone's pardon** See **apologize**
See also: **appeal, ask, press, request, urge**

beggar *noun* **1 = panhandler** (*informal*), bum (*informal*), tramp, bag lady, pauper, down-and-out, vagrant
2 = scrounger (*informal*), supplicant, sponger (*informal*), mendicant, cadger

beggarly *adjective* = **poor**, impoverished, needy, poverty-

stricken, destitute, indigent

begin *verb* = **start**, institute, originate, initiate, commence (*formal*), inaugurate, set about • *She began to move around the room.*
OPPOSITE: end
See also: **proceed**

beginner *noun* = **novice**, rookie (*informal*), starter, amateur, apprentice, trainee, intern, neophyte, learner, tyro, newbie, noob (*slang*) • *a course for beginners*
OPPOSITE: expert
See also: **recruit**

beginning *noun* **1 = start**, birth, opening, origin, onset, outset, commencement (*formal*) • *the beginning of the city*
OPPOSITE: end
2 = seed, root, germ, fount
See also: **head, source**

begrudge *verb* = **resent**, envy, grudge, be jealous, be reluctant, be stingy

begrudging See **bitter**

beguile *verb* **1 = fool**, trick, mislead, cheat, dupe, deceive, delude, hoodwink, take for a ride (*informal*)
2 = charm, occupy, divert, entertain, distract, amuse, engross

beguiling *adjective* = **charming**, attractive, alluring, bewitching, captivating, enchanting, enthralling, intriguing

behave *verb* **1 = act**, work, run, operate, perform, function
2 = conduct oneself properly, act correctly, keep one's nose clean, mind one's manners
▷ **behave toward** See **treat**

behaviour *noun* **1 = conduct**, manner, bearing, demeanour, actions, deportment, manners, ways
2 = action, operation, performance, functioning

behind *preposition* **1 = after**, following, at the back of, at the heels of, at the rear of, later than
2 = causing, at the bottom of, initiating, instigating, responsible for
3 = supporting, for, backing, in

b

agreement, on the side of
▷ **behind time** See **late**
▶ adverb **4** = **after**, next,
following, subsequently,
afterwards, in the wake or in the
wake of
5 = **overdue**, behindhand, in
arrears, in debt
▶ noun **6** (Informal) = **bottom**,
butt, bum, posterior, buttocks
behold verb = **look at**, survey,
watch, view, witness, regard,
observe, perceive
beholden adjective = **indebted**,
grateful, bound, obliged, owing,
under obligation
being noun **1** = **existence**, life,
reality
2 = **nature**, substance, spirit,
soul, entity, essence
3 = **creature**, individual, human
being, living thing
belated adjective = **late**, delayed,
overdue, behindhand, behind
time, late in the day, tardy
belch verb **1** = **burp** (informal)
2 = **emit**, erupt, discharge, vent,
disgorge, give off, spew forth
beleaguered adjective
1 = **harassed**, badgered, hassled
(informal), persecuted, pestered,
plagued, put upon, vexed
2 = **besieged**, beset, assailed,
blockaded, hemmed in,
surrounded
belief noun **1** = **opinion**, trust,
view, confidence, conviction,
judgment • belief in reincarnation
2 = **faith**, principle, ideology,
doctrine, tenet, creed, dogma
• the culture and beliefs of ancient
times
See also: **idea, viewpoint**
believable adjective = **credible**,
likely, possible, probable,
imaginable, plausible • The book
is full of believable characters.
OPPOSITE: unbelievable
believe verb **1** = **accept**, trust,
assume, swallow (informal),
presume • Don't believe everything
you read in the papers.
OPPOSITE: doubt
2 = **think**, judge, gather,
suppose, assume, imagine,

speculate, presume, reckon
See also: **consider, expect, feel,
suspect, understand**
believed See **supposed**
believer noun = **follower**,
supporter, convert, devotee,
adherent, zealot, disciple,
upholder
belittle verb = **disparage**, deride,
minimize, scorn, downgrade,
undervalue, decry, denigrate,
deprecate, scoff at, sneer at • He
belittles my opinions.
OPPOSITE: praise
See also: **put down**
belligerent adjective
1 = **aggressive**, hostile,
combative, unfriendly,
pugnacious, bellicose, warlike,
warring
▶ noun **2** = **fighter**, combatant,
warring nation
bellow noun, verb = **shout**,
cry, scream, roar, yell, howl,
clamour, shriek, bawl
belly noun **1** = **stomach**,
abdomen, gut, tummy, insides
(informal), paunch, potbelly
▶ verb **2** = **swell out**, spread, fill,
swell, bulge, billow
bellyful noun = **surfeit**, enough,
plenty, excess, glut, satiety,
plateful, too much
belong See **fit**
▷ **belong to** = **be the property
of**, be at the disposal of, be held
by, be owned by; = **be a member
of**, be affiliated to, be allied to,
associated with, be included in
belonging noun = **relationship**,
association, acceptance,
loyalty, attachment, inclusion,
fellowship, affinity, rapport
belongings plural noun
= **possessions**, stuff, gear,
paraphernalia, accoutrements,
chattels, effects, goods, personal
property, things
beloved adjective = **darling**,
precious, cherished, adored,
dearest, treasured • His beloved pet
died last year.
OPPOSITE: despised
See also: **dear**
below preposition, adverb

1 = under, down, lower, beneath, underneath • *about 6 m below sea level*
OPPOSITE: above
▶ *preposition* **2 = lesser**, subject, inferior, subordinate
3 = less than, lower than

belt *noun* **1 = waistband**, band, girth, sash, girdle, cummerbund
2 (*Geography*) **= zone**, area, region, stretch, district, strip, layer, tract

bemoan *verb* **= lament**, mourn, regret, deplore, rue, bewail, grieve for, weep for

bemused *adjective* **= puzzled**, confused, at sea, bewildered, flummoxed, muddled, nonplussed, perplexed

bench *noun* **= worktable**, board, table, counter, trestle table, workbench
▷ **the bench = court**, tribunal, courtroom, judiciary, judges, magistrates

benchmark *noun* **= reference point**, level, measure, standard, model, par, criterion, gauge, norm, yardstick

bend *verb* **1 = curve**, turn, twist, buckle, warp • *Bend the bar into a horseshoe.*
2 = stoop, bow, lean, incline, arch, crouch • *I bent over and picked up the loonie.*
▷ **bend down** See **crouch**
▶ *noun* **3 = curve**, turn, corner, twist, angle, loop, arc, arch • *a bend in the road*
See also: **fold**

beneath *preposition* **1 = under**, below, underneath, lower than
2 = inferior to, below, less than
3 = unworthy of, unbefitting
▶ *adverb* **4 = underneath**, below, in a lower place

benefactor *noun* **= supporter**, donor, sponsor, patron, backer, philanthropist, helper

beneficial *adjective* **= advantageous**, healthy, useful, helpful, wholesome, good for you • *Calcium is beneficial to the bones.*
See also: **favourable**, **valuable**

beneficiary *noun* **= recipient**, receiver, heir, inheritor, payee

benefit *noun* **1 = good**, advantage, help, use, profit, gain, asset, boon • *the benefits of relaxation*
OPPOSITE: disadvantage
▶ *verb* **2 = help**, profit, further, assist, aid, enhance • *The experience will benefit you.*
OPPOSITE: harm
See also: **beauty**, **blessing**, **value**

benevolence *noun* **= kindness**, charity, understanding, humanity, sympathy, tolerance, grace, compassion, goodwill, clemency, decency, goodness, generosity, altruism, indulgence, philanthropy, magnanimity, beneficence, kind-heartedness, kindliness, gentleness, fellow feeling
OPPOSITE: ill will

benevolent *adjective* **= kind**, charitable, benign, compassionate, humane, philanthropic, altruistic, beneficent • *a benevolent ruler*

benign *adjective* **1 = kindly**, kind, friendly, sympathetic, amiable, genial, obliging
2 (*Medical*) **= harmless**, curable, remediable

bent *adjective* **1 = curved**, twisted, crooked, arched, angled, bowed, hunched, stooped
▷ **bent on = determined to**, disposed to, fixed on, inclined to, insistent on, predisposed to, resolved on, set on
▶ *noun* **2 = inclination**, ability, preference, tendency, penchant, leaning, propensity, aptitude

bequeath *verb* **= leave**, will, give, grant, bestow, entrust, endow, impart, hand down, pass on

bequest *noun* **= legacy**, settlement, gift, estate, inheritance, endowment, bestowal

berate *verb* **= scold**, criticize, rebuke, reprimand, censure, castigate, chide, upbraid, harangue, reprove, tell off (*informal*)

bereavement *noun* **= loss**, death, deprivation, misfortune, affliction, tribulation

bereft adjective = **deprived**, devoid, lacking, parted from, robbed of, wanting

berserk adverb = **frenzied**, wild, mad, crazy, frantic, enraged, raging, amok • *The protester went berserk and started attacking the crowd.*

berth noun 1 = **bunk**, bed, hammock, billet
2 (*Nautical*) = **anchorage**, port, dock, haven, wharf, pier, harbour, quay
▶ verb 3 (*Nautical*) = **anchor**, land, dock, moor, drop anchor, tie up

beseech verb = **beg**, ask, plead, pray, solicit, implore, call upon, entreat

beset verb = **plague**, trouble, harass, bedevil, pester

beside preposition = **next to**, near, alongside, adjacent to, close to
• *In the photo, I'm standing beside my father and my uncle.*
▷ **beside oneself** = **distraught**, apoplectic, at the end of one's tether, desperate, frantic, frenzied, out of one's mind, unhinged

besides adverb 1 = **too**, also, further, otherwise, moreover, furthermore, as well, in addition, into the bargain, what's more
▶ preposition 2 = **apart from**, without, barring, excepting, excluding, in addition to, other than, over and above

besiege verb 1 = **surround**, blockade, encircle, hem in, lay siege to, shut in
2 = **harass**, plague, hound, nag, hassle (*informal*), badger, harry, pester

besotted adjective = **infatuated**, doting, hypnotized, smitten, spellbound

best adjective 1 = **finest**, principal, outstanding, foremost, supreme, pre-eminent, unsurpassed, leading, most excellent • *the best TV series I have seen in a long time*
OPPOSITE: worst

▷ **best part** See **majority**
▶ adverb 2 = **most highly**, extremely, greatly, most deeply, most fully
▶ noun 3 = **finest**, top, pick, prime, cream, flower, elite, crème de la crème (*French*) • *Of all my presents, this is the best.*
OPPOSITE: worst
See also: **senior**

bestial adjective = **brutal**, savage, inhuman, barbaric, sordid, beastly, brutish

best-loved See **favourite**

bestow verb = **present**, give, award, commit, grant, lavish, impart, hand out

bet noun 1 = **gamble**, risk, stake, speculation, venture, wager, long shot
▶ verb 2 = **gamble**, risk, chance, stake, venture, speculate, hazard, wager

betoken verb = **indicate**, suggest, promise, represent, signify, bode, denote

betray verb 1 = **be unfaithful**, break your promise, double-cross (*informal*), inform on • *I was betrayed by someone I had thought was a friend.*
2 = **reveal**, show, expose, manifest • *My voice betrayed little emotion.*

betrayal noun 1 = **disloyalty**, back-stabbing (*informal*), treason, deception, sell-out (*informal*), treachery, trickery, double-cross (*informal*)
2 = **giving away**, disclosure, revelation, divulgence

better adjective 1 = **superior**, preferable, higher-quality, excelling, finer, greater, more desirable, surpassing • *Today was much better than yesterday.*
OPPOSITE: inferior
2 = **well**, cured, fully recovered, on the mend (*informal*), recovering, stronger • *I hope you feel better soon.*
OPPOSITE: worse
▷ **better part** See **majority**
▶ adverb 3 = **in a more excellent manner**, in a superior way,

more advantageously, more
attractively, more competently,
more effectively
4 = to a greater degree, more
completely, more thoroughly
▶ verb **5 = improve**, raise,
further, enhance
See also: **reform, senior, top**
between preposition = **amidst**,
among, mid, betwixt, in the
middle of
beverage noun = **drink**, liquid,
liquor, refreshment
bevy noun = **group**, company,
crowd, band, collection, pack,
gathering, bunch (informal),
troupe
bewail verb = **lament**, mourn,
regret, bemoan, deplore, moan,
cry over, grieve for
beware verb = **be careful**, be
cautious, be wary, guard against,
look out, watch out • Beware of
the dog.
bewilder verb = **confound**,
puzzle, confuse, baffle, mystify,
perplex, flummox, bemuse,
nonplus
bewildered adjective = **confused**,
at a loss, at sea, baffled,
flummoxed, mystified,
nonplussed, perplexed,
puzzled
bewildering See **confusing**
bewitch verb = **enchant**,
entrance, charm, fascinate,
captivate, hypnotize, beguile,
enrapture
bewitched adjective = **enchanted**,
charmed, entranced, fascinated,
mesmerized, spellbound, under
a spell
bewitching See **magical**
beyond preposition **1 = past**, over,
above, apart from, at a distance,
away from
2 = exceeding, out of reach of,
superior to, surpassing
bias noun **1 = prejudice**, bigotry,
favouritism • Some employers show
bias against younger workers.
▶ verb **2 = prejudice**, weight,
influence, twist, sway,
predispose, distort, slant, warp
See also: **colour, injustice**

biased adjective = **prejudiced**,
partial, one-sided, weighted,
slanted • biased attitudes
OPPOSITE: neutral
See also: **narrow-minded**
bicker verb = **quarrel**, fight,
dispute, argue, disagree,
squabble, wrangle
bid verb **1 = offer**, propose,
submit, tender, proffer,
counterbid
2 = say, call, tell, wish, greet
3 = tell, ask, order, require,
direct, command, instruct
▶ noun **4 = offer**, price, advance,
amount, proposal, tender, sum
5 = attempt, go (informal), try,
effort, crack (informal), stab
(informal)
bidding noun = **order**, request,
direction, command,
instruction, summons, beck
and call
big adjective **1 = large**, great, huge,
massive, extensive, substantial,
enormous, immense, supersize,
vast • a big house
OPPOSITE: small
2 = important, main,
significant, powerful,
prominent, influential,
eminent, leading • a big name in
the world of hockey
OPPOSITE: unimportant
3 = grown-up, adult, mature,
elder, grown
4 = generous, noble, gracious,
unselfish, benevolent, altruistic,
magnanimous, hospitable
• That's very big of him.
▷ **big cheese** (Informal)
= **manager**, alpha male,
boss (informal), supervisor,
superintendent, foreman,
overseer, bossman (slang), head
honcho (slang), muckymuck
▷ **big name** See **celebrity,
personality**
bighead noun (Informal) = **boaster**,
know-it-all (informal), braggart
bigheaded adjective = **boastful**,
arrogant, cocky, overconfident,
conceited, egotistic, immodest,
swollen-headed
bigmouth See **braggart**

bigot noun = **fanatic**, sectarian, racist, zealot

bigoted adjective = **intolerant**, sectarian, opinionated, narrow-minded, dogmatic, biased, prejudiced

bigotry noun = **intolerance**, discrimination, bias, prejudice, sectarianism, fanaticism, dogmatism, narrow-mindedness

bigwig noun (Informal) = **important person**, celebrity, somebody, mogul, dignitary, big shot (informal), personage, V.I.P., muckymuck

bill noun 1 = **charge**, statement, account, invoice • a huge hotel bill
2 = **proposal**, measure, piece of legislation, projected law
3 = **list**, program, schedule, card, inventory, agenda, roster, listing, catalogue
4 = **advertisement**, notice, poster, handout, bulletin, circular, leaflet, placard, handbill
▶ verb 5 = **charge**, debit, invoice
6 = **advertise**, announce, slate, give advance notice of

billet verb 1 = **quarter**, station, berth, accommodate
▶ noun 2 = **quarters**, accommodation, lodging, barracks

billow verb 1 = **surge**, roll, swell, balloon, belly, puff up, rise up
▶ noun 2 = **wave**, surge, swell, tide, roller, crest, breaker

bind verb 1 = **secure**, lash, hitch, fasten, tie, strap
2 = **oblige**, force, require, engage, compel, constrain, necessitate
▶ noun 3 = **difficulty**, spot (informal), dilemma, quandary

binding adjective = **compulsory**, necessary, mandatory, obligatory, irrevocable, indissoluble, unalterable

binge noun (Informal) = **bout**, feast, spree, fling, orgy

biography noun = **life story**, account, bio (informal), record, life, profile, memoir

birth noun 1 = **childbirth**, delivery, nativity, parturition
2 = **ancestry**, stock, blood, background, pedigree, lineage, parentage, breeding

bisect verb = **cut in two**, cross, separate, split, halve, intersect, cut across, divide in two

bit noun = **piece**, part, grain, scrap, fragment, crumb, speck, iota, jot • a bit of bread
See also: **portion**

bitch noun 1 = **vixen**, cow, dragon (informal), nag, scold, fury, spitfire, shrew, harridan, virago, termagant (rare), harpy, ballbreaker (slang), biach, biatch (slang)
▶ verb 2 (Informal) = **complain**, object, lament, bemoan, grumble, gripe (informal), grouse

bitchy adjective (Informal) = **spiteful**, mean, nasty, vindictive, catty (informal), snide, backbiting

bite verb 1 = **nip**, chew, nibble, gnaw • His cat bit me when I tried to pat it.
▶ noun 2 = **wound**, nip, pinch, prick, sting, tooth marks
3 = **snack**, food, piece, taste, mouthful, refreshment, light meal, morsel
See also: **savage**

> INFORMALLY SPEAKING
> **bite someone's head off**: be sharply angry with someone
> **bite your tongue**: keep from saying something
> **put the bite on**: demand money from
> **take a bite out of**: use up a large part of

biting adjective 1 = **piercing**, sharp, bitter, harsh, cutting, penetrating
2 = **sarcastic**, scathing, cutting, vitriolic, caustic, incisive, mordant, stinging, trenchant

bitter adjective 1 = **resentful**, sour, acrimonious, rancorous, begrudging, embittered • a bitter argument
2 = **sour**, sharp, acid, tart, acrid, astringent • the pill

has a bitter taste
OPPOSITE: sweet
3 = freezing, severe, intense, fierce, biting, stinging
See also: **cold**

bitterness noun **1 = sourness**, acidity, sharpness, acerbity, tartness
2 = resentment, hostility, grudge, animosity, sarcasm, acrimony, asperity, rancour

bizarre adjective **= strange**, odd, unusual, extraordinary, fantastic, weird, curious, eccentric, ludicrous, peculiar, outlandish, zany, queer, freakish • He has some bizarre ideas about gardening.
OPPOSITE: ordinary

blab verb **= tell**, reveal, disclose, divulge, blurt out, give away, let slip, let the cat out of the bag, spill the beans (informal)

black adjective **1 = dark**, jet, raven, dusky, ebony, sable, swarthy
2 = hopeless, sad, dismal, gloomy, ominous, sombre, depressing, foreboding
3 = angry, hostile, furious, sullen, resentful, menacing, threatening
4 = wicked, bad, evil, nefarious, villainous, iniquitous • a black day for the livestock industry
▷ **black magic = witchcraft**, sorcery, wizardry, black art, diabolism, necromancy, voodoo
▷ **black sheep = disgrace**, dropout, bad egg (old-fashioned informal), renegade, outcast, prodigal, reprobate, wastrel

---

SHADES OF BLACK

ebony	pitch
inky	black
jet	raven
jet black	sable

---

blacken verb **1 = darken**, cloud, soil, dirty, smudge, befoul, begrime, make black
2 = discredit, smear, defame, vilify, malign, slander, denigrate, smirch

blackguard noun **= scoundrel**, bastard (offensive), rogue, villain, swine, rascal

blacklist verb **= exclude**, ban, reject, bar, boycott, expel, snub, debar

blackmail noun **1 = threat**, ransom, intimidation, extortion, hush money (slang)
▶ verb **2 = threaten**, demand, squeeze, compel, intimidate, coerce, extort, hold to ransom

blackness noun **= darkness**, gloom, duskiness, murkiness, swarthiness

blackout noun **1 = power failure** or **power outage**, blown fuse, electricity failure
2 = unconsciousness, coma, faint, oblivion, swoon, loss of consciousness
3 = noncommunication, censorship, secrecy, suppression, radio silence, withholding news

blame verb **1 = hold responsible**, charge, accuse • Don't blame me for this trouble.
▶ noun **2 = responsibility**, fault, accountability, liability, culpability, incrimination • I'm not going to take the blame for that!
See also: **censure, condemn**

blameless adjective **= innocent**, clean, perfect, impeccable, immaculate, unblemished, virtuous, above suspicion, faultless, guiltless, irreproachable

blameworthy adjective **= reprehensible**, shameful, inexcusable, indefensible, discreditable, disreputable, iniquitous, reproachable

bland adjective **= dull**, flat, boring, tasteless, humdrum, insipid, unexciting, uninspiring, vapid

blank adjective **1 = unmarked**, clear, clean, empty, plain, bare • a blank sheet of paper
2 = impassive, empty, vacant, dull, deadpan • a blank expression on his face
▶ noun **3 = empty space**, space,

b

b

gap, void, vacuum, vacancy, emptiness, nothingness
See also: **ignore**

blanket *noun* **1 = cover**, coverlet
2 = covering, sheet, layer, coat, carpet, cloak, mantle
▸ *verb* **3 = cover**, hide, mask, coat, cloak, suppress, conceal, obscure

blare *verb* **= sound out**, blast, scream, roar, trumpet, resound, clamour, clang

blaring *See* **loud**

blaspheme *verb* **= curse**, abuse, swear, damn, desecrate, profane, revile, execrate

blasphemous *adjective*
= irreverent, profane, sacrilegious, godless, impious, irreligious, ungodly

blasphemy *noun* **= irreverence**, profanity, desecration, swearing, cursing, execration, impiety, sacrilege

blast *noun* **1 = explosion**, crash, burst, bang, discharge, outburst, eruption, salvo, volley, detonation
2 = blare, blow, scream, wail, honk, clang, peal, toot
3 = launch, shot, firing, projection, discharge, liftoff, expulsion, launching
▸ *verb* **4 = blow up**, destroy, explode, burst, ruin, shatter, demolish, break up, put paid to

blasé *adjective* **= indifferent**, lukewarm, apathetic, unconcerned, nonchalant, offhand

blatant *adjective* **= obvious**, brazen, flagrant, overt, glaring, conspicuous, obtrusive, ostentatious

blaze *noun* **1 = fire**, bonfire, conflagration, flames
2 = glare, light, flash, flare, beam, glow, glitter, brilliance, gleam, radiance
▸ *verb* **3 = burn**, fire, flame
4 = shine, flash, flare, beam, glow, glare, gleam

bleach *verb* **= whiten**, fade, lighten, blanch, grow pale, wash out

bleached *See* **light**

bleak *adjective* **1 = bare**, exposed, barren, desolate, windswept, unsheltered, weather-beaten
2 = dismal, grim, gloomy, dreary, hopeless, sombre, cheerless, depressing, discouraging, joyless

bleary *adjective* **= blurred**, misty, murky, dim, fuzzy, hazy, blurry, foggy, indistinct

bleed *verb* **1 = hemorrhage**, run, flow, spurt, gush, ooze, lose blood, shed blood
2 = draw blood *or* **take blood**, extract, leech
3 (*Informal*) **= extort**, milk, drain, squeeze, exhaust, fleece

blemish *noun* **1 = mark**, flaw, defect, fault, taint, stain, blot, smudge, imperfection, disfigurement
▸ *verb* **2 = stain**, mark, damage, injure, spoil, taint, impair, mar, tarnish, disfigure, sully

blend *verb* **1 = mix**, combine, merge, mingle • *Blend the butter with the sugar.*
OPPOSITE: separate
2 = harmonize, match, suit, co-ordinate, complement, go well • *The colours blend with the rest of the decor.*
▸ *noun* **3 = mixture**, mix, combination, compound, alloy, fusion, amalgamation • *a blend of juice and sparkling water*
See also: **cross, union**

bless *verb* **1 = consecrate**, dedicate, hallow • *The priest blessed the congregation.*
OPPOSITE: curse
2 = grant, give, provide, favour, grace, bestow

blessed *adjective* **= holy**, sacred, divine, hallowed, adored, beatified, revered, sanctified

blessing *noun* **1 = benefit**, help, gift, boon, godsend • *Good health is a blessing.*
OPPOSITE: disadvantage
2 = approval, leave, support, permission, consent, backing • *They got married with their parents' blessing.*

OPPOSITE: disapproval
3 = benediction, dedication, grace, commendation, benison, consecration, invocation, thanksgiving
See also: **sanction**

blight noun **1 = curse**, pollution, corruption, contamination, plague, evil, woe, scourge, affliction, bane
2 = disease, fungus, infestation, pest, decay, rot, canker, mildew, pestilence
▶ verb **3 = frustrate**, disappoint, crush, ruin, spoil, wreck, mar, dash, undo

blind adjective **1 = visually impaired**, sightless, eyeless, unseeing, unsighted, visionless
2 = unaware of, ignorant, oblivious, careless, indifferent, insensitive, heedless, inattentive, inconsiderate, unconscious of
3 = unreasoning, indiscriminate, prejudiced
▶ noun **4 = cover**, front, screen, mask, cloak, camouflage, masquerade, façade, feint, smoke screen

blindly adverb **1 = thoughtlessly**, recklessly, carelessly, heedlessly, inconsiderately, senselessly
2 = aimlessly, indiscriminately, instinctively, at random

blink verb **1 = wink**, bat, flutter
2 = flicker, shine, flash, gleam, glimmer, wink, twinkle
▶ noun
▷ **on the blink** (Slang)
= broken, faulty, not working or not working properly, malfunctioning, out of action, out of order, playing up

bliss noun **= joy**, happiness, heaven, paradise, ecstasy, euphoria, nirvana, rapture, beatitude, blessedness, blissfulness, felicity, gladness

blissful adjective **= joyful**, happy, ecstatic, heavenly (informal), euphoric, elated, enraptured, rapturous

blister noun **= sore**, boil, abscess, pimple, carbuncle, cyst, pustule, swelling

blithe adjective **= heedless**, casual, careless, indifferent, thoughtless, unconcerned, nonchalant, untroubled

blitz noun **= attack**, strike, campaign, assault, offensive, raid, bombardment, onslaught, blitzkrieg

blizzard noun **= snowstorm**, storm, blast, squall, tempest, gale

bloat verb **= puff up**, expand, swell, balloon, inflate, enlarge, dilate, blow up, distend

blob noun **= drop**, bead, droplet, dab • He had a blob of pudding on his tie.

bloc noun **= group**, union, league, coalition, alliance, faction, axis

block noun **1 = piece**, bar, brick, chunk, lump, ingot • a block of wood
2 = obstruction, bar, barrier, jam, obstacle, impediment, blockage, hindrance
▶ verb **3 = obstruct**, choke, plug, clog • Mud blocked the river.
OPPOSITE: unblock
4 = prevent, stop, check, bar, halt, thwart, obstruct • The committee blocked his plans.
See also: **close, frustrate, hinder, impede**

blockade noun **= stoppage**, block, restriction, barrier, obstacle, obstruction, siege, barricade, impediment, hindrance

blockage noun **= obstruction**, block • a blockage in the pipe

blockhead noun **= idiot**, fool, chump (informal), dork (slang), dunce, nitwit, schmuck (slang), thickhead, idiot, dummy, moron, halfwit, jackanapes, lemming, bozo

blond, blonde adjective **= fair**, light, fair-haired, fair-skinned, flaxen, golden-haired, tow-headed
See also: **fair, light**

blood noun **1 = lifeblood**, gore, vital fluid
2 = family, birth, descent, extraction, ancestry, lineage,

b

kinship, relations

bloodcurdling *adjective*
= **terrifying**, fearful,
horrendous, appalling,
dreadful, hair-raising, chilling,
frightening, horrifying, scaring,
spine-chilling

bloodshed *noun* = **killing**,
murder, slaughter, massacre,
slaying, carnage, gore, blood
bath, blood-letting, butchery

bloodthirsty *adjective* = **cruel**,
brutal, vicious, murderous,
ferocious, savage, gory,
barbarous, cut-throat, warlike

bloody *adjective* 1 = **bloodstained**,
raw, blood-soaked, bleeding,
blood-spattered, gaping
2 = **cruel**, fierce, ferocious,
savage, sanguinary

bloom *noun* 1 = **flower**, opening
(of flowers), blossom, bud,
blossoming, efflorescence
2 = **prime**, health, beauty, glow,
heyday, vigour, lustre, freshness,
flourishing, radiance
▶ *verb* 3 = **blossom**, open, blow,
burgeon, bud, sprout
4 = **flourish**, grow, develop,
succeed, thrive, wax, prosper,
fare well

blooming See **well**

blossom *noun* 1 = **flower**, bloom,
bud, floret, flowers
▶ *verb* 2 = **flower**, burgeon,
bloom
3 = **grow**, develop, progress,
mature, thrive, flourish, bloom,
prosper

blot *noun* 1 = **spot**, mark, patch,
smear, speck, smudge, blotch,
splodge
2 = **stain**, spot, flaw, defect,
fault, taint, scar, blemish
▶ *verb* 3 = **stain**, mark, spot,
spoil, disgrace, tarnish, smudge,
sully, smirch
4 = **soak up**, dry, absorb, take up
▷ **blot out** = **obliterate**, destroy,
shadow, eclipse, obscure,
darken, efface; = **erase**, cancel,
expunge

blotch See **spot**

blow[1] *verb* 1 = **gust**, drive, sweep,
buffet, flutter, whirl, waft • *The*
wind blew his papers away.
2 = **exhale**, breathe, pant, puff
3 = **play**, sound, mouth, pipe,
trumpet, blare, vibrate, toot
▷ **blow out** = **put out**, snuff,
extinguish; = **burst**, explode,
erupt, shatter, rupture, fracture,
break, split open
▷ **blow up** = **explode**, bomb,
blast, burst, detonate, shatter,
rupture, blow sky-high;
= **inflate**, fill, expand, swell,
enlarge, bloat, distend, puff
up, pump up; (*Informal*) = **lose**
one's temper, erupt, rage,
become angry, fly off the handle
(*informal*), hit the roof (*informal*),
see red (*informal*)
See also: **sound**

INFORMALLY SPEAKING
blow away: astonish
blow over: pass by or be
forgotten
blow your mind: amaze you

blow[2] *noun* 1 = **knock**, bang,
thump, smack, whack • *a blow to*
the head
2 = **shock**, upset, setback,
disappointment, jolt,
catastrophe, bombshell,
calamity, misfortune • *Our third*
loss in overtime was a major blow.
See also: **hit**

bludgeon *noun* 1 = **club**,
truncheon, cudgel
▶ *verb* 2 = **club**, beat up, strike,
cudgel, knock down
3 = **bully**, force, coerce, railroad
(*informal*), bulldoze (*informal*),
steamroller

blue *adjective* 1 = **azure**, navy,
cobalt, sapphire, cerulean, cyan,
sky-coloured, ultramarine
2 = **depressed**, low, sad,
unhappy, dejected, melancholy,
despondent, downcast
3 = **smutty**, obscene, indecent,
lewd, X-rated (*informal*), risqué

blueprint *noun* = **plan**, design,
draft, outline, pattern, sketch,
prototype, pilot scheme

blues *plural noun* = **depression**,
gloom, unhappiness, doldrums,
melancholy, dumps (*informal*),
low spirits

bluff[1] *verb* **1 = deceive**, fake, mislead, con, pretend, delude, feign, pull the wool over someone's eyes
▶ *noun* **2 = deception**, fraud, sham, deceit, pretense, bravado, bluster, subterfuge, humbug

bluff[2] *noun* **1 = precipice**, bank, peak, cliff, ridge, escarpment, headland, crag, promontory
▶ *adjective* **2 = hearty**, open, outspoken, blunt, good-natured, genial, blustering, plain-spoken

blunder *noun* **1 = mistake**, blooper (*informal*), foul-up (*slang*), faux pas, indiscretion
2 = error, slip, mistake, fault, oversight, inaccuracy, slip-up (*informal*), screw-up
▶ *verb* **3 = make a mistake**, err, botch, bungle, screw up, mess up, foul up (*slang*), slip up (*informal*)
4 = stumble, flounder, bumble

blunt *adjective* **1 = dull**, rounded, unsharpened • *blunt scissors*
OPPOSITE: sharp
2 = frank, outspoken, straightforward, forthright, brusque • *a blunt speaker*
OPPOSITE: tactful
▶ *verb* **3 = dull**, weaken, soften, dampen, numb, deaden, take the edge off, water down
See also: **candid, direct, straight**

blur *verb* **1 = make indistinct**, cloud, mask, obscure, darken, make hazy, make vague
▶ *noun* **2 = indistinctness**, confusion, fog, haze, obscurity

blurt *verb* **blurt out = exclaim**, reveal, disclose, let the cat out of the bag, spill the beans (*informal*), tell all, utter suddenly

blush *verb* **1 = go red**, flush • *I felt myself blushing.*
▶ *noun* **2 = reddening**, colour, glow, flush, pink tinge, rosiness, rosy tint, ruddiness

bluster *verb* **1 = roar**, storm, bully, rant, domineer, hector
▶ *noun* **2 = hot air** (*informal*), bluff, bravado, bombast

blustery *adjective* **= gusty**, violent, wild, stormy, windy, boisterous, inclement, tempestuous, squally

board *noun* **1 = plank**, panel, lumber, timber, slat, piece of timber
2 = directors, committee, panel, council, conclave, advisers, trustees
3 = meals, daily meals, provisions, victuals
▶ *verb* **4 = get on**, enter, mount, embark
5 = lodge, quarter, room, put up

boast *verb* **= brag**, crow • *He boasted about his high marks.*

boaster See **braggart**

boastful *adjective* **= cocky**, conceited, crowing, egotistical, swaggering • *a boastful skateboarder*
OPPOSITE: modest

bob *verb* **= bounce**, duck, nod, hop, wobble, wiggle, oscillate

bode *verb* **= portend**, threaten, predict, signify, augur, foretell, forebode, be an omen of

bodily *adjective* **= physical**, material, substantial, actual, tangible, corporal, carnal, corporeal

body *noun* **1 = physique**, build, figure, form, shape, frame • *My*

SHADES OF BLUE

aqua	gentian	robin's-egg blue
aquamarine	indigo	royal blue
azure	lapis lazuli	sapphire
cerulean	midnight blue	sky blue
cobalt	navy	teal
cyan	peacock blue	turquoise
electric blue	periwinkle	

whole body hurts!
RELATED WORDS
adjectives: corporal, physical
2 = **corpse**, carcass, dead body,
remains • *a body buried in the forest*
3 = **organization**, company,
band, society, association,
corporation, confederation
• *local voluntary bodies*
4 = **torso**, trunk
5 = **main part**, matter, material,
mass, substance, bulk, essence
bog *noun* = **marsh**, swamp, mire,
quagmire, slough, muskeg
(*Canad*), morass, fen, wetlands
bogey *noun* = **bugbear**,
nightmare, bête noire, bugaboo
boggle *See* **wonder**
bogus *adjective* = **fake**, false,
counterfeit, artificial,
fraudulent, phony (*informal*),
sham, imitation, forged
bohemian *adjective*
1 = **unconventional**, alternative,
artistic, unorthodox, offbeat,
artsy or artsy-fartsy (*informal*),
left bank, nonconformist
▶ *noun* **2** = **nonconformist**,
dropout, hippie, beatnik,
iconoclast
boil[1] *verb* = **bubble**, foam, froth,
fizz • *The water is boiling.*
See also: **cook**

> INFORMALLY SPEAKING
> **boil down**: reduce to essentials
> **boil over**: let excitement or
> anger show

boil[2] *noun* = **swelling**, tumour,
blister • *a boil on my neck*
boiling *See* **hot**
boisterous *adjective* = **unruly**,

wild, loud, noisy, disorderly,
rowdy, vociferous, unrestrained,
riotous, rollicking
bold *adjective* **1** = **impudent**,
forward, confident, brazen,
cheeky, brash • *a bold question*
OPPOSITE: shy
2 = **fearless**, brave, daring,
courageous, valiant,
adventurous, intrepid • *a bold
attempt*
OPPOSITE: cowardly
3 = **bright**, strong, loud, striking,
vivid, flashy • *bold colours*
OPPOSITE: dull
boldness *noun* = **daring**, bravery,
impudence
bolster *verb* = **support**, help,
boost, strengthen, reinforce,
augment, shore up
bolt *verb* **1** = **run away**, fly, rush,
escape, flee, dash, run off, take
off • *I bolted toward the exit.*
2 = **lock**, bar, secure, latch, fasten
3 = **gobble**, stuff, wolf, cram,
guzzle, devour, gorge, gulp,
swallow whole
▶ *noun* **4** = **bar**, catch, lock, latch,
fastener, deadbolt, sliding bar
5 = **pin**, peg, rod, rivet
See also: **run**
bomb *noun* **1** = **explosive**, device,
mine, rocket, missile, shell,
grenade, firebomb, torpedo,
projectile • *The bomb exploded near
the city.*
▶ *verb* **2** = **bombard**, attack,
destroy, shell, firebomb, torpedo,
blow up • *London, England, was
heavily bombed during World War II.*
bombard *verb* **1** = **bomb**, assault,

TYPES OF BOAT

barge	gondola	punt
canoe	houseboat	rowboat
coracle	iceboat	sailboat
cruiser or	junk	speedboat
cabin cruiser	kayak	umiak (*Canad*)
dinghy	ketch	yacht
dugout	longliner	
ferry	motorboat	

b

```
┌──────────────────────────────────────────────────────────────┐
│                     PARTS OF A BOOK                          │
│                                                              │
│   acknowledgments      dust jacket        introduction       │
│   appendix             footnote           layout             │
│   bibliography         foreword           line               │
│   blurb                glossary           page               │
│   caption              heading            preface            │
│   chapter              illustration       table of contents  │
│   cover                index              title              │
│                                                              │
└──────────────────────────────────────────────────────────────┘
```

pound, shell, blitz, strafe, fire
upon, open fire
2 = attack, harass, hound, assail,
beset, besiege, pester

bombardment noun = **bombing**,
attack, assault, blitz, barrage,
fusillade, shelling

bombastic adjective
= **grandiloquent**, inflated,
grandiose, pompous, verbose,
high-flown, wordy

bombshell noun **1 = complete
surprise**, shock, revelation, jolt,
bolt from the blue
2 (Slang) = **beautiful woman**,
beauty, knockout, babe (informal),
hottie (slang), vixen, cutie,
temptress, looker (old-fashioned,
informal)

bona fide adjective = **genuine**,
real, true, actual, legitimate,
honest, authentic, kosher
(informal)

bond noun **1 = tie**, link, union,
connection, relationship,
attachment, affinity • a special
bond between us
2 = agreement, contract,
promise, word, pledge,
obligation • the bonds of marriage

3 = fastening, tie, chain, cord,
shackle, fetter, ligature, manacle
▶ verb **4 = fix**, tape, bind, paste,
glue, fuse, fasten • strips of wood
bonded together
See also: **association, relation,
stick**

bondage noun = **slavery**,
imprisonment, confinement,
captivity, enslavement,
subjugation

bonds See **stock**

bonus noun = **extra**, gift, reward,
plus, dividend, premium, prize,
icing on the cake

bony adjective = **thin**, lean, skinny,
gaunt, scrawny, emaciated, skin
and bone

book noun **1 = work**, title, volume,
publication, textbook, tome
(formal) • I'm reading a great book.
2 = notebook, album, pad, diary,
exercise book, jotter, scribbler
(Canad)
▶ verb **3 = reserve**, schedule,
organize, engage, charter • The
tickets for the cruise are booked.
4 = note, record, list, enter,
register, log, mark down, put
down, write down

```
┌──────────────────────────────────────────────────────────────┐
│                     TYPES OF BOOK                            │
│                                                              │
│   anthology            fiction            novel              │
│   atlas                gazetteer          phrasebook         │
│   autobiography        glossary           short stories      │
│   biography            guidebook          textbook           │
│   dictionary           handbook           thesaurus          │
│   directory            manual                                │
│   encyclopedia         nonfiction                            │
│                                                              │
└──────────────────────────────────────────────────────────────┘
```

b

by the book: according to the rules
in my book: in my opinion
throw the book at: punish as severely as the law allows

booklet noun = **brochure**, leaflet, pamphlet

boom verb **1** = **bang**, crash, blast, roll, explode, roar, rumble, thunder, resound, reverberate
2 = **flourish**, increase, grow, develop, expand, strengthen, swell, intensify, thrive, prosper
▶ noun **3** = **bang**, crash, blast, explosion, burst, roar, rumble, thunder, clap
4 = **expansion**, increase, growth, boost, jump, development, improvement, upswing, upsurge, upturn

boon noun = **benefit**, advantage, favour, gift, blessing, windfall, godsend, manna from heaven

boorish adjective = **loutish**, crude, vulgar, coarse, uncivilized, churlish, oafish, uncouth

boost noun **1** = **help**, praise, promotion, encouragement
2 = **rise**, increase, jump, addition, expansion, improvement, increment
▶ verb **3** = **increase**, raise, develop, expand, heighten, amplify, enlarge, add to
4 = **advertise**, further, promote, encourage, praise, foster, hype, plug (informal)

boot verb = **kick**, drive, knock, punt, drop-kick, shove

booty noun = **plunder**, haul, loot, prey, swag (slang), gains, spoils, takings, winnings

booze See **alcohol, drink**

border noun **1** = **frontier**, line, boundary, borderline • the border between two countries
2 = **edge**, margin, rim, bounds, limits • plain tiles with a bright border
▶ verb **3** = **edge**, trim, rim, fringe • Tall trees bordered the fields.
See also: **coast**

borderline See **border**

bore¹ verb = **drill**, mine, sink,

tunnel, penetrate, pierce, burrow, gouge out, perforate

bore² verb **1** = **tire**, fatigue, weary, be tedious, jade, pall on, send to sleep, wear out
▶ noun **2** = **nuisance**, pain (informal), geek (slang), nudnik (informal)
3 = **pain** (informal), yawn (informal)

bored adjective = **fed up**, tired, uninterested, wearied • I am bored with this movie.
OPPOSITE: interested
See also: **sick of**

boredom noun = **weariness**, apathy, dullness, flatness, monotony, tedium • the boredom of long trips
OPPOSITE: interest

boring adjective = **dull**, flat, stale, tedious, tiresome, monotonous, humdrum, meh (slang), insipid, repetitious • a boring job
OPPOSITE: interesting
See also: **dreary**

borrow verb **1** = **take on loan**, mooch, scrounge (informal), use temporarily
2 = **steal**, take, adopt, copy, obtain, plagiarize, usurp

CONFUSABLES
Borrow means get.
Lend means give.

bosom noun **1** = **breast**, bust, chest
▶ adjective **2** = **intimate**, close, confidential, boon, dear, cherished, very dear

boss¹ noun = **head**, leader, director, chief, manager, employer, big cheese (informal) • His boss insisted he get to work on time.
▶ verb
▷ **boss around** (Informal) = **domineer**, order, dominate, bully, oppress, push around (slang)
See also: **superior**

boss² noun = **stud**, point, tip, knob, protuberance

bosses See **management**

bossy adjective = **domineering**, arrogant, authoritarian, dictatorial, imperious,

overbearing • *a rather bossy little child*
See also: **pushy**

botch verb = **mess up**, mar, bungle • *a botched operation*
▷ **botch up** See **mess**

bother verb 1 = **disturb**, concern, worry, trouble, upset, distress, harass, inconvenience, annoy, irritate, agitate, pester, get on someone's nerves (*informal*), piss off (*taboo slang*), tee off (*slang*) • *His lack of money bothers him.*
▶ noun 2 = **trouble**, concern, worry, strain, difficulty, distress, inconvenience, fuss, hassle, nuisance, irritation, annoyance • *I hate the bother of shopping.*

bothered See **anxious, worried**

bottle noun
▶ verb
bottle up = **suppress**, contain, check, restrict, trap, curb, keep back, shut in

bottleneck noun = **hold-up**, block, jam or traffic jam, obstacle, obstruction, congestion, impediment, blockage

bottom noun 1 = **base**, foot, floor, bed, depths • *the bottom of the stairs*
OPPOSITE: top
2 = **underside**, sole, underneath, lower side
3 = **buttocks**, behind (*informal*), seat, butt, rear, informal, bum, backside, posterior, rump, tush (*slang*), buns
▶ adjective 4 = **lowest**, ground, basement • *the bottom drawer*
OPPOSITE: highest

bottomless adjective
= **unlimited**, deep, infinite, immeasurable, unfathomable, inexhaustible, boundless, fathomless

bounce verb 1 = **rebound**, jump, bump, bound, bob, ricochet • *I bounced a ball against the wall.*
▶ noun 2 (*Informal*) = **life**, go (*informal*), energy, zip (*informal*), vigour, dynamism, liveliness, vivacity

3 = **springiness**, give, spring, resilience, recoil, elasticity
See also: **glance, leap**

bound¹ adjective 1 = **tied**, secured, fastened, fixed, pinioned, tied up
2 = **certain**, sure, doomed, destined, fated
3 = **obliged**, committed, required, forced, beholden, compelled, constrained, duty-bound, pledged

bound² verb = **limit**, surround, restrict, restrain, confine, enclose, encircle, demarcate, hem in

bound³ verb, noun = **leap**, jump, spring, bounce, skip, hurdle, vault, bob, gambol

boundary noun = **limits**, border, edge, margin, barrier, brink, fringe, frontier, borderline, extremity

boundless adjective = **unlimited**, vast, endless, immense, infinite, untold, inexhaustible, incalculable, unconfined

bounds plural noun = **boundary**, border, limit, edge, rim, verge, confine, extremity

bountiful adjective (*Literary*)
1 = **plentiful**, prolific, lavish, ample, abundant, exuberant, copious, bounteous, luxuriant
2 = **generous**, liberal, magnanimous, open-handed, prodigal, unstinting

bounty noun (*Literary*)
1 = **generosity**, charity, kindness, largesse or largess, philanthropy, benevolence, liberality
2 = **reward**, present, gift, bonus

bouquet noun 1 = **bunch of flowers**, spray, wreath, garland, buttonhole, corsage, nosegay, posy
2 = **aroma**, scent, perfume, savour, fragrance, redolence

bourgeois adjective = **middle-class**, traditional, conventional, materialistic, hidebound

bout noun 1 = **period**, term, turn, fit, spell, stint

b

2 = **fight**, match, struggle, competition, contest, encounter, engagement, boxing match, set-to

boutique See **store**

bovine See **cow**

bow[1] verb 1 = **bend**, nod, bob, stoop, droop, genuflect
2 = **give in**, submit, surrender, comply, concede, yield, defer, succumb, relent, acquiesce, kowtow
▶ noun 3 = **bending**, nod, bob, genuflexion, kowtow, obeisance

bow[2] noun (Nautical) = **prow**, head, stem, beak, fore

bowels plural noun 1 = **guts**, entrails, innards (informal), insides (informal), intestines, viscera, vitals
2 = **depths**, inside, deep, core, interior, belly

bowl noun = **basin**, vessel, dish

box[1] noun = **carton**, case, container, chest, trunk • All her possessions were packed in boxes.

box[2] verb = **fight**, spar, exchange blows

boxer noun = **fighter**, pugilist, prizefighter, sparring partner

boy noun = **lad**, fellow, schoolboy • I knew him several years ago, when he was a boy.

boycott verb = **spurn**, reject, exclude, embargo, blacklist, proscribe, refrain from • Some voters are boycotting the election. See also: **sanctions**

boyfriend noun = **sweetheart**, man, date, lover, suitor, admirer, beau

boyish adjective = **youthful**, young, adolescent, juvenile, childish, immature, puerile

brace noun 1 = **support**, stay, bolster, prop, bracket, reinforcement, truss, buttress, strut
▶ verb 2 = **support**, strengthen, steady, bolster, reinforce, fortify, buttress

bracing adjective = **refreshing**, fresh, crisp, brisk, exhilarating, invigorating, stimulating

brag verb = **boast**, crow • They never stop bragging about their achievements.

braggart noun = **boaster**, bigmouth (slang), bragger, show-off • He's a braggart and a liar.

bragger See **braggart**

bragging See **boastful**

braid verb = **interweave**, weave, lace, intertwine, entwine, interlace, twine, plait

brain noun 1 = **cerebrum**, mind, grey matter (informal)
2 (Informal) = **intellectual**, mastermind, scholar, sage, pundit, genius, intellect, prodigy, egghead (informal), highbrow, bluestocking (usually derogatory), brainbox
RELATED WORD
adjective: cerebral

brainless adjective = **stupid**, foolish, senseless, mindless, idiotic, thoughtless, inane, witless

brains plural noun = **intelligence**, sense, understanding, intellect

brainteaser See **puzzle**

brainwave noun = **idea**, thought, bright idea, stroke of genius

brainy adjective (Informal) = **intelligent**, smart, bright, brilliant, clever

brake noun 1 = **control**, check, curb, rein, restraint, constraint
▶ verb 2 = **slow**, stop, check, halt, moderate, decelerate, slacken, reduce speed

branch noun 1 = **bough**, shoot, arm, spray, limb, offshoot, sprig
2 = **division**, part, office, department, section, wing, chapter, subdivision, subsection

brand noun 1 = **label**, sign, mark, stamp, symbol, marker, trademark, logo, hallmark, emblem
2 = **kind**, make, type, quality, class, cast, sort, variety, species, grade
▶ verb 3 = **mark**, burn, label, stamp, scar, burn in
4 = **stigmatize**, mark, expose, denounce, disgrace, discredit, censure

brandish verb = **wave**, raise,

display, shake, exhibit, swing, parade, flourish, wield, flaunt

brash *adjective* = **bold**, rude, brazen, cocky, impertinent, impudent, insolent, pushy (*informal*)

bravado *noun* = **swagger**, bluster, swashbuckling, boastfulness, boasting, bombast, vaunting

brave *adjective* 1 = **courageous**, bold, heroic, daring, valiant, plucky, fearless, intrepid, valorous • *a brave attempt to stop the attack*
OPPOSITE: cowardly
▶ *verb* 2 = **face**, stand up to • *Fans braved the rain to hear him sing.*

bravery *noun* = **courage**, pluck, valour, heroism, mettle, fortitude, boldness, fearlessness • *He deserves praise for his bravery.*
OPPOSITE: cowardice
See also: **daring**

brawl *noun* 1 = **fight**, dispute, clash, scuffle, skirmish, altercation, melee, fray, fracas, punch-up (*informal*), affray (*law*), rumpus
▶ *verb* 2 = **fight**, scrap (*informal*), wrestle, scuffle, tussle

brawn *noun* = **muscle**, power, might, beef (*informal*), strength, vigour, muscles

brawny *adjective* = **muscular**, strong, powerful, hefty (*informal*), beefy (*informal*), sturdy, lusty, strapping, well-built

brazen *adjective* = **bold**, defiant, audacious, shameless, brash, unabashed, barefaced, impudent, insolent, unashamed

breach *noun* 1 = **infringement**, offence, violation • *a breach of confidence*
2 = **crack**, opening, hole, split, gap, rift • *the breach in the wall*
See also: **break, division**

bread *noun* 1 = **food**, fare,

TYPES OF BREAD

bagel	farmhouse	pita
baguette	flatbread	plait
bannock (*Canad*)	focaccia	poppadom *or*
batch loaf	French bread	poppadum
black bread	French stick	pumpernickel
bloomer	fruit loaf	puri
bridge roll	fry bread	quartern
brioche	garlic bread	roll
brown bread	griddlebread	roti
bun	half-quartern	rusk
butterhorn	injera	rye bread
buttery (*Scot*)	johnny cake	schnecken
challah *or*	kaiser roll	soda bread
hallah	loaf	sourdough
chapati *or*	matzo	split tin
chapatti	Montreal	square tin
ciabatta	bagel (*Canad*)	stollen
cob	muffin	tortilla
coburg	multigrain	touton
cornbread	nan	(*Newfoundland*)
cottage loaf	pan bread *or*	unleavened bread
cracked wheat	loaf (*Scot*)	white bread
crescent roll	panettone	whole grain
croissant	panino	whole-wheat
egg bread	paratha	zwieback
English muffin	paska (*Canad*)	

nourishment, sustenance

2 (*Slang*) = **money**, cash, dough (*slang*)

breadth *noun* **1** = **width**, spread, span, latitude, broadness, wideness

2 = **extent**, range, scale, scope, compass, expanse

break *verb* **1** = **fracture**, destroy, crack, split, burst, smash, shatter, fragment, snap, disintegrate, separate • *I broke a plate.*

2 = **breach**, violate, infringe, contravene • *He broke his promise to attend.*

3 = **reveal**, tell, announce, disclose, inform, proclaim, divulge, impart, let out, make public

4 = **stop**, cut, rest, suspend, abandon, pause, interrupt, discontinue, give up

5 = **weaken**, undermine, subdue, tame, demoralize, dispirit

6 (~ *a record, etc.*) = **beat**, top, surpass, exceed, better, excel, outstrip, outdo, go beyond

▷ **break down** = **collapse**, stop, fail, malfunction, come unstuck, seize up, stop working; = **be overcome**, crack up (*informal*), go to pieces

▷ **break free** *See* **escape**

▷ **break into** *See* **raid**

▷ **break off** = **detach**, part, separate, divide, sever, splinter, pull off, snap off; = **stop**, end, finish, suspend, halt, cease, terminate, discontinue, desist, pull the plug on

▷ **break out** = **begin**, start, appear, happen, occur, emerge, arise, commence, set in, spring up

▷ **break up** = **separate**, part, split, divorce, divide, dissolve, scatter, sever; = **stop**, end, suspend, dismantle, adjourn, terminate, disband

▷ **break your promise** *See* **betray**

▶ *noun* **7** = **interval**, rest, pause, intermission, recess, hiatus, respite, interlude • *I took a five-minute break from work.*

8 = **division**, opening, hole, tear, split, crack, gap, fracture, fissure

9 (*Informal*) = **stroke of luck**, chance, opportunity, advantage, opening, fortune

▷ **break-in** = **burglary**, robbery, breaking and entering

See also: **burst, dash, disobey, holiday, ruin**

> **INFORMALLY SPEAKING**
> **break down**: stop functioning
> **break even**: gain nothing and lose nothing
> **break off**: stop suddenly

breakable *adjective* = **fragile**, delicate, frail, brittle, flimsy, crumbly, frangible, friable

breakdown *noun* = **collapse**, failure, malfunction, disruption, stoppage, mishap, disintegration

breaker *See* **wave**

breakfast *See* **eat**

breakneck *See* **furious**

breakthrough *noun* = **development**, find, advance, progress, discovery, invention, leap, quantum leap, step forward

breakup *See* **split**

breast *noun* = **bosom**, front, bust, chest, udder, teat

breath *noun* = **respiration**, pant, breathing, wheeze, inhalation, gasp, gulp, exhalation

breathe *verb* **1** = **inhale and exhale**, pant, wheeze, puff, gasp, gulp, draw in, respire

2 = **whisper**, sigh, murmur

breather *noun* (*Informal*) = **rest**, break, halt, pause, recess, respite, breathing space

breathing *See* **alive**

breathless *adjective* **1** = **out of breath**, spent, gasping, gulping, panting, short-winded, wheezing

2 = **excited**, eager, open-mouthed, on tenterhooks, wired (*slang*), with bated breath

breathtaking *adjective* = **amazing**, cool (*informal*), impressive, exciting, thrilling, sensational, magnificent, awe-inspiring, astonishing, phat (*slang*), stunning (*informal*)

breed *noun* **1 = variety**, stock, kind, type, strain, species • *What breed of dog shall we get?*
2 = kind, type, brand, sort, variety, stamp
▶ *verb* **3 = rear**, keep, raise, develop, nurture, cultivate • *They breed dogs at the farm.*
4 = reproduce, produce, multiply, propagate • *Frogs can breed in most ponds.*
5 = produce, cause, create, generate, arouse, bring about, give rise to, stir up

breeding *noun* **1 = upbringing**, development, training, reproduction, nurture, cultivation, ancestry, raising, lineage, rearing
2 = refinement, conduct, culture, courtesy, polish, cultivation, sophistication, urbanity

breeze *noun* **1 = light wind**, air, draft, gust, waft, breath of wind, current of air, zephyr
▶ *verb* **2 = move briskly**, pass, sweep, sail, hurry, glide, flit

breezy *adjective* **1 = windy**, fresh, gusty, blustery, airy, blowy, squally
2 = carefree, casual, lively, easy-going, light-hearted, jaunty, blithe, free and easy, sprightly

brevity *noun* **1 = shortness**, briefness, impermanence, transience, transitoriness
2 = conciseness, economy, crispness, curtness, pithiness, succinctness, terseness

brew *verb* **1 = make** (beer), boil, soak, steep, stew, infuse (tea), ferment
2 = develop, start, form, gather, foment, stir up
▶ *noun* **3 = drink**, preparation, beverage, liquor, blend, mixture, infusion, concoction

bribe *verb* **1 = buy off**, reward, corrupt, grease the palm of *or* grease the hand of (*slang*), pay off (*informal*), suborn
▶ *noun* **2 = inducement**,

kickback, backhander (*slang*), allurement, enticement, sweetener (*slang*), pay-off (*informal*)

bribery *noun* **= buying off**, corruption, payola (*informal*), inducement, palm-greasing (*slang*)

bric-a-brac *noun* **= knick-knacks**, baubles, curios, ornaments, trinkets

brick *See* **block**

bridal *adjective* **= matrimonial**, marriage, wedding, marital, conjugal, connubial, nuptial

bridge *noun* **1 = arch**, span, overpass, fixed link (*Canad*), ice bridge (*Canad*), viaduct
▶ *verb* **2 = connect**, link, join, span

bridle *noun* **1 = curb**, control, check, rein, restraint
▶ *verb* **2 = get angry**, bristle, be indignant, draw (oneself) up, get one's back up, raise one's hackles, rear up

brief *adjective* **1 = short**, quick, swift, momentary, fleeting • *a brief appearance on television*
OPPOSITE: long
▶ *verb* **2 = inform**, prime, prepare, advise, instruct, fill in • *The press secretary briefed reporters.*
▶ *noun* **3 = summary**, outline, sketch, abstract, digest, synopsis, epitome, abridgment, précis
See also: **concise**

briefing *noun* **= instructions**, conference, information, preparation, guidance, rundown, directions, priming

briefly *adverb* **= quickly**, shortly, hastily, momentarily, hurriedly, concisely, in a nutshell, in brief

brigade *noun* **= group**, company, team, force, troop, organization, unit, band, squad, corps, outfit

brigand *noun* **= bandit**, robber, outlaw, gangster, desperado, freebooter, highwayman, marauder, plunderer

bright *adjective* **1 = brilliant**, vivid, glowing, luminous,

radiant, dazzling, shining • *a bright light*
OPPOSITE: dull

2 = intelligent, smart, brilliant, clever, ingenious, brainy • *my brightest student*
OPPOSITE: dim

3 = cheerful, happy, lively, merry, jolly, light-hearted • *a bright smile*

4 = sunny, clear, fair, transparent, pleasant, lucid, translucent, cloudless, limpid, unclouded
See also: **acute, astute, bold, colourful, gaudy, glossy, sharp**

brighten *verb* = **make brighter**, shine, glow, illuminate, lighten, gleam, light up

brightness *noun* **1 = shine**, light, intensity, glare, brilliance, incandescence, luminosity, radiance, vividness

2 = intelligence, quickness, sharpness, acuity, cleverness, smartness

brilliance *noun* **1 = brightness**, intensity, dazzle, sparkle, lustre, luminosity, radiance, vividness

2 = talent, excellence, wisdom, distinction, genius, greatness, inventiveness, cleverness

3 = splendour, glamour, grandeur, éclat, illustriousness, magnificence

brilliant *adjective* **1 = bright**, sparkling, vivid, glowing, luminous, radiant, dazzling, gleaming • *a brilliant light*
OPPOSITE: dull

2 = intelligent, sharp, smart, bright, acute, clever, perceptive, sophisticated • *a brilliant student*
OPPOSITE: stupid

3 = splendid, famous, notable, celebrated, outstanding, glorious, magnificent, superb, illustrious
See also: **colourful, glossy, keen, shining, witty**

brim *noun* **1 = rim**, border, edge, margin, brink, lip, verge, skirt

▶ *verb* **2 = be full**, fill, spill, overflow, fill up, hold no more, run over, well over

bring *verb* **1 = take**, lead, carry, transport, convey • *Bring a friend to the party.*

2 = cause, create, produce, effect, occasion, wreak, inflict, result in • *Bring the water to a boil.*

▷ **bring about = cause**, create, produce, generate, make happen • *Her suggestions brought about several big improvements.*

▷ **bring around** See **persuade, reason**

▷ **bring back to** See **remind**

▷ **bring down** See **overthrow, depress**

▷ **bring forward** See **produce**

▷ **bring in** See **earn**

▷ **bring off = accomplish**, perform, achieve, execute, succeed, carry off, pull off

▷ **bring out** See **publish**

▷ **bring to an end** See **end**

▷ **bring to a standstill** See **cripple**

▷ **bring to bear** See **employ**

▷ **bring to light = reveal**, show, discover, unveil, expose, disclose, uncover, unearth, show up, lay bare

▷ **bring up = rear**, support, raise, develop, form, train, teach, breed, educate, nurture; = **mention**, move, raise, propose, introduce, broach, allude to, put forward

brink *noun* = **edge**, border, limit, margin, rim, lip, boundary, verge, skirt, threshold, fringe, frontier, brim

briny See **salty**

brisk *adjective* **1 = lively**, quick, active, busy, energetic, vigorous, spry, bustling, sprightly

2 = invigorating, fresh, sharp, keen, crisp, biting, stimulating, bracing, refreshing, exhilarating, nippy • *The breeze was cool, brisk and invigorating.*

briskly *adverb* = **quickly**, rapidly, actively, promptly, readily, efficiently, smartly, apace, energetically

bristle noun **1** = **hair**, spine, barb, thorn, stubble, whisker, prickle
▶ verb **2** = **stand up**, rise, stand on end
3 = **be angry**, rage, seethe, bridle, flare up, see red

bristling See **thick**

bristly adjective = **hairy**, rough, prickly, stubbly

brittle adjective = **fragile**, delicate, crisp, frail, crumbly, breakable, crumbling, frangible, friable

broach verb **1** = **bring up**, suggest, propose, introduce, mention, open up, raise the subject, speak of, talk of, touch on
2 = **open**, start, crack, tap, puncture, pierce, uncork, draw off

broad adjective **1** = **wide**, large, extensive, vast, thick, ample, spacious, expansive • *His shoulders were broad and his waist narrow*.
OPPOSITE: narrow
2 = **comprehensive**, general, wide, extensive, universal, wide-ranging, sweeping • *A broad range of issues was discussed*.
3 = **general**, rough, vague, approximate, non-specific, sweeping • *a broad outline of Canadian politics*
See also: **widespread**

broadcast noun
1 = **transmission**, show, program, telecast, podcast, webcast
▶ verb **2** = **transmit**, show, air, radio, cable, relay, beam, televise, put on the air
3 = **make public**, report, announce, publish, spread, advertise, circulate, proclaim

broaden verb = **expand**, increase, develop, extend, spread, stretch, supplement, widen, swell, enlarge

broad-minded adjective
= **tolerant**, liberal, unbiased, open-minded, indulgent, permissive, free-thinking, unbigoted, unprejudiced

broadside noun = **attack**, assault, criticism, censure, bombardment, diatribe, denunciation, battering

brochure noun = **booklet**, flyer, circular, leaflet, pamphlet • *a travel brochure*

broke adjective (*Informal*)
= **penniless**, short, bust (*informal*), impoverished, bankrupt, insolvent, down and out, down on one's luck (*informal*), in the red, ruined

broken adjective **1** = **smashed**, burst, fractured, shattered, fragmented, demolished • *a broken window*
2 = **infringed**, violated • *a broken promise*
3 = **interrupted**, incomplete, erratic, intermittent, discontinuous, fragmentary, spasmodic
4 = **not working**, defective, imperfect, kaput (*informal*), on the blink (*slang*), out of order
5 = **imperfect**, disjointed, halting, hesitating, stammering

broken-down See **worn out**

brokenhearted adjective
= **heartbroken**, miserable, devastated, desolate, grief-stricken, inconsolable, wretched, disconsolate, sorrowful

broker noun = **dealer**, agent, factor, negotiator, middleman, intermediary, go-between

bronze adjective = **reddish-brown**, copper, tan, rust, chestnut, brownish

brood noun **1** = **offspring**, family, issue, litter, clutch, progeny
▶ verb **2** = **think upon**, ponder, muse, agonize, dwell upon, mope, mull over, ruminate

brook noun = **stream**, creek, rill, rivulet, watercourse

brother noun **1** = **sibling**, relative, relation, kin, blood brother, kinsman
2 = **monk**, cleric, friar

brotherhood noun
1 = **fellowship**, camaraderie, companionship, friendliness,

kinship, brotherliness, comradeship
2 = association, order, community, union, league, society, alliance, guild, fraternity
brotherly *adjective* = **kind**, friendly, sympathetic, cordial, neighbourly, affectionate, fraternal, amicable, philanthropic, benevolent, altruistic
browbeat *verb* = **bully**, threaten, intimidate, coerce, badger, dragoon, hector, ride roughshod over, tyrannize
brown *adjective* **1 = brunette**, bronze, chocolate, coffee, bay, tan, chestnut, auburn, dun, hazel, sunburned, tanned, tawny, umber
▶ *verb* **2 = fry**, cook, grill, sear, sauté
browse *verb* **1 = skim**, survey, scan, peruse, dip into, examine cursorily, flip through, glance at, leaf through, look around, look through
2 = graze, eat, feed, nibble, chow down (*slang*)
bruise *verb* **1 = discolour**, mark, damage, injure, pound, mar
▶ *noun* **2 = discoloration**, injury, mark, blemish, contusion, black mark, swelling
bruised *See* **tender**
brunt *noun* = **full force**, force, violence, pressure, impact, stress, shock, strain, burden, thrust
brush¹ *noun* **1 = broom**, sweeper, besom

2 = encounter, conflict, clash, confrontation, skirmish, tussle
▶ *verb* **3 = clean**, sweep, paint, wash, buff, polish
4 = touch, sweep, stroke, kiss, flick, glance, scrape, graze
▷ **brush off** (*Slang*) = **ignore**, reject, dismiss, snub, scorn, disregard, spurn, disdain, repudiate, blow off (*slang*)
▷ **brush up** = **review**, study, cram, bone up (*informal*), go over, polish up, read up, refresh one's memory, relearn
brush² *noun* = **shrubs**, scrub, thicket, brushwood, bushes, copse, undergrowth
brusque *adjective* = **curt**, short, sharp, abrupt, terse, gruff, surly, discourteous, impolite
brutal *adjective* **1 = cruel**, vicious, savage, inhuman, ruthless, heartless, bloodthirsty, uncivilized, animalistic
2 = harsh, severe, rough, rude, insensitive, callous, gruff, impolite
brutality *noun* = **cruelty**, atrocity, ferocity, savagery, inhumanity, viciousness, barbarism, bloodthirstiness, ruthlessness
brute *noun* **1 = savage**, devil, monster, beast, swine, barbarian, fiend, sadist
2 = animal, creature, beast, wild animal
▶ *adjective* **3 = mindless**, physical, bodily, senseless, carnal, fleshly, instinctive, unthinking
bubble *noun* **1 = air ball**, drop,

SHADES OF BROWN

auburn	chestnut	khaki	sandy
beige	chocolate	mahogany	sepia
bronze	cinnamon	mocha	tan
buff	coffee	oatmeal	taupe
burnt sienna	dun	ochre	tawny
burnt umber	fawn	putty	terracotta
café au lait	ginger	russet	umber
camel	hazel	rust	

bead, blister, droplet, blob, globule

▷ *verb* **2 = foam**, boil, sparkle, froth, percolate, seethe, effervesce, fizz

3 = gurgle, trickle, ripple, murmur, babble, burble

bubbles See **foam**

bubbly *adjective* **1 = lively**, happy, animated, excited, merry, bouncy, elated, wired (*slang*)
2 = frothy, sparkling, effervescent, carbonated, fizzy, foamy

buccaneer *noun* = **pirate**, corsair, freebooter, privateer, sea-rover

buckle *noun* **1 = fastener**, catch, clip, clasp, hasp

▷ *verb* **2 = fasten**, close, secure, hook, clasp

3 = distort, collapse, twist, fold, bend, bulge, warp, crumple, contort, cave in

bud *noun* **1 = shoot**, embryo, germ, sprout

▷ *verb* **2 = develop**, shoot, grow, burgeon, sprout, burst forth

budding *adjective* = **developing**, potential, beginning, promising, embryonic, fledgling, nascent, burgeoning, growing, incipient

buddy *noun* (*Informal*) = **chum** (*informal*), friend, pal (*informal*), crony (*old-fashioned*) • *We've been buddies since we were kids.*

budge *verb* = **move**, push, shift, stir, dislodge

budget *noun* **1 = allowance**, cost, means, allocation, finances, funds, resources

▷ *verb* **2 = plan**, cost, estimate, allocate, ration, apportion

budgetary See **economic**

budgeting See **finance**

buff[1] *adjective* **1 = yellowish-brown**, tan, straw, sandy, yellowish

▷ *verb* **2 = polish**, shine, brush, smooth, rub, burnish

buff[2] *noun* (*Informal*) = **expert**, fan, addict, enthusiast, admirer, devotee, aficionado, connoisseur

buffer *noun* = **safeguard**, screen, shield, cushion, bumper, intermediary, fender, bulwark, shock absorber

buffet *verb* = **batter**, strike, beat, pound, knock, bump, thump, pummel, wallop (*informal*)

buffoon *noun* = **clown**, comedian, comic, fool, harlequin, wag, joker, jester

bug *noun* **1 = insect**, creepy-crawly (*informal*), beastie (*informal*) • *Bugs destroyed my garden last year.*

2 (*Informal*) = **illness**, disease, infection, virus

3 = fault, error, flaw, defect, glitch, gremlin

▷ *verb* **4** (*Informal*) = **annoy**, disturb, bother, irritate, hassle (*informal*), vex, pester, get on one's nerves (*informal*)

5 = tap, spy, wiretap, eavesdrop, listen in

bugbear *noun* = **pet hate**, bogey, horror, nightmare, dread, bane, bête noire

build *verb* **1 = construct**, make, form, assemble, erect, fabricate • *The house was built last year.* OPPOSITE: dismantle

2 = develop, increase, extend, strengthen, intensify • *I want to build a relationship with them.*

▷ **build up** See **reconstruct**

▷ *noun* **3 = physique**, body, figure, form, shape, frame • *He is of medium build.* See also: **base**

building *noun* = **structure**, edifice • *a glass building* See also: **house**, **making**

build-up *noun* = **increase**, gain, growth, development, expansion, escalation, accumulation, enlargement

bulbous *adjective* = **bulging**, bloated, rounded, convex, swelling, swollen

bulge *verb* **1 = stick out**, expand, swell, distend, protrude • *He bulges out of his black T-shirt.*

▷ *noun* **2 = lump**, bump, hump, protrusion, swelling • *My wallet made a bulge in my pocket.*

3 = increase, rise, boost, surge, intensification

b

bulk *noun* **1 = size**, weight, volume, substance, magnitude, dimensions, immensity, largeness

2 = main part, most, body, majority, mass, preponderance, better part, lion's share, nearly all

bulky *adjective* **= large**, big, heavy, massive, substantial, cumbersome, weighty, unwieldy, voluminous, hulking

bull See **nonsense**

bulldoze *verb* **= demolish**, level, flatten, raze

bullet *noun* **= projectile**, shot, ball, missile, pellet, slug

bulletin *noun* **= announcement**, report, statement, account, message, communication, dispatch, notification, communiqué, news flash

bully *noun* **1 = persecutor**, oppressor • *the class bully*
▶ *verb* **2 = persecute**, intimidate, tease, oppress, torment, pick on • *I wasn't going to let him bully me.*

3 = force, pressure, intimidate • *bullied into doing his work for him*

bulwark *noun* **1 = fortification**, defence, bastion, buttress, embankment, partition, rampart

2 = defence, support, security, guard, safeguard, mainstay, buffer

bumbling *adjective* **= clumsy**, awkward, inept, incompetent, inefficient, blundering, bungling, maladroit, muddled

bump *verb* **1 = knock**, hit, strike, collide, bang, jolt • *He bumped his head on the wall.*

2 = jerk, shake, bounce, jolt, rattle
▷ **bump into** See **meet**
▶ *noun* **3 = knock**, bang, thump, thud • *He heard a bump outside.*

4 = lump, bulge, hump, knob, swelling • *a bump in the road*
See also: **crash**

bumper *adjective* **= exceptional**, massive, excellent, whopping

(*informal*), abundant, jumbo (*informal*), bountiful

bumpkin *noun* **= yokel**, rustic, peasant, redneck (*slang*), hick (*informal*), hillbilly, country bumpkin

bumptious *adjective* **= cocky**, forward, arrogant, brash, overconfident, conceited, full of oneself, pushy (*informal*), self-assertive

bumpy *adjective* **= rough**, jerky, uneven, choppy, bouncy, jarring, jolting, rutted

bunch *noun* **1 = group**, lot, crowd, band, gang, multitude, gaggle • *The players were a great bunch.*

2 = bouquet, spray, posy

3 = cluster, set, load, pile, batch, bundle, heap • *He took out a bunch of keys.*
▶ *verb* **4 = group**, mass, collect, pack, cluster, assemble, bundle, huddle

bundle *noun* **1 = bunch**, group, mass, collection, pile, stack, batch, heap, assortment
▶ *verb* **2** (with *out*, *off*, *into*, etc.) **= push**, throw, rush, thrust, shove, hurry, hustle
▷ **bundle up = wrap up**, swathe, swaddle

bungle *verb* **= mess up**, blow (*slang*), ruin, spoil, blunder, botch, muff, foul up, make a mess of

bungling *adjective* **= incompetent**, blundering, clumsy, inept, maladroit

bunk *noun* **1 = cot**, bed, berth

2 (*Informal*) **= nonsense**, garbage (*informal*), BS or bull shit, baloney (*informal*), hogwash, balderdash, hot air (*informal*), moonshine, poppycock (*informal*), twaddle

buoy *noun* **= marker**, guide, signal, float, beacon
▶ *verb*
▷ **buoy up = encourage**, support, raise, lift, boost, cheer, sustain, hearten, cheer up, keep afloat

buoyancy *noun* **1 = lightness**, weightlessness

2 = cheerfulness, bounce

(*informal*), animation, good
humour, high spirits, liveliness

buoyant *adjective* **1 = floating**,
light, weightless, afloat

2 = cheerful, happy, upbeat
(*informal*), light-hearted,
carefree, jaunty, chirpy (*informal*)

burble *See* **babble**

burden *noun* **1 = load**, weight • *My
wet clothes were an added burden*.

2 = trouble, care, worry, stress,
strain, anxiety • *the burden of
looking after a sick parent*

▶ *verb* **3 = weigh down**, tax,
worry, load, bother, oppress,
handicap, saddle with

RELATED WORD
adjective: onerous

bureau *noun* **1 = office**, service,
agency, division, department,
branch

2 = desk, writing desk

bureaucracy *noun* **1 = red tape**,
administration, officialdom,
regulations • *Is there too much
bureaucracy in government?*

2 = government,
administration, authorities,
civil service, corridors of power,
officials, the system

bureaucrat *noun* **= official**,
officer, administrator,
mandarin, functionary, civil
servant, public servant

burglar *noun* **= housebreaker**,
thief, robber, cat burglar, filcher,
pilferer, sneak thief

burglarize *See* **rob**

burglary *noun* **= breaking and
entering**, theft, robbery, break-
in, larceny, housebreaking,
stealing, thieving

burial *noun* **= interment**,
funeral, entombment, exequies,
obsequies

buried *adjective* **1 = interred**,
entombed, laid to rest

2 = hidden, private, concealed,
sequestered, tucked away

burlesque *noun* **1 = parody**,
satire, caricature, mockery, send-
up (*informal*), takeoff (*informal*),
spoof (*informal*), travesty, piss-
take (*informal*)

2 = striptease, strip, lap dance

3 = cabaret, vaudeville, music-
hall

▶ *verb* **4 = satirize**, mock,
caricature, ape, parody,
exaggerate, ridicule, imitate,
lampoon, make a monkey out of,
make fun of, send up (*informal*),
spoof (*informal*), travesty

burly *adjective* **= brawny**, big,
hefty, beefy (*informal*), bulky,
sturdy, stocky, stout, hulking,
thickset, well-built

burn *verb* **1 = be on fire**, flame,
blaze, flare, flicker, be ablaze • *a
fire burning in the fireplace*

2 = scorch, char, singe,
incinerate, shrivel • *The old house
burned down.*

3 = be passionate, simmer,
fume, smoulder, seethe, be
angry, be aroused, be inflamed

| INFORMALLY SPEAKING
| **burn out**: wear out through
| much use
| **burn up**: make angry or
| annoyed

burning *adjective* **1 = intense**,
eager, passionate, impassioned,
ardent, vehement, fervent

2 = crucial, important,
significant, critical, essential,
vital, urgent, acute, pressing,
compelling

3 = blazing, fiery, glowing,
flaming, flashing, gleaming,
illuminated, scorching,
smouldering

burnish *verb* **= polish**, shine,
smooth, brighten, buff, glaze,
furbish, rub up

burrow *noun* **1 = hole**, retreat,
shelter, tunnel, den, lair

▶ *verb* **2 = dig**, tunnel, delve,
excavate, hollow out, scoop out

burst *verb* **1 = explode**, break,
split, crack, rupture, puncture
• *The balloon burst.*

2 = rush, break, erupt, barge,
gush • *to burst into flames*

▶ *noun* **3 = rush**, outbreak, surge,
fit, spate, torrent • *a burst of energy*

4 = explosion, break, blast, split,
crack, bang, discharge, blowout,
rupture

▶ *adjective* **5 = ruptured**, split,

rent, punctured
See also: **broken, flash**

bury verb 1 = **inter**, entomb, consign to the grave, inhume, lay to rest
2 = **embed**, engulf, submerge
3 = **hide**, cover, conceal, secrete, enshroud, stow away

bush noun = **shrub**, plant, hedge, shrubbery, thicket
▷ **the bush** = **the wild**, forest, brush, scrub, woodland, scrubland, backwoods, woods

bushy adjective = **thick**, rough, fuzzy, unruly, fluffy, shaggy, bristling, luxuriant

busily adverb = **actively**, briskly, strenuously, diligently, purposefully, assiduously, energetically, industriously, speedily

business noun 1 = **trade**, industry, transaction, commerce, trading, dealings • *a career in business*
2 = **establishment**, company, firm, organization, corporation, enterprise • *a family business*
3 = **matter**, issue, problem, question, affair, subject • *This business has upset me.*
4 = **profession**, work, trade, job, line, career, function, employment, occupation, vocation
See also: **concern, event, scene, undertaking**

businesslike adjective = **efficient**, professional, organized, practical, thorough, systematic, orderly, methodical, well-ordered

businessman noun = **executive**, employer, merchant, tycoon, entrepreneur, financier, capitalist, industrialist, tradesman

bust[1] noun = **bosom**, front, breast, chest, torso

bust[2] (*Informal*) ▷ verb 1 = **break**, burst, fracture, rupture
2 = **arrest**, search, catch, raid
▷ **go bust** = **go bankrupt**, fail, become insolvent, be ruined

bustle verb 1 = **hurry**, rush, dash, scuttle, fuss, scurry • *Salespeople bustled about the store.*
▶ noun 2 = **activity**, flurry, excitement, hurry, fuss, commotion • *the bustle of modern life*
OPPOSITE: peace

bustling adjective = **busy**, full, active, crowded, lively, buzzing, humming, swarming, teeming

busy adjective 1 = **occupied**, active, working, employed, engaged (in), engrossed • *What is it? I'm busy.*
OPPOSITE: idle
2 = **hectic**, full, active, lively, restless • *Halifax is a busy port.*
▶ verb 3 = **occupy**, engage, employ, absorb, immerse • *We busied ourselves in the kitchen.*
See also: **industrious**

busybody noun = **meddler** • *the neighbourhood busybody*

but conjunction 1 = **although**, while, though, yet • *Heat the cider until it is very hot but not boiling.*
▶ preposition 2 = **except**, save, except for, other than • *The crew gave them nothing but bread to eat.*
3 = **only**, just, simply, merely, solely, singly

butcher noun 1 = **murderer**, killer, destroyer, slaughterer, slayer
▶ verb 2 = **slaughter**, cut, prepare, clean, dress, joint, carve, cut up
3 = **kill**, destroy, slay, slaughter, massacre, assassinate, liquidate, exterminate, cut down, put to the sword

butt[1] noun 1 = **end**, stock, handle, shaft, shank, haft, hilt
2 = **stub**, tip, cigarette (*slang*), leftover, butt end, cigarette end
3 (*Informal*) = **buttocks**, behind (*informal*), bottom, derrière (*euphemistic*), bum (*informal*), rump (*informal*), tush (*slang*), buns (*slang*)

butt[2] noun = **target**, victim, dupe, laughing stock

butt[3] verb, noun (with or of the head or horns) = **knock**, push,

bump, poke, thrust, shove, ram, prod, bunt
▶ *verb*
▷ **butt in** = **interfere**, interrupt, meddle, intrude, cut in, put one's oar in, stick one's nose in

butt[4] *noun* = **cask**, barrel, firkin

buttocks *plural noun* = **butt** (*informal*), behind, bottom, bum (*informal*), backside, posterior, rear (end), buns (*slang*) • *exercises for your buttocks*

buttonhole *verb* = **detain**, catch, grab, bore, accost, importune, take aside, waylay

buttress *noun* **1** = **support**, brace, prop, reinforcement, mainstay, strut, stanchion
▶ *verb* **2** = **support**, strengthen, uphold, sustain, bolster, reinforce, back up, prop up, shore up

buxom *adjective* = **plump**, healthy, ample, well-rounded, voluptuous, busty, bosomy, curvaceous

buy *verb* = **purchase**, acquire, obtain, procure, invest in, pay for • *I'd like to buy him lunch.*
OPPOSITE: sell

▷ **buy off** See **corrupt**
| CONFUSABLES
| *Buy* means *purchase*.
| *By* means *beside*.

buyer See **customer**

by *preposition* **1** = **via**, over, by way of
2 = **through**, through the agency of
3 = **near**, past, along, beside, close to, next to
▶ *adverb* **4** = **near**, close, handy, at hand, in reach
5 = **past**, away, aside, to one side

bygone *adjective* = **past**, former, lost, extinct, antiquated, forgotten, of old, olden

bypass *verb* = **go around**, avoid, circumvent, depart from, detour around, deviate from, get around, give a wide berth to, pass around

bystander *noun* = **onlooker**, witness, viewer, observer, watcher, spectator, eyewitness, passer-by, looker-on

byword *noun* = **saying**, slogan, adage, motto, maxim, proverb, precept

Cc

cab *noun* = **taxi**, taxicab, hackney carriage, minicab

cabal *noun* 1 = **clique**, set, party, league, caucus, faction, conclave, golden circle
2 = **plot**, scheme, conspiracy, intrigue, machination

cabin *noun* 1 = **room**, berth, compartment, quarters
2 = **hut**, shed, cottage, lodge, shack, chalet, shanty

cabinet *noun* = **cupboard**, case, locker, closet, dresser, chiffonier, commode, escritoire

Cabinet *noun* = **council**, administration, ministry, assembly, counsellors

cache *noun* = **store**, fund, reserve, supply, treasury, stockpile, stash (*informal*), hoard, accumulation

cad *noun* (*Old-fashioned, informal*) = **scoundrel**, rat (*informal*), heel (*slang*)

caddish *adjective* = **ungentlemanly**, low, despicable, lousy (*slang*), ill-bred, scuzzy (*slang*), unmannerly

cadence See **beat**

cadge See **scrounge**

café *noun* = **snack bar**, restaurant, cafeteria, brasserie, coffee bar, coffee shop, lunchroom, tearoom

cage *noun* = **enclosure**, pound, pen

cagey *adjective* (*Informal*) = **wary**, careful, cautious, wily, shrewd, discreet, guarded, noncommittal, chary

cajole *verb* = **persuade**, flatter, coax, seduce, brown-nose (*slang*), sweet-talk (*informal*), wheedle

cake *noun* 1 = **block**, bar, mass, lump, cube, slab, loaf
▶ *verb* 2 = **encrust**, bake, solidify, coagulate, congeal

cakewalk *noun* = **walkover**, pushover (*slang*), breeze (*informal*), child's play (*informal*), picnic (*informal*), piece of cake (*informal*), laugher (*informal*), slam dunk (*informal*), cinch (*slang*), no-brainer (*slang*)

calamitous *adjective* = **disastrous**, deadly, fatal, tragic, dire, catastrophic, ruinous, cataclysmic, devastating

calamity *noun* = **disaster**, tragedy, ruin, catastrophe, mishap, misadventure, misfortune, tribulation, cataclysm

calculate *verb* 1 = **work out**, count, determine, reckon • *how to calculate the cost of setting up a business*
2 = **plan**, aim, design, intend

calculated *adjective* = **deliberate**, planned, intended, aimed, designed • *Everything they said was calculated to hurt his feelings.*
OPPOSITE: unplanned

calculating *adjective* = **scheming**, sharp, crafty, shrewd, manipulative, sly, cunning, devious, Machiavellian

calculation *noun* 1 = **working out**, result, estimate, answer, forecast, judgment, reckoning, computation
2 = **planning**, deliberation, precaution, discretion, foresight, contrivance, forethought

calibre *noun* 1 = **worth**, standard, quality, ability, capacity, talent, merit, distinction, stature
2 = **diameter**, measure, gauge, bore

call *verb* **1** = **name**, term, label, style, dub, entitle, designate, christen, describe as • *We called our dog Bandit.*
2 = **phone**, telephone • *He called me at my office.*
3 = **cry**, hail, shout, yell • *Did someone call my name?*
4 = **summon**, rally, gather, assemble, convene, muster
▷ **call for** = **require**, need, suggest, involve, demand, occasion, entail, necessitate
▷ **call off** See **cancel**
▷ **call on** = **visit**, see, drop in on, look in on, look up
▷ **call to mind** See **remember**
▷ **call upon** See **appeal**
▶ *noun* **5** = **cry**, hail, shout, scream, yell, whoop • *a call for help*
6 = **summons**, order, demand, appeal, request, notice, plea, command, invitation
7 = **need**, cause, reason, occasion, excuse, justification, grounds

calling *noun* = **profession**, trade, career, mission, vocation, life's work

callous *adjective* = **heartless**, cold, indifferent, insensitive • *his callous disregard for other people's safety*
OPPOSITE: caring
See also: **cruel, merciless**

callousness See **cruelty**

callow *adjective* = **inexperienced**, green, raw, naive, immature, unsophisticated, guileless

calm *adjective* **1** = **cool**, collected, composed, impassive, relaxed • *Try to keep calm.*
OPPOSITE: worried
2 = **still**, mild, balmy, tranquil • *Tuesday was a clear and calm day.*
OPPOSITE: rough
▶ *noun* **3** = **peacefulness**, peace, quiet, serenity, calmness, stillness • *He liked the calm of the evening.*
▶ *verb* **4** = **soothe**, relax • *We were trying to calm the puppy.*
See also: **ease, pacify, patient, peaceful, silence**

calmness *noun* **1** = **coolness**, cool (*slang*), poise, composure,

equanimity, impassivity, sang-froid, self-possession
2 = **peacefulness**, quiet, calm, hush, serenity, repose, stillness, tranquillity, restfulness

camaraderie See **fellowship**

camouflage *noun* **1** = **disguise**, cover, screen, mask, blind, cloak, masquerade, subterfuge, concealment
▶ *verb* **2** = **disguise**, cover, screen, hide, mask, cloak, veil, conceal, obscure, obfuscate

camp[1] *noun* = **camp site**, encampment, bivouac, camping ground, tents

camp[2] *adjective* (*Informal*) = **effeminate**, artificial, affected, mannered, ostentatious, posturing

campaign *noun* = **operation**, push, movement, crusade, blitz • *a campaign to educate people*
See also: **agitate**

canal *noun* = **waterway**, channel, passage, duct, conduit, watercourse

cancel *verb* **1** = **call off**, abandon • *We're going to have to cancel our picnic.*
2 = **annul**, quash, revoke, repeal • *They were forced to cancel their contract.*
▷ **cancel out** = **make up for**, offset, neutralize, nullify, counterbalance, balance out, compensate for
See also: **lift**

cancellation *noun* = **abandonment**, elimination, repeal, abolition, annulment, revocation, deletion

cancer *noun* = **growth**, corruption, tumour, sickness, malignancy, pestilence

candid *adjective* = **honest**, open, blunt, straightforward, frank, truthful • *a candid interview*
See also: **direct, natural, straight**

candidate *noun* = **contender**, competitor, applicant • *a candidate for the presidency of the debating team*

candour *noun* = **honesty**,

openness, truthfulness, directness, forthrightness, frankness, outspokenness, straightforwardness

candy noun = **sweets**, confectionery • *I ate too many candies and I feel sick.*

cane *See* **stick**

canine *See* **dog**

canker noun = **disease**, cancer, infection, corruption, sore, scourge, ulcer, rot, blight, bane

cannon noun = **gun**, mortar, big gun, field gun

canny adjective = **shrewd**, careful, cautious, wise, prudent, clever, astute, judicious

canon noun 1 = **rule**, regulation, standard, principle, formula, criterion, dictate, statute, yardstick, precept
2 = **list**, roll, catalogue

canopy noun = **awning**, shade, marquee, covering, sunshade

cant¹ noun 1 = **hypocrisy**, pretense, humbug, insincerity, lip service, pretentiousness, sanctimoniousness
2 = **jargon**, lingo, slang, vernacular, argot, patter

cant² verb = **tilt**, rise, slope, angle, incline, slant, bevel

cantankerous adjective = **bad-tempered**, contrary, testy, grumpy, irritable, irascible, choleric, disagreeable, waspish

canter noun 1 = **jog**, amble, dogtrot, lope
▶ verb 2 = **jog**, amble, lope

canvass verb 1 = **campaign**, solicit, electioneer, solicit votes
2 = **poll**, study, investigate, examine, inspect, scrutinize
▶ noun 3 = **poll**, investigation, survey, tally, scrutiny, examination

cap verb = **beat**, top, crown, surpass, exceed, eclipse, better, outstrip, outdo, transcend

capability noun = **ability**, power, potential, capacity, means, qualification *or* qualifications, competence, proficiency, wherewithal

capable adjective = **able**, efficient,

competent, accomplished, adept, proficient, skilful • *a capable leader*
OPPOSITE: incompetent
▷ **capable of** *See* **equal to**

capacious adjective = **spacious**, wide, broad, extensive, substantial, vast, sizable *or* sizeable, expansive, voluminous, roomy, commodious

capacity noun 1 = **size**, space, room, volume, dimensions • *the vehicle's fuel capacity*
2 = **ability**, power, potential, facility, gift, capability • *Our capacity for giving care, love, and attention is limited.*
3 = **function**, post, province, office, role, position, sphere
See also: **part**, **talent**

cape noun = **headland**, point, head, peninsula, promontory

caper noun 1 = **escapade**, stunt, mischief, prank, antic, lark (*informal*), high jinks, jape, practical joke
▶ verb 2 = **dance**, jump, trip, spring, skip, bound, frolic, cavort, gambol

capital noun 1 = **money**, cash, investment *or* investments, principal, wealth, means, wherewithal, assets, funds, resources, finances, venture capital
▶ adjective 2 = **principal**, major, prime, vital, cardinal
3 (*Old-fashioned*) = **first-rate**, fine, excellent, superb, splendid, sterling

capitalism noun = **private enterprise**, free enterprise, laissez faire *or* laisser faire, private ownership

capitalize verb **capitalize on** = **take advantage of**, exploit, benefit from, cash in on (*informal*), gain from, make the most of, profit from

capitulate verb = **give in**, submit, surrender, yield, succumb, relent, come to terms, give up

capitulation *See* **surrender**

caprice noun = **whim**, notion, impulse, fancy, fad, whimsy,

fickleness, inconstancy
capricious adjective
= **unpredictable**, inconsistent,
variable, erratic, whimsical,
wayward, fickle, impulsive,
mercurial, changeful, fitful,
inconstant
capsize verb = **overturn**, upset,
invert, keel over, tip over, turn
over, turn turtle
capsule noun 1 = **pill**, tablet,
lozenge
2 (*Botany*) = **pod**, case, vessel,
shell, sheath, receptacle, seed
case
captain noun = **leader**, head,
chief, commander, boss
(*informal*), master, skipper
captivate verb = **charm**, attract,
entrance, fascinate, allure,
mesmerize, enchant, enthrall,
bewitch, beguile, enrapture,
infatuate
captive noun 1 = **prisoner**,
convict, hostage, detainee, slave,
internee, prisoner of war
▶ adjective 2 = **confined**,
restricted, caged, enslaved,
ensnared, imprisoned,
incarcerated, locked up, penned,
subjugated
captivity noun = **confinement**,
custody, detention,
imprisonment, slavery,
incarceration, internment,
bondage
capture verb 1 = **catch**, take,
arrest, seize, apprehend
• *captured by rebels*
OPPOSITE: release
▶ noun 2 = **catching**, arrest,
seizure, taking, trapping • *She
evaded capture for eight years.*
See also: **kidnap**
car noun 1 = **automobile**, vehicle
• *I finally left the car at the garage*
2 = **carriage** or **railway carriage**,
coach, van, buffet car, cable car,
dining car, sleeping car
carcass noun = **body**, shell,
skeleton, framework, corpse,
hulk, cadaver (*medical*), dead
body, remains
cardinal adjective = **principal**,
first, chief, key, capital, main,

central, primary, essential,
fundamental, paramount,
leading
care verb 1 = **be concerned**,
mind, be bothered, be interested
• *a company that cares about the
environment*
▷ **care for** = **look after**, protect,
attend, nurse, tend, foster, take
care of, minister to, provide for,
watch over; = **like**, want, love,
enjoy, desire, prize, be fond of,
take to
▶ noun 2 = **worry**, concern,
stress, trouble, woe, anxiety
• *without a care in the world*
3 = **caution**, attention, pains • *We
took great care in choosing a location.*
4 = **protection**, charge,
control, management, custody,
supervision, guardianship,
keeping
See also: **burden**
career noun 1 = **occupation**,
employment, pursuit, calling,
livelihood, vocation, life's work
▶ verb 2 = **rush**, race, barrel or
barrel along (*informal*), speed,
tear, bolt, dash, hurtle
carefree adjective = **untroubled**,
cheerful, easy-going, breezy,
light-hearted, happy-go-lucky,
blithe, halcyon
careful adjective 1 = **cautious**,
prudent • *Be careful what you say
to him.*
OPPOSITE: careless
2 = **thorough**, precise,
painstaking, meticulous • *It
needs careful planning.*
OPPOSITE: careless
See also: **deliberate,
economical, thrifty**
careless adjective 1 = **slapdash**,
irresponsible, sloppy (*informal*),
neglectful • *careless driving*
OPPOSITE: careful
2 = **nonchalant**, casual, offhand
• *careless laughter*
3 = **negligent**, hasty,
thoughtless, remiss, absent-
minded, forgetful, unthinking
carelessness noun = **negligence**,
neglect, omission, indiscretion,
irresponsibility, laxity,

slackness, sloppiness (*informal*), thoughtlessness

caress *verb* 1 = **stroke**, pet, embrace, neck (*informal*), kiss, hug, cuddle, fondle, make out (*informal*), nuzzle
▶ *noun* 2 = **stroke**, embrace, kiss, hug, pat, cuddle, fondling

caretaker *noun* = **warden**, curator, keeper, superintendent, concierge, janitor, custodian, porter, watchman

cargo *noun* = **load**, shipment, merchandise, freight, baggage, consignment, contents, goods

caricature *noun* 1 = **parody**, cartoon, satire, distortion, farce, lampoon, burlesque, travesty, piss-take (*informal*)
▶ *verb* 2 = **parody**, mock, mimic, ridicule, distort, satirize, lampoon, burlesque

caring *adjective* = **compassionate**, warm, sensitive, soft, tender, loving, sympathetic, responsive, receptive, kindly, considerate, softhearted, tenderhearted, touchy-feely (*informal*), warmhearted

carnage *noun* = **slaughter**, murder, massacre, havoc, bloodshed, holocaust, shambles, blood bath, butchery, mass murder

carnal *adjective* = **sexual**, erotic, lewd, sensual, fleshly, lascivious, libidinous, lustful

carnival *noun* = **festival**, holiday, fair, celebration, gala, jamboree, revelry, fête, fiesta, jubilee, merrymaking

carol *noun* = **song**, lay, chorus, hymn, ditty

carp *verb* = **find fault**, criticize, complain, reproach, quibble, cavil, pick holes

carpenter *noun* = **joiner**, cabinet-maker, woodworker

carping See **critical**

carriage *noun* 1 = **coach**, railway car, cab, conveyance
2 = **bearing**, air, conduct, manner, behaviour, posture, gait, demeanour, comportment, deportment

carry *verb* 1 = **transport**, take, bear, convey (*formal*), lug • *She was carrying a briefcase.*
2 = **win**, gain, effect, capture, secure, accomplish
▷ **carry on** = **continue**, last, maintain, endure, persist, perpetuate, persevere, keep going
▷ **carry out** = **perform**, achieve, accomplish, fulfill • *the surgeon who carried out the operation*
See also: **administer**, **commit**, **conduct**, **do**, **keep**
See also: **bring**, **hold**

carton *noun* = **box**, case, package, pack, container, packet

cartoon *noun* 1 = **drawing**, sketch, satire, caricature, parody, lampoon, comic strip
2 = **animation**, animated cartoon, animated film

cartridge *noun* 1 = **shell**, charge, round
2 = **container**, case, magazine, capsule, cylinder, cassette

carve *verb* = **cut**, sculpt, engrave, inscribe, chisel • *He carves his figures from pine.*
See also: **model**

cascade *noun* 1 = **waterfall**, flood, avalanche, shower, cataract, fountain, outpouring, deluge, downpour, torrent, falls
▶ *verb* 2 = **flow**, fall, pitch, surge, flood, tumble, spill, plunge, pour, descend, overflow, teem, gush

case¹ *noun* 1 = **instance**, example, occasion, occurrence, illustration • *a case of mistaken identity*
2 = **lawsuit**, trial, action, proceedings • *a libel case*
See also: **argument**, **patient**, **situation**

case² *noun* 1 = **container**, box • *an eyeglass case*
2 = **covering**, jacket, shell, capsule, envelope, casing, wrapper, sheath
See also: **cover**

cash *noun* = **money**, silver, currency, dough (*slang*), coinage, funds, notes, ready money

cashier¹ *noun* = **teller**, banker,

clerk, treasurer, bank
clerk, bursar, purser

cashier² verb = **dismiss**,
expel, discharge, discard,
drum out, give the boot to (slang)

casket noun = **box**, case, chest,
coffer, jewel box

cast noun **1** = **actors**, company,
troupe, characters, dramatis
personae, players
2 = **type**, style, stamp, manner,
complexion
▶ verb **3** = **choose**, name, pick,
select, appoint, assign, allot
4 = **give out**, spread, distribute,
shed, deposit, emit, scatter,
bestow, radiate, diffuse
5 = **form**, set, model, shape,
found, mould
6 = **throw**, launch, pitch, toss,
hurl, thrust, fling, sling
▷ **cast aside** See **discard**
▷ **cast a vote** See **vote**

caste noun = **class**, order, status,
rank, estate, grade, stratum,
social order

castigate verb = **reprimand**,
criticize, rebuke, chastise,
censure, scold, berate, lambast or
lambaste

cast-iron adjective = **certain**,
established, definite, copper-
bottomed, fixed, guaranteed,
settled

castle noun = **fortress**, keep,
tower, palace, stronghold,
chateau, citadel

cast-off adjective **1** = **unwanted**,
useless, unneeded, discarded,
rejected, scrapped, surplus to
requirements
▶ noun **2** = **reject**, second, failure,
discard, outcast

castrate verb = **neuter**,
emasculate, geld

casual adjective **1** = **chance**,
accidental, incidental • *a casual
remark*
OPPOSITE: deliberate
2 = **careless**, cursory,
nonchalant, offhand, relaxed • *a
casual look over his shoulder*
OPPOSITE: concerned
3 = **informal**, sporty, non-
dressy

casualty noun = **victim**, death,
loss, wounded, fatality, sufferer

cat noun = **feline**, kitty, puss or
pussy (cat) (informal) • *sharing his
apartment with four cats*
RELATED WORDS
adjective: feline
male: tom
female: tabby
young: kitten

catacombs plural noun = **vault**,
tomb, crypt

catalogue noun **1** = **list**, record,
schedule, roll, index, register,
inventory, roster, directory,
gazetteer
▶ verb **2** = **list**, file, index,
register, inventory, classify,
tabulate, accession, alphabetize

catapult noun **1** = **sling**,
slingshot (US)
▶ verb **2** = **shoot**, pitch, plunge,
propel, hurl, heave

catastrophe noun = **disaster**,
trouble, tragedy, fiasco,
adversity, calamity, misfortune,
cataclysm

catastrophic See **fatal**

catcall noun = **jeer**, boo, whistle,
raspberry, hiss, gibe

catch verb **1** = **capture**, arrest,
trap, snare, apprehend • *another
technique for catching criminals*
2 = **seize**, take, get, grab, grip,
clutch, snatch, grasp, lay hold
of
3 = **discover**, surprise, expose,
detect, unmask, catch in the act,
find out, take unawares
4 = **contract**, get, develop, incur,
go down with, succumb to,
suffer from
5 = **make out**, get, hear,
recognize, sense, perceive, grasp,
comprehend, discern, take in
▷ **catch on** = **understand**, see,
grasp, comprehend, find out, get
the picture, see through
▶ noun **6** = **fastener**, clip, bolt,
latch, clasp • *windows fitted with
safety catches*
7 = **drawback**, snag,
disadvantage • *The catch is that
you have to change planes twice.*
See also: **stick**, **tangle**

C

catch it: be scolded or
punished
catch on: understand; be
popular

catching adjective = **infectious**,
contagious, communicable,
transferable, transmittable

catchword noun = **slogan**,
password, motto, byword,
watchword

catchy adjective = **memorable**,
popular, haunting, captivating

categorical adjective = **absolute**,
positive, express, explicit,
downright, unconditional,
emphatic, unequivocal,
unqualified, unambiguous,
unreserved

categorize verb = **classify**, class,
sort, peg (informal)

category noun = **class**, group, set,
type, sort, genre, classification,
subgenre • The items were organized
into six different categories.
See also: **kind, variety**

cater verb = **provide**, supply,
outfit, furnish, purvey

cattle plural noun = **cows**, stock,
livestock, beasts, bovines

catty adjective = **spiteful**,
malicious, venomous,
malevolent, rancorous, snide,
backbiting, bitchy (informal),
shrewish

cause noun **1** = **origin**, source,
root • the most common cause of
back pain
2 = **aim**, movement, ideal
• dedication to the cause of peace
3 = **reason**, basis, motivation,
motive, justification, grounds
• They gave us no cause to believe
that.
▶ verb **4** = **produce**, create,
generate, provoke, bring about
• This may cause delays.
See also: **bring, factor, lead to,
prompt, result in**

caustic adjective **1** = **burning**,
vitriolic, corrosive, acrid,
astringent, biting, corroding,
mordant
2 = **sarcastic**, scathing, virulent,
cutting, acrimonious, vitriolic,
pungent, stinging, trenchant

caution noun **1** = **care**, prudence
• Drivers are urged to exercise extreme
caution in icy weather.
2 = **warning**, advice, counsel,
injunction, admonition
▶ verb **3** = **warn**, reprimand • The
two men were cautioned, but police
say they will not be charged.
See also: **advise**

cautious adjective = **careful**,
tentative, wary, guarded • a
cautious approach
OPPOSITE: daring
See also: **deliberate**

cavalcade noun = **parade**, train,
array, procession, spectacle,
march-past

cavalier adjective = **haughty**, lofty,
arrogant, disdainful, lordly,
offhand, scornful, supercilious

cavalry noun = **horsemen**, horse,
mounted troops

cave noun = **hollow**, cavity, den,
grotto, cavern
▶ verb
▷ **cave in** See **give**

cavern noun = **cave**, hollow,
pothole

cavernous adjective = **deep**,
sunken, hollow, yawning

cavity noun = **hollow**, hole, gap,
pit, dent, crater

cease verb **1** = **stop**, end, finish,
be over, come to an end, die away
• Almost miraculously, the noise
ceased.
OPPOSITE: begin
2 = **discontinue**, stop, finish,
suspend, desist from, give up
• A small number of companies have
ceased doing business.
OPPOSITE: start
See also: **disappear, fail, halt,
vanish**

ceaseless adjective = **continual**,
constant, endless, eternal,
perpetual, nonstop, incessant,
interminable, everlasting,
never-ending, twenty-four-
seven (slang), unremitting

cede verb = **surrender**, resign,
transfer, concede, yield,
renounce, relinquish, hand over,
make over

ceiling See **maximum**

celebrate verb 1 = **rejoice**, party, commemorate • I was in a mood to celebrate.
OPPOSITE: mourn
2 = **perform**, bless, honour, solemnize

celebrated adjective = **well-known**, popular, famous, prominent, acclaimed, renowned, notable, marquee, illustrious, distinguished, eminent

celebration noun 1 = **party**, festival, gala, festivity • his eightieth birthday celebration
2 = **performance**, anniversary, remembrance, commemoration, observance, honouring, solemnization

celebrity noun 1 = **personality**, name, star, superstar, VIP, big name • At the age of twelve, he was already a celebrity.
2 = **fame**, reputation, distinction, prominence, stardom, prestige, renown, repute, notability
See also: **success**

celestial adjective = **heavenly**, spiritual, astral, divine, supernatural, sublime, ethereal, angelic

celibacy noun = **chastity**, purity, virginity, continence

cell noun 1 = **room**, tank (slang), stall, chamber, cavity, compartment, cubicle, dungeon
2 = **unit**, group, core, caucus, nucleus, coterie

cement noun 1 = **mortar**, gum, paste, glue, plaster, adhesive, sealant
▶ verb 2 = **stick together**, join, bond, combine, seal, bind, unite, attach, glue, plaster, weld

cemetery noun = **graveyard**, necropolis, burial ground, churchyard, God's acre

censor verb = **cut**, blue-pencil, bowdlerize, expurgate

censorious adjective = **critical**, severe, scathing, captious, carping, cavilling, condemnatory, disapproving, disparaging, fault-finding, hypercritical

censure noun 1 = **disapproval**, blame, criticism, condemnation, reproach • a controversial policy that has attracted international censure
▶ verb 2 = **criticize**, condemn, denounce, pan (informal), reproach • He should not have been censured for his personal opinions.
See also: **abuse, accuse, attack, fault**

CONFUSABLES
Censure means criticize severely.
Censor means delete something considered unsuitable.

central adjective 1 = **middle**,

TYPES OF CELEBRATION

BUDDHIST	HINDU	
Wesak	Diwali	Shavuot
	Durga	Succoth
CHRISTIAN	Holi	Yom Kippur
Advent	Puja	
Christmas		**MUSLIM**
Easter	**JEWISH**	Bairam
Good Friday	Hannukkah	Eid-ul-Adha
Lent	Passover	Eid-ul-Fitr
Palm	Purim	Ramadan
Sunday	Rosh	
Pentecost	Hashana	**SIKH**
		Baisakhi

mean, interior, inner, median, mid

2 = main, chief, key, primary, principal, essential, fundamental, focal

centralize verb = **unify**, concentrate, incorporate, streamline, rationalize, condense

centre noun **1 = middle**, heart, focus, core, hub, pivot, nucleus, kernel, midpoint • *the centre of the room*
OPPOSITE: edge
▶ verb **2 = focus**, concentrate, cluster, revolve, converge • *All his thoughts were centred around himself.*
See also: **base**

ceremonial adjective **1 = ritual**, formal, solemn, stately, liturgical, ritualistic
▶ noun **2 = ritual**, ceremony, rite, formality, solemnity

ceremonious adjective = **formal**, civil, stiff, solemn, dignified, stately, courteous, deferential, punctilious

ceremony noun **1 = ritual**, service, rite, observance, pomp • *The awards ceremony was followed by a banquet.*
2 = formality, protocol, etiquette, decorum, niceties • *He hung up without ceremony.*

certain adjective **1 = definite**, inevitable, definitive, established, guaranteed, sure, undeniable, known • *One thing is certain - they respect each other.*
OPPOSITE: uncertain
2 = sure, clear, positive, confident, convinced, definite, satisfied • *She's absolutely certain she's going to win.*
OPPOSITE: uncertain
3 = known, true, conclusive, unequivocal, undeniable, irrefutable, incontrovertible
4 = inevitable, sure, bound, definite, inescapable, destined, fated
See also: **necessary**

certainly adverb = **definitely**, undoubtedly, undeniably,

unquestionably, without doubt • *I'll certainly do all I can to help.*
▷ **certainly not** See **no**
See also: **really**

certainty noun **1 = sureness**, trust, confidence, conviction, faith, assurance, validity, positiveness
2 = fact, reality, truth, sure thing (*informal*)

certificate noun = **document**, warrant, license, authorization, credential *or* credentials, diploma, voucher, testimonial

certified See **official**

certify verb = **confirm**, declare, testify, guarantee, assure, verify, authenticate, validate, attest

chafe verb **1 = rub**, scratch, scrape, rasp, abrade
2 = be annoyed, worry, rage, fume, fret, be impatient

chaff¹ noun = **waste**, refuse, garbage, trash, dregs, remains, husks

chaff² verb = **tease**, mock, rib (*informal*), taunt, scoff, ridicule

chain noun **1 = link**, bond, shackle, coupling, fetter, manacle
2 = series, set, train, string, sequence, progression, succession
▶ verb **3 = bind**, handcuff, restrain, confine, tether, shackle, enslave, fetter, manacle

chairman noun = **director**, president, spokesman, speaker, chairwoman, chairperson, master of ceremonies

challenge noun **1 = dare** • *They issued a challenge to their rivals.*
2 = test, trial, question, confrontation, provocation, ultimatum, throwdown (*slang*)
▶ verb **3 = dare**, defy • *He challenged his rival to a duel.*
4 = question, dispute, throw down (*slang*) • *challenging the authority of the government*
5 = test, question, dispute, tackle, defy, confront, object to, throw down the gauntlet
See also: **contest**, **query**

challenger See **competitor, rival**

challenging See **formidable**

chamber noun 1 = **room**, apartment, hall, bedroom, compartment, enclosure, cubicle
2 = **council**, legislature, assembly, legislative body

champion noun 1 = **winner**, hero, victor, title holder • *the world chess champion*
2 = **defender**, advocate, guardian, protector • *He received acclaim as a champion of the oppressed.*
▸ verb 3 = **support**, defend, promote, uphold, stick up for (*informal*), fight for • *He passionately championed the poor.*
See also: **supporter**

championship See **competition**

chance noun 1 = **probability**, possibility, prospect, likelihood, odds • *a good chance of success*
2 = **opportunity**, time, opening, occasion • *He didn't give me a chance to explain.*
3 = **luck**, accident, fortune, coincidence • *events that were merely the result of chance*
RELATED WORD
adjective: fortuitous
4 = **risk**, speculation, gamble, uncertainty, hazard, jeopardy
▸ verb 5 = **risk**, try, stake, gamble, venture, hazard, endanger, jeopardize, wager
See also: **accidental, casual, fate, turn, unexpected, unpredictable**

chances See **probability**

chancy adjective (*Slang*) = **dangerous**, difficult, risky, hazardous, perilous

change noun 1 = **alteration**, difference, transformation, modification • *a change in her attitude*
2 = **variety**, break (*informal*), departure, variation, diversion, novelty
3 = **exchange**, trade, swap, conversion, substitution, interchange
▸ verb 4 = **alter**, reform, convert, moderate, modify, transform • *My views have changed since I began working here.*
5 = **exchange**, trade, replace, swap, substitute, interchange, barter • *Can I change this sweater for one a size bigger?*
See also: **adapt, affect, reverse, turn, vary**

changeable adjective = **variable**, volatile, unpredictable, unstable, irregular, erratic, fickle • *changeable weather*
OPPOSITE: constant

channel noun 1 = **route**, way, medium, course, approach, path, means, artery, avenue
2 = **passage**, route, canal, groove, duct, strait, gutter, conduit, furrow
▸ verb 3 = **direct**, conduct, guide, transmit, convey

chant verb 1 = **sing**, chorus, recite, carol, intone, descant, warble
▸ noun 2 = **song**, chorus, melody, carol, psalm

chaos noun = **disorder**, confusion, mayhem, lawlessness, pandemonium, anarchy, tumult, bedlam, disorganization

chaotic adjective = **disordered**, confused, tumultuous, lawless, uncontrolled, topsy-turvy, anarchic, deranged, disorganized, riotous

chap noun (*Informal*) = **fellow**, man, person, guy (*informal*), individual, character

chaperone noun 1 = **escort**, companion, plus-one (*informal*)
▸ verb 2 = **escort**, protect, attend, accompany, safeguard, shepherd, watch over

chapter noun = **section**, part, period, stage, division, phase, episode, topic, clause

char See **burn**

character noun 1 = **personality**, makeup, temperament, nature • *He has a dark side to his character.*
2 = **integrity**, honour, strength • *She showed real character in her attempt to win over the crowd.*
3 = **role**, part, portrayal, persona

c

4 = eccentric, card (*informal*), original, oddball (*informal*)
5 = symbol, sign, mark, figure, letter, device, hieroglyph, rune
See also: **individual, name, reputation**
characteristic noun **1 = feature**, quality, property, attribute, trait
• *His chief characteristic is honesty.*
▶ adjective **2 = typical**, distinctive, distinguishing
• *She responded with characteristic generosity.*
OPPOSITE: uncharacteristic
See also: **individual, point, representative, special**
characterize verb **= identify**, mark, represent, indicate, brand, stamp, distinguish, typify
charade noun **= pretense**, fake, parody, farce, travesty, pantomime
charge verb **1 = ask (for)**, bill, levy
• *Most electricians charge a fair price.*
2 = rush, storm, dash, stampede
• *He charged into the room.*
3 = accuse, blame, indict, arraign, incriminate, impeach
4 = fill, load
5 = command, order, bid, demand, require, commit, instruct, entrust
▶ noun **6 = price**, cost, fee, payment • *We can arrange this for a small charge.*
7 = accusation, allegation, indictment, imputation
8 = rush, attack, assault, onset, stampede, onslaught, sortie
9 = care, office, trust, duty, responsibility, custody, safekeeping
10 = ward
11 = instruction, order, demand, direction, command, mandate, injunction, precept
See also: **rate, tear**
charges See **bill**
charisma noun **= charm**, lure, personality, attraction, allure, magnetism, mojo (*slang*)
charismatic adjective
= charming, attractive, influential, magnetic, alluring, enticing

charitable adjective **1 = tolerant**, understanding, sympathetic, humane, lenient, kindly, considerate, favourable, forgiving, indulgent, magnanimous
2 = generous, liberal, kind, lavish, bountiful, philanthropic, benevolent, beneficent
charity noun **1 = donations**, help, fund, relief, gift, assistance, endowment, largesse or largess, philanthropy, benefaction, contributions, hand-out
2 = kindness, humanity, compassion, goodwill, generosity, altruism, indulgence, benevolence, fellow feeling
charlatan noun **= fraud**, fake, cheat, phony (*informal*), sham, impostor, quack, pretender, con man (*informal*), swindler
charm noun **1 = attraction**, appeal, allure, fascination, magnetism, mojo (*slang*) • *a man of great charm*
2 = spell, magic, sorcery, enchantment
3 = talisman, trinket, fetish, mojo, amulet
▶ verb **4 = enchant**, entrance, delight, captivate, bewitch • *He charmed the entire audience.*
See also: **beauty, entertain, please**
charmed See **lucky**
charming adjective **= attractive**, cute, appealing, pleasing, delightful, likable or likeable, seductive, captivating, fetching, winsome
chart noun **1 = table**, plan, map, blueprint, graph, diagram, road map
▶ verb **2 = plot**, draft, shape, outline, sketch, delineate, map out
charter noun **1 = document**, contract, permit, license, deed, prerogative
▶ verb **2 = hire**, commission, employ, rent, lease
3 = authorize, sanction
chase verb **1 = pursue**, hunt • *She*

chased the thief until he surrendered.
2 = drive, hound • *Angry protestors chased him away.*
▶ *noun* **3 = pursuit**, race, hunt, hunting

chasm *noun* **= gulf**, gap, crater, ravine, fissure, abyss, gorge, crevasse

chaste *adjective* **= pure**, simple, modest, innocent, unaffected, immaculate, virtuous, undefiled

chasten *verb* **= subdue**, correct, humble, discipline, tame, humiliate, chastise, put in one's place

chastise *verb* **1 = scold**, correct, discipline, censure, castigate, berate, upbraid
2 (*Old-fashioned*) **= beat**, punish, lash, whip, lick (*informal*), scourge, flog

chastity *noun* **= purity**, innocence, virtue, celibacy, virginity, modesty, continence, maidenhood

chat *noun* **1 = talk**, conversation • *We sat around and had a chat.*
▶ *verb* **2 = talk**, gossip • *He was chatting to his father.*
See also: **word**

chatter *noun* **1 = prattle**, chat, gossip, gab (*informal*), babble, blather
▶ *verb* **2 = prattle**, chat, gossip, gab (*informal*), babble, blather, chew the fat (*slang*), schmooze (*slang*)

chatty *See* **talkative**

chauvinism *See* **prejudice**

cheap *adjective* **1 = inexpensive**, bargain, reasonable, economical • *Cheap flights are available.*
OPPOSITE: expensive
2 = inferior, tacky, second-rate • *a suit made of some cheap material*
See also: **petty**

cheapen *verb* **= degrade**, lower, discredit, disparage, demean, denigrate, devalue, belittle, depreciate, debase

cheat *verb* **1 = deceive**, con (*informal*), rip off (*slang*), defraud, dupe, swindle, fleece • *the people he cheated out of their life savings*
2 = deceiver, shark, trickster,

charlatan, con man (*informal*), double-crosser (*informal*), sharper, swindler
3 = deception, fraud, scam (*slang*), swindle, deceit, trickery, rip-off (*slang*)
See also: **crook**

cheating *See* **dishonesty**

check *verb* **1 = examine**, check out (*informal*), test, inspect, crosscheck • *Check all the details first.*
2 = stop, control, halt, curb, restrain, inhibit • *a policy to check the inflation rate*
▷ **check out** *See* **check, try**
▶ *noun* **3 = examination**, test, inspection • *a thorough check of the equipment*
4 = stoppage, control, curb, restraint, obstacle, obstruction, limitation, constraint, impediment, damper, hindrance
See also: **block, delay, foil, frustrate, hinder, slow (down)**

checkup *See* **examination**

cheek *noun* (*Informal*)
= impudence, audacity, chutzpah (*informal*), nerve, lip (*slang*), disrespect, effrontery, impertinence, insolence, temerity

cheeky *adjective* **= impudent**, forward, disrespectful, audacious, saucy, impertinent, insolent, insulting, pert

cheer *verb* **1 = applaud**, hail, acclaim, clap, root for (*sports*)
2 = cheer up, encourage, comfort, brighten, uplift, hearten, gladden, buoy up
▷ **cheer up = comfort**, encourage, hearten, gladden, enliven; **= take heart**, rally, buck up (*informal*), perk up
▶ *noun* **3 = applause**, ovation, acclamation, plaudits

cheerful *adjective* **= happy**, bright, merry, buoyant, jolly, light-hearted, cheery, jaunty • *She was very cheerful despite her illness.*
OPPOSITE: miserable

cheerfulness *noun* **= happiness**, exuberance, buoyancy, gaiety, geniality, good cheer, good humour, high spirits, jauntiness, light-heartedness

cheerless *adjective* = **gloomy**, dismal, bleak, woeful, miserable, dreary, drab, desolate, sombre, forlorn

cheery *adjective* = **cheerful**, happy, sunny, upbeat, jolly, chirpy, good-humoured • *He is loved by everyone for his cheery disposition.*

cherish *verb* **1** = **cling to**, encourage, sustain, treasure, foster, entertain, nurture, prize, harbour, cleave to, hold dear **2** = **care for**, support, love, nurse, shelter, comfort, hold dear

cherished *See* **beloved, dear**

chest *noun* = **box**, case, casket, trunk, coffer, crate, strongbox

chew *verb* = **munch**, crunch, chomp, gnaw • *Eat slowly and chew your food properly.*
See also: **bite**

> **INFORMALLY SPEAKING**
> **chew out**: scold
> **chew the fat**: chat

chewy *adjective* = **tough**, as tough as old boots, leathery

chic *adjective* = **stylish**, cool (*informal*), smart, elegant, trendy (*informal*), fashionable, phat (*slang*), designer (*informal*)

chicken *See* **coward, cowardly**

chide *verb* (Old-fashioned) = **scold**, criticize, rebuke, lecture, reprimand, censure, berate, admonish, reproach, reprove, tell off (*informal*)

chief *noun* **1** = **head**, leader, director, manager, boss, warden, chieftain • *the chief of the fire department*
▶ *adjective* **2** = **primary**, key, prime, main, principal, foremost, prevailing • *The job went to one of her chief rivals.*
See also: **first, leading, supreme, top**

chiefly *adverb* **1** = **especially**, essentially, primarily, principally, above all **2** = **mainly**, usually, mostly, largely, predominantly, in

general, in the main, on the whole

chieftain *See* **chief**

child *noun* = **youngster**, baby, kid (*informal*), infant, minor, toddler, offspring, juvenile, tot • *I lived in Manitoba as a child.*
OPPOSITE: adult
RELATED WORDS
adjective: filial
prefix: pedo-

childbirth *noun* = **child-bearing**, delivery, confinement, labour, travail, lying-in, parturition

childhood *noun* = **youth**, minority, infancy, boyhood *or* girlhood, immaturity, schooldays

childish *adjective* = **immature**, juvenile, infantile, puerile • *I don't have time for this childish behaviour.*
OPPOSITE: mature

> **CONFUSABLES**
> *Childish* means *immature*, like a child.
> *Childlike* means *innocent*, like a child.

childlike *adjective* = **innocent**, simple, naive, artless, guileless, ingenuous, trusting

chill *noun* **1** = **cold**, bite, nip, sharpness, coolness, crispness, coldness, frigidity, rawness
▶ *verb* **2** = **cool**, freeze, refrigerate **3** = **dishearten**, discourage, depress, dampen, dismay, deject
▶ *adjective* **4** = **cold**, sharp, raw, bleak, frigid, chilly, wintry, freezing, biting

chilled *See* **cool, frozen**

chilling *See* **scary**

chilly *adjective* **1** = **cool**, fresh, sharp, crisp, brisk, drafty, nippy, penetrating **2** = **unfriendly**, hostile, frigid, unresponsive, unsympathetic, unwelcoming

chime *verb, noun* = **ring**, sound, toll, jingle, clang, peal, tinkle

china *noun* = **pottery**, service, ware, porcelain, ceramics, crockery, tableware

chink *noun* = **opening**, crack, gap,

fissure, cleft, cranny, crevice, aperture

chip noun **1 = scratch**, notch, fragment, shaving, nick, shard, sliver, wafer
▶ verb **2 = nick**, damage, whittle, gash, chisel

chirp verb **= chirrup**, pipe, peep, twitter, cheep, tweet, warble

chirpy See **cheery**

chisel See **carve**

chivalrous adjective **= courteous**, brave, bold, courageous, valiant, gallant, honourable, gentlemanly

chivalry noun **= courtesy**, courage, knighthood, politeness, gallantry, gentlemanliness, knight-errantry

choice noun **1 = range**, variety, selection • available in a choice of colours
2 = option, say, alternative • They had little choice in the matter.
▶ adjective **3 = best**, prime, rare, select, excellent, exclusive, elite
See also: **superior, will**

choke verb **1 = strangle**, overpower, stifle, suppress, gag, smother, throttle, suffocate, asphyxiate
2 = block, stop, bar, clog, bung, obstruct, congest, constrict

choose verb **= pick**, take, select, opt for • a number of foods from which to choose
See also: **decide, determine**

choosy adjective **= fussy**, particular, selective, picky (informal), finicky, discriminating, faddy, fastidious

chop verb **= cut**, hack, fell, lop • I heard him chopping wood in the yard.

chore noun **= task**, job, duty, burden, errand, joe job (Canad informal)

chortle verb, noun **= chuckle**, crow, guffaw, cackle

chorus noun **1 = choir**, ensemble, choristers, singers, vocalists
2 = refrain, response, strain, burden
3 = unison, accord, concert, harmony

christen verb **1 = baptize**

2 = name, call, term, title, style, dub, designate

Christmas noun **= festive season**, Noel, Xmas, Yule, Yuletide

chronicle noun **1 = record**, history, story, account, register, journal, blog (informal), diary, narrative, weblog, annals
▶ verb **2 = record**, report, tell, enter, relate, register, recount, narrate, put on record, set down

chubby adjective **= plump**, buxom, flabby, round, portly, stout, rotund, tubby

chuck verb (Informal) **= throw**, pitch, cast, toss, hurl, fling, sling, heave

chuckle verb **= laugh**, crow, giggle, exult, chortle, snigger, titter

chum noun (Informal) **= friend**, comrade, companion, crony, homeboy (slang), homegirl (slang), pal (informal)

chunk noun **= piece**, block, mass, portion, lump, slab, nugget, dollop (informal), hunk

chunky See **stocky**

churlish adjective **= rude**, harsh, surly, sullen, brusque, ill-tempered, impolite, uncivil

churn verb **= stir up**, beat, toss, swirl, agitate, convulse

chutzpah noun (Informal) **= impudence**, nerve, lip (slang), disrespect, audacity, effrontery, impertinence, insolence, temerity

cinema noun **= films**, big screen (informal), flicks (slang), motion pictures, movies, pictures

cipher noun **1 = code**, cryptograph
2 = nobody, nonentity

circle noun **1 = ring**, globe, disc, sphere, orb
2 = group, company, set, club, society, clique, coterie
▶ verb **3 = go round**, ring, surround, enclose, envelop, encircle, circumnavigate, circumscribe

circuit noun **= course**, track, tour, route, journey, orbit, revolution, lap

circuitous adjective **= indirect**,

oblique, roundabout, rambling, tortuous, labyrinthine, meandering, winding

circular *adjective* **1** = **round**, rotund, ring-shaped, spherical **2** = **orbital**, cyclical, circuitous ▶ *noun* **3** = **advertisement**, notice

circulate *verb* **1** = **spread**, distribute, propagate • *He circulated rumours about everyone.* **2** = **flow**, revolve, rotate, radiate, gyrate

circulation *noun* **1** = **bloodstream** **2** = **flow**, motion, rotation, circling **3** = **distribution**, spread, currency, transmission, dissemination

circumference *noun* = **boundary**, border, edge, outline, rim, perimeter, extremity, periphery, limits

circumstance *noun* = **event**, condition, situation, incident, accident, respect, particular, contingency, occurrence, happening

circumstances *plural noun* = **situation**, state, station, position, status, means, state of affairs

cistern *noun* = **tank**, sink, reservoir, basin, vat

citadel *noun* = **fortress**, keep, tower, stronghold, bastion, fortification

cite *verb* = **quote**, name, advance, mention, extract, specify, adduce, enumerate, allude to

citizen *noun* = **inhabitant**, resident, subject, dweller, denizen, townsman

city *noun* = **town**, municipality, metropolis • *the city of Regina* RELATED WORD *adjective*: civic

civic *adjective* = **public**, local, municipal, communal

civil *adjective* **1** = **civic**, political, domestic, municipal **2** = **polite**, refined, affable, courteous, obliging, urbane, well-mannered

civility *See* **courtesy, politeness**

civilization *noun* **1** = **culture**, development, education, progress, advancement, cultivation, sophistication, refinement, enlightenment **2** = **society**, people, community, nation, polity

civilize *verb* = **cultivate**, educate, refine, tame, enlighten, sophisticate

civilized *adjective* = **cultured**, enlightened • *a highly civilized society* *See also*: **refined**

claim *verb* **1** = **assert**, hold, allege, maintain, insist, profess • *He claims to have lived here all his life.* **2** = **demand**, need, ask, require, insist, call for ▶ *noun* **3** = **assertion**, allegation • *He rejected claims that he had taken bribes.* **4** = **demand**, call, request, application, requirement, petition **5** = **right**, title *See also*: **argue**

clairvoyant *noun* **1** = **psychic**, visionary, diviner, fortune-teller ▶ *adjective* **2** = **psychic**, visionary, extrasensory, second-sighted, telepathic

clamber *verb* = **climb**, scale, scramble, claw, shin, scrabble

clammy *adjective* = **moist**, close, sticky, damp, sweaty, dank

clamour *noun* = **noise**, outcry, uproar, racket, commotion, din, hubbub, shouting

clamp *noun* **1** = **vice**, press, grip, bracket, fastener ▶ *verb* **2** = **fasten**, fix, secure, brace, make fast

clan *noun* = **family**, group, society, faction, tribe, fraternity, brotherhood

clandestine *adjective* = **secret**, private, underground, covert, stealthy, surreptitious, cloak-and-dagger, concealed, furtive

clang *See* **ring, sound**

clap *verb* = **applaud**, cheer, acclaim

clarification *noun* = **explanation**,

interpretation, illumination, exposition, elucidation, simplification

clarify verb = **explain**, interpret, illuminate, simplify, clear up, elucidate, make plain, throw light on or shed light on

clarity noun = **clearness**, definition, transparency, precision, simplicity, lucidity, limpidity

clash verb 1 = **fight**, battle, wrangle, quarrel • A group of 400 demonstrators clashed with police. 2 = **conflict**, contradict, disagree, differ, jar, go against • Their decisions clashed with company policy. 3 = **crash**, bang, rattle, jar, clang, clank, clatter, jangle ▶ noun 4 = **fight**, battle, struggle, conflict, confrontation, skirmish (informal), squabble • a number of clashes between rival parties See also: **argument, dispute, game, war**

clasp verb 1 = **grip**, hold, press, embrace, clutch, hug, squeeze • I clasped the winning ticket tightly. 2 = **fasten**, connect ▶ noun 3 = **fastening**, catch, clip, buckle, fastener • She undid the clasp of her necklace. 4 = **grasp**, hold, embrace, grip, hug

class noun 1 = **group**, set, kind, type, sort, category, grade, genre • a new class of SUV ▶ verb 2 = **classify**, rate, rank, designate, grade, categorize • He is classed as a comedian. See also: **family, form, lesson, polish, range, variety**

classes See **course**

classic adjective 1 = **definitive**, standard, model, ideal, exemplary, quintessential, archetypal 2 = **typical**, standard, regular, usual, characteristic, time-honoured 3 = **best**, world-class, consummate, first-rate, finest, masterly

4 = **lasting**, enduring, immortal, abiding, ageless, deathless, undying 5 (Informal) = **hilarious**, comical, ludicrous, hysterical, uproarious ▶ noun 6 = **standard**, model, masterpiece, prototype, paradigm, exemplar

classical adjective = **pure**, elegant, refined, restrained, harmonious, symmetrical, understated, well-proportioned

classification noun = **categorization**, analysis, arrangement, grading, sorting, taxonomy, profiling

classify verb = **categorize**, rank, sort, arrange, grade • We can classify frogs according to family. See also: **class, group**

classy adjective (Informal) = **high-class**, exclusive, elegant, superior, stylish, swanky, ritzy, up-market, top-drawer

clause noun = **section**, part, condition, article, passage, chapter, paragraph

claw noun 1 = **nail**, tentacle, talon, pincer ▶ verb 2 = **scratch**, tear, rip, dig, maul, scrape, lacerate

clay See **earth, soil**

clean adjective 1 = **spotless**, impeccable, immaculate, laundered, washed • clean shoes OPPOSITE: dirty 2 = **hygienic**, antiseptic, uncontaminated, purified, sterilized, unpolluted • a lack of clean water and sanitation OPPOSITE: contaminated 3 = **moral**, good, innocent, pure, decent, upright, respectable, honourable, chaste, virtuous 4 = **complete**, final, total, whole, perfect, entire, decisive, thorough, conclusive, unimpaired ▶ verb 5 = **cleanse**, wash, wipe, dust, scrub, scour, swab, sponge, deep clean • We cleaned the house from top to bottom. OPPOSITE: soil See also: **blank, simple**

cleanliness See **hygiene**

cleanse *verb* = **clean**, clear, wash, scrub, purge, scour, purify, rinse, absolve

cleanser *noun* = **detergent**, soap, solvent, disinfectant, purifier, scourer

clear *adjective* **1** = **obvious**, apparent, plain, explicit, evident, blatant, definite, manifest, unequivocal, palpable, conspicuous • *He made it clear that he did not want to talk.*

2 = **transparent**, translucent, crystalline, glassy • *a clear liquid*
OPPOSITE: cloudy

3 = **certain**, sure, positive, convinced, definite, satisfied, decided, resolved

4 = **bright**, light, fine, fair, sunny, luminous, cloudless, shining, unclouded

5 = **unobstructed**, open, free, empty, smooth, unimpeded, unhindered

6 = **unblemished**, clean, innocent, pure, immaculate, untarnished

▶ *verb* **7** = **absolve**, acquit • *She was cleared of all suspicion.*
OPPOSITE: convict

8 = **unblock**, open, free, rid, unload, loosen, extricate, disentangle

9 = **pass over**, miss, jump, leap, vault

10 = **brighten**, lighten, break up

11 = **clean**, wipe, erase, refine, cleanse, tidy *or* tidy up, purify, sweep away

12 = **gain**, make, earn, acquire, secure, reap

▷ **clear up** = **tidy (up)**, order, straighten, rearrange, put in order; = **solve**, explain, resolve, clarify, unravel, elucidate, straighten out
See also: **blank, visible**

> **INFORMALLY SPEAKING**
> **clear out (or off)**: leave
> **in the clear**: free of guilt or blame

clear-cut *adjective*
= **straightforward**, specific, plain, explicit, precise, definite, black-and-white, unequivocal, unambiguous, cut-and-dried (*informal*)

clearly *adverb* = **obviously**, openly, undoubtedly, markedly, evidently, distinctly, undeniably, overtly, beyond doubt

cleft *noun* = **opening**, break, crack, breach, gap, rent, fracture, fissure, cranny, chink, crevice

clergy *noun* = **priesthood**, ministry, churchmen, clergymen, clerics, holy orders, the cloth

clergyman *noun* = **minister**, cleric, priest, pastor, chaplain, padre, vicar, man of God, man of the cloth, parson

clever *adjective* = **intelligent**, smart, bright, shrewd, brainy (*informal*) • *Today's contestants are all quite clever.*
See also: **astute, brilliant, witty**

cleverness *noun* = **intelligence**, ability, ingenuity, brains, quick wits, resourcefulness, shrewdness, smartness

cliché *noun* = **platitude**, stereotype, commonplace, truism, banality, hackneyed phrase

clichéd See **hackneyed**

client *noun* = **customer**, consumer, patient, shopper, buyer, patron, applicant

clientele *noun* = **customers**, market, trade, business, following, patronage, clients, regulars

cliff *noun* = **rock face**, scar, bluff, overhang, rampart, precipice, escarpment, crag, scarp

climactic *adjective* = **crucial**, critical, peak, decisive, paramount

climate *noun* = **weather**, temperature

climax *noun* = **culmination**, top, summit, highlight, peak, height, zenith, high point

climb *verb* = **ascend**, scale, mount, clamber • *Climbing the first hill took half an hour.*
▷ **climb down** = **descend**, dismount; = **back down**, retreat, retract, eat one's words

▷ **climb to** See **reach**
See also: **rise**

clinch verb = **settle**, confirm, decide, determine, conclude, secure, seal, set the seal on, sew up (informal)

cling verb = **stick**, embrace, grip, clutch, hug, adhere, grasp, clasp

clinical adjective = **unemotional**, cold, scientific, objective, dispassionate, analytic, detached, impersonal

clip[1] verb 1 = **trim**, cut, crop, shorten, curtail, pare, prune, shear, snip
▶ noun, verb 2 (Informal) = **smack**, strike, knock, punch, thump, wallop (informal), whack, cuff, clout (informal)

clip[2] verb 1 = **attach**, hold, fix, pin, staple, fasten

clique noun = **group**, set, gang, circle, faction, cabal, coterie

cloak noun 1 = **cape**, wrap, coat, mantle
▶ verb 2 = **cover**, screen, hide, mask, veil, conceal, obscure, disguise, camouflage

clog verb = **obstruct**, block, jam, hinder, impede, congest

close[1] verb 1 = **shut**, secure, lock
• Close the gate behind you.
OPPOSITE: open
2 = **block**, bar, seal, plug, obstruct, stop up • The northbound road is closed due to an accident.
3 = **end**, finish, complete, conclude, cease, terminate, shut down, wind up
4 = **connect**, join, couple, unite, fuse, come together
▶ noun 5 = **end**, finish, finale, conclusion, completion, ending, culmination, denouement
See also: **halt**

close[2] adjective 1 = **near**, nearby, adjacent, handy, adjoining, nigh, at hand, cheek by jowl, impending, neighbouring • The restaurant was close to their home.
OPPOSITE: distant
2 = **intimate**, confidential, familiar, loving, dear, devoted, inseparable, attached • We became close friends.

OPPOSITE: distant
3 = **careful**, minute, intense, detailed, thorough, rigorous, painstaking
4 = **compact**, tight, crowded, packed, dense, jam-packed, impenetrable, congested
5 = **stifling**, heavy, oppressive, humid, stuffy, muggy, airless, suffocating, sweltering
6 = **secretive**, private, secret, reticent, taciturn, uncommunicative
▷ **close to** See **almost**
See also: **alike, beside, friendly, immediate, imminent**

closed adjective 1 = **shut**, sealed, locked, fastened, out of service
2 = **exclusive**, restricted
3 = **finished**, over, concluded, decided, ended, resolved, settled, terminated

closely See **immediately, well**

closeness See **friendship**

closest See **next**

closet See **secret**

closing See **final, last**

clot See **thicken**

cloth noun = **fabric**, material, textiles • a piece of red cloth

clothe verb = **dress**, cover, array, equip, drape, robe, attire, garb, swathe, fit out

clothes plural noun = **clothing**, wear, dress, gear (informal), costume, outfit, wardrobe, attire, garments • They spend too much money on clothes.

clothing noun = **clothes**, wear, dress, gear (informal), costume, outfit, wardrobe, apparel, attire, garb, garments

clotted See **thick**

cloud noun 1 = **mist**, fog, haze, billow, vapour • The sky was dark with clouds.
▶ verb 2 = **confuse**, distort, muddle • Anger has clouded his judgment.
3 = **obscure**, shadow, eclipse, shade, overshadow, darken, dim, obfuscate, becloud, veil

cloudy adjective 1 = **dull**, gloomy, overcast, leaden • a cloudy sky
OPPOSITE: clear

2 = opaque, murky, muddy • *a glass of cloudy liquid*
OPPOSITE: clear
See also: **dark**

clout (*Informal*) ▶ *noun*
1 = influence, power, authority, pull, weight, prestige
▶ *verb* **2 = hit**, strike, punch, thump, wallop (*informal*), clobber (*slang*), sock (*slang*)

clown *noun* **1 = comedian**, comic, fool, prankster, harlequin, buffoon, joker, jester
▶ *verb* **2 = play the fool**, jest, act the fool, mess around

cloying *See* **sweet**

club *noun* **1 = association**, group, union, society, circle, guild • *a swimming club*
2 = stick, bat • *pictures of cave dwellers armed with clubs*
▶ *verb* **3 = beat**, batter, bash, bludgeon • *Two thugs clubbed him with baseball bats.*
See also: **fellowship**

clue *noun* **= indication**, lead, sign, evidence, hint, trace, suggestion, suspicion, pointer

clueless *adjective* **= stupid**, dim, slow, simple, thick, dull, half-witted, unintelligent, witless

clump *noun* **1 = cluster**, group, mass, bunch, bundle
▶ *verb* **2 = stomp**, lumber, thump, plod, thud, tramp

clumsiness *noun*
= awkwardness, ungainliness • *The accident was entirely the result of his own clumsiness.*

clumsy *adjective* **= awkward**, lumbering, ungainly, gauche, unco-ordinated • *He is big and clumsy in his movements.*
OPPOSITE: graceful

cluster *noun* **1 = gathering**, group, collection, bunch, knot, batch, clump, assemblage
▶ *verb* **2 = gather**, group, collect, bunch, assemble, flock

clutch *verb* **= seize**, catch, grab, embrace, grip, snatch, grasp, clasp, cling to

clutches *plural noun* **= power**, control, custody, possession, grip, sway, grasp, claws, hands, keeping

clutter *verb* **1 = litter**, scatter, strew
▶ *noun* **2 = untidiness**, disorder, confusion, disarray, mess, litter, muddle, jumble

cluttered *See* **untidy**

coach *noun* **1 = bus**, car, vehicle, carriage, charabanc
2 = instructor, teacher, trainer, handler, tutor
▶ *verb* **3 = instruct**, prepare, train, exercise, drill, tutor

coaching *See* **education, lesson**

coalesce *verb* **= blend**, combine, mix, unite, merge, incorporate, integrate, fuse, amalgamate

coalition *noun* **= alliance**, union, merger, association, combination, bloc, conjunction, fusion, amalgamation, confederation

coarse *adjective* **1 = rough**, crude, unfinished, homespun, unrefined, unprocessed, impure, unpolished, unpurified
2 = vulgar, improper, rude, indecent, earthy, indelicate, ribald, smutty

coarseness *noun* **1 = roughness**, crudity, unevenness
2 = vulgarity, bawdiness, crudity, earthiness, indelicacy, ribaldry, smut, uncouthness

coast *noun* **1 = shore**, border, beach, coastline, seaside • *a holiday by the coast*
2 = cruise, taxi, sail, drift, glide, freewheel

coastline *See* **coast**

coat *noun* **1 = fur**, hide, skin, hair, pelt, wool, fleece • *She gave the dog's coat a brush.*
2 = layer, coating, covering, overlay
▶ *verb* **3 = cover**, spread, apply, smear, plaster

coating *noun* **= layer**, coat, covering • *a thin coating of ice*
See also: **cover**

coax *verb* **= persuade**, cajole, talk into • *We coaxed her into coming with us.*
See also: **prompt**

cocktail *noun* **= mixture**, mix,

combination, blend

cocky adjective = **overconfident**, arrogant, brash, conceited • *He was a bit cocky because he was winning all the time.*
See also: **boastful**

code noun 1 = **cipher**, cryptograph
2 = **principles**, system, convention, custom, etiquette, maxim, canon, ethics, manners, regulations, rules

cogent adjective = **convincing**, strong, powerful, effective, potent, influential, forceful, weighty, compelling

cogitate verb = **think**, consider, reflect, ponder, deliberate, contemplate, muse, meditate, mull over, ruminate

coherent adjective 1 = **consistent**, organized, meaningful, logical, systematic, rational, orderly, lucid, reasoned
2 = **intelligible**, articulate, comprehensible

coil verb = **wind**, curl, twist, spiral, loop, twine • *a coiled spring*

coin noun 1 = **money**, change, cash, silver, specie, copper
▶ verb 2 = **invent**, create, originate, forge, mint, fabricate, mould, make up

coincide verb 1 = **occur simultaneously**, synchronize, coexist, be concurrent
2 = **agree**, accord, match, square, tally, correspond, harmonize, concur

coincidence noun 1 = **chance**, accident, luck, fluke, happy accident, stroke of luck
2 = **coinciding**, correspondence, conjunction, correlation, concurrence

coincidental adjective = **chance**, accidental, casual, unintentional, unplanned, fortuitous, fluky (*informal*)

cold adjective 1 = **chilly**, bitter, raw, icy, bleak, arctic, wintry, freezing, biting • *the coldest winter in ten years*
OPPOSITE: hot
2 = **unfriendly**, distant, frigid,

lukewarm, reserved, aloof, stony • *a cold, unfeeling individual*
OPPOSITE: warm
▶ noun 3 = **coldness**, chill, frigidity, frostiness, iciness
See also: **callous, cool, impersonal, remote, stiff**

> INFORMALLY SPEAKING
> **cold feet**: loss of nerve or courage
> **out cold**: unconscious
> **out in the cold**: alone or neglected

cold-blooded adjective = **callous**, ruthless, steely, heartless, dispassionate, unemotional, stony-hearted, unfeeling

collaborate verb 1 = **work together**, participate, cooperate, join forces, play ball (*informal*), team up
2 = **conspire**, collude, cooperate, fraternize

collaboration noun = **teamwork**, association, alliance, partnership, cooperation

collaborator noun 1 = **co-worker**, partner, associate, colleague, confederate, team-mate
2 = **traitor**, turncoat, fraternizer, quisling

collapse verb 1 = **fall down**, give way • *The whole building is about to collapse.*
2 = **fail**, founder, fold • *Thousands of small businesses collapsed last year.*
▶ noun 3 = **failure**, downfall • *the collapse of their marriage*
4 = **faint**, breakdown, exhaustion, prostration
See also: **crash, fall, give**

collar verb (*Informal*) = **seize**, arrest, catch, capture, grab, apprehend, nail (*informal*)

colleague noun = **fellow worker**, partner, associate, workmate • *I'll have to consult my colleagues.*
See also: **assistant**

collect verb 1 = **gather**, raise, assemble, accumulate • *collecting signatures for a petition*
OPPOSITE: scatter
2 = **assemble**, rally, cluster, convene, converge,

congregate, flock together
See also: **concentrate, stockpile**

collected adjective = **calm**, cool, serene, composed, poised, self-possessed, unperturbed, unruffled

collection noun
1 = **accumulation**, group, store, assortment • my CD collection
2 = **group**, company, crowd, assembly, cluster, assortment
3 = **contribution**, offering, alms, offertory
See also: **number, variety**

collective adjective = **combined**, corporate, joint, aggregate, composite, shared, unified, cumulative, united

collectively See **together**

collide verb 1 = **crash**, clash, come into collision, meet head-on
2 = **conflict**, clash
▷ **collide with** See **hit**

collision noun 1 = **crash**, impact, accident, bump, pile-up (informal), smash, wreck
2 = **conflict**, opposition, clash, encounter, confrontation, skirmish

colloquial adjective = **conversational**, everyday, informal • a colloquial expression

colony noun 1 = **dominion**, territory, dependency • a former British colony
2 = **community**, settlement, outpost • an artists' colony

colossal adjective = **huge**, massive, vast, enormous, mammoth, immense, gigantic • a colossal statue
OPPOSITE: tiny
See also: **large, unbelievable**

colour noun 1 = **hue**, shade, tint, pigmentation • Her favourite colour is blue.
2 = **paint**, dye, pigment • food colour
▶ verb 3 = **tint**, paint, dye, stain • men and women who colour their hair
4 = **bias**, prejudice, distort, slant • The experience coloured his opinion of lawyers.
5 = **blush**, flush, redden

colourful adjective 1 = **bright**, rich, intense, brilliant, vibrant, vivid, psychedelic, jazzy (informal), multicoloured, kaleidoscopic • colourful clothes
OPPOSITE: dull
2 = **interesting**, rich, graphic, vivid, lively • a colourful character
OPPOSITE: dull

colourless adjective 1 = **drab**, anemic, wan, achromatic, ashen, bleached, faded, washed out
2 = **uninteresting**, dull, dreary, lacklustre, characterless, insipid, vapid

column noun 1 = **pillar**, post, support, shaft, upright, obelisk
2 = **line**, file, row, rank, procession, cavalcade

coma noun = **unconsciousness**, oblivion, stupor, trance

comb verb 1 = **untangle**, dress, arrange, groom
2 = **search**, hunt, rake, scour, forage, sift, ransack, rummage

combat noun 1 = **fight**, action, war, battle, struggle, contest, conflict, encounter, engagement, skirmish, warfare
▶ verb 2 = **fight**, oppose, resist, defy, withstand, do battle with

combatant noun = **fighter**, soldier, opponent, enemy, warrior, adversary, antagonist

combination noun 1 = **mixture**, mix, blend, amalgamation • a combination of charm and skill
2 = **association**, union, coalition, alliance, federation, consortium, syndicate, confederation
See also: **cross**

combine verb = **mix**, unite, merge, blend, integrate, fuse, amalgamate • trying to combine business with pleasure
OPPOSITE: separate

combustion See **fire**

come verb 1 = **arrive**, appear, enter, materialize, show up (informal), turn up (informal) • Two young children came into the room.
2 = **happen**, fall, occur, take place • It's too bad that birthdays

come only once a year.
3 = move towards, near, advance, approach, draw near
4 = result, issue, emerge, flow, arise, originate, emanate
5 = reach, extend
6 = be available, be made, be offered, be on offer, be produced
▷ **come about = happen**, result, occur, arise, transpire (*informal*), befall, come to pass, take place
▷ **come across = find**, meet, discover, notice, encounter, unearth, bump into (*informal*), chance upon, stumble upon
▷ **come after** See **follow**
▷ **come apart** See **split**
▷ **come back = return**, recur, re-enter, reappear
▷ **come between** See **divide**
▷ **come first** See **win**
▷ **come on** See **flourish**
▷ **come out** See **appear**
▷ **come to = revive**, rally, recover, come around, regain consciousness; = **amount to**, total, add up to
▷ **come together** See **assemble**
▷ **come upon** See **meet**
▷ **come up with** See **invent**
▷ **come with** See **accompany**
comeback *noun* **1** (*Informal*)
= **return**, rally, rebound, recovery, triumph, revival, resurgence
2 = response, reply, retaliation, retort, rejoinder, riposte
comedian *noun* = **comic**, card (*informal*), clown, wit, wag, joker, humorist, jester, funny man
comedown *noun* **1 = decline**, reverse, demotion, deflation
2 (*Informal*) = **disappointment**, blow, humiliation, letdown, anticlimax
comedy *noun* = **humour**, fun, farce, hilarity, jesting, joking, light entertainment
comeuppance *noun* (*Informal*)
= **punishment**, retribution, chastening, deserts, due reward, recompense
comfort *noun* **1 = ease**, luxury, well-being • *I settled back in comfort.*

2 = relief, help, support, satisfaction, consolation • *Her words gave him some comfort.*
▶ *verb* **3 = console**, cheer, reassure, soothe • *trying to comfort the upset child*
comfortable *adjective*
1 = relaxing, easy, cozy, restful, homey • *a comfortable chair*
OPPOSITE: uncomfortable
2 = at ease, happy, contented, at home, relaxed • *I don't feel comfortable around him.*
OPPOSITE: uneasy
3 (*Informal*) = **well-off**, affluent, prosperous, well-to-do, in clover (*informal*)
See also: **leisurely, wealthy**
comforting *adjective* = **consoling**, soothing, heart-warming, encouraging, cheering, consolatory, reassuring
comic *adjective* **1 = funny**, humorous, amusing, witty, comical, farcical, droll, jocular
▶ *noun* **2 = comedian**, clown, wit, buffoon, wag, humorist, jester, funny man
comical *adjective* = **funny**, comic, hilarious, humorous, amusing, priceless, farcical, droll, side-splitting
coming *adjective*
1 = approaching, near, imminent, forthcoming, nigh, at hand, impending, in store
▶ *noun* **2 = arrival**, approach, advent
command *verb* **1 = order**, bid (*formal*), demand, direct • *I commanded the dog to lie down.*
2 = control, lead, head, manage, supervise • *the general who commanded the UN troops*
▶ *noun* **3 = order**, instruction, injunction, decree, directive, bidding • *The punishment was carried out at the emperor's command.*
4 = knowledge, grasp, mastery • *a good command of English*
5 = authority, government, charge, power, rule, control, management, supervision, mastery

See also: **administer, direction, exact, instruct, tell**

commandeer *verb* = **seize**, appropriate, confiscate, sequester, requisition, sequestrate

commander *noun* = **officer**, head, leader, chief, captain, boss (*informal*), ruler, alpha male, commanding officer

commanding *adjective* = **controlling**, decisive, dominant, superior, advantageous, dominating

commemorate *verb* = **celebrate**, honour • *concerts to commemorate the anniversary of his birth*

commemoration *noun* = **remembrance**, ceremony, tribute, honouring, memorial service

commence *verb* = **begin**, start, open, originate, origin, initiate, embark on, enter upon

commencement *noun* = **beginning**, start, launch, birth, opening, origin, dawn, onset, inauguration, outset, inception, initiation, embarkation

commend *verb* = **praise**, approve, recommend, applaud, acclaim, compliment, extol, speak highly of

commendable *adjective* = **praiseworthy**, worthy, exemplary, deserving, admirable, laudable, meritorious, creditable, estimable

commendation *noun* = **praise**, credit, approval, recommendation, acclaim, kudos, encouragement, acclamation, approbation, good opinion, panegyric

comment *verb* **1** = **remark**, say, note, mention, observe, point out • *He refused to comment on the rumours.*
2 = **annotate**, explain, interpret, elucidate
▶ *noun* **3** = **remark**, statement, observation • *sarcastic comments*
4 = **note**, explanation,

commentary, illustration, exposition, annotation
See also: **word**

commentary *noun*
1 = **narration**, description, voice-over
2 = **notes**, review, analysis, explanation, critique, treatise

commentator *noun*
1 = **reporter**, sportscaster, special correspondent
2 = **critic**, interpreter, annotator

commerce *noun* = **trade**, business, traffic, exchange, dealing

commercial *adjective*
1 = **mercantile**, trading
2 = **materialistic**, mercenary, profit-making
▶ *noun* **3** = **advertisement**, ad (*informal*), announcement, plug (*informal*)

commiserate *verb* = **sympathize**, console, pity, feel for

commission *noun* **1** = **duty**, mission, task, mandate, errand
2 = **fee**, cut, percentage, rake-off (*slang*), royalties
3 = **committee**, board, delegation, commissioners, deputation, representatives
▶ *verb* **4** = **appoint**, order, contract, select, nominate, engage, delegate, authorize, empower, depute

commit *verb* **1** = **do**, perform, perpetrate, carry out • *A crime has been committed.*
2 = **put in custody**, imprison, confine

commitment *noun*
1 = **dedication**, involvement, loyalty, devotion
2 = **responsibility**, tie, duty, obligation, liability, engagement

committed *See* **fervent**
committee *See* **council**

commode *noun* = **washroom**, lavatory, latrine, loo, powder room, convenience *or* public convenience, toilet, water closet, W.C., restroom, bathroom

commodity *See* **product**

common adjective 1 = **general**, popular, widespread, universal, prevalent, prevailing • *a common complaint*
OPPOSITE: rare
2 = **ordinary**, average, standard, usual, everyday, plain, commonplace • *the common cold*
3 = **vulgar**, rude, coarse • *a common, rude guest*
OPPOSITE: refined
4 = **collective**, public, popular, social, communal, shared • *the common good*
▷ **common sense** = **good sense**, judgment, prudence, level-headedness • *Use your common sense.*
See also: **head, sense**
See also: **frequent, low, natural**

commonplace adjective
1 = **everyday**, common, obvious, ordinary, mundane, banal, humdrum, widespread
▶ noun 2 = **cliché**, truism, banality, platitude

commotion noun = **disturbance**, disorder, turmoil, excitement, uproar, fuss, upheaval, furor, tumult, hue and cry, rumpus

communal adjective = **public**, general, joint, collective, shared

commune noun = **community**, collective, cooperative, kibbutz
▶ verb
▷ **commune with**
= **contemplate**, ponder, meditate on, muse on, reflect on

communicate verb 1 = **contact**, correspond, be in contact, be in touch • *We communicate mainly by email.*
2 = **pass on**, spread, inform, transmit, convey, impart • *The results will be communicated by mail.*
▷ **communicate with** See contact
See also: **express**

communication noun
1 = **passing on**, link, contact, transmission, conversation, correspondence, dissemination
2 = **message**, report, news, statement, information, word, announcement, disclosure, dispatch

communicative adjective
= **talkative**, open, outgoing, forthcoming, frank, expansive, informative, chatty, loquacious, voluble

Communism noun = **socialism**, Bolshevism, collectivism, Marxism, state socialism

Communist noun = **socialist**, Red (informal), Marxist, Bolshevik, collectivist

community noun = **society**, people, company, public, state, commonwealth, populace, brotherhood, general public, residents

commuter noun = **daily traveller**, straphanger (informal), suburbanite

compact[1] adjective 1 = **closely packed**, solid, thick, dense, condensed, compressed, pressed together
2 = **brief**, terse, concise, succinct, compendious, to the point
▶ verb 3 = **pack closely**, stuff, cram, compress, condense, tamp

compact[2] noun = **agreement**, deal, contract, bond, treaty, bargain, understanding, pact, arrangement, covenant

companion noun 1 = **friend**, partner, comrade, pal (informal), crony • *They've been constant companions for the past six years.*
2 = **escort**, assistant, aide, attendant, chaperon, squire, plus-one (informal)

companionship noun
= **fellowship**, company, friendship, camaraderie, rapport, togetherness, comradeship, conviviality, esprit de corps

company noun 1 = **business**, house, firm, corporation, establishment, numbered company (Canad) • *a publishing company*
2 = **group**, party, community, crowd, band, circle, assembly, troupe, ensemble • *the Canadian Opera Company.*

3 = companionship, presence • *I could do with some company*
4 = guests, party, callers, visitors
See also: **association, body, enterprise, organization**
comparable *adjective* **1 = on a par**, equivalent, equal, tantamount, proportionate, commensurate, a match for, as good as, in a class with, on a level playing field (*informal*)
2 = similar, related, alike, akin, analogous, cognate, corresponding, cut from the same cloth, of a piece
comparative *adjective* = **relative**, qualified, by comparison
compare *verb* **1 = contrast**, weigh, juxtapose • *Compare these two illustrations.*
2 (usually with *with*) = **be on a par with**, match, approach, equal, bear comparison, be in the same class as, be the equal of, compete with, hold a candle to
▷ **compare to** = **liken to**, resemble, parallel, correlate to, equate to, identify with, mention in the same breath as
comparison *noun* **1 = contrast**, distinction, juxtaposition
2 = similarity, likeness, correlation, resemblance, analogy, comparability
compartment *noun* **1 = car** • *We shared our compartment with a group of tourists.*
2 = section, division, chamber, bay • *the freezer compartment of the fridge*
compass *noun* = **range**, area, reach, field, limit, extent, scope, boundary, realm, circumference
compassion *noun* = **sympathy**, understanding, humanity, condolence, mercy, sorrow, pity, kindness, tenderness, fellow feeling, tender-heartedness
compassionate *adjective* = **sympathetic**, kind, caring, humane, merciful, empathetic, kind-hearted, tender • *My father is a deeply compassionate man.*

See also: **benevolent, understanding**
compassionately *See* **well**
compatibility *noun* = **harmony**, agreement, sympathy, empathy, affinity, rapport, concord, like-mindedness
compatible *adjective* = **harmonious**, consistent, congenial, in keeping • *Business partners should be compatible.*
OPPOSITE: incompatible
compel *verb* = **force**, make, pressure, coerce, oblige, railroad (*informal*), obligate, pressurize, constrain, impel, dragoon
compelling *adjective*
1 = fascinating, irresistible, hypnotic, enchanting, enthralling, gripping, mesmeric, spellbinding
2 = pressing, urgent, binding, imperative, unavoidable, coercive, overriding, peremptory
3 = convincing, powerful, forceful, conclusive, weighty, irrefutable, cogent, telling
compensate *verb* **1 = repay**, reward, refund, atone • *You will be properly compensated for your loss.*
2 = cancel out, balance, offset, counteract, make up for • *His lack of skill was compensated for by his enthusiasm.*
See also: **pay**
compensation *noun* = **amends**, payment, atonement, damages • *compensation for his injuries*
compete *verb* = **contend**, fight, contest, vie • *companies competing for business*
See also: **play**
competence *noun* = **ability**, capacity, skill, fitness, capability, expertise, proficiency, suitability
competent *adjective* = **able**, fit, capable, adequate, suitable, qualified, proficient
competently *See* **well**
competition *noun* **1 = rivalry**, opposition, struggle, contest, contention • *There's a lot of competition for this year's Gemini Awards.*

2 = contest, event, championship, tournament • *a surfing competition*

3 = opposition, field, challengers, rivals

See also: **competitor, match**

competitive *adjective* **1 = cut-throat**, rival, aggressive, antagonistic, at odds, dog-eat-dog, opposing

2 = ambitious, combative

competitor *noun* **= contestant**, opposition, competition, rival, opponent, challenger, adversary • *one of the youngest competitors in the event*

See also: **candidate**

compilation *noun* **= collection**, treasury, accumulation, assortment, anthology, assemblage

compile *verb* **= put together**, gather, collect, organize, garner, accumulate, amass, cull, marshal

complacency *noun* **= self-satisfaction**, satisfaction, contentment, smugness

complacent *adjective* **= self-satisfied**, satisfied, smug, serene, contented, unconcerned, pleased with oneself, resting on one's laurels

complain *verb* **= find fault**, whine, carp, grumble, moan, grouse, make a fuss, kick up a fuss (*informal*), kvetch (*informal*) • *They always complain about the noise.*

See also: **protest**

complaint *noun* **1 = grumble**, protest, criticism, objection, grievance • *There have been a number of complaints about the food.*

2 = illness, disease, upset, disorder, ailment, sickness, malady, affliction

complement *noun*
1 = completion, supplement, counterpart, companion, consummation, finishing touch, rounding-off

2 = total, capacity, aggregate, quota, entirety, totality, wholeness

▶ *verb* **3 = complete**, cap (*informal*), crown, round off, set off

complementary *adjective* **= completing**, companion, reciprocal, corresponding, interdependent, interrelating, matched

complete *adjective* **1 = total**, perfect, absolute, outright, utter, thorough, consummate • *a complete transformation*

2 = whole, full, entire, intact, undivided • *a complete set of tools*
OPPOSITE: incomplete

3 = finished, accomplished, achieved, concluded, ended

▶ *verb* **4 = finish**, end, conclude • *He has just completed his first novel.*

See also: **accomplish, achieve, ideal, over, perform, pure, rank, sheer**

completely *adverb* **= totally**, fully, absolutely, entirely, perfectly, altogether, thoroughly, wholly, utterly, every inch, hook, line and sinker, in full, lock, stock and barrel, one hundred per cent

completion *noun* **= finishing**, end, close, conclusion, culmination, fruition, fulfillment, bitter end

complex *adjective*
1 = complicated, difficult, involved, tangled, intricate • *complex issues*
OPPOSITE: simple

2 = compound, multiple, composite, manifold, heterogeneous, multifarious

▶ *noun* **3 = obsession**, problem, thing, preoccupation, phobia, fixation • *I have never had a complex about my height.*

4 = structure, system, network, organization, scheme, aggregate, composite

See also: **elaborate, hard, sophisticated, tricky**

complexion *noun* **1 = skin**, colour, hue, pigmentation, colouring, skin tone

2 = nature, look, light, appearance, character,

aspect, guise, make-up

complexity noun
= **complication**, involvement, ramification, intricacy, entanglement, elaboration

complicate verb = **make difficult**, involve, confuse, entangle, muddle, ravel

complicated adjective
1 = **complex**, elaborate, involved, intricate, convoluted • *a complicated situation*
OPPOSITE: simple
2 = **difficult**, problematic, involved, troublesome, perplexing, puzzling
See also: **confusing, hard, sophisticated, tricky**

complication noun
1 = **complexity**, web, confusion, intricacy, entanglement
2 = **problem**, difficulty, snag, obstacle, embarrassment, drawback

compliment noun 1 = **praise**, tribute, honour, eulogy, bouquet, commendation, congratulations, flattery
▶ verb 2 = **praise**, congratulate, salute, commend, flatter, extol, brown-nose (slang), pay tribute to, speak highly of

complimentary adjective
1 = **flattering**, appreciative, congratulatory, approving, commendatory, laudatory
2 = **free**, courtesy, honorary, gratuitous, donated, gratis, on the house

compliments plural noun
= **greetings**, salutation, good wishes, regards, remembrances, respects

comply verb = **obey**, follow, submit, observe, acquiesce, abide by, adhere to, conform to, toe the line

component noun 1 = **part**, unit, piece, item, ingredient, element, constituent
▶ adjective 2 = **constituent**, inherent, intrinsic

compose verb 1 = **create**, write, produce, invent, devise • *She has composed a symphony.*

2 = **put together**, make, build, form, fashion, construct, constitute, comprise, make up
3 = **calm**, control, collect, quiet, soothe, placate, pacify
4 = **arrange**, adjust

composed adjective = **calm**, cool, sedate, serene, unflappable, at ease, collected, level-headed, poised, relaxed, self-possessed

composition noun 1 = **creation**, production, formation, making, compilation, formulation, fashioning, putting together
2 = **design**, organization, structure, arrangement, formation, layout, configuration, make-up
3 = **essay**, work, exercise, piece, opus, treatise, literary work

composure noun = **calmness**, poise, serenity, aplomb, equanimity, sang-froid, self-assurance, self-possession

compound noun
1 = **combination**, composite, blend, mixture, alloy, fusion, medley, amalgam, synthesis
▶ verb 2 = **combine**, mix, unite, blend, amalgamate, synthesize, intermingle
3 = **intensify**, worsen, aggravate, complicate, exacerbate, heighten, magnify, augment, add to
▶ adjective 4 = **complex**, multiple, composite, intricate

comprehend verb = **understand**, see, appreciate, grasp, fathom, take in, work out • *I just cannot comprehend your attitude.*
See also: **know, read, realize**

comprehensible adjective
= **understandable**, clear, plain, explicit, coherent, conceivable, intelligible

comprehension noun
= **understanding**, intelligence, perception, grasp, conception, realization, discernment

comprehensive adjective
= **broad**, complete, full, blanket, thorough, inclusive, exhaustive, all-inclusive, encyclopedic, all-embracing

compress *verb* = **squeeze**, contract, press, crush, concentrate, shorten, squash, abbreviate, condense

compressed *See* **firm**

comprise *verb* 1 = **be composed of**, include, contain, embrace, encompass, consist of, take in
2 = **make up**, form, compose, constitute

compromise *noun* 1 = **give-and-take**, agreement, settlement, concession, adjustment, accommodation, trade-off
▶ *verb* 2 = **meet halfway**, agree, settle, adjust, concede, give and take, go fifty-fifty (*informal*), strike a balance
3 = **dishonour**, expose, weaken, embarrass, jeopardize, prejudice, discredit

compulsion *noun* 1 = **urge**, need, drive, obsession, necessity, preoccupation
2 = **force**, demand, pressure, obligation, urgency, constraint, coercion, duress

compulsive *adjective* = **irresistible**, urgent, obsessive, uncontrollable, neurotic, compelling, driving, overwhelming

compulsory *adjective* = **obligatory**, mandatory, required, requisite • *School attendance is compulsory.*
OPPOSITE: voluntary

compute *verb* = **calculate**, total, count, tally, reckon, enumerate, add up, figure out

comrade *noun* = **companion**, friend, partner, associate, colleague, fellow, ally, co-worker, homeboy (*slang*), homegirl (*slang*)

con *verb* 1 = **swindle**, trick, mislead, cheat, deceive • *He claimed that he'd been conned out of his life savings.*
▶ *noun* 2 = **swindle**, fraud, scam, trick, bluff, deception • *Snacks that offer miraculous weight loss are a con.*
See also: **dupe, fool, rob, take in**

concave *adjective* = **hollow**, indented

conceal *verb* = **hide**, cover, screen, bury, mask, obscure, disguise, camouflage

concealed *See* **invisible**

concede *verb* 1 = **admit**, allow, own, accept, grant, acknowledge, confess
2 = **give up**, surrender, yield, relinquish, cede, hand over

conceit *noun* = **self-importance**, pride, vanity, egotism • *his insufferable conceit*

conceited *adjective* = **self-important**, vain, cocky, bigheaded (*informal*), egotistical • *She's smart and beautiful, but not conceited.*
OPPOSITE: modest
See also: **boastful, haughty, pretentious, smug, stuck-up**

conceivable *adjective* = **imaginable**, possible, credible, believable, thinkable

conceivably *See* **maybe, perhaps**

conceive *verb* 1 = **imagine**, think, believe, understand, suppose, fancy, comprehend, envisage
2 = **think up**, create, design, devise, formulate, contrive
3 = **become pregnant**, become impregnated

▷ **conceive of** *See* **picture**

concentrate *verb* 1 = **focus your attention on**, be engrossed in, give your attention to, put your mind to • *Concentrate on your studies.*
2 = **gather**, collect, accumulate • *Condominiums are mostly concentrated in urban areas.*
3 = **focus**, cluster, centre, converge, bring to bear
See also: **essence**

concentrated *adjective* 1 = **intense**, hard, deep, intensive, all-out (*informal*)
2 = **condensed**, rich, boiled down, evaporated, reduced, thickened, undiluted

concentration *noun* 1 = **single-mindedness**, application, heed, absorption
2 = **focusing**, consolidation,

C

convergence, centring, intensification, bringing to bear, centralization

3 = convergence, mass, collection, cluster, accumulation, horde, aggregation

concept noun = **idea**, view, image, theory, notion, hypothesis, conception, abstraction, conceptualization

conception noun **1 = idea**, plan, design, image, concept, notion

2 = impregnation, fertilization, insemination, germination

concern noun **1 = worry**, anxiety, apprehension, disquiet • *public concern about violence*

2 = business, responsibility, affair • *His private life is not my concern.*

3 = importance, interest, bearing, relevance

4 = company, business, firm, organization, corporation, establishment, enterprise

▶ *verb* **5 = worry**, trouble, disturb, bother, distress • *It concerns me that he doesn't want to go.*

6 = involve, affect, apply to, be relevant to • *This concerns both of us.*

See also: **care, consideration, issue, job**

concerned *adjective* **1 = involved**, active, interested, implicated, mixed up, privy to

2 = worried, upset, troubled, anxious, distressed, uneasy, disturbed, bothered

concerning *preposition* = **regarding**, about, touching, re, apropos of, as regards, on the subject of, relating to, respecting, with reference to

concession noun **1 = grant**, permit, compromise, adjustment, allowance, privilege, boon, indulgence, sop

2 = conceding, surrender, confession, admission, acknowledgment, assent, yielding

conciliate *verb* = **pacify**, mediate,

reconcile, appease, soothe, placate, mollify, clear the air, win over

conciliation noun = **pacification**, reconciliation, soothing, appeasement, mollification, placation

conciliatory *adjective* = **pacifying**, pacific, appeasing, mollifying, peaceable, placatory

concise *adjective* = **brief**, short, terse, succinct • *a concise guide*
OPPOSITE: long

conclude *verb* **1 = decide**, judge, suppose, reckon (*informal*), infer, surmise, deduce • *He concluded that she had been right.*

2 = finish, end, close, round off, wind up • *He concluded the letter with a request.*
OPPOSITE: begin

3 = accomplish, effect, bring about, carry out, pull off
See also: **complete, gather, stop**

concluding *See* **final, last**

conclusion noun **1 = deduction**, verdict, judgment, inference • *I've come to the conclusion that he was telling the truth.*

2 = end, close, finish, ending, termination • *the conclusion of the program*
OPPOSITE: beginning
See also: **decision**

conclusive *adjective* = **decisive**, final, ultimate, definite, irrefutable, clinching, convincing, unanswerable

concoct *verb* = **make up**, prepare, invent, brew, hatch, devise, formulate, contrive, think up

concoction noun = **mixture**, combination, creation, compound, preparation, blend, brew

concrete *adjective* **1 = specific**, explicit, definite

2 = real, material, substantial, actual, factual, tangible, sensible

concur *verb* = **agree**, consent, assent, acquiesce

concurrently *See* **together**

condemn *verb* **1 = criticize**, blame, denounce, damn,

censure • *He was condemned for his
violent actions.*
2 = sentence, doom • *condemned
to life in prison*
See also: **disapprove**

condemnation *noun*
1 = disapproval, blame, censure,
denunciation, reproach, reproof,
stricture
2 = sentence, conviction,
judgment, doom,
damnation

condemned See **doomed**

condensation *noun*
1 = distillation, precipitation,
precipitate, liquefaction
2 = abridgment, digest,
contraction, synopsis, précis
3 = concentration, reduction,
consolidation, compression,
crystallization, curtailment

condense *verb* **1 = abridge**,
concentrate, shorten, compress,
summarize, epitomize,
abbreviate
2 = concentrate, reduce,
thicken, boil down

condensed *adjective*
1 = abridged, potted (*informal*),
concentrated, summarized,
shortened, compressed,
shrunken, slimmed-down
2 = concentrated, reduced,
boiled down, thickened

condescend *verb* **1 = patronize**,
talk down to
2 = lower oneself, bend, stoop,
deign, humble oneself or
demean oneself, see fit

condescending *adjective*
= patronizing, superior, lofty,
disdainful, lordly, snobbish,
snooty (*informal*), supercilious

condition *noun* **1 = state**, form,
shape • *The house is in good
condition.*
2 = requirement, provision,
qualification, stipulation,
requisite, prerequisite,
proviso, terms • *terms and
conditions of the contract*
3 = health, order, shape, trim,
fitness, fettle, kilter, state of
health
4 = ailment, problem,

complaint, weakness, malady,
infirmity
▶ *verb* **5 = accustom**, prepare,
train, ready, adapt, equip, tone
up, work out
See also: **disorder**

conditional *adjective*
= dependent, limited,
contingent, qualified,
provisional, subject to, with
reservations

conditions *plural noun*
= circumstances, situation,
environment, surroundings,
milieu, way of life

condone *verb* **= overlook**, excuse,
pardon, forgive, let pass, look the
other way, make allowance for,
turn a blind eye to

conduct *verb* **1 = carry out**, do,
run, perform, manage, direct,
organize • *to conduct an experiment*
2 = accompany, lead, guide,
steer, escort, usher, convey
▶ **conduct yourself = behave**, act
• *The way she conducts herself reflects
on the school.*
▶ *noun* **3 = behaviour**, attitude,
manners, ways • *Other people
judge you by your conduct.*
4 = management, control,
organization, administration,
direction, handling, guidance,
supervision, running
See also: **handle, manner, take,
way**

confectionery See **candy**

confederacy *noun* **= union**,
league, coalition, alliance,
federation, confederation

confederation *noun* **= union**,
body, organization, association

confer *verb* **1 = discuss**, talk,
consult, deliberate, discourse,
converse
2 = grant, give, accord, award,
present, bestow, hand out
▶ **confer with** See **consult**

conference *noun* **= meeting**,
discussion, convention, forum,
congress • *a conference on education*

confess *verb* **1 = admit**,
acknowledge, own up • *He
confessed his love.*
OPPOSITE: deny

2 = **declare**, confirm, reveal, assert, affirm, profess

confession noun = **admission**, acknowledgment • *a confession of her guilt*

confidant, confidante noun = **close friend**, familiar, intimate, crony, alter ego, bosom friend

confide verb **1** = **tell**, reveal, admit, disclose, confess, divulge, whisper, impart
2 (*Formal*) = **entrust**, commit, commend, consign

confidence noun **1** = **trust**, faith, belief, reliance • *I have complete confidence in you.*
OPPOSITE: distrust
2 = **self-assurance**, assurance, aplomb, self-possession • *I've never had much confidence.*
OPPOSITE: shyness
▷ **in confidence** = **in secrecy**, privately, between you and me or between you and me and the gatepost, confidentially

confident adjective **1** = **certain**, sure, positive, secure, convinced, satisfied • *confident of success*
OPPOSITE: uncertain
2 = **self-assured**, assured, self-possessed • *a confident attitude*
OPPOSITE: shy
See also: **bold, optimistic**

confidential adjective = **secret**, private, classified, intimate, privy, hush-hush (*informal*), off the record

confidentially adverb = **in secret**, personally, privately, behind closed doors, between ourselves, in camera, in confidence, sub rosa

confine verb **1** = **limit**, restrict • *They confined themselves to talking about the weather.*
2 = **imprison**, restrict, incarcerate, hem in, shut up, lock down • *confined to bed for two days*

confinement noun = **imprisonment**, custody, detention, lockdown, incarceration, internment

confines plural noun = **limits**, edge, circumference, boundaries, bounds, precincts

confirm verb **1** = **prove**, endorse, verify, validate, substantiate, bear out • *Police confirmed that they had received a call.*
2 = **fix**, settle • *Can we confirm the arrangements for tomorrow?*
3 = **strengthen**, fix, establish, reinforce, fortify, buttress
See also: **determine**

confirmation noun **1** = **proof**, evidence, testimony, verification, validation, authentication, corroboration, substantiation
2 = **sanction**, agreement, approval, endorsement, acceptance, ratification, assent

confirmed adjective = **long-established**, chronic, seasoned, habitual, hardened, ingrained, dyed-in-the-wool, inveterate

confiscate verb = **seize**, appropriate, commandeer, sequester, impound, sequestrate

confiscation noun = **seizure**, takeover, forfeiture, appropriation, sequestration, impounding

conflict noun **1** = **disagreement**, opposition, hostility, strife, friction, discord, antagonism • *conflict between workers and management*
2 = **battle**, war, combat, strife, fighting • *the conflict in the Middle East*
▷ verb **3** = **be incompatible**, clash, disagree, differ, be at variance • *conflicting ideas*
See also: **dispute, interfere**

conflicting adjective = **incompatible**, contrary, inconsistent, contradictory, paradoxical, antagonistic, clashing, discordant, opposing

conform verb **1** = **comply**, follow, adjust, adapt, obey, fall in with, toe the line
2 = **agree**, accord, match, suit, tally, correspond, harmonize

conformist noun = **traditionalist**, stick-in-the-mud (*informal*), yes man

conformity *noun* = **compliance**, observance, orthodoxy, conventionality, traditionalism

confound *verb* = **bewilder**, confuse, baffle, astound, mystify, perplex, flummox, dumbfound, nonplus

confront *verb* = **face**, challenge, oppose, tackle, encounter, defy, accost, stand up to

confrontation *noun* = **conflict**, fight, contest, encounter, head-to-head, showdown (*informal*)

confuse *verb* **1** = **mix up**, mistake, muddle up • *confusing fact with fiction*
2 = **bewilder**, puzzle, baffle, mystify • *Politics confuse me.*
3 = **disconcert**, upset, rattle (*informal*), disorient, unnerve, fluster, discompose, throw off balance
▷ **confuse with** *See* **mistake**
See also: **cloud**, **muddle**

confused *adjective*
1 = **bewildered**, baffled, muddled, perplexed, puzzled • *confused about health risks*
2 = **disordered**, chaotic, disorganized, untidy • *The clothes lay in a confused heap.*
OPPOSITE: tidy
See also: **dazed**, **garbled**, **unclear**

confusing *adjective*
= **bewildering**, complicated, baffling, puzzling • *a confusing situation*

confusion *noun* **1** = **disorder**, chaos, mess, disarray, disorganization • *My life is in confusion.*
OPPOSITE: order
2 = **bewilderment**, puzzlement, disorientation, mystification, perplexity
See also: **fuss**, **muddle**

congeal *See* **thicken**
congealed *See* **firm**
congenial *adjective* **1** = **pleasant**, friendly, kindly, affable, favourable, agreeable, genial, companionable
2 = **compatible**, sympathetic, like-minded, well-suited, kindred

congenital *adjective* = **inborn**, natural, inherent, innate, immanent, inbred

congested *adjective*
1 = **overcrowded**, crowded, teeming
2 = **clogged**, packed, jammed, blocked-up, crammed, overfilled, overflowing, stuffed

congestion *noun*
1 = **overcrowding**, crowding
2 = **clogging**, jam, bottleneck, surfeit

congratulate *verb*
= **compliment**, pat on the back, wish joy to

congratulation *See* **praise**
congratulations *plural noun, interjection* = **good wishes**, best wishes, compliments, felicitations, greetings

congregate *verb* = **come together**, meet, gather, mass, collect, assemble, convene, flock, converge

congregation *noun* = **assembly**, crowd, flock, throng, multitude, fellowship, brethren

congress *noun* = **meeting**, conference, parliament, council, legislature, convention, assembly, caucus, conclave

conjecture *noun* **1** = **guess**, speculation, theory, hypothesis, surmise, supposition, shot in the dark
▶ *verb* **2** = **guess**, suppose, imagine, speculate, theorize, hypothesize, surmise

conjugal *adjective* = **marital**, married, bridal, connubial, matrimonial, nuptial, wedded

conjure *verb* = **perform tricks**, juggle
▷ **conjure up** = **bring to mind**, create, recall, evoke, contrive, produce as if by magic, recollect

conjurer, conjuror *noun*
= **magician**, wizard, sorcerer, illusionist

connect *verb* **1** = **join**, link, couple, attach, fasten, affix
• *Connect the pipe to the tap.*
OPPOSITE: separate
2 = **associate**, link, relate, ally

• evidence connecting them with the crime

connected adjective = **linked**, combined, related, akin, allied, affiliated, associated, coupled, joined, united

connection noun
1 = **association**, link, relationship, bond, relation, affiliation, correspondence, correlation • a connection between good health and lots of exercise
2 = **link**, junction, coupling, fastening • The fault was just a loose connection.
3 = **contact**, friend, associate, ally, sponsor, acquaintance, homeboy (slang), homegirl (slang)
See also: **tie**

connivance noun = **collusion**, complicity, abetting, conspiring, tacit consent

connive verb = **conspire**, plot, scheme, intrigue, collude, cook up (informal)
▷ **connive at** = **turn a blind eye to**, overlook, disregard, abet, let pass, look the other way, wink at

connoisseur noun = **expert**, judge, authority, buff (informal), devotee, aficionado, appreciator

conquer verb 1 = **defeat**, beat, overcome, crush, master, overpower, quell, overthrow, vanquish, subjugate, get the better of
2 = **seize**, win, acquire, obtain, occupy, overrun, annex

conqueror noun = **winner**, master, victor, conquistador, defeater, subjugator, vanquisher

conquest noun 1 = **defeat**, victory, rout, triumph, overthrow, mastery
2 = **takeover**, invasion, occupation, coup, annexation, subjugation

conscience noun = **principles**, scruples, sense of right and wrong • He had a guilty conscience.
See also: **principle**

CONFUSABLES
Conscience means knowing right from wrong.
Conscious means aware.

conscientious adjective
= **thorough**, particular, careful, exact, faithful, painstaking, meticulous, diligent, punctilious

conscious adjective 1 = **aware**, alive, alert, awake, responsive, sensible, sentient
2 = **deliberate**, intentional, calculated, self-conscious, wilful, knowing, premeditated, studied

consciousness noun
= **awareness**, knowledge, recognition, sensibility, realization, apprehension

consecrate verb = **sanctify**, devote, dedicate, ordain, venerate, hallow, set apart

consecrated See **holy**

consecutive adjective
= **successive**, running, uninterrupted, in sequence, in turn, sequential, succeeding

consensus noun = **agreement**, unity, harmony, assent, unanimity, common consent, concord, general agreement

consent noun 1 = **agreement**, approval, sanction, permission, go-ahead (informal), compliance, assent, acquiescence, O.K. or okay (informal)
▶ verb 2 = **agree**, allow, approve, permit, concur, assent, acquiesce

consequence noun 1 = **result**, issue, effect, outcome, sequel, repercussion, upshot, end result
2 = **importance**, concern, account, value, weight, moment, import, significance

consequent adjective
= **following**, subsequent, successive, resultant, ensuing, resulting

consequently adverb = **as a result**, therefore, thus, subsequently, accordingly, hence, ergo

conservation noun = **protection**, saving, maintenance, preservation, safekeeping, upkeep, guardianship, husbandry, safeguarding

Conservative adjective 1 = **Tory**, right-wing

▶ *noun* **2 = Tory**, right-winger, righty (*informal*)

conservative *adjective*
1 = traditional, conventional
• *People sometimes become more conservative as they grow older.*
OPPOSITE: radical
2 = traditionalist, reactionary, stick-in-the-mud (*informal*)
See also: **right-wing**

conserve *verb* **= protect**, keep, save, husband, nurse, preserve, hoard, store up, take care of, use sparingly

consider *verb* **1 = think**, rate, believe, judge, deem, regard as
• *They do not consider him a suitable candidate.*
2 = think about, reflect, ponder, deliberate, contemplate, muse, meditate • *I will consider your offer.*
3 = bear in mind, respect, make allowances for, take into account, think about • *We should consider her feelings.*
See also: **feel, reckon, regard, view**

considerable *adjective* **= large**, great, substantial, marked, sizable *or* sizeable, plentiful, noticeable, appreciable, goodly, supersize

considerably *adverb* **= greatly**, significantly, substantially, remarkably, markedly, noticeably, appreciably, very much

considerate *adjective*
= thoughtful, patient, concerned, mindful, kindly, attentive, unselfish, obliging, tactful

considerately *See* **well**

consideration *noun* **1 = thought**, study, attention, deliberation, contemplation • *a decision requiring careful consideration*
2 = thoughtfulness, concern, respect, kindness, tact • *Show some consideration for the other passengers.*
3 = factor, point, issue • *Safety is a major consideration.*
4 = payment, fee, tip, reward, remuneration, recompense

See also: **aspect**

considering *preposition* **= taking into account**, in the light of, in view of

consignment *noun* **= shipment**, delivery, batch, goods

consist *verb*
▷ **consist in = lie in**, be expressed by, be found in *or* be contained in, inhere in, reside in
▷ **consist of = be made up of**, include, involve, contain, incorporate, comprise, embody, amount to, be composed of

consistency *noun* **1 = texture**, density, thickness, firmness, compactness, viscosity
2 = constancy, regularity, uniformity, evenness, steadfastness, steadiness

consistent *adjective*
1 = unchanging, regular, steady, persistent, constant, dependable, true to type, undeviating
2 = agreeing, logical, compatible, coherent, harmonious, congruous, consonant

consolation *noun* **= comfort**, help, support, relief, cheer, solace, encouragement, succour

console *verb* **= comfort**, encourage, cheer, calm, soothe, express sympathy for

consolidate *verb* **1 = strengthen**, secure, stabilize, reinforce, fortify
2 = combine, join, unite, fuse, amalgamate, federate

consort *verb* **1 = associate**, fraternize, go around with, hang out with *or* hang around with, mix, keep company
▶ *noun* **2 = spouse**, wife, partner, husband, companion

conspicuous *adjective*
1 = obvious, apparent, evident, blatant, noticeable, perceptible
• *Her conspicuous lack of warmth confirmed her disapproval.*
2 = noteworthy, signal, prominent, remarkable, notable, outstanding, striking, illustrious, salient

See also: **clear, manifest, visible**

conspiracy noun = **plot**, scheme, intrigue, treason, collusion, machination

conspirator noun = **plotter**, traitor, conspirer, intriguer, schemer

conspire verb **1** = **plot**, plan, scheme, intrigue, manoeuvre, contrive, machinate
2 = **work together**, contribute, combine, tend, cooperate, concur

constant adjective
1 = **continuous**, relentless, eternal, perpetual, continual, nonstop • a government under constant attack from the media
OPPOSITE: periodic
2 = **unchanging**, even, regular, stable, steady, uniform, fixed • a constant temperature
OPPOSITE: changeable
3 = **faithful**, true, loyal, stalwart, staunch, devoted, trustworthy, trusty
See also: **permanent, steadfast**

constantly adverb
= **continuously**, always, continually, invariably, perpetually, nonstop, endlessly, incessantly, all the time, interminably, twenty-four-seven (slang)

consternation noun = **dismay**, fear, alarm, anxiety, distress, dread, trepidation

constituent noun **1** = **voter**, elector
2 = **component**, part, unit, factor, ingredient, element
▶ adjective **3** = **component**, basic, essential, integral, elemental

constitute verb = **make up**, form, establish, found, compose, comprise, set up

constitution noun **1** = **health**, build, character, disposition, physique
2 = **structure**, form, nature, composition, make-up

constitutional adjective
1 = **statutory**, chartered, vested
▶ noun **2** = **walk**, turn, stroll, airing

constrain verb **1** = **force**, bind, compel, coerce, oblige, pressurize, necessitate, impel
2 = **restrict**, check, curb, restrain, confine, constrict, straiten

constraint noun **1** = **restriction**, check, curb, rein, limitation, deterrent, hindrance
2 = **force**, pressure, restraint, necessity, coercion, compulsion

constricted See **tight**

construct verb = **build**, make, create, assemble, erect, put together, put up • to construct a model plane
See also: **fashion, produce**

construction noun **1** = **building**, creation, composition, edifice
2 = **interpretation**, reading, explanation, rendering, inference

constructive adjective = **helpful**, positive, valuable, useful, productive, practical

consult verb = **ask for advice**, confer with, refer to • Consult your doctor before beginning an exercise program.
See also: **refer**

consultant noun = **specialist**, authority, adviser, counsellor, consigliere

consultation noun = **meeting**, conference, interview, hearing, discussion, council, appointment, dialogue, deliberation, examination, seminar, session

consume verb **1** = **eat**, swallow, gobble or gobble up, devour, chow down (slang), eat up, put away
2 = **use up**, spend, waste, absorb, exhaust, squander, dissipate, expend
3 = **destroy**, devastate, ravage, demolish, annihilate, lay waste
4 (often passive) = **obsess**, dominate, absorb, preoccupy, monopolize, engross, eat up

consumer noun = **buyer**, customer, user, shopper, purchaser

consummate verb 1 = **complete**,
end, finish, conclude, crown,
accomplish, fulfill
▶ adjective 2 = **skilled**, perfect,
accomplished, supreme, superb,
polished, matchless, practised
3 = **complete**, total, extreme,
absolute, utter, supreme,
conspicuous

consumption noun 1 = **using
up**, loss, waste, expenditure,
exhaustion, depletion,
diminution, dissipation
2 (Old-fashioned) = **tuberculosis**,
T.B.

contact noun 1 = **communication**,
touch, correspondence • We keep
in daily contact.
2 = **acquaintance**, connection • a
contact in the music business
3 = **touch**, contiguity
▶ verb 4 = **get in touch with**,
reach, approach, communicate
with, get hold of • We contacted
the company to complain.

contagious adjective
= **infectious**, communicable,
transmissible, catching,
spreading

contain verb 1 = **include**,
comprise • My diary contains
personal information.
2 = **restrain**, control, curb, stifle,
repress • efforts to contain the
disease
3 = **hold**, seat, incorporate,
accommodate, enclose, have
capacity for
See also: **restrict, suppress**

container noun = **holder**, vessel
• a plastic container for food
See also: **box, case**

contaminate verb = **pollute**,
infect, taint, corrupt, stain,
tarnish, defile, adulterate,
befoul

contamination noun
= **pollution**, infection,
corruption, taint, poisoning,
contagion, defilement, impurity

contemplate verb 1 = **think
about**, consider, ponder,
examine, muse on, reflect on
• She carefully contemplated her next
move.

2 = **consider**, plan, envisage,
think of • He contemplated a
career as a doctor.
3 = **look at**, study, survey, view,
examine, regard, inspect, eye up,
gaze at, stare at
See also: **think**

contemplation See
consideration, thought

contemplative See **thoughtful**

contemporary adjective
1 = **coexisting**, concurrent,
contemporaneous
2 = **modern**, recent, current,
present, up-to-date, present-day,
à la mode, newfangled
▶ noun 3 = **peer**, fellow

contempt noun = **scorn**,
disregard, disrespect, disdain,
derision • I shall treat that remark
with the contempt it deserves.
OPPOSITE: respect

contemptible adjective
= **despicable**, shameful, lousy
(slang), paltry, worthless,
pitiful, ignominious, measly,
detestable, scuzzy (slang)

contemptuous adjective
= **scornful**, arrogant, derisive,
condescending, disdainful,
haughty, sneering, supercilious,
withering

contend verb 1 = **compete**, fight,
struggle, contest, clash, vie,
strive, jostle
2 = **argue**, hold, dispute, allege,
maintain, assert, affirm

contender See **candidate**

content[1] noun 1 = **meaning**,
substance, significance, essence,
gist
2 = **amount**, measure, size,
capacity, volume, load

content[2] adjective 1 = **satisfied**,
comfortable, agreeable,
contented, at ease, fulfilled,
willing to accept
▶ verb 2 = **satisfy**, please,
indulge, appease, placate,
humour, mollify
▶ noun 3 = **satisfaction**, ease,
comfort, pleasure, gratification,
contentment, peace of mind

contented adjective = **satisfied**,
content, happy, comfortable,

glad, thankful, pleased, serene, gratified

contention See **competition**

contentious adjective
= **argumentative**, bickering, captious, cavilling, disputatious, quarrelsome, querulous, wrangling

contentment noun
= **satisfaction**, content, peace, ease, comfort, happiness, pleasure, serenity, fulfillment, equanimity

contents plural noun
= **constituents**, load, elements, ingredients

contest noun 1 = **competition**, game, match, tournament • first prize in the spelling contest
2 = **struggle**, fight, battle
• a bitter contest over the party's leadership
▶ verb 3 = **dispute**, question, challenge, oppose • Your former employer has 14 days to contest the case.
OPPOSITE: accept
4 = **compete**, fight, vie, contend, strive
See also: **event**

contestant noun = **competitor**, player, candidate, participant, contender, entrant

context noun 1 = **circumstances**, situation, ambience, conditions
2 = **frame of reference**, connection, relation, background, framework

contingency noun = **possibility**, event, chance, emergency, incident, accident, happening, eventuality

continual adjective = **frequent**, regular, repeated, recurrent • the continual ringing of his cellphone
OPPOSITE: occasional
See also: **constant**

> **CONFUSABLES**
> Continual means often repeated.
> Continuous means without interruption.

continually adverb = **constantly**, always, repeatedly, forever, nonstop, persistently, incessantly, all the time,

interminably, twenty-four-seven (slang)

continuation noun
1 = **continuing**, resumption, perpetuation, prolongation
2 = **addition**, extension, supplement, sequel, postscript, furtherance

continue verb 1 = **keep on**, persist, carry on, go on • He continued to work for another year.
2 = **remain**, last, survive, endure, persist, carry on • The discussion continued after they'd left.
3 = **resume**, recommence, carry on • After a moment, she continued speaking.
See also: **extend, proceed, stretch**

continued See **continuous**

continuing adjective = **lasting**, ongoing, sustained, enduring, in progress

continuity noun = **sequence**, connection, flow, progression, succession, cohesion

continuous adjective = **constant**, continued, extended, prolonged, endless, eternal, perpetual, uninterrupted, nagging
• continuous growth
OPPOSITE: periodic
See also: **continual, gradual, steady**

continuously See **always**

contours plural noun = **outline**, figure, form, relief, shape, profile, curve, silhouette, lines

contraband noun 1 = **smuggling**, trafficking, black-marketing, bootlegging
▶ adjective 2 = **smuggled**, hot (informal), illegal, illicit, unlawful, bootleg, banned, forbidden, prohibited

contract noun 1 = **agreement**, settlement, commitment, bargain, pact, arrangement, covenant
▶ verb 2 = **agree**, pledge, negotiate, bargain, covenant, come to terms, commit oneself
3 = **shorten**, reduce, shrink, narrow, diminish, dwindle, curtail, lessen,

abbreviate, shrivel
4 = catch, get, develop, acquire, incur, be afflicted with, go down with

contraction *noun* = **shortening**, reduction, compression, shrinkage, abbreviation, narrowing, shrivelling, tightening

contradict *verb* = **deny**, challenge, negate, belie, rebut, be at variance with, controvert, fly in the face of

contradiction *noun* = **denial**, conflict, opposite, inconsistency, contravention, incongruity, negation

contradictory *adjective* = **inconsistent**, opposite, contrary, incompatible, conflicting, paradoxical, opposed

contraption *noun* (*Informal*) = **device**, gadget, instrument, mechanism, apparatus, contrivance

contrary *noun* **1 = opposite**, reverse, converse, antithesis
▶ *adjective* **2 = opposed**, counter, opposite, hostile, adverse, inconsistent, contradictory, paradoxical, clashing, discordant
3 = perverse, difficult, awkward, cantankerous, intractable, disobliging, obstinate, unaccommodating

contrast *noun* **1 = difference**, opposition, comparison, foil, distinction, disparity, divergence, dissimilarity
▶ *verb* **2 = differentiate**, compare, oppose, differ, distinguish, set in opposition, set off

contrasting *See* **different**, **opposite**

contravene *See* **break**

contribute *verb* = **give**, add, provide, supply, donate, subscribe, bestow, chip in (*informal*)
▷ **contribute to = be partly responsible for**, help, be conducive to, be instrumental in, lead to, tend to

contribution *noun* = **gift**, grant, addition, offering, donation, input, subscription

contributor *noun* = **giver**, supporter, donor, subscriber, patron

contrite *adjective* = **sorry**, humble, remorseful, chastened, conscience-stricken, penitent, regretful, repentant, sorrowful

contrivance *noun* **1 = device**, machine, implement, gadget, invention, instrument, mechanism, appliance, contraption, apparatus
2 = plan, plot, trick, scheme, intrigue, ruse, machination, stratagem

contrive *verb* **1 = bring about**, plan, effect, plot, manage, scheme, succeed, arrange, manoeuvre
2 = devise, create, design, manufacture, construct, invent, improvise, fabricate, concoct

contrived *adjective* = **forced**, planned, artificial, elaborate, strained, unnatural, laboured, overdone

control *noun* **1 = power**, government, rule, authority, management, direction, command, supremacy • *He was forced to give up control of the company.*
2 = restraint, check, regulation, curb, brake, limitation
▶ *verb* **3 = have power over**, rule, manage, direct, govern, command, administer, be in charge of • *trying to control your mind*
4 = restrain, contain, limit, check, curb, subdue, constrain, repress, hold back
See also: **determine, grip, head, hold, influence, possess, possession, restriction, run**

controls *plural noun* = **instruments**, console, dash, dashboard, control panel, dials

controversial *adjective* = **disputed**, contentious, debatable, at issue, disputable,

open to question, under
discussion, third-rail

controversy noun = **argument**,
debate, dispute, row, altercation,
squabble, quarrel, wrangling,
third rail (politics chiefly US),
wedge issue

conundrum See **mystery**,
problem

convalesce See **recover**

convalescence noun = **recovery**,
improvement, rehabilitation,
recuperation, return to health

convalescent adjective
= **recovering**, getting better,
improving, mending, on the
mend, recuperating

convene verb = **gather**, call, meet,
assemble, summon, congregate,
bring together, come together,
convoke

convenience noun
1 = **availability**, benefit,
advantage, fitness, utility,
accessibility, usefulness,
suitability, appropriateness
2 = **appliance**, help, facility,
comfort, amenity, labour-saving
device

convenient adjective 1 = **useful**,
helpful, handy • a convenient mode
of transport
OPPOSITE: inconvenient
2 = **nearby**, available, accessible,
handy, at hand, close at hand,
just round the corner, within
reach
See also: **ready**

convention noun 1 = **custom**,
practice, code, tradition,
etiquette • It's a social convention
that men don't wear skirts.
2 = **assembly**, conference,
meeting, congress • the annual
convention of the Canadian
Association of Journalists
3 = **agreement**, contract, treaty,
bargain, pact, protocol
See also: **habit**

conventional adjective
1 = **conservative**, conformist,
unadventurous • His opinions are
generally quite conventional.
2 = **ordinary**, customary,
orthodox, standard, regular,

traditional • the conventional
treatment for diabetes
3 = **unoriginal**, routine, banal,
hackneyed, prosaic, stereotyped
See also: **formal, normal,
popular, proper**

converge verb = **come together**,
meet, join, gather, combine,
merge, coincide

conversation noun = **talk**,
conference, discussion, chat,
dialogue, gossip, discourse,
tête-à-tête

conversational See **colloquial**

converse[1] verb = **talk**, chat,
confer, discourse, commune,
chew the fat (slang), exchange
views

converse[2] noun 1 = **opposite**,
reverse, contrary, antithesis,
obverse, other side of the coin
▶ adjective 2 = **opposite**, counter,
reverse, contrary, reversed,
transposed

conversion noun 1 = **change**,
transformation, metamorphosis
2 = **adaptation**, reconstruction,
reorganization, modification,
alteration, remodelling

convert verb 1 = **change**, turn,
alter, transform, transpose
2 = **adapt**, apply, modify, revise,
reorganize, customize, remodel,
restyle
3 = **reform**, convince, proselytize
▶ noun 4 = **neophyte**, disciple,
proselyte

convex adjective = **rounded**,
bulging, gibbous, protuberant

convey verb 1 = **communicate**,
express, impart, get across • She
conveyed her enthusiasm to her
friends.
2 = **carry**, move, bring, send,
bear, conduct, guide, transport,
fetch
See also: **take**

convict verb 1 = **find guilty**,
sentence, condemn, imprison,
pronounce guilty
▶ noun 2 = **prisoner**, criminal,
lag (slang), culprit, felon, jailbird,
perp (informal)

convicted See **guilty**

conviction noun 1 = **belief**, view,

opinion, principle, faith, tenet, persuasion, creed
2 = confidence, assurance, certainty, reliance, firmness, certitude
convince verb = **persuade**, satisfy, assure • *I convinced him of my innocence.*
convinced adjective = **sure**, positive, certain, confident
convincing adjective
= **persuasive**, powerful, effective, conclusive, plausible, telling • *a convincing argument*
OPPOSITE: unconvincing
convoluted See **complicated**
convulse verb = **shake**, work, disorder, twist, disturb, agitate, derange, churn up
convulsion noun = **spasm**, fit, seizure, cramp, contraction, paroxysm
cook verb = **heat**, boil, fry, steam, bake, microwave, grill, roast, barbecue, toast, stew, poach, sauté, stir fry • *I enjoy cooking for friends.*
cool adjective **1 = cold**, chilly, chilled, refreshing • *a gust of cool air*
OPPOSITE: warm
2 = calm, serene, collected, composed, level-headed, relaxed • *He kept cool through the whole thing.*
OPPOSITE: nervous
3 = unfriendly, distant, indifferent, lukewarm, aloof, offhand, standoffish, unenthusiastic, unwelcoming
4 (*Informal*) = **fashionable**, hip, trendy (*informal*), phat (*slang*)
▶ verb **5 = chill**, freeze, refrigerate, cool off • *Put the cookies on a wire rack to cool.*
OPPOSITE: heat
▷ **cool off** See **cool**
▶ noun **6** (*Slang*) = **calmness**, control, poise, temper, composure, self-control, self-discipline, self-possession
See also: **apathetic, patience**
cooperate verb = **work together**, combine, collaborate, conspire, coordinate, join forces, pool

resources, pull together
• *The family cooperated with the author of the book.*
See also: **team**
cooperation noun = **teamwork**, unity, collaboration, combined effort, esprit de corps, give-and-take
cooperative adjective **1 = helpful**, supportive, responsive, onside (*informal*), accommodating, obliging
2 = shared, joint, collective, combined
coordinate verb = **bring together**, match, organize, integrate, synchronize, harmonize, systematize
cope verb = **manage**, survive, carry on, get by (*informal*), hold one's own, make the grade, struggle through
▷ **cope with = deal with**, weather, handle, contend with, grapple with, struggle with, wrestle with
copious adjective = **abundant**, full, extensive, lavish, ample, plentiful, bountiful, profuse
copy noun **1 = reproduction**, fake, counterfeit, replica, forgery, duplicate, imitation • *He kept a copy of the letter.*
▶ verb **2 = imitate**, follow, mimic, ape, emulate • *She tried to copy the author's writing style.*
3 = reproduce, counterfeit, duplicate • *documents copied by hand*
See also: **issue**
cord noun = **rope**, line, string, twine
cordial adjective = **warm**, friendly, hearty, cheerful, affable, agreeable, sociable, genial, congenial
cordon noun = **chain**, line, ring, barrier
▶ verb
▷ **cordon off = surround**, separate, picket, isolate, enclose, encircle, close off, fence off
core noun = **centre**, heart, essence, nucleus, kernel, crux, gist, nub, pith

cork See **plug**

corner noun 1 = **angle**, joint, bend, crook
2 = **space**, retreat, hideout, nook, hideaway
▶ verb 3 = **trap**, run to earth
4 (~ a market) = **monopolize**, dominate, hog (slang), engross

corny adjective = **unoriginal**, stale, sentimental, banal, trite, hackneyed, maudlin, stereotyped • corny old love songs

corporation noun 1 = **business**, society, association, corporate body
2 = **town council**, council, civic authorities, municipal authorities

corps noun = **team**, company, troop, unit, division, band, regiment, detachment, squadron

corpse noun = **body**, stiff (slang), carcass, cadaver, remains

correct adjective 1 = **accurate**, right, true, exact, precise, flawless, faultless • a correct diagnosis
OPPOSITE: wrong
2 = **proper**, OK (informal), appropriate, acceptable, fitting, seemly • correct behaviour
OPPOSITE: unacceptable
▶ verb 3 = **rectify**, right, improve, reform, cure, amend, remedy
• trying to correct his faults
4 = **punish**, discipline, rebuke, chastise, reprimand, chide, admonish, chasten, reprove
See also: **fix, formal, revise, standard**

correction noun
1 = **rectification**, amendment, adjustment, righting • The newspaper printed a correction of the story.
2 = **punishment**, discipline, reformation, admonition, castigation, chastisement, reproof
See also: **reform**

correctly adverb = **rightly**, right, properly, perfectly, precisely, accurately

correctness noun 1 = **truth**, precision, accuracy, regularity, fidelity, exactitude, exactness, faultlessness, preciseness
2 = **decorum**, civility, good breeding, propriety, seemliness

correlate See **correspond**

correlation noun
= **correspondence**, link, connection, relation, equivalence, interrelationship

correspond verb 1 = **match**, agree, fit, tally, coincide, correlate, be related • The two maps correspond closely.
2 = **communicate**, write, exchange letters, keep in touch
See also: **suit**

correspondence
noun 1 = **letters**, post, communication, mail, writing
2 = **relation**, agreement, match, comparison, similarity, coincidence, harmony, correlation, conformity

correspondent noun 1 = **letter writer**, pen friend or pen pal
2 = **reporter**, journalist, contributor

corresponding adjective
= **related**, similar, equivalent, complementary, reciprocal, analogous, answering, matching

corridor noun = **passage**, alley, hallway, aisle, passageway

corroborate verb = **support**, confirm, endorse, ratify, authenticate, validate, substantiate, back up, bear out

corrode verb = **eat away**, consume, corrupt, erode, rust, oxidize, gnaw, wear away

corrosion See **wear**

corrosive adjective = **corroding**, virulent, wasting, vitriolic, caustic, consuming, erosive, wearing

corrupt adjective 1 = **dishonest**, unethical, fraudulent, crooked, shady (informal), unscrupulous, unprincipled, venal • corrupt politicians
OPPOSITE: honest
2 = **depraved**, vicious,

degenerate, debased, dissolute, profligate

3 = distorted, altered, doctored, falsified

▶ verb **4 = bribe**, fix (informal), buy off • Power is said to corrupt some people.

5 = deprave, pervert • Is TV really corrupting our children?

6 = distort, doctor, tamper with

See also: **criminal, dirty**

corruption noun **1 = dishonesty**, fraud, bribery • charges of corruption

2 = depravity, evil, vice, perversion, immorality, decadence, wickedness

3 = distortion, falsification, doctoring

corset noun **= girdle**, belt, bodice

cosmetic adjective **= beautifying**, surface, superficial, nonessential

cosmic adjective **= universal**, stellar

cosmopolitan adjective

1 = sophisticated, universal, open-minded, broad-minded, catholic, urbane, well-travelled, worldly-wise

▶ noun **2 = man of the world** or **woman of the world**, jet-setter, sophisticate

cosset See **spoil**

cost noun **1 = price**, charge, rate, payment, expense, outlay • The cost of fuel has increased.

2 = loss, penalty, expense, detriment • the total cost in human misery

▶ verb **3 = sell at**, come to, set someone back (informal) • The air fares were going to cost a lot.

4 = lose, injure, hurt, harm, do disservice to

See also: **value**

cost-effective See **economical**

costly adjective **1 = expensive**, stiff, steep (informal), dear, exorbitant, extortionate, highly-priced

2 = damaging, harmful, disastrous, catastrophic, ruinous, deleterious, loss-making

costs plural noun **= expenses**, budget, outgoings, overheads

costume noun **= outfit**, dress, uniform, ensemble, apparel, attire, garb, clothing, livery

cosy adjective (Esp. Brit) variant of **cozy**

cottage noun **= cabin**, lodge, hut, shack, chalet

couch See **express**

cough noun **1 = frog in one's throat** or **tickle in one's throat**, hack, bark

▶ verb **2 = clear one's throat**, hack, bark

council noun **= committee**, board, panel, assembly • the city council

> **CONFUSABLES**
> Council is a noun that refers to a group of people.
> Counsel means advice (n) or advise (v).

counsel noun **1 = advice**, information, warning, recommendation, direction, suggestion, guidance

2 = legal adviser, lawyer, advocate, attorney, barrister

▶ verb **3 = advise**, warn, urge, recommend, advocate, instruct, exhort

count verb **1 = add up**, tally, calculate • He counted the votes.

2 = matter, rate, weigh, signify, carry weight • Our opinions don't count.

3 = consider, think, rate, judge, regard, deem, look upon

4 = take into account or **take into consideration**, include, number among

▷ **count on, count upon**
= depend on, trust, bank on, believe in, lean on, pin one's faith on, reckon on, rely on, take for granted, take on trust

▷ **count up = add**, total, tally, sum, reckon up

▶ noun **5 = calculation**, tally, sum, reckoning • The count revealed that our party had the majority.

See also: **reckon**

INFORMALLY SPEAKING
count for: be worth
count on: rely on

countenance See **expression, face**

counter verb **1 = retaliate**, meet, answer, respond, oppose, resist, parry, hit back, ward off
▶ adverb **2 = opposite to**, against, versus, conversely, at variance with, contrariwise, in defiance of

counteract verb **= act against**, offset • *pills to counteract high blood pressure*
See also: **compensate**

counterbalance verb **= offset**, balance, compensate, make up for, set off

counterfeit adjective **1 = fake**, false, bogus, phony (informal), sham, simulated, imitation, forged
▶ noun **2 = fake**, fraud, copy, reproduction, forgery, phony (informal), sham, imitation
▶ verb **3 = fake**, copy, forge, pretend, fabricate, simulate, sham, imitate, impersonate, feign

countermand verb **= cancel**, reverse, revoke, retract, rescind, repeal, override, annul

counterpart noun **= equivalent**, match, fellow, supplement, twin, tally, equal, mate, complement

countless adjective **= innumerable**, myriad, infinite, untold • *the star of countless movies*
See also: **many**

country noun **1 = nation**, state, land, kingdom • *the boundary between the two countries*
2 = countryside, outdoors, bush • *He lives right out in the country.*
RELATED WORDS
adjectives: pastoral, rural
3 = territory, region, land, terrain
4 = people, public, community, nation, society, populace, citizens, inhabitants

countryside noun **= country**, outdoors, farmland, outback (Austral & NZ), green belt, sticks (informal)

county noun **= province**, shire

coup noun **= masterstroke**, action, stunt, exploit, accomplishment, feat, deed, manoeuvre

couple noun **1 = pair**, two, brace, duo, twosome
▶ verb **2 = link**, join, pair, connect, marry, unite, wed, hitch, yoke

coupling See **connection**

coupon noun **= slip**, card, ticket, certificate, token, voucher

courage noun **= bravery**, nerve, pluck, daring, grit, valour, heroism, guts (informal) • *Her courage impressed everyone.*
OPPOSITE: fear

courageous adjective **= brave**, bold, gritty, daring, valiant, fearless, gallant, intrepid, lion-hearted, stouthearted

courier noun **1 = guide**, representative
2 = messenger, carrier, envoy, runner, bearer

course noun **1 = classes**, curriculum • *a course in information technology*
2 = procedure, plan, policy • *The premier took the only course left open to her.*
3 = route, way, line, direction, path, trajectory • *She sensed the plane had changed course.*
4 = progression, order, development, progress, movement, flow, sequence, unfolding
5 = racecourse, circuit, cinder track
6 = period, time, term, sweep, passage, passing, lapse, duration
▷ **course of action** See **process**
▷ **of course = naturally**, certainly, obviously, definitely, undoubtedly, indubitably, needless to say, without a doubt
▶ verb **7 = run**, race, speed, surge, flow, stream, gush
8 = hunt, follow, pursue, chase, stalk

See also: **pour**

CONFUSABLES
Course has nothing to do with roughness.
Coarse means *rough*.

court noun **1** = **law court**, bench, tribunal • *He ended up in court for theft.*

2 = **courtyard**, yard, square, quad (*informal*), plaza, piazza, cloister, quadrangle

3 = **palace**, hall, manor

4 = **royal household**, train, suite, entourage, cortege, attendants, retinue

▶ *verb* **5** (*Old-fashioned*) = **go steady** • *My grandparents courted for five years before they married.*

6 = **cultivate**, seek, solicit, flatter, brown-nose (*slang*), curry favour with, fawn upon, pander to

7 = **invite**, seek, prompt, attract, provoke, incite, bring about

courteous *adjective* = **polite**, civil, refined, respectful, gracious, gallant, attentive, affable, urbane, well-mannered

courteousness *See* **courtesy**

courtesy noun **1** = **politeness**, grace, civility, courteousness, gallantry, good manners, graciousness • *a lack of courtesy to other drivers*

2 = **favour**, kindness, indulgence, benevolence

courtier noun = **attendant**, follower, squire

courtly *adjective* = **ceremonious**, formal, elegant, refined, dignified, polished, gallant, stately, chivalrous, urbane

courtyard noun = **yard**, quad, enclosure, quadrangle

cove noun = **bay**, sound, inlet, anchorage

covenant noun **1** = **promise**, contract, agreement, pledge, commitment, pact, arrangement

▶ *verb* **2** = **promise**, agree, contract, pledge, undertake, stipulate

cover *verb* **1** = **conceal**, screen, hide, mask, cloak, shade,

obscure, cover up • *He covered his face.*

OPPOSITE: **reveal**

2 = **overlay**, coat • *Tears covered his face.*

3 = **clothe**, dress, wrap, envelop, put on

4 = **submerge**, flood, overrun, engulf, wash over

5 = **travel over**, cross, traverse, pass through *or* pass over

6 = **protect**, defend, guard, shield

7 = **report**, investigate, describe, relate, narrate, tell of, write up

▷ **cover up** = **conceal**, hide, suppress, whitewash (*informal*), draw a veil over, hush up, sweep under the carpet

▶ *noun* **8** = **covering**, case, screen, jacket, mask, coating, wrapper • *quilts, blankets, and other covers*

9 = **disguise**, front, screen, mask, veil, pretext, façade, smoke screen

10 = **protection**, guard, shelter, shield, defence, camouflage, concealment

11 = **insurance**, protection, compensation, reimbursement, indemnity

See also: **defence, include, safeguard, spread, stretch**

covering *adjective*

1 = **explanatory**, introductory, descriptive, accompanying

▶ *noun* **2** = **cover**, layer, blanket, casing, coating, wrapping

covert *See* **secret**

cover-up noun = **concealment**, front, conspiracy, complicity, whitewash (*informal*), smoke screen

covet *verb* = **long for**, desire, envy, crave, aspire to, lust after, set one's heart on, yearn for

covetous *adjective* = **envious**, greedy, jealous, yearning, acquisitive, avaricious, close-fisted, grasping, rapacious

cow noun = **bovine**, cattle • *a herd of dairy cows*

coward noun = **wimp** (*informal*), chicken (*slang*), wuss (*informal*)

• *too much of a coward to fight*
cowardice *noun* = **faint-heartedness**, weakness, fearfulness, spinelessness
cowardly *adjective* = **faint-hearted**, chicken (*slang*), gutless (*informal*) • *too cowardly to tell the truth*
OPPOSITE: brave
See also: **timid**
cowboy *noun* = **cowhand**, rancher, cattleman, gaucho, herdsman, drover, stockman
cower *verb* = **cringe**, shrink, quail
• *The hostages cowered in their seats.*
coy *adjective* = **shy**, modest, timid, reserved, demure, bashful, retiring, shrinking
cozy *adjective* = **snug**, warm, comfortable, intimate, comfy (*informal*), sheltered, homey, homely, tucked up
crack *verb* **1** = **break**, snap, fracture • *A gas main has cracked.*
2 = **solve**, decipher, work out
• *We've managed to crack the problem.*
3 = **snap**, crash, ring, pop, explode, burst, detonate
4 = **give in**, collapse, yield, succumb, break down, give way, go to pieces, lose control
5 (*Informal*) = **hit**, clip (*informal*), slap, smack, whack, cuff, clout (*informal*)
▶ *noun* **6** = **break**, fracture, cleft, crevice • *a large crack in the wall*
7 = **snap**, report, crash, explosion, pop, burst, clap
8 (*Informal*) = **blow**, clip (*informal*), slap, smack, whack, cuff, clout (*informal*)
9 (*Informal*) = **joke**, dig, gag (*informal*), quip, jibe, wisecrack (*informal*), funny remark, witticism
See also: **attempt, bang, breach, fissure, gap, leak, opening, split**

| INFORMALLY SPEAKING
crack down: impose stricter discipline
crack up: respond with laughter; suffer a breakdown
get cracking: hurry up

crackdown *noun* = **suppression**, clampdown, repression, crushing
cracked *adjective* = **broken**, split, faulty, damaged, flawed, defective, imperfect, chipped
cracking See **excellent, splendid**
cradle *noun* **1** = **crib**, cot, bassinet
2 = **birthplace**, source, spring, beginning, origin, fount, fountainhead, wellspring
▶ *verb* **3** = **hold**, support, rock, nurse, lull, nestle
craft *noun* **1** = **occupation**, work, trade, business, employment, pursuit, vocation, handicraft
2 = **skill**, art, ability, technique, expertise, know-how (*informal*), artistry, ingenuity, workmanship, aptitude
3 = **vessel**, plane, ship, aircraft, boat, spacecraft
craftsman *noun* = **skilled worker**, maker, master, technician, artisan, smith, wright
craftsmanship *noun* = **workmanship**, technique, expertise, mastery, artistry
crafty *adjective* = **cunning**, slippery, wily, sly, devious, artful, scheming • *That crafty old devil has taken us for a ride!*
See also: **shrewd, sneaky**
crag *noun* = **rock**, peak, bluff, pinnacle, tor
craggy See **jagged, rough**
cram *verb* **1** = **stuff**, pack, jam, squeeze • *She crammed the towel into her gym bag.*
2 = **overeat**, stuff, glut, gorge, satiate
3 = **study**, bone up (*informal*), review
See also: **fill**
cramp[1] *noun* = **spasm**, pain, ache, stitch, contraction, convulsion, pang, twinge
cramp[2] *verb* = **restrict**, hamper, hinder, obstruct, impede, inhibit, handicap, constrain
cramped *adjective* = **closed in**, crowded, packed,

uncomfortable, confined, congested, hemmed in, overcrowded

crank See **eccentric**

cranny noun = **crevice**, opening, hole, crack, gap, fissure, cleft, chink

crash noun 1 = **collision**, accident, bump, smash, pile-up (informal) • a plane crash
2 = **bang**, clash, smash, din • There was a sudden crash outside.
3 = **collapse**, failure, depression, bankruptcy, ruin • a stock-market crash
▶ verb 4 = **collide**, bump, wreck, drive into, have an accident, hurtle into, plow into • His car crashed into the rear of a minivan.
5 = **collapse**, fail, fold, be ruined, fold up, go belly up (informal), go bust (informal), go to the wall, go under
6 = **hurtle**, plunge, topple, lurch, fall headlong, give way, overbalance
See also: **dash**

crass adjective = **insensitive**, gross, stupid, boorish, unrefined, indelicate, oafish, witless

crate noun = **container**, case, box, packing case, tea chest

crater noun = **hollow**, depression, dip

crave verb 1 = **long for**, want, desire, hanker for, hope for, lust after, yearn for
2 = **beg**, ask, seek, petition, solicit, implore, beseech, entreat, plead for, pray for, supplicate

craving noun = **longing**, hope, desire, hunger, appetite, yen (informal), thirst, yearning, hankering

crawl verb 1 = **be full of**, swarm, teem, be alive with, be overrun (slang) • The place is crawling with tourists.
2 = **creep**, inch, wriggle, writhe, slither, advance slowly, worm one's way
3 = **grovel**, creep, fawn, brown-nose (slang), humble oneself, kiss

ass (slang), toady

craze noun = **fad**, trend, fashion, vogue • the latest fitness craze
See also: **whim**

crazy adjective 1 (Informal) = **ridiculous**, wild, mad, foolish, insane, zany • a crazy idea
OPPOSITE: sensible
2 (Informal) = **fanatical**, wild, mad, passionate, obsessed, smitten • He's crazy about figure skating.
OPPOSITE: uninterested
3 = **insane**, mad, unbalanced, crazed, demented, deranged, nuts (slang), out of one's mind
See also: **absurd, idiotic, irrational**

creak verb = **squeak**, grind, scratch, scrape, grate, screech, groan

cream noun 1 = **lotion**, oil, cosmetic, paste, essence, ointment, emulsion, liniment, salve, unguent
2 = **best**, pick, prime, flower, elite, crème de la crème (French)
▶ adjective 3 = **off-white**, yellowish-white

creamy adjective = **smooth**, rich, soft, buttery, milky, velvety

crease noun 1 = **line**, fold, wrinkle, groove, ridge, corrugation
▶ verb 2 = **wrinkle**, fold, crumple, corrugate, rumple, double up, screw up

create verb 1 = **cause**, occasion, bring about, lead to • The new factory created hundreds of jobs.
2 = **invent**, coin, compose, originate, devise, formulate • creating a new style of painting
3 = **appoint**, make, establish, invest, install, constitute, set up
See also: **bring, construct, fashion, form, produce, start**

creation noun 1 = **making**, generation, formation, conception, genesis, procreation
2 = **setting up**, production, development, institution, foundation, formation, establishment, inception
3 = **invention**, production,

achievement, brainchild (*informal*), concoction, handiwork, magnum opus, *pièce de résistance* (French)
4 = universe, world, nature, cosmos
creative *adjective* = **imaginative**, inspired, fertile, inventive • *her creative talents*
creativity *noun* = **imagination**, inspiration, ingenuity, originality, inventiveness, cleverness
creator *noun* = **maker**, author, father, designer, architect, inventor, originator, prime mover
creature *noun* 1 = **living thing**, animal, being, beast, brute
2 = person, man, woman, individual, soul, mortal, human being
credentials *plural noun* = **certification**, document, passport, licence, reference or references, authorization, testimonial, papers
credibility *noun* = **believability**, integrity, reliability, plausibility, trustworthiness
credible *adjective* 1 = **believable**, likely, possible, reasonable, probable, imaginable, plausible, conceivable, thinkable
2 = reliable, honest, sincere, dependable, trustworthy, trusty
credit *noun* 1 = **praise**, recognition, glory, acclaim, kudos, commendation, thanks, Brownie points, full marks (*Brit & Canad*), props (*informal*) • *He took all the credit for my idea.*
2 = source of satisfaction or **source of pride**, honour, feather in one's cap
3 = prestige, position, status, influence, regard, standing, reputation, esteem, repute, good name
4 = belief, trust, confidence, faith, reliance, credence
▷ **on credit = on account**, by deferred payment, by instalments, on the card
▶ *verb* **5 = believe**, trust, accept,

have faith in, rely on
▷ **credit with = attribute to**, ascribe to, assign to, impute to
See also: **loan**
creditable *adjective* = **praiseworthy**, worthy, respectable, admirable, reputable, honourable, commendable, laudable
credulity *noun* = **gullibility**, blind faith, credulousness, naivety
creed *noun* = **belief**, doctrine, dogma, credo, articles of faith, catechism, principles
creek *noun* (*US, Canad, Austral, & NZ*) = **stream**, tributary, bayou, brook, rivulet, runnel, watercourse
creep *verb* 1 = **sneak**, steal, tiptoe, slink, approach unnoticed, skulk
2 = crawl, glide, wriggle, squirm, writhe, slither
▶ *noun* **3** (*Slang*) = **toady**, sneak, bootlicker, brown-noser (*slang*), crawler (*slang*), scuzzbucket (*slang*), sycophant
4 (*Slang*) = **jerk** (*slang*), loser, pervert, scumbag (*slang*), lowlife, scuzzbucket (*slang*)
creeper *noun* = **climbing plant**, runner, vine, rambler, trailing plant
creeps *plural noun*
▷ **give one the creeps** (*Informal*) = **disgust**, scare, frighten, repel, repulse, make one's hair stand on end, make one squirm
creepy *adjective* (*Informal*) = **disturbing**, scary (*informal*), eerie, sinister, spooky, macabre, unnatural • *This place is really creepy at night.*
crescent *noun* = **meniscus**, sickle, new moon
crest *noun* 1 = **top**, summit, crown, peak, ridge, pinnacle, apex, highest point
2 = tuft, crown, comb, plume, mane
3 = emblem, device, symbol, badge, insignia, bearings
crestfallen *adjective* = **disappointed**, depressed, dejected, despondent, discouraged, downcast,

disheartened, downhearted

crevice noun = **gap**, opening, hole, crack, fissure, slit, cleft, cranny, chink

crew noun 1 = **company** or **ship's company**, complement or ship's complement, hands
2 = **team**, gang, squad, corps, posse
3 (Informal) = **crowd**, set, band, pack, gang, bunch (informal), mob, horde

crib noun 1 = **cradle**, bed, cot, bassinet
2 = **manger**, stall, rack
▶ verb 3 (Informal) = **copy**, steal, pirate, cheat, plagiarize, purloin

crime noun 1 = **offence**, wrong, violation, misdemeanour • the problem of organized crime
2 = **lawbreaking**, corruption, vice, wrongdoing, misconduct, illegality
See also: **pity, sin**

criminal noun 1 = **lawbreaker**, offender, culprit, villain, crook (informal), perp (informal), felon, malefactor • the country's most dangerous criminals
▶ adjective 2 = **unlawful**, illegal, illicit, corrupt, crooked • criminal activities
3 = **disgraceful**, ridiculous, foolish, senseless, scandalous, deplorable, preposterous
See also: **guilty**

crimson See **blush**

cringe verb = **shrink**, shy, flinch, wince, recoil, cower, draw back

cripple verb 1 = **disable**, paralyze, maim • She was crippled in a car accident.
2 = **impair**, bring to a standstill, put out of action • The crisis may cripple the provincial economy.

crippled adjective = **disabled**, paralyzed, lame, handicapped, challenged, incapacitated, laid up (informal)

crisis noun 1 = **critical point**, crunch (informal), height, climax, culmination, crux, moment of truth, turning point
2 = **emergency**, trouble, plight, meltdown (informal),

predicament, deep water, dire straits, panic stations (informal)

crisp adjective 1 = **crunchy**, firm, fresh, crispy, brittle, crumbly
2 = **clean**, trim, smart, tidy, neat, spruce, well-groomed, well-pressed
3 = **bracing**, fresh, brisk, invigorating, refreshing

crisscross See **cross**

criterion noun = **standard**, test, rule, measure, principle, gauge, touchstone, yardstick, bench mark

critic noun 1 = **judge**, expert, authority, analyst, commentator, reviewer, pundit, connoisseur
2 = **fault-finder**, attacker, detractor, knocker (informal)

critical adjective 1 = **crucial**, decisive, vital, pivotal, momentous, deciding • a critical point in history
OPPOSITE: unimportant
2 = **serious**, grave, precarious • a critical illness
3 = **disparaging**, scathing, derogatory, carping, disapproving • critical remarks
OPPOSITE: complimentary
4 = **analytical**, judicious, perceptive, discerning, discriminating, fastidious, penetrating
See also: **acute, major, severe**

criticism noun 1 = **fault-finding**, censure, flak (informal), disapproval • The finance minister faced criticism over the budget.
OPPOSITE: praise
2 = **analysis**, comment, assessment, judgment, commentary, appreciation, evaluation, critique, appraisal
See also: **complaint, review**

criticize verb = **find fault with**, knock (informal), condemn, censure, disparage, lambaste, put down, excoriate • The dictatorial regime has been harshly criticized.
OPPOSITE: praise
See also: **attack, fault**

croak verb = **squawk**, wheeze,

caw, grunt, utter huskily *or* speak huskily

croaky *See* **hoarse**

crony *See* **companion, friend**

crook *noun* (*Informal*) = **criminal**, thief, shark, cheat, rogue, villain, scoundrel (*old-fashioned*), swindler • *The man is a crook and a liar.*

crooked *adjective* **1** = **bent**, twisted, irregular, distorted, deformed, out of shape, warped • *a crooked tree*
OPPOSITE: straight
2 = **dishonest**, criminal, illegal, corrupt, fraudulent, shady (*informal*), nefarious, unprincipled • *crooked business practices*
OPPOSITE: honest
3 = **at an angle**, lopsided, awry, askew, off-centre, uneven, squint, slanting
See also: **dirty, dubious, wrong**

croon *verb* = **sing**, hum, purr, warble

crop *noun* **1** = **produce**, yield, gathering, harvest, vintage, fruits, reaping
▶ *verb* **2** = **cut**, clip, trim, pare, prune, shear, lop, snip
3 = **graze**, browse, nibble
▷ **crop up** = **happen**, appear, occur, emerge, arise, spring up, turn up

cross *verb* **1** = **go across**, span, traverse, ford • *the bridge that crosses the river*
2 = **intersect**, crisscross • *the intersection where the roads cross*
3 = **oppose**, block, resist, interfere, obstruct, impede
4 = **interbreed**, mix, blend, crossbreed, cross-fertilize, cross-pollinate, hybridize, intercross, mongrelize
▷ **cross out, cross off** = **strike off** *or* **strike out**, cancel, eliminate, delete, blue-pencil, score out *or* score off
▷ **cross your mind** *See* **occur**
▶ *noun* **5** = **mixture**, combination, hybrid, blend • *a cross between a collie and a retriever*
6 = **crucifix**, rood

7 = **trouble**, trial, worry, load, burden, woe, grief, misfortune, affliction, tribulation
▶ *adjective* **8** = **angry**, fractious, grumpy, annoyed, irritable, fretful, in a bad mood • *I'm really cross with you.*
9 = **transverse**, oblique, diagonal, crosswise, intersecting

cross-examine *verb* = **question**, pump, quiz, grill (*informal*), interrogate

crossing *noun* = **crossroads**, intersection, junction

crouch *verb* = **bend down**, squat • *crouching behind the car*
See also: **bend**

crow *verb* = **gloat**, triumph, boast, brag, swagger, strut, exult, blow one's own trumpet

crowd *noun* **1** = **multitude**, host (*formal*), mass, mob, swarm, throng, horde • *a large crowd at the garage sale*
2 = **group**, set, lot, circle, bunch (*informal*), clique
3 = **audience**, house, attendance, gate, spectators
▶ *verb* = **gather**, swarm, throng, congregate • *Thousands of fans crowded into the stadium.*
4 = **squeeze**, pack, pile, bundle, cram, congest
See also: **band, company, jam, number**

crowded *adjective* = **packed**, full, congested, overflowing • *a crowded room*

crowing *See* **boastful**

crown *noun* **1** = **coronet**, tiara, circlet, diadem
2 = **laurel wreath**, trophy, wreath, honour, prize, garland, laurels
3 = **high point**, top, tip, summit, crest, pinnacle, apex
▶ *verb* **4** = **honour**, adorn, festoon, dignify
5 = **cap**, top, finish, complete, perfect, be the climax of *or* be the culmination of, put the finishing touch to, round off
6 (*Slang*) = **strike**, belt (*informal*), box, punch, hit over the head

Crown noun 1 = **monarchy**, royalty, sovereignty
2 = **monarch**, king or queen, ruler, sovereign, emperor or empress

crucial adjective 1 = **vital**, central, critical, decisive, pivotal, momentous • a crucial moment in her career
2 = **critical**, central, decisive, pivotal
See also: **essential, major, serious**

crucify verb = **execute**, torture, persecute, torment

crude adjective 1 = **rough**, simple, primitive, rudimentary • a crude weapon
2 = **vulgar**, dirty, obscene, indecent, tasteless, coarse • a crude sense of humour
OPPOSITE: refined
3 = **unrefined**, natural, raw, unprocessed

crudely adverb = **vulgarly**, roughly, bluntly, coarsely, rudely, impolitely, tastelessly

crudity noun 1 = **roughness**, clumsiness, crudeness
2 = **vulgarity**, obscenity, indecency, impropriety, coarseness, indelicacy, smuttiness

cruel adjective 1 = **brutal**, vicious, inhumane, sadistic, callous, heartless, cold-blooded, barbarous • I can't understand why people are cruel to animals.
OPPOSITE: kind
2 = **merciless**, ruthless, unrelenting, pitiless
See also: **harsh, malicious, savage, spiteful, unkind, violent**

cruelly adverb 1 = **brutally**, mercilessly, barbarously, callously, heartlessly, in cold blood, pitilessly, sadistically, spitefully
2 = **bitterly**, deeply, severely, fearfully, grievously, monstrously

cruelty noun = **brutality**, savagery, inhumanity, viciousness, barbarity, callousness • an act of unbelievable cruelty
OPPOSITE: kindness
See also: **violence**

cruise noun 1 = **sail**, voyage, boat trip, sea trip
▶ verb 2 = **sail**, coast, voyage
3 = **travel along**, coast, drift, keep a steady pace

crumb noun = **bit**, grain, scrap, shred, fragment, morsel, soupçon (French)

crumble verb 1 = **disintegrate**, collapse, deteriorate, decay, degenerate, fall apart, go to pieces, go to rack and ruin, tumble down
2 = **crush**, pound, grind, powder, fragment, granulate, pulverize

crummy adjective (Informal)
1 = **despicable**, mean, lousy (slang), contemptible, scuzzy (slang)
2 = **inferior**, poor, inadequate, lousy (slang), deficient, substandard, of poor quality
3 = **unwell**, below par, off colour, under the weather (informal)

crumple verb 1 = **crush**, crease, wrinkle • She crumpled the paper in her hand.
2 = **collapse**, fall, break down, cave in, give way, go to pieces
See also: **fold**

crunch verb 1 = **chomp**, grind, champ, munch, chew noisily
▶ noun 2 (Informal) = **critical point**, test, emergency, crisis, crux, moment of truth

crusade noun = **campaign**, cause, drive, push, movement

crush verb 1 = **squash**, crumble, mash, crumple • Their car was crushed, but nobody was seriously hurt.
2 = **overcome**, quell, vanquish, put down, stamp out • The Blue Jays crushed the Yankees.
3 = **humiliate**, shame, quash, mortify, abash, put down (slang)
▶ noun 4 = **crowd**, jam, huddle
See also: **dash, defeat, press, subdue, suppress**

crust noun = **layer**, skin, surface, shell, coating, covering

crusty adjective **1** = **crispy**, hard
2 = **irritable**, cross, testy, cantankerous, prickly, gruff, short-tempered

cry verb **1** = **weep**, sob, blubber, shed tears, snivel • *Stop crying and tell me what's wrong.*
2 = **shout**, call, scream, roar, yell, howl, exclaim, shriek, bellow, bawl, call out • *"See you soon!" they cried.*
▷ **cry off** (*Informal*) = **back out**, quit, withdraw, excuse oneself
▶ noun **3** = **shout**, call, howl, bellow, exclamation, scream, roar, screech, shriek
4 = **weeping**, weep, sob, blubbering, snivelling, sobbing • *the act of weeping*
5 = **appeal**, plea
See also: **bay**

cryptic See **mysterious, obscure**

crystalline See **clear, transparent**

cub noun = **young**, offspring, whelp

cuckoo adjective (*Slang*) = **insane**, crazy, stupid, foolish, idiotic, bonkers (*informal*), daft (*informal*), nuts (*slang*), out of one's mind

cuddle verb = **hug**, pet, embrace, snuggle, fondle, bill and coo, cosset

cudgel noun = **club**, nightstick, billy club, stick, truncheon

cue noun = **signal**, sign, key, hint, suggestion, reminder, catchword, prompting

cul-de-sac noun = **dead end**, blind alley

culminate verb = **end up**, close, finish, conclude, climax, come to a climax, come to a head, wind up

culmination noun = **climax**, peak, conclusion, finale, pinnacle, zenith, acme, consummation

culpable adjective
= **blameworthy**, guilty, wrong, at fault, found wanting, in the wrong, to blame

culprit noun = **offender**, criminal, wrongdoer, felon,
miscreant, evildoer, guilty party, perp (*informal*), transgressor

cult noun **1** = **sect**, school, religion, faction, clique
2 = **devotion**, worship, idolization

cultivate verb **1** = **farm**, work, plant, tend, plow, till
2 = **develop**, improve, promote, foster, refine
3 = **court**, dance attendance upon, run after, seek out

cultivated See **educated, sophisticated**

cultivation noun **1** = **farming**, gardening, husbandry, planting, plowing, tillage
2 = **development**, support, promotion, nurture, encouragement, patronage, fostering, furtherance

cultural adjective = **artistic**, liberal, educational, humane, civilizing, edifying, enlightening, enriching

culture noun **1** = **civilization**, society, lifestyle, mores, customs, way of life
2 = **refinement**, education, sophistication, enlightenment, good taste, urbanity
3 = **farming**, cultivation, husbandry

cultured adjective = **refined**, sophisticated, enlightened, well-informed, educated, highbrow, urbane, well-read

culvert noun = **drain**, channel, gutter, conduit, watercourse

cumbersome adjective
= **awkward**, heavy, bulky, weighty, unwieldy, unmanageable, burdensome

cunning adjective **1** = **crafty**, wily, sly, devious, artful • *a cunning and ruthless plot*
OPPOSITE: open
2 = **skilful**, imaginative, ingenious
▶ noun **3** = **deviousness**, guile
• *the cunning of today's criminals*
4 = **skill**, ingenuity, subtlety, artifice, cleverness

cup noun **1** = **mug**, bowl, chalice,

beaker, goblet, teacup
2 = **trophy**
curb verb 1 = **restrain**, control, contain, limit, check, suppress
• *He must learn to curb that temper of his.*
▶ noun 2 = **restraint**, control, limit, brake, limitation • *She called for stricter curbs on government spending.*
See also: **halt, moderate, restriction**
curdled See **sour**
cure verb 1 = **remedy**, heal
• *Doctors are still seeking a treatment that will cure the common cold.*
▶ noun 2 = **remedy**, treatment, medicine • *a cure for the disease*
See also: **correct**
curiosity noun
1 = **inquisitiveness**, interest, infomania (*informal*) • *a curiosity about the past*
2 = **oddity**, freak, marvel, novelty, rarity • *a museum displaying relics and curiosities*
curious adjective 1 = **inquisitive**, interested, nosy (*informal*), inquiring • *He was curious about my family.*
2 = **strange**, odd, unusual, extraordinary, bizarre, singular, peculiar • *a curious mixture of the old and the new*
OPPOSITE: ordinary
See also: **weird**
curl verb 1 = **twirl**, turn, wind, twist, spiral, bend, curve, loop, coil
▶ noun 2 = **twist**, spiral, coil, kink, ringlet, whorl
curly adjective = **curling**, fuzzy, wavy, crinkly, curled, frizzy, winding
currency noun 1 = **money**, coinage, coins, notes
2 = **acceptance**, exposure, popularity, circulation, prevalence, vogue
current noun 1 = **flow**, tide, undertow • *swept away by the strong current*
2 = **mood**, trend, feeling, atmosphere, tendency, undercurrent

▶ adjective 3 = **present**, ongoing, contemporary, fashionable, present-day, up-to-the-minute, today's • *current trends*
OPPOSITE: past
4 = **prevalent**, popular, common, widespread, customary, topical, accepted, in circulation
See also: **modern, recent**
currently See **now**
curriculum See **course**
curriculum vitae See **résumé**
curse verb 1 = **swear**, blaspheme, cuss (*informal*), take the Lord's name in vain
2 = **damn**, excommunicate, anathematize
▶ noun 3 = **oath**, obscenity, expletive, blasphemy, swearing, swearword
4 = **denunciation**, ban, jinx, anathema, excommunication, hoodoo (*informal*)
5 = **affliction**, trouble, plague, hardship, scourge, torment, bane
cursed adjective = **damned**, doomed, ill-fated, accursed, bedevilled
cursory See **casual, quick**
curt adjective = **short**, brief, blunt, abrupt, terse, gruff, succinct, brusque, monosyllabic
curtail verb = **cut short**, reduce, decrease, dock, diminish, shorten, lessen, cut back, truncate
curtain noun = **hanging**, drape
curve noun 1 = **bend**, turn, arc, trajectory, incurve (*baseball*) • *a curve in the road*
RELATED WORD
adjective: sinuous
▶ verb 2 = **bend**, arc, arch, swerve
• *The road curved sharply to the left.*
curved adjective = **bent**, twisted, rounded, arched, serpentine, bowed, sinuous
cushion noun 1 = **pillow**, pad, bolster, beanbag, hassock, headrest
▶ verb 2 = **soften**, stifle, suppress, dampen, muffle, deaden

cushy adjective (Informal) = **easy**, comfortable, soft, undemanding

custody noun 1 = **safekeeping**, charge, care, protection, supervision, keeping
2 = **imprisonment**, detention, confinement, incarceration

custom noun 1 = **tradition**, practice, convention, ritual • *a family custom to have a birthday picnic*
2 = **habit**, practice, wont (formal) • *It was his custom to start work at 8:30.*
3 = **customers**, trade, patronage *See also:* **way**

customary adjective = **usual**, common, traditional, normal, routine, conventional, ordinary, established, accepted, accustomed

customer noun = **client**, consumer, shopper, buyer, patron, purchaser • *The store was filled with customers.*

customs plural noun = **duty**, tax, toll, tariff, import charges

cut verb 1 = **penetrate**, score, wound, slash, slice, chop, sever, pierce, slit • *He accidentally cut his chin while he was shaving.*
2 = **divide**, split, slice, dissect, bisect
3 = **trim**, clip, shave, lower, prune, lop, snip, hew
4 = **abridge**, shorten, delete, curtail, abbreviate, condense
5 = **reduce**, contract, lower, decrease, slash, slim or slim down, diminish, downsize, rationalize, cut back • *The department's first priority is to cut costs.*
OPPOSITE: increase
6 = **shape**, form, fashion, carve, sculpt, whittle, engrave, chisel
7 = **hurt**, wound, insult, sting, snub, put down
▷ **cut back** *See* **cut**
▷ **cut down** = **fell**, level, lop, hew; = **reduce**, lower, decrease, lessen
▷ **cut in** = **interrupt**, intervene, intrude, break in, butt in

▷ **cut off** = **separate**, isolate, sever; = **interrupt**, intercept, disconnect
▷ **cut out** = **stop**, cease, give up, refrain from
▷ **cut short** *See* **halt**
▷ **cut up** *See* **divide**
▶ noun 8 = **incision**, wound, stroke, slash, gash, nick, slit, laceration • *a cut on his left eyebrow*
9 = **reduction**, fall, saving, decrease, cutback, lowering • *another cut in interest rates*
OPPOSITE: increase
10 (Informal) = **share**, piece, percentage, section, portion, slice
11 = **style**, look, fashion, shape

> **INFORMALLY SPEAKING**
> **cut down to size**: humiliate
> **cut it fine**: leave no room for error
> **cut it out**: stop it
> **make the cut**: be one of a limited number selected

cutback noun = **reduction**, cut, economy, decrease, lessening, retrenchment

cute adjective = **appealing**, pretty, attractive, dear, charming, gorgeous, good-looking • *You were such a cute baby!*

cutthroat adjective
1 = **competitive**, fierce, relentless, ruthless, dog-eat-dog, unprincipled
▶ noun 2 = **murderer**, killer, assassin, butcher, executioner, hit man (slang)

cutting adjective = **hurtful**, bitter, scathing, malicious, barbed, acrimonious, vitriolic, sarcastic, caustic, wounding

cycle noun = **era**, period, circle, phase, revolution, rotation

cylindrical *See* **round**

cynic noun = **skeptic**, doubter, pessimist, misanthrope, misanthropist, scoffer

cynical adjective = **skeptical**, distrustful • *a cynical attitude*

cynicism noun = **skepticism**, doubt, disbelief, pessimism, misanthropy

Dd

dab *verb* **1 = pat**, touch, tap, daub, stipple
▶ *noun* **2 = spot**, drop, bit, pat, speck, smudge
3 = pat, touch, stroke, tap, flick
dabble *verb* **1 = play at**, tinker, putter, trifle *or* trifle with, dip into
2 = splash, dip
daft *adjective* (*Informal*) **1 = foolish**, crazy, stupid, silly, absurd, idiotic, asinine, bonkers (*informal*), crackpot (*informal*), witless
2 = crazy, bonkers (*slang*), insane, demented, deranged, nuts (*slang*), touched, unhinged
dagger *noun* **= knife**, stiletto, bayonet, dirk
daily *adjective* **1 = everyday**, diurnal, quotidian
▶ *adverb* **2 = every day**, day by day, once a day
dainty *adjective* **= delicate**, fine, pretty, elegant, charming, neat, exquisite, graceful, petite
dam *noun* **1 = barrier**, wall, obstruction, barrage, embankment
▶ *verb* **2 = block up**, restrict, barricade, obstruct, hold back
damage *verb* **1 = harm**, injure, hurt • *A fire had severely damaged the school.*
▶ *noun* **2 = harm**, injury • *The flood caused extensive damage to the restaurant.*
3 (*Informal*) **= cost**, charge, bill, expense
See also: **ruin, spoil**
damaged See **imperfect**
damages *plural noun* (*Law*) **= compensation**, fine, satisfaction, reimbursement, reparation

damaging *adjective* **= harmful**, detrimental, hurtful, ruinous, deleterious, injurious, disadvantageous
dame *noun* **= noblewoman**, lady, baroness, dowager, *grande dame* (*French*), peeress
damn *verb* **1 = condemn**, blast, criticize, denounce, censure, put down
2 = sentence, condemn, doom
damnation *noun* **= condemnation**, doom, denunciation, anathema, damning
damned *adjective* **1 = doomed**, lost, accursed, condemned
2 (*Slang*) **= detestable**, hateful, confounded, infernal, loathsome
damp *adjective* **1 = moist**, wet, soggy, humid, sodden, clammy, dank • *a damp towel*
▶ *noun* **2 = moisture**, drizzle, dampness, dankness
▶ *verb* **3 = moisten**, wet, dampen
▷ **damp down = reduce**, check, curb, stifle, diminish, inhibit, allay, pour cold water on
dampen *verb* **1 = reduce**, check, moderate, stifle, restrain, lessen, dull
2 = moisten, spray, wet, make damp
damper *noun* **= discouragement**, restraint, hindrance, cold water (*informal*), wet blanket (*informal*)
dampness *noun* **= moisture**, humidity • *There was dampness all over the walls.*
See also: **wet**
dance *verb* **1 = prance**, trip, skip, hop, sway, whirl, jig
▶ *noun* **2 = ball**, hop (*informal, dated*), disco, discotheque, social

dancer noun = **ballerina**, Terpsichorean

danger noun = **peril**, risk, threat, hazard, menace, jeopardy • *Your life is in danger!*
OPPOSITE: safety

dangerous adjective = **perilous**, risky, hazardous, treacherous • *It's dangerous to ride a bike without a helmet.*
OPPOSITE: safe
See also: **fierce, serious**

dangerously adverb = **perilously**, recklessly, alarmingly, precariously, hazardously, riskily, unsafely

dangle verb 1 = **hang**, trail, swing, sway, flap, hang down
2 = **wave**, flourish, brandish, flaunt

dank See **damp**

dapper adjective = **neat**, trim, smart, spruce, spry, soigné or soignée, well-groomed, well turned out

dare verb 1 = **challenge**, defy • *I dare you to ask him for a date.*
2 = **risk**, venture • *Nobody dared to complain.*
▶ noun 3 = **challenge**, taunt, provocation

daredevil noun 1 = **adventurer**, desperado, exhibitionist, show-off (*informal*), stunt man
▶ adjective 2 = **daring**, bold, audacious, adventurous, death-defying, reckless

daring adjective 1 = **brave**, bold, audacious, adventurous, fearless • *a daring escape by helicopter*
OPPOSITE: cautious
▶ noun 2 = **bravery**, nerve (*informal*), courage, audacity, boldness, guts (*informal*) • *His daring may have cost him his life.*
OPPOSITE: caution

dark adjective 1 = **dim**, murky, cloudy, shadowy, overcast, dingy • *It was too dark to see what was happening.*
OPPOSITE: light
2 = **black**, swarthy • *a dark suit*
3 = **gloomy**, sad, dismal, bleak, grim, mournful, sombre, morose

4 = **evil**, foul, wicked, sinister, vile, infernal
5 = **secret**, mysterious, hidden, concealed
▶ noun 6 = **darkness**, dusk, gloom, dimness • *I've always been afraid of the dark.*
OPPOSITE: light
7 = **night**, evening, twilight, nightfall, night-time

| **INFORMALLY SPEAKING**
in the dark: not knowing or not understanding
keep dark: keep secret

darken verb = **make dark**, overshadow, obscure, dim, blacken

darkness noun = **dark**, shade, gloom, nightfall, blackness, duskiness, murk, shadows

darling noun 1 = **beloved**, love, dear, sweetheart, dearest, truelove
▶ adjective 2 = **beloved**, precious, dear, cherished, adored, treasured

darn verb 1 = **mend**, repair, patch, stitch, cobble up, sew up
▶ noun 2 = **mend**, patch, reinforcement, invisible repair

dart verb = **dash**, run, shoot, race, fly, spring, rush, tear, sprint

dash verb 1 = **rush**, run, race, fly, tear, sprint, bolt • *Suddenly, the dog dashed into the street.*
2 = **smash**, break, crash, throw, slam, hurl • *The waves dashed against the rocks.*
3 = **frustrate**, destroy, disappoint, crush, thwart, foil, shatter • *They had their hopes raised and then dashed.*
▶ noun 4 = **rush**, run, race, sprint, bolt, stampede • *a dash to the hospital*
5 = **drop**, splash, pinch, sprinkling • *a dash of vinegar*
6 = **style**, spirit, flourish, flair, panache, verve, brio, élan
See also: **bustle, charge, hurry, trace**

dashing adjective 1 = **bold**, spirited, lively, gallant, swashbuckling, debonair
2 = **stylish**, smart, elegant,

flamboyant, showy, sporty, jaunty

data noun = **information**, details, facts, figures, statistics

date noun 1 = **time**, period, age, stage, era, epoch
2 = **appointment**, meeting, engagement, rendezvous, tryst, assignation
3 = **partner**, friend, escort
▶ verb 4 = **put a date on**, assign a date to, fix the period of
5 = **become old-fashioned**, be dated, show one's age
▷ **date from**, **date back to** = **come from**, bear a date of, belong to, exist from, originate in

dated adjective = **old-fashioned**, outdated, obsolete, outmoded, old hat, out of date, passé, unfashionable

daub verb = **smear**, cover, paint, coat, plaster, slap on (informal)

daunt See **discourage**

daunting adjective = **intimidating**, alarming, demoralizing, disconcerting, discouraging, disheartening, frightening, unnerving

dauntless adjective = **fearless**, bold, unflinching, gallant, resolute, intrepid, undaunted, indomitable, doughty, stouthearted

dawdle verb = **waste time**, delay, trail, idle, loaf, loiter, dally, drag one's feet or drag one's heels, hang about

dawn noun 1 = **daybreak**, morning, daylight, aurora (poetic), sunrise, cockcrow, crack of dawn, sunup
2 = **beginning**, start, rise, birth, origin, emergence, advent, genesis
▶ verb 3 = **grow light**, break, brighten, lighten
4 = **begin**, rise, appear, develop, emerge, originate, unfold
▷ **dawn on**, **dawn upon** = **hit**, strike, occur, register (informal), become apparent, come into one's head, come to mind

day noun 1 = **twenty-four hours**, daylight, daytime
2 = **point in time**, time, date
3 = **time**, period, age, era, heyday, epoch, zenith
▷ **days gone by** See **the past**

daybreak noun = **dawn**, morning, sunrise, break of day, cockcrow, crack of dawn, first light, sunup

daydream noun 1 = **fantasy**, dream • He learned to escape into daydreams.
▶ verb 2 = **fantasize**, dream • She daydreams of being a famous journalist.
See also: **vision**

daylight noun = **sunlight**, sunshine, light of day

day-to-day See **everyday**

daze verb 1 = **stun**, shock, paralyze, numb, benumb, stupefy
▶ noun 2 = **shock**, confusion, distraction, bewilderment, stupor, trance, trancelike state

dazed adjective = **stunned**, confused, dizzy, bewildered, light-headed, numbed • At the end of the interview, I was dazed and exhausted.

dazzle verb 1 = **impress**, overwhelm, overpower, astonish, amaze, bowl over (informal), take one's breath away
2 = **blind**, confuse, blur, daze, bedazzle
▶ noun 3 = **splendour**, sparkle, glitter, brilliance, magnificence, razzmatazz (slang)

dazzling adjective = **splendid**, brilliant, sensational (informal), sparkling, glorious, virtuoso, glittering, scintillating, stunning

de facto adverb 1 = **in fact**, really, actually, in effect, in reality
▶ adjective 2 = **actual**, real, existing

de jure adverb = **legally**, rightfully, by right

dead adjective 1 = **deceased**, late, extinct, departed • Our cat's been dead a year now.
OPPOSITE: alive
2 = **not working**, defunct • a dead language

3 = numb, paralyzed, inert
4 = total, complete, absolute, outright, utter, thorough, unqualified
5 (*Informal*) **= exhausted**, tired, spent, worn out
6 = boring, flat, dull, uninteresting
▷ **dead body** *See* **body**
▷ **dead ringer** *See* **look-alike**
▶ *noun* **7 = middle**, depth, midst

| INFORMALLY SPEAKING
| **dead in the water**: totally defeated
| **dead to the world**: deeply asleep
| **over my dead body**: I will resist to the end
| **wouldn't be caught dead**: be extremely unwilling to do

deaden *verb* **= reduce**, weaken, stifle, diminish, cushion, suppress, blunt, alleviate, smother, lessen, dull, muffle
deadline *noun* **= time limit**, limit, cutoff point, target date
deadlock *noun* **= impasse**, standoff, standstill, gridlock, stalemate
deadlocked *adjective* **1 = even**, level, equal, neck and neck, on a level playing field (*informal*)
2 = gridlocked, at an impasse, at a standstill
deadly *adjective* **= lethal**, fatal, destructive, mortal • *a deadly disease*
deadpan *adjective*
= expressionless, blank, impassive, inexpressive, inscrutable, poker-faced, straight-faced
deaf *adjective* **1 = hard of hearing**, stone deaf, without hearing
2 = oblivious, indifferent, unmoved, unconcerned, unhearing
deafen *verb* **= make deaf**, din, drown out, split the eardrums *or* burst the eardrums
deafening *adjective* **= ear-piercing**, thunderous, piercing, ringing, ear-splitting, booming, overpowering, resounding
deal *noun* **1 = agreement**, contract, transaction, bargain, understanding, pact, arrangement
2 = amount, share, degree, portion, extent, quantity
▶ *verb* **3 = sell**, trade, stock, traffic, negotiate, bargain, buy and sell, do business
▷ **deal out = distribute**, give, share, assign, dispense, allot, apportion, dole out, mete out
▷ **deal with = cope with**, manage, handle, attend to, see to, take care of • *He must learn to deal with stress;* **= be concerned with**, consider
See also: **administer**
dealer *noun* **= trader**, supplier, merchant, wholesaler, purveyor, tradesman
dealings *See* **business**
dear *noun* **1 = darling**, treasure (*informal*), sweetheart • *What's the matter, dear?*
▶ *adjective* **2 = beloved**, precious, prized, darling, cherished, esteemed, treasured • *a dear friend of mine*
3 = expensive, costly, pricey (*informal*), high-priced, overpriced, at a premium
See also: **cute**
dearest *See* **beloved**, **favourite**
dearly *adverb* **1 = very much**, extremely, greatly, profoundly
2 = at great cost, at a high price
dearth *noun* **= scarcity**, want, lack, shortage, poverty, deficiency, inadequacy, insufficiency, paucity
death *noun* **1 = dying**, end, exit, departure, passing, demise
2 = destruction, finish, ruin, extinction, downfall, undoing
deathly *adjective* **= deathlike**, grim, pale, ghastly, pallid, wan
debacle *noun* **= disaster**, defeat, collapse, rout, catastrophe, reversal, fiasco
debase *verb* **= degrade**, reduce, lower, devalue, cheapen
debatable *adjective* **= doubtful**, controversial, uncertain, questionable, problematic, dubious, moot, arguable

debate noun 1 = **discussion**, dispute, controversy, argument, contention
  ▶ verb 2 = **discuss**, question, dispute, argue
  3 = **consider**, reflect, weigh, ponder, deliberate, ruminate

debauchery noun = **depravity**, excess, indulgence, overindulgence, dissipation, dissoluteness, intemperance, lewdness

debonair adjective = **elegant**, smooth, charming, refined, courteous, suave, dashing, urbane, well-bred

debrief verb = **interrogate**, question, probe, examine, quiz, cross-examine

debris noun = **remains**, waste, wreckage, rubble, detritus, bits, fragments, ruins

debt noun = **debit**, commitment, obligation, liability
  ▷ **in debt** = **owing**, liable, in arrears, in the red (informal)

debtor noun = **borrower**, mortgagor

debunk verb = **expose**, mock, deflate, ridicule, disparage, cut down to size, show up

debut noun = **introduction**, beginning, bow, presentation, entrance, initiation, coming out, first appearance

decadence noun = **degeneration**, decline, corruption, deterioration, decay, dissolution, dissipation

decadent adjective = **degenerate**, corrupt, immoral, self-indulgent, decaying, declining, dissolute

decapitate verb = **behead**, execute, guillotine

decay verb 1 = **decline**, deteriorate, crumble, dwindle, wane, wither, disintegrate, shrivel, waste away
  2 = **rot**, perish, decompose, corrode, putrefy
  ▶ noun 3 = **decline**, collapse, degeneration, deterioration, fading, wasting, failing, withering

4 = **rot**, decomposition, caries, gangrene, putrefaction

decayed See **rotten**

decease noun (Formal) = **death**, release, departure, demise, dying

deceased adjective = **dead**, former, late, defunct, departed, lifeless, expired

deceit noun = **dishonesty**, fraud, deception, pretense, treachery, trickery, back-stabbing (informal), cheating, chicanery, lying

deceitful adjective = **dishonest**, false, fraudulent, treacherous, deceptive, sneaky, untrustworthy, down and dirty (informal), two-faced

deceive verb = **fool**, trick, mislead, con (informal), dupe, double-cross, take in • I was really hurt that he had deceived me.
  See also: **cheat**

deceiver noun = **liar**, fraud, cheat, impostor, trickster, con man (informal), double-dealer, swindler

decelerate See **slow (down)**

decency noun = **respectability**, courtesy, correctness, etiquette, civility, decorum, modesty, propriety

decent adjective 1 = **adequate**, reasonable, respectable, satisfactory, tolerable, passable • to earn a decent salary
  2 = **respectable**, proper • the decent thing to do
  OPPOSITE: improper
  3 = **proper**, appropriate, suitable, fitting, becoming, befitting, seemly
  4 (Informal) = **kind**, friendly, helpful, generous, thoughtful, gracious, courteous, accommodating, obliging

deception noun 1 = **trickery**, fraud, deceit, cunning, treachery, guile, legerdemain
  2 = **trick**, lie, hoax, illusion, bluff, ruse, subterfuge, decoy

deceptive adjective = **misleading**, false, fraudulent, illusory, unreliable • First impressions can be deceptive.

decide verb = **reach a decision**, choose, determine (formal), elect (formal), resolve (formal), come to a decision, make up your mind • *She decided to write her autobiography.*
▷ **decide on** See **select, settle**
See also: **conclude, settle**

decided See **definite**

decidedly adverb = **definitely**, clearly, positively, downright, distinctly, unequivocally, unmistakably

deciding See **critical**

decimate verb = **devastate**, ravage, wreak havoc on

decipher verb = **figure out** (informal), read, crack, solve, interpret, decode, deduce, make out

decision noun 1 = **judgment**, ruling, finding, resolution, verdict, conclusion • *The umpire's decision is final.*
2 = **decisiveness**, resolution, resolve, purpose, determination, firmness, strength of mind or strength of will

decisive adjective 1 = **influential**, significant, critical, crucial, conclusive, momentous, fateful
2 = **resolute**, firm, determined, forceful, incisive, decided, strong-minded, trenchant

deck verb = **decorate**, dress, clothe, array, adorn, embellish, festoon, beautify

declaim verb = **orate**, speak, lecture, proclaim, rant, recite, harangue, hold forth
▷ **declaim against** = **protest against**, attack, rail, denounce, decry, inveigh

declaration noun 1 = **statement**, testimony, affirmation, protestation (formal) • *a declaration of war*
2 = **announcement**, profession, proclamation, pronouncement, notification, edict

declare verb 1 = **state**, announce, pronounce, assert, certify, proclaim, affirm, profess (formal) • *He declared that he was*
going to be famous.
2 = **make known**, show, reveal, disclose, confess

decline verb 1 = **decrease**, fall, drop, plummet, diminish, go down • *a declining birth rate*
OPPOSITE: increase
2 = **refuse**, abstain, excuse yourself, turn down • *He declined their invitation.*
OPPOSITE: accept
3 = **deteriorate**, worsen, weaken, pine, decay, languish, degenerate, droop
▶ noun 4 = **decrease**, fall, drop, slump, recession, downturn, shrinkage • *economic decline*
5 = **deterioration**, degeneration, decay, failing, weakening, worsening
OPPOSITE: increase
See also: **fail, reject, wither**

decode verb = **decipher**, crack, solve, interpret, unscramble, decrypt, work out

decompose verb = **rot**, crumble, decay, fester, break up, fall apart, putrefy

decomposed See **rotten**

decor noun = **decoration**, colour scheme, furnishing style, ornamentation

decorate verb 1 = **adorn**, paper, paint, colour, deck, renovate, wallpaper, do up (informal), furbish, pimp (up) (slang) • *He decorated his room with pictures.*
2 = **pin a medal on**, cite, confer an honour on or confer an honour upon
See also: **honour**

decorated See **fancy**

decoration noun 1 = **adornment**, enrichment, trimming, embellishment, elaboration, beautification, ornamentation
2 = **ornament**, garnish, frill, bauble, trimmings
3 = **medal**, award, star, ribbon, badge

decorative adjective = **ornamental**, pretty, fancy, beautifying, nonfunctional

decorous adjective = **proper**, correct, decent, fitting, polite, dignified, becoming, seemly, well-behaved

decorum noun = **propriety**, protocol, dignity, decency, etiquette, respectability, politeness, good manners

decoy noun 1 = **lure**, trap, bait, inducement, pretense, enticement
▶ verb 2 = **lure**, entice, deceive, tempt, seduce, ensnare, entrap

decrease verb 1 = **lessen**, drop, reduce, decline, lower, shrink, diminish, dwindle, cut down
• *Population growth is decreasing by 1.4 per cent each year.*
OPPOSITE: increase
▶ noun 2 = **lessening**, drop, decline, reduction, cutback • *a decrease in the number of unemployed*
OPPOSITE: increase
See also: **abate**, **cut**, **fall**

decree noun 1 = **law**, order, act, ruling, command, proclamation, statute, edict
▶ verb 2 = **order**, rule, demand, command, prescribe, pronounce, proclaim, ordain

decrepit adjective 1 = **weak**, frail, feeble, infirm, aged, doddering
2 = **worn-out**, battered, dilapidated, rickety, ramshackle, run-down, beat-up (*informal*), broken-down, tumbledown, weather-beaten

decry verb = **condemn**, criticize, denounce, discredit, disparage, denigrate, belittle, put down, run down

dedicate verb 1 = **devote**, commit, pledge, surrender, give over to
2 = **inscribe**, address

dedicated adjective = **devoted**, enthusiastic, committed, zealous, purposeful, single-minded, wholehearted

dedication noun 1 = **devotion**, commitment, loyalty, allegiance, adherence, faithfulness, single-mindedness, wholeheartedness
2 = **inscription**, message, address

deduce verb = **conclude**, draw, reason, understand, gather, glean, infer, take to mean

deduct verb = **subtract**, remove, decrease by, knock off (*informal*), reduce by, take away, take off

deduction noun 1 = **subtraction**, reduction, withdrawal, decrease, discount, diminution
2 = **conclusion**, result, finding, assumption, reasoning, inference

deed noun 1 = **action**, act, fact, performance, achievement, exploit, feat
2 (*Law*) = **document**, contract, title

deem verb = **consider**, think, hold, believe, judge, account, estimate, regard, suppose, imagine, conceive, reckon, esteem

deep adjective 1 = **bottomless**, yawning • *a deep hole*
OPPOSITE: shallow
2 = **intense**, great, serious, extreme, grave, profound • *his deep love of his country*
3 = **low**, bass • *a deep voice*
OPPOSITE: high
4 = **mysterious**, secret, abstract, obscure, hidden, arcane, esoteric, abstruse, recondite
5 = **absorbed**, lost, engrossed, immersed, preoccupied, rapt
6 = **dark**, strong, rich, intense, vivid
▷ **the deep** (*Poetic*) = **ocean**, main, sea, briny (*informal*), high seas
See also: **far**, **heavy**, **severe**

deepen verb = **intensify**, increase, grow, strengthen, reinforce, magnify

deeply adverb 1 = **thoroughly**, completely, seriously, severely, profoundly, gravely, to the core, to the heart, to the quick
2 = **intensely**, sadly, passionately, acutely, affectingly, distressingly, feelingly, mournfully, movingly

deface verb = **vandalize**, damage, spoil, mar, tarnish, disfigure, mutilate, deform

defame verb = **slander**, knock

(*informal*), smear, libel, discredit, disparage, malign, denigrate, bad-mouth (*slang*), cast aspersions on

default noun **1 = failure**, neglect, lapse, evasion, deficiency, omission, dereliction, nonpayment
▶ *verb* **2 = fail**, neglect, evade, dodge

defeat verb **1 = beat**, crush, rout, trounce, conquer, vanquish (*formal*), whitewash (*informal*), whup (*informal*) • *to defeat the enemy*
2 = frustrate, ruin, thwart, foil, baffle, balk, confound, get the better of
▶ *noun* **3 = conquest**, rout, debacle (*formal*), whitewash (*informal*), trouncing • *a 2-1 defeat by Russia*
OPPOSITE: victory
4 = frustration, failure, reverse, setback, rebuff, thwarting
See also: **subdue**

defeatist noun **1 = pessimist**, quitter, prophet of doom
▶ *adjective* **2 = pessimistic**

defect noun **1 = fault**, flaw, weakness, deficiency, shortcoming, failing, imperfection • *A defect in the aircraft caused the crash.*
▶ *verb* **2 = desert**, rebel, abandon, revolt, change sides, go over, walk out on (*informal*)
See also: **handicap, hole**

defection noun **= desertion**, rebellion, apostasy

defective adjective **= faulty**, flawed, deficient, imperfect, broken, not working, on the blink (*slang*), out of order

defector noun **= deserter**, renegade, apostate, turncoat

defence noun **1 = protection**, security, cover, resistance, safeguard • *The high walls around the city made a good defence against attackers.*
2 = argument, plea, excuse, explanation, justification • *the mayor's defence of her position*
3 = shield, barricade, buttress,

fortification, rampart, bulwark
4 (*Law*) **= plea**, testimony, denial, rebuttal, alibi

defenceless adjective **= helpless**, vulnerable, naked, unarmed, unprotected, powerless, exposed, unguarded, wide open

defend verb **1 = protect**, cover, guard, shelter, shield, safeguard • *The wolves defended their cubs.*
2 = support, endorse, uphold, justify, stick up for (*informal*) • *I can't defend what he did.*
See also: **champion**

defendant noun **= the accused**, defence, offender, respondent, prisoner at the bar

defender noun **1 = supporter**, champion, advocate • *a committed defender of human rights*
2 = protector, guard, escort, bodyguard

defensive adjective **= on guard**, protective, watchful, uptight (*informal*), on the defensive

defer[1] verb **= postpone**, delay, suspend, shelve, procrastinate, hold over, put off, put on ice

defer[2] verb **= comply**, submit, yield, bow, accede, capitulate, give in, give way to

deference noun **= respect**, attention, regard, courtesy, consideration, honour, civility, politeness, reverence

deferential adjective **= respectful**, polite, obedient, submissive, ingratiating, obeisant, obsequious, reverential

defiance noun **= resistance**, opposition, confrontation, contempt, disregard, disobedience, insubordination, insolence, rebelliousness

defiant adjective **= resisting**, bold, provocative, daring, audacious, rebellious, disobedient, insolent, insubordinate, mutinous

deficiency noun **1 = lack**, deficit, deprivation, inadequacy • *signs of a vitamin deficiency*
OPPOSITE: abundance
2 = failing, flaw, weakness, defect, fault, shortcoming, frailty, imperfection, demerit

See also: **failure, shortage, want**

deficient *adjective* **1 = lacking**, short, poor, inadequate, wanting • *a diet deficient in vitamins*
2 = unsatisfactory, weak, faulty, incomplete, impaired, flawed, defective, lousy (*slang*), inferior, imperfect
See also: **insufficient**

deficit *noun* = **shortfall**, loss, shortage, deficiency, arrears

define *verb* **1 = describe**, explain, designate, characterize, specify, interpret, expound, spell out
2 = mark out, limit, outline, bound, delineate, circumscribe, demarcate

definite *adjective* **1 = certain**, assured, decided, fixed, guaranteed, settled • *It's too soon to give a definite answer.*
2 = clear, positive • *The police had nothing definite against them.*
See also: **final, sure**

definitely *adverb* = **certainly**, clearly, absolutely, surely, positively, categorically, undeniably, unquestionably, unmistakably, without doubt
▷ **definitely not** See **no**

definition *noun* **1 = explanation**, clarification, exposition, elucidation, statement of meaning
2 = sharpness, focus, contrast, precision, clarity, distinctness

definitive *adjective* **1 = final**, complete, decisive, absolute, conclusive
2 = authoritative, perfect, ultimate, reliable, exhaustive

deflate *verb* **1 = collapse**, shrink, empty, exhaust, flatten, puncture
2 = humiliate, humble, squash, disconcert, mortify, dispirit, chasten, put down (*slang*)
3 (*Economics*) **= reduce**, diminish, depress, devalue

deflect *verb* = **turn aside**, bend, veer, swerve, ricochet, deviate, diverge, glance off

deflection *noun* = **deviation**, bend, swerve, divergence

deform *verb* **1 = distort**, twist, buckle, mangle, warp, contort, gnarl, misshape
2 = disfigure, ruin, spoil, mar, mutilate, maim, deface

deformed See **distorted**

deformity *noun* = **abnormality**, defect, malformation, disfigurement

defraud *verb* = **cheat**, con (*informal*), trick, swindle, fleece, pilfer, embezzle, rip off (*slang*)

deft *adjective* = **skilful**, expert, neat, adept, nimble, agile, proficient, adroit, dexterous

defunct *adjective* **1 = dead**, extinct, deceased, departed, gone
2 = obsolete, invalid, expired, bygone, nonexistent, inoperative, out of commission

defy *verb* = **resist**, slight, confront, brave, scorn, disregard, spurn, flout

degenerate *adjective*
1 = depraved, low, corrupt, immoral, decadent, perverted, debauched, dissolute
▷ *verb* **2 = worsen**, decline, slip, sink, decrease, deteriorate, lapse, decay, fall off

degradation *noun* **1 = disgrace**, shame, humiliation, discredit, dishonour, ignominy, mortification
2 = deterioration, decline, degeneration, demotion, downgrading

degrade *verb* **1 = disgrace**, humble, shame, humiliate, discredit, demean, debase, dishonour
2 = demote, lower, downgrade

degrading *adjective*
= demeaning, dishonourable, humiliating, shameful, unworthy, undignified

degree *noun* = **stage**, point, step, unit, notch, grade, rung

dehydrate See **dry**

deity *noun* = **god**, idol, goddess, immortal, divinity, godhead, supreme being

dejected *adjective*
= downhearted, sad, depressed, miserable, despondent,

d

glum, downcast, crestfallen, disconsolate, disheartened

dejection noun = **low spirits**, depression, sadness, sorrow, despair, gloom, unhappiness, doldrums, melancholy, despondency, downheartedness

delay verb 1 = **put off**, suspend, postpone, shelve, defer, procrastinate • *the decision to delay the announcement until tomorrow*
2 = **hinder**, check, obstruct, impede, set back • *Various setbacks delayed production.*
OPPOSITE: hurry
▶ noun 3 = **hold-up**, setback, obstruction, interruption • *a seven-hour work stoppage that caused delays on most flights*
4 = **putting off**, suspension, postponement, procrastination, deferment
See also: **pause, wait**

delayed See **late**

delectable See **delicious**

delegate noun
1 = **representative**, agent, commissioner, ambassador, deputy, envoy, legate
▶ verb 2 = **entrust**, give, transfer, assign, devolve, consign, hand over, pass on
3 = **appoint**, commission, mandate, designate, authorize, empower, accredit, depute

delegation noun 1 = **deputation**, mission, commission, embassy, contingent, envoys, legation
2 = **devolution**, commitment, assignment, deputation, transference

delete verb = **remove**, erase, cross out, rub out, cancel, blue-pencil, edit out, strike out • *I accidentally deleted the email.*

deliberate adjective
1 = **intentional**, conscious, calculated, premeditated, studied • *a deliberate act of sabotage*
OPPOSITE: accidental
2 = **careful**, cautious, measured, methodical • *His movements were gentle and deliberate.*
OPPOSITE: casual
▶ verb 3 = **ponder**, debate,

reflect, meditate, mull over • *The jury deliberated for five days before reaching a verdict.*
See also: **consider, think**

deliberately adverb
= **intentionally**, knowingly, consciously, willfully, by design, calculatingly, in cold blood, on purpose, wittingly

deliberation noun
1 = **consideration**, thought, reflection, calculation, meditation, circumspection, forethought
2 = **discussion**, conference, debate, consultation

delicacy noun 1 = **fineness**, precision, accuracy, lightness, elegance, subtlety, daintiness, exquisiteness
2 = **fragility**, weakness, frailty, tenderness, flimsiness, slenderness
3 = **treat**, luxury, tidbit, dainty, savoury
4 = **fastidiousness**, taste, discrimination, sensibility, finesse, purity, refinement
5 = **sensitivity**, tact, sensitiveness

delicate adjective 1 = **fine**, skilled, subtle, precise, elegant, exquisite, graceful, deft
2 = **subtle**, fine, choice, tender, delicious, yummy (*informal*), dainty, savoury
3 = **fragile**, weak, slight, tender, frail, slender, flimsy
4 = **considerate**, diplomatic, sensitive, discreet, tactful

delicately adverb 1 = **finely**, precisely, deftly, gracefully, elegantly, subtly, exquisitely, daintily, skillfully
2 = **tactfully**, diplomatically, sensitively

delicious adjective = **delectable**, tasty, luscious, appetizing • *a wide selection of delicious foods*

delight noun 1 = **pleasure**, happiness, joy, satisfaction, glee, rapture • *To my great delight, it worked.*
▶ verb 2 = **please**, thrill, charm, amuse, captivate,

enchant • *The report has delighted environmentalists.*

▷ **delight in** = **take pleasure in**, like, love, enjoy, appreciate, relish, feast on, revel in, savour
See also: **ecstasy, entertain, entrance, pride, rejoice**

delighted *adjective* = **pleased**, happy, ecstatic, jubilant, joyous, elated, enchanted, overjoyed, thrilled, jazzed (*slang*)

delightful *adjective* = **pleasant**, thrilling, charming, enjoyable, delectable, agreeable, pleasurable, enchanting, rapturous

delinquent *noun* = **criminal**, offender, culprit, villain, wrongdoer, lawbreaker, miscreant

delirious *adjective* **1** = **mad**, crazy, insane, incoherent, demented, raving, deranged, unhinged
2 = **ecstatic**, wild, excited, frantic, frenzied, hysterical, beside oneself, carried away, wired (*slang*)

delirium *noun* **1** = **madness**, insanity, hallucination, raving, derangement
2 = **frenzy**, fever, passion, ecstasy, hysteria

deliver *verb* **1** = **carry**, bring, bear, distribute, transport, cart, convey
2 = **hand over**, commit, grant, transfer, surrender, yield, relinquish, give up, make over, turn over
3 = **give**, announce, present, read, declare, utter
4 = **release**, save, free, rescue, loose, ransom, liberate, emancipate
5 = **strike**, give, deal, launch, aim, direct, administer, inflict

deliverance *noun* = **release**, rescue, escape, ransom, redemption, liberation, salvation, emancipation

delivery *noun* **1** = **handing over**, distribution, transfer, transmission, surrender, dispatch, consignment, conveyance
2 = **speech**, utterance, articulation, elocution, enunciation, intonation
3 = **childbirth**, confinement, labour, parturition

delude *verb* = **deceive**, kid (*informal*), mislead, fool, dupe, hoodwink, beguile, trick

deluge *noun* **1** = **flood**, spate, downpour, torrent, cataclysm, inundation, overflowing
2 = **rush**, flood, avalanche, barrage, spate, torrent
▶ *verb* **3** = **flood**, drown, soak, swamp, douse, drench, inundate, submerge
4 = **overwhelm**, swamp, overrun, overload, engulf, inundate

delusion *noun* = **misconception**, mistake, error, fancy, illusion, hallucination, fallacy, false impression, misapprehension

deluxe *adjective* = **luxurious**, special, select, expensive, grand, costly, exclusive, superior, splendid, opulent

delve *verb* = **research**, search, probe, investigate, explore, forage, burrow, rummage, ferret out, look into

demagogue *noun* = **agitator**, firebrand, rabble-rouser

demand *verb* **1** = **require**, take, want, need, involve • *This situation demands hard work.*
2 = **request**, ask, question, challenge, interrogate, inquire
3 = **claim**, expect, order, exact, insist on
▶ *noun* **4** = **request**, order, question, inquiry, requisition
5 = **need**, call, want, market, claim, requirement
See also: **command, insist**

demanding *adjective* = **difficult**, hard, tough, exacting, challenging, high-maintenance, taxing, trying, wearing

demarcation *noun* = **delimitation**, division, separation, distinction, differentiation

demean *verb* = **humiliate**
• *I wasn't going to demean myself*

by becoming possessive.
See also: **reduce**

demeanour *noun* = **behaviour**, air, conduct, manner, carriage, bearing, comportment, deportment

demented *adjective* = **mad**, crazy, insane, frenzied, unbalanced, crazed, deranged, maniacal, unhinged

demise *noun* **1** = **failure**, end, fall, collapse, ruin, downfall
2 (*Euphemistic*) = **death**, departure, decease

democracy *noun* = **self-government**, republic, commonwealth

democratic *adjective* = **self-governing**, popular, representative, populist, autonomous, egalitarian

demolish *verb* **1** = **knock down**, level, destroy, dismantle, flatten, raze, bulldoze, tear down
2 = **defeat**, destroy, overturn, wreck, overthrow, undo, annihilate

demolished *See* **broken**

demolition *noun* = **knocking down**, explosion, destruction, bulldozing, levelling, razing, tearing down, wrecking

demon *noun* **1** = **evil spirit**, devil, fiend, goblin, ghoul, malignant spirit
2 = **wizard**, master, ace (*informal*), fiend

demonic, demoniac, demoniacal *adjective*
1 = **devilish**, satanic, diabolical, hellish, diabolic, fiendish, infernal
2 = **frenzied**, furious, frantic, hectic, frenetic, manic, crazed, maniacal

demonstrable *adjective* = **provable**, obvious, evident, unmistakable, palpable, verifiable, self-evident, irrefutable

demonstrate *verb* **1** = **prove**, show, indicate, display, exhibit, manifest, testify to
2 = **show how**, describe, explain, teach, illustrate, make clear
3 = **march**, rally, protest, parade, picket

demonstration *noun* **1** = **march**, rally, protest, parade, picket, sit-in, mass lobby
2 = **explanation**, test, trial, presentation, description, exposition
3 = **proof**, evidence, display, testimony, exhibition, expression, confirmation, illustration

demoralize *verb* = **dishearten**, weaken, undermine, discourage, depress, unnerve, dispirit, deject

demote *verb* = **downgrade**, relegate, degrade, kick downstairs (*slang*), lower in rank

demur *verb* **1** = **object**, protest, refuse, dispute, balk, hesitate, waver, take exception
▶ *noun* **2** = **objection**, protest, dissent, hesitation, qualm, misgiving, compunction

demure *adjective* = **shy**, modest, sedate, reserved, reticent, unassuming, diffident, retiring

den *noun* **1** = **lair**, hole, shelter, cave, haunt, hideout, cavern
2 (*Chiefly US*) = **study**, retreat, sanctuary, hideaway, sanctum, cubbyhole, living room

denial *noun* **1** = **negation**, dissent, contradiction, retraction, repudiation, renunciation
2 = **refusal**, veto, rejection, rebuff, prohibition, repulse

denigrate *verb* = **disparage**, knock (*informal*), malign, belittle, bad-mouth (*slang*), vilify, slander, run down

denomination *noun*
1 = **religious group**, school, belief, sect, persuasion, creed
2 = **unit**, value, size, grade

denote *verb* = **indicate**, show, mean, mark, express, designate, imply, signify, betoken

denounce *verb* = **condemn**, attack, accuse, censure, vilify, revile, stigmatize, denunciate

dense *adjective* **1** = **thick**, heavy, solid, compact, condensed, close-knit, opaque, impenetrable

2 = **stupid**, thick, dull, obtuse, slow-witted, stolid

density noun **1** = **tightness**, mass, bulk, consistency, thickness, compactness, denseness, impenetrability, solidity

dent noun **1** = **hollow**, chip, depression, dip, pit, impression, crater, dimple, indentation
▶ verb **2** = **make a dent in**, gouge, hollow, press in, push in

deny verb **1** = **contradict**, refute
• She denied both accusations.
OPPOSITE: admit
2 = **refuse**, reject, withhold
• denied access to the property
3 = **renounce**, retract, recant, repudiate, disown, disclaim
▷ **deny oneself** See **abstain**
See also: **dispute**

depart verb **1** = **leave**, go, retire, quit, withdraw, exit, disappear, retreat, absent (oneself), go away
2 = **deviate**, vary, differ, veer, stray, swerve, diverge, digress, turn aside

departed See **dead**, **late**

department noun = **section**, office, unit, division • the marketing department
See also: **field**

departure noun **1** = **leaving**, retirement, exit, withdrawal, exodus, going, moving, going away, leave-taking
2 = **divergence**, variation, deviation, digression
3 = **shift**, change, difference, innovation, novelty, whole new ball game (informal)

depend verb **1** = **rely on**, trust, bank on, count on • You can depend on me.
2 = **be determined by**, hinge on
• Success depends on the dedication of the team.
▷ **depend on** See **require**, **trust**

dependable adjective = **reliable**, responsible, sure, steady, faithful, staunch, trustworthy, reputable, trusty, unfailing

dependant noun = **relative**, child, minor, subordinate, protégé

dependence See **habit**

dependency See **colony**

dependent adjective = **relying on**, weak, vulnerable, helpless, reliant, defenceless
▷ **dependent on, dependent upon** = **determined by**, conditional on, contingent on, depending on, influenced by, subject to

depict verb **1** = **draw**, picture, paint, outline, portray, sketch, illustrate, delineate
2 = **describe**, represent, outline, characterize, narrate

depiction noun = **representation**, picture, portrayal, description, sketch, delineation

deplete verb = **use up**, reduce, consume, empty, drain, exhaust, lessen, expend, impoverish

deplorable adjective
1 = **regrettable**, sad, unfortunate, grievous, lamentable, wretched, pitiable
2 = **disgraceful**, shameful, scandalous, reprehensible, dishonourable

deplore verb = **disapprove of**, condemn, denounce, censure, abhor, object to, take a dim view of

deploy verb = **position**, use, station, arrange, utilize, set out

deployment noun = **position**, use, organization, spread, arrangement, utilization, stationing

deport verb = **expel**, oust, exile, extradite, banish, expatriate
▷ **deport oneself** = **behave**, act, acquit oneself, bear oneself, carry oneself, comport oneself, conduct oneself, hold oneself

depose verb **1** = **remove from office**, dismiss, oust, displace, demote, dethrone
2 (Law) = **testify**, declare, avouch, make a deposition

deposit verb **1** = **put**, leave, place, drop, lay, put down • The waiter deposited a hamburger in front of him.

d

2 = store, bank, lodge, entrust, consign
▶ *noun* **3 = down payment**, security, pledge, stake, instalment, retainer, part payment
4 = sediment, accumulation, precipitate, silt, dregs, lees
See also: **dump, keep, payment, set**

depot *noun* **1 = storehouse**, warehouse, repository, depository
2 = bus station, garage, terminus

deprave *See* **corrupt**

depraved *adjective* **= corrupt**, evil, vicious, wicked, immoral, degenerate, vile, sinful, dissolute

depravity *noun* **= corruption**, evil, vice, immorality, debauchery, sinfulness, wickedness

depreciate *verb* **1 = devalue**, reduce, lower, decrease, lessen, deflate, lose value
2 = disparage, scorn, deride, detract, denigrate, belittle, run down, sneer at

depreciation *noun*
1 = devaluation, fall, drop, slump, depression, deflation
2 = disparagement, denigration, belittlement, deprecation, detraction

depress *verb* **1 = sadden**, discourage, oppress, dishearten, dispirit, deject, make despondent, weigh down, harsh someone's buzz (*slang*)
2 = lower, reduce, diminish, downgrade, lessen, devalue, cheapen, depreciate
3 = press down, level, lower, flatten, push down

depressed *adjective* **1 = low-spirited**, blue, sad, unhappy, dejected, despondent, discouraged, downcast, dispirited, downhearted, fed up
2 = poverty-stricken, poor, disadvantaged, needy, run-down, deprived
3 = lowered, weakened, cheapened, depreciated, devalued
4 = sunken, hollow, concave, indented, recessed

depressing *adjective* **= bleak**, sad, dismal, gloomy, discouraging, disheartening, dispiriting, harrowing, saddening

depression *noun* **1 = low spirits**, sadness, despair, melancholy, despondency, dejection, downheartedness, dumps (*informal*), gloominess, the blues
2 = recession, slump, inactivity, stagnation, economic decline, hard times *or* bad times, credit crunch
3 = hollow, dip, pit, bowl, dent, valley, cavity, dimple, indentation

deprivation *noun*
1 = withholding, withdrawal, removal, denial, expropriation, dispossession
2 = want, need, distress, hardship, destitution, privation

deprive *verb* **= withhold**, strip, rob, bereave, despoil, dispossess

deprived *adjective* **= poor**, disadvantaged, needy, destitute, bereft, down at heel, in need, lacking

depth *noun* **1 = deepness**, drop, measure, extent
2 = insight, wisdom, penetration, discernment, astuteness, profoundness, profundity, sagacity

depths *See* **bottom**

deputation *noun* **= delegation**, commission, embassy, envoys, legation

deputize *verb* **= stand in for**, understudy, act for, take the place of

deputy *noun* **= substitute**, representative, delegate, lieutenant, proxy, surrogate, second-in-command, legate, number two

deranged *adjective* **= mad**, crazy, insane, irrational, unbalanced, crazed, demented, distracted, unhinged

derelict *adjective* **1 = abandoned**,
dilapidated, neglected, ruined
• *a derelict warehouse*
▶ *noun* **2 = tramp**, outcast, bag
lady, down and out, vagrant
deride *verb* = **mock**, insult, scorn,
taunt, scoff, jeer, ridicule,
disparage, disdain, sneer
derision *noun* = **mockery**, insult,
laughter, scorn, contempt,
ridicule, disrespect, disdain,
denigration, contumely,
disparagement, raillery,
scoffing, sneering
derisory *adjective* = **ridiculous**,
outrageous, lousy (*slang*),
ludicrous, laughable,
preposterous, contemptible,
insulting
derivation *noun* = **origin**, source,
beginning, root, foundation
derive *verb* **derive from** = **come
from**, arise from, emanate from,
flow from, issue from, originate
from, proceed from, spring from,
stem from
derogatory *adjective*
= **disparaging**, offensive,
unflattering, defamatory,
belittling, slighting,
uncomplimentary, unfavourable
descend *verb* **1 = go down**, fall,
sink, dive, dip, plummet • *as we
descend to the basement*
OPPOSITE: ascend
2 = slope, dip, incline, slant
3 = lower oneself, deteriorate,
degenerate, stoop
▷ **be descended = originate**,
issue, spring, proceed, derive, be
handed down, be passed down
▷ **descend on = attack**, arrive,
raid, invade, swoop
See also: **drop**
descendants See **family**
descent *noun* **1 = coming down**,
fall, drop, plunge, swoop
2 = slope, drop, dip, incline,
slant, declivity
3 = ancestry, origin, extraction,
genealogy, lineage, parentage,
family tree
4 = decline, degeneration,
deterioration
describe *verb* **1 = relate**, define,

portray, depict • *Describe what you
do in your spare time.*
2 = trace, draw, outline,
delineate, mark out
See also: **explain, report,
represent**
description *noun* **1 = account**,
report, explanation, portrayal,
representation, sketch,
depiction, narrative
2 = kind, order, type, class,
brand, sort, category, variety
descriptive *adjective* = **graphic**,
detailed, pictorial, vivid,
picturesque, expressive,
explanatory, illustrative
desert[1] *noun* = **wilderness**, waste,
solitude, wasteland, wilds
desert[2] *verb* = **abandon**, leave,
quit, strand, maroon, jilt,
forsake, abscond, leave stranded,
walk out on (*informal*)
deserted *adjective* = **abandoned**,
empty, vacant, derelict, desolate,
neglected, unoccupied, forsaken
deserter *noun* = **defector**,
runaway, fugitive, renegade,
traitor, escapee, absconder,
truant
desertion *noun* = **abandonment**,
flight, escape, evasion,
betrayal, defection, dereliction,
absconding, apostasy,
relinquishment
deserve *verb* = **merit**, earn,
warrant, justify, be entitled
to, be worthy of • *He deserves a rest.*
deserved *adjective* = **well-earned**,
due, proper, fitting, justified,
rightful, earned, merited,
warranted
deserving *adjective* = **worthy**,
commendable, righteous,
laudable, meritorious,
estimable, praiseworthy
design *verb* **1 = plan**, draft,
outline, draw up • *They wanted to
design a new product that was both
attractive and practical.*
2 = create, fashion, originate,
invent, conceive, fabricate,
think up
3 = intend, plan, mean, aim,
propose, purpose
▶ *noun* **4 = plan**, draft, model,

outline • *her design for a new office*
5 = **style**, form, shape, pattern • *a new design of clock*
6 = **intention**, end, goal, target, aim, object, purpose, objective
See also: **layout, structure**

designate *verb* **1** = **name**, call, term, label, style, dub, entitle
2 = **appoint**, choose, select, nominate, delegate, assign, depute

designation *noun* = **name**, mark, title, label, description

designed See **calculated**

designer *noun* = **creator**, architect, inventor, planner, originator, deviser

desirable *adjective*
1 = **worthwhile**, good, profitable, beneficial, preferable, win-win (*informal*), advantageous, advisable
2 = **attractive**, sexy (*informal*), glamorous, alluring, seductive, adorable, fetching

desire *verb* **1** = **want**, wish, fancy, crave, yearn, long for • *We can stay longer if you desire.*
▶ *noun* **2** = **wish**, appetite, yen (*informal*), longing, craving, yearning, hankering • *a strong desire to help people*
3 = **lust**, passion, appetite, libido
See also: **urge**

desist *verb* = **stop**, end, cease, pause, discontinue, break off, forbear, leave off, refrain from

desolate *adjective*
1 = **uninhabited**, wild, bare, bleak, solitary, barren, dreary, godforsaken
2 = **miserable**, gloomy, dejected, despondent, downcast, wretched, disconsolate, forlorn
▶ *verb* **3** = **lay waste**, destroy, devastate, ruin, ravage, plunder, pillage, depopulate, despoil, lay low
4 = **deject**, discourage, grieve, distress, depress, dismay, dishearten

desolation *noun* **1** = **ruin**, destruction, havoc, devastation
2 = **bleakness**, isolation, solitude, barrenness

3 = **misery**, woe, distress, sadness, despair, anguish, gloom, dejection, wretchedness

despair *noun* **1** = **hopelessness**, gloom, despondency, dejection • *feelings of despair*
▶ *verb* **2** = **lose hope**, feel dejected, feel despondent, lose heart • *Don't despair. I know things will be all right.*
See also: **misery**

despairing *adjective* = **hopeless**, desperate, frantic, miserable, dejected, grief-stricken, despondent, inconsolable, wretched, disconsolate

desperado *noun* = **criminal**, outlaw, villain, bandit, lawbreaker

desperate *adjective* **1** = **reckless**, risky, furious, frantic, daring, audacious
2 = **grave**, extreme, urgent, drastic

desperately *adverb* **1** = **gravely**, seriously, badly, severely, perilously, dangerously
2 = **hopelessly**, shockingly, appallingly, fearfully, frightfully

desperation *noun*
1 = **recklessness**, frenzy, madness, foolhardiness, impetuosity, rashness
2 = **misery**, worry, trouble, despair, anguish, agony, unhappiness, hopelessness

despicable *adjective*
= **contemptible**, mean, disgraceful, shameful, lousy (*slang*), worthless, hateful, vile, sordid, detestable, wretched, scuzzy (*slang*)

despise *verb* = **look down on**, scorn, loathe, detest, revile, abhor

despite *preposition* = **in spite of**, notwithstanding (*formal*), regardless of • *Despite its condition, he bought the car anyway.*

despondency *noun* = **dejection**, depression, misery, sadness, despair, desperation, gloom, melancholy, low spirits

despondent *adjective* = **dejected**,

sad, depressed, glum, disconsolate, disheartened, dispirited, downhearted, in despair, sorrowful

despot *noun* = **tyrant**, dictator, autocrat, oppressor

despotic *adjective* = **tyrannical**, authoritarian, oppressive, autocratic, dictatorial, imperious, domineering

despotism *noun* = **tyranny**, dictatorship, oppression, totalitarianism, autocracy

destination *noun* = **journey's end**, stop, station, haven, resting-place, terminus

destined *adjective* = **fated**, certain, doomed, bound, intended, meant, predestined

destiny *noun* = **fate**, lot, portion, fortune, doom, karma, kismet

destitute *adjective* = **penniless**, poor, impoverished, insolvent, poverty-stricken, down and out, down on one's luck (*informal*), indigent, moneyless, penurious

destitution *See* **hardship, poverty**

destroy *verb* = **ruin**, devastate, wreck, demolish, annihilate, raze, obliterate • *The building was completely destroyed.*
See also: **bomb, dash, eat away, erode, kill, put down, spoil**

destruction *noun* = **ruin**, devastation, demolition, annihilation, obliteration • *the destruction of the ozone layer*

destructive *adjective* = **damaging**, deadly, fatal, harmful, lethal, catastrophic, ruinous, calamitous, devastating

detach *verb* = **separate**, remove, divide, sever, disconnect, disengage, cut off, tear off, unfasten

detached *adjective* 1 = **separate**, unconnected, disconnected, discrete
2 = **uninvolved**, objective, neutral, impartial, unbiased, reserved, disinterested, hands-off, dispassionate, impersonal

detachment *noun*
1 = **indifference**, remoteness, coolness, aloofness, nonchalance, unconcern
2 = **impartiality**, neutrality, fairness, objectivity
3 (*Military*) = **unit**, force, party, body, patrol, squad, task force

detail *noun* 1 = **point**, respect, particular, element, aspect • *We discussed every detail of the performance.*
2 = **fine point**, particular, nicety, triviality
3 (*Military*) = **party**, force, body, duty, squad, fatigue, assignment, detachment
▶ *verb* 4 = **list**, relate, recount, rehearse, recite, catalogue, tabulate, enumerate, itemize
5 = **appoint**, charge, send, commission, delegate, assign, allocate

detailed *adjective*
= **comprehensive**, minute, full, particular, thorough, exhaustive, intricate, blow-by-blow

detain *verb* 1 = **delay**, check, hinder, impede, hold up, keep back, retard, slow up *or* slow down
2 = **hold**, arrest, restrain, confine, intern

detect *verb* 1 = **notice**, note, spot, identify, recognize, observe, perceive, ascertain
2 = **discover**, find, uncover, unmask, track down

detective *noun* = **investigator**, cop (*slang*), gumshoe (*slang*), sleuth (*informal*), private eye, private investigator, skip tracer, peeper (*slang*)

detention *noun*
= **imprisonment**, custody, quarantine, confinement, incarceration

deter *verb* = **discourage**, stop, prevent, intimidate, frighten, dissuade, inhibit from, put off, talk out of

detergent *noun* = **cleaner**, cleanser

deteriorate *verb* = **decline**, lower, slump, worsen, degenerate, go downhill (*informal*)

deterioration See **rot, wear**

determination *noun*
= **resolution**, resolve (*formal*), perseverance, persistence, tenacity • *the government's determination to improve health care*
See also: **drive, will**

determine *verb* **1** = **affect**, control, decide, shape, govern, dictate • *The size of the chicken pieces will determine the cooking time.*
2 = **decide**, choose, settle, fix, resolve, arrange • *The final wording had not yet been determined.*
3 = **find out**, confirm, discover, establish, verify, ascertain (*formal*) • *The investigation will determine what really happened.*
See also: **calculate, learn, see**

determined *adjective* = **resolute**, persistent, dogged, tenacious, purposeful, single-minded, bent on, intent on • *She was determined not to repeat the error.*
See also: **firm, set on**

deterrent *noun*
= **discouragement**, check, curb, restraint, obstacle, impediment, hindrance, disincentive

detest *verb* = **hate**, loathe, despise, abhor, abominate, dislike intensely, recoil from

detested See **unpopular**

detonate *verb* = **explode**, blast, trigger, discharge, blow up, set off

detonation See **bang**

detour *noun* = **diversion**, bypass, circuitous route *or* indirect route, roundabout way

detract *verb*
▷ **detract from** = **lessen**, reduce, lower, diminish, devaluate, take away from

detriment *noun* = **damage**, injury, loss, hurt, harm, disadvantage, impairment, disservice

detrimental *adjective*
= **damaging**, harmful, adverse,

destructive, prejudicial, deleterious, disadvantageous, unfavourable

devastate *verb* = **destroy**, level, sack, ruin, wreck, ravage, demolish, raze, lay waste

devastating *adjective*
= **overwhelming**, cutting, savage, vitriolic, overpowering, trenchant, withering

devastation *noun* = **destruction**, ruin, havoc, demolition, desolation

develop *verb* **1** = **grow**, result, advance, spring, progress, evolve, mature • *to develop at different rates*
2 = **fall ill with**, contract (*formal*), catch, succumb, come down with, pick up • *He developed a bad cold.*
3 = **form**, establish, generate, breed, originate, invent
4 = **expand**, elaborate, broaden, unfold, augment, amplify, enlarge, work out
See also: **build, enlarge on, expand on, extend**

development *noun* **1** = **growth**, increase, advance, spread, progress, expansion, improvement, evolution
2 = **event**, result, incident, occurrence, happening, upshot, turn of events

deviant *adjective* **1** = **perverted**, sick (*informal*), twisted, kinky (*slang*), warped
▷ *noun* **2** = **pervert**, freak, degenerate, misfit, weirdo *or* weirdie (*informal*), sicko *or* sickie (*informal*)

deviate *verb* = **differ**, depart, wander, veer, stray, swerve, diverge

deviation *noun* = **departure**, shift, irregularity, variation, discrepancy, disparity, inconsistency, divergence, digression

device *noun* **1** = **gadget**, tool, machine, implement, instrument, appliance, contraption, apparatus
2 = **ploy**, plan, trick, scheme,

gambit, manoeuvre, stratagem, wile

devil noun 1 = **brute**, terror, monster, beast, demon, ogre, fiend

2 = **scamp**, rogue, rascal, scoundrel

3 = **person**, thing, creature, beggar, wretch

▷ **the Devil** = **Satan**, Beelzebub, Evil One, Lucifer, Mephistopheles, Prince of Darkness

devilish adjective = **fiendish**, wicked, atrocious, satanic, diabolical, detestable, hellish, damnable, infernal

devious adjective = **sly**, wily, scheming, calculating, underhand • devious ways of getting the starring role in the play See also: **crafty, cunning, sneaky**

deviousness See **cunning**

devise verb = **work out**, design, construct, invent, conceive, formulate, contrive, dream up, think up

devoid adjective = **lacking**, without, empty, deficient, destitute, bereft, free from, wanting

devote verb = **dedicate**, give, reserve, commit, pledge, apply, assign, allot, set apart

devoted adjective = **dedicated**, true, constant, loyal, faithful, loving, doting • a devoted parent See also: **ardent, enthusiastic, fond**

devotee noun = **enthusiast**, fan, supporter, follower, buff (informal), fanatic, admirer, aficionado, adherent, disciple

devotion noun 1 = **dedication**, commitment, loyalty, allegiance, adherence, fidelity, constancy, faithfulness

2 = **love**, passion, affection, attachment, fondness

3 = **devoutness**, holiness, spirituality, reverence, piety, godliness

▷ **devotions** = **prayers**, church

service, divine office, religious observance

devotional See **religious**

devour verb 1 = **eat**, consume, swallow, wolf, gobble, guzzle, gulp, chow down (slang), polish off (informal)

2 = **destroy**, waste, consume, ravage, annihilate, wipe out

3 = **enjoy**, read compulsively or read voraciously, take in

devout adjective = **religious**, holy, pure, orthodox, pious, godly, prayerful, reverent, saintly

dexterity noun 1 = **skill**, touch, expertise, finesse, proficiency, adroitness, deftness, nimbleness

2 = **cleverness**, ability, ingenuity, aptitude

diabolical adjective (Informal) = **dreadful**, terrible, shocking, outrageous, appalling, atrocious, abysmal, hellish

diagnose verb = **identify**, determine, recognize, analyze, pronounce, interpret, pinpoint, distinguish

diagnosis noun 1 = **examination**, investigation, analysis, scrutiny

2 = **opinion**, conclusion, interpretation, pronouncement

diagonal adjective = **slanting**, cross, oblique, angled, crossways, crosswise

diagonally adverb = **aslant**, obliquely, at an angle, cornerwise, crosswise

diagram noun = **plan**, figure, chart, drawing, representation, sketch, graph

dialect noun = **language**, speech, jargon, vernacular, brogue, idiom, patois, provincialism

dialogue noun = **conversation**, conference, discussion, communication, discourse

diary noun = **journal**, blog (informal), chronicle, weblog, appointment book, daily record, engagement book, Filofax (trademark)

dictate verb 1 = **speak**, say, utter, read out

2 = **order**, demand, direct, impose, command, pronounce,

decree, lay down the law
▶ *noun* **3 = command**, order, demand, direction, injunction, decree, edict, fiat
4 = principle, rule, law, code
dictator *noun* **= absolute ruler**, tyrant, despot, autocrat, oppressor
dictatorial *adjective* **1 = absolute**, unlimited, unrestricted, arbitrary, autocratic, despotic, totalitarian, tyrannical
2 = domineering, authoritarian, oppressive, imperious, bossy (*informal*), overbearing
dictatorship *noun* **= absolute rule**, tyranny, totalitarianism, absolutism, authoritarianism, autocracy, despotism
diction *noun* **= pronunciation**, speech, delivery, inflection, fluency, articulation, elocution, enunciation, intonation
dictionary *noun* **= wordbook**, vocabulary, glossary, lexicon
die *verb* **1 = pass away**, expire (*formal*), depart, perish (*formal*), pass on, bite the big one (*slang*), buy it (*slang*), check out (*slang*), kick it (*slang*), croak (*slang*), give up the ghost, go belly-up (*slang*), snuff it (*slang*), peg out (*informal*), kick the bucket (*slang*), buy the farm (*slang*), peg it (*informal*), pop your clogs (*informal*), breathe your last • *to die in an accident*
2 = fade away, fade out, peter out • *My love for you will never die.*
3 = stop, fail, halt, break down, fade out *or* fade away, fizzle out, lose power, peter out, run down
▶ **be dying = long**, desire, hunger, ache, yearn, be eager, pine for
▶ **die away** *See* **cease, fade**
▶ **die out = disappear**, fade, vanish • *That custom has died out now.*

┃ **INFORMALLY SPEAKING**
┃ **die down**: become calmer
┃ **die hard**: resist to the end
┃ **to die for**: excellent
die-hard *noun* **= reactionary**, fanatic, old fogey, stick-in-the-mud (*informal*)

diet¹ *noun* **1 = food**, fare, nourishment, sustenance, nutriment, provisions, rations, victuals
2 = regime, fast, regimen, abstinence
▶ *verb* **3 = slim**, fast, abstain, eat sparingly, lose weight
diet² *noun* **= council**, meeting, parliament, legislature, convention, chamber, congress
differ *verb* **1 = be dissimilar**, contrast, vary, contradict, diverge, depart from, run counter to, stand apart
2 = disagree, debate, dispute, oppose, clash, contend, dissent, demur, take exception, take issue
difference *noun*
1 = dissimilarity, contrast, variation, discrepancy, distinction, disparity, divergence • *the vast difference in size*
OPPOSITE: similarity
2 = remainder, balance • *The difference is 853.*
3 = disagreement, debate, dispute, conflict, clash, argument, quarrel, contretemps
▶ **difference of opinion** *See* **division**
See also: **change, gap**
different *adjective* **1 = unlike**, disparate (*formal*), divergent (*formal*), dissimilar, contrasting, opposed • *We have totally different views.*
OPPOSITE: similar
2 = unusual, special, unique • *The result is interesting and different.*
3 = various, another, individual, separate, distinct, discrete (*formal*) • *to support a different charity each year*
▶ **different from** *See* **unlike**
differentiate *verb*
1 = distinguish, separate, contrast, discriminate, make a distinction, mark off, set off *or* set apart, tell apart
2 = make different, change,

convert, modify, alter, adapt, transform

difficult *adjective* **1 = hard**, uphill, arduous, demanding, intractable (*formal*), laborious • *a difficult decision to make*
OPPOSITE: easy

2 = troublesome, demanding, trying • *I hope they're not going to be difficult.*

3 = problematic, complex, complicated, obscure, involved, intricate, abstruse, baffling, knotty
See also: **formidable, rough, serious, stiff, tough, tricky**

difficulty *noun* **1 = problem**, trouble, hurdle, complication, snag, obstacle, pitfall, hassle (*informal*) • *The main difficulty is his inability to get along with others.*

2 = hardship, strain, tribulation (*formal*) • *a problem of great difficulty*

3 = predicament, trouble, jam (*informal*), mess, plight, embarrassment, dilemma, quandary, hot water (*informal*)
See also: **bother, distress, drawback, fix**

diffidence *noun* **= shyness**, reserve, insecurity, modesty, hesitancy, bashfulness, self-consciousness, timidity

diffident *adjective* **= shy**, modest, doubtful, hesitant, timid, insecure, reserved, unassuming, self-conscious, bashful, unassertive

diffuse See **distribute**

diffusion See **spread**

dig *verb* **1 = excavate**, tunnel, till, gouge, burrow, quarry, hollow out • *to dig a hole in the ground*

2 = poke, thrust, jab • *He could feel the coins digging into his palm.*

3 = investigate, research, search, probe, delve, dig down, go into

4 (with *out* or *up*) **= find**, discover, expose, uncover, unearth, uproot

▶ *noun* **5 = poke**, thrust, jab, prod • *a dig in the ribs*

6 = cutting remark, barb, insult, taunt, jeer, wisecrack (*informal*), sneer, gibe
See also: **stick**

INFORMALLY SPEAKING
dig in: begin to eat heartily
dig up: find by searching thoroughly

digest *verb* **1 = ingest**, absorb, incorporate, dissolve, assimilate

2 = take in, study, consider, understand, absorb, contemplate, grasp

▶ *noun* **3 = summary**, abstract, synopsis, epitome, abridgment, précis, résumé

digestion *noun* **= ingestion**, conversion, transformation, absorption, assimilation, incorporation

digit See **figure, number**

dignified *adjective*
= distinguished, formal, grave, solemn, noble, stately, reserved, imposing

dignitary *noun* **= public figure**, notable, worthy, high-up (*informal*), personage, pillar of society, V.I.P.

dignity *noun* **1 = decorum**, gravity, loftiness, majesty, grandeur, nobility, courtliness, solemnity, stateliness

2 = honour, status, rank, standing, importance, respectability, eminence

3 = self-importance, pride, self-esteem, self-respect

digress *verb* **= wander**, depart, drift, stray, ramble, deviate, diverge, get off the point *or* get off the subject, go off at a tangent

digression *noun* **= departure**, aside, diversion, detour, deviation, divergence, straying, wandering

dilapidated *adjective* **= ruined**, rickety, decrepit, ramshackle, run-down, broken-down, crumbling, in ruins, tumbledown, raggedy

dilate *verb* **= enlarge**, expand, stretch, widen, swell, broaden, puff out

dilatory *adjective* **= time-wasting**, slow, sluggish, delaying, lingering, procrastinating, tardy, tarrying

dilemma noun = **predicament**, problem, spot (informal), difficulty, puzzle, mess, plight, quandary

dilettante noun = **amateur**, aesthete, dabbler, trifler

diligence noun = **application**, industry, care, attention, perseverance, laboriousness

diligent adjective = **hard-working**, careful, persistent, painstaking, conscientious, tireless, attentive, industrious, assiduous, studious

dilute verb 1 = **water down**, cut, weaken, thin or thin out, adulterate, make thinner
2 = **reduce**, decrease, weaken, diminish, temper, lessen, mitigate, diffuse, attenuate

diluted See **thin**

dim adjective 1 = **dull**, dark, grey, murky, shadowy, poorly lit • the dim light of the streetlamp
2 = **vague**, faint, obscure, hazy, shadowy, indistinct • a dim memory
OPPOSITE: clear
3 (Informal) = **stupid**, slow, thick (informal), dense, obtuse • He is rather dim.
OPPOSITE: bright
▷ **take a dim view** = **disapprove**, suspect, reject, be displeased, be skeptical, look askance, take exception, view with disfavour
▶ verb 4 = **dull**, cloud, fade, obscure, darken, blur
See also: **soft**

dimension noun (often plural) = **measurement**, size, capacity, volume, extent, bulk, amplitude, proportions

diminish verb 1 = **reduce**, lower, decrease, weaken, lessen • This scandal has diminished her credibility.
2 = **dwindle**, contract, decline, shrink, wane, recede, subside, die out
See also: **abate, drop, fall**

diminutive adjective = **small**, minute, little, tiny, mini, miniature, petite, undersized

dimness See **dark**

din noun = **noise**, crash, row, uproar, clamour, racket, commotion, pandemonium, clatter
▶ verb
▷ **din (something) into (someone)** = **instill**, teach, instruct, drum into, go on at, hammer into, inculcate

dine verb = **eat**, lunch, feast, banquet, chow down (slang), sup

dingy adjective = **dull**, dark, obscure, gloomy, murky, dim, dreary, drab, sombre

dinner noun = **meal**, spread (informal), feast, banquet, main meal, repast

dip verb 1 = **plunge**, duck, dunk, douse, immerse, bathe
2 = **slope**, fall, drop or drop down, decline, lower, sink, descend, subside
▷ **dip into** = **sample**, browse, skim, peruse, glance at
▶ noun 3 = **plunge**, immersion, douche, drenching, ducking, soaking
4 = **bathe**, swim, plunge, dive
5 = **hollow**, hole, depression, slope, basin, incline, concavity
6 = **drop**, fall, decline, slip, slump, sag, lowering

diplomacy noun
1 = **statesmanship**, international negotiation, statecraft
2 = **tact**, skill, craft, discretion, delicacy, finesse, subtlety, artfulness, savoir-faire

diplomat noun = **negotiator**, politician, mediator, conciliator, moderator, go-between, tactician

diplomatic adjective = **tactful**, sensitive, subtle, prudent, polite, adept, discreet, politic

dire adjective 1 = **disastrous**, terrible, horrible, awful, catastrophic, woeful, ruinous, calamitous
2 = **desperate**, critical, crucial, extreme, urgent, drastic, pressing, now or never
3 = **grim**, dismal, gloomy, fearful, ominous, dreadful, portentous

direct adjective **1** = **straight**, personal, immediate, first-hand, uninterrupted • the direct route
OPPOSITE: indirect
2 = **straightforward**, straight, blunt, frank, candid, forthright • He can sometimes be very direct.
OPPOSITE: devious
3 = **immediate**, personal, head-on, face-to-face, first-hand
4 = **explicit**, express, absolute, plain, blunt, point-blank, downright, unequivocal, unambiguous, categorical
▶ verb **5** = **control**, lead, run, manage, guide, oversee, supervise • She will direct day-to-day operations at work.
6 = **order**, charge, bid, demand, command, dictate, instruct
7 = **guide**, lead, show, indicate, point in the direction of, point the way
8 = **address**, send, label, route, mail
9 = **aim**, point, level, focus, train
See also: **administer, conduct, head, influence, require, tell**

direction noun **1** = **way**, course, route, path • five kilometres in the opposite direction
2 = **management**, charge, control, leadership, command, guidance • He was chopping vegetables under the chef's direction.

directions plural noun = **instructions**, plan, recommendation, guidance, briefing, guidelines, regulations

directive noun = **order**, ruling, regulation, command, mandate, instruction, injunction, decree, edict

directly adverb **1** = **straight**, exactly, precisely, by the shortest route, in a beeline, unswervingly, without deviation
2 = **honestly**, openly, point-blank, unequivocally, truthfully, plainly, straightforwardly
3 = **at once**, immediately, promptly, straightaway, as soon as possible, forthwith, right away

director noun = **controller**, head, leader, chief, executive, manager, governor, administrator, supervisor

directors See **management**

directory See **list**

dirge noun = **lament**, requiem, dead march, elegy, funeral song, threnody

dirt noun **1** = **filth**, dust, mud, muck, grime • I started to scrub off the dirt.
2 = **soil**, earth • He drew a circle in the dirt with the stick.
3 = **obscenity**, pornography, indecency, sleaze, smut
See also: **gossip, ground**

dirty adjective **1** = **filthy**, muddy, grimy, unclean, grubby, mucky, soiled • The kids' clothes are dirty.
OPPOSITE: clean
2 = **dishonest**, corrupt, crooked • a dirty fight
OPPOSITE: honest
3 = **obscene**, blue, rude, pornographic, filthy • a dirty joke
4 (~ look) = **angry**, bitter, annoyed, resentful, choked, indignant, offended, scorching
▶ verb **5** = **soil**, foul, spoil, pollute, stain, muddy, blacken, defile, smirch
See also: **crude, indecent, shabby, vulgar**

disability noun **1** = **handicap**, complaint, disorder, defect, ailment, impairment, malady, affliction, infirmity
2 = **incapacity**, inability, unfitness

disable verb **1** = **handicap**, damage, impair, paralyze, cripple, incapacitate, immobilize, enfeeble
2 = **disqualify**, invalidate, render incapable or declare incapable

disabled adjective = **handicapped**, paralyzed, weakened, lame, crippled, infirm, challenged (informal), incapacitated

disadvantage noun
1 = **drawback**, weakness, minus, handicap • the advantages and disadvantages of changing the law
OPPOSITE: advantage

2 = harm, injury, loss, damage, hurt, prejudice, detriment, disservice
See also: **catch, snag**

disagree verb **1 = differ**, dispute, dissent • *They can communicate even when they disagree.*
OPPOSITE: agree

2 = object, oppose, take issue with • *I disagree with that policy in general.*

3 = conflict, counter, vary, differ, contradict, diverge, be dissimilar, run counter to

4 = make ill, hurt, trouble, upset, sicken, bother, distress, discomfort, nauseate
See also: **argue, clash, protest**

disagreeable adjective
1 = unpleasant, nasty, horrible, objectionable, horrid, obnoxious • *a disagreeable odour*
OPPOSITE: agreeable

2 = rude, difficult, unpleasant, unfriendly, irritable, surly, bad-tempered, churlish, disobliging
See also: **sour, uncomfortable**

disagreement noun
1 = argument, dispute, difference, row, altercation (formal), squabble, quarrel, tiff • *My driving instructor and I had a brief disagreement.*
OPPOSITE: agreement

2 = objection, opposition, dissent • *Britain and France have expressed some disagreement with the proposal.*

3 = incompatibility, difference, discrepancy, disparity, variance, divergence, incongruity, dissimilarity
See also: **conflict**

disallow verb **= reject**, refuse, dismiss, rebuff, disavow, repudiate, disown

disappear verb **1 = vanish**, fade, recede, be lost to view, drop out of sight • *The aircraft disappeared off the radar.*
OPPOSITE: appear

2 = cease, pass, vanish, die out, go away, melt away • *The pain has finally disappeared.*
See also: **melt**

disappearance noun
= vanishing, departure, eclipse, passing, going, evaporation, evanescence, melting

disappoint verb **= let down**, fail, dismay, dissatisfy, disillusion, dishearten, disgruntle, disenchant

disappointed adjective **= let down**, dejected, despondent, disenchanted, downcast, disillusioned, saddened • *I was disappointed that my best friend was not there.*
OPPOSITE: satisfied

disappointing adjective
= unsatisfactory, sorry, sad, inadequate, insufficient, lousy (slang), depressing, disconcerting, discouraging

disappointment noun
1 = regret, despondency, dejection • *Book early to avoid disappointment.*

2 = let-down, blow, setback • *The reunion was a bitter disappointment.*
See also: **failure**

disapproval noun
= condemnation, criticism, censure • *their disapproval of his coaching style*
OPPOSITE: approval
See also: **opposition**

disapprove verb **= condemn**, dislike, deplore (formal), find unacceptable, take a dim view of • *Everyone disapproved of their marrying so young.*
OPPOSITE: approve
See also: **protest**

disapproving See **critical, severe**

disarm verb **1 = render defenceless**, disable

2 = win over, persuade, set at ease

3 = demilitarize, disband, deactivate, demobilize

disarmament noun **= arms reduction**, arms limitation, de-escalation, demilitarization, demobilization

disarming adjective **= charming**, winning, irresistible, likable or likeable, persuasive

disarrange verb = **disorder**, shake or shake up, mess or mess up, disturb, confuse, shuffle, scatter, jumble or jumble up, disorganize

disarray noun **1** = **confusion**, disorder, disorganization, disunity, indiscipline, unruliness
2 = **untidiness**, chaos, clutter, mess, muddle, jumble, shambles

disaster noun = **catastrophe**, tragedy, calamity (formal), misfortune, train wreck, car crash, perfect storm • another air disaster

disastrous adjective = **terrible**, fatal, tragic, catastrophic, ruinous, cataclysmic, calamitous, devastating

disbelief noun = **skepticism**, doubt, distrust, mistrust, dubiety, incredulity, unbelief

discard verb = **get rid of**, dump (informal), shed, jettison, cast aside, dispose of, throw away, throw out • Read the instructions before discarding the box.
See also: **banish**

discern verb (Formal) = **see**, spot, notice, detect, observe, perceive, make out • trying to discern a pattern in his behaviour
See also: **distinguish, tell**

discernment See **wisdom**

discharge verb **1** = **emit**, release, empty, expel, flush, give off • The motorboat discharged fuel into the lake.
2 = **release**, free, liberate, let go, set free • He has a broken nose, but may be discharged today.
3 = **dismiss**, fire, remove, oust, sack (informal), expel, eject, discard, cashier, give (someone) the boot (slang), give (someone) the sack (informal) • discharged when caught stealing a computer
4 = **fire**, shoot, explode, detonate, let loose (informal), let off, set off
5 = **carry out**, do, perform, execute, observe, accomplish, fulfil

6 = **pay**, meet, clear, settle, satisfy, relieve, honor, square up
▶ noun **7** = **dismissal**, ejection, expulsion, the sack (informal) • a dishonourable discharge from the army
8 = **release**, pardon, clearance, acquittal, liberation
9 = **firing**, report, shot, blast, explosion, burst, salvo, volley, detonation
10 = **emission**, ooze, secretion, seepage, excretion, pus, suppuration
See also: **drain, dump**

disciple noun = **follower**, student, supporter, pupil, devotee, apostle, adherent

disciplinarian noun = **authoritarian**, tyrant, stickler, despot, martinet, taskmaster

discipline noun **1** = **training**, practice, regulation, exercise, drill, method, regimen
2 = **punishment**, correction, castigation, chastisement
3 = **self-control**, control, conduct, regulation, restraint, orderliness, strictness
4 = **field of study**, area, course, subject, specialty, curriculum, branch of knowledge
▶ verb **5** = **train**, prepare, exercise, drill, educate, bring up
6 = **punish**, correct, penalize, chastise, reprimand, castigate, chasten, bring to book, reprove

disclose verb **1** = **make known**, publish, broadcast, reveal, relate, communicate, confess, divulge, let slip
2 = **show**, reveal, unveil, expose, uncover, bring to light, lay bare

disclosure noun = **revelation**, announcement, leak, publication, declaration, confession, admission, acknowledgment, divulgence

discolour verb = **stain**, mark, streak, soil, fade, tarnish, tinge

discomfort noun **1** = **pain**, hurt, ache, malaise, irritation, soreness
2 = **uneasiness**, trouble, distress,

hardship, nuisance, irritation, annoyance

disconcert verb = **disturb**, worry, upset, rattle (informal), unsettle, faze, fluster, perturb, take aback

disconcerting adjective = **disturbing**, confusing, awkward, alarming, bewildering, distracting, embarrassing, perplexing, upsetting

disconnect verb = **cut off**, part, separate, divide, sever, detach, disengage, take apart, uncouple

disconnected adjective = **illogical**, confused, incoherent, rambling, disjointed, unintelligible, jumbled, mixed-up

disconsolate adjective = **inconsolable**, miserable, crushed, dejected, heartbroken, desolate, grief-stricken, wretched, forlorn

discontent noun = **dissatisfaction**, regret, displeasure, envy, unhappiness, restlessness, uneasiness

discontented adjective = **dissatisfied**, unhappy, disgruntled, disaffected, displeased, exasperated, fed up, vexed

discontinue verb = **stop**, end, drop, suspend, quit, abandon, cease, terminate, break off, give up

discord noun 1 = **disagreement**, division, conflict, strife, friction, dissension, incompatibility, disunity
2 = **disharmony**, racket, cacophony, din, tumult, harshness, dissonance, jarring

discordant adjective
1 = **disagreeing**, different, contrary, contradictory, incompatible, conflicting, at odds, clashing
2 = **inharmonious**, harsh, strident, shrill, grating, cacophonous, dissonant, jarring

discount verb 1 = **leave out**, ignore, overlook, disregard, disbelieve, brush off (slang), pass over
2 = **deduct**, reduce, lower, mark down, take off
▶ noun 3 = **deduction**, cut, reduction, concession, rebate

discourage verb 1 = **put off**, deter, dissuade, daunt • Don't let these problems discourage you.
2 = **dishearten**, intimidate, depress, dampen, demoralize, dispirit, deject, overawe, put a damper on
OPPOSITE: encourage

discouraged adjective = **put off**, glum, dismayed, downcast, crestfallen, deterred, disheartened, dispirited, down in the mouth

discouragement noun 1 = **loss of confidence**, depression, disappointment, dismay, despair, despondency, dejection, downheartedness
2 = **deterrent**, opposition, setback, obstacle, impediment, damper, hindrance, disincentive

discouraging adjective = **disheartening**, daunting, dampening, depressing, disappointing, dispiriting, unfavourable

discourse noun 1 = **conversation**, talk, speech, discussion, communication, chat, dialogue, seminar
2 = **speech**, lecture, essay, sermon, homily, treatise, dissertation, oration
▶ verb 3 = **hold forth**, talk, speak, expatiate

discourteous adjective = **rude**, disrespectful, boorish, bad-mannered, ill-mannered, impolite, insolent, offhand, ungentlemanly, ungracious

discourtesy noun 1 = **rudeness**, bad manners, disrespectfulness, impertinence, impoliteness, incivility, insolence
2 = **insult**, slight, snub, rebuff, affront, cold shoulder, kick in the teeth (slang)

discover verb 1 = **find**, unearth, come across, stumble on or

stumble across • *to discover a new
planet*
2 = find out, learn, recognize,
notice, realize, detect, uncover,
perceive, ascertain
See also: **determine, hear,
observe, see**
discovery *noun* **1 = finding**,
location, disclosure, exploration,
revelation, detection,
uncovering
2 = breakthrough, find, secret,
invention, innovation
discredit *verb* **1 = disgrace**,
smear, defame, disparage, vilify,
slander, dishonour, bring into
disrepute
2 = doubt, question, deny,
challenge, dispute, discount,
distrust, mistrust, disbelieve
▶ *noun* **3 = disgrace**, scandal,
shame, stigma, disrepute,
dishonour, ignominy, ill-repute
discreditable *adjective*
= **disgraceful**, shameful,
scandalous, reprehensible,
ignominious, unworthy,
dishonourable
discreet *adjective* = **tactful**,
diplomatic, careful, cautious,
wary, prudent, considerate,
guarded, judicious,
circumspect
discrepancy *noun*
= **disagreement**, difference,
conflict, variation, disparity,
inconsistency, contradiction,
divergence, incongruity
discrete *adjective* = **separate**,
individual, distinct,
disconnected, detached,
discontinuous, unattached
discretion *noun* **1 = tact**, caution,
consideration, diplomacy,
prudence, wariness, carefulness,
judiciousness
2 = choice, will, pleasure,
preference, inclination, volition
discretionary See **flexible**
discriminate *verb* **1 = show
prejudice**, favour, victimize,
show bias, single out, treat as
inferior, treat differently
2 = differentiate, separate,
distinguish, segregate, draw a

distinction, tell the difference
discriminating *adjective*
= **discerning**, particular,
refined, selective, tasteful,
cultivated, fastidious
discrimination *noun*
1 = prejudice, bias, intolerance,
bigotry, unfairness, favouritism
2 = discernment, taste,
judgment, perception,
refinement, subtlety
discuss *verb* = **talk about**, debate,
exchange views on, go into • *I
will be discussing the situation with
students tomorrow.*
discussion *noun* = **talk**, debate,
conversation, dialogue,
consultation, discourse • *informal
discussions*
See also: **conference, word**
disdain *noun* **1 = contempt**,
scorn, arrogance, derision,
haughtiness, superciliousness
▶ *verb* **2 = scorn**, reject, slight,
disregard, spurn, deride, look
down on, sneer at
disdainful *adjective*
= **contemptuous**, proud,
superior, arrogant, aloof,
derisive, haughty, scornful,
sneering, supercilious
disease *noun* = **illness**, condition,
infection, complaint, disorder,
ailment, sickness, malady,
affliction, infirmity
diseased *adjective* = **sick**,
infected, ailing, unhealthy,
rotten, unwell, sickly, unsound,
unwholesome
disembark *verb* = **land**, arrive,
alight, get off, go ashore, step
out of
disenchanted *adjective*
= **disillusioned**, disappointed,
indifferent, cynical, soured,
jaundiced, let down, sick of
disenchantment *noun*
= **disillusionment**,
disappointment, disillusion,
rude awakening
disengage *verb* = **release**,
free, loosen, extricate, untie,
disentangle, set free, unloose
disentangle *verb* = **untangle**,
free, loose, unravel, disconnect,

d

extricate, disengage

disfavour noun = **disapproval**, dislike, displeasure, disapprobation

disfigure verb = **damage**, mar, scar, distort, mutilate, blemish, deface, deform

disfigured See **distorted**

disgorge verb = **vomit**, empty, expel, discharge, eject

disgrace noun 1 = **shame**, scandal
• to bring disgrace upon the whole team
OPPOSITE: credit
2 = **stain**, scandal, stigma, slur, blemish, blot, reproach
▶ verb 3 = **shame**, discredit • to disgrace their family's name
See also: **humble, humiliate**

disgraceful adjective = **shameful**, shocking, scandalous • disgraceful behaviour

disgruntled adjective = **discontented**, grumpy, annoyed, irritated, dissatisfied, displeased, peeved, put out, vexed

disguise verb 1 = **hide**, cover, screen, mask, cloak, veil, conceal, shroud, camouflage
2 = **misrepresent**, fake, falsify
▶ noun 3 = **costume**, cover, screen, mask, veil, camouflage
4 = **façade**, front, deception, pretense, trickery, veneer, semblance, dissimulation

disguised adjective = **in disguise**, fake, false, undercover, covert, masked, camouflaged, feigned, incognito

disgust noun 1 = **revulsion**, nausea, repulsion • his disgust at the incident
▶ verb 2 = **sicken**, revolt, repel
• He disgusted many with his behaviour.
See also: **horrify, horror, shock**

disgusted adjective = **sickened**, appalled, nauseated, offended, repulsed, scandalized

disgusting adjective = **sickening**, foul, gross, repellent, vile, obnoxious, revolting • one of the most disgusting sights I had ever seen
See also: **nasty**

dish noun 1 = **bowl**, plate, platter, salver
2 = **food**, fare, recipe

dishearten verb = **discourage**, deter, depress, dismay, dispirit, cast down, deject, put a damper on

dishevelled adjective = **untidy**, messy, bedraggled, disordered, ruffled, rumpled, tousled, uncombed, unkempt

dishonest adjective = **deceitful**, corrupt, fraudulent, crooked, hypocritical, lying • It would be dishonest to mislead people.
OPPOSITE: honest
See also: **dubious, insincere, sneaky, two-faced**

dishonesty noun = **deceit**, corruption, trickery, cheating
• She accused the government of dishonesty.
OPPOSITE: honesty
See also: **lying**

dishonour verb 1 = **shame**, disgrace, defame, discredit, degrade, sully, debase, debauch
▶ noun 2 = **shame**, scandal, disgrace, discredit, disrepute, infamy, reproach, ignominy, obloquy
3 = **insult**, abuse, slight, outrage, offence, indignity, affront, discourtesy, sacrilege

dishonourable adjective
1 = **shameful**, infamous, disgraceful, despicable, scandalous, lousy (slang), ignominious, contemptible, discreditable, scuzzy (slang)
2 = **untrustworthy**, corrupt, treacherous, shameless, unscrupulous, disreputable, unprincipled

disillusioned adjective = **disenchanted**, disappointed, enlightened, disabused, undeceived

disinclination noun = **reluctance**, opposition, resistance, objection, dislike, unwillingness, aversion, hesitance, repugnance

disinclined adjective = **reluctant**, resistant, unwilling, loath, averse, hesitating, not in the mood, opposed

disinfect verb = **sterilize**, clean, sanitize, cleanse, purify, decontaminate, deodorize, fumigate

disinfectant noun = **antiseptic**, germicide, sterilizer

disinherit verb (Law) = **cut off**, oust, repudiate, disown, dispossess

disintegrate verb = **break up**, crumble, fragment, fall apart, fall to pieces • *The sculpture fell off the table and disintegrated.* See also: **erode**

disinterest noun = **impartiality**, neutrality, fairness, detachment

disinterested adjective = **impartial**, objective, neutral, unbiased, even-handed, dispassionate, detached, impersonal, unprejudiced

disjointed adjective = **incoherent**, confused, rambling, disconnected, disordered

dislike verb 1 = **hate**, loathe, detest, abhor (formal), be averse to, not be able to abide, not be able to bear, not be able to stand • *We don't serve it often because many people dislike it.* OPPOSITE: like
▶ noun 2 = **hatred**, hostility, animosity, distaste, aversion, loathing, antipathy • *She looked at him with dislike.* OPPOSITE: liking See also: **disapprove, resent**

disliked See **unpopular**

dislodge verb = **displace**, remove, oust, disturb, uproot, extricate, force out, knock loose

disloyal adjective = **treacherous**, false, subversive, untrustworthy, unfaithful, faithless, traitorous, two-faced

disloyalty noun = **treachery**, treason, infidelity, backstabbing (informal), breach of trust, deceitfulness, double-dealing, falseness, inconstancy, unfaithfulness

dismal adjective = **gloomy**, dark, bleak, dreary, sombre, wretched, cheerless, depressing, discouraging, forlorn

dismantle verb = **take apart**, strip, demolish, disassemble, take to pieces

dismay verb 1 = **alarm**, scare, paralyze, terrify, frighten, distress, horrify, appall, unnerve
2 = **disappoint**, discourage, disillusion, dishearten, daunt, dispirit, put off
▶ noun 3 = **alarm**, fear, horror, anxiety, dread, apprehension, trepidation, consternation
4 = **disappointment**, disillusionment, chagrin, discouragement

dismember verb = **cut into pieces**, sever, amputate, mutilate, dissect

dismiss verb 1 = **discharge**, fire (informal), remove, sack (informal), axe (informal), cashier, give notice to, give (someone) their marching orders, lay off
2 = **let go**, release, free, dissolve, disperse, send away
3 = **put out of one's mind**, reject, banish, dispel, discard, disregard, lay aside, set aside

dismissal noun = **the sack** (informal), notice, removal, expulsion, marching orders (informal), the boot (slang)

disobedience noun = **defiance**, revolt, insubordination, mutiny, indiscipline, noncompliance, nonobservance, recalcitrance, unruliness, waywardness

disobedient adjective = **defiant**, contrary, undisciplined, naughty, disorderly, unruly, wayward, intractable, insubordinate, refractory

disobey verb = **defy**, break, violate, infringe, flout • *He was forever disobeying the rules.* OPPOSITE: obey

disorder noun 1 = **untidiness**, disarray, clutter, muddle • *Inside, all was disorder.* OPPOSITE: order
2 = **confusion**, chaos, turmoil, disarray • *Regular fire drills prevent disorder in a real emergency.*

d

3 = **illness**, disease, condition, complaint, ailment, affliction
• *a rare nerve disorder*
4 = **disturbance**, riot, turmoil, unrest, uproar, commotion, unruliness
See also: **mess**

disordered *See* **confused**

disorderly *adjective* 1 = **untidy**, chaotic, confused, disorganized, messy, jumbled
2 = **unruly**, turbulent, tumultuous, disruptive, lawless, rowdy, indisciplined, riotous, ungovernable

disorganization *See* **confusion**, **muddle**

disorganized *adjective* = **muddled**, chaotic, confused, haphazard, disordered, jumbled, unsystematic

disown *verb* = **deny**, reject, renounce, disavow, repudiate, cast off, disclaim

disparage *verb* = **run down**, ridicule, deride, vilify, malign, slander, denigrate, belittle, deprecate, put down

disparagement *See* **criticism**

disparaging *See* **abusive**, **critical**

disparate *See* **different**, **various**

disparity *See* **difference**, **gap**

dispassionate *adjective*
1 = **unemotional**, cool, calm, serene, collected, composed, imperturbable, unruffled
2 = **objective**, fair, neutral, impartial, unbiased, disinterested, detached, impersonal, unprejudiced

dispatch *verb* 1 = **send**, dismiss, hasten, consign
2 = **carry out**, finish, perform, settle, discharge, dispose of
3 = **murder**, kill, slay, execute, slaughter, assassinate
▶ *noun* 4 = **message**, report, news, story, account, communication, bulletin, communiqué

dispel *verb* = **drive away**, eliminate, dismiss, expel, banish, disperse, chase away

dispense *verb* 1 = **distribute**, share, assign, allocate, allot, apportion, deal out, dole out
2 = **prepare**, supply, measure, mix
3 = **administer**, operate, apply, execute, implement, enforce, discharge, carry out
▷ **dispense with = do away with**, cancel, abolish, brush aside, dispose of, get rid of; = **do without**, relinquish, forgo, abstain from, give up

disperse *verb* 1 = **scatter**, broadcast, spread, distribute, strew, disseminate, diffuse
2 = **break up**, separate, dissolve, scatter, disband

dispirited *adjective* = **disheartened**, sad, depressed, gloomy, dejected, despondent, glum, discouraged, downcast, crestfallen

displace *verb* 1 = **move**, shift, disturb, misplace, transpose
2 = **replace**, oust, succeed, supplant, supersede, take the place of

display *verb* 1 = **show**, reveal, present, expose, exhibit, disclose, demonstrate, manifest
2 = **show off**, parade, flourish, flaunt, vaunt
▶ *noun* 3 = **exhibition**, show, demonstration, presentation, array, revelation
4 = **show**, parade, flourish, spectacle, pageant, pomp, ostentation

displease *verb* = **annoy**, upset, anger, offend, irk, pique, irritate, vex, put out

displeasure *noun* = **annoyance**, anger, dissatisfaction, resentment, irritation, disapproval, indignation, distaste

disposable *adjective*
1 = **throwaway**, biodegradable, nonreturnable
2 = **available**, expendable, consumable

disposal *noun* = **throwing away**, removal, ejection, riddance,

discarding, dumping (*informal*), jettisoning, scrapping
▷ **at one's disposal = available**, expendable, consumable, at one's service, free for use

dispose *verb* = **arrange**, group, put, place, order, distribute, array, marshal
▷ **dispose of = get rid of**, dump, discard, jettison, dispense with, throw away • *Dispose of your garbage in the proper containers.*
See also: **process, settle**

disposed See **prone**

disposition *noun* 1 = **character**, nature, spirit, constitution, temper, make-up, temperament
2 = **tendency**, habit, bias, bent, inclination, leaning, propensity, proclivity
3 = **arrangement**, organization, distribution, placement, classification, grouping, ordering

disproportion *noun* = **inequality**, imbalance, discrepancy, disparity, asymmetry, lopsidedness, unevenness

disproportionate *adjective* = **unequal**, excessive, unreasonable, uneven, unbalanced, inordinate, out of proportion

disprove *verb* = **prove false**, refute, discredit, invalidate, give the lie to • *the statistics that will prove or disprove the statement*
OPPOSITE: prove

dispute *noun* 1 = **argument**, conflict, row, clash, feud, disagreement, wrangle, turf war (*informal*) • *The dispute between them is settled.*
2 = **disagreement**, debate, discussion, controversy, argument, contention, dissension
▶ *verb* 3 = **contest**, question, deny, challenge, contradict, query • *He disputed the allegations.*
OPPOSITE: accept
4 = **argue**, debate, clash, squabble, quarrel, cross swords
See also: **disagree, fight**

disqualification *noun* = **ban**, elimination, rejection, exclusion, ineligibility, DQ

disqualified *adjective* = **ineligible**, debarred, eliminated, knocked out, out of the running

disqualify *verb* = **ban**, prohibit, preclude, debar, declare ineligible, rule out

disquiet *noun* 1 = **uneasiness**, concern, worry, alarm, anxiety, disturbance, nervousness, trepidation, foreboding
▶ *verb* 2 = **make uneasy**, concern, worry, trouble, upset, disturb, bother, unsettle, perturb

disregard *verb* 1 = **ignore**, discount, overlook, neglect, brush aside *or* brush away, make light of, pass over, pay no heed to, turn a blind eye to
▶ *noun* 2 = **inattention**, negligence, oversight, neglect, contempt, disrespect, indifference, disdain

disrepair *noun* = **dilapidation**, collapse, deterioration, decay, ruination

disreputable *adjective* = **discreditable**, notorious, infamous, shameful, scandalous, shady (*informal*), ignominious, dishonourable, louche

disrepute *noun* = **discredit**, shame, disgrace, infamy, unpopularity, dishonour, ignominy, ill repute, obloquy

disrespect *noun* = **contempt**, sauce, cheek, irreverence, impertinence, impoliteness, impudence, insolence, lack of respect, rudeness

disrespectful *adjective* = **rude**, impertinent, impudent, insolent • *They were disrespectful to the older workers.*

disrupt *verb* 1 = **disturb**, upset, disorder, spoil, confuse, disorganize
2 = **interrupt**, upset, obstruct, unsettle, intrude, break up *or* break into, interfere with

disruption *noun* = **disturbance**,

interference, stoppage,
interruption

disruptive *adjective* = **disturbing**,
troublesome, disorderly,
unruly, distracting, unsettling,
upsetting

dissatisfaction *noun*
= **discontent**, frustration,
disappointment, displeasure,
resentment, irritation,
unhappiness, annoyance,
chagrin

dissatisfied *adjective*
= **discontented**, frustrated,
unhappy, disappointed,
disgruntled, displeased, fed up,
unsatisfied

dissect *verb* 1 = **cut up** *or* **cut
apart**, dismember, anatomize,
lay open
2 = **analyze**, study, research,
investigate, explore, inspect,
scrutinize, break down

disseminate *verb* = **spread**,
broadcast, distribute, circulate,
scatter, disperse, publicize

dissension *noun* = **disagreement**,
dispute, conflict, row, dissent,
strife, friction, quarrel, discord

dissent *verb* 1 = **disagree**, protest,
refuse, object, differ, withhold
assent *or* withhold approval
▷ *noun* 2 = **disagreement**,
opposition, resistance, refusal,
objection, discord, dissension

dissenter *noun* = **objector**,
dissident, nonconformist

dissertation *noun* = **thesis**, essay,
critique, discourse, exposition,
treatise, disquisition

disservice *noun* = **bad turn**,
injury, wrong, harm, injustice,
unkindness

dissident *adjective*
1 = **dissenting**, disagreeing,
discordant, heterodox,
nonconformist
▷ *noun* 2 = **protester**, rebel,
dissenter, agitator

dissimilar *adjective* = **different**,
various, unlike, diverse,
unrelated, disparate, divergent,
heterogeneous

dissipate *verb* 1 = **squander**,
spend, waste, consume, deplete,

expend, fritter away, run
through
2 = **disperse**, disappear,
dissolve, vanish, scatter, dispel,
evaporate, drive away

dissipation *noun* 1 = **dispersal**,
disappearance, dissolution,
disintegration, scattering,
vanishing
2 = **debauchery**, waste, excess,
indulgence, extravagance,
dissoluteness, intemperance,
prodigality, profligacy,
wantonness

dissociate *verb* 1 = **break away**,
quit, break off, part company
2 = **separate**, divorce, distance,
isolate, disconnect, detach,
segregate, set apart

dissolute *adjective* = **immoral**,
wild, degenerate, wanton,
debauched, depraved,
dissipated, profligate, rakish

dissolution *noun* 1 = **breaking
up**, division, separation,
parting, disintegration
2 = **adjournment**, end, finish,
suspension, termination,
discontinuation

dissolve *verb* 1 = **melt**, soften,
thaw, fuse, liquefy, deliquesce
2 = **end**, suspend, terminate,
discontinue, break up, wind up

dissuade *verb* = **deter**, warn,
discourage, advise against, put
off, remonstrate, talk out of

distance *noun* 1 = **space**, range,
stretch, gap, length, span,
extent, interval
2 = **reserve**, restraint, stiffness,
remoteness, coolness, aloofness,
coldness
▷ **in the distance** = **far off**, afar,
far away, on the horizon, yonder
▷ *verb*
▷ **distance oneself** = **separate
oneself**, be distanced from,
dissociate oneself

distant *adjective* 1 = **far**, remote,
outlying, out-of-the-way • *a
distant land*
OPPOSITE: close
2 = **reserved**, aloof, detached,
withdrawn • *He is polite, but
distant.*

OPPOSITE: friendly
3 = **apart**, separate, distinct, scattered, dispersed
See also: **cold, foreign**

distaste noun = **dislike**, horror, disgust, revulsion, aversion, loathing, odium, repugnance

distasteful adjective
= **unpleasant**, offensive, objectionable, repulsive, repugnant, unpalatable, disagreeable, scuzzy (slang), uninviting, unsavoury

distill verb = **extract**, refine, purify, condense

distilled See **refined**

distinct adjective 1 = **different**, individual, separate, unconnected, discrete, detached
2 = **definite**, clear, obvious, evident, marked, noticeable, unmistakable, palpable, well-defined, decided
▷ **distinct from** See **unlike**

distinction noun
1 = **differentiation**, discrimination, perception, separation, discernment
2 = **feature**, mark, quality, characteristic, individuality, distinctiveness, particularity, peculiarity
3 = **difference**, division, contrast, separation, differential
4 = **excellence**, fame, importance, merit, honour, prominence, greatness, repute, eminence

distinctive adjective
= **characteristic**, special, individual, original, unique, typical, singular, peculiar, idiosyncratic

distinctly adverb = **definitely**, obviously, clearly, markedly, noticeably, decidedly, patently, plainly, unmistakably

distinguish verb
1 = **differentiate**, tell, discriminate, tell apart, tell the difference • Could he distinguish right from wrong?
2 = **make out**, recognize, discern, pick out • I heard shouting, but was unable to distinguish the words.

3 = **characterize**, mark, separate, classify, categorize, set apart, single out

distinguishable See **visible**

distinguished adjective
= **eminent**, famous, acclaimed, famed, renowned, well-known, celebrated, illustrious, noted

distinguishing See **characteristic, peculiar**

distort verb 1 = **misrepresent**, colour, twist, bias, falsify, slant, pervert
2 = **deform**, twist, bend, disfigure, buckle, warp, contort, misshape

distorted adjective = **deformed**, disfigured • the distorted image caused by the projector
See also: **crooked, garbled**

distortion noun
1 = **misrepresentation**, bias, slant, perversion, falsification
2 = **deformity**, twist, bend, buckle, warp, malformation, contortion, crookedness

distract verb 1 = **divert**, draw away • Playing computer games distracts him from his homework.
2 = **amuse**, occupy, entertain, engross, beguile

distracted adjective = **agitated**, troubled, at sea, flustered, harassed, in a flap (informal), perplexed, puzzled

distraction noun 1 = **diversion**, interference, disturbance, interruption
2 = **entertainment**, diversion, recreation, amusement, pastime
3 = **agitation**, disorder, confusion, disturbance, commotion, discord, bewilderment

distraught adjective = **frantic**, desperate, distressed, overwrought, agitated, beside oneself, distracted, out of one's mind, worked-up

distress noun 1 = **suffering**, pain, sorrow, heartache • Kindness eased their distress.
2 = **need**, trouble, difficulty, straits • The ship might be in distress.

d

▷ **distress signal** See **alarm**

▶ verb **3** = **upset**, worry, pain, trouble, disturb, bother, grieve, sadden • *Our fight greatly distressed me.*

See also: **agitate, alarm, concern, grief, hurt, shake, shock**

distressed adjective **1** = **upset**, troubled, worried, distraught, wretched, agitated, distracted, tormented

2 = **poverty-stricken**, poor, needy, destitute, down at heel, indigent, straitened

distressing adjective = **upsetting**, sad, painful, heart-breaking, disturbing, harrowing, worrying

distribute verb **1** = **hand out**, circulate, pass around • *They publish and distribute flyers.*

2 = **spread**, scatter, disperse, diffuse • *Distribute the berries evenly over the cake.*

3 = **share**, divide, allocate, dispense, allot, dole out • *Distribute chores equally among all family members.*

distribution noun **1** = **delivery**, handling, transportation, dealing, mailing

2 = **sharing**, division, allocation, allotment, apportionment

3 = **classification**, organization, arrangement, placement, grouping

district noun = **area**, quarter, region, sector, neighbourhood, parish, locale, vicinity, locality

distrust verb **1** = **suspect**, question, doubt, mistrust, disbelieve, be suspicious of, be wary of, smell a rat (*informal*)

▶ noun **2** = **suspicion**, question, doubt, skepticism, disbelief, mistrust, misgiving, wariness

distrustful adjective = **suspicious**, skeptical, wary, doubtful, dubious, cynical, uneasy, leery (*slang*), chary, disbelieving, distrusting, doubting, mistrustful

disturb verb **1** = **interrupt**, disrupt, bother, intrude on

• *Don't disturb me while I'm studying.*

2 = **upset**, worry, trouble, shake, distress, agitate, unsettle • *Some scenes in the movie may disturb you.*

3 = **muddle**, disorder, disarrange

See also: **concern**

disturbance noun

1 = **interruption**, bother, distraction, intrusion, annoyance

2 = **disorder**, brawl, fray, commotion, fracas, rumpus

disturbed adjective **1** (*Psychiatry*) = **unbalanced**, upset, troubled, neurotic, disordered, maladjusted

2 = **worried**, upset, troubled, nervous, anxious, concerned, uneasy, apprehensive, bothered, wired (*slang*)

disturbing adjective = **worrying**, startling, alarming, disconcerting, distressing, frightening, harrowing, unsettling, upsetting

disuse noun = **neglect**, decay, abandonment, idleness

ditch noun **1** = **channel**, drain, trench, gully, moat, furrow, dyke, watercourse

▶ verb **2** (*Slang*) = **get rid of**, drop, dump (*informal*), abandon, scrap, discard, jettison, dispose of, throw out or throw overboard

dither verb **1** = **vacillate**, hesitate, waver, teeter, hum and haw, shillyshally (*informal*)

▶ noun **2** = **flutter**, flap (*informal*), tizzy (*informal*), fluster

dive verb **1** = **plunge**, jump, leap, submerge • *She was standing by the pool, about to dive in.*

▶ noun **2** = **plunge**, jump, spring, leap, lunge, nose dive

See also: **descend**

diverge verb **1** = **separate**, part, spread, split, divide, branch, fork

2 = **deviate**, depart, wander, stray, meander, digress, turn aside

divergence See **difference, split**

divergent See **different**

divergent from See **unlike**

diverse adjective **1** = **various**,

several, assorted, varied, miscellaneous, manifold, of every description, sundry
2 = different, separate, unlike, distinct, disparate, divergent, dissimilar, discrete, varying
diversify verb = **vary**, change, expand, branch out, have a finger in every pie, spread out
diversion noun **1 = distraction**, deflection, deviation, digression
2 = pastime, game, play, sport (old-fashioned), entertainment, delight, distraction, pleasure, recreation, amusement, hobby, relaxation, enjoyment, gratification, divertissement, beguilement
diversity noun = **difference**, range, variety, distinctiveness, diverseness, heterogeneity, multiplicity
divert verb **1 = redirect**, switch, avert, deflect, turn aside
2 = distract, sidetrack, draw away from or lead away from, lead astray
3 = entertain, delight, amuse, gratify, regale, beguile
diverting adjective
= **entertaining**, fun, pleasant, enjoyable, humorous, amusing, beguiling
divide verb **1 = separate**, split, partition, segregate, cut up, split up • Divide the pizza into six slices. OPPOSITE: join
2 = bisect, separate • the border dividing the countries
3 = split, come between, set against one another • the enormous differences that still divide them
4 = share, distribute, allocate, dispense, allot, deal out
See also: **sort**
dividend noun = **bonus**, share, cut (informal), gain, extra, surplus, plus, portion, divvy (informal)
divine adjective **1 = heavenly**, holy, spiritual, celestial, supernatural, superhuman, angelic, godlike
2 = sacred, religious, holy, spiritual, consecrated, sanctified

3 (Informal) = **wonderful**, perfect, beautiful, excellent, glorious, splendid, marvellous, superlative
▶ verb **4 = infer**, suppose, guess, perceive, apprehend, discern, surmise, deduce
divinity noun **1 = theology**, religion, religious studies
2 = god or **goddess**, spirit, deity, guardian spirit
3 = godliness, holiness, sanctity, deity, divine nature
divisible adjective = **dividable**, separable, splittable
division noun **1 = separation**, partition • equal division of the money
2 = disagreement, split, breach, rupture, difference of opinion • There were divisions in the club over who should be in charge.
3 = section, sector, department • the research division of the toy company
4 = sharing, distribution, allotment, apportionment
See also: **compartment**
divorce noun **1 = separation**, dissolution, annulment, split-up, talaq or talak
▶ verb **2 = separate**, part, divide, dissolve (marriage), sever, disconnect, dissociate, split up
divorced See **separate**
divulge verb = **make known**, tell, reveal, declare, disclose, confess, proclaim, let slip
dizzy adjective **1 = giddy**, lightheaded • He kept getting dizzy spells.
2 = confused, bemused, at sea, befuddled, bewildered, dazed, dazzled, muddled
See also: **faint**
do verb **1 = perform**, execute (formal), undertake, carry out • He just didn't want to do any work.
2 = be sufficient, suffice (formal), be adequate • Homemade soup is best, but canned soup will do.
3 = get on, manage, fare • She did well at school.
4 = get ready, prepare, fix, arrange, look after, see to

d

5 = solve, resolve, decode, decipher, figure out, puzzle out, work out

6 = cause, create, produce, effect, bring about

▷ **do away with = kill**, murder, slay, exterminate; **= get rid of**, remove, eliminate, abolish, discard, discontinue, put an end to, put paid to

▷ **do business** See **trade**

▷ **do up** See **decorate, renovate**

▷ **do well = succeed**, thrive, flourish

▷ **do without = manage without**, kick (informal), forgo, abstain from, dispense with, get along without, give up

▷ **do wrong** See **sin**

▷ **do your best** See **strive**

See also: **accomplish, achieve, commit, conduct, practise, suit**

docile adjective **= submissive**, manageable, compliant, amenable, obedient, biddable, pliant

docility noun **= submissiveness**, compliance, obedience, manageability, meekness

dock¹ noun **1 = wharf**, waterfront, pier, harbour, quay

▶ verb **2 = moor**, land, berth, anchor, drop anchor, put in, tie up

3 (Of a spacecraft) **= link up**, join, couple, unite, rendezvous, hook up

dock² verb **1 = deduct**, reduce, decrease, withhold, diminish, lessen, subtract

2 = cut off, clip, crop, shorten, curtail, cut short

doctor noun **1 = G.P.**, physician, medic (informal), general practitioner, medical practitioner

▶ verb **2 = change**, alter, disguise, misrepresent, falsify, pervert, tamper with

3 = add to, cut, spike, dilute, adulterate, mix with, water down

doctrinaire adjective **= dogmatic**, rigid, opinionated, fanatical, inflexible, insistent, biased

doctrinal See **religious**

doctrine noun **= teaching**, opinion, conviction, principle, belief, tenet, creed, dogma, article of faith, precept

document noun **1 = paper**, report, record, certificate

▶ verb **2 = support**, detail, verify, certify, authenticate, validate, substantiate, corroborate

dodge verb **1 = duck**, swerve • *We dodged to the side as the joggers approached.*

2 = avoid, elude, evade, sidestep, shirk, get out of • *dodging responsibilities by pretending to be ill*

See also: **escape, manoeuvre**

dog noun **1 = canine**, pooch, mutt, mongrel • *a children's book about dogs*

RELATED WORDS

adjective: canine

female: bitch

young: pup, puppy

▷ **go to the dogs** (Informal) **= go to ruin**, deteriorate, degenerate, go down the drain, go to pot

▶ verb **2 = trouble**, follow, track, trail, pursue, plague, haunt, hound, stalk

> **INFORMALLY SPEAKING**
> **a dog's life**: a miserable life
> **go to the dogs**: be ruined
> **let sleeping dogs lie**: avoid stirring up unnecessary trouble

dogged adjective **= determined**, persistent, stubborn, steadfast, resolute, tenacious, unshakable, indefatigable, obstinate, unflagging

dogma noun **= doctrine**, opinion, belief, creed, credo, teachings

dogmatic adjective **= opinionated**, arrogant, emphatic, assertive, doctrinaire, obdurate, overbearing

doldrums noun

▷ **the doldrums = inactivity**, depression, gloom, malaise, dumps (informal), listlessness

dole verb

▷ **dole out = give out**, distribute, assign, allocate, dispense, allot, apportion, hand out

dollop noun = **lump**, portion, scoop, serving, helping

dolt noun = **idiot**, ass, chump (informal), blockhead, dope (informal), fool, dork (slang), dunce, oaf, schmuck (slang)

domain See **field**, **territory**

domestic adjective **1** = **home**, family, private, household
2 = **home-loving**, stay-at-home, homey, domesticated, housewifely
3 = **domesticated**, pet, tame, trained, house-trained
4 = **native**, internal, indigenous
▶ noun **5** = **servant**, help, daily, maid, charwoman

dominance See **advantage**, **hold**

dominant adjective
1 = **controlling**, ruling, superior, supreme, authoritative, assertive, commanding, governing
2 = **main**, chief, primary, prominent, principal, pre-eminent, predominant

dominate verb **1** = **control**, rule, direct, govern, monopolize, have the whip hand over, tyrannize
2 = **tower above**, survey, overlook, loom over, stand head and shoulders above, stand over

domination noun = **control**, power, rule, authority, influence, command, supremacy, superiority, ascendancy

domineering adjective
= **overbearing**, arrogant, authoritarian, oppressive, dictatorial, tyrannical, imperious, high-handed, bossy (informal)

dominion noun **1** = **control**, power, rule, authority, command, sovereignty, jurisdiction, supremacy
2 = **kingdom**, country, territory, empire, domain, realm

don verb = **put on**, clothe oneself in, dress in, get into, pull on, slip on or slip into

donate verb = **give**, present,

contribute, subscribe, make a gift of

donation noun = **contribution**, present, grant, gift, offering, subscription, hand-out

done See **over**, **right**

donor noun = **giver**, contributor, benefactor, philanthropist, donator

doom noun **1** = **destruction**, lot, fate, ruin, fortune, catastrophe, downfall
▶ verb **2** = **condemn**, sentence, destine, damn, consign

doomed adjective = **hopeless**, ill-fated, condemned • a doomed attempt to rescue the miners

door noun = **opening**, exit, entry, entrance, doorway

doorway See **entrance**, **entry**

dope noun **1** (Slang) = **drug**, narcotic, opiate
2 (Informal) = **idiot**, fool, dimwit (informal), doofus (slang), dork (slang), dunce, dweeb (slang), nitwit (informal), schmuck (slang)
▶ verb **3** = **drug**, sedate, anesthetize, knock out, narcotize, stupefy

dork noun (Slang) = **idiot**, dope (slang), fool, geek (slang), nerd, doofus (slang), dunce, dweeb (slang)

dormant adjective = **inactive**, asleep, suspended, sleeping, latent, hibernating, inert, inoperative, slumbering

dose noun = **quantity**, measure, draft, prescription, portion, dosage, potion

dot noun **1** = **spot**, point, mark, speck, jot, speckle, fleck
▷ **on the dot** = **on time**, exactly, promptly, precisely, on the button (informal), punctually, to the minute
▶ verb **2** = **spot**, sprinkle, dabble, stud, dab, speckle, fleck, stipple

dotage noun = **senility**, weakness, decrepitude, feebleness, imbecility, old age, second childhood

dote on, **dote upon** verb = **adore**, treasure, admire, prize, idolize, hold dear, lavish affection on

doting *adjective* = **adoring**, fond, foolish, devoted, indulgent, lovesick

double *adjective* 1 = **twice**, twofold • *a double scoop*
2 = **twofold**, twin, dual • *a double check of her work*
▶ *verb* 3 = **multiply**, increase, grow, duplicate, magnify, enlarge
▶ *noun* 4 = **twin**, clone, replica, duplicate, lookalike, dead ringer (*slang*), Doppelgänger, spitting image (*informal*)
▷ **on the double** = **quickly**, immediately, briskly, at full speed, posthaste, without delay

double-cross *verb* = **betray**, trick, mislead, two-time (*informal*), cheat, defraud, swindle, hoodwink

doubt *noun* 1 = **uncertainty**, skepticism, qualm, misgiving • *This raises doubts about the point of advertising.*
OPPOSITE: certainty
2 = **suspicion**, skepticism, apprehension, distrust, mistrust, qualm, misgiving
▶ *verb* 3 = **be dubious**, question, query, be skeptical • *No one doubted his ability.*
OPPOSITE: believe
4 = **suspect**, fear, discredit, distrust, mistrust, lack confidence in

doubtful *adjective* 1 = **unlikely**, uncertain, questionable, dubious, debatable • *It is doubtful whether she will compete in the next Olympics.*
OPPOSITE: certain
2 = **unsure**, tentative, suspicious, skeptical, uncertain, unconvinced, distrustful, hesitating, in two minds (*informal*), wavering
See also: **hesitant, improbable, suspect, unpredictable**

doubtless *adverb* 1 = **certainly**, surely, undoubtedly, unquestionably, assuredly, indisputably, of course, without doubt

2 = **probably**, apparently, seemingly, presumably, supposedly, ostensibly, most likely

dough See **money**

dour *adjective* = **gloomy**, sour, dismal, grim, dreary, unfriendly, sullen, forbidding, morose

dovetail See **fit**

dowdy *adjective* = **frumpy**, drab, dingy, dumpy (*informal*), frowzy, shabby, homely (US), unfashionable

down *adverb* 1 = **downward**, downstairs • *We went down in the elevator.*
OPPOSITE: up
▶ *adjective* 2 = **depressed**, miserable, dejected, melancholy, despondent, glum, dispirited, fed up (*informal*), morose • *He sounded really down.*
▶ *verb* 3 (*Informal*) = **swallow**, drink *or* drink down, drain, gulp, put away, toss off
▶ *noun*
▷ **have a down on, be down on** (*Informal*) = **be antagonistic to** *or* **be hostile to**, bear a grudge towards, be prejudiced against, be set against, have it in for (*slang*)
See also: **below, gloomy, pile, sad, unhappy**

INFORMALLY SPEAKING
come down with: get sick with (a short-term illness)
down on: disapprovingly critical

down-and-out *adjective*
1 = **destitute**, impoverished, derelict, down on one's luck (*informal*), short, poor, distressed, needy, insolvent, poverty-stricken, penniless, without two pennies to rub together (*informal*), ruined, dirt-poor (*informal*), flat broke (*informal*), on the rocks, indigent, impecunious, on the breadline (*informal*), penurious, necessitous, moneyless
▶ *noun* 2 = **tramp**, derelict, beggar, bag lady, pauper, vagabond, vagrant

downcast adjective = **dejected**, depressed, disappointed, despondent, dismayed, discouraged, crestfallen, disconsolate, disheartened, dispirited

downer noun (Informal) = **moaner**, pessimist, killjoy, prophet of doom, sourpuss (informal), spoilsport, wet blanket (informal), buzzkill (slang)

downfall noun = **ruin**, fall, collapse • Lack of support led to the team's downfall.
See also: **failure**

downgrade verb = **demote**, humble, degrade, lower in rank or reduce in rank, take down a peg (informal)

downhearted adjective = **dejected**, sad, unhappy, depressed, despondent, discouraged, downcast, crestfallen, disheartened, dispirited

downpour noun = **rainstorm**, flood, deluge, cloudburst, inundation, torrential rain

downright adjective = **complete**, total, absolute, plain, outright, utter, unqualified, out-and-out, thoroughgoing, undisguised

downstairs See **down**

down-to-earth adjective = **sensible**, realistic, practical, no-nonsense, sane, unsentimental, matter-of-fact, plain-spoken

downtrodden adjective = **oppressed**, helpless, subservient, exploited, subjugated, tyrannized

downturn See **decline**, **recession**

downward adjective = **descending**, declining, earthward, heading down, sliding, slipping

doze verb 1 = **nap**, sleep, snooze (informal), slumber, nod off (informal)
▶ noun 2 = **nap**, catnap, forty winks (informal), snooze (informal), siesta, shuteye (slang)

drab adjective = **dull**, grey, dismal, sombre, gloomy, dreary, dingy • the same drab grey outfit
OPPOSITE: bright

draft[1] noun 1 = **outline**, plan, version, rough, sketch, abstract
2 = **order**, check, bill of exchange, money order
▶ verb 3 = **outline**, plan, draw, design, compose, sketch, formulate, draw up

draft[2] noun 1 = **breeze**, current, movement, flow, puff
2 = **drink**, cup, dose, quantity, potion

drag verb 1 = **pull**, draw, trail, haul, tow, lug • He dragged his chair toward the table.
▷ **drag on**, **drag out** = **last**, extend, persist, prolong, lengthen, draw out, keep going, protract, spin out, stretch out
▶ noun 2 (Informal) = **nuisance**, pain (informal), bother, bore, pest, downer (informal), annoyance
See also: **tug**

| INFORMALLY SPEAKING
| **drag in**: bring something irrelevant into a discussion
| **drag on**: be boringly long
| **drag your feet**: act slowly on purpose

dragoon verb = **force**, drive, bully, compel, intimidate, coerce, railroad (informal), constrain, browbeat, impel

drain verb 1 = **pump** • We drained the pipes till the water ran clear.
2 = **flow**, empty, discharge, seep • rivers that drain into lakes
3 = **exhaust**, tax, consume, sap, use up • The prolonged feud drained him of energy.
4 = **drink up**, finish, swallow, quaff, gulp down
▶ noun 5 = **pipe**, sink, channel, ditch, trench, sewer, duct, culvert, conduit
6 = **reduction**, strain, withdrawal, drag, exhaustion, sap, depletion
See also: **dry**, **tire**

drained See **tired**, **weary**

drama noun 1 = **play**, show, dramatization, stage show

2 = **theatre**, acting, dramaturgy, stagecraft

3 = **excitement**, scene, crisis, turmoil, spectacle, histrionics

dramatic adjective **1** = **theatrical**, dramaturgical, Thespian

2 = **powerful**, impressive, striking, vivid, expressive, moving

3 = **exciting**, thrilling, tense, sensational, breathtaking, climactic, suspenseful, electrifying, melodramatic

dramatist noun = **playwright**, screenwriter, scriptwriter, dramaturge

dramatize verb = **exaggerate**, overstate, overdo, lay it on or lay it on thick (slang), play to the gallery

drape verb = **cover**, wrap, fold, cloak, swathe

drastic adjective = **extreme**, severe, harsh, radical • It's time for drastic action.

draw verb **1** = **sketch**, paint, trace • to draw pictures of flowers

2 = **move**, pull • as the car drew away

3 = **pull**, drag, haul • He drew his chair nearer the fire.

4 = **take out**, extract, pull out

5 = **attract**, influence, invite, persuade, induce, entice, allure, evoke, elicit

6 = **deduce**, make, take, derive, infer

▷ **draw away** See **distract**

▷ **draw back** See **retreat**

▷ **draw off** See **drain**

▷ **draw on** = **make use of**, use, employ, extract, exploit, fall back on, have recourse to, rely on, take from

▷ **draw out** = **extend**, stretch, prolong, lengthen, drag out, make longer, protract, spin out, string out

▷ **draw up** = **draft**, prepare, frame, compose, formulate, write out; = **halt**, stop, bring to a stop, pull up

▶ noun **7** (Informal) = **attraction**, pull (informal), lure, enticement

8 = **tie**, deadlock, gridlock, impasse, stalemate, dead heat, saw-off (Canad)

See also: **earn, tug**

INFORMALLY SPEAKING
beat to the draw: manage to do something before someone else
draw out: extend too much
draw the line: set a limit

drawback noun = **problem**, trouble, difficulty, snag, hitch • The only drawback was that the apartment was too small.

See also: **catch, disadvantage, fault, handicap**

drawing noun = **picture**, study, cartoon, outline, portrayal, representation, sketch, depiction, illustration

drawn adjective = **tense**, tired, haggard, pinched, stressed, worn

dread verb **1** = **fear**, quail, tremble, shudder, cringe at, have cold feet (informal), shrink from

▶ noun **2** = **fear**, terror, alarm, horror, dismay, apprehension, trepidation, fright

dreadful adjective = **terrible**, awful, horrendous, appalling, atrocious, ghastly, frightful • He told us the dreadful news

OPPOSITE: wonderful

See also: **horrible**

dream noun **1** = **vision**, hallucination, trance • He had a dream about horses.

2 = **daydream**, fantasy • rich beyond her wildest dreams

3 = **ambition**, goal, hope, aim, wish, desire, aspiration

4 = **delight**, beauty, treasure, joy, gem, pleasure, marvel

▶ verb **5** = **have dreams**, think, imagine, fancy, envisage, visualize, conjure up, hallucinate

6 = **daydream**, fantasize, build castles in the air or build castles in Spain, stargaze

INFORMALLY SPEAKING
a dream come true: exactly what one would have wanted
dream up: have an idea, especially an unusual one
like a dream: perfectly

dreamer noun = **idealist**, visionary, utopian, escapist, daydreamer, fantasist, Walter Mitty

dreamy adjective **1** = **vague**, absent, faraway, abstracted, daydreaming, pensive, preoccupied, with one's head in the clouds
2 = **impractical**, speculative, imaginary, fanciful, airy-fairy, quixotic

dreary adjective = **dull**, boring, drab, uneventful, tedious, monotonous, humdrum • *the dreary winter months*
OPPOSITE: exciting
See also: **gloomy**

dregs plural noun **1** = **sediment**, waste, deposit, residue, scum, dross, grounds, lees, residuum
2 = **scum**, rabble, good-for-nothings, riffraff

drench verb = **soak**, flood, wet, drown, steep, saturate, swamp, inundate, souse

drenched See **wet**

dress noun **1** = **garment**, gown, robe • *a black dress*
2 = **clothing**, clothes, costume, attire (formal), garb (formal) • *casual dress*
▶ verb **3** = **put on**, clothe, attire, garb (formal) • *She often dressed in black.*
OPPOSITE: undress
4 = **bandage**, treat, wrap, swathe, Band-Aid (trademark), bind up
5 = **arrange**, prepare, adjust, align, straighten, get ready

dressmaker noun = **seamstress**, tailor, couturier

dribble verb **1** = **run**, drop, leak, trickle, drip, seep, ooze, fall in drops
2 = **drool**, drivel, slaver, slobber

dried-up See **dry**

drift verb **1** = **float**, go or go aimlessly, coast, wander, stray, meander, waft, be carried along
2 = **pile up**, drive, gather, accumulate, amass, bank up
▶ noun **3** = **pile**, bank, mass, mound, heap, accumulation

4 = **meaning**, import, direction, intention, significance, thrust, tendency, purport, gist

drifter noun = **wanderer**, bum (informal), beachcomber, hobo, itinerant, rolling stone, vagrant

drill noun **1** = **boring tool**, bit, borer, gimlet
2 = **training**, practice, exercise, preparation, discipline, instruction, repetition
▶ verb **3** = **bore**, penetrate, puncture, pierce, perforate, sink in
4 = **train**, coach, practise, exercise, teach, discipline, instruct, rehearse

drink verb **1** = **swallow**, sip, guzzle, gulp, imbibe, quaff, sup • *I drank some water.*
2 = **booze** (informal), tipple • *He drinks little and eats carefully.*
▶ noun **3** = **beverage**, liquid, potion, refreshment
4 = **alcohol**, booze (informal), hooch or hootch (informal), liquor, spirits, the bottle (informal)
5 = **glass**, draft, cup

drip verb **1** = **drop**, splash, trickle, dribble • *water dripping from the kitchen tap*
▶ noun **2** = **drop**, bead, droplet • *drips of water*
3 (Informal) = **weakling**, mama's boy (informal)

drive verb **1** = **operate**, work, power, pilot, propel, steer • *Don't drive a car after taking this medication.*
2 = **force**, lead, push, prompt, spur, motivate, compel • *Her love of acting drove her into a life in the theatre.*
3 = **thrust**, sink, knock, hammer, ram • *I used the sledgehammer to drive in the pegs.*
4 = **push**, send, urge, propel, herd, hurl, impel
▷ **drive into** See **crash**
▷ **drive off** See **repel**
▷ **drive someone up the wall** See **pester**
▶ noun **5** = **run**, trip, ride, journey, spin, excursion, jaunt • *We might go for a drive on Sunday.*

6 = determination, energy, initiative, motivation, ambition, enterprise, vigour • *We remember her great drive and enthusiasm.*
7 = campaign, action, effort, push (*informal*), appeal, crusade
See also: **blow**, **chase**, **go**, **make**, **reduce**

drivel noun **1 = nonsense**, garbage (*informal*), trash, rubbish, hogwash, gibberish, hot air (*informal*), poppycock (*informal*)
▶ *verb* **2 = babble**, ramble, gab (*informal*), blether, prate

driving adjective **= forceful**, violent, energetic, dynamic, vigorous, compelling, sweeping

drizzle noun **1 = fine rain**, mist
▶ *verb* **2 = rain**, spray, shower, sprinkle, spot with rain *or* spit with rain

droll adjective **= amusing**, funny, humorous, whimsical, comical, entertaining, jocular, waggish

drone verb **1 = hum**, buzz, purr, vibrate, thrum, whirr
▷ **drone on = speak monotonously**, chant, spout, intone, be boring, talk interminably
▶ *noun* **2 = hum**, buzz, vibration, purr, murmuring, thrum, whirring

drool verb **= dribble**, salivate, drivel, slaver, slobber, water at the mouth
▷ **drool over = gloat over**, gush, dote on, make much of, rave about (*informal*)

droop verb **= sag**, drop, sink, hang *or* hang down, bend, dangle, fall down

drooping See **limp**

drop verb **1 = fall**, sink, tumble, plummet, descend • *She let her head drop.*
2 = decrease, fall, decline, sink, slump, tumble, plummet, diminish • *Temperatures can drop to freezing at night.*
OPPOSITE: rise
3 = drip, trickle, dribble, fall in drops
4 = discontinue, kick (*informal*),

quit, axe (*informal*), relinquish, give up
▷ **drop off = set down**, leave, deliver, let off; (*Informal*) **= fall asleep**, nod *or* nod off, snooze (*informal*), doze *or* doze off, have forty winks (*informal*); **= decrease**, decline, diminish, dwindle, lessen, slacken, fall off
▷ **drop out = leave**, stop, quit, withdraw, abandon, fall by the wayside, give up
▷ **drop out of sight** See **disappear**
▶ *noun* **5 = droplet**, bead, drip • *a drop of blue ink*
6 = dash, shot (*informal*), spot, sip, mouthful, swig (*informal*), trace, trickle
7 = decrease, cut, decline, slump, reduction, downturn, deterioration, fall-off, lowering
8 = fall, plunge, descent
See also: **ball**, **blob**, **deposit**, **dump**, **lose**, **lower**

INFORMALLY SPEAKING
a drop in the bucket: a comparatively small amount
drop out: leave school without finishing courses
drop the ball: make a mess of what one is doing

droplet noun **= drop**, drip, blob

drought noun **= dry spell**, dehydration, dryness, aridity

drove noun **= herd**, company, crowd, collection, mob, flock, swarm, throng, multitude, horde

drown verb **1 = drench**, flood, sink, swamp, engulf, inundate, deluge, submerge, immerse, go under
2 = overpower, overcome, overwhelm, stifle, obliterate, muffle, deaden, swallow up, wipe out

drowsy adjective **= sleepy**, heavy, tired, lethargic, dopey (*slang*), dozy, half asleep, somnolent, torpid

drudge noun **= menial**, servant, factotum, worker, slave, toiler

drudgery noun **= menial labour**, donkey-work, grind (*informal*), labour, hard work, toil, slog

drug noun **1** = **medication**, medicine • *a new drug in the fight against AIDS*
RELATED WORD
combining form: pharmaco-
2 = **dope** (*slang*), narcotic, stimulant • *She was sure her cousin was taking drugs.*
▶ verb **3** = **dose**, treat, dope (*slang*), medicate, administer a drug
4 = **knock out**, poison, numb, deaden, anesthetize, stupefy

drum verb **1** = **beat**, tap, tattoo, rap, reverberate, throb, pulsate
▷ **drum into** = **drive home**, reiterate, din into, hammer away, harp on, instill into

drunk adjective **1** = **intoxicated** (*formal*), tipsy • *He got drunk.*
OPPOSITE: sober
▶ noun **2** = **drunkard**, alcoholic, boozer (*informal*) • *A drunk lay in the alley.*

drunkard noun = **drinker**, drunk, alcoholic, lush (*slang*), wino (*informal*), dipsomaniac, tippler

drunkenness noun = **intoxication**, alcoholism, bibulousness, dipsomania, inebriation, insobriety, intemperance

dry adjective **1** = **dehydrated**, arid, parched, dried-up • *The path was dry after the sunshine.*
OPPOSITE: wet
2 = **dull**, plain, boring, dreary, tedious, tiresome, monotonous, uninteresting
3 = **sarcastic**, low-key, sly, deadpan, droll
▶ verb **4** = **dehydrate**, drain • *Wash and dry the lettuce.*
OPPOSITE: moisten
▷ **dry out**, **dry up** = **become dry**, wither, wilt, harden, shrivel up, wizen
See also: **barren**

dual adjective = **twofold**, double, twin, duplicate, duplex, binary, matched, paired

dub See **name**

dubious adjective **1** = **suspect**, suspicious, questionable, unreliable, crooked, dishonest • *a rather dubious claim*
2 = **unsure**, nervous, suspicious, skeptical, undecided, doubtful, unconvinced • *My parents were a bit dubious about it all.*
See also: **improbable**, **uncertain**

duck verb **1** = **bob**, drop, lower, bow, bend, dodge, crouch, stoop
2 = **plunge**, dive, dip, wet, dunk, douse, submerge, immerse, souse
3 (*Informal*) = **dodge**, avoid, escape, shun, evade, sidestep, shirk
▷ **duck out of** See **avoid**

dud (*Informal*) ▶ noun **1** = **failure**, flop (*informal*), washout (*informal*)
▶ adjective **2** = **useless**, broken, failed, worthless, inoperative

dudgeon noun
▷ **in high dudgeon** = **indignant**, angry, resentful, choked, fuming, offended, ticked off (*informal*), vexed

due adjective **1** = **expected**, scheduled
2 = **payable**, outstanding, unpaid, in arrears, owed, owing
3 = **fitting**, appropriate, proper, suitable, justified, rightful, deserved, merited, well-earned
▶ noun **4** = **right** or **rights**, privilege, deserts, merits
▶ adverb **5** = **directly**, dead, straight, exactly, undeviatingly

duel noun **1** = **single combat**, affair of honour
2 = **contest**, fight, competition, clash, encounter, engagement, rivalry, head-to-head
▶ verb **3** = **fight**, struggle, rival, contest, compete, clash, contend, lock horns, vie with

dues plural noun = **membership fee**, charge, fee, contribution, levy, charges

dull adjective **1** = **boring**, drab, tedious, monotonous, humdrum, uninteresting • *I found the play rather dull.*
OPPOSITE: interesting
2 = **drab**, sombre, gloomy,

d

d

muted, subdued • *a dark, dull blue colour*
OPPOSITE: bright
3 = **cloudy**, murky, overcast, leaden • *It seems as if it's always dull and raining.*
4 = **stupid**, dense, dim-witted (*informal*), slow, thick, unintelligent
5 = **lifeless**, blank, listless, indifferent, apathetic, unresponsive, passionless
6 = **blunt**, blunted, unsharpened
▶ *verb* **7** = **relieve**, moderate, soften, blunt, alleviate, lessen, allay, take the edge off
See also: **dim, dreary, fade, flat, numb, sleepy, stuffy**

dullness *See* **boredom**

duly *adverb* **1** = **properly**, correctly, appropriately, accordingly, suitably, rightfully, fittingly, deservedly, befittingly, decorously
2 = **on time**, at the proper time, punctually

dumb *adjective* **1** = **mute**, silent, speechless • *We were all struck dumb for a minute.*
2 (*Informal*) = **stupid**, thick, dense, dull, foolish, asinine, dim-witted (*informal*), unintelligent

dumbfounded *adjective* = **amazed**, speechless, staggered, overwhelmed, astonished, astounded, flabbergasted (*informal*), lost for words, nonplussed, stunned

dumbness *See* **silence**

dummy *noun* **1** = **model**, figure, form, mannequin, manikin
2 = **copy**, counterfeit, substitute, duplicate, sham, imitation
3 (*Slang*) = **fool**, idiot, blockhead, dork (*slang*), dunce, nitwit (*informal*), oaf, schmuck (*slang*), simpleton
▶ *adjective* **4** = **imitation**, fake, false, artificial, mock, bogus, phony (*informal*), sham, simulated

dump *verb* **1** = **get rid of**, discharge, jettison, dispose of, throw away, throw out • *The*

thieves were arrested when they dumped the stolen car in the police station's parking lot.
2 = **drop**, deposit • *We dumped our bags at the hotel and went for a walk.*
▶ *noun* **3** = **landfill**, transfer station, rubbish heap, junkyard, refuse heap, garbage dump, nuisance grounds (*Canad*), dumping ground, slag pit
4 (*Informal*) = **pigsty**, mess, slum, hovel
See also: **discard**

dumpy *adjective* (*Informal*) = **dowdy**, frowzy, frumpy, homely (*US*), unfashionable

dunce *noun* = **simpleton**, blockhead, moron, dunderhead, ignoramus, thickhead

dungeon *noun* = **prison**, cell, vault, cage, oubliette

dupe *verb* = **trick**, fool, con (*informal*), cheat, deceive, delude, play a trick on • *I was duped into believing the autograph was authentic.*
See also: **take in, trap**

duplicate *adjective* **1** = **identical**, twin, twofold, corresponding, matched, matching
▶ *noun* **2** = **copy**, double, clone, reproduction, replica, photocopy, facsimile, carbon copy
▶ *verb* **3** = **copy**, double, repeat, clone, replicate, reproduce

durability *noun* = **durableness**, endurance, persistence, constancy, imperishability, permanence

durable *adjective* = **long-lasting**, strong, tough, persistent, reliable, resistant, enduring, sturdy, dependable, hard-wearing

duration *noun* = **length**, time, term, period, stretch, span, spell, extent

duress *noun* = **pressure**, threat, constraint, coercion, compulsion

dusk *noun* = **twilight**, evening, dark, sunset, nightfall,

sundown, eventide, gloaming
(*Scot, poetic*)

dusky *adjective* **1 = dark**, dark-
complexioned, sable, swarthy
2 = dim, obscure, gloomy,
murky, shady, cloudy, shadowy,
tenebrous, twilit

dust *noun* **1 = grime**, powder, grit,
particles
▶ *verb* **2 = sprinkle**, cover,
spread, spray, powder, scatter,
sift, dredge

dusty *adjective* **= dirty**, unclean,
grubby, scuzzy (*slang*), sooty,
unswept

dutiful *adjective* **= conscientious**,
respectful, devoted, obedient,
submissive, reverential

duty *noun* **1 = responsibility**,
obligation • *Citizens have a duty
to vote.*
2 = job, role, responsibility,
assignment • *He carried out his
duties conscientiously.*
3 = tax, tariff, levy, excise
• *customs duties*
4 = loyalty, respect, allegiance,
deference, obedience, reverence
▷ **on duty = at work**, busy,
engaged, on active service, on
the job (*informal*)
See also: **function, part, task,
work**

dwarf *verb* **1 = tower above**
or **tower over**, dominate,
diminish, overshadow
▶ *adjective* **2 = miniature**,
small, baby, tiny, diminutive,
undersized, bonsai
▶ *noun* **3 = midget**, pygmy *or*
pigmy, Lilliputian, Tom
Thumb

dweeb *noun* (*Slang*) **= idiot**, dope
(*slang*), fool, geek, nerd, slang,
doofus (*slang*), dunce

dwell *verb* **= live**, abide, lodge,
reside, inhabit

dwelling *noun* **= home**, house,
pad (*slang*), residence, lodging,
abode, habitation, domicile,
quarters

dwindle *verb* **= lessen**, decline,
decrease, shrink, fade, diminish,
wane, subside, die away, peter
out, taper off

dye *noun* **1 = colouring**, colour,
stain, pigment, tint, tinge,
colourant
▶ *verb* **2 = colour**, stain, pigment,
tint, tinge

dying *adjective* **= expiring**, failing,
moribund, at death's door, *in
extremis* (*Latin*), not long for this
world
▷ **be dying for = long for**, ache
for, hunger for, pine for, yearn
for • *I'm dying for a breath of fresh air!*

dynamic *adjective* **= energetic**,
powerful, vital, go-ahead, lively,
high-powered, forceful, go-
getting (*informal*)

dynasty *noun* **= empire**,
government, rule, house,
regime, sovereignty

d

Ee

each *adjective* **1** = **every**
▶ *pronoun* **2** = **every one**, each and every one, each one, one and all
▶ *adverb* **3** = **apiece**, respectively, individually, for each, per capita, per head, per person, to each

eager *adjective* = **keen**, anxious, enthusiastic, avid, ardent, raring to go (*informal*) • *She is eager to earn some extra money*
See also: **impatient, ready, willing**

eagerness *noun* = **keenness**, hunger, enthusiasm, thirst, zeal, impatience, yearning, ardour, fervour

ear *noun* = **sensitivity**, taste, discrimination, perception, appreciation

earlier *adverb* **1** = **before**, previously
▶ *adjective* **2** = **previous**, former, past, prior, preceding

earliest *See* **first**

early *adjective* **1** = **premature**, advance, untimely • *You're not late - I'm early!*
OPPOSITE: late
2 = **primitive**, primeval • *the early 1990s*
▶ *adverb* **3** = **ahead of time**, prematurely, beforehand, in advance, in good time • *We left early so we wouldn't have to line up*

earmark *verb* = **set aside**, reserve, label, flag, designate, allocate, mark out

earn *verb* **1** = **make**, get, obtain, bring in • *He earns a lot more than I do.*
2 = **win**, acquire, attain (*formal*) • *She earned the respect of her team.*
See also: **deserve, gain, merit**

earnest *adjective* = **serious**, grave, intent, solemn, sincere, thoughtful, resolute, resolved
▶ *noun*
▷ **in earnest** = **seriously**, sincerely, truthfully

earnings *plural noun* = **income**, pay, salary, remuneration, proceeds, profits, receipts, takings, wages

earth *noun* **1** = **world**, planet, globe • *the tallest mountain on earth*
RELATED WORD
adjective: terrestrial **72** = **soil**, ground, dirt, turf, clay, topsoil, loam • *He filled a pot with earth and planted the seeds in it.*

earthenware *noun* = **crockery**, pottery, terracotta, ceramics, pots

earthly *adjective* = **worldly**, human, material, secular, mortal, temporal

earthy *adjective* = **crude**, robust, raunchy (*slang*), coarse, bawdy, unsophisticated, ribald, uninhibited

ease *noun* **1** = **easiness**, facility, simplicity, readiness, effortlessness • *He passed his test with ease.*
2 = **content**, peace, quiet, comfort, happiness, leisure, serenity, tranquillity, peace of mind
3 = **rest**, leisure, relaxation, repose, restfulness
▶ *verb* **4** = **relieve**, calm, relax, abate, slacken • *The doctor gave him medication to ease the pain.*
5 = **edge**, lower, guide, inch, creep, squeeze, manoeuvre • *He eased the door open and peered outside.*
See also: **moderate**

easily *adverb* = **without difficulty**, smoothly, readily, comfortably, effortlessly, with ease, with one hand tied behind one's back

▷ **easily offended** See **sensitive, touchy**

▷ **easily upset** See **sensitive**

easy adjective **1 = simple**, light, smooth, straightforward, painless • *The software is very easy to install.*

OPPOSITE: hard

2 = carefree, quiet, comfortable, leisurely, relaxed • *He has not had an easy life.*

3 = tolerant, mild, lenient, easy-going, indulgent, permissive, unoppressive

See also: **fluent, informal**

| INFORMALLY SPEAKING
| **easy come, easy go**: easily obtained and easily lost
| **easy does it**: act gently
| **take it easy**: relax

easy-going adjective **= relaxed**, easy, casual, tolerant, laid-back (*informal*), carefree, happy-go-lucky, nonchalant, even-tempered, placid, undemanding

eat verb **1 = consume**, swallow, ingest, chew, gobble, scoff (*slang*), devour, munch • *For lunch he ate a cheese sandwich.*

2 = have a meal, feed, dine, picnic, chow down (*slang*), take nourishment • *We like to eat early.*

3 = destroy, dissolve, erode, decay, rot, corrode, waste away, wear away

▷ **eat away = destroy**, dissolve, erode, rot, corrode, wear away • *The front of the car had been eaten away by rust.*

eavesdrop verb **= listen in**, monitor, spy, overhear, snoop (*informal*)

eavesdropping See **nosy**

ebb verb **1 = flow back**, retire, withdraw, retreat, wane, recede, subside, go out

2 = decline, flag, decrease, diminish, dwindle, lessen, fade away, fall away, peter out

▶ noun **3 = flowing back**, withdrawal, retreat, wane,

going out, low tide, low water, subsidence

eccentric adjective **1 = strange**, bizarre, weird, outrageous, quirky, outlandish, screwball (*slang*), ding-a-ling (*slang*) • *His math teacher was considered a bit eccentric.*

▶ noun **2 = crank** (*informal*), character (*informal*), screwball (*slang*), ding-a-ling (*slang*) • *He's always been regarded as a bit of an eccentric.*

eccentricity noun **= oddity**, irregularity, abnormality, quirk, foible, caprice, capriciousness, idiosyncrasy, peculiarity

ecclesiastic noun **1 = clergyman**, minister, cleric, priest, pastor, churchman, holy man, man of the cloth, parson

▶ adjective **2** Also **ecclesiastical** **= clerical**, religious, holy, spiritual, divine, pastoral, priestly

echelon See **rank**

echo noun **1 = repetition**, answer, reverberation

2 = copy, parallel, reflection, reproduction, imitation, mirror image, reiteration

▶ verb **3 = repeat**, resound, reverberate

4 = copy, recall, reflect, mirror, resemble, parallel, ape, imitate

eclipse noun **1 = obscuring**, extinction, darkening, dimming, shading

▶ verb **2 = surpass**, exceed, outshine, excel, outdo, transcend, put in the shade (*informal*)

economic adjective **1 = financial**, commercial, budgetary • *the need for economic reform*

2 = profitable, productive, viable, money-making, profit-making, remunerative

See also: **economical**

economical adjective

1 = economic, cheap, inexpensive, cost-effective • *Our car may not be fast, but it's very economical.*

2 = thrifty, careful, prudent,

frugal • *He's never been very economical about shopping for clothes.*
3 = efficient, cost-effective, money-saving, sparing, time-saving

economics *See* **finance**

economize *verb* = **cut back**, save, be economical, be frugal, draw in one's horns, retrench, scrimp, tighten one's belt, cheap out (*informal*)

economy *noun* = **thrift**, restraint, prudence, frugality (*formal*) • *improvements in the fuel economy of new cars*

ecstasy *noun* = **rapture**, delight, joy, bliss, euphoria, elation, exaltation • *his feeling of ecstasy after winning the medal*
See also: **happiness, heaven**

ecstatic *adjective* = **rapturous**, joyous, euphoric, blissful, elated, enraptured, entranced, in seventh heaven, on cloud nine (*informal*), overjoyed

eddy *noun* **1 = swirl**, undertow, whirlpool, vortex, counter-current, counterflow
▶ *verb* **2 = swirl**, whirl

edge *noun* **1 = border**, margin, rim, lip, boundary, fringe, perimeter, brim, periphery • *on the edge of the forest*
OPPOSITE: centre
2 = sharpness, point, force, bite, effectiveness, incisiveness, keenness
3 = advantage, lead, dominance, superiority, ascendancy, upper hand
on edge = nervous, tense, impatient, edgy, apprehensive, irritable, ill at ease, keyed up, on tenterhooks, wired (*slang*)
▶ *verb* **4 = inch**, creep, sidle • *He edged toward the phone, ready to grab it if it rang.*
5 = border, fringe, hem
See also: **bank, ease, outskirts, side**

| INFORMALLY SPEAKING
on edge: nervous and tense
take the edge off: take away the sharpness of; blunt

edgy *adjective* = **nervous**, anxious,

tense, restive, irritable, ill at ease, keyed up, on edge, on tenterhooks, wired (*slang*)

edible *adjective* = **eatable**, good, harmless, palatable, wholesome, digestible, fit to eat

edict *noun* = **decree**, order, law, act, ruling, command, injunction, proclamation

edifice *noun* = **building**, house, construction, structure, erection

edify *verb* = **instruct**, school, improve, guide, teach, inform, educate, nurture, enlighten

edit *verb* = **revise**, correct, adapt, rewrite, polish, condense, emend

edition *noun* = **version**, issue, program (*TV, radio*), number, copy, volume, impression, printing

educate *verb* = **teach**, school, develop, improve, train, inform, discipline, instruct, enlighten, tutor, civilize

educated *adjective* **1 = cultured**, intellectual, cultivated, learned • *an educated, tolerant, and reasonable person*
2 = taught, informed, coached, instructed, nurtured, schooled, tutored

education *noun* = **teaching**, training, instruction, schooling, coaching • *the importance of a good education*
See also: **knowledge**

educational *adjective* = **instructive**, cultural, informative, edifying, educative, enlightening, improving

eerie *adjective* = **frightening**, mysterious, strange, scary (*informal*), weird, spooky (*informal*), creepy (*informal*), ghostly, uncanny, unearthly

efface *verb* = **obliterate**, cancel, destroy, erase, delete, eradicate, blot out, expunge, rub out, wipe out

effect *noun* **1 = result**, fruit, consequence, upshot, end result • *the effect that divorce has on children*
See also: **influence**

2 = **operation**, force, action, execution, enforcement, implementation
3 = **impression**, impact, sense, tenor, significance, essence
▶ *verb* **4** = **bring about**, complete, produce, perform, achieve, execute, accomplish, fulfill

| CONFUSABLES
Effect means *result*, and is usually a noun.
Affect means *influence*, and is a verb.

effective *adjective* **1** = **efficient**, active, capable, useful, adequate, productive, competent, serviceable
2 = **in operation**, current, active, operative, in effect, in force
3 = **powerful**, impressive, forceful, persuasive, cogent, compelling, convincing, telling
effectively *See* **well**
effectiveness *See* **value**
effects *plural noun* = **belongings**, property, gear, paraphernalia, goods, possessions, things
effeminate *adjective* = **womanly**, camp (*informal*), weak, soft, tender, feminine, sissy, unmanly, womanish
effervescent *adjective*
1 = **bubbling**, sparkling, frothy, carbonated, fizzy, foaming
2 = **lively**, animated, enthusiastic, bubbly, exuberant, irrepressible, ebullient, vivacious
effete *adjective* = **decadent**, weak, feeble, ineffectual, dissipated, enfeebled, spoiled
efficacious *adjective* = **effective**, powerful, successful, efficient, potent, useful, adequate, productive, operative
efficiency *noun* = **competence**, power, economy, capability, productivity, effectiveness, proficiency, adeptness
efficient *adjective* = **competent**, effective, organized, economical, businesslike, productive • *The new hatchback has a much more efficient engine.*
OPPOSITE: inefficient

See also: **able, capable, proficient**
efficiently *See* **well**
effigy *noun* = **likeness**, figure, guy, picture, image, icon, portrait, statue, representation, idol, dummy
effluent *noun* = **waste**, pollutant, sewage, effluvium
effort *noun* **1** = **exertion**, work, energy, trouble, application • *It took a lot of effort, but we managed in the end.*
2 = **attempt**, bid, struggle, stab (*informal*), blitz • *an unsuccessful effort to ban Sunday shopping*
See also: **enterprise, hassle, labour, try**
effortless *adjective* = **easy**, simple, smooth, painless, uncomplicated, plain sailing, undemanding
effrontery *noun* = **insolence**, nerve, arrogance, cheek (*informal*), presumption, audacity, brazenness, impertinence, impudence, temerity
effusive *adjective*
= **demonstrative**, lavish, expansive, exuberant, ebullient, unrestrained, gushing, unreserved
egg *verb*
▷ **egg on** = **encourage**, urge, push, prompt, spur, incite, prod, goad, exhort
egocentric *adjective* = **self-centred**, selfish, egoistic, egoistical, egotistic, egotistical
egoistic *See* **selfish**
egoistical *See* **selfish**
egotism, egoism *noun* = **self-centredness**, self-esteem, vanity, selfishness, self-interest, narcissism, self-importance, conceitedness, self-absorption
egotist, egoist *noun*
= **egomaniac**, bighead (*informal*), boaster, braggart, narcissist
egotistic, egotistical, egoistic, egoistical
▶ *adjective* = **self-centred**, vain, self-absorbed, egocentric, narcissistic, boasting, conceited,

full of oneself, self-important

egress noun (Formal) = **exit**, withdrawal, departure, exodus, way out

eject verb = **throw out**, remove, oust, expel, banish, evict, drive out, turn out

ejection noun = **expulsion**, deportation, exile, removal, eviction, banishment

eke verb
▷ **eke out** = **be sparing with**, husband, economize on, stretch out

elaborate adjective
1 = **complicated**, complex, detailed, involved, intricate • an elaborate research project
OPPOSITE: simple
2 = **ornate**, fancy, fussy • elaborate wooden carvings
▶ verb 3 = **expand**, develop, enlarge • He promised to elaborate on what had been said last night.
▷ **elaborate on** See **enlarge on**, **expand on**
See also: **sophisticated**

elapse verb = **pass**, lapse, glide by, go by, roll by, slip away

elastic adjective 1 = **stretchy**, plastic, resilient, rubbery, supple, pliable, pliant, springy, tensile
2 = **adaptable**, flexible, variable, tolerant, compliant, adjustable, supple, accommodating, yielding

elated adjective = **joyful**, ecstatic, jubilant, delighted, euphoric, gleeful, exhilarated, overjoyed

elation noun = **joy**, delight, ecstasy, bliss, euphoria, glee, jubilation, exhilaration, rapture, high spirits

elbow noun 1 = **joint**, angle
▷ **elbow room** = **scope**, play, space, room, freedom, latitude, leeway
▶ verb 2 = **push**, knock, nudge, shove, jostle

elder adjective 1 = **older**, senior, first-born
▶ noun 2 = **older person**, senior

elect verb = **choose**, vote, pick, determine, select, appoint,

prefer, opt for, settle on

election noun = **voting**, vote, choice, selection, appointment, judgment, preference

elector noun = **voter**, constituent, selector

electric adjective = **charged**, exciting, thrilling, tense, dynamic, rousing, stimulating, stirring

electrify verb = **startle**, shock, excite, stir, thrill, jolt, astound, invigorate, galvanize

electrifying See **exciting**

elegance noun = **style**, taste, luxury, dignity, grace, grandeur, refinement, exquisiteness, gracefulness

elegant adjective = **stylish**, fine, delicate, chic, refined, handsome, exquisite, polished, graceful, tasteful

element noun = **component**, part, unit, factor, section, ingredient, constituent, subdivision
▷ **be in one's element** = **be in one's natural environment**, be in one's domain, be in one's field, be in one's habitat, be in one's medium, be in one's milieu, be in one's sphere, feel at home

elementary adjective
= **simple**, clear, easy, plain, straightforward, rudimentary, uncomplicated

elements plural noun 1 = **basics**, essentials, foundations, fundamentals, nuts and bolts (informal), principles, rudiments
2 = **weather conditions**, atmospheric conditions, powers of nature

elevate verb 1 = **raise**, lift, heighten, hoist, uplift, lift up
2 = **promote**, advance, upgrade, prefer, exalt, aggrandize

elevated adjective = **high-minded**, grand, inflated, lofty, dignified, noble, sublime, exalted, high-flown

elevation noun 1 = **promotion**, advancement, aggrandizement, exaltation, preferment, upgrading

2 = **altitude**, pitch, height

elicit *verb* **1** = **bring about**, cause, evolve, derive, bring forth, bring out, bring to light, call forth, give rise to

2 = **obtain**, exact, extract, evoke, extort, wrest, draw out

eligible *adjective* = **qualified**, fit, appropriate, proper, acceptable, worthy, suitable, desirable, preferable

eliminate *verb* **1** = **get rid of**, remove, eradicate, cut out, do away with, stamp out • *We've eliminated two of the four options so far.*

2 = **knock out**, put out • *Our team was eliminated in the first round.* See also: **banish, exclude**

elite *noun* = **best**, pick, cream, flower, nobility, aristocracy, *crème de la crème* (French), upper class

elitist *adjective* = **snobbish**, exclusive, selective

elixir *noun* = **panacea**, nostrum

elocution *noun* = **diction**, speech, delivery, pronunciation, oratory, articulation, declamation, enunciation, speechmaking

elongate *verb* = **make longer**, extend, stretch, prolong, lengthen, draw out, protract

elope *verb* = **run away**, leave, escape, disappear, bolt, abscond, decamp, run off, slip away, steal away

eloquence *noun* = **expressiveness**, expression, rhetoric, oratory, fluency, forcefulness, persuasiveness, way with words

eloquent *adjective* **1** = **silver-tongued**, articulate, fluent, forceful, moving, persuasive, stirring, well-expressed

2 = **expressive**, meaningful, vivid, suggestive, telling

elsewhere *adverb* = **in another place** *or* **to another place**, away, abroad, hence (*archaic*), not here, somewhere else

elucidate *verb* = **clarify**, explain, illustrate, illuminate, expound, clear up, explicate, make plain,

shed light on *or* throw light on, spell out

elude *verb* **1** = **escape**, duck (*informal*), avoid, flee, evade, dodge, outrun, get away from

2 = **baffle**, escape, frustrate, puzzle, thwart, foil, stump, confound, be beyond (someone)

elusive *adjective* **1** = **difficult to catch**, slippery, tricky, shifty

2 = **indefinable**, subtle, intangible, fleeting, transient, transitory

emaciated *adjective* = **skeletal**, thin, lean, gaunt, scrawny, cadaverous, haggard, pinched, undernourished, wasted

emanate *verb* = **flow**, issue, spring, emerge, stem, proceed, arise, originate, derive, come forth

emancipate *verb* = **free**, release, deliver, liberate, set free, unchain, unfetter

emancipation *noun* = **freedom**, release, liberty, liberation, deliverance

embalm *verb* = **preserve**, mummify

embargo *noun* **1** = **ban**, bar, restriction, boycott, restraint, stoppage, prohibition, interdiction

▶ *verb* **2** = **ban**, stop, block, bar, prohibit, restrict, boycott

embark *verb* = **go aboard**, board ship, take ship

▷ **embark on, embark upon** = **begin**, start, launch, enter, commence, plunge into, set about, set out, take up

embarrass *verb* = **shame**, humiliate, disconcert, fluster • *You always embarrass me in front of my friends!*

embarrassed *adjective* = **ashamed**, awkward, red-faced, self-conscious, sheepish, humiliated • *I was embarrassed about making a fool of myself in public.* See also: **uncomfortable**

embarrassing *adjective* = **humiliating**, sensitive, uncomfortable, awkward,

shameful, compromising,
discomfiting, disconcerting,
mortifying, toe-curling (*informal*)
embarrassment *noun*
1 = **shame**, humiliation,
awkwardness, bashfulness, self-
consciousness • *I laughed loudly to
cover my embarrassment.*
2 = **predicament**, difficulty, bind
(*informal*), mess, scrape (*informal*),
pickle (*informal*)
embellish *verb* = **decorate**,
enhance, elaborate, enrich,
adorn, ornament, embroider,
festoon, beautify
embellishment *noun*
= **decoration**, enrichment,
ornament, enhancement,
exaggeration, embroidery,
adornment, elaboration,
ornamentation
embezzle *verb* = **misappropriate**,
steal, appropriate, misuse,
pilfer, filch, peculate, purloin,
rip off (*slang*)
embezzlement *noun*
= **misappropriation**, fraud,
theft, misuse, appropriation,
filching, peculation, pilfering,
stealing
embittered *adjective* = **resentful**,
angry, bitter, disaffected,
rancorous, soured, disillusioned,
with a chip on one's shoulder
(*informal*)
emblem *noun* = **symbol**, sign,
mark, image, crest, badge,
token, insignia
embodiment *noun*
= **personification**, example,
symbol, expression,
representation, avatar,
incarnation, epitome, exemplar
embody *verb* **1** = **personify**,
represent, symbolize, manifest,
exemplify, typify, stand for
2 = **incorporate**, include,
contain, combine, comprise,
encompass
embolden *verb* = **encourage**,
fire, strengthen, stir, stimulate,
inflame, invigorate, rouse
embrace *verb* **1** = **hug**, hold,
seize, squeeze, envelop, cuddle,
clasp, take in one's arms *or*

hold in one's arms
2 = **accept**, welcome, seize,
adopt, espouse, take on board,
take up
3 = **include**, involve, contain,
cover, comprise, encompass,
comprehend, take in
▶ *noun* **4** = **hug**, clinch (*slang*),
squeeze, cuddle, clasp
embroil *verb* = **involve**, implicate,
incriminate, mire, entangle,
ensnare, enmesh, mix up
embryo *noun* = **germ**, beginning,
root, nucleus, rudiment
emend *verb* = **revise**, improve,
correct, edit, amend, rectify
emendation *noun* = **revision**,
improvement, amendment,
correction, editing, rectification
emerge *verb* **1** = **come into view**,
issue, rise, appear, surface, arise,
emanate, come forth, spring up
2 = **become apparent**, transpire,
become known, come out, come
out in the wash, come to light,
crop up
emergence *noun* = **coming**,
rise, development, appearance,
arrival, advent, materialization
emergency *noun* = **crisis**, pinch
• *This is an emergency!*
emergent *See* **in the making**
emigrate *verb* = **move abroad**,
move, migrate
emigration *noun* = **departure**,
migration, exodus
eminence *noun* = **prominence**,
note, fame, importance,
distinction, greatness, prestige,
esteem, renown, repute
eminent *adjective* = **prominent**,
famous, renowned, well-known,
celebrated, high-ranking,
illustrious, distinguished,
noted, esteemed
emission *noun* = **giving off** *or*
giving out, transmission,
radiation, discharge, ejection,
ejaculation, exhalation,
shedding
emit *verb* = **give out**, release,
utter, exude, give off, send out
• *She blinked and emitted a long sigh.*
See also: **discharge**
emotion *noun* = **feeling**,

passion, sentiment, sensation, excitement, warmth, ardour, fervour, vehemence

emotional *adjective* **1** = **sensitive**, passionate, sentimental, temperamental, hot-blooded, demonstrative, excitable
2 = **moving**, poignant, sentimental, touching, heart-warming, emotive, affecting, stirring

emotive *adjective* = **sensitive**, controversial, delicate, touchy

empathize *verb*
▷ **empathize with** *See* **identify with**

empathy *See* **sympathy**

emphasis *noun* = **importance**, weight, accent, prominence • *too much emphasis on materialism*

emphasize *verb* = **stress**, highlight, underline, accent, accentuate, play up • *He emphasized the need for everyone to remain calm.*
See also: **feature**

emphatic *adjective* = **forceful**, positive, vigorous, pronounced, definite, unmistakable, unequivocal, insistent, categorical, resounding

empire *noun* = **kingdom**, domain, realm, commonwealth

empirical *adjective* = **first-hand**, experimental, practical, pragmatic, observed, experiential

employ *verb* **1** = **hire**, commission, appoint, engage (*formal*), take on • *He was employed by the singer as a bodyguard.*
2 = **use**, utilize, bring to bear, make use of • *the tactics employed by the police*
3 = **keep busy**, fill, engage, occupy, make use of, take up, use up
▶ *noun*
▷ **in the employ of** = **in the service of**, employed by, engaged by, hired by
See also: **busy**

employed *adjective* = **working**, active, busy, occupied, engaged, in a job, in employment, in work

employee *noun* = **worker**, hand • *the way they look after their employees*

employees *See* **labour**, **staff**

employer *noun* = **boss** • *a meeting with her employer to discuss the issue*

employers *See* **management**

employment *noun* **1** = **hiring**, engagement, recruitment, enlistment, taking on • *the employment of teenagers to work in restaurants*
2 = **use**, exercise, application, utilization, exertion
3 = **job**, work, trade, line, occupation, profession, vocation

emporium *noun* (*Old-fashioned*) = **store**, market, shop, warehouse, bazaar, mart

empower *verb* = **enable**, allow, commission, warrant, sanction, qualify, permit, delegate, license, entitle, authorize

emptiness *noun* **1** = **bareness**, waste, void, vacuum, vacancy, blankness, desolation
2 = **purposelessness**, futility, vanity, banality, hollowness, inanity, meaninglessness, senselessness, worthlessness
3 = **insincerity**, cheapness, hollowness, idleness

empty *adjective* **1** = **bare**, clear, blank, vacant, uninhabited, deserted, unfurnished • *The roads were empty.*
OPPOSITE: full
2 = **meaningless**, worthless, inane • *My life is empty without you.*
3 = **insincere**, cheap, hollow, idle
▶ *verb* **4** = **evacuate**, clear, drain, unload • *He emptied all the drawers before the guests arrived.*
OPPOSITE: fill
See also: **barren**, **discharge**, **fond**

empty-headed *adjective* = **scatterbrained**, silly, dizzy (*informal*), brainless, featherbrained, harebrained, vacuous

emulate *verb* = **imitate**, follow, rival, copy, echo, mimic, compete with

en masse *See* **together**

en route *adverb* = **on the way** *or*

along the way, in transit, on the road

enable *verb* = **allow**, warrant, sanction, qualify, permit, license, entitle, authorize, empower

enact *verb* **1** = **establish**, order, sanction, command, authorize, proclaim, legislate, decree, ordain
2 = **perform**, play, represent, portray, depict, act out, play the part of

enamoured *adjective* = **in love**, fond, captivated, charmed, enraptured, infatuated, smitten, taken

encampment *noun* = **camp**, base, campsite, bivouac, camping ground, cantonment, quarters, tents

encapsulate *verb* = **sum up**, digest, compress, summarize, epitomize, condense, abridge, précis

enchant *verb* = **fascinate**, charm, delight, captivate, enthrall, bewitch, spellbind, beguile, enrapture, ravish

enchanter *noun* = **sorcerer**, wizard, witch, magician, conjurer, magus, necromancer, warlock

enchanting *adjective*
= **fascinating**, attractive, lovely, pleasant, charming, delightful, alluring, bewitching, captivating, entrancing

encircle See **enclose, surround**

enclose *verb* **1** = **surround**, border, wrap, encircle, fence off, hem in • *The CDs arrived enclosed in a small brown box.*
2 = **send with**, include, insert, put in

encompass *verb* **1** = **surround**, ring, circle, enclose, envelop, encircle
2 = **include**, hold, contain, cover, admit, embrace, incorporate, comprise, take in

encounter *verb* **1** = **meet**, face, experience, confront, bump into (*informal*), chance upon, come upon, run across

▶ *noun* **2** = **meeting**, brush, confrontation, rendezvous
3 = **battle**, contest, conflict, clash, head-to-head, run-in (*informal*)

encourage *verb* **1** = **hearten**, cheer, reassure • *We were very encouraged by the response.*
OPPOSITE: discourage
2 = **support**, help, boost, aid, favour, incite • *the need to encourage people to be sensible*
See also: **back, push, strengthen**

encouragement *noun*
= **inspiration**, support, cheer, promotion, stimulus, stimulation, incitement, reassurance

encouraging *adjective*
= **promising**, good, bright, hopeful, rosy, cheerful, comforting, heartening, reassuring

encroach *verb* = **intrude**, invade, infringe, trespass, overstep, usurp, impinge, make inroads

encumber *verb* = **burden**, hamper, hinder, inconvenience, saddle, obstruct, impede, handicap, weigh down

end *noun* **1** = **finish**, close, stop, closure, ending, cessation, expiration, termination, expiry • *the end of the 20th century*
OPPOSITE: beginning
RELATED WORDS
adjectives: final, terminal, ultimate
2 = **extremity**, point, limit, edge, tip, extreme, extent, boundary, terminus • *the room at the end of the hallway*
3 = **purpose**, point, goal, aim, reason, object, intention, objective • *The army is being used for political ends.*
4 = **conclusion**, resolution, finale, ending, culmination, denouement
5 = **remnant**, scrap, butt, remainder, fragment, leftover, stub, oddment
6 = **destruction**, death, ruin, extinction, doom,

demise, extermination

▷ **end result** See **effect**

▶ verb 7 = **finish**, close, stop, conclude, cease, terminate, culminate, bring to an end, put a stop to, lower the boom (slang) • talks being held to end the players' strike

OPPOSITE: begin

See also: **back, complete, halt, lift, use**

| INFORMALLY SPEAKING
| **at loose ends**: not doing anything in particular
| **end up**: do or be, eventually
| **jump** or **go off the deep end**: act rashly
| **make both ends meet**: spend no more than you have
| **no end**: very much or very many

endanger verb = **put at risk**, risk, threaten, compromise, jeopardize • a dispute that could endanger the peace talks

endearing adjective = **attractive**, winning, sweet, cute, charming, engaging, lovable, captivating

endearment noun = **loving word**, sweet nothing

endeavour verb 1 = **try**, attempt, aim, struggle, strive, aspire, labour, make an effort, take pains

▶ noun 2 = **effort**, try, trial, attempt, venture, enterprise, undertaking

See also: **attempt, enterprise, seek, strive, try, undertaking**

ending noun = **finish**, end, close, conclusion, finale, completion, cessation, culmination, denouement

endless adjective = **eternal**, unlimited, infinite, continual, incessant, boundless, interminable, everlasting

endorse verb 1 = **approve**, back, support, champion, promote, recommend, advocate, authorize, ratify

2 = **sign**, countersign

endorsement noun 1 = **approval**, support, recommendation, advocacy, authorization, backing, favour, ratification, approbation, seal of approval

2 = **signature**, countersignature

endow verb = **provide**, give, award, fund, finance, donate, bestow, confer, bequeath

endowment noun = **provision**, award, grant, gift, donation, legacy, bequest, benefaction

endurable adjective = **bearable**, acceptable, sustainable, tolerable, sufferable

endurance noun 1 = **staying power**, strength, resolution, patience, stamina, perseverance, persistence, tenacity, fortitude, toleration

2 = **permanence**, stability, duration, longevity, continuity, durability

endure verb 1 = **go through**, stand, suffer, experience, cope with • He had to endure hours of discomfort.

2 = **last**, remain, survive, live on • Our friendship has endured through everything.

See also: **bear, continue, have, tolerate, undergo**

enduring adjective = **long-lasting**, persistent, lasting, perennial, steadfast, abiding, continuing, unfaltering, unwavering

enemy noun = **foe**, opponent, adversary, antagonist • She has many enemies in the government.

OPPOSITE: friend

energetic adjective = **vigorous**, animated, dynamic, spirited, tireless, indefatigable • She is an able, energetic, and very determined politician.

See also: **active, alive, lively, vital**

energy noun = **vigour**, life, drive, strength, spirit, vitality • I'm saving my energy for tomorrow.

See also: **activity, effort**

enforce verb = **impose**, apply, execute, implement, prosecute, administer, carry out, insist on, put into effect

engage verb 1 = **participate**, join, undertake, embark on, enter into, set about, take part

2 = occupy, involve, grip, absorb, preoccupy, engross
3 = captivate, arrest, gain, catch, fix
4 = employ, hire, appoint, retain, enlist, enrol, take on
5 (*Military*) = **begin battle with**, attack, meet, encounter, assail, fall on, join battle with, take on
6 = set going, apply, activate, energize, bring into operation, switch on

engaged *adjective* **1 = betrothed** (*archaic*), promised, affianced, pledged, spoken for
2 = occupied, busy, unavailable, employed, in use, tied up

engagement *noun*
1 = appointment, meeting, date, commitment, arrangement
2 = betrothal, troth (*archaic*)
3 = battle, fight, action, conflict, combat, encounter

engaging *adjective* = **charming**, winning, attractive, pleasing, likable *or* likeable, agreeable, fetching (*informal*), winsome

engender *verb* = **produce**, cause, create, generate, breed, induce, instigate, give rise to, lead to

engine *noun* = **machine**, mechanism, motor

engineer *verb* = **bring about**, plan, create, effect, plot, scheme, mastermind, devise, contrive

engrave *verb* **1 = carve**, cut, etch, inscribe, chisel
2 = fix, impress, embed, lodge, imprint, ingrain

engraving *noun* = **carving**, plate, inscription, etching, woodcut

engross *verb* = **absorb**, involve, engage, occupy, immerse, preoccupy

engrossed *adjective* = **absorbed**, lost, caught up, enthralled, fascinated, gripped, immersed, preoccupied, rapt, riveted

engulf *verb* = **immerse**, overwhelm, swamp, overrun, inundate, envelop, submerge, swallow up

enhance *verb* = **improve**, increase, lift, boost, strengthen, swell, reinforce, heighten, add to

enhancement *See* **improvement**

enigma *noun* = **mystery**, problem, puzzle, riddle, teaser, conundrum

enigmatic *adjective* = **mysterious**, obscure, cryptic, ambiguous, unfathomable, equivocal, inscrutable, puzzling

enjoy *verb* **1 = take pleasure in**, like, love, appreciate, relish, delight in, revel in, take pleasure from • *I haven't enjoyed a movie as much as that in ages!*
2 = have, use, own, experience, possess, be blessed with *or* be favoured with, have the benefit of, reap the benefits of

enjoyable *adjective* = **pleasurable**, pleasant, delightful, agreeable, entertaining, gratifying, satisfying, to one's liking

enjoyment *noun* = **pleasure**, fun, entertainment, delight, happiness, joy, amusement, relish, gratification, delectation

enlarge *verb* = **expand**, increase, extend, magnify, add to • *plans to enlarge the stadium*
▷ **enlarge on = expand on**, develop, elaborate on • *I'd like you to enlarge on that last point.*
See also: **elaborate**

enlargement *See* **growth**

enlighten *verb* = **inform**, advise, teach, counsel, educate, instruct, cause to understand, edify, make aware

enlightened *adjective* = **informed**, aware, reasonable, sophisticated, civilized, knowledgeable, open-minded, cultivated, educated

enlightenment *noun* = **understanding**, education, knowledge, awareness, instruction, insight, wisdom, learning, comprehension

enlist *verb* **1 = join up**, join, enter *or* enter into, register, volunteer, muster, enrol, sign up
2 = obtain, engage, recruit, procure

enlistment See **employment**

enliven verb = **cheer up**, spark, inspire, excite, stimulate, animate, invigorate, rouse, pep up, vitalize

enmity noun = **hostility**, hatred, animosity, bitterness, acrimony, malice, bad blood, ill will

ennoble verb = **dignify**, raise, enhance, honour, elevate, glorify, magnify, exalt, aggrandize

enormity noun 1 = **wickedness**, atrocity, depravity, monstrousness, outrageousness, vileness, villainy

2 = **atrocity**, crime, outrage, evil, horror, disgrace, abomination, monstrosity

3 (Informal) = **hugeness**, magnitude, greatness, vastness, immensity

enormous adjective = **huge**, massive, vast, tremendous, immense, gigantic, colossal • an enormous dust cloud
OPPOSITE: tiny
See also: **excessive, large**

enough adjective 1 = **sufficient**, plenty, adequate, ample, abundant
▶ noun 2 = **sufficiency**, plenty, abundance, adequacy, ample supply, right amount
▶ adverb 3 = **sufficiently**, adequately, reasonably, abundantly, satisfactorily, amply, tolerably

enquire see **inquire**
enquiry see **inquiry**

enrage verb = **anger**, inflame, incense, infuriate, exasperate, madden

enraged adjective = **furious**, wild, mad (informal), angry, irate, raging or raging mad, incandescent, irritated, incensed, angered, infuriated, inflamed, fuming, exasperated, aggravated, choked, boiling mad, fit to be tied, on the warpath, very angry

enrich verb 1 = **enhance**, develop, improve, supplement, refine, augment

2 = **make rich**, make wealthy

enrol verb = **enlist**, accept, admit, register, recruit, join up, sign up or sign on, take on
See also: **join, recruit**

enrolment noun = **enlistment**, admission, registration, engagement, acceptance, recruitment, matriculation

ensemble noun 1 = **whole**, set, total, collection, aggregate, sum, entirety, totality

2 = **outfit**, suit, costume, get-up (informal)

3 = **group**, company, band, cast, troupe, chorus

ensign noun = **flag**, standard, banner, pennant, jack, streamer, colours, pennon

ensue verb = **follow**, issue, result, stem, flow, proceed, arise, derive, come next

ensuing See **next**

ensure verb 1 = **make sure**, guarantee, make certain • We must ensure that this never happens again.

2 = **protect**, guard, secure, safeguard, make safe

> **CONFUSABLES**
> Ensure means make sure.
> Assure means instill confidence.
> Insure means arrange for payment in case of accident or loss.

entail verb = **involve**, demand, require, occasion, necessitate, bring about, call for, give rise to

entangle verb 1 = **tangle**, catch, trap, snag, implicate, embroil, snare, ensnare, enmesh, entrap

2 = **mix up**, puzzle, confuse, complicate, perplex, muddle, jumble

enter verb 1 = **come in, come into, go in**, or **go into**, arrive, penetrate, pierce, make an entrance, pass into

2 = **join**, start, enlist, enrol, commence, embark upon, set out on, take up

3 = **record**, list, note, register, log, inscribe, set down, take down

▷ **enter into** See **participate**

enterprise noun 1 = **business**,

company, concern, operation, firm, establishment • *a small enterprise that grew into a major corporation*
2 = undertaking, effort, project, operation, venture, endeavour • *a creative enterprise such as painting or photography*
3 = initiative, drive, energy, enthusiasm, daring, boldness, adventurousness, resourcefulness
See also: **racket**

enterprising *adjective* = **resourceful**, go-ahead, bold, energetic, enthusiastic, daring, spirited, adventurous, intrepid

entertain *verb* **1 = amuse**, please, charm, delight, enthrall • *things that might entertain children during the spring break*
2 = show hospitality to, treat, accommodate, lodge, harbour, be host to, have company, put up
3 = consider, imagine, contemplate, conceive, keep in mind, think about
See also: **receive**
▷ **entertain oneself** *See* **play**

entertaining *adjective* = **enjoyable**, funny, pleasant, humorous, amusing, interesting, pleasurable, cheering, diverting

entertainment *noun* = **enjoyment**, fun, pleasure, recreation, amusement • *Their main form of entertainment is TV.*
See also: **festival**

enthrall *verb* = **fascinate**, grip, entrance, charm, captivate, mesmerize, enchant, enrapture
See **entertain, entrance, fascinate**

enthuse *See* **rave**

enthusiasm *noun* = **keenness**, interest, excitement, warmth, eagerness • *We were disappointed by their lack of enthusiasm.*
See also: **spirit**

enthusiast *noun* = **fan**, supporter, lover, follower, buff (*informal*), jock (*slang*), fanatic, devotee, aficionado, keener (*Canad informal*), groupie (*slang*)

enthusiastic *adjective* = **keen**, eager, passionate, excited, avid, devoted, ardent • *He was very enthusiastic about the new plan.*
OPPOSITE: apathetic
See also: **active, fervent**

entice *verb* = **attract**, lure, persuade, allure, coax, tempt, seduce, cajole, lead on

entire *adjective* = **whole**, complete, full, total, gross

entirely *adverb* = **completely**, fully, absolutely, totally, altogether, thoroughly, wholly, utterly, in every respect

entitle *verb* **1 = give the right to**, allow, permit, license, enable, authorize, empower
2 = call, term, name, title, label, dub, christen

entity *noun* = **thing**, individual, object, substance, being, creature, organism

entourage *noun* = **retinue**, company, court, train, staff, escort, associates, attendants, followers

entrails *plural noun* = **intestines**, bowels, guts, innards (*informal*), insides (*informal*), offal, viscera

entrance[1] *noun* **1 = way in**, door, entry, gate, doorway • *I met my cousin in front of the arena entrance.*
2 = appearance, entry, arrival • *The actors made their entrance when the curtain went up.*
3 = admission, access, entry • *His happy manner gained him entrance to the group.*

entrance[2] *verb* **1 = charm**, delight, fascinate, captivate, enthrall, bewitch • *The audience was entranced by her voice.*
2 = mesmerize, hypnotize, put in a trance

entrant *noun* = **competitor**, player, candidate, participant, entry, contestant

entreaty *noun* = **plea**, appeal, request, prayer, petition, earnest request, exhortation, supplication

entrenched *adjective* = **fixed**, set, deep-rooted, well-established, ingrained, deep-seated, unshakable, ineradicable, rooted

entrepreneur noun
= **businessman** or
businesswoman, tycoon,
magnate, impresario,
industrialist

entrust verb = **give custody
of**, deliver, commit, delegate,
assign, confide, hand over, turn
over

entry noun 1 = **appearance**,
arrival, entrance • her dramatic
entry
2 = **way in**, door, entrance, gate,
doorway • He was hanging around
at the entry to the station.
3 = **record**, note, item • the final
entry in his journal
4 = **admission**, access, entrance,
entrée, permission to enter

entwine verb = **twist**, wind,
weave, knit, interweave,
interlace, twine, plait

enumerate verb = **list**, name,
cite, relate, quote, mention,
recount, recite, itemize, spell out

enunciate verb 1 = **pronounce**,
say, speak, sound, voice, utter,
articulate, enounce, vocalize
2 = **state**, publish, declare,
pronounce, proclaim,
promulgate, propound

envelop verb = **enclose**, cover,
surround, wrap, cloak, shroud,
engulf, encircle, encase

envelope noun = **wrapping**, case,
cover, jacket, casing, wrapper,
covering

enviable adjective = **desirable**,
lucky, fortunate, privileged, win-
win (informal), advantageous,
favoured, to die for (informal)

envious adjective = **covetous**,
jealous, resentful, green with
envy, grudging

environment noun
= **surroundings**, medium,
situation, background,
atmosphere, setting, habitat,
conditions

environmental adjective
= **ecological**, green,
conservationist • Children and
adolescents are now aware of
environmental issues.

environmentalist noun
= **conservationist**, green,
ecologist

environs plural noun
= **surrounding area**, district,
neighbourhood, vicinity,
locality, outskirts, precincts,
suburbs

envisage verb 1 = **imagine**,
picture, contemplate, conceive
or conceive of, fancy, visualize,
conceptualize, think up
2 = **foresee**, see, predict,
anticipate, envision

envoy noun = **messenger**, agent,
ambassador, representative,
diplomat, delegate, courier,
intermediary, emissary

envy noun 1 = **jealousy**,
resentment • his feelings of envy
toward his cousin
▶ verb 2 = **be jealous**, covet,
resent, be envious, begrudge • I
don't envy you one bit.

ephemeral adjective = **brief**,
temporary, passing, short-lived,
momentary, fleeting, transient,
transitory

epidemic noun = **spread**,
growth, outbreak, wave, plague,
rash, upsurge, contagion

epigram noun = **witticism**, quip,
aphorism, bon mot

epilogue noun = **conclusion**,
postscript, coda, concluding
speech

episode noun 1 = **event**,
experience, matter, incident,
affair, adventure, occurrence,
happening, escapade
2 = **part**, scene, section, passage,
chapter, instalment, webisode

epistle noun = **letter**, note,
message, communication,
missive

epitaph noun = **monument**,
inscription

epithet noun = **name**, title,
tag, description, nickname,
designation, moniker or
monicker (slang), appellation,
sobriquet

epitome noun = **personification**,
type, representation, essence,
embodiment, archetype,

e

quintessence, typical example
epitomize verb = **typify**,
represent, illustrate, symbolize,
embody, exemplify, personify
epoch noun = **era**, time, period,
age, date
equable adjective = **even-tempered**, calm, easy-going,
serene, unflappable (informal),
composed, imperturbable, level-headed, placid
equal adjective 1 = **identical**,
equivalent, the same • equal
numbers of men and women
2 = **regular**, uniform,
symmetrical, unvarying
3 = **even**, balanced, evenly
matched, fifty-fifty (informal)
4 = **fair**, just, impartial,
unbiased, even-handed,
egalitarian, on a level playing
field (informal)
▷ **equal to** = **capable of**, up to
• She was equal to any task they gave
her.
▶ verb 5 = **match**, be equal to • the
runner's time equalled her previous
record
▶ noun 6 = **match**, rival, twin,
counterpart, equivalent
See also: **same**
equality noun 1 = **sameness**,
balance, identity, similarity,
correspondence, likeness,
uniformity, equivalence,
evenness
2 = **fairness**, parity,
egalitarianism, equal
opportunity
equalize verb = **make equal**, level,
match, balance, square, equal,
smooth, standardize, even up,
regularize
equally See **alike**
equate verb = **make equal** or be
equal, compare, parallel, liken,
be commensurate, correspond
with or correspond to, mention
in the same breath
equation noun = **equating**,
comparison, parallel,
correspondence
equilibrium noun = **stability**,
rest, balance, symmetry,
equipoise, evenness, steadiness

equine See **horse**
equip verb = **supply**, provide,
arm, endow, fit out • The boat was
equipped with an outboard motor.
See also: **issue**
equipment noun = **apparatus**,
tackle, stuff, gear, paraphernalia
• a shed full of gardening equipment
See also: **supplies**
equitable adjective = **fair**, just,
proper, reasonable, honest,
impartial, unbiased, even-handed
equity noun = **fairness**, justice,
integrity, honesty, impartiality,
reasonableness, equitableness,
even-handedness, fair-mindedness, fair play, rectitude,
righteousness, uprightness
OPPOSITE: unfairness
equivalence noun = **equality**,
parity, similarity,
correspondence, likeness,
evenness, sameness
equivalent noun 1 = **equal**,
match, twin, counterpart,
parallel, opposite number
▶ adjective 2 = **equal**, same,
similar, comparable, alike,
tantamount, interchangeable,
commensurate, corresponding,
of a piece, on a level playing field
(informal)
equivocal adjective = **ambiguous**,
uncertain, vague, obscure,
indefinite, oblique, evasive,
indeterminate, misleading
era noun = **age**, time, day or days,
period, date, generation, epoch
eradicate verb = **wipe out**,
remove, destroy, eliminate,
erase, extinguish, annihilate,
obliterate, exterminate, root out
erase verb = **wipe out**, remove,
cancel, delete, blot, obliterate,
expunge, rub out
erect verb 1 = **build**, raise,
construct, put up, set up
2 = **found**, create, form,
establish, organize, institute,
initiate, set up
▶ adjective 3 = **upright**, straight,
stiff, elevated, vertical,
perpendicular, pricked-up
erode verb = **wear away**, destroy,

deteriorate, disintegrate, corrode, eat away, wear down • *The cliffs were being eroded by the constant pounding of the waves.*
See also: **wash, wear**

erosion *noun* = **deterioration**, destruction, attrition, disintegration, abrasion, eating away, grinding down, wearing down *or* wearing away

erotic *adjective* = **sexual**, sexy (*informal*), seductive, sensual, voluptuous, amatory, carnal, lustful

err *verb* = **make a mistake**, blunder, miscalculate, go wrong • *The builders had erred in their original estimate.*

errand *noun* = **job**, charge, mission, message, commission, task

erratic *adjective* = **unpredictable**, inconsistent, unstable, irregular, unreliable, variable, uneven, wayward, changeable

erroneous *adjective* = **incorrect**, wrong, false, faulty, mistaken, flawed, invalid, unsound, fallacious

error *noun* = **lapse**, slip, mistake, fault, blunder • *a mathematical error*
See also: **hole**

erstwhile *adjective* = **former**, late, past, old, once, previous, one-time, sometime, bygone

erudite *adjective* = **learned**, knowledgeable, scholarly, cultured, well-educated, cultivated, educated, well-read

erupt *verb* 1 = **explode**, gush, spout, belch forth, blow up, burst out, pour forth, spew forth *or* spew out, throw off
2 (*Medical*) = **break out**, appear

eruption *noun* 1 = **explosion**, outbreak, discharge, outburst, ejection, flare-up
2 (*Medical*) = **inflammation**, outbreak, rash

escalate *verb* = **increase**, rise, grow, extend, expand, mount, intensify, heighten

escapade *noun* = **adventure**, stunt, scrape (*informal*),

prank, antic, caper

escape *verb* 1 = **get away**, break free, break out, make your escape, run away, run off • *Three prisoners who escaped have given themselves up.*
2 = **avoid**, duck, elude, evade, dodge • *He was lucky to escape injury.*
3 = **leak**, issue, flow, seep, gush, exude, emanate, pour forth
▸ *noun* 4 = **distraction**, relief, diversion • *Cycling gives her an escape from the routine of work.*
5 = **getaway**, break, flight, break-out
6 = **avoidance**, evasion, circumvention
7 = **leak**, emission, seepage, emanation
See also: **bolt, flee**

eschew See **avoid**

escort *noun* 1 = **guard**, train, convoy, bodyguard, entourage, cortege, retinue
2 = **companion**, partner, guide, attendant, beau, chaperon, plus-one (*informal*)
▸ *verb* 3 = **accompany**, lead, conduct, partner, guide, usher, shepherd, chaperon

especial *adjective* (*Formal*) = **exceptional**, special, unusual, principal, outstanding, uncommon, noteworthy

especially *adverb* = **exceptionally**, notably, unusually, remarkably, specially, markedly, strikingly, conspicuously, uncommonly, outstandingly

espionage *noun* = **spying**, intelligence, surveillance, counter-intelligence, undercover work

espousal *noun* = **support**, championship, promotion, advocacy, adoption, defence, backing, championing, embracing, taking up

espouse *verb* = **support**, back, champion, promote, advocate, adopt, uphold, embrace, stand up for, take up

essay *noun* 1 = **composition**, paper, article, piece, tract,

discourse, treatise, dissertation
▶ verb 2 (Formal) = **attempt**, try, aim, undertake, endeavour
essence noun 1 = **nature**, heart, core, spirit, soul • *The essence of good manners is the ability to listen.*
2 = **concentrate**, extract, distillate, spirits, tincture
essential adjective 1 = **vital**, crucial, indispensable • *Good ventilation is essential in a greenhouse.*
2 = **fundamental**, key, main, basic, principal, cardinal • *an essential part of any child's development*
See also: **necessary, requirement**
essentials plural noun = **necessities**, basics, fundamentals, prerequisites, rudiments • *We had only enough food money for the essentials.*
establish verb 1 = **create**, form, ground, settle, found, institute, constitute, inaugurate, set up
2 = **prove**, confirm, demonstrate, verify, certify, authenticate, substantiate, corroborate
established adjective
1 = **accepted**, traditional, historic, conventional, customary, time-honoured, officially recognized
2 = **famous**, prominent, acclaimed, legendary, remarkable, renowned, well-known, notable, celebrated, glorious, illustrious, distinguished, conspicuous, eminent, noted, much-publicized, honoured, lionized
establishment noun
1 = **creation**, organization, institution, foundation, formation, installation, inauguration, founding, setting up
2 = **organization**, company, business, concern, firm, institution, corporation, outfit (*informal*), enterprise
▷ the Establishment = the **authorities**, ruling class, the powers that be, the system

estate noun 1 = **lands**, area, property, domain, manor, holdings
2 (*Law*) = **property**, wealth, fortune, assets, belongings, effects, goods, possessions
esteem noun 1 = **respect**, regard, admiration, estimation, reverence • *held in high esteem by her students*
▶ verb 2 = **respect**, love, value, treasure, admire, revere, prize, regard highly, think highly of
3 = **consider**, think, believe, judge, view, estimate, regard, deem, reckon
See also: **approval, favour**
esteemed See **dear**
estimate noun 1 = **reckoning**, quote, guess, assessment, valuation, appraisal, estimation • *This figure is five times the original estimate.*
2 = **opinion**, assessment, judgment, belief, appraisal, estimation
▶ verb 3 = **calculate roughly**, number, judge, value, guess, assess, evaluate, gauge, reckon
4 = **form an opinion**, rate, believe, consider, judge, rank, reckon, conjecture, surmise
See also: **price, tender**
estimated See **approximate, rough**
estimation noun = **opinion**, view, assessment, judgment, belief, consideration, appreciation, appraisal, considered opinion
estuary noun = **inlet**, mouth, creek, fjord, firth
et cetera adverb 1 = **and so on**, and so forth
▶ noun 2 = **and the rest**, and others, and the like, et al.
etch verb = **cut**, stamp, impress, carve, engrave, imprint, inscribe, eat into
etching noun = **print**, impression, imprint, carving, inscription, engraving
eternal adjective 1 = **everlasting**, immortal, unchanging • *the secret of eternal life*
2 = **permanent**, lasting,

enduring, unchanging, indestructible, deathless, immutable, imperishable
See also: **constant, continual, infinite**

eternity noun 1 = **infinity**, immortality, perpetuity, ages, endlessness, timelessness 2 (*Theology*) = **the afterlife**, heaven, paradise, the hereafter, the next world

ethical adjective = **moral**, good, just, right, fair, proper, upright, principled, conscientious, honourable, virtuous

ethics plural noun = **moral code**, conscience, morality, moral philosophy, moral values, principles, rules of conduct, standards

ethnic adjective = **cultural**, national, native, traditional, folk, racial, indigenous • *They appeared in full ethnic costume.*
▷ **ethnic group** See **race**

etiquette noun = **good behaviour** or **proper behaviour**, courtesy, protocol, civility, decorum, politeness, formalities, manners, propriety

euphoria noun = **elation**, joy, ecstasy, intoxication, jubilation, exhilaration, rapture, exaltation

evacuate verb = **clear**, leave, quit, withdraw, abandon, desert, vacate, forsake, move out, pull out

evacuation See **retreat**

evade verb 1 = **avoid**, duck, escape, elude, dodge, sidestep, get away from, steer clear of 2 = **avoid answering**, hedge, fudge, parry, equivocate, fend off

evaluate verb = **assess**, rate, judge, estimate, weigh, calculate, gauge, reckon, appraise, size up (*informal*)

evaporate verb 1 = **dry up**, dry, dehydrate, vaporize, desiccate 2 = **disappear**, dissolve, vanish, dematerialize, fade away, melt away

evasion noun 1 = **avoidance**, escape, dodging 2 = **deception**, equivocation,

evasiveness, prevarication

evasive adjective = **deceptive**, slippery, indirect, cagey (*informal*), oblique, shifty, equivocating, prevaricating

eve noun 1 = **night before**, vigil, day before 2 = **brink**, point, edge, verge, threshold

even adjective 1 = **level**, flat, smooth, horizontal • *I need an even surface to write on.*
OPPOSITE: uneven
2 = **regular**, steady, uniform, constant, smooth • *an even flow of liquid*
3 = **equal**, identical, neck and neck • *At half-time, the scores were still even.*
4 = **calm**, cool, well-balanced, composed, even-tempered, imperturbable, placid, unruffled
▷ **even though** See **in spite of**
▷ **get even, get even with** = **pay back**, repay, retaliate, reciprocate, give tit for tat, requite
See also: **straight**

| INFORMALLY SPEAKING
break even: have equal gains and losses
even out: become more level or balanced
get even: take revenge

evening noun = **dusk**, twilight, gloaming (*Scot, poetic*)

event noun 1 = **incident**, business, experience, matter, affair, circumstance, episode • *still amazed at the events of last week*
2 = **competition**, contest, bout • *The next event is the long jump.*
See also: **occasion**

even-tempered adjective = **calm**, cool, tranquil, composed, imperturbable, level-headed, placid, unexcitable, unruffled

eventful adjective = **exciting**, full, active, dramatic, busy, remarkable, memorable, lively

eventual adjective = **final**, overall, ultimate, concluding

eventuality noun = **possibility**, case, event, chance, likelihood, contingency, probability

eventually *adverb* = **in the end**, finally, ultimately, after all, at the end of the day, one day, some time, when all is said and done

ever *adverb* **1** = **at any time**, at all, at any period, at any point, by any chance, in any case, on any occasion

2 = **always**, constantly, continually, perpetually, at all times, evermore, for ever, twenty-four-seven (*slang*)

everlasting *adjective* = **eternal**, endless, timeless, perpetual, immortal, indestructible, never-ending, undying

evermore *adverb* = **for ever**, always, ever, eternally, to the end of time

every *adjective* = **each**, all, each one

▷ **every now and then** *See* **sometimes**

▷ **every one** *See* **all**

▷ **every so often** *See* **sometimes**

▷ **every time** *See* **always**

everybody *pronoun* = **everyone**, all and sundry, each one, each person, every person, one and all, the whole world

everyday *adjective* = **ordinary**, common, daily, routine, day-to-day, mundane • *the drudgery of everyday life*
See also: **colloquial, frequent, natural, regular**

everyone *pronoun* = **everybody**, all and sundry, each one, each person, every person, one and all, the whole world

everything *pronoun* = **all**, each thing, the lot, the whole lot, the whole schmear (*informal*), the whole enchilada (*slang*)

everywhere *adverb* = **to every place** *or* **in every place**, all around, all over, far and wide *or* far and near, high and low, in every nook and cranny, the world over, ubiquitously

evict *verb* = **expel**, remove, oust, eject, boot out (*informal*), kick out (*informal*), throw out, turn out

evidence *noun* **1** = **proof**, sign,

testimony, demonstration, indication, confirmation, corroboration, grounds, substantiation

▶ *verb* **2** = **show**, reveal, prove, witness, indicate, display, exhibit, demonstrate, signify

evident *adjective* = **obvious**, clear, apparent, visible, plain, noticeable, palpable • *He spoke with evident emotion about his ordeal.*
See also: **conspicuous, naked**

evidently *adverb* **1** = **obviously**, clearly, undoubtedly, plainly, manifestly, unmistakably, without question

2 = **apparently**, seemingly, ostensibly, outwardly, to all appearances

evil *noun* **1** = **wickedness**, vice, sin, immorality, badness • *the conflict between good and evil*
OPPOSITE: good

2 = **harm**, ill, misery, sorrow, affliction • *a lecture on the evils of alcohol*

▶ *adjective* **3** = **wicked**, bad, vile, sinful, malevolent, depraved • *an utterly evil person*
OPPOSITE: good

4 = **harmful**, disastrous, dire, catastrophic, destructive, ruinous, calamitous, pernicious

5 = **offensive**, foul, unpleasant, noxious, vile, pestilential
See also: **sinister, wrong**

evoke *verb* = **recall**, call, induce, awaken, rekindle, arouse, give rise to, stir up, summon up

evolution *noun* = **development**, increase, growth, progress, expansion, maturation, unfolding, working out

evolve *verb* = **develop**, increase, grow, expand, progress, mature, unfold, work out

exact *adjective* **1** = **accurate**, true, faithful, authentic, precise, faultless • *It's an exact reproduction of the first steam engine.*
OPPOSITE: approximate

▶ *verb* **2** (*Formal*) = **demand**, command, impose, extract, wring, insist on, insist upon • *They are certain to exact a high price*

for their co-operation.
See also: **correct, particular, right, strict**

exacting adjective = **demanding**, hard, tough, difficult, severe, strict, harsh, rigorous, stringent, taxing

exactly adverb 1 = **precisely**, just, accurately, faithfully, on the dot, quite • *He arrived at exactly five o'clock.*
OPPOSITE: approximately
2 = **in every respect**, quite, absolutely, indeed, specifically, precisely, to the letter
▶ interjection 3 = **indeed**, quite, absolutely, precisely • *"We'll never know the answer." – "Exactly. So let's stop speculating."*
See also: **prompt**

exactness noun = **precision**, accuracy, correctness, veracity, exactitude, rigorousness, scrupulousness, strictness

exaggerate verb = **overstate**, overestimate, overdo • *He thinks I'm exaggerating, but I'm not!*

exaggerated See **excessive**

exaggeration noun = **overstatement**, embellishment, enlargement, hyperbole, amplification, overemphasis, overestimation

exalt verb 1 = **praise**, acclaim, worship, glorify, idolize, extol, set on a pedestal
2 = **raise**, advance, promote, upgrade, honour, elevate, ennoble

exaltation noun 1 = **praise**, tribute, acclaim, worship, glorification, reverence, idolization
2 = **rise**, promotion, advancement, elevation, ennoblement, upgrading

exalted adjective = **high-ranking**, grand, prestigious, lofty, dignified, eminent, honoured

exam noun = **test**, examination • *a final exam*

examination noun
1 = **inspection**, study, analysis • *a careful examination of all the evidence*

2 = **check**, physical, checkup • *The doctor suggested an immediate examination of his ear.*
3 = **questioning**, test, probe, inquiry, quiz, inquisition
See also: **exam, research, review**

examine verb 1 = **inspect**, study, analyze, go over, go through, look over • *Police are examining the scene of the crash.*
2 = **check**, test, look at • *I was examined by several specialists.*
3 = **question**, test, quiz, grill (*informal*), interrogate, inquire, cross-examine
See also: **contemplate, investigate, research, scrutinize**

example noun 1 = **specimen**, sample, illustration • *some examples of well-made horror movies*
2 = **ideal**, model, prototype, paragon • *His dedication is an example to us all.*
3 = **warning**, caution, lesson
See also: **case**

exasperate verb = **irritate**, anger, annoy, inflame, pique, incense, infuriate, enrage, madden

exasperation noun = **irritation**, anger, rage, wrath, pique, provocation, fury, annoyance

excavate verb = **dig out**, mine, uncover, tunnel, unearth, delve, burrow, quarry, dig up

exceed verb 1 = **surpass**, top, beat, pass, cap (*informal*), eclipse, overtake, better, outstrip, outdo
2 = **go over the limit of**, overstep, go over the top

exceeding See **above, over**

exceedingly adverb = **extremely**, very, unusually, hugely, extraordinarily, exceptionally, enormously, superlatively, surpassingly

excel verb = **be superior**, beat, surpass, eclipse, outshine, outdo, transcend
▷ **excel in, excel at** = **be good at**, be proficient in, be skillful at, be talented at, shine at, show talent in

excellence noun = **high quality**, merit, distinction, greatness, goodness, supremacy, superiority, eminence, pre-eminence

excellent *adjective*
= **outstanding**, great, fine, brilliant, superb, first-class, peachy-keen (*slang, now usu. facetious*) • *It's an excellent book, one of my favourites.*
OPPOSITE: terrible
See also: **exceptional, first-rate, marvellous, splendid, wonderful**

except *preposition* 1 = **apart from**, but, save (*formal*), other than, with the exception of • *I don't eat dessert, except for the occasional slice of pie.*
▷ **except for** See **but**
▶ *verb* 2 = **exclude**, omit, leave out, pass over

| CONFUSABLES
| *Except* means *other than*, and is a preposition.
| *Accept* means *receive*, and is a verb.

exception *noun* 1 = **special case**, irregularity, oddity, freak, inconsistency, anomaly, deviation, peculiarity
2 = **exclusion**, omission, leaving out, passing over

exceptional *adjective*
1 = **remarkable**, excellent, extraordinary, talented, outstanding, phenomenal • *Her piano playing is exceptional.*
OPPOSITE: mediocre
2 = **unusual**, special, rare, isolated, unheard-of, out of the ordinary • *The traffic is exceptional for this time of day.*
OPPOSITE: common
See also: **extreme, first-rate, particular, singular, superior, uncommon**

excerpt *noun* = **extract**, part, piece, section, selection, passage, fragment, quotation

excess *noun* 1 = **overindulgence**, indulgence, extravagance, debauchery, dissipation, intemperance • *a life of excess*
2 = **surfeit**, surplus, glut, plethora, overabundance,
superabundance, superfluity • *An excess of houseplants made the room look like a jungle.*
OPPOSITE: shortage
▶ *adjective* 3 = **surplus**, extra, superfluous • *travelling with excess baggage*

excessive *adjective*
= **immoderate**, enormous, exaggerated, unreasonable, needless, undue • *an excessive reliance on government funding*
See also: **extreme, steep**

excessively See **too**

exchange *verb* 1 = **interchange**, change, trade, switch, swap, barter • *We exchanged phone numbers.*
▷ **exchange views on** See **discuss**
▶ *noun* 2 = **interchange**, trade, switch, swap • *a ceasefire to allow the exchange of prisoners*
See also: **substitute**

excise See **duty, tax**

excitable *adjective* = **nervous**, emotional, volatile, mercurial, temperamental, highly strung, hot-headed, quick-tempered, wired (*slang*)

excite *verb* 1 = **thrill**, agitate, animate, titillate • *The idea of travelling across Canada really excited the kids.*
2 = **arouse**, inspire, provoke, incite, evoke, elicit, stir up • *The meeting failed to excite strong feelings in anyone.*

excited *adjective* = **thrilled**, enthusiastic, feverish, agitated, jazzed (*slang*) • *We are very excited about getting a new dog.*
OPPOSITE: bored

excitement *noun* = **thrill**, activity, adventure, enthusiasm, agitation, commotion • *The release of her latest book has caused great excitement.*
See also: **bustle, heat, passion**

exciting *adjective* = **thrilling**, dramatic, rousing, electrifying, exhilarating, stimulating, kicky (*slang*) • *the most exciting race I've ever seen*
OPPOSITE: boring

See also: **impressive**

exclaim *verb* = **cry out**, declare, shout, yell, utter, proclaim, call out

exclamation *noun* = **cry**, call, shout, yell, outcry, utterance, interjection

exclude *verb* 1 = **leave out**, eliminate, ignore, omit, rule out
• *We cannot exclude this possibility altogether.*
OPPOSITE: include
2 = **keep out**, ban, bar, forbid
• *Nobody is excluded from this club.*
See also: **boycott**

exclusion *noun* 1 = **ban**, bar, boycott, veto, embargo, prohibition, disqualification, interdict
2 = **elimination**, rejection, omission

exclusive *adjective* 1 = **select**, upscale, chic, posh (*informal*), classy • *one of the city's most exclusive golf clubs*
2 = **sole**, complete, full, total, whole, entire, absolute, undivided
3 = **limited**, unique, restricted, peculiar, confined
See also: **private**

excommunicate *verb* = **expel**, ban, exclude, denounce, banish, repudiate, anathematize, cast out

excruciating *adjective* = **agonizing**, violent, severe, intense, unbearable, piercing, harrowing, insufferable

exculpate *verb* = **absolve**, clear, excuse, acquit, discharge, pardon, exonerate, vindicate

excursion *noun* = **trip**, tour, journey, outing, expedition, ramble, jaunt, day trip, pleasure trip

excusable *adjective* = **forgivable**, allowable, understandable, justifiable, permissible, defensible, pardonable, warrantable

excuse *noun* 1 = **justification**, reason, explanation, pretext
• *Stop making excuses and get on with it!*
▶ *verb* 2 = **forgive**, overlook, pardon, turn a blind eye to
• *Please excuse my late arrival.*
3 = **justify**, defend, explain, mitigate, vindicate, apologize for
4 = **free**, release, relieve, spare, discharge, exempt, absolve, let off
▷ **excuse yourself** *See* **decline**
See also: **defence**, **grounds**

excused *See* **exempt**

execute *verb* 1 = **put to death**, kill, shoot, hang, behead, electrocute, guillotine
2 = **carry out**, effect, perform, implement, accomplish, prosecute, administer, discharge, enact

execution *noun* 1 = **carrying out**, operation, performance, administration, prosecution, enforcement, accomplishment, implementation, enactment
2 = **killing**, hanging, capital punishment

executioner *noun* 1 = **hangman**, headsman
2 = **killer**, murderer, assassin, exterminator, hit man (*slang*), liquidator, slayer

executive *noun*
1 = **administrator**, official, director, manager
2 = **administration**, government, leadership, management, hierarchy, directorate, directors
▶ *adjective* 3 = **administrative**, decision-making, managerial, controlling, directing, governing

exemplary *adjective* 1 = **ideal**, good, fine, model, excellent, admirable, commendable, praiseworthy
2 = **warning**, cautionary

exemplify *verb* = **show**, represent, display, exhibit, demonstrate, illustrate, embody, serve as an example of

exempt *adjective* 1 = **immune**, excused, not liable • *exempt from paying the tax*
▶ *verb* 2 = **grant immunity**,

release, free, excuse, relieve, spare, discharge, absolve, let off

exemption noun = **immunity**, release, freedom, exception, discharge, exoneration, absolution, dispensation

exercise noun 1 = **exertion**, work, activity, training • *I need to get more exercise.*

2 = **task**, problem, practice, drill, lesson

3 = **use**, practice, application, discharge, implementation, utilization, fulfillment

▶ verb 4 = **put to use**, use, apply, employ, exert, utilize, bring to bear

5 = **train**, practice, work out

exert verb = **use**, exercise, apply, employ, wield, utilize, bring to bear, make use of

▷ **exert oneself** = **make an effort**, work, struggle, strain, strive, labour, toil, endeavour, apply oneself, do one's best

exertion noun = **effort**, industry, struggle, exercise, strain, toil, endeavour, elbow grease (*facetious*)

exhaust verb 1 = **tire out**, drain, fatigue, wear out • *Don't exhaust yourself by taking on too many projects.*

2 = **use up**, consume, deplete, run through • *She has exhausted all my patience.*

See also: **tax, tire**

exhausted adjective 1 = **worn out**, debilitated, done in (*informal*), drained, fatigued, beat (*informal*), spent, tired out, whipped (*informal*)

2 = **used up**, finished, spent, consumed, depleted, dissipated, expended, squandered, wasted

exhausting adjective = **tiring**, strenuous, gruelling, backbreaking, debilitating, laborious, punishing, sapping, taxing

exhaustion noun 1 = **tiredness**, fatigue, debilitation, weariness

2 = **depletion**, consumption, emptying, using up

exhaustive adjective = **thorough**, complete, extensive, comprehensive, intensive, full-scale, in-depth, all-embracing

exhibit verb = **display**, show, reveal, indicate, express, demonstrate, parade, manifest, put on view

exhibition noun = **display**, show, performance, demonstration, presentation, representation, spectacle, ex (*Canad*), exposition

exhilarating adjective = **exciting**, thrilling, breathtaking, enlivening, invigorating, stimulating

exhort verb = **urge**, press, advise, spur, persuade, beseech, call upon, entreat

exhume verb = **dig up**, unearth, disentomb, disinter

exigency noun = **need**, demand, requirement, necessity, constraint

exile noun 1 = **banishment**, deportation, expulsion, expatriation

2 = **expatriate**, refugee, outcast, deportee, émigré

▶ verb 3 = **banish**, deport, expel, eject, expatriate, drive out

exist verb 1 = **be**, live, survive, occur, endure, be present

2 = **survive**, subsist, eke out a living, get along *or* get by, keep one's head above water, stay alive

existence noun = **being**, life, actuality, subsistence

existent adjective = **in existence**, present, alive, standing, living, existing, extant, surviving

exit noun 1 = **way out**, door, outlet, gate

2 = **departure**, withdrawal, retreat, farewell, exodus, going, good-bye, leave-taking

▶ verb 3 = **depart**, leave, retire, withdraw, retreat, go away, go offstage (*theatre*), go out, make tracks, take one's leave

exodus noun = **departure**, flight, exit, evacuation, withdrawal, retreat, migration, going out, leaving

exonerate verb = **clear**, excuse, acquit, justify, discharge, pardon, vindicate, absolve, exculpate

exorbitant adjective = **excessive**, outrageous, unreasonable, extravagant, inordinate, preposterous, extortionate, immoderate

exorcise verb = **drive out**, deliver or deliver from, expel, purify, cast out

exotic adjective 1 = **unusual**, mysterious, strange, glamorous, striking, unfamiliar, colourful, fascinating
2 = **foreign**, external, alien, imported, naturalized

expand verb 1 = **increase**, develop, extend, enlarge
OPPOSITE: decrease
2 = **grow**, swell, fill out • *The rails expanded and buckled in the fierce heat.*
3 = **spread** or **spread out**, stretch or stretch out, unfold, unravel, unfurl, diffuse, unroll
See also: **bulge, elaborate**
▷ **expand on** = **go into detail about**, develop, elaborate on, enlarge on • *an idea that I will expand on later*

expanse noun = **area**, space, sweep, range, stretch, extent, tract, breadth

expansion noun = **increase**, growth, development, spread, enlargement, amplification, magnification, opening out

expansive adjective 1 = **wide**, broad, widespread, extensive, wide-ranging, far-reaching, voluminous
2 = **talkative**, open, friendly, outgoing, affable, effusive, sociable, communicative, loquacious, unreserved

expatriate adjective 1 = **exiled**, banished, emigrant, émigré
▶ noun 2 = **exile**, refugee, emigrant, émigré

expect verb 1 = **think**, believe, assume, anticipate, imagine, presume, reckon • *The trial is expected to last several weeks.*
2 = **require**, demand, rely on • *I was expecting to have a bit of time to myself.*
3 = **look forward to**, predict, await, anticipate, contemplate, envisage, hope for, watch for
See also: **figure, suppose**

expectant adjective
1 = **expecting**, ready, hopeful, eager, watchful, apprehensive, anticipating, in suspense
2 = **pregnant**, expecting (*informal*), gravid

expectation noun
1 = **probability**, forecast, belief, likelihood, assumption, presumption, conjecture, supposition
2 = **anticipation**, hope, promise, suspense, expectancy, apprehension

expected See **likely, supposed**

expediency noun = **suitability**, benefit, utility, profitability, convenience, usefulness, prudence, pragmatism, advisability

expedient noun 1 = **means**, measure, device, resort, scheme, method, makeshift, stopgap, contrivance
▶ adjective 2 = **advantageous**, effective, appropriate, useful, helpful, practical, beneficial, suitable, convenient, win-win (*informal*), opportune

expedition noun = **journey**, mission, tour, quest, trek, voyage, excursion, safari

expel verb 1 = **drive out**, remove, discharge, eject, spew, belch, cast out
2 = **dismiss**, ban, exclude, exile, banish, evict, chuck out (*slang*), drum out, throw out

expend verb = **spend**, use or use up, consume, exhaust, dissipate, go through, pay out

expendable adjective = **dispensable**, unnecessary, unimportant, nonessential, inessential, replaceable

expenditure noun = **spending**, cost, payment, expense, consumption, output,

e

e

outlay, expenses, outgoings

expense noun = **cost**, charge, loss, payment, expenditure, spending, outlay

expensive adjective = **costly**, pricey, dear • *a very expensive suit*
OPPOSITE: inexpensive
See also: **precious, valuable**

experience noun 1 = **knowledge**, training, understanding, expertise, know-how • *They're looking for someone with experience.*
2 = **incident**, affair, episode, encounter, adventure, ordeal • *a terrifying experience that they still talk about*
▶ verb 3 = **undergo**, have, meet, encounter • *We are experiencing a few technical problems.*
See also: **endure, event, feel, go through, suffer**

experienced adjective = **knowledgeable**, expert, seasoned, practised, well versed • *an experienced diver*
OPPOSITE: inexperienced
See also: **practical, skilled**

experiment noun 1 = **test**, trial, research, investigation, procedure, proof, examination, experimentation, trial run
▶ verb 2 = **test**, try, research, investigate, examine, sample, verify, put to the test

experimental adjective = **test**, trial, pilot, tentative, preliminary, provisional, speculative, exploratory, probationary, trial-and-error

expert noun 1 = **specialist**, authority, professional, ace (*informal*), wizard, buff (*informal*), guru • *A team of experts will be on hand to offer advice.*
OPPOSITE: beginner
▶ adjective 2 = **skilful**, able, skilled, experienced, knowledgeable, adept, proficient • *Her expert approach impressed everyone.*
See also: **perfect**

expertise noun = **skill**, facility, knowledge, command, judgment, mastery, know-how (*informal*), proficiency, adroitness

expertly See **well**

expire verb 1 = **finish**, end, close, stop, conclude, cease, terminate, lapse, come to an end, run out
2 = **breathe out**, expel, emit, exhale
3 = **die**, depart, perish, kick the bucket (*informal*), pass away or pass on

explain verb 1 = **make clear**, describe, define, illustrate • *He explained to us how the system worked.*
2 = **account for**, excuse, justify, give a reason for

explanation noun
1 = **description**, definition, clarification, exposition • *her clear explanation of the parliamentary system*
2 = **reason**, account, answer, excuse, motive, justification, vindication
See also: **defence, statement**

explanatory adjective = **descriptive**, interpretive, illustrative

explicit adjective = **clear**, specific, precise, straightforward, frank, definite, unambiguous, categorical

explode verb 1 = **blow up**, burst, detonate, go off, set off • *the sound of fireworks exploding in the air*
2 = **go mad**, blow up, go berserk • *I asked him if he'd finished, and he just exploded.*
3 = **shoot up**, soar, skyrocket • *Sales of digital cameras have exploded in recent years.*
4 = **disprove**, refute, discredit, debunk, invalidate, repudiate, give the lie to
See also: **fire**

exploit verb 1 = **take advantage of**, abuse, milk, manipulate, misuse, play on or play upon
2 = **make the best use of**, use, utilize, capitalize on, cash in on (*informal*), profit by or profit from
▶ noun 3 = **feat**, achievement, adventure, stunt, accomplishment, deed, escapade, attainment

exploitation noun = **misuse**,

abuse, manipulation
exploration noun
1 = investigation, research, search, inquiry, analysis, inspection, scrutiny, examination
2 = expedition, survey, travel, trip, tour, reconnaissance
exploratory adjective
= investigative, trial, experimental, fact-finding, probing, searching
explore verb **1 = investigate**, research, search, probe, examine, inspect, inquire into, look into
2 = travel, survey, tour, scout, reconnoitre
explosion noun **1 = bang**, blast • *The explosion shattered windows all along the street.*
2 = outburst, outbreak, fit, eruption
explosive adjective **1 = unstable**, volatile
2 = violent, fiery, stormy, vehement, touchy
exponent noun **1 = advocate**, champion, supporter, defender, promoter, backer, proponent, upholder
2 = performer, player
expose verb **1 = uncover**, show, reveal • *The original floor was exposed as we began sanding.*
2 = reveal, uncover, unearth, bring to light, show up • *He has been exposed as a liar and a cheat.*
3 = make vulnerable, subject, endanger, jeopardize, imperil, lay open, leave open
See also: **betray**
exposed adjective
1 = unconcealed, bare, uncovered, on display, on show, on view, revealed
2 = unsheltered, open, unprotected
3 = vulnerable, susceptible, in peril, laid bare, wide open
exposition See **explanation**
exposure noun **= publicity**, display, exhibition, showing, presentation, revelation, unveiling, uncovering

expound verb **= explain**, describe, unfold, interpret, elucidate, set forth, spell out
express verb **1 = state**, communicate, couch, put, voice, phrase, put across • *She expressed interest in trying out for the part.*
2 = show, represent, reveal, indicate, exhibit, intimate, convey, signify, symbolize, make known, stand for
▷ **express regret** See **apologize**
▶ adjective **3 = fast**, direct, high-speed, non-stop • *express delivery service*
4 = explicit, clear, plain, distinct, definite, unambiguous, categorical
5 = specific, special, particular, singular, clear-cut, especial
See also: **swift**
expression noun **1 = look**, face, countenance • *a pleasant expression*
2 = phrase, term, remark, idiom • *It's my grandmother's favourite expression.*
3 = statement, announcement, communication, declaration, utterance
4 = indication, show, sign, demonstration, exhibition, symbol, representation, token, manifestation
expressive adjective **= vivid**, poignant, striking, eloquent, moving, telling
expressly adverb **1 = definitely**, clearly, explicitly, categorically, distinctly, plainly, unambiguously, in no uncertain terms
2 = specifically, especially, particularly, specially
expulsion noun **= ejection**, removal, dismissal, eviction, exclusion, banishment
exquisite adjective **1 = beautiful**, attractive, lovely, charming, striking, pleasing, comely
2 = fine, beautiful, precious, delicate, elegant, lovely, dainty
3 = intense, sharp, acute, keen
extempore adverb
1 = impromptu, freely,

spontaneously, ad lib, offhand, off the cuff (*informal*)
▷ *adjective* **2 = impromptu**, unprepared, unpremeditated, ad-lib, offhand, off-the-cuff (*informal*)

extend *verb* **1 = reach**, continue, hang, stretch • *The city will soon extend way beyond its present borders.*
2 = stick out, project, protrude, jut out • *She extended her hand and shook mine.*
3 = enlarge, develop, expand, widen, add to • *We'd like to extend the house and build a sunroom.*
4 = make longer, stretch, prolong, lengthen, drag out, draw out, spin out, spread out
5 = last, continue, carry on, go on
6 = offer, present, confer, impart, proffer
▷ **extend to** *See* **reach**
See also: **build, increase, range, spread**

extended *See* **continuous**

extension *noun* **1 = annex**, addition, supplement, appendage, appendix
2 = lengthening, increase, development, spread, expansion, enlargement, broadening, widening

extensive *adjective* **1 = large**, wide, broad, vast, spacious, expansive, sweeping • *the mansion's extensive grounds*
2 = widespread, great, comprehensive, considerable, far-reaching, untold, pervasive • *The blast caused extensive damage.*
See also: **full**

extent *noun* **= size**, level, measure, degree, scale • *The full extent of the damage was revealed yesterday.*
See also: **area, length, quantity, range, spread, stretch**

extenuating *adjective* **= mitigating**, justifying, moderating, qualifying

exterior *noun* **1 = outside**, face, skin, surface, shell, coating, covering, façade
▷ *adjective* **2 = outside**, external,

surface, outer, outward, outermost

exterminate *verb* **= destroy**, eliminate, eradicate, abolish, annihilate

external *adjective* **1 = outer**, outside, surface, exterior, outward, outermost
2 = outside, foreign, alien, extrinsic

extinct *adjective* **= dead**, lost, defunct, gone, vanished

extinction *noun* **= dying out**, destruction, eradication, abolition, oblivion, extermination, annihilation, obliteration

extinguish *verb* **1 = put out**, stifle, douse, smother, quench, blow out, snuff out
2 = destroy, end, remove, eliminate, eradicate, annihilate, exterminate, wipe out

extol *verb* **= praise**, acclaim, commend, glorify, eulogize, exalt, sing the praises of

extort *verb* **= force**, bully, squeeze, extract, coerce, blackmail

extortionate *adjective* **= exorbitant**, excessive, outrageous, inflated, unreasonable, sky-high, extravagant, preposterous

extra *adjective* **1 = additional**, more, new, further, excess, added, supplementary, auxiliary, ancillary • *The company is taking on extra staff for the summer.*
2 = surplus, excess, spare, unused, leftover, redundant, superfluous
▷ *noun* **3 = addition**, bonus, accessory • *The cost of the extras added to the price of the vacation.*
▷ *adverb* **4 = exceptionally**, especially, particularly, extremely, unusually, remarkably, extraordinarily, uncommonly
See also: **luxury, supplement**

extract *verb* **1 = take out**, draw, remove, mine, obtain, pull out • *Citric acid can be extracted from orange juice.*
2 = elicit, get, draw, obtain,

glean • *She tried to extract further information from the witness.*
▶ *noun* **3 = passage**, section, reading, snatch, excerpt, snippet • *an extract from his latest novel*
4 = concentrate • *vanilla extract*
See also: **exact, quote, withdraw**
extraction See **origin, stock**
extraneous *adjective*
= **irrelevant**, inappropriate, unrelated, unconnected, immaterial, beside the point, off the subject
extraordinary *adjective*
= **unusual**, odd, amazing, strange, bizarre, singular, surprising • *He really is an extraordinary man.*
OPPOSITE: ordinary
See also: **curious, exceptional, incredible, uncommon, weird**
extravagance *noun* **1 = waste**, wastefulness, lavishness, overspending, prodigality, profligacy, squandering
2 = excess, exaggeration, wildness, outrageousness, preposterousness
extravagant *adjective*
1 = wasteful, lavish, spendthrift, prodigal, profligate
2 = excessive, reckless, outrageous, unreasonable, preposterous, over the top (*slang*)
extreme *adjective* **1 = great**, acute, deep, severe, intense, dire, profound • *living in extreme poverty*
2 = excessive, exceptional, drastic, extravagant, radical, unreasonable • *I think that's rather an extreme reaction.*
3 = maximum, great, severe, intense, ultimate, acute, supreme, utmost, highest
4 = farthest, far-off, most distant, outermost, remotest
▶ *noun* **5 = limit**, end, depth, height, ultimate, boundary • *We're just going from one extreme to the other.*
See also: **serious, uncommon**
extremely *adverb* = **very**, severely, unusually, terribly,

extraordinarily, exceptionally, awfully (*informal*), exceedingly, uncommonly
extremist *noun* = **fanatic**, radical, die-hard, zealot
extremity *noun* **1 = limit**, border, edge, tip, extreme, boundary, frontier, pinnacle
2 = crisis, emergency, trouble, disaster, adversity, dire straits, exigency
▷ **extremities = hands and feet**, fingers and toes, limbs
extricate *verb* = **free**, release, remove, rescue, disengage, disentangle, get out, wriggle out of
extrovert *adjective* = **outgoing**, exuberant, gregarious, sociable
exuberance *noun* **1 = high spirits**, spirit, enthusiasm, vitality, zest, cheerfulness, ebullience, liveliness, vivacity
2 = luxuriance, abundance, copiousness, lavishness, profusion
exuberant *adjective* **1 = high-spirited**, animated, energetic, enthusiastic, spirited, lively, cheerful, ebullient, vivacious
2 = luxuriant, lavish, abundant, plentiful, copious, profuse
exude See **emit**
exult *verb* = **be joyful**, celebrate, rejoice, be overjoyed, jump for joy
eye *noun* **1 = eyeball**, optic (*informal*), peeper (*informal, often plural*)
2 = appreciation, taste, judgment, recognition, discrimination, perception, discernment
▶ *verb* **3 = look at**, study, survey, watch, view, inspect, contemplate, check out (*informal*)
eye-catching See **prominent**
eyesight *noun* = **vision**, sight, perception
eyesore *noun* = **mess**, sight (*informal*), horror, blemish, blot, disfigurement, monstrosity
eyewitness *noun* = **observer**, witness, viewer, spectator, bystander, onlooker, passer-by

e

Ff

fable *noun* **1** = **story**, legend, tale, myth, allegory, parable
2 = **fiction**, invention, fantasy, fabrication, yarn (*informal*), fish story (*informal*), tall tale (*informal*), urban legend
fabric *noun* **1** = **cloth**, material, web, stuff, textile
2 = **framework**, organization, construction, structure, constitution, make-up, foundations
fabricate *verb* **1** = **make up**, forge, invent, devise, falsify, concoct, feign, trump up
2 = **build**, make, form, manufacture, shape, assemble, construct, erect
fabrication *noun* **1** = **forgery**, lie, fake, fiction, invention, myth, concoction, falsehood
2 = **construction**, production, building, manufacture, assembly, erection
fabulous *adjective* **1** (*Informal*) = **wonderful**, spectacular, brilliant, fantastic (*informal*), sensational (*informal*), superb, marvellous, out-of-this-world (*informal*)
2 = **astounding**, amazing, incredible, unbelievable, phenomenal, breathtaking, inconceivable
3 = **legendary**, fantastic, fictitious, imaginary, mythical, unreal, made-up, apocryphal, invented
façade *noun* = **appearance**, show, face, front, mask, exterior, guise, pretense, semblance
See also: **outside**
face *noun* **1** = **countenance**, mug (*slang*), features, lineaments, physiognomy • *A strong wind was blowing in my face.*
2 = **side**, front, surface, aspect, exterior • *the north face of Everest*
3 = **expression**, look, appearance, aspect
4 = **scowl**, grimace, frown, pout, smirk
5 = **façade**, show, front, appearance, display, mask, exterior
6 = **self-respect**, authority, image, status, standing, reputation, dignity, honour, prestige
▷ **face down** See **prone**
▶ *verb* **7** = **look onto**, overlook, be opposite • *a room that faces on to the street*
8 = **meet**, experience, oppose, tackle, encounter, confront, brave, come up against, deal with
9 = **coat**, finish, cover, dress, clad
See also: **outside**
▷ **face up to** = **accept**, acknowledge, tackle, confront, come to terms with, cope with, deal with, meet head-on

> **INFORMALLY SPEAKING**
> **face someone down**: confront someone and make that person lose confidence or feel embarrassed
> **face to face**: in person
> **face up to**: meet bravely and boldly
> **get in someone's face**: be aggressive

faceless *adjective* = **impersonal**, remote, anonymous
facet *noun* = **aspect**, part, face, side, plane, surface, phase, angle, slant
facetious *adjective* = **funny**, humorous, amusing, frivolous,

playful, comical, droll, flippant, jocular, tongue in cheek

facile *adjective* = **superficial**, slick, shallow, hasty, cursory, glib

facilitate *verb* = **promote**, help, forward, further, expedite, make easy, pave the way for, speed up

facility *noun* 1 = **skill**, ability, ease, efficiency, proficiency, dexterity, fluency, adroitness, effortlessness
2 (*often plural*) = **equipment**, aid, opportunity, advantage, resource, means, convenience, appliance, amenity

facsimile *noun* = **copy**, print, transcript, reproduction, replica, fax, duplicate, photocopy, carbon copy

fact *noun* 1 = **truth**, reality, certainty • *a statement of fact*
OPPOSITE: lie
2 = **event**, act, performance, incident, occurrence, deed, happening, fait accompli (*French*)

faction *noun* 1 = **group**, set, party, gang, bloc, contingent, clique, cabal, coterie, splinter group
2 = **dissension**, division, conflict, rebellion, disagreement, infighting, discord, disunity

factor *noun* = **element**, part, cause, influence, aspect, consideration • *Physical activity is an important factor in maintaining fitness.*

factory *noun* = **works**, plant, mill • *He owned furniture factories in several locations.*

facts See **information**

factual *adjective* = **true**, real, correct, exact, genuine, authentic, precise, true-to-life

faculties *plural noun* = **powers**, reason, intelligence, capabilities, senses, wits

faculty *noun* 1 = **ability**, power, facility, capacity, skill, propensity, aptitude
2 = **department**, school

fad *noun* = **craze**, trend, fashion, rage, mania, vogue, whim

fade *verb* 1 = **dull**, dim, discolour, wash out • *The fabric had faded in the bright sunlight.*
2 = **dwindle**, decline, disappear, dissolve, vanish, wane, die away, melt away
▷ **fade away** See **die, vanish**
▷ **fade out** See **die**
See also: **die out, wither**

faded *adjective* = **discoloured**, dull, pale, bleached, indistinct, washed out

fading *adjective* = **declining**, decreasing, disappearing, dying, on the decline, vanishing

fail *verb* 1 = **be unsuccessful**, flunk (*informal*), be defeated, be in vain, come to grief, fall through, go belly up (*informal*) • *He failed in his attempt to fire the coach.*
OPPOSITE: succeed
2 = **omit**, neglect • *They failed to email her.*
3 = **give out**, decline, sink, cease, wane, stop working • *His eyesight began to fail.*
4 = **disappoint**, forget, abandon, desert, neglect, forsake, let down
5 = **go bankrupt**, fold (*informal*), become insolvent, close down, go broke (*informal*), go bust (*informal*), go into receivership, go out of business, go to the wall, go under
▷ **fail to notice** See **miss**
▷ **fail to remember** See **forget**
▶ *noun*
▷ **without fail** = **regularly**, constantly, religiously, conscientiously, dependably, like clockwork, punctually, twenty-four-seven (*slang*), without exception
See also: **collapse, weaken**

failing *noun* 1 = **weakness**, flaw, defect, fault, deficiency, shortcoming, blemish, drawback, imperfection
▶ *preposition* 2 = **in the absence of**, in default of, lacking

failure *noun* 1 = **defeat**, breakdown, miscarriage, downfall, fiasco, flameout (*informal*) • *to end in failure*
OPPOSITE: success

2 = **disappointment**, loser, turkey (*slang*), flop (*informal*), incompetent, ne'er-do-well • *The new business was a complete failure.*
3 = **shortcoming**, deficiency • *a failure in the insurance system*
4 = **bankruptcy**, crash, ruin, downfall, liquidation, insolvency
See also: **collapse**

faint *adjective* **1** = **dim**, low, vague, muted, faded, indistinct • *a faint smell of perfume*
OPPOSITE: strong
2 = **dizzy**, giddy, light-headed • *Feeling faint is one of the symptoms of lack of food.*
3 = **slight**, weak, remote, feeble, unenthusiastic
▸ *verb* **4** = **pass out**, collapse, black out • *to faint from shock*
▸ *noun* **5** = **blackout**, collapse, swoon (*literary*), unconsciousness
See also: **slender, soft**

faint-hearted See **cowardly**

faintly *adverb* **1** = **softly**, weakly, feebly, in a whisper, indistinctly
2 = **slightly**, somewhat, dimly, a little

fair¹ *adjective* **1** = **unbiased**, equal, proper, legitimate, upright, impartial, equitable • *a fair trial*
OPPOSITE: unfair
2 = **light**, blonde or blond • *long, fair hair*
OPPOSITE: dark
3 = **respectable**, average, moderate, reasonable, decent, adequate, satisfactory, tolerable, passable, O.K. or okay (*informal*)
4 = **beautiful**, pretty, lovely, handsome, bonny, comely
5 = **fine**, clear, dry, bright, sunny, cloudless, unclouded
See also: **acceptable, all right**

fair² *noun* = **carnival**, show, festival, exhibition, fete, bazaar • *a country fair*
See also: **market**

fairly *adverb* **1** = **moderately**, rather, quite, somewhat, adequately, reasonably, pretty well, tolerably
2 = **deservedly**, properly, honestly, objectively, equitably,

impartially, justly, without fear or favour
3 = **positively**, really, absolutely

fairness *noun* = **impartiality**, justice, equity, legitimacy, decency, disinterestedness, equitableness, rightfulness

fairy *noun* = **sprite**, brownie, elf, pixie, imp, leprechaun, peri, Robin Goodfellow
▷ **fairy tale, fairy story**
= **folk tale**, romance;
= **lie**, fiction, invention, fabrication, cock-and-bull story (*informal*), tall tale (*informal*), untruth

faith *noun* **1** = **trust**, confidence • *to have great faith in something*
2 = **religion**, belief, persuasion, creed • *the faith of their family*
3 = **allegiance**, loyalty, fidelity, constancy, faithfulness

faithful *adjective* **1** = **loyal**, true, staunch, devoted • *a faithful dog*
OPPOSITE: unfaithful
2 = **accurate**, true, strict, exact • *The play was faithful to the novel.*
See also: **realistic, reliable, steadfast, trusty**

faithfully See **exactly**

faithless *adjective* = **disloyal**, false, unreliable, treacherous, fickle, unfaithful, inconstant, traitorous

fake *noun* **1** = **fraud**, copy, reproduction, forgery, sham, imitation • *These paintings are fakes.*
▸ *adjective* **2** = **artificial**, false, counterfeit, phony (*informal*), imitation • *fake fur*
OPPOSITE: real
▸ *verb* **3** = **pretend**, simulate, feign • *He faked his own death.*
See also: **mock**

fall *verb* **1** = **drop**, trip, collapse, plunge, topple • *The tile fell from the roof.*
OPPOSITE: rise
2 = **decrease**, decline, plummet, diminish, dwindle, subside, abate, ebb, depreciate • *The value of the Canadian dollar fell last week.*
OPPOSITE: increase
3 = **be overthrown**, surrender,

succumb, capitulate, pass into enemy hands

4 = die, perish, be killed, meet one's end

5 = occur, happen, chance, befall, come about, come to pass, take place

6 = slope, incline, fall away

7 = lapse, offend, sin, err, trespass, go astray, transgress

▷ **fall apart** See **disintegrate**

▷ **fall behind** See **lag**

▷ **fall down** See **collapse**

▷ **fall ill** See **develop**

▷ **fall out = argue**, fight, clash, disagree, differ, squabble, quarrel, come to blows, throw down (*slang*)

▷ **fall over** See **trip**

▷ **fall to** See **reach**

▷ **fall to pieces** See **disintegrate**

▶ *noun* **8 = decrease**, drop, decline, slump, reduction • *a fall in the exchange rate*

OPPOSITE: rise

9 = descent, drop, slip, tumble, plunge, dive, plummet, nose dive, face-plant (*informal*)

10 = collapse, defeat, destruction, ruin, overthrow, downfall, capitulation

11 = lapse, sin, transgression

See also: **descend**

| INFORMALLY SPEAKING
fall all over yourself: be extremely eager
fall for: be fooled by; fall in love with
fall off: decline
fall through: fail

fallacy *noun* **= error**, mistake, flaw, misconception, delusion, falsehood, misapprehension, untruth

fallible *adjective* **= imperfect**, weak, uncertain, ignorant, frail, erring

fallow *adjective* **= uncultivated**, idle, unused, dormant, inactive, resting, unplanted

false *adjective* **1 = untrue**, fictitious • *He gave a false name and address.*

OPPOSITE: true

2 = incorrect, wrong, faulty,

inaccurate, mistaken, invalid, erroneous, inexact • *false information*

3 = artificial, fake, bogus, simulated, forged • *false eyelashes*

OPPOSITE: genuine

4 = deceitful, unfaithful, disloyal, insincere • *They turned out to be false friends.*

See also: **deceptive, lying, mock, phony, two-faced**

falsehood *noun*

1 = untruthfulness, deception, deceit, dishonesty, dissimulation, mendacity

2 = lie, story, fiction, fabrication, fib, untruth

falsify *verb* **= forge**, doctor, fake, counterfeit, alter, misrepresent, distort, tamper with

falter *verb* **= hesitate**, stumble, waver, stutter, vacillate, stammer, totter

faltering *adjective* **= hesitant**, weak, tentative, uncertain, timid, broken, irresolute, stammering

fame *noun* **= prominence**, reputation, glory, renown, eminence • *The movie brought her international fame.*

See also: **success**

familiar *adjective* **1 = acquainted with**, aware of, knowledgeable about, versed in • *Most children are familiar with fairy tales.*

OPPOSITE: unfamiliar

2 = well-known, common, routine, frequent, ordinary, recognizable, customary, accustomed

3 = friendly, close, easy, intimate, amicable, relaxed

4 = disrespectful, forward, bold, intrusive, presumptuous, impudent

▷ **familiar with** See **aware of**

See also: **informal**

familiarity *noun*

1 = acquaintance, experience, understanding, awareness, grasp

2 = friendliness, ease, openness, intimacy, informality, sociability

f

3 = disrespect, presumption, boldness, forwardness

familiarize *verb* = **accustom**, season, school, train, instruct, inure, habituate

family *noun* **1 = relations**, descendants, relatives • *My family is always supportive of me.*
RELATED WORD
adjective: familial
2 = class, kind, classification
• *Tigers are members of the cat family.*
3 = clan, house, race, tribe, dynasty
See also: **kin, young**

famine *noun* = **hunger**, starvation, scarcity, dearth

famished *adjective* = **starving**, voracious, ravenous

famous *adjective* = **well-known**, legendary, renowned, celebrated, illustrious, distinguished, noted • *She was undoubtedly the most famous singer of her time.*
OPPOSITE: unknown
▷ **famous name** *See* **personality**
See also: **prominent**

fan[1] *noun* **1 = blower**, ventilator, air conditioner
▶ *verb* **2 = blow**, cool, refresh, ventilate, air-condition
▷ **fan out** *See* **spread**

fan[2] *noun* = **enthusiast**, supporter, lover, buff (*informal*), admirer, devotee, aficionado, adherent, zealot, groupie (*slang*) • *a fan of the new band*
See also: **follower**

fanatic *noun* = **extremist**, militant, activist, devotee, zealot
• *a soccer fanatic*

fanatical *adjective* = **obsessive**, wild, passionate, rabid, fervent
• *a fanatical supporter of the baseball team*
See also: **crazy**

fanciful *adjective* = **unreal**, wild, romantic, visionary, imaginary, whimsical, mythical

fancy *verb* **1 = want**, be attracted to, hanker after, have a yen for, would like • *He fancied an ice-cream cone.*

2 = suppose, think, believe, imagine, reckon, conjecture, think likely
▶ *adjective* **3 = elaborate**, extravagant, intricate, ornate, decorated • *dressed up in fancy clothes*
OPPOSITE: plain
▶ *noun* **4 = whim**, urge, idea, thought, desire, notion, impulse, inclination, humour, caprice
5 = delusion, dream, vision, fantasy, chimera, daydream
See also: **illusion**

fantasize *verb* = **daydream**, dream, imagine, envision

fantastic *adjective* **1** (*Informal*)
= **excellent**, wonderful, awesome (*slang*), sensational (*informal*), superb, marvellous, first-rate
2 = strange, grotesque, outlandish, fanciful
3 = unrealistic, wild, ridiculous, ludicrous, extravagant, far-fetched
4 = implausible, unlikely, incredible, absurd, preposterous, cock-and-bull (*informal*)

fantasy *noun* **1 = imagination**, invention, fancy, creativity, originality
2 = daydream, dream, vision, illusion, mirage, reverie, flight of fancy, pipe dream

far *adverb* **1 = a long way**, deep, afar, a great distance • *The ocean was far below us.*
2 = much, considerably, incomparably, very much • *far better than the others*
▷ **far from** *See* **unlike**
▶ *adjective* **3 = remote**, long, distant, outlying • *in the far south of the country*
OPPOSITE: near

farce *noun* **1 = comedy**, satire, burlesque, slapstick, buffoonery
2 = mockery, joke, nonsense, parody, sham, travesty

farcical *adjective* = **ludicrous**, comic, ridiculous, absurd, laughable, preposterous, nonsensical, derisory, risible

fare noun 1 = **charge**, price, ticket money
2 = **food**, sustenance, provisions, rations, victuals
▶ verb 3 = **get on**, do, manage, prosper, get along, make out

farewell noun = **good-bye**, departure, adieu, parting, sendoff (informal), leave-taking, valediction

far-fetched adjective = **unconvincing**, unlikely, incredible, fantastic, unbelievable, unrealistic, preposterous, implausible, cock-and-bull (informal)

farm noun 1 = **smallholding**, ranch, plantation, homestead, farmstead, grange
▶ verb 2 = **cultivate**, work, plant

fascinate verb = **entrance**, absorb, intrigue, captivate, bewitch, enthral • He was fascinated by the new discovery.
See also: **appeal, interest**

fascinating adjective = **entrancing**, engaging, irresistible, alluring, captivating, compelling, engrossing, enticing, gripping, intriguing, riveting

fascination noun = **attraction**, pull, lure, magic, charm, allure, magnetism, enchantment

fashion noun 1 = **style**, trend, vogue, fad, craze • changing fashions in clothing
2 = **manner**, way, method, mode • It works in a similar fashion.
▶ verb 3 = **make**, work, create, shape, construct, mould • fashioned from rough wood
See also: **form, model**

fashionable adjective = **popular**, in (informal), current, designer (informal), latest, chic, trendsetting, prevailing, in vogue, kicky (slang) • a fashionable restaurant
OPPOSITE: old-fashioned
See also: **trendy**

fast[1] adjective 1 = **quick**, rapid, speedy, swift, hurried, accelerated • a fast train
OPPOSITE: slow

2 = **fixed**, close, firm, sound, secure, tight, steadfast, fastened, immovable
3 = **dissipated**, wild, loose, reckless, extravagant, wanton, self-indulgent, dissolute, profligate
▶ adverb 4 = **quickly**, rapidly, swiftly, hastily, hurriedly • You'll have to move fast.
OPPOSITE: slowly
5 = **firmly**, tightly, securely • Hold fast to the rail.
See also: **express**

fast[2] verb 1 = **go hungry**, abstain, deny oneself, go without food
▶ noun 2 = **fasting**, abstinence

fasten verb = **secure**, join, tie, fix, lock, attach • Fasten your seatbelts.
See also: **bond, connect, hang, link, shut**

fastened See **secure, shut**

fastener See **clasp**

fastening See **clasp, connection**

fastidious adjective = **particular**, difficult, critical, nice, picky (informal), meticulous, fussy, squeamish, finicky, choosy, dainty, pernickety, punctilious, hypercritical, nit-picky (informal), hard to please, discriminating, overdelicate, overnice
OPPOSITE: careless

fat adjective 1 = **overweight**, heavy, obese, portly, plump, stout, rotund, pudgy, corpulent, tubby • a fat cat
OPPOSITE: thin
2 = **fatty**, oily, greasy, adipose, oleaginous
▶ noun 3 = **fatness**, obesity, bulk, flesh, lard (slang), blubber, corpulence, flab, paunch, spare tire (informal), saddlebags (informal), muffin top (informal)
See also: **thick**

fatal adjective 1 = **lethal**, deadly, terminal, incurable, mortal • fatal injuries
2 = **disastrous**, catastrophic, calamitous • The mistake was fatal to my plans.

fatality noun = **death**, loss, casualty, mortality

fate noun **1 = destiny**, chance, fortune, providence • *the fickleness of fate*
2 = fortune, lot, cup, portion, horoscope, stars
See also: **luck**

fated adjective **= destined**, sure, inevitable, doomed, inescapable, foreordained, predestined, preordained, written

fateful adjective **1 = crucial**, important, significant, critical, decisive, portentous
2 = disastrous, deadly, fatal, lethal, destructive, ominous, ruinous

father noun **1 = parent**, dad (*informal*), pa (*informal*), daddy (*informal*), papa (*old-fashioned, informal*), old man (*informal*), pop (*informal*), sire, pater (*old-fashioned, informal, chiefly Brit*)
2 = forefather, predecessor, ancestor, progenitor, forebear
3 = founder, author, maker, creator, architect, inventor, originator, prime mover
4 = priest, pastor, padre (*informal*)
▸ verb **5 = sire**, get, beget, procreate

fatherland noun **= homeland**, motherland, native land

fatherly adjective **= paternal**, protective, supportive, benign, kindly, affectionate, benevolent, patriarchal

fathom verb **= understand**, interpret, grasp, comprehend, get to the bottom of

fatigue noun **1 = tiredness**, lethargy, heaviness, languor, listlessness
▸ verb **2 = tire**, drain, exhaust, weaken, weary, take it out of (*informal*), wear out

fatigued adjective **= tired**, weary, overtired, zonked (*slang*), bushed (*informal*), wasted, tired out, exhausted, (dead) beat (*informal*), all in (*slang*)

fatten verb **1 = grow fat**, spread, expand, swell, thicken, gain weight, put on weight
2 (*often with* up) **= feed up**, feed, stuff, nourish, build up, overfeed

fatty adjective **= greasy**, fat, rich, oily, adipose, oleaginous

fatuous adjective **= foolish**, stupid, silly, ludicrous, mindless, idiotic, inane, moronic, brainless, witless

fault noun **1 = responsibility**, blame, liability • *It was all my fault!*
2 = flaw, weakness, defect, deficiency, blemish, drawback, failing, imperfection • *a minor technical fault*
OPPOSITE: strength
3 = mistake, slip, error, oversight, lapse, blunder, indiscretion
at fault = guilty, responsible, culpable, answerable, blamable, in the wrong, to blame
find fault with = criticize, complain, quibble, carp at, pick holes in, pull to pieces, take to task
to a fault = excessively, unduly, immoderately, in the extreme, overmuch
▸ verb **4 = criticize**, blame, censure • *Her conduct cannot be faulted.*
See also: **fissure, hole**

INFORMALLY SPEAKING
at fault: deserving the blame
find fault with: criticize in a negative way
to a fault: to a great degree

faultfinding *See* **criticism**

faultless adjective **= flawless**, model, perfect, correct, exemplary, impeccable, foolproof, unblemished

faulty adjective **= defective**, flawed, invalid, imperfect, buggy (*informal*), unsound, imprecise, fallacious, malfunctioning • *Faulty goods should be sent back.*
See also: **weak, wrong**

favour noun **1 = approval**, support, grace, esteem • *The proposals met with favour.*
OPPOSITE: disapproval
2 = good turn, service, courtesy, kindness • *Can you do me a favour?*
OPPOSITE: wrong

▶ *verb* **3** = **prefer**, single out
• *They favoured the cuter puppy.*
4 = **advocate**, support, approve,
champion, encourage, prefer,
commend, incline towards
See also: **back**, **goodwill**

favourable *adjective*
1 = **advantageous**, good,
beneficial, suitable, opportune
• *favourable conditions*
OPPOSITE: unfavourable
2 = **positive**, friendly,
sympathetic, affirmative,
amicable, approving, welcoming
• *a positive response*
OPPOSITE: unfavourable

favourably *adverb*
1 = **advantageously**, well,
fortunately, conveniently,
profitably, auspiciously,
opportunely, to one's advantage
2 = **positively**, enthusiastically,
helpfully, approvingly, with
approval
See also: **well**

favoured See **favourite**

favourite *adjective* **1** = **preferred**,
best-loved, dearest, favoured
• *my favourite teacher*
▶ *noun* **2** = **darling**, pick, pet, idol
• *The collie was always her favourite.*
See also: **popular**

favouritism *noun* = **bias**, one-
sidedness • *There was never a hint of
favouritism.*
OPPOSITE: impartiality

fawn¹ *verb* (often with *on* or *upon*)
= **ingratiate oneself**, creep,
crawl, flatter, cringe, curry
favour, brown-nose (*slang*),
dance attendance, grovel, kiss
ass (*slang*), kowtow, pander to

fawn² *adjective* = **beige**, neutral,
buff, greyish-brown

fawning *adjective* = **obsequious**,
deferential, crawling, cringing,
flattering, grovelling, servile,
sycophantic

fear *noun* **1** = **dread**, terror, alarm,
panic, awe, trepidation, fright,
apprehensiveness, cravenness
• *shivering with fear*
2 = **bugbear**, bogey, horror,
nightmare, bête noire, spectre
▶ *verb* **3** = **be afraid**, dread, be

frightened, be scared, take fright
• *There is nothing to fear.*
▷ **fear for** = **worry about**, be
anxious about, feel concern for
See also: **anxiety**, **worry**

fearful *adjective* **1** = **scared**,
afraid, nervous, frightened,
uneasy, timid, alarmed, jumpy,
timorous, wired (*slang*)
2 = **frightful**, terrible, dire,
awful, horrific, gruesome,
horrendous, dreadful, hair-
raising

fearfully *adverb* **1** = **nervously**,
apprehensively, diffidently,
timidly, timorously, uneasily
2 = **very**, terribly, excessively,
tremendously, awfully,
exceedingly, frightfully

fearless *adjective* = **brave**, bold,
courageous, valiant, plucky,
intrepid, undaunted, unafraid,
indomitable, dauntless

fearsome *adjective* = **terrifying**,
daunting, formidable, awe-
inspiring, frightening,
horrifying, menacing,
unnerving

feasible *adjective* = **possible**,
likely, reasonable, viable,
achievable, attainable,
workable, practicable

feast *noun* **1** = **banquet**, treat,
spread (*informal*), dinner, repast
2 = **festival**, holiday, celebration,
fête, holy day, red-letter day,
saint's day
3 = **treat**, delight, pleasure,
enjoyment, gratification
▶ *verb* **4** = **eat one's fill**, indulge,
gorge, overindulge, gormandize,
pig out (*slang*), wine and dine

feat *noun* = **accomplishment**,
act, performance, achievement,
exploit, deed, attainment

feathers *plural noun* = **plumage**,
down, plumes

feature *noun* **1** = **aspect**, mark,
quality, property, attribute,
characteristic • *an unusual feature
of the room*
2 = **article**, report, story, piece,
item, blog, column • *a news
feature*
3 = **highlight**, attraction,

specialty, main item
▶ *verb* **4** = **spotlight**, emphasize, give prominence to, star
• *featuring an interview with the premier*
See also: **point**

features *plural noun* = **face**, countenance, lineaments, physiognomy

feckless *adjective* = **irresponsible**, incompetent, worthless, hopeless, ineffectual, good-for-nothing, shiftless

fed up *adjective* = **dissatisfied**, bored, tired, depressed, glum, discontented, down in the mouth, sick and tired (*informal*)

federation *noun* = **union**, league, coalition, association, combination, alliance, syndicate, amalgamation

fee *noun* = **charge**, bill, payment, toll, remuneration

feeble *adjective* **1** = **weak**, frail, infirm, sickly, puny, weedy (*informal*), debilitated, doddering, effete
2 = **unconvincing**, poor, thin, inadequate, tame, insufficient, pathetic, lousy (*slang*), lame, paltry, flimsy

feebleness *noun* = **weakness**, frailty, effeteness, infirmity, languor, lassitude, sickliness

feed *verb* **1** = **cater for**, supply, sustain, provision, nourish, provide for, victual, wine and dine
2 (sometimes with *on*) = **eat**, devour, chow down (*slang*), exist on, live on, partake of
▶ *noun* **3** = **food**, fodder, pasturage, provender
4 (*Informal*) = **meal**, feast, spread (*informal*), repast

feedback *See* **reaction**

feel *verb* **1** = **experience**, suffer, undergo • *I felt enormous happiness.*
2 = **believe**, think, consider, judge, deem • *She feels she is in control of her life.*
3 = **touch**, stroke, finger, fondle • *Feel this lovely material!*
4 = **sense**, be convinced, intuit
▷ **feel dejected** *See* **despair**

▷ **feel despondent** *See* **despair**
▷ **feel for** *See* **identify with**, **pity**
▷ **feel sorry for** *See* **pity**
▷ **feel uneasy** *See* **worry**
▶ *noun* **5** = **texture**, finish, touch, surface
6 = **impression**, air, quality, sense, feeling, atmosphere, ambience
See also: **handle, have, suspect**

| INFORMALLY SPEAKING
feel for: sympathize with
feel like: have a desire for
feel out: find out about, in a cautious way

feeler *noun* **1** = **antenna**, tentacle, whisker
2 = **approach**, probe, advance

feeling *noun* **1** = **emotion**, heat, passion, sentiment, fervour
• *feelings of envy*
2 = **sensation**, sense • *a feeling of pain*
3 = **opinion**, view, perspective, inclination, point of view • *strong feelings on politics*
4 = **impression**, idea, sense, suspicion, notion, hunch, inkling, presentiment
5 = **sympathy**, concern, understanding, sensitivity, compassion, empathy, pity, sensibility
6 = **atmosphere**, feel, air, quality, mood, aura, ambience
See also: **guess, instinct**

feign *See* **fake, pretend**
feigned *See* **mock**
feline *See* **cat**
fell *verb* = **cut down**, cut, level, demolish, hew, knock down
fellow *noun* **1** = **man**, person, guy (*informal*), individual, character, chap (*informal*)
2 = **associate**, partner, colleague, peer, comrade, companion
▶ *adjective*
▷ **fellow worker** *See* **colleague**
fellowship *noun*
1 = **camaraderie**, companionship • *a sense of community and fellowship*
2 = **society**, order, club, league,

association, guild, fraternity, brotherhood

female noun **1** = **woman**, girl, lady • Hay fever affects males more than females.

▶ adjective **2** = **feminine** • the world's greatest female skater

feminine adjective = **womanly**, soft, tender, delicate, gentle, ladylike

fen noun = **marsh**, swamp, bog, quagmire, slough, morass

fence noun **1** = **barrier**, wall, hedge, defense, barricade, rampart, palisade, railings

▶ verb **2** (often with in or off) = **enclose**, protect, surround, pen, confine, bound, encircle **3** = **evade**, dodge, equivocate, parry

ferment noun = **commotion**, stir, disruption, turmoil, unrest, excitement, frenzy, uproar, furor, tumult

ferocious adjective **1** = **fierce**, violent, wild, savage, predatory, rapacious, ravening **2** = **cruel**, brutal, vicious, barbaric, ruthless, bloodthirsty

ferocity noun = **savagery**, cruelty, brutality, viciousness, wildness, bloodthirstiness, fierceness

ferret noun

▶ verb

▷ **ferret out** = **track down**, discover, trace, unearth, elicit, dig up, root out, search out

ferry noun **1** = **ferry boat**, packet, packet boat

▶ verb **2** = **carry**, run, ship, shuttle, transport, convey, chauffeur

fertile adjective = **productive**, rich, prolific, fruitful • fertile soil OPPOSITE: barren
See also: **creative**

fertility noun = **fruitfulness**, abundance, richness, fecundity, luxuriance, productiveness

fertilizer noun = **compost**, manure, dressing, dung

fervent adjective = **ardent**, passionate, enthusiastic, committed, devout, zealous,

impassioned • a fervent admirer of her work
See also: **fanatical, intense**

fervour noun = **intensity**, passion, excitement, enthusiasm, warmth, zeal, ardour, vehemence
See also: **feeling, heat, violence**

fester verb **1** = **decay**, putrefy, suppurate, ulcerate **2** = **intensify**, aggravate, smoulder

festival noun **1** = **fair**, entertainment, gala, fete, carnival • the Toronto Film Festival **2** = **holiday** • different religious festivals
See also: **celebration**

festive adjective = **celebratory**, happy, jubilant, merry, joyful, joyous, cheery, jovial, convivial

festivity noun (often plural) = **celebration**, party, festival, entertainment

festoon verb = **decorate**, hang, array, deck, drape, swathe, garland, wreathe

fetch verb **1** = **bring**, get, carry, deliver, obtain, transport, retrieve, convey, go for **2** = **sell for**, make, earn, realize, yield, bring in, go for

fetching adjective = **attractive**, cute, charming, alluring, captivating, enticing, winsome

fete See **fair, festival**

fetish noun **1** = **fixation**, thing (informal), obsession, mania **2** = **talisman**, amulet

feud noun **1** = **hostility**, conflict, row, argument, rivalry, disagreement, quarrel, vendetta, enmity

▶ verb **2** = **quarrel**, war, dispute, row, clash, contend, squabble, bicker, fall out

fever noun = **excitement**, frenzy, agitation, delirium, ferment, restlessness, fervour

feverish adjective **1** = **hot**, febrile, fevered, flushed, inflamed, pyretic (medical) **2** = **excited**, frantic, frenzied, restless, frenetic, overwrought, agitated, wired (*slang*)

few *adjective* = **not many**, scarce, meagre, sparse, infrequent • *a few moments ago*
OPPOSITE: many
See also: **rare, uncommon**

> **CONFUSABLES**
> *Fewer* means *not so many.*
> *Less* means *not so much.*

fewest *See* **least**

fiasco *noun* = **failure**, disaster, mess, catastrophe, debacle, washout (*informal*)

fib *noun* = **lie**, story, fiction, untruth, white lie

fibbing *See* **lying**

fibre *noun* 1 = **thread**, strand, pile, texture, filament, wisp
2 = **essence**, quality, nature, substance, spirit
▷ **moral fibre** = **strength of character**, strength, resolution, toughness, stamina

fickle *adjective* = **changeable**, volatile, variable, temperamental, capricious, unfaithful, faithless, inconstant, irresolute

fiction *noun* 1 = **tale**, story, novel, legend, fantasy, romance, myth, yarn (*informal*)
2 = **lie**, invention, fabrication, falsehood, cock and bull story (*informal*), tall tale (*informal*), untruth, urban legend

fictional *adjective* = **imaginary**, legendary, unreal, nonexistent, made-up, invented

fictitious *adjective* = **false**, bogus, untrue, imaginary, mythical, made-up, make-believe, fabricated, invented

fiddle *verb* 1 = **fidget**, play, finger, tinker, interfere with, mess around with, tamper with
▶ *noun* 2 = **violin**
▷ **fit as a fiddle** = **healthy**, strong, sound, blooming, hale and hearty, in fine fettle, in good form, in good shape, in rude health, in the pink

fiddling *adjective* = **trivial**, petty, insignificant, futile, pettifogging, trifling

fidelity *noun* 1 = **loyalty**, devotion, allegiance, dependability, constancy, faithfulness, staunchness, trustworthiness
2 = **accuracy**, precision, correspondence, closeness, exactness, faithfulness, scrupulousness

fidget *verb* = **twitch**, fiddle (*informal*), squirm, jiggle • *fidgeting in his seat*
▶ *noun*
▷ **the fidgets** = **restlessness**, nervousness, unease, uneasiness, fidgetiness, jitters (*informal*)
See also: **fuss**

fidgety *adjective* = **restless**, nervous, impatient, uneasy, jittery (*informal*), restive, jumpy, twitchy (*informal*), antsy (*slang*), on edge, wired (*slang*)

field *noun* 1 = **meadow**, pasture • *a field full of sheep*
2 = **area**, province, department, territory, specialty, domain • *a breakthrough in the field of physics*
3 = **competitors**, competition, applicants, candidates, contestants, entrants, possibilities, runners
▶ *verb* 4 = **retrieve**, return, stop, catch, pick up
5 = **deal with**, handle, deflect, turn aside
See also: **range**

fiend *noun* 1 = **demon**, devil, evil spirit
2 = **brute**, monster, beast, savage, barbarian, ogre, ghoul
3 (*Informal*) = **enthusiast**, addict, freak (*informal*), fanatic, maniac

fiendish *adjective* = **wicked**, cruel, malignant, satanic, monstrous, unspeakable, diabolical, devilish, hellish, infernal

fierce *adjective* 1 = **ferocious**, dangerous, aggressive, murderous • *a fierce lion*
OPPOSITE: gentle
2 = **intense**, strong, keen, relentless • *fierce competition*
3 = **stormy**, strong, powerful, violent, furious, raging,

inclement, tempestuous, howling
See also: **wild**

fiercely adverb = **ferociously**, passionately, furiously, viciously, savagely, tempestuously, tigerishly, tooth and nail, with no holds barred

fiery adjective **1** = **burning**, ablaze, flaming, aflame, afire, blazing, on fire
2 = **excitable**, fierce, passionate, irritable, irascible, hot-headed, impetuous

fight verb **1** = **battle**, struggle, brawl, grapple, throw down (slang) • He fought the world boxing champion.
2 = **oppose**, dispute, contest, resist, defy, withstand, make a stand against, stand up to
3 = **engage in**, conduct, wage, prosecute, carry on
▷ **fight against** See **oppose**
▷ **fight for** See **champion**
▷ **fight off** = **repel**, resist, repress, repulse, beat off, keep at bay or hold at bay, stave off, ward off
▶ noun **4** = **battle**, action, combat, bout, duel, skirmish, slugfest (informal), throwdown (slang) • a fight between gladiators
5 = **argument**, dispute, row, squabble • a fight with my best friend
6 = **resistance**, spirit, pluck, militancy, belligerence
See also: **argue, clash, compete, quarrel, war**

fighter noun **1** = **soldier**, warrior, mercenary • killing 15 rebel fighters
2 = **boxer**, pugilist, prize fighter

fighting See **conflict, war**

figure noun **1** = **number**, total, amount, statistic, digit, numeral • No one really knows the true figures.
2 = **shape**, body, build, form, silhouette, physique • A figure appeared in the doorway.
3 = **person**, player, character, personality, dignitary • international political figures
4 = **amount**, price, cost, total, value, sum

5 = **diagram**, design, pattern, drawing, representation, sketch, illustration
▶ verb **6** (Informal) = **suppose**, expect, guess, reckon (informal) • I figure I'll learn from experience
7 = **calculate**, count, tally, compute, reckon, tot up, work out
8 (usually with in) = **feature**, appear, act, be featured, contribute to, play a part
▷ **figure out** = **calculate**, compute, reckon, work out; = **understand**, see, comprehend, decipher, fathom, make out
See also: **outline, symbol**

figurehead noun = **front man**, puppet, mouthpiece, titular head or nominal head

filch verb = **steal**, take, pinch (informal), misappropriate, pilfer, embezzle, thieve, walk off with

file[1] noun **1** = **folder**, case, information, portfolio, data, dossier, documents
2 = **line**, row, column, queue
▶ verb **3** = **register**, record, enter, document, pigeonhole, put in place
4 = **march**, troop, parade

file[2] verb = **smooth**, shape, scrape, rub, polish, rasp, abrade

fill verb **1** = **pack**, stock, stuff, cram, gorge • Fill the bottle with water.
OPPOSITE: empty
2 = **saturate**, charge, pervade, imbue, impregnate, suffuse
3 = **plug**, close, stop, block, seal, cork, bung
4 = **perform**, hold, execute, occupy, fulfill, discharge, carry out
▷ **fill in** = **complete**, answer, fill out (US), fill up; (Informal) = **inform**, acquaint, apprise, bring up to date, give the facts or give the background; = **replace**, represent, sub, substitute, deputize, stand in, take the place of
▷ **fill out** = **complete**, answer, fill in, fill up

f

▶ *noun*
▷ **one's fill = sufficient**, enough, plenty, ample, all one wants
See also: **load**

> **INFORMALLY SPEAKING**
> **fill someone in**: bring someone up to date
> **fill the bill**: be just what is needed

filled *See* **full**
filler *noun* = **padding**, stopgap, makeweight
filling *noun* **1** = **stuffing**, inside, filler, contents, insides, padding, wadding
▶ *adjective* **2** = **satisfying**, heavy, square, substantial, ample
film *noun* **1** = **layer**, skin, tissue, coating, membrane, covering, dusting
2 = **movie**, flick (*slang*), motion picture
▶ *verb* **3** = **photograph**, take, shoot, video, videotape
filter *noun* **1** = **sieve**, mesh, riddle, membrane, gauze, strainer
▶ *verb* **2** = **purify**, screen, strain, refine, clarify, sift, winnow, sieve, filtrate
3 = **trickle**, escape, leak, penetrate, dribble, seep, ooze, exude, percolate
filtered *See* **refined**
filth *noun* **1** = **dirt**, refuse, sewage, sludge, muck, excrement, grime, squalor, slime
2 = **obscenity**, pornography, indecency, vulgarity, impurity, smut
filthy *adjective* **1** = **dirty**, foul, polluted, slimy, squalid, unclean, putrid
2 = **muddy**, grimy, grubby, begrimed, blackened, scuzzy (*slang*)
3 = **obscene**, corrupt, pornographic, indecent, lewd, X-rated, depraved, impure, licentious, smutty
final *adjective* **1** = **last**, ultimate, eventual, closing, concluding • *the fifth and final day*
OPPOSITE: first
2 = **definitive**, absolute, definite,

conclusive • *The judges' decision is final.*
finale *noun* = **ending**, close, conclusion, climax, culmination, epilogue, denouement
finalize *verb* = **complete**, decide, settle, conclude, clinch, tie up, wind up, work out, wrap up (*informal*)
finally *adverb* **1** = **eventually**, at last, at the last moment, in the end, in the long run • *It finally arrived.*
2 = **in conclusion**, lastly, in summary • *Finally, I'd like to talk about safety measures.*
finance *verb* **1** = **pay for**, back, support, fund • *financed by the government*
▶ *noun* **2** = **economics**, investment, banking, commerce, budgeting • *the world of high finance*
finances *plural noun* = **resources**, money, capital, cash, pocketbook (*informal*), wherewithal, affairs, assets, funds
financial *adjective* = **economic**, fiscal, monetary • *financial difficulties*
find *verb* **1** = **discover**, locate, unearth, come across, track down, turn up, scare up (*informal*), descry, espy, ferret out • *I can't find that computer file.*
OPPOSITE: lose
2 = **realize**, learn, discover, detect, become aware • *We found that we had a lot in common.*
▷ **find a solution to** *See* **resolve**
▷ **find fault** *See* **complain**, **put down**
▷ **find fault with** *See* **criticize**
▷ **find out = learn**, note, discover, realize, detect, observe, perceive; = **detect**, catch, reveal, expose, disclose, uncover, unmask
▷ **find unacceptable** *See* **disapprove**
▶ *noun* **3** = **discovery**, catch, acquisition, asset, bargain, good buy
finding *See* **decision**, **verdict**

fine¹ adjective **1 = excellent**, beautiful, outstanding, magnificent, splendid, admirable • fine clothes
2 = delicate, slender, powdery • powder with very fine particles
3 = thin, light, sheer, lightweight, flimsy, diaphanous, gauzy, gossamer • fine fabrics
4 = subtle, sensitive, keen, precise, refined, fastidious • the fine details
5 = sunny, clear, fair, dry, bright, pleasant, balmy, cloudless, clement
6 = satisfactory, good, acceptable, suitable, convenient, all right, O.K. or okay (informal)
See also: **narrow, sound**

fine² noun **1 = penalty**, punishment, forfeit, damages
▶ verb **2 = penalize**, punish

finery noun **= splendour**, gear (informal), frippery, glad rags (informal), ornaments, showiness, Sunday best, trappings, trinkets

finesse noun **= skill**, craft, diplomacy, discretion, delicacy, sophistication, tact, subtlety, adeptness, adroitness, savoir-faire

finger verb **= touch**, feel, handle, manipulate, maul, paw (informal), fiddle with (informal), toy with

finish verb **1 = complete**, end, close, conclude, finalize • I have to finish a report.
OPPOSITE: start
2 = consume, eat, empty, exhaust, devour, dispose of, use up
3 = destroy, defeat, overcome, rout, ruin, exterminate, bring down, knock down, dispose of, put an end to, put paid to
4 = perfect, refine, polish
5 = coat, stain, polish, wax, texture, veneer, lacquer, gild
▶ noun **6 = end**, close, conclusion, finale, completion, ending • to see it through to the finish
OPPOSITE: start

7 = surface, grain, shine, polish, texture, lustre • a glossy finish
8 = defeat, end, death, ruin, annihilation, curtains (informal), end of the road
See also: **cease, stop**

finished adjective **1 = polished**, professional, accomplished, refined, perfected
2 = over, through, complete, closed, done, ended, finalized
3 = spent, empty, done, drained, exhausted, used up
4 = ruined, through, lost, doomed, defeated, done for (informal), undone, wiped out

finite adjective **= limited**, restricted, bounded, circumscribed, delimited, demarcated

fire noun **1 = flames**, blaze, combustion, inferno • a ball of fire
2 = bombardment, hail, barrage, salvo, volley, flak, cannonade, fusillade, shelling, sniping
3 = passion, spirit, intensity, excitement, enthusiasm, sparkle, eagerness, vigour, verve, ardour, fervour
▶ verb **4 = shoot**, launch, explode, detonate, set off • to fire a starter's pistol
5 (Informal) **= dismiss**, sack (informal), discharge, lay off, make redundant • She was fired yesterday.
6 = inspire, excite, stir, inflame, animate, galvanize, rouse, enliven, impassion

> **INFORMALLY SPEAKING**
> **fire away**: go ahead and ask
> **light a fire under**: encourage someone to act more quickly
> **play with fire**: meddle with something dangerous

firebrand noun **= rabble-rouser**, instigator, incendiary, agitator, demagogue, tub-thumper

fireworks plural noun
1 = pyrotechnics, illuminations
2 = rage, storm, trouble, row, uproar, hysterics

firm¹ adjective **1 = hard**, set, solid, stiff, rigid, compressed,

congealed • *Freeze the ice cream until it is firm.*
OPPOSITE: soft

2 = determined, staunch, adamant, resolute, inflexible, unshakable • *The debating team needs a firm coach.*

3 = secure, fast, tight, stable, steady, unshakable, embedded, fixed, immovable, rooted
See also: **positive, steadfast, strict, trusty**

firm² noun = **company**, business, organization, corporation, enterprise • *a firm of builders*

firmly adverb **1 = securely**, steadily, tightly, immovably, like a rock, unflinchingly, unshakably

2 = resolutely, steadfastly, staunchly, unchangeably, unwaveringly

firmness noun **1 = hardness**, resistance, stiffness, rigidity, inelasticity, inflexibility, solidity

2 = resolve, resolution, constancy, inflexibility, staunchness, steadfastness

first adjective **1 = earliest**, opening, original, initial, primeval • *the first moon landing*
OPPOSITE: last

2 = foremost, chief, prime, principal, leading • *our first responsibility*

3 = elementary, key, primary, basic, fundamental, cardinal, rudimentary

▶ adverb **4 = to begin with**, earlier, initially, beforehand, firstly • *You must do that first.*

▶ noun

▷ **from the first = from the start**, from the beginning, from the commencement, from the inception, from the introduction, from the outset, from the starting point

first-class adjective = **excellent**, prime, premium, exceptional, world-class, outstanding, superb, exemplary, marvellous, blue-chip, five-star, top-notch (*informal*), superlative, A1 or A-one (*informal*), tiptop,

twenty-four carat or 24-carat, tops (*slang*), second to none
OPPOSITE: terrible

first-hand See **direct**

first-rate adjective = **excellent**, exceptional, outstanding, superb, marvellous, splendid, first-class • *They were dealing with a first-rate professional.*
See also: **able, prime, prize, select, superior**

fiscal See **financial**

fishy adjective **1** (*Informal*) = **suspicious**, suspect, odd, unlikely, funny (*informal*), questionable, dubious, implausible

2 = fishlike, piscatorial, piscatory, piscine

fissure noun = **crack**, split, fault, rift, pothole, cleft, crevice • *There was a rumbling, and a fissure opened up.*
See also: **abyss, leak**

fit¹ verb **1 = match**, go, belong, correspond, dovetail • *made to fit a child*

2 = position, place, arrange • *a fitted carpet*

3 = prepare, arm, equip, fit out, provide

4 = adapt, shape, adjust, modify, alter, arrange, customize

▷ **fit out** See **equip**

▶ adjective **5 = healthy**, well, trim, robust, buff (*informal*), in good condition • *a reasonably fit person*
OPPOSITE: unfit

6 = appropriate, right, correct, proper, suitable, fitting, apt, becoming, seemly
See also: **burst, sound**

fit² noun **1 = seizure**, attack, bout, spasm, convulsion, paroxysm

2 = outbreak, burst, spell, bout, outburst

fitful adjective = **irregular**, uneven, sporadic, intermittent, disturbed, desultory, broken, inconstant, spasmodic

fitness noun

1 = appropriateness, readiness, eligibility, competence,

suitability, aptness, propriety
2 = **health**, strength, vigour, good condition, good health, robustness

fitting adjective 1 = **appropriate**, right, correct, proper, suitable • a fitting thank-you speech
▶ noun 2 = **accessory**, part, unit, component, attachment • fixtures and fittings

fix verb 1 = **fasten**, stick, secure, bind, attach • fixed to the wall
2 = **repair**, correct, mend, patch up • They fixed the broken window.
3 = **place**, set, plant, position, establish, locate, install, implant, embed
4 = **decide**, set, determine, settle, establish, arrange, specify, agree on, arrive at
5 = **focus**, direct
6 (Informal) = **manipulate**, influence, rig
▷ **fix up** = **arrange**, plan, settle, fix, organize, agree on, sort out; (often with with) = **provide**, arrange for, bring about, lay on
▶ noun 7 (informal) = **difficulty**, mess, predicament, quandary • in a bit of a fix
See also: **confirm, corrupt, glue, hang, hole, jam, limit**

fixation noun = **preoccupation**, thing (informal), complex, obsession, mania, hang-up (informal), idée fixe (French), infatuation

fixed adjective 1 = **permanent**, set, secure, established, rigid, immovable, rooted
2 = **intent**, steady, resolute, unwavering
3 = **agreed**, planned, established, definite, arranged, decided, resolved, settled

fixture See **attachment**

fizz verb = **bubble**, sparkle, fizzle, froth, sputter, hiss, effervesce

fizzy adjective = **bubbly**, sparkling, effervescent, bubbling, carbonated, gassy

flabbergasted adjective = **astonished**, speechless, staggered, overwhelmed, dumbfounded, amazed, astounded, lost for words, stunned

flabby adjective = **limp**, slack, floppy, sagging • a flabby stomach
OPPOSITE: taut

flag[1] noun 1 = **banner**, standard, pennant, streamer, colours, ensign, pennon
▶ verb 2 = **mark**, note, indicate, label
3 (sometimes with down) = **hail**, warn, wave, signal

flag[2] verb = **weaken**, fade, wane, sag, languish, weary, abate, wilt, droop, peter out

flagging adjective = **fading**, declining, deteriorating, faltering, waning, weakening, wilting

flagrant adjective = **outrageous**, brazen, scandalous, blatant, shameless, heinous, glaring, barefaced

flagstone noun = **paving stone**, block, flag, slab

flail verb = **thrash**, beat, windmill, thresh

flair noun 1 = **ability**, feel, gift, talent, faculty, mastery, genius, knack, aptitude
2 = **style**, taste, dash, chic, elegance, panache, discernment, stylishness

flak See **criticism**

flake noun 1 = **wafer**, scale, layer, shaving, sliver, peeling
▶ verb 2 = **blister**, chip, peel or peel off
▷ **flake out** = **collapse**, faint, keel over, pass out

flamboyant adjective
1 = **extravagant**, elaborate, theatrical, showy, ornate, swashbuckling, dashing, florid, ostentatious
2 = **colourful**, brilliant, glamorous, glitzy (slang), dazzling

flame noun 1 = **fire**, light, blaze, brightness
2 (Informal) = **sweetheart**, lover, girlfriend, boyfriend, beau, heart-throb (Brit)
▶ verb 3 = **burn**, blaze, shine,

flash, flare, glow, glare

flames See **fire**

flaming adjective = **burning**, red-hot, fiery, ablaze, glowing, raging, blazing

flank noun 1 = **side**, hip, thigh, loin
2 = **wing**, side

flap verb 1 = **flutter**, beat, wave, shake, thrash, vibrate, flail, wag
▶ noun 2 = **flutter**, beating, swish, shaking, swinging, waving

flare verb 1 = **blaze**, glare, flicker, burn up
2 = **widen**, broaden, spread out
▷ **flare up** = **lose one's temper**, explode, blow one's top (informal), boil over, fly off the handle (informal), throw a tantrum
▶ noun 3 = **flame**, blaze, burst, flash, glare, flicker

flash noun 1 = **flare**, burst, sparkle • a flash of lightning
2 = **moment**, second, instant, jiffy (informal), split second, trice, twinkling of an eye
▶ verb 3 = **flare**, sparkle, glitter, twinkle, glint • They signalled by flashing a light.
4 = **speed**, shoot, race, fly, streak, whistle, dash, zoom, dart
5 = **show**, display, expose, exhibit, flourish, flaunt
See also: **minute**

flashy adjective = **showy**, flamboyant, tacky (informal), garish • flashy clothes
OPPOSITE: modest
See also: **bold, gaudy, loud, ostentatious, tasteless, vulgar**

flat adjective 1 = **level**, smooth, horizontal, unbroken • a flat surface
OPPOSITE: uneven
2 = **dull**, weak, boring, monotonous, insipid • a dreadfully flat speech
3 = **absolute**, positive, explicit, downright, unequivocal, unqualified, categorical, out-and-out
4 = **punctured**, burst, empty, collapsed, blown out, deflated
▶ adverb 5 = **completely**, exactly,

absolutely, precisely, utterly, categorically, point blank
▷ **flat out = at full speed**, all out, at full tilt, for all one is worth
See also: **even, stale**

flatly adverb = **absolutely**, completely, positively, categorically, unhesitatingly

flatness noun 1 = **evenness**, uniformity, smoothness
2 = **dullness**, monotony, tedium

flatten verb = **level**, squash, trample, compress, raze, even out, iron out, smooth off

flatter verb 1 = **compliment**, fawn • flattering remarks
2 = **suit**, enhance, set off • clothes that flatter your figure
See also: **humour**

flattering adjective 1 = **becoming**, kind, effective, well-chosen, enhancing
2 = **ingratiating**, complimentary, fulsome, adulatory, fawning, laudatory

flattery noun = **fawning**, adulation • susceptible to flattery

flaunt verb = **show off**, sport (informal), display, exhibit, parade, flourish, brandish, flash around

flavour noun 1 = **taste**, smack, aroma, relish, seasoning, zest, flavouring, piquancy, savour, tang
2 = **quality**, feel, character, style, feeling, tone, essence, tinge
▶ verb 3 = **season**, spice, infuse, imbue, ginger up, leaven
See also: **taste**

flaw noun = **imperfection**, defect, fault, blemish • a flaw in his argument
See also: **hole, weakness**

flawed adjective = **damaged**, faulty, defective, erroneous, imperfect, unsound, blemished

flawless adjective = **perfect**, spotless, impeccable, unblemished, faultless, unsullied

flee verb = **run away**, leave, fly, escape, bolt, take flight • to flee the country

fleece See **cheat, coat**

fleet noun = **navy**, flotilla, armada, task force

fleeting adjective = **momentary**, brief, temporary, passing, short-lived, transient, ephemeral, transitory

flesh noun 1 = **meat**, weight, fat, tissue, brawn
2 = **human nature**, carnality, flesh and blood
▷ **one's own flesh and blood** = **family**, blood, kin, kinsfolk, kith and kin, relations, relatives

flexibility noun = **adaptability**, give (informal), resilience, elasticity, adjustability, pliability, pliancy, springiness

flexible adjective 1 = **supple**, elastic, lithe, pliable • flexible wire
2 = **adaptable**, open, discretionary • flexible working hours
See also: **soft**

flick verb = **strike**, hit, touch, tap, flip, dab
▷ **flick through** = **browse**, skip, thumb, skim, flip through, glance at

flicker verb 1 = **twinkle**, flash, flare, sparkle, shimmer, glimmer, gutter
2 = **flutter**, waver, vibrate, quiver
▶ noun 3 = **glimmer**, spark, flash, flare, gleam
4 = **trace**, spark, breath, glimmer, iota

flight[1] noun 1 = **journey**, trip, voyage
2 = **aviation**, aeronautics, flying
3 = **flock**, unit, cloud, formation, swarm, squadron

flight[2] noun = **escape**, exit, retreat, departure, getaway, exodus, fleeing, running away

flimsy adjective 1 = **fragile**, shaky, delicate, makeshift, frail, rickety, insubstantial
2 = **thin**, light, transparent, sheer, gauzy, gossamer
3 = **unconvincing**, poor, weak, inadequate, pathetic, lousy (slang), unsatisfactory, feeble, implausible

flinch verb = **wince**, start, shrink, cringe • The sharp pain made me flinch.

fling verb 1 = **throw**, cast, toss, propel, hurl, catapult, sling, heave
▶ noun 2 = **binge** (informal), party, bash, good time, spree

flip verb, noun = **toss**, throw, snap, spin, flick

flippancy noun = **frivolity**, irreverence, impertinence, levity, pertness, sauciness

flippant adjective = **frivolous**, disrespectful, cheeky, superficial, irreverent, glib, impertinent, offhand

flirt verb 1 = **lead on**, hit on (slang), make advances, make eyes at, philander
2 (usually with with) = **toy with**, consider, entertain, dabble in, expose oneself to, give a thought to, play with, trifle with
▶ noun 3 = **tease**, coquette, heart-breaker, hussy, philanderer

flirtatious adjective = **teasing**, provocative, coy, amorous, come-hither, coquettish, enticing, flirty, sportive

flit See **fly**

float verb 1 = **stay afloat**, drift, bob, be on the surface, lie on the surface • leaves floating on the river
OPPOSITE: sink
2 = **glide**, hang, hover, drift
• floating on the breeze
3 = **launch**, promote, get going, set up

floating adjective 1 = **buoyant**, afloat, sailing, buoyed up, swimming
2 = **fluctuating**, free, variable, movable, unattached, wandering

flock noun 1 = **herd**, flight, colony, drove, gaggle, skein
2 = **crowd**, company, group, host, mass, collection, gathering, herd, congregation
▶ verb 3 = **gather**, crowd, mass, collect, herd, converge, throng, huddle, congregate

flog verb = **beat**, lash, whip, trounce, whack, scourge, thrash, flagellate, flay

flood noun 1 = **deluge**, spate, downpour, torrent • *Many people were drowned in the floods.*
2 = **rush**, stream, spate, torrent • *a flood of angry letters*
▶ verb 3 = **immerse**, swamp, overflow, deluge, submerge • *The river flooded its banks.*
4 = **engulf**, sweep, surge, overwhelm, swarm
5 = **oversupply**, fill, choke, saturate, glut
See also: **flow, rash, wave**

floor noun 1 = **tier**, level, stage, story
▶ verb 2 = **knock down**, deck (*slang*), prostrate
3 (*Informal*) = **bewilder**, defeat, throw (*informal*), puzzle, baffle, stump, perplex, disconcert, confound, dumbfound

flop verb 1 = **fall**, drop, collapse, slump, sag, dangle, droop
2 (*Informal*) = **fail**, founder, fold (*informal*), misfire, come unstuck, fall flat, go belly-up (*slang*)
▶ noun 3 (*Informal*) = **failure**, disaster, debacle, fiasco, washout (*informal*), nonstarter

floppy adjective = **droopy**, loose, soft, limp, baggy, flaccid, pendulous, sagging

floral adjective = **flowery**, flower-patterned

florid adjective 1 = **flushed**, blowsy, high-coloured, rubicund, ruddy
2 = **flowery**, flamboyant, ornate, baroque, fussy, high-flown, overelaborate

flotsam noun = **debris**, wreckage, junk, detritus, jetsam, odds and ends

flounder verb = **fumble**, struggle, toss, stumble, thrash, grope

flourish verb 1 = **thrive**, boom, succeed, bloom, prosper, do well • *Business was flourishing.*
OPPOSITE: fail
2 = **wave**, display, brandish (*literary*), hold aloft • *She flourished her scarf for dramatic effect.*
▶ noun 3 = **wave**, sweep, flick • *with a flourish of his hand*
4 = **ornamentation**, sweep, decoration, plume, embellishment, curlicue
See also: **grow, shake**

flourishing adjective = **successful**, rampant, blooming, going places, in the pink, luxuriant, prospering, thriving

flout verb = **defy**, mock, scorn, spurn, laugh in the face of, scoff at, sneer at

flow verb 1 = **run**, roll, slide, circulate, glide • *a river flowing gently down into the valley*
2 = **pour**, sweep, surge, flood, rush, stream, cascade, gush
3 = **result**, issue, spring, emerge, proceed, arise, emanate
▶ noun 4 = **stream**, current, flood, tide, drift, outrush • *traffic flow*
See also: **drain, movement**

flower noun 1 = **bloom**, blossom, efflorescence
2 = **elite**, French, pick, cream, best, crème de la crème
▶ verb 3 = **blossom**, open, mature, flourish, unfold, bloom

flowery adjective = **ornate**, fancy, baroque, embellished, florid, high-flown

flowing adjective 1 = **streaming**, smooth, falling, gushing, rolling, rushing, sweeping
2 = **fluent**, easy, smooth, continuous, uninterrupted, unbroken

fluctuate verb = **change**, shift, swing, vary, alternate, veer, waver, seesaw, oscillate

fluctuating See **uneven**

fluency noun = **ease**, control, facility, command, assurance, readiness, articulateness, glibness, slickness, smoothness

fluent adjective = **articulate**, ready, easy, effortless, flowing • *a fluent speaker of Italian*
OPPOSITE: hesitant

fluff noun = **fuzz**, down, pile, nap

fluffy adjective = **soft**, fuzzy, downy, feathery, fleecy

fluid noun 1 = **liquid**, solution, liquor

▶ *adjective* **2** = **liquid**, runny, watery, flowing, liquefied, melted, molten

fluke *noun* = **lucky break**, chance, accident, coincidence, serendipity, quirk of fate, stroke of luck

flunk See **fail**

flurry *noun* **1** = **commotion**, stir, excitement, disturbance, fuss, bustle, flutter, ado
2 = **gust**, squall

flush[1] *verb* **1** = **blush**, glow, colour, go red, redden
2 = **rinse out**, flood, cleanse, hose down, wash out
▶ *noun* **3** = **blush**, glow, colour, redness, rosiness

flush[2] *adjective* **1** = **level**, even, true, square, flat
2 (*Informal*) = **wealthy**, rich, well-heeled (*informal*), well-off, moneyed, in the money (*informal*)

flushed *adjective* = **blushing**, hot, red, rosy, embarrassed, glowing, crimson, ruddy

fluster *verb* **1** = **upset**, disturb, confuse, bother, rattle (*informal*), agitate, ruffle, unnerve, perturb
▶ *noun* **2** = **turmoil**, flurry, flap (*informal*), disturbance, furor, flutter, dither

flutter *verb* **1** = **beat**, flap, ripple, waver, vibrate, tremble, quiver, palpitate
▶ *noun* **2** = **vibration**, tremor, shiver, tremble, palpitation, shudder, quiver, twitching
3 = **agitation**, confusion, excitement, commotion, dither, fluster

fly *verb* **1** = **soar**, sail, flutter, flit
• *to fly to Paris*
2 = **rush**, race, dash, hurry, dart, speed, tear • *She flew down the stairs.*
3 = **pilot**, control, operate, manoeuvre
4 = **display**, show, wave, float, flap, flutter
5 = **pass**, glide, elapse, flit, pass swiftly, roll on, run its course, slip away
6 = **flee**, escape, get away, run for

it, skedaddle (*informal*), take to one's heels
See also: **bolt**, **go**

flying *adjective* = **hurried**, brief, short-lived, hasty, fleeting, transitory, rushed

foam *noun* **1** = **froth**, head, bubbles, lather • *waves tipped with foam*
▶ *verb* **2** = **froth**, bubble, fizz • *a foaming river*
See also: **boil**

focal point See **focus**

focus *verb* **1** = **concentrate**, aim, direct, fix • *His eyes began to focus.*
▷ **focus your attention on** See **concentrate**
▶ *noun* **2** = **centre**, target, hub, focal point • *the focus of the conversation*

foe *noun* = **enemy**, rival, opponent, adversary, antagonist

fog *noun* = **mist**, gloom, miasma, murk, smog

foggy *adjective* = **misty**, murky, dim, cloudy, hazy, smoggy, indistinct, vaporous

foil[1] *verb* = **thwart**, defeat, check, frustrate, counter • *The police foiled an armed robbery.*
See also: **dash**, **prevent**

foil[2] *noun* = **contrast**, background, complement, antithesis • *a perfect foil for his personality*

foist *verb* = **impose**, unload, fob off, palm off, pass off, sneak in

fold *verb* **1** = **bend**, crease, tuck, crumple, turn under • *He folded the paper carefully.*
2 (*Informal*) = **go bankrupt**, crash, fail, collapse, go bust (*informal*), go to the wall, go under, shut down
▶ *noun* **3** = **crease**, bend, wrinkle, pleat • *hanging in folds*

folder *noun* = **file**, portfolio, envelope, binder

folk *noun* = **people**, family, race, tribe, clan, kin, kindred

follow *verb* **1** = **pursue**, track, hound, stalk • *We were being followed.*
2 = **come after**, succeed, supersede • *Night follows day.*
OPPOSITE: **precede**

3 = **obey**, comply, observe, conform • *Follow the instructions carefully.*
4 = **accompany**, attend, escort, tag along
5 = **understand**, realize, appreciate, grasp, comprehend, fathom, catch on (*informal*), take in
6 = **result**, issue, develop, spring, flow, proceed, arise, ensue
7 = **be interested in**, support, cultivate, keep abreast of
See also: **copy, happen, heed, practise, see**

follower *noun* = **supporter**, fan, believer, disciple • *a loyal follower of the team*
OPPOSITE: leader

following *adjective* 1 = **next**, later, subsequent, successive, consequent, ensuing, succeeding
▶ *noun* 2 = **supporters**, train, suite, clientele, entourage, coterie, fans, retinue

folly *noun* = **foolishness**, nonsense, madness, stupidity, indiscretion, lunacy, imprudence, rashness

fond *adjective* 1 = **loving**, devoted, affectionate, adoring, doting, having a liking for • *a fond greeting*
2 = **foolish**, empty, naive, vain, deluded, delusive, overoptimistic
▷ **fond of** = **keen on**, into (*informal*), addicted to, attached to, enamoured of, having a soft spot for, hooked on, partial to

fondle *verb* = **caress**, pet, stroke, pat, cuddle, dandle

fondly *adverb* 1 = **lovingly**, dearly, affectionately, indulgently, possessively, tenderly, with affection
2 = **foolishly**, stupidly, credulously, naively, vainly

fondness *noun* 1 = **liking**, love, taste, weakness, fancy, attachment, penchant, partiality, soft spot
2 = **devotion**, love, affection, attachment, kindness, tenderness

food *noun* = **nourishment**, diet, fare, grub (*informal*), refreshment, foodstuffs, provisions • *our favourite food*
RELATED WORDS
adjective: alimentary
noun: gastronomy

foodstuffs *See* **food**

fool *noun* 1 = **idiot**, moron, dunce, ignoramus • *I felt like such a fool!*
2 = **dupe**, mug (*Brit slang*), sucker (*slang*), stooge (*slang*), fall guy (*informal*), laughing stock
3 = **clown**, harlequin, buffoon, jester
▶ *verb* 4 = **deceive**, trick, mislead, con (*informal*), dupe • *Don't let him fool you.*
See also: **take in**

foolhardy *adjective* = **rash**, irresponsible, reckless, imprudent, hot-headed, impetuous

foolish *adjective* = **unwise**, silly, senseless, nonsensical, inane, unintelligent, stunned (*Canad informal*) • *feeling foolish*
OPPOSITE: wise
See also: **crazy, fond, frivolous, idiotic, mad, stupid**

foolishly *adverb* = **unwisely**, mistakenly, stupidly, idiotically, ill-advisedly, imprudently, injudiciously

foolishness *noun* = **stupidity**, weakness, folly, indiscretion, absurdity, silliness, irresponsibility, imprudence

foolproof *adjective* = **infallible**, safe, certain, unassailable, unbreakable, sure-fire (*informal*), guaranteed

foot *See* **base, bottom**

footing *noun* 1 = **basis**, foundation, groundwork
2 = **relationship**, position, status, rank, standing, grade

footling *adjective* (*Informal*) = **trivial**, minor, silly, petty, insignificant, unimportant, fiddling, hairsplitting, trifling

footpath *See* **path**

footstep *noun* = **step**, tread, footfall

for that reason *See* **therefore**

forage *verb* 1 = **search**, seek, hunt, explore, scour, rummage, cast about
▶ *noun* 2 (Cattle, etc.) = **fodder**, food, feed, provender

foray *noun* = **raid**, invasion, incursion, swoop, inroad, sortie, sally

forbear *verb* = **refrain**, stop, cease, abstain, desist, hold back, keep from, restrain oneself

forbearance *noun* = **patience**, resignation, restraint, tolerance, moderation, long-suffering, self-control, temperance

forbearing *adjective* = **patient**, moderate, lenient, merciful, tolerant, long-suffering, forgiving, indulgent

forbid *verb* = **prohibit**, ban, exclude, veto, outlaw • *forbidden to go out*
OPPOSITE: allow

forbidden *adjective* = **prohibited**, taboo, outlawed, banned, out of bounds, proscribed, vetoed

forbidding *adjective* = **threatening**, hostile, daunting, ominous, sinister, unfriendly, frightening, menacing

force *verb* 1 = **compel**, make, drive, pressure, coerce, oblige, obligate • *We were forced to turn right.*
2 = **break open**, blast, wrest, pry, wrench
3 = **push**, propel, thrust
▶ *noun* 4 = **compulsion**, pressure, duress • *They made him agree by force.*
5 = **power**, might, pressure, impact, strength • *the force of the explosion*
6 = **intensity**, emphasis, vigour, fierceness, vehemence
7 = **army**, troop, host, unit, patrol, squad, regiment, legion
▷ **in force** = **valid**, current, effective, working, binding, operative, in operation; = **in**

great numbers, all together, in full strength
See also: **bully, jam, reduce, spirit, stuff, violence**

forced *adjective* 1 = **compulsory**, mandatory, involuntary, obligatory, conscripted, enforced
2 = **false**, artificial, stiff, affected, wooden, strained, contrived, unnatural, insincere, laboured

forceful *adjective* 1 = **assertive**, aggressive, ambitious, bossy, obtrusive, pushy (*informal*) • *She is notorious for her forceful nature.*
2 = **powerful**, effective, dynamic, persuasive, cogent, compelling, convincing

forcible *adjective* 1 = **violent**, aggressive, armed, compulsory, coercive
2 = **strong**, powerful, potent, energetic, forceful, weighty, compelling

ford *See* **cross**

forebear *noun* = **ancestor**, father, predecessor, forerunner, forefather

foreboding *noun* = **dread**, fear, chill, anxiety, apprehension, misgiving, apprehensiveness, premonition, presentiment

forecast *verb* 1 = **predict**, anticipate, foresee, divine, augur, foretell, prophesy
▶ *noun* 2 = **prediction**, guess, prognosis, prophecy, conjecture

forefather *noun* = **ancestor**, father, predecessor, forerunner, forebear

forefront *noun* = **lead**, front, centre, spearhead, prominence, fore, foreground, vanguard

foregoing *adjective* = **preceding**, former, previous, above, prior, anterior, antecedent

foreign *adjective* = **alien**, overseas, distant, exotic • *foreign travel*
See also: **strange, unfamiliar**

foreigner *noun* = **alien**, immigrant, stranger, incomer

foremost *adjective* = **leading**, first, top, chief, prime, principal, best, greatest, most important
• *one of the world's foremost scholars*

See also: **important, main, supreme**

forensic *See* **legal**

forerunner *noun* = **precursor**, envoy, herald, prototype, harbinger, point-man

foresee *verb* = **anticipate**, forecast, predict, envisage, foretell, prophesy

foreshadow *verb* = **predict**, promise, indicate, signal, augur, presage, forebode, portend, prefigure

foresight *noun* = **anticipation**, precaution, preparedness, prudence, far-sightedness, forethought, prescience

forest *noun* = **wood** or **woods**, trees, bush (*Canad*), grove, woodland, bushland, rainforest, thicket, copse

---

TYPES OF FOREST

bush (*Canad*)	thicket
grove	woodland
jungle	woods
rainforest	

---

foretell *verb* = **predict**, forecast, forewarn, presage, prognosticate, prophesy

forethought *noun* = **anticipation**, provision, precaution, foresight, prudence, providence, far-sightedness

forever *adverb* **1** = **evermore**, always, for all time, for keeps, in perpetuity, till Doomsday, till the cows come home (*informal*) **2** = **constantly**, continually, perpetually, endlessly, eternally, incessantly, all the time, interminably, twenty-four-seven (*slang*), unremittingly

forewarn *verb* = **caution**, alert, advise, apprise, give fair warning, put on guard, tip off

foreword *See* **introduction**

forfeit *noun* **1** = **penalty**, loss, fine, forfeiture, damages ▸ *verb* **2** = **lose**, surrender,

renounce, relinquish, be deprived of, be stripped of, give up, say good-bye to

forge *verb* **1** = **create**, make, work, form, fashion, shape, frame, construct, devise, mould **2** = **falsify**, copy, fake, counterfeit, imitate, feign

forged *See* **false, phony**

forgery *noun* **1** = **fraudulence**, falsification, coining, counterfeiting, fraudulent imitation **2** = **fake**, counterfeit, phony (*informal*), sham, imitation, falsification

forget *verb* = **fail to remember**, overlook, omit • *I forgot to lock the door.* OPPOSITE: remember *See also*: **neglect**

forgetful *adjective* = **absent-minded**, vague, oblivious, careless, inattentive, neglectful, unmindful

forgive *verb* = **pardon**, excuse, condone, absolve • *Can you ever forgive me?* OPPOSITE: blame

forgiveness *noun* = **pardon**, mercy, acquittal • *I ask for your forgiveness.*

forgiving *adjective* = **merciful**, compassionate, lenient, tolerant, clement, forbearing, magnanimous, soft-hearted

forgo *verb* = **give up**, resign, abandon, surrender, yield, renounce, waive, relinquish, do without

forgotten *adjective* = **unremembered**, past, lost, bygone, left behind, omitted, past recall

fork *verb* = **branch**, part, split, divide, diverge, bifurcate

forked *adjective* = **branching**, split, divided, angled, bifurcate or bifurcated, branched, pronged, zigzag

forlorn *adjective* = **miserable**, unhappy, pathetic, helpless, hopeless, pitiful, wretched, disconsolate, down in the dumps (*informal*), woebegone

form noun **1** = **kind**, type, class, sort, variety, variant • *a rare form of the illness*

2 = **shape**, structure, outline, layout, contours • *Valleys often take the form of deep canyons*.

3 = **condition**, health, shape, trim, fitness, fettle

4 = **procedure**, convention, protocol, custom, etiquette

5 = **document**, paper, application, sheet

6 = **class**, rank, grade

▶ verb **7** = **constitute**, compose, make up, serve as • *the ideas that formed the basis of the argument*

8 = **make**, create, develop, establish, fashion, assemble • *The bowl was formed out of clay*.

9 = **arrange**, combine, organize, draw up

10 = **take shape**, rise, grow, appear, materialize, crystallize, become visible, come into being

11 = **develop**, contract, acquire, cultivate, pick up

See also: **body, build, design, figure, model**

formal adjective **1** = **conventional**, correct, stiff, precise • *a formal dinner*

OPPOSITE: informal

2 = **official**, legal, regular, prescribed, approved • *No formal announcement has been made*.

See also: **impersonal, stuffy**

formality noun **1** = **convention**, procedure, custom, ritual, rite, red tape

2 = **correctness**, protocol, etiquette, decorum

format noun = **style**, plan, look, form, type, construction, appearance, arrangement, layout, make-up

formation noun

1 = **establishment**, production, development, manufacture, generation, constitution, genesis, forming

2 = **pattern**, design, structure, arrangement, configuration, grouping

formative adjective

= **developmental**, influential • *her formative years*

former adjective = **previous**, past, old, ancient, bygone • *a former tennis champion*

▷ **former times** *See* **the past**

formerly adverb = **previously**, before, once, lately, at one time

formidable adjective **1** = **difficult**, mammoth, daunting, onerous, challenging, intimidating • *They faced formidable obstacles*.

2 = **impressive**, great, powerful, cool (*informal*), tremendous, terrific (*informal*), awesome, mighty, phat (*slang*), redoubtable

See also: **stiff**

formula noun = **method**, rule, procedure, principle, recipe, blueprint, precept

formulate verb **1** = **define**, detail, express, frame, specify, give form to, set down, systematize

2 = **devise**, plan, develop, originate, forge, invent, map out, work out

forsake verb **1** = **desert**, abandon, strand, disown, leave in the lurch

2 = **give up**, surrender, yield, renounce, relinquish, forgo, set aside

forsaken adjective = **deserted**, abandoned, outcast, disowned, forlorn, left in the lurch, marooned, stranded

fort noun = **fortress**, castle, fortification, citadel • *They had to abandon the fort*.

▷ **hold the fort** = **stand in**, carry on, keep things on an even keel, take over the reins

forte noun = **specialty**, gift, strength, talent, métier, strong point

forth adverb = **forward**, out, away, ahead, outward, onward

forthcoming adjective

1 = **approaching**, future, upcoming, imminent, prospective, coming, expected, impending

2 = **accessible**, available, ready, at hand, in evidence, obtainable, on tap (*informal*)

3 = **communicative**, open, free, expansive, informative, sociable, talkative, chatty, unreserved

forthright *adjective* = **outspoken**, open, direct, blunt, straightforward, frank, candid, upfront (*informal*), plain-spoken

forthwith *adverb* = **at once**, immediately, quickly, directly, instantly, straightaway, right away, without delay

fortification *noun* **1** = **defence**, protection, stronghold, fort, fortress, bastion, fastness
2 = **strengthening**, reinforcement

fortified *See* **secure**

fortify *verb* = **strengthen**, support, protect, reinforce, augment, buttress, shore up

fortitude *noun* = **courage**, strength, resolution, backbone, grit, bravery, perseverance, fearlessness, valour

fortress *noun* = **castle**, stronghold, fort, citadel, fastness, redoubt

fortuitous *See* **lucky**

fortunate *adjective* **1** = **lucky**, favoured, in luck, successful, well-off
2 = **favourable**, timely, helpful, convenient, win-win (*informal*), opportune, fortuitous, advantageous, expedient, felicitous, providential

fortunately *adverb* = **luckily**, happily, by a happy chance, by good luck, providentially

fortune *noun* **1** = **wealth**, property, treasure, prosperity, affluence, riches, opulence, possessions
2 = **luck**, chance, fate, destiny, providence, kismet
▷ **fortunes** = **destiny**, lot, history, success, adventures, experiences

forum *See* **conference**

forward *adjective* **1** = **leading**, first, head, front, advance, foremost
2 = **presumptuous**, familiar, bold, brazen, cheeky, brash,

impertinent, impudent, pushy (*informal*)
3 = **well-developed**, advanced, premature, precocious
▶ *adverb* **4** = **ahead**, on, forth, onward
▶ *verb* **5** = **promote**, further, assist, advance, hurry, expedite, hasten
6 = **send**, mail, dispatch, send on

foster *verb* **1** = **promote**, support, feed, encourage, uphold, stimulate, nurture, cultivate
2 = **bring up**, raise, mother, nurse, rear, take care of

foul *adjective* **1** = **dirty**, funky (*slang*), filthy, squalid, repulsive, unclean, putrid, fetid, malodorous, nauseating, scuzzy (*slang*), stinking
2 = **obscene**, blue, abusive, indecent, vulgar, lewd, profane, coarse, scurrilous
3 = **offensive**, disgraceful, despicable, shameful, wicked, scandalous, lousy (*slang*), abhorrent, detestable, scuzzy (*slang*)
4 = **unfair**, fraudulent, crooked, shady (*informal*), dishonest, unscrupulous, underhand
▶ *verb* **5** = **pollute**, contaminate, taint, dirty, stain, besmirch, defile, sully

found *verb* = **establish**, start, create, organize, institute, originate, constitute, inaugurate, set up

foundation *noun*
1 = **groundwork**, base, bottom, basis, footing, bedrock, underpinning, substructure
2 = **setting up**, organization, settlement, institution, establishment, inauguration, endowment

founder[1] *noun* = **initiator**, author, father, architect, inventor, beginner, originator

founder[2] *verb* **1** = **sink**, submerge, be lost, go down, go to the bottom
2 = **fail**, collapse, misfire,

miscarry, break down, come to grief, come unstuck, fall through
3 = stumble, trip, sprawl, stagger, lurch
foundling noun = **stray**, orphan, outcast, waif
fountain noun **1 = jet**, well, spring, spray, reservoir, spout, font, fount
2 = source, cause, origin, derivation, fount, fountainhead, wellspring
foyer noun = **entrance hall**, lobby, antechamber, anteroom, reception area, vestibule
fracas noun = **brawl**, riot, scuffle, skirmish, disturbance, melee or mêlée, affray (law), rumpus
fraction noun = **piece**, part, share, percentage, section, portion, segment, slice
fractious adjective = **irritable**, cross, testy, touchy, captious, petulant, querulous, refractory, tetchy
fracture noun **1 = break**, opening, split, crack, rift, rupture, fissure, cleft
▶ verb **2 = break**, split, crack, rupture, splinter
fractured See **broken**
fragile adjective = **delicate**, frail, flimsy, dainty, breakable • fragile china
OPPOSITE: tough
fragility See **weakness**
fragment noun **1 = piece**, bit, chip, portion, scrap, particle, shred, sliver
▶ verb **2 = break**, shatter, crumble, splinter, disintegrate, break up, come apart, come to pieces, split up
fragmentary adjective = **incomplete**, partial, scattered, sketchy, scrappy, piecemeal, incoherent, disconnected, bitty, broken
fragmented See **broken**
fragrance noun = **aroma**, smell, scent, perfume, bouquet • the fragrance of the roses
fragrant adjective = **aromatic**,

perfumed, sweet-smelling
• fragrant oils
OPPOSITE: smelly
See also: **sweet**
frail adjective = **weak**, vulnerable, delicate, fragile, feeble, flimsy, infirm, puny, insubstantial
frailty noun = **feebleness**, weakness, susceptibility, fallibility, frailness, infirmity
frame noun **1 = casing**, construction, structure, shell, framework
2 = physique, body, build, anatomy, carcass
▷ **frame of mind = mood**, state, outlook, attitude, temper, disposition, humour
▶ verb **3 = construct**, make, build, manufacture, assemble, put together
4 = draft, compose, sketch, devise, formulate, draw up, map out
5 = mount, case, surround, enclose
framework noun = **structure**, plan, frame, foundation, shell, skeleton, groundwork, the bare bones
frank adjective = **honest**, open, plain, blunt, straightforward, candid • a frank discussion
See also: **direct, natural, straight**
frankly adverb **1 = honestly**, candidly, in truth, to be honest
2 = openly, directly, freely, bluntly, plainly, without reserve
frankness noun = **outspokenness**, openness, truthfulness, bluntness, candour, forthrightness, plain speaking
frantic adjective **1 = furious**, wild, distraught, berserk, at the end of one's tether, beside oneself, distracted
2 = hectic, desperate, fraught (informal), frenzied, frenetic
fraternity noun **1 = club**, company, union, league, association, circle, guild, brotherhood
2 = companionship, fellowship,

brotherhood, camaraderie, kinship

fraternize *verb* = **associate**, mix, cooperate, mingle, socialize, hobnob, consort, keep company

fraud *noun* 1 = **deception**, hoax, deceit, trickery, guile • *The votes were recounted because of electoral fraud.*
2 = **fake**, forgery, cheater, quack, imposter, charlatan • *Many psychics are frauds.*
See also: **con, corruption, racket**

fraudulent *adjective* = **deceitful**, sham, crooked (*informal*), treacherous, dishonest, double-dealing, duplicitous, swindling

fray *verb* = **wear thin**, wear, rub, chafe

freak *noun* 1 = **oddity**, anomaly, aberration, malformation, weirdo *or* weirdie (*informal*), monstrosity
2 = **enthusiast**, fan, addict, nut (*slang*), buff (*informal*), fanatic, devotee, aficionado, fiend (*informal*)
▶ *adjective* 3 = **abnormal**, unusual, exceptional, unparalleled

free *adjective* 1 = **at liberty**, loose, liberated, at large, on the street • *a free person*
OPPOSITE: captive
2 = **without charge**, unpaid, complimentary, gratis • *a free brochure*
3 = **allowed**, able, clear, unrestricted, unimpeded, permitted
4 = **available**, empty, spare, idle, vacant, unused, unemployed, unoccupied
5 = **generous**, liberal, lavish, unsparing, unstinting
▷ **free time** See **leisure**
▶ *verb* 6 = **release**, discharge, liberate, set at liberty, set loose • *to free the caged animals*
OPPOSITE: imprison
7 = **extricate**, rescue, disengage, cut loose, disentangle
See also: **immune, independent, wild**

INFORMALLY SPEAKING
a free hand: freedom to behave as you see fit
free and easy: with little attention to rules and customs
make free (with): act as if you had complete rights to something

freedom *noun* 1 = **licence**, scope, discretion, latitude, leeway • *freedom of action*
2 = **liberty**, release, emancipation • *gaining their freedom after months of captivity*
OPPOSITE: captivity
3 = **exemption**, immunity • *freedom from pain*

free-for-all *noun* = **fight**, brawl, row, riot, melee *or* mêlée, scrimmage, fracas, throwdown (*slang*)

freely *adverb* 1 = **willingly**, voluntarily, spontaneously, of one's own accord, of one's own free will, without prompting
2 = **openly**, frankly, plainly, candidly, unreservedly, without reserve
3 = **abundantly**, liberally, lavishly, amply, copiously, extravagantly, unstintingly

freeze *verb* 1 = **chill**, stiffen, harden, ice over *or* ice up
2 = **suspend**, stop, fix, peg, inhibit, hold up

freezing *adjective* = **icy**, bitter, raw, chill, arctic, frosty, glacial, wintry, biting

freight *noun* 1 = **transportation**, shipment, carriage, conveyance
2 = **cargo**, load, burden, merchandise, payload, consignment, goods

French *adjective* = **Gallic**

frenzied *adjective* = **furious**, wild, frantic, feverish, frenetic, rabid, uncontrolled, distracted

frenzy *noun* = **fury**, rage, madness, agitation, hysteria • *The room was a frenzy of activity.*

frequency See **rate**

frequent *adjective* 1 = **common**, repeated, everyday, habitual, continual, recurrent • *his frequent visits*

OPPOSITE: rare
▶ *verb* **2 = visit**, attend, haunt, patronize • *a restaurant that we frequent*
OPPOSITE: avoid

frequently *adverb* **= often**, much, repeatedly, commonly, habitually, many times, not infrequently

fresh *adjective* **1 = new**, recent, different, original, novel, modern, up-to-date
2 = additional, more, other, further, extra, added, supplementary, auxiliary
3 = invigorating, clean, cool, pure, crisp, brisk, bracing, refreshing, unpolluted
4 = lively, alert, keen, energetic, vigorous, spry, refreshed, sprightly
5 = natural, unprocessed
6 (*Informal*) **= cheeky**, forward, familiar, disrespectful, presumptuous, impudent, insolent

freshen *verb* **= refresh**, restore, revitalize, enliven, freshen up, liven up

freshness *noun* **1 = novelty**, originality, inventiveness, newness
2 = cleanness, shine, glow, sparkle, vigour, brightness, clearness, wholesomeness

fret *verb* **= worry**, grieve, brood, agonize, lose sleep over, upset oneself *or* distress oneself

fretful *adjective* **= irritable**, uneasy, edgy, fractious, testy, touchy, crotchety, querulous, short-tempered

friction *noun* **1 = rubbing**, resistance, rasping, abrasion, grating, chafing, scraping
2 = hostility, conflict, disagreement, resentment, animosity, discord, dissension, bad blood

friend *noun* **1 = companion**, buddy, pal, confidant *or* confidante, crony • *lifelong friends*
OPPOSITE: enemy
2 = supporter, associate, ally, patron, well-wisher

friendliness *noun* **= kindliness**, warmth, affability, amiability, congeniality, conviviality, geniality, neighbourliness, sociability

friendly *adjective* **= amiable**, close, cordial, affectionate, genial, welcoming • *a very friendly group of people*
OPPOSITE: unfriendly
See also: **cozy, favourable, pleasant, sociable, warm**

friendship *noun* **= goodwill**, affection, attachment, closeness • *I value our friendship.*
OPPOSITE: hostility

fright *noun* **= fear**, shock, scare, alarm, panic, horror, dread, trepidation, consternation

frighten *verb* **= scare**, alarm, intimidate, terrify, terrorize, startle, unnerve • *trying to frighten us*

frightened *adjective* **= afraid**, scared, alarmed, petrified, startled, terrified • *frightened of thunder*

frightening *adjective* **= terrifying**, hair-raising, alarming, intimidating, menacing • *a frightening experience*
See also: **scary, spooky**

frightful *adjective* **= terrifying**, terrible, horrible, awful, fearful, traumatic, horrendous, dreadful, ghastly, alarming

frigid *adjective* **1 = cold**, icy, arctic, frosty, glacial, wintry, frozen
2 = forbidding, formal, austere, aloof, unresponsive, unapproachable, unfeeling

frills *plural noun* **= trimmings**, fuss, additions, bells and whistles, embellishments, extras, frippery, ornamentation, ostentation

fringe *noun* **1 = border**, hem, trimming, edging
2 = edge, margin, perimeter, borderline, periphery, limits, outskirts
▶ *adjective* **3 = unofficial**, unconventional, unorthodox

frisk *verb* **1 = frolic**, play, jump, trip, skip, caper, prance, cavort, gambol

2 = search, check, inspect, run over, shake down (US slang)

frisky adjective = **lively**, playful, coltish, frolicsome, high-spirited, kittenish, sportive

fritter verb

▷ **fritter away = waste**, squander, misspend, dissipate, idle away, run through, spend like water

frivolity noun = **fun**, silliness, flippancy, frivolousness, gaiety, levity, light-heartedness, superficiality, triviality

frivolous adjective **1 = flippant**, silly, juvenile, foolish, puerile • a frivolous remark
OPPOSITE: serious

2 = trivial, minor, shallow, petty, unimportant, trifling

frolic verb **1 = play**, sport, romp, caper, cavort, frisk, lark, gambol, make merry

▶ noun **2 = revel**, game, romp, spree, antic, lark

frolicsome adjective = **playful**, lively, merry, coltish, frisky, kittenish, sportive

from time to time See **sometimes**

front noun **1 = exterior**, face, frontage • the front of the house
OPPOSITE: back

2 = appearance, show, face, exterior • She put on a brave front.

3 = forefront, lead, head, vanguard, front line

4 = disguise, show, cover, mask, blind, cover-up, pretext, façade

▷ **in front = ahead**, before, leading • too close to the car in front

▶ adjective **5 = first**, lead, head, foremost, cutting edge, leading, topmost

▶ verb **6 = face onto**, overlook, look over or look into

frontage See **front**

frontier noun = **boundary**, limit, edge, verge, perimeter, borderline

frost noun = **hoarfrost**, freeze, rime

frosty adjective **1 = cold**, icy, chilly, wintry, frozen

2 = unfriendly, frigid, discouraging, standoffish, unenthusiastic, unwelcoming

froth noun **1 = foam**, head, scum, suds, bubbles, effervescence, lather, spume

▶ verb **2 = fizz**, foam, bubble over, come to a head, effervesce, lather

frothy adjective = **foamy**, foaming, sudsy

frown verb = **scowl**, glare, glower
• She frowned in displeasure.

▷ **frown on = disapprove of**, discourage, dislike, look askance at, take a dim view of

frozen adjective = **icy**, arctic, frigid, numb, chilled • I was frozen in the arena.

frugal adjective = **thrifty**, careful, prudent, economical, abstemious, niggardly, parsimonious, sparing

frugality See **economy**

fruit noun **1 = produce**, product, crop, yield, harvest

2 = result, return, profit, effect, benefit, advantage, reward, consequence, outcome, end result

fruitful adjective = **useful**, effective, successful, productive, profitable, beneficial, worthwhile, rewarding, win-win (informal), advantageous

fruition noun = **maturity**, completion, realization, perfection, fulfillment, attainment, materialization, ripeness

fruitless adjective = **useless**, unsuccessful, pointless, vain, futile, unproductive, unprofitable, ineffectual, profitless, unavailing

frustrate verb = **thwart**, block, check, foil • His efforts were frustrated.
See also: **dash, hamper, hinder**

frustrated adjective
= **disappointed**, discouraged, resentful, disheartened, embittered

frustration noun

1 = obstruction, blocking, circumvention, foiling, thwarting
2 = annoyance, disappointment, grievance, dissatisfaction, resentment, irritation, vexation
fry See **cook**
fuddy-duddy noun
= **conservative**, square (informal), fogey or old fogey, stick-in-the-mud (informal), stuffed shirt (informal)
fudge verb = **misrepresent**, change, fake, cook (slang), alter, forge, distort, falsify, misstate, tamper with, tinker with
fuel noun = **incitement**, ammunition, provocation
fugitive noun **1 = runaway**, refugee, runner, deserter, escapee
▶ adjective **2 = momentary**, brief, temporary, passing, short-lived, fleeting, transient, ephemeral, transitory
fulfill verb **1 = achieve**, perform, realize, satisfy, accomplish, carry out • He decided to fulfill his dream and become a photographer.
2 = comply with, meet, fill, answer, observe, obey, conform to
See also: **keep**
fulfillment noun = **achievement**, accomplishment, completion, implementation, realization, attainment, consummation
full adjective **1 = filled**, packed, loaded, saturated • full of books
OPPOSITE: empty
2 = comprehensive, maximum, extensive, detailed, thorough, exhaustive • I want a full account of what happened.
3 = loose, baggy, voluminous • a full skirt
4 = plentiful, extensive, comprehensive, adequate, generous, ample, abundant, exhaustive
5 = rich, clear, deep, loud, distinct, rounded, resonant
6 = plump, rounded, voluptuous, buxom, curvaceous
▷ **full of life** See **alive**

▶ noun
▷ **in full = completely**, in its entirety, in total, without exception
See also: **busy, complete, crowded, whole**
full-blooded adjective = **vigorous**, hearty, lusty, red-blooded, virile
full-grown See **mature**
fullness noun **1 = plenty**, fill, abundance, saturation, satiety, sufficiency, copiousness, profusion
2 = richness, strength, resonance, clearness, loudness
full-scale adjective = **major**, comprehensive, wide-ranging, thorough, in-depth, all-out, exhaustive, sweeping, thoroughgoing
fully adverb = **totally**, completely, entirely, perfectly, altogether, thoroughly, wholly, utterly, in all respects, one hundred per cent
fully-fledged See **mature**
fulsome adjective = **insincere**, excessive, extravagant, inordinate, immoderate, sycophantic, unctuous
fumble verb = **grope**, flounder, scrabble, feel around
fume verb = **rage**, storm, rant, smoulder, seethe, get hot under the collar (informal), see red (informal)
fumes plural noun = **smoke**, gas, pollution, exhaust, smog, vapour
fumigate verb = **disinfect**, sanitize, cleanse, purify, sterilize, clean out or clean up
fuming adjective = **furious**, angry, enraged, raging, incensed, seething, in a rage, on the warpath (informal), up in arms
fun noun **1 = enjoyment**, entertainment, pleasure, recreation, amusement • It was great fun.
▷ **make fun of = mock**, taunt, ridicule, deride, laugh at • Don't make fun of him.
▶ adjective **2 = enjoyable**, lively, amusing, witty, convivial, diverting, entertaining

f

function noun 1 = **purpose**, job, duty, responsibility, role • *What is the function of this software?*
2 = **reception**, party, dinner, gathering • *We were going to a function downtown.*
▶ verb 3 = **work**, go, run, operate, perform • *The furnace was not functioning properly.*
See also: **act, behave, part**

functional adjective 1 = **practical**, useful, utilitarian, serviceable, hard-wearing
2 = **working**, operative

fund noun 1 = **reserve**, supply, capital, pool, foundation • *the pension fund*
2 = **store**, reserve, mine, reservoir, hoard • *an extraordinary fund of energy*
▶ verb 3 = **finance**, support, subsidize, pay for • *to raise money to fund scientific research*
See also: **bank**

fundamental adjective
1 = **essential**, key, central, primary, basic, principal, cardinal, elementary, rudimentary, underlying
▶ noun 2 = **principle**, rule, law, cornerstone, axiom, rudiment

fundamentally adverb
= **essentially**, basically, primarily, radically, intrinsically, at bottom, at heart

fundamentals See **essentials**

funds plural noun = **money**, capital, cash, finance, ready money, resources, savings, the wherewithal

funeral noun = **burial**, cremation, interment, inhumation, obsequies

funnel verb = **channel**, move, pass, conduct, direct, pour, filter, convey

funny adjective 1 = **strange**, odd, unusual, mysterious, peculiar, puzzling • *They heard a funny noise.*
2 = **amusing**, comic, hilarious, humorous, witty, comical • *a funny story*
OPPOSITE: serious
▷ **funny feeling** See **premonition**

See also: **suspicious, weird**

fur See **coat, pile**

furious adjective 1 = **enraged**, mad, raging, livid, fuming, infuriated • *furious about the poor service they received*
2 = **frantic**, intense, fierce, frenzied, breakneck, manic • *a furious battle*
See also: **angry, violent**

furnish verb 1 = **decorate**, stock, equip, fit out
2 = **supply**, give, offer, provide, present, grant, hand out

furniture noun = **household goods**, appliances, fittings, furnishings, goods, possessions, things (*informal*)

furor noun = **disturbance**, stir, outcry, uproar, commotion, to-do, hullabaloo

furrow noun 1 = **groove**, line, channel, crease, wrinkle, trench, seam, hollow, rut
▶ verb 2 = **wrinkle**, crease, knit, corrugate, draw together

further adverb 1 = **in addition**, also, besides, moreover, furthermore, additionally, into the bargain, to boot
▶ adjective 2 = **additional**, more, new, other, extra, fresh, supplementary
▶ verb 3 = **promote**, help, forward, assist, advance, encourage, lend support to, work for

furthermore adverb = **besides**, too, further, moreover, additionally, as well, in addition, into the bargain, to boot

furthest adjective = **most distant**, extreme, ultimate, farthest, furthermost, outmost, remotest

furtive adjective = **sly**, clandestine, secretive, sneaky, stealthy, surreptitious, conspiratorial, underhand, under-the-table

fury noun 1 = **anger**, rage, passion, frenzy, wrath, madness, impetuosity
2 = **violence**, force, intensity, severity, ferocity, savagery, fierceness, vehemence

fuse verb 1 = **join**, combine,

unite, merge, dissolve, blend, integrate, amalgamate, meld, coalesce, intermix, intermingle, federate (*politics*), commingle, agglutinate, run together, put together
OPPOSITE: separate
2 = **bond**, join, stick, melt, smelt, weld, solder
fusion *noun* = **merging**, union, merger, blend, federation (*politics*), integration, mixture, amalgamation, synthesis, blending, coalescence, uniting, commixture, commingling
fuss *noun* **1** = **bother**, stir, confusion, agitation, commotion, to-do • *What's all the fuss about?*
2 = **argument**, trouble, complaint, row, objection, squabble, furor
▸ *verb* **3** = **fret**, bustle, fidget, carry on (*informal*) • *The servers fussed and hovered around our table.*
fussy *adjective* **1** = **particular**, exacting, choosy (*informal*), discriminating, fastidious • *fussy about his food*

2 = **overelaborate**, busy, cluttered, overworked, rococo
See also: **elaborate**
fusty *adjective* = **stale**, damp, stuffy, airless, mildewed, mouldering, musty
futile *adjective* = **useless**, unsuccessful, vain, abortive, forlorn • *a futile effort to run away*
OPPOSITE: successful
See also: **hopeless**
futility *noun* = **uselessness**, emptiness, ineffectiveness, hollowness
future *adjective* **1** = **forthcoming**, later, forward, prospective, approaching, coming, impending • *to predict future growth*
OPPOSITE: past
▸ *noun* **2** = **hereafter**, time to come
3 = **outlook**, expectation, prospect
fuzzy *adjective* **1** = **fluffy**, woolly, downy, frizzy
2 = **indistinct**, unclear, vague, obscure, distorted, bleary, blurred, ill-defined, out of focus

Gg

gabble *verb* **1 = prattle**, gush, spout, babble, blabber, gibber, jabber
▷ *noun* **2 = gibberish**, chatter, babble, drivel, blabber, prattle, twaddle

gadabout *noun* **= pleasure-seeker**, rover, wanderer, gallivanter, rambler

gadget *noun* **= device**, tool, machine, appliance • *kitchen gadgets such as blenders and can openers*

gaffe *noun* **= blunder**, bloomer (*informal*), faux pas, slip, mistake, lapse, indiscretion, solecism

gag¹ *verb* **1 = suppress**, quiet, silence, curb, stifle, muzzle, muffle, stop up
2 = retch, vomit, spew, heave, puke (*slang*), barf (*slang*), throw up (*informal*), toss one's cookies (*slang*)

gag² *noun* **= joke**, crack (*slang*), funny (*informal*), hoax, jest, wisecrack (*informal*), witticism

gaggle *See* **bunch**

gaiety *noun* **1 = cheerfulness**, glee, exhilaration, merriment, blitheness, high spirits, jollity, light-heartedness, mirth
2 = merrymaking, fun, festivity, revelry, conviviality, jollification

gaily *adverb* **1 = cheerfully**, happily, gleefully, blithely, joyfully, light-heartedly, merrily
2 = colourfully, brightly, brilliantly, flamboyantly, flashily, gaudily, showily

gain *verb* **1 = acquire**, win, secure, obtain, achieve, earn • *Students can gain valuable experience by working.*
2 = benefit, profit • *Would any areas of the world gain from global warming?*
3 = reach, attain, arrive at, come to, get to
▷ **gain on = get nearer**, close, approach, overtake, catch up with, narrow the gap
▷ *noun* **4 = increase**, rise, growth, advance, improvement • *Our party has made substantial gains in local elections.*
5 = profit, return, benefit, advantage, dividend, yield

gainful *adjective* **= profitable**, lucrative, useful, productive, beneficial, worthwhile, rewarding, win-win (*informal*), fruitful, advantageous, remunerative

gains *plural noun* **= profits**, revenue, prize, earnings, proceeds, takings, winnings

gainsay *verb* **= contradict**, deny, dispute, retract, contravene, rebut, controvert, disagree with

gait *noun* **= walk**, step, pace, stride, carriage, tread, bearing

gala *noun* **= festival**, celebration, festivity, pageant, carnival, jamboree, fête

gale *noun* **1 = storm**, blast, hurricane, tornado, cyclone, typhoon, squall, tempest
2 = outburst, outbreak, explosion, fit, burst, shout, eruption, howl, shriek, peal

gall¹ *noun* **1** (*Informal*) **= impudence**, nerve (*informal*), cheek (*informal*), chutzpah (*informal*), brazenness, effrontery, impertinence, insolence
2 = bitterness, hostility, animosity, acrimony, bile, rancour

gall² *verb* **1 = scrape**, irritate, chafe, abrade

2 = annoy, provoke, irk, irritate, vex, exasperate, rankle

gallant adjective **1 = brave**, bold, heroic, courageous, valiant, noble, honourable, manly, intrepid

2 = chivalrous, polite, noble, gracious, attentive, courteous, gentlemanly

gallantry noun **1 = bravery**, spirit, courage, heroism, boldness, intrepidity, manliness, valour

2 = attentiveness, courtesy, nobility, politeness, chivalry, courteousness, gentlemanliness, graciousness

galling adjective **= annoying**, bitter, exasperating, irksome, irritating, provoking, vexatious

gallivant verb **= wander**, roam, rove, ramble, gad about

gallop verb **= run**, race, career, speed, rush, sprint, bolt, dash, hurry

galore adverb **= in abundance**, everywhere, aplenty, all over the place, in great quantity, in great numbers, in profusion, to spare

galvanize verb **= stimulate**, spur, inspire, provoke, excite, stir, jolt, electrify, invigorate

gamble verb **1 = bet** • *He gambled on the horses.*

2 = risk, chance, stake • *Few networks seem willing to gamble on new TV series.*

▶ noun **3 = risk**, chance, lottery, wager • *We are taking a gamble on a young player.*

4 = bet, wager

gambol verb **1 = frolic**, jump, skip, hop, caper, prance, cavort, frisk

▶ noun **2 = frolic**, jump, skip, hop, caper, prance

game noun **1 = pastime**, sport, entertainment, distraction, diversion, recreation, amusement, lark

2 = match, contest, clash • *the Blue Jays' first game of the season*

3 = wild animals, prey, quarry

4 = scheme, plan, design, plot, trick, tactic, ploy, stratagem

▶ adjective **5 = brave**, persistent, gritty, spirited, courageous, plucky, gallant, intrepid

6 = willing, ready, interested, eager, keen, prepared, desirous

See also: **agreeable**

> **INFORMALLY SPEAKING**
> **ahead of the game**: winning rather than losing
> **game over**: final defeat
> **off your game**: not performing well
> **play the game**: follow the rules

gamut noun **= range**, area, series, field, sweep, scale, scope, compass, catalogue

gang noun **= group**, company, team, club, crowd, band, pack, squad, mob, clique, coterie

gangling adjective **= tall**, awkward, lanky, angular, rangy, rawboned, spindly

gangster noun **= racketeer**, hood (*slang*), mobster (*slang*), crook (*informal*), hoodlum

gap noun **1 = opening**, break, space, hole, clearing, chink • *They squeezed through a gap in the fence.*

2 = interval, pause, hiatus (*formal*), lull, interlude • *After a gap of nearly a decade, she returned to politics.*

3 = difference, disparity (*formal*), inconsistency • *the gap between rich and poor*

See also: **breach**

gape verb **1 = stare**, gawk, wonder, goggle

2 = open, split, crack, yawn

gaping adjective **= wide**, open, great, broad, vast, cavernous, wide open, yawning

garb See **dress**

garbage noun **1 = trash**, refuse, waste, debris, junk (*informal*), litter • *piles of garbage*

2 (*Informal*) **= nonsense**, rubbish, drivel, gibberish • *I personally think this is complete garbage.*

garbled adjective **= jumbled**, confused, distorted, incomprehensible, unintelligible • *a garbled voice-mail message*

gardens *See* **grounds**

garish *adjective* = **gaudy**, loud, tasteless, flashy, showy, tacky (*informal*), vulgar, brash, brassy

garland *noun* 1 = **wreath**, crown, honours, festoon, bays, chaplet, laurels
▶ *verb* 2 = **adorn**, crown, deck, festoon, wreathe

garments *plural noun* = **clothes**, dress, gear (*slang*), costume, uniform, outfit, apparel, attire, garb, clothing

garner *verb* = **collect**, save, store, gather, stockpile, accumulate, amass, hoard, stow away

garnish *verb* 1 = **decorate**, trim, enhance, adorn, ornament, embellish, set off
▶ *noun* 2 = **decoration**, enhancement, trimming, embellishment, adornment, ornamentation

garrison *noun* 1 = **troops**, unit, command, detachment, armed force
2 = **fort**, post, base, station, camp, stronghold, fortress, fortification, encampment
▶ *verb* 3 = **station**, post, position, assign, put on duty

garrulous *adjective* = **talkative**, chatty, verbose, gossiping, loquacious, prattling, voluble

gash *verb* 1 = **cut**, wound, tear, split, slash, gouge, slit, lacerate
▶ *noun* 2 = **cut**, wound, tear, split, slash, gouge, slit, laceration, incision

gasp *verb* 1 = **gulp**, pant, puff, choke • *She gasped for air.*
▶ *noun* 2 = **gulp**, puff • *An audible gasp went through the theatre.*

gate *noun* = **barrier**, opening, door, exit, passage, entrance, portal, gateway

gather *verb* 1 = **assemble**, mass, flock, congregate, round up, convene, muster, marshal • *We gathered around the fireplace.*
OPPOSITE: scatter
2 = **collect**, stockpile, accumulate, amass, hoard • *I suggest we gather enough firewood to last the night.*
3 = **learn**, hear, understand, conclude, assume • *"He speaks English." "I gathered that."*
4 = **pick**, select, harvest, garner, reap, cull, pluck, glean
5 = **intensify**, increase, rise, grow, expand, swell, deepen, heighten, thicken
6 = **fold**, tuck, pleat
See also: **concentrate, crowd, imagine, meet**

gathering *noun* = **assembly**, meeting, rally, congregation, muster, get-together (*informal*), conference, convention, congress • *polite social gatherings*
See also: **function, party**

gauche *adjective* = **awkward**, clumsy, unsophisticated, ill-mannered, inelegant, tactless

gaudy *adjective* = **garish**, bright, loud, flashy, showy • *gaudy fake jewellery*
See also: **tasteless, vulgar**

gauge *verb* 1 = **measure**, check, count, determine, weigh, calculate, compute, ascertain
2 = **judge**, rate, value, estimate, guess, assess, evaluate, reckon, appraise, adjudge
▶ *noun* 3 = **indicator**, test, measure, standard, guide, guideline, criterion, meter, touchstone, yardstick

gaunt *adjective* = **emaciated**, lean, spare, skinny, anorexic, skeletal, bony, angular, scrawny, cadaverous, pinched

gawky *adjective* = **awkward**, clumsy, lumbering, ungainly, gauche, loutish, maladroit

gay *adjective* 1 = **homosexual**, lesbian, bent (*informal, offensive*), queer (*informal, offensive*)
2 = **carefree**, sparkling, lively, merry, cheerful, light-hearted, jovial, blithe
3 = **colourful**, rich, bright, brilliant, flamboyant, vivid, flashy, showy
▶ *noun* 4 = **homosexual**, lesbian

gaze verb 1 = **stare**, look, watch, view, wonder, regard, gape
▶ noun 2 = **stare**, look, fixed look

gazette noun = **newspaper**, paper, journal, periodical, news-sheet

gear noun 1 = **cog**, cogwheel, gearwheel
2 = **mechanism**, machinery, cogs, works
3 = **equipment**, tackle, apparatus, paraphernalia, accoutrements, instruments, supplies, tools
4 = **clothing**, wear, dress, clothes, costume, outfit, garments, togs
▶ verb 5 = **equip**, fit, adjust, adapt

geek noun (Slang) = **nerd**, bore, drip (informal), obsessive, wonk (informal), anorak (informal), dork (slang), trainspotter (informal)

gelatinous adjective = **jelly-like**, sticky, gummy, gluey, glutinous, viscous

gelid adjective = **cold**, icy, arctic, frigid, chilly, frosty, glacial, ice-cold, freezing, frozen

gem noun 1 = **precious stone**, stone, jewel
2 = **prize**, treasure, jewel, masterpiece, pearl

general adjective 1 = **overall**, broad, comprehensive • a general decline in employment
OPPOSITE: specific
2 = **widespread**, common, broad, universal, accepted • The project should raise general awareness about animal rights.
OPPOSITE: special
3 = **imprecise**, loose, vague, indefinite, approximate, inexact, ill-defined, unspecific
See also: **mass, popular, public**

generally adverb 1 = **usually**, normally, typically, ordinarily, customarily, as a rule, by and large, on the whole
2 = **commonly**, publicly, widely, extensively, universally, popularly

generate verb = **produce**, make,

cause, create, breed, engender, propagate, give rise to

generation noun 1 = **production**, creation, formation, reproduction, genesis, propagation
2 = **age group**, crop, breed
3 = **age**, time, period, era, epoch

generic adjective = **collective**, general, common, wide, comprehensive, blanket, universal, inclusive

generosity noun 1 = **charity**, kindness, benevolence • She is well known for her generosity.
OPPOSITE: meanness
2 = **unselfishness**, goodness, high-mindedness, magnanimity, nobleness

generous adjective 1 = **charitable**, liberal, kind, lavish, hospitable, munificent, open-handed, prodigal, unstinting • Not all wealthy people are so generous.
OPPOSITE: stingy
2 = **plentiful**, ample, abundant • a generous portion of spaghetti
OPPOSITE: meagre
3 = **unselfish**, good, lofty, noble, big-hearted, high-minded, magnanimous
See also: **handsome**

genesis noun = **beginning**, start, birth, creation, origin, formation, inception

genial adjective = **cheerful**, warm, friendly, pleasant, affable, good-natured, agreeable, amiable, jovial, congenial

geniality noun = **cheerfulness**, warmth, friendliness, affability, agreeableness, amiability, conviviality, cordiality, good cheer, joviality

genius noun 1 = **master**, brain, mastermind, virtuoso • a mathematical genius
2 = **brilliance**, intellect, brains • a poet of genius
See also: **talent**

genre noun = **type**, group, kind, class, style, sort, category, species

genteel adjective = **refined**, elegant, polite, respectable,

g

courteous, gentlemanly, cultured, ladylike, urbane, well-mannered

gentle *adjective* 1 = **kind**, soft, tender, benign, kindly, meek, placid • *a quiet and gentle man*
OPPOSITE: cruel
2 = **moderate**, light, mild, slight, soft, muted, soothing
3 = **gradual**, light, slow, easy, moderate, mild, slight, imperceptible
4 = **tame**, manageable, docile, biddable, broken, placid, tractable
See also: **leisurely**

gentleman See **man**

gentlemanly *adjective* = **polite**, civil, refined, gallant, honourable, courteous, genteel, urbane, well-mannered

gentleness *noun* = **tenderness**, compassion, kindness, softness, sweetness, mildness

gentry *noun* = **nobility**, elite, aristocracy, upper class, upper crust (*informal*)

genuine *adjective* 1 = **authentic**, real, bona fide • *They're convinced the picture is genuine.*
OPPOSITE: fake
2 = **sincere**, honest, earnest, heartfelt, frank, candid, unaffected, unfeigned
See also: **actual, natural, right, serious, true**

germ *noun* 1 = **microbe**, virus, bacterium, bug (*informal*), microorganism
2 = **beginning**, source, spark, seed, root, origin, embryo, rudiment

germane *adjective* = **relevant**, material, appropriate, related, fitting, pertinent, connected, apposite, apropos, to the point or to the purpose

germ-free See **pure, sterile**

germinate *verb* = **sprout**, shoot, grow, develop, generate, swell, originate, bud, vegetate

gesticulate *verb* = **signal**, sign, indicate, wave, motion, gesture, make a sign

gesture *noun* 1 = **signal**, sign,

action, motion, indication, gesticulation
▶ *verb* 2 = **signal**, sign, indicate, wave, motion, gesticulate

get *verb* 1 = **obtain**, receive, acquire, secure (*formal*), fetch, procure (*formal*) • *I'll get us all something to eat.*
2 = **become**, turn, grow • *People draw the curtains once it gets dark.*
3 = **contract**, take, catch, come down with, fall victim to
4 = **capture**, grab, lay hold of, take, seize
5 = **understand**, see, follow, catch, perceive, comprehend, fathom, take in, work out
6 = **persuade**, influence, convince, induce, prevail upon
7 (*Informal*) = **annoy**, upset, bug (*informal*), irritate, gall, vex

get across = **cross**, negotiate, traverse, ford, pass over;
= **communicate**, transmit, convey, impart, bring home to, make clear or make understood, put over
▷ **get along** = **be friendly**, agree, click (*slang*), concur, be compatible, hit it off (*informal*)
▷ **get at** = **gain access to**, reach, acquire, attain, come to grips with, get hold of; = **imply**, suggest, mean, intend, hint, lead up to • *What are you getting at?*; = **criticize**, attack, blame, nag, find fault with, pick on
▷ **get away** See **escape**
▷ **get back** See **recover**
▷ **get back at** See **retaliate**
▷ **get better** See **recover**
▷ **get by** = **manage**, survive, exist, fare, cope, get along, keep one's head above water, make both ends meet
▷ **get even** See **revenge**
▷ **get even with** See **retaliate**
▷ **get going** See **start**
▷ **get hold of** See **contact, obtain**
▷ **get in the way** See **impede**
▷ **get in touch with** See **contact**
▷ **get off** = **leave**, escape, exit, depart, descend, disembark, dismount, alight

g

▷ **get off your chest** See **reveal**

▷ **get on** = **board**, climb, mount, embark, ascend, enter • *Hurry up and get on the boat!*

▷ **get on someone's nerves** = **annoy**, provoke, plague, aggravate (*informal*), bug (*informal*), irk, rile, irritate, ruffle, exasperate, peeve, madden, make someone's blood boil, rub someone up the wrong way (*informal*), get in someone's hair (*informal*), get someone's goat (*slang*), piss off (*taboo slang*), tee off (*slang*)

▷ **get out of** See **dodge**

▷ **get over** = **recover from**, rally, survive, revive, mend, get better, pull through

▷ **get rid of** = **dispose of**, remove, eliminate, dump, expel, eject, throw away *or* throw out

▷ **get through** See **pass**

▷ **get to** See **reach**

▷ **get together** See **meet**

▷ **get well** See **recover**

See also: **develop, do, earn, extract, win**

getaway *noun* = **escape**, break, flight, break-out

get-together *noun* = **gathering**, party, meeting, social, function, celebration, reception, bash (*informal*), festivity, rave (*slang*), do (*informal*), shindig (*informal*), soirée, social gathering

ghastly *adjective* = **horrible**, terrible, shocking, gruesome, horrendous, dreadful, hideous, frightful, loathsome, terrifying

ghost *noun* 1 = **spirit**, spectre, phantom, apparition • *the ghost in the haunted house*
RELATED WORD
adjective: spectral
2 = **trace**, possibility, hint, suggestion, shadow, glimmer, semblance

ghostly *adjective* = **supernatural**, eerie, spooky (*informal*), phantom, ghostlike, spectral, unearthly, wraithlike

ghoulish *adjective* = **macabre**, sick (*informal*), gruesome, grisly, morbid, disgusting, unwholesome

giant *noun* 1 = **ogre**, monster, titan, colossus
▶ *adjective* 2 = **huge**, vast, enormous, mammoth, immense, titanic, gigantic, colossal, gargantuan

gibberish *noun* = **nonsense**, babble, drivel, gobbledygook (*informal*), mumbo jumbo, twaddle

gibe, jibe *verb* 1 = **taunt**, mock, scorn, scoff, jeer, ridicule, sneer, make fun of, poke fun at
▶ *noun* 2 = **taunt**, crack (*slang*), dig, barb, jeer, sarcasm, sneer, scoffing, cheap shot (*informal*)

giddiness *noun* = **dizziness**, vertigo, faintness, light-headedness

giddy *adjective* = **dizzy**, faint, unsteady, dizzying, light-headed, reeling, vertiginous

gift *noun* 1 = **donation**, present, contribution, legacy, bequest (*formal*) • *He showered us with gifts.*
2 = **talent**, ability, flair, aptitude • *a gift for comedy*
See also: **blessing, capacity**

gifted *adjective* = **talented**, expert, able, capable, brilliant, skilled, accomplished, clever, ingenious, masterly

gigantic *adjective* = **enormous**, huge, giant, tremendous, mammoth, immense, titanic, colossal, stupendous

giggle *verb*, *noun* = **laugh**, chuckle, chortle, twitter, cackle, snigger, titter

gild *verb* = **adorn**, coat, enhance, brighten, ornament, embellish, embroider, beautify, dress up

gimmick *noun* = **stunt**, device, scheme, dodge, ploy, contrivance

gingerly *adverb* = **cautiously**, carefully, reluctantly, suspiciously, warily, charily, circumspectly, hesitantly, timidly

gird *verb* = **surround**, ring, encompass, enclose, encircle, enfold, hem in

girdle *noun* 1 = **belt**, band,

waistband, sash, cummerbund
▶ *verb* **2 = surround**, ring, bound, encompass, enclose, encircle, gird

girl *noun* **= female child**, schoolgirl • *She was a strong girl, and quite tall.*
See also: **female**

girth *noun* **= circumference**, measure, size, bulk

gist *noun* **= point**, force, idea, sense, core, substance, meaning, significance, essence

give *verb* **1 = present**, award, provide, supply, deliver, grant, donate, hand • *I gave her a CD.*
OPPOSITE: take
2 = collapse, yield, buckle, cave in, give way • *My knees gave out under me.*
3 = announce, issue, notify, communicate, transmit, pronounce, utter
4 = concede, grant, surrender, yield, relinquish, hand over
5 = produce, make, cause, occasion, engender
▷ **give a talk** See **lecture**
▷ **give away = reveal**, expose, leak, disclose, uncover, betray, divulge, let out, let slip
▷ **give back** See **return**
▷ **give in = surrender**, submit, concede, yield, succumb, capitulate • *Who do you think will give in first?*
▷ **give off = emit**, release, produce, discharge, exude, send out, throw out
▷ **give out = emit**, release, produce, discharge, exude, send out, throw out
▷ **give up = abandon**, stop, quit, surrender, cease, renounce, relinquish, desist, call it a day or call it a night, leave off
▷ **give way** See **collapse, give**
See also: **hand down, spare**

given See **prone**

glad *adjective* **1 = happy**, pleased, delighted, joyful, overjoyed • *They'll be glad to get away from it all.*
OPPOSITE: sorry
2 = pleasing, pleasant,

cheerful, cheering, gratifying

gladden *verb* **= please**, cheer, delight, gratify, hearten

gladly *adverb* **= happily**, freely, readily, willingly, gleefully, cheerfully, with pleasure

gladness *noun* **= happiness**, delight, joy, pleasure, glee, cheerfulness, gaiety, high spirits, mirth

glamorous *adjective* **= elegant**, smart, exciting, prestigious, attractive, glossy, dazzling, fascinating, glittering

glamour *noun* **= charm**, appeal, beauty, attraction, allure, fascination, prestige, enchantment

glance *noun* **1 = peek**, look, glimpse, peep • *The boys exchanged glances.*
▶ *verb* **2 = peek**, look, glimpse, peep, scan • *He glanced at his watch.*
3 = bounce, brush, skim • *The car glanced off the guardrail.*
4 = gleam, reflect, shine, flash, shimmer, glitter, glimmer, twinkle, glisten, glint
▷ **glance at** See **read**

glare *verb* **1 = scowl**, frown, glower • *He glared at his brother.*
2 = blaze, flame, flare, dazzle
▶ *noun* **3 = scowl**, frown • *The server lowered his eyes to avoid my furious glare.*
4 = blaze, flare, glow, dazzle, brilliance • *the glare of the headlights*
See also: **light**

glaring *adjective* **1 = conspicuous**, obvious, gross, outrageous, blatant, flagrant, manifest, unconcealed
2 = dazzling, bright, glowing, garish, blazing

glassy *adjective* **1 = transparent**, clear, smooth, slippery, shiny, glossy
2 = expressionless, cold, blank, empty, vacant, dull, lifeless, fixed, glazed

glaze *verb* **1 = coat**, polish, gloss, enamel, varnish, lacquer
▶ *noun* **2 = coat**, finish, shine,

g

polish, gloss, enamel, varnish, lacquer, patina, lustre

gleam noun **1** = **glow**, flash, ray, beam, sparkle, glimmer
2 = **trace**, hint, suggestion, flicker, glimmer, inkling
▶ verb **3** = **shine**, flash, glow, sparkle, shimmer, glitter, glimmer, glisten, glint

gleaming See **brilliant, shining**

glean See **extract**

glee noun = **delight**, triumph, joy, exuberance, elation, exhilaration, merriment, exultation

gleeful adjective = **delighted**, triumphant, jubilant, joyful, exuberant, elated, exultant, overjoyed

glib adjective = **smooth**, ready, easy, quick, slick, fluent, plausible, suave, insincere, voluble

glide verb = **slide**, run, roll, coast, skate, slip, flow, float, sail, drift

glimmer verb **1** = **flicker**, shine, glow, sparkle, shimmer, glitter, blink, gleam, twinkle, glisten
▶ noun **2** = **gleam**, ray, glow, sparkle, shimmer, blink, flicker, twinkle
3 = **trace**, hint, suggestion, gleam, flicker, inkling

glimpse noun **1** = **look**, sight, glance, peek, sighting, peep
▶ verb **2** = **catch sight of**, view, spot, spy, sight, espy

glint verb **1** = **gleam**, shine, flash, sparkle, glitter, glimmer, twinkle
▶ noun **2** = **gleam**, shine, flash, sparkle, glitter, glimmer, twinkle, twinkling

glisten verb = **gleam**, shine, flash, glance, sparkle, shimmer, glitter, glare, glimmer, twinkle, glint

glitch noun = **problem**, difficulty, malfunction, snag, hitch, interruption, blip, gremlin

glitter verb **1** = **shine**, flash, sparkle, shimmer, glare, gleam, glimmer, twinkle, glisten, glint
▶ noun **2** = **shine**, flash, sparkle, shimmer, glare, gleam, brightness, sheen, radiance
3 = **glamour**, show, display, tinsel, pageantry, splendour, gaudiness, showiness

gloat verb = **relish**, triumph, glory, brag, crow, drool, exult, revel in, rub it in (informal)

global adjective **1** = **worldwide**, world, international, universal, planetary
2 = **comprehensive**, general, total, unlimited, exhaustive, all-inclusive

globe noun = **sphere**, world, ball, planet, earth, orb

globule noun = **droplet**, drop, particle, bead, bubble, pellet, pearl

gloom noun **1** = **darkness**, dark, shadow, shade, dusk, twilight, obscurity, blackness, murk
2 = **depression**, woe, sorrow, unhappiness, melancholy, despondency, dejection, low spirits

gloomy adjective **1** = **miserable**, down, sad, dejected, glum • *They are gloomy about the team's chances of success.*
OPPOSITE: cheerful
2 = **dark**, dismal, dull, dreary • *a gloomy house on the edge of the park*
OPPOSITE: sunny
3 = **depressing**, bad, sad, dismal, dreary, sombre, cheerless, disheartening, dispiriting
See also: **cloudy, drab, pessimistic**

glorify verb **1** = **enhance**, elevate, magnify, aggrandize, dignify, ennoble
2 = **worship**, bless, honour, revere, adore, idolize, venerate, exalt, pay homage to
3 = **praise**, celebrate, extol, eulogize, sing the praises of or sound the praises of

glorious adjective **1** = **famous**, renowned, celebrated, magnificent, illustrious, distinguished, majestic, eminent, honoured
2 = **splendid**, beautiful, brilliant, gorgeous, superb, dazzling, shining

g

3 = **delightful**, fine, excellent, wonderful, gorgeous, marvellous

glory noun **1** = **honour**, praise, fame, immortality, prestige • *It was her moment of glory.*
OPPOSITE: disgrace
2 = **splendour**, majesty, grandeur, magnificence • *Spring arrived in all its glory.*
▶ verb **3** = **revel**, relish, gloat • *The curling team was glorying in its unexpected win.*
See also: **credit, rejoice**

gloss[1] noun = **shine**, polish, brilliance, gleam, sheen • *paper with a high gloss finish*

gloss[2] noun **1** = **comment**, note, explanation, commentary, translation, interpretation, footnote, annotation, elucidation
▶ verb **2** = **interpret**, comment, explain, translate, annotate, elucidate

glossy adjective = **shiny**, bright, brilliant, sleek, polished, lustrous • *glossy paint*
See also: **smooth**

glow noun **1** = **light**, gleam, glimmer • *the glow of the fire*
2 = **radiance**, brilliance, brightness, splendour, effulgence, vividness
▶ verb **3** = **shine**, smoulder, gleam, glimmer • *A light glowed behind the curtains.*
See also: **blush, glare**

glower verb **1** = **scowl**, glare, frown, give a dirty look, look daggers at, lour or lower
▶ noun **2** = **scowl**, glare, frown, black look, dirty look, lour or lower

glowing adjective **1** = **bright**, flaming, luminous, radiant, aglow
2 = **complimentary**, enthusiastic, ecstatic, rave (informal), adulatory, laudatory, rhapsodic

glue verb **1** = **stick**, fix, seal, paste • *Glue the two halves together.*
▶ noun **2** = **adhesive**, gum, paste, cement

See also: **bond**

glum adjective = **gloomy**, low, pessimistic, dejected, sullen, crestfallen, doleful, morose

glut noun **1** = **surfeit**, surplus, excess, plethora, oversupply, saturation, superfluity
▶ verb **2** = **saturate**, flood, choke, clog, overload, inundate, deluge, oversupply

glutton noun = **gourmand**, pig (informal)

gluttonous adjective = **greedy**, voracious, insatiable, ravenous, gormandizing, piggish

gluttony noun = **greed**, gormandizing, greediness, voracity

gnarled adjective = **twisted**, rough, rugged, knotted, contorted, knotty, weather-beaten, wrinkled

gnaw verb = **bite**, chew, nibble, munch

go verb **1** = **move**, drive, travel, advance, fly, proceed (formal), journey (formal) • *I went home on the weekend.*
2 = **function**, work • *stuck on the highway in a car that won't go*
3 = **leave**, withdraw, depart, make tracks, move out, set off, slope off
4 = **contribute**, serve, tend, lead to, work towards
5 = **harmonize**, agree, match, suit, fit, blend, complement, correspond, chime
6 = **elapse**, pass, flow, expire, lapse, slip away
▷ **go across** See **cross**
▷ **go against** See **clash**
▷ **go as far as** See **reach**
▷ **go away** See **disappear, vanish**
▷ **go back** See **return**
▷ **go beyond** See **pass, top**
▷ **go down** See **decline, descend**
▷ **go for** = **favour**, like, choose, prefer, admire, be attracted to, be fond of; = **attack**, assault, assail, launch oneself at, rush upon, set about or set upon, spring upon
▷ **go into** See **discuss**

▷ **go off = explode**, fire, detonate, blow up; **= leave**, part, quit, depart, decamp, go away, move out, slope off

▷ **go on = happen**, occur, take place; **= continue**, last, proceed, keep going, carry on; **= ramble on**, chatter, carry on, prattle

▷ **go on at** See **hassle**

▷ **go out = leave**, exit, depart; **= be extinguished**, expire, die out, fade out

▷ **go over = examine**, study, review, revise, reiterate, inspect, rehearse, work over

▷ **go through = suffer**, experience, undergo, endure • *I was going through a very difficult time*; **= examine**, look, search, check, hunt, explore, forage

▷ **go together with** See **accompany**

▷ **go up** See **rise**

▷ **go well** See **blend**

▷ **go with = match**, suit, fit, blend, complement, harmonize, correspond with, agree with

▷ **go wrong** See **err**

▶ *noun* 7 **= attempt**, try, shot (*informal*), stab (*informal*) • *I always wanted to have a go at waterskiing.*
8 (*Informal*) **= energy**, force, life, drive, spirit, vitality, vigour, verve, vivacity

▷ **go-ahead** See **permission**

▷ **go-between = intermediary**, medium, agent, dealer, broker, mediator, middleman

See also: **range, turn, work out**

goad *verb* 1 **= provoke**, drive, prompt, spur, incite, prod, exhort, egg on

▶ *noun* 2 **= provocation**, urge, spur, incentive, stimulus, incitement, impetus, irritation

goal *noun* **= aim**, end, target, object, purpose, intention, objective • *The goal seems to be to make as much money as possible.*
See also: **point**

gobble *verb* **= devour**, wolf • *I gobbled all the beef stew.*

gobbledygook *noun* **= nonsense**, cant, jargon, babble, gabble, gibberish, hocus-pocus, mumbo jumbo, twaddle

godforsaken *adjective* **= desolate**, remote, dismal, bleak, gloomy, abandoned, lonely, dreary, wretched, deserted, forlorn

godlike *adjective* **= divine**, celestial, heavenly, superhuman, transcendent

godly *adjective* **= devout**, good, religious, holy, righteous, pious, god-fearing, saintly

godsend *noun* **= blessing**, boon, windfall, manna, stroke of luck

golden *adjective* 1 **= yellow**, blond or blonde, flaxen
2 **= successful**, happy, rich, glorious, prosperous, flourishing, halcyon
3 **= promising**, excellent, opportune, favourable

gone *adjective* 1 **= finished**, over, past, elapsed, ended
2 **= missing**, away, lost, absent, astray, lacking, vanished

good *adjective* 1 **= excellent**, great, fine, acceptable, superior, satisfactory, splendid, pleasing, first-class, admirable, first-rate • *We had a really good time.*
OPPOSITE: bad
2 **= praiseworthy**, moral, ethical, honest, worthy, upright, admirable, trustworthy, honourable, righteous, virtuous
3 **= expert**, able, skilled, talented, competent, accomplished, clever, adept, proficient, adroit • *I'm not very good at waterskiing.*
OPPOSITE: incompetent
4 **= beneficial**, useful, profitable, helpful, suitable, fitting, convenient, win-win (*informal*), wholesome, favourable, advantageous
5 **= kind**, friendly, charitable, humane, merciful, kindly, benevolent, altruistic, kind-hearted, obliging • *You are so good to me.*
OPPOSITE: unkind
6 **= valid**, real, true, proper, legitimate, genuine, authentic, bona fide
7 **= well-behaved**, polite,

g

orderly, obedient, dutiful, well-mannered

8 = full, large, complete, extensive, substantial, adequate, considerable, sufficient, ample

▶ *noun* **9 = benefit**, use, interest, profit, gain, advantage, welfare, usefulness, wellbeing

10 = virtue, right, worth, excellence, merit, morality, goodness, rectitude, righteousness

▷ **for good = permanently**, finally, for ever, irrevocably, once and for all

See also: **favourable, respectable, sound**

| CONFUSABLES
| *Good* is an adjective, and so always describes a noun.
| *Well* is an adverb, and so always describes a verb.
| *Well* can be used as an adjective, but only to mean *in good health*.

good-bye *noun* **= farewell**, adieu, parting, leave-taking

good-for-nothing *noun*
1 = idler, couch potato (*slang*), slacker (*informal*), waster, wastrel

▶ *adjective* **2 = worthless**, idle, irresponsible, useless, feckless

good-looking See **cute, handsome**

goodly *adjective* **= considerable**, large, significant, substantial, sizable *or* sizeable, ample, tidy (*informal*)

goodness *noun* **1 = excellence**, value, worth, quality, merit, superiority

2 = kindness, mercy, goodwill, generosity, friendliness, benevolence, humaneness, kind-heartedness, kindliness

3 = virtue, integrity, merit, honesty, honour, morality, probity, rectitude, righteousness, uprightness

4 = benefit, advantage, salubriousness, wholesomeness

goods *plural noun* **1 = property**, gear, paraphernalia, belongings, chattels, effects, possessions, things, trappings

2 = merchandise, stock, stuff, commodities, wares

goodwill *noun* **= friendliness**, favour, benevolence • *They invited us to dinner as a gesture of goodwill.*
See also: **friendship**

gore[1] *noun* **= blood**, slaughter, carnage, bloodshed, butchery

gore[2] *verb* **= pierce**, wound, impale, transfix

gorge *noun* **1 = ravine**, pass, canyon, fissure, chasm, defile, cleft

▶ *verb* **2 = overeat**, feed, stuff, wolf, gobble, cram, guzzle, devour, glut, gulp

gorgeous *adjective* **1 = beautiful**, elegant, magnificent, superb, splendid, sumptuous, dazzling, ravishing, stunning (*informal*)

2 (*Informal*) **= pleasing**, good, fine, lovely, glorious, enjoyable, exquisite, delightful

gory *adjective* **= bloodthirsty**, bloody, murderous, blood-soaked, bloodstained, sanguinary

gospel *noun* **1 = truth**, fact, certainty, the last word

2 = doctrine, news, message, revelation, creed, credo, tidings

gossip *noun* **1 = hearsay**, dirt • *Gossip doesn't interest me.*

2 = busybody, telltale, chatterbox (*informal*), chatterer, gossipmonger, scandalmonger, tattler

▶ *verb* **3 = chat**, jaw (*slang*), blether, chew the fat (*slang*), gabble, prate, prattle, tattle
See also: **rumour**

gouge *verb* **1 = scoop**, cut, dig *or* dig out, claw, hollow *or* hollow out, chisel

▶ *noun* **2 = gash**, cut, scratch, scoop, groove, trench, hollow, furrow

gourmet *noun* **= connoisseur**, foodie (*informal*), bon vivant (*French*), epicure, gastronome

govern *verb* **1 = rule**, lead, order, control, manage, direct, handle, guide, command, administer

2 = restrain, control, check, regulate, curb, master, discipline, subdue, tame, hold in check

government noun 1 = **rule**, authority, administration, sovereignty, governance, statecraft
2 = **executive**, administration, regime, ministry, powers-that-be

governor noun = **leader**, head, director, chief, executive, manager, commander, controller, administrator, ruler

gown noun = **dress**, habit, costume, robe, garment, garb, frock

grab verb = **snatch**, seize, clutch, grasp • *I grabbed him by the arm.*

grace noun 1 = **elegance**, poise • *the grace of a ballet dancer*
OPPOSITE: clumsiness
2 = **goodwill**, favour, goodness, kindness, generosity, benefaction, benevolence, kindliness
3 = **manners**, consideration, decency, etiquette, decorum, tact, propriety
4 = **indulgence**, pardon, reprieve, mercy
5 = **prayer**, blessing, benediction, thanks, thanksgiving
▶ verb 6 = **honour**, enhance, enrich, decorate, adorn, favour, ornament, embellish, dignify, set off
See also: **courtesy, favour, polish**

graceful adjective = **elegant**, easy, beautiful, charming, pleasing, tasteful, comely

gracious adjective = **kind**, civil, friendly, charitable, polite, cordial, considerate, courteous, well-mannered

graciousness See **courtesy**

grade verb 1 = **classify**, group, rate, class, sort • *Eggs are graded according to quality.*
2 = **level**, group, stage, class, rank, category, degree, echelon
See also: **kind, quality**

gradient noun = **slope**, rise, bank, hill, grade, incline, declivity

gradual adjective = **steady**, slow, continuous, progressive • *the gradual improvement in communications*
OPPOSITE: sudden

gradually adverb = **steadily**, slowly, gently, progressively, by degrees, little by little, step by step, unhurriedly

graduate verb 1 = **mark off**, regulate, grade, proportion, calibrate, measure out
2 = **classify**, group, order, rank, sort, arrange, grade

graft noun 1 = **shoot**, implant, bud, sprout, splice, scion
▶ verb 2 = **transplant**, join, implant, insert, splice, affix, ingraft

grain noun 1 = **cereals**, crops
2 = **seed**, kernel, grist
3 = **bit**, piece, trace, scrap, particle, fragment, speck, modicum, granule, morsel
4 = **texture**, surface, pattern, weave, nap, fibre
5 = **inclination**, character, temper, disposition, make-up, humour

grand adjective 1 = **impressive**, magnificent, splendid, monumental, majestic, imposing • *a grand building in the centre of town*
2 (Informal) = **wonderful**, great (informal), terrific, marvellous • *It was a grand day.*

grandeur noun = **splendour**, dignity, majesty, pomp, nobility, magnificence, stateliness, sublimity

grandiose adjective
1 = **pretentious**, affected, flamboyant, showy, extravagant, pompous, bombastic, high-flown, ostentatious
2 = **imposing**, grand, impressive, lofty, magnificent, monumental, majestic, stately

grant noun 1 = **award**, subsidy, allocation, bursary • *My application for a grant has been accepted.*
▶ verb 2 = **give**, allow, award, permit, allocate • *France has agreed*

g

to grant him political asylum.
OPPOSITE: deny
3 = admit, allow, accept, acknowledge, concede • *I grant that you had some justification for your actions.*
OPPOSITE: deny
4 = consent to, allow, permit, accede to, agree to
See also: **present**

granule *noun* = **grain**, scrap, particle, fragment, molecule, atom, crumb, speck

graphic *adjective* **1 = vivid**, clear, detailed, explicit, striking, lively, expressive, lucid
2 = pictorial, visual, diagrammatic

grapple *verb* **1 = grip**, grab, seize, clutch, wrestle, grasp
2 = deal with, struggle, tackle, confront, address oneself to, get to grips with, take on

grasp *verb* **1 = grip**, hold, grab, seize, clutch, snatch • *He grasped both my hands.*
2 = understand, realize, appreciate, absorb, assimilate, take in • *Has anybody grasped the seriousness of the problem?*
▶ *noun* **3 = grip**, hold, embrace, clasp • *She slipped her hand from my grasp.*
4 = understanding, knowledge, grip, awareness, comprehension • *They have a good grasp of languages.*
5 = control, power, reach, scope
See also: **command, comprehend, handle, learn, master, see**

grasping *adjective* = **greedy**, acquisitive, avaricious, covetous, rapacious

grate *verb* **1 = shred**, grind, mince, pulverize, triturate
2 = scrape, grind, scratch, rub, creak, rasp
3 = annoy, jar, irritate, rankle, exasperate, get on one's nerves (*informal*), set one's teeth on edge

grateful *adjective* = **thankful**, appreciative, indebted • *I am grateful to you for your help.*
OPPOSITE: ungrateful

gratification *noun* = **satisfaction**, reward, thrill, delight, pleasure, relish, enjoyment, indulgence, fulfilment

gratified See **proud**

gratify *verb* = **please**, satisfy, delight, humour, gladden, give pleasure, requite

grating[1] *adjective* = **irritating**, offensive, harsh, raucous, strident, unpleasant, annoying, discordant, displeasing, jarring

grating[2] *noun* = **grille**, grid, grate, gridiron, lattice, trellis

gratis See **free**

gratitude *noun* = **thankfulness**, recognition, appreciation, thanks • *We wish to express our gratitude to the coach.*
OPPOSITE: ingratitude

gratuitous *adjective* **1 = free**, voluntary, unpaid, spontaneous, complimentary, gratis, unasked-for, unrewarded
2 = unjustified, unnecessary, baseless, unwarranted, needless, groundless, wanton, superfluous, causeless, uncalled-for, unmerited

gratuity *noun* = **tip**, gift, reward, donation, bonus, largesse *or* largess

grave[1] *noun* = **tomb**, pit, mausoleum • *They visited the grave twice a year.*
RELATED WORD
adjective: sepulchral

grave[2] *adjective* **1 = critical**, serious, acute • *The situation in his country is very grave.*
2 = solemn, serious, sombre, sober, earnest, dignified, dour, unsmiling
See also: **deep, grim, heavy, severe**

graveyard *noun* = **cemetery**, necropolis, burial ground, charnel house, churchyard

gravity *noun* **1 = importance**, severity, significance, urgency, seriousness, acuteness, momentousness, perilousness, weightiness
2 = solemnity, dignity,

seriousness, sobriety, gravitas, earnestness

graze[1] *verb* = **feed**, crop, browse, pasture

graze[2] *verb* 1 = **scratch**, skin, scrape • *He fell and grazed his left arm.*

2 = **touch**, brush, scrape, shave, rub, skim, glance off

▶ *noun* 3 = **scratch**, abrasion (*informal*), road rash (*informal*) • *He has just a slight graze on his elbow.*

greasy *adjective* = **fatty**, slippery, oily, slimy, oleaginous

great *adjective* 1 = **large**, big, huge, vast, enormous, immense, gigantic, voluminous, prodigious, supersize • *great columns of ice*
OPPOSITE: small

2 = **important**, serious, significant, critical, crucial, momentous • *the great events of the 20th century*

3 = **famous**, prominent, remarkable, renowned, outstanding, illustrious, noteworthy, eminent

4 (*Informal*) = **excellent**, fine, wonderful, tremendous (*informal*), fantastic (*informal*), terrific (*informal*), superb, marvellous • *I thought it was a great idea.*
OPPOSITE: terrible

▷ **great deal** *See* **plenty**
See also: **acute, brilliant, deep, extensive, extreme, grand, intense, splendid, uncommon**

greatest *adjective* = **supreme**, ultimate, foremost

greatly *adverb* = **very much**, considerably, remarkably, hugely, vastly, tremendously, enormously, immensely, exceedingly

greatness *noun* 1 = **immensity**, size, magnitude, enormity, vastness, hugeness, prodigiousness

2 = **importance**, weight, gravity, significance, urgency, seriousness, momentousness

3 = **fame**, note, celebrity, glory, distinction, kudos, renown, grandeur, eminence, illustriousness

greed, greediness *noun*
1 = **gluttony**, hunger, edacity, esurience, gormandizing, voracity

2 = **avarice**, desire, longing, craving, selfishness, acquisitiveness, avidity, covetousness

greedy *adjective* 1 = **grasping**, materialistic • *greedy people who take more than their fair share*

2 = **gluttonous**, hungry, voracious, insatiable, ravenous, gormandizing, piggish

green *adjective* 1 = **leafy**, grassy, verdant

2 = **ecological**, conservationist, environment-friendly, non-polluting, ozone-friendly, green-collar

3 = **immature**, new, raw, naive, inexperienced, gullible, untrained, wet behind the ears (*informal*)

4 = **jealous**, envious, resentful, covetous, grudging

▶ *noun* 5 = **lawn**, common, turf, sward

g

SHADES OF GREEN

avocado	olive
chartreuse	pea green
emerald	sage
jade	sea green
khaki	turquoise
lime	

---

greet *verb* = **welcome**, meet, receive (*formal*) • *The champions were greeted by their fans.*

greeting *noun* = **welcome**, address, reception, salute, salutation

gregarious *adjective* = **outgoing**, social, friendly, cordial, affable, sociable, companionable, convivial

grey *adjective* 1 = **pale**, pallid, wan, ashen

2 = **dismal**, dark, gloomy, dull, dim, dreary, drab, depressing
3 = **characterless**, anonymous, dull, colourless
See also: **dim, drab**

SHADES OF GREY

ash	platinum
charcoal	silver
gunmetal	silvery
hoary	slate
leaden	stone
pewter	taupe

---

gridlock noun = **standstill**, deadlock, impasse, stalemate
grief noun = **sadness**, distress, misery, sorrow, unhappiness, heartache • *a huge outpouring of national grief*
OPPOSITE: happiness
See also: **pain, regret**
grief-stricken See **sad**
grievance noun = **complaint**, injury, injustice, gripe (*informal*), axe to grind
grieve verb 1 = **mourn**, lament • *He still grieves for his wife.*
2 = **sadden**, pain, upset, distress • *It grieved us to be separated from our loved ones.*
OPPOSITE: cheer
See also: **regret**
grievous adjective 1 = **painful**, severe, grave, harmful, dreadful
2 = **deplorable**, offensive, shocking, outrageous, shameful, atrocious, dreadful, monstrous
grill See **cook, interrogate**
grim adjective = **stern**, severe, grave, solemn • *Her face was grim.*
See also: **horrible, serious**
grimace noun 1 = **scowl**, face, frown, sneer
▶ verb 2 = **scowl**, frown, sneer, lour or lower, make a face or make faces
grime noun = **dirt**, grease, filth, soot, smut
grimy adjective = **dirty**, foul, filthy, unclean, grubby, scuzzy

(*slang*), soiled, sooty
grin See **smile**
grind verb 1 = **crush**, pound, mill, powder, grate, granulate, pulverize, abrade, triturate, kibble
2 = **smooth**, sand, polish, sharpen, whet
3 = **scrape**, grate, gnash
▶ noun 4 (*Informal*) = **hard work**, sweat (*informal*), chore, labour, toil, drudgery
grip noun 1 = **grasp**, hold, clasp • *He tightened his grip on the wallet.*
2 = **control**, power, influence, clutches • *The dictator maintains an iron grip on his country.*
3 = **understanding**, command, grasp, mastery, comprehension
▶ verb 4 = **grasp**, hold, clutch • *I gripped the steering wheel and stared straight ahead.*
5 = **engross**, hold, entrance, absorb, fascinate, mesmerize, rivet, enthrall
See also: **handle**
gripping adjective = **fascinating**, exciting, thrilling, compelling, engrossing, enthralling, entrancing, riveting, spellbinding
grisly adjective = **gruesome**, horrible, shocking, awful, appalling, dreadful, macabre, ghastly, terrifying
grit noun 1 = **gravel**, dust, sand, pebbles
2 = **courage**, resolution, spirit, determination, backbone, perseverance, tenacity, fortitude, guts (*informal*)
▶ verb 3 = **grind**, grate, clench, gnash
gritty adjective 1 = **rough**, dusty, sandy, rasping, gravelly, granular
2 = **courageous**, brave, spirited, plucky, determined, steadfast, resolute, dogged, tenacious
groan noun 1 = **moan**, cry, whine, sigh
▶ verb 2 = **moan**, cry, whine, sigh
groggy adjective = **dizzy**, weak, shaky, faint, confused,

unsteady, wobbly, dazed

groom noun 1 = **stableman**, stableboy
▶ verb 2 = **smarten up**, clean, tidy, preen, primp, spruce up
3 = **rub down**, clean, tend, brush, curry
4 = **train**, coach, prime, prepare, ready, drill, educate, nurture, make ready

groove noun = **indentation**, cut, channel, trench, hollow, rut, trough, flute, furrow

grope verb = **feel**, search, fish, fumble, flounder, forage, scrabble, cast about

gross adjective 1 = **fat**, overweight, obese, corpulent, hulking
2 = **total**, whole, entire, aggregate, before deductions, before tax
3 = **vulgar**, crude, offensive, obscene, coarse, indelicate
4 = **blatant**, rank, utter, sheer, flagrant, heinous, grievous, unmitigated
▶ verb = **earn**, make, take, bring in, rake in (informal)

grotesque adjective = **unnatural**, strange, bizarre, fantastic, distorted, outlandish, preposterous, deformed, freakish

ground noun 1 = **earth**, land, soil, dirt, terrain • We slid down the roof and dropped to the ground.
2 = **stadium**, field, park, arena
3 (usually plural) = **dregs**, deposit, sediment, lees
▶ verb 4 = **base**, set, settle, fix, establish, found
5 = **instruct**, train, teach, initiate, tutor, acquaint with, familiarize with
See also: **bottom**

> INFORMALLY SPEAKING
> **break new ground**: do something original
> **get off the ground**: make a successful start
> **lose ground**: give up what has been gained
> **stand your ground**: refuse to give in or retreat

groundless adjective

= **unjustified**, empty, idle, baseless, unwarranted, unfounded, uncalled-for

grounds plural noun 1 = **land**, estate • the grounds of the university
2 = **basis**, cause, reason, excuse, justification • I'm against it on the grounds of expense.
See also: **argument**

groundwork noun
= **preliminaries**, foundation, preparation, fundamentals, spadework, underpinnings

group noun 1 = **set**, party, crowd, band, collection, pack, gang, bunch, platoon, coterie, aggregation, assemblage • a group of football fans
▶ verb 2 = **arrange**, class, sort, organize, classify, marshal, assort • Their responses are grouped into 11 categories.
See also: **association**, **category**, **club**, **company**, **grade**, **lot**, **mass**, **movement**, **organization**, **society**, **team**, **type**

grouping See **party**

grouse verb 1 = **complain**, whine, carp, grumble, moan, gripe (informal), bellyache (slang)
▶ noun 2 = **complaint**, protest, objection, grievance, grumble, moan, gripe (informal), grouch (informal)

grove noun = **wood**, covert, plantation, thicket, coppice, copse, spinney

grovel verb = **humble oneself**, creep, crawl, cringe, fawn, abase oneself, bow and scrape, brown-nose (slang), demean oneself, kiss ass (slang), kowtow, toady

grow verb 1 = **increase**, develop, expand, multiply • Bacteria grow more quickly once food is contaminated.
OPPOSITE: shrink
2 = **flourish**, sprout, germinate • Trees and bushes grew down to the water's edge.
3 = **become**, get, turn • The puppy grew more comfortable with us.
4 = **originate**, issue, spring, stem, arise

5 = improve, advance, progress, succeed, thrive, flourish, prosper
6 = cultivate, raise, produce, farm, breed, nurture, propagate
▷ **grow up** See **mature**
See also: **rise, spread**
grown See **mature**
grown-up adjective **1 = mature** • *I didn't hear*
adult, fully-grown, of age
▶ noun **2 = adult**, man, woman
growth noun **1 = increase**, development, expansion, enlargement • *the growth of the sport-fishing industry*
2 = improvement, rise, advance, success, progress, expansion, prosperity
3 (*Medical*) **= tumour**, lump
See also: **gain, spread**
grub noun **1 = larva**, caterpillar, maggot
2 (*Slang*) **= food**, sustenance, rations, victuals
▶ verb **3 = dig up**, root (*informal*), burrow, pull up
4 = search, hunt, uncover, unearth, scour, forage, ferret, rummage
grubby adjective **= dirty**, messy, filthy, grimy, mucky, shabby, sordid, squalid, seedy, unwashed, scuzzy (*slang*)
grudge verb **1 = resent**, mind, complain, covet, envy, begrudge
▶ noun **2 = resentment**, grievance, dislike, animosity, bitterness, enmity, antipathy, rancour
grudging See **unwilling**
gruelling adjective **= exhausting**, severe, arduous, strenuous, demanding, backbreaking, laborious, punishing, taxing, tiring
gruesome adjective **= horrific**, terrible, horrible, shocking, grim, grisly, macabre, ghastly
gruff adjective **1 = surly**, rough, rude, grumpy, sullen, bad-tempered, brusque, churlish, ungracious
2 = hoarse, low, rough, harsh, husky, rasping, croaking, guttural, throaty
grumble verb **1 = complain**,

whine, carp, moan, groan, mutter • *"This is very inconvenient,"*
he grumbled.
2 = rumble, roar, mutter, growl, murmur, gurgle
▶ noun **3 = complaint**, protest, objection, murmur • *I didn't hear*
any grumbles from anyone at the time.
4 = rumble, roar, growl, murmur, gurgle, muttering
grumpy adjective **= irritable**, surly, sullen, sulky • *a grumpy*
old dog
See also: **cross**
grunt See **moan**
guarantee noun **1 = assurance**, promise, word, pledge, undertaking • *a guarantee of job*
security
▶ verb **2 = ensure**, promise, pledge • *Remarks of this kind are*
guaranteed to cause anxiety
guaranteed See **certain,.**
definite
guard verb **1 = protect**, defend, shelter, shield, safeguard, watch over • *Police were guarding his home*
yesterday.
2 = supervise, police, patrol
• *Soldiers were guarding the prisoners.*
▷ **guard against** See **beware**
▶ noun **3 = sentry**, warden, sentinel, watchman, warder
• *The prisoners overpowered their*
guards and locked them in a cell.
4 = protection, security, screen, shield, safeguard, defence, buffer
▷ **off guard = unprepared**, unwary, napping, unready
▷ **on guard = prepared**, ready, alert, cautious, wary, vigilant, watchful, circumspect, on the alert, on the lookout
See also: **watch**
guarded adjective **= cautious**, careful, suspicious, wary, prudent, cagey (*informal*), reserved, reticent, noncommittal, circumspect
guardian noun **= keeper**, champion, guard, defender, curator, warden, protector, custodian
guerrilla noun **= freedom fighter**,

g

partisan, underground fighter

guess *verb* 1 = **estimate**, speculate • *I guessed that he was in the movie business.*
2 = **suppose**, think, believe, suspect, judge, imagine, fancy, reckon, conjecture
▶ *noun* 3 = **speculation**, feeling, reckoning • *My guess is that the answer will be no.*
See also: **assume**, **figure**, **idea**

guesswork *noun* = **speculation**, theory, estimation, conjecture, surmise, supposition

guest *noun* = **visitor**, company, caller, boarder, lodger, visitant

guffaw See **laugh**

guidance *noun* = **advice**, help, leadership, management, direction, instruction, teaching, counselling

guide *verb* 1 = **lead**, direct, accompany, escort • *He took the child by the arm and guided him to safety.*
2 = **influence**, govern, counsel (*formal*) • *He should have let his instinct guide him.*
3 = **steer**, control, manage, direct, handle, command, manoeuvre
▶ *noun* 4 = **escort**, leader, teacher, adviser, conductor, usher, mentor, counsellor
5 = **model**, standard, example, ideal, inspiration, paradigm
6 = **pointer**, sign, landmark, marker, beacon, signpost, guiding light, lodestar
7 = **guidebook**, key, manual, directory, catalogue, handbook, Baedeker, instructions
See also: **ease**, **take**

guideline See **rule**, **standard**

guild *noun* = **society**, company, order, union, club, league, organization, association, corporation, lodge, fellowship, fraternity, brotherhood

guile *noun* = **cunning**, craft, deceit, trickery, artifice, cleverness, slyness, wiliness

guileless See **innocent**

guilt *noun* 1 = **culpability**, blame, responsibility, wrongdoing, misconduct, guiltiness, sinfulness, wickedness
2 = **remorse**, regret, shame, stigma, contrition, guilty conscience, self-reproach

guiltless *adjective* = **innocent**, clean (*slang*), pure, spotless, untainted, blameless, irreproachable, sinless, squeaky-clean

guilty *adjective* 1 = **responsible**, criminal, convicted • *They were found guilty of the crime.*
OPPOSITE: innocent
2 = **ashamed**, sorry, remorseful (*formal*), regretful • *When she saw me, she looked guilty.*

guise *noun* = **form**, appearance, shape, aspect, mode, disguise, pretense, semblance, demeanour

gulf *noun* 1 = **bay**, bight, sea inlet
2 = **chasm**, opening, split, gap, separation, void, rift, abyss

gullibility *noun* = **credulity**, innocence, simplicity, naivety

gullible *adjective* = **naive**, trusting • *I'm so gullible I would have believed him.*
OPPOSITE: suspicious
See also: **impressionable**

gully *noun* = **channel**, ditch, gutter, watercourse

gulp *verb* 1 = **swallow**, wolf, gobble, guzzle, devour, swig (*informal*), quaff, swill
2 = **gasp**, choke, swallow
▶ *noun* 3 = **swallow**, draft, mouthful, swig (*informal*)

gum *noun* 1 = **glue**, paste, cement, resin, adhesive
▶ *verb* 2 = **stick**, paste, cement, glue, affix

gumption *noun* (*Informal*) = **resourcefulness**, initiative, enterprise, savvy (*slang*), wit or wits, acumen, astuteness, common sense, mother wit

gun *noun* = **firearm**, piece (*slang*), rifle, handgun, pistol, revolver, saturday night special (*slang*)

gunman *noun* = **terrorist**, killer, bandit, gunslinger (*slang*)

gurgle *verb* 1 = **murmur**, lap, splash, bubble, ripple,

babble, plash, purl
▶ *noun* **2** = **murmur**, ripple, babble, purl
guru *noun* = **teacher**, leader, authority, master, sage, mentor, tutor, Svengali
gush *verb* **1** = **flow**, pour, stream, spurt • *Water gushed out of the broken pipe.*
2 = **enthuse**, overstate, chatter, spout, babble, effervesce, effuse
▶ *noun* **3** = **stream**, flood, rush, jet, flow, spurt, cascade, torrent, spout
See also: **rave**
gust *noun* **1** = **blast**, blow, rush, breeze, puff, squall
▶ *verb* **2** = **blow**, blast, squall
gusto *noun* = **relish**, delight, pleasure, enthusiasm, enjoyment, zeal, verve, fervour
gut *noun* **1** (*Informal*) = **paunch**, belly, potbelly, spare tire (*slang*)
▷ **guts** = **intestines**, stomach, belly, bowels, entrails, innards (*informal*), insides (*informal*), viscera; (*Informal*) = **courage**, backbone, audacity, spirit, nerve, pluck, daring, mettle

▶ *verb* **2** = **disembowel**, clean
3 = **ravage**, empty, clean out, despoil
▶ *adjective* **4** (*~ reaction*)
= **instinctive**, natural, basic, heartfelt, spontaneous, involuntary, visceral, intuitive, unthinking
gutless *See* **cowardly**
gutsy *adjective* = **brave**, bold, gritty, spirited, courageous, plucky, determined, resolute, indomitable
gutter *noun* = **drain**, channel, ditch, trench, conduit, trough, sluice
guttural *adjective* = **throaty**, deep, rough, thick, husky, rasping, gruff, gravelly, hoarse
guy *noun* (*Informal*) = **man**, person, fellow, dude (*slang*), lad, chap
guzzle *verb* = **devour**, drink, bolt, wolf, gobble, cram, swill, stuff (oneself)
Gypsy, Gipsy *noun* = **traveler**, rover, nomad, Bohemian, wanderer, rambler, roamer, Romany

Hh

habit *noun* **1** = **custom**, practice, convention, tradition, routine • *his habit of smiling at everyone he sees*
2 = **addiction**, dependence • *a drug habit*
habitat *noun* = **home**, environment, territory • *the habitat of the spotted owl*
habitation *noun* **1** = **dwelling**, home, house, residence, lodging, abode, domicile, living quarters, quarters
2 = **occupancy**, occupation, inhabitance, tenancy
habitual *adjective* = **customary**, standard, regular, traditional, normal, usual, routine, familiar, accustomed
hack¹ *verb* = **cut**, slash, chop, mutilate, mangle, lacerate, hew
hack² *noun* **1** = **scribbler**, literary hack, penny-a-liner
2 = **horse**, nag, crock
hackneyed *adjective* = **clichéd**, tired, stale, banal, trite • *hackneyed phrases like "tried and true"*
OPPOSITE: original
See also: **corny, stock**
hag *noun* = **witch**, crone, harridan
haggard *adjective* = **gaunt**, thin, wan, careworn, drawn, emaciated, pinched
haggle *verb* = **bargain**, barter, beat down
hail¹ *noun* **1** = **shower**, storm, barrage, volley, bombardment • *a hail of bullets*
▶ *verb* **2** = **rain down on**, rain, batter, shower, pelt, bombard, beat down upon
hail² *verb* **1** = **call**, flag down, signal to • *He hailed me from across the street.*
2 = **greet**, welcome,

acknowledge, cheer, applaud, salute, honour, acclaim
▷ **hail from** = **come from**, be a native of, be born in, originate in
hair *noun* = **locks**, shock, mop, mane, head of hair, tresses
hairdresser *noun* = **stylist**, barber, coiffeur or coiffeuse
hair-raising *adjective* = **frightening**, shocking, scary, alarming, bloodcurdling, horrifying, spine-chilling, terrifying
hairstyle *noun* = **haircut**, cut, style, hairdo, coiffure
hairy *adjective* = **shaggy**, furry, woolly, unshaven, bushy, hirsute, stubbly
halcyon *adjective* **1** = **peaceful**, quiet, calm, gentle, tranquil, serene, undisturbed
2 (~ *days*) = **happy**, golden, prosperous, carefree, flourishing, palmy
hale *adjective* = **healthy**, well, strong, sound, fit, robust, vigorous, able-bodied, flourishing, in the pink
half *noun* **1** = **equal part**, section, portion, hemisphere, fifty per cent
▶ *adjective* **2** = **partial**, moderate, limited, halved
▶ *adverb* **3** = **partially**, partly, in part
half-baked *adjective* = **ill-judged**, impractical, short-sighted, ill-conceived, poorly planned, unformed, unthought out or unthought through
half-hearted *adjective* = **unenthusiastic**, tame, listless, indifferent, lukewarm, apathetic, lacklustre, perfunctory

halfway adverb **1** = **midway**, to the middle or in the middle
▶ adjective **2** = **midway**, central, middle, mid, intermediate, equidistant
▷ **halfway point** See **middle**

halfwit noun = **fool**, idiot, moron, imbecile (informal), airhead (slang), dork (slang), dunderhead, schmuck (slang), simpleton

hall noun **1** = **entrance hall**, lobby, entry, passage, corridor, hallway, foyer, passageway, vestibule
2 = **meeting place**, chamber, auditorium, assembly room, concert hall

hallmark noun **1** = **seal**, sign, mark, device, stamp, symbol, endorsement
2 = **indication**, sure sign, telltale sign

hallow See **bless**

hallowed See **holy**

hallucination noun = **illusion**, dream, vision, fantasy, delusion, mirage, apparition, figment of the imagination

halo noun = **ring of light**, aura, corona, nimbus, radiance

halt verb **1** = **stop**, draw up, pull up • She held her hand out to halt him.
2 = **end**, check, curb, cease, terminate, cut short • Production was halted on the movie.
OPPOSITE: begin
▶ noun **3** = **stop**, end, close, pause, standstill, stoppage • He brought the car to a halt.
See also: **block**

halting adjective = **faltering**, awkward, hesitant, laboured, stammering, stumbling, stuttering

halve verb = **bisect**, cut in half, divide equally, share equally, split in two

hammer verb **1** = **hit**, strike, beat, drive, knock, tap, bang
2 (Informal) = **defeat**, beat, trounce, drub, thrash, run rings around (informal), wipe the floor with (informal)

hamper verb = **hinder**, restrict, frustrate, obstruct, impede

• I was hampered by a lack of information.
See also: **handicap, restrain**

hand noun **1** = **palm**, fist, paw (informal), mitt (slang)
2 = **hired man**, worker, employee, operative, artisan, craftsman, labourer, workman
3 = **penmanship**, script, handwriting, calligraphy
4 = **ovation**, clap, round of applause
▷ **at hand, on hand** = **nearby**, close, near, available, ready, handy, at one's fingertips, within reach
▷ **hand-out** = **charity**, alms; = **leaflet**, literature (informal), bulletin, circular, mailshot, press release
▶ verb **5** = **pass**, deliver, hand over
▷ **hand down** = **pass on**, will, give, bestow, bequeath, pass down • stories handed down from parents to children
▷ **hand in** See **submit, tender**
▷ **hand out** See **distribute, present**
▷ **hand-pick** See **pick**

handbook noun = **guidebook**, guide, manual, Baedeker, instruction book

handcuff verb = **shackle**, fetter, manacle

handcuffs plural noun = **shackles**, cuffs (informal), fetters, manacles

handful noun = **few**, smattering, sprinkling, small number

handicap noun **1** = **disadvantage**, barrier, obstacle, impediment, drawback, hindrance • Being short was a slight handicap for the basketball player.
2 = **advantage**, head start
3 = **disability**, defect, impairment
▶ verb **4** = **hinder**, restrict, burden, hamper, impede
• Greater levels of stress may handicap some students.

handicraft noun = **craftsmanship**, art, skill, craft, workmanship, handiwork

handiwork noun = **creation**,

product, production, design, achievement, invention

handle noun **1 = grip**, knob, hilt
• a broom handle
▶ verb **2 = hold**, feel, touch, finger, grasp • Wear protective gloves when handling chemicals.
3 = control, manage, direct, guide, manipulate, manoeuvre
• The truck is difficult to handle on the road.
4 = deal with, manage, administer, supervise, cope with, take care of • Can you handle the situation?
See also: **deal, process**
handsome adjective **1 = good-looking**, attractive • a handsome man
OPPOSITE: ugly
2 = generous, liberal, considerable, sizable, ample, plentiful • a handsome profit
OPPOSITE: small
handwriting noun
= penmanship, hand, script, scrawl, calligraphy
handy adjective **1 = convenient**, close, nearby, at hand, at your fingertips, on hand • Keep a pencil and paper handy.
2 = useful, helpful, practical, convenient, neat, easy to use
• handy hints on looking after indoor plants
3 = skilful, expert, skilled, adept, deft, proficient, adroit, dexterous
See also: **available, ready**
hang verb **1 = dangle**, sag, droop
• His jacket hung from a hook behind the door.
2 = suspend, fix, attach, drape, fasten • to hang clothes on a line
3 = execute, lynch, string up (informal)
▷ **hang around** See **stay**
▷ **hang back = hesitate**, recoil, be reluctant, demur, hold back
▷ **hang out** See **associate**
▶ noun
▷ **get the hang of = grasp**, understand, comprehend
▷ **hang-up = preoccupation**, problem, thing (informal), block,

difficulty, obsession, inhibition
See also: **extend, float, stretch**

INFORMALLY SPEAKING
get the hang of: learn how to do or to operate
hang around: loiter aimlessly
hang back: be unwilling to go forward
hang in (there): be persistent
hang out: spend time with someone or in some place
hang together: be consistent

hangdog adjective **= guilty**, downcast, wretched, cowed, cringing, defeated, furtive, shamefaced
hangover noun **= aftereffects**, crapulence, morning after (informal)
hank noun **= coil**, roll, piece, length, loop, skein
hanker verb (with for or after)
= desire, long, hunger, pine, thirst, crave, itch, lust, yearn
hankering noun **= desire**, hope, urge, wish, hunger, ache, longing, craving, thirst, itch, yearning, pining
haphazard adjective
= disorganized, random, casual, indiscriminate, aimless, hit or miss (informal), slapdash
haphazardly See **at random**
hapless See **unlucky**
happen verb **1 = occur**, follow, result, come about, take place • The accident happened on Wednesday.
2 = chance, turn out
See also: **come, work out**
happening noun **= event**, experience, incident, affair, episode, proceeding, occurrence
happily adverb **1 = willingly**, freely, gladly, with pleasure
2 = joyfully, gleefully, blithely, cheerfully, joyously, gaily, merrily
3 = luckily, fortunately, opportunely, providentially
happiness noun **= joy**, delight, pleasure, satisfaction, ecstasy, elation, contentment • Money can't buy happiness.
OPPOSITE: sadness

h

happy adjective 1 = **joyful**, content, glad, ecstatic, jubilant, merry, pleased, delighted, cheerful, blissful, elated, overjoyed, thrilled • *a happy atmosphere*
OPPOSITE: sad
2 = **fortunate**, lucky, timely, win-win (*informal*), favourable, advantageous, auspicious • *a happy coincidence*
OPPOSITE: unlucky
See also: **agreeable, bright, cheery, comfortable, ready, satisfied, willing**

happy-go-lucky adjective = **carefree**, easy-going, light-hearted, unconcerned, nonchalant, blithe, untroubled

harangue verb 1 = **rant**, address, lecture, spout (*informal*), exhort, declaim, hold forth
▶ noun 2 = **speech**, address, tirade, diatribe, declamation, exhortation

harass verb = **annoy**, trouble, plague, bother, hound, hassle (*informal*), persecute, vex, harry, pester

harassed adjective = **worried**, troubled, strained, distraught, careworn, hassled (*informal*), tormented, under pressure, vexed

harassment noun = **trouble**, bother, persecution, hassle (*informal*), nuisance, irritation, annoyance, pestering

harbour noun 1 = **port**, haven, anchorage
▶ verb 2 = **shelter**, protect, hide, shield, provide refuge
3 = **maintain**, hold, nurse, retain, foster, entertain, nurture, cling to
See also: **bear, refuge**

hard adjective 1 = **solid**, strong, firm, tough, stiff, rigid • *a hard piece of cheese*
OPPOSITE: soft
2 = **strenuous**, rigorous, arduous, exhausting, laborious, tough • *hard work*
OPPOSITE: easy
3 = **difficult**, complex, complicated, baffling, puzzling • *That's a very hard question.*
OPPOSITE: simple
4 = **unfeeling**, cold, cruel, stern, callous, unsympathetic, unkind, hardhearted, pitiless
5 = **painful**, unpleasant, intolerable, grievous, disagreeable, distressing
▷ **hard up** = **poor**, short, impoverished, broke (*informal*), penniless, impecunious, on the breadline, out of pocket, strapped for cash (*informal*)
▶ adverb 6 = **energetically**, heavily, sharply, strongly, severely, vigorously, fiercely, violently, intensely, forcibly, forcefully, powerfully, with all one's might, with might and main
7 = **diligently**, steadily, persistently, doggedly, industriously, untiringly
See also: **harsh, rough, severe, tricky**

hard-boiled adjective = **tough**, realistic, practical, cynical, hard-nosed (*informal*), unsentimental, matter-of-fact

harden verb 1 = **solidify**, set, freeze, bake, cake, stiffen • *The cement finally hardened.*
OPPOSITE: soften
2 = **accustom**, season, train, inure, habituate
See also: **strengthen**

hardened adjective 1 = **habitual**, chronic, shameless, incorrigible, inveterate
2 = **accustomed**, seasoned, habituated, inured, toughened

hard-headed adjective = **sensible**, tough, realistic, practical, pragmatic, shrewd, unsentimental, level-headed

hardhearted adjective = **unsympathetic**, hard, cold, insensitive, callous, heartless, uncaring, unfeeling

hardiness noun = **resilience**, resolution, toughness, robustness, ruggedness, sturdiness

hardly adverb = **barely**, just,

scarcely, only just • *I could hardly believe what I was seeing.*

hardship *noun* = **suffering**, want, difficulty, adversity, misfortune, destitution • *Many people are suffering economic hardship.*
See also: **ordeal, poverty, sorrow**

hardy *adjective* = **strong**, tough, sound, robust, rugged, sturdy, stout

hark See **listen**

harm *verb* 1 = **injure**, damage, abuse, hurt, wound, ruin, ill-treat • *The robbers seemed anxious not to harm anyone.*
▶ *noun* 2 = **injury**, damage, abuse, hurt • *Even friendly bears are capable of doing harm to human beings.*
See also: **spoil**

harmful *adjective* = **damaging**, destructive, detrimental, hurtful • *Most stress is harmful, but some is beneficial.*
OPPOSITE: harmless
See also: **unhealthy**

harmless *adjective* = **safe**, innocuous, nontoxic, not dangerous • *This experiment was harmless to the animals.*
OPPOSITE: harmful

harmonious *adjective*
1 = **melodious**, musical, agreeable, concordant, consonant, dulcet, mellifluous, sweet-sounding, tuneful
2 = **friendly**, sympathetic, compatible, cordial, amicable, agreeable, congenial

harmonize *verb* = **match**, tally, blend, correspond, coordinate, chime with, cohere, tone in with

harmony *noun* 1 = **agreement**, accord, peace, sympathy, friendship, compatibility, cooperation, rapport, amicability, concord
2 = **tunefulness**, tune, melody, unison, euphony

harness *noun* 1 = **equipment**, tackle, gear, tack
▶ *verb* 2 = **exploit**, control, channel, employ, mobilize, utilize

harrowing *adjective*
= **distressing**, painful, traumatic, nerve-racking, agonizing, disturbing, heart-rending, terrifying, tormenting

harry *verb* = **pester**, plague, bother, molest, harass, hassle (*informal*), badger, chivvy

harsh *adjective* 1 = **severe**, hard, cruel, stern, ruthless, austere • *harsh weather conditions*
OPPOSITE: mild
2 = **raucous**, rough, strident, rasping, grating, discordant, dissonant, guttural
See also: **drastic**

harshly *adverb* = **severely**, strictly, roughly, brutally, cruelly, sternly

harshness *noun* = **severity**, brutality, austerity, roughness, rigour, asperity, sternness

harvest *noun* 1 = **crop**, produce, yield
▶ *verb* 2 = **gather**, pick, reap, pluck, mow

hash *noun*
▷ **make a hash of** (*Informal*)
= **mess up**, mishandle, botch, bungle, muddle, mismanage, make a pig's ear of (*informal*)

hassle *noun* 1 (*Informal*) = **trouble**, effort, bother, inconvenience, upheaval • *It's not worth the hassle.*
2 = **argument**, fight, dispute, row, disagreement, squabble, quarrel, bickering
▶ *verb* 3 (*Informal*) = **bother**, harass, nag, badger, pester • *The picky customer hassled the server.*
See also: **annoy, difficulty, nuisance, stress, worry**

haste *noun* 1 = **speed**, urgency, velocity, quickness, alacrity, rapidity, swiftness
2 = **rush**, hurry, hustle, impetuosity

hasten *verb* = **rush**, race, fly, speed, dash, hurry *or* hurry up, scurry, make haste

hastily *adverb* 1 = **speedily**, quickly, rapidly, promptly
2 = **hurriedly**, impetuously, precipitately, rashly

hasty *adjective* 1 = **speedy**, prompt, rapid, swift, brisk,

hurried • *The signs of their hasty departure could be seen everywhere.*
2 = impetuous, rash, precipitate, impulsive, thoughtless
See also: **quick, sudden**

hatch *verb* **1 = incubate**, breed, brood, bring forth
2 = devise, design, conceive, concoct, contrive, cook up (*informal*), dream up (*informal*), think up

hate *verb* **1 = detest**, dislike, loathe, despise, abhor, be sick of • *Most people hate him, but they don't care to say so.*
OPPOSITE: love
2 = be unwilling, dislike, be loath, be reluctant, be sorry, feel disinclined, shrink from
▷ *noun* **3 = hatred**, hostility, dislike, animosity, aversion, loathing • *a violent bully, destructive and full of hate*
OPPOSITE: love

hateful *adjective* = **horrible**, offensive, despicable, abhorrent, obnoxious, loathsome • *It was a hateful thing to say to me.*

hatred *noun* = **hate**, dislike, animosity, revulsion, aversion, antipathy • *He has been accused of inciting racial hatred.*
OPPOSITE: love
See also: **horror, hostility**

haughty *adjective* = **proud**, arrogant, conceited, disdainful, snobbish, stuck-up (*informal*) • *He spoke in a haughty tone.*
OPPOSITE: humble
See also: **superior**

haul *verb* **1 = drag**, pull, draw, tug, heave, lug
▷ *noun* **2 = gain**, catch, yield, harvest, loot, booty, spoils, takings

haunt *verb* **1 = plague**, trouble, possess, recur, obsess, torment, prey on, stay with, weigh on
▷ *noun* **2 = meeting place**, hangout (*informal*), rendezvous, stamping ground

haunted *adjective* **1 = possessed**, eerie, spooky (*informal*), ghostly, cursed, jinxed
2 = preoccupied, troubled,

worried, obsessed, plagued, tormented

haunting *adjective* = **poignant**, persistent, nostalgic, unforgettable, evocative

have *verb* **1 = own**, hold, keep, possess • *We have two tickets for the concert.*
2 = experience, feel, enjoy, undergo, endure, sustain • *He had a marvellous time.*
3 = receive, take, get, gain, accept, acquire, secure, obtain, procure
4 = give birth to, bear, deliver, beget, bring forth
▷ **have fun** See **play**
▷ **have on = wear**, be clothed in, be dressed in; = **tease**, kid (*informal*), deceive, pull someone's leg, trick
▷ **have to = be obliged**, should, must, ought, be bound, be compelled, be forced, have got to

haven *noun* = **sanctuary**, retreat, shelter, refuge, asylum, sanctum

havoc *noun* = **disorder**, chaos, confusion, disruption, mayhem, shambles

hawk See **sell**

haywire *adjective* = **topsy-turvy**, chaotic, confused, disordered, disorganized, mixed up, out of order, shambolic (*informal*)

hazard *noun* **1 = danger**, risk, threat, peril, jeopardy, pitfall
▷ *verb* **2 = jeopardize**, risk, threaten, expose, endanger, imperil
3 (~ *a guess*) = **conjecture**, offer, advance, volunteer, venture, presume, throw out

hazardous *adjective* = **dangerous**, difficult, unsafe, risky, perilous, precarious, insecure

haze *noun* = **mist**, cloud, fog, obscurity, vapour

hazy *adjective* **1 = misty**, dull, dim, cloudy, foggy, overcast
2 = vague, unclear, uncertain, indefinite, fuzzy, nebulous, ill-defined, indistinct, muddled

head *noun* **1 = mind**, brain, intelligence, aptitude, common sense, wits • *I don't*

have a head for business.
2 = top, start, front, source, beginning • *the head of the line*
OPPOSITE: tail
3 = leader, president, director, chief, manager, boss, principal • *heads of government*
4 = skull, crown, nut (*slang*), noodle (*slang*), pate
▷ **go to one's head = excite**, intoxicate, make conceited, puff up
▷ **head of state** See **ruler**
▷ **head over heels**
= uncontrollably, completely, thoroughly, utterly, intensely, wholeheartedly
▶ *verb* **5 = be in charge of**, lead, run, control, manage, direct • *She heads the department.*
6 = lead, top, cap, crown, precede, be first or go first, lead the way
7 = make for, point, turn, aim, steer, go to, make a beeline for, set off for, set out, start towards
▶ *adjective* **8 = chief**, first, prime, main, premier, principal, supreme, arch, pre-eminent, leading
See also: **command, foam**

> INFORMALLY SPEAKING
> **come to a head**: reach a climax
> **head off**: successfully turn something back or aside
> **keep your head**: remain calm
> **lose your head**: lose control of yourself
> **put heads together**: discuss

headache *noun* **1 = migraine**, neuralgia
2 = problem, worry, trouble, bother, inconvenience, nuisance, bane, vexation
heading *noun* **= title**, name, headline, caption, rubric
headlong *adverb, adjective*
1 = headfirst, head-on
▶ *adverb* **2 = hastily**, hurriedly, heedlessly, helter-skelter, pell-mell, precipitately, rashly, thoughtlessly
▶ *adjective* **3 = hasty**, dangerous, reckless, precipitate, breakneck,

impulsive, thoughtless, impetuous, inconsiderate
headquarters See **base**
headstrong *adjective* **= obstinate**, stubborn, unruly, perverse, foolhardy, impulsive, wilful, heedless, pig-headed, self-willed
headway *noun* **= progress**, way, advance, improvement, progression
heady *adjective* **1 = inebriating**, strong, potent, intoxicating
2 = exciting, thrilling, exhilarating, intoxicating, stimulating
heal *verb* **= cure**, treat, restore, remedy, mend, regenerate, make well
healing See **recovery**
health *noun* **1 = condition**, shape, constitution • *Smoking is bad for your health.*
2 = well-being, fitness, good condition • *In hospital they nursed me back to health.*
OPPOSITE: illness
healthy *adjective* **1 = well**, strong, fit, active, robust, in good shape • *a very healthy child*
OPPOSITE: ill
2 (*Informal*) **= wholesome**, beneficial, nutritious, bracing, good for you, nourishing • *a healthy diet*
OPPOSITE: unhealthy
See also: **sound**

> CONFUSABLES
> The word *healthy* means *in good health*, and *healthful* means *good for the health*, but, in everyday speech, most people use *healthy* for both meanings.

heap *noun* **1 = pile**, mass, mound, stack, hoard • *a heap of garbage*
2 (*often plural*) **= a lot**, great deal, mass, pot or pots (*informal*), plenty, stack or stacks, lots (*informal*), tons
▶ *verb* **3 = pile**, stack • *She heaped vegetables onto his plate.*
4 = shower upon, load, assign, bestow, confer
See also: **bunch**
hear *verb* **1 = listen to**, catch, heed, overhear, eavesdrop,

h

listen in • *I heard the sound of a car backfiring.*

2 = **learn**, discover, understand, gather, ascertain, find out • *I heard that he was forced to resign.*

3 (*Law*) = **try**, judge, investigate, examine

See also: **listen**

hearing *noun* = **inquiry**, trial, review, investigation, industrial tribunal, sentencing circle (*chiefly Canad*)

hearsay *noun* = **rumour**, report, talk, gossip, idle talk, tittle-tattle, word of mouth

heart *noun* **1** = **nature**, character, soul, disposition, temperament

2 = **bravery**, will, resolution, purpose, spirit, courage, pluck, fortitude

3 = **centre**, middle, core, hub, nucleus, quintessence

▷ **by heart** = **by memory**, pat, by rote, off pat, parrot-fashion (*informal*), word for word

heartache *noun* = **sorrow**, pain, torture, suffering, grief, distress, remorse, despair, anguish, heartbreak, agony, torment

heartbreak *noun* = **grief**, pain, suffering, misery, sorrow, despair, anguish, desolation

heartbreaking *adjective* = **tragic**, sad, poignant, pitiful, agonizing, distressing, harrowing, heart-rending

heartbroken *adjective* = **miserable**, crushed, desolate, despondent, brokenhearted, disconsolate, dispirited, heartsick

hearten *See* **encourage**

heartfelt *adjective* = **sincere**, deep, honest, profound, genuine, earnest, devout, unfeigned, wholehearted

heartily *adverb* = **enthusiastically**, vigorously, eagerly, resolutely, earnestly, zealously

heartless *adjective* = **cruel**, hard, cold, callous, merciless, hardhearted, pitiless, uncaring, unfeeling

heart-rending *adjective* = **moving**, sad, tragic, poignant, heartbreaking, affecting, distressing, harrowing

hearty *adjective* **1** = **friendly**, warm, enthusiastic, effusive, genial, jovial, ebullient, back-slapping

2 = **substantial**, solid, square, filling, sizable *or* sizeable, ample, nourishing

heat *noun* **1** = **warmth**, high temperature • *the heat of the sun*

OPPOSITE: cold

RELATED WORD

adjective: thermal

2 = **passion**, intensity, excitement, fervour, vehemence • *in the heat of the election campaign*

▶ *verb* **3** = **warm up**, reheat • *Heat the oil in a frying pan.*

OPPOSITE: cool

▷ **heat up** *See* **warm**

See also: **feeling, warm**

heated *adjective* = **angry**, intense, fierce, passionate, stormy, furious, excited, frenzied, impassioned, vehement

heathen *noun* **1** = **unbeliever**, infidel, pagan

▶ *adjective* **2** = **pagan**, godless, idolatrous, irreligious

heave *verb* **1** = **lift**, raise, pull *or* pull up, drag *or* drag up, haul *or* haul up, hoist, tug

2 = **throw**, send, pitch, cast, toss, hurl, fling, sling

3 = **sigh**, puff, groan

4 = **vomit**, barf (*slang*), gag, spew, retch, throw up (*informal*)

heaven *noun* **1** (*Informal*) = **bliss**, paradise, ecstasy, rapture • *I was in cinematic heaven.*

2 = **paradise**, bliss, Zion (*Christianity*), nirvana (*Buddhism, Hinduism*), Elysium *or* Elysian fields (*Greek myth*), hereafter, life everlasting, next world

▷ **the heavens** = **sky**, ether, firmament

heavenly *adjective* **1** = **wonderful**, beautiful, lovely, divine (*informal*), exquisite, delightful, sublime, blissful, ravishing

2 = **celestial**, holy, divine,

immortal, angelic, blessed

heavily adverb 1 = **ponderously**, awkwardly, clumsily, weightily
2 = **densely**, closely, thickly, compactly
3 = **considerably**, excessively, a great deal, copiously, to excess, very much

heaviness noun = **weight**, gravity, heftiness, ponderousness

heavy adjective 1 = **weighty**, massive, bulky • *a heavy frying pan*
OPPOSITE: light
2 = **serious**, deep, grave, profound, solemn, weighty • *a heavy speech*
OPPOSITE: trivial
3 = **considerable**, large, excessive, abundant, copious, profuse
See also: **stuffy**

heckle verb = **jeer**, disrupt, boo, interrupt, taunt, shout down

hectic adjective = **frantic**, animated, heated, turbulent, chaotic, feverish, frenetic

hedge noun 1 = **barrier**, screen, boundary, windbreak
▶ verb 2 = **dodge**, duck, evade, equivocate, sidestep, prevaricate, temporize
3 = **insure**, protect, cover, guard, shield, safeguard

heed verb 1 = **pay attention to**, follow, listen to, take notice of • *Few at the conference heeded his warning.*
▶ noun 2 = **attention**, notice • *He paid little heed to her warning.*
See also: **hear**

heedless adjective = **careless**, oblivious, foolhardy, thoughtless, inattentive, unmindful

heel¹ noun (Slang) = **swine**, rat, louse, skunk, scumbag, scuzzbucket (slang)

heel² verb
▷ **heel over** = **lean over**, list, tilt, keel over

hefty adjective = **big**, strong, massive, robust, muscular, burly, hulking, strapping

height noun 1 = **altitude**, loftiness, stature, elevation,

highness, tallness
2 = **peak**, top, summit, crown, crest, pinnacle, apex, zenith
3 = **culmination**, limit, maximum, ultimate, climax

heighten verb = **intensify**, increase, improve, strengthen, enhance, sharpen, magnify, amplify, add to

heir noun = **successor**, heiress (feminine), beneficiary, inheritor, next in line

heirloom See **legacy**

heirlooms See **valuables**

hell noun 1 (Informal) = **torment**, anguish, agony, nightmare, ordeal, misery • *Bullies can make your life hell.*
2 = **underworld**, abyss, inferno, hellfire, fire and brimstone, Hades (Greek myth), nether world

> **INFORMALLY SPEAKING**
> **from hell**: of the worst possible kind
> **like hell**: strenuously
> **raise hell**: cause a lot of trouble

hellish adjective = **devilish**, diabolical, damnable, fiendish, infernal

hello interjection = **hi** (informal), good afternoon, good evening, good morning, greetings, how do you do? (formal) • *I dropped by to say hello.*
OPPOSITE: goodbye

helm noun = **tiller**, wheel, rudder
▷ **at the helm** = **in charge**, at the wheel, in command, in control, in the driving seat, in the saddle

help verb 1 = **assist**, support, aid, lend a hand • *He began to help with the chores.*
2 = **improve**, ease, relieve, facilitate, alleviate, mitigate, ameliorate
3 = **refrain from**, prevent, avoid, resist, keep from
▶ noun 4 = **assistance**, support, aid, advice, guidance, helping hand • *The books were not much help.*
See also: **benefit, blessing, comfort, encourage**

helper noun = **assistant**, supporter, deputy, aide • *There is* *an adult helper for every two children.*

helpful *adjective* **1 = co-operative**, kind, supportive, accommodating • *The staff in the office are very helpful.*
OPPOSITE: unhelpful
2 = beneficial, useful, profitable, constructive, advantageous • *Having the right equipment will be enormously helpful.*
See also: **convenient, handy, positive, valuable**

helping *noun* = **portion**, piece, ration, serving, dollop (*informal*), plateful
▶ *adjective*
▷ **helping hand** *See* **help**

helpless *adjective* = **powerless**, weak, vulnerable, unprotected, defenceless • *a helpless baby*

helter-skelter *adjective*
1 = haphazard, confused, disordered, random, topsy-turvy, hit-or-miss, jumbled, muddled
▶ *adverb* **2 = carelessly**, wildly, hastily, anyhow, recklessly, headlong, hurriedly, pell-mell, rashly

hem *noun* = **edge**, border, margin, fringe, trimming
▶ *verb*
▷ **hem in** = **surround**, restrict, confine, enclose, beset, circumscribe, shut in

hence *conjunction* = **therefore**, thus, ergo, for this reason, on that account

henchman *noun* = **attendant**, supporter, associate, follower, bodyguard, subordinate, sidekick (*slang*), minder (*slang*), right-hand man

henpecked *adjective* = **bullied**, timid, meek, browbeaten, dominated, subjugated, pussy-whipped or whipped (*slang*)

herald *noun* **1 = messenger**, crier
2 = forerunner, sign, signal, indication, precursor, token, omen, harbinger
▶ *verb* **3 = indicate**, show, promise, presage, portend, foretoken, usher in

herd *noun* **1 = multitude**, crowd, mass, collection, mob, flock, swarm, throng, drove, horde
▶ *verb* **2 = congregate**, rally, gather, collect, assemble, flock, muster, huddle

here *See* **present**

hereafter *adverb* **1 = in future**, hence, from now on, henceforth, henceforward
▶ *noun* **2 = afterlife**, life after death, next world

hereditary *adjective* **1 = genetic**, transmissible, inborn, inbred, inheritable
2 = inherited, traditional, ancestral

heredity *noun* = **genetics**, constitution, inheritance, genetic make-up

heresy *noun* = **unorthodoxy**, apostasy, dissidence, heterodoxy, iconoclasm

heretic *noun* = **nonconformist**, dissident, renegade, dissenter, apostate, revisionist

heretical *adjective* = **unorthodox**, heterodox, iconoclastic, idolatrous, impious, revisionist

heritage *noun* = **inheritance**, tradition, legacy, bequest, endowment, birthright

hermit *noun* = **recluse**, monk, loner (*informal*), anchorite, eremite

hero *noun* **1 = star**, champion, superstar, idol, victor, conqueror
2 = leading man, protagonist

heroic *adjective* = **courageous**, brave, daring, valiant, fearless, gallant, intrepid, lion-hearted

heroine *noun* = **leading lady**, diva, protagonist, prima donna

heroism *noun* = **bravery**, spirit, courage, fearlessness, courageousness, gallantry, intrepidity, valour

hesitant *adjective* = **uncertain**, reluctant, unsure, doubtful, diffident, wavering • *At first he was hesitant to accept the role.*

hesitate *verb* **1 = waver**, pause, dither • *She hesitated before replying.*
2 = be reluctant, balk, be unwilling, demur, hang back,

scruple, shrink from, think
twice

hesitation noun **1 = indecision**,
delay, doubt, uncertainty,
hesitancy, irresolution,
vacillation
2 = reluctance, unwillingness,
qualm or qualms, misgiving or
misgivings, scruple or scruples

hew verb **1 = cut**, split, axe, chop,
hack, lop
2 = carve, make, form, model,
fashion, shape, sculpture,
smooth, sculpt

heyday noun **= prime**, pink,
bloom, prime of life, salad days

hi See **hello**

hiatus noun **= pause**, break, space,
gap, interruption, interval,
respite, discontinuity

hibernate See **sleep**

hibernation See **sleep**

hidden adjective **= concealed**,
secret, clandestine, covert,
unseen, latent, veiled, under
wraps

hide¹ verb **1 = conceal**, stash
(informal), secrete • The pirates hid
the gold in a cave.
2 = go into hiding, go to ground,
go underground, hole up, lie low,
take cover
3 = disguise, cover, mask, cloak,
veil, conceal, obscure, shroud,
camouflage
4 = suppress, withhold, draw
a veil over, hush up, keep dark,
keep secret, keep under one's hat
See also: **cover, obscure, shelter**

hide² noun **= skin**, pelt • the process
of tanning hides
See also: **coat**

hidebound adjective
= conventional, rigid, narrow-
minded, ultraconservative, set
in one's ways, strait-laced

hideous adjective **= ugly**, grim,
gruesome, grisly, grotesque,
monstrous, ghastly, unsightly,
repulsive, revolting, scuzzy
(slang)

hideout noun **= hiding place**,
shelter, den, hideaway, lair

hiding noun (Informal) **= beating**,
drubbing, thrashing, whipping,

spanking, licking (informal),
walloping (informal)

hierarchy noun **= grading**,
ranking, pecking order

high adjective **1 = tall**, steep,
elevated, lofty, towering, soaring
• a high tower
OPPOSITE: low
2 = extreme, great, strong,
sharp, excessive, extraordinary,
intensified • There is a high risk of
heart disease.
OPPOSITE: low
3 = important, chief, powerful,
superior, arch, eminent, exalted
4 (Informal) **= intoxicated**, stoned
(slang), tripping (informal)
5 = high-pitched, sharp, acute,
strident, piercing, shrill, piping,
penetrating
▷ **high point** See **peak, top**
▷ **high temperature** See **heat**
▶ adverb **6 = aloft**, at great
height, far up, way up
See also: **excited, thrill**

highbrow noun **1 = intellectual**,
scholar, egghead (informal),
aesthete
▶ adjective **2 = intellectual**,
sophisticated, cultured, bookish,
cultivated

higher adjective
▷ **higher than** See **above**

highest See **supreme, top**

high-flown adjective
= extravagant, elaborate,
exaggerated, inflated, lofty,
overblown, grandiose,
pretentious, florid

high-handed adjective
= dictatorial, oppressive,
despotic, tyrannical, wilful,
imperious, domineering,
overbearing

highlight noun **1 = feature**, focus,
peak, climax, focal point, high
point, high spot
▶ verb **2 = emphasize**, stress,
flag, spotlight, underline,
accent, accentuate, bring to the
fore, show up

highly adverb **= extremely**, very,
greatly, vastly, exceptionally,
tremendously, immensely, very
much

▷ **highly strung** = **nervous**, sensitive, tense, edgy, temperamental, neurotic, twitchy (*informal*), excitable, stressed, wired (*slang*) • *a highly strung individual*

high-ranking See **senior**

high-speed See **express**

hijack *verb* = **seize**, expropriate, commandeer, take over

hike *noun* **1** = **walk**, stroll, excursion, ramble • *They went for a hike through the woods.*

▶ *verb* **2** = **walk**, wander, stroll, backpack, stray, amble • *We hiked through the ravine.*

▷ **hike up** = **raise**, lift, hitch up, jack up, pull up

hilarious *adjective* = **funny**, humorous, amusing, comical, entertaining, rollicking, side-splitting, uproarious

hilarity *noun* = **laughter**, amusement, glee, exhilaration, merriment, high spirits, jollity, mirth

hill *noun* = **mount**, height, mound, hilltop, fell, knoll, hillock, tor

---

TYPES OF HILL

bluff (*Canad*)
butte (*Canad*)
dune
foothill
height
height of land (*Canad*)
knoll
moraine
mound
prominence

---

hillock *noun* = **mound**, knoll, hummock

hilly *adjective* = **mountainous**, rolling, undulating

hilt *noun* = **handle**, grip, haft, handgrip

hinder *verb* = **obstruct**, prevent, delay, block, check, frustrate, hamper, stymie, impede, encumber • *A thigh injury*

hindered her mobility.

See also: **handicap**, **interfere**, **restrain**

hindmost *adjective* = **last**, final, furthest, furthest behind, rearmost, trailing

hindrance *noun* = **obstacle**, restriction, difficulty, barrier, snag, obstruction, hitch, deterrent, impediment, handicap, drawback, stumbling block

hinge *verb* = **depend**, turn, rest, hang, pivot, be contingent, revolve around

hint *noun* **1** = **suggestion**, indication, clue, intimation • *He gave a strong hint that I would make the team.*

2 = **advice**, tip, suggestion, pointer • *I hope to get some fashion hints.*

3 = **trace**, touch, suggestion, suspicion, dash, undertone, tinge

▶ *verb* **4** = **suggest**, indicate, intimate, imply, insinuate • *Criticism is merely hinted at.*

▷ **hint at** See **promise**

See also: **idea**, **mention**, **note**, **sign**

hip See **fashionable**

hippie *noun* = **bohemian**, dropout, beatnik

hire *verb* **1** = **employ**, commission, appoint, engage, sign up • *I was hired for a summer job.*

2 = **rent**, let, engage, charter, lease

hiring See **employment**

hiss *noun* **1** = **sibilation**, buzz, hissing

2 = **catcall**, boo, jeer

▶ *verb* **3** = **whistle**, wheeze, whiz, sibilate, whirr

4 = **jeer**, boo, mock, deride, hoot

historic *adjective* = **significant**, famous, remarkable, extraordinary, notable, outstanding, ground-breaking, momentous, epoch-making

historical *adjective* = **factual**, real, actual, authentic, attested, documented

history *noun* **1** = **chronicle**,

record, story, account, narrative, recital, annals
2 = the past, yesterday, antiquity, yesteryear, olden days
histrionic See **melodramatic**
hit verb **1 = strike**, beat, pop (informal), knock, slap, bang, thump, smack, wallop (informal), whack, clout (informal) • *He had been hit with a baseball bat.*
2 = collide with, bump, bang into, meet head-on, run into, smash into, bang into, clash with, crash against • *The car had apparently hit a traffic sign.*
3 = reach, gain, achieve, accomplish, attain, arrive at
4 = affect, damage, touch, influence, overwhelm, devastate, impact on, leave a mark on
▷ **hit it off** (Informal) **= get on** or **get on well**, click (slang), be on good terms, get on like a house on fire (informal)
▶ noun **5 = blow**, stroke, knock, slap, belt (informal), rap, smack, wallop (informal), clout (informal) • *Give the nail a good hard hit with the hammer.*
6 = success, winner, triumph, smash (informal), sensation
hitch noun **1 = problem**, catch, difficulty, snag, obstacle, impediment, drawback, hindrance, hold-up
▶ verb **2 = fasten**, join, couple, tie, connect, attach, harness, tether
3 (Informal) **= hitchhike**, thumb a lift
▷ **hitch up = pull up**, yank, jerk, tug
hitherto adverb **= previously**, heretofore, so far, thus far, until now
hit-or-miss adjective **= haphazard**, random, casual, uneven, indiscriminate, aimless, disorganized, undirected
hoard verb **1 = store**, save, stockpile • *People have begun to hoard food and gasoline.*
▶ noun **2 = store**, fund, reserve, supply, stockpile, cache • *a hoard*

of silver and jewels
See also: **bank, gather, heap, pile**

| **CONFUSABLES**
Hoard means *store.*
Horde means *crowd.*

hoarse adjective **= husky**, rasping, gruff, croaky • *He became hoarse from shouting.*
OPPOSITE: clear
hoax noun **1 = trick**, fraud, con (informal), prank, spoof (informal), deception, swindle, practical joke
▶ verb **2 = deceive**, fool, con (slang), dupe, swindle, hoodwink, trick
hobbling See **lame**
hobby noun **= pastime**, diversion, leisure activity, leisure pursuit • *My hobbies are music and photography.*
See also: **activity, interest**
hobnob verb **= socialize**, associate, mix, mingle, consort, fraternize, hang around, hang out (informal), keep company
hodgepodge noun **= mixture**, mess, medley, jumble, mishmash, farrago, *mélange* (French), potpourri
hog See **pig**
hoist verb **1 = raise**, lift, erect, elevate, heave
▶ noun **2 = lift**, elevator, crane, winch
hold verb **1 = grasp**, carry, embrace, grip, clutch, clasp • *Hold the baby while I load the car.*
2 = own, have, keep, maintain, retain, occupy, possess
3 = restrain, detain, imprison, confine, impound
4 = consider, think, believe, judge, regard, assume, deem, presume, reckon
5 = convene, call, run, conduct, preside over
6 = accommodate, take, contain, seat, have a capacity for
▷ **hold back** See **restrain**
▷ **hold forth = speak**, lecture, preach, discourse, spout (informal), declaim, go on, spiel (informal)

▷ **hold out** *See* **offer**
▷ **hold up** = **delay**, stop, detain, hinder, retard, set back, slow down; = **support**, sustain, prop, shore up; = **rob**, mug (*informal*), waylay
▶ *noun* **7** = **control**, sway, dominance • *The leader has a considerable hold over his people.*
8 = **grip**, grasp • *He grabbed the rope and got a hold on it.*
9 = **foothold**, support, footing
See also: **claim, handle, influence, reserve**

> **INFORMALLY SPEAKING**
> **get hold of**: get in contact with
> **hold against**: continue to resent
> **on hold**: inactive

holder *noun* **1** = **owner**, keeper, proprietor, bearer, possessor
2 = **case**, cover, container
hold-up *noun* **1** = **delay**, wait, snag, setback, stoppage, hitch, bottleneck, traffic jam
2 = **robbery**, theft, mugging (*informal*), stick-up (*slang*)

hole *noun* **1** = **opening**, tear, split, gap • *to punch holes in the paper*
2 = **flaw**, error, defect, fault, loophole • *There are some holes in that theory.*
3 (*Informal*) = **predicament**, fix (*informal*), mess, hot water (*informal*), tight spot • *He admitted that the company was in a financial hole.*
4 = **cavity**, pit, chamber, cave, hollow, cavern
5 = **burrow**, earth, shelter, den, lair
6 (*Informal*) = **hovel**, dump (*informal*), dive (*slang*), slum
See also: **breach, jam, leak**

> **INFORMALLY SPEAKING**
> **hole up**: go into hiding
> **in the hole**: in debt
> **make a hole in**: use up a large amount of
> **pick holes in**: find fault with

holiday *noun* **1** = **vacation**, leave, break, recess, time off,

---

NAMES OF CANADIAN HOLIDAYS

NATIONAL		NEWFOUNDLAND & LABRADOR	
Jan 1	New Year's Day	Mar	St. Patrick's Day
Mar/Apr	Good Friday	Apr	St. George's Day
Mar/Apr	Easter Sunday	Jun 24	Discovery Day
Mar/Apr	Easter Monday	Jul 1	Memorial Day
May	Victoria Day	Jul 12	Orangemen's Day
Jul 1	Canada Day	variable	Regatta Day
Sep	Labour Day	**NOVA SCOTIA**	
Oct	Thanksgiving	Jul/Aug	Natal Day
Nov 11	Remembrance Day	**NORTHWEST TERRITORIES**	
Dec 25	Christmas Day	Aug	Civic Holiday
Dec 26	Boxing Day	**ONTARIO**	
		Aug	Civic Holiday
PROVINCES/TERRITORIES		**PRINCE EDWARD ISLAND**	
ALBERTA		Aug	Natal Day
Feb	Family Day	**QUÉBEC**	
Aug	Heritage Day	Jun 24	Fête nationale
BRITISH COLUMBIA		**SASKATCHEWAN**	
Aug	B.C. Day	Aug	Civic Holiday
MANITOBA		**YUKON**	
Aug	Civic Holiday	Aug	Discovery Day
NEW BRUNSWICK			
Aug	New Brunswick Day		

staycation (*informal*) • *They were in Paris on a holiday.*

2 = statutory holiday (*Canad*), anniversary, celebration, gala, festivity, feast, public holiday (*US*), fête, red-letter day, mela, name day, saint's day, stat holiday (*Canad*)

3 = festival, celebration • *The Thanksgiving holiday always falls on a Monday.*
See also: **rest**

holiness *noun* = **divinity**, purity, spirituality, sanctity, piety, godliness, righteousness, sacredness, saintliness

hollow *adjective* **1 = empty**, void, vacant, unfilled

2 = deep, low, dull, muted, reverberant

3 = worthless, useless, meaningless, pointless, vain, futile, fruitless

▶ *noun* **4 = cavity**, hole, depression, pit, bowl, crater, basin, trough

5 = valley, glen, dell, dale, dingle

▶ *verb* **6 = scoop**, dig, gouge, excavate

▷ **hollow out** See **dig**

holocaust *noun* = **genocide**, destruction, massacre, devastation, annihilation, conflagration

holy *adjective* **1 = sacred**, hallowed, consecrated, sacrosanct, venerated • *We visited the city's holy places.*

2 = devout, religious, pious, saintly • *There are holy people in all religions.*

homage *noun* = **respect**, honour, devotion, worship, deference, adoration, adulation, reverence

home *noun* **1 = dwelling**, house, residence, abode • *They stayed home and watched TV.*

2 = birthplace, home town

▷ **at home = in**, available, present; **at ease**, comfortable, familiar, relaxed

▷ **bring home to = make clear**, emphasize, drive home, impress upon, press home

▶ *adjective* **3 = domestic**,

national, native, internal • *The home team is in town.*
OPPOSITE: foreign

INFORMALLY SPEAKING
bring (or drive) home: make clear or convincing
hit home: make a forceful impression
home free: sure of success
home in on: narrow the attention to

homeboy, home girl ▶ *noun* (*Slang*) = **friend**, comrade, buddy (*informal*), pal (*informal*), chum (*informal*), crony

homeland *noun* = **native land**, motherland, country of origin, fatherland, mother country

homeless *adjective* = **destitute**, displaced, dispossessed, down-and-out, down on one's luck (*informal*)

▶ *noun*

▷ **the homeless = vagrants**, squatters

homely *adjective* = **dowdy**, dumpy (*informal*), frowzy, ugly, unattractive, frumpy, unfashionable

homespun *adjective* = **unsophisticated**, rough, plain, coarse, home-made, homey (*US*), dumpy (*informal*)

homey *adjective* = **comfortable**, simple, friendly, modest, ordinary, plain, cozy, homespun, welcoming • *The room was small and homey.*
OPPOSITE: grand

homicidal *adjective* = **murderous**, deadly, lethal, mortal, maniacal

homicide *noun* **1 = murder**, killing, manslaughter, slaying, bloodshed

2 = murderer, killer, slayer

homily *noun* = **sermon**, address, lecture, discourse, preaching

homogeneity *noun* = **uniformity**, similarity, correspondence, consistency, sameness

homogeneous *adjective* = **uniform**, similar, consistent, comparable, identical, alike, akin, analogous, unvarying

h

hone verb = **sharpen**, point, file, edge, grind, polish, whet

honest adjective 1 = **trustworthy**, truthful, law-abiding, reputable, virtuous • *He is a very honest, decent man.*
OPPOSITE: dishonest
2 = **open**, direct, plain, sincere, frank, candid, upfront (*informal*), forthright
See also: **real, serious, straight, straightforward**

honestly adverb 1 = **ethically**, legally, lawfully, cleanly, by fair means, honourably
2 = **frankly**, straight or straight out, truthfully, plainly, candidly, in all sincerity, to one's face

honesty noun 1 = **integrity**, honour, virtue, morality, truthfulness, incorruptibility, probity, rectitude, scrupulousness, trustworthiness, uprightness
2 = **frankness**, openness, sincerity, bluntness, candour, outspokenness, straightforwardness

honorary adjective = **nominal**, unofficial, unpaid, complimentary, titular, in name only or in title only

honour noun 1 = **integrity**, honesty, decency, goodness • *I can no longer serve with honour in your government.*
OPPOSITE: dishonour
2 = **tribute**, praise, recognition, homage, accolade, commendation • *He was showered with honours - among them a Gemini award.*
3 = **glory**, credit, reputation, fame, dignity, distinction, kudos, prestige, renown
4 = **privilege**, credit, pleasure, compliment
▶ verb 5 = **acclaim**, praise, commemorate, decorate, commend, glorify • *She was honoured by the club with a gold medal.*
6 = **respect**, value, appreciate, prize, adore, esteem
7 = **fulfill**, keep, observe, discharge, be true to, carry out, live up to
8 = **accept**, take, pay, pass, acknowledge
See also: **character, recognize, right, worship**

honourable adjective = **respected**, respectable, reputable, virtuous, creditable, estimable
See also: **noble, respectable**

honoured See **proud**

hoodlum noun = **thug**, tough, vandal, hooligan, lout • *The hoodlums hurled rocks at the building.*

hoodwink verb = **deceive**, trick, mislead, fool, con (*informal*), dupe, swindle, delude

hook noun 1 = **fastener**, link, catch, peg, clasp
▶ verb 2 = **fasten**, fix, secure, clasp
3 = **catch**, trap, snare, ensnare, entrap

hooked adjective 1 = **bent**, aquiline, curved, hook-shaped
2 = **addicted**, devoted, obsessed, enamoured, taken, turned on (*slang*)

hooligan noun = **delinquent**, vandal, lager lout, ruffian

hooliganism noun = **delinquency**, violence, disorder, vandalism, loutishness, rowdiness

hoop noun = **ring**, band, wheel, loop, girdle, circlet

hoot noun = **cry**, call, toot
2 = **catcall**, boo, jeer, hiss
▶ verb 3 = **jeer**, boo, hiss, howl down

hop verb 1 = **jump**, trip, spring, skip, leap, vault, bound, caper
▶ noun 2 = **jump**, step, spring, bounce, skip, leap, vault, bound

hope noun 1 = **ambition**, expectation, dream • *There was little hope of recovery.*
▶ verb 2 = **desire**, long, aspire, cross one's fingers, look forward to, set one's heart on
See also: **possibility, prospect**

hopeful adjective 1 = **optimistic**, confident, expectant, buoyant, sanguine, looking forward to

2 = promising, bright, rosy, auspicious, encouraging, heartening, reassuring

hopefully adverb
= **optimistically**, confidently, expectantly

hopeless adjective
1 = impossible, useless, pointless, vain, futile, forlorn • Our situation is hopeless.
2 = inadequate, poor, useless (informal), pathetic • I don't drive, and the buses are hopeless.
See also: **doomed, pessimistic**

hopelessness See **despair**

horde noun = **crowd**, host, band, pack, gang, mob, swarm, throng, multitude, drove

horizon noun = **skyline**, vista

horizontal adjective = **level**, flat, parallel

horrendous adjective = **horrific**, shocking, awful, grim, appalling, grisly, dreadful, ghastly, frightful, frightening, terrifying, horrifying

horrible adjective **1 = unpleasant**, mean, nasty, awful, horrid, disagreeable • a horrible person to work with
2 = appalling, grim, gruesome, dreadful, terrifying • horrible crimes
See also: **hateful, terrible**

horrid adjective **1 = unpleasant**, terrible, horrible, awful, dreadful, disagreeable
2 (Informal) = **unkind**, mean, nasty, cruel, beastly (informal)

horrific adjective = **horrifying**, shocking, awful, horrendous, appalling, grisly, dreadful, ghastly, frightful, terrifying

horrify verb **1 = shock**, outrage, sicken, disgust, dismay, appal • a crime wave that horrified the city
2 = terrify, scare, alarm, intimidate, frighten, petrify, make one's hair stand on end

horror noun **1 = terror**, fear, alarm, panic, dread, fright • He gazed in horror at the knife.
2 = hatred, disgust, revulsion, aversion, loathing, abhorrence • his horror of speaking in public

horse noun = **equine**, pony, nag (informal) • a fall from a horse
RELATED WORDS
adjectives: equestrian, equine, horsey
noun: equitation
male: stallion
female: mare
young: foal, colt, filly

horseman noun = **rider**, cavalier, equestrian, cavalryman, dragoon

horseplay noun = **fooling around**, rough-and-tumble, buffoonery, clowning, high jinks, pranks, romping, skylarking (informal)

hospitable adjective
= **welcoming**, liberal, kind, friendly, generous, gracious, cordial, sociable

hospitality noun = **welcome**, warmth, friendliness, conviviality, cordiality, neighbourliness, sociability

host[1] noun **1 = master of ceremonies**, entertainer, landlord or landlady, proprietor, innkeeper
2 = presenter, anchorman or anchorwoman
▶ verb **3 = present**, front (informal), introduce

host[2] noun = **multitude**, army, array, swarm, throng, legion, myriad, drove, horde

hostage noun = **prisoner**, captive, pawn

hostel See **shelter**

hostile adjective **1 = unfriendly**, belligerent, antagonistic, malevolent, unkind • The umpire faced a hostile crowd.
OPPOSITE: friendly
2 = opposed, against, contrary, antagonistic, ill-disposed
See also: **aggressive**

hostilities plural noun = **warfare**, war, conflict, fighting

hostility noun = **ill will**, hatred, resentment, animosity, antagonism, malice • hostility toward the rival team
OPPOSITE: friendship

h

See also: **conflict, dislike, hate, opposition**

hot *adjective* **1** = **heated**, warm, boiling, scalding, scorching • *a hot climate*
OPPOSITE: cold
2 = **spicy**, peppery • *a hot, aromatic curry*
OPPOSITE: bland
3 = **fierce**, violent, intense, passionate, fiery, stormy, raging
4 = **recent**, new, fresh, latest, just out, up to the minute
5 = **popular**, sought-after, approved, favoured, in demand, in vogue
▷ **hot air** = **empty talk**, wind, bombast, claptrap (*informal*), guff (*slang*), verbiage
▷ **hot water** (usually preceded by *in*) (*Informal*) = **predicament**, spot (*informal*), fix (*informal*), jam (*informal*), mess, scrape (*informal*), dilemma, tight spot

| INFORMALLY SPEAKING
| **hot and bothered**: angry and upset
| **hot under the collar**: angry
| **in the hot seat**: in a potentially embarrassing position

hot-blooded *adjective* = **passionate**, wild, fiery, spirited, ardent, impulsive, temperamental, excitable
hot-headed *adjective* = **rash**, volatile, fiery, reckless, hasty, foolhardy, hot-tempered, impetuous, quick-tempered
hound *verb* = **harass**, provoke, persecute, badger, goad, harry, pester, impel
house *noun* **1** = **home**, building, residence, dwelling, abode • *They live in a large house with eight rooms.*
2 = **family**, household
3 = **dynasty**, tribe, clan
4 = **firm**, company, business, organization, outfit (*informal*)
5 = **assembly**, Commons, parliament, legislative body
on the house = **free**, for nothing, gratis
▶ *verb* **6** = **accommodate**, quarter, lodge, harbour, billet, put up, take in

7 = **contain**, keep, store, protect, cover, shelter, sheathe
See also: **accommodation**

| INFORMALLY SPEAKING
| **bring down the house**: be loudly applauded
| **like a house on fire**: very well or very fast
| ▷ **on the house**: free

household *noun* = **family**, home, house
▷ **household name** *See* **personality**
householder *noun* = **occupant**, resident, homeowner, tenant
housing *noun*
1 = **accommodation**, dwellings, homes, houses
2 = **case**, cover, container, enclosure, casing, sheath, covering
hovel *noun* = **hut**, hole, shed, cabin, den, shack, shanty
hover *verb* **1** = **float**, fly, hang, drift, flutter
2 = **linger**, hang about
3 = **waver**, fluctuate, dither, vacillate, oscillate
how do you do? *See* **hello**
however *adverb* = **nevertheless**, but, still, though, yet, notwithstanding, nonetheless, anyhow, after all
howl *noun* **1** = **cry**, scream, roar, bay, wail, clamour, groan, shriek, bawl
▶ *verb* **2** = **cry**, scream, roar, yell, weep, wail, shriek, bellow, bawl
howler *noun* = **mistake**, blunder, bloomer (*informal*), error, malapropism
howling *See* **wild**
hub *noun* = **centre**, heart, focus, middle, core, focal point, nerve centre
hubbub *noun* **1** = **noise**, uproar, racket, cacophony, din, ruckus (*informal*), tumult, babel
2 = **confusion**, disorder, riot, disturbance, clamour, brouhaha, pandemonium, bedlam, hullabaloo, rumpus, ruction (*informal*), hurly-burly
huddle *verb* **1** = **crowd**, gather, press, cluster,

flock, converge, throng
2 = curl up, crouch, hunch up
▶ noun **3** (*Informal*) **= conference**, meeting, discussion, powwow
hue noun **= colour**, tone, shade, dye, tint, tinge
huff *See* **resentment**
huffy *See* **resentful, sulky**
hug verb **1 = embrace**, squeeze, cuddle, clasp • *We hugged each other.*
▶ noun **2 = embrace** • *She gave him a hug.*
huge adjective **= enormous**, giant, massive, vast, immense, colossal • *a huge crowd*
OPPOSITE: tiny
See also: **large, spacious**
hulk noun **1 = wreck**, frame, shell, hull, shipwreck
2 = oaf, lump (*informal*), lout, lubber
hull noun **= frame**, body, framework, casing, covering
hum verb **1 = murmur**, buzz, drone, purr, vibrate, throb, whir, thrum
2 = be busy, stir, buzz, pulse, bustle, pulsate
human adjective **1 = mortal**, manlike
▶ noun **2 = human being**, man or woman, person, individual, soul, creature, mortal
humane adjective **= kind**, charitable, thoughtful, compassionate, caring, merciful, benevolent • *a more just and humane society*

CONFUSABLES
Humane refers to compassion towards others.
Human refers to qualities belonging specially to people rather than animals.

humanely *See* **well**
humanitarian adjective
1 = compassionate, charitable, humane, philanthropic, benevolent, altruistic, public-spirited
▶ noun **2 = philanthropist**, benefactor, altruist, Good Samaritan
humanity noun **1 = human**

race, people, man, mankind, humankind, Homo sapiens
2 = human nature, mortality
3 = sympathy, charity, mercy, compassion, kindness, philanthropy, fellow feeling, kind-heartedness
humanize verb **= civilize**, improve, educate, soften, tame, enlighten
humankind noun **= humanity**, human race • *the evolution of humankind*
See also: **people**
humans *See* **people**
humble adjective **1 = modest**, unassuming, meek • *He gave a great performance, but he was very humble.*
OPPOSITE: haughty
2 = ordinary, simple, modest • *Some fresh herbs will transform a humble stew.*
▶ verb **3 = humiliate**, disgrace • *the little car company that humbled the industry giants*
See also: **unknown**
humbug noun **1 = fraud**, phony (*informal*), impostor, trickster, charlatan, con man (*informal*), faker, swindler
2 = nonsense, garbage, hypocrisy, cant, baloney (*informal*), quackery, claptrap (*informal*)
3 = killjoy, scrooge (*informal*), spoilsport, wet blanket (*informal*)
humdrum adjective **= dull**, ordinary, boring, dreary, mundane, uneventful, tedious, tiresome, banal, monotonous
humid adjective **= damp**, steamy, sticky, muggy, clammy • *a hot, humid summer*
See also: **wet**
humidity noun **= damp**, moisture, clamminess, dampness, dankness, moistness, mugginess, wetness
humiliate verb **= embarrass**, humble, shame, disgrace, put down • *Why do you enjoy humiliating me?*
humiliated *See* **ashamed, embarrassed**

h

humiliating *adjective*
= **embarrassing**, degrading, ignominious, crushing, humbling, mortifying, shaming

humiliation *noun*
= **embarrassment**, shame, disgrace, indignity, degradation, dishonour, humbling, ignominy, loss of face, mortification, put-down

humility *noun* = **modesty**, humbleness, lowliness, meekness, submissiveness, unpretentiousness

humorist *noun* = **comedian**, card (*informal*), comic, wit, wag, joker, jester, funny man

humorous *adjective* = **funny**, comic, amusing, playful, witty, comical, droll, entertaining, jocular, waggish

humour *noun* 1 = **comedy**, wit • *The movie's humour contains a serious message.*
2 = **mood**, temper, frame of mind, spirits • *He hasn't been in a good humour lately.*
▶ *verb* 3 = **indulge**, flatter, mollify • *I nodded, partly to humour him.*

humourless *See* **serious**

hump *noun* = **lump**, bump, projection, mound, bulge, protrusion, protuberance, swelling

hunch *noun* 1 = **feeling**, idea, suspicion, impression, intuition, inkling, premonition, presentiment
▶ *verb* 2 = **draw in**, bend, curve, arch

hunger *noun* 1 = **famine**, starvation
2 = **appetite**, emptiness, hungriness, ravenousness
3 = **desire**, appetite, ache, craving, thirst, itch, lust, yearning
▶ *verb* 4 = **want**, long, wish, desire, ache, thirst, crave, itch, yearn, hanker

hungry *adjective* 1 = **starving**, ravenous, famished, peckish (*informal*) • *I didn't have any lunch, so I'm really hungry.*

2 = **eager**, keen, avid, greedy, craving, yearning, athirst, covetous, desirous

hunk *noun* = **lump**, block, piece, mass, chunk, wedge, slab, nugget

hunt *verb* 1 = **stalk**, track, trail, pursue, chase, hound
2 = **search**, look, seek, scour, forage, ferret about
▶ *noun* 3 = **search**, investigation, chase, hunting, pursuit, quest

hurdle *noun* 1 = **fence**, barrier, barricade
2 = **obstacle**, difficulty, barrier, hazard, obstruction, impediment, handicap, hindrance, stumbling block

hurl *verb* = **throw**, launch, pitch, cast, toss, propel, fling, sling, heave, let fly

hurricane *noun* = **storm**, tornado, cyclone, twister, tempest, gale, typhoon

hurried *adjective* = **hasty**, short, quick, brief, speedy, swift, cursory, perfunctory, rushed

hurriedly *See* **fast, quickly**

hurry *verb* 1 = **rush**, fly, dash, scurry, get a move on (*informal*) • *She hurried through the empty streets.*
2 = **speed up**, accelerate, hasten, quicken • *an attempt to hurry the building process*
OPPOSITE: **slow down**
▶ *noun* 3 = **rush**, speed, flurry, urgency, haste, quickness
See also: **bustle, race**

hurt *verb* 1 = **injure**, wound, harm • *I didn't mean to hurt anyone.*
2 = **upset**, wound, distress, sadden • *What you said really hurt me.*
3 = **ache**, burn, smart, sting, throb, be sore, be tender
▶ *adjective* 4 = **upset**, wounded, aggrieved, offended • *He felt hurt by all the lies.*
5 = **injured**, cut, wounded, damaged, bruised, harmed, scarred
▶ *noun* 6 = **distress**, pain, suffering, discomfort, soreness, pang

See also: **abuse, damage**

hurtful *adjective* = **unkind**, nasty, cruel, destructive, malicious, cutting, damaging, spiteful, upsetting, wounding

hurtle *verb* = **rush**, charge, shoot, crash, race, fly, speed, tear, plunge, stampede
▷ **hurtle into** *See* **crash**

husband *noun* 1 = **partner**, mate, spouse, better half (*humorous*)
▶ *verb* 2 = **economize**, save, store, budget, conserve, hoard

husbandry *noun* 1 = **farming**, agriculture, cultivation, tillage
2 = **thrift**, economy, frugality

hush *verb* 1 = **quieten**, silence, mute, muzzle, shush
▶ *noun* 2 = **quiet**, peace, silence, calm, stillness, tranquillity

hushed *See* **quiet, silent**

hush-hush *adjective* = **secret**, confidential, classified, restricted, top-secret, under wraps

husky *adjective* 1 = **hoarse**, rough, harsh, raucous, gruff, croaky, guttural, throaty
2 = **muscular**, powerful, hefty, rugged, burly, stocky, strapping, thickset

hustle *verb* = **jostle**, force, push, elbow, shove, jog

hut *noun* = **shed**, shelter, cabin, tilt (*Canad Nfld*), den, shanty, hovel, lean-to, caboose (*Canad*), fish hut (*Canad*), ice-fishing hut (*Canad*), ice hut (*Canad*)

hybrid *noun* = **crossbreed**, cross, compound, composite, mixture, amalgam, half-breed, mongrel

hygiene *noun* = **cleanliness**, sanitation • *Be extra careful about personal hygiene.*

hygienic *adjective* = **clean**, healthy, pure, sterile, sanitary, aseptic, disinfected, germ-free

hymn *noun* = **anthem**, chant, carol, psalm, paean

hype *noun* = **publicity**, promotion, brouhaha, ballyhoo (*informal*), plugging (*informal*), razzmatazz (*slang*)

hypnotic *adjective* = **mesmerizing**, soothing, mesmeric, sleep-inducing, soporific, spellbinding

hypnotize *verb* = **put in a trance**, put to sleep • *She said he would be hypnotized at the count of three.*

hypocrisy *noun* = **insincerity**, cant, deception, pretense, deceitfulness, duplicity

hypocrite *noun* = **fraud**, phony (*informal*), impostor, pretender, deceiver, charlatan

hypocritical *adjective* = **insincere**, false, fraudulent, phony (*informal*), deceitful, canting, duplicitous, sanctimonious, two-faced

hypothesis *noun* = **theory**, assumption, premise, proposition, thesis, postulate, supposition

hypothetical *adjective* = **theoretical**, academic, speculative, imaginary, assumed, supposed, conjectural, putative

hysteria *noun* = **frenzy**, panic, madness, agitation, delirium, hysterics

hysterical *adjective* 1 = **frenzied**, frantic, raving, overwrought • *Calm down! Don't become hysterical.*
2 (*Informal*) = **hilarious**, comical • *His stand-up routine was hysterical.*

h

Ii

icy *adjective* **1 = cold**, bitter, raw, chill, chilly, frosty, ice-cold, freezing, biting
2 = slippery, glassy, slippy (*informal dialect*)
3 = unfriendly, cold, distant, frigid, frosty, aloof, unwelcoming

idea *noun* **1 = plan**, recommendation, solution, scheme, suggestion • *She said she'd had a brilliant idea.*
2 = opinion, view, conviction, belief, impression, notion • *old-fashioned ideas about health care*
3 = impression, hint, guess, suspicion, clue, inkling • *They had no idea where they were.*
See also: **intention, object, thought**

> **INFORMALLY SPEAKING**
> **don't get ideas:** don't plan for things you shouldn't
> **have no idea:** not know at all
> **the (very) idea!:** Outrageous!

ideal *noun* **1 = principle**, value, standard • *Live up to your ideals.*
2 = model, standard, example, epitome, paragon • *That rose is the ideal of beauty.*
▶ *adjective* **3 = perfect**, complete, model, classic, supreme, consummate • *the ideal person for the job*
See also: **cause, vision**

idealist *noun* **= romantic**, visionary, dreamer, Utopian

idealistic *adjective* **= perfectionist**, optimistic, romantic, visionary, impracticable, starry-eyed, Utopian

idealize *verb* **= romanticize**, worship, glorify, magnify, exalt, apotheosize, ennoble, put on a pedestal

ideally *adverb* **= in a perfect world**, all things being equal, if one had one's way

ideals *See* **standards**

identical *adjective* **= alike**, twin, duplicate, interchangeable, indistinguishable, matching

identification *noun*
1 = recognition, naming, pinpointing
2 = understanding, connection, relationship, association, involvement, sympathy, empathy, rapport, fellow feeling

identify *verb* **= recognize**, name, place, label, diagnose, pinpoint • *I tried to identify the perfume.*
▷ **identify with = relate to**, associate with, empathize with, feel for, respond to • *I can't identify with the characters in the play.*
See also: **associate**

identity *noun* **1 = existence**, personality, self, individuality
2 = sameness, unity, correspondence

ideology *See* **belief**

idiocy *noun* **= foolishness**, insanity, lunacy, asininity, fatuousness, imbecility, inanity, senselessness

idiom *noun* **1 = phrase**, expression, turn of phrase
2 = language, style, jargon, parlance, vernacular

idiosyncrasy *noun* **= peculiarity**, trick, oddity, characteristic, quirk, mannerism, eccentricity

idiosyncratic *See* **individual**

idiot *noun* **= fool**, moron, imbecile, oaf, twit (*informal*), mouth-breather (*slang*), ding-a-ling (*slang*) • *You're an idiot!*

idiotic *adjective* = **foolish**, crazy, stupid, senseless • *an idiotic thing to do*
See also: **silly, unwise**

idle *adjective* **1** = **inactive**, jobless, unemployed • *idle, wealthy people*
OPPOSITE: busy
2 = **lazy**, sluggish, lackadaisical, good-for-nothing, indolent, shiftless, slothful
3 = **useless**, ineffective, unsuccessful, pointless, vain, worthless, futile, fruitless, groundless, unavailing
▶ *verb* **4** (often with *away*) = **laze**, lounge, putter, dawdle, loaf, loiter, dally, kill time
See also: **rest**

idleness *noun* **1** = **inactivity**, unemployment, leisure, inaction, time on one's hands
2 = **laziness**, sluggishness, sloth, inertia, shiftlessness, torpor

idol *noun* **1** = **graven image**, god, deity
2 = **hero**, pet, beloved, favorite, darling, pin-up (*slang*)

idolatry *noun* = **adoration**, glorification, adulation, exaltation

idolize *verb* = **worship**, love, revere, glorify, adore, venerate, exalt, dote upon, hero-worship, look up to

idyllic *adjective* = **idealized**, ideal, charming, picturesque, heavenly, unspoiled, halcyon

if *conjunction* = **provided**, providing, assuming, on condition that, supposing

ignite *verb* **1** = **catch fire**, burn, inflame, burst into flames, flare up, take fire
2 = **set fire to**, light, torch, kindle, set alight

ignominious *adjective* = **humiliating**, sorry, disgraceful, shameful, undignified, discreditable, dishonourable, indecorous, inglorious

ignominy *noun* = **disgrace**, shame, stigma, humiliation, discredit, disrepute, infamy, dishonour, obloquy

ignoramus See **fool**

ignorance *noun* = **unawareness**, innocence, inexperience, unconsciousness, unfamiliarity

ignorant *adjective* **1** = **unaware**, innocent, unconscious, inexperienced, oblivious • *He was completely ignorant of the rules.*
2 = **naive**, green, unaware
• *People are afraid to appear ignorant.*
3 = **uneducated**, illiterate
4 = **insensitive**, rude, crass, half-baked (*informal*)

ignore *verb* = **disregard**, discount, overlook, neglect • *Her cousin ignored her.*
See also: **exclude**

ill *adjective* **1** = **unwell**, sick, ailing, unhealthy, queasy • *She was seriously ill with pneumonia.*
OPPOSITE: healthy
2 = **harmful**, bad, foul, evil, unfortunate, detrimental, deleterious, injurious, damaging
▷ **ill at ease** See **uncomfortable**
▷ **ill will** = **hostility**, hatred, venom, dislike, resentment, animosity, enmity, malice, bad blood, rancour
▶ *noun* **3** = **harm**, injury, hurt, trouble, woe, misery, hardship, misfortune, affliction, unpleasantness
▶ *adverb* **4** = **badly**, unfortunately, poorly, inauspiciously, unfavourably, unluckily
5 = **hardly**, barely, scantily, by no means

ill-advised *adjective* = **misguided**, reckless, rash, foolhardy, unwise, imprudent, thoughtless, ill-considered, ill-judged, incautious, injudicious

ill-disposed *adjective* = **unfriendly**, hostile, antagonistic, disobliging, inimical, uncooperative, unwelcoming

illegal *adjective* = **unlawful**, criminal, illicit, outlawed, banned, prohibited • *an illegal organization*
OPPOSITE: legal

See also: **crooked, wrong**

illegality *noun* = **crime**, wrong, felony, lawlessness, illegitimacy

illegible *adjective* = **indecipherable**, obscure, scrawled, unreadable

illegitimate *adjective*
1 = **unlawful**, illegal, unauthorized, illicit, improper
2 = **born out of wedlock**, bastard

ill-fated *adjective* = **doomed**, unfortunate, hapless, unhappy, unlucky, ill-omened, ill-starred, luckless, star-crossed

ill-fitting *See* **uncomfortable**

illicit *adjective* 1 = **illegal**, criminal, unauthorized, unlawful, unlicensed, illegitimate, felonious, prohibited
2 = **forbidden**, guilty, improper, clandestine, immoral, furtive

illiterate *adjective* = **uneducated**, ignorant, uncultured, untaught, untutored

ill-mannered *adjective* = **rude**, boorish, badly behaved, churlish, discourteous, impolite, insolent, loutish, uncouth

illness *noun* = **sickness**, disease, complaint, disorder, ailment • *a mystery illness*

illogical *adjective* = **irrational**, inconsistent, unreasonable, absurd, meaningless, senseless, invalid, unscientific, unsound

ill-treat *verb* = **abuse**, damage, injure, harm, misuse, mishandle, oppress, maltreat

ill-treatment *See* **abuse**

illuminate *verb* 1 = **light up**, brighten
2 = **explain**, clarify, interpret, enlighten, clear up, elucidate, make clear, shed light on

illuminating *adjective* = **informative**, helpful, revealing, instructive, explanatory, enlightening

illumination *noun* 1 = **light**, brightness, lighting, radiance
2 = **enlightenment**, revelation, insight, clarification

illusion *noun* 1 = **hallucination**, semblance, mirage • *Artists create the illusion of space.*
2 = **delusion**, fancy, misconception, fallacy • *Their hopes proved to be an illusion.*
See also: **vision**

> **CONFUSABLES**
> *Illusion* means *misleading appearance.*
> *Allusion* means *indirect reference.*

illusory *adjective* = **unreal**, false, mistaken, sham, deceptive, chimerical, delusive, fallacious, hallucinatory

illustrate *verb* = **demonstrate**, show, explain, emphasize, bring home, elucidate, point up

illustrated *adjective* = **pictorial**, graphic, decorated

illustration *noun* 1 = **example**, case, instance, specimen
2 = **picture**, figure, plate, sketch, decoration

illustrative *See* **representative**

illustrious *adjective* = **famous**, great, prominent, renowned, notable, celebrated, glorious, distinguished, eminent

image *noun* 1 = **representation**, figure, picture, icon, portrait, statue, idol, likeness, avatar, effigy
2 = **replica**, double, counterpart, ringer *or* dead ringer (*slang*), facsimile, Doppelgänger, spitting image (*informal*)
3 = **concept**, idea, perception, impression, mental picture

imaginable *adjective* = **possible**, likely, credible, plausible, conceivable, believable, comprehensible

imaginary *adjective* = **fictional**, ideal, hypothetical, fictitious, mythological, illusory, invented • *an imaginary friend*
OPPOSITE: real

imagination *noun* 1 = **creativity**, vision, ingenuity, originality, inventiveness • *a student who lacks imagination*
2 = **unreality**, illusion, supposition
See also: **mind**

imaginative *adjective* = **creative**, original, inspired, clever, ingenious, inventive, enterprising

imagine verb 1 = **envisage**, picture, conceive, visualize, fantasize, ideate • *He could not imagine a more peaceful scene.*
2 = **believe**, suspect, gather, suppose, guess (*informal*), assume • *I imagine you're talking about my brother.*
See also: **expect, think**

imbecile noun 1 = **idiot**, fool, moron, chump, cretin (*offensive*), dork (*slang*), halfwit, schmuck (*slang*), thickhead
▶ adjective 2 = **stupid**, thick, foolish, idiotic, moronic, asinine, fatuous, feeble-minded, witless

imbibe verb 1 = **drink**, sink (*informal*), consume, swallow, swig (*informal*), quaff, knock back (*informal*)
2 (*Literary*) = **absorb**, receive, gain, acquire, gather, ingest, assimilate, take in

imbroglio noun = **complication**, involvement, embarrassment, misunderstanding, quandary, entanglement

imitate verb = **copy**, mimic, ape, simulate, emulate, impersonate • *She imitated her parents.*

imitation noun 1 = **mimicry**, simulation, duplication, likeness, resemblance, counterfeiting
2 = **replica**, fake, impression, reproduction, forgery, sham, substitution, impersonation
▶ adjective 3 = **artificial**, synthetic, mock, reproduction, phony (*informal*), dummy, sham, man-made, simulated, ersatz

imitative adjective = **derivative**, second-hand, copycat (*informal*), simulated, mimetic, parrot-like, unoriginal

imitator noun = **impersonator**, mimic, impressionist, parrot, copycat (*informal*), copier

immaculate adjective 1 = **clean**, neat, spruce, spotless, spick-and-span, squeaky-clean
2 = **flawless**, perfect, impeccable, unblemished, above reproach, faultless, unexceptionable, untarnished

immaterial adjective = **irrelevant**, insignificant, trivial, unimportant, inconsequential, extraneous, inessential, of no importance

immature adjective 1 = **young**, adolescent, undeveloped, unripe, unformed
2 = **childish**, juvenile, inexperienced, callow, infantile, puerile

immaturity noun
1 = **unripeness**, imperfection, greenness, rawness, unpreparedness
2 = **childishness**, inexperience, callowness, puerility

immediate adjective 1 = **instant**, instantaneous • *My immediate reaction was fear.*
2 = **nearest**, close, near, direct • *my immediate family*
See also: **prompt, urgent**

immediately adverb 1 = **at once**, now, directly, promptly, instantly, straightaway, right away • *She answered my email immediately.*
2 = **right**, directly, closely • *immediately behind the house*

immense adjective = **huge**, giant, massive, vast, enormous, gigantic, colossal • *an immense cloud of smoke*
OPPOSITE: tiny
See also: **large**

immensity noun = **size**, extent, bulk, magnitude, greatness, expanse, enormity, vastness, hugeness

immerse verb 1 = **plunge**, duck, sink, dip, dunk, douse, submerge, bathe
2 = **engross**, involve, busy, engage, occupy, absorb, take up

immersed See **preoccupied**

immersion noun 1 = **dipping**, dousing, ducking, dunking, plunging, submerging
2 = **involvement**, concentration, preoccupation, absorption

immigrant noun = **settler**,

newcomer, incomer

imminent *adjective* = **coming**, close, near, forthcoming, impending, looming • *my sister's imminent arrival*

> **CONFUSABLES**
> *Imminent* means *expected soon*.
> *Eminent* means *outstanding*.

immobile *adjective* = **stationary**, still, static, rigid, motionless, at a standstill, at rest, fixed, immovable, rooted, stock-still, unmoving

immobility *noun* = **stillness**, stability, fixity, inertness, motionlessness, steadiness

immobilize *verb* = **paralyze**, stop, halt, freeze, cripple, disable, transfix, bring to a standstill

immoderate *adjective* = **excessive**, extreme, exaggerated, unreasonable, unjustified, undue, extravagant, exorbitant, inordinate, over the top (*slang*)

immoral *adjective* = **wicked**, bad, wrong, corrupt, unethical, indecent, sinful, debauched, depraved, dissolute, unprincipled

immorality *noun* = **wickedness**, wrong, corruption, vice, sin, depravity, debauchery, dissoluteness

immortal *adjective* **1** = **eternal**, lasting, perennial, enduring, everlasting, deathless, imperishable, undying
▶ *noun* **2** = **god**, goddess (*feminine*)
3 = **hero**, great, genius

immortality *noun* **1** = **eternity**, perpetuity, everlasting life
2 = **fame**, celebrity, glory, greatness, renown

immortalize *verb* = **commemorate**, celebrate, glorify, exalt

immovable *adjective* **1** = **fixed**, set, firm, secure, stable, stationary, stuck, jammed, immutable
2 = **inflexible**, adamant, steadfast, resolute, unyielding, unshakable, obdurate, unwavering

immune *adjective* = **unaffected**, free, safe, resistant, exempt, protected • *She seems immune to pressure.*

immunity *noun* **1** = **exemption**, release, freedom, licence, amnesty, indemnity, invulnerability
2 = **resistance**, protection, immunization

immunize *verb* = **vaccinate**, protect, safeguard, inoculate

imp *noun* **1** = **demon**, devil, sprite
2 = **rascal**, rogue, brat, scamp, minx

impact *noun* **1** = **collision**, crash, blow, contact, stroke, knock, bump, smash, thump, jolt
2 = **effect**, influence, impression, significance, consequences, repercussions
▶ *verb* **3** = **hit**, strike, crash, clash, crush, collide

impair *verb* = **worsen**, reduce, damage, injure, harm, decrease, weaken, undermine, diminish, hinder, blunt, lessen

impaired *adjective* = **damaged**, faulty, flawed, defective, imperfect, unsound

impart *verb* **1** = **communicate**, tell, reveal, relate, disclose, convey, divulge, make known, pass on
2 = **give**, accord, grant, afford, lend, yield, bestow, confer

impartial *adjective* = **neutral**, just, fair, objective, equitable, unbiased, open-minded, disinterested, even-handed, detached, unprejudiced

impartiality *noun* = **neutrality**, equity, fairness, detachment, objectivity, disinterestedness, dispassion, even-handedness, open-mindedness

impassable *adjective* = **blocked**, closed, impenetrable, obstructed

impasse *noun* = **deadlock**, standoff, standstill, gridlock, stalemate, dead end

impassioned *adjective* = **intense**, animated, heated, passionate, fiery, inspired, rousing, fervent, stirring

impassive *adjective*
= **unemotional**, indifferent, unfazed (*informal*), callous, unmoved, reserved, serene, apathetic, aloof, stoic, unconcerned, dispassionate, stolid, unruffled, emotionless, poker-faced (*informal*), phlegmatic, imperturbable, impassible (*rare*), composed, unexcitable

impatience *noun* **1** = **haste**, intolerance, impetuosity, rashness
2 = **restlessness**, anxiety, agitation, nervousness, eagerness, uneasiness, edginess, fretfulness

impatient *adjective* **1** = **irritable**, brusque, curt • *You are too impatient with others.*
OPPOSITE: patient
2 = **eager**, restless • *He was impatient for the play to end.*
3 = **hasty**, demanding, hot-tempered, impetuous

impeach *verb* = **charge**, accuse, indict, arraign

impeccable *adjective* = **faultless**, perfect, flawless, immaculate, unblemished, blameless, irreproachable, unimpeachable

impecunious *adjective* = **poor**, broke (*informal*), insolvent, poverty-stricken, destitute, penniless, down and out, down on one's luck (*informal*), indigent

impede *verb* = **hinder**, delay, block, disrupt, hamper, obstruct, get in the way • *Fallen rocks are impeding the progress of rescue workers.*
See also: **handicap, interfere, prevent, restrict**

impediment *noun* = **obstacle**, difficulty, barrier, snag, obstruction, hindrance, encumbrance, stumbling block

impel *verb* = **force**, drive, push, require, compel, induce, oblige, constrain

impending *adjective* = **imminent**, near, upcoming, gathering, forthcoming, looming, approaching, coming, in the pipeline

impenetrable *adjective* **1** = **solid**, thick, dense, impassable, impervious, impermeable, inviolable
2 = **incomprehensible**, mysterious, obscure, enigmatic, arcane, unfathomable, unintelligible, inscrutable

imperative *adjective* = **urgent**, crucial, essential, vital, pressing

imperceptible *adjective* = **undetectable**, minute, small, tiny, slight, subtle, faint, microscopic, indiscernible

imperfect *adjective* = **flawed**, faulty, damaged, defective, broken • *We live in an imperfect world.*
OPPOSITE: perfect

imperfection *noun* = **flaw**, weakness, defect, fault, taint, deficiency, shortcoming, blemish, failing, frailty

imperial *adjective* = **royal**, sovereign, majestic, regal, princely, kingly, queenly

imperil *verb* = **endanger**, risk, expose, jeopardize

imperious *See* **bossy**

impersonal *adjective* = **detached**, cold, remote, formal, neutral, aloof • *I found him strangely distant and impersonal.*

impersonate *verb* = **imitate**, do (*informal*), mimic, ape, masquerade as, pass oneself off as, pose as (*informal*)

impersonation *noun* = **imitation**, impression, caricature, parody, mimicry

impertinence *noun* = **rudeness**, front, nerve (*informal*), cheek (*informal*), disrespect, presumption, brazenness, effrontery, impudence, insolence

impertinent *adjective* = **rude**, brazen, disrespectful, cheeky (*informal*), presumptuous, impolite, impudent, insolent

imperturbable *adjective* = **calm**, cool, serene, unflappable (*informal*), collected, composed, nerveless, self-possessed, unexcitable, unruffled

impervious *adjective*
1 = **resistant**, sealed, impassable, impenetrable, impermeable
2 = **unaffected**, immune, untouched, unmoved, invulnerable, proof against

impetuosity *noun* = **haste**, impulsiveness, precipitateness, rashness

impetuous *adjective* = **rash**, precipitate, hasty, impulsive, unthinking

impetus *noun* 1 = **incentive**, push, spur, motivation, stimulus, impulse, catalyst, goad
2 = **force**, power, energy, momentum

impinge *verb* 1 = **encroach**, violate, invade, infringe, trespass, obtrude
2 = **affect**, impact, touch, influence, bear upon, have a bearing on, relate to

impious *adjective* = **sacrilegious**, wicked, profane, irreverent, blasphemous, sinful, godless, irreligious, ungodly, unholy

impish *adjective* = **mischievous**, devilish, puckish, rascally, roguish, sportive, waggish

implacable *adjective*
= **unyielding**, uncompromising, merciless, inflexible, intractable, pitiless, unbending, unforgiving

implant *verb* 1 = **instill**, infuse, inculcate
2 = **insert**, fix, graft

implausible *adjective*
= **improbable**, suspect, unlikely, incredible, unbelievable, dubious, far-fetched, flimsy, unconvincing, cock-and-bull (*informal*)

implement *verb* 1 = **carry out**, complete, effect, perform, realize, execute, enforce, fulfill, bring about
▶ *noun* 2 = **tool**, device, gadget, instrument, appliance, apparatus, utensil

implicate *verb* = **incriminate**, include, involve, associate, embroil, entangle, inculpate

implication *noun* = **suggestion**, meaning, significance, presumption, inference, overtone, innuendo

implicit *adjective* 1 = **implied**, undeclared, tacit, latent, unspoken, inferred, taken for granted, understood
2 = **absolute**, firm, full, constant, steadfast, unqualified, fixed, unreserved, wholehearted

implied *adjective* = **unspoken**, indirect, undeclared, implicit, suggested, tacit, hinted at, unexpressed, unstated

implore *verb* = **beg**, beseech (*literary*), plead with • *"Tell me what to do!" he implored us.*
See also: **ask**, **plead**, **press**, **urge**

imply *verb* 1 = **hint**, suggest, intimate, signify, insinuate
2 = **involve**, mean, indicate, entail, point to, presuppose

impolite *adjective* = **bad-mannered**, rude, disrespectful, discourteous, ill-mannered, insolent, loutish, uncouth

impoliteness *noun* = **bad manners**, disrespect, boorishness, churlishness, discourtesy, insolence, rudeness

import *verb* 1 = **bring in**, introduce
▶ *noun* 2 = **meaning**, sense, intention, implication, drift, significance, thrust, gist
3 = **importance**, weight, moment, substance, consequence, magnitude, significance

importance *noun*
1 = **significance**, concern, interest, value, weight, moment, import, substance, consequence, usefulness
2 = **prestige**, status, influence, standing, distinction, prominence, esteem, eminence

important *adjective*
1 = **significant**, serious, momentous, weighty • *Their*

puppies are the most important thing to them.

OPPOSITE: unimportant

2 = powerful, influential, notable, foremost, eminent, leading • *the most important person in the country*

See also: **prominent, special, valuable, vital**

importunate *adjective*
= **persistent**, urgent, pressing, dogged, demanding, insistent

impose *verb* **1 = enforce**, dictate, inflict • *Fines were imposed on the culprits.*

2 = establish, introduce, fix, institute, levy, decree, ordain

▷ **impose on = take advantage of**, use, abuse • *I should stop imposing on your hospitality.*

See also: **administer, exact**

imposing *adjective* = **impressive**, grand, striking, dignified, majestic, stately, commanding

imposition *noun* **1 = application**, introduction, levying

2 = intrusion, liberty, presumption

impossibility *noun*
= **hopelessness**, inability, impracticality

impossible *adjective*
1 = unthinkable, inconceivable, hopeless, out of the question • *You shouldn't promise impossible things.*

OPPOSITE: possible

2 = absurd, outrageous, unreasonable, ludicrous, preposterous • *We are in an impossible situation.*

impostor, imposter *noun*
= **impersonator**, fraud, fake, phony (*informal*), sham, trickster, pretender, deceiver, charlatan

impotence *noun*
= **powerlessness**, weakness, inability, paralysis, incompetence, frailty, helplessness, incapacity, ineffectiveness, feebleness, uselessness

impotent *adjective* = **powerless**, weak, ineffective, paralyzed,

helpless, frail, incompetent, incapable, feeble, incapacitated

impound *See* **seize**

impoverish *verb* **1 = bankrupt**, break, ruin, beggar

2 = deplete, reduce, drain, diminish, exhaust, sap, use up, wear out

impoverished *adjective* = **poor**, needy, bankrupt, destitute, impecunious, poverty-stricken, penurious

impracticable *adjective*
= **unfeasible**, impossible, unworkable, unattainable, out of the question, unachievable

impractical *adjective*
1 = unworkable, wild, impossible, inoperable, unrealistic, impracticable, nonviable

2 = idealistic, romantic, unrealistic, starry-eyed

imprecise *adjective* = **indefinite**, loose, rough, vague, inexact, woolly, hazy, indeterminate, equivocal, ill-defined, inexplicit

impregnable *adjective*
= **invulnerable**, secure, unbeatable, invincible, unassailable, impenetrable, indestructible, unconquerable

impregnate *verb* **1 = saturate**, soak, steep, infuse, permeate, suffuse

2 = make pregnant, inseminate, fertilize

impress *verb* **1 = excite**, move, strike, affect, touch, inspire, stir, make an impression

2 = stress, fix, emphasize, bring home to, inculcate, instill into

3 = imprint, mark, print, stamp, engrave, emboss, indent

impression *noun* **1 = feeling**, idea, sense, notion, hunch • *your first impressions of high school*

2 = effect, impact, reaction, influence, feeling

3 = mark, stamp, outline, dent, hollow, imprint, indentation

4 = imitation, parody, impersonation

▷ **make an impression = make an impact**, influence, cause

a stir • *He certainly made an impression on his teachers.*

impressionable *adjective*
= **susceptible**, open, vulnerable, sensitive, receptive, gullible • *impressionable minds of children*

impressive *adjective* = **grand**, powerful, exciting, awesome, striking, stirring • *an impressive achievement*
See also: **significant**, **splendid**

imprint *noun* 1 = **mark**, sign, stamp, impression, indentation
▶ *verb* 2 = **fix**, print, stamp, impress, engrave, etch

imprison *verb* = **jail**, detain, confine, incarcerate, lock up, send to prison • *imprisoned for murder*
OPPOSITE: free

imprisoned *adjective* = **jailed**, inside (*slang*), captive, behind bars, confined, incarcerated, in jail, locked up, under lock and key

imprisonment *noun*
= **confinement**, custody, detention, incarceration

improbability *noun*
= **unlikelihood**, doubt, uncertainty, dubiety

improbable *adjective* = **unlikely**, unbelievable, doubtful, dubious, far-fetched, implausible • *improbable stories*
OPPOSITE: probable
See also: **incredible**

impromptu *adjective*
= **spontaneous**, unprepared, unscripted, ad-lib, extemporaneous, improvised, offhand, off the cuff (*informal*), unrehearsed

improper *adjective* 1 = **indecent**, vulgar, suggestive, unbecoming, untoward, unseemly, risqué, smutty
2 = **inappropriate**, unfit, unwarranted, unsuitable, out of place, uncalled-for

impropriety *noun* = **indecency**, vulgarity, incongruity, bad taste

improve *verb* 1 = **get better**, develop, advance, progress, look up (*informal*) • *The situation has*
improved since then.
OPPOSITE: worsen
2 = **enhance**, reform, upgrade, upscale, better, ameliorate • *They improved their house over the years.*
▷ **improve on** See **top**
See also: **correct**, **perfect**, **polish**, **recover**

improvement *noun* = **advance**, development, progress, enhancement, upturn • *dramatic improvements in conditions*
See also: **gain**, **recovery**, **reform**, **rise**

improvident *adjective*
= **imprudent**, reckless, negligent, careless, spendthrift, wasteful, short-sighted, thoughtless, prodigal, profligate

improvisation *noun*
1 = **spontaneity**, invention, ad-libbing, extemporizing
2 = **makeshift**, expedient, ad-lib

improvise *verb* 1 = **extemporize**, invent, ad-lib, busk, play it by ear (*informal*), speak off the cuff (*informal*), wing it (*informal*)
2 = **devise**, concoct, contrive, throw together

imprudent *adjective* = **unwise**, irresponsible, reckless, rash, careless, ill-advised, foolhardy, ill-considered, ill-judged, injudicious

impudence *noun*
= **impertinence**, nerve, gall, audacity, chutzpah (*informal*), boldness, insolence • *Have you ever heard such impudence?*

impudent *adjective* = **rude**, bold, brazen, audacious, shameless, cheeky (*informal*), presumptuous, impertinent, insolent, pert

impulse *noun* = **urge**, wish, feeling, notion, whim, inclination, caprice

impulsive *adjective* = **instinctive**, passionate, rash, spontaneous, precipitate, hasty, intuitive, devil-may-care, impetuous

impunity *noun* = **immunity**, security, freedom, licence, permission, exemption, liberty, dispensation

impure *adjective* **1 = unrefined**, mixed, adulterated, debased
2 = contaminated, tainted, infected, dirty, polluted, defiled
3 = immoral, corrupt, obscene, indecent, lewd, lascivious, licentious, unchaste

impurity *noun* **= contamination**, infection, pollution, taint, defilement, dirtiness

imputation *noun* **= blame**, accusation, slur, censure, slander, reproach, insinuation, aspersion

in *See* **fashionable, trendy**
▷ **in addition** *See* **too**
▷ **in advance** *See* **before, early**
▷ **in charge** *See* **responsible**
▷ **in fact** *See* **really**
▷ **in favour** *See* **popular**
▷ **in keeping** *See* **compatible**
▷ **in part** *See* **partly**
▷ **in sight** *See* **visible**
▷ **in spite of** *See* **despite**
▷ **in the end** *See* **finally**
▷ **in the long run** *See* **finally**
▷ **in the middle of** *See* **among**

inability *noun* **= ineptitude**, impotence, incompetence, inadequacy • *an inability to concentrate*
OPPOSITE: ability

inaccessible *adjective* **= out of reach**, remote, impassable, unattainable, out of the way, unapproachable, unreachable

inaccuracy *noun* **= error**, mistake, defect, fault, lapse, erratum

inaccurate *adjective* **= incorrect**, out, wrong, faulty, mistaken, unreliable, defective, erroneous, imprecise, unsound

inactive *adjective* **= unused**, idle, dormant, unemployed, unoccupied, inoperative

inactivity *noun* **= immobility**, unemployment, inaction, hibernation, passivity, dormancy

inadequacy *noun* **1 = shortage**, poverty, dearth, insufficiency, meagreness, paucity, scantiness
2 = incompetence, inability,

deficiency, incapacity, ineffectiveness
3 = shortcoming, weakness, defect, failing, imperfection

inadequate *adjective*
1 = insufficient, short, poor, scarce, lacking • *Supplies of medicine are inadequate.*
2 = incompetent, useless, pathetic, inept, incapable, deficient • *We felt painfully inadequate in the crisis.*
OPPOSITE: adequate
See also: **hopeless, meagre, unsatisfactory, weak**

inadmissible *adjective*
= unacceptable, inappropriate, irrelevant, unallowable

inadvertent *See* **accidental**

inadvertently *adverb*
= unintentionally, accidentally, mistakenly, unwittingly, involuntarily, by accident, by mistake

inadvisable *adjective* **= unwise**, ill-advised, imprudent, impolitic, inexpedient, injudicious

inane *adjective* **= senseless**, empty, stupid, silly, frivolous, futile, mindless, idiotic, fatuous, vacuous

inanimate *adjective* **= lifeless**, dead, cold, extinct, defunct, inert

inanity *See* **nonsense, stupidity**

inapplicable *adjective*
= irrelevant, inappropriate, unsuitable

inappropriate *noun*
= unsuitable, unfit, untimely, unseemly, incongruous, improper • *This behaviour is inappropriate.*
OPPOSITE: appropriate

inarticulate *adjective* **= poorly spoken**, hesitant, faltering, halting

inattention *noun* **= neglect**, preoccupation, carelessness, absent-mindedness, daydreaming, inattentiveness, thoughtlessness

inattentive *adjective*
= preoccupied, vague,

negligent, careless, dreamy, distracted, unobservant

inaudible adjective = **indistinct**, low, unheard, mumbling, out of earshot, stifled

inaugural adjective = **first**, opening, initial, maiden, introductory

inaugurate verb **1** = **launch**, begin, introduce, institute, initiate, commence, get under way, set in motion
2 = **invest**, install, induct

inauguration noun **1** = **launch**, opening, institution, initiation, setting up
2 = **investiture**, installation, induction

inauspicious adjective = **unpromising**, bad, unfortunate, ominous, unlucky, discouraging, ill-omened, unfavourable, unpropitious

inborn adjective = **natural**, native, congenital, inherent, innate, intuitive, ingrained, hereditary, inbred, instinctive

inbred adjective = **innate**, natural, native, constitutional, inherent, ingrained, deep-seated

incalculable adjective = **countless**, vast, infinite, untold, limitless, innumerable, boundless, numberless

incantation noun = **chant**, formula, spell, charm, invocation

incapable adjective
1 = **incompetent**, weak, inadequate, ineffective, unfit, insufficient, lousy (informal), inept, feeble, unqualified, inexpert
2 = **unable**, helpless, powerless, impotent

incapacitate verb = **disable**, paralyze, cripple, immobilize, lay up (informal), put out of action (informal)

incapacitated adjective = **indisposed**, unfit, hors de combat (French), immobilized, laid up (informal), out of action (informal)

incapacity noun = **inability**, weakness, impotence, inadequacy, ineffectiveness, powerlessness, incapability, incompetency, unfitness

incarcerate verb = **imprison**, jail, detain, confine, intern, impound, lock up, throw in jail

incarceration noun = **imprisonment**, detention, confinement, captivity, internment

incarnate adjective = **personified**, embodied, typified

incarnation noun = **embodiment**, type, personification, epitome, manifestation

incense verb = **anger**, rile (informal), inflame, irritate, infuriate, enrage, madden, make one's hackles rise

incensed adjective = **angry**, furious, enraged, irate, fuming, indignant, infuriated, maddened, steamed up (slang), up in arms

incentive noun = **inducement**, motivation, stimulus, encouragement • the incentive to work
See also: **reason**

inception noun = **beginning**, start, birth, origin, dawn, outset, initiation, commencement

incessant adjective = **constant**, endless, eternal, perpetual, continual, nonstop, unending, interminable, ceaseless, never-ending, twenty-four-seven (slang), unceasing

incessantly adverb = **constantly**, continually, perpetually, nonstop, endlessly, persistently, eternally, ceaselessly, interminably, twenty-four-seven (slang)

inch See **ease**, **edge**

incident noun **1** = **event**, circumstance, episode, occasion, occurrence, happening • Little incidents can shape our lives.
2 = **disturbance**, scene, clash, confrontation, commotion, contretemps
See also: **experience**

incidental *adjective* = **secondary**, minor, subsidiary, occasional, subordinate, nonessential, ancillary

incidentally *adverb* – **by the way**, by the bye, in passing, parenthetically

incinerate *verb* = **burn up**, char, cremate, carbonize, reduce to ashes

incipient *adjective* = **beginning**, embryonic, nascent, commencing, developing, inchoate, starting

incision *noun* = **cut**, opening, slash, notch, gash, slit

incisive *adjective* = **penetrating**, acute, keen, piercing, perspicacious, trenchant

incite *verb* = **provoke**, instigate, goad, agitate for, stir up
• *Protestors tried to incite a riot.*
See also: **encourage, excite**

incitement *noun* = **provocation**, spur, stimulus, encouragement, agitation, impetus, instigation, prompting

incivility *noun* = **rudeness**, disrespect, bad manners, boorishness, discourteousness, discourtesy, ill-breeding, impoliteness

inclement *adjective* = **stormy**, severe, foul, rough, harsh, tempestuous, intemperate

inclination *noun* 1 = **tendency**, penchant, disposition, liking, propensity, predisposition, predilection, partiality, proclivity, proneness
2 = **slope**, pitch, grade, angle, tilt, incline, slant, gradient

incline *verb* 1 = **predispose**, influence, persuade, sway, prejudice
2 = **slope**, tip, lean, tilt, veer, slant
▷ **incline toward** *See* **prefer**
▶ *noun* 3 = **slope**, rise, dip, grade, descent, ascent, gradient

inclined *adjective* = **disposed**, likely, willing, prone, liable, apt, given, minded, predisposed

include *verb* 1 = **contain**, involve, cover, embrace, incorporate, encompass • *Breakfast always*
includes pancakes with maple syrup.
OPPOSITE: exclude
2 = **introduce**, add, enter, insert

inclusion *noun* = **addition**, insertion, incorporation

inclusive *adjective* = **comprehensive**, general, global, blanket, umbrella, across-the-board, all-embracing, sweeping

incognito *adjective* = **in disguise**, unknown, unrecognized, disguised, under an assumed name

incoherence *noun* = **unintelligibility**, disjointedness, inarticulateness

incoherent *adjective* = **unintelligible**, inconsistent, confused, rambling, disjointed, disordered, inarticulate, jumbled, muddled, stammering, stuttering

income *noun* = **earnings**, pay, salary, profits, wages • *a two-income family*

incoming *adjective* = **arriving**, new, landing, approaching, entering, homeward, returning

incomparable *adjective* = **unequalled**, supreme, unparalleled, superlative, unrivalled, inimitable, peerless
• *an area of incomparable beauty*

incomparably *See* **far**

incompatible *adjective* = **inconsistent**, contradictory, conflicting, incongruous, mismatched, unsuited

incompetence *noun* = **ineptitude**, inability, inadequacy, incapacity, ineffectiveness, incapability, unfitness, uselessness

incompetent *adjective* = **inept**, unable, useless, incapable, bungling • *You are incompetent, and you know it.*
OPPOSITE: competent
See also: **inadequate, inefficient**

incomplete *adjective* = **unfinished**, partial, insufficient, deficient • *an incomplete book*
OPPOSITE: complete

incomprehensible *adjective*
= **unintelligible**, obscure, opaque, unfathomable, impenetrable, baffling, beyond one's grasp, perplexing, puzzling

inconceivable *adjective*
= **unimaginable**, incredible, unbelievable, unthinkable, incomprehensible, mind-boggling (*informal*), unheard-of, beyond belief, out of the question

inconclusive *adjective*
= **indecisive**, open, vague, undecided, ambiguous, indeterminate, unconvincing, up in the air (*informal*)

incongruity *noun*
= **inappropriateness**, conflict, discrepancy, disparity, inconsistency, incompatibility, unsuitability

incongruous *adjective*
= **inappropriate**, improper, incompatible, unsuitable, unbecoming, discordant, out of keeping, out of place

inconsiderable *adjective*
= **insignificant**, small, minor, slight, negligible, trivial, unimportant, inconsequential, trifling

inconsiderate *adjective* = **selfish**, rude, insensitive, thoughtless, unkind, indelicate, tactless, unthinking

inconsistency *noun*
1 = **incompatibility**, disagreement, discrepancy, disparity, variance, divergence, incongruity
2 = **unreliability**, instability, unsteadiness, unpredictability, fickleness

inconsistent *adjective*
1 = **incompatible**, contradictory, irreconcilable, conflicting, incongruous, at odds, discordant, out of step
2 = **changeable**, unpredictable, unstable, variable, erratic, unsteady, fickle, capricious

inconsolable *adjective*
= **heartbroken**, desolate, brokenhearted, despairing

inconspicuous *adjective*
= **unobtrusive**, ordinary, plain, insignificant, hidden, unassuming, camouflaged, unnoticeable, unostentatious

incontrovertible *adjective*
= **indisputable**, sure, positive, certain, established, undeniable, irrefutable, incontestable, indubitable, unquestionable

inconvenience *noun* 1 = **trouble**, difficulty, disruption, bother, disturbance, fuss, disadvantage, nuisance, hindrance, awkwardness
▶ *verb* 2 = **trouble**, upset, disrupt, disturb, bother, discommode, put out

inconvenient *adjective*
= **troublesome**, awkward, untimely, unsuitable, bothersome, inopportune, disadvantageous, disturbing

incorporate *verb* = **include**, combine, merge, absorb, blend, integrate, assimilate, subsume

incorrect *adjective* = **false**, wrong, faulty, inaccurate, mistaken, flawed, untrue, erroneous

incorrigible *adjective* = **incurable**, hardened, hopeless, intractable, inveterate, irredeemable, unreformed

incorruptible *adjective*
1 = **honest**, straight, upright, trustworthy, above suspicion
2 = **imperishable**, everlasting, undecaying

increase *verb* 1 = **grow**, extend, expand, swell, escalate, multiply, augment, enlarge, supersize, step up, turn up • *The population continues to increase.*
OPPOSITE: decrease
▶ *noun* 2 = **growth**, rise, gain, upsurge, increment • *a pay increase*
OPPOSITE: decrease
See also: **addition, build, jump, spread**

increasingly *adverb*
= **progressively**, more and more

incredible *adjective* 1 = **amazing**, extraordinary, sensational,

marvellous, astonishing, astounding • *a champion with incredible skill*
2 = unbelievable, improbable, absurd, unthinkable, unimaginable, far-fetched • *the incredible stories of some children*
See also: **unlikely, wonderful**

> **CONFUSABLES**
> *Incredible* means *hard to believe.*
> *Incredulous* means *not willing to believe.*

incredulity *noun* = **disbelief**, doubt, skepticism, distrust
incredulous *adjective* = **disbelieving**, suspicious, skeptical, doubtful, dubious, unconvinced, distrustful, unbelieving
increment *noun* = **increase**, gain, addition, supplement, advancement, accrual, enlargement, augmentation, step up
incriminate *verb* = **implicate**, charge, accuse, involve, blame, impeach, inculpate
incumbent *adjective* = **obligatory**, necessary, mandatory, binding, compulsory
incur *verb* = **earn**, bring or bring upon oneself, gain, draw, provoke, arouse, expose oneself to, meet with
incurable *adjective* = **fatal**, terminal, inoperable, irremediable
indebted *adjective* = **grateful**, beholden, in debt, obligated, obliged, under an obligation
indecency *noun* = **obscenity**, pornography, impropriety, vulgarity, immodesty, impurity, indelicacy, lewdness, licentiousness
indecent *adjective* **1 = obscene**, crude, dirty, improper, rude, vulgar, lewd • *indecent lyrics*
2 = unbecoming, vulgar, unseemly, in bad taste, indecorous
indecipherable *adjective* = **illegible**, indistinguishable, unintelligible, unreadable
indecision *noun* = **hesitation**,

doubt, dithering, indecisiveness, uncertainty, vacillation, wavering
indecisive *adjective* = **hesitating**, tentative, uncertain, undecided, dithering, faltering, in two minds (*informal*), vacillating, wavering
indeed *adverb* = **really**, actually, certainly, truly, undoubtedly, in truth
indefatigable See **energetic**
indefensible *adjective* = **unforgivable**, wrong, inexcusable, untenable, unjustifiable, unpardonable, unwarrantable
indefinable *adjective* = **inexpressible**, indescribable, impalpable
indefinite *adjective* = **unclear**, uncertain, vague, doubtful, inexact, indeterminate, equivocal, imprecise, ill-defined, unfixed
indefinitely *adverb* = **endlessly**, continually, ad infinitum, for ever
indelible *adjective* = **permanent**, lasting, enduring, ingrained, indestructible, ineradicable
indelicate *adjective* = **offensive**, crude, rude, tasteless, vulgar, coarse, suggestive, embarrassing, immodest, off-colour, risqué
indemnify *verb* **1 = insure**, protect, secure, guarantee, underwrite
2 = compensate, repair, reimburse, repay, remunerate
indemnity *noun* **1 = insurance**, security, protection, guarantee
2 = compensation, redress, restitution, reimbursement, reparation, remuneration
independence *noun* = **freedom**, sovereignty, liberty, autonomy, self-sufficiency, self-rule, self-reliance
independent *adjective*
1 = separate, free, unrelated, liberated • *an independent politician*
2 = self-sufficient, liberated, individualistic, unaided • *a*

fiercely independent woman
3 = self-governing, sovereign, autonomous, nonaligned, self-determining
See also: **individual**

independently adverb
= separately, alone, solo, individually, autonomously, by oneself, on one's own, unaided

indescribable adjective = **beyond description**, beyond words, indefinable, inexpressible, unutterable

indestructible adjective
= permanent, lasting, enduring, indelible, immortal, unbreakable, everlasting, imperishable, incorruptible, indissoluble

indeterminate adjective
= uncertain, unspecified, vague, indefinite, inexact, undefined, imprecise, unfixed, unstipulated

index See **list**

indicate verb **1 = show**, reveal, signal, signify, denote • *a gesture that indicates his relief*
2 = point out, designate, specify
3 = register, show, record, read, express, display
See also: **hint, mean, promise, suggest**

indication noun = **sign**, warning, signal, hint, suggestion, clue • *She gave no indication that she had heard me.*
See also: **lead, trace**

indicative adjective = **suggestive**, significant, symptomatic, pointing to

indicator noun = **sign**, mark, guide, signal, symbol, marker, gauge, meter, pointer

indict verb = **charge**, accuse, prosecute, arraign, summon, impeach

indictment noun = **charge**, allegation, prosecution, accusation, summons, impeachment

indifference noun = **disregard**, negligence, detachment, apathy, inattention, coolness, aloofness, coldness, nonchalance, unconcern

indifferent adjective
1 = unconcerned, cold, cool, callous, unmoved, aloof, impervious, unsympathetic, uninterested, detached, inattentive
2 = mediocre, moderate, ordinary, so-so (*informal*), passable, undistinguished

indigestion noun = **heartburn**, dyspepsia, upset stomach, acid reflux

indignant adjective = **resentful**, angry, disgruntled, irate, incensed, exasperated, peeved (*informal*), riled, scornful, ticked off (*informal*), up in arms (*informal*)

indignation noun = **resentment**, anger, rage, scorn, pique, exasperation, umbrage

indignity noun = **humiliation**, injury, insult, slight, snub, disrespect, affront, dishonour, opprobrium

indirect adjective **1 = roundabout**, oblique, rambling, tortuous, meandering, wandering • *an indirect route to school*
OPPOSITE: direct
2 = incidental, subsidiary, secondary, unintended

indiscreet adjective = **tactless**, reckless, rash, naive, unwise, imprudent, impolitic, incautious, injudicious

indiscretion noun = **mistake**, slip, error, gaffe, lapse, folly, foolishness, faux pas

indiscriminate adjective
= random, general, wholesale, careless, desultory, uncritical, undiscriminating, unsystematic

indiscriminately See at **random**

indispensable adjective
= essential, key, necessary, crucial, vital, needed, imperative, requisite

indisposed adjective = **ill**, ailing, sick, unwell, under the weather

indisposition noun = **illness**, ailment, sickness, ill health

indisputable adjective
= undeniable, certain,

irrefutable, incontrovertible, beyond doubt, incontestable, indubitable, unquestionable

indistinct adjective = **unclear**, vague, faint, fuzzy, hazy, shadowy, indeterminate, undefined, blurred, ill-defined

indistinguishable See **same**

individual adjective 1 = **separate**, single, independent, discrete (formal) • individual servings of pie 2 = **special**, personal, original, unique, characteristic, distinctive, idiosyncratic • Develop your own individual writing style.
▶ noun 3 = **person**, party, character, soul, human being • the rights of the individual
See also: **different, peculiar, private**

individualist noun = **nonconformist**, independent, original, maverick, loner, freethinker, lone wolf

individualistic See **independent**

individuality noun = **distinctiveness**, character, personality, originality, uniqueness, separateness, singularity

individually adverb = **separately**, apart, independently, one at a time, one by one, singly

indoctrinate verb = **train**, school, ground, teach, drill, instruct, initiate, brainwash, imbue

indoctrination noun = **training**, instruction, schooling, drilling, grounding, brainwashing, inculcation

indolent adjective = **lazy**, sluggish, idle, listless, inactive, lethargic, inert, languid, slothful, workshy

indomitable adjective = **invincible**, bold, staunch, unbeatable, unflinching, steadfast, resolute, unyielding, unconquerable

indubitable adjective = **certain**, sure, obvious, undeniable, indisputable, irrefutable, incontrovertible, incontestable, unquestionable

induce verb 1 = **persuade**, prompt, encourage, influence, convince, incite, instigate, prevail upon, talk into 2 = **cause**, produce, effect, generate, occasion, engender, bring about, give rise to, lead to

inducement noun = **incentive**, reward, lure, carrot (informal), attraction, bait, encouragement, incitement

indulge verb 1 = **gratify**, feed, satisfy, give way to, pander to, yield to 2 = **spoil**, humour, cosset, give in to, go along with, pamper

indulgence noun 1 = **gratification**, satisfaction, fulfillment, appeasement, satiation 2 = **luxury**, treat, privilege, favour, extravagance 3 = **tolerance**, understanding, patience, forbearance

indulgent adjective = **lenient**, liberal, understanding, tolerant, easy-going, kindly, compliant, permissive, forbearing

industrialist noun = **capitalist**, manufacturer, tycoon, magnate, big businessman, captain of industry

industrious adjective = **hard-working**, busy, conscientious, diligent, tireless • industrious students
OPPOSITE: lazy
See also: **active**

industry noun 1 = **business**, trade, production, commerce, manufacturing 2 = **effort**, activity, application, labour, diligence, toil, zeal, tirelessness

inebriated adjective = **drunk**, crocked (slang), intoxicated, paralytic (informal), plastered (slang), three sheets to the wind (slang), tipsy, under the influence (informal)

ineffective adjective = **useless**, idle, vain, worthless, inefficient, futile, impotent, fruitless, unproductive, unavailing

ineffectual adjective = **weak**,

inadequate, ineffective, lousy
(*slang*), inept, incompetent,
feeble, impotent

inefficiency *noun*
= **incompetence**, muddle,
carelessness, disorganization,
slackness, sloppiness

inefficient *adjective*
= **incompetent**, sloppy, inept,
incapable, disorganized • *an
inefficient retrieval system*
OPPOSITE: efficient

ineligible *adjective* = **unqualified**,
unacceptable, unfit, unsuitable,
disqualified, ruled out

inept *adjective* = **incompetent**,
clumsy, bumbling, bungling,
inexpert, maladroit

ineptitude *noun*
= **incompetence**, clumsiness,
inexpertness, unfitness

inequality *noun* = **disparity**,
difference, irregularity,
bias, diversity, prejudice,
disproportion, unevenness

inequitable *adjective* = **unfair**,
partial, partisan, discriminatory,
unjust, one-sided, preferential,
biased, prejudiced

inert *adjective* = **inactive**, still,
dead, dormant, static, lifeless,
motionless, unresponsive,
immobile, unreactive

inertia *noun* = **inactivity**, apathy,
sloth, lethargy, passivity,
immobility, listlessness,
unresponsiveness

inescapable *adjective*
= **unavoidable**, sure, certain,
inevitable, inexorable, destined,
fated, ineluctable

inestimable *adjective*
= **incalculable**, precious,
invaluable, priceless,
immeasurable, prodigious

inevitable *adjective*
= **unavoidable**, sure, certain,
assured, inescapable,
inexorable, destined, fixed,
ineluctable

inevitably *adverb* = **unavoidably**,
certainly, necessarily,
automatically, surely, as a result,
of necessity, perforce, willy-nilly

inexact *See* **approximate**

inexcusable *adjective*
= **unforgivable**, outrageous,
indefensible, unjustifiable,
unpardonable, unwarrantable

inexhaustible *See* **infinite**

inexorable *adjective*
= **unrelenting**, relentless,
inescapable, unyielding,
remorseless, unbending

inexpensive *adjective* = **cheap**,
budget, modest, bargain,
reasonable, economical

inexperience *noun*
= **unfamiliarity**, ignorance,
newness, callowness, greenness,
rawness

inexperienced *adjective* = **new**,
green (*informal*), raw, novice,
unaccustomed, raggedy ass
(*offensive slang*) • *inexperienced
drivers*
OPPOSITE: experienced
See also: **ignorant**

inexpert *adjective* = **amateurish**,
bungling, inept, unprofessional,
clumsy, unskilled, maladroit,
unpracticed

inexplicable *adjective*
= **unaccountable**,
mysterious, strange,
enigmatic, incomprehensible,
unfathomable, unintelligible,
baffling, insoluble, mystifying

inextricably *adverb*
= **inseparably**, totally,
irretrievably, intricately,
indissolubly, indistinguishably

infallibility *noun* = **perfection**,
supremacy, impeccability,
omniscience, unerringness

infallible *adjective* = **foolproof**,
sure, certain, reliable,
unbeatable, dependable,
trustworthy, sure-fire (*informal*),
unfailing

infamous *adjective* = **notorious**,
ignominious, disreputable,
ill-famed

infancy *noun* = **beginnings**, start,
dawn, outset, inception, cradle,
origins

infant *noun* = **baby**, babe, child,
minor, toddler, tot

infantile *adjective* = **childish**,
immature, babyish, puerile

infatuate verb = **obsess**,
fascinate, captivate, enchant,
bewitch, besot, enrapture

infatuated adjective = **obsessed**,
besotted, bewitched, captivated,
carried away, enamoured,
enraptured, fascinated,
possessed, smitten (informal),
spellbound

infatuation noun = **obsession**,
thing (informal), crush (informal),
passion, madness, fixation

infect verb = **contaminate**, affect,
taint, blight • One mosquito can
infect many people.
See also: **pollute**

infection noun = **contamination**,
virus, poison, pollution,
corruption, contagion,
defilement

infectious adjective = **catching**,
contagious • infectious diseases

infer verb = **deduce**, understand,
gather, conclude, derive,
presume, surmise

inference noun = **deduction**,
reading, conclusion,
assumption, presumption,
surmise

inferior adjective **1** = **lower**,
minor, secondary, lesser,
subordinate, second-class, bush
league (informal) • Young people are
considered to have inferior status.
OPPOSITE: superior
2 = **second-rate**, poor, hack,
mediocre, shoddy, second-class
• inferior-quality DVDs
OPPOSITE: superior
▶ noun **3** = **subordinate**, junior,
underling • Don't treat me like an
inferior.
OPPOSITE: superior
See also: **cheap, rotten**

inferiority noun **1** = **inadequacy**,
deficiency, mediocrity,
imperfection, insignificance,
shoddiness, worthlessness
2 = **subservience**,
subordination, abasement,
lowliness

infernal adjective = **devilish**,
damned, satanic, diabolical,
hellish, accursed, damnable,
fiendish

inferno See **fire, hell**

infertile adjective = **barren**,
sterile, unproductive, unfruitful

infertility noun = **sterility**,
barrenness, infecundity,
unproductiveness

infest verb = **overrun**, invade,
ravage, swarm, penetrate,
throng, beset, permeate

infested adjective = **overrun**,
alive, crawling, ravaged, ridden,
swarming, teeming

infiltrate verb = **penetrate**,
permeate, pervade, percolate,
filter through, insinuate
oneself, make inroads or make
inroads into, sneak in (informal)

infinite adjective = **limitless**,
eternal, untold, perpetual,
inexhaustible, boundless,
everlasting • an infinite number of
possibilities
See also: **countless, plentiful**

infinitesimal adjective
= **microscopic**, minute, tiny,
insignificant, negligible,
minuscule, teeny, unnoticeable

infinity noun = **eternity**, vastness,
boundlessness, endlessness,
immensity

infirm adjective = **frail**, weak,
ailing, failing, feeble, decrepit,
debilitated, doddering,
enfeebled

infirmity noun = **frailty**,
vulnerability, decrepitude, ill
health, sickliness

inflame verb = **enrage**, anger,
provoke, excite, stimulate,
incense, infuriate, arouse, rouse,
madden

inflamed adjective = **sore**, hot, red,
infected, fevered, swollen

inflammable adjective
= **flammable**, incendiary,
combustible

inflammation noun = **soreness**,
rash, redness, tenderness,
painfulness

inflammatory adjective
= **provocative**, explosive, fiery,
intemperate, like a red rag to a
bull, rabble-rousing

inflate verb = **expand**, increase,
swell, enlarge, bloat, dilate, blow

up, distend, puff up or puff out,
pump up

inflated adjective = **exaggerated**,
overblown, ostentatious,
swollen

inflation noun = **expansion**,
increase, rise, spread, extension,
escalation, enlargement,
swelling

inflexibility noun = **obstinacy**,
intransigence, obduracy

inflexible adjective **1** = **obstinate**,
stubborn, steadfast, resolute,
uncompromising, intractable,
implacable, obdurate, set in
one's ways, unbending
2 = **inelastic**, hard, stiff, rigid,
taut

inflict verb = **impose**, visit,
deliver, apply, administer, levy,
wreak, mete out or deal out

infliction noun = **imposition**,
administration, perpetration,
wreaking

influence noun **1** = **power**,
control, authority, importance,
sway, domination, ascendancy,
peer pressure • *They have quite a lot
of influence.*
2 = **effect**, hold, weight, spell,
magnetism • *under the influence
of alcohol*
▶ verb **3** = **affect**, control, direct,
guide, sway, manipulate • *His
parents never try to influence him.*
See also: **factor, grip**

influential adjective = **important**,
significant, powerful, potent,
instrumental, authoritative,
weighty, leading, telling

influx noun = **arrival**, rush,
invasion, incursion, inrush,
inundation

inform verb = **tell**, advise (formal),
notify, enlighten • *Please inform
me of your progress.*
▷ **inform of** See **report**
▷ **inform on** = **betray**, denounce,
tell on (informal) • *Somebody must
have informed on the thieves.*
See also: **alert, brief,
communicate**

informal adjective = **casual**,
easy, natural, familiar,
colloquial, relaxed • *His manner

was informal and relaxed.*
OPPOSITE: formal
See also: **cozy**

informality noun = **familiarity**,
ease, simplicity, relaxation,
casualness, naturalness

information noun = **facts**, news,
word, material, notice, data • *I
would never give any information
about you.*

informative adjective
= **instructive**, educational,
forthcoming, revealing, chatty,
communicative, edifying,
enlightening, illuminating

informed adjective
= **knowledgeable**, expert,
familiar, enlightened, erudite,
in the picture, learned, up to
date, versed, well-read

informer noun = **betrayer**, sneak,
accuser, Judas, stool pigeon,
finger man (slang)

infrequent adjective = **occasional**,
rare, unusual, uncommon,
sporadic, few and far between,
once in a blue moon

infringe verb = **break**, violate,
contravene, disobey, transgress

infringed See **broken**

infringement noun
= **contravention**, breach,
violation, infraction, trespass,
transgression

infuriate verb = **enrage**, anger,
provoke, rile, irritate, incense,
exasperate, madden

infuriated See **furious, mad**

infuriating adjective = **annoying**,
galling, maddening,
exasperating, irritating,
mortifying, provoking,
vexatious

ingenious adjective = **creative**,
original, bright, brilliant,
clever, crafty, shrewd, inventive,
resourceful

ingenuity noun = **originality**,
gift, genius, flair, inventiveness,
sharpness, cleverness,
resourcefulness, shrewdness

ingenuous adjective = **naive**,
open, simple, innocent, honest,
plain, sincere, unsophisticated,
artless, guileless, trusting

inglorious adjective
= **dishonourable**, infamous, disgraceful, shameful, ignominious, discreditable, disreputable, ignoble, unheroic

ingratiate verb = **pander to**, crawl, flatter, fawn, brown-nose (slang), curry favour, grovel, insinuate oneself, kiss ass (slang), toady

ingratiating adjective
= **sycophantic**, humble, crawling, fawning, flattering, obsequious, servile, toadying, unctuous

ingratitude noun
= **ungratefulness**, thanklessness

ingredient noun = **component**, element, constituent • Place all the ingredients in a pan.

inhabit verb = **live**, occupy, lodge, populate, reside (formal), dwell • the people who inhabit these islands

inhabitant noun = **resident**, native, citizen, inmate, occupant • an inhabitant of Norway

inhabitants See **people**

inhabited adjective = **populated**, developed, occupied, colonized, peopled, settled, tenanted

inhale verb = **breathe in**, gasp, draw in, respire, suck in

inherent adjective = **innate**, natural, native, essential, built-in, ingrained, hereditary, intrinsic, inborn, inbred, inherited

inherit verb = **be left**, come into, fall heir to, succeed to

inheritance noun = **legacy**, heritage, bequest • This gold watch is my inheritance from my grandfather.

inhibit verb = **restrain**, check, frustrate, curb, discourage, hinder, obstruct, impede, constrain, hold back or hold in

inhibited adjective = **shy**, subdued, reserved, guarded, reticent, self-conscious, repressed, constrained

inhibition noun = **shyness**, reserve, block, restraint, reticence, hang-up (informal), self-consciousness

inhospitable adjective
1 = **unfriendly**, cool, xenophobic, uncongenial, unreceptive, unsociable, unwelcoming
2 = **bleak**, hostile, barren, desolate, forbidding, godforsaken

inhuman adjective = **cruel**, brutal, savage, barbaric, ruthless, heartless, cold-blooded, merciless, pitiless, unfeeling

inhumane adjective
= **cruel**, brutal, heartless, unsympathetic, unkind, pitiless, unfeeling

inhumanity noun = **cruelty**, atrocity, brutality, barbarism, heartlessness, pitilessness, ruthlessness, unkindness

inimical adjective = **hostile**, adverse, unfriendly, antagonistic, ill-disposed, opposed, unfavourable, unwelcoming

inimitable adjective = **unique**, unparalleled, consummate, incomparable, unrivalled, matchless, peerless

iniquitous adjective = **wicked**, criminal, evil, immoral, unjust, reprehensible, sinful

iniquity noun = **wickedness**, wrong, evil, sin, injustice, abomination

initial adjective = **first**, opening, beginning, primary, introductory, incipient

initially adverb = **at first**, first, originally, primarily, firstly, at the beginning or in the beginning

initiate verb **1** = **begin**, start, open, launch, originate, commence, get under way, kick off (informal), set in motion
2 = **induct**, introduce, invest, indoctrinate
3 = **instruct**, coach, train, teach, acquaint with, familiarize with
▶ noun **4** = **novice**, member, convert, entrant, beginner, learner, probationer

initiation noun = **introduction**,

debut, entrance, installation,
inauguration, induction,
enrolment, investiture

initiative noun 1 = **first step**,
lead, advantage, first move
2 = **resourcefulness**, drive,
leadership, ambition,
enterprise, dynamism, get-up-
and-go (informal)

inject verb 1 = **vaccinate**,
inoculate
2 = **introduce**, insert, infuse,
instill, bring in

injection noun 1 = **vaccination**,
inoculation, shot (informal)
2 = **introduction**, dose, infusion,
insertion

injudicious adjective = **unwise**,
rash, foolish, ill-advised,
imprudent, ill-judged, impolitic,
incautious, inexpedient,
unthinking

injunction noun = **order**,
ruling, command, mandate,
instruction, exhortation,
precept

injure verb = **hurt**, wound, harm,
maim • Five people were injured in
the ferry accident.
See also: **damage**

injured adjective = **hurt**, disabled,
wounded, damaged, weakened,
broken, challenged, undermined

injury noun = **wound**, damage,
harm • He sustained serious injuries
in the accident.

injustice noun = **unfairness**,
wrong, discrimination, bias,
prejudice, inequality • the
injustice of the system
OPPOSITE: justice

inkling noun = **suspicion**, idea,
hint, suggestion, indication,
clue, notion, conception,
whisper, intimation

inland adjective = **interior**,
domestic, internal, upcountry

inlet noun = **bay**, passage, creek,
fjord, bight, firth or frith (Scot)

inmate See **inhabitant**

inmost, innermost adjective
= **deepest**, private, personal,
central, secret, basic, essential,
intimate

innards See **insides**

innate adjective = **inborn**, natural,
native, constitutional, essential,
congenital, inherent, intuitive,
ingrained, inbred, instinctive

inner adjective 1 = **inside**, central,
middle, internal, interior,
inward
2 = **private**, personal, secret,
intimate, hidden, repressed,
unrevealed

innermost See **inside**

innkeeper noun = **publican**, host
or hostess, landlord or landlady,
hotelier, mine host

innocence noun
1 = **inexperience**, simplicity,
gullibility, naivety • the innocence
of babies
2 = **guiltlessness**, virtue,
purity, blamelessness, clean
hands, incorruptibility, probity,
uprightness
3 = **harmlessness**,
innocuousness, inoffensiveness

innocent adjective 1 = **not guilty**,
clear, spotless, blameless • the
arrest of innocent suspects
OPPOSITE: guilty
2 = **naive**, pure, childlike,
guileless • They seem so young and
innocent.
3 = **harmless**, innocuous,
well-intentioned, inoffensive,
unobjectionable, well-meant
See also: **ignorant**

innocuous See **harmless, safe**

innovation noun
= **modernization**, change,
departure, introduction,
variation, novelty, alteration,
newness

innuendo noun = **insinuation**,
hint, suggestion, implication,
whisper, overtone, aspersion,
imputation, intimation

innumerable adjective
= **countless**, numerous, myriad,
infinite, untold, incalculable,
beyond number, multitudinous,
numberless, unnumbered

inoffensive adjective
= **harmless**, quiet, innocent,
mild, innocuous, retiring,
unobjectionable, unobtrusive

inoperative adjective = **out of**

action, ineffective, useless, defective, invalid, broken, null and void, out of order, out of service

inopportune *adjective* = **inconvenient**, inappropriate, unfortunate, untimely, unsuitable, unseasonable, ill-chosen, ill-timed, unfavourable, unpropitious

inordinate *adjective* = **excessive**, unreasonable, unwarranted, disproportionate, undue, extravagant, unconscionable, preposterous, immoderate, intemperate

inorganic *adjective* = **artificial**, chemical, man-made

inquest *noun* = **inquiry**, investigation, probe, inquisition

inquire *verb* 1 = **investigate**, research, probe, explore, examine, look into, make inquiries
2 *Also* **enquire** = **ask**, question, query

inquiring *See* **curious**

inquiry *noun* 1 = **investigation**, study, research, survey, probe, inquest, exploration, interrogation, examination
2 *Also* **enquiry** = **question**, query

inquisition *noun* = **investigation**, inquiry, inquest, examination, cross-examination, grilling (*informal*), questioning, third degree (*informal*)

inquisitive *adjective* = **curious**, inquiring, nosy (*informal*), probing, prying, questioning

inquisitiveness *See* **curiosity**

insane *adjective* 1 = **mad**, crazy, crazed, demented, deranged, unbalanced, out of one's mind, unhinged
2 = **stupid**, irresponsible, foolish, senseless, irrational, impractical, idiotic, preposterous, bonkers (*informal*), daft (*informal*)

insanitary *adjective* = **unhealthy**, dirty, polluted, filthy, unclean, disease-ridden, infested, insalubrious, scuzzy (*slang*), unhygienic

insanity *noun* 1 = **madness**, dementia, delirium, mental disorder, mental instability
2 = **stupidity**, folly, lunacy, irresponsibility, senselessness

insatiable *adjective* = **unquenchable**, greedy, voracious, ravenous, intemperate, rapacious

inscribe *verb* = **carve**, cut, impress, engrave, imprint, etch

inscription *noun* = **engraving**, legend, dedication, words

inscrutable *adjective*
1 = **enigmatic**, blank, impenetrable, deadpan, poker-faced (*informal*)
2 = **mysterious**, hidden, incomprehensible, inexplicable, unfathomable, unintelligible, unexplainable

insecure *adjective* 1 = **anxious**, afraid, uncertain, unsure
2 = **unsafe**, vulnerable, unprotected, wide-open, exposed, unguarded, defenseless

insecurity *noun* = **anxiety**, fear, worry, uncertainty

insensible *adjective* = **unaware**, unconscious, oblivious, unaffected, impervious, unmindful

insensitive *adjective* = **unfeeling**, tough, indifferent, callous, hardened, unconcerned, thick-skinned, uncaring

inseparable *adjective*
1 = **indivisible**, indissoluble
2 = **devoted**, close, intimate, bosom

insert *verb* = **put**, set, place, enter, introduce, implant • *He inserted the key into the lock.*
See also: **stick**

insertion *noun* = **inclusion**, addition, supplement, introduction, implant, interpolation

inside *adjective* 1 = **inner**, internal, interior, innermost
• *We booked an inside cabin.*
OPPOSITE: outside
2 = **confidential**, private, secret, internal, exclusive, classified, restricted

▶ *adverb* **3 = indoors**, within, under cover

▶ *noun* **4 = interior**, contents

insides *plural noun (Informal)* **= guts**, entrails, innards, internal organs • *My insides ached from eating too much.*

insidious *adjective* **= stealthy**, smooth, subtle, deceptive, sly, surreptitious, sneaking

insight *noun* **= understanding**, vision, judgment, perception, awareness, observation, penetration, comprehension, discernment, perspicacity

insignia *noun* **= badge**, symbol, crest, emblem

insignificance *noun* **= unimportance**, irrelevance, inconsequence, meaninglessness, pettiness, triviality, worthlessness

insignificant *adjective* **= unimportant**, little, minor, petty, irrelevant, trivial, trifling • *a small, insignificant flaw in the sweater*
OPPOSITE: significant
See also: **slight**

insincere *adjective* **= deceitful**, false, dishonest, two-faced • *insincere flattery*
OPPOSITE: sincere

insincerity *noun* **= deceitfulness**, hypocrisy, pretense, dishonesty, dissimulation, duplicity, untruthfulness

insinuate *verb* **1 = imply**, suggest, indicate, hint, intimate, allude
2 = ingratiate, curry favour, get in with, worm one's way in *or* work one's way in

insinuation *noun* **= implication**, hint, suggestion, slur, innuendo, allusion, aspersion

insipid *adjective* **1 = bland**, anemic, characterless, colourless, prosaic, uninteresting, vapid, wishy-washy *(informal)*
2 = tasteless, bland, watery, flavourless, unappetizing

insist *verb* **1 = demand**, urge, press • *My family insisted I should not give in.*
2 = assert, claim, maintain, vow, repeat, swear, reiterate, aver

insistence *noun* **= persistence**, stress, emphasis, importunity

insistent *adjective* **= persistent**, urgent, emphatic, unrelenting, incessant, dogged, importunate, persevering

insist on, insist upon See **exact**

insolence *noun* **= rudeness**, cheek *(informal)*, disrespect, boldness, effrontery, impertinence, impudence

insolent *adjective* **= rude**, bold, contemptuous, impertinent, impudent, insubordinate, insulting

insoluble *adjective* **= inexplicable**, mysterious, unfathomable, unaccountable, impenetrable, baffling, indecipherable, unsolvable

insolvency *noun* **= bankruptcy**, failure, ruin, liquidation

insolvent *adjective* **= bankrupt**, failed, broke *(informal)*, gone bust *(informal)*, gone to the wall, in receivership, ruined

insomnia *noun* **= sleeplessness**, wakefulness

inspect *verb* **= examine**, survey, investigate, eye, check, scan • *the right to inspect company files*
See also: **scrutinize**

inspection *noun* **= examination**, review, investigation, search, survey, check, scrutiny, checkup, once-over *(informal)*

inspector *noun* **= examiner**, investigator, censor, supervisor, superintendent, overseer, scrutinizer

inspiration *noun* **1 = influence**, spur, stimulus, muse
2 = revelation, insight, creativity, illumination

inspire *verb* **1 = stimulate**, encourage, influence, spur, animate, galvanize, enliven
2 = arouse, produce, excite, enkindle, give rise to

inspired *adjective* **1 = brilliant**, cool *(informal)*, impressive, wonderful, thrilling,

memorable, outstanding,
superlative, dazzling, phat
(*slang*)
2 = uplifted, elated, enthused,
exhilarated, stimulated
inspiring *adjective* = **uplifting**,
exciting, rousing, moving,
exhilarating, heartening,
stimulating, stirring
instability *noun*
= **unpredictability**, volatility,
fluctuation, insecurity,
unsteadiness, variability,
changeableness, fickleness,
impermanence, inconstancy,
wavering
install *verb* **1 = set up**, place,
station, position, lay, fix, lodge,
put in
2 = institute, introduce,
establish, invest, induct,
inaugurate
3 = settle, position, ensconce
installation *noun* **1 = setting
up**, establishment, fitting,
instalment, placing, positioning
2 = inauguration, induction,
investiture
3 = equipment, system, plant,
machinery
instalment *noun* **1 = repayment**,
part payment
See also: **payment**
2 = part, division, section,
episode, chapter
See also: **issue**
instance *noun* **1 = example**, case,
situation, occasion, occurrence,
illustration
▶ *verb* **2 = quote**, name, cite,
mention, specify, adduce
instant *noun* **1 = moment**,
second, minute, flash, split
second, trice • *The pain disappeared
in an instant.*
2 = point, time, moment,
occasion, juncture
▶ *adjective* **3 = immediate**,
prompt, instantaneous • *He had
taken an instant dislike to me.*
4 = precooked, fast,
convenience, ready-mixed
instantaneous *adjective*
= **immediate**, direct, prompt,
instant, on-the-spot

instantaneously *adverb*
= **immediately**, promptly,
instantly, at once, in the
twinkling of an eye (*informal*), on
the spot, straight away
instantly *adverb* = **immediately**,
now, directly, at once,
instantaneously, right away,
straight away, this minute
instead *adverb* = **rather**,
preferably, alternatively, in
lieu, in preference, on second
thoughts
▷ **instead of** = **in place of**, in lieu
of, rather than
instigate *verb* = **provoke**, start,
prompt, trigger, influence,
stimulate, initiate, incite, bring
about, set off
instigation *noun* = **prompting**,
incentive, encouragement,
incitement, bidding, urging,
behest
instigator *noun* = **ringleader**,
leader, troublemaker, motivator,
agitator, prime mover
instill *verb* = **introduce**, implant,
infuse, imbue, engender,
insinuate, inculcate
instinct *noun* = **intuition**, urge,
feeling, impulse, sixth sense
• *My first instinct was to protect
myself.*
instinctive *adjective* = **inborn**,
natural, automatic, inherent,
spontaneous, reflex, innate,
involuntary, visceral, intuitive,
unpremeditated
instinctively *adverb*
= **intuitively**, automatically,
naturally, involuntarily, by
instinct, without thinking
institute *noun* **1 = society**,
school, college, institution,
association, foundation,
academy, guild
▶ *verb* **2 = establish**, start,
launch, introduce, fix, organize,
found, pioneer, originate,
initiate, set up
institution *noun*
1 = establishment, school,
society, college, foundation,
institute, academy
2 = custom, rule, law, practice,

i

convention, tradition, ritual

institutional adjective
= **conventional**, formal,
established, orthodox, accepted

instruct verb 1 = **order**, tell,
direct, command • *They have
instructed their lawyers to sue.*
2 = **teach**, school, coach, train,
educate, tutor • *He instructs people
in computer technology.*
See also: **brief, require, show**

instruction noun 1 = **teaching**,
training, education, lesson
or lessons, tuition, guidance,
schooling, grounding, coaching
2 = **order**, demand, ruling,
command, mandate, injunction,
directive

instructions plural noun
= **orders**, information, key,
advice, guidance, directions,
recommendations, rules

instructive adjective
= **informative**, useful,
educational, helpful, revealing,
edifying, enlightening,
illuminating

instructor noun = **teacher**, coach,
guide, adviser, demonstrator,
trainer, mentor, tutor

instrument noun 1 = **tool**, device,
implement, gadget, mechanism,
appliance, contraption (*informal*),
apparatus
2 = **means**, medium, agency,
vehicle, agent, organ,
mechanism

instrumental adjective = **active**,
influential, useful, helpful,
involved, contributory

insubordinate adjective
= **disobedient**, defiant,
undisciplined, disorderly,
unruly, rebellious, recalcitrant,
mutinous, refractory,
ungovernable

insubordination noun
= **disobedience**, rebellion,
revolt, defiance, insurrection,
mutiny, indiscipline,
recalcitrance

insubstantial adjective = **flimsy**,
poor, weak, thin, slight, frail,
tenuous, feeble

insufferable adjective

= **unbearable**, impossible,
dreadful, intolerable, detestable,
insupportable, unendurable

insufficient adjective
= **inadequate**, short, scant,
deficient, lacking • *insufficient
information*
OPPOSITE: sufficient
See also: **incomplete**

insular adjective = **narrow-
minded**, provincial, limited,
narrow, petty, parochial,
blinkered, circumscribed,
inward-looking

insulate verb = **isolate**, protect,
shield, cushion, cocoon,
sequester, close off, cut off

insult verb 1 = **offend**, abuse,
slight, snub, affront, put down,
rip on (*slang*), bag on (*slang*) • *I did
not mean to insult you.*
OPPOSITE: compliment
▶ noun 2 = **offence**, abuse, slight,
snub, affront • *The two men
exchanged insults.*
See also: **provoke**

insulting adjective = **offensive**,
rude, abusive, degrading,
contemptuous, disparaging,
insolent, scurrilous

insults See **abuse**

insuperable adjective
= **insurmountable**, invincible,
impassable, unconquerable

insupportable adjective
1 = **intolerable**, unbearable,
insufferable, unendurable
2 = **unjustifiable**, untenable,
indefensible

insurance noun = **protection**,
security, cover, guarantee,
safeguard, warranty, assurance,
indemnity

insure verb = **protect**, cover,
guarantee, warrant, assure,
underwrite, indemnify

insurgent noun 1 = **rebel**,
revolutionary, rioter,
insurrectionist, mutineer
▶ adjective 2 = **rebellious**,
revolutionary, revolting,
disobedient, insubordinate,
mutinous, riotous, seditious

insurmountable adjective
= **insuperable**, impossible,

invincible, hopeless, impassable, overwhelming, unconquerable

insurrection noun = **rebellion**, riot, insurgency, revolution, coup, uprising, revolt, mutiny

intact adjective = **undamaged**, complete, sound, whole, perfect, entire, unharmed, unscathed, unbroken, unimpaired

integral adjective = **essential**, necessary, basic, component, fundamental, constituent, indispensable, intrinsic

integrate verb = **combine**, join, unite, merge, incorporate, blend, fuse, amalgamate, assimilate

integration noun = **assimilation**, unification, combining, amalgamation, incorporation, blending, fusing, mixing

integrity noun 1 = **honesty**, principle, honour, virtue, goodness, purity, incorruptibility, probity, rectitude, uprightness
2 = **unity**, cohesion, soundness, coherence, completeness, wholeness

intellect noun = **intelligence**, reason, sense, mind, judgment, understanding, brains (informal)

intellectual adjective
1 = **scholarly**, intelligent, cerebral, thoughtful, bookish, highbrow, studious, pointy-headed (informal)
▶ noun 2 = **thinker**, academic, egghead (informal), highbrow, pointy-head (informal)

intelligence noun 1 = **intellect**, sense, understanding, perception, wit, comprehension, cleverness • students of high intelligence
2 = **information**, report, news, knowledge, data, notification, facts, findings
See also: **head, word**

intelligent adjective = **clever**, quick, sharp, smart, bright, acute, brainy (informal) • Dolphins are intelligent animals.
OPPOSITE: stupid
See also: **brilliant**

intelligentsia noun = **intellectuals**, highbrows, literati

intelligible adjective = **understandable**, open, clear, plain, distinct, lucid, comprehensible

intemperate adjective = **excessive**, wild, extreme, self-indulgent, unrestrained, unbridled, immoderate, profligate

intend verb 1 = **plan**, mean, aim, propose, resolve, be determined • She intended to move back to Saskatoon.
2 = **mean**, aim, design, earmark • a book intended for serious students

intended See **calculated**

intense adjective 1 = **extreme**, great, deep, powerful, severe, fierce, acute, profound • intense heat
2 = **passionate**, fierce, earnest, impassioned, ardent, vehement, fervent • She was very intense before the important game.
See also: **colourful, furious, serious, uncommon, violent**

intensify verb = **increase**, strengthen, aggravate, escalate, deepen, reinforce, heighten, sharpen, magnify, redouble, add to

intensity noun = **force**, strength, emotion, passion, vigour, fanaticism, ardour, fervour, fierceness, vehemence

intensive adjective = **concentrated**, comprehensive, thorough, in-depth, exhaustive, demanding, thoroughgoing

intent noun 1 = **intention**, plan, end, goal, aim, design, object, purpose, objective, meaning
▶ adjective 2 = **absorbed**, eager, watchful, determined, steadfast, attentive, engrossed, preoccupied, rapt, resolved

intention noun = **aim**, goal, idea, object, purpose, objective • He announced his intention of retiring.
See also: **point**

intentional adjective = **deliberate**, planned, intended, calculated, wilful, meant, premeditated

intentionally adverb
= **deliberately**, wilfully, designedly, on purpose

inter verb = **bury**, entomb, lay to rest

intercede verb = **mediate**, plead, intervene, arbitrate

intercept verb = **catch**, stop, block, seize, interrupt, obstruct, cut off, head off

interchange verb 1 = **switch**, trade, exchange, swap, alternate, reciprocate
▶ noun 2 = **junction**, crossing, intersection, crossroads

interchangeable adjective
= **identical**, equivalent, synonymous, reciprocal, exchangeable

intercourse noun
1 = **communication**, contact, commerce, dealings
2 = **sexual intercourse**, sex, carnal knowledge, coitus, copulation

interest noun 1 = **curiosity**, concern, attention, fascination • I have a great interest in that period of history.
2 = **hobby**, activity, pursuit, pastime • He has a wide range of interests.
3 = **advantage**, good, profit, benefit
4 = **stake**, right, share, claim, investment
▶ verb 5 = **intrigue**, appeal, stimulate, fascinate, captivate • This part of the book interests me most.
OPPOSITE: bore
See also: **enthusiasm**

interested adjective 1 = **curious**, keen, excited, attracted, drawn, fascinated
2 = **involved**, concerned, implicated

interesting adjective
= **intriguing**, absorbing, compelling, entertaining, gripping, stimulating • an interesting hobby
OPPOSITE: boring

See also: **colourful**

interface noun = **connection**, link, border, boundary, frontier

interfere verb 1 = **meddle**, intervene, tamper, intrude, butt in • Stop interfering and leave me alone.
2 = **conflict**, disrupt, hinder, obstruct, impede, inhibit • His problems interfered with his work.
See also: **pry**

interference noun 1 = **meddling**, intervention, intrusion, prying
2 = **conflict**, opposition, collision, obstruction, clashing

interim adjective = **temporary**, acting, makeshift, provisional, caretaker, stopgap, improvised

interior noun 1 = **inside**, heart, core, centre
▶ adjective 2 = **inside**, internal, inner, inward
3 = **mental**, private, personal, secret, spiritual, intimate, inner, hidden

interloper noun = **trespasser**, intruder, gate-crasher (informal), meddler

interlude noun = **interval**, break, delay, rest, spell, pause, stoppage, intermission, hiatus, respite, breathing space

intermediary noun = **mediator**, agent, broker, middleman, go-between

intermediate adjective
= **middle**, midway, halfway, mid, transitional, in-between (informal), intervening

interment noun = **burial**, funeral

interminable adjective = **endless**, protracted, infinite, perpetual, everlasting, long-winded, ceaseless, long-drawn-out, never-ending

intermingle verb = **mix**, combine, merge, blend, fuse, interweave, intermix, interlace

intermission noun = **interval**, break, rest, pause, stoppage, recess, respite, interlude

intermittent adjective = **periodic**, occasional, irregular, sporadic, broken, fitful, spasmodic

intern verb = **imprison**, hold,

detain, confine, hold in custody
internal *adjective* **1** = **inner**,
inside, interior
2 = **domestic**, home, civic, in-
house, intramural • *the new head
of internal affairs*
▷ **internal organs** *See* **insides**
international *adjective*
= **global**, worldwide, universal,
cosmopolitan, intercontinental
internet *noun* = **information
superhighway**, cyberspace, the
net (*informal*), the web (*informal*),
World Wide Web, interweb
(*humorous*)
interpose *verb* = **interrupt**,
insert, interject, put one's oar
in
interpret *verb* = **explain**,
translate, render, decode,
decipher, construe, elucidate,
make sense of
interpretation *noun*
= **explanation**, version, analysis,
portrayal, translation, rendition,
clarification, exposition,
elucidation
interpreter *noun* = **translator**,
commentator
interrogate *verb* = **question**,
examine, quiz, grill • *I interrogated
everyone even slightly involved.*
See also: **ask**
interrogation *noun*
= **questioning**, inquiry,
examination, cross-
examination, inquisition,
grilling (*informal*), third degree
(*informal*)
interrupt *verb* **1** = **butt in**,
heckle • *He tried to speak, but she
interrupted him.*
2 = **suspend**, break, discontinue
• *The game was interrupted by rain.*
See also: **intrude**
interruption *noun* = **stoppage**,
break, suspension, disruption,
pause, disturbance, hitch,
intrusion
intersect *See* **cross**
intersection *noun* = **junction**,
crossing, interchange,
crossroads
interval *noun* = **break**, gap, pause,
hiatus, interlude • *There was a*

long interval of silence.
See also: **period, space, time,
wait**
intervene *verb* **1** = **mediate**,
arbitrate • *I relied on them to
intervene if anything happened.*
2 = **happen**, occur, ensue, befall,
come to pass, take place
See also: **interfere**
intervention *noun* = **mediation**,
agency, interference, intrusion
interview *noun* **1** = **meeting**,
talk, conference, audience,
dialogue, consultation, press
conference
▶ *verb* **2** = **question**, examine,
interrogate, talk to
interviewer *noun* = **questioner**,
reporter, investigator,
interrogator, examiner
intestines *plural noun* = **guts**,
bowels, entrails, innards
(*informal*), insides (*informal*),
viscera
intimacy *noun* = **familiarity**,
confidentiality, closeness
intimate[1] *adjective* **1** = **close**, near,
confidential, thick (*informal*),
dear, bosom, buddy-buddy
(*informal*)
2 = **personal**, private, secret,
confidential
3 = **detailed**, deep, immediate,
profound, thorough, first-hand,
in-depth, exhaustive
4 = **snug**, warm, friendly, cozy,
comfy (*informal*), homey
▶ *noun* **5** = **friend**, companion
or constant companion,
confidant or confidante
(*feminine*), crony, close friend,
homeboy (*slang*), homegirl
(*slang*), soul mate
intimate[2] *verb* **1** = **suggest**,
indicate, hint, imply, insinuate
2 = **announce**, state, declare,
communicate, make known
intimately *adverb*
1 = **confidingly**, personally,
warmly, affectionately,
confidentially, familiarly,
tenderly
2 = **in detail**, fully, thoroughly,
inside out, very well
intimation *noun* **1** = **hint**,

warning, suggestion, indication, reminder, inkling, allusion, insinuation

2 = announcement, communication, notice, declaration

intimidate verb = **frighten**, threaten, scare, bully, subdue, coerce, terrorize, daunt, browbeat, overawe

intimidating See **formidable, frightening**

intimidation noun = **bullying**, pressure, threat or threats, coercion, arm-twisting (informal), browbeating, menaces, terrorization

into See **keen**

intolerable adjective = **unbearable**, impossible, painful, excruciating, insufferable, insupportable, unendurable

intolerance noun = **narrow-mindedness**, discrimination, prejudice, bigotry, fanaticism, chauvinism, dogmatism, illiberality

intolerant adjective = **narrow-minded**, dictatorial, chauvinistic, fanatical, dogmatic, bigoted, illiberal, prejudiced, small-minded

intone verb = **chant**, recite

intoxicated adjective **1 = drunk**, drunken, inebriated, paralytic (informal), plastered (slang), tipsy, under the influence (informal)

2 = euphoric, high (informal), excited, dizzy, elated, enraptured, exhilarated, wired (slang)

intoxicating adjective

1 = alcoholic, strong

2 = exciting, thrilling, heady, exhilarating

intoxication noun

1 = drunkenness, inebriation, insobriety, tipsiness

2 = excitement, delirium, euphoria, elation, exhilaration

intractable See **difficult, obstinate**

intransigent adjective = **uncompromising**, hardline,

stubborn, intractable, unyielding, obdurate, obstinate, stiff-necked, unbending

intrepid adjective = **fearless**, brave, bold, daring, courageous, audacious, valiant, plucky, gallant, stouthearted

intricacy noun = **complexity**, complication, convolutions, elaborateness

intricate adjective = **complicated**, complex, elaborate, fancy, involved, tangled, tortuous, convoluted, labyrinthine

intrigue verb **1 = interest**, attract, fascinate, rivet, titillate

2 = plot, scheme, conspire, manoeuvre, connive, machinate

▶ noun **3 = plot**, scheme, conspiracy, collusion, machination, manoeuvre, chicanery, stratagem, wile

4 = affair, romance, liaison, intimacy, amour

intriguing adjective = **interesting**, exciting, beguiling, compelling, diverting, fascinating, tantalizing, titillating

intrinsic adjective = **inborn**, natural, native, basic, constitutional, essential, fundamental, built-in, congenital, inherent, inbred

introduce verb **1 = present**, acquaint, familiarize, make known

2 = bring in, start, launch, establish, found, pioneer, institute, initiate, set up

3 = bring up, air, advance, submit, moot, broach, put forward

4 = insert, add, inject, put in, throw in (informal)

introduction noun **1 = launch**, institution, establishment, inauguration, initiation • *the introduction of the loonie in 1987*

2 = foreword, preface, prologue • *The book contains a new introduction by the author.*
See also: **appearance**

introductory adjective = **preliminary**, first, opening, initial, inaugural, preparatory

introspective adjective
= **inward-looking**, meditative, contemplative, brooding, introverted, pensive

introverted adjective
= **introspective**, self-contained, inner-directed, inward-looking, withdrawn

intrude verb = **butt in**, violate, interrupt, infringe, trespass, encroach • *I don't want to intrude on your parents.*
▷ **intrude on** See **disturb**
See also: **interfere, pry**

intruder noun = **trespasser**, invader, interloper, gate-crasher (*informal*), infiltrator, prowler

intrusion noun = **invasion**, violation, infringement, interference, interruption, trespass, encroachment

intrusive adjective = **interfering**, unwanted, presumptuous, impertinent, importunate, meddlesome, nosy (*informal*), pushy (*informal*), uncalled-for

intuition noun = **instinct**, perception, insight, hunch, presentiment, sixth sense

intuitive adjective = **instinctive**, spontaneous, innate, untaught

inundate verb = **flood**, overwhelm, drown, swamp, overflow, overrun, engulf, submerge, immerse

invade verb 1 = **attack**, enter, violate, occupy • *The allies invaded the mainland.*
2 = **infest**, overrun, permeate, pervade, swarm over
See also: **raid**

invader noun = **attacker**, raider, aggressor, plunderer, trespasser

invalid[1] adjective 1 = **disabled**, ill, sick, ailing, frail, bedridden, infirm, challenged
▶ noun 2 = **patient**, convalescent, valetudinarian, sickie (*informal*)

invalid[2] adjective = **null and void**, false, void, unfounded, irrational, worthless, illogical, unsound, fallacious, inoperative

invalidate verb = **nullify**, cancel, undermine, overthrow, undo, annul

invaluable adjective = **precious**, valuable, priceless, inestimable, worth one's weight in gold *or* worth its weight in gold

invariably adverb = **always**, regularly, consistently, perpetually, customarily, day in, day out, habitually, unfailingly, without exception

invasion noun 1 = **attack**, campaign, assault, offensive, raid, foray, incursion, onslaught, inroad
2 = **intrusion**, breach, violation, infringement, infraction, encroachment, usurpation

invective noun = **abuse**, tirade, censure, diatribe, denunciation, tongue-lashing, vilification, vituperation

invent verb 1 = **create**, coin, originate, conceive, formulate, come up with (*informal*) • *He invented the first electric clock.*
2 = **make up**, manufacture, fabricate, concoct • *I tried to invent a plausible excuse.*
See also: **compose, produce**

invented See **imaginary**

invention noun 1 = **creation**, design, device, discovery, gadget, instrument, contraption, brainchild (*informal*), contrivance
2 = **creativity**, imagination, genius, ingenuity, originality, inventiveness, resourcefulness
3 = **fiction**, lie, fantasy, forgery, fabrication, yarn, falsehood, untruth

inventive adjective = **creative**, original, innovative, inspired, fertile, imaginative, ingenious, resourceful

inventiveness See **imagination**

inventor noun = **creator**, author, maker, designer, architect, originator, coiner

inventory noun = **list**, record, file, account, roll, register, roster, catalogue

inverse adjective = **opposite**, reverse, contrary, reversed, converse, transposed

invert verb = **overturn**, upset, reverse, upturn, transpose

i

invest verb **1 = spend**, advance, sink, devote, lay out, put in **2 = empower**, charge, sanction, license, authorize, vest in ▷ **invest in** See **buy**

investigate verb **= examine**, study, research, probe, explore, sift • *Police are still investigating the incidents.* See also: **inspect**

investigation noun **= examination**, study, review, search, survey, probe, inquiry, inspection, inquest, exploration

investigator noun **= examiner**, researcher, detective or private detective, gumshoe (*slang*), sleuth, inquirer, private eye (*informal*)

investiture noun **= installation**, inauguration, induction, ordination, enthronement

investment noun **1 = transaction**, speculation, venture **2 = stake**, contribution, ante (*informal*)

investments See **stock**

inveterate adjective **= long-standing**, chronic, incurable, habitual, entrenched, hardened, deep-seated, confirmed, dyed-in-the-wool, incorrigible

invidious adjective **= undesirable**, hateful

invigilate verb **= watch over**, run, conduct, oversee, supervise, keep an eye on, preside over, superintend

invigorate verb **= refresh**, stimulate, fortify, energize, revitalize, exhilarate, galvanize, enliven, liven up

invincible adjective **= unbeatable**, indomitable, impregnable • *When the skating pair is at their best, they're invincible.*

inviolable adjective **= sacrosanct**, holy, sacred, hallowed, inalienable, unalterable

inviolate adjective **= intact**, whole, entire, pure, untouched, unhurt, unbroken, undefiled, unpolluted, unsullied

invisible adjective **= unseen**, hidden, concealed, disguised, inconspicuous • *His face was invisible beneath his hat.* OPPOSITE: visible

invitation noun **= request**, call, invite (*informal*), summons

invite verb **1 = request**, ask, bid, beg, summon **2 = encourage**, court, welcome, attract, provoke, entice, tempt, ask for (*informal*)

inviting adjective **= tempting**, attractive, appealing, alluring, seductive, enticing, mouthwatering, welcoming

invocation noun **= appeal**, prayer, petition, entreaty, supplication

invoice See **bill**

invoke verb **1 = call upon**, pray, petition, beg, implore, beseech, appeal to, entreat, supplicate **2 = apply**, use, implement, initiate, put into effect, resort to

involuntary adjective **= unintentional**, automatic, unconscious, spontaneous, reflex, uncontrolled, instinctive, unthinking

involve verb **1 = require**, incorporate, take in • *Running a kitchen involves a great deal of organization.* **2 = concern**, affect, touch, implicate, draw in See also: **demand**, **include**

involved adjective **1 = complicated**, complex, elaborate, confusing, tangled, intricate, tortuous, convoluted, labyrinthine **2 = concerned**, caught or caught up, implicated, mixed up in or mixed up with, participating, taking part

involvement noun **= connection**, interest, commitment, association, participation

invulnerable adjective **= safe**, secure, invincible, unassailable, impenetrable, indestructible, insusceptible, proof against

inward adjective **1 = incoming**, inbound, entering, ingoing **2 = internal**, inside, interior, inner

3 = **private**, personal, secret, confidential, hidden, innermost, inmost

inwardly adverb = **privately**, inside, secretly, at heart, deep down

irate adjective = **angry**, cross, furious, enraged, annoyed, livid, incensed, indignant, infuriated

irksome adjective = **irritating**, troublesome, tiresome, bothersome, annoying, disagreeable, exasperating, trying, vexing, wearisome

iron adjective **1** = **ferrous**, chalybeate, ferric
2 = **inflexible**, strong, hard, tough, adamant, rigid, steely, unyielding, implacable, indomitable, unbending
▸ verb
▷ **iron out** = **settle**, resolve, reconcile, clear up, get rid of, put right, smooth over, sort out, straighten out

ironic adjective **1** = **sarcastic**, satirical, wry, double-edged, sardonic, mocking, with tongue in cheek
2 = **paradoxical**, incongruous

irony noun **1** = **sarcasm**, satire, mockery
2 = **paradox**, incongruity

irrational adjective = **illogical**, crazy, absurd, nonsensical, unsound • *irrational fears*

irrefutable adjective = **undeniable**, sure, certain, indisputable, incontrovertible, incontestable, indubitable, unquestionable

irregular adjective **1** = **uneven**, lopsided, bumpy, jagged, ragged, asymmetrical • *an irregular surface*
OPPOSITE: regular
2 = **variable**, random, occasional, erratic, patchy, haphazard • *She worked irregular hours.*
OPPOSITE: regular
3 = **unconventional**, unusual, extraordinary, unofficial, exceptional, abnormal, peculiar, unorthodox
See also: **changeable, crooked**

irregularity noun
1 = **inconsistency**, desultoriness, disorganization, haphazardness
2 = **abnormality**, oddity, anomaly, peculiarity, unorthodoxy
3 = **unevenness**, roughness, asymmetry, bumpiness, jaggedness, lopsidedness, raggedness

irrelevant adjective
= **unconnected**, inappropriate, unrelated, immaterial, extraneous, beside the point, impertinent, inapplicable, neither here nor there

irreparable adjective = **beyond repair**, incurable, irreversible, irremediable, irretrievable

irrepressible adjective
= **unstoppable**, boisterous, buoyant, ebullient, effervescent

irreproachable adjective
= **blameless**, perfect, innocent, pure, impeccable, beyond reproach, faultless, unimpeachable

irresistible adjective
= **overwhelming**, urgent, compulsive, compelling, overpowering

irresponsible adjective
= **thoughtless**, wild, reckless, careless • *an irresponsible attitude*
OPPOSITE: responsible
See also: **unwise**

irreverent adjective
= **disrespectful**, cheeky (*informal*), tongue-in-cheek, flippant, iconoclastic, impertinent, impudent, mocking

irreversible adjective
= **irrevocable**, final, incurable, irreparable, unalterable

irrevocable adjective = **fixed**, irreversible, fated, immutable, predestined, predetermined, settled, unalterable

irrigate verb = **water**, flood, wet, inundate, moisten

irritability noun = **bad temper**, impatience, ill humour, irascibility, prickliness,

testiness, tetchiness, touchiness
irritable *adjective* = **bad-tempered**, cantankerous, crabby, petulant • *He's unusually tense and irritable.*
See also: **grumpy, impatient, moody**
irritate *verb* **1** = **annoy**, anger, needle (*informal*), bother, ruffle, exasperate, piss off (*taboo slang*), tee off (*slang*) • *Their attitude irritates me.*
2 = **inflame**, pain, rub, chafe
See also: **provoke**
irritated *adjective* = **annoyed**, cross, angry, bothered, exasperated, nettled, piqued, put out, vexed
irritating *adjective* = **annoying**, troublesome, maddening, disturbing, infuriating, irksome, nagging, trying
irritation *noun* **1** = **annoyance**, anger, displeasure, resentment, indignation, exasperation, testiness, vexation
2 = **nuisance**, drag (*informal*), irritant, pain in the neck (*informal*), thorn in one's flesh
island *noun* = **isle**, islet, atoll, cay or key
isolate *verb* = **separate**, disconnect, detach, insulate, segregate, cut off, set apart
isolated *adjective* = **remote**, lonely, outlying, hidden, secluded, off the beaten track, out-of-the-way
isolation *noun* = **separation**, detachment, segregation, solitude, seclusion, remoteness
issue *noun* **1** = **topic**, problem, question, concern, matter, subject • *important issues of the day*
2 = **edition**, copy, instalment • *the latest issue of* Maclean's *magazine*
3 = **outcome**, result, effect, consequence, upshot, end result
4 = **children**, offspring, progeny,

descendants, heirs
▷ **take issue** = **disagree**, challenge, dispute, oppose, object, raise an objection, take exception
▶ *verb* **5** = **pronounce**, make, give, release, deliver, read out • *They have issued a statement denying the allegations.*
OPPOSITE: withdraw
6 = **provide**, supply, equip, furnish, give out • *Staff will be issued with badges.*
See also: **affair, business, consideration**

> INFORMALLY SPEAKING
> **a burning issue**: a matter of great importance
> **make an issue (out) of**: make into a point of argument
> **take issue**: disagree

isthmus *noun* = **strip**, spit
it could be *See* **maybe, perhaps**
itch *noun* **1** = **irritation**, itchiness, prickling, tingling
2 = **desire**, passion, hunger, yen (*informal*), longing, craving, lust, yearning, hankering
▶ *verb* **3** = **prickle**, irritate, tickle, tingle
4 = **long**, hunger, pine, ache, crave, lust, yearn, hanker
itching *adjective* = **longing**, eager, avid, impatient, raring, spoiling for
itchy *adjective* = **impatient**, eager, edgy, restive, restless, unsettled, fidgety
item *noun* **1** = **article**, point, matter • *an item on the agenda*
2 = **report**, feature, article, piece, notice • *There was an item in the paper about them.*
See also: **entry**
itinerant *adjective* = **wandering**, migratory, nomadic, peripatetic, roaming, roving, travelling, vagrant
itinerary *noun* = **schedule**, program, route, timetable

Jj

jab *verb, noun* = **poke**, tap, stab, punch, dig, nudge, thrust, prod, lunge

jabber *verb* = **chatter**, mumble, babble, blether, gabble, ramble, yap (*informal*)

jack *verb*
▷ **jack up** = **raise**, lift, hoist, elevate, lift up

jacket *noun* = **covering**, case, skin, coat, casing, wrapper, sheath, wrapping

jackpot *noun* = **prize**, award, reward, bonanza, winnings

jaded *adjective* = **tired**, weary, spent, exhausted, fatigued

jagged *adjective* = **uneven**, rough, barbed, craggy, serrated • *jagged cliffs*
OPPOSITE: smooth
See also: **irregular, sharp**

jail *noun* **1** = **prison** • *sentenced to six months in jail*
▶ *verb* **2** = **imprison**, detain, incarcerate • *He was jailed for 20 years.*

jailer *noun* = **guard**, keeper, warden

jam *noun* **1** = **mass**, crowd, crush, mob, throng, multitude • *There was quite a traffic jam on the highway.*
2 = **predicament**, hole (*slang*), fix (*informal*), trouble, plight, dilemma, quandary • *We're in a real jam now.*
▶ *verb* **3** = **cram**, force, stuff, ram • *She jammed on the brakes.*
4 = **stick**, stall • *The paper has jammed in the photocopier again.*
5 = **crowd**, crush, throng
See also: **mess**

jamboree *noun* = **festival**, celebration, festivity, spree, carnival, revelry, fête

jangle *verb* = **rattle**, clash, chime, vibrate, jingle, clank, clatter

janitor *noun* = **caretaker**, concierge, custodian, porter, doorkeeper

jar¹ *noun* = **pot**, pitcher, container, vase, jug, urn, crock

jar² *verb* **1** = **jolt**, rock, shake, bump, rattle, vibrate, convulse
2 = **irritate**, offend, irk, annoy, grate, get on one's nerves (*informal*), nettle
▶ *noun* **3** = **jolt**, shock, bump, vibration, convulsion

jargon *noun* = **parlance**, usage, argot, idiom

jaundiced *adjective* **1** = **cynical**, skeptical
2 = **bitter**, suspicious, hostile, jealous, envious, resentful, spiteful

jaunt *noun* = **outing**, trip, tour, expedition, stroll, airing, excursion, ramble

jaunty *adjective* = **sprightly**, lively, buoyant, carefree, perky, high-spirited, self-confident, sparky

jaw *verb* = **talk**, chat, gossip, chatter, spout, chew the fat (*slang*)

jaws *plural noun* = **opening**, mouth, entrance

jazz *noun*
▶ *verb*
▷ **jazz up** = **enliven**, improve, enhance, animate

jazzy *adjective* = **flashy**, fancy, gaudy, snazzy (*informal*)

jealous *adjective* **1** = **envious**, resentful • *He was jealous of my success.*
2 = **wary**, suspicious, protective, vigilant, watchful, mistrustful

jealousy *noun* = **envy**, suspicion, spite, resentment, mistrust, covetousness, possessiveness

jeans *plural noun* = **denims**, Levis (*trademark*)

jeer *verb* **1** = **scoff**, mock, taunt, barrack, heckle, ridicule, deride, gibe
▶ *noun* **2** = **taunt**, abuse, boo, ridicule, derision, catcall, gibe

jeering See **mockery**

jell *verb* **1** = **solidify**, set, thicken, harden, congeal
2 = **take shape**, materialize, crystallize, come together

jeopardize *verb* = **endanger**, risk, chance, stake, expose, gamble, venture, imperil

jeopardy *noun* = **danger**, risk, peril, vulnerability, insecurity

jerk *verb, noun* = **tug**, pull, jolt, yank, thrust, wrench, lurch, twitch

jerky *adjective* = **bumpy**, shaky, jumpy, twitchy, convulsive, jolting, spasmodic

jerry-built *adjective* = **ramshackle**, cheap, defective, shabby, flimsy, rickety, slipshod, thrown together

jest *noun* **1** = **joke**, crack (*slang*), prank, quip, wisecrack (*informal*), bon mot, jape, pleasantry, witticism
▶ *verb* **2** = **joke**, kid (*informal*), mock, quip, tease

jester *noun* = **clown**, fool, harlequin, buffoon

jet[1] *adjective* = **black**, raven, inky, coal-black, ebony, pitch-black, sable

jet[2] *noun* **1** = **stream**, spring, flow, spray, fountain, gush, spout
2 = **sprayer**, sprinkler, nozzle, atomizer
▶ *verb* **3** = **fly**, soar, zoom

jettison *verb* = **discard**, dump, abandon, scrap, expel, eject, unload, throw overboard

jetty *noun* = **pier**, dock, mole, wharf, breakwater, groyne, quay

jewel *noun* **1** = **gemstone**, rock (*slang*), ornament, sparkler (*informal*)
2 = **treasure**, find, gem, collector's item, wonder, pearl, rarity

jewellery *noun* = **jewels**, treasure, regalia, finery, gems, ornaments, trinkets

jib *verb* = **refuse**, retreat, shrink, balk, recoil, stop short

jibe see **gibe**

jiffy *noun* (*Slang*) = **instant**, second, flash, heartbeat (*informal*), blink of an eye (*informal*), two shakes of a lamb's tail (*slang*)

jig *verb* = **skip**, bounce, bob, caper, wiggle, prance

jiggle See **fidget**

jilt See **abandon**

jingle *noun* **1** = **rattle**, clang, ringing, clink, reverberation, tinkle
2 = **song**, tune, chorus, melody, ditty
▶ *verb* **3** = **ring**, rattle, chime, clatter, clink, jangle, tinkle

jinx *noun* **1** = **curse**, nemesis, hex (*informal*), evil eye (*informal*), hoodoo (*informal*)
▶ *verb* **2** = **curse**, hex (*informal*), bewitch

jitters *plural noun* = **nerves**, anxiety, nervousness, butterflies *or* butterflies in one's stomach (*informal*), cold feet (*informal*), fidgets, the shakes (*informal*)

jittery *adjective* = **nervous**, shaky, anxious, fidgety, jumpy, twitchy (*informal*), agitated, trembling, wired (*slang*)

job *noun* **1** = **occupation**, post, trade, position, employment, profession • *I'm still looking for a job.*
2 = **duty**, concern, role, responsibility, function, task • *It's your job to find out what's going on.*
See also: **appointment, undertaking, work**

jobless *adjective* = **unemployed**, idle, inactive, unoccupied, out of work

jocular *adjective* = **humorous**, funny, amusing, playful, jovial, droll, facetious, joking, sportive, teasing, waggish

jog *verb* **1** = **nudge**, push, shake, stir, prod

2 = run, trot, canter, lope
▷ **jog someone's memory** *See* **remind**

John Doe *noun* (*Informal*) = **man in the street**, average guy, average person, know-nothing (*slang*)

joie de vivre *noun* = **enthusiasm**, relish, enjoyment, zest, gusto, ebullience

join *verb* **1 = enrol**, enlist, sign up • *He joined the team last year.*
OPPOSITE: resign
2 = connect, link, couple, tie, attach, fasten • *two sticks joined together by a chain*
OPPOSITE: separate
▷ **join forces = co-operate**, unite, team up
▷ **join in** *See* **participate, take part in**
See also: **piece together, unite**

joint *adjective* **1 = shared**, collective, combined, mutual, communal, cooperative, joined, united
▶ *noun* **2 = junction**, connection, intersection, hinge, node, nexus
▶ *verb* **3 = divide**, segment, carve, sever, dissect, cut up

jointly *adverb* = **collectively**, together, mutually, as one, in common, in conjunction, in league, in partnership

joke *noun* **1 = jest**, gag (*informal*), prank, quip, wisecrack, lark, witticism • *I heard a great joke today.*
2 = laughing stock, clown, buffoon
▶ *verb* **3 = jest**, kid (*informal*), quip, tease, banter, chaff • *She was always joking about her friends.*

joker *noun* = **comedian**, comic, clown, wit, prankster, buffoon, wag, trickster, humorist, jester

jolly *adjective* = **happy**, upbeat (*informal*), merry, playful, cheerful, genial, jovial, chirpy (*informal*), sprightly

jolt *noun* **1 = jerk**, start, jump, shake, bump, jar, jog, lurch
2 = surprise, blow, shock, setback, bombshell, bolt from the blue
▶ *verb* **3 = jerk**, push, knock,

shake, shove, jar, jog, jostle
4 = surprise, stun, disturb, stagger, startle, discompose, perturb

jostle *verb* = **push**, shake, bump, elbow, jolt, shove, jog, hustle

jot *verb* **1 = note down**, record, list, scribble
▶ *noun* **2 = bit**, grain, scrap, fraction, speck, morsel

jotting *See* **note**

journal *noun* **1 = newspaper**, magazine, daily, weekly, monthly, periodical, gazette
2 = diary, record, blog (*informal*), log, chronicle, weblog

journalist *noun* = **reporter**, broadcaster, columnist, commentator, correspondent, hack, newsman *or* newswoman, pressman

journey *noun* **1 = trip**, tour, expedition, trek, voyage, excursion • *the journey across the continent*
▶ *verb* **2 = travel**, go, tour, proceed, trek, voyage • *Last year, she journeyed through South America.*
See also: **drive**

jovial *adjective* = **cheerful**, happy, animated, merry, jolly, cheery, convivial, mirthful

joy *noun* = **delight**, ecstasy, bliss, elation, rapture • *Her face shone with joy.*
OPPOSITE: misery
See also: **happiness, pleasure**

joyful *adjective* = **delighted**, jubilant, elated, over the moon (*informal*) • *a joyful smile*
See also: **glad**

joyless *adjective* = **unhappy**, sad, dismal, depressed, gloomy, miserable, dreary, cheerless

joyous *adjective* = **joyful**, merry, festive, rapturous

jubilant *adjective* = **overjoyed**, triumphant, exuberant, euphoric, elated, enraptured, exultant, thrilled

jubilation *noun* = **joy**, celebration, triumph, excitement, festivity, ecstasy, elation, exultation

jubilee *noun* = **celebration**, holiday, festival, festivity

judge noun **1 = justice** • *The judge sentenced her to three years in prison.*
RELATED WORD
adjective: judicial
2 = referee, umpire • *A panel of judges are selecting the finalists.*
3 = critic, expert, authority, arbiter, connoisseur, assessor
▶ *verb* **4 = consider**, rate, estimate, assess, evaluate, appraise • *Don't judge people by their looks.*
5 = referee, umpire • *Entrants will be judged in two categories.*
See also: **conclude, feel, reckon, regard, think, view**

judgment noun **1 = opinion**, view, ruling, verdict, assessment, conclusion, appraisal • *It's hard to form a judgment without all the facts.*
2 = sense, understanding, discrimination, wisdom, prudence, acumen, discernment, shrewdness
3 = verdict, decision, sentence, ruling, finding, arbitration, decree
See also: **belief, common sense, reason**

judicial *adjective* **= legal**, official
judiciary *See* **legal**
judicious *adjective* **= sensible**, careful, wise, prudent, thoughtful, shrewd, enlightened, astute, discriminating, well-judged

jug noun **= container**, pitcher, vessel, jar, urn, crock, carafe, ewer

juggle *verb* **= manipulate**, change, modify, alter, manoeuvre

juice noun **= liquid**, liquor, extract, fluid, sap, nectar

juicy *adjective* **1 = moist**, lush, succulent
2 = interesting, sensational, provocative, vivid, colourful, spicy (*informal*), racy, suggestive, risqué

jumble noun **1 = muddle**, disorder, mess, confusion, mixture, disarray, clutter, mishmash

▶ *verb* **2 = mix**, mistake, disorder, confuse, shuffle, muddle, disorganize

jumbled *See* **garbled, untidy**

jumbo *adjective* **= giant**, large, huge, immense, gigantic, oversized, supersize

jump *verb* **1 = leap**, clear, spring, hurdle, vault, bound • *I jumped over the fence.*
2 = increase, rise, surge, escalate • *Sales jumped by 25 per cent last year.*
3 = recoil, start, jerk, flinch, wince
4 = miss, avoid, skip, evade, omit
▶ *noun* **5 = leap**, vault, bound • *the longest-ever jump by a human being*
6 = interruption, break, space, gap, hiatus, lacuna
7 = rise, increase, advance, upsurge, increment, upturn
See also: **bounce, dive**

> INFORMALLY SPEAKING
> **have the jump on**: have the advantage over
> **jump at**: accept eagerly
> **jump out of your skin**: be very startled
> **jump the gun**: start doing something too soon

jumped-up *adjective* **= conceited**, arrogant, pompous, presumptuous, insolent, overbearing

jumpy *adjective* **= nervous**, anxious, tense, jittery (*informal*), restless, apprehensive, fidgety, agitated, on edge, wired (*slang*)

junction noun **1 = connection**, union, coupling, linking
2 = intersection, crossing, underpass, crossroads, overpass

juncture noun **= moment**, time, point, occasion

junior *adjective* **= inferior**, lower, lesser, subordinate • *a junior counsellor*
OPPOSITE: senior
See also: **young**

junk noun **= garbage**, refuse, scrap, trash, clutter, rubbish, odds and ends • *What are you going to do with all that junk?*

jurisdiction *noun* **1** = **authority**, power, rule, control, influence, command
2 = **range**, province, area, field, scope, compass, sphere, bounds
just *adverb* **1** = **exactly**, completely, absolutely, entirely, perfectly, precisely
2 = **recently**, hardly, lately, scarcely, only now
3 = **merely**, only, simply, solely, by the skin of one's teeth
▷ **just about** *See* **nearly**
▶ *adjective* **4** = **fair**, good, honest, upright, equitable, conscientious, fair-minded, virtuous
5 = **proper**, due, appropriate, fitting, apt, justified, rightful, deserved, merited
justice *noun* **1** = **fairness**, equity, impartiality • *We want freedom, justice, and equality.*
OPPOSITE: injustice
2 = **judge** • *his appointment as a justice of the Supreme Court*
See also: **right**
justifiable *adjective* = **reasonable**, legitimate, acceptable, valid, sensible, understandable, defensible, excusable, warrantable
justification *noun*
1 = **explanation**, excuse, defence, vindication, rationalization
2 = **reason**, basis, warrant, grounds, reasonable cause *or* probable cause
justify *verb* = **defend**, explain, warrant, excuse, vindicate • *How can you justify what you've done?*
See also: **deserve**
justly *adverb* = **properly**, fairly, correctly, lawfully, equitably
jut *verb* = **stick out**, project, extend, poke, bulge, protrude, overhang
jutting *See* **prominent**
juvenile *adjective* **1** = **young**, youthful, inexperienced, childish, immature, babyish, callow, infantile, puerile
▶ *noun* **2** = **child**, girl, boy, youth, infant, minor, adolescent
juxtapose *See* **compare**
juxtaposition *noun* = **proximity**, contact, vicinity, closeness, adjacency, nearness, propinquity

j

Kk

kamikaze adjective = **self-destructive**, suicidal, foolhardy

keel verb
▷ **keel over** = **collapse**, faint, black out (informal), pass out

keen adjective 1 = **eager**, into (informal), enthusiastic, avid, ardent, fond of • a keen amateur photographer
2 = **perceptive**, quick, brilliant, shrewd, astute • a keen intellect
3 = **sharp**, cutting, incisive, razor-like
See also: **acute, fierce, fine, ready**

keenness noun = **eagerness**, passion, intensity, enthusiasm, zest, zeal, ardour, fervour

keep verb 1 = **care for**, maintain, preserve • I'd like to keep horses.
2 = **store**, hold, deposit • He keeps his money under the mattress.
3 = **carry out**, honour, fulfil • I always keep my promises.
4 = **retain**, hold, control, maintain, preserve, possess, conserve
5 = **support**, maintain, feed, sustain, subsidize, provide for
6 = **detain**, prevent, delay, hinder, restrain, obstruct, hold back, keep back
▷ **keep an eye on** See **mind, supervise**
▷ **keep on** See **continue**
▷ **keep out** See **exclude**
▷ **keep safe** See **save**
▷ **keep up** = **maintain**, continue, preserve, sustain, keep pace
▷ **keep your eyes open** See **watch out**
▶ noun 7 = **board**, food, living, maintenance
8 = **tower**, castle

See also: **breed, have, own, reserve, save, upkeep**

keeper noun = **guardian**, guard, curator, attendant, caretaker, warden, preserver, steward, janitor, custodian, groundskeeper

keeping noun = **care**, charge, protection, custody, possession, safekeeping, guardianship
▷ **in keeping with** = **in agreement with**, in accord with, in balance with, in compliance with, in conformity with, in correspondence with, in harmony with, in observance with

keepsake noun = **souvenir**, symbol, reminder, relic, token, memento

keg noun = **barrel**, drum, cask, vat

kernel noun = **essence**, core, substance, germ, gist, nub, pith

key noun 1 = **opener**, latchkey
2 = **answer**, solution, explanation
▶ adjective 3 = **essential**, major, important, main, crucial, principal, decisive, fundamental, pivotal, cutting-edge, leading
▶ verb
▷ **key in** = **type**, enter, input, keyboard

keynote noun = **heart**, core, substance, theme, centre, essence, gist

kick verb 1 = **boot**, punt

2 (*Informal*) = **give up**, stop, quit, abandon, desist from, leave off

▷ **kick off = begin**, start, open, initiate, commence, get the show on the road

▷ **kick out = dismiss**, remove, sack (*informal*), axe, expel, eject, evict, get rid of

▷ **kick up a fuss** *See* **complain**

▶ *noun* **3** (*Informal*) = **thrill**, buzz (*slang*), pleasure, stimulation

kid¹ *noun* (*Informal*) = **child**, baby, youth, infant, teenager, minor, youngster, tot

kid² *verb* = **tease**, joke, trick, fool, pretend, hoax, jest, delude

kidnap *verb* = **abduct**, capture, seize • *Four tourists have been kidnapped by rebels.*

kill *verb* **1** = **slay**, murder, destroy, execute, slaughter, massacre, assassinate, butcher, exterminate • *The earthquake killed 62 people.*

2 = **suppress**, stop, halt, quash, stifle, quell, smother, scotch, extinguish

See also: **put down**

killer *noun* = **murderer**, gunman, assassin, butcher, executioner, exterminator, cut-throat, hit man (*slang*), slayer

killing *noun* **1** = **murder**, homicide, slaughter, massacre, manslaughter, slaying, carnage, bloodshed, extermination

2 (*Informal*) = **profit**, gain, success, cleanup (*informal*), coup, windfall, bonanza

killjoy *noun* = **spoilsport**, grinch (*informal*), dampener, wet blanket (*informal*), buzzkill (*slang*)

kin *noun* = **family**, people, relations, relatives • *"Next of kin" means the person most closely related to you.*

See also: **relation**

kind¹ *noun* = **type**, class, brand, sort, category, variety, species, grade, breed, genre, classification • *I don't like that kind of movie.*

See also: **breed, class, family, form, sort, type, variety**

kind² *adjective* = **considerate**, good, charitable, benign, thoughtful, compassionate, humane, kindly, unselfish, benevolent, kind-hearted • *Thank you for being so kind to me.*

OPPOSITE: cruel

See also: **accommodating, generous, gentle, helpful, merciful, tender**

kind-hearted *adjective* = **sympathetic**, kind, helpful, generous, compassionate, humane, considerate, good-natured, altruistic, tender-hearted

kindle *verb* **1** = **set fire to**, light, ignite, inflame

2 = **arouse**, inspire, provoke, stir, stimulate, induce, awaken, rouse

kindliness *noun* = **kindness**, charity, humanity, compassion, friendliness, amiability, benevolence, gentleness, kind-heartedness

kindly *adjective* **1** = **benevolent**, kind, warm, helpful, benign, pleasant, sympathetic, compassionate, good-natured

▶ *adverb* **2** = **benevolently**, politely, graciously, thoughtfully, cordially, agreeably, tenderly

kindness *noun* = **benevolence**, charity, humanity, compassion, gentleness • *Everyone has treated me with great kindness.*

OPPOSITE: cruelty

See also: **consideration, favour, generosity, mercy, pity**

kindred *adjective* **1** = **similar**, like, related, akin, corresponding, matching

▶ *noun* **2** = **family**, kin, kinsfolk, relations, relatives

king *noun* = **monarch**, sovereign • *the next king of England*

RELATED WORDS

adjectives: royal, regal, monarchical

k

kingdom noun = **country**, state, nation, territory, realm

kink noun **1** = **twist**, bend, wrinkle, coil
2 = **quirk**, whim, foible, fetish, vagary, eccentricity, idiosyncrasy

kinky adjective **1** (Slang) = **weird**, odd, strange, quirky, eccentric, peculiar, outlandish, queer
2 = **twisted**, tangled, coiled, curled

kinship noun **1** = **relationship**, kin, consanguinity, ties of blood
2 = **similarity**, connection, relationship, association, correspondence, affinity

kinsman See **relation**

kinswoman See **relation**

kiosk noun = **booth**, stand, stall, counter, newsstand, bookstall

kiss verb **1** = **osculate**, neck (informal), peck (informal)
2 = **brush**, touch, glance, scrape, graze
▷ noun **3** = **osculation**, peck (informal), smooch (slang), smacker (slang)

kit noun = **equipment**, tackle, gear, apparatus, paraphernalia, tools, fit-out (Canad Nfld)

kitty See **cat**

knack noun = **skill**, facility, ability, gift, capacity, trick, talent, expertise, propensity, aptitude

knave noun = **rogue**, rascal, villain, scoundrel

knead verb = **squeeze**, work, form, press, shape, manipulate, massage, rub, mould

kneel verb = **genuflect**, stoop, get on one's knees or get down on one's knees

knell noun = **ringing**, sound, toll, chime, peal

knick-knack noun = **trinket**, plaything, trifle, bauble, bagatelle, bric-a-brac

knife noun **1** = **blade**, cutter
▷ verb **2** = **cut**, wound, stab, slash, pierce, lacerate

knit verb **1** = **join**, link, tie, bind, unite, weave, intertwine, fasten
2 = **wrinkle**, knot, crease, pucker, furrow

▷ **knit your brows** See **frown**

knob noun = **lump**, bump, knot, projection, stud, hump, protrusion

knock verb **1** = **hit**, strike, punch, belt (informal), rap, thump, smack, cuff
2 (Informal) = **criticize**, abuse, condemn, censure, disparage, denigrate, belittle, deprecate, find fault, run down
▷ **knock around** = **hit**, strike, abuse, batter, maul, mistreat, manhandle, maltreat, beat up (informal)
▷ **knock down** = **demolish**, level, destroy, raze, fell
▷ **knock out** See **eliminate**
▷ **knock over** See **overturn**, **upset**
▶ noun **3** = **blow**, clip, slap, rap, thump, smack, cuff, clout (informal)
4 = **setback**, defeat, failure, rejection, rebuff, reversal

knockabout adjective = **boisterous**, farcical, slapstick, riotous, rollicking

knockout noun **1** = **killer blow**, KO or K.O. (slang), coup de grâce (French)
2 = **success**, hit, winner, triumph, smash, sensation, smash hit

knot noun **1** = **connection**, tie, bond, joint, loop, ligature
2 = **cluster**, collection, bunch, clump
▶ verb **3** = **tie**, secure, bind, loop, tether

know verb **1** = **understand**, see, perceive, apprehend, comprehend, be aware of • I don't know a lot about cars.
2 = **be acquainted with**, recognize, be familiar with • I believe you know my brother.

INFORMALLY SPEAKING
in the know: aware of information few people have
know the ropes: understand what to do
know what's what: be well informed

know-how noun = **capability**,

ability, knowledge, skill, talent, expertise, knack, ingenuity, aptitude, savoir-faire

knowing *adjective* = **meaningful**, significant, expressive

knowingly *adverb* = **deliberately**, intentionally, purposely, consciously, wilfully, on purpose, wittingly

knowledge *noun* **1** = **learning**, education, wisdom, scholarship • *She had no knowledge of world history.*
2 = **acquaintance**, familiarity, intimacy, cognizance
See also: **command, experience, grasp, understanding**

knowledgeable *adjective*
1 = **well-informed**, aware, familiar, experienced, cognizant, *au fait (French)*, clued-up *(informal)*, conversant, in the know *(informal)*
2 = **intelligent**, scholarly, educated, erudite, learned

known *adjective* = **famous**, well-known, celebrated, noted, acknowledged, avowed, recognized

knuckle *noun*
▶ *verb*
▷ **knuckle under** = **give in**, submit, surrender, yield, succumb, acquiesce, accede, capitulate, cave in *(informal)*, give way

kudos *noun* = **credit**, praise, recognition, applause, acclaim, laudation, plaudits, props *(informal)*

Ll

label *noun* **1 = tag**, ticket, sticker
• *He checked the label on the bottle.*
  ▶ *verb* **2 = tag**, flag, sticker • *The
  shirt was labelled "Made in Canada."*
See also: **identify**
laborious *adjective* = **hard**, tough,
arduous, strenuous, onerous,
backbreaking, exhausting,
tiring, wearisome
labour *noun* **1 = work**, effort,
toil, exertion, industry • *the
labour involved in weeding and
digging*
  2 = workers, workforce,
  employees • *unskilled labour*
  3 = childbirth, delivery,
  parturition
  ▶ *verb* **4 = work**, slave, toil
  • *harvesters labouring in the fields*
  5 (usually with *under*) = **be
  disadvantaged**, suffer, be a
  victim of, be burdened by
  6 = overemphasize, strain,
  elaborate, overdo, dwell on
  OPPOSITE: relax
See also: **struggle**
laboured *adjective* = **forced**,
difficult, heavy, stiff, strained,
awkward
labourer *noun* = **worker**, hand,
blue-collar worker, drudge,
manual worker, roustabout
See also: **worker**
labyrinth *noun* = **maze**, jungle,
tangle, intricacy
lace *noun* **1 = netting**, filigree,
openwork
  2 = cord, tie, string, shoelace,
  bootlace
  ▶ *verb* **3 = fasten**, tie, bind,
  thread, do up
  4 = mix in, spike, fortify, add to
lacerate *verb* = **tear**, cut, wound,
slash, rip, claw, mangle, gash
laceration *noun* = **cut**, wound,
tear, slash, rent, rip, gash

lack *noun* **1 = shortage**, want
(*formal*), absence, deficiency,
scarcity • *a lack of funds*
OPPOSITE: abundance
  ▶ *verb* **2 = be short of**, miss,
  be deficient in • *She lacks
  confidence.*
lackadaisical *adjective*
  1 = lethargic, listless, dull,
  indifferent, apathetic, half-
  hearted, languid
  2 = lazy, idle, dreamy, abstracted,
  indolent, inert
lackey *noun* **1 = hanger-on**,
minion, brown-noser (*slang*),
flatterer, sycophant, toady, yes
man
  2 = manservant, attendant,
  valet, flunky, footman
lacking *adjective* = **deficient**,
missing, inadequate, minus
(*informal*), impaired, flawed,
wanting, needing, sans
(*archaic*)
lacklustre *adjective* = **dull**,
flat, muted, lifeless, drab,
uninspired, leaden, prosaic,
vapid
laconic *adjective* = **terse**, short,
brief, concise, succinct, curt,
monosyllabic, pithy
lad *noun* = **boy**, kid (*informal*),
guy (*informal*), youth, fellow,
youngster, juvenile
laden *adjective* = **loaded**,
full, charged, burdened,
encumbered, weighed down
lady *noun* **1 = gentlewoman**,
dame
  2 = woman, female
lady-killer *noun* (*Informal*)
= **womanizer**, rake, libertine,
Casanova, heartbreaker, Don
Juan, ladies' man, philanderer,
roué
ladylike *adjective* = **refined**,

modest, proper, sophisticated, elegant, polite, respectable, genteel, well-bred

lag verb = **fall behind**, trail • *He is now lagging a metre behind the champion.*

laggard noun = **straggler**, dawdler, idler, loiterer, snail, slowpoke (*informal*), sluggard

laid-back adjective = **relaxed**, casual, easy-going, unflappable (*informal*), unhurried, free and easy

lair noun = **nest**, hole, earth, den, burrow

laissez faire noun = **nonintervention**, free enterprise, free trade

lake noun = **pond**, basin, lagoon, pool, mere, reservoir, tarn

---

TYPES OF LAKE

lagoon	slough (*Canad*)
pond	tarn
reservoir	

---

lame adjective 1 = **limping** • *lame in one leg*
2 = **unconvincing**, poor, weak, pathetic, feeble, flimsy • *a lame excuse*

lament verb 1 = **grieve**, mourn, weep, wail • *She lamented the death of her friend.*
▶ noun 2 = **moan**, wail • *a lament for his vanished youth*
3 = **dirge**, requiem, elegy, threnody
See also: **regret**

lamentable adjective = **regrettable**, tragic, unfortunate, woeful, deplorable, mournful, grievous, distressing

lampoon noun 1 = **satire**, caricature, parody, burlesque, takeoff (*informal*), spoof (*informal*), piss-take (*informal*)
▶ verb 2 = **ridicule**, mock, caricature, parody, satirize, make fun of

lance See **pierce**

land noun 1 = **property**, estate, grounds • *a dispute over land*
2 = **country**, province, region, nation, territory • *the land of opportunity*
3 = **ground**, earth, dry land, terra firma
4 = **soil**, ground, dirt, loam
5 = **countryside**, farmland
▶ verb 6 = **arrive**, dock, alight, touch down • *We landed in New York at noon.*
7 = **end up**, turn up, wind up
8 (*Informal*) = **obtain**, win, get, gain, acquire, secure
See also: **state**

landlord noun 1 = **innkeeper**, host, hotelier
2 = **owner**, proprietor, freeholder, lessor

landmark noun 1 = **feature**, monument
2 = **milestone**, watershed, turning point

landscape noun = **scenery**, view, scene, prospect, outlook, countryside, vista, panorama

landslide noun 1 = **rockfall**, avalanche, mudslide, landslip
▶ adjective 2 = **overwhelming**, decisive, runaway, conclusive

lane noun = **road**, way, street, path, alley, pathway, passageway, footpath

language noun 1 = **tongue**, dialect, vocabulary, lingo (*informal*), jargon, vernacular, idiom • *She speaks four languages.*
2 = **style**, wording, phrasing • *He explained the process in plain language.*

languid adjective 1 = **lazy**, listless, indifferent, lackadaisical, languorous, unenthusiastic
2 = **lethargic**, heavy, sluggish, dull, torpid

languish verb 1 = **decline**, fail, flag, weaken, fade, faint, wither, wilt, droop
2 (often with *for*) = **pine**, long, desire, hunger, yearn, hanker

3 = **waste away**, suffer, rot, be abandoned, be neglected

lank *adjective* **1** = **limp**, lifeless, straggling
2 = **thin**, lean, slim, spare, skinny, slender, gaunt, scrawny, emaciated

lanky *adjective* = **gangling**, tall, spare, gaunt, bony, angular, rangy

lap[1] *noun* = **circuit**, tour, circle, orbit, loop

lap[2] *verb* **1** = **ripple**, wash, splash, swish, gurgle, plash, purl
2 = **drink**, lick, sip, sup

lapse *noun* **1** = **mistake**, slip, error, fault, negligence, oversight, omission, failing, indiscretion
2 = **interval**, break, gap, pause, intermission, interruption, lull, breathing space
3 = **decline**, fall, drop, deterioration
▶ *verb* **4** = **decline**, fall, drop, slip, sink, slide, deteriorate, degenerate
5 = **end**, stop, expire, terminate, run out

lapsed *adjective* = **expired**, finished, invalid, discontinued, ended, out of date, run out

large *adjective* = **big**, great, huge, giant, massive, vast, enormous, immense, gigantic, colossal • *a large room*
OPPOSITE: small
▷ **at large** = **free**, at liberty, on the loose, on the run, unconfined; = **in general**, generally, mainly, chiefly, as a whole, in the main; = **at length**, greatly, exhaustively, in full detail
▷ **large numbers** See **many**
See also: **broad, extensive, spacious**

largely *adverb* = **mainly**, mostly, generally, primarily, predominantly, principally, chiefly, as a rule, by and large, to a great extent

large-scale *adjective* = **wide-ranging**, global, wide, broad, extensive, vast, wholesale, far-reaching, sweeping

lark *noun* = **prank**, game, fun, mischief, escapade, caper, jape
▶ *verb*
▷ **lark about** = **play**, caper, cavort, have fun, make mischief

lash[1] *noun* **1** = **blow**, hit, stroke, swipe (*informal*), stripe
▶ *verb* **2** = **whip**, beat, scourge, thrash, flog, birch
3 = **pound**, strike, beat, hammer, smack, dash, drum, buffet
4 = **criticize**, attack, blast, censure, scold, put down, upbraid

lash[2] *verb* = **fasten**, tie, secure, bind, strap, make fast

lass *noun* = **girl**, damsel, maiden, maid, young woman

last[1] *adjective* **1** = **most recent**, previous, latest, preceding • *last year*
OPPOSITE: first
2 = **final**, ultimate, closing, concluding • *the last three chapters of the book*
OPPOSITE: first
3 = **hindmost**, at the end, rearmost
See also: **remainder**

> **INFORMALLY SPEAKING**
> **at last**: after a long or seemingly long time
> **breathe your last**: die
> **see the last of**: not see ever again

last[2] *verb* = **continue**, remain, survive, endure, persist • *The movie lasted for two and a half hours.*
See also: **stretch, ultimate**

lasting *adjective* = **continuing**, long-term, permanent, long-standing, perennial, durable, enduring, abiding

lastly See **finally**

last-minute See **late**

latch *noun* **1** = **fastening**, catch, bar, lock, hook, bolt, hasp
▶ *verb* **2** = **fasten**, bar, secure, bolt, make fast

late *adjective* **1** = **overdue**, behind, last-minute, delayed, belated, behind schedule • *The train was late.*

OPPOSITE: early

2 = dead, deceased, departed • *my late husband*

3 = recent, new, fresh, modern, advanced

▶ *adverb* **4 = belatedly**, at the last minute, behindhand, behind time, dilatorily, tardily

lately *adverb* = **recently**, in recent times, just now, latterly, not long ago, of late

lateness *noun* = **delay**, tardiness, belatedness

latent *adjective* = **hidden**, potential, invisible, dormant, undeveloped, unrealized, concealed

later *adverb* = **afterwards**, after, subsequently, thereafter, by and by, in a while, in time, later on

lateral *adjective* = **sideways**, edgeways, flanking

latest *adjective* = **up-to-date**, current, cool (*informal*), modern, fashionable, up-to-the-minute, most recent, newest, phat (*slang*)

lather *noun* **1 = froth**, foam, suds, bubbles, soapsuds

▶ *verb* **2 = froth**, foam, soap

latitude *noun* = **scope**, play, freedom, license, liberty, leeway, elbowroom, laxity

latter *adjective* = **last-mentioned**, last, second, closing, concluding

latterly *adverb* = **recently**, lately, of late

lattice *noun* = **grid**, grating, grille, trellis

laudable *adjective* = **praiseworthy**, excellent, worthy, admirable, commendable, meritorious, creditable, of note

laugh *verb* **1 = chuckle**, guffaw, giggle, chortle, snigger, titter, be in stitches, split one's sides • *You never laugh at my jokes.*

▷ **laugh at** *See* **make fun of, mock**

▷ **laugh off = disregard**, dismiss, ignore, minimize, pooh-pooh, brush aside, shrug off

▶ *noun* **2 = chuckle**, guffaw, giggle, chortle, snigger, titter • *She has a very infectious laugh.*

3 (*Informal*) **= joke**, scream (*informal*), hoot (*informal*), lark

> **INFORMALLY SPEAKING**
> **laugh at**: make fun of
> **laugh off**: dismiss with a
> laugh

laughable *adjective* = **ridiculous**, absurd, ludicrous, preposterous, farcical, nonsensical, derisory, risible

laughing stock *noun* = **figure of fun**, target, victim, butt

laughter *noun* = **amusement**, glee, merriment, hilarity, mirth

launch *verb* **1 = propel**, fire, project, dispatch, discharge, send off, set in motion

2 = begin, start, open, introduce, initiate, commence, inaugurate, instigate, embark upon

launder *See* **wash**

laundered *See* **clean**

laurels *plural noun* = **glory**, credit, praise, recognition, fame, honour, distinction, kudos, prestige, renown

lavatory *noun* = **washroom**, bathroom, loo, latrine, toilet, convenience *or* public convenience, restroom, powder room, water closet, W.C., commode

lavish *adjective* **1 = plentiful**, prolific, abundant, copious, profuse

2 = generous, liberal, free, bountiful, munificent, open-handed, unstinting

3 = extravagant, wild, excessive, exaggerated, wasteful, unrestrained, immoderate, prodigal

▶ *verb* **4 = spend**, waste, pour, shower, squander, heap, deluge, dissipate, expend

law *noun* **1 = constitution**, code, charter • *The sale of lottery tickets to minors is against the law.*

RELATED WORDS
adjectives: legal, judicial

2 = rule, act, regulation, code,

bylaw, decree, statute • *He was charged under the anti-stalking law.*
3 = **principle**, canon, axiom, precept

law-abiding *adjective* = **obedient**, good, honest, lawful, orderly, compliant, honourable, dutiful, peaceable

law-breaker *noun* = **criminal**, convict, offender, culprit, villain, crook (*informal*), delinquent, wrongdoer, felon, miscreant, perp (*informal*)

law court *See* **court**

lawful *adjective* = **legal**, constitutional, legitimate, valid, authorized, rightful, permissible, legalized, licit, warranted

lawless *adjective* = **disorderly**, wild, chaotic, unruly, rebellious, anarchic, riotous

lawlessness *noun* = **disorder**, chaos, anarchy, mob rule

lawsuit *noun* = **case**, trial, action, dispute, suit, prosecution, litigation, industrial tribunal, proceedings

lawyer *noun* = **legal adviser**, advocate, attorney, counsel, solicitor, barrister and solicitor (*Canad*) • *I'm discussing the matter with my lawyer.*

lax *adjective* = **slack**, casual, negligent, careless, lenient, remiss, overindulgent, slapdash, slipshod

lay¹ *verb* **1** = **place**, set, put, spread, set down • *Lay a sheet of newspaper on the floor.*
2 = **arrange**, set out • *to lay the carpet*
3 = **produce**, bear, deposit
4 = **put forward**, offer, advance, present, submit, lodge, bring forward
5 = **attribute**, assign, allocate, allot, ascribe, impute
6 = **devise**, plan, prepare, design, plot, hatch, concoct, contrive, work out
7 = **bet**, risk, stake, gamble, hazard, give odds, wager
▷ **lay off** = **dismiss**, discharge, let go, pay off

▷ **lay on** = **provide**, give, supply, cater or cater for, furnish, purvey

▷ **lay out** = **arrange**, plan, design, display, exhibit, spread out; (*informal*) = **spend**, pay, invest, expend, disburse, fork out (*slang*), shell out (*informal*); (*informal*) = **knock out**, KO or K.O. (*slang*), knock for six (*informal*), knock unconscious

> **INFORMALLY SPEAKING**
> **lay away**: put away for future use
> **lay in**: put aside for an emergency
> **lay it on thick**: flatter or exaggerate
> **lay off**: give up something or stop doing something
> **lay on**: supply with something
> **lay yourself out**: make a big effort

lay² *adjective* **1** = **nonclerical**, secular
2 = **nonspecialist**, amateur, inexpert, nonprofessional

layabout *noun* = **idler**, loafer, couch potato (*slang*), good-for-nothing, lounger, wastrel

layer *noun* **1** = **covering**, film, sheet, coat, blanket, coating • *A fresh layer of snow covered the street.*
2 = **tier**, row, seam, thickness, stratum • *the layers of rock on the canyon wall*

layman *noun* = **amateur**, outsider, lay person, nonprofessional

layoff *noun* = **unemployment**, discharge, dismissal

layout *noun* = **arrangement**, plan, design, format • *the layout of the pages*
See also: **form**

laze *verb* = **idle**, lounge, loaf • *We spent a few days lazing around by the pool.*
OPPOSITE: work
See also: **relax, rest**

laziness *noun* = **idleness**, inactivity, sluggishness, sloth, indolence, slackness

lazy *adjective* **1** = **idle**, slack • *a lazy and incompetent employee*

2 = lethargic, sluggish, drowsy, sleepy, slow-moving, languid, languorous, somnolent, torpid
OPPOSITE: industrious

leach verb = **extract**, strain, drain, filter, seep, percolate

lead verb **1 = guide**, conduct, steer, escort, usher • She led him into the house.
2 = command, head, manage, direct, govern, supervise • Lester B. Pearson led the country between 1963 and 1968.
3 = persuade, cause, draw, prompt, influence, prevail, dispose, induce, incline
4 = come first, surpass, exceed, excel, outstrip, outdo, transcend, be ahead or be ahead of, blaze a trail
5 = live, have, spend, pass, experience, undergo
▷ **lead on = entice**, lure, deceive, tempt, seduce, beguile, draw on, string along (informal)
▷ **lead to = cause**, produce, contribute to • A proper diet can lead to better health.
See also: **create, result in**
▷ **lead up to = introduce**, pave the way, prepare for
▶ noun **6 = clue**, trace, indication • The police are following up several leads.
7 = first place, priority, supremacy, precedence, vanguard, primacy
8 = advantage, start, edge, margin
9 = example, leadership, model, direction, guidance
10 = leading role, principal, protagonist, title role
▶ adjective **11 = main**, first, head, chief, prime, premier, primary, principal, foremost, cutting-edge, leading
See also: **bring, drive, motivate, rule, take, top**

| INFORMALLY SPEAKING
| **lead nowhere**: have no effect
| **lead off**: begin or start
| **lead on**: influence; deceive
| **lead up to**: prepare the way for

leaden See **cloudy, dull**

leader noun = **head**, director, chief, captain, commander, boss (informal), principal, ringleader, point-man • the leader of the New Democratic Party
OPPOSITE: follower
See also: **ruler**

leadership noun **1 = guidance**, management, direction, domination, running, superintendency
2 = authority, control, influence, initiative, command, supremacy, pre-eminence

leading adjective = **main**, top, major, chief, key, prominent, principal, eminent • a leading industrial nation
See also: **first, foremost, important, in front, prime, supreme**

leaf noun **1 = frond**, blade
2 = page, sheet, folio
▷ verb
▷ **leaf through = browse**, flip, thumb or thumb through, glance, skim, riffle

leaflet noun = **booklet**, flyer, brochure, circular, pamphlet • Protesters were handing out leaflets in the street.

leafy adjective = **green**, shady, shaded, verdant, bosky (literary)

league noun **1 = association**, group, union, coalition, alliance, partnership, federation, consortium, guild, fraternity, confederation
2 = class, level, category

leak verb **1 = escape**, spill, seep, ooze • The gas had leaked.
2 = disclose, tell, reveal, divulge, give away, let slip, make known, make public, pass on
▶ noun **3 = hole**, crack, puncture, fissure • Have you plugged the leaks?
4 = drip, leakage, seepage, percolation
5 = disclosure, divulgence

leaky adjective = **leaking**, split, porous, perforated, cracked, holey, punctured

lean[1] verb **1 = rest**, prop, recline, repose, be supported

2 = bend, tip, heel, slope, tilt, incline, slant
3 = tend, prefer, favor, be disposed to, be prone to
▷ **lean on = depend on**, trust, count on, have faith in, rely on

lean² adjective **1 = thin**, slim, spare, skinny, slender, gaunt, bony, angular, rangy, wiry
2 = unproductive, poor, barren, meager, scanty, unfruitful

leaning noun **= tendency**, bias, bent, penchant, disposition, inclination, propensity, predilection, partiality, proclivity

leap verb **1 = jump**, spring, bounce, vault, bound • *The deer leaped into the air.*
▶ noun **2 = jump**, spring, bound • *a leap of 2.37 m.*
3 = increase, rise, surge, escalation, upswing, upsurge
See also: **dive**

learn verb **1 = master**, grasp, pick up • *I am trying to learn Spanish.*
2 = discover, hear, determine, understand, gather, ascertain, find out • *On learning who she was, I asked to meet her.*
See also: **find, study**

| CONFUSABLES
Learn means *come to know.*
Teach means *instruct.*

learned adjective **= scholarly**, academic, intellectual, literate, erudite • *a very learned person*
See also: **educated**

learner noun **= beginner**, apprentice, novice, neophyte, tyro

learning noun **= knowledge**, study, information, culture, education, wisdom, scholarship, lore, erudition

lease verb **= rent** • *She leases her house for the summer.*

leash noun **= lead**, rein, tether

least adjective **= smallest**, minimum, fewest, lowest, slightest • *Stick to foods with the least fat.*
OPPOSITE: most
▷ **least possible** See **minimum**

leathery adjective **= tough**, hard, rough

leave¹ verb **1 = depart**, go, quit, withdraw, abandon, desert, forsake, bail on (slang) • *He is not allowed to leave the country.*
2 = forget, leave behind, mislay
3 = cause, produce, generate, deposit, result in
4 = give up, drop, abandon, surrender, renounce, relinquish
5 = entrust, commit, refer, assign, cede, allot, consign, give over
6 = bequeath, will, hand down
▷ **leave behind** See **abandon**
▷ **leave out = omit**, reject, ignore, exclude, overlook, neglect, disregard, blow off (slang), cast aside
See also: **flee, resign**

leave² noun **1 = vacation**, holiday, sabbatical, furlough, time off • *Why don't you take a few days' leave?*
2 = permission, freedom, sanction, concession, consent, allowance, authorization, liberty, dispensation
3 = parting, retirement, withdrawal, departure, farewell, adieu, good-bye, leave-taking
See also: **blessing**

lecherous adjective **= lustful**, lewd, lascivious, libidinous, licentious, prurient, salacious

lecture noun **1 = talk**, speech, address, presentation, sermon, discourse • *In his lecture, he covered several topics.*
2 = scolding, warning, reprimand • *The police gave us a stern lecture on safety.*
▶ verb **3 = talk**, speak, teach, give a talk • *She has lectured all over the world.*
4 = scold, reprimand, censure, castigate, berate, admonish, reprove, tell off (informal)
See also: **lesson**

lecturer See **teacher**

ledge noun **= shelf**, step, projection, ridge, mantle, sill

leer noun, verb **= grin**, stare, goggle, ogle, gloat, smirk, squint

lees plural noun = **sediment**, deposit, dregs, grounds

leeway noun = **room**, play, space, margin, scope, latitude, elbowroom

left adjective **1** = **left-hand**, port, larboard (nautical), sinistral
2 (Of politics) = **socialist**, radical, leftist, left-wing

leftist See **left-wing**

leftover noun = **remnant**, scrap, oddment

leftovers See **remains**

left-wing adjective = **socialist**, liberal, radical, leftist • a left-wing demonstration

leg noun **1** = **limb**, member, pin (informal), stump (informal), lower limb
2 = **support**, brace, prop, upright
3 = **stage**, part, stretch, section, portion, segment, lap
▷ **pull someone's leg** (Informal) = **tease**, kid (informal), trick, fool, make fun of

legacy noun = **bequest**, estate, inheritance, heirloom • He left his children a generous legacy.
See also: **gift**

legal adjective **1** = **judicial**, forensic, judiciary • the Dutch legal system
2 = **lawful**, legitimate, valid, authorized, rightful, permissible • The strike was perfectly legal.
OPPOSITE: illegal
See also: **formal**

legality noun = **lawfulness**, legitimacy, validity, rightfulness

legalize verb = **allow**, approve, sanction, permit, license, authorize, legitimate, validate, legitimize, decriminalize

legation noun = **delegation**, embassy, representation, consulate

legend noun **1** = **myth**, story, tale, fiction, saga, fable, folk tale
2 = **celebrity**, phenomenon, luminary, prodigy, megastar (informal)
3 = **inscription**, motto, caption

legendary adjective **1** = **mythical**, traditional, romantic, fabulous, fictitious, fabled, apocryphal
2 = **famous**, famed, renowned, well-known, celebrated, illustrious, immortal

legibility noun = **readability**, clarity, neatness

legible adjective = **readable**, clear, distinct, neat, decipherable, easy to read

legion noun **1** = **army**, company, force, troop, division, brigade
2 = **multitude**, number, host, mass, throng, myriad, drove, horde

legislation noun **1** = **lawmaking**, regulation, prescription, enactment
2 = **law**, bill, act, measure, ruling, regulation, charter, statute

legislative adjective = **law-making**, judicial, law-giving

legislator noun = **lawmaker**, lawgiver

legislature noun = **parliament**, assembly, chamber, congress, senate

legitimate adjective **1** = **lawful**, legal, genuine, authentic, authorized, kosher (informal), rightful, licit
2 = **reasonable**, correct, valid, logical, sensible, justifiable, admissible, well-founded, warranted
▶ verb **3** = **legalize**, sanction, permit, authorize, legitimize, pronounce lawful

legitimize verb = **legalize**, sanction, permit, authorize

leisure noun = **free time**, recreation, relaxation, time off • There wasn't a lot of time for leisure.
OPPOSITE: work
See also: **ease**, **rest**

leisurely adjective = **unhurried**, easy, comfortable, gentle, relaxed • a leisurely walk along the beach
See also: **slow**

lend verb **1** = **loan**, advance
2 = **add**, give, provide, supply, grant, bestow, confer, impart

▷ **lend a hand** See **help**
▷ **lend itself to** = **suit**, be appropriate, be serviceable
length noun 1 = **distance**, span, extent • *The length of the box is 45 cm.*
2 = **duration**, term, period, space, span • *The movie is over two hours in length.*
3 = **piece**, measure, section, portion, segment
▷ **at length** = **in detail**, completely, fully, thoroughly, in depth, to the full; = **for a long time**, for ages, for hours, interminably; = **at last**, finally, eventually, at long last, in the end
lengthen verb = **extend**, stretch, prolong, make longer • *The airport runway had to be lengthened.*
OPPOSITE: shorten
lengthy adjective = **long**, extended, prolonged, protracted, drawn-out, tedious, interminable, long-winded, long-drawn-out
leniency noun = **mercy**, quarter, tolerance, compassion, clemency, pity, moderation, indulgence, forbearance
lenient adjective = **merciful**, kind, compassionate, tolerant, forgiving, indulgent, forbearing, sparing
lesbian adjective = **homosexual**, gay, sapphic
less adjective 1 = **smaller**, shorter
▶ preposition 2 = **minus**, without, excepting, lacking, subtracting

> **CONFUSABLES**
> *Less than* means *not so much as*, and refers only to amount. *Fewer than* means *not so many as*, and refers to countable things.

lessen verb = **decrease**, reduce, lower, shrink, diminish, minimize, dwindle, abate • *changes to their diet that would lessen the risk of disease*
OPPOSITE: increase
See also: **weaken**
lessening See **decrease**
lesser adjective = **minor**, lower,

secondary, inferior, less important
lesson noun 1 = **class**, period, lecture, coaching, tutoring • *I'm taking piano lessons.*
2 = **example**, message, moral, deterrent
lessons See **study**
let[1] verb = **allow**, sanction, permit, give permission • *Don't let the cat out of the house.*
OPPOSITE: forbid
▷ **let down** = **disappoint**, fail, dissatisfy, disillusion, disenchant, fall short, leave in the lurch, leave stranded
▷ **let go** See **discharge**
▷ **let in** See **admit**
▷ **let off** = **fire**, explode, detonate, discharge; = **emit**, release, leak, exude, give off; = **excuse**, release, spare, discharge, pardon, forgive, exempt, exonerate, absolve
▷ **let on** = **reveal**, say, admit, disclose, divulge, give away, let the cat out of the bag (*informal*), make known
▷ **let out** = **emit**, produce, give vent to; = **release**, free, discharge, liberate, let go
▷ **let up** = **stop**, ease or ease up, decrease, moderate, relax, diminish, subside, abate, slacken

> **INFORMALLY SPEAKING**
> **let down**: disappoint
> **let off**: release or allow to go free
> **let off steam**: give way to feelings
> **let someone in for**: involve someone in something unpleasant
> **let up**: stop or pause

let[2] noun (*Archaic*) = **hindrance**, restriction, interference, obstacle, obstruction, prohibition, constraint, impediment
letdown noun = **disappointment**, blow, setback, washout (*informal*), anticlimax, comedown (*informal*)
lethal adjective = **deadly**, dangerous, fatal, destructive,

murderous, virulent, mortal,
devastating

lethargic adjective = **sluggish**,
listless, dull, drowsy, sleepy,
apathetic, languid, slothful

lethargy noun = **sluggishness**,
sleepiness, apathy, drowsiness,
sloth, inertia, languor, lassitude,
listlessness

letter noun 1 = **character**, sign,
symbol
2 = **message**, note, line,
communication, dispatch,
missive, epistle

let-up noun = **lessening**, break,
pause, lull, interval, respite,
remission, breathing space,
slackening

level adjective 1 = **flat**, horizontal
• *a plateau of level ground*
OPPOSITE: uneven
2 = **even**, uniform, consistent,
smooth, plain
3 = **equal**, even, equivalent,
balanced, comparable,
proportionate, commensurate,
neck and neck, on a level playing
field (*informal*), on a par
▶ verb 4 = **flatten**, plane, smooth
• *We levelled the ground*.
5 = **equalize**, balance, even up
6 = **raze**, destroy, devastate,
demolish, flatten, bulldoze,
knock down, pull down, tear
down
7 = **direct**, point, aim, focus,
train
▶ noun 8 = **grade**, stage,
standard, status, rank • *Crime
levels have started to decline.*
▷ **on the level** (*informal*) = **honest**,
straight, fair, square, genuine,
above board
See also: **extent**

level-headed adjective = **steady**,
cool, calm, balanced, sensible,
unflappable (*informal*), collected,
composed

level-headedness *See*
common sense

levelled *See* **flat**

lever noun 1 = **handle**, bar
▶ verb 2 = **pry**, force

leverage noun = **influence**,
authority, pull (*informal*),

weight, clout (*informal*)

levity noun = **light-heartedness**,
silliness, facetiousness,
flippancy, frivolity, skittishness,
triviality

levy verb 1 = **impose**, charge,
demand, collect, exact
2 = **conscript**, raise, muster,
mobilize, call up
▶ noun 3 = **imposition**,
collection, assessment,
gathering, exaction
4 = **tax**, fee, duty, toll, tariff,
excise

lewd adjective = **indecent**,
obscene, pornographic, bawdy,
wanton, X-rated, lascivious,
libidinous, licentious, lustful,
smutty

lewdness noun = **indecency**,
pornography, obscenity,
depravity, debauchery,
bawdiness, carnality,
lasciviousness, lechery,
licentiousness, wantonness

liability noun 1 = **responsibility**,
accountability, culpability,
answerability
2 = **debt**, obligation, debit
3 = **disadvantage**, burden,
inconvenience, nuisance,
handicap, drawback, hindrance,
encumbrance, millstone

liable adjective 1 = **responsible**,
accountable, answerable,
obligated
2 = **vulnerable**, open, subject,
susceptible, exposed
3 = **likely**, prone, apt, inclined,
disposed, tending

liaise verb = **communicate**, link,
mediate, keep contact

liaison noun 1 = **communication**,
connection, contact,
interchange, hook-up
2 = **affair**, romance, intrigue,
entanglement, amour, love
affair

liar noun = **falsifier**, fabricator,
fibber, perjurer

libel noun 1 = **defamation**, smear,
denigration, aspersion, calumny
▶ verb 2 = **defame**, smear, slur,
blacken, vilify, malign, revile

libellous adjective = **defamatory**,

false, malicious, untrue,
derogatory, injurious, scurrilous
liberal *adjective* **1 = progressive**,
radical, reformist, libertarian
2 = generous, kind, charitable,
bountiful, beneficent, open-
handed, open-hearted,
unstinting
3 = tolerant, indulgent,
permissive, broad-minded
4 = abundant, rich, lavish,
handsome, ample, plentiful,
bountiful, copious, munificent,
profuse
liberality *noun* **1 = generosity**,
charity, bounty, kindness,
largesse *or* largess, philanthropy,
beneficence, benevolence,
munificence
2 = tolerance, latitude,
liberalism, broad-mindedness,
libertarianism, permissiveness
liberalize *verb* **= relax**, ease,
moderate, modify, soften,
loosen, slacken
liberate *verb* **= free**, release,
deliver, rescue, emancipate, let
loose, let out, set free
liberated *See* **free,
independent**
liberation *noun* **= deliverance**,
release, freedom, liberty,
emancipation, freeing
liberator *noun* **= deliverer**,
rescuer, emancipator, freer,
redeemer, savior
libertine *noun* **= reprobate**, rake,
womanizer, debauchee, lecher,
profligate, roué, sensualist,
voluptuary
liberty *noun* **1 = freedom**, release,
independence, sovereignty,
immunity, autonomy,
liberation, self-determination,
emancipation
2 = impertinence, impropriety,
presumption, impudence,
insolence
▷ **at liberty = free**, unrestricted,
on the loose
libidinous *adjective* **= lustful**,
carnal, debauched, lascivious,
lecherous, sensual, wanton
licence *noun* **1 = certificate**,
warrant, permit, charter

2 = permission, right,
leave, authority, exemption,
immunity, authorization,
liberty, entitlement,
dispensation, blank check, carte
blanche
3 = freedom, independence,
liberty, latitude, leeway
4 = excess, indulgence,
irresponsibility, immoderation,
laxity
license *verb* **= permit**, allow,
warrant, sanction, authorize,
certify, empower, accredit
licensed *See* **official**
licentious *adjective*
= promiscuous, abandoned,
immoral, sensual, wanton,
debauched, dissolute, lascivious,
lustful
lick *verb* **1 = taste**, lap, tongue
2 (*Of a flame*) **= flicker**, touch,
flick, ripple, dart, play over
3 (*Slang*) **= beat**, defeat, overcome,
master, rout, trounce, outstrip,
outdo, vanquish
▶ *noun* **4 = dab**, bit, touch, stroke
5 (*Informal*) **= pace**, rate, speed,
clip (*informal*)
lid *See* **top**
lie[1] *verb* **1 = fib**, perjure oneself,
tell a lie • *He always lies about his
age.*
▶ *noun* **2 = falsehood**,
fabrication, deceit, fiction, fib
• *His whole story was a lie.*
lie[2] *verb* **1 = recline**, sprawl,
lounge, loll • *I like to lie on my back
when I sleep.*
2 = be situated, be, remain,
exist, be placed

> **CONFUSABLES**
> *Lie* and *lay* both mean *rest on a
> surface.*
> *Lie* does not take an object: *to lie
> on the floor.*
> *Lay* always has an object: *to lay a
> new floor.*

life *noun* **1 = existence**, lifetime,
lifespan • *a long and active life*
RELATED WORDS
adjectives: animate, vital
2 = being, vitality, sentience
3 = biography, history, story,
autobiography, confessions,

life story, memoirs
4 = behaviour, conduct, life style, way of life
5 - liveliness, energy, spirit, animation, vitality, zest, vigor, verve, high spirits, vivacity
▷ **life force** See **spirit**

INFORMALLY SPEAKING
as large as life: in person
get a life: find something worthwhile to do
not on your life: under no circumstances
to save your life: even if your life depended on it

lifeless adjective **1 = dead**, extinct, deceased, defunct, inanimate
2 = dull, flat, sluggish, wooden, lacklustre, listless, lethargic, colourless
3 = unconscious, comatose, dead to the world (informal), insensible
lifelike adjective **= realistic**, natural, exact, faithful, authentic, vivid, true-to-life
lifelong adjective **= long-standing**, persistent, lasting, long-lasting, perennial, enduring
lifespan See **life**
lifetime noun **= existence**, time, day or days, career, span
lift verb **1 = raise**, hoist, elevate, pick up • straining to lift heavy weights
OPPOSITE: lower
2 = revoke, end, remove, cancel, relax, rescind • the decision to lift sanctions against the country
3 = disappear, vanish, disperse, dissipate, be dispelled
▷ noun **4 = ride**, run, drive
5 = boost, encouragement, pick-me-up, shot in the arm (informal)
light¹ noun **1 = brightness**, glow, glare, brilliance, illumination, radiance, incandescence, luminescence, luminosity, phosphorescence • Cracks of light filtered through the shutters.
OPPOSITE: dark
RELATED WORD
prefix: photo-
2 = lamp, torch, flare, candle, flashlight, beacon, lantern, taper

3 = aspect, viewpoint, context, angle, interpretation, slant, point of view, vantage point
4 = match, flame, lighter
▷ adjective **5 = pale**, fair, pastel, bleached, blonde or blond • a light blue shirt
OPPOSITE: dark
6 = bright, brilliant, luminous, illuminated, lustrous, shining, well-lit
OPPOSITE: dark
▷ verb **7 = illuminate**, brighten, light up • The room was lit by many candles.
OPPOSITE: darken
8 = ignite, kindle • It's time to light the bonfire.
OPPOSITE: extinguish
light² adjective **1 = insubstantial**, slight, portable, lightweight, flimsy • working out with light weights
OPPOSITE: heavy
2 = weak, moderate, mild, slight, soft, faint, gentle, indistinct
3 = insignificant, small, slight, trivial, inconsequential, inconsiderable, scanty, trifling
4 = nimble, graceful, agile, lithe, sprightly, sylphlike
5 = light-hearted, funny, humorous, amusing, frivolous, witty, entertaining
6 = digestible, modest, frugal
▷ verb **7 = settle**, land, perch, alight
▷ **light on, light upon = come across**, find, discover, encounter, chance upon, happen upon, hit upon, stumble on
▷ **light up** See **light**
See also: **easy**
lighten¹ verb **= brighten**, illuminate, irradiate, become light, light up
lighten² verb **1 = ease**, reduce, relieve, alleviate, lessen, mitigate, allay, assuage, ameliorate
2 = cheer, lift, revive, brighten, buoy up, perk up
light-headed adjective **= faint**, dizzy, hazy, giddy, woozy (informal), vertiginous

light-hearted *adjective*
= **carefree**, upbeat (*informal*),
playful, jolly, cheerful, jovial,
happy-go-lucky, blithe
lightly *adverb* **1** = **gently**, slightly,
softly, delicately, faintly
2 = **moderately**, thinly, sparsely,
sparingly
3 = **easily**, simply, readily,
effortlessly
4 = **carelessly**, breezily,
flippantly, frivolously,
heedlessly, thoughtlessly
lightweight *adjective*
= **unimportant**, slight, petty,
insignificant, paltry, worthless,
trivial, inconsequential, trifling
like[1] *adjective* = **similar**, same,
parallel, identical, alike, akin,
analogous • *He looks just like his
father.*
OPPOSITE: unlike

> INFORMALLY SPEAKING
> **and the like**: and similar
> things
> **like crazy (mad, etc.)**: with
> great speed, effort, etc.
> **nothing like**: not nearly
> **something like**: almost like
> **the likes of**: someone or
> something like

like[2] *verb* **1** = **enjoy**, love,
appreciate, relish, adore
(*informal*), be fond of, be keen on,
be partial to, go for (*informal*),
have a soft spot for, have a
weakness for, revel in • *I really like
this music.*
OPPOSITE: dislike
2 = **admire**, approve, appreciate,
cherish, prize, esteem, hold dear,
take to
3 = **wish**, want, choose, prefer,
desire, fancy, care to, feel
inclined
4 (*Informal*) = **be attracted to**, be
captivated by, be turned on by
(*informal*), lust after, take a liking
to, take to
▷ **like better** *See* **prefer**
likeable *adjective* = **pleasant**,
nice, attractive, charming,
sympathetic, engaging,
appealing, agreeable, amiable
See **pleasant**

likelihood *noun* = **probability**,
chance, possibility, prospect
likely *adjective* **1** = **probable**,
possible, anticipated, liable,
expected • *It seems likely that he will
come back.*
OPPOSITE: unlikely
2 = **inclined**, prone, liable, apt,
disposed, tending
3 = **plausible**, possible,
reasonable, credible, feasible,
believable
4 = **promising**, hopeful, up-and-
coming
See also: **potential, probably**
liken *verb* = **compare**, match,
relate, parallel, equate, set
beside
likeness *noun* **1** = **resemblance**,
similarity, correspondence,
affinity
2 = **portrait**, picture, image,
representation, depiction, effigy
likewise *adverb* = **similarly**, in
like manner, in the same way
liking *noun* = **fondness**, love,
taste, weakness, affection,
preference, penchant,
inclination, partiality, soft spot
limb *noun* **1** = **part**, member, arm,
leg, wing, extremity, appendage
2 = **branch**, spur, projection,
offshoot, bough
limelight *noun* = **publicity**,
attention, celebrity, recognition,
fame, prominence, stardom,
public eye, the spotlight
limit *noun* **1** = **bounds**, deadline,
maximum, ultimate, utmost
• *the speed limit*
2 = **boundary**, border, edge,
frontier, perimeter
▶ *verb* **3** = **restrict**, fix, curb,
confine, ration • *Limit yourself to
one evening out a week.*
See also: **extreme**
limitation *noun* = **restriction**,
control, condition, check,
curb, restraint, reservation,
qualification, constraint
limited *adjective* = **restricted**,
controlled, finite, bounded,
checked, circumscribed,
confined, constrained, curbed
limitless *adjective* = **infinite**,

vast, unlimited, countless, endless, untold, inexhaustible, boundless, unbounded

limits See **border, range**

limp¹ *verb* **1 = hobble**, falter, hop, shuffle, shamble
▶ *noun* **2 = lameness**, hobble

limp² *adjective* **= floppy**, drooping, flabby, soft • *a limp lettuce leaf*
OPPOSITE: stiff

limping See **lame**

line *noun* **1 = rule**, streak, stripe • *Draw a line down the centre of the page.*
2 = row, file, rank, column, queue • *a long line at the box office*
3 = course, track, route, path, trajectory • *the line of flight*
4 = wrinkle, mark, crease, furrow, crow's foot
5 = boundary, border, limit, edge, frontier, borderline
6 = string, cable, wire, cord, rope, thread
7 = job, trade, business, area, field, employment, occupation, profession, calling, specialization
▷ **in line for = due for**, in the running for
▶ *verb* **8 = mark**, score, rule, crease, furrow
9 = border, edge, fringe, bound

> INFORMALLY SPEAKING
> **bring into line**: cause to conform
> **cross the line**: do something unacceptable
> **hold the line**: stand firm against an attack or challenge
> **in line with**: in agreement with
> **lay it on the line**: state firmly and clearly
> **on the line**: at risk
> **out of line**: not suitable or proper

lineage See **origin, stock**

lineaments *plural noun* **= features**, face, countenance, physiognomy

lined *adjective* **1 = ruled**, feint
2 = wrinkled, furrowed, wizened, worn

lines *plural noun* **= words**, part, script

line-up *noun* **= arrangement**, team, row, selection, array

linger *verb* **1 = stay**, remain, stop, wait, loiter, hang around, tarry
2 = delay, idle, dawdle, dally, drag one's feet *or* drag one's heels, take one's time

lingering See **slow**

lingo See **language**

link *noun* **1 = connection**, tie, relationship, bond, association, affiliation, attachment • *the link between diet and health*
2 = component, part, member, piece, element, constituent
▶ *verb* **3 = connect**, join, couple, tie, attach, fasten • *He was linked to the crime.*
OPPOSITE: separate
4 = associate, identify, relate, connect, bracket
▷ **link up** See **team, unite**
See also: **relation**

lip *noun* **1 = edge**, margin, rim, brink, brim
2 (*Slang*) **= impudence**, cheek (*informal*), backchat (*informal*), effrontery, impertinence, insolence

liquid *noun* **1 = fluid**, solution • *a clear liquid*
▶ *adjective* **2 = fluid**, runny, molten • *wash in warm water with liquid detergent*
3 (~ *assets*) **= convertible**, negotiable

liquidate *verb* **1 = pay**, clear, settle, square, discharge, honour, pay off
2 = annul, cancel, dissolve, terminate, abolish
3 = kill, murder, destroy, eliminate, dispatch, exterminate, get rid of, wipe out (*informal*)

liquor *noun* **1 = alcohol**, drink, booze (*informal*), hard stuff (*informal*), spirits, strong drink
2 = juice, stock, liquid, extract, broth

list¹ *noun* **1 = record**, index, register, inventory, catalogue, listing, directory, laundry list

• *There were six names on the list.*
▶ *verb* **2 = record**, index, register, catalogue • *All the ingredients are listed on the label.*

list² *verb* **1 = lean**, tip, tilt, incline, careen, heel over
▶ *noun* **2 = tilt**, cant, slant, leaning

listen *verb* **1 = hear** • *She was listening to the radio.*
2 = pay attention • *Nobody listens to a word I say.*
▷ **listen in** See **hear**

listing See **list**

listless *adjective* = **languid**, sluggish, indifferent, lethargic, apathetic, indolent

literacy *noun* = **education**, knowledge, learning

literal *adjective* **1 = exact**, close, strict, accurate, faithful, verbatim, word for word
2 = actual, real, true, simple, plain, genuine, bona fide, unvarnished

literally *adverb* = **exactly**, really, actually, strictly, truly, precisely, faithfully, verbatim, to the letter, word for word

literary *adjective* = **well-read**, formal, scholarly, bookish, erudite, learned

literate *adjective* = **educated**, informed, knowledgeable

literature *noun* = **writings**, lore, letters

lithe *adjective* = **supple**, flexible, limber, lissom *or* lissome, loose-limbed, pliable

litigant *noun* = **claimant**, party, plaintiff

litigate *verb* = **go to court**, sue, prosecute, press charges

litigation *noun* = **lawsuit**, case, action, prosecution

litter *noun* **1 = trash**, garbage, debris, detritus, refuse, rubbish, muck
2 = brood, young, offspring, progeny
▶ *verb* **3 = clutter**, disorder, derange, disarrange, mess up
4 = scatter, strew

little *adjective* **1 = small**, minute, short, tiny, miniature, wee,

diminutive, petite • *a little kitten*
OPPOSITE: large
2 = young, junior, infant, immature, undeveloped, babyish
▷ **little ones** See **young**
▶ *adverb* **3 = hardly**, barely
4 = rarely, seldom, scarcely, hardly ever, not often
▶ *noun* **5 = bit**, spot, touch, hint, trace, particle, fragment, speck
• *Would you like a little juice?*
See also: **insignificant, low**

live¹ *verb* **1 = dwell**, reside, inhabit
• *She has lived here for 20 years.*
2 = be alive, exist • *She has lived a happy life.*
3 = persist, last, prevail
4 = survive, endure, subsist, get along, make ends meet, support oneself
5 = thrive, flourish, prosper
▷ **live on** See **endure**

INFORMALLY SPEAKING
live it up: enjoy life to the full
live up to: act according to
live with: accept or tolerate

live² *adjective* **1 = living**, alive, animate • *a live spider*
2 = topical, current, controversial, hot, burning, prevalent, pressing, pertinent
3 = burning, hot, active, glowing, alight, blazing, ignited, smouldering

livelihood *noun* = **occupation**, work, job, living, employment, bread and butter (*informal*)

liveliness *noun* = **energy**, spirit, animation, vitality, dynamism, boisterousness, sprightliness, vivacity

lively *adjective* **1 = energetic**, active, animated, sparkling, perky, vivacious, sprightly • *a lively personality*
OPPOSITE: dull
2 = vivid, bright, exciting, colourful, forceful, invigorating, refreshing, stimulating
See also: **alive, busy, colourful, vital**

liven up *verb* = **stir**, brighten, animate, rouse, enliven, buck up (*informal*), perk up

liverish adjective 1 = **sick**, bilious, queasy
2 = **irritable**, grumpy, crusty, irascible, crotchety, disagreeable, ill-humoured, splenetic, tetchy

livery noun = **costume**, suit, dress, uniform, attire, garb, regalia, clothing

livid adjective 1 (Informal) = **angry**, furious, outraged, enraged, incensed, beside oneself, fuming, indignant, infuriated
2 = **discoloured**, purple, black-and-blue, bruised, contused

living adjective 1 = **alive**, active, breathing, existing
2 = **current**, active, contemporary, extant, in use
▶ noun 3 = **existence**, life, being, existing, subsistence
4 = **life style**, way of life
▷ **living soul** See **person**

load noun 1 = **cargo**, shipment, freight, consignment • *This truck can carry a large load.*
2 = **burden**, worry, weight, trouble, onus, albatross, encumbrance, millstone
▶ verb 3 = **fill**, pack, pile, stack • *The trucks were loaded with blankets and supplies.*
4 = **burden**, worry, oppress, encumber, saddle with, weigh down
5 (~a firearm) = **make ready**, charge, prime
See also: **bunch, mass, stuff**

loaded adjective 1 = **biased**, distorted, weighted
2 = **tricky**, manipulative, insidious, prejudicial, artful
3 (Slang) = **rich**, wealthy, affluent, flush (informal), well-heeled (informal), well-to-do, moneyed, well off

loads plural noun (Informal) = **plenty**, heaps, lots, stacks, tons (informal), scads • *I've got loads of money.*

loaf[1] noun = **lump**, block, cake, cube, slab

loaf[2] verb = **idle**, loiter, laze, lie around, lounge around, take it easy

loan noun 1 = **advance**, credit, mortgage • *a small business loan*
▶ verb 2 = **lend**, advance • *He loaned us the painting for our exhibition.*

CONFUSABLES
Loan and lend are both verbs that mean give something temporarily. Loan is also a noun, but lend isn't.

loath, loth adjective = **unwilling**, reluctant, averse, disinclined, opposed

loathe verb = **hate**, dislike, detest, despise, abhor, abominate

loathing noun = **hatred**, disgust, revulsion, aversion, antipathy, abhorrence, detestation, repugnance, repulsion

loathsome adjective = **hateful**, offensive, abhorrent, vile, obnoxious, repulsive, repugnant, disgusting, odious, detestable, revolting, nauseating, scuzzy (slang)

lob See **throw**

lobby noun 1 = **corridor**, passage, hallway, porch, foyer, entrance hall, vestibule
2 = **pressure group**, committee, organization, activist, coalition, movement, advocate, association, initiative, agenda, demonstrator, faction, lobbyist, campaigner, special interest group, public interest group
▶ verb 3 = **campaign**, urge, push, pressure, press, promote, influence, persuade

local adjective
1 = **neighbourhood**, community, district, regional • *We shop at our local stores.*
2 = **confined**, limited, restricted (chiefly US)
▶ noun 3 = **resident**, inhabitant • *That's what the locals call the place.*

locality noun
1 = **neighbourhood**, area, region, district, vicinity, neck of the woods (informal)
2 = **site**, place, position, spot, scene, location, setting, locale

localize verb = **restrict**, contain,

limit, confine, circumscribe,
delimit

locate verb **1** = **find**, pinpoint,
track down • *We have been unable
to locate him.*
2 = **place**, set, put, seat, settle,
fix, establish, situate
See also: **position, trace**

located adjective = **situated**,
placed • *The restaurant is located
near the park.*

location noun = **place**, point,
site, position, situation, spot,
whereabouts • *a house in a
beautiful location*
See also: **scene, surroundings**

lock¹ verb **1** = **fasten**, latch,
padlock • *Are you sure you locked
the door?*
OPPOSITE: unlock
2 = **unite**, link, join, engage,
entangle, clench, entwine
3 = **embrace**, press, clutch, hug,
grasp, enclose, encircle, clasp
▷ **lock up** = **imprison**,
jail, detain, confine, cage,
incarcerate, put behind bars,
shut up
▶ noun **4** = **fastening**, latch,
padlock • *The lock had been forced
open.*
See also: **secure**

lock² noun = **strand**, curl, tress,
tuft, ringlet

locked See **secure**

lockup noun = **prison**, jail, cell

lodge noun **1** = **cabin**, shelter,
shed, cottage, hut, chalet,
gatehouse
2 = **society**, group, club, branch,
chapter
▶ verb **3** = **stay**, board, room
4 = **stick**, implant, come to rest,
imbed
5 = **register**, file, submit, put on
record

lodger noun = **tenant**, resident,
boarder, paying guest

lodging noun (often plural)
= **accommodation**, abode,
apartments, shelter, residence,
quarters, rooms

lofty adjective **1** = **high**, elevated,
towering, raised, soaring
2 = **noble**, grand, renowned,

elevated, illustrious,
distinguished, dignified,
exalted
3 = **haughty**, proud, arrogant,
condescending, disdainful,
patronizing, supercilious

log noun **1** = **stump**, block, chunk,
trunk
2 = **record**, account, journal,
logbook
▶ verb **3** = **chop**, cut, fell, hew
4 = **record**, note, register, chart,
set down

loggerheads plural noun
▷ **at loggerheads** = **quarrelling**,
at daggers drawn, at each other's
throats, at odds, feuding, in
dispute, opposed

logic noun = **reason**, sense, good
sense

logical adjective **1** = **rational**,
sound, consistent, valid,
reasoned • *a logical theory*
2 = **reasonable**, obvious, wise,
sensible, plausible, judicious • *a
logical deduction*
OPPOSITE: illogical

logo See **sign, symbol**

loiter verb = **linger**, idle, dawdle,
loaf, dally, dilly-dally (*informal*),
hang about *or* hang around,
skulk

loll verb **1** = **lounge**, slump,
relax, sprawl, recline, loaf,
slouch
2 = **droop**, drop, hang, flap, sag,
dangle, flop

lone adjective = **solitary**, one, only,
single, sole, unaccompanied

loneliness noun = **solitude**,
isolation, seclusion, desolation

lonely adjective **1** = **lonesome**,
alone, forlorn, forsaken • *He's
lonely and just wants to talk.*
2 = **desolate**, remote, isolated,
secluded, uninhabited, deserted
• *a lonely hillside*
3 = **solitary**, single, alone, apart,
lone, isolated, companionless,
withdrawn

loner noun = **individualist**,
maverick, outsider, recluse, lone
wolf

lonesome adjective = **lonely**,
gloomy, dreary, desolate,

companionless, forlorn,
friendless

long¹ *adjective* **1 = prolonged**,
lengthy, sustained, protracted,
interminable, lingering, long-
drawn-out • *a long interval when
nobody spoke*
OPPOSITE: short
2 = elongated, extensive,
lengthy, extended, expanded,
far-reaching, stretched, spread
out • *a long line of people*
OPPOSITE: short
▷ **long ago** *See* **past, the past**
▷ **long shot = outsider**, dark
horse
See also: **far**

long² *verb* **= desire**, want, wish,
hunger, pine, ache, covet, crave,
itch, lust, yearn, hanker • *He
longed for peace and quiet.*

longing *noun* **= desire**, hunger,
craving, thirst, yearning,
hankering • *her longing to return
home*
See also: **urge, wish**

long-lived *adjective* **= long-
lasting**, enduring

long-standing *adjective*
= established, long-lasting,
enduring, long-established,
abiding, fixed, time-honoured,
timeless

long-suffering *adjective*
= uncomplaining, patient,
tolerant, easy-going, forgiving,
forbearing, resigned, stoical

long-winded *adjective*
= rambling, lengthy, prolonged,
tedious, tiresome, verbose, long-
drawn-out, prolix, repetitious,
wordy

look *verb* **1 = see**, study, survey,
watch, view, eye, read, examine,
scan, observe, contemplate,
glance, gaze • *She looked at me with
affection.*
2 = seem, appear, look like, seem
to be, strike one as • *the desire to
look older*
3 = face, front, overlook
4 = hope, expect, await,
anticipate, reckon on
5 = search, seek, hunt, forage
▷ **look after = take care of**,

watch, mind, nurse, tend, care
for • *Will you look after my cats this
weekend?*
See also: **run, safeguard**
▷ **look down on = disdain**, scorn,
spurn, despise, sneer, contemn
▷ **look for = search**, seek, hunt,
forage • *I'm looking for my winter
boots.*
▷ **look forward to = anticipate**,
expect, await, hope for, long for,
look for, wait for
▷ **look like = resemble**, echo,
take after, be the image of,
remind one of, make one think
of, put one in mind of
▷ **look on** *See* **regard**
▷ **look out = be careful**, beware,
keep an eye out, pay attention,
watch out
▷ **look up = research**, find, hunt
for, search for, seek out, track
down; **= improve**, progress, get
better, perk up, pick up, shape up
(*informal*); **= visit**, call on, drop in
on (*informal*), look in on
▷ **look up to = respect**, admire,
honour, revere, esteem, defer to
▶ *noun* **6 = gaze**, view,
inspection, sight, examination,
glimpse, observation, glance,
peek • *He took a last look in the
mirror.*
7 = appearance, face, air,
aspect, manner, expression,
bearing, demeanour, semblance,
countenance • *He had the look of a
confident man.*
See also: **regard, stare**

INFORMALLY SPEAKING
look around: consider many possibilities
look bad: appear improper or unsuitable
look down on: despise
look into: investigate
look out for: take care of or protect
look over: examine or inspect
look up to: respect or admire

look-alike *noun* **= double**,
spitting image (*informal*), dead
ringer (*informal*) • *an Elvis look-alike*

lookout *noun* **1 = watch**, guard,
vigil, readiness

2 = watchman, guard, sentry, sentinel

3 = watchtower, post, observatory, observation post

looks See **appearance**

loom verb = **appear**, threaten, emerge, bulk, hover, menace, impend, take shape

looming See **imminent, near**

loony See **mad**

loop noun **1 = curve**, ring, curl, circle, twist, spiral, coil, twirl, whorl

▶ verb **2 = twist**, turn, roll, curl, knot, spiral, coil, wind round

loophole noun = **let-out**, escape, excuse

loose adjective **1 = unsecured**, free, wobbly • a loose tooth
OPPOSITE: secure

2 = slack, baggy • Wear loose clothes for comfort.
OPPOSITE: tight

3 = vague, random, inaccurate, inexact, rambling, imprecise, ill-defined, indistinct

4 = promiscuous, fast, abandoned, immoral, debauched, dissipated, dissolute, profligate

▶ verb **5 = free**, release, unleash, disconnect, detach, liberate, untie, set free, unfasten
See also: **approximate, full**

| CONFUSABLES
| _Loose_ means not tight.
| _Lose_ usually means misplace or
| fail to keep.

loosen verb **1 = untie**, undo, slacken • He loosened his tie.

2 = free, release, liberate, set free
▷ **loosen up = relax**, soften, de-stress, ease up or ease off, go easy (informal), let up
OPPOSITE: tighten

loot verb **1 = plunder**, raid, ransack, pillage • Gangs began breaking windows and looting stores.
▶ noun **2 = plunder**, haul, booty, spoils • The loot was never recovered.
See also: **rob**

lop See **chop**

lopsided adjective = **crooked**, disproportionate, awry, asymmetrical, askew, cockeyed,

uneven, unbalanced, squint, warped

lord noun **1 = master**, leader, commander, governor, superior, ruler, overlord, liege

2 = nobleman, peer, noble, earl, viscount

▷ **Our Lord = Jesus**, Jesus Christ, the Lord God, Christ, Jehovah, the Almighty
▶ verb
▷ **lord it over = order around**, swagger, boss around (informal), domineer, pull rank, put on airs

lordly adjective = **proud**, lofty, arrogant, imperious, high-handed, condescending, disdainful, domineering, haughty, overbearing

lore noun = **traditions**, teaching, wisdom, doctrine, beliefs, sayings

lose verb **1 = mislay**, drop, misplace • I've lost my keys.
OPPOSITE: find

2 = be beaten, be defeated • We lost the game.
OPPOSITE: win

3 = forfeit, miss, yield, pass up (informal)
▷ **lose hope** See **despair**
▷ **lose your nerve** See **panic**
▷ **lose your temper** See **rage**

loser noun **1 = failure**, flop (informal), dud (informal), also-ran

2 = nerd, drip (informal), geek (slang), dork (slang), dweeb (slang)

loss noun **1 = defeat**, failure, waste, forfeiture, mislaying, squandering

2 = damage, injury, cost, hurt, harm, destruction, ruin

3 (sometimes plural) **= deficit**, debt, debit, deficiency, depletion
▷ **at a loss = confused**, helpless, at one's wits' end, baffled, bewildered, nonplussed, perplexed, puzzled, stumped

lost adjective **1 = off course**, adrift, astray • I think we're lost.

2 = missing, mislaid, misplaced • I wonder if my lost keys will ever turn up.

lot noun **1 = group**, set, crowd,

bunch (*informal*), quantity, batch • *We've just sacked one lot of builders.*

2 = destiny, chance, accident, fate, fortune, doom

▷ **a lot, lots = plenty**, abundance, piles (*informal*), a great deal, masses (*informal*), quantities, scores • *Remember to drink lots of water.*

See also: **loads, many, numerous, whole**

loth *See* **loath**

lotion *noun* = **cream**, solution, balm, embrocation, liniment, salve

lottery *noun* **1 = raffle**, drawing, sweepstakes

2 = gamble, risk, chance, hazard, toss-up (*informal*)

loud *adjective* **1 = noisy**, strident, thunderous, blaring, deafening, resounding • *a loud explosion*
OPPOSITE: quiet

2 = garish, flamboyant, flashy, lurid, gaudy • *a loud tie*
OPPOSITE: dull
See also: **bold**

loudly *adverb* = **noisily**, vigorously, vehemently, lustily, deafeningly, fortissimo (*music*), shrilly, uproariously, vociferously

lounge *verb* = **relax**, sprawl, loaf, loiter, laze, lie around, loll, take it easy

lousy *adjective* (*Informal*) = **awful**, terrible, inadequate, shoddy, inferior, crappy (*slang*), shabby, crummy

lout *noun* = **oaf**, boor, dolt, lummox (*informal*), schlub (*slang*)

lovable *adjective* = **adorable**, sweet, charming, enchanting, endearing • *His vulnerability makes him very lovable.*
OPPOSITE: hateful

love *verb* **1 = adore**, worship, cherish • *They loved each other very much.*
OPPOSITE: hate

2 = enjoy, like, appreciate, relish • *We both love fishing.*
OPPOSITE: hate

▶ *noun* **3 = adoration**, passion, affection, devotion, ardour,

infatuation • *their love for their children*
OPPOSITE: hatred

4 = liking, weakness, devotion, fondness • *her love of animals*
OPPOSITE: hatred

5 = beloved, lover, dear, sweetheart, darling, dearest, truelove

▷ **in love = enamoured**, besotted, charmed, enraptured, infatuated, smitten

▷ **love affair = romance**, relationship, affair, intrigue, liaison, amour
See also: **attachment**

loveliness *See* **beauty**

lovely *adjective* **1 = attractive**, pretty, beautiful, pleasant, enjoyable, delightful • *You look lovely.*
OPPOSITE: horrible

2 = enjoyable, nice, pleasant, engaging, pleasing, delightful, agreeable

lover *noun* = **sweetheart**, flame (*informal*), beloved, boyfriend *or* girlfriend, suitor, admirer, mistress, main squeeze (*slang*)

loving *adjective* = **affectionate**, warm, tender, fond, devoted, doting • *their loving parents*
OPPOSITE: cold
See also: **romantic**

low *adjective* = **small**, little, short, sunken, squat, stunted • *a low bench*
OPPOSITE: high

1 = meagre, small, poor, modest, minimal, scant, reduced • *low prices*
OPPOSITE: high

2 = inferior, poor, inadequate, shoddy, lousy (*slang*), deficient, second-rate

3 = coarse, common, crude, rough, rude, vulgar, undignified, disreputable

4 = dejected, depressed, gloomy, miserable, despondent, glum, downcast, disheartened, down in the dumps (*informal*), fed up

5 = ill, weak, frail, stricken, debilitated

6 = quiet, soft, gentle, muted,

subdued, hushed, muffled,
whispered
See also: **deep, faint,
reasonable, sad**
lowdown *noun* (*Informal*)
= **information**, intelligence,
info (*informal*), inside story
lower *verb* 1 = **drop**, let down,
take down • *They lowered the coffin
into the grave.*
OPPOSITE: raise
2 = **lessen**, cut, reduce, decrease,
slash, diminish, minimize • *a
commitment to lower taxes*
OPPOSITE: increase
▶ *adjective* 3 = **minor**, junior,
secondary, lesser, inferior,
subordinate, second-class,
smaller
4 = **reduced**, diminished,
curtailed, decreased, lessened
See also: **below, ease**
lowering *See* **cut**
lowest *See* **bottom, least**
low-key *adjective* = **subdued**,
quiet, muted, restrained, toned
down, understated
lowly *adjective* 1 = **disreputable**,
despicable, vulgar, contemptible
• *his lowly status*
2 = **humble**, modest, mild,
unassuming, meek
low-spirited *adjective*
= **depressed**, down, low, sad,
dismal, miserable, dejected,
despondent, down-hearted,
fed up
loyal *adjective* = **faithful**, true,
constant, staunch, dependable,
trusty • *a loyal friend*
OPPOSITE: treacherous
See also: **devoted**
loyalty *noun* = **faithfulness**,
devotion, allegiance, fidelity,
dependability, constancy,
staunchness, steadfastness,
trustworthiness
lubricate *verb* = **oil**, smear, grease
lucid *adjective* 1 = **clear**, explicit,
transparent, comprehensible,
intelligible
2 = **translucent**, clear,
transparent, crystalline, glassy,
diaphanous, limpid, pellucid
3 = **clear-headed**, rational, sane,

all there, *compos mentis* (*Latin*), in
one's right mind
luck *noun* 1 = **fortune**, chance,
accident, fate, destiny • *It was just
luck that we happened to meet.*
2 = **good fortune**, advantage,
success, blessing, prosperity,
windfall, serendipity, godsend
luckily *adverb* = **fortunately**,
happily, favourably, opportunely,
propitiously, providentially
luckless *adjective* = **unlucky**,
unfortunate, hapless, doomed,
ill-fated, hopeless, cursed,
jinxed
lucky *adjective* 1 = **fortunate**,
blessed, charmed • *He had always
been lucky at cards.*
OPPOSITE: unlucky
2 = **opportune**, fortunate,
timely, fortuitous • *a lucky break*
OPPOSITE: unlucky
lucrative *adjective* = **profitable**,
productive, fruitful,
advantageous, well-paid,
remunerative
lucre *noun* = **money**, profit, gain,
wealth, riches, mammon, pelf,
spoils
ludicrous *adjective* = **ridiculous**,
crazy, silly, absurd, laughable,
outlandish, preposterous,
farcical, nonsensical
lug *See* **carry, drag**
luggage *noun* = **baggage**, gear,
paraphernalia, bags, cases,
impedimenta, suitcases, things
lugubrious *adjective* = **gloomy**,
serious, sad, mournful,
melancholy, somber, doleful,
sorrowful, woebegone
lukewarm *adjective* 1 = **tepid**,
warm
2 = **half-hearted**, cool,
indifferent, apathetic,
unresponsive, unenthusiastic
lull *verb* 1 = **calm**, subdue, quell,
allay, soothe, pacify, tranquilize
▶ *noun* 2 = **respite**, quiet, silence,
calm, pause, hush, let-up
(*informal*)
lumber *noun, verb* 1 = **trundle**,
career, barrel, shuffle, rumble,
bound, thunder, stagger, barge,
lunge, meander, lurch, chug,

amble, waddle, totter, canter
2 = timber, wood, planks, boards

lumber² verb = **plod**, shuffle, stump, clump, trudge, trundle, waddle, shamble

lumbering adjective = **awkward**, heavy, clumsy, ungainly, hulking, ponderous

luminary See **star**

luminous adjective = **bright**, glowing, luminescent, radiant, illuminated, lustrous, shining

lump noun **1 = piece**, ball, chunk, cake, wedge, hunk • *a big lump of clay*
2 = bump, bulge, hump, swelling • *I've got a big lump on my head.*
▶ verb **3 = group**, mass, collect, combine, pool, consolidate, conglomerate
See also: **block**

lumpy adjective = **bumpy**, uneven, knobbly

lunacy noun **1 = insanity**, dementia, madness, mania, psychosis, derangement
2 = foolishness, madness, stupidity, folly, craziness, absurdity, foolhardiness

lunatic adjective **1 = mad**, crazy, insane, irrational, bonkers (*informal*), crackbrained (*informal*), crackpot (*informal*), daft, deranged
▶ noun **2 = madman**, psychopath, maniac, nutcase (*slang*), sicko (*informal*), sickie (*informal*), ding-a-ling (*slang*)

lunch See **eat**

lunge noun **1 = thrust**, charge, spring, swing, pounce, jab
▶ verb **2 = pounce**, charge, plunge, dive, leap, thrust

lurch verb **1 = tilt**, list, rock, pitch, roll, lean, heel, heave
2 = stagger, stumble, reel, sway, weave, totter

lure verb **1 = tempt**, draw, attract, entice, beckon • *We are being lured into a trap.*
▶ noun **2 = temptation**, pull, attraction, magnet, bait • *the lure of rural life*

lurid adjective **1 = sensational**, shocking, graphic, vivid, melodramatic
2 = glaring, intense

lurk verb = **hide**, sneak, prowl, slink, conceal oneself, lie in wait, skulk

luscious adjective = **delicious**, sweet, juicy, palatable, yummy (*informal*), succulent, appetizing, mouth-watering, toothsome

lush adjective **1 = abundant**, green, rank, dense, verdant, flourishing
2 = luxurious, grand, elaborate, lavish, plush (*informal*), extravagant, ornate, sumptuous, opulent, palatial

lust noun **1 = lechery**, lasciviousness, lewdness, sensuality
2 = appetite, desire, passion, greed, longing, craving, thirst
▶ verb **3 = desire**, want, covet, crave, yearn, hunger for or hunger after

lustre noun **1 = sparkle**, shine, glow, shimmer, glitter, gloss, gleam, sheen, glint
2 = glory, fame, honour, distinction, kudos, prestige, renown
See also: **finish**

lustful adjective = **lascivious**, lewd, carnal, lecherous • *lustful thoughts*

lusty adjective = **vigorous**, strong, healthy, powerful, robust, energetic, hearty, sturdy, virile

luxuriant See **thick**

luxurious adjective = **sumptuous**, lavish, posh, plush (*informal*), deluxe, opulent • *a luxurious lifestyle*
OPPOSITE: plain

> **CONFUSABLES**
> Luxurious usually means *full of luxury.*
> Luxuriant means *growing thickly.*

luxury noun **1 = opulence**, affluence, sumptuousness • *a life of luxury*
2 = extravagance, treat, extra,

indulgence • *Telephones are still a luxury in some countries.*
See also: **comfort**

lying *noun* **1** = **dishonesty**, perjury, fabrication, deceit, fibbing • *I've had enough of your lying.*

▸ *adjective* **2** = **deceitful**, false, dishonest, untruthful • *The man is just a lying cheat.*
OPPOSITE: honest

lyrical *adjective* = **enthusiastic**, inspired, impassioned, poetic, effusive, rhapsodic

Mm

macabre *adjective* = **gruesome**, grim, eerie, grisly, dreadful, morbid, ghostly, ghoulish, ghastly, frightening

mace *See* **stick**

machiavellian *adjective* = **scheming**, cynical, crafty, unscrupulous, opportunist, sly, cunning, astute, double-dealing, underhand

machine *noun* **1 = appliance**, device, instrument, mechanism, contraption, apparatus • *a washing machine*
2 = system, organization, structure, setup (*informal*), machinery
See also: **gadget**

machinery *noun* = **equipment**, tackle, gear, apparatus, instruments, tools

macho *adjective* = **manly**, masculine, chauvinist, virile

mad *adjective* **1 = insane**, crazy (*informal*), unstable, psychotic, demented, raving, deranged, *non compos mentis* (*Latin*), nuts (*slang*), of unsound mind, out of one's mind, unhinged
2 = foolish, crazy (*informal*), stupid, foolhardy • *He'd be mad to refuse.*
3 = angry, crazy, furious, enraged, irate, livid, incensed, fuming, infuriated • *They both got mad at me for interfering.*
4 = enthusiastic, wild, crazy (*informal*), avid, impassioned, ardent, fanatical, infatuated
5 = frenzied, wild, excited, frenetic, uncontrolled, unrestrained, wired (*slang*)
▷ **like mad** (*Informal*) = **energetically**, rapidly, wildly, violently, enthusiastically, furiously, excitedly, speedily

madcap *adjective* = **reckless**, crazy, rash, foolhardy, impulsive, imprudent, thoughtless, hare-brained

madden *verb* = **infuriate**, upset, annoy, inflame, irritate, incense, enrage, derange, drive one crazy

madly *adverb* **1 = insanely**, frantically, hysterically, crazily, deliriously, distractedly, frenziedly
2 = foolishly, wildly, absurdly, irrationally, ludicrously, senselessly
3 = energetically, wildly, recklessly, furiously, excitedly, like mad (*informal*), speedily
4 (*Informal*) = **passionately**, desperately, intensely, devotedly, to distraction

madman madwoman
▶ *noun* = **lunatic**, psychopath, psycho (*slang*), maniac, nutcase (*slang*)

madness *noun* **1 = insanity**, dementia, distraction, mania, delusion, craziness, aberration, lunacy, psychosis, derangement, mental instability
2 = foolishness, nonsense, folly, idiocy, absurdity, wildness, daftness (*informal*), foolhardiness, preposterousness

maelstrom *noun* **1 = whirlpool**, vortex
2 = turmoil, disorder, chaos, confusion, upheaval, tumult

maestro *noun* = **master**, expert, genius, virtuoso

magazine *noun* **1 = journal**, pamphlet, periodical
2 = storehouse, store, warehouse, arsenal, depot

magic *noun* **1 = sorcery**, witchcraft • *They believe in magic.*
2 = conjuring, illusion, trickery,

legerdemain, prestidigitation, sleight of hand
3 = charm, power, glamour, fascination, magnetism, mojo (*slang*), enchantment, allurement
▶ *adjective* **4 = enchanting**, charming, miraculous, marvellous, bewitching, entrancing, fascinating, spellbinding

magical *adjective* **= enchanting**, bewitching • *Paris is a magical city.*

magician *noun* **1 = sorcerer**, wizard, witch, illusionist, conjurer, enchanter *or* enchantress, necromancer, warlock

magisterial *adjective* **= authoritative**, masterful, commanding, lordly

magistrate *noun* **= judge**, justice, J.P., justice of the peace

magnanimity *noun* **= generosity**, largesse *or* largess, nobility, selflessness, benevolence, big-heartedness, unselfishness

magnanimous *adjective* **= generous**, kind, charitable, noble, selfless, bountiful, unselfish, big-hearted

magnate *noun* **= tycoon**, mogul, baron, captain of industry, plutocrat

magnet See **lure**

magnetic *adjective* **= attractive**, charismatic, charming, irresistible, seductive, hypnotic, captivating, fascinating, mesmerizing

magnetism *noun* **= attraction**, pull, appeal, magic, charm, allure, charisma, mojo (*slang*), seductiveness, drawing power

magnification *noun* **= increase**, expansion, enhancement, enlargement, amplification, intensification, heightening

magnificence *noun* **= splendour**, glory, brilliance, majesty, grandeur, nobility, opulence, stateliness, sumptuousness

magnificent *adjective*
1 = splendid, cool (*informal*), impressive, glorious, gorgeous, sublime, majestic, sumptuous, regal, imposing
2 = excellent, fine, brilliant, outstanding, superb, splendid, phat (*slang*)

magnify *verb* **1 = enlarge**, increase, boost, expand, intensify, heighten, amplify, dilate, blow up (*informal*)
2 = exaggerate, inflate, overstate, overplay, overemphasize

magnitude *noun*
1 = importance, note, weight, moment, consequence, significance, greatness
2 = size, amount, mass, volume, extent, quantity, amplitude

maid *noun* **1 = girl**, damsel, lass, maiden, wench
2 = servant, housemaid, maidservant, serving-maid

maiden *noun* **1 = girl**, damsel, lass, virgin, maid, wench
▶ *adjective* **2 = unmarried**, unwed
3 = first, initial, inaugural, introductory

maidenly *adjective* **= modest**, pure, decent, demure, chaste, decorous, virginal

mail *noun* **1 = letters**, post, correspondence, junk mail
2 = postal service, collection, delivery, post office
▶ *verb* **3 = send**, post, forward, transmit, dispatch

maim *verb* **= cripple**, injure, hurt, wound, disable, mutilate

main *adjective* **1 = chief**, major, prime, primary, principal, cardinal, foremost, predominant, leading • *the main reason*
▶ *noun* **2 = conduit**, line, cable, channel, pipe, duct
▷ **in the main = on the whole**, mostly, generally, mainly, for the most part, in general
See also: **essential**

mainly *adverb* **= chiefly**, mostly, largely, generally, primarily, predominantly, principally • *The staff members were mainly young.*

See also: **as a rule**

mainstay *noun* **1** = **pillar**, anchor, prop, backbone, buttress, bulwark, lynchpin

mainstream *adjective* = **conventional**, general, current, established, orthodox, accepted, prevailing, received, lamestream (*informal*)

maintain *verb* **1** = **continue**, preserve, retain, sustain, prolong, perpetuate, carry on, keep up
2 = **support**, supply, care for, look after, provide for, take care of
3 = **assert**, claim, state, declare, insist, contend, profess, avow

maintenance *noun*
1 = **continuation**, carrying-on, perpetuation, prolongation
2 = **upkeep**, care, conservation, nurture, preservation, repairs, keeping
3 = **allowance**, keep, support, alimony

majestic *adjective* = **grand**, impressive, magnificent, superb, splendid, monumental, sublime, stately, grandiose, regal

majesty *noun* = **grandeur**, glory, pomp, nobility, splendour, magnificence, stateliness

major *adjective* **1** = **important**, significant, critical, crucial, outstanding, leading • *a major problem*
OPPOSITE: minor
2 = **main**, chief, senior, higher, supreme, bigger, greater, leading
See also: **principal**

majority *noun* **1** = **most**, bulk, best part, better part • *The majority of our cheeses are made with cow's milk.*
2 = **adulthood**, maturity, manhood *or* womanhood, seniority

make *verb* **1** = **create**, build, produce, form, manufacture, fashion, assemble, construct, fabricate • *She makes all her own clothes.*
2 = **force**, drive, compel, coerce, oblige, impel • *He tried to make me lie for him.*

3 = **produce**, cause, create, effect, generate, accomplish, bring about, give rise to, lead to
4 = **amount to**, form, compose, constitute, add up to
5 = **perform**, do, effect, execute, carry out
6 = **earn**, win, get, gain, clear, net, obtain
▷ **make a difference** *See* **matter**
▷ **make a mistake** *See* **err**
▷ **make an attempt** *See* **try**
▷ **make an effort** *See* **strive, try**
▷ **make certain** *See* **ensure**
▷ **make for** = **head for**, aim for, be bound for, head towards
▷ **make fun of** *See* **mock, tease**
▷ **make it** (*Informal*) = **succeed**, arrive (*informal*), prosper, get on
▷ **make known** *See* **advise, announce**
▷ **make off** = **flee**, bolt, clear out (*informal*), run away *or* run off, take to one's heels
▷ **make off with** = **steal**, kidnap, abduct, carry off, filch, pinch (*informal*), run away with *or* run off with
▷ **make out** = **see**, discover, recognize, detect, perceive, distinguish, discern;
= **understand**, follow, grasp, comprehend, decipher, fathom, work out; = **write out**, complete, draw up, fill in *or* fill out;
= **pretend**, claim, assert, let on, make as if *or* make as though;
= **fare**, manage, get on
▷ **make sure** *See* **ensure**
▷ **make up** = **form**, compose, constitute, comprise • *Westerners make up the majority of the team*;
= **invent**, manufacture, fabricate, formulate, concoct • *It's very unkind of you to make up stories about him*; = **complete**, supply, fill; = **settle**, reconcile, bury the hatchet, call it quits
▷ **make up for** = **compensate for**, balance, offset, atone for, make amends for, recompense
▷ **make up your mind** *See* **decide, resolve**
▷ **make use of** *See* **employ**
▶ *noun* **7** = **brand**, model • *a*

m

certain make of wristwatch
See also: **issue, reach, shape, sort, type**

> **INFORMALLY SPEAKING**
> **make it**: succeed
> **make like**: imitate
> **make something of**: start an argument
> **on the make**: ambitiously trying for success

make-believe noun = **fantasy**, imagination, pretense, play-acting, unreality

maker noun = **manufacturer**, producer, builder, constructor

makeshift adjective = **temporary**, substitute, provisional, expedient, stopgap

make-up noun **1** = **cosmetics**, face (informal), paint (informal), powder, greasepaint (theatre) **2** = **structure**, organization, construction, constitution, assembly, format, arrangement, composition, configuration **3** = **nature**, character, constitution, disposition, temperament

making noun = **creation**, production, building, construction, manufacture, assembly, fabrication • the making of this movie
▷ **in the making** = **budding**, potential, up-and-coming, emergent • a captain in the making
▷ **makings** = **beginnings**, potential, capacity, ingredients

maladjusted adjective = **disturbed**, unstable, neurotic, alienated

maladministration noun = **mismanagement**, corruption, inefficiency, incompetence, malpractice, dishonesty, misrule

maladroit adjective = **clumsy**, awkward, inept, inexpert, unskilful

malady noun = **disease**, complaint, illness, disorder, ailment, sickness, affliction, infirmity

malaise noun = **unease**, depression, anxiety, melancholy, disquiet

malcontent noun = **troublemaker**, rebel, agitator, mischief-maker, stirrer (informal)

male noun **1** = **man**, boy, gentleman • a pride of lions with three males, ten females, and six cubs
▶ adjective **2** = **masculine** • the finest male actor in movies today

malefactor noun = **wrongdoer**, criminal, offender, villain, delinquent, miscreant, evildoer

malevolence noun = **malice**, hate, hatred, spite, ill will, rancour, vindictiveness

malevolent adjective (Formal) = **malicious**, hostile, malign, vengeful, vindictive, ill-natured, spiteful

malformation noun = **deformity**, distortion, misshapenness

malformed adjective = **misshapen**, twisted, abnormal, irregular, crooked, distorted, deformed

malfunction verb **1** = **break down**, fail, go wrong
▶ noun **2** = **fault**, failure, flaw, defect, glitch, breakdown

malice noun = **ill will**, hate, hatred, spite, animosity, enmity, evil intent, malevolence, vindictiveness

malicious adjective = **spiteful**, mean, vicious, cruel, malevolent (formal) • She described the charges as malicious.
See also: **unkind**

malign verb **1** = **disparage**, abuse, smear, libel, defame, vilify, slander, denigrate, run down
▶ adjective **2** = **evil**, bad, harmful, hostile, destructive, wicked, malignant, injurious, malevolent, pernicious

malignant adjective **1** = **harmful**, hostile, destructive, hurtful, malign, malevolent, pernicious, spiteful **2** (Medical) = **uncontrollable**, deadly, dangerous, fatal, cancerous, irremediable

malleable adjective **1** = **workable**, plastic, soft, ductile, tensile **2** = **manageable**, compliant, impressionable, adaptable,

m

biddable, pliable, tractable

malodorous *adjective* = **smelly**, offensive, funky (*slang*), putrid, fetid, mephitic, nauseating, noisome, reeking, stinking

malpractice *noun* = **misconduct**, abuse, negligence, mismanagement, dereliction

maltreat *verb* = **abuse**, injure, hurt, harm, bully, mistreat, ill-treat

mammoth *adjective* = **gigantic**, huge, giant, massive, enormous, mountainous, immense, monumental, colossal, prodigious

man *noun* **1** = **male**, guy (*informal*), gentleman • *a young man*
2 = **human**, person, individual, soul, human being
3 = **mankind**, people, humanity, humankind, Homo sapiens, human race
4 = **manservant**, servant, attendant, retainer, valet
▶ *adjective*
▷ **man-made** = **artificial**, synthetic, mock, ersatz, manufactured
▶ *verb* **5** = **staff**, people, crew, occupy, garrison

manacle *noun* **1** = **handcuff**, bond, chain, iron, shackle, fetter
▶ *verb* **2** = **handcuff**, chain, bind, shackle, fetter, put in chains

manage *verb* **1** = **succeed in**, effect, engineer, accomplish, arrange, contrive • *We managed to find somewhere to sit.*
2 = **be in charge of**, run, control, direct, command • *Within two years, he was managing the store.*
3 = **handle**, use, control, operate, manipulate
4 = **cope**, survive, carry on, get by (*informal*), make do, muddle through
See also: **administer, conduct, deal, do, head, lead, oversee, supervise, take care of**

manageable *adjective* = **docile**, easy, compliant, amenable, submissive

management *noun* **1** = **running**, control, direction • *The zoo needed better management.*
2 = **directors**, board, administration, bosses (*informal*), employers • *The management is doing its best.*

manager *noun* = **supervisor**, director, executive, boss (*informal*) • *the manager of the company's Atlantic division*
See also: **chief, head, superior**

mandate *noun* = **command**, order, commission, instruction, decree, directive, edict

mandatory *adjective* = **compulsory**, binding, required, requisite, obligatory

manfully *adverb* = **bravely**, hard, boldly, valiantly, resolutely, courageously, determinedly, gallantly, stoutly

mangle *verb* = **crush**, destroy, tear, ruin, spoil, wreck, distort, disfigure, mutilate, deform

mangy *adjective* = **scruffy**, dirty, shoddy, shabby, squalid, seedy, moth-eaten, scuzzy (*slang*)

manhandle *verb* = **rough up**, maul, paw (*informal*), knock about *or* knock around

manhood *noun* = **manliness**, masculinity, virility

mania *noun* **1** = **madness**, dementia, insanity, delirium, lunacy, derangement
2 = **obsession**, thing (*informal*), passion, preoccupation, fad (*informal*), craze, fixation, fetish

maniac *noun* **1** = **madman** *or* **madwoman**, lunatic, psychopath, psycho (*slang*)
2 = **fanatic**, fan, enthusiast, freak (*informal*), fiend (*informal*)

manic See **furious**

manifest *adjective* **1** (*Formal*) = **obvious**, clear, patent, plain, blatant, glaring, conspicuous • *the manifest failure of the policy*
▶ *verb* **2** = **display**, show, reveal, express, expose, exhibit, demonstrate
See also: **betray, visible**

manifestation *noun* = **display**, show, sign, mark, symptom, demonstration, exhibition, indication, expression

m

manifold *adjective* = **numerous**, many, various, multiple, diverse, assorted, varied, copious, multifarious

manipulate *verb* 1 = **operate**, use, work, handle
2 = **influence**, control, direct, engineer, maneuver

mankind *noun* = **people**, man, humanity, humankind, Homo sapiens, human race

manliness *noun* = **virility**, courage, bravery, masculinity, vigour, boldness, fearlessness, valour

manly *adjective* = **virile**, strong, brave, bold, vigorous, courageous, fearless, masculine, manful, strapping

manner *noun* 1 = **way**, fashion, style, mode • *She smiled again in a friendly manner.*
2 = **behaviour**, conduct, bearing, demeanour • *her kind manner*
3 = **type**, form, kind, brand, sort, category, variety

mannered *adjective* = **affected**, artificial, pretentious, stilted

mannerism *noun* = **habit**, trick, characteristic, trait, quirk, foible, idiosyncrasy, peculiarity

manners *plural noun*
1 = **behaviour**, conduct, demeanour
2 = **politeness**, courtesy, etiquette, decorum, refinement, p's and q's

manoeuvre *verb* 1 = **steer**, negotiate, guide, navigate • *It took expertise to manoeuvre the boat so close to the shore.*
2 = **manipulate**, engineer, scheme, contrive, machinate, pull strings, wangle (*informal*)
▶ *noun* 3 = **tactic**, dodge, ploy, ruse • *manoeuvres to block the changes on the team*
4 = **movement**, operation, exercise
See also: **ease, measure**

mansion *noun* = **residence**, seat, hall, villa, manor

manslaughter *See* **murder**

mantle *noun* 1 = **cloak**, wrap, hood, cape, shawl
2 = **covering**, screen, blanket, veil, curtain, shroud, pall, canopy

manual *adjective* 1 = **hand-operated**, human, physical
▶ *noun* 2 = **handbook**, bible, instructions

manufacture *verb* 1 = **make**, process, produce, assemble, fabricate, mass-produce • *Several models are being manufactured here.*
2 = **concoct**, invent, devise, fabricate, cook up (*informal*), make up, think up, trump up
▶ *noun* 3 = **making**, production, assembly, fabrication, mass production • *the manufacture of cardboard boxes*

manufacturer *noun* = **maker**, producer, creator, builder, industrialist, constructor

manure *noun* = **compost**, fertilizer, droppings, dung, muck, excrement, ordure, road apple (*slang*)

many *adjective* 1 = **numerous**, countless, myriad, innumerable, umpteen (*informal*) • *Cooking is one of his many hobbies.*
OPPOSITE: few
▶ *noun* 2 = **a lot**, plenty, a mass, a multitude, large numbers, lots (*informal*), scores, millions (*informal*) • *in many of these neighbourhoods*
OPPOSITE: few

mar *verb* = **spoil**, damage, hurt, ruin, taint, impair, stain, scar, tarnish, disfigure, blemish, detract from

maraud *verb* = **raid**, loot, ravage, forage, ransack, plunder, pillage

marauder *noun* = **raider**, bandit, outlaw, buccaneer, plunderer

march *verb* 1 = **walk**, file, pace, parade, stride, strut
▶ *noun* 2 = **walk**, trek, routemarch
3 = **progress**, advance, development, evolution, progression

margin *noun* = **edge**, border, side, rim, brink, boundary, verge, perimeter, periphery

marginal *adjective*

1 = borderline, peripheral, bordering, on the edge
2 = insignificant, small, minor, slight, minimal, negligible
marijuana noun = **cannabis**, pot (slang), dope (slang), grass (slang), hemp
marinate See **steep**
marine adjective = **nautical**, naval, maritime, seagoing, seafaring
mariner noun = **sailor**, salt, seaman, seafarer, sea dog
marital adjective = **matrimonial**, conjugal, connubial, nuptial
maritime adjective **1 = nautical**, marine, naval, oceanic, seafaring
2 = coastal, seaside, littoral
mark noun **1 = stain**, line, spot, streak, scratch, fingerprint, scar, blemish, blot, smudge, handprint • *I can't get this mark off the curtain.*
2 = sign, device, label, flag, symbol, hallmark, badge, token, emblem
3 = criterion, measure, standard, norm, yardstick
4 = target, goal, aim, object, purpose, objective
▸ verb **5 = stain**, streak, scratch, scar, blemish, blot, smudge • *to stop the shoes from marking the floor*
6 = characterize, identify, label, brand, flag, stamp
7 = distinguish, show, illustrate, exemplify, denote
8 = observe, note, watch, attend, mind, notice, pay attention, pay heed
9 = grade, assess, correct, evaluate, appraise
See also: **feature, quality**

> **INFORMALLY SPEAKING**
> **make your mark**: succeed
> **miss the mark**: fail to do what you tried to do
> **up to the mark**: meeting a certain standard

marked adjective = **noticeable**, clear, patent, prominent, obvious, distinct, striking, pronounced, blatant, conspicuous, decided
markedly adverb = **noticeably**, obviously, clearly, considerably, decidedly, distinctly, strikingly, conspicuously
market noun **1 = fair**, bazaar, farmers' market • *the local market*
▷ **market price** See **value**
▸ verb **2 = sell**, retail, vend
See also: **shop**
marketable adjective = **in demand**, wanted, salable, sought after
marksman, markswoman noun = **sharpshooter**, crack shot (informal), good shot
maroon verb = **abandon**, leave, strand, desert, leave high and dry (informal)
marriage noun = **matrimony** (formal), wedlock (formal) • *six years of marriage*
RELATED WORDS
adjectives: conjugal, connubial, marital, nuptial
marry verb **1 = wed**, get hitched (slang), tie the knot (informal)
2 = unite, link, join, bond, ally, merge, unify, knit, yoke
marsh noun = **swamp**, bog, quagmire, slough, morass, fen

TYPES OF MARSH

bayou
bog
fen
marshland
mire
morass
mud flat
muskeg (Canad)
quagmire
quicksand
swamp
swampland
wetland

---

marshal verb **1 = arrange**, group, order, organize, deploy, array, align, draw up, line up
2 = conduct, lead, guide, escort, usher, shepherd
marshy adjective = **swampy**, wet,

waterlogged, boggy, quaggy

martial *adjective* = **military**, belligerent, bellicose, warlike

martinet *noun* = **disciplinarian**, stickler

martyrdom *noun* = **persecution**, suffering, ordeal

marvel *verb* **1** = **wonder**, gape, be amazed, be awed
▶ *noun* **2** = **wonder**, phenomenon, miracle, prodigy, portent

marvellous *adjective* = **excellent**, wonderful, remarkable, brilliant, magnificent, superb, splendid, first-rate • *a marvellous actor*
OPPOSITE: terrible
See also: **grand, incredible**

masculine *adjective* = **male**, manly, manlike, mannish, virile

mash See **crush, press**

mask *noun* **1** = **disguise**, front, cover, screen, veil, camouflage, guise, façade
▶ *verb* **2** = **disguise**, cover, screen, hide, cloak, veil, conceal, obscure, camouflage

masquerade *noun* **1** = **masked ball**, revel, fancy dress party
2 = **pretense**, screen, pose, mask, cloak, disguise, deception, cover-up, subterfuge
▶ *verb* **3** = **pose**, pretend *or* pretend to be, disguise, impersonate, dissemble, dissimulate, pass oneself off

mass *noun* **1** = **lot**, crowd, load, pile, mob, lump, throng, heap • *a mass of papers*
2 = **piece**, block, chunk, lump, hunk
3 = **size**, bulk, magnitude, greatness
▶ *adjective* **4** = **widespread**, general, popular, universal • *mass unemployment*
▷ **mass production** See **manufacture**
▶ *verb* **5** = **gather**, group, assemble, congregate • *The crowd began to mass in the square.*
See also: **jam, majority, tangle**

massacre *noun* **1** = **slaughter**, murder, carnage, holocaust, extermination, annihilation, blood bath, butchery
▶ *verb* **2** = **slaughter**, kill, murder, butcher, exterminate, cut to pieces, mow down, wipe out

massage *noun* **1** = **rub-down**, manipulation
▶ *verb* **2** = **rub down**, manipulate, knead

masses See **lot, public**

massive *adjective* = **huge**, big, enormous, hefty, mammoth, whopping (*informal*), immense, monumental, gigantic, colossal

mass-produce See **manufacture**

master *verb* **1** = **learn**, grasp, become proficient in, get the hang of (*informal*) • *She found it easy to master the latest technology.*
2 = **overcome**, defeat, tame, conquer, vanquish, triumph over
3 = **ruler**, director, chief, manager, commander, governor, boss (*informal*), controller, lord
4 = **expert**, ace (*informal*), wizard, genius, maestro, virtuoso, doyen, past master
5 = **teacher**, guide, instructor, guru, tutor
▶ *adjective* **6** = **main**, chief, prime, principal, foremost, predominant, leading

masterful *adjective* **1** = **skilful**, expert, fine, world-class, supreme, consummate, superlative, first-rate, adroit, masterly
2 = **domineering**, arrogant, imperious, high-handed, bossy (*informal*), overbearing, overweening

masterly *adjective* = **skilful**, expert, crack (*slang*), world-class, supreme, masterful, consummate, first-rate, adroit

mastermind *verb* **1** = **plan**, manage, direct, organize, conceive, devise
▶ *noun* **2** = **organizer**, director, manager, brain *or* brains (*informal*), engineer, architect, planner

masterpiece *noun* = **classic**,

jewel, magnum opus, *pièce de résistance* (French), *tour de force* (French)

mastery noun 1 = **expertise**, skill, prowess, know-how (*informal*), finesse, proficiency, virtuosity
2 = **control**, command, domination, supremacy, superiority, ascendancy, upper hand, whip hand

mat See **tangle**

match noun 1 = **game**, competition, contest • *a tennis match*
2 = **equal**, rival, counterpart, peer
3 = **marriage**, alliance, partnership, pairing
▶ verb 4 = **correspond**, agree, suit, fit, tally, go with • *The shoes matched her dress.*
5 = **rival**, compare, compete, equal, emulate, measure up to
See also: **blend**

matching adjective = **identical**, like, twin, equivalent, coordinating, corresponding

matchless adjective = **unequalled**, supreme, unparalleled, unmatched, superlative, incomparable, unsurpassed, unrivalled, inimitable

mate noun 1 = **partner**, husband or wife, spouse
2 = **colleague**, associate, companion
3 = **assistant**, helper, subordinate
▶ verb 4 = **couple**, pair, breed

material noun 1 = **cloth**, fabric • *the thick material of her skirt*
2 = **substance**, matter, stuff • *the materials needed to build the shed*
3 = **information**, evidence, data, facts, notes
▶ adjective 4 = **physical**, substantial, concrete, bodily, tangible, palpable, corporeal
5 = **important**, serious, significant, essential, vital, meaningful, momentous, weighty
6 = **relevant**, applicable, pertinent, apposite, apropos, germane

materialistic See **greedy**

materialize verb = **occur**, appear, happen, come about, come to pass, take shape, turn up

materially adverb = **significantly**, much, seriously, essentially, greatly, substantially, gravely

maternal adjective = **motherly**

maternity noun = **motherhood**, motherliness (*informal*)

matrimonial adjective = **marital**, conjugal, connubial, nuptial

matrimony noun = **marriage**, nuptials, wedlock, wedding ceremony

matted adjective = **tangled**, knotted, tousled, uncombed

matter noun 1 = **situation**, issue, business, question, affair, subject • *business matters*
2 = **substance**, material, stuff • *The atom is the smallest divisible particle of matter.*
3 = **problem**, worry, trouble, difficulty, complication, distress
▶ verb 4 = **be important**, count, be of consequence, make a difference • *It doesn't matter what you wear to the party.*
See also: **event**, **item**

matter-of-fact adjective = **unsentimental**, plain, sober, mundane, down-to-earth, deadpan, unimaginative, emotionless, prosaic

mature verb 1 = **grow up**, come of age, reach adulthood • *Some children mature earlier than others.*
▶ adjective 2 = **grown-up**, adult, full-fledged, full-grown, grown • *He's very mature for his age.*
See also: **develop**

maturity noun = **adulthood**, experience, wisdom, manhood or womanhood, ripeness

maudlin adjective = **sentimental**, slushy (*informal*), mawkish, overemotional, tearful, weepy (*informal*)

maul verb 1 = **ill-treat**, abuse, molest, paw, manhandle
2 = **tear**, batter, claw, mangle, lacerate

m

mausoleum *See* **grave, tomb**

maverick *noun* **1 = rebel**, protester, radical, eccentric, dissenter, heretic, iconoclast, individualist, nonconformist
▸ *adjective* **2 = rebel**, radical, eccentric, heretical, dissenting, iconoclastic, individualistic, nonconformist

mawkish *adjective* **= sentimental**, emotional, slushy (*informal*), maudlin, schmaltzy (*slang*)

maxim *noun* **= saying**, rule, adage, motto, dictum, proverb, aphorism, axiom

maximum *noun* **1 = most**, height, ceiling, utmost, upper limit • *The restaurant can seat a maximum of 30 people.*
OPPOSITE: minimum
▸ *adjective* **2 = top**, utmost • *the maximum recommended dosage*
OPPOSITE: minimum
See also: **full, limit**

maybe *adverb* **= perhaps**, possibly, conceivably, it could be • *Maybe I should have done a bit more.*

mayhem *noun* **= chaos**, violence, trouble, disorder, destruction, confusion, havoc, commotion, fracas

maze *noun* **1 = labyrinth**
2 = web, confusion, tangle, imbroglio

meadow *noun* **= field**, pasture, grassland, lea (*poetic*)

meagre *adjective* **= inadequate**, sparse, paltry, scant, measly (*informal*) • *a meagre pension*
See also: **few**

meal *noun* **= repast**, dinner, feast, banquet • *She sat next to me throughout the meal.*

mean¹ *verb* **1 = signify**, indicate, denote • *The flashing signal means stop.*
2 = intend, plan, aim • *I meant to phone you, but didn't have time.*
See also: **represent**

mean² *adjective* **1 = spiteful**, nasty, malicious, hurtful • *Why are you being so mean to me?*
2 = miserly, tight (*informal*), stingy, parsimonious, penny-pinching, tight-fisted • *Don't*
be mean with the tip.
3 = despicable, petty, shameful, lousy (*slang*), callous, shabby, vile, sordid, contemptible, hard-hearted, scuzzy (*slang*)
See also: **horrible, sneaky, unkind**

mean³ *noun* **1 = average**, middle, balance, compromise, norm, midpoint, happy medium
▸ *adjective* **2 = average**, standard, middle

meander *verb* **1 = wind**, turn, snake, zigzag
2 = wander, stroll, ramble
▸ *noun* **3 = curve**, turn, twist, bend, loop, coil, zigzag

meandering *See* **indirect**

meaning *noun* **= significance**, message, sense, drift, gist • *the meaning of this dream*

meaningful *adjective* **= significant**, important, material, useful, relevant, valid, worthwhile, purposeful

meaningless *adjective* **= pointless**, empty, useless, senseless, vain, insignificant, worthless, futile, inconsequential, inane

meanness *noun* **1 = miserliness**, selfishness, niggardliness, parsimony, stinginess
2 = pettiness, disgracefulness, ignobility, narrow-mindedness, shabbiness, shamefulness

means *plural noun* **1 = method**, way, medium, agency, process, instrument, mode
2 = money, income, capital, wealth, fortune, affluence, wherewithal, funds, resources
▷ **by all means = certainly**, definitely, surely, doubtlessly, of course
▷ **by no means = in no way**, definitely not, not in the least, on no account

meant *See* **supposed**

meantime, meanwhile *adverb* **= at the same time**, simultaneously, concurrently, in the interim

measly *adjective* **= meagre**, poor, pathetic, miserable, paltry, pitiful, skimpy, puny, scanty

measurable *adjective*
= **quantifiable**, significant, assessable, perceptible

measure *verb* 1 = **gauge**, survey • *We measured the size of the room.*
▷ **measure up to** = **achieve**, be equal to, be suitable, come up to scratch (*informal*), fit the bill or fill the bill, make the grade (*informal*)
▶ *noun* 2 = **amount**, degree, portion, proportion • *There has been a measure of agreement.*
3 = **action**, step, procedure, means, manoeuvre, expedient • *Tough measures are needed to maintain safety.*
4 = **gauge**, rule, scale, metre, yardstick
5 = **law**, bill, act, resolution, statute
6 = **rhythm**, beat, meter, verse, cadence
See also: **extent, quantity**

measured *adjective* 1 = **steady**, even, slow, regular, solemn, dignified, sedate, leisurely, stately, unhurried
2 = **considered**, deliberate, sober, calculated, reasoned, studied, well-thought-out

measurement *noun*
= **calculation**, assessment, evaluation, valuation, calibration, computation, mensuration

meat *noun* = **flesh**

meaty *adjective* 1 = **brawny**, heavy, solid, beefy (*informal*), muscular, sturdy, burly, heavily built, strapping
2 = **interesting**, significant, rich, substantial, meaningful, profound

mechanical *adjective*
1 = **automatic**, automated
2 = **unthinking**, routine, automatic, involuntary, cursory, perfunctory, impersonal, instinctive, unfeeling

mechanism *noun* 1 = **machine**, device, tool, instrument, appliance, apparatus, contrivance

2 = **process**, system, agency, operation, procedure, method, technique, means

meddle *verb* = **interfere**, intervene, tamper, pry, intrude, butt in

meddler *noun* = **busybody**, snooper • *a meddler in everyone's personal affairs*

meddlesome *adjective*
= **interfering**, intrusive, mischievous, meddling, officious, prying

mediate *verb* = **intervene**, referee, umpire, reconcile, arbitrate, conciliate, intercede, step in (*informal*)

mediation *noun* = **intervention**, arbitration, reconciliation, conciliation, intercession

mediator *noun* = **negotiator**, referee, arbitrator, umpire, middleman, peacemaker, intermediary, arbiter, go-between, honest broker

medical *See* **examination**

medication *See* **drug, medicine**

medicinal *adjective*
= **therapeutic**, medical, healing, remedial, restorative, curative

medicine *noun* = **remedy**, drug, medication • *Don't forget to take your medicine.*
See also: **cure**

mediocre *adjective* = **second-rate**, average, ordinary, pedestrian, indifferent, inferior, passable, middling, so-so (*informal*), undistinguished, meh (*slang*)

mediocrity *noun*
= **insignificance**, indifference, inferiority, ordinariness, unimportance

meditate *verb* 1 = **reflect**, think, consider, ponder, deliberate, contemplate, muse, cogitate, ruminate
2 = **plan**, intend, purpose, scheme, have in mind

meditation *noun* = **reflection**, study, thought, musing, contemplation, cogitation, pondering, rumination

medium *adjective* 1 = **average**,

m

medium-sized, middling • *He was of medium height.*
▸ *noun* **2** = **means**, vehicle, channel • *the medium of television*
3 = **middle**, mean, average, compromise, centre, midpoint
4 = **environment**, atmosphere, setting, surroundings, milieu, conditions
5 = **spiritualist**
See also: **moderate**
medium-sized *See* **medium**
medley *noun* = **mixture**, assortment, jumble, mishmash, hodgepodge, farrago, *mélange* (French), miscellany, mixed bag (*informal*), potpourri
meek *adjective* = **submissive**, timid, unassuming, docile, deferential • *a meek, mild-mannered young man*
OPPOSITE: bold
See also: **gentle, humble, mild**
meekness *noun*
= **submissiveness**, compliance, humility, deference, modesty, acquiescence, docility, gentleness, mildness, timidity
meet *verb* **1** = **encounter**, bump into (*informal*), come upon, run across, run into • *I met him at the mall yesterday.*
2 = **gather**, assemble, convene, congregate, get together • *We meet for lunch once a week.*
3 = **fulfill**, answer, satisfy • *services intended to meet the needs of the elderly*
4 = **converge**, join, cross, touch, connect, intersect, come together, link up
5 = **experience**, face, bear, suffer, undergo, endure, encounter, go through
See also: **greet, receive**
▹ **meet head-on** *See* **hit**
meeting *noun* **1** = **gathering**, conference, convention, reunion, congress, get-together (*informal*) • *a business meeting*
2 = **encounter**, rendezvous, tryst • *a chance meeting*
See also: **appointment**
melancholy *noun* **1** = **sadness**, depression, misery, sorrow,

gloom, unhappiness, despondency, dejection, low spirits
▸ *adjective* **2** = **sad**, depressed, gloomy, miserable, mournful, despondent, glum, dispirited, downhearted, sorrowful
melee, mêlée *noun* = **fight**, brawl, scuffle, scrimmage, fracas, free-for-all (*informal*), rumpus, skirmish, tussle
mellifluous *adjective* = **sweet**, soft, smooth, soothing, silvery, dulcet, euphonious, honeyed, sweet-sounding
mellow *adjective* **1** = **soft**, rich, sweet, mature, delicate, ripe, full-flavoured
▸ *verb* **2** = **mature**, season, develop, improve, soften, sweeten, ripen
melodious *adjective* = **tuneful**, musical, melodic, harmonious, dulcet, euphonious, sweet-sounding
melodramatic *adjective* = **theatrical**, sensational, histrionic • *Don't you think you're being rather melodramatic?*
melody *noun* **1** = **tune**, music, air, song, strain, theme
2 = **tunefulness**, harmony, euphony, melodiousness, musicality
melt *verb* **1** = **dissolve**, thaw • *The snow had melted.*
2 = **disappear**, dissolve, vanish, disperse, evaporate • *My inhibitions melted.*
3 = **soften**, relax, disarm, mollify
See also: **warm**
member *noun*
1 = **representative**, associate, fellow
2 = **limb**, part, arm, leg, extremity, appendage
membership *noun* **1** = **members**, body, associates, fellows
2 = **participation**, belonging, fellowship, enrolment
memento *noun* = **souvenir**, memorial, trophy, reminder, remembrance, relic, token, keepsake
memo *See* **message, note**

memoir noun = **account**, record, life, journal, biography, essay, narrative, monograph

memoirs plural noun = **autobiography**, diary, experiences, journals, life story, memories, recollections, reminiscences

memorable adjective = **notable**, historic, striking, catchy, unforgettable • a memorable victory

memorandum noun = **note**, minute, message, communication, memo, reminder, jotting

memorial noun 1 = **monument**, record, plaque, souvenir, remembrance, memento
▶ adjective 2 = **commemorative**, monumental

memorize verb = **remember**, learn, commit to memory, learn by heart, learn by rote

memory noun 1 = **recall**, remembrance (formal) • Every detail is fresh in my memory.
2 = **commemoration**, honor, remembrance

menace noun 1 = **threat**, warning, intimidation
2 (Informal) = **nuisance**, plague, pest, troublemaker, annoyance
▶ verb 3 = **threaten**, loom, bully, intimidate, frighten, terrorize, lour or lower

menacing adjective = **threatening**, ominous, forbidding, frightening, intimidating, looming, louring or lowering

mend verb 1 = **repair**, fix, restore, patch, renovate • to mend a broken chain
2 = **improve**, reform, correct, amend, rectify, ameliorate, emend
3 = **heal**, recover, recuperate, convalesce, get better
▶ noun 4 = **repair**, patch, stitch, darn
▷ **on the mend** = **convalescent**, getting better, improving, recovering, recuperating
See also: **piece together**

mendacious adjective = **lying**, false, fraudulent, deceptive, dishonest, deceitful, duplicitous, fallacious, insincere, untruthful

menial adjective 1 = **unskilled**, routine, boring, dull, humdrum, low-status
▶ noun 2 = **servant**, attendant, lackey, drudge, flunky, underling

mental adjective 1 = **intellectual**, cerebral
2 (Informal) = **insane**, mad, unstable, psychotic, disturbed, unbalanced, deranged, unhinged

mentality noun = **attitude**, character, outlook, personality, psychology, disposition, make-up, cast of mind

mentally adverb = **in the mind**, psychologically, intellectually, in one's head, inwardly

mention verb 1 = **refer to**, hint, intimate, broach, allude to, bring up, touch on, touch upon • I may not have mentioned it to her.
▶ noun 2 = **reference**, allusion • There was no mention of elections.
3 = **acknowledgment**, tribute, recognition, citation
See also: **comment, note, observe, refer, remark**

mentor noun = **guide**, coach, teacher, adviser, instructor, guru, tutor, counselor

menu noun = **bill of fare**, carte du jour (French)

mercantile adjective = **commercial**, trading

mercenary adjective 1 = **greedy**, sordid, acquisitive, avaricious, grasping, money-grubbing (informal), venal
▶ noun 2 = **hireling**, soldier of fortune

merchandise noun = **goods**, stock, produce, commodities, products, wares

merchant noun = **tradesman**, retailer, dealer, supplier, trader, seller, broker, vendor, trafficker, salesman, wholesaler, shopkeeper, purveyor

m

merciful adjective
 1 = **compassionate**, kind, humane • merciful and sympathetic to others
 OPPOSITE: merciless
 2 = **forgiving**, lenient • We can only hope the court is merciful.
 OPPOSITE: merciless
merciless adjective = **cruel**, ruthless, callous, heartless, implacable • a merciless dictator
 OPPOSITE: merciful
mercurial adjective = **changeable**, mobile, active, volatile, unpredictable, spirited, lively, impulsive, irrepressible, capricious, quicksilver, sprightly
mercy noun 1 = **compassion**, quarter, pity, kindness • She showed no mercy.
 2 = **forgiveness**, leniency • He threw himself upon the mercy of the court.
 3 = **blessing**, boon, godsend
mere adjective 1 = **simple**, common, pure, plain, bare, sheer, nothing more than
merely See **only**
meretricious adjective = **trashy**, flashy, showy, gaudy, garish, tinsel, gimcrack, tawdry
merge verb = **combine**, meet, join, mix, unite, blend, converge, fuse, mingle, amalgamate, coalesce
merger noun = **union**, coalition, combination, consolidation, fusion, amalgamation, incorporation
merit noun 1 = **worth**, value, excellence, virtue • Box-office success mattered more than artistic merit.
 2 = **advantage**, asset, strength, virtue, strong point • Despite its merits, the work would never be used.
 ▶ verb 3 = **deserve**, earn, warrant, be entitled to, be worthy of • Such ideas merit careful consideration.
 See also: **quality**
meritorious adjective
 = **praiseworthy**, good, excellent, worthy, deserving, admirable, commendable, laudable, virtuous, creditable
merriment noun = **fun**, laughter, festivity, amusement, glee, revelry, hilarity, jollity, joviality, mirth
merry adjective = **cheerful**, happy, festive, jolly, joyous, carefree, blithe, convivial
mesh noun 1 = **net**, network, web, netting, tracery
 ▶ verb 2 = **engage**, connect, combine, knit, coordinate, harmonize, interlock, dovetail
mesmerize verb = **entrance**, grip, fascinate, captivate, enthrall, hypnotize, hold spellbound
mess noun 1 = **disorder**, chaos, disarray • I'll clear up the mess later.
 2 = **difficulty**, fix (informal), jam (informal), turmoil, muddle • the reasons why the economy is in such a mess
 ▶ verb 3 (often with up) = **bungle**, botch up (informal), make a hash of (informal), muck up (slang) • He had messed up his career.
 4 (often with up) = **dirty**, clutter, dishevel, disarrange, scramble, pollute, muddle
 5 (often with with) = **interfere**, play, tamper, meddle, tinker
 ▷ **mess around** = **putter**, fool, dabble, amuse oneself or fool around, play around, trifle, toy with
 See also: **confusion, hole**

 | INFORMALLY SPEAKING
 | **mess around**: be busy without seeming to accomplish anything
 | **mess up**: spoil; do wrong
 | **mess with**: defy; provoke
message noun
 1 = **communication**, note, word, dispatch, memo, bulletin, memorandum • He left a voice-mail message.
 2 = **point**, moral, meaning, theme • the story's anti-violence message
messenger noun = **courier**, envoy • A messenger will deliver the documents.
messy adjective = **untidy**, dirty, sloppy (informal), chaotic,

m

confused, cluttered, dishevelled, disordered, disorganized, muddled, scuzzy (*slang*), shambolic

metamorphosis *noun* = **transformation**, change, conversion, mutation, alteration, transmutation

metaphor *noun* = **figure of speech**, image, symbol, analogy, allegory, trope

metaphorical *adjective* = **figurative**, symbolic, emblematic, allegorical

mete *verb* = **distribute**, deal, assign, administer, dispense, apportion, portion

meteoric *adjective* = **spectacular**, fast, overnight, sudden, rapid, brilliant, speedy, swift, dazzling

method *noun* **1** = **way**, approach, procedure, technique, mode • *her favourite method of making popcorn*
2 = **orderliness**, system, order, organization, purpose, pattern, regularity, planning
See also: **fashion, plan, practice, process, style**

methodical *adjective* = **orderly**, regular, organized, deliberate, precise, systematic, structured, disciplined, meticulous, businesslike

meticulous *adjective* = **thorough**, particular, strict, exact, precise, painstaking, fussy, scrupulous, fastidious, punctilious

meticulously See **well**

metre See **beat**

metropolis See **city**

mettle *noun* = **courage**, life, resolution, spirit, nerve, pluck, bravery, fortitude, vigour, gallantry, valour

microbe *noun* = **microorganism**, virus, bacterium, bug (*informal*), germ, bacillus

microscopic *adjective* = **tiny**, minute, invisible, negligible, minuscule, imperceptible, infinitesimal

microwave See **cook**

midday *noun* = **noon**, noonday, twelve o'clock

middle *noun* **1** = **centre**, midst,

halfway point • *in the middle of the room*
▶ *adjective* **2** = **central**, halfway
• *the middle house*

middle-class *adjective*
= **bourgeois**, traditional, conventional

middling *adjective* **1** = **mediocre**, indifferent, so-so (*informal*), tolerable, unremarkable, unexceptional
2 = **moderate**, medium, average, fair, modest, ordinary, adequate, passable, serviceable, all right, O.K. or okay (*informal*)

midget *noun* = **dwarf**, shrimp (*informal*), pygmy *or* pigmy, Tom Thumb

midnight *noun* = **twelve o'clock**, dead of night, middle of the night, the witching hour

midst *noun*
▷ **in the midst of** = **among**, during, amidst, in the middle of, in the thick of, surrounded by

midway *adjective, adverb*
= **halfway**, betwixt and between, in the middle

might *noun* = **power**, force, energy, strength, vigor
▷ **with might and main**
= **forcefully**, vigorously, mightily, lustily, manfully

mightily *adverb* **1** = **very**, much, highly, extremely, greatly, hugely, intensely, decidedly, exceedingly
2 = **powerfully**, strongly, vigorously, forcefully, lustily, energetically, manfully

mighty *adjective* = **powerful**, strong, robust, vigorous, forceful, sturdy, lusty, strapping

migrant *noun* **1** = **wanderer**, immigrant, rover, traveller, nomad, itinerant, drifter, emigrant
▶ *adjective* **2** = **travelling**, immigrant, migratory, nomadic, transient, itinerant, drifting, roving, shifting, vagrant, wandering

migrate *verb* = **move**, travel, journey, wander, roam, trek, voyage, emigrate, rove

m

migration noun = **wandering**, travel, movement, journey, trek, voyage, emigration, roving

migratory adjective = **nomadic**, migrant, transient, itinerant, peripatetic, roving

mild adjective 1 = **weak**, insipid • *a mild shampoo*
OPPOSITE: strong
2 = **gentle**, meek, placid • *a mild approach*
3 = **temperate**, balmy • *The area is famous for its mild winter climate.*
See also: **calm, quiet**

mildness noun = **gentleness**, clemency, warmth, moderation, calmness, tranquillity, docility, placidity

miles See **far**

milieu noun = **surroundings**, environment, scene, location, element, background, setting, locale

militant adjective = **aggressive**, active, vigorous, combative, assertive

military adjective 1 = **warlike**, armed, martial, soldierly
▶ noun 2 = **armed forces**, army, forces, services

militate verb
▷ **militate against** = **counteract**, oppose, counter, resist, be detrimental to, conflict with, tell against, weigh against

milk verb = **exploit**, pump, extract, take advantage of

mill noun 1 = **factory**, plant, foundry, works
2 = **grinder**, crusher
▶ verb 3 = **grind**, pound, crush, powder, grate
4 = **swarm**, crowd, throng

millstone noun 1 = **grindstone**, quernstone
2 = **burden**, weight, load, affliction, albatross, encumbrance

mime verb = **act out**, represent, gesture, simulate

mimic verb 1 = **imitate**, do (informal), caricature, ape, parody, impersonate
▶ noun 2 = **imitator**, impressionist, copycat (informal), impersonator, caricaturist

mimicry noun = **imitation**, caricature, parody, mockery, impersonation, burlesque, mimicking

mince verb 1 = **cut**, grind, chop, crumble, hash
2 (~ words) = **tone down**, moderate, weaken, spare, soften

mincing adjective = **affected**, camp (informal), precious, pretentious, dainty, effeminate, foppish, sissy

mind noun 1 = **brain**, head, imagination, psyche, intellect
• *You have a very suspicious mind.*
RELATED WORD
adjective: mental
2 = **memory**, remembrance, recollection
3 = **intention**, urge, wish, desire, notion, fancy, disposition, inclination, leaning
4 = **sanity**, reason, judgment, marbles (informal), mental balance, rationality, senses, wits
▷ **make up one's mind** = **decide**, choose, determine, resolve
▶ verb 5 = **be bothered**, care, object • *I don't mind what you do.*
6 = **look after**, watch, keep an eye on, take care of • *My mother is minding the store.*
7 = **pay attention**, note, mark, observe, heed, obey, listen to, pay heed to, take heed
8 = **be careful**, watch, be cautious, be on guard or be on one's guard, be wary, take care
See also: **will**

INFORMALLY SPEAKING
have a mind to: intend to
keep in mind: remember
make up your mind: decide
never mind: pay no attention to
on your mind: much in your thoughts
take someone's mind off: distract someone from something unpleasant

mindful adjective = **aware**, alert, careful, wary, conscious, watchful, alive to, heedful

mindless adjective = **stupid**,

foolish, idiotic, thoughtless, inane, moronic, unthinking, witless

mine noun 1 = **pit**, deposit, shaft, excavation, colliery
2 = **source**, fund, stock, store, reserve, supply, wealth, treasury, abundance, hoard
▶ verb 3 = **dig up**, extract, unearth, quarry, excavate, dig for, hew

miner noun = **coalminer**

mingle verb 1 = **mix**, join, combine, unite, merge, blend, interweave, intermingle
2 = **associate**, socialize, hobnob, consort, fraternize, hang about or hang around, rub shoulders (informal)

miniature adjective = **small**, minute, little, toy, tiny, diminutive, minuscule, scaled-down

minimal adjective = **minimum**, least, token, nominal, least possible, slightest, smallest

minimize verb 1 = **reduce**, decrease, shrink, diminish, curtail, prune, miniaturize
2 = **play down**, discount, decry, disparage, underrate, belittle, deprecate, make light of or make little of

minimum adjective 1 = **least possible**, minimal • the minimum requirements for the job
OPPOSITE: maximum
▶ noun 2 = **least**, lowest, nadir

minion noun = **follower**, henchman, underling, lackey, flunky, hanger-on, hireling, yes man

minister noun 1 = **clergyman**, cleric, priest, pastor, preacher, vicar, rector, parson
▶ verb 2 = **attend**, serve, tend, administer, cater to, pander to, take care of

ministry noun 1 = **department**, office, council, bureau, quango
2 = **holy orders**, the church, the priesthood

minor adjective = **lesser**, slight, secondary, petty, trivial, trifling • a minor injury

OPPOSITE: major
See also: **child, inferior, insignificant, unimportant**

minstrel noun = **musician**, singer, bard, songstress, troubadour

mint verb = **make**, strike, produce, cast, stamp, punch, coin

minus See **disadvantage**

minuscule adjective = **tiny**, minute, little, miniature, diminutive, microscopic, infinitesimal

minute¹ noun = **moment**, second, flash, instant • I'll be with you in just a minute.

minute² adjective 1 = **tiny**, small, negligible, microscopic, slender • Only a minute amount is needed.
OPPOSITE: vast
2 = **precise**, close, critical, detailed, exact, exhaustive, painstaking, meticulous, punctilious

minutes plural noun = **record**, transcript, memorandum, notes, proceedings, transactions

minutiae plural noun = **details**, finer points, ins and outs, niceties, particulars, subtleties, trifles, trivia

minx noun = **flirt**, coquette, hussy

miracle noun = **wonder**, marvel • It was a miracle that nobody was seriously hurt in the crash.

miraculous adjective = **wonderful**, amazing, extraordinary, incredible, unbelievable, phenomenal, unaccountable, prodigious, astonishing, astounding

mirage noun = **illusion**, hallucination, optical illusion

mire noun 1 = **swamp**, bog, quagmire, marsh, morass
2 = **mud**, dirt, ooze, muck, slime

mirror noun 1 = **looking-glass**, glass, reflector
▶ verb 2 = **reflect**, follow, copy, echo, emulate

mirth noun = **merriment**, fun, laughter, amusement, glee, revelry, cheerfulness, gaiety, hilarity, jollity, joviality

mirthful adjective = **merry**, happy, festive, playful, jolly, cheerful,

m

light-hearted, cheery, jovial, blithe, sportive

misadventure *noun*
= **misfortune**, accident, disaster, reverse, setback, catastrophe, debacle, mishap, calamity, bad luck

misanthropic *adjective*
= **antisocial**, cynical, unfriendly, malevolent

misapprehend *verb*
= **misunderstand**, mistake, misinterpret, misread, misconstrue

misapprehension *noun*
= **misunderstanding**, mistake, error, misconception, delusion, fallacy, misinterpretation

misappropriate *verb* = **steal**, pocket, misuse, misspend, embezzle, peculate

misbehave *verb* = **act up**, be disobedient, make a fuss, make trouble, make waves

miscalculate *verb* = **misjudge**, underestimate, err, blunder, overrate, overestimate, underrate, slip up

miscarriage *noun* = **failure**, error, breakdown, mishap, perversion

miscarry *verb* = **fail**, misfire, come to grief, fall through, go awry, go wrong

miscellaneous *adjective*
= **assorted**, various, mixed, diverse, varied, jumbled, motley, sundry

miscellany *noun* = **assortment**, collection, variety, mixture, medley, jumble, anthology, hodgepodge, *mélange (French)*, mixed bag, potpourri

mischance *noun* = **misfortune**, accident, disaster, mishap, misadventure, calamity

mischief *noun* 1 = **misbehavior**, trouble, impishness, monkey business *(informal)*, naughtiness, shenanigans *(informal)*, waywardness
2 = **harm**, injury, damage, hurt, trouble, evil, misfortune

mischievous *adjective*
1 = **naughty**, troublesome, playful, wayward, impish,

puckish, rascally, roguish, sportive
2 = **malicious**, harmful, evil, vicious, destructive, wicked, hurtful, damaging, spiteful

misconception *noun* = **delusion**, error, misunderstanding, fallacy, misapprehension

misconduct *noun* = **immorality**, wrongdoing, mismanagement, impropriety, malpractice

miscreant *noun* = **wrongdoer**, criminal, rogue, villain, rascal, sinner, reprobate, scoundrel, vagabond

misdeed *noun* = **offence**, crime, wrong, fault, misconduct, sin, misdemeanor, transgression

misdemeanour *noun* = **offence**, fault, infringement, misdeed, transgression, peccadillo
See also: **crime**

miser *noun* = **skinflint**, cheapskate *(informal)*, niggard, penny-pincher *(informal)*, Scrooge

miserable *adjective* 1 = **unhappy**, down, low, sad, depressed, mournful, dejected, melancholy, downcast, wretched • *a job that made me miserable*
OPPOSITE: cheerful
2 = **gloomy**, sorry, pathetic, wretched • *It's a miserable job, but someone has to do it.*

miserly *adjective* = **mean**, stingy, avaricious, grasping, niggardly, parsimonious, penny-pinching *(informal)*, tightfisted, ungenerous

misery *noun* = **unhappiness**, depression, woe, grief, sadness, sorrow, despair, melancholy
• *All that money brought nothing but misery.*
OPPOSITE: joy
See also: **evil, hell, pain**

misfire *verb* = **fail**, miscarry, fall through, go wrong

misfit *noun* = **nonconformist**, eccentric, oddball *(informal)*, fish out of water *(informal)*, square peg *or* square peg in a round hole *(informal)*

misfortune *noun* 1 = **mishap**, disaster, tragedy, reverse, setback, calamity, affliction • *I had the misfortune of seeing that movie.*

2 = bad luck, trouble, adversity, tribulation

See also: **blow, hardship, sorrow**

misgiving *noun* = **unease**, worry, doubt, suspicion, uncertainty, anxiety, reservation, apprehension, distrust, qualm, trepidation

misguided *adjective* = **unwise**, mistaken, unwarranted, erroneous, ill-advised, imprudent, deluded, injudicious, misplaced

mishandle *verb* = **mismanage**, botch, bungle, muff, make a mess of, mess up (*informal*)

mishap *noun* = **accident**, misadventure, calamity, misfortune, mischance

misinform *verb* = **mislead**, deceive, misdirect, misguide

misinterpret *verb* = **misunderstand**, mistake, misrepresent, distort, misread, misconstrue, misjudge, misapprehend, misconceive

misjudge *verb* = **miscalculate**, underestimate, overrate, overestimate, underrate

mislaid *See* **lost**

mislay *verb* = **lose**, misplace, lose track of

mislead *verb* = **deceive**, fool, misinform, misdirect, delude, hoodwink, misguide

misleading *adjective* = **confusing**, false, deceptive, ambiguous, disingenuous, evasive

mismanage *verb* = **mishandle**, misconduct, botch, misdirect, bungle, make a mess of, mess up, misgovern

misplace *verb* = **lose**, lose track of, mislay

misplaced *See* **lost**

misprint *noun* = **mistake**, literal, typo (*informal*), corrigendum, erratum

misquote *verb* = **misrepresent**, twist, falsify

misrepresent *verb* = **distort**, twist, falsify • *The salesperson deliberately misrepresented the condition of the used printer.*

misrule *noun* = **disorder**, chaos, confusion, turmoil, lawlessness, anarchy

miss *verb* **1 = fail to notice**, mistake, overlook • *It's on the second floor. You can't miss it.*

2 = long for, pine for, yearn for • *We missed our friends when we moved.*

3 = avoid, escape, evade

4 = mistake, failure, error, oversight, blunder, omission

See also: **lack**

misshapen *adjective* = **deformed**, twisted, grotesque, crooked, distorted, contorted, malformed, warped

missile *noun* = **rocket**, weapon, projectile

missing *adjective* = **absent**, lost, astray, lacking, left out, mislaid, misplaced, unaccounted-for

mission *noun* = **task**, job, commission, duty, quest, assignment, undertaking, errand, vocation

missionary *noun* = **evangelist**, preacher, apostle

missive *noun* = **letter**, report, note, message, communication, dispatch, memorandum, epistle

misspent *adjective* = **wasted**, imprudent, dissipated, profitless, squandered

mist *noun* = **fog**, film, spray, cloud, steam, smog, haze, vapour

mistake *noun* **1 = error**, oversight, gaffe, blunder, blooper (*informal*), slip-up • *spelling mistakes*

▶ *verb* **2 = confuse with**, misinterpret as, mix up with, take for • *I mistook her for the owner of the house.*

3 = misunderstand, misinterpret, misread, misconstrue, misjudge, misapprehend

See also: **confuse, miss, mix-up**

mistaken *adjective* = **wrong**, false, faulty, incorrect, inaccurate, misguided, erroneous, unsound, wide of the mark

mistakenly *adverb* = **incorrectly**, wrongly, falsely, erroneously, inaccurately, by mistake, fallaciously, misguidedly

mistimed *adjective* = **inopportune**, untimely, badly timed, ill-timed

mistreat *verb* = **ill-treat**, abuse
• *The dog had been mistreated by its former owner*

mistress *noun* = **lover**, girlfriend, concubine, kept woman, paramour

mistrust *verb* 1 = **doubt**, suspect, fear, distrust, be wary of
▶ *noun* 2 = **suspicion**, doubt, uncertainty, skepticism, distrust, misgiving, wariness

mistrustful *adjective* = **suspicious**, skeptical, wary, uncertain, fearful, doubtful, cynical, hesitant, chary, distrustful

misty *adjective* = **foggy**, obscure, murky, dim, cloudy, hazy, overcast, opaque, blurred, indistinct

misunderstand *verb* = **misinterpret**, mistake, misread, misconstrue, misjudge, be at cross-purposes, get the wrong end of the stick, misapprehend

misunderstanding *noun* = **mistake**, error, mix-up, misconception, misjudgment, misinterpretation

misuse *noun* 1 = **waste**, abuse, desecration, misapplication, squandering
▶ *verb* 2 = **waste**, abuse, prostitute, squander, desecrate, misapply

mitigate *verb* = **ease**, moderate, soften, subdue, temper, lessen, lighten, extenuate

mitigation *noun* = **alleviation**, relief, moderation, remission, diminution, extenuation

mix *verb* 1 = **combine**, merge, blend, mingle, amalgamate • *Mix the ingredients together slowly.*
2 = **socialize**, associate, mingle, hobnob, consort, fraternize, hang out (*informal*)

▷ **mix up** = **confuse**, muddle
• *People often mix us up*; = **combine**, mix, blend
▷ **mix up with** *See* **mistake**
▶ *noun* 3 = **mixture**, combination, compound, blend, alloy, fusion, medley, assortment, amalgam

mixed *adjective* 1 = **combined**, joint, compound, composite, amalgamated, blended, mingled, united
2 = **varied**, diverse, assorted, cosmopolitan, miscellaneous, heterogeneous, motley

mixed-up *adjective* = **confused**, upset, distraught, disturbed, at sea, bewildered, maladjusted, muddled, perplexed, puzzled

mixture *noun* = **combination**, compound, hybrid, blend, alloy, fusion, medley, amalgamation
• *a sticky mixture of flour and water*
See also: **cross**, **union**, **variety**

mix-up *noun* = **mistake**, misunderstanding, muddle • *a mix-up in the hotel reservations*

moan *verb* 1 = **groan**, grunt • *He moaned in his sleep.*
2 = **complain**, whine, grumble, groan • *He's always moaning about how much homework he has.*
▶ *noun* 3 = **groan**, grunt • *He let out a moan when he heard the sad news.*
4 = **complaint**, protest, whine, grumble, gripe (*informal*), grouse, grouch (*informal*)
See also: **lament**

mob *noun* 1 = **crowd**, host, mass, pack, flock, swarm, throng, multitude, drove, horde
2 (*Slang*) = **gang**, group, set, lot, crew (*informal*)
▷ **mob violence** *See* **riot**
▶ *verb* 3 = **surround**, jostle, crowd around, set upon, swarm around

mobile *adjective* = **movable**, portable, moving, itinerant, peripatetic, travelling, wandering

mobilize *verb* = **prepare**, rally, ready, organize, activate, marshal, call to arms, call up, get ready or make ready

mock verb 1 = **make fun of**, ridicule, deride (formal), laugh at, poke fun at, scoff at • Don't mock me when I'm only trying to help.
2 = **mimic**, caricature, ape, parody, satirize, imitate, lampoon
▶ adjective 3 = **imitation**, fake, false, counterfeit, artificial, bogus, phony (informal), dummy, sham, feigned, pretended • mock laughter
See also: **tease**

mockery noun 1 = **derision**, ridicule, jeering • Was there a hint of mockery in his eyes?
2 = **farce**, apology (informal), joke, disappointment, letdown
See also: **scorn**

mocking adjective = **derisive**, satirical, disrespectful, sarcastic, sardonic, contemptuous, disdainful, scoffing, scornful

mode noun 1 = **method**, way, system, process, form, style, procedure, technique, manner
2 = **fashion**, look, trend, style, rage, vogue, craze

model noun 1 = **representation**, replica, dummy • an architect's model of the new art gallery
2 = **paragon**, example, ideal, epitome • The essay is a model of clarity.
3 = **sitter**, subject, poser
▶ verb 4 = **shape**, form, fashion, carve, mould, sculpt • clay modelled into the shape of a bear
5 = **show off**, sport (informal), wear, display
See also: **design, make**

moderate adjective 1 = **average**, medium, fair, reasonable, middling • moderate exercise
2 = **mild**, steady, limited, modest, reasonable, gentle, controlled, restrained, middle-of-the-road
▶ verb 3 = **tone down**, ease, curb, relax, soften, temper, abate • They are hoping he will moderate his views.
See also: **change**

moderately adverb = **reasonably**, rather, quite, slightly, somewhat, fairly, passably, tolerably

moderation noun = **restraint**, fairness, reasonableness, temperance

modern adjective 1 = **current**, recent, present, contemporary, present-day • modern society
2 = **up-to-date**, new, latest, up-to-the-minute • modern technology
OPPOSITE: old-fashioned

modernity noun = **newness**, currency, innovation, novelty, freshness

modernize verb = **update**, renew, revamp, renovate, remake, rejuvenate, remodel, make over

modest adjective 1 = **small**, moderate, limited, middling • a modest improvement
2 = **humble**, unassuming • Although an award-winning writer, she is modest about her achievements.
OPPOSITE: conceited
See also: **low, reasonable**

modesty noun = **reserve**, humility, reticence, bashfulness, coyness, demureness, diffidence, shyness, timidity

modicum noun = **little**, drop, bit, touch, scrap, shred, fragment, crumb

modification noun = **change**, variation, adjustment, revision, qualification, alteration, refinement

modify verb 1 = **change**, reform, convert, adjust, revise, alter, adapt, rework, remodel
2 = **tone down**, lower, ease, qualify, moderate, soften, temper, restrain, lessen

modish adjective = **fashionable**, in, current, cool (informal), smart, contemporary, stylish, chic, chic, trendy (informal), up-to-the-minute, phat (slang), voguish

modulate verb = **adjust**, balance, regulate, tune, vary, attune

mogul noun = **tycoon**, baron, big cheese (informal), magnate, big shot (informal), V.I.P.

moist adjective = **damp**, wet, soggy, humid, clammy, dewy

moisten verb = **dampen**, water, wet, soak, damp, moisturize

moisture noun = **dampness**, water, liquid, dew, wetness

molecule noun = **particle**, speck, jot

molest verb **1** = **annoy**, worry, disturb, plague, bother, harass, persecute, beset, torment, badger, pester
2 = **abuse**, attack, hurt, harm, maltreat, ill-treat, interfere with

mollify verb = **pacify**, quiet, calm, sweeten, appease, soothe, placate, conciliate, de-stress

mollycoddle verb = **pamper**, baby, spoil, indulge, cosset

molten See **liquid**

moment noun **1** = **instant**, second, minute, split second • *He paused for a moment.*
2 = **point**, time, instant • *At that moment, the doorbell rang.*

momentarily adverb = **briefly**, temporarily, for a moment

momentary adjective = **brief**, short, temporary, passing, short-lived, fleeting, transitory

momentous adjective = **significant**, important, critical, historic, crucial, vital, pivotal, fateful, weighty

momentum noun = **impetus**, force, power, drive, energy, push, strength, thrust, propulsion

monarch noun = **ruler**, king, queen, prince or princess, sovereign, emperor or empress, potentate

monarchy noun **1** = **sovereignty**, autocracy, kingship, monocracy, royalism
2 = **kingdom**, empire, realm, principality

monastery noun = **abbey**, convent, cloister, friary, nunnery, priory

monastic adjective = **monkish**, reclusive, secluded, contemplative, ascetic, cloistered, hermit-like, sequestered, withdrawn

monetary adjective = **financial**, capital, cash, fiscal, budgetary, pecuniary

money noun = **cash**, capital, dough (*informal*), funds • *I needed to earn some money.*
RELATED WORD
adjective: pecuniary
See also: **financial**, **wealth**

> **INFORMALLY SPEAKING**
> **for my money**: in my opinion
> **on the money**: correct, or exact

mongrel noun **1** = **hybrid**, cross, crossbreed, half-breed
▶ adjective **2** = **hybrid**, crossbred

monitor noun **1** = **watchdog**, guide, invigilator, supervisor
▶ verb **2** = **check**, follow, survey, watch, observe, stalk, keep an eye on, keep tabs on, keep track of, bird dog (*informal*)

monk noun = **friar**, brother

monkey noun **1** = **simian**, primate
2 = **rascal**, devil, rogue, scamp, imp
▶ verb **3** = **tinker**, play, mess, fool, meddle

monolithic adjective = **huge**, massive, solid, monumental, colossal, impenetrable, intractable

monologue noun = **speech**, lecture, sermon, harangue, soliloquy

monopolize verb = **control**, dominate, hog (*slang*), corner the market in, keep to oneself, take over

monotonous adjective = **tedious**, boring, dull, repetitive, tiresome, unchanging, mind-numbing, humdrum, wearisome

monotony noun = **tedium**, routine, boredom, monotonousness, repetitiveness, sameness, tediousness

monster noun **1** = **brute**, devil, beast, villain, demon, fiend
2 = **freak**, mutant, monstrosity
3 = **giant**, mammoth, titan, colossus
▶ adjective **4** = **huge**, massive, tremendous, enormous, mammoth, immense, gigantic,

colossal, stupendous
monstrosity noun = **eyesore**,
horror, monster, freak
monstrous adjective
  1 = **unnatural**, horrible,
gruesome, grotesque, hideous,
frightful, fiendish, freakish
  2 = **outrageous**, foul, shocking,
disgraceful, scandalous,
inhuman, intolerable, diabolical
  3 = **huge**, massive, tremendous,
enormous, mammoth,
immense, colossal, prodigious,
stupendous
monument noun
  = **memorial**, marker, shrine,
commemoration, tombstone,
mausoleum, cenotaph,
headstone, gravestone, cairn
monumental adjective
  1 = **important**, significant,
historic, enormous, memorable,
awesome, unforgettable,
majestic, epoch-making
  2 (Informal) = **immense**, great,
massive, colossal, staggering
mood noun = **state of mind**,
humour, frame of mind, spirits,
temper • She was in a really cheerful
mood.
moody adjective **1** = **sulky**,
irritable, sullen, morose • Despite
his charm, he could sulk and be
moody.
  2 = **temperamental**, volatile
• What a moody person - cheerful one
moment and miserable the next.
moon noun **1** = **satellite**
  ▶ verb **2** = **idle**, languish,
daydream, mope, waste time
moor¹ noun = **moorland**, heath
moor² verb = **tie up**, secure, berth,
anchor, dock, lash, make fast
moot adjective **1** = **debatable**,
controversial, undecided,
doubtful, unresolved, unsettled,
arguable, contestable,
disputable
  ▶ verb **2** = **bring up**, suggest,
propose, broach, put forward
mop noun **1** = **squeegee**, swab,
sponge
  2 = **mane**, shock, tangle, thatch
  ▶ verb
  ▷ **mop up** = **clean up**, wash,

wipe, swab, sponge, soak up
mope verb = **brood**, moon, pine,
languish, fret, pout, sulk
moral adjective **1** = **good**, just,
right, ethical, decent, noble,
principled, honorable, virtuous,
high-minded
  ▶ noun **2** = **lesson**, point,
message, meaning, significance
morale noun = **confidence**, heart,
spirit, self-esteem, esprit de
corps
morality noun **1** = **integrity**,
justice, honesty, virtue, decency,
goodness, righteousness
  2 = **standards**, conduct,
philosophy, mores, ethics,
manners, morals, principles
morals plural noun = **morality**,
conduct, integrity, behaviour,
mores, ethics, habits, manners,
principles, scruples, standards
morass noun **1** = **marsh**, swamp,
bog, quagmire, slough, fen
  2 = **mess**, confusion, mix-up,
tangle, muddle
moratorium noun
  = **postponement**, halt, freeze,
suspension, standstill
morbid adjective
  1 = **unwholesome**, sick,
unhealthy, gloomy, melancholy,
sombre, ghoulish
  2 = **gruesome**, grisly, dreadful,
macabre, horrid, hideous,
ghastly
mordant adjective = **sarcastic**,
scathing, cutting, caustic,
pungent, incisive, biting,
stinging, trenchant
more adjective **1** = **extra**, further,
additional, added • I have more
fries than you.
  OPPOSITE: less
  ▶ adverb **2** = **to a greater extent**,
further, longer, better
  ▷ **more than** See **over**
moreover adverb = **furthermore**,
also, too, further, besides,
additionally, as well, in addition
morgue noun = **mortuary**
moribund adjective = **declining**,
weak, stagnant, on its last legs,
waning
morning noun **1** = **dawn**, sunrise,

m

daybreak, morn (*poetic*), break of day
2 = **forenoon**, a.m.
moron noun = **fool**, idiot, imbecile, blockhead, cretin (*offensive*), dork (*slang*), dunce, dunderhead, halfwit, oaf, schmuck (*slang*)
moronic adjective = **idiotic**, stupid, foolish, mindless, cretinous (*offensive*), halfwitted, imbecilic, unintelligent
morose adjective = **sullen**, sour, depressed, gloomy, moody, surly, dour, glum, ill-tempered, sulky, taciturn
morsel noun = **piece**, part, bit, taste, bite, scrap, crumb, tidbit, mouthful, soupçon (*French*)
mortal adjective **1** = **human**, passing, transient, temporal, ephemeral, worldly, impermanent
2 = **fatal**, deadly, killing, terminal, lethal, destructive, murderous, death-dealing
▷ noun **3** = **human being**, man, woman, human, person, individual, being, earthling
mortality noun **1** = **humanity**, impermanence, transience
2 = **death**, killing, destruction, fatality, carnage, bloodshed
mortgage See **loan**
mortification noun
1 = **humiliation**, shame, embarrassment, annoyance, chagrin, discomfiture, vexation
2 = **discipline**, control, denial, abasement, chastening, subjugation
3 (*Medical*) = **gangrene**, corruption, festering
mortified adjective = **humiliated**, ashamed, crushed, embarrassed, chagrined, chastened, deflated, humbled, shamed
mortify verb **1** = **humiliate**, crush, humble, embarrass, shame, deflate, chagrin, chasten
2 = **discipline**, control, deny, subdue, chasten, abase
3 (Of flesh) = **putrefy**, die, fester, deaden

mortuary noun = **morgue**, funeral parlour
most See **majority**, **maximum**
▷ **most important** See **foremost**
▷ **most recent** See **last**
mostly adverb = **generally**, usually, largely, mainly, primarily, predominantly, principally, chiefly, as a rule, on the whole
moth-eaten adjective = **decayed**, dilapidated, shabby, ragged, decrepit, worn-out, tattered, threadbare
mother noun **1** = **parent**, mom (*informal*), dam, mater (*old-fashioned, informal, chiefly Brit*), ma (*informal*), mommy (*informal*), mama or momma (*old-fashioned, informal*), old lady (*informal*)
▶ adjective **2** = **native**, natural, innate, inborn
▶ verb **3** = **nurture**, raise, protect, nurse, tend, rear, cherish, care for
motherly adjective = **maternal**, protective, loving, caring, affectionate, comforting, sheltering
motif noun **1** = **theme**, idea, subject, concept, leitmotif
2 = **design**, shape, decoration, ornament
motion noun **1** = **movement**, move, travel, progress, flow, mobility, locomotion
2 = **proposal**, recommendation, suggestion, submission, proposition
▶ verb **3** = **gesture**, direct, wave, signal, nod, beckon, gesticulate
motionless adjective = **still**, standing, paralyzed, stationary, static, immobile, frozen, fixed, stock-still, transfixed, unmoving
motivate verb = **drive**, lead, move, prompt, inspire, provoke
• *What motivates athletes to excel?*
motivation noun = **incentive**, reason, spur, inspiration, motive, stimulus, incitement, inducement
motive noun = **reason**, ground or grounds, object, purpose,

incentive, inspiration, stimulus, rationale, inducement

motley *adjective*
1 = **miscellaneous**, mixed, disparate, assorted, varied, heterogeneous
2 = **multicolored**, checkered, variegated

mottled *adjective* = **blotchy**, spotted, dappled, flecked, piebald, speckled, stippled, streaked

motto *noun* = **saying**, rule, slogan, adage, maxim, dictum, proverb, precept, watchword

mould[1] *noun* 1 = **cast**, shape, pattern
2 = **design**, build, form, kind, construction, fashion, style, shape, pattern, format
3 = **nature**, kind, type, quality, character, sort, stamp, calibre
▶ *verb* 4 = **shape**, make, work, create, form, model, fashion, forge, construct, sculpt
5 = **influence**, make, control, form, affect, direct, shape

mould[2] *noun* = **fungus**, blight, mildew, mustiness
See also: **rot**

mouldy *adjective* = **stale**, bad, rotten, blighted, decaying, fusty, mildewed, musty *See* **rotten**

mound *noun* 1 = **heap**, pile, drift, stack, rick
2 = **hill**, rise, bank, dune, embankment, knoll, hillock

mount *verb* 1 = **climb**, scale, ascend, clamber up, go up
2 = **climb onto**, bestride, jump on
3 = **increase**, grow, build, swell, escalate, intensify, accumulate, multiply, pile up
▶ *noun* 4 = **backing**, support, base, stand, frame, setting
5 = **horse**, steed (*archaic or literary*)

mountain *noun* 1 = **peak**, mount, fell (*Brit*), alp
2 = **heap**, mass, pile, mound, ton, stack, abundance

mountainous *adjective* 1 = **high**, steep, alpine, rocky, towering, highland, soaring, upland
2 = **huge**, great, enormous, mammoth, mighty, immense, daunting, monumental, gigantic

mourn *verb* = **grieve**, lament, weep, bemoan, deplore, wail, rue, bewail

mournful *adjective* 1 = **sad**, tragic, unhappy, woeful, melancholy, piteous, plaintive, sorrowful
2 = **dismal**, gloomy, miserable, somber, downcast, disconsolate, grieving, heavy-hearted, lugubrious, rueful

mourning *noun* 1 = **grieving**, woe, grief, bereavement, lamentation, weeping
2 = **black**, sackcloth and ashes, widow's weeds

mouth *noun* 1 = **lips**, jaws, maw
2 = **opening**, door, entrance, gateway, inlet, aperture, orifice

mouthful *noun* = **taste**, little, bit, sample, bite, swallow, spoonful, morsel

mouthpiece *noun*
= **spokesperson**, spokesman or spokeswoman, agent, representative, delegate

movable *adjective* = **portable**, mobile, transferable, detachable, transportable

move *verb* 1 = **go**, advance, progress, shift, proceed, stir, budge • *The train began to move.*
2 = **change**, transfer, shift, switch, transpose
3 = **relocate**, leave, remove, quit, migrate, pack one's bags (*informal*) • *She had often considered moving to the Maritimes.*
4 = **drive**, start, turn, operate, shift, propel, activate
5 = **touch**, affect, excite, impress • *The story moved us to tears.*
6 = **incite**, cause, prompt, influence, inspire, persuade, motivate, induce, rouse
7 = **propose**, suggest, urge, recommend, advocate, put forward
▷ **move to** *See* **settle**
▷ **move up** *See* **rise**
▶ *noun* 8 = **action**, turn, step, measure, stroke, ploy, manoeuvre, stratagem

m

9 = transfer, shift, removal, relocation
See also: **draw**

INFORMALLY SPEAKING
get a move on: hurry
make your move: take action
on the move: moving about

moved See **sorry**

movement noun 1 = **motion**, flow • *They monitor the movement of the fish swimming upstream.*
2 = **group**, campaign, organization, faction • *the peace movement*
3 = **workings**, action, mechanism, machinery, works
4 (*Music*) = **section**, part, division, passage
See also: **cause**, **wave**

movie noun = **film**, feature, picture, flick (*slang*)

moving adjective 1 = **emotional**, poignant, touching, affecting, stirring • *It was a moving moment.*
2 = **mobile**, portable, running, unfixed
See also: **sad**

mow verb = **cut**, crop, trim, shear, scythe
▷ **mow down** = **massacre**, slaughter, butcher, cut down, cut to pieces, shoot down

much adjective 1 = **a lot of**, great, substantial, considerable, sizable or sizeable, ample, abundant, copious, plenty of
▶ noun 2 = **a lot**, a good deal, a great deal, heaps (*informal*), scads (*informal*), tons (*informal*), plenty, lots (*informal*)
▶ adverb 3 = **greatly**, considerably, decidedly, exceedingly, a great deal, a lot

muck noun 1 = **manure**, dung, ordure
2 = **dirt**, filth, mud, mire, sludge, ooze, slime
▶ verb
▷ **muck up** = **ruin**, blow (*slang*), spoil, botch, bungle, muff, make a mess of, make a pig's ear of (*informal*), mess up

mucky adjective = **dirty**, messy, muddy, filthy, grimy, begrimed, scuzzy (*slang*)

mud noun = **dirt**, clay, mire, sludge, ooze, silt, slime

muddle noun 1 = **disorder**, chaos, mess, confusion, tangle, disarray, jumble, disorganization • *Our finances are in a muddle.*
▶ verb 2 = **mix up**, confuse, jumble • *Their names are so similar, they often get muddled.*
3 = **jumble**, disorder, scramble, mess, spoil, tangle, disorganize, disarrange
4 = **confuse**, daze, bewilder, perplex, disorient, confound, befuddle, stupefy
▷ **muddle up** See **confuse**
See also: **cloud**, **mix-up**

muddled See **confused**

muddy adjective 1 = **dirty**, grimy, bespattered, mucky, mud-caked, scuzzy (*slang*), soiled
2 = **boggy**, swampy, marshy, quaggy

muffle verb 1 = **wrap up**, cover, cloak, shroud, envelop, swathe, swaddle
2 = **deaden**, silence, stifle, soften, suppress, muzzle, quieten

muffled adjective = **indistinct**, faint, muted, subdued, stifled, strangled, suppressed

mug[1] noun = **cup**, pot, beaker, flagon, tankard

mug[2] noun 1 = **face**, visage, countenance, features
2 = **fool**, dork (*slang*), schmuck (*slang*), sucker (*slang*)
▶ verb 3 = **attack**, assault, rob, beat up, set about or set upon

mug[3] verb
▷ **mug up** (*Brit slang*) = **study**, review, cram (*informal*), bone up on (*informal*), burn the midnight oil (*informal*)

mugger See **thief**

muggy adjective = **humid**, close, sticky, oppressive, moist, sultry, stuffy, clammy

mull verb = **ponder**, consider, weigh, deliberate, contemplate, meditate, reflect on, ruminate, think over

multifarious adjective = **diverse**,

many, different, multiple, numerous, legion, varied, miscellaneous, manifold, sundry

multiple *adjective* = **many**, several, various, numerous, manifold, multitudinous, sundry

multiply *verb* **1** = **increase**, spread, proliferate • *The problems with my old computer just seem to multiply.*
2 = **reproduce**, breed, propagate
See also: **grow**

multitude *noun* = **mass**, host, crowd, army, mob, swarm, throng, myriad, horde

mumble *verb* = **murmur**, mutter • *He mumbled a few words.*

munch *verb* = **chew**, crunch, champ, chomp

mundane *adjective* **1** = **ordinary**, routine, everyday, day-to-day, commonplace, banal, humdrum, prosaic, workaday
2 = **earthly**, secular, mortal, terrestrial, temporal, worldly

municipal *adjective* = **civic**, public, urban

municipality *noun* = **town**, city, district, borough, township

munificence *noun* = **generosity**, bounty, largesse *or* largess, philanthropy, beneficence, benevolence, liberality, magnanimousness

munificent *adjective* = **generous**, liberal, lavish, bountiful, philanthropic, benevolent, beneficent, magnanimous, open-handed, unstinting

murder *noun* **1** = **killing**, assassination, homicide, slaughter, manslaughter, slaying (*literary*) • *after being found guilty of murder*
▶ *verb* **2** = **kill**, slay (*literary*), slaughter, assassinate, take the life of • *a book about two men who murder a third*

murderer *noun* = **killer**, homicide, assassin, butcher, cut-throat, hit man (*slang*), slaughterer, slayer

murderous *adjective* = **deadly**, brutal, lethal, cruel, ferocious, savage, bloodthirsty, cut-throat

murky *adjective* = **dark**, misty, gloomy, dull, dim, gray, cloudy, overcast

murmur *verb* **1** = **mumble**, whisper, mutter
2 = **grumble**, complain, moan (*informal*)
▶ *noun* **3** = **drone**, rumble, whisper, purr, buzzing, humming

muscle *noun* **1** = **tendon**, sinew
2 = **strength**, power, might, weight, clout (*informal*), stamina, brawn, forcefulness

muscular *adjective* = **strong**, powerful, robust, athletic, vigorous, sturdy, sinewy, strapping

muse *verb* = **ponder**, consider, reflect, deliberate, contemplate, brood, meditate, cogitate, mull over, ruminate

mushy *adjective* **1** = **soft**, slushy, pulpy, semi-solid, squashy, squelchy
2 (*Informal*) = **sentimental**, sloppy (*informal*), slushy (*informal*), maudlin, mawkish, saccharine, schmaltzy (*slang*)

musical *adjective* = **melodious**, lyrical, melodic, harmonious, dulcet, euphonious, sweet-sounding, tuneful

must *noun* = **necessity**, requirement, essential, fundamental, imperative, requisite, prerequisite, *sine qua non* (*Latin*)

muster *verb* **1** = **assemble**, rally, gather, convene, marshal, summon, mobilize, call together
▶ *noun* **2** = **assembly**, meeting, rally, collection, convention, gathering, roundup, congregation

musty *adjective* = **stale**, old, funky (*slang*), smelly, stuffy, airless, dank, fusty, mildewed, moldy

mutability *noun* = **change**, transition, variation, evolution, alteration, metamorphosis, vicissitude

mutable *adjective* = **changeable**, volatile, inconsistent, unstable,

m

variable, fickle, unsettled, adaptable, alterable, inconstant

mutate See **turn**

mutation noun = **change**, variation, evolution, transformation, modification, alteration, metamorphosis, transfiguration

mute adjective = **silent**, dumb, mum, speechless, unspoken, voiceless, wordless

muted adjective = **subdued**, delicate, subtle, low-key, discreet, restrained, pastel, understated, toned down, faded

muteness See **silence**

mutilate verb 1 = **maim**, damage, injure, amputate, disfigure, dismember, mangle, lacerate, cut up
2 = **distort**, cut, damage, censor, adulterate, bowdlerize, expurgate

mutinous adjective = **rebellious**, insurgent, subversive, unruly, unmanageable, disobedient, insubordinate, refractory, riotous

mutiny noun 1 = **rebellion**, riot, revolution, uprising, revolt, disobedience, insurrection, insubordination
▶ verb 2 = **rebel**, resist, revolt, disobey, rise up

mutt See **dog**

mutter verb = **grumble**, complain, rumble, mumble, murmur, grouse

mutual adjective = **shared**, common, joint, interchangeable, reciprocal, requited, returned

muzzle noun 1 = **jaws**, mouth, nose, snout
▶ verb 2 = **suppress**, silence, curb, censor, stifle, restrain, gag

myopic adjective = **short-sighted**, near-sighted

myriad adjective (Formal)

1 = **innumerable**, countless, untold, immeasurable, incalculable, multitudinous
▶ noun 2 = **multitude**, host, army, swarm, horde

mysterious adjective
1 = **mystifying**, cryptic, enigmatic, arcane (formal), baffling • He died in mysterious circumstances.
2 = **secretive**, furtive • Stop being so mysterious.
See also: **funny**

mystery noun = **puzzle**, riddle, conundrum, enigma • the mystery surrounding her fortune

mystic, mystical adjective
= **supernatural**, mysterious, paranormal, occult, otherworldly, inscrutable, metaphysical, preternatural, transcendental

mystify verb = **puzzle**, confuse, baffle, stump, bewilder, perplex, confound, flummox, nonplus

mystifying See **mysterious**

mystique noun = **fascination**, magic, spell, charm, awe, glamour, charisma, mojo (slang)

myth noun 1 = **legend**, story, fiction, saga, allegory, fable, fairy story, folk tale, urban legend or urban myth
2 = **imagination**, fantasy, fancy, illusion, delusion, superstition, figment, tall tale (informal)

mythical adjective 1 = **legendary**, fabulous, fabled, fairy-tale, mythological
2 = **imaginary**, fantasy, untrue, fictitious, unreal, nonexistent, made-up, make-believe, fabricated, invented, pretended

mythological adjective
= **legendary**, traditional, fabulous, mythical, mythic

mythology noun = **legend**, tradition, lore, folklore

Nn

nab *verb* = **catch**, arrest, capture, grab, seize, snatch, collar (*informal*), apprehend

nadir *noun* = **bottom**, minimum, depths, lowest point, rock bottom

naevus *noun* = **birthmark**, mole

naff *adjective* = **bad**, poor, shoddy, low-grade, inferior, worthless, shabby, second-rate, rubbishy

nag¹ *verb* **1** = **scold**, worry, plague, harass, annoy, irritate, hassle (*informal*), badger, pester, upbraid, henpeck
▶ *noun* **2** = **scold**, shrew, harpy, tartar, virago

nag² *noun* = **horse**, hack

nagging *adjective* **1** = **persistent**, irritating, worrying
2 = **scolding**, shrewish

nail *verb* = **fasten**, join, fix, secure, hammer, attach, pin, tack

naive *adjective* **1** = **gullible**, green, callow, credulous, unsuspicious, wet behind the ears (*informal*)
2 = **innocent**, open, simple, unsophisticated, artless, guileless, ingenuous, trusting, unworldly

naivety, naïveté *noun*
1 = **gullibility**, callowness, credulity
2 = **innocence**, simplicity, openness, inexperience, artlessness, guilelessness, ingenuousness, naturalness

naked *adjective* **1** = **nude**, bare, unclothed • *a naked body*
OPPOSITE: clothed
2 = **open**, evident, blatant, manifest, unmistakable • *naked aggression*
OPPOSITE: secret

nakedness *noun* = **nudity**, undress, bareness

namby-pamby *adjective* = **feeble**, weak, sentimental, spineless, weedy (*informal*), insipid, vapid, wimpish *or* wimpy (*informal*), wishy-washy (*informal*)

name *noun* **1** = **title**, term, nickname, designation, epithet • *My name is Joe.*
RELATED WORD
adjective: nominal
2 = **reputation**, character • *to protect his good name*
▶ *verb* **3** = **call**, term, dub • *a little girl named Anna*
4 = **nominate**, choose, select, appoint, designate, specify
See also: **celebrity**, **identify**

INFORMALLY SPEAKING
call names: insult by swearing at
name after: give someone the same name as
name of the game: the main objective

named *adjective* **1** = **called**, baptized, christened, dubbed, entitled, known as, labelled, styled, termed
2 = **nominated**, selected, specified, appointed, chosen, designated, mentioned, picked, singled out

nameless *adjective*
1 = **anonymous**, unnamed, untitled
2 = **unknown**, obscure, unsung, unheard-of, incognito, undistinguished
3 = **horrible**, unspeakable, indescribable, abominable, unmentionable, unutterable

namely *adverb* = **specifically**, to wit, viz.

naming *See* **appointment**

nap¹ noun **1** = **sleep**, catnap, forty winks (*informal*), rest, siesta
▶ verb **2** = **sleep**, doze, catnap, drop off (*informal*), rest, snooze (*informal*), nod off (*informal*)
nap² noun = **pile**, down, grain, weave, fibre
napkin noun = **cloth**, linen, wipe
narc, nark noun (*Slang*)
= **informer**, sneak, accuser, traitor, Judas, betrayer, double-crosser, quisling, stool pigeon, snake in the grass, two-timer, squealer (*slang*)
narcissism noun = **egotism**, vanity, self-love
narcotic noun **1** = **drug**, painkiller, anesthetic, sedative, opiate, tranquilizer, analgesic, anodyne
▶ adjective **2** = **sedative**, analgesic, hypnotic, calming, painkilling, soporific
narrate verb = **tell**, report, detail, describe, relate, recount, chronicle, recite
narration noun = **telling**, account, relation, reading, explanation, description, recital
narrative noun = **story**, report, statement, history, account, blog (*informal*), tale, chronicle, weblog
narrator noun = **storyteller**, reporter, author, writer, commentator, chronicler
narrow adjective **1** = **thin**, fine, slim, slender • *a narrow stream*
OPPOSITE: wide
2 = **limited**, close, tight, restricted, meagre, confined, constricted, contracted
3 = **insular**, partial, intolerant, narrow-minded, dogmatic, illiberal, prejudiced, small-minded
▶ verb **4** = **restrict**, reduce, limit, tighten, constrict
See also: **shrink**
narrowly adverb = **just**, barely, scarcely, by the skin of one's teeth, only just
narrow-minded adjective

= **intolerant**, insular, opinionated, biased, bigoted, prejudiced • *their own narrow-minded view of the world*
OPPOSITE: tolerant
nastiness noun = **spitefulness**, malice, meanness
nasty adjective **1** = **unpleasant**, foul, horrible, repellent, vile, disgusting, disagreeable • *a nasty taste*
OPPOSITE: pleasant
2 = **spiteful**, mean, vicious, malicious, despicable, lousy (*slang*), unpleasant, vile, distasteful, disagreeable, scuzzy (*slang*)
3 = **serious**, bad, dangerous, critical, severe
See also: **unkind**
nation noun = **country**, people, state, race, society, tribe, realm
national adjective **1** = **nationwide**, public, widespread, countrywide
▶ noun **2** = **citizen**, resident, native, subject, inhabitant
nationalism noun = **patriotism**, loyalty, allegiance, chauvinism, jingoism
nationality noun = **race**, nation, birth
nationwide adjective = **national**, general, widespread, countrywide
native adjective **1** = **local**, home, domestic, indigenous
2 = **inborn**, natural, congenital, innate, ingrained, hereditary, intrinsic, inbred, instinctive
▶ noun **3** = **inhabitant**, national, resident, citizen, dweller, countryman, aborigine
natter See **chat**
natty adjective = **smart**, trim, elegant, stylish, fashionable, neat, spruce, dapper, snazzy (*informal*), phat (*slang*)
natural adjective **1** = **normal**, common, usual, typical, ordinary, everyday • *the natural reaction to such sad news*
OPPOSITE: unnatural
2 = **unaffected**, real, genuine,

frank, candid • *He was so natural with the children.*
OPPOSITE: false

3 = **innate**, inherent, intuitive, inborn, instinctive • *He's a natural comedian.*

4 = **pure**, whole, organic, plain, unrefined
See also: **automatic, informal, wild**

naturalist *noun* = **biologist**, ecologist, zoologist, botanist

naturalistic *adjective* = **realistic**, lifelike, true-to-life

naturally *adverb* **1** = **of course**, certainly

2 = **genuinely**, simply, normally, typically, spontaneously, unaffectedly, unpretentiously

nature *noun* **1** = **personality**, character, makeup • *It's not in my nature to sit still.*

2 = **creation**, world, environment, earth, universe, cosmos

3 = **kind**, type, style, sort, category, variety, species, description

4 = **character**, constitution, makeup, essence, complexion

naught *noun* (*archaic*) = **nothing**, nothing, zero, zip (*informal*), nil, zilch (*informal*), nada (*slang*), diddley-squat (*slang*)

naughty *adjective*
1 = **disobedient**, bad, wayward, mischievous, impish • *a naughty child*
OPPOSITE: well-behaved

2 = **obscene**, vulgar, lewd, bawdy • *naughty song lyrics*
See also: **wicked**

nausea *noun* = **sickness**, biliousness, queasiness, retching, squeamishness, vomiting

nauseate *verb* = **sicken**, offend, disgust, revolt, repel, repulse, turn one's stomach

nauseous *adjective* = **sickening**, offensive, abhorrent, distasteful, repulsive, repugnant, disgusting, revolting, nauseating, scuzzy (*slang*)

nautical *adjective* = **maritime**, marine, naval

naval *adjective* = **nautical**, marine, maritime

navigable *adjective* **1** = **passable**, clear, unobstructed, negotiable

2 = **sailable**, controllable, dirigible

navigate *verb* = **steer**, drive, pilot, handle, guide, sail, voyage, manoeuvre

navigation *noun* = **sailing**, helmsmanship, seamanship, voyaging

navigator *noun* = **pilot**, mariner, seaman

navvy *noun* (*Informal*) = **labourer**, worker, workman

navy *noun* = **fleet**, flotilla, armada

near *adjective* **1** = **close**, nearby, adjacent, adjoining • *The Rockies are near.*
OPPOSITE: far

2 = **imminent**, upcoming, forthcoming, approaching, looming • *The time of birth is near.*
▶ *preposition* **3** = **close to**, alongside, adjacent to, next to, not far from • *Take a chair near the*
See also: **beside, immediate**

nearby *adjective* = **neighbouring**, adjacent, convenient, handy, adjoining

nearest See **next**

nearly *adverb* = **almost**, virtually, practically, as good as, just about • *The beach was nearly empty.*
See also: **about**

nearness *noun* = **closeness**, proximity, availability, accessibility, vicinity, handiness

near-sighted *adjective* = **short-sighted**, myopic

neat *adjective* **1** = **tidy**, trim, smart, orderly • *The house was clean and neat.*
OPPOSITE: untidy

2 = **graceful**, efficient, elegant, stylish, adept, deft, nimble, skilful, adroit, dexterous

3 (*~ alcoholic drinks*) = **undiluted**, straight, pure, unmixed
See also: **handy**

neatly *adverb* **1** = **tidily**,

systematically, methodically, smartly, daintily, fastidiously, sprucely
2 = gracefully, efficiently, deftly, expertly, elegantly, adeptly, adroitly, dexterously, nimbly, skillfully

neatness noun **1 = tidiness**, daintiness, orderliness, smartness, spruceness, trimness
2 = grace, skill, style, efficiency, elegance, dexterity, adroitness, deftness, nimbleness

nebulous adjective **= vague**, unclear, uncertain, indefinite, confused, dim, hazy, shadowy, imprecise, indistinct

necessarily adverb **= inevitably**, certainly, automatically, naturally, undoubtedly, compulsorily, incontrovertibly, inexorably, of necessity

necessary adjective **1 = needed**, essential, vital, required, imperative, indispensable • *Make the necessary arrangements.*
OPPOSITE: unnecessary
2 = certain, inevitable, unavoidable, inexorable • *a necessary consequence of overindulgence*
See also: **basic**

necessitate verb **= compel**, force, demand, require, coerce, oblige, constrain, call for, impel

necessities plural noun **= essentials**, exigencies, fundamentals, needs, requirements

necessity noun **1 = inevitability**, obligation, compulsion, inexorableness
2 = need, requirement, essential, fundamental, requisite, prerequisite, desideratum, *sine qua non* (Latin)

neck and neck See **even**

necromancy noun **= magic**, sorcery, witchcraft, wizardry, black magic, divination, enchantment

necropolis noun **= cemetery**, graveyard, burial ground, churchyard

need verb **1 = require**, want, demand • *You need some fresh air.*
▶ noun **2 = poverty**, lack, shortage, deprivation, inadequacy, insufficiency, destitution, paucity, penury
3 = requirement, demand, essential, requisite, desideratum
4 = emergency, want, obligation, urgency, necessity, exigency
See also: **distress**

needed adjective **= necessary**, wanted, required, called for, desired, lacked

needful adjective **= necessary**, essential, vital, needed, required, indispensable, requisite, stipulated

needle verb **= irritate**, provoke, harass, taunt, rile, annoy, nag, goad, pester, get on one's nerves (informal)

needless adjective **= unnecessary**, unwanted, useless, pointless, redundant, groundless, gratuitous, superfluous, uncalled-for

needlework noun **= embroidery**, needlecraft, sewing, stitching, tailoring

needy adjective **= poor**, impoverished, disadvantaged, poverty-stricken, underprivileged, destitute, penniless, deprived

ne'er-do-well noun **= good-for-nothing**, black sheep, couch potato (slang), idler, loser, loafer, wastrel

nefarious adjective **= wicked**, criminal, foul, evil, heinous, villainous, depraved, infernal

negate verb **1 = invalidate**, cancel, reverse, neutralize, annul, nullify, countermand, obviate, wipe out
2 = deny, oppose, contradict, refute, disallow, disprove, rebut, gainsay (archaic or literary)

negation noun **1 = cancellation**, neutralization, nullification
2 = denial, reverse, opposite, rejection, contradiction,

converse, inverse, renunciation, disavowal

negative adjective
1 = contradictory, contrary, denying, dissenting, opposing, refusing, rejecting, resisting
2 = pessimistic, unwilling, gloomy, cynical, jaundiced, uncooperative, unenthusiastic
▶ noun **3 = contradiction**, refusal, denial

neglect verb **1 = disregard**, ignore, overlook, turn your back on • *unhappy and neglected children*
2 = fail, forget, omit • *He had neglected to give her his address.*
▶ noun **3 = disregard**, indifference, unconcern • *Most of her plants died from neglect.*
4 = negligence, failure, oversight, dereliction, carelessness, laxity, slackness

neglected adjective
1 = abandoned, derelict, overgrown
2 = disregarded, unappreciated, undervalued, underestimated

neglectful adjective **= careless**, lax, negligent, indifferent, thoughtless, remiss, heedless, inattentive, uncaring

negligence noun **= carelessness**, neglect, disregard, indifference, dereliction, inattention, laxity, slackness, thoughtlessness

negligent adjective **= careless**, slack, thoughtless, remiss, forgetful, heedless, inattentive, neglectful, slapdash, unthinking

negligible adjective
= insignificant, minute, small, minor, trivial, unimportant, inconsequential, imperceptible, trifling

negotiable adjective **= debatable**, variable

negotiate verb **1 = bargain**, deal, debate, discuss, arrange, mediate, haggle, conciliate, transact, work out
2 = get round, pass, clear, cross, surmount, get over, get past

negotiation noun **= bargaining**, transaction, debate, discussion, arbitration, diplomacy, mediation, haggling, wheeling and dealing (*informal*)

negotiator noun **= mediator**, ambassador, diplomat, delegate, moderator, intermediary, honest broker

neighbourhood noun **= district**, quarter, community, region, locale, vicinity, locality, environs

neighbouring adjective **= nearby**, near, adjacent, adjoining, connecting, next to, surrounding, bordering

neighbourly adjective **= helpful**, kind, friendly, considerate, sociable, harmonious, hospitable, obliging

nemesis noun **= retribution**, fate, destruction, destiny, vengeance

nepotism noun **= favoritism**, bias, patronage, partiality, preferential treatment

nerd, nurd noun **= bore**, drip (*informal*), geek (*slang*), egghead (*informal*), doofus (*slang*), dork (*slang*), dweeb (*slang*), goober (*informal*)

nerve noun **1 = impudence**, gall, audacity, insolence, rudeness • *I'm amazed they had the nerve to ask in the first place.*
2 = bravery, will, resolution, courage, pluck, daring, grit, fearlessness, guts (*informal*)
▶ verb
▷ **nerve oneself = brace oneself**, fortify oneself, steel oneself

nerveless adjective **= calm**, cool, controlled, unemotional, composed, impassive, imperturbable, self-possessed

nerve-racking adjective **= tense**, difficult, stressful, white-knuckle (*informal*), distressing, frightening, harrowing, trying, worrying

nerves plural noun **= tension**, worry, stress, strain, anxiety, nervousness, butterflies or butterflies in one's stomach (*informal*), cold feet (*informal*), fretfulness

nervous *adjective*
= **apprehensive**, anxious, tense, worried, edgy, jittery, uptight, jumpy • *She had been nervous before the finals.*
OPPOSITE: calm
See also: **afraid, dubious, timid, uneasy**

nervousness *noun* = **anxiety**, worry, tension, agitation, fluster, excitability, disquiet, touchiness

nervy *adjective* = **anxious**, nervous, tense, jittery (*informal*), fidgety, jumpy, twitchy (*informal*), agitated, on edge, wired (*slang*)

nest *noun* = **refuge**, retreat, haunt, den, hideaway
▷ **nest egg** *noun* = **savings**, fund *or* funds, store, reserve, deposit, cache, fall-back

nestle *verb* = **snuggle**, huddle, cuddle, curl up, nuzzle

nestling *noun* = **chick**, fledgling

net[1] *noun* 1 = **mesh**, network, web, lattice, netting, openwork, tracery
▶ *verb* 2 = **catch**, capture, bag, trap, entangle, ensnare, enmesh

net[2] *adjective* 1 = **after taxes**, final, clear, take-home
▶ *verb* 2 = **earn**, make, gain, clear, realize, reap, accumulate, bring in

nether *adjective* = **lower**, under, below, bottom, underground, beneath, inferior

nettled *adjective* = **irritated**, annoyed, incensed, exasperated, galled, harassed, peeved, put out, riled, vexed

network *noun* 1 = **web**, grid, maze, labyrinth, lattice
2 = **system**, organization, complex, structure, arrangement

neurosis *noun* = **obsession**, abnormality, instability, phobia, affliction, derangement, maladjustment, mental illness

neurotic *adjective* = **unstable**, nervous, unhealthy, abnormal,

compulsive, obsessive, disturbed, manic, maladjusted

neuter *verb* = **castrate**, doctor (*informal*), fix (*informal*), spay, emasculate, geld

neutral *adjective* 1 = **impartial**, disinterested, dispassionate, nonaligned • *We stayed neutral during their dispute.*
OPPOSITE: biased
2 = **indeterminate**, dull, intermediate, undefined, indistinct
See also: **impersonal**

neutrality *noun* = **impartiality**, detachment, nonalignment, noninterference, noninvolvement, nonpartisanship

neutralize *verb* = **counteract**, cancel, frustrate, offset, undo, negate, nullify, counterbalance, compensate for

never *adverb* = **at no time**, not ever • *I never said I was leaving.*

nevertheless *adverb* = **even so**, but, still, however, though *or* even though, yet, regardless, notwithstanding, nonetheless

new *adjective* 1 = **modern**, recent, current, original, novel, fresh, contemporary, latest, state-of-the-art, unfamiliar, up-to-date, ground-breaking • *a new invention*
OPPOSITE: old
2 = **changed**, renewed, altered, modernized, improved, redesigned, restored
3 = **extra**, more, added, supplementary
See also: **inexperienced, strange**

newcomer *noun* = **beginner**, arrival, Johnny-come-lately (*informal*), new kid in town (*informal*), novice, parvenu, cheechako (*Canad*)

newfangled *adjective* = **new**, recent, novel, cool (*informal*), modern, contemporary, state-of-the-art, fashionable, gimmicky, phat (*slang*)

newly *adverb* = **recently**, just,

lately, freshly, anew, latterly

newness noun = **novelty**,
innovation, oddity, freshness,
originality, uniqueness,
unfamiliarity, strangeness

news noun = **information**,
word, intelligence, disclosure,
dispatch, latest (informal),
bulletin, tidings (formal) • news
about the trial

newsworthy adjective
= **interesting**, important,
significant, remarkable,
notable, noteworthy,
stimulating

next adjective 1 = **following**,
subsequent, ensuing,
succeeding • Their next car will be a
convertible.
2 = **nearest**, adjacent, adjoining,
closest, neighbouring • in the
next room
▷ **next world** See **heaven**
▶ adverb 3 = **afterwards**,
subsequently • My brother arrived
next.
▷ **next to** See **beside, near**

nib See **point**

nibble verb 1 = **bite**, eat, nip, peck,
munch, gnaw, pick at
▶ noun 2 = **snack**, taste, bite,
peck, crumb, tidbit, morsel,
soupçon (French)

nice adjective 1 = **pleasant**, good,
attractive, charming, delightful,
agreeable, pleasurable • We had a
nice vacation.
2 = **kind**, friendly, polite, likable
or likeable, courteous, well-
mannered
3 = **neat**, fine, trim, tidy, dainty
4 = **subtle**, fine, strict, careful,
delicate, precise, meticulous,
fastidious

nicely adverb 1 = **pleasantly**,
well, attractively, charmingly,
delightfully, acceptably,
agreeably, pleasurably
2 = **kindly**, politely, amiably,
commendably, courteously
3 = **neatly**, finely, daintily, tidily,
trimly

niceties See **ceremony**

nicety noun = **subtlety**,
discrimination, distinction,

delicacy, nuance, refinement,
daintiness

niche noun 1 = **alcove**, opening,
corner, recess, hollow, nook
2 = **position**, place, slot (informal),
calling, vocation, pigeonhole
(informal)

nick verb 1 = **cut**, score, mark,
chip, notch, scratch, dent, scar,
snick
▶ noun 2 = **cut**, mark, chip,
notch, scratch, dent, scar

nickname noun = **pet name**,
label, moniker or monicker
(slang), diminutive, epithet,
sobriquet

nifty adjective = **neat**, smart,
attractive, stylish, chic,
pleasing, deft

niggard noun = **miser**,
cheapskate (informal), Scrooge,
skinflint

niggardly adjective = **stingy**,
mean, frugal, miserly,
avaricious, grudging,
parsimonious, tightfisted,
ungenerous

niggle verb 1 = **worry**, annoy,
irritate, rankle
2 = **criticize**, fuss, carp, cavil,
find fault

niggling adjective 1 = **persistent**,
gnawing, irritating, troubling,
worrying
2 = **petty**, picky (informal), fussy,
finicky, nit-picking (informal),
pettifogging, quibbling

nigh See **near**

night noun = **darkness**, dark,
night-time

nightfall noun = **evening**, sunset,
dusk, twilight, sundown

nightly adjective 1 = **nocturnal**,
night-time
▶ adverb 2 = **every night**, each
night, night after night, nights
(informal)

nightmare noun 1 = **bad dream**,
hallucination
2 = **ordeal**, trial, horror, torment,
tribulation

nil noun = **nothing**, love, none,
zero, naught

nimble adjective = **agile**, quick,
swift, brisk, lively, deft,

n

spry, dexterous, sprightly

nimbly adverb = **agilely**, quickly, easily, readily, swiftly, briskly, deftly, smartly, dexterously, spryly

nincompoop noun = **idiot**, fool, chump, blockhead, dork (slang), nitwit (informal), schmuck (slang)

nip[1] verb = **pinch**, bite, squeeze, tweak

nip[2] noun = **dram**, drop, shot (informal), draft, sip, mouthful, snifter (informal)

nipper noun (Informal) = **child**, girl, baby, boy, kid (informal), infant, tot

nippy adjective = **chilly**, sharp, biting, stinging

nirvana noun = **paradise**, peace, joy, bliss, serenity, tranquillity

nit-picking adjective = **fussy**, finicky, captious, carping, hairsplitting, pedantic, pettifogging, quibbling

nitty-gritty noun = **basics**, core, substance, crux, gist, brass tacks (informal), essentials, fundamentals

nitwit noun (Informal) = **fool**, dummy (slang), dimwit (informal), doofus (slang), dork (slang), halfwit, oaf, schmuck (slang), simpleton

no interjection **1** = **not at all**, absolutely not, certainly not, definitely not, of course not, in a pig's eye (informal) • "Any problems?" "No, everything's fine."
OPPOSITE: yes
2 = **refusal**, denial, negation
▷ **no go** = **impossible**, futile, hopeless, vain

nob noun = **aristocrat**, toff (Brit, slang), V.I.P.

nobble verb = **bribe**, influence, intimidate, get at, win over

nobility noun **1** = **integrity**, honour, virtue, incorruptibility, uprightness
2 = **aristocracy**, elite, lords, nobles, patricians, peerage, upper class

noble adjective **1** = **worthy**, generous, upright, honourable, virtuous, magnanimous • a good and noble thing to do
OPPOSITE: ignoble
2 = **aristocratic**, blue-blooded, highborn, lordly, patrician, titled
3 = **great**, grand, impressive, lofty, distinguished, dignified, splendid, stately, imposing
▶ noun **4** = **aristocrat**, nobleman • He claims to come from a family of British nobles.

nobleman See **noble**

nobody pronoun **1** = **no-one**
▶ noun **2** = **nonentity**, lightweight (informal), cipher, menial

nocturnal adjective = **nightly**, night-time

nod verb **1** = **gesture**, indicate, acknowledge, signal, bow
2 = **sleep**, nap, doze, drowse
▶ noun **3** = **gesture**, sign, signal, indication, greeting, acknowledgment

noggin noun **1** = **cup**, nip, mug, tot, dram
2 (Informal) = **head**, block (informal), nut (slang), noodle (slang)

noise noun = **din**, uproar, racket, commotion, pandemonium, hubbub • He is making an awful noise.
OPPOSITE: silence
See also: **sound**

noiseless adjective = **silent**, still, quiet, mute, inaudible, hushed, soundless

noisome adjective **1** = **poisonous**, bad, harmful, unhealthy, pernicious, pestilential, unwholesome
2 = **disgusting**, offensive, foul, funky (slang), noxious, smelly, putrid, fetid, malodorous, stinking

noisy adjective = **loud**, tumultuous, strident, piercing, vociferous, deafening • a noisy audience of schoolchildren
OPPOSITE: quiet
See also: **rowdy**

nomad noun = **wanderer**, rover, migrant, itinerant,

drifter, rambler, vagabond

nomadic adjective = **wandering**, migrant, itinerant, peripatetic, roaming, roving, traveling, vagrant

nom de plume noun = **pseudonym**, alias, assumed name, nom de guerre, pen name

nomenclature noun = **terminology**, classification, vocabulary, codification, phraseology, taxonomy

nominal adjective **1** = **so-called**, formal, purported, puppet, theoretical, titular, supposed, ostensible, professed **2** = **small**, symbolic, minimal, insignificant, token, trivial, inconsiderable, trifling

nominate verb = **propose**, name, suggest, recommend, select, submit • *The party refused to nominate him as its candidate.*

nomination noun = **choice**, election, proposal, recommendation, selection, appointment, suggestion, designation

nominee noun = **candidate**, runner, contestant, entrant, aspirant, protégé

nonaligned adjective = **neutral**, undecided, impartial, uncommitted

nonchalance noun = **indifference**, calm, composure, equanimity, imperturbability, sang-froid, self-possession, unconcern

nonchalant adjective = **indifferent**, calm, casual, careless, laid-back (informal), unconcerned, blasé, insouciant, offhand, unperturbed

noncombatant noun = **civilian**, neutral, nonbelligerent

noncommittal adjective = **evasive**, tentative, cautious, wary, neutral, vague, guarded, politic, equivocal, circumspect, temporizing

nonconformist noun = **dissenter**, protester, rebel, radical, maverick, eccentric, heretic, iconoclast, individualist

nonconformity noun = **dissent**, heresy, eccentricity, heterodoxy

nondescript adjective = **ordinary**, dull, commonplace, featureless, unremarkable, undistinguished, unexceptional

none pronoun = **not any**, nothing, nobody, zero, nil, no-one, not one

nonentity noun = **nobody**, lightweight (informal), mediocrity, cipher, small fry

nonessential adjective = **unnecessary**, peripheral, expendable, unimportant, extraneous, superfluous, dispensable, inessential

nonetheless adverb = **nevertheless**, however, yet, despite that, even so, in spite of that

nonevent noun = **failure**, disappointment, flop (informal), fiasco, dud (informal), washout

nonexistent adjective = **imaginary**, legendary, fictional, hypothetical, mythical, unreal, illusory, chimerical

nonsense noun = **garbage** (informal), garbage (informal), rubbish, drivel, inanity • *I say the accusation is complete nonsense.*

nonsensical adjective = **senseless**, crazy, ridiculous, silly, absurd, foolish, meaningless, irrational, incomprehensible, inane

non-specific See **broad**

nonstarter noun = **dead loss**, loser, lemon (informal), turkey (informal), dud (informal), washout (informal), no-hoper (informal)

nonstop adjective **1** = **continuous**, constant, endless, relentless, uninterrupted, incessant, unbroken, interminable, twenty-four-seven (slang) ▶ adverb **2** = **continuously**, constantly, relentlessly, perpetually, endlessly, incessantly, ceaselessly, interminably, twenty-four-

n

seven (*slang*), unremittingly

noodle *noun* (*Slang*) = **head**, common sense, sense, intuition, gut feeling (*informal*)

nook *noun* = **niche**, opening, corner, retreat, recess, hideout, alcove, cubbyhole

noon *noun* = **midday**, high noon, noonday, noontide, twelve noon

norm *noun* = **standard**, rule, average, par, pattern, benchmark, criterion, yardstick

normal *adjective* 1 = **usual**, average, standard, regular, routine, conventional, typical, ordinary, habitual • *my normal routine*
OPPOSITE: unusual
2 = **sane**, reasonable, rational, well-adjusted
See also: **natural**

normality *noun* 1 = **regularity**, conventionality, naturalness
2 = **sanity**, reason, balance, rationality

normally *adverb* = **usually**, generally, regularly, typically, commonly, ordinarily, as a rule, habitually

north *adjective* 1 = **northern**, Arctic, polar, boreal, northerly
▶ *adverb* 2 = **northward** or **northwards**, northerly

nose *noun* 1 = **snout**, bill, beak, honker (*slang*), proboscis
▶ *verb* 2 = **ease forward**, push, nudge, shove, nuzzle
3 = **pry**, meddle, snoop (*informal*)

nosegay *noun* = **posy**, bouquet

nostalgia *noun* = **reminiscence**, remembrance, longing, yearning, homesickness, pining, regretfulness, wistfulness

nostalgic *adjective*
= **sentimental**, emotional, homesick, longing, wistful, maudlin, regretful

nostrum *noun* = **medicine**, drug, treatment, cure, remedy, elixir, potion, panacea

nosy *adjective* = **inquisitive**, curious, eavesdropping, prying
• *nosy neighbours watching us*

through the curtains

notability *noun* = **fame**, celebrity, distinction, esteem, renown, eminence

notable *adjective* 1 = **remarkable**, rare, unusual, extraordinary, memorable, outstanding, uncommon, striking, noteworthy, conspicuous
▶ *noun* 2 = **celebrity**, dignitary, big name, personage, V.I.P.

notably *adverb* = **particularly**, especially, strikingly, outstandingly

not at all *See* **no**

notation *noun* = **symbols**, system, code, script, characters, signs

not be able to abide *See* **dislike**

not be able to bear *See* **dislike**

not be able to stand *See* **dislike**

notch *noun* 1 = **cut**, score, mark, nick, incision, cleft, indentation
2 (*Informal*) = **grade**, level, step, degree
▶ *verb* 3 = **cut**, score, mark, scratch, nick, indent
▷ **notch up** = **achieve**, make, score, gain, register

not dangerous *See* **harmless**

note *noun* 1 = **message**, email, letter, communication (*formal*), memo, reminder, memorandum
• *I wrote him a note asking him to visit.*
2 = **record**, account, jotting • *I made a note of his address.*
3 = **tone**, touch, hint, trace • *I detected a note of bitterness in his voice.*
4 = **symbol**, sign, mark, indication, token
▶ *verb* 5 = **notice**, see, register, observe, perceive • *I noted that the rain had stopped.*
6 = **mention**, remark • *The report noted a rise in the unemployment figures.*
7 = **indicate**, record, mark, register, designate, denote
See also: **comment**, **entry**

notebook *noun* = **notepad**, journal, diary, exercise book, jotter

noted adjective = **famous**, prominent, acclaimed, renowned, well-known, notable, celebrated, illustrious, distinguished, eminent

not ever See **never**

noteworthy adjective = **remarkable**, important, significant, unusual, extraordinary, notable, exceptional, outstanding

not far from See **near**

not guilty See **innocent**

nothing noun = **naught**, zero, void, nil, emptiness, nada (informal), nothingness, nullity

nothingness noun **1** = **oblivion**, nonbeing, nonexistence, nullity **2** = **insignificance**, unimportance, worthlessness

notice verb **1** = **observe**, see, note, spot, detect, perceive, discern • Then I noticed he wasn't laughing. ▶ noun **2** = **sign**, bill, poster, advertisement • a handwritten notice posted on the wall **3** = **advance warning**, warning, notification, intimation • She was transferred without notice. **4** = **observation**, note, interest, regard, consideration, heed, cognizance **5** = **attention**, respect, civility See also: **information**, **item**, **review**

noticeable adjective = **obvious**, evident, unmistakable, conspicuous, perceptible • a noticeable improvement See also: **prominent**, **visible**

notification noun = **announcement**, statement, information, warning, message, notice, intelligence, advice, declaration, heads-up

notify verb **1** = **inform**, tell, warn, advise (formal) • The skipper notified the coastguard of the difficulty. See also: **alert**, **report**

notion noun **1** = **idea**, view, opinion, belief, concept, sentiment, impression, inkling **2** = **whim**, wish, desire, impulse,

fancy, inclination, caprice

notional adjective = **hypothetical**, abstract, speculative, imaginary, theoretical, unreal, conceptual

not level See **uneven**

not liable See **exempt**

not many See **few**

notoriety noun = **infamy**, scandal, disrepute, dishonour, obloquy, opprobrium

notorious adjective = **infamous**, scandalous, disreputable • The district was notorious for violent crime.

notoriously adverb = **infamously**, dishonorably, disreputably, opprobriously, scandalously

not quite See **almost**

not smooth See **uneven**

not well See **unhealthy**

notwithstanding preposition = **despite**, in spite of

nought noun (archaic) = **naught**, nothing, zero, zip (informal), nil, zilch (informal), nada (slang)

nourish verb **1** = **feed**, supply, nurse, tend, sustain, nurture **2** = **encourage**, support, maintain, promote, comfort, foster, cultivate

nourishing adjective = **nutritious**, beneficial, wholesome, nutritive

nourishment noun = **food**, nutrition, sustenance, nutriment

novel[1] noun = **story**, tale, fiction, romance, narrative

novel[2] adjective = **new**, different, original, fresh, unusual, strange, innovative, uncommon, unfamiliar

novelty noun **1** = **newness**, surprise, innovation, oddity, freshness, originality, uniqueness, unfamiliarity, strangeness **2** = **gimmick**, gadget, curiosity **3** = **knick-knack**, souvenir, memento, trinket, trifle, bauble

novice noun = **beginner**, amateur, newcomer, pupil, apprentice, trainee, learner, probationer

now adverb **1** = **at the moment**,

n

currently, nowadays • *I'm feeling much better now.*
2 = **immediately**, straightaway, at once, right now, without delay • *Tell her I need to see her now.*
▷ **now and then, now and again** = **occasionally**, sometimes, sporadically, infrequently, intermittently, from time to time, on and off

nowadays *adverb* = **now**, today, anymore, at the moment, in this day and age

noxious *adjective* = **harmful**, deadly, foul, unhealthy, destructive, poisonous, hurtful, injurious, unwholesome

nuance *noun* = **subtlety**, degree, shade, distinction, refinement, nicety, tinge, gradation

nubile *adjective* = **marriageable**, ripe (*informal*)

nucleus *noun* = **centre**, heart, focus, basis, core, pivot, kernel, nub

nude *adjective* = **naked**, bare, disrobed, in one's birthday suit, stark-naked, stripped, unclad, unclothed, undressed, without a stitch on (*informal*)

nudge *verb* = **push**, touch, bump, elbow, dig, poke, shove, jog, prod

nudity *noun* = **nakedness**, undress, bareness, deshabille, nudism

nugget *noun* = **lump**, piece, mass, chunk, clump, hunk

nuisance *noun* = **bother**, pain (*informal*), inconvenience, pest, hassle, irritation, annoyance • *Sorry to be a nuisance.*

null *adjective*
▷ **null and void** = **invalid**, void, useless, worthless, inoperative, valueless

nullify *verb* = **cancel**, veto, neutralize, negate, counteract, invalidate, obviate, render null and void

nullity *noun* = **nonexistence**, powerlessness, invalidity, uselessness, worthlessness

numb *adjective* **1** = **frozen**, paralyzed, insensitive • *Your right arm goes numb.*
▷ *verb* **2** = **deaden**, freeze, stun, paralyze, dull • *The cold numbed my fingers.*
See also: **shock**

numbed *See* **dazed**

number *noun* **1** = **numeral**, figure, digit • *Pick a number between one and ten.*
2 = **collection**, crowd, multitude, horde • *She has introduced me to a large number of people.*
3 = **issue**, copy, edition, printing, imprint
▷ *verb* **4** = **count**, include, add, total, account, calculate, compute, reckon, enumerate
See also: **quantity**

> **INFORMALLY SPEAKING**
> **do a number on someone**: treat someone unfairly or harshly
> **have someone's number**: know someone's character
> **someone's number is up**: someone is doomed

numberless *adjective* = **infinite**, countless, endless, myriad, untold, innumerable, multitudinous, unnumbered

numbness *noun* = **deadness**, paralysis, insensitivity, dullness, torpor

numbskull, numskull *noun* = **fool**, blockhead, dummy (*slang*), dolt, dork (*slang*), dunce, oaf, schmuck (*slang*)

numeral *noun* = **number**, figure, digit, integer

numerous *adjective* = **many**, several, lots • *on numerous occasions*

nuncio *noun* = **ambassador**, envoy, messenger, legate

nunnery *noun* = **convent**, house, abbey, cloister

nuptial *adjective* = **marital**, bridal, conjugal, connubial, matrimonial

nuptials *plural noun* = **wedding**, marriage, matrimony

nurse *verb* **1** = **look after**, treat, tend, care for, minister to
2 = **breast-feed**, feed, nurture, nourish, suckle, wet-nurse

3 = **foster**, support, promote, encourage, preserve, cultivate, cherish, harbour, succour

nursery noun = **nursery school**, daycare, kindergarten, playroom

nurture noun **1** = **upbringing**, development, training, education, discipline, instruction, rearing
▶ verb **2** = **bring up**, school, develop, train, discipline, educate, instruct, rear

nut noun (Slang) = **lunatic**, crank (informal), madman, psycho (slang), maniac, nutcase (slang)

nutrition noun = **food**, nourishment, sustenance, nutriment

nutritious adjective = **nourishing**, beneficial, wholesome, health-giving, invigorating, nutritive, strengthening

nuts adjective (Slang) = **insane**, mad, unstable, psychotic, disturbed, unbalanced, deranged, unhinged

nuzzle verb = **snuggle**, pet, burrow, nestle, cuddle, fondle

nymph noun = **sylph**, girl, maiden, dryad, naiad

n

Oo

oaf *noun* = **lout**, brute • *You stupid oaf!*
See also: **idiot**

oafish *adjective* = **loutish**, stupid, thick, dense, dumb (*informal*), moronic, dim-witted (*informal*), doltish

oath *noun* **1** = **promise**, pledge, vow • *an oath of loyalty to the government*
2 = **swearword**, curse, profanity, expletive, blasphemy
See also: **word**

obdurate *adjective* = **stubborn**, dogged, inflexible, unyielding, implacable, hard-hearted, immovable, obstinate, pig-headed

obedience *noun*
= **submissiveness**, respect, compliance, observance, reverence, acquiescence, docility, subservience

obedient *adjective* = **submissive**, law-abiding, subservient • *He was always very obedient to his parents.*
OPPOSITE: disobedient

obelisk *noun* = **column**, needle, monument, shaft, pillar, monolith

obese *adjective* = **fat**, heavy, overweight, gross, portly, plump, stout, rotund, corpulent, paunchy, tubby

obesity *noun* = **fatness**, bulk, corpulence, grossness, portliness, stoutness, tubbiness

obey *verb* = **abide by**, follow, observe, adhere to, comply with • *Most people obey the law.*
OPPOSITE: disobey

obfuscate *verb* = **confuse**, cloud, obscure, darken, perplex, befog, muddy the waters

object[1] *noun* **1** = **thing**, article • *everyday objects such as wooden spoons*
2 = **purpose**, goal, aim, idea, intention, objective • *The object of the exercise is to raise money for the charity.*
3 = **target**, victim, focus, recipient
See also: **point, subject, use**

object[2] *verb* = **protest against**, oppose • *A lot of people will object to the book.*
OPPOSITE: approve
▷ **object to** See **query, resent**
See also: **disagree, mind, protest**

objection *noun* = **protest**, opposition • *despite objections by the committee*
OPPOSITE: support
See also: **complaint, disagreement, grumble**

objectionable *adjective*
= **unpleasant**, offensive, regrettable, deplorable, intolerable, obnoxious, unseemly, repugnant, disagreeable

objective *noun* **1** = **purpose**, end, goal, target, mark, aim, object, intention, ambition
▶ *adjective* **2** = **unbiased**, fair, impartial, open-minded, disinterested, even-handed, dispassionate, detached, unprejudiced

objectively *adverb* = **impartially**, disinterestedly, dispassionately, even-handedly, with an open mind

objectivity *noun* = **impartiality**, detachment, disinterestedness, dispassion

obligation *noun* = **duty**, charge,

responsibility, requirement, burden, accountability, liability, compulsion

obligatory *adjective*
= **compulsory**, necessary, mandatory, essential, binding, required, imperative, unavoidable, requisite, de rigueur (*French*)

oblige *verb* 1 = **compel**, make, force, require, bind, constrain, necessitate, impel
2 = **indulge**, benefit, please, accommodate, gratify

obliged *adjective* 1 = **grateful**, thankful, appreciative, indebted, beholden, in (someone's) debt
2 = **forced**, bound, required, compelled

obliging *adjective* = **cooperative**, kind, willing, helpful, polite, considerate, good-natured, agreeable, accommodating

oblique *adjective* 1 = **slanting**, tilted, angled, aslant, sloping
2 = **indirect**, implied, backhanded, roundabout, circuitous, sidelong

obliterate *verb* = **destroy**, erase, eradicate, annihilate, blot out, efface, expunge, extirpate, root out, wipe out

obliteration *noun*
= **annihilation**, elimination, eradication, extirpation, wiping out

oblivion *noun* 1 = **neglect**, disregard, forgetfulness, abeyance
2 = **unconsciousness**, insensibility, obliviousness, unawareness

oblivious *adjective* = **unaware**, regardless, unconscious, ignorant, negligent, unconcerned, forgetful, heedless, insensible, neglectful, unmindful

obloquy *noun* 1 = **abuse**, attack, blame, criticism, censure, slander, reproach, vilification, aspersion, invective
2 = **disgrace**, shame, stigma, humiliation, discredit,

infamy, dishonour, ignominy

obnoxious *adjective*
= **objectionable**, offensive, nasty, unpleasant, repulsive, odious, revolting, disagreeable, insufferable, loathsome, nauseating, scuzzy (*slang*)

obscene *adjective* 1 = **indecent**, blue, dirty, pornographic, lewd, filthy, bawdy • *obscene pictures*
2 = **disgusting**, evil, shocking, outrageous, wicked, atrocious, heinous, sickening, vile, loathsome
See also: **crude, naughty**

obscenity *noun* 1 = **indecency**, pornography, impropriety, coarseness, dirtiness, lewdness, licentiousness, smut
2 = **swearword**, profanity, four-letter word, vulgarism
3 = **outrage**, wrong, evil, atrocity, offense, blight, affront, abomination

obscure *adjective* 1 = **little-known**, unknown • *an obscure Canadian law*
OPPOSITE: famous
2 = **arcane**, cryptic, opaque
• *The news was shrouded in obscure language.*
OPPOSITE: simple
3 = **indistinct**, faint, gloomy, murky, dim, cloudy, shadowy, blurred
▶ *verb* 4 = **hide**, screen, cloud, mask, cloak, conceal, shroud
• *His view was obscured by trees.*
OPPOSITE: expose
See also: **blot out, cover**

obscurity *noun* 1 = **darkness**, dusk, haze, gloom, dimness, shadows
2 = **insignificance**, lowliness, unimportance

obsequious *adjective*
= **sycophantic**, deferential, submissive, cringing, fawning, flattering, grovelling, ingratiating, servile, unctuous

observable *adjective*
= **noticeable**, apparent, obvious, visible, evident, recognizable, detectable, discernible, perceptible

o

observance *noun* = **carrying out**, performance, compliance, fulfillment, honouring

observant *adjective* = **alert**, vigilant, watchful, attentive, perceptive • *Painting makes you really observant of things.*
See also: **sharp**

observation *noun* **1** = **study**, review, inspection, surveillance, scrutiny, examination, monitoring, watching
2 = **remark**, note, comment, opinion, thought, reflection, pronouncement, utterance

observe *verb* **1** = **watch**, study, survey, view, monitor, scrutinize, bird dog (*informal*) • *He has spent years observing the habits of frogs.*
2 = **notice**, see, note, spot, discover, witness • *I observed a number of strange phenomena.*
3 = **remark**, say, state, comment, mention • *"You've had your hair cut," he observed.*
4 = **abide by**, keep, follow, respect, comply, heed, honour, obey, adhere to, conform to
See also: **discern, practise**

observer *noun* = **spectator**, witness, viewer, watcher, bystander, eyewitness, onlooker, beholder, fly on the wall, looker-on

obsessed *adjective* = **preoccupied**, troubled, haunted, dominated, gripped, hung up on (*slang*), infatuated

obsession *noun* = **preoccupation**, thing (*informal*), complex, fixation • *Chess is an obsession of mine.*

obsessive *adjective* = **compulsive**, haunting, besetting, consuming, gripping

obsolescent *adjective* = **outdated**, ageing, declining, dying out, on the wane, on the way out, past its prime, waning

obsolete *adjective* = **outdated**, old, old-fashioned, extinct, antiquated, archaic, outmoded, discarded, disused, out of date, passé

obstacle *noun* = **difficulty**, hurdle, barrier, obstruction, impediment, hindrance • *a large obstacle to improving the team's standing*
See also: **handicap**

obstinacy *noun* = **stubbornness**, persistence, tenacity, intransigence, doggedness, inflexibility, obduracy, pig-headedness, wilfulness

obstinate *adjective* = **stubborn**, wilful, dogged, inflexible, intractable, headstrong • *He is obstinate and will not give up.*
OPPOSITE: flexible

obstreperous *adjective* = **unruly**, wild, loud, turbulent, noisy, disorderly, rowdy, unmanageable, riotous

obstruct *verb* = **block**, bar, choke, clog • *Trucks obstructed the road.*
See also: **close, delay, hamper, impede, interfere**

obstruction *noun* = **obstacle**, bar, difficulty, barrier, barricade, impediment, blockage, hindrance

obstructive *adjective* = **uncooperative**, awkward, restrictive, unhelpful, blocking, delaying, hindering, stalling

obtain *verb* **1** = **get**, acquire, secure (*formal*), procure (*formal*), get hold of, get your hands on (*informal*) • *to obtain a false passport*
2 = **exist**, hold, prevail, be in force, be prevalent, be the case
See also: **buy, earn, extract, gain**

obtainable *adjective* = **available**, achievable, attainable, on tap (*informal*), to be had

obtrusive *adjective* = **noticeable**, prominent, obvious, blatant, protruding, protuberant, sticking out

obtuse *adjective* = **stupid**, slow, thick, dense, dull, stolid, uncomprehending

obviate *verb* = **prevent**, remove, avert, preclude

obvious *adjective* = **clear**, apparent, plain, evident, blatant, overt, palpable, self-evident • *an obvious injustice*

See also: **conspicuous, logical, manifest, noticeable, prominent, visible**

obviously *adverb* = **clearly**, undeniably, patently, plainly, unquestionably, manifestly, of course, palpably, unmistakably, without doubt

occasion *noun* 1 = **event**, affair • *The launch of a ship was a big occasion.*
2 = **opportunity**, time, chance • *an important occasion for celebrating our friendship*
3 = **reason**, call, cause, ground or grounds, excuse, motive, justification, provocation, prompting
▶ *verb* 4 (*Formal*) = **cause**, produce, prompt, provoke, induce, bring about, give rise to • *damage occasioned by fire*
See also: **case, create, incident**

occasional *adjective* = **infrequent**, odd, sporadic, periodic, intermittent • *an occasional fumble of the ball*
OPPOSITE: frequent
See also: **irregular**

occasionally *adverb* = **sometimes**, periodically, irregularly, at times, from time to time, now and again, once in a while

occult *adjective* = **supernatural**, mysterious, magical, mystical, arcane, esoteric

occupancy *noun* = **tenancy**, use, possession, residence, tenure

occupant *noun* = **resident**, inmate, incumbent, tenant, inhabitant, occupier, indweller, lessee

occupation *noun* 1 = **job**, trade, business, line or line of work, employment, pursuit, profession, calling, vocation, walk of life
2 = **occupancy**, control, possession, holding, residence, tenure, tenancy
3 = **invasion**, seizure, conquest, subjugation

occupied *adjective* 1 = **busy**, working, engaged, employed

2 = **in use**, full, unavailable, engaged, taken
3 = **inhabited**, lived-in, peopled, settled, tenanted

occupy *verb* 1 (*often passive*) = **take up**, involve, engage, employ, divert, preoccupy, monopolize, engross, tie up
2 = **live in**, own, possess, inhabit, dwell in, reside in
3 = **fill**, cover, permeate, pervade, take up
4 = **invade**, capture, seize, overrun, take over

occur *verb* 1 = **happen**, appear, arise, take place • *The changes occurred over a long period.*
2 = **exist**, be present • *The disease occurs more commonly among the over-50s.*
▷ **occur to** = **cross your mind**, strike, dawn on • *It didn't occur to me to check.*
See also: **come**

occurrence *noun* 1 = **incident**, event, affair, circumstance, episode, instance, adventure, happening
2 = **existence**, development, appearance, manifestation, materialization

odd *adjective* 1 = **strange**, funny, bizarre, weird, curious, singular (*formal*), peculiar • *an odd coincidence*
OPPOSITE: frequent
2 = **occasional**, various, random, casual, irregular, periodic, incidental, sundry
3 = **spare**, surplus, leftover, solitary, unmatched, remaining, unpaired
See also: **extraordinary**

oddity *noun* 1 = **irregularity**, freak, abnormality, quirk, anomaly, eccentricity, idiosyncrasy, peculiarity
2 = **misfit**, maverick, crank (*informal*), oddball (*informal*)

oddment *noun* = **leftover**, bit, scrap, remnant, fragment, snippet, fag end, off cut

odds *plural noun* = **probability**, likelihood, chances
▷ **at odds** = **in conflict**, at

daggers drawn, at loggerheads, at sixes and sevens, at variance, out of line

odds and ends *plural noun* = **scraps**, debris, bits, bits and pieces, oddments, remnants

odious *adjective* = **offensive**, unpleasant, horrid, obnoxious, repulsive, detestable, revolting, loathsome, scuzzy (*slang*)

odour *noun* = **smell**, stink, scent, perfume, essence, aroma, fragrance, bouquet, stench, redolence
See also: **smell**

odyssey *noun* = **journey**, quest, trek, voyage, pilgrimage, crusade

of course not See **no**

off *adverb* 1 = **away**, out, aside, apart, elsewhere
▶ *adjective* 2 = **unavailable**, finished, gone, canceled, postponed
3 = **bad**, sour, rotten, rancid, moldy, turned
▷ **off colour** = **ill**, sick, poorly (*informal*), unwell, out of sorts, peaky, queasy, run down, under the weather (*informal*)

offbeat *adjective* = **unusual**, novel, strange, eccentric, left-field (*informal*), unconventional, unorthodox, outré, way-out (*informal*)

offence *noun* 1 = **crime**, fault, wrongdoing, sin, trespass, misdemeanour, misdeed, transgression
2 = **insult**, hurt, slight, outrage, snub, injustice, indignity, affront
3 = **annoyance**, anger, wrath, pique, displeasure, resentment, indignation, umbrage

offend *verb* = **upset**, insult, outrage, affront • *He says he had no intention of offending the community.*
OPPOSITE: please
See also: **repel, shock**

offended *adjective* = **upset**, disgruntled, outraged, resentful, affronted, displeased, piqued, put out

(*informal*), smarting, stung

offender *noun* = **criminal**, culprit, villain, crook, delinquent, wrongdoer, lawbreaker, miscreant, sinner, perp (*informal*), transgressor

offensive *adjective* 1 = **insulting**, abusive, objectionable • *offensive behaviour*
2 = **disagreeable**, repellent, unpleasant, vile, obnoxious, disgusting, odious, revolting, nauseating
3 = **aggressive**, attacking, invading
▶ *noun* 4 = **attack**, drive, campaign, push (*informal*), onslaught
See also: **hateful**

offer *verb* 1 = **bid**, tender, hold out • *I offered him an apple.*
2 = **provide**, present, afford, furnish
3 = **propose**, suggest, advance, submit
4 = **volunteer**, come forward, offer one's services
▶ *noun* 5 = **bid**, tender, proposition • *She had refused several excellent job offers.*

offering *noun* = **donation**, present, gift, contribution, sacrifice, subscription, hand-out

offhand *adjective* 1 = **casual**, careless, aloof, glib, brusque, curt
▶ *adverb* 2 = **impromptu**, ad lib, extempore, off the cuff (*informal*)

office *noun* = **post**, place, role, situation, responsibility, function, occupation

officer *noun* = **official**, executive, agent, representative, appointee, functionary, office-holder

official *adjective* 1 = **authorized**, formal, licensed, certified • *the official figures*
OPPOSITE: unofficial
▶ *noun* 2 = **officer**, executive, representative • *a senior UN official*

| CONFUSABLES
Official means *authorized*.
Officious means *self-important*.

officialdom See **bureaucracy**

officiate verb = **preside**, serve, conduct, manage, chair, oversee, superintend

officious adjective = **interfering**, intrusive, overzealous, dictatorial, meddlesome, obtrusive, pushy (informal), self-important

offing noun
▷ **in the offing** = **imminent**, upcoming, in prospect, on the horizon

off-putting adjective = **discouraging**, daunting, formidable, disconcerting, dispiriting, disturbing, intimidating, unnerving, unsettling

offset verb = **cancel out**, neutralize, counteract, counterbalance, balance out, compensate for, make up for

offshoot noun = **by-product**, development, spin-off, adjunct, appendage

offspring noun 1 = **child**, successor, heir, descendant, scion
2 = **children**, family, issue, young, brood, progeny, descendants, heirs

often adverb = **frequently**, repeatedly • They often spent their summers at the lake.

ogle verb = **leer**, eye up (informal)

ogre noun = **monster**, giant, devil, demon, bogeyman, bugbear, spectre

oil verb = **lubricate**, grease

oily adjective = **greasy**, fatty, oleaginous

ointment noun = **lotion**, cream, balm, embrocation, emollient, liniment, salve, unguent

OK adjective 1 = **all right**, acceptable • Is it OK if I show up early?
▶ interjection 2 = **all right**, right, yes, roger, agreed, very good, very well
▶ verb 3 = **approve**, endorse, sanction, authorize, rubber-stamp (informal), agree to, give the green light
▶ noun 4 = **approval**, agreement, sanction, permission, go-ahead (informal), consent, authorization, assent, green light, say so (informal), seal of approval
See also: **all right, correct, right, safe, tolerable, yes**

old adjective 1 = **aged**, elderly, ancient, mature, venerable, decrepit, senile • an old turtle
OPPOSITE: young
2 = **dated**, antique, obsolete, antiquated, antediluvian, timeworn
OPPOSITE: new
3 = **former**, previous, earlier, one-time, erstwhile • my old art teacher
OPPOSITE: new
See also: **stale**

olden See **past**

old-fashioned adjective = **out of date**, outdated, obsolete, antiquated, archaic, dated, outmoded, passé • old-fashioned shoes
OPPOSITE: fashionable
See also: **stuffy**

omen noun = **sign**, warning • Her showing up at this moment is an omen of disaster.
See also: **premonition**

ominous adjective = **sinister**, threatening • an ominous silence

omission noun 1 = **exclusion**
2 = **failure**, lack, oversight, neglect

omit verb = **leave out**, skip, exclude • Omit the salt in this recipe.
See also: **fail, forget, neglect**

omnipotence noun = **supremacy**, mastery, invincibility

omnipotent adjective = **all-powerful**, supreme, almighty

omniscient adjective = **all-knowing**, all-wise

on preposition
▷ **on account of** See **by virtue of**
▷ **on edge** See **restless**
▷ **on guard** See **alert**
▷ **on hand** See **handy**
▷ **on the dot** See **exactly, prompt**

▷ **on the whole** See **as a rule**
▷ **on time** See **punctual**
once adverb = **at one time**, previously, formerly, long ago, once upon a time
▷ **at once** = **immediately**, now, directly, instantly, forthwith, right away, straight away, this minute or this very minute; = **at the same time**, together, simultaneously
▷ **once in a while** See **sometimes**
▷ **once more** See **again**
oncoming adjective = **approaching**, forthcoming, onrushing, advancing, looming
one See **only, single**
onerous adjective = **difficult**, hard, heavy, oppressive, demanding, exacting, burdensome, laborious, taxing
one-sided adjective = **biased**, unfair, partial, partisan, lopsided, unjust, prejudiced
one-sidedness See **favouritism**
one-time See **previous**
ongoing adjective = **in progress**, continuous, unfinished, developing, evolving, progressing, unfolding
onlooker noun = **observer**, witness, viewer, watcher, spectator, bystander, eyewitness, looker-on
only adverb 1 = **solely**, just, simply, merely, purely • Only the singer herself knows whether she will make a comeback.
▷ **only just** See **hardly**
▶ adjective 2 = **sole**, one • their only hit single
See also: **single**
onset noun = **beginning**, start, outbreak, inception
onslaught noun = **attack**, charge, assault, offensive, blitz, onset, onrush
onus noun = **burden**, responsibility, task, load, obligation, liability
onward, onwards adverb = **forward**, on, ahead, beyond, forth, in front

ooze[1] verb = **seep**, escape, leak, drain, filter, drip, dribble
ooze[2] noun = **mud**, mire, sludge, silt, slime, alluvium
opaque adjective = **cloudy**, dull, murky, dim, muddy, hazy, impenetrable, filmy
open verb 1 = **unfasten**, uncover, unlock, undo • She opened the door.
OPPOSITE: shut
2 = **start**, begin, launch, initiate, commence, inaugurate, kick off (informal), set in motion
3 = **unfold**, spread or spread out, expand, unfurl, unroll
▶ adjective 4 = **unfastened**, uncovered, ajar, undone, unlocked • an open box of chocolates
OPPOSITE: shut
5 = **frank**, honest, candid • He had always been open with her.
6 = **accessible**, public, free, available, vacant, unrestricted, unoccupied
7 = **unresolved**, undecided, moot, debatable, unsettled, arguable
See also: **bare, flexible, impressionable, straightforward**

| INFORMALLY SPEAKING
| **be open with**: speak candidly
| **into the open**: not concealed
| **open up**: fully reveal

open-air adjective = **outdoor**, alfresco
open-handed adjective = **generous**, liberal, free, lavish, bountiful, munificent, unstinting
opening adjective 1 = **first**, initial, inaugural, introductory • the opening day of the fishing season
OPPOSITE: closing
▶ noun 2 = **beginning**, start, commencement (formal) • The opening was the best part of the movie.
OPPOSITE: conclusion
3 = **hole**, space, crack, gap, slot, vent, cleft, chink • a narrow opening in the fence
4 = **opportunity**, chance, occasion, vacancy
See also: **breach**

openly adverb = **frankly**, overtly, plainly, candidly, unreservedly, forthrightly, unhesitatingly

open-minded adjective = **broad-minded**, liberal, reasonable, receptive, impartial, tolerant, unbiased, undogmatic, unprejudiced

operate verb 1 = **work**, go, run, act, perform, function
2 = **handle**, use, work, manage, maneuver, be in charge of

operation noun = **procedure**, action, process, performance, course, exercise, motion, movement

operational adjective = **working**, ready, viable, operative, prepared, functional, going, workable, usable, up and running

operative adjective 1 = **in operation**, effective, active, operational, functioning, in force
▶ noun 2 = **worker**, employee, artisan, laborer

operator noun = **worker**, driver, conductor, mechanic, technician, operative, handler, practitioner

opinion noun = **belief**, view, assessment, judgment, viewpoint, estimation, point of view • *I wasn't asking for your opinion.*
See also: **advice, feeling, idea, thought, verdict**

opinionated adjective = **dogmatic**, single-minded, bigoted, cocksure, doctrinaire, overbearing, pig-headed, prejudiced

opponent noun = **adversary**, rival, competitor, enemy, contestant, challenger, foe, antagonist

opportune adjective = **timely**, appropriate, suitable, fitting, convenient, apt, favourable, advantageous, auspicious, well-timed

opportunism noun = **expediency**, exploitation, pragmatism, unscrupulousness

opportunity noun = **chance**, time, moment, opening, occasion, scope

oppose verb = **be against**, resist, fight against, speak out against • *students opposing the new rules*
OPPOSITE: support
See also: **contest, disagree, object, protest**

opposed adjective = **contrary**, hostile, conflicting, averse, antagonistic, clashing, dissentient

opposing adjective = **conflicting**, rival, enemy, opposite, contrary, hostile, incompatible

opposite adjective 1 = **reverse**, contrary, conflicting, contrasting, opposed • *I take a completely opposite view.*
2 = **facing**, fronting
▶ noun 3 = **reverse**, contrary, converse, antithesis • *He was the complete opposite of his cousin.*

opposition noun 1 = **hostility**, resistance, disapproval • *Much of the opposition to this plan has come from the media.*
OPPOSITE: support
2 = **opponent**, competition, rival, foe, antagonist, other side
See also: **competitor, conflict, disagreement, objection**

oppress verb 1 = **depress**, burden, sadden, harass, afflict, torment, vex, dispirit
2 = **persecute**, abuse, wrong, subdue, suppress, maltreat, subjugate

oppressed adjective = **downtrodden**, abused • *a member of an oppressed minority*

oppression noun = **persecution**, tyranny • *the oppression of slaves*
See also: **abuse**

oppressive adjective 1 = **tyrannical**, severe, harsh, brutal, cruel, unjust, inhuman, repressive, despotic
2 = **stifling**, close, sultry, stuffy, muggy, airless

oppressor noun = **persecutor**, bully, scourge, tyrant, despot, autocrat, slave-driver, tormentor

opt verb (often with *for*) = **choose**,

decide *or* decide on, elect, prefer, go for, plump for

optimistic *adjective* = **hopeful**, positive, confident, buoyant, sanguine • *He is in an optimistic mood.*
OPPOSITE: pessimistic

optimum *adjective* = **ideal**, perfect, peak, best, optimal, superlative, highest

option *noun* = **choice**, alternative, selection, preference

optional *adjective* = **voluntary**, open, possible, extra, discretionary, elective

opulence *noun* 1 = **wealth**, plenty, luxury, prosperity, affluence, riches, luxuriance
2 = **abundance**, richness, fullness, cornucopia, copiousness, profusion, superabundance

opulent *adjective* 1 = **wealthy**, rich, affluent, lavish, prosperous, luxurious, sumptuous, well-off, well-to-do, moneyed
2 = **abundant**, prolific, lavish, plentiful, copious, luxuriant, profuse

opus *noun* = **work**, production, piece, creation, composition, brainchild, *oeuvre (French)*

oracle *noun* 1 = **prophecy**, prediction, revelation, prognostication, divination
2 = **authority**, adviser, mastermind, wizard, guru, mentor, pundit

oral *adjective* = **spoken**, verbal • *oral history*
See also: **exam**

SHADES OF ORANGE

amber
apricot
carrot
peach
tangerine

oration *noun* = **speech**, address, lecture, discourse, homily, harangue

orator *noun* = **public speaker**, speaker, lecturer, declaimer, rhetorician

oratorical *adjective* = **rhetorical**, eloquent, bombastic, declamatory, grandiloquent, high-flown, magniloquent, sonorous

oratory *noun* = **rhetoric**, eloquence, declamation, elocution, grandiloquence, public speaking, speech-making

orb *noun* = **sphere**, ball, ring, circle, globe

orbit *noun* 1 = **path**, course, cycle, circle, revolution, rotation, trajectory
2 = **sphere of influence**, reach, sweep, range, influence, domain, scope, compass, ambit
▸ *verb* 3 = **circle**, encircle, circumnavigate, revolve around

orchestra See **band**

orchestrate *verb* 1 = **score**, arrange
2 = **organize**, arrange, coordinate, put together, set up, stage-manage

ordain *verb* 1 = **appoint**, invest, nominate, anoint, consecrate
2 = **order**, will, rule, demand, fix, prescribe, dictate, legislate, decree, lay down

ordeal *noun* = **hardship**, trial, torture, nightmare, tribulation • *the ordeal of being arrested*
See also: **experience**, **hell**

order *noun* 1 = **command**, instruction, dictate, decree, directive • *I don't take orders from them any more.*
2 = **harmony**, regularity, symmetry • *the wish to impose order upon confusion*
OPPOSITE: disorder
3 = **sequence**, series, structure, arrangement, array, progression, layout, line-up, grouping
4 = **discipline**, law, control, peace, quiet, calm, tranquillity, law and order
5 = **request**, commission, application, reservation,

booking, requisition
6 = class, position, status, rank, grade, caste
7 = kind, family, type, class, sort, genre, ilk
8 = society, company, community, organization, association, guild, fraternity, brotherhood
▶ verb **9 = command**, direct, instruct, decree, ordain • *The troops were ordered to withdraw.*
OPPOSITE: forbid
10 = request, book, reserve, apply for, send away for
11 = arrange, group, organize, classify, marshal, catalog, sort out, systematize
See also: **require, routine, rule, tell**

> **INFORMALLY SPEAKING**
> **in short order**: quickly
> **order around**: constantly command
> **out of order**: not arranged properly or not working properly

orderly adjective **1 = neat**, regular, tidy • *Their bicycles were parked in orderly rows.*
OPPOSITE: disorderly
2 = well-behaved, quiet, controlled, disciplined, restrained, law-abiding, peaceable
ordinarily adverb **= usually**, generally, normally, commonly, customarily, as a rule, habitually, in general
ordinary adjective **1 = usual**, standard, regular, normal, routine, conventional • *an ordinary day*
OPPOSITE: special
2 = commonplace, modest, humble, plain, mundane, banal, humdrum, unremarkable, workaday
See also: **common, everyday, natural**
organ noun **1 = part**, unit, structure, element
2 = mouthpiece, medium, vehicle, voice, forum
organic adjective **1 = natural**, live,

living, biological, animate
2 = systematic, organized, integrated, structured, methodical, ordered
organism noun **= creature**, body, animal, structure, being, entity
organization noun **1 = group**, company, body, institution, association, outfit, confederation • *charitable organizations*
2 = organizing, planning, structuring • *We were involved in the organization of the picnic.*
3 = structure, pattern, format, unity, arrangement, chemistry, composition, make-up
See also: **business, firm, movement, society**
organize verb **= arrange**, plan, establish, set up • *Organizing a wedding takes time.*
See also: **book, conduct, group, stage**
organized See **efficient, ready**
organizing See **organization**
orgy noun **1 = revel**, revelry, bacchanalia, carousal, debauch, Saturnalia
2 = spree, excess, binge (*informal*), bout, splurge, indulgence, overindulgence, surfeit
orient verb **= familiarize**, adjust, adapt, align, acclimatize, get one's bearings, orientate
orientation noun **1 = position**, location, direction, bearings
2 = familiarization, introduction, adjustment, adaptation, assimilation, acclimatization, settling in
orifice noun **= opening**, hole, rent, mouth, vent, pore, cleft, aperture
origin noun **1 = root**, source, derivation • *the origins of the custom*
2 = ancestry, stock, descent, extraction, lineage • *She was of Swedish origin.*
3 = beginning, start, launch, birth, foundation, creation, emergence, inception, genesis
See also: **cause**
original adjective **1 = first**, initial

o

• *the original owner of the cottage*
2 = new, novel, fresh • *a stunningly original idea*
OPPOSITE: unoriginal
3 = creative, fertile, imaginative, ingenious, inventive, resourceful
▶ *noun* **4 = prototype**, standard, model, pattern, master, precedent, paradigm, archetype
See also: **individual**

originality *noun* = **novelty**, innovation, imagination, creativity, ingenuity, freshness, inventiveness, newness, unorthodoxy

originally *adverb* = **at first**, first, initially, in the beginning, to begin with

originate *verb* **1 = begin**, come, start, rise, result, spring, emerge, stem, arise, derive
2 = invent, launch, create, introduce, generate, pioneer, institute, formulate, bring about

originator *noun* = **creator**, author, father *or* mother, maker, founder, pioneer, architect, inventor

ornament *noun* **1 = decoration**, trinket, adornment, bauble, knick-knack • *a shelf containing ornaments*
▶ *verb* **2 = decorate**, grace, adorn, embellish, festoon, beautify, prettify

ornamental *adjective* = **decorative**, attractive, showy, beautifying, embellishing, for show

ornamentation *noun* = **decoration**, embellishment, embroidery, adornment, elaboration, frills, ornateness

ornate *adjective* = **elaborate**, busy, fancy, baroque, fussy, decorated, florid, ornamented, overelaborate, rococo

orthodox *adjective* = **established**, official, traditional, conventional, customary, accepted, well-established, approved, received

orthodoxy *noun* = **conformity**, authority, conventionality,

received wisdom, traditionalism

oscillate *verb* = **fluctuate**, swing, vary, sway, waver, seesaw, vibrate, vacillate

oscillation *noun* = **fluctuation**, swing, variation, instability, vacillation, wavering

ossify *verb* = **harden**, solidify, stiffen, fossilize

ostensible *adjective* = **apparent**, so-called, purported, superficial, seeming, outward, supposed, pretended, professed

ostensibly *adverb* = **apparently**, seemingly, supposedly, on the face of it, professedly

ostentation *noun* = **display**, show, parade, pomp, affectation, exhibitionism, flamboyance, flashiness, flaunting, pretentiousness, showing off (*informal*)

ostentatious *adjective* = **showy**, flamboyant, flashy, extravagant, grandiose, pretentious • *an ostentatious lifestyle*
See also: **pompous, vain**

ostracism *noun* = **exclusion**, exile, rejection, isolation, banishment

ostracize *verb* = **exclude**, reject, exile, banish, cast out, cold-shoulder, give (someone) the cold shoulder, shun

other *adjective* **1 = additional**, more, further, extra, alternative, spare, added, supplementary, auxiliary
2 = different, separate, distinct, diverse, unrelated, variant, dissimilar, contrasting

others *See* **remainder, rest**

otherwise *conjunction* **1 = or else**, if not, or then
▶ *adverb* **2 = differently**, any other way, contrarily

ounce *noun* = **shred**, drop, grain, trace, scrap, atom, crumb, speck

oust *verb* = **expel**, topple, displace, depose, eject, unseat, dislodge, dispossess, throw out, turn out

out *adjective* **1 = away**, outside, elsewhere, abroad, absent, gone, not at home
2 = extinguished, dead,

finished, expired, at an end,
ended, exhausted, used up
▷ **out loud** See **aloud**
▷ **out of danger** See **safe**
▷ **out of shape** See **crooked**
▷ **out of the ordinary** See
exceptional, uncommon
▷ **out of the question** See
impossible

out-and-out See **total, utter**

outback See **country**

outbreak noun = **eruption**,
explosion • *the outbreak of war*
See also: **burst, rash**

outburst noun = **eruption**,
outbreak, surge, explosion,
outpouring, flare-up, spasm,
paroxysm

outcast noun = **pariah**, refugee,
exile, Latin, castaway, leper,
persona non grata, vagabond,
wretch

outclass verb = **surpass**, eclipse,
overshadow, outshine, excel,
outstrip, outdo, leave standing
(*informal*), run rings around
(*informal*)

outcome noun = **result**, end,
issue, consequence, conclusion,
payoff (*informal*), upshot

outcry noun = **protest**,
complaint, outburst, uproar,
clamour, commotion, hue and
cry, hullaballoo

outdated adjective = **old-
fashioned**, obsolete, antiquated,
archaic, outmoded, out of date,
passé, unfashionable

outdo verb = **surpass**, top,
outshine, go one better than
• *She would love to outdo the previous
champion.*
See also: **beat, pass**

outdoor adjective = **open-air**,
outside, alfresco, out-of-door or
out-of-doors

outdoors See **country**

outer adjective = **external**,
outside, surface, exterior,
exposed, outlying, peripheral,
outward

outfit noun 1 = **costume**, clothes,
ensemble, garb, get-up (*informal*),
suit
2 = **group**, company, team,

organization, unit, crew, squad,
setup (*informal*)

outgoing adjective 1 = **leaving**,
former, departing, retiring,
withdrawing
2 = **sociable**, open, warm,
friendly, expansive, gregarious,
approachable, extrovert,
communicative

outing noun = **trip**, spin (*informal*),
expedition, excursion, jaunt

outlandish adjective = **strange**,
bizarre, fantastic, weird, exotic,
preposterous, unheard-of, far-
out (*slang*), freakish, outré

outlaw noun 1 = **bandit**, fugitive,
robber, outcast, desperado,
highwayman, marauder
▷ verb 2 = **forbid**, ban, bar,
prohibit, exclude, disallow,
proscribe

outlawed See **illegal**

outlay noun = **expenditure**,
investment, spending,
cost(s), expenses, outgoings,
overhead(s)

outlet noun 1 = **release**, opening,
exit, channel, vent, avenue, duct
2 = **store**, market, shop

outline verb 1 = **summarize**,
sketch • *The mayor outlined his plan
to clean up the town.*
▷ noun 2 = **summary**, rundown,
synopsis • *an outline of the
archaeologist's findings*
3 = **shape**, figure, form,
silhouette, contours • *the hazy
outline of the buildings*

outlive verb = **outlast**, survive

outlook noun 1 = **attitude**, view,
perspective • *I adopted a positive
outlook on life.*
2 = **prospects**, future • *The
economic outlook is one of rising
unemployment.*
See also: **prospect**

outlying adjective = **remote**,
provincial, distant, peripheral,
far-flung, out-of-the-way

outmoded adjective = **old-
fashioned**, obsolete,
antiquated, archaic, out-of-date,
anachronistic, outworn, passé,
unfashionable • *Fax machines are
an outmoded technology.*

out-of-date *adjective* = **outdated**, old-fashioned, invalid, obsolete, antiquated, expired, archaic, dated, outmoded, lapsed, outworn, passé
OPPOSITE: modern

out-of-the-way *See* **distant**

outpost *See* **colony**

outpouring *noun* = **stream**, flow, spate, spurt, cascade, torrent, effusion

output *noun* = **production**, manufacture, yield, achievement, productivity

outrage *noun* 1 = **violation**, violence, abuse, insult, offense, desecration, indignity, affront, sacrilege
2 = **indignation**, hurt, shock, anger, wrath, resentment, fury
▶ *verb* 3 = **offend**, shock, incense, infuriate, affront, scandalize, madden

outrageous *adjective*
1 = **atrocious**, offensive, disgraceful, wicked, flagrant, heinous, unspeakable, nefarious, villainous, iniquitous
2 = **unreasonable**, steep (*informal*), shocking, scandalous, extravagant, exorbitant, preposterous, immoderate

outré *adjective* = **eccentric**, odd, bizarre, fantastic, weird, unconventional, outlandish, off-the-wall (*slang*), freakish

outright *adjective* 1 = **absolute**, complete, total, perfect, thorough, unconditional, unqualified, unmitigated, out-and-out, thoroughgoing
2 = **direct**, flat, straightforward, definite, unequivocal, unqualified
▶ *adverb* 3 = **absolutely**, completely, openly, thoroughly, overtly, straightforwardly, to the full

outset *noun* = **beginning**, start, opening, onset, kickoff (*informal*), inauguration, inception, commencement

outshine *verb* = **outclass**, surpass, eclipse, overshadow, upstage, outstrip, outdo, transcend, leave in the shade *or* put in the shade

outside *noun* 1 = **exterior**, face, surface, facade • *The moth was on the outside of the glass.*
OPPOSITE: inside
▶ *adjective* 2 = **exterior**, external, surface, outdoor, outer, outward
• *an outside water tap*
OPPOSITE: inside
3 (~ *chance*) = **unlikely**, small, remote, slight, slim, distant, faint, marginal

> INFORMALLY SPEAKING
> **at the outside**: at the most
> **outside of**: with the exception of

outsider *noun* = **interloper**, stranger, newcomer, intruder, incomer, odd man out

outsize *adjective* = **extra-large**, huge, giant, monster, mammoth, gigantic, oversized, jumbo (*informal*), supersize

outskirts *plural noun* = **edge**, perimeter, periphery • *the outskirts of Toronto*

outspoken *adjective* = **forthright**, open, explicit, blunt, abrupt, frank, unequivocal, plain-spoken, unceremonious

outstanding *adjective*
1 = **excellent**, great, brilliant, exceptional, superb, first-class, first-rate • *an outstanding tennis player*
2 = **unpaid**, due, overdue, payable, owing • *The total debt outstanding is $2 billion.*
See also: **fine**, **major**, **prize**

outstrip *verb* = **surpass**, exceed, eclipse, overtake, better, excel, outdo, transcend, outdistance

outward *adjective* = **apparent**, surface, obvious, visible, noticeable, observable, ostensible, perceptible

outwardly *adverb* = **apparently**, seemingly, ostensibly, externally, on the face of it, on the surface, superficially, to all intents and purposes

outweigh *verb* = **override**,

cancel or cancel out, eclipse, compensate for, prevail over, take precedence over, tip the scales

outwit verb = **outthink**, fool, cheat, dupe, outsmart (informal), get the better of, outfox, outmanoeuvre, swindle

outworn adjective = **outdated**, discredited, obsolete, antiquated, out-of-date, worn-out, outmoded, disused, hackneyed, threadbare

oval adjective = **elliptical**, egg-shaped, ovoid

ovation noun = **applause**, tribute, acclaim, acclamation, big hand, cheers, clapping, plaudits

over preposition 1 = **more than**, above, exceeding, in excess of • It cost over a million dollars.

2 = **on top of**, on, above, upon

▷ **over the moon** See **joyful**

RELATED WORDS
prefixes: hyper-, super-, supra-, sur-

▶ adjective 3 = **finished**, up, past, complete, gone, at an end, done • I am glad it's all over.

▶ adverb 4 = **above**, overhead, aloft, on high

5 = **extra**, beyond, in addition, in excess, left over

> INFORMALLY SPEAKING
> **over again**: once more
> **over and over**: again and again
> **over with** or **over and done with**: finished

over- See **too**

overact verb = **exaggerate**, ham or ham up (informal), overdo, overplay

overall adjective 1 = **total**, general, global, complete, comprehensive, blanket, inclusive, all-embracing

▶ adverb 2 = **in general**, on the whole

overawe verb = **intimidate**, scare, alarm, terrify, frighten, daunt, abash

overbalance verb = **overturn**, slip, tumble, capsize, keel over, tip over, topple over, turn turtle

overbearing adjective = **domineering**, superior, arrogant, dictatorial, imperious, high-handed, bossy (informal), haughty, supercilious

overblown adjective = **excessive**, inflated, disproportionate, undue, immoderate, overdone, over the top

overcast adjective = **cloudy**, dismal, dull, murky, gray, dreary, leaden, louring or lowering

overcharge verb = **cheat**, sting (informal), surcharge, fleece, short-change, rip off (slang)

overcome verb 1 = **conquer**, master, vanquish (formal), surmount, get the better of, triumph over • I had overcome my fear of flying.

▶ adjective 2 = **overwhelmed**, affected, speechless, at a loss for words, bowled over (informal), swept off one's feet

See also: **beat, crush, resolve, subdue**

overconfident adjective = **cocky**, brash, foolhardy, presumptuous, cocksure, overweening

overcrowded adjective = **packed**, jam-packed, bursting at the seams, choked, congested, overloaded, overpopulated, packed out, swarming

overdo verb = **exaggerate**, overstate, overindulge, overreach, belabour, gild the lily, go overboard (informal)

▷ **overdo it** = **overwork**, overload, bite off more than one can chew, burn the candle at both ends (informal), strain oneself or overstrain oneself, wear oneself out

overdone adjective 1 = **excessive**, unnecessary, exaggerated, undue, inordinate, fulsome, immoderate, overelaborate, too much

2 = **overcooked**, burnt, charred, dried up, spoiled

overdose See **excess**

overdue adjective = **late**, belated, behindhand, behind schedule, owing, tardy, unpunctual

overeat verb = **gorge**, binge (informal), guzzle, overindulge, gormandize, pig out (slang), stuff oneself

overemphasize verb = **exaggerate**, belabour, blow up out of all proportion, make a mountain out of a molehill (informal), overdramatize, overstress

overestimate See **exaggerate**

overflow verb 1 = **spill**, brim over, bubble over, pour over, run over, well over
▶ noun 2 = **surplus**, overabundance, spilling over

overflowing See **crowded**

overhang verb = **stick out**, project, extend, loom, protrude, jut

overhaul verb 1 = **check**, service, repair, restore, examine, inspect, refurbish, do up (informal), recondition
2 = **overtake**, pass, catch up with, get ahead of
▶ noun 3 = **checkup**, check, examination, service, inspection, reconditioning

overhead adverb 1 = **above**, upward, aloft, skyward, in the sky, on high, up above
▶ adjective 2 = **raised**, upper, aerial, overhanging

overheads plural noun = **running costs**, operating costs

overhear See **hear**

overindulgence noun = **excess**, immoderation, intemperance, overeating, surfeit

overjoyed adjective = **delighted**, jubilant, euphoric, elated, on cloud nine (informal), over the moon (informal), thrilled

overlay See **cover**, **spread**

overload verb = **weigh down**, strain, burden, saddle or saddle with, oppress, overburden, overtax, encumber

overlook verb 1 = **ignore**, neglect, disregard, turn a blind eye to
• We tend to overlook warning signals about our health.
2 = **miss**, forget • One crucial detail was overlooked.

3 = **have a view of**, look over or look out on
See also: **excuse**, **face**

overly See **too**

overpower verb = **overwhelm**, defeat, overcome, crush, master, subdue, quell, overthrow, conquer, vanquish, subjugate

overpowering adjective = **overwhelming**, strong, powerful, forceful, irresistible, invincible, irrefutable

overrate verb = **overestimate**, exaggerate, overvalue

override verb = **overrule**, cancel, outweigh, annul, nullify, supersede, countermand

overriding adjective = **major**, primary, dominant, ultimate, supreme, paramount, predominant

overrule verb = **overturn**, reverse • The Court of Appeal overruled this decision.

overrun verb 1 = **invade**, overwhelm, rout, occupy
2 = **infest**, choke, ravage, inundate, permeate, spread over, swarm over
3 = **exceed**, overshoot, go beyond, run over or run on

overseas See **foreign**

oversee verb = **supervise**, manage, direct, co-ordinate, preside, be in charge of • Get a supervisor to oversee the work.

overseer noun = **supervisor**, chief, boss (informal), master, superintendent, foreman

overshadow verb 1 = **outshine**, dominate, surpass, eclipse, dwarf, leave in the shade or put in the shade, tower above
2 = **spoil**, ruin, temper, mar, blight, put a damper on

oversight noun = **mistake**, slip, error, fault, neglect, lapse, blunder, omission, carelessness

overstate See **exaggerate**

overt adjective = **open**, public, obvious, plain, blatant, manifest, observable, unconcealed, undisguised

overtake verb 1 = **pass**, overhaul, outstrip, outdo, outdistance, catch up with, get past, leave behind

2 = befall, hit, strike, happen, overwhelm, engulf

overthrow *verb* **1 = depose**, oust, topple, bring down • *The government was overthrown in a military coup.*

▶ *noun* **2 = downfall**, fall, defeat, destruction, undoing, dethronement, ousting, unseating

overtone *noun* **= connotation**, sense, hint, suggestion, implication, nuance, innuendo, undercurrent, intimation

overture *noun* (*Music*) **= introduction**, opening, prelude

▷ **overtures = approach**, offer, advance, proposal, invitation, proposition

overturn *verb* **1 = tip over**, upset, topple, capsize, knock over • *to overturn a can of paint*

2 = overrule, reverse • *The referee's decision was overturned.* *See also:* **abolish**

overused *See* **stock**

overweight *adjective* **= fat**, obese, hefty, stout • *Being overweight increases your risk of heart problems.*

overwhelm *verb* **1 = overcome**, devastate, stagger, bowl over (*informal*), knock (someone) for six (*informal*), sweep (someone) off his feet *or* sweep (someone) off her feet, take (someone's) breath away

2 = destroy, crush, rout, overpower, massacre, overrun, cut to pieces

overwhelming *adjective* **= overpowering**, towering,

breathtaking, irresistible, crushing, devastating, shattering, stunning

overwork *verb* **1 = wear oneself out**, strain, sweat (*informal*), burn the midnight oil, work one's fingers to the bone

2 = exploit, fatigue, exhaust, weary, oppress, overuse, wear out

overwrought *adjective* **= agitated**, tense, excited, frantic, uptight (*informal*), overexcited, distracted, keyed up, on edge, wired (*slang*)

owe *verb* **= be in debt**, be in arrears, be obligated *or* be indebted

owing *adjective* **= unpaid**, due, overdue, outstanding, payable, unsettled, owed

owing to *preposition* **= because of**, as a result of, on account of

own *adjective* **1 = personal**, private • *I have my own website.*

▶ *verb* **2 = possess**, have • *His parents own a hardware store.*

3 = acknowledge, allow, admit, recognize, grant, concede, confess

▷ **hold one's own = keep going**, compete, keep one's end up, keep one's head above water

▷ **on one's own = alone**, independently, by oneself, unaided • *I work best on my own.*

▷ **own up = confess**, admit, come clean, make a clean breast, tell the truth

owner *noun* **= possessor**, proprietor • *the owner of the store*

ownership *noun* **= possession**, title, dominion

o

Pp

pace noun 1 = **step**, walk, stride, gait
2 = **speed**, rate, velocity, tempo
▶ verb 3 = **stride**, pound, march, patrol, tread
▷ **pace out** = **measure**, step, count, mark out

pacifist noun = **peace lover**, dove, conscientious objector

pacify verb = **calm**, appease, soothe, placate, mollify • *They tried to pacify the upset fans.*

pack verb 1 = **package**, store, load, bundle, stow
2 = **cram**, crowd, fill, press, stuff, jam, ram, compress
▷ **pack off** = **send away**, dismiss, send packing (*informal*)
▷ **pack up** = **put away**, store; (*Informal*) = **stop**, finish, give up, pack it in (*informal*); = **break down**, fail, conk out (*informal*)
▶ noun 3 = **bundle**, load, burden, backpack, knapsack, back pack, kitbag, nunny-bag (*Canad Nfld*), rucksack
4 = **package**, package, parcel, packet
5 = **group**, company, troop, crowd, band, gang, bunch, herd, mob, flock

package noun 1 = **parcel**, box, container, carton, packet
2 = **collection**, unit, whole, combination
▶ verb 3 = **pack**, box, wrap, parcel *or* parcel up

packed adjective = **full**, crowded, jam-packed, jammed, chock-a-block, chock-full, crammed, filled

packet noun = **package**, bag, container, carton, parcel

pact noun = **agreement**, deal, alliance, treaty, bargain, understanding, covenant

pad¹ noun 1 = **cushion**, protection, buffer, stuffing, wad
2 = **notepad**, block, jotter, writing pad
3 = **paw**, foot, sole
4 (*Slang, dated*) = **home**, place, apartment, flat
▶ verb 5 = **pack**, protect, fill, stuff, cushion
▷ **pad out** = **lengthen**, stretch, elaborate, fill out, flesh out, protract, spin out

pad² verb = **sneak**, steal, creep, go barefoot

padding noun 1 = **filling**, packing, stuffing, wadding
2 = **wordiness**, hot air (*informal*), verbiage, verbosity

paddle¹ noun 1 = **oar**, scull
▶ verb 2 = **row**, pull, propel, scull

paddle² verb 1 = **wade**, splash *or* splash about, slop
2 = **dabble**, stir

padlock See **lock**

pagan adjective 1 = **heathen**, infidel, idolatrous, polytheistic, pre-Christian
▶ noun 2 = **heathen**, infidel, idolater, polytheist

page¹ noun = **folio**, side, leaf, sheet

page² noun 1 = **attendant**, servant, pageboy, squire
▶ verb 2 = **call**, summon, send for

pageant noun = **show**, display, parade, procession, spectacle, tableau

pageantry noun = **spectacle**, show, display, parade, grandeur, pomp, splendour, theatricality

pain noun 1 = **soreness**, trouble, ache, discomfort, irritation, twinge • *I felt a sharp pain in my lower back.*
2 = **distress**, grief, misery, anguish, agony • *the pain of rejection*

▷ **pain in the neck** See
annoyance, pest
▶ verb **3** = **hurt**, smart, sting,
throb
4 = **distress**, hurt, torture,
grieve, sadden, agonize,
torment, cut to the quick
See also: **annoyance, nuisance,
pest, sorrow**
pained adjective = **distressed**,
hurt, upset, injured, wounded,
aggrieved, offended
painful adjective **1** = **distressing**,
unpleasant, grievous, saddening
• painful memories
2 = **sore**, tender, aching,
excruciating • a painful cramp in
the stomach
See also: **uncomfortable**
painfully adverb = **distressingly**,
clearly, unfortunately, sadly,
dreadfully
painkiller noun = **analgesic**, drug,
anesthetic, anodyne
painless adjective = **simple**, easy,
fast, quick, effortless
pains plural noun = **trouble**, effort,
care, bother, diligence
painstaking adjective
= **thorough**, careful,
conscientious, meticulous,
diligent, scrupulous, assiduous
paint noun **1** = **colouring**, dye,
stain, colour, pigment, tint
▶ verb **2** = **depict**, draw,
represent, picture, portray,
sketch
3 = **coat**, cover, apply, colour,
daub
painting See **picture**
pair noun **1** = **couple**, brace, duo,
twins
▶ verb **2** = **couple**, team, join,
match or match up, twin,
bracket
▷ **pair up** See **team**
pal noun (Informal) = **friend**,
comrade, companion, buddy
(informal), chum (informal), crony,
homeboy (slang), homegirl (slang)
palatable adjective = **delicious**,
tasty, yummy (informal), luscious,
appetizing, mouthwatering
palate noun = **taste**, stomach,
appetite

palatial adjective = **magnificent**,
grand, splendid, majestic,
stately, regal, opulent, imposing
palaver noun = **fuss**, big deal
(informal), performance (informal),
to-do, rigmarole, song and dance
(informal)
pale adjective **1** = **light**, colourless,
wan, ashen, faded, sallow
• Migrating birds filled the pale sky.
▶ verb **2** = **become pale**, whiten,
blanch, go white, lose colour
See also: **soft**
pall[1] noun **1** = **cloud**, shadow, veil,
shroud, mantle
2 = **gloom**, check, damper, damp
pall[2] verb = **become boring**, tire,
sicken, weary, become dull,
become tedious, cloy, jade
pallid adjective = **pale**, anemic,
pasty, wan, ashen, colourless
pallor noun = **paleness**, lack of
colour, pallidness, wanness,
whiteness
palm off verb = **fob off**, foist off,
pass off
palpable adjective = **obvious**,
clear, visible, plain, evident,
manifest, unmistakable,
conspicuous
palpitate verb = **beat**, pound,
flutter, tremble, throb, pulsate
paltry adjective = **insignificant**,
despicable, lousy (slang), meagre,
contemptible, inconsiderable,
small, poor, minor, slight, petty,
miserable, worthless, trivial,
unimportant, measly, puny,
scuzzy (slang), trifling
pamper verb = **spoil**, indulge,
coddle, cater to, cosset, pet,
overindulge
pamphlet noun = **booklet**, tract,
brochure, circular, leaflet
pan[1] noun **1** = **pot**, container,
saucepan
▶ verb **2** = **sift out**, look for,
search for
3 (Informal) = **criticize**, slam
(slang), knock (informal), censure
pan[2] verb = **move**, follow, track,
sweep
panacea noun = **cure-all**,
nostrum, universal cure
panache noun = **style**, dash,

P

élan, flamboyance

pandemonium *noun* = **uproar**, chaos, confusion, turmoil, racket, din, bedlam, hullabaloo, rumpus

pander *verb*
▷ **pander to** = **indulge**, please, satisfy, gratify, cater to, play up to (*informal*)

panel *See* **council**

pang *noun* = **twinge**, pain, stab, sting, ache, spasm, prick
▷ **pang of conscience** *See* **regret**

panic *noun* **1** = **terror**, fear, alarm, dismay, hysteria, fright • *The earthquake caused panic among the population.*
▶ *verb* **2** = **go to pieces**, become hysterical, lose your nerve • *I panicked when the elevator came to a sudden stop between floors and didn't move.*
3 = **alarm**, scare, unnerve
See also: **horror**

panic-stricken *adjective* = **terrified**, frightened, scared, hysterical, panicky, frightened out of one's wits, in a cold sweat (*informal*), scared stiff

panoply *noun* = **array**, dress, attire, garb, regalia, trappings

panorama *noun* = **view**, prospect, vista

panoramic *adjective* = **wide**, overall, extensive, comprehensive, sweeping

pant *verb* = **puff**, blow, breathe, wheeze, gasp, heave

pantomime *See* **play**

pants *plural noun* = **trousers**, slacks

paper *noun* **1** = **newspaper**, daily, journal, gazette
2 = **essay**, report, article, treatise, dissertation
▷ **papers** = **documents**, certificates, deeds, records; = **letters**, file, archive, dossier, diaries, documents, records
▶ *verb* **3** = **wallpaper**, hang

par *noun*
▷ **above par** = **excellent**, superior, exceptional, outstanding, first-rate (*informal*)
▷ **below** *or* **under par** = **inferior**,

poor, substandard, imperfect, second-rate, lacking, wanting, below average, two-bit (*slang*), not up to scratch (*informal*), dime-a-dozen (*informal*), bush-league (*informal*), not up to snuff (*informal*), tinhorn (*US slang*)
▷ **on a par with** = **equal to**, the same as, much the same as, well-matched with
▷ **par for the course** = **usual**, average, standard, typical, ordinary, predictable, expected
▷ **up to par** = **satisfactory**, acceptable, adequate, passable, good enough, up to scratch (*informal*), up to the mark

parable *noun* = **lesson**, story, allegory, fable, moral tale

parade *noun* **1** = **procession**, march, motorcade, pageant • *the Grey Cup parade*
2 = **show**, display, spectacle
▶ *verb* **3** = **flaunt**, display, exhibit, show off (*informal*)
4 = **march**, process

paradigm *noun* = **model**, example, pattern, ideal

paradise *noun* **1** = **heaven**, Elysian fields, Happy Valley, Promised Land
2 = **bliss**, delight, heaven, utopia, felicity

paradox *noun* = **contradiction**, puzzle, oddity, anomaly, enigma

paradoxical *adjective* = **contradictory**, enigmatic, baffling, confounding, puzzling

paragon *noun* = **model**, pattern, ideal, epitome, exemplar, nonpareil, quintessence

paragraph *noun* = **section**, part, item, passage, clause, subdivision

---

PARTS OF A PARAGRAPH

clause
phrase
sentence
word

---

parallel *adjective* **1** = **equidistant**,

alongside, side by side
2 = **matching**, like, similar, analogous, corresponding, resembling
▶ *noun* **3** = **equivalent**, match, twin, counterpart, equal, analogue
4 = **similarity**, comparison, likeness, resemblance, analogy

paralysis *noun* **1** = **immobility**, palsy
2 = **standstill**, halt, breakdown, stoppage

paralytic *adjective* = **paralyzed**, disabled, lame, crippled, challenged, incapacitated, palsied

paralyze *verb* **1** = **disable**, cripple, lame, incapacitate
2 = **immobilize**, halt, freeze, stun, numb, petrify

paralyzed *See* **numb**

parameter *noun* = **limit**, restriction, framework, limitation, specification

paramount *adjective* = **principal**, first, chief, prime, main, primary, cardinal, foremost, supreme

paranoid *adjective* **1** = **mentally ill**, psychotic, disturbed, neurotic, manic, deluded, paranoiac
2 (*Informal*) = **suspicious**, nervous, fearful, worried, wired (*slang*)

paraphernalia *noun*
= **equipment**, tackle, stuff, gear, baggage, apparatus, belongings, effects, things, trappings

paraphrase *noun* **1** = **rewording**, restatement, rephrasing
▶ *verb* **2** = **reword**, restate, express in other words *or* express in one's own words, rephrase

parasite *noun* = **sponger** (*informal*), leech, bloodsucker (*informal*), hanger-on, scrounger (*informal*)

parasitic, parasitical *adjective* = **sponging** (*informal*), bloodsucking (*informal*), scrounging (*informal*)

parcel *noun* **1** = **package**, pack, bundle

▶ *verb* **2** (often with *up*) = **wrap**, package, pack, do up, tie up

parch *verb* = **dry up**, evaporate, wither, dehydrate, shrivel, desiccate

parched *adjective* = **dried out** *or* **dried up**, dry, thirsty, arid, dehydrated

pardon *verb* **1** = **forgive**, excuse, acquit, overlook, exonerate, absolve, let off (*informal*)
▶ *noun* **2** = **forgiveness**, amnesty, acquittal, exoneration, absolution

pardonable *adjective*
= **forgivable**, minor, understandable, excusable, venial

pare *verb* **1** = **peel**, cut, skin, clip, trim, shave
2 = **cut back**, cut, reduce, decrease, crop, dock

parent *noun* = **father** *or* **mother**, progenitor, sire, procreator

parentage *noun* = **family**, stock, birth, descent, pedigree, ancestry, lineage

pariah *noun* = **outcast**, exile, undesirable, untouchable

parish *noun* = **community**, church, flock, congregation

parity *noun* = **equality**, unity, consistency, uniformity, equivalence

park *noun* = **parkland**, estate, garden, woodland, grounds, parkette (*Canad*)

parlance *noun* = **language**, talk, speech, tongue, jargon, idiom, phraseology

parliament *noun* = **assembly**, council, legislature, convention, congress, senate

parliamentary *adjective*
= **governmental**, legislative, law-making

parlor *noun* (*Old-fashioned*)
= **sitting room**, lounge, drawing room, front room, living room

parlous *adjective* (*Archaic or humorous*) = **dangerous**, risky, hazardous

parochial *adjective* = **provincial**, limited, narrow, petty, insular, narrow-minded, small-minded

parody noun 1 = **takeoff** (informal), satire, skit, spoof (informal), imitation, lampoon, piss-take (informal) • a parody of the newscast
▶ verb 2 = **take off** (informal), satirize (informal), caricature, burlesque

paroxysm noun = **outburst**, attack, fit, seizure, spasm, convulsion

parrot verb = **repeat**, copy, echo, mimic, imitate

parry verb 1 = **ward off**, block, deflect, rebuff, repel, repulse
2 = **evade**, avoid, dodge, sidestep

parsimonious adjective = **mean**, close, stingy, frugal, miserly, niggardly, penny-pinching (informal), tightfisted

parson noun = **clergyman**, minister, cleric, priest, pastor, preacher, vicar, churchman

part noun 1 = **piece**, bit, section, portion, fraction, fragment • I like that part of Hamilton.
2 = **involvement**, role, duty, capacity, function • He tried to conceal his part in the accident.
3 = **component**, member, unit, division, branch, constituent
4 (Theatre) = **role**, character, lines
5 = **side**, cause, concern, interest, behalf
6 (often plural) = **region**, area, quarter, district, neighbourhood, vicinity
▷ **in good part** = **good-naturedly**, well, cheerfully, without offence
▷ **in part** = **partly**, somewhat, partially, a little, in some measure
▷ **take part in** = **participate in**, be instrumental in, be involved in, have a hand in, join in, play a part in • Thousands took part in the celebrations.
▶ verb 7 = **divide**, break, separate, tear, split, sever, detach, come apart, rend
8 = **separate**, go, leave, withdraw, depart, go away, split up
See also: **aspect, attachment, factor, fitting, quantity**

INFORMALLY SPEAKING
for my part: as far as I am concerned
for the most part: mostly
in part: to some extent
part and parcel: a necessary or essential part
part with: give up or let go
play a part: be a contributing factor

partake verb
▷ **partake of** = **consume**, take, eat, chow down (slang)
▷ **partake in** = **participate in**, engage in, share in, take part in

partial adjective 1 = **incomplete**, unfinished, imperfect, uncompleted
2 = **biased**, unfair, partisan, discriminatory, unjust, one-sided, prejudiced

partiality noun 1 = **bias**, preference, prejudice, favouritism
2 = **liking**, love, taste, weakness, penchant, fondness, inclination, predilection

partially adverb = **partly**, somewhat, fractionally, incompletely, in part, not wholly

participant noun = **participator**, player, member, stakeholder, contributor

participate verb = **take part**, be involved in, engage in, enter into, join in • More than half the class participated in the event.
See also: **play**
▷ **participate in** See **take part in**

participation noun = **taking part**, contribution, involvement, joining in, partaking, sharing in

particle noun = **bit**, piece, grain, scrap, shred, mite, speck, iota, jot

particular adjective 1 = **specific**, express, exact, distinct, precise, peculiar, discrete • That particular place is dangerous.
2 = **special**, notable, exceptional, marked, uncommon, singular • Pay particular attention to the instructions.
3 = **fussy**, meticulous, exacting, choosy (informal), fastidious • He

was very particular about the colours he used.

▶ *noun* 4 (*usually plural*) = **detail**, fact, feature, item, circumstance, specification

▷ **in particular** = **especially**, particularly, exactly, specifically, distinctly

See also: **personal, strict**

particularly *adverb*

1 = **especially**, notably, unusually, exceptionally, uncommonly, singularly

2 = **specifically**, especially, explicitly, distinctly, expressly, in particular

parting *noun* 1 = **farewell**, going, good-bye

2 = **division**, split, separation, rift, rupture, breaking

partisan *noun* 1 = **supporter**, devotee, adherent, upholder

2 = **underground fighter**, guerrilla, resistance fighter

▶ *adjective* 3 = **prejudiced**, interested, sectarian, partial, one-sided, biased

partition *noun* 1 = **screen**, wall, barrier

2 = **division**, separation, segregation

3 = **allotment**, distribution, apportionment

▶ *verb* 4 = **separate**, screen, divide

partly *adverb* = **partially**, half-, in part, to some degree, to some extent • *This is partly my fault.*

partner *noun* 1 = **spouse**, wife, husband, mate • *My partner moved in with me last year.*

PARTS OF SPEECH

adjective
adverb
conjunction
interjection
noun
preposition
pronoun
verb

---

2 = **companion**, teammate • *my tennis partner*

See also: **colleague**

partnership *noun* = **company**, house, firm, union, society, alliance, cooperative

party *noun* 1 = **get-together**, function, celebration, reception, gathering, afterparty • *Most teenagers like to go to parties.*

2 = **faction**, coalition, alliance • *his resignation as chairman of the party*

3 = **team**, unit, crew, band, gang, squad • *a search party looking for the lost child*

4 = **person**, someone, individual

See also: **celebrate, company, group, side**

pass *verb* 1 = **exceed**, surpass, overtake, outstrip, outdo, go beyond • *She gave a triumphant wave as she passed the finish line.*

2 = **qualify**, succeed, graduate, get through • *I just passed my driving test.*

OPPOSITE: **fail**

3 = **go by** *or* **go past**, go, run, move, proceed, lapse, elapse

4 = **spend**, fill, occupy, while away

5 = **give**, send, hand, deliver, transfer, convey

6 = **approve**, accept, ratify, enact, legislate, decree, ordain

7 = **end**, go, cease, blow over

▷ **pass around** *See* **distribute**

▷ **pass away, pass on** (*Euphemistic*) = **die**, expire, kick the bucket (*slang*), pass over, shuffle off this mortal coil, snuff it (*informal*)

▷ **pass down** *See* **hand down**

▷ **pass off** = **fake**, counterfeit, make a pretense of, palm off

▷ **pass on** = **hand down**, will; = **communicate**

▷ **pass out** = **faint**, become unconscious, black out (*informal*), lose consciousness

▷ **pass over** = **disregard**, ignore, overlook, take no notice of

▷ **pass round** *See* **distribute**

▷ **pass up** = **miss**, decline, abstain, forgo, neglect, let slip

P

▸ noun 8 = **licence**, ticket, passport, identification • *a free pass to the movies*

9 = **gap**, route, ravine, canyon, gorge

See also: **disappear, permit, vanish**

| INFORMALLY SPEAKING
| **pass out**: lose consciousness
| **pass over**: fail to notice
| **pass up**: give up or renounce

passable adjective = **adequate**, average, fair, acceptable, mediocre, so-so (informal), tolerable, all right

passage noun 1 = **way**, road, course, route, channel, path • *He cleared a passage through the crowd.*

2 = **corridor**, hall, aisle • *up some stairs and along a narrow passage toward a door*

3 = **extract**, section, excerpt, quotation • *a passage from Shakespeare*

4 = **journey**, trip, crossing, trek, voyage

5 = **safe-conduct**, right, freedom, permission

passageway noun = **corridor**, hall, passage, lane, alley, hallway, aisle

passé adjective = **out-of-date**, old-fashioned, outdated, obsolete, dated, outmoded, old hat, unfashionable

passenger noun = **traveller**, fare, rider

passer-by noun = **bystander**, witness, onlooker

passing adjective 1 = **momentary**, brief, temporary, short-lived, fleeting, transient, ephemeral, transitory

2 = **superficial**, short, quick, casual, cursory, glancing

passion noun 1 = **emotion**, fire, intensity, excitement, warmth, zeal • *She spoke with great passion.*

2 = **love**, desire, lust, ardour, infatuation

3 = **rage**, storm, fit, anger, outburst, frenzy, fury, paroxysm

4 = **mania**, bug (informal), enthusiasm, obsession, craving, fascination, craze

See also: **feeling, heat, weakness**

passionate adjective
1 = **emotional**, strong, intense, heartfelt, impassioned, ardent • *I'm a passionate believer in equal rights.*

2 = **loving**, hot, erotic, ardent, amorous, lustful

See also: **crazy, enthusiastic, fanatical, fervent, romantic**

passive adjective = **submissive**, receptive, docile, resigned • *His passive attitude made things easier for me.*

See also: **apathetic, uninterested**

passport See **pass, permit**

password noun = **watchword**, signal, key word

past adjective 1 = **former**, previous, ancient, bygone, olden • *details of his past activities*

OPPOSITE: future

2 = **over**, finished, gone, done, ended

▸ noun 3 = **background**, life, history, past life

▷ **the past** = **former times**, antiquity, days gone by, long ago • *We would like to put the past behind us.*

▸ preposition 4 = **beyond**, by, over • *It's just past the station.*

5 = **after**, beyond, later than

paste noun 1 = **adhesive**, gum, cement, glue

▸ verb 2 = **stick**, gum, cement, glue

pastel adjective = **pale**, light, soft, delicate, muted

pasteurized See **pure**

pastiche noun = **medley**, blend, mixture, hodgepodge, mélange (French), miscellany

pastime noun = **activity**, diversion, recreation, hobby • *Her favourite pastime is curling.*

See also: **interest**

pastor noun = **clergyman**, minister, priest, vicar, rector, churchman, ecclesiastic, parson

pastoral adjective 1 = **rustic**, country, rural, bucolic

2 = **ecclesiastical**, ministerial, clerical, priestly

pasture noun = **grassland**, grass, grazing, meadow

pasty adjective = **pale**, anemic, sickly, pallid, wan

pat verb 1 = **stroke**, pet, touch, tap, fondle, caress
▶ noun 2 = **stroke**, tap, clap

patch noun 1 = **reinforcement**
2 = **spot**, bit, scrap, shred, small piece
3 = **plot**, area, land, ground, tract
▶ verb 4 = **mend**, cover, repair, reinforce, sew up
▷ **patch together** See **piece together**
▷ **patch up** See **fix**, **repair**

patchwork noun = **mixture**, medley, jumble, hodgepodge, pastiche

patchy adjective = **uneven**, irregular, variable, erratic, spotty, sketchy, fitful

patent noun 1 = **copyright**, licence
▶ adjective 2 = **obvious**, clear, apparent, evident, manifest, glaring

paternal adjective = **fatherly**, protective, concerned, solicitous

paternity noun 1 = **fatherhood**
2 = **parentage**, family, descent, extraction, lineage

path noun 1 = **pathway**, track, trail, footpath • We followed the paths alongside the river.
2 = **route**, way, course, direction, passage • A group of reporters stood in his path.
See also: **line**

pathetic adjective 1 = **sad**, heartbreaking • small, shrunken, and looking pathetic
2 = **poor**, sorry, feeble, pitiful, lamentable • pathetic excuses
See also: **hopeless**, **inadequate**, **lame**, **miserable**

pathos noun = **sadness**, poignancy, pitifulness, plaintiveness

pathway See **path**

patience noun 1 = **forbearance**, cool (informal), restraint, tolerance, composure, calmness • It was exacting work and required all her patience.

2 = **endurance**, resignation, submission, perseverance, long-suffering, fortitude, constancy, stoicism

patient adjective 1 = **long-suffering**, calm, philosophical, serene, composed • Please be patient - your cheque will arrive.
OPPOSITE: impatient
2 = **forbearing**, understanding, mild, lenient, tolerant, forgiving, indulgent, even-tempered
▶ noun 3 = **sick person**, case, sufferer, invalid, sickie (informal) • patients who wish to change their doctor

patriarch See **parent**

patriot noun = **nationalist**, loyalist, chauvinist

patriotic adjective = **nationalistic**, loyal, chauvinistic, jingoistic

patriotism noun = **nationalism**, jingoism

patrol noun 1 = **policing**, vigilance, protecting, guarding, watching
2 = **guard**, watch, sentinel, watchman, patrolman
▶ verb 3 = **police**, guard, safeguard, inspect, keep guard, keep watch

patron noun 1 = **supporter**, friend, champion, sponsor, backer, benefactor, philanthropist, helper
2 = **customer**, shopper, client, buyer, frequenter, habitué

patronage noun 1 = **support**, help, aid, sponsorship, assistance, promotion, backing
2 = **custom**, trade, business, traffic, commerce, trading, clientele

patronize verb 1 = **talk down to**, look down on
2 = **be a customer of** or **be a client of**, frequent, do business with, shop at
3 = **support**, help, back, fund, maintain, promote, sponsor

patronizing adjective
= **condescending**, superior, gracious, disdainful, haughty,

snobbish, supercilious

patter[1] verb **1** = **tap**, beat, pat, pitter-patter

2 = **walk lightly**, trip, skip, scuttle, scurry

▶ noun **3** = **tapping**, pattering, pitter-patter

patter[2] noun **1** = **spiel** (informal), line, pitch

2 = **chatter**, gabble, jabber, nattering, prattle

3 = **jargon**, cant, lingo (informal), slang, vernacular, argot, patois

▶ verb **4** = **chatter**, spout (informal), jabber, prate, rattle on

pattern noun **1** = **design**, motif
• red and purple thread stitched into a pattern of flames

2 = **plan**, design, blueprint, template, stencil, diagram
• sewing patterns

3 = **order**, plan, system, method, sequence

▶ verb **4** = **model**, follow, form, copy, style, imitate, mold
See also: **routine**

paucity noun (Formal) = **scarcity**, lack, shortage, deficiency, rarity, dearth, scantiness, sparseness

paunch noun = **belly**, pot, potbelly, spare tire (slang), muffin top (informal)

pauper noun = **down-and-out**, bankrupt, mendicant, poor person

pause verb **1** = **stop**, break, wait, delay, rest, halt, take a break • On leaving, she paused for a moment at the door.

▶ noun **2** = **stop**, break, rest, halt, stoppage, intermission, interruption, interval • There was a pause between the first and second acts.
See also: **gap, hesitate**

pave verb = **cover**, floor, surface, concrete, tile

paw verb = **manhandle**, grab, molest, maul, handle roughly

pawn[1] verb = **hock** (informal), pledge, mortgage, deposit

pawn[2] noun = **tool**, instrument, puppet, plaything, stooge (slang), cat's-paw

pay verb **1** = **settle**, honour,

compensate, reimburse, remunerate, recompense, pony up (informal) • You can pay by credit card.

2 = **be advantageous**, be worthwhile • It pays to be honest.

3 = **give**, extend, present, grant, bestow, hand out

4 = **be profitable**, make a return, make money

5 = **yield**, return, produce, bring in

▷ **pay attention** See **listen, watch**

▷ **pay attention to** See **heed**

▷ **pay back** = **repay**, square, refund, reimburse, settle up; = **get even with** (informal), retaliate, hit back

▷ **pay for** = **buy**, fund, finance; = **suffer for**, answer for, atone for, be punished for, compensate for, get one's just deserts, make amends for, suffer the consequences of

▷ **pay off** = **settle**, clear, square, discharge, pay in full; = **succeed**, work, be effective

▷ **pay out** = **spend**, expend, disburse, fork out, fork over, or fork up (slang), shell out (informal)

▷ **pay tribute to** See **praise**

▶ noun **6** = **wages**, income, fee, payment, salary, earnings • their complaints about pay and conditions

INFORMALLY SPEAKING
pay back: give the same treatment as you receive
pay off: give all the money that is owed
pay up: pay in full

payable adjective = **due**, outstanding, owed, owing

payment noun **1** = **remittance**, advance, premium, deposit, instalment • mortgage payments

2 = **paying**, settlement, discharge, remittance

3 = **wage**, fee, salary, reward, remuneration
See also: **charge, compensation, cost, pay**

peace noun **1** = **stillness**, quiet, silence, calm, tranquility • They

left me in peace to recover from my
exhaustion.
2 = truce, armistice, cessation
of hostilities • *The people do not
believe that the leaders want peace.*
OPPOSITE: war
3 = serenity, calm, composure,
repose, contentment
4 = harmony, accord,
agreement, concord
peaceable *adjective* = **peace-
loving**, friendly, peaceful, mild,
gentle, conciliatory, unwarlike
peaceful *adjective* **1 = calm**, still,
quiet, tranquil, serene, placid
• *a peaceful house in the heart of the
countryside*
2 = at peace, friendly, amicable,
harmonious, nonviolent
3 = peace-loving, conciliatory,
peaceable, unwarlike
See also: **relaxed**
peacefulness See **calm**
peacemaker *noun* = **mediator**,
arbitrator, conciliator, pacifier
peak *noun* **1 = high point**, climax,
culmination, zenith • *the peak of
the morning rush hour*
2 = summit, top, crest, brow,
pinnacle • *snow-covered peaks*
▶ *verb* **3 = culminate**, climax,
be at its height, come to a head,
reach its highest point • *Her
career peaked when she was in her
40s.*
See also: **ultimate**
peal *noun* **1 = ring**, crash, blast,
roar, rumble, clap, chime, clang,
reverberation
▶ *verb* **2 = ring**, crash, roar,
rumble, resound, chime
peasant *noun* = **rustic**,
countryman
peccadillo *noun* = **misdeed**, slip,
error, lapse, misdemeanour,
indiscretion
peck *verb, noun* = **pick**, hit, strike,
tap, dig, poke, jab, prick
peculiar *adjective* **1 = strange**,
odd, funny, bizarre, weird,
curious • *a very peculiar sense of
humour*
2 = special, personal,
individual, unique, distinctive,
distinguishing • *He has his own

peculiar way of doing things.*
See also: **particular**
peculiarity *noun*
1 = eccentricity, oddity,
abnormality, quirk, foible,
mannerism, idiosyncrasy
2 = characteristic, mark,
feature, quality, property,
attribute, trait, particularity
pedagogue *noun* = **teacher**,
master *or* mistress, instructor,
schoolmaster *or* schoolmistress
pedant *noun* = **hairsplitter**, nit-
picker (*informal*), quibbler
pedantic *adjective*
= **hairsplitting**, particular,
formal, academic, precise, fussy,
bookish, donnish, nit-picking
(*informal*), punctilious
pedantry *noun* = **hairsplitting**,
punctiliousness, quibbling
peddle *verb* = **sell**, market, trade,
push (*informal*), hawk
peddler *noun* = **seller**, vendor,
door-to-door salesman, hawker,
huckster
pedestal *noun* = **support**, base,
stand, foot, mounting, plinth
pedestrian *noun* **1 = walker**,
foot-traveller
▶ *adjective* **2 = dull**, ordinary,
mediocre, boring, commonplace,
mundane, banal, humdrum,
prosaic, uninspired
pedigree *noun* **1 = lineage**,
family, line, stock, race, blood,
breed, descent, extraction,
genealogy, ancestry, family tree
▶ *adjective* **2 = purebred**,
thoroughbred, full-blooded
peek *verb* **1 = glance**, peep, catch a
glimpse, sneak a look • *She peeked
at him through a crack in the wall.*
▶ *noun* **2 = glance**, look, glimpse,
peep • *He took his first peek at the
new stadium.*
peel *verb* **1 = skin**, scale, pare,
flake off, strip off
▶ *noun* **2 = skin**, rind, peeling
peep[1] *verb* **1 = peek**, look, sneak a
look, steal a look
▶ *noun* **2 = peek**, look, glimpse,
look-see (*slang*)
peep[2] *verb, noun* = **squeak**, chirp,
cheep, tweet

P

peephole noun = **spyhole**, opening, hole, crack, chink, aperture

peer[1] noun 1 = **aristocrat**, lord, noble, nobleman
2 = **equal**, like, fellow, compeer

peer[2] verb = **squint**, spy, scan, inspect, gaze, snoop, peep

peerage noun = **aristocracy**, nobility, lords and ladies, peers

peerless adjective = **unequalled**, excellent, outstanding, unparalleled, unmatched, incomparable, unrivalled, beyond compare, matchless

peevish adjective = **irritable**, cross, fractious, childish, grumpy, cantankerous, surly, snappy, sullen, churlish, crotchety, fretful, petulant, querulous, sulky

peg verb = **fasten**, join, fix, secure, attach

pejorative adjective = **derogatory**, negative, unpleasant, deprecatory, depreciatory, disparaging, uncomplimentary

pellet See **ball**

pelt[1] verb 1 = **throw**, strike, cast, batter, pepper, shower, hurl, bombard, sling
2 = **rush**, charge, shoot, speed, tear, belt (slang), dash, hurry, run fast
3 = **pour**, teem, bucket down (informal), rain cats and dogs (informal), rain hard

pelt[2] noun = **coat**, hide, skin, fell

pen[1] verb = **write**, draft, compose, draw up, jot down
▷ noun
▷ **pen name** noun = **pseudonym**, nom de plume

pen[2] noun 1 = **enclosure**, pound, fold, cage, coop, hutch, sty
▷ verb 2 = **enclose**, hedge, confine, cage, coop up, fence in, shut up or shut in

penal adjective = **disciplinary**, punitive, corrective

penal institution See **prison**

penalize verb = **punish**, discipline, handicap, impose a penalty on

penalties See **sanctions**

penalty noun = **punishment**, price, fine, forfeit, handicap

penance noun = **atonement**, penalty, reparation, sackcloth and ashes

penchant noun = **liking**, taste, bias, tendency, bent, fondness, inclination, leaning, propensity, predilection, partiality, proclivity

pending adjective = **undecided**, imminent, undetermined, unsettled, awaiting, impending, in the balance, tba or to be announced

penetrate verb 1 = **pierce**, enter, stab, bore, prick, go through
2 = **work out**, grasp, comprehend, decipher, fathom, figure out (informal), get to the bottom of

penetrating adjective
1 = **piercing**, sharp, harsh, shrill, carrying
2 = **perceptive**, quick, sharp, acute, keen, intelligent, shrewd, astute, incisive, perspicacious, sharp-witted

penetration noun 1 = **piercing**, entry, entrance, incision, puncturing
2 = **perception**, insight, sharpness, acuteness, astuteness, keenness, shrewdness

penitence noun = **repentance**, regret, shame, sorrow, remorse, contrition, compunction

penitent adjective = **repentant**, sorry, remorseful, apologetic, abject, contrite, conscience-stricken, regretful

pennant noun = **flag**, banner, streamer, ensign, pennon

penniless adjective = **poor**, impoverished, broke (informal), poverty-stricken, destitute, dirt-poor (informal), down and out, down on one's luck (informal), flat broke (informal), impecunious, indigent, penurious

pension noun = **allowance**, benefit, annuity, superannuation, old age security (Canad), social security (US)

P

pensioner noun = **senior citizen**, O.A.P., retired person

pensive adjective = **thoughtful**, serious, sad, solemn, musing, reflective, dreamy, meditative, contemplative, wistful, preoccupied

pent-up adjective = **suppressed**, repressed, inhibited • *a lot of pent-up anger to release*

penury noun = **poverty**, want, need, beggary, destitution, indigence, privation

people plural noun 1 = **human beings**, humanity, humankind, humans • *Hundreds of people lost their homes in the earthquake.*
2 = **inhabitants**, public, population, citizens • *It's a triumph for the Canadian people.*
3 = **family**, race, tribe, clan
▶ verb 4 = **inhabit**, settle, occupy, populate, colonize
See also: **kin**

pepper noun 1 = **seasoning**, spice, flavour
▶ verb 2 = **sprinkle**, dot, speck, spatter, fleck
3 = **pelt**, shower, bombard

peppery See **hot**

perceive verb 1 = **see**, note, spot, discover, recognize, notice, observe, behold, discern, espy, make out
2 = **understand**, see, learn, gather, realize, grasp, comprehend

percentage See **proportion**

perceptible adjective = **visible**, clear, apparent, obvious, evident, recognizable, tangible, noticeable, detectable, discernible, appreciable, observable

perception noun
= **understanding**, idea, sense, feeling, awareness, impression, notion, sensation, consciousness, grasp, conception

perceptive adjective = **astute**, sharp, aware, acute, penetrating • *a perceptive account of the poet's life*
See also: **brilliant, keen, observant, shrewd, wise**

perch noun 1 = **resting place**, post, branch, pole
▶ verb 2 = **sit**, land, rest, settle, balance, roost, alight

percussion noun = **impact**, crash, blow, knock, clash, bump, smash, collision, thump

peremptory adjective
1 = **imperative**, final, decisive, absolute, binding, obligatory, compelling
2 = **imperious**, authoritative, dictatorial, dogmatic, bossy (*informal*), domineering, overbearing

perennial adjective = **continual**, persistent, constant, lasting, enduring, incessant, recurrent, abiding, twenty-four-seven (*slang*)

perfect adjective 1 = **faultless**, expert, skilled, flawless, polished, masterly • *His English was perfect.*
OPPOSITE: imperfect
2 = **complete**, absolute, utter, sheer, consummate, unmitigated • *They have a perfect right to say so.*
3 = **excellent**, ideal, supreme, superb, splendid, sublime, superlative
4 = **exact**, true, correct, accurate, faithful, precise, unerring
▶ verb 5 = **improve**, refine, polish, hone • *The technique was perfected last year.*
6 = **accomplish**, finish, complete, perform, achieve, fulfill, carry out

perfection noun
1 = **completeness**, maturity
2 = **purity**, integrity, perfectness, wholeness
3 = **excellence**, superiority, exquisiteness, sublimity
4 = **exactness**, precision, faultlessness

perfectionist noun = **stickler**, purist, precisionist

perfectly adverb 1 = **completely**, quite, fully, absolutely, totally, altogether, thoroughly, wholly, utterly
2 = **flawlessly**, ideally,

P

wonderfully, superbly, impeccably, supremely, faultlessly

perfidious *adjective (Literary)*
= **treacherous**, unfaithful, disloyal, double-dealing, traitorous, two-faced

perforate *verb* = **pierce**, drill, punch, penetrate, bore, puncture

perform *verb* 1 = **carry out**, do, complete, execute, fulfill • *people who have performed acts of bravery*
2 = **present**, do, play, act, stage, put on • *students performing Shakespeare's Macbeth*
See also: **achieve, administer, appear, commit, conduct, function**

performance *noun* 1 = **carrying out**, work, act, execution, achievement, accomplishment, completion, fulfillment
2 = **presentation**, play, show, production, appearance, exhibition, portrayal, gig (*informal*), acting

performer *noun* = **artiste**, player, actor *or* actress, Thespian, trouper

perfume *noun* = **fragrance**, smell, scent, aroma, bouquet, odor

perfumed See **fragrant, sweet**

perfunctory *adjective* = **offhand**, routine, mechanical, indifferent, superficial, sketchy, cursory, heedless

perhaps *adverb* = **maybe**, possibly, conceivably, it could be • *Perhaps you're right.*

peril *noun* = **danger**, risk, uncertainty, hazard, menace, jeopardy

perilous *adjective* = **dangerous**, unsafe, risky, hazardous, precarious, threatening

perimeter *noun* = **boundary**, border, limit, edge, margin, circumference, periphery, ambit, bounds, confines

period *noun* = **time**, while, term, stretch, spell, interval • *a period of a few months*
See also: **length, lesson, round, space, stage**

periodic *adjective* = **recurrent**, regular, repeated, occasional, cyclical, sporadic, intermittent

periodical *noun* = **publication**, paper, magazine, journal, quarterly, weekly, monthly

peripheral *adjective*
1 = **secondary**, minor, marginal, irrelevant, unimportant, incidental, inessential
2 = **outermost**, outside, external, outer, exterior

periphery See **outskirts**

perish *verb* 1 = **die**, expire, be killed, lose one's life, pass away
2 = **be destroyed**, fall, decline, collapse, disappear, vanish
3 = **rot**, waste, decay, disintegrate, decompose, moulder

perishable *adjective* = **short-lived**, decaying, decomposable

perjure *verb*
▷ **perjure oneself** (*Criminal law*)
= **commit perjury**, bear false witness, forswear, give false testimony, lie under oath, swear falsely

perjury *noun* = **lying under oath**, bearing false witness, false statement, forswearing, giving false testimony

perk *noun* (*Informal*) = **bonus**, benefit, extra, plus, fringe benefit, perquisite

perky See **lively**

permanence *noun* = **continuity**, stability, endurance, durability, perpetuity, finality, continuance, constancy, indestructibility

permanent *adjective* = **lasting**, constant, enduring, eternal, perpetual, abiding • *a permanent end to the hostilities*
OPPOSITE: temporary

permeate *verb* = **pervade**, charge, fill, saturate, penetrate, infiltrate, imbue, impregnate, spread through

permissible *adjective*
= **permitted**, legal, legitimate, acceptable, authorized, lawful, allowable, all right, O.K. *or* okay (*informal*)

permission noun
= **authorization**, approval,
licence, go-ahead, consent,
assent • *He asked permission to leave
the room.*
OPPOSITE: ban
See also: **blessing, permit,
sanction**

permissive adjective = **tolerant**,
liberal, free, lax, lenient, easy-
going, indulgent, forbearing

permit verb 1 = **allow**, grant,
sanction, enable, authorize,
give the green light to • *We aren't
permitted to bring our own food to the
movies.*
OPPOSITE: ban
▶ noun 2 = **licence**, pass,
passport, warrant, permission,
authorization • *a work permit*
See also: **approve, let**

permutation noun
= **transformation**, change,
alteration, transposition

pernicious adjective = **harmful**,
bad, deadly, dangerous, fatal,
evil, destructive, poisonous,
detrimental, wicked, hurtful,
malign, damaging

pernickety adjective (*Old-fashioned,
informal*) = **fussy**, particular,
picky (*informal*), exacting, finicky,
fastidious, overprecise

perpendicular adjective
= **upright**, straight, vertical,
plumb, at right angles to, on end

perpetrate verb = **commit**, do,
perform, execute, enact, wreak,
carry out

perpetual adjective
1 = **everlasting**, permanent,
lasting, endless, perennial,
eternal, infinite, unchanging,
unending, never-ending
2 = **continual**, persistent,
constant, repeated, continuous,
endless, incessant, recurrent,
interminable, never-ending,
twenty-four-seven (*slang*)

perpetually *See* **always**

perpetuate verb = **maintain**,
preserve, immortalize, keep
going

perplex verb = **puzzle**, confuse,
baffle, stump, mystify, bewilder,
confound

perplexed *See* **confused**

perplexing adjective = **puzzling**,
hard, difficult, complex,
complicated, confusing,
enigmatic, inexplicable,
baffling, bewildering,
mystifying

perplexity noun 1 = **puzzlement**,
confusion, bewilderment,
bafflement, incomprehension,
mystification
2 = **puzzle**, fix (*informal*),
difficulty, mystery, paradox

perquisite noun (*Formal*) = **bonus**,
benefit, extra, plus, dividend,
perk (*informal*)

persecute verb 1 = **victimize**,
torture, hound, oppress,
torment, ill-treat, pick on
• *persecuted for religious beliefs*
2 = **harass**, bother, annoy, hassle
(*informal*), tease, badger, pester
See also: **bully**

| CONFUSABLES
| *Persecute* means *harass.*
| *Prosecute* means *take legal action
| against.*

persecution *See* **oppression**

persecutor *See* **bully**

perseverance noun
= **persistence**, resolution,
determination, endurance,
diligence, tenacity, doggedness,
pertinacity

persevere verb = **keep going**,
continue, remain, persist, carry
on, go on, hang on, stick at *or*
stick to

persist verb 1 = **continue**, last,
remain, linger, carry on, keep up
2 = **persevere**, continue, insist,
stand firm

persistence noun
= **determination**, resolution,
endurance, grit, perseverance,
tenacity, doggedness,
pertinacity, tirelessness

persistent adjective
1 = **continuous**, constant,
repeated, endless, perpetual,
continual, incessant, never-
ending, twenty-four-seven
(*slang*)
2 = **determined**, steady,

p

stubborn, steadfast, tireless, dogged, tenacious, obdurate, obstinate, persevering, pertinacious, unflagging

person noun = **individual**, human, soul, human being, living soul • *The amount of sleep we need varies from person to person.*
▷ **in person** = **personally**, bodily, oneself, in the flesh
See also: **figure**

personable adjective = **pleasant**, nice, attractive, charming, handsome, good-looking, likable or likeable, agreeable, amiable

personage noun = **personality**, celebrity, somebody, notable, dignitary, luminary, big shot (informal), megastar (informal), public figure, V.I.P.

personal adjective 1 = **individual**, own, special, private, particular, unique, peculiar • *personal belongings*
2 = **offensive**, nasty, derogatory, disparaging, insulting
See also: **direct**

personality noun 1 = **nature**, character, identity, makeup, individuality, psyche • *She has such a kind, friendly personality.*
2 = **celebrity**, star, big name, famous name, household name • *television personalities*
See also: **figure**

personally adverb 1 = **by oneself**, alone, solely, independently, on one's own
2 = **in one's opinion**, for one's part, from one's own viewpoint, in one's books, in one's own view
3 = **individually**, privately, specially, individualistically, subjectively

personification noun = **embodiment**, image, portrayal, representation, incarnation, epitome

personify verb = **embody**, represent, symbolize, exemplify, epitomize, typify

personnel noun = **employees**, people, staff, workforce, helpers, human resources, workers

perspective noun 1 = **outlook**, attitude, context, angle, frame of reference
2 = **objectivity**, relation, proportion, relativity, relative importance

perspicacious adjective = **perceptive**, alert, sharp, acute, keen, shrewd, astute, discerning, percipient

perspiration noun = **sweat**, moisture, wetness

perspire verb = **sweat**, glow, swelter, exude, secrete, pour with sweat

persuade verb 1 = **talk into**, bring around (informal), sway, induce, coax, win over • *He persuaded the company to sign her up.*
2 = **convince**, satisfy, cause to believe
See also: **push, reason**

persuasion noun 1 = **urging**, inducement, cajolery, enticement, wheedling
2 = **persuasiveness**, force, power, potency, cogency
3 = **belief**, opinion, conviction, faith, tenet, creed, credo, views
4 = **faction**, party, school, side, camp, denomination, school of thought

persuasive adjective = **convincing**, sound, effective, influential, valid, credible, forceful, plausible, eloquent, weighty, cogent, compelling, telling

pert adjective = **impudent**, forward, bold, cheeky, saucy, sassy (informal), impertinent, insolent

pertain verb = **relate**, concern, apply, refer, regard, belong, befit, be relevant

pertinent adjective = **relevant**, material, fit, appropriate, proper, fitting, applicable, apt, apposite, germane, to the point

pertness noun = **impudence**, front, cheek (informal), audacity, cheekiness, effrontery, forwardness, impertinence, insolence, sauciness

perturb verb = **disturb**, worry,

trouble, bother, agitate, ruffle, unsettle, faze, disconcert, vex, fluster

perturbed *adjective* = **disturbed**, troubled, anxious, worried, uncomfortable, uneasy, shaken, agitated, disconcerted, flustered

peruse *verb* = **read**, study, check, examine, scan, browse, inspect, scrutinize

pervade *verb* = **spread through**, charge, fill, penetrate, infuse, permeate, imbue, suffuse

pervasive *adjective* = **widespread**, general, common, extensive, universal, prevalent, ubiquitous, rife, omnipresent

perverse *adjective* 1 = **abnormal**, contrary, unhealthy, improper, troublesome, rebellious, deviant, disobedient, refractory
2 = **wilful**, contrary, dogged, intractable, intransigent, wrong-headed, headstrong, obdurate
3 = **stubborn**, contrary, wayward, mulish, obstinate, pig-headed, stiff-necked
4 = **ill-natured**, cross, fractious, churlish, ill-tempered, peevish, surly

perversion *noun* 1 = **deviation**, vice, abnormality, kink (*informal*), aberration, immorality, depravity, debauchery, kinkiness (*slang*), unnaturalness
2 = **distortion**, corruption, misrepresentation, falsification, misinterpretation, twisting

perversity *noun* = **contrariness**, intransigence, contradictoriness, obduracy, refractoriness, waywardness, wrong-headedness

pervert *noun* 1 = **deviant**, degenerate, weirdo *or* weirdie (*informal*), sicko (*informal*), sickie (*informal*)
▷ *verb* 2 = **distort**, abuse, twist, misrepresent, misuse, falsify, warp, garble
3 = **corrupt**, degrade, debase, debauch, deprave, lead astray

perverted *adjective* = **deviant**, unhealthy, immoral, depraved

• *perverted phone calls and letters*

pessimism *noun* = **gloominess**, depression, despair, distrust, gloom, melancholy, hopelessness, despondency, dejection

pessimist *noun* = **prophet of doom**, cynic, defeatist, killjoy, wet blanket (*informal*), worrier

pessimistic *adjective* = **gloomy**, hopeless, despondent, glum • *a pessimistic view of life*
OPPOSITE: optimistic

pest *noun* 1 = **blight**, scourge, bane • *Aphids and other pests destroyed much of the crop.*
2 = **nuisance**, pain (*informal*), bore, bane, pain in the neck (*informal*) • *I didn't want to be a cry baby or a pest.*
See also: **annoyance**

pester *verb* = **annoy**, bother, bug (*informal*), badger, drive someone up the wall (*informal*), get on someone's nerves (*informal*) • *He gets fed up with people pestering him for money.*
See also: **hassle, worry**

pestilence *noun* = **plague**, epidemic, visitation

pestilent *adjective* 1 = **annoying**, tiresome, bothersome, irksome, irritating, vexing
2 = **harmful**, evil, detrimental, injurious, pernicious
3 = **contaminated**, infected, infectious, contagious, diseased, catching, disease-ridden

pestilential *adjective* = **deadly**, dangerous, harmful, hazardous, destructive, detrimental, injurious, pernicious

pet *noun* 1 = **favourite**, treasure, jewel, idol, darling
▷ *adjective* 2 = **favourite**, cherished, dearest, dear to one's heart
▷ *verb* 3 = **pamper**, baby, coddle, cosset, spoil
4 = **fondle**, stroke, pat, caress
5 = **cuddle**, neck (*informal*), kiss, smooch (*informal*), make out

peter *verb*
peter out = **die out**, stop, fail, fade, dwindle, wane,

ebb, run out, taper off

petite adjective = **small**, little, slight, delicate, dainty, elfin

petition noun **1** = **appeal**, request, suit, plea, prayer, solicitation, entreaty, supplication
▶ verb **2** = **appeal**, ask, plead, pray, beg, solicit, beseech, adjure, entreat, supplicate

petrified See **frightened**

petrify verb **1** = **terrify**, stun, paralyze, horrify, immobilize, transfix, stupefy
2 = **fossilize**, harden, calcify, turn to stone

petty adjective **1** = **trivial**, insignificant, unimportant, measly (informal), trifling • endless rules and petty regulations
2 = **small-minded**, mean, cheap, childish • I think that attitude is a bit petty.
See also: **minor**

petulance noun = **sulkiness**, pique, irritability, bad temper, ill humour, peevishness, sullenness

petulant adjective = **sulky**, moody, sullen, bad-tempered, huffy, ill-humoured, peevish

phantom noun **1** = **specter**, spirit, shade (literary), ghost, spook (informal), apparition, phantasm, wraith
2 = **illusion**, vision, hallucination, figment of the imagination

phase noun = **stage**, time, point, period, step, position, development, chapter, juncture
▶ verb
▷ **phase out** = **eliminate**, close, remove, withdraw, terminate, ease off, pull out, run down, wind down, wind up

phenomenal adjective = **extraordinary**, unusual, remarkable, fantastic, exceptional, outstanding, miraculous, marvellous, prodigious

phenomenon noun
1 = **occurrence**, event, fact, incident, circumstance, episode, happening

2 = **wonder**, exception, sensation, miracle, marvel, rarity, prodigy, black swan

philanderer noun = **womanizer** (informal), flirt, Casanova, Don Juan, gigolo, ladies' man, wolf (informal), stud (slang), playboy

philanthropic adjective = **humanitarian**, kind, charitable, humane, benevolent, kind-hearted, beneficent, munificent, public-spirited

philanthropist noun = **humanitarian**, donor, patron, contributor, benefactor, giver

philanthropy noun = **humanitarianism**, charity, generosity, almsgiving, beneficence, benevolence, brotherly love, charitableness, kind-heartedness

philistine noun **1** = **boor**, yahoo, barbarian, ignoramus, lout, lowbrow, vulgarian
▶ adjective **2** = **uncultured**, ignorant, tasteless, boorish, uneducated, unrefined, lowbrow, uncultivated

philosopher noun = **thinker**, sage, theorist, logician, metaphysician, wise man

philosophical adjective **1** = **wise**, abstract, logical, rational, thoughtful, theoretical, sagacious
2 = **stoical**, cool, calm, tranquil, serene, collected, composed, unruffled

philosophy noun **1** = **thought**, knowledge, wisdom, logic, reasoning, thinking, metaphysics, rationalism
2 = **outlook**, viewpoint, ideology, doctrine, thinking, beliefs, convictions, principles, tenets, values, world view
3 = **stoicism**, composure, serenity, calmness, equanimity, self-possession

phlegmatic adjective = **unemotional**, indifferent, apathetic, impassive, placid, stoical, stolid, undemonstrative, unfeeling

phobia noun = **terror**, thing

(*informal*), fear, horror, hatred, dread, revulsion, aversion, loathing, detestation, repulsion

phone *noun* **1** = **telephone**, landline, cell, horn (*informal*), iPhone (*trademark*), blower (*informal*), cell phone, camera phone, smart phone, video phone, carphone, internet phone
2 = **call**, phone, message, phone-call
▶ *verb* **3** = **call**, get on the blower (*informal*), get on the horn (*informal*), give someone a call, make a call, telephone

phony *adjective* **1** = **fake**, false, counterfeit, bogus, sham, forged
• *a phony accent*
OPPOSITE: genuine
▶ *noun* **2** = **fake**, fraud, counterfeit, forgery, sham, impostor, pseud (*informal*)
See also: **mock**

photograph *noun* **1** = **picture**, shot, photo (*informal*), snap (*informal*), print, transparency, snapshot
▶ *verb* **2** = **take a picture of**, record, film, shoot, snap (*informal*), take (someone's) picture

photographic *adjective*
1 = **lifelike**, natural, visual, realistic, graphic, pictorial, vivid
2 (~ *memory*) = **accurate**, exact, faithful, precise, retentive

phrase *noun* **1** = **expression**, remark, saying, group of words, idiom
▶ *verb* **2** = **express**, say, put, word, voice, put into words

phraseology *noun* = **wording**, speech, language, style, expression, phrase, phrasing, parlance, choice of words, idiom, syntax

phrasing See **language**

physical *adjective* **1** = **bodily**, corporal, mortal, earthly, corporeal, fleshly, incarnate
2 = **material**, real, natural, solid, substantial, tangible, palpable

physician *noun* = **doctor**, medic (*informal*), doc (*informal*), doctor of

medicine, general practitioner, G.P., M.D., medical practitioner

physique *noun* = **build**, body, figure, form, shape, frame, structure, constitution

pick *verb* **1** = **choose**, select, decide upon, hand-pick, opt for, settle on • *She picked ten people to interview for six sales jobs.*
2 = **gather**, harvest, pluck • *I picked the most beautiful rose.*
3 = **nibble**, have no appetite, peck at, play with *or* toy with, push the food round the plate
4 = **provoke**, start, incite, instigate
5 = **open**, force, crack, break into, break open
▷ **pick on** = **torment**, bait, tease
• *Bullies pick on weaker children.*
See also: **bully, persecute**
▷ **pick out** = **identify**, recognize, perceive, discriminate, distinguish, make out, tell apart
▷ **pick up** = **lift**, raise, gather, grasp, uplift, take up; = **obtain**, find, buy, purchase, come across; = **recover**, improve, rally, mend, be on the mend, get better, take a turn for the better, turn the corner; = **learn**, acquire, master, get the hang of (*informal*)
▶ *noun* **6** = **the best**, elite, pride
• *the pick of the country's young athletes*
7 = **choice**, decision, option, selection, preference
See also: **favourite**

> INFORMALLY SPEAKING
> **pick and choose**: be very fussy
> **pick apart**: find many flaws in
> **pick up on**: notice and understand

picket *noun* **1** = **protester**, demonstrator, picketer
2 = **stake**, post, upright, pale, paling, stanchion
▶ *verb* **3** = **blockade**, demonstrate, boycott

pickle *noun* **1** (*Informal*)
= **predicament**, fix (*informal*), difficulty, bind (*informal*), jam (*informal*), scrape (*informal*), dilemma, quandary, hot water (*informal*), tight spot

p

▶ *verb* **2** = **preserve**, steep, marinade

pick-me-up *noun* (*Informal*) = **tonic**, stimulant, restorative, refreshment, bracer (*informal*), shot in the arm (*informal*)

pickpocket *See* **thief**

picnic *noun* = **outdoor meal**, outing, excursion

pictorial *adjective* = **graphic**, picturesque, scenic, illustrated, representational

pick-up *noun* = **improvement**, rise, rally, recovery, revival, upswing, upturn, change for the better, strengthening

picture *noun* **1** = **representation**, painting, photograph, portrait, drawing, sketch, illustration • *I have a picture of you as my screen saver.*
RELATED WORD
adjective: pictorial
2 = **description**, report, account, image, impression, depiction
3 = **double**, image, copy, twin, replica, duplicate, likeness, lookalike, carbon copy, dead ringer (*slang*), spitting image (*informal*)
4 = **personification**, essence, epitome, embodiment
5 = **film**, movie, flick (*slang*), motion picture
▶ *verb* **6** = **imagine**, see, visualize, conceive of • *He pictured her with long black hair.*
7 = **represent**, show, draw, paint, photograph, depict, sketch, illustrate

> INFORMALLY SPEAKING
> **get the picture**: understand without further explanation
> **out of the picture**: not part of a certain situation

picturesque *adjective* **1** = **pretty**, beautiful, attractive, charming, striking, scenic, quaint
2 = **vivid**, graphic, colorful

piebald *adjective* = **dappled**, spotted, black and white, brindled, flecked, mottled, pied, speckled

piece *noun* **1** = **bit**, part, portion, slice, chunk, fragment • *a piece of cheese*
2 = **work**, study, article, creation, composition • *I read his piece on hockey parents.*
See also: **block, feature, item, lump, section**
▶ *verb*
▷ **piece together** = **assemble**, join, repair, restore, mend, patch together • *Doctors painstakingly pieced together the broken bones.*
See also: **reconstruct**

> INFORMALLY SPEAKING
> **go to pieces**: break down or collapse
> **piece of cake**: a very easy task
> **piece of my mind**: a scolding
> **piece of work**: a difficult person to deal with
> **speak your piece**: express your opinion

piecemeal *adverb* = **bit by bit**, gradually, by degrees, little by little

pier *noun* **1** = **jetty**, wharf, promenade, landing place, quay
2 = **pillar**, post, support, column, pile, upright, buttress

pierce *verb* = **penetrate**, drill, bore, puncture, lance • *Pierce the potato with a fork.*

piercing *adjective* **1** (~ *sound*) = **penetrating**, sharp, loud, high-pitched, shrill, ear-splitting
2 = **perceptive**, alert, sharp, keen, shrewd, penetrating, perspicacious, quick-witted
3 (~ *wind, etc.*) = **cold**, bitter, arctic, wintry, freezing, biting, nippy
4 = **sharp**, severe, intense, painful, acute, stabbing, agonizing, excruciating

piety *noun* = **holiness**, faith, religion, reverence, godliness, piousness

pig *noun* **1** = **hog**, swine, piggy (*informal*) • *the number of pigs at the trough*
RELATED WORDS
adjective: porcine
male: boar
female: sow
young: piglet

collective noun: litter

habitation: sty

2 (*Informal*) = **brute**, hog (*informal*), swine, boor, glutton, slob (*slang*)

pigeonhole noun

1 = **compartment**, place, section, locker, niche, cubbyhole

▶ verb **2** = **classify**, label, slot (*informal*), characterize, categorize, compartmentalize, ghettoize

3 = **postpone**, shelve, defer, put off

pig-headed adjective = **stubborn**, contrary, inflexible, unyielding, mulish, obstinate, self-willed, stiff-necked

pigment noun = **colour**, paint, dye, stain, tint, colouring, tincture

pigmentation See **colour**

pile[1] noun **1** = **heap**, mountain, mound, stack, hoard • *a pile of books*

2 (*Informal, often plural*) = **a lot**, ocean, quantity, great deal, stacks

3 = **building**, structure, erection, edifice

▶ verb **4** = **heap**, stack • *A few newspapers were piled on the table.*

5 = **collect**, gather, assemble, accumulate, amass, hoard

6 = **crowd**, flood, rush, pack, crush, stream, jam, flock

See also: **bunch, load, mass**

pile[2] noun = **foundation**, post, support, column, beam, upright, pillar

pile[3] noun = **nap**, down, hair, fur • *the carpet's thick pile*

pile-up noun (*Informal*) = **collision**, crash, accident, smash, multiple collision, smash-up (*informal*)

pilfer verb = **steal**, appropriate, embezzle, filch, lift (*informal*), pinch (*informal*), purloin, take, swipe (*slang*)

pilgrim noun = **traveller**, wanderer, wayfarer

pilgrimage noun = **journey**, mission, trip, tour, expedition, excursion

pill noun = **tablet**, capsule, pellet

▷ **the pill** = **oral contraceptive**

pillage verb **1** = **plunder**, raid, sack, loot, ravage, ransack, maraud, despoil

▶ noun **2** = **plunder**, robbery, sack, marauding, spoliation

pillar noun **1** = **support**, post, column, prop, shaft, upright, pier, stanchion

2 = **supporter**, follower, mainstay, upholder

pillory verb = **ridicule**, brand, denounce, stigmatize

pilot noun **1** = **airman**, flyer, aviator

2 = **helmsman**, navigator, steersman

▶ adjective **3** = **trial**, test, model, experimental

▶ verb **4** = **fly**, drive, operate, conduct, direct, handle, guide, steer, navigate

pimple noun = **spot**, boil, pustule, zit (*slang*)

pin verb **1** = **fasten**, join, fix, secure, attach, affix

2 = **hold fast**, fix, immobilize, hold down, pinion

▷ **pin down** = **force**, make, press, compel, pressurize, constrain; = **determine**, name, identify, locate, specify, pinpoint

pinch verb **1** = **squeeze**, press, nip, grasp, compress

2 = **hurt**, pain, crush, cramp

3 (*Informal*) = **steal**, filch, lift (*informal*), pilfer, purloin, swipe (*slang*)

▶ noun **4** = **squeeze**, nip

5 = **dash**, bit, mite, speck, jot, soupçon (*French*)

6 = **hardship**, emergency, crisis, difficulty, plight, necessity, strait, predicament

pinched adjective = **thin**, gaunt, drawn, haggard, peaky, worn

pine verb **1** (often with *for*) = **long**, desire, ache, crave, hanker, eat one's heart out over, hunger for, thirst for, wish for, yearn for

2 = **waste**, decline, sicken, fade, languish

pinion verb = **immobilize**, tie, chain, bind, shackle, fasten, fetter, manacle

P

pink *adjective* = **rosy**, salmon, rose, flushed, reddish, roseate

---

SHADES OF PINK

coral
flesh
fuchsia
rose
salmon
shell pink
shocking pink

---

pinnacle *noun* = **peak**, top, summit, crown, height, crest, apex, zenith, vertex

pinpoint *verb* = **identify**, locate, define, distinguish

pioneer *noun* 1 = **settler**, explorer, colonist
2 = **founder**, leader, developer, innovator, trailblazer
▶ *verb* 3 = **develop**, start, create, discover, establish, institute, originate, invent, initiate, instigate, show the way

pious *adjective* = **religious**, holy, devout, righteous, God-fearing, godly, reverent, saintly

pipe *noun* 1 = **tube**, line, main, pipeline, passage, hose, duct, conduit
▶ *verb* 2 = **whistle**, play, sound, sing, peep, cheep, warble
3 = **convey**, conduct, channel
▷ **pipe down** (*Informal*) = **be quiet**, hush, hold one's tongue, quieten down, shush, shut one's mouth, shut up (*informal*)

pipeline *noun* = **tube**, pipe, passage, duct, conduit

piquant *adjective* 1 = **spicy**, sharp, tart, tangy, pungent, zesty, biting, savory
2 = **interesting**, provocative, sparkling, lively, scintillating, stimulating

pique *noun* 1 = **resentment**, offence, displeasure, huff, irritation, annoyance, hurt feelings, umbrage, wounded pride

▶ *verb* 2 = **displease**, get (*informal*), sting, offend, irk, rile, annoy, irritate, affront, nettle
3 = **arouse**, spur, excite, stir, stimulate, rouse, whet

piracy *noun* = **robbery**, theft, buccaneering, freebooting, stealing

pirate *noun* 1 = **buccaneer**, rover, raider, corsair, freebooter, marauder
2 = **plagiarist**, infringer, plagiarizer
▶ *verb* 3 = **copy**, appropriate, steal, reproduce, poach, plagiarize

pirouette *See* **spin**

pit *noun* 1 = **hole**, pothole, chasm
• *He lost his footing and began to slide into the pit.*
▶ *verb* 2 = **scar**, mark, dent, pockmark, indent
See also: **abyss, grave**

pitch *verb* 1 = **throw**, cast, toss, hurl, lob (*informal*), fling, sling, heave, chuck (*informal*)
2 = **set up**, raise, settle, erect, put up
3 = **fall**, drop, tumble, dive, topple
4 = **toss**, roll, plunge, lurch
▷ **pitch in** = **help**, contribute, participate, cooperate, chip in (*informal*), do one's bit, join in, lend a hand
▷ **pitch into** (*Informal*) = **attack**, assault, assail, get stuck into (*informal*), tear into (*informal*)
▶ *noun* 5 = **sports field**, ground, park, field of play
6 = **level**, point, summit, degree, height, highest point
7 = **slope**, grade, angle, tilt, incline, gradient
8 = **tone**, sound, timbre, modulation
9 = **sales talk**, patter, spiel (*informal*)

pitch-black *adjective* = **dark**, unlit, inky, jet-black, pitch-dark

piteous *adjective* = **pathetic**, sad, poignant, heartbreaking, pitiful, moving, affecting, distressing, harrowing, heart-rending, pitiable, plaintive

pitfall noun = **danger**, catch, trap, difficulty, hazard, snag, peril, drawback

pith noun = **essence**, point, heart, core, kernel, crux, gist, nub, quintessence, salient point

pithy adjective = **succinct**, short, brief, pointed, terse, concise, cogent, epigrammatic, laconic, to the point, trenchant

pitiful adjective 1 = **pathetic**, sad, heartbreaking, grievous, wretched, distressing, harrowing, heart-rending, piteous, pitiable
2 = **contemptible**, low, base, mean, sorry, miserable, lousy (slang), paltry, shabby, abject

pitiless adjective = **merciless**, cruel, relentless, ruthless, callous, heartless, cold-blooded, implacable, cold-hearted, hardhearted, unmerciful

pittance noun = **slave wages**, drop, mite, trifle, chicken feed (slang), peanuts (slang)

pity verb 1 = **feel sorry for**, feel for, sympathize with • I don't know whether to hate or pity him.
▶ noun 2 = **compassion**, charity, understanding, sympathy, mercy, kindness • She saw no pity in their faces.
3 = **shame**, crime, crying shame • It's a pity they can't all have the same opportunities.

pivot noun 1 = **axis**, swivel, spindle, axle, fulcrum
2 = **centre**, heart, hub, hinge, kingpin
▶ verb 3 = **turn**, spin, revolve, rotate, twirl, swivel
4 = **rely**, hang, depend, hinge, be contingent

pivotal adjective = **crucial**, central, critical, decisive, vital

pixie noun = **elf**, brownie, fairy, sprite

placard noun = **notice**, bill, poster, advertisement

placate verb = **calm**, appease, soothe, pacify, assuage, humour, mollify, conciliate, de-stress, propitiate

place noun 1 = **spot**, point, site, area, position, location • The pain is always in the same place.
2 = **region**, quarter, district, neighbourhood, locale, vicinity, locality
3 = **rank**, station, position, status, grade
4 = **space**, room, accommodation
5 = **home**, house, property, pad (slang, dated), residence, dwelling, abode, domicile
6 = **duty**, charge, right, concern, role, responsibility, affair, function, prerogative
7 = **job**, post, position, appointment, employment
▷ **take place** = **happen**, occur, come about, go on • The meeting took place on Thursday.
▶ verb 8 = **put**, plant, position, locate, deposit, situate • Chairs were placed in rows for the parents.
9 = **classify**, group, order, class, rank, sort, arrange, grade
10 = **identify**, know, remember, recognize, put one's finger on
11 = **assign**, give, charge, appoint, allocate, entrust
See also: **fit, insert, lay, scene, set**

> **INFORMALLY SPEAKING**
> **all over the place**: everywhere; disorderly
> **go places**: achieve success
> **put someone in his or her place**: tell or show that someone is conceited

placed See **located**

placid adjective = **calm**, tranquil, serene, collected, composed, equable, even-tempered, imperturbable, unexcitable, unruffled, untroubled

plagiarism noun = **copying**, borrowing, theft, infringement, piracy

plagiarize verb = **copy**, borrow, lift (informal), steal, pirate

plague noun 1 = **disease**, infection, epidemic, pestilence
2 = **affliction**, evil, curse, scourge, blight, torment, bane
▶ verb 3 = **pester**, trouble, torture, bother, harass, annoy, hassle (informal), tease,

torment, vex, badger, harry

plain adjective **1 = simple**, bare, stark, austere, bare-bones, spartan • *It was a plain, grey stone house.*
OPPOSITE: fancy
2 = obvious, clear, evident, distinct, unmistakable, comprehensible • *It was plain to him that I was bored.*
3 = honest, open, direct, outspoken, blunt, straightforward, frank, candid, upfront (*informal*), downright, forthright
4 = ugly, unattractive, dumpy (*informal*), frowzy, homely, ill-favoured, no oil painting (*informal*), not beautiful, unlovely, unprepossessing
5 = ordinary, common, simple, everyday, commonplace, unaffected, unpretentious
▶ noun **6 = flatland**, prairie, plateau, grassland, steppe, veld
See also: **blank, manifest, straight, visible**

TYPES OF PLAIN

flat	plateau
flatland	prairie
grassland	savannah
llano	steppe
lowland	tableland
mesa	

---

plain-spoken adjective **= blunt**, direct, outspoken, frank, candid, downright, forthright

plaintive adjective **= sorrowful**, sad, pathetic, mournful, pitiful, heart-rending, piteous

plan noun **1 = scheme**, system, proposal, strategy, method, gameplan • *a plan to merge the two teams*
2 = diagram, blueprint, layout, scale drawing • *a detailed plan of the science project*
▶ verb **3 = devise**, design, draft, arrange, formulate • *when we plan road construction*
4 = intend, mean, aim, propose, purpose
See also: **contemplate, course, idea, organize, pattern, plot, suggestion**

plane noun **1 = airplane**, jet, aircraft
2 = flat surface, level surface
3 = level, condition, position, degree
▶ adjective **4 = level**, even, regular, flat, smooth, horizontal
▶ verb **5 = skim**, skate, sail, glide

planet See **earth**

planned See **calculated**

planning See **organization**

plant noun **1 = flower**, vegetable, weed, bush, herb, shrub
2 = factory, yard, shop, mill, foundry, works
3 = machinery, equipment, gear, apparatus
▶ verb **4 = sow**, seed, transplant, scatter, put in the ground
5 = place, set, put, fix, establish, found, insert

plaster noun **1 = mortar**, stucco, gypsum, plaster of Paris
2 (*Brit*) **= bandage**, dressing, adhesive plaster, Band-Aid (*trademark*), sticking plaster
▶ verb **3 = cover**, spread, coat, smear, overlay, daub

plastic adjective **1 = manageable**, responsive, receptive, docile, malleable, pliable, tractable
2 = pliant, soft, flexible, supple, ductile, mouldable, pliable

plate noun **1 = platter**, dish, trencher (*archaic*)
2 = helping, course, portion, dish, serving
3 = layer, panel, sheet, slab
4 = illustration, print, lithograph
▶ verb **5 = coat**, cover, laminate, overlay, gild

plateau noun **1 = upland**, table, highland, tableland
2 = levelling off, level, stage, stability

platform noun **1 = stage**, stand, podium, dais, rostrum
2 = policy, program, principle,

objective or objectives,
manifesto, party line

platitude noun = **cliché**,
commonplace, truism, banality

platoon noun = **squad**, company,
team, group, patrol, outfit
(informal), squadron

platter noun = **plate**, dish, tray,
salver, trencher (archaic)

plaudits plural noun = **praise**,
approval, applause, acclaim,
acclamation, approbation

plausible adjective 1 = **believable**,
likely, possible, reasonable,
credible, probable, conceivable,
persuasive, tenable
2 = **glib**, smooth, smooth-
talking, smooth-tongued,
specious

play verb 1 = **amuse oneself**,
frolic, entertain oneself, have
fun • *The child was playing with her
teddy bear.*
2 = **take part**, compete,
participate, take on, vie with • *I
was playing cards with my friends.*
3 = **act**, represent, perform,
portray, act the part of
▷ **play a part** See **appear**
▷ **play a part in** See **take part in**
▷ **play a trick on** See **dupe**
▷ **play down** = **minimize**, gloss
over, make light of, make little
of, underrate, underplay
▷ **play on** = **take advantage of**,
abuse, exploit, capitalize on,
impose on, trade on
▷ **play the part of** See **act**
▷ **play up** = **emphasize**, stress,
highlight, underline, accentuate
▶ noun 4 = **drama**, show, comedy,
tragedy • *Shakespeare's most
popular play*
5 = **amusement**, game, sport,
fun, entertainment, diversion,
recreation, pastime
6 = **fun**, sport, prank, jest,
humour, lark (informal), joking
7 = **space**, room, margin, scope,
latitude, leeway, elbowroom
See also: **appear**

| INFORMALLY SPEAKING
play for time: delay in order to
gain an advantage
play it safe (or **smart**, or **cool**,

| etc.): act in a safe (or smart,
etc.) way to achieve a certain
result
play on: take advantage of
play up to: try to get some
benefit through flattery

playboy noun = **womanizer**,
ladies' man, rake, philanderer,
roué

player noun 1 = **sportsman** or
sportswoman, participant,
competitor, contestant
2 = **musician**, artist, performer,
virtuoso, instrumentalist
3 = **performer**, actor or actress,
entertainer, Thespian, trouper

playful adjective = **lively**, spirited,
merry, mischievous, impish,
vivacious, frisky, sportive,
sprightly

playmate noun = **friend**,
comrade, companion, pal
(informal), chum (informal),
playfellow

plaything noun = **toy**, game,
amusement, pastime, trifle

plea noun 1 = **appeal**, request,
suit, prayer, petition, entreaty,
intercession, supplication
2 = **excuse**, explanation, defence,
justification

plead verb = **beg**, ask, appeal,
implore, beseech (formal) • *I
pleaded with them to come home.*
▷ **plead with** See **implore**
See also: **press**, **urge**

pleasant adjective 1 = **enjoyable**,
nice, lovely, delightful,
agreeable, pleasurable • *a
pleasant little apartment*
OPPOSITE: unpleasant
2 = **friendly**, nice, charming,
likable, affable, amiable • *an
extremely pleasant and obliging
person*
OPPOSITE: unpleasant
See also: **warm**

pleasantry noun = **joke**, quip,
jest, banter, badinage,
witticism

please verb = **delight**, charm,
entertain, amuse • *I was tidying
my bedroom to please my parents.*
See also: **appeal**, **satisfy**, **suit**

pleased adjective = **happy**, glad,

delighted, satisfied, contented
• *I'm pleased with the way things have been going.*
See also: **proud**

pleasing *adjective* = **enjoyable**, charming, engaging, delightful, likable *or* likeable, agreeable, pleasurable, gratifying, satisfying

pleasurable *adjective* = **enjoyable**, good, fun, nice, lovely, pleasant, delightful, agreeable

pleasure *noun* = **enjoyment**, happiness, joy, satisfaction, amusement • *Almost everybody takes pleasure in eating.*
See also: **delight, entertainment, fun, pride**

pleat See **fold**

plebeian *adjective* 1 = **common**, low, base, working-class, vulgar, coarse, unrefined, lower-class, proletarian, uncultivated
▶ *noun* 2 = **commoner**, common man, man in the street, pleb, proletarian

plebiscite See **vote**

pledge *noun* 1 = **promise**, word, vow, warrant, assurance, oath, undertaking, covenant
2 = **guarantee**, security, bail, deposit, collateral, pawn, surety
▶ *verb* 3 = **promise**, contract, vow, engage, swear, give one's oath, give one's word

plentiful *adjective* = **abundant**, ample, infinite, bountiful, copious • *a plentiful supply*
OPPOSITE: scarce
See also: **generous, handsome, rich**

plenty *noun* 1 = **lots**, enough, great deal, loads (*informal*), plethora • *There's plenty to go around.*
2 = **abundance**, wealth, prosperity, fertility, affluence, copiousness, fruitfulness, plenitude, profusion
▷ **plenty of** See **ample**
See also: **many**

plethora *noun* = **excess**, surplus, glut, overabundance, profusion, superabundance, surfeit

pliable *adjective* 1 = **flexible**, plastic, supple, bendable, bendy, malleable, pliant
2 = **easily led**, susceptible, responsive, receptive, compliant, impressionable, docile, adaptable, pliant, tractable

pliant *adjective* 1 = **flexible**, plastic, supple, bendable, bendy, pliable
2 = **easily led**, susceptible, compliant, impressionable, biddable, pliable, tractable

plight *noun* = **difficulty**, state, condition, situation, spot (*informal*), trouble, jam (*informal*), scrape (*informal*), predicament

plod *verb* 1 = **trudge**, lumber, drag, clump, slog, tramp
2 = **slog**, grind (*informal*), labour, persevere, plow through, toil, soldier on

plot[1] *noun* 1 = **scheme**, plan, conspiracy, intrigue • *the plot to assassinate the dictator*
2 = **story**, scenario, narrative, storyline • *This book has a ludicrously complicated plot.*
▶ *verb* 3 = **scheme**, plan, conspire, hatch • *Prosecutors allege that the defendants plotted to overthrow the government.*
4 = **devise**, design, lay, conceive, hatch, concoct, contrive, cook up (*informal*)
5 = **chart**, mark, locate, map, outline, calculate

plot[2] *noun* = **patch**, area, lot, ground, tract, parcel, allotment

plow *verb* 1 = **turn over**, dig, till, cultivate
2 (usually with *through*) = **push**, cut, drive, press, plunge, forge, wade

ploy *noun* = **tactic**, move, device, trick, scheme, dodge, ruse, maneuver, stratagem, wile

pluck *verb* 1 = **pull out** *or* **pull off**, pick, gather, harvest
2 = **tug**, catch, clutch, yank, snatch, tweak, jerk, pull at
3 = **strum**, pick, finger, twang
▶ *noun* 4 = **courage**, backbone, boldness, nerve, grit, bravery, guts (*informal*)

plucky adjective = **courageous**, game, brave, bold, daring, gutsy (slang), intrepid

plug noun 1 = **stopper**, cork • She put the plug in the sink.
2 (Informal) = **mention**, push, publicity, advertisement, hype
▶ verb 3 = **seal**, block, fill, stop (up) • working to plug a major oil leak
4 (Informal) = **mention**, push, promote, advertise, hype, publicize, build up

plum adjective = **choice**, best, prize, first-class

plumb verb 1 = **delve**, probe, explore, gauge, unravel, penetrate, fathom, go into
▶ noun 2 = **weight**, lead, plummet, plumb bob
▶ adverb 3 = **exactly**, slap, bang, precisely

plume noun = **feather**, crest, pinion, quill

plummet verb = **plunge**, fall, crash, tumble, dive, descend, drop down, nose-dive

plump adjective = **chubby**, fat, beefy, burly, stout • a plump chicken

plunder verb 1 = **loot**, raid, strip, sack, rifle, rob, ransack, pillage
▶ noun 2 = **loot**, swag (slang), prize, booty, pillage, ill-gotten gains, spoils

plunge verb 1 = **throw**, pitch, cast
2 = **hurtle**, charge, career, jump, rush, tear, dash
3 = **descend**, fall, drop, sink, tumble, dive, dip, plummet, nose-dive
▶ noun 4 = **dive**, fall, drop, jump, descent

plus preposition 1 = **and**, with, added to, coupled with
▶ adjective 2 = **additional**, extra, added, supplementary, add-on
▶ noun 3 = **advantage**, gain, benefit, extra, asset, bonus, good point

plush adjective = **luxurious**, rich, luxury, lavish, deluxe, sumptuous, opulent

ply verb 1 = **work at**, follow, practice, exercise, pursue, carry on

2 = **use**, handle, employ, manipulate, wield

poach verb = **infringe**, trespass, encroach, intrude

pocket noun 1 = **pouch**, bag, sack, compartment, receptacle
▶ verb 2 = **steal**, take, lift (informal), appropriate, pilfer, filch, purloin
▶ adjective 3 = **small**, little, portable, compact, miniature, concise, abridged

pod noun, verb = **shell**, hull, shuck, husk

podium noun = **platform**, stage, dais, rostrum

poem noun = **verse**, song, lyric, ode, rhyme, sonnet

poet noun = **bard**, lyricist, rhymer, versifier

poetic adjective = **lyrical**, lyric, elegiac, metrical

poetry noun = **verse**, rhyme, poems, rhyming

poignancy noun 1 = **sadness**, feeling, emotion, sentiment, tenderness, pathos
2 = **sharpness**, intensity, bitterness, keenness

poignant adjective = **moving**, intense, sad, bitter, painful, pathetic, touching, distressing, heart-rending

point noun 1 = **purpose**, goal, aim, object, intention • Cutting costs is not the point of the exercise.
2 = **feature**, attribute, characteristic, side, quality, trait • Tact was never her strong point.
3 = **tip**, nib, prong • the point of a needle
4 = **essence**, question, heart, import, subject, drift, meaning, thrust, crux, gist, nub, pith
5 = **item**, feature, detail, particular, aspect
6 = **place**, site, stage, position, spot, location
7 = **headland**, head, cape, promontory
8 = **stage**, condition, position, degree, circumstance, extent
9 = **moment**, time, instant, juncture, very minute
10 = **score**, unit, tally

p

▷ **point of view = opinion**, view, idea, approach, thought, feeling, judgment, belief, attitude, viewpoint, sentiment, way of thinking, way of looking at it; **= perspective**, position, outlook, viewpoint, stance, angle, orientation, standpoint, slant, frame of reference

▶ *verb* **11 = indicate**, show, direct, designate, signify, denote, call attention to

12 = aim, level, train, direct

▷ **point out = mention**, show, identify, indicate, specify, allude to, bring up

See also: **consideration, message, use**

point-blank *adjective* **1 = direct**, express, plain, explicit, blunt, downright

▶ *adverb* **2 = directly**, straight, frankly, openly, explicitly, bluntly, plainly, candidly, forthrightly

pointed *adjective* **1 = sharp**, acute, barbed, edged

2 = cutting, sharp, acute, keen, pertinent, incisive, biting, penetrating, telling

pointer *noun* **1 = hint**, information, tip, recommendation, advice, caution, suggestion

2 = indicator, hand, guide, needle

pointless *adjective* **= senseless**, stupid, silly, useless, irrelevant, absurd, meaningless, futile, fruitless, aimless, inane

poise *noun* **= composure**, cool (*slang*), presence, assurance, dignity, calmness, aplomb, sang-froid, self-possession

poised *adjective* **1 = ready**, prepared, waiting, all set, standing by

2 = composed, together (*informal*), calm, dignified, collected, self-confident, self-possessed

poison *noun* **1 = toxin**, venom
• *Mercury is a known poison.*
RELATED WORD
adjective: toxic

▶ *verb* **2 = murder**, kill, give (someone) poison

3 = contaminate, infect, pollute

4 = corrupt, undermine, taint, warp, pervert, subvert, defile, deprave

poisonous *adjective* **1 = toxic**, venomous, noxious • *a large cloud of poisonous gas*

2 = evil, malicious, noxious, baleful, corrupting, pernicious

poke *verb* **1 = jab**, stab, elbow, dig, nudge, prod • *She poked a fork into the turkey skin*

▷ **poke fun at** *See* **mock**

▷ **poke your nose in** *See* **pry**

▶ *noun* **2 = jab**, dig, nudge, prod
• *She gave him a playful poke.*
See also: **stick**

poky *adjective* **= small**, tiny, narrow, cramped, confined

pole *noun* **= rod**, post, staff, bar, stick, shaft, spar, mast

police *noun* **1 = cops** (*slang*), boys in blue (*informal*), constabulary, fuzz (*slang*), police force, the law (*informal*)

▶ *verb* **2 = control**, watch, protect, guard, patrol, regulate

policeman *noun* **= cop** (*slang*), officer, captain, copper (*slang*), detective, constable, policewoman (*feminine*), fuzz (*slang*), police officer, patrol man, traffic cop

policy *noun* **= procedure**, plan, rule, action, course, approach, practice, code, scheme, custom

polish *verb* **1 = shine**, buff, wax
• *polishing the furniture*

2 = improve, perfect, refine, brush up • *Polish your writing skills.*

▶ *noun* **3 = style**, class (*informal*), grace, elegance, finesse, refinement • *The early stories lacked the polish of his later work.*

4 = varnish, wax

5 = sheen, finish, gloss, glaze, brightness, lustre
See also: **practise**

polished *adjective*

1 = accomplished, expert, fine, professional, adept, superlative, skilful, masterly

2 = shining, bright, smooth,

glossy, burnished, gleaming

3 = elegant, sophisticated, refined, polite, cultivated, well-bred

polite *adjective* **1 = well-mannered**, civil, respectful, courteous, well-behaved • *It's not polite to point at people.*
OPPOSITE: rude

2 = refined, sophisticated, cultured, genteel, urbane • *Certain words are not acceptable in polite society.*

politeness *noun* **= courtesy**, decency, etiquette, civility • *She listened to him, but only out of politeness.*

politic *adjective* **= wise**, diplomatic, prudent, sensible, advisable, judicious, expedient

political *adjective* **= governmental**, parliamentary, policy-making

politician *noun* **= statesman**, legislator, bureaucrat, congressman, minister (*Canad, Brit*), representative, office bearer, public servant, junior minister (*Canad, Brit*)

politics *noun* **= statesmanship**, government, affairs of state, civics, political science

poll *noun* **1 = canvass**, survey, count, ballot, census, sampling

2 = vote, tally, voting, figures, returns

▶ *verb* **3 = tally**, register

4 = question, survey, interview, ballot, sample, canvass

polls *See* **vote**

pollute *verb* **1 = contaminate**, infect, poison, taint • *Heavy industry pollutes our rivers with noxious chemicals.*

2 = defile, corrupt, desecrate, profane, sully, debase, dishonour, debauch, deprave
See also: **soil**

pollution *noun* **= contamination**, corruption, taint, defilement, dirtying, foulness, impurity, uncleanness, carbon footprint

pomp *noun* **1 = ceremony**, state, flourish, pageant, grandeur, pageantry, splendour, magnificence

2 = show, display, grandiosity, ostentation

pomposity *noun* **= self-importance**, pretension, affectation, airs, grandiosity, pompousness, portentousness, pretentiousness

pompous *adjective* **1 = self-important**, arrogant, grandiose, pretentious, ostentatious, puffed up • *a pompous man with a high opinion of his own capabilities*

2 = grandiloquent, inflated, bombastic, boastful, high-flown

pond *noun* **= pool**, duck pond, fish pond, millpond, small lake, tarn

ponder *verb* **= think**, consider, reflect, contemplate, brood, mull over • *I'm continually pondering how to improve the team.*
See also: **deliberate, wonder**

ponderous *adjective* **1 = dull**, heavy, tedious, long-winded, pedantic

2 = unwieldy, huge, heavy, massive, bulky, cumbersome, weighty

3 = clumsy, awkward, lumbering, heavy-footed

pontificate *verb* **= hold forth**, pronounce, preach, expound, lay down the law, sound off

pony *See* **horse**

pooch *See* **dog**

pool[1] *noun* **1 = pond**, lake, mere, puddle, tarn

2 = swimming pool, swimming bath

pool[2] *noun* **1 = syndicate**, team, group, trust, collective, consortium

2 = kitty, bank, pot, jackpot, funds

▶ *verb* **3 = combine**, share, league, merge, amalgamate, join forces, put together

poor *adjective* **1 = impoverished**, broke (*informal*), poverty-stricken, destitute, penniless, hard up (*informal*) • *a poor family*
OPPOSITE: rich

2 = inferior, mediocre, shoddy, unsatisfactory, feeble, second-rate • *He was a poor actor.*

3 = inadequate, incomplete, insufficient, lousy (*slang*), scant, deficient, skimpy, meagre, measly, lacking, scanty
See also: **hopeless, lame, low, pathetic, remote, rotten, sorry, worthless**

poorly *adverb* **= badly**, unsuccessfully, inadequately, incompetently, inexpertly, insufficiently, unsatisfactorily

pop *verb* **1 = burst**, snap, crack, explode, bang, go off
2 = put, push, stick, slip, insert, tuck, thrust, shove
▷ *noun* **3 = bang**, report, explosion, crack, burst, noise

pope *noun* **= Holy Father**, pontiff, Bishop of Rome, Vicar of Christ

populace *noun* **= people**, mob, multitude, general public, hoi polloi, masses

popular *adjective* **1 = well-liked**, favourite, fashionable, sought-after, in demand, in favour
• *These delicious pastries will be very popular.*
OPPOSITE: unpopular
2 = common, general, conventional, universal, prevalent • *the popular press*
See also: **mass, public**

popularity *noun* **= favour**, approval, currency, regard, acceptance, acclaim, vogue, esteem

popularize *verb* **= make popular**, spread, disseminate, give currency to, give mass appeal, make available to all, universalize

popularly *adverb* **= generally**, usually, widely, commonly, traditionally, universally, ordinarily, customarily, conventionally

populate *verb* **= inhabit**, settle, occupy, colonize, live in

population *noun* **= inhabitants**, people, community, society, folk, denizens, natives, residents

populous *adjective* **= heavily populated**, crowded, packed, populated, overpopulated, swarming, teeming

pore¹ *noun* **= opening**, hole, outlet, orifice

pore² *verb*
▷ **pore over = study**, read, examine, ponder, scrutinize, peruse

pornographic *adjective* **= obscene**, blue, dirty, indecent, lewd, filthy, X-rated, salacious, scuzzy (*slang*), smutty

pornography *noun* **= obscenity**, porn (*informal*), dirt, indecency, filth, smut

porous *adjective* **= permeable**, spongy, absorbent, absorptive, penetrable

port *noun* **= harbour**, haven, seaport, anchorage

portable *adjective* **= light**, compact, convenient, manageable, handy, movable, easily carried

portend *verb* **= foretell**, promise, indicate, predict, herald, bode, foreshadow, augur, betoken, prognosticate, warn of

portent *noun* **= omen**, sign, warning, indication, prognostication, augury, forewarning

portentous *adjective*
1 = significant, important, crucial, ominous, momentous, fateful, menacing
2 = pompous, solemn, ponderous, self-important

porter¹ *noun* **= baggage attendant**, carrier, bearer

porter² *noun* **= doorman**, caretaker, concierge, janitor, gatekeeper

portion *noun* **1 = part**, bit, piece, segment, chunk, serving, helping • *I have spent a considerable portion of my life here.*
2 = share, lot, measure, quota, quantity, allowance, ration, allocation, allotment
3 = helping, piece, serving
4 = destiny, lot, fate, luck, fortune
▷ *verb*
▷ **portion out = divide**, deal, distribute, allocate, allot, apportion, dole out, share out

p

See also: **section**

portly *adjective* = **stout**, large, heavy, fat, plump, burly, fleshy, corpulent

portrait *noun* **1** = **picture**, image, painting, photograph, representation, likeness
2 = **description**, profile, portrayal, depiction, characterization, thumbnail sketch

portray *verb* **1** = **represent**, figure, draw, picture, paint, depict, sketch, illustrate
2 = **describe**, depict, characterize, put in words
3 = **play**, represent, act the part of

portrayal *noun*
= **representation**, performance, picture, interpretation, depiction, characterization

pose *verb* **1** = **ask**, put, submit • *When I finally posed the question "Why?" he merely shrugged.*
2 = **impersonate**, masquerade as, pass oneself off as, pretend to be • *The police officers posed as gamblers.*
3 = **position oneself**, sit, model
4 = **put on airs**, posture, show off (*informal*)
▶ *noun* **5** = **posture**, position, attitude, stance, bearing
6 = **act**, air, front, pretense, mannerism, affectation, façade, posturing
See also: **show**

poser *noun* = **puzzle**, problem, question, riddle, enigma

posh *adjective* (*informal*) = **smart**, exclusive, upscale, elegant, stylish, fashionable, classy (*informal*) • *a posh hotel*

posit *verb* = **put forward**, state, advance, assume, presume, postulate, propound

position *noun* **1** = **location**, point, place, whereabouts • *The ship's name and position were reported to the coastguard.*
2 = **posture**, pose, attitude, arrangement, stance
3 = **attitude**, view, opinion, outlook, belief, viewpoint,

stance, slant, point of view
4 = **status**, place, station, rank, standing, reputation, importance, stature, prestige
5 = **job**, post, place, office, role, situation, duty, employment, occupation
▶ *verb* **6** = **put**, place, locate, arrange, lay out • *Position the plants near the edge of the garden.*
See also: **appointment, fit, set, spot, state**

positive *adjective* **1** = **certain**, sure, confident, convinced • *I was positive he'd known about that money.*
2 = **definite**, clear, firm, concrete, conclusive, clear-cut • *positive evidence*
3 = **helpful**, constructive • *I anticipate a positive response.*
See also: **favourable, optimistic**

positively *adverb* = **definitely**, certainly, absolutely, firmly, surely, categorically, emphatically, unequivocally, unquestionably, assuredly

possess *verb* **1** = **be endowed with**, have, enjoy, be blessed with, be born with • *He possesses both stamina and creativity.*
2 = **own**, hold, acquire • *He was said to possess a huge fortune.*
3 = **control**, seize, occupy, take over • *They thought he was possessed by a demon.*

possessed *adjective* = **crazed**, frenzied, obsessed, demented, raving, berserk

possession *noun* = **ownership**, control, custody, tenure • *How did this picture come into your possession?*

possessions *plural noun*
= **belongings**, property, estate, assets, effects, things • *People had lost all their possessions.*

possessive *adjective* = **jealous**, selfish, controlling, covetous, dominating, domineering, overprotective

possessor *See* **owner**

possibility *noun* **1** = **likelihood**, risk, hope, chance, prospect, odds • *the possibility of a strike*
2 = **feasibility**, likelihood,

P

potentiality, practicability, workableness

3 (*often plural*) = **potential**, promise, talent, prospects, capabilities, potentiality

possible *adjective* **1** = **feasible**, viable, attainable, workable, practicable • *I am grateful to my teachers for making this project possible.*

2 = **conceivable**, potential, imaginable • *It's just possible that he did it deliberately.*

3 = **likely**, potential, hopeful, promising, probable
See also: **believable**

possibly *adverb* = **perhaps**, maybe, perchance (*archaic*)

post[1] *noun* **1** = **support**, stake, pole, column, picket, shaft, upright, pillar
▶ *verb* **2** = **put up**, display, affix, pin up

post[2] *noun* **1** = **mail**, collection, delivery, postal service
▶ *verb* **2** = **send**, mail, transmit, dispatch
▷ **keep someone posted** = **notify**, advise, brief, inform, fill in on (*informal*), report to

post[3] *noun* **1** = **job**, place, office, position, situation, appointment, employment, assignment
2 = **station**, place, beat, position
▶ *verb* **3** = **station**, put, place, position, assign, situate

poster *noun* = **notice**, bill, announcement, sticker, advertisement, placard, public notice

posterior See **bottom**

posterity *noun* **1** = **future**, succeeding generations
2 = **descendants**, family, issue, offspring, progeny, children, heirs

postpone *verb* = **put off**, delay, shelve, adjourn, defer, put back • *The visit has been postponed until tomorrow.*

postponement *noun* = **delay**, stay, suspension, adjournment, deferral, deferment

postscript *noun* = **P.S.**, addition,

supplement, afterthought

postulate *verb* = **presuppose**, propose, suppose, assume, theorize, hypothesize, posit, take for granted

posture *noun* **1** = **bearing**, set, attitude, stance, carriage, disposition
▶ *verb* **2** = **show off** (*informal*), affect, pose, put on airs

pot *noun* = **container**, vessel, bowl, pan

potency *noun* = **power**, force, might, strength, influence, effectiveness

potent *adjective* **1** = **powerful**, dominant, influential, dynamic, authoritative, commanding
2 = **strong**, powerful, mighty, vigorous, forceful

potential *adjective* **1** = **possible**, likely, probable • *potential sources of funding*
▶ *noun* **2** = **ability**, power, capacity, capability, wherewithal, aptitude
• *recognizing the potential of solar energy*
See also: **in the making**

pothole See **pit**

potion *noun* = **concoction**, draft, dose, mixture, brew, elixir, philtre

pottery *noun* = **ceramics**, terracotta, earthenware, stoneware

pouch *noun* = **bag**, pocket, sack, container, purse

pounce *verb* **1** = **spring**, attack, strike, jump, swoop, fall upon, leap at
▶ *noun* **2** = **spring**, attack, jump, assault, leap, bound, swoop

pound[1] *verb* **1** = **beat**, strike, batter, hammer, thump, pummel, clobber (*slang*), thrash, belabour
2 = **crush**, powder, pulverize
3 = **pulsate**, beat, pulse, throb, palpitate
4 = **stomp** (*informal*), march, thunder, tramp

pound[2] *noun* = **enclosure**, yard, compound, pen

pour *verb* **1** = **flow**, run, course,

stream, gush, spout • *Blood was pouring from his broken nose.*
2 = let flow, spill, splash, decant
3 = rain, pelt *or* pelt down, teem, bucket down (*informal*)
4 = stream, crowd, swarm, throng, teem
pout *verb* **1 = sulk**, glower, look petulant, pull a long face
▶ *noun* **2 = sullen look**, glower, long face
poverty *noun* **1 = destitution**, want, hardship, insolvency • *The artist died in loneliness and poverty.*
2 = scarcity, lack, shortage, deficiency, dearth, insufficiency, paucity
poverty-stricken *adjective*
= penniless, poor, impoverished, broke (*informal*), destitute, down and out, down on one's luck (*informal*), flat broke (*informal*), impecunious, indigent
powder *noun* **1 = dust**, fine grains, loose particles, talc
▶ *verb* **2 = dust**, cover, scatter, sprinkle, strew, dredge
powdery *adjective* **= fine**, dry, dusty, grainy, granular, crumbly
power *noun* **1 = control**, sovereignty, supremacy, dominion, ascendancy • *a position of great power and influence*
2 = authority, right, licence, authorization, privilege • *the power to change the rules*
3 = strength, might, vigour, brawn • *Power and speed are vital to success in hockey.*
4 = ability, potential, capacity, capability, faculty, competence, competency
See also: **drive, force, grip, influence**
powerful *adjective*
1 = influential, dominant, commanding • *a large, powerful country*
2 = strong, mighty, vigorous, sturdy, strapping • *It's such a powerful dog.*
OPPOSITE: weak
3 = effective, forceful, persuasive, compelling,

convincing, telling • *a powerful argument*
See also: **important, impressive, intense, violent**
powerless *adjective* **1 = helpless**, incapable, impotent • *I was powerless to do anything.*
2 = defenceless, subject, vulnerable, ineffective, unarmed, dependent, tied
See also: **weak**
practicability *noun* **= feasibility**, use, advantage, possibility, viability, usefulness, practicality
practicable *adjective* **= feasible**, possible, viable, achievable, attainable, doable
practical *adjective* **1 = pragmatic**, applied • *practical suggestions for a nutritious diet*
2 = useful, functional, sensible
• *The clothes are lightweight and practical for camping.*
OPPOSITE: impractical
3 = feasible, useful, doable, workable, serviceable, practicable
4 = skilled, efficient, experienced, accomplished, proficient
See also: **handy, realistic**
practically *adverb* **1 = almost**, nearly, basically, virtually, essentially, fundamentally, all but, in effect, just about, very nearly, well-nigh
2 = sensibly, clearly, reasonably, realistically, rationally, matter-of-factly
practice *noun* **1 = custom**, way, method, routine, habit • *My usual practice is to wake up early.*
2 = training, exercise, drill, preparation, rehearsal • *I need more practice in this area.*
3 = profession, work, business, career, vocation
4 = use, action, operation, experience, exercise, application
See also: **convention, procedure**
practise *verb* **1 = rehearse**, train, polish • *She practises the piano every day.*
2 = work at, pursue, carry on, engage in

practised *adjective* = **skilled**, expert, able, experienced, trained, accomplished, seasoned, proficient, versed
See also: **experienced**

pragmatic *adjective* = **practical**, realistic, sensible, down-to-earth, utilitarian, businesslike, hard-headed

praise *verb* 1 = **approve**, applaud, congratulate, pay tribute to • *Many others praised her for taking a strong stand.*
OPPOSITE: criticize
2 = **give thanks to**, bless, worship, glorify, adore, exalt
▶ *noun* 3 = **approval**, tribute, accolade, congratulation, commendation • *She is full of praise for her co-workers.*
OPPOSITE: criticism
4 = **thanks**, glory, homage, worship, kudos, adoration
See also: **credit, honour**

praiseworthy *adjective* = **creditable**, worthy, admirable, commendable, laudable, meritorious

prance *verb* 1 = **dance**, skip, romp, caper, cavort, frisk, gambol
2 = **strut**, parade, stalk, swagger, show off (*informal*)

prank *noun* = **trick**, antic, escapade, lark (*informal*), jape, practical joke

prattle *verb* = **chatter**, babble, blather, blether, gabble, jabber

pray *verb* 1 = **say one's prayers**, offer a prayer, recite the rosary
2 = **beg**, ask, plead, request, petition, solicit, implore, beseech, adjure, entreat
▷ **pray to** See **worship**

prayer *noun* 1 = **orison**, devotion, litany, invocation, supplication
2 = **plea**, appeal, request, petition, entreaty, supplication

preach *verb* 1 = **deliver a sermon**, address, evangelize
2 = **lecture**, advocate, exhort, moralize, sermonize

preacher *noun* = **clergyman**, minister, missionary, evangelist, parson

preamble *noun* = **introduction**, prelude, preface, foreword, opening statement *or* opening remarks

precarious *adjective* = **dangerous**, unsafe, shaky, risky, hazardous, unsure, tricky, unreliable, perilous, insecure

precaution *noun* 1 = **safeguard**, insurance, protection, provision, preventive measure • *taking precautions against accidents*
2 = **forethought**, care, caution, prudence, wariness, providence

precede *verb* = **go before**, lead, head, introduce, preface, antedate, come first

precedence *noun* = **priority**, rank, seniority, supremacy, superiority, primacy, antecedence, pre-eminence

precedent *noun* = **instance**, standard, model, example, pattern, prototype, paradigm, antecedent

preceding *adjective* = **previous**, former, past, above, earlier, prior, aforementioned, aforesaid, foregoing

precept *noun* = **rule**, order, law, regulation, principle, command, instruction, decree, statute, commandment, canon

precinct *noun* 1 = **limits**, confines
2 = **area**, quarter, sector, zone, district, section

precious *adjective* 1 = **valuable**, expensive, prized, invaluable, priceless • *precious jewels*
OPPOSITE: worthless
2 = **loved**, beloved, dear, prized, darling, cherished, adored, treasured
3 = **affected**, artificial, overnice, overrefined

precipice *noun* = **cliff**, height, bluff, crag, rock face

precipitate *verb* 1 = **quicken**, advance, trigger, accelerate, hurry, expedite, hasten, bring on, speed up
2 = **throw**, launch, cast, hurl, fling, let fly
▶ *adjective* 3 = **hasty**, reckless, rash, impulsive, precipitous,

heedless, impetuous
4 = swift, rapid, breakneck, headlong, rushing
5 = sudden, quick, brief, unexpected, abrupt, without warning

> **TYPES OF PRECIPITATION**
>
> | | |
> |---|---|
> | drizzle | shower |
> | freezing | sleet |
> | rain | snow |
> | hail | |

precipitous *adjective* **1 = sheer**, high, steep, abrupt, dizzy, perpendicular
2 = hasty, reckless, rash, hurried, precipitate, heedless
précis *noun* **1 = summary**, outline, synopsis, abridgment, résumé
▶ *verb* **2 = summarize**, outline, shorten, abridge, sum up
precise *adjective* **1 = exact**, very, specific, particular, correct, actual, accurate • *We may never know the precise details*.
OPPOSITE: vague
2 = strict, particular, formal, careful, exact, stiff, rigid, meticulous, scrupulous, finicky, fastidious, punctilious
See also: **fine**, **right**
precisely *adverb* **= exactly**, square, absolutely, strictly, smack (*informal*), correctly, accurately, squarely, plumb (*informal*), just so
precision *noun* **= exactness**, care, accuracy, meticulousness, particularity, preciseness
preclude *verb* **= prevent**, stop, check, prohibit, exclude, inhibit, forestall, debar, obviate, rule out
precocious *adjective* **= advanced**, forward, ahead, quick, smart, bright, developed
preconceived *adjective* **= presumed**, forejudged, prejudged, presupposed
preconception *noun*

= **preconceived idea** *or* **preconceived notion**, bias, notion, prejudice, predisposition, presupposition
precursor *noun* **1 = herald**, forerunner, harbinger, vanguard
2 = forerunner, predecessor, antecedent, forebear
predatory *adjective* **= hunting**, carnivorous, predacious, raptorial
predecessor *noun* **1 = previous job holder**, precursor, forerunner, antecedent
2 = ancestor, forefather, antecedent, forebear
predestination *noun* **= fate**, destiny, foreordainment, foreordination, predetermination
predestined *adjective* **= fated**, doomed, meant, preordained
predetermined *adjective* **= prearranged**, set, agreed, fixed, preplanned
predicament *noun* **= fix** (*informal*), jam (*informal*), scrape, hot water (*informal*), tight spot • *He found himself in a peculiar predicament.*
See also: **hole**, **problem**, **state**
predict *verb* **= foretell**, forecast, foresee, prophesy • *The opinion polls are predicting a very close vote.*
predictable *adjective* **= likely**, sure, certain, reliable, anticipated, foreseeable, expected
prediction *noun* **= prophecy**, forecast • *He was unwilling to make a prediction for the coming year.*
predilection *noun* **= liking**, love, taste, weakness, bias, preference, penchant, fondness, inclination, leaning, propensity, partiality
predispose *verb* **= incline**, lead, affect, prompt, influence, bias, dispose, prejudice
predisposed *adjective* **= inclined**, ready, subject, willing, liable, susceptible, given, minded
predominant *adjective* **= main**, chief, prime, principal, dominant, prevalent, paramount, ascendant,

p

leading, prevailing

predominantly adverb = **mainly**, mostly, largely, generally, primarily, principally, chiefly, for the most part

predominate verb = **prevail**, outweigh, overshadow, overrule, be most noticeable, carry weight, hold sway

pre-eminence noun = **superiority**, excellence, distinction, prominence, prestige, supremacy, renown, predominance

pre-eminent adjective = **outstanding**, chief, excellent, renowned, superior, foremost, supreme, distinguished, predominant, incomparable, matchless

pre-empt verb = **forestall**, assume, anticipate, appropriate, usurp

preen verb **1** (Of a bird) = **clean**, plume
2 = **smarten**, dress up, spruce up, titivate
▷ **preen oneself, preen oneself on** = **pride oneself**, congratulate oneself

preface noun **1** = **introduction**, preliminary, prelude, preamble, prologue, foreword
▶ verb **2** = **introduce**, open, begin, prefix

prefer verb = **like better**, favour, be partial to, go for, incline toward • *Does she prefer a particular type of music?*

preferable adjective = **better**, superior, best, chosen, favoured, more desirable

preferably adverb = **rather**, first, sooner, by choice, in preference or for preference

preference noun **1** = **first choice**, pick, option, choice, selection, desire, favorite, predilection, partiality
2 = **priority**, precedence, favoured treatment, favouritism, first place

preferential adjective = **privileged**, special, better, advantageous, favoured

preferment noun = **promotion**, rise, advancement, elevation, exaltation, upgrading

preferred See **favourite**

pregnant adjective **1** = **expectant**, big with child or heavy with child, expecting (*informal*), with child
2 = **meaningful**, significant, loaded, pointed, charged, expressive, eloquent, weighty, telling

prehistoric adjective = **earliest**, early, primitive, primordial, primeval

prejudge verb = **jump to conclusions**, anticipate, presume, presuppose

prejudice noun **1** = **bias**, preconception • *prejudice against workers over 55*

PREFIXES

ante-	extra-	multi-	semi-
anti-	hyper-	neo-	step-
auto-	in-	non-	sub-
bi-	inter-	over-	super-
centi-	intra-	poly-	tele-
co-	mega-	post-	trans-
contra-	micro-	pre-	tri-
de-	mid-	pro-	ultra-
demi-	milli-	pseudo-	un-
dis-	mini-	re-	under-
ex-	mono-	self-	vice-

2 = discrimination, racism, sexism, bigotry, chauvinism
• *racial prejudice*
▶ *verb* **3 = bias**, influence, poison, colour, predispose, distort, slant
4 = harm, damage, injure, hurt, undermine, spoil, impair, mar, hinder
See also: **colour, injustice**

prejudiced *adjective* = **biased**, unfair, one-sided, intolerant, opinionated, narrow-minded, bigoted, influenced

prejudicial *adjective* = **harmful**, detrimental, hurtful, deleterious, injurious, damaging, disadvantageous, unfavourable

preliminary *adjective* **1 = first**, test, trial, opening, pilot, initial, prior, preparatory, introductory, prefatory
▶ *noun* **2 = introduction**, start, opening, beginning, prelude, overture, preamble, preface

prelude *noun* = **introduction**, start, beginning, overture, preamble, preface, prologue, foreword

premature *adjective* **1 = early**, forward, untimely, unseasonable
2 = hasty, ill-timed, overhasty, rash, untimely, too soon

prematurely *See* **early**

premeditated *adjective* = **planned**, deliberate, conscious, intentional, calculated, considered, wilful

premeditation *noun* = **planning**, design, purpose, intention, forethought, plotting, prearrangement, predetermination

premier *noun* **1 = head of government**, chancellor, chief minister, chief officer, prime minister
▶ *adjective* **2 = chief**, first, head, prime, main, primary, principal, foremost, alpha male, highest, leading

premiere *noun* = **first night**, debut, opening

premise *noun* = **assumption**, argument, assertion, hypothesis, proposition, supposition, postulation, presupposition

premises *plural noun* = **building**, place, site, property, establishment

premium *noun* = **bonus**, fee, reward, perk (*informal*), bounty, prize, perquisite
▷ **at a premium = in great demand**, rare, scarce, hard to come by, in short supply

premonition *noun* = **foreboding**, funny feeling (*informal*), omen
• *He had a premonition that he would die.*
See also: **warning**

preoccupation *noun*
1 = obsession, fixation, bee in one's bonnet
2 = absorption, immersion, abstraction, reverie, absent-mindedness, daydreaming, engrossment, woolgathering

preoccupied *adjective* = **absorbed**, oblivious, engrossed, immersed, wrapped up • *I am preoccupied with my tennis career.*

preparation *noun*
1 = groundwork, preparing, getting ready
2 (*often plural*) = **arrangement**, plan, measure, provision
3 = mixture, medicine, compound, concoction

preparatory *adjective* = **introductory**, opening, primary, preliminary, prefatory

prepare *verb* = **make ready** *or* **get ready**, prime, train, practise, adjust, arrange, adapt, warm up

prepared *adjective* **1 = ready**, set, arranged, in order, in readiness, primed
2 = willing, inclined, disposed

preponderance *noun* = **predominance**, mass, dominance, domination, prevalence, supremacy, extensiveness, greater numbers, greater part, lion's share

prepossessing *adjective* = **attractive**, charming,

handsome, good-looking, engaging, appealing, pleasing, likable or likeable, fetching

preposterous *adjective*
= **ridiculous**, crazy, incredible, outrageous, absurd, insane, ludicrous, laughable, unthinkable, nonsensical, out of the question

prerequisite *noun*
1 = **requirement**, must, condition, essential, necessity, qualification, precondition, requisite, *sine qua non* (*Latin*)
▶ *adjective* 2 = **required**, necessary, mandatory, essential, vital, indispensable, requisite, obligatory

prerogative *noun* = **right**, due, advantage, exemption, immunity, privilege, liberty

presage *verb* = **portend**, signify, bode, foreshadow, augur, betoken, foretoken

prescience *noun* = **foresight**, clairvoyance, foreknowledge, precognition, second sight

prescribe *verb* = **order**, set, rule, direct, recommend, dictate, specify, decree, stipulate, ordain, lay down

prescribed *See* **formal**

prescription *noun*
1 = **instruction**, direction, formula, recipe
2 = **medicine**, drug, preparation, remedy, mixture

presence *noun* 1 = **being**, residence, attendance, existence, occupancy, inhabitance
2 = **personality**, air, appearance, poise, aspect, aura, carriage, bearing, demeanour, self-assurance
▷ **presence of mind** = **level-headedness**, cool (*slang*), composure, calmness, coolness, self-possession, wits

present[1] *adjective* 1 = **there**, here, at hand, in attendance • *He had been present at the meeting.*
OPPOSITE: absent
2 = **current**, immediate, contemporary, existing,

present-day, existent
▶ *noun*
▷ **the present** = **now**, today, here and now, the present moment, the time being
▷ **at present** = **just now**, now, at the moment, right now
▷ **for the present** = **for now**, temporarily, for the moment, for the time being, in the meantime
See also: **modern**

present[2] *noun* 1 = **gift**, offering, donation • *a birthday present*
▶ *verb* 2 = **give**, award, grant, donate, bestow, hand out • *The mayor presented the prizes.*
3 = **introduce**, acquaint with, make known
4 = **put on**, show, give, stage, display, exhibit
See also: **perform, submit**

presentable *adjective*
= **satisfactory**, acceptable, decent, suitable, respectable, passable, becoming, fit to be seen, O.K. *or* okay (*informal*)

presentation *noun* 1 = **giving**, award, offering, donation, bestowal, conferral
2 = **performance**, show, production, display, demonstration, exhibition

present-day *adjective* = **current**, recent, present, modern, contemporary, up-to-date, latter-day, newfangled

presently *adverb* = **soon**, shortly, anon (*archaic*), before long, by and by

preservation *noun* = **protection**, support, safety, conservation, maintenance, salvation, safekeeping, safeguarding

preserve *verb* 1 = **protect**, keep, save, defend, shelter, shield, safeguard, conserve, care for
2 = **maintain**, continue, keep, uphold, sustain, perpetuate, keep up
▶ *noun* 3 = **area**, field, domain, realm, sphere

preside *verb* = **run**, lead, head, control, conduct, manage, direct, chair, govern, administer, officiate

president *See* **head**

press *verb* 1 = **compress**, push, crush, squeeze, mash • *Press the blue button.*

2 = **urge**, pressure, plead, petition, beg, implore • *The journalist was pressed to reveal her sources.*

3 = **hug**, crush, embrace, squeeze, clasp, fold in one's arms, hold close

4 = **smooth**, iron, flatten

5 = **crowd**, push, gather, surge, herd, flock, swarm, throng, seethe

▷ **press on** *See* **advance**

▶ *noun*

▷ **the press** = **newspapers**, Fleet Street, fourth estate, news media, the papers;

= **journalists**, columnists, correspondents, newsmen, pressmen, reporters

See also: **insist, rush**

pressing *adjective* = **urgent**, important, serious, crucial, vital, imperative, high-priority, importunate

pressure *noun* 1 = **force**, weight, compression, compressing, crushing, squeezing

2 = **power**, force, influence, sway, constraint, coercion, compulsion

3 = **stress**, heat, strain, load, burden, urgency, hassle (*informal*), demands

prestige *noun* = **status**, credit, standing, reputation, fame, importance, honour, distinction, kudos, renown, eminence

prestigious *adjective* = **celebrated**, great, important, prominent, renowned, notable, respected, illustrious, eminent, esteemed

presumably *adverb* = **apparently**, probably, seemingly, in all likelihood, in all probability, it would seem, on the face of it

presume *verb* 1 = **believe**, think, suppose, guess (*informal*), assume, infer, conjecture, surmise, postulate, take for granted

2 = **dare**, venture, go so far, make so bold, take the liberty

presumed *See* **supposed**

presumption *noun* 1 = **cheek** (*informal*), nerve (*informal*), gall (*informal*), audacity, boldness, effrontery, impudence, insolence

2 = **probability**, chance, basis, likelihood

presumptuous *adjective* = **pushy** (*informal*), forward, bold, audacious, overconfident, insolent, too big for one's boots

presuppose *verb* = **presume**, assume, imply, postulate, posit, take as read, take for granted

presupposition *noun* = **assumption**, belief, premise, presumption, preconception, supposition

pretend *verb* 1 = **feign**, fake, counterfeit, falsify, pass oneself off as • *Sometimes the boy pretended to be asleep.*

2 = **make believe**, act, suppose, imagine, make up

▷ **pretend to be** *See* **pose**

pretended *adjective* = **feigned**, fake, false, so-called, counterfeit, pretend (*informal*), bogus, phony (*informal*), sham, pseudo (*informal*)

pretender *noun* = **claimant**, aspirant

pretense *noun* 1 = **deception**, acting, simulation, sham, deceit, charade, trickery, falsehood, feigning

2 = **show**, display, veneer, affectation, artifice, façade

pretension *noun* 1 = **claim**, demand, assumption, profession, aspiration, pretense

2 = **affectation**, show, vanity, snobbery, self-importance, airs, conceit, ostentation, pretentiousness

pretentious *adjective* = **affected**, pompous, conceited, ostentatious, snobbish • *Many critics thought his work and ideas pretentious and empty.*

P

pretext noun = **guise**, show, cover, excuse, cloak, ploy, ruse, pretense

pretty adjective **1** beautiful, attractive, cute, lovely • *a very charming and very pretty girl*
▶ adverb **2** = **fairly**, rather, quite, kind of (informal) • *He's a pretty good card player.*

prevail verb **1** = **win**, overcome, succeed, triumph, overrule, be victorious
2 = **be widespread**, abound, be current, be prevalent, exist generally, predominate

prevailing adjective
1 = **widespread**, general, current, popular, common, cool (informal), usual, ordinary, prevalent, established, fashionable, customary, in vogue, phat (slang)
2 = **predominating**, main, ruling, principal, dominant

prevalence noun = **commonness**, currency, popularity, frequency, universality

prevalent adjective = **common**, general, current, popular, usual, widespread, frequent, universal, established, customary

prevaricate verb = **evade**, dodge, deceive, cavil, beat about the bush, equivocate, hedge

prevent verb = **stop**, thwart, foil, avert, hinder, impede • *the most practical way of preventing crime*
See also: **bar, prohibit**

prevention noun = **elimination**, precaution, safeguard, avoidance, deterrence, thwarting

preventive adjective
1 = **hindering**, obstructive, hampering, impeding
2 = **protective**, precautionary, deterrent, counteractive
▷ **preventive measure** See **precaution**
▶ noun **3** = **hindrance**, block, obstacle, obstruction, impediment
4 = **protection**, prevention, shield, safeguard, remedy, deterrent

preview noun = **advance showing**, trailer, foretaste, sneak preview, taster

previous adjective = **earlier**, former, past, prior, one-time, preceding • *the previous year*
See also: **last**

previously adverb = **before**, once, earlier, formerly, beforehand, hitherto, in the past

prey noun **1** = **quarry**, game, kill
2 = **victim**, target, mug (Brit slang), dupe, fall guy (informal)

price noun **1** = **cost**, charge, figure, value, amount, fee • *a sharp increase in the price of gasoline*
2 = **consequences**, cost, penalty, toll
▶ verb **3** = **value**, cost, estimate, appraise, put a price on • *I just can't imagine why it has been priced at this level.*
See also: **rate**

priceless adjective **1** = **valuable**, expensive, costly, precious, dear, invaluable
2 (Informal) = **hilarious**, comic, funny, amusing, droll, rib-tickling, side-splitting

pricey adjective = **expensive**, costly, steep (informal), dear, high-priced

prick verb **1** = **pierce**, stab, punch, jab, puncture, lance, perforate
2 = **sting**, bite, smart, itch, tingle, prickle
▶ noun **3** = **puncture**, wound, hole, perforation, pinhole

prickle noun **1** = **spike**, point, spur, needle, spine, barb, thorn
▶ verb **2** = **tingle**, smart, sting, itch
3 = **prick**, stick, jab

prickly adjective **1** = **spiny**, barbed, thorny, bristly
2 = **itchy**, sharp, scratchy, crawling, smarting, stinging, tingling

pride noun **1** = **satisfaction**, delight, pleasure • *We take pride in offering you the highest standards in the industry.*
2 = **conceit**, arrogance, vanity, snobbery, egotism, smugness • *His pride may still be his downfall.*

P

OPPOSITE: humility

3 = self-respect, dignity, honour, self-esteem, self-worth

4 = gem, treasure, jewel, pride and joy

See also: **pick**

priest noun = **clergyman**, minister, father, cleric, pastor, divine, curate, vicar, ecclesiastic

prig noun = **goody-goody** (informal), prude, puritan, stuffed shirt (informal)

priggish adjective = **self-righteous**, prim, puritanical, goody-goody (informal), holier-than-thou, prudish

prim adjective = **prudish**, proper, puritanical, straitlaced • We tend to assume our great-grandparents were very prim and proper.

prima donna noun = **diva**, star, leading lady

primarily adverb **1 = chiefly**, mostly, largely, generally, mainly, essentially, fundamentally, principally, above all

2 = at first, initially, originally, at the start or from the start, first and foremost, in the beginning, in the first place

primary adjective **1 = chief**, first, prime, main, principal, cardinal, paramount, cutting-edge, greatest, highest

2 = elementary, simple, introductory, rudimentary

prime adjective **1 = main**, chief, principal, leading • a prime cause of traffic accidents

2 = best, choice, select, superior, first-rate • prime beef

▶ noun **3 = peak**, height, flower, bloom, heyday, zenith

▶ verb **4 = inform**, tell, brief, notify, clue in (informal), fill in (informal)

5 = prepare, coach, train, get ready, make ready

See also: **first, foremost, top**

primed See **ready**

primeval adjective = **earliest**, first, early, old, ancient, prehistoric, primitive, primal, primordial

primitive adjective = **crude**, simple, rough, rude, rudimentary • a primitive shack

See also: **early**

prince noun = **ruler**, monarch, lord, sovereign

princely adjective **1 = regal**, royal, sovereign, noble, majestic, imperial

2 = generous, liberal, rich, lavish, gracious, bounteous, munificent, open-handed

principal adjective **1 = main**, first, major, chief, prime, primary, foremost • His principal concern is that of winning the school election.

▶ noun **2 = head teacher**, head (informal), dean, superintendent, headmaster or headmistress

3 = leader, lead, star, alpha male

4 = capital, money, assets

See also: **essential, leading, supreme, top**

principally adverb = **mainly**, especially, mostly, largely, primarily, predominantly, chiefly, above all

principle noun **1 = morals**, integrity, conscience, scruples, sense of duty • a person of principle

2 = rule, law, fundamental, doctrine, canon, axiom • the basic principles of capitalism

▷ **in principle = in theory**, ideally, theoretically

See also: **basis, belief, ideal**

principles See **conscience, standards**

print verb **1 = publish**, issue, mark, stamp, impress, engrave, imprint

▶ noun **2 = publication**, book, newspaper, magazine, newsprint, periodical, printed matter

3 = reproduction, photo (informal), picture, copy, photograph, engraving

prior adjective = **earlier**, former, previous, preceding, foregoing, pre-existent, pre-existing

▷ **prior to = before**, preceding, earlier than, previous to

priority noun = **precedence**, rank, preference, seniority, pre-eminence, right of way

priory noun = **monastery**, convent, abbey, nunnery, religious house

prison noun = **jail**, penitentiary, dungeon, penal institution • *a high-security prison*

prisoner noun 1 = **convict** • *top-security prisoners*
2 = **captive**, hostage • *concentration-camp prisoners*

prissy adjective = **prim**, old-maidish (*informal*), prim and proper, prudish, strait-laced

pristine adjective = **new**, pure, untouched, unspoiled, immaculate, uncorrupted, undefiled, unsullied, virginal

privacy noun = **seclusion**, retirement, retreat, isolation, solitude

private adjective 1 = **exclusive**, special, personal, individual • *a private bathroom*
2 = **secret**, confidential, clandestine • *a private wedding*
OPPOSITE: public
3 = **secluded**, separate, secret, isolated, solitary, concealed, sequestered
See also: **own**

privilege noun = **right**, claim, due, advantage, freedom, concession, liberty, entitlement, prerogative

privileged adjective = **special**, elite, advantaged, entitled, favoured, honoured

privy adjective
▷ **privy to** = **informed of**, apprised of, aware of, cognizant of, in on, in the know about (*informal*), wise to (*slang*)
▶ noun = **lavatory**, bathroom, washroom, latrine, outhouse, outside toilet

prize[1] noun 1 = **award**, honour, trophy, accolade • *first prize at the piano competition*
2 = **winnings**, haul, jackpot, purse, stakes
▶ adjective 3 = **champion**, top, award-winning, outstanding, first-rate • *a prize bull*
See also: **reward**

prize[2] verb = **value**, treasure, cherish, esteem • *These ornaments are prized by collectors.*
See also: **appreciate**

prized adjective = **treasured**, beloved, precious, cherished, valued, much loved

probability noun = **likelihood**, prospect, chances, odds • *the probability of a serious earthquake*
See also: **chance**

probable adjective = **likely**, apparent, feasible, plausible, in the cards • *a misunderstanding about the probable cost*
OPPOSITE: improbable
See also: **believable**, **potential**

probably adverb = **likely**, presumably, doubtless, in all probability • *The wedding is probably going to be in late August.*

probation noun = **trial period**, trial, apprenticeship

probe verb 1 = **examine**, search, investigate, explore, scrutinize, go into, look into
2 = **explore**, poke, prod, feel around
▶ noun 3 = **examination**, study, investigation, inquiry, exploration, scrutiny, detection

problem noun 1 = **difficulty**, trouble, bitch (*informal*), predicament, quandary • *the economic problems of the city*
2 = **puzzle**, riddle, conundrum • *a mathematical problem*
See also: **business**, **complex**, **drawback**, **issue**, **snag**

problematic adjective = **tricky**, doubtful, dubious, debatable, problematical, puzzling

procedure noun = **method**, policy, system, process, practice, strategy • *He did not follow the correct procedure in applying for a permit.*
See also: **course**, **measure**, **routine**, **way**

proceed verb 1 = **begin**, start, get under way • *I had no idea how to proceed.*
OPPOSITE: cease
2 = **continue**, carry on, go on • *They proceeded with the trial.*

OPPOSITE: cease
3 = go on, continue, travel, advance, progress, make your way • *She proceeded along the hallway.*
4 = arise, come, issue, result, spring, stem, flow, originate, derive, emanate
See also: **go, journey**

| CONFUSABLES
Proceed means *move forward.*
Precede means *go before.*

proceeding noun = **action**, move, step, process, act, measure, procedure, deed
▷ **proceedings = business**, report, account, archives, doings, affairs, minutes, records, transactions
See also: **case**

proceeds plural noun = **income**, profit, gain, revenue, yield, earnings, products, returns, takings

process noun **1 = procedure**, system, method, means, course of action • *The building process was spread over three years.*
2 = development, growth, advance, progress, movement, evolution, progression
▶ verb **3 = deal with**, handle, dispose of, take care of • *Your application is being processed.*
See also: **action, manufacture**

processed See **refined**

procession noun = **parade**, file, train, march, cortege, cavalcade

proclaim verb = **declare**, announce, publish, indicate, advertise, circulate, herald, profess, make known

proclamation noun
= **declaration**, announcement, notice, publication, decree, pronouncement, notification, edict

procrastinate verb = **delay**, postpone, stall, dally, drag one's feet (*informal*), gain time, play for time, put off, temporize

procure verb = **obtain**, win, get, find, score (*slang*), buy, gain, purchase, acquire, secure, come by, pick up

prod verb **1 = poke**, drive, push, dig, nudge, shove, jab
2 = prompt, move, urge, spur, motivate, stimulate, incite, rouse, goad, egg on, impel
▶ noun **3 = poke**, push, dig, nudge, shove, jab
4 = prompt, signal, reminder, stimulus, cue

prodigal adjective = **extravagant**, excessive, reckless, spendthrift, wasteful, immoderate, improvident, profligate

prodigious adjective **1 = huge**, giant, massive, vast, enormous, immense, gigantic, colossal, monstrous
2 = wonderful, amazing, remarkable, extraordinary, fantastic (*informal*), exceptional, fabulous, phenomenal, marvelous, staggering

prodigy noun **1 = genius**, talent, mastermind, wizard, whizz (*informal*)
2 = wonder, phenomenon, sensation, miracle, marvel

produce verb **1 = make**, create, manufacture, construct, invent, scare up (*informal*)
• *clothing produced from the finest materials*
2 = show, advance, bring forward, bring to light, put forward • *To rent a car, you must produce a driver's licence.*
3 = cause, effect, generate, bring about, give rise to
4 = bring forth, bear, deliver, breed, beget
5 = present, do, show, stage, direct, exhibit, mount, put on
▶ noun **6 = fruit and vegetables**, product, crop, yield, harvest, greengrocery
See also: **bring, compose, lead to, occasion, provoke**

producer noun **1 = director**, impresario
2 = maker, farmer, manufacturer, grower

product noun **1 = goods**, produce, commodity, merchandise • *Many household products give off noxious fumes.*

p

2 = result, effect, consequence, outcome, upshot

production noun **1 = producing**, construction, manufacture, creation, formation, making, fabrication, manufacturing

2 = presentation, management, direction, staging

productive adjective **1 = fertile**, prolific, fruitful • *Training makes workers highly productive.*
OPPOSITE: unproductive

2 = useful, valuable, constructive, worthwhile • *I'm hopeful the talks will be productive.*
OPPOSITE: unproductive
See also: **economic, efficient**

productivity noun **= output**, production, yield, work rate

profane adjective
1 = sacrilegious, wicked, disrespectful, irreverent, sinful, godless, impious, impure, irreligious, ungodly

2 = crude, foul, obscene, vulgar, coarse, blasphemous, filthy
▶ verb **3 = desecrate**, violate, defile, debase, commit sacrilege

profanity noun **1 = sacrilege**, blasphemy, impiety, profaneness

2 = swearing, curse, obscenity, irreverence, cursing

profess verb **1 = claim**, allege, fake, pretend, purport, feign, make out

2 = state, announce, admit, declare, confess, assert, proclaim, affirm, vouch, avow

professed adjective **1 = supposed**, alleged, so-called, would-be, purported, self-styled, ostensible, pretended

2 = declared, proclaimed, self-confessed, avowed, confessed, confirmed, self-acknowledged

profession noun **1 = occupation**, business, career • *a teacher by profession*

2 = declared, proclaimed, self-confessed, avowed, confessed, confirmed, self-acknowledged
See also: **job, trade, work**

professional adjective **1 = expert**, efficient, skilled, experienced, competent, qualified, adept,

proficient, masterly
▶ noun **2 = expert**, specialist, master, pro (*slang*), maestro, adept, virtuoso, past master

professionally See **well**

professor noun **= teacher**, fellow (Brit), don (Brit), prof (*informal*)

proficiency noun **= skill**, ability, expertise, mastery, knack, competence, know-how (*informal*), dexterity, aptitude

proficient adjective **= skilled**, able, capable, efficient, competent, accomplished, adept, skilful • *They tend to be proficient in foreign languages.*
OPPOSITE: incompetent
See also: **expert, practical**

profile noun **1 = outline**, figure, form, drawing, sketch, silhouette, contour, side view

2 = biography, sketch, characterization, vignette, thumbnail sketch

profit noun **1 = earnings**, revenue, surplus, proceeds, takings • *The bank made pre-tax profits of $3.5 million.*
OPPOSITE: loss

2 = benefit, good, use, gain, value, advantage, advancement
▶ verb **3 = take advantage of**, exploit, capitalize on, make the most of • *He profited shamefully at the expense of my family.*

4 = benefit, help, serve, gain, improve, promote, be of advantage to

profitable adjective
1 = moneymaking, productive, viable, economical • *Our new venture has proved highly profitable.*

2 = beneficial, valuable, useful, productive, worthwhile, rewarding, win-win (*informal*), fruitful, advantageous
See also: **helpful, successful**

profiteer noun **1 = racketeer**, exploiter
▶ verb **2 = exploit**, racketeer, make a quick buck (*slang*)

profits See **income**

profligate adjective
1 = extravagant, reckless, spendthrift, wasteful,

immoderate, improvident, prodigal

2 = depraved, wild, wicked, immoral, shameless, degenerate, wanton, debauched, dissolute, licentious

▸ *noun* **3 = spendthrift**, squanderer, waster, wastrel

4 = degenerate, rake, libertine, debauchee, reprobate, roué

profound *adjective* **1 = wise**, deep, sage, philosophical, abstruse, learned, penetrating, sagacious

2 = intense, great, extreme, acute, keen, heartfelt, deeply felt

profuse *adjective* **= plentiful**, prolific, ample, abundant, bountiful, copious, luxuriant, overflowing

profusion *noun* **= abundance**, surplus, excess, wealth, quantity, bounty, glut, plethora, extravagance

progeny *noun* **= children**, family, issue, young, stock, race, offspring, lineage, descendants, posterity

prognosis *noun* **= forecast**, prediction, diagnosis, projection, prognostication

program *noun* **1 = schedule**, agenda, timetable • *We attended several training programs.*

2 = broadcast, show • *local news programs*

See also: **routine**

progress *noun* **1 = advance**, improvement, breakthrough, headway • *progress in the fight against cancer*

2 = movement, way, advance, course, passage

▹ **in progress = going on**, proceeding, happening, being done, occurring, taking place, under way

▸ *verb* **3 = advance**, develop, improve, blossom • *His piano playing is progressing well.*

4 = move on, continue, travel, advance, proceed, go forward, make headway

progression *noun* **1 = progress**, gain, advance, advancement, headway, furtherance,

movement forward

2 = sequence, series, course, chain, string, cycle, succession

progressive *adjective*

1 = enlightened, liberal, modern, advanced, radical, revolutionary, reformist, avant-garde, forward-looking

2 = growing, ongoing, advancing, continuing, developing, increasing

prohibit *verb* **1 = forbid**, ban, prevent, outlaw, interdict • *a law that prohibits parking during certain hours*

OPPOSITE: allow

2 = prevent, stop, restrict, hamper, hinder, impede

See also: **veto**

prohibited *See* illegal

prohibition *noun* **1 = prevention**, restriction, obstruction, exclusion, constraint

2 = ban, bar, boycott, injunction, veto, embargo, interdict, proscription, interdict

prohibitive *adjective*

= exorbitant, excessive, steep (*informal*), extortionate

project *noun* **1 = scheme**, work, plan, job, activity, task, venture, occupation, assignment, enterprise, undertaking

▸ *verb* **2 = forecast**, estimate, predict, calculate, gauge, reckon, extrapolate

3 = stick out, extend, bulge, protrude, jut, overhang, stand out

projectile *noun* **= missile**, rocket, bullet, shell

projection *noun* **1 = protrusion**, shelf, bulge, ridge, ledge, overhang, protuberance

2 = forecast, estimate, calculation, estimation, reckoning, computation, extrapolation

proletarian *adjective*

1 = working-class, common, plebeian

▸ *noun* **2 = worker**, commoner, man of the people, pleb, plebeian

proletariat *noun* **= working class**, commoners, hoi polloi, labouring classes, lower classes, plebs, the common people, the masses

proliferate verb = **increase**, expand, breed, multiply, grow rapidly

proliferation noun = **increase**, spread, expansion, multiplication

prolific adjective = **productive**, abundant, fertile, fruitful, copious, fecund, luxuriant, profuse

prologue noun = **introduction**, preliminary, prelude, preamble, preface, foreword

prolong verb = **lengthen**, continue, delay, extend, stretch, perpetuate, drag out, draw out, protract, spin out

prolonged See **continuous**

promenade noun 1 = **walkway**, parade, prom, esplanade
2 = **stroll**, turn, walk, constitutional, saunter
▶ verb 3 = **stroll**, walk, saunter, perambulate, take a walk

prominence noun
1 = **conspicuousness**, markedness
2 = **fame**, name, celebrity, reputation, importance, distinction, prestige, eminence

prominent adjective 1 = **famous**, important, renowned, well-known, notable, eminent, noted
• a prominent journalist
2 = **noticeable**, obvious, striking, pronounced, conspicuous, eye-catching, jutting • a prominent feature of the landscape
See also: **leading**

promiscuity noun
= **licentiousness**, immorality, debauchery, looseness, permissiveness, promiscuousness, wantonness

promiscuous adjective
= **licentious**, fast, wild, loose, abandoned, immoral, libertine, wanton, debauched

promise verb 1 = **guarantee**, pledge, vow, assure, give your word • I promise not to be back too late.

2 = **show signs of**, indicate, hint at • This promised to be a very long night.
▶ noun 3 = **guarantee**, pledge, vow, assurance, undertaking
• If you make a promise, you should keep it.
4 = **potential**, ability, capacity, talent, capability, flair, aptitude
See also: **bond, oath, prospect, word**

promising adjective
1 = **encouraging**, likely, bright, hopeful, rosy, favourable, auspicious, propitious, reassuring
2 = **talented**, able, gifted, rising

promontory noun = **point**, head, cape, headland, foreland

promote verb 1 = **support**, back
• All attempts to promote interest in putting on a school musical have failed.
2 = **advertise**, plug (informal), publicize • She's in Europe promoting her new movie.
3 = **elevate**, upgrade • He has been promoted twice in two years.
See also: **advocate, champion**

promotion noun 1 = **rise**, honor, advancement, elevation, exaltation, move up, preferment, upgrading
2 = **publicity**, advertising, plugging (informal)
3 = **encouragement**, support, advancement, boosting, furtherance

prompt verb 1 = **cause**, spur, inspire, motivate, induce • The uncertain economy has prompted consumers to stop buying new cars.
2 = **remind**, coax • "What was that you were saying about a guided tour?" he prompted her.
▶ adjective 3 = **immediate**, quick, rapid, instant, swift, instantaneous • a serious condition that needs prompt treatment
▶ adverb 4 (Informal) = **exactly**, sharp, promptly, on the dot, punctually
See also: **drive, hasty, occasion, provoke, punctual**

promptly adverb = **exactly**, sharp,

precisely, on the dot • *He showed up for the interview promptly at ten.* See also: **immediately**

promptness noun = **swiftness**, speed, willingness, haste, quickness, eagerness, briskness, punctuality

promulgate verb = **make known**, publish, broadcast, spread, promote, communicate, circulate, proclaim, disseminate, make public

prone adjective 1 = **liable**, susceptible, given, inclined, disposed • *He is prone to depression.* 2 = **face down**, prostrate • *We were lying prone on the grass.*

prong noun = **point**, spike, tine

pronounce verb 1 = **say**, speak, sound, accent, articulate, enunciate
2 = **declare**, announce, deliver, proclaim, affirm, decree

pronounced adjective = **noticeable**, obvious, evident, distinct, marked, striking, definite, conspicuous, decided

pronouncement noun = **announcement**, statement, judgment, declaration, decree, proclamation, edict, dictum

pronunciation noun = **intonation**, speech, stress, accent, inflection, articulation, diction, enunciation

proof noun 1 = **evidence**, testimony, confirmation, verification • *We were asked for proof of our age.*
▶ adjective 2 = **impervious**, strong, resistant, repellent, impenetrable

prop verb 1 = **support**, stay, uphold, brace, sustain, bolster, buttress, hold up
▶ noun 2 = **support**, stay, brace, mainstay, buttress, stanchion

propaganda noun = **information**, promotion, publicity, hype, advertising, disinformation

propagate verb 1 = **spread**, publish, broadcast, promote, transmit, circulate, disseminate, promulgate
2 = **reproduce**, increase, produce, generate, breed, multiply, engender, beget, procreate

propel verb = **drive**, force, launch, shoot, send, push, thrust, shove, impel

propensity noun = **tendency**, liability, bent, penchant, disposition, inclination, predisposition, proclivity

proper adjective 1 = **suitable**, appropriate, apt, right, fitting • *the proper course of action* OPPOSITE: improper
2 = **correct**, conventional, orthodox, accepted • *It seemed the proper thing to do.*
3 = **polite**, decent, respectable, gentlemanly, genteel, ladylike, decorous, mannerly, seemly See also: **fair**, **prim**

properly adverb 1 = **suitably**, appropriately, rightly, fittingly, aptly
2 = **correctly**, accurately
3 = **politely**, decently, respectably

property noun 1 = **possessions**, estate, assets, belongings, effects • *her personal property*
2 = **quality**, feature, attribute, characteristic, trait, hallmark • *Mint is said to have powerful healing properties.*
3 = **land**, estate, holding, freehold, real estate

prophecy noun = **prediction**, forecast, prognostication, augury, divination, second sight, soothsaying

prophesy verb = **predict**, forecast, foresee, divine, augur, foretell, prognosticate

prophet noun = **soothsayer**, forecaster, diviner, oracle, prophesier, seer, sibyl

prophetic adjective = **predictive**, prescient, oracular, prognostic, sibylline

propitious adjective = **favourable**, happy, bright, lucky, promising, fortunate, auspicious, encouraging

proportion noun 1 = **part**, share,

P

percentage, segment, quota • *a tiny proportion of the population*
2 = relative amount, relationship, ratio
3 = balance, correspondence, harmony, symmetry, congruity
▷ **proportions = dimensions**, size, capacity, volume, extent, expanse
See also: **measure**

proportional, proportionate *adjective* = **corresponding**, even, consistent, balanced, compatible, equitable, commensurate, in proportion

proposal *noun* = **suggestion**, plan, offer, program, bid, project, recommendation, scheme, presentation

propose *verb* **1 = put forward**, suggest, advance, present, submit
2 = nominate, name, present, recommend
3 = intend, plan, mean, aim, design, scheme, have in mind
4 = offer marriage, ask for someone's hand *or* ask for someone's hand in marriage, pop the question (*informal*)

proposition *noun* **1 = proposal**, plan, recommendation, scheme, suggestion
▷ *verb* **2 = make a pass at**, solicit, accost, make an improper suggestion

propound *verb* = **put forward**, suggest, propose, advance, present, submit, postulate

proprietor, proprietress *noun* = **owner**, landlord *or* landlady, titleholder

propriety *noun* **1 = correctness**, fitness, aptness, rightness, seemliness
2 = decorum, courtesy, decency, etiquette, respectability, politeness, manners, seemliness

propulsion *noun* = **propelling force**, drive, push, thrust, impulse, impetus

prosaic *adjective* = **dull**, routine, ordinary, everyday, pedestrian, boring, mundane, matter-

of-fact, trite, unimaginative, humdrum

proscribe *verb* **1 = prohibit**, ban, forbid, embargo, interdict
2 = outlaw, deport, exclude, exile, expel, banish, expatriate, ostracize

prosecute *verb* (*Law*) = **take to court**, try, sue, indict, arraign, litigate, bring to trial, put on trial

prospect *noun* **1 = expectation**, hope, promise, outlook • *There was no prospect of going home.*
2 (*sometimes plural*) = **likelihood**, chance, possibility
3 = view, scene, outlook, sight, landscape, spectacle, vista
▷ *verb* **4 = look for**, seek, search for
See also: **probability**

prospective *adjective* = **future**, likely, possible, potential, anticipated, imminent, forthcoming, intended, coming, destined, expected

prospects See **outlook**

prospectus *noun* = **catalogue**, program, list, outline, synopsis, syllabus

prosper *verb* = **succeed**, advance, progress, thrive, flourish, do well, get on

prosperity *noun* = **success**, plenty, luxury, wealth, fortune, affluence, riches, good fortune, prosperousness

prosperous *adjective* **1 = wealthy**, rich, affluent, well-heeled (*informal*), well-off, well-to-do, moneyed
2 = successful, lucky, fortunate, booming, doing well, flourishing, thriving

prostitute *noun* **1 = whore**, ho (*slang*), hooker (*slang*), call girl, fallen woman, harlot, loose woman, tart (*informal*), streetwalker, strumpet, trollop
▷ *verb* **2 = cheapen**, degrade, demean, profane, devalue, pervert, debase, misapply

prostrate *adjective* **1 = prone**, flat, horizontal
2 = exhausted, overcome,

depressed, dejected, desolate, spent, inconsolable, drained, worn out
▶ *verb* **3** = **exhaust**, tire, drain, fatigue, weary, sap, wear out
▷ **prostrate oneself** = **bow down to**, kneel, abase oneself, fall at (someone's) feet, grovel, kiss ass (*slang*), kowtow

protagonist *noun* **1** = **supporter**, champion, advocate, exponent
2 = **leading character**, hero or heroine, principal, central character

protect *verb* = **keep safe**, defend, guard, shelter, shield, safeguard
• *Bank tellers are protected by security barrier shields.*
See also: **save, take care of**

protected *adjective* = **safe**, secure, immune

protection *noun* **1** = **safeguard**, cover, shelter, barrier, buffer
• *a diet believed to offer protection against some diseases*
2 = **safety**, security, care, custody, safeguard, defense, safekeeping, protecting, aegis
See also: **defence, precaution**

protective *adjective* = **protecting**, defensive, vigilant, watchful, maternal, paternal, motherly, fatherly

protector *noun* = **defender**, champion, guard, patron, bodyguard, guardian

protest *verb* **1** = **object**, complain, disagree, disapprove, oppose
• *She protested that the new hours of work were unfair.*
2 = **assert**, declare, maintain, insist, affirm, profess, attest, avow
▶ *noun* **3** = **objection**, complaint, outcry • *The council has ignored their protests by granting a building permit.*
See also: **agitate, grumble**

protestation *noun*
= **declaration**, vow, profession, affirmation, avowal

protester *noun* = **demonstrator**, rebel, agitator

protocol *noun* = **code of behaviour**, etiquette, decorum,

conventions, customs, manners, propriety

prototype *noun* = **original**, first, type, standard, model, example, pattern

protracted *adjective* = **extended**, prolonged, drawn-out, dragged out, long-drawn-out, spun out

protrude *verb* = **stick out**, project, extend, bulge, jut, come through, obtrude, stand out

protrusion *noun* = **protuberance**, bump, projection, lump, bulge, outgrowth

protuberance *noun* = **bulge**, process, bump, lump, prominence, hump, knob, excrescence, outgrowth, protrusion, swelling

proud *adjective* **1** = **satisfied**, pleased, gratified, honoured • *I was proud of our players today.*
2 = **conceited**, arrogant, boastful, imperious, disdainful, haughty, lordly, overbearing, self-satisfied, snobbish, supercilious
See also: **stuck-up, vain**

prove *verb* **1** = **verify**, confirm, establish, demonstrate, ascertain • *History will prove him to have been right all along.*
OPPOSITE: disprove
2 = **test**, try, check, examine, analyze, assay
3 = **turn out**, result, come out, end up
▷ **prove false** See **disprove**
See also: **show**

proven *adjective* = **verified**, reliable, established, definite, proved, attested, confirmed, tested

proverb *noun* = **saying**, saw, adage, maxim, dictum

proverbial *adjective*
= **conventional**, current, traditional, famous, famed, legendary, typical, notorious, well-known, acknowledged, axiomatic

provide *verb* **1** = **supply**, contribute, equip, outfit, furnish
• *I'll be glad to provide a copy of this.*

P

2 = **give**, add, bring, serve, produce, present, afford, lend, yield, render, impart
▷ **provide for, provide against** = **take precautions against**, anticipate, forearm, plan ahead, plan for, prepare for
▷ **provide for** = **support**, keep, maintain, sustain, care for, take care of
See also: **issue**

providence noun = **fate**, fortune, destiny

provident adjective **1** = **thrifty**, prudent, economical, frugal
2 = **foresighted**, careful, cautious, vigilant, wise, shrewd, discreet, well-prepared, far-seeing, forearmed

providential adjective = **lucky**, happy, fortunate, timely, opportune, fortuitous, heaven-sent

provider noun **1** = **supplier**, source, donor, giver
2 = **breadwinner**, supporter, earner, wage earner

providing, provided conjunction = **on condition that**, given, as long as

province noun **1** = **region**, division, department, zone, district, section, patch, domain, colony
2 = **area**, business, concern, line, role, field, duty, responsibility, capacity, function, sphere

provincial adjective **1** = **rural**, country, local, rustic, homespun, hick (informal)
2 = **narrow-minded**, limited, narrow, small-town, insular, parochial, inward-looking, small-minded, unsophisticated
▶ noun **3** = **yokel**, country cousin, hayseed, rustic, hick (informal)

provision noun **1** = **supplying**, furnishing, catering, providing, equipping
2 = **condition**, term, demand, requirement, rider, clause, stipulation, proviso

provisional adjective
1 = **temporary**, interim

2 = **conditional**, tentative, limited, contingent, qualified

provisions plural noun = **food**, fare, edibles, foodstuff, comestibles, eatables, rations, stores, supplies, victuals

proviso noun = **condition**, requirement, rider, clause, qualification, stipulation

provocation noun **1** = **cause**, reason, motivation, stimulus, incitement, grounds
2 = **offence**, injury, challenge, insult, dare, taunt, grievance, indignity, affront, annoyance

provocative adjective
= **offensive**, galling, annoying, goading, insulting, provoking, stimulating

provoke verb **1** = **anger**, insult, annoy, irritate, tease, enrage, goad • I didn't want to do anything to provoke him.
2 = **cause**, produce, prompt, evoke, spark, rouse, set off
• His comments have provoked an unexpected response.
See also: **bring about, excite, incite, motivate, occasion**

prowess noun **1** = **skill**, talent, excellence, accomplishment, expertise, mastery, genius, adeptness, aptitude
2 = **bravery**, courage, daring, heroism, mettle, fearlessness, valiance, valor

prowl verb = **move stealthily**, steal, sneak, stalk, slink, skulk

proximity noun = **nearness**, closeness

proxy noun = **representative**, agent, factor, deputy, delegate, substitute

prudence noun = **common sense**, care, caution, judgment, wisdom, discretion, vigilance, wariness, good sense

prudent adjective **1** = **sensible**, careful, cautious, wary, vigilant, wise, shrewd, discreet, politic, judicious, discerning
2 = **thrifty**, careful, economical, frugal, canny, far-sighted, provident, sparing

prudish adjective = **prim**, proper,

Victorian, stuffy, starchy (*informal*), puritanical, old-maidish (*informal*), overmodest, priggish, prissy (*informal*), strait-laced

prune *verb* = **cut**, reduce, shape, clip, trim, dock, shorten, snip

pry *verb* = **be inquisitive**, interfere, snoop (*informal*), intrude, poke your nose in (*informal*) • *We do not want people prying into our business.*

prying *adjective* = **inquisitive**, curious, interfering, meddlesome, meddling, nosy (*informal*), snooping (*informal*), spying

psalm *noun* = **hymn**, chant

pseudo- *adjective* = **false**, fake, artificial, mock, phony (*informal*), sham, imitation, spurious, pretended

pseudonym *noun* = **false name**, alias, assumed name, incognito, nom de plume, pen name

psyche *noun* = **soul**, mind, spirit, personality, self, individuality, anima

psychiatrist *noun* = **psychotherapist**, analyst, shrink (*slang*), psychologist, therapist, psychoanalyst, headshrinker (*slang*)

psychic *adjective*
1 = **supernatural**, occult, mystic
2 = **mental**, psychological, spiritual

psychological *adjective*
1 = **mental**, intellectual, cerebral
2 = **imaginary**, irrational, unreal, all in the mind, psychosomatic

psychology *noun*
1 = **behaviourism**, science of mind, study of personality
2 = **way of thinking**, attitude, mental make-up, mental processes, thought processes, what makes one tick

psychopath *noun* = **madman**, lunatic, maniac, headcase (*informal*), nutcase (*slang*), psychotic, sociopath, sickie (*informal*), sicko (*informal*)

psychotic *adjective* = **mad**, insane, loony (*informal*), lunatic, demented, certifiable, deranged, unbalanced, non compos mentis (*Latin*)

pub *noun* (*Informal*) = **tavern**, bar, inn, brasserie (*Canad Queb*), public house

puberty *noun* = **adolescence**, pubescence, teens

public *noun* 1 = **people**, nation, society, populace, masses • *the public's confidence in health care*
▶ *adjective* 2 = **general**, popular, civic, universal • *public support for the idea*
3 = **communal**, community, universal, open to the public • *public transit*
OPPOSITE: private
4 = **well-known**, important, prominent, respected
5 = **plain**, patent, obvious, overt, acknowledged, known

publication *noun* 1 = **pamphlet**, issue, title, newspaper, magazine, brochure, leaflet, periodical
2 = **announcement**, disclosure, declaration, proclamation, notification, broadcasting, publishing, reporting

publicity *noun* = **advertising**, promotion, plug (*informal*) • *The book's publicity campaign included television and newspaper interviews.*

publicize *verb* = **advertise**, promote, plug (*informal*) • *The author appeared on TV to publicize her book.*

public-spirited *adjective* = **altruistic**, humanitarian, charitable, philanthropic, unselfish

publish *verb* 1 = **bring out**, print • *We publish a range of titles.*
2 = **announce**, broadcast, reveal, spread, advertise, disclose, circulate, proclaim, publicize, divulge
See also: **release**

pucker *verb* 1 = **wrinkle**, contract, gather, tighten, crease, purse, knit, draw together, screw up
▶ *noun* 2 = **wrinkle**, fold, crease

P

pudgy *adjective* = **tubby**, fat, plump, chubby, stout, rotund, dumpy, roly-poly

puerile *adjective* = **childish**, silly, juvenile, foolish, immature, trivial, babyish

puff *noun* **1** = **blast**, draft, breath, gust, whiff
2 = **smoke**, pull, drag (*slang*)
▶ *verb* **3** = **blow**, breathe, pant, wheeze, gasp, exhale, gulp
4 = **smoke**, draw, drag (*slang*), suck, inhale, pull at *or* pull on
5 (usually with *up*) = **swell**, expand, inflate, bloat, dilate, distend

puffed up *See* **pompous**

puffy *adjective* = **swollen**, enlarged, bloated, distended, puffed up

pugilist *noun* = **boxer**, fighter, prizefighter

pugnacious *adjective* = **aggressive**, combative, belligerent, hot-tempered, quarrelsome

pull *verb* **1** = **draw**, drag, haul, yank, tow, tug • *a wooden plough pulled by oxen*
OPPOSITE: push
2 = **strain**, tear, stretch, rip, sprain, dislocate, wrench
3 = **extract**, pick, remove, gather, pluck, uproot, draw out, take out
▷ **pull back** *See* **retreat**
▷ **pull down** = **demolish**, remove, destroy, raze, bulldoze
▷ **pull off** = **succeed**, manage, accomplish, carry out, do the trick
▷ **pull out** = **withdraw**, leave, quit, evacuate, retreat, depart
▷ **pull through** = **survive**, rally, recover, get better
▷ **pull together** *See* **co-operate, unite**
▷ **pull up** = **stop**, halt, brake
▶ *noun* **4** = **attraction**, lure, magnetism • *The pull of Mexico was too strong to resist.*
5 = **tug**, yank, jerk, twitch
6 = **puff**, drag (*slang*), inhalation
7 (*Informal*) = **influence**, power, weight, muscle, clout (*informal*)
See also: **attract**

| INFORMALLY SPEAKING
| **pull down**: receive as a salary
| **pull for**: give help to
| **pull off**: successfully complete

pulp *noun* **1** = **paste**, mash, mush
2 = **flesh**, soft part
▶ *verb* **3** = **crush**, squash, mash, pulverize
▶ *adjective* **4** = **cheap**, lurid, trashy, rubbishy

pulsate *verb* = **throb**, beat, pound, thump, pulse, quiver, palpitate

pulse *noun* **1** = **beat**, beating, rhythm, vibration, throb, pulsation, throbbing
▶ *verb* **2** = **beat**, vibrate, throb, pulsate

pulverize *verb* **1** = **crush**, pound, mill, grind, granulate
2 = **defeat**, destroy, crush, smash, wreck, demolish, flatten, annihilate

pummel *verb* = **beat**, strike, pound, batter, hammer, punch, thump

pump *verb* **1** (often with *into*) = **drive**, force, send, push, supply, pour, inject
2 = **interrogate**, probe, quiz, cross-examine

pun *noun* = **play on words**, quip, double entendre, witticism

punch[1] *verb* **1** = **hit**, strike, box, smash, belt (*informal*), pummel, sock (*slang*), bop (*informal*)
▶ *noun* **2** = **blow**, hit, wallop (*informal*), sock (*slang*), jab, bop (*informal*)
3 (*Informal*) = **effectiveness**, drive, impact, bite, vigour, verve, forcefulness

punch[2] *verb* = **pierce**, cut, drill, stamp, bore, puncture, prick, perforate

punctilious *adjective* = **particular**, nice, formal, strict, proper, exact, precise, meticulous, fussy, finicky

punctual *adjective* = **on time**, prompt, in good time • *The most punctual airline last year was Swissair.*

punctuality *noun* = **promptness**, readiness, promptitude

punctuate *verb* **1** = **interrupt**,

break, pepper, sprinkle, intersperse
2 = emphasize, stress, underline, accentuate

PUNCTUATION MARKS

apostrophe
asterisk
bracket
colon
comma
dash
exclamation mark
hyphen
period
question mark
quotation marks
semicolon

---

puncture noun **1 = hole**, break, cut, damage, opening, leak, nick, slit
2 = flat tire, flat
▶ verb **3 = pierce**, cut, penetrate, bore, rupture, nick, prick, perforate

pungent adjective **= strong**, hot, sharp, bitter, sour, spicy, tart, acrid, peppery, piquant

punish verb **= discipline**, sentence, penalize, grounded, rap someone's knuckles, throw the book at, lower the boom (slang) • *The child was punished for teasing the puppy.*

punishable adjective **= culpable**, criminal, indictable, blameworthy

punishing adjective **= hard**, arduous, strenuous, gruelling, backbreaking, exhausting, taxing, tiring, wearing

punishment noun **= penalty**, retribution • *a punishment that fits the crime*

punitive adjective **= retaliatory**, in reprisal, retaliative

punt verb **1 = bet**, back, lay, stake, gamble, wager
▶ noun **2 = bet**, stake, gamble, wager

punter noun **1 = gambler**, backer, better
2 (*Informal*) **= person**, man in the street

puny adjective **= feeble**, weak, skinny, frail, sickly • *It's hard to believe he was a puny child.*

pupil noun **= learner**, student, novice, beginner, schoolboy or schoolgirl, disciple

puppet noun **1 = marionette**, doll, ventriloquist's dummy
2 = pawn, tool, instrument, mouthpiece, stooge, cat's-paw

purchase verb **1 = buy**, get, score (slang), gain, acquire, obtain, come by, pay for, pick up
▶ noun **2 = buy**, gain, investment, property, acquisition, asset, possession
3 = grip, hold, support, leverage, foothold

purchaser See **customer**

pure adjective **1 = clean**, spotless, germ-free, pasteurized, sterilized • *The water is pure enough to drink.*
OPPOSITE: impure
2 = complete, absolute, outright, utter, sheer, unmitigated • *a matter of pure luck*
3 = unmixed, real, straight, natural, simple, genuine, authentic, neat, flawless, unalloyed
4 = innocent, modest, impeccable, chaste, virtuous, blameless, uncorrupted, unsullied, virginal
See also: **refined**

purely adverb **= absolutely**, just, only, simply, completely, entirely, merely, exclusively, solely, wholly

purge verb **1 = get rid of**, remove, expel, eradicate, exterminate, do away with, wipe out
▶ noun **2 = removal**, elimination, eradication, ejection, expulsion

purified See **clean, refined**

purify verb **1 = clean**, wash, refine, clarify, sanitize, cleanse, disinfect, decontaminate, detoxify

P

2 = **absolve**, redeem, cleanse, sanctify

purist noun = **stickler**, formalist, pedant

puritan noun **1** = **moralist**, fanatic, zealot, prude, rigorist
▶ adjective **2** = **strict**, severe, austere, narrow-minded, ascetic, moralistic, prudish, strait-laced

puritanical adjective = **strict**, severe, proper, austere, narrow-minded, ascetic, prudish, puritan, strait-laced

purity noun **1** = **cleanness**, cleanliness, faultlessness, immaculateness, pureness, wholesomeness
2 = **innocence**, integrity, honesty, virtue, decency, virginity, chastity, chasteness, virtuousness

purloin verb = **steal**, appropriate, filch, pinch (informal), swipe (slang), pilfer, thieve

---

SHADES OF PURPLE

amethyst	lilac
aubergine	magenta
gentian	mauve
heather	mulberry
heliotrope	plum
indigo	puce
lavender	violet

---

purport verb **1** = **claim**, allege, assert, profess
▶ noun **2** = **significance**, idea, import, implication, drift, meaning, gist

purpose noun **1** = **reason**, point, aim, function, object, intention • What is the purpose of this meeting?
2 = **aim**, plan, end, goal, hope, wish, object, intention, desire, ambition
3 = **determination**, will, resolution, resolve, persistence, tenacity, firmness, single-mindedness

▷ **on purpose** = **deliberately**, knowingly, intentionally, purposely, by design • Did you do that on purpose?
See also: **use**

purposeful See **determined**

purposeless adjective
= **pointless**, empty, unnecessary, senseless, needless, aimless, motiveless, uncalled-for

purposely adverb = **deliberately**, knowingly, intentionally, consciously, expressly, on purpose, with intent

purse noun **1** = **pouch**, wallet, money-bag
2 = **funds**, money, wealth, means, treasury, exchequer, resources
▶ verb **3** = **pucker**, contract, tighten, pout, press together

pursue verb **1** = **follow**, track, dog, hunt, chase, shadow, tail (informal), hound, stalk, hunt down, run after
2 = **try for**, seek, desire, aim for, strive for, work towards
3 = **engage in**, perform, conduct, practise, carry on
4 = **continue**, maintain, proceed, carry on, keep on, persevere in, persist in

pursuit noun **1** = **pursuing**, search, hunt, chase, quest, seeking, trailing
2 = **occupation**, interest, line, activity, pleasure, hobby, pastime

purvey verb = **supply**, sell, provide, cater, furnish, deal in, trade in

push verb **1** = **shove**, press, thrust, ram • She pushed the door open. OPPOSITE: pull
2 = **urge**, press, encourage, persuade • They tried to push me into playing street hockey.
3 = **make one's way** or **force one's way**, move, shoulder, elbow, squeeze, thrust, shove, jostle
▶ noun **4** = **shove**, butt, nudge, thrust
5 = **drive**, go (informal), energy, initiative, ambition, enterprise,

vitality, dynamism, vigour
See also: **advertise**, **agitate**,
campaign, **rush**, **stick**, **stuff**

> **INFORMALLY SPEAKING**
> **push around**: treat roughly or
> with contempt
> **pushed for**: limited by some
> lack
> **push for**: promote strongly

pushed *adjective* (often *with for*)
= **short of**, hurried, pressed,
rushed, under pressure

pushover *noun* **1** = **child's play**
(*informal*), breeze (*informal*), cinch
(*slang*), picnic (*informal*), piece
of cake (*informal*), plain sailing,
walkover (*informal*) • *Last night's
playoff certainly was no pushover.*
2 = **sucker** (*slang*), mug (*Brit
slang*), easy game (*informal*), easy
mark or soft mark (*informal*),
walkover (*informal*)

pushy *adjective* (*informal*)
= **forceful**, forward, aggressive,
ambitious, assertive, bossy,
obtrusive • *a pushy salesperson*

puss See **cat**

pussy See **cat**

pussycat See **cat**

pussyfoot *verb* = **hedge**,
beat about the bush, be
noncommittal, equivocate, hum
and haw, prevaricate, sit on the
fence

put *verb* **1** = **place**, position,
rest, lay, deposit • *She put the
photograph on the desk.*
2 = **express**, word, phrase • *I think
you put that very well.*
See also: **insert**, **pose**, **set**, **stick**

▷ **put across** = **communicate**,
explain, convey, get across, make
clear, make oneself understood

▷ **put aside**, **put by** = **save**, store,
deposit, stockpile, lay by

▷ **put away** = **save**, keep, deposit,
put by; = **lock up**, commit,
certify, institutionalize;
= **consume**, gobble, devour,
eat up, wolf down; = **put back**,
replace, tidy away • *Now it's time
to put your toys away.*

▷ **put back** See **postpone**, **put
off**

▷ **put by** See **reserve**, **save**

▷ **put down** = **humiliate**,
criticize, belittle, find fault
• *Racist jokes come from wanting
to put down other people;* = **put to
sleep**, kill, destroy, put out of its
misery • *The judge ordered the dog to
be put down immediately;* = **record**,
enter, set down, take down,
write down; = **stamp out**, crush,
quash, quell, suppress, repress;
(usually *with to*) = **attribute**,
ascribe, impute, set down
See also: **attack**, **insult**

▷ **put forward** = **recommend**,
suggest, propose, advance,
nominate, submit, tender

▷ **put off** = **postpone**, delay,
defer, reschedule, put back, put
on ice • *The House of Commons has
put off the vote until next month;*
= **disconcert**, throw (*informal*),
confuse, dismay, unsettle, faze,
discomfit, nonplus, perturb;
= **discourage**, dishearten,
dissuade

▷ **put on** = **don**, dress, change
into, get dressed in, slip into;
= **fake**, affect, assume, pretend,
simulate, sham, feign;
= **present**, do, show, stage,
produce, mount; = **add**, gain,
increase by

▷ **put out** = **annoy**, anger, irk,
irritate, vex, exasperate, nettle;
= **extinguish**, douse, quench,
blow out; = **inconvenience**,
trouble, bother, discomfit,
discommode, impose upon,
incommode

▷ **put through** See **subject**

▷ **put to sleep** See **hypnotize**,
put down

▷ **put together** See **assemble**,
construct

▷ **put up** = **build**, raise,
construct, erect, fabricate;
= **accommodate**, board, house,
lodge, take in; = **nominate**, offer,
propose, present, recommend,
submit, put forward

▷ **put up with** = **stand**, bear,
stomach, tolerate, abide, brook,
countenance, stand for • *They
won't put up with a return to the bad
old days.*

putrid *adjective* = **rotten**, bad, decayed, decomposed, rancid, putrefied, rotting, spoiled

putter *verb* = **mess around**, dabble, dawdle, tinker, monkey around (*informal*)

puzzle *verb* **1** = **perplex**, confuse, baffle, stump, mystify, bewilder
• *There was something about her that puzzled me.*
▶ *noun* **2** = **problem**, riddle, brainteaser • *a crossword puzzle*
See also: **mystery, wonder**

puzzled *adjective* = **perplexed**, lost, confused, at a loss, at sea, baffled, bewildered, mystified

puzzlement *noun* = **perplexity**, doubt, confusion, bewilderment, bafflement, mystification

puzzling *adjective* = **perplexing**, involved, enigmatic, incomprehensible, abstruse, baffling, bewildering, mystifying

P

Qq

quack *noun* = **charlatan**, fraud, fake, phony (*informal*), impostor, pretender, humbug, mountebank

quaff *verb* = **drink**, down, swallow, gulp, imbibe, swig (*informal*)

quagmire *noun* = **bog**, swamp, mire, marsh, slough, morass, fen, quicksand

quail *verb* = **cringe**, shrink, falter, flinch, shudder, recoil, blanch, cower, blench, have cold feet (*informal*)

quaint *adjective* **1** = **unusual**, odd, bizarre, curious, old-fashioned, eccentric, peculiar, fanciful, queer, droll, strange, singular
2 = **old-fashioned**, picturesque, antiquated, old-world

quake *verb* = **shake**, move, rock, shiver, vibrate, tremble, shudder, quiver

qualification *noun*
1 = **capability**, quality, ability, skill, achievement, accomplishment • *Her qualifications are impressive.*
2 = **condition**, exception, reservation, modification • *The argument is not true without qualification.*

qualified *adjective* **1** = **capable**, expert, able, fit, efficient, experienced, competent, trained, adept, proficient, skilful, practised
2 = **restricted**, limited, contingent, conditional, provisional, modified, reserved, bounded, confined

qualify *verb* **1** = **be certified**, graduate, become licensed • *She qualified as a doctor 20 years ago.*
2 = **restrict**, reduce, limit, ease, regulate, moderate, soften, diminish, temper, restrain, lessen
See also: **pass**

quality *noun* **1** = **standard**, value, worth, grade, merit, distinction, calibre • *The quality of food is very poor.*
2 = **characteristic**, mark, feature, property, aspect, trait • *These qualities are essential for success.*
3 = **nature**, make, kind, character, sort
See also: **attribute, point, qualification**

qualm *noun* = **misgiving**, doubt, anxiety, apprehension, hesitation, uneasiness, compunction, disquiet, scruple, twinge of conscience *or* pang of conscience

quandary *noun* = **difficulty**, Catch-22, puzzle, plight, impasse, dilemma, strait, predicament

quantities *See* **lot**

quantity *noun* **1** = **amount**, part, number, sum • *a large quantity of candy*
2 = **size**, measure, volume, extent • *emphasis on quality rather than quantity*
See also: **lot**

quarrel *noun* **1** = **argument**, fight, dispute, row, feud, disagreement, squabble • *I had a terrible quarrel with my brother.*
▶ *verb* **2** = **argue**, fight, clash, squabble, bicker • *My brother quarrelled with my cousin.*

quarrelsome *adjective* = **argumentative**, contentious, combative, belligerent, pugnacious, disputatious

quarry noun = **prey**, game, goal, victim, aim, objective, prize

quarter noun 1 = **district**, part, place, province, area, side, region, zone, neighbourhood, locality
2 = **mercy**, compassion, clemency, forgiveness, pity, leniency
▶ verb 3 = **accommodate**, post, place, board, house, station, lodge, billet

quarters plural noun = **lodgings**, residence, dwelling, abode, habitation, barracks, billet, chambers, rooms

quash verb 1 = **annul**, cancel, reverse, revoke, overthrow, rescind, overrule, invalidate
2 = **suppress**, beat, crush, subdue, quell, overthrow, squash, repress, put down

quasi- adjective = **pseudo-**, so-called, would-be, apparent, seeming, semi-

quaver verb 1 = **tremble**, shake, quake, waver, flutter, flicker, vibrate, quiver
▶ noun 2 = **trembling**, shake, vibration, tremor, tremble, quiver

queasy adjective 1 = **sick**, ill, nauseous, unwell • *He already felt queasy.*
2 = **uneasy**, troubled, anxious, uncertain, worried, restless, fidgety, ill at ease

queen noun 1 = **sovereign**, monarch, ruler, consort
2 = **star**, model, ideal, mistress

queer adjective 1 = **strange**, odd, unusual, funny, extraordinary, weird, curious, abnormal, uncommon, peculiar, droll
2 = **faint**, dizzy, giddy, light-headed, queasy

quell verb 1 = **suppress**, defeat, overcome, crush, overpower, quash, subdue, conquer, vanquish, put down
2 = **calm**, quiet, appease, allay, soothe, pacify, assuage, mollify

quench verb 1 = **satisfy**, appease, allay, sate, satiate, slake
2 = **put out**, crush, stifle,

suppress, douse, smother, extinguish

querulous adjective = **complaining**, critical, dissatisfied, captious, carping, discontented, fault-finding, grumbling, peevish, whining

query noun 1 = **question**, problem, inquiry, doubt, suspicion, objection
▶ verb 2 = **doubt**, suspect, challenge, dispute, distrust, mistrust, disbelieve
3 = **ask**, question, inquire or enquire

quest noun = **search**, mission, hunt, journey, adventure, expedition, enterprise, crusade

question noun 1 = **inquiry**, query • *If you have any questions, please contact us.*
OPPOSITE: response
2 = **issue**, point, motion, subject, topic • *Can we get back to the question of the car?*
3 = **difficulty**, problem, dispute, doubt, controversy, argument, contention, query
▷ **in question** = **under discussion**, at issue, in doubt, open to debate
▷ **out of the question** = **impossible**, unthinkable, inconceivable
▶ verb 4 = **dispute**, challenge, query, object to • *No one questioned my decision.*
5 = **interrogate**, probe, examine, quiz • *A man is being questioned by police.*
OPPOSITE: answer
6 = **doubt**, suspect, dispute, distrust • *She questioned his ability to do his job.*
See also: **affair, ask, business, contest, matter**

questionable adjective = **dubious**, controversial, debatable, suspect, suspicious, doubtful, moot, iffy (*informal*), sketchy (*informal*)

queue noun = **line**, file, series, train, chain, string, sequence

quibble verb 1 = **split hairs**, carp, cavil

▶ noun **2 = objection**, complaint, criticism, cavil, nicety, niggle

quick adjective **1 = fast**, rapid, speedy, swift, brisk, hasty • *You'll have to be quick to catch the flight.*
OPPOSITE: slow
2 = brief, fast, hurried, cursory, perfunctory • *a quick chat*
OPPOSITE: long
3 = immediate, prompt, sudden, hasty • *a quick response*
4 = intelligent, alert, sharp, smart, bright (*informal*), acute, clever, shrewd, astute, perceptive, quick-witted
5 = deft, adept, skilful, adroit, dexterous
6 = excitable, passionate, testy, irritable, touchy, irascible
See also: **keen**

quicken verb **1 = speed up**, accelerate, hurry, expedite, hasten, precipitate, impel
2 = stimulate, inspire, revive, excite, incite, energize, arouse, invigorate, vitalize

quickly adverb **= swiftly**, fast, rapidly, hastily, hurriedly, speedily • *Stop me if I'm speaking too quickly.*
OPPOSITE: slowly

quick-tempered adjective **= hot-tempered**, fiery, irritable, irascible, choleric, quarrelsome, testy

quick-witted adjective **= clever**, alert, sharp, smart, bright (*informal*), keen, shrewd, astute, perceptive

quiet adjective **1 = silent**, low, soft, inaudible, hushed • *The children were quiet for a change.*
OPPOSITE: noisy
2 = calm, peaceful, mild, tranquil, serene, restful • *a quiet evening at home*
3 = undisturbed, private, isolated, secluded, sequestered, unfrequented
4 = reserved, mild, shy, gentle, sedate, meek, retiring
▶ noun **5 = peace**, silence, serenity, tranquility, calmness, stillness • *The teacher called for quiet.*

OPPOSITE: noise
See also: **easy, sleepy**

quieten verb **1 = silence**, still, stop, quiet, stifle, compose, subdue, quell, mute, hush, muffle
2 = soothe, calm, blunt, dull, appease, allay, deaden

quietly adverb **1 = silently**, softly, in an undertone, inaudibly, in silence, mutely, noiselessly
2 = calmly, patiently, mildly, serenely, placidly

quietness noun **= peace**, quiet, silence, calm, hush, stillness, tranquillity

quilt noun **= bedspread**, comforter, duvet, continental quilt, counterpane, coverlet, eiderdown

quintessence noun **= essence**, spirit, soul, distillation

quintessential adjective **= ultimate**, typical, definitive, prototypical, archetypal

quip noun **= joke**, jest, retort, wisecrack (*informal*), gibe, pleasantry, riposte, sally, witticism

quirk noun **= peculiarity**, habit, oddity, characteristic, trait, kink, aberration, foible, mannerism, eccentricity, idiosyncrasy

quirky adjective **= odd**, unusual, eccentric, peculiar, offbeat, idiosyncratic

quit verb **1 = resign**, leave, retire • *He quit his job at the pizza place.*
2 = stop, discontinue, give up • *Let's just quit talking about it.*

quite adverb **1 = somewhat**, rather, fairly, reasonably, moderately • *He is quite old.*
2 = absolutely, completely, fully, totally, entirely, perfectly • *The dog lay quite still.*
3 = truly, really, in fact, in reality, in truth
See also: **exactly, pretty**

quiver verb **1 = shake**, quake, shiver, vibrate, tremble, shudder, oscillate, quaver
▶ noun **2 = shake**, vibration, tremor, shiver, tremble, shudder, oscillation

q

quixotic *adjective* = **unrealistic**, romantic, impractical, fanciful, dreamy, idealistic

quiz *noun* 1 = **examination**, test, investigation, questioning
▶ *verb* 2 = **question**, ask, investigate, examine, interrogate

quizzical *adjective* = **mocking**, arch, sardonic, questioning, teasing

quota *noun* = **share**, part, portion, slice, assignment, allowance, ration

quotation *noun* 1 = **passage**, quote (*informal*), reference, extract, excerpt, citation
2 (*Commerce*) = **estimate**, charge, price, rate, figure, quote (*informal*), tender, costing

quote *verb* = **repeat**, cite, extract, recite • *She quoted a great line from Shakespeare.*
See also: **estimate**

q

Rr

rabble noun = **mob**, crowd, herd, swarm, throng, horde, canaille

rabid adjective **1** = **fanatical**, extreme, irrational, zealous, fervent, narrow-minded
2 = **mad**, hydrophobic

race¹ noun **1** = **contest**, competition, chase, pursuit, rivalry, dash
▶ verb **2** = **run**, fly, speed, tear, dash, hurry • *She raced out of the house.*
See also: **rush**

race² noun = **people**, nation, ethnic group • *Discrimination on the grounds of race is illegal.*

racial adjective = **ethnic**, national, genetic, folk, tribal, ethnological, genealogical

racism *See* **prejudice**

rack noun **1** = **frame**, stand, structure, framework
▶ verb **2** = **torture**, pain, afflict, harrow, oppress, agonize, torment, crucify

racket noun **1** = **noise**, clamour, commotion, din, hubbub, rumpus • *The racket went on past midnight.*
2 = **fraud**, scam, scheme, con (*informal*), enterprise • *an investment racket*
See also: **sound**

racy adjective **1** = **risqué**, blue, naughty, bawdy, suggestive, smutty
2 = **lively**, exciting, animated, energetic, sparkling, spirited, entertaining

radiance noun **1** = **happiness**, delight, joy, pleasure, warmth, rapture, gaiety
2 = **brightness**, light, shine, glow, glare, brilliance, gleam, lustre

radiant adjective **1** = **happy**, ecstatic, delighted, glowing, joyful, joyous, blissful, on cloud nine (*informal*), rapturous
2 = **bright**, brilliant, glowing, luminous, gleaming, glittering, lustrous, shining

radiate verb **1** = **spread out**, issue, diverge, branch out
2 = **emit**, spread, pour, shed, scatter, diffuse, give off *or* give out, send out

radical adjective
1 = **fundamental**, natural, basic, profound, innate, deep-seated
2 = **extreme**, complete, entire, severe, extremist, thorough, drastic, fanatical, sweeping
▶ noun **3** = **extremist**, militant, revolutionary, fanatic

raffle noun = **draw**, sweep, lottery, sweepstake

ragamuffin noun = **urchin**, guttersnipe

rage noun **1** = **fury**, anger, frenzy, wrath • *trembling with rage*
▶ verb **2** = **be furious**, storm, fume, rave, lose your temper • *He was raging at their lack of response.*
3 = **be at its height**, storm, surge, rampage • *The fire raged out of control.*
▷ **all the rage** = **in fashion**, trendy, fashionable, *du jour* (*French*), the latest thing, voguish, culty

ragged adjective **1** = **tattered**, shabby, in rags, in tatters, tatty, threadbare, torn, unkempt
2 = **rough**, rugged, uneven, unfinished, jagged, serrated

raging adjective = **furious**, mad, enraged, incensed, seething, raving, beside oneself, fuming, infuriated

r

rags *plural noun* = **tatters**, castoffs, old clothes, tattered clothing

raid *verb* **1** = **attack**, assault, invade, plunder, break into • *Soldiers raided the capital.*
▶ *noun* **2** = **attack**, break-in, foray • *Our raid on the kitchen provided enough food for the hike.*
See also: **loot**

raider *noun* = **attacker**, thief, robber, invader, marauder, plunderer

rail *See* **bar**

railing *noun* = **fence**, barrier, balustrade, paling, rails

rain *noun* **1** = **rainfall**, deluge, downpour, drizzle, showers • *A few drops of rain fell on her hand.*
▶ *verb* **2** = **pour**, drizzle, teem • *It rained the whole weekend.*
3 = **fall**, drop, deposit, shower, sprinkle

rainfall *See* **rain**

rainy *adjective* = **wet**, damp, drizzly, showery

raise *verb* **1** = **lift**, hoist, elevate, heave • *a drive to raise standards of literacy*
OPPOSITE: lower
2 = **bring up**, rear, nurture • *the house where she was raised*
3 = **mention**, advance, bring up, suggest, introduce, broach • *He had raised no objections at the time.*
4 = **increase**, boost, advance, strengthen, intensify, enhance, heighten, inflate, magnify, amplify, enlarge
5 = **collect**, rally, form, gather, mass, obtain, recruit, assemble • *They raised money for their work in Afghanistan.*
6 = **cause**, start, create, produce, occasion, provoke, originate, engender
See also: **breed**
┃ CONFUSABLES
┃ *Raise* means *lift up.*
┃ *Rise* means *get up* or *go up.*

rake¹ *verb* **1** = **gather**, remove, collect
2 = **search**, scrutinize, comb, scour

rake² *noun* = **libertine**, playboy, debauchee, lecher, roué

rakish *adjective* = **dashing**, dapper, jaunty, debonair, devil-may-care, raffish

rally *noun* **1** = **gathering**, meeting, convention, assembly, congress
2 = **recovery**, improvement, revival, recuperation
▶ *verb* **3** = **reassemble**, unite, regroup, reorganize
4 = **gather**, collect, unite, assemble, convene, muster, marshal, round up
5 = **recover**, improve, revive, recuperate, get better

ram *verb* **1** = **hit**, force, drive, crash, impact, smash, butt, dash
2 = **cram**, force, crowd, stuff, jam, thrust

ramble *verb* **1** = **walk**, range, wander, roam, stroll, stray, rove, saunter
2 = **babble**
▶ *noun* **3** = **walk**, tour, hike, stroll, saunter, roaming, roving

rambler *noun* = **walker**, rover, hiker, wanderer, wayfarer

rambling *adjective* = **long-winded**, incoherent, disjointed, disconnected, circuitous, digressive, discursive, wordy

ramification *noun*
▷ **ramifications** = **consequences**, sequel, upshot, developments, results

ramp *noun* = **slope**, rise, grade, incline, gradient

rampage *verb* = **go berserk**, rage, run amok, run riot • *children rampaging around the garden*
▶ *noun*
▷ **on the rampage** = **berserk**, wild, amok • *a wild animal on the rampage*
See also: **riot**

rampant *adjective*
1 = **widespread**, prevalent, unchecked, rife, uncontrolled, unrestrained, profuse, spreading like wildfire
2 (*Heraldry*) = **upright**, standing, erect, rearing

rampart *noun* = **defence**, wall, fence, bastion, fortification, bulwark

r

ramshackle adjective = **rickety**, unsafe, shaky, unsteady, derelict, flimsy, decrepit, crumbling, tumbledown

rancid adjective = **rotten**, bad, foul, fetid, rank, tainted, sour, stale, putrid, strong-smelling

rancorous See **bitter**

rancour noun = **hatred**, hate, animosity, bitterness, bad blood, ill feeling, ill will

random adjective = **chance**, spot, arbitrary, indiscriminate, haphazard, aimless • *random acts of kindness*
  ▷ **at random** = **haphazardly**, randomly, indiscriminately, arbitrarily, aimlessly • *chosen at random*
  See also: **absent-minded**, **accidental**, **irregular**

randomly See **at random**

randy adjective (Informal) = **lustful**, hot, amorous, horny (slang), aroused, lascivious, turned-on (slang)

range noun 1 = **limits**, province, field, extent, scope, bounds • *What is the range of your cellphone?*
  2 = **series**, class, variety, selection, assortment, gamut • *a wide range of colours*
  ▶ verb 3 = **vary**, go, run, extend, stretch • *items ranging between the everyday and the exotic*
  4 = **roam**, wander, rove, ramble, traverse
  See also: **area**, **choice**

rangy adjective = **long-limbed**, lanky, leggy, gangling, long-legged

rank[1] noun 1 = **status**, level, station, class, standing, grade, echelon • *She rose to the rank of captain.*
  2 = **row**, file, line, column • *ranks of police*
  ▷ **rank and file** = **general public**, majority, mass, masses
  ▶ verb 3 = **arrange**, order, sort, array, dispose, align, line up
  See also: **classify**, **rate**

rank[2] adjective 1 = **absolute**, complete, utter, sheer, downright, unmitigated • *It was rank stupidity to go there alone.*
  2 = **foul**, bad, offensive, funky (slang), noxious, smelly, rancid, disgusting, revolting, noisome, stinking
  3 = **abundant**, dense, lush, luxuriant, profuse

rankle verb = **annoy**, anger, irk, rile, irritate, gall, get on one's nerves (informal)

ransack verb 1 = **search**, explore, comb, scour, rummage, go through, turn inside out
  2 = **plunder**, raid, strip, loot, pillage

ransom noun = **payment**, price, money, payoff

rant verb = **shout**, cry, roar, yell, rave, declaim

rap verb 1 = **hit**, strike, knock, crack, tap
  ▷ **rap someone's knuckles** See **punish**
  ▶ noun 2 = **blow**, knock, crack, tap, clout (informal)
  3 (Slang) = **punishment**, blame, responsibility

rapacious adjective = **greedy**, predatory, voracious, insatiable, avaricious, grasping, preying

rape verb 1 = **sexually assault**, force, abuse, violate, outrage, ravish
  ▶ noun 2 = **sexual assault**, violation, outrage, ravishment
  3 = **desecration**, abuse, violation, defilement

rapid adjective = **quick**, fast, prompt, express, speedy, swift, brisk, hurried, hasty

rapidity noun = **speed**, rush, hurry, velocity, haste, quickness, alacrity, briskness, fleetness, promptness, swiftness

rapidly adverb = **quickly**, fast, promptly, swiftly, briskly, hastily, hurriedly, in haste, pronto (informal), speedily

rapport noun = **bond**, link, tie, relationship, understanding, sympathy, empathy, harmony, affinity

rapprochement noun = **reconciliation**, reunion, detente

r

rapt adjective = **spellbound**, absorbed, engrossed, enthralled, entranced, fascinated, gripped

rapture noun = **ecstasy**, transport, delight, joy, bliss, euphoria, rhapsody, seventh heaven

rapturous adjective = **ecstatic**, joyful, euphoric, blissful, in seventh heaven, overjoyed, over the moon (informal), transported

rare adjective 1 = **uncommon**, few, unusual, exceptional, scarce, sparse, sporadic • a rare species of bird
OPPOSITE: common
2 = **superb**, great, fine, choice, excellent, superlative, peerless
See also: **singular**

rarefied adjective = **exalted**, high, spiritual, elevated, lofty, noble, sublime

rarely adverb = **seldom**, hardly, infrequently, hardly ever

raring adjective
▷ **raring to** = **eager to**, desperate to, enthusiastic to, impatient to, keen to, longing to, ready to
▷ **raring to go** See **eager**

rarity noun 1 = **curio**, find, treasure, gem, collector's item
2 = **uncommonness**, shortage, scarcity, infrequency, sparseness, strangeness, unusualness

rascal noun = **rogue**, devil, good-for-nothing, imp, villain, scamp, scoundrel

rash[1] adjective = **reckless**, hasty, foolhardy, impulsive, impetuous • It would be rash to act on such flimsy evidence.
See also: **unwise**

rash[2] noun 1 = **outbreak**, eruption • I noticed a rash on my leg.
2 = **spate**, flood, wave, epidemic, plague • a rash of computer viruses

rashness noun = **recklessness**, indiscretion, carelessness, foolhardiness, hastiness, heedlessness, thoughtlessness

rasp See **scrape**

rasping See **hoarse**

rate noun 1 = **speed**, pace, frequency, velocity, tempo • appearing at the rate of one a week

2 = **charge**, price, cost, fee, tariff • cheap telephone rates
3 = **degree**, standard, scale, proportion, ratio
▷ **at any rate** = **in any case**, anyway, anyhow, at all events
▶ verb 4 = **evaluate**, consider, count, class, regard, rank, appraise • He was rated as one of the best.
5 = **deserve**, merit, be entitled to, be worthy of
See also: **grade, judge**
▷ **rate highly** See **appreciate, value**

| INFORMALLY SPEAKING
at any rate: under any circumstances
at this (or that) rate: under such circumstances

rather adverb 1 = **quite**, pretty, slightly, relatively, somewhat, fairly • We got along rather well.
2 = **preferably**, sooner, more readily, more willingly

ratify verb = **approve**, confirm, endorse, establish, sanction, uphold, authorize, affirm

rating noun = **position**, rate, order, class, status, rank, degree, grade, placing

ratio noun = **proportion**, rate, percentage, relation, fraction

ration noun 1 = **allowance**, part, share, measure, portion, quota, allotment, helping
▶ verb 2 = **limit**, control, budget, restrict

rational adjective = **logical**, reasonable, sensible, enlightened • to arrive at a rational conclusion
See also: **sane, wise**

rationale noun = **reason**, principle, theory, motivation, philosophy, logic, grounds, raison d'être (French)

rationality See **reason**

rationalize verb = **justify**, excuse, vindicate, account for

rations See **supplies**

rattle verb 1 = **clatter**, bang, jangle
2 = **shake**, bounce, jolt, jar, vibrate

3 (*Informal*) = **fluster**, upset, shake, disturb, faze, disconcert, perturb

raucous *adjective* = **harsh**, rough, loud, noisy, strident, hoarse, grating

raunchy *adjective* (*Slang*) = **sexy**, sexual, steamy (*informal*), coarse, earthy, lusty

ravage *verb* = **destroy**, devastate, ruin, spoil, demolish, ransack, despoil, lay waste
▷ *noun*
▷ **ravages** = **damage**, destruction, ruin, havoc, devastation, ruination, spoliation

rave *verb* **1** = **rant**, rage, babble • *He started raving about being treated badly.*
2 (*informal*) = **enthuse**, gush, be wild about (*informal*) • *She raved about the facilities there.*

ravenous *adjective* = **starving**, famished, starved

ravine *noun* = **canyon**, gorge, defile, gulch, pass, gully

raving *adjective* = **mad**, wild, crazy, insane, irrational, delirious, hysterical, crazed

ravish *verb* **1** = **enchant**, entrance, charm, delight, fascinate, captivate, spellbind, enrapture
2 = **rape**, force, abuse, violate, sexually assault

ravishing *adjective* = **enchanting**, beautiful, lovely, charming, gorgeous, bewitching, entrancing

raw *adjective* **1** = **uncooked**, natural, fresh
2 = **unrefined**, natural, crude, basic, rough, unfinished, coarse, unprocessed
3 = **inexperienced**, new, green, immature, callow
4 = **chilly**, cold, bitter, freezing, biting, piercing

ray *noun* = **beam**, bar, flash, shaft, gleam

raze *verb* = **destroy**, level, ruin, demolish, flatten, knock down, pull down

razor-sharp *See* **sharp**

re *preposition* = **concerning**, about, regarding, apropos, with reference to, with regard to

reach *verb* **1** = **arrive at**, get as far as, get to, make it to • *He did not stop until he reached the door.*
2 = **extend to**, touch • *Her coat nearly reached to the ground.*
3 = **attain**, climb to, fall to, rise to • *Unemployment has reached record levels.*
4 = **contact**, communicate with, get hold of, get in touch with, get through to
▷ *noun* **5** = **range**, power, extension, stretch, influence, capacity, distance, extent, scope, grasp
See also: **extend**

react *verb* **1** = **respond**, answer, reply
2 = **act**, work, operate, proceed, function, behave

reaction *noun* **1** = **response**, answer, feedback, acknowledgment • *Reaction to the visit was mixed.*
2 = **backlash**, counterbalance • *a reaction against rising prices*
3 = **conservatism**, the right

reactionary *adjective*
1 = **conservative**, right-wing
▷ *noun* **2** = **conservative**, right-winger, die-hard

read *verb* **1** = **look at**, study, scan, peruse, glance at, pore over • *I love to read in bed.*
2 = **interpret**, comprehend, decipher • *as if he could read my thoughts*
3 = **register**, show, record, indicate, display
▷ **read out** *See* **issue**
▷ **read up** *See* **study**

> **INFORMALLY SPEAKING**
> **read between the lines**: find a meaning not actually expressed
> **read into**: interpret in a certain way
> **read up on**: research by reading

readable *adjective* **1** = **enjoyable**, interesting, entertaining, enthralling, gripping

2 = **legible**, clear, comprehensible, decipherable

readily adverb 1 = **willingly**, quickly, promptly, freely, eagerly, gladly
2 = **easily**, quickly, smoothly, effortlessly, speedily, unhesitatingly

readiness noun 1 = **willingness**, eagerness, keenness
2 = **ease**, facility, dexterity, adroitness, promptness

reading noun 1 = **perusal**, study, inspection, scrutiny, examination
2 = **recital**, performance, lesson, sermon
3 = **interpretation**, version, impression, grasp
4 = **learning**, education, knowledge, scholarship, erudition

ready adjective 1 = **prepared**, set, organized, ripe, primed • *The plums are ready to eat now.*
2 = **willing**, happy, eager, keen, agreeable • *She was always ready to give interviews.*
3 = **available**, accessible, convenient, handy • *ready cash*
4 = **prompt**, quick, alert, sharp, smart, bright, keen, intelligent, clever, perceptive
See also: **fluent**

real adjective 1 = **actual**, true, legitimate, concrete, genuine, authentic, factual, tangible • *You're dealing with real life now.*
OPPOSITE: imaginary
2 = **genuine**, true, honest, authentic, sincere, unaffected, rightful, bona fide • *Is that a real diamond?*
OPPOSITE: fake
See also: **natural**

realism See **reality**

realistic adjective 1 = **practical**, sober, sensible, down-to-earth, matter-of-fact, level-headed • *It's only realistic to admit that things will go wrong.*
2 = **lifelike**, true, faithful, authentic • *His novels are more realistic than his short stories.*
See also: **actual**

reality noun = **truth**, fact, authenticity, realism • *Fiction and reality were increasingly blurred.*

realization noun 1 = **awareness**, understanding, recognition, perception, grasp, conception, comprehension, cognizance
2 = **achievement**, accomplishment, fulfillment

realize verb 1 = **become aware of**, understand, recognize, appreciate, grasp, comprehend • *People don't realize how serious it is.*
2 = **achieve**, do, complete, effect, perform, accomplish, fulfill, carry out or carry through
See also: **discover, find, see, sense**

really adverb 1 = **very**, extremely, absolutely, truly, remarkably, terribly • *I've had a really good time.*
2 = **in fact**, actually, truly, in reality • *He didn't really understand the question.*

realm noun 1 = **kingdom**, country, land, empire, domain, dominion
2 = **sphere**, world, province, area, field, department, territory, branch

reap verb 1 = **collect**, cut, gather, harvest, garner, bring in
2 = **get**, gain, acquire, derive, obtain

reappear See **return**

rear¹ noun 1 = **back**, end, tail, stern, rearguard, tail end
▶ adjective 2 = **back**, last, following, hind

rear² verb 1 = **bring up**, raise, train, breed, foster, educate, nurture
2 = **rise**, soar, tower, loom

reason noun 1 = **cause**, purpose, incentive, motive, grounds • *for a multitude of reasons*
2 = **sense**, judgment, reasoning, intellect, rationality • *a conflict between emotion and reason*
▶ verb 3 = **persuade**, bring around, win over • *It's better to reason with them than to use force.*
4 = **deduce**, think, conclude, infer, make out, work out
See also: **argue, excuse, wisdom**

reasonable adjective 1 = **sensible**,

fair, moderate, wise, sober,
rational, sane • *a reasonable sort
of person*
2 = logical, sound, legitimate,
sensible, understandable,
justifiable • *It seems reasonable to
expect rapid urban growth.*
3 = inexpensive, low, fair, cheap,
competitive, modest • *His fees
were quite reasonable.*
See also: **decent, respectable,
tolerable**
reasonably *See* **quite**
reasoned *adjective =* **sensible**,
clear, logical, well-thought-out
reasoning *noun =* **thinking**,
thought, analysis, logic
reassure *verb =* **encourage**,
bolster, comfort, cheer up • *She
reassured me that everything was
fine.*
See also: **satisfy**
reassured *See* **secure**
rebate *noun =* **refund**, reduction,
discount, bonus, allowance,
deduction, tax credit
rebel *verb* **1 = revolt**, resist,
mutiny • *I rebelled against
everything when I was younger.*
2 = defy, dissent, disobey
▶ *noun* **3 = revolutionary**,
insurgent, secessionist,
revolutionist
4 = nonconformist, dissenter,
apostate, heretic, schismatic
▶ *adjective* **5 = rebellious**,
insurgent, revolutionary,
insurrectionary
rebellion *noun* **1 = revolt**,
revolution, uprising,
insurrection, mutiny • *the
ruthless suppression of the rebellion*
2 = nonconformity, defiance,
heresy, schism
rebellious *adjective*
1 = revolutionary, rebel,
insurgent, disorderly, unruly,
disloyal, disobedient, mutinous,
seditious
2 = defiant, difficult, resistant,
unmanageable, refractory
rebound *verb* **1 = bounce**,
ricochet, recoil
2 = misfire, backfire, recoil,
boomerang

rebuff *verb* **1 = reject**, cut, refuse,
slight, snub, spurn, repulse,
cold-shoulder, knock back
(*slang*), turn down
▶ *noun* **2 = rejection**, slight,
refusal, snub, repulse, cold
shoulder, kick in the teeth
(*slang*), knock-back (*slang*), slap in
the face (*informal*)
rebuild *See* **reconstruct,
restore**
rebuke *verb* **1 = scold**, censure,
castigate, chide, admonish,
reprimand, reprove, tell off
(*informal*)
▶ *noun* **2 = scolding**, censure,
admonition, row, reprimand,
telling-off (*informal*)
rebut *verb =* **disprove**, overturn,
refute, negate, invalidate,
confute, prove wrong
rebuttal *noun =* **disproof**,
confutation, invalidation,
negation, refutation
recalcitrant *adjective*
= disobedient, defiant, unruly,
wayward, unmanageable,
wilful, insubordinate, refractory
recall *verb* **1 = recollect**,
remember, evoke, bring to mind
or call to mind
2 = annul, cancel, withdraw,
revoke, retract, repeal,
countermand
▶ *noun* **3 = recollection**,
memory, remembrance
4 = annulment, withdrawal,
cancellation, repeal, retraction,
rescindment
recant *verb =* **withdraw**, revoke,
retract, renege, repudiate,
disclaim, forswear, take back
recapitulate *verb =* **repeat**,
outline, recount, restate, recap
(*informal*), summarize
recapture *See* **recover,
recovery**
recede *verb =* **fall back**, return,
retire, withdraw, retreat,
subside, abate, ebb, regress
receipt *noun* **1 = sales slip**, stub,
proof of purchase
2 = receiving, delivery,
reception, acceptance
receive *verb* **1 = get**, take, accept,

r

be given, pick up • *Did they receive my letter?*
2 = experience, suffer, undergo, sustain, encounter • *We received a very warm welcome.*
3 = greet, meet, welcome, entertain, take in • *She was officially received by the prime minister.*
See also: **admit**
recent *adjective* = **new**, current, fresh, up-to-date, present-day • *his most recent acquisition*
See also: **modern**
recently *adverb* = **newly**, currently, lately, freshly, latterly, not long ago, of late
receptacle *noun* = **container**, holder, repository
reception *noun* **1** = **party**, function, levee, soirée
2 = **response**, treatment, welcome, reaction, greeting, acknowledgment
receptive *adjective* = **open**, interested, susceptible, sympathetic, open-minded, amenable, open to suggestions
recess *noun* **1** = **alcove**, corner, bay, niche, hollow, nook
2 = **break**, rest, holiday, vacation, intermission, interval, respite
recession *noun* = **depression**, decline, slump, downturn • *companies that survived the recession*
recipe *noun* **1** = **directions**, ingredients, instructions
2 = **method**, process, procedure, prescription, formula, technique
reciprocal *adjective*
= **mutual**, equivalent, alternate, complementary, interchangeable, correlative, corresponding, exchanged
reciprocate *verb* = **return**, trade, respond, exchange, reply, swap, requite
recital *noun* **1** = **performance**, rehearsal, rendering
2 = **account**, statement, relation, narrative, telling
3 = **recitation**, reading
recitation *noun* = **recital**,

performance, piece, reading, passage, lecture
recite *verb* = **repeat**, speak, perform, deliver, narrate, declaim
reckless *adjective* = **careless**, wild, rash, precipitate, mindless, hasty, headlong, imprudent, thoughtless, heedless
recklessness See **abandon**
reckon *verb* **1** (*informal*) = **think**, believe, suppose, assume • *I reckon they're still fond of each other.*
2 = **consider**, rate, judge, account, count, regard, deem, esteem
3 = **count**, estimate, calculate, figure out, work out • *The figure is now reckoned to be 20 per cent.*
See also: **conclude, expect, figure, guess**
reckoning *noun* **1** = **count**, estimate, addition, calculation
2 = **bill**, charge, score, due, account
reclaim *verb* = **regain**, recover, reform, salvage, retrieve, redeem, recapture
reclamation See **recovery**
recline *verb* = **lean**, rest, lie or lie down, sprawl, lounge, repose, loll
recluse *noun* = **hermit**, monk, solitary, anchoress, anchorite
reclusive *adjective* = **solitary**, isolated, hermit-like, retiring, withdrawn
recognition *noun*
1 = **identification**, discovery, remembrance, recollection
2 = **acceptance**, confession, admission, realization
3 = **appreciation**, respect, notice, props (*informal*)
recognize *verb* **1** = **identify**, know, place, spot • *I recognized him at once.*
2 = **acknowledge**, honour, appreciate, salute • *She was recognized as an outstanding pilot.*
3 = **appreciate**, respect, notice
See also: **distinguish, realize, remember**
recoil *verb* **1** = **jerk back**, rebound, kick, react, spring back

2 = draw back, shrink, falter, quail
3 = backfire, rebound, misfire, boomerang
▶ *noun* **4 = reaction**, rebound, kick, backlash, repercussion
recollect *verb* = **remember**, place, recall, summon up
recollection *noun* = **memory**, recall, impression, remembrance, reminiscence
recommence See **continue, renew**
recommend *verb* **1 = advise**, suggest, propose, advance, advocate, counsel, prescribe, put forward
2 = commend, approve, endorse, praise
recommendation *noun*
1 = advice, proposal, counsel, suggestion
2 = commendation, approval, praise, sanction, reference, advocacy, endorsement, testimonial
recompense *verb* **1 = reward**, pay, remunerate
2 = compensate, reimburse, repay, redress, make up for, pay for, requite
▶ *noun* **3 = compensation**, payment, repayment, amends, restitution, reparation, remuneration, damages, requital
4 = reward, return, payment, wages
reconcile *verb* **1 = resolve**, settle, square, adjust, compose, rectify, put to rights
2 = reunite, appease, conciliate, make peace between, propitiate
3 = accept, submit, yield, put up with (*informal*), resign oneself
reconciliation *noun* = **reunion**, conciliation, pacification, reconcilement
recondite *adjective* = **obscure**, difficult, deep, secret, dark, mysterious, profound, hidden, arcane, occult, concealed
recondition *verb* = **restore**, repair, renew, revamp, overhaul,

renovate, remodel, do up (*informal*)
reconnaissance *noun*
= **inspection**, investigation, exploration, observation, survey, scan
reconnoitre *verb* = **inspect**, case (*slang*), survey, investigate, explore, scan, observe, spy out
reconsider *verb* = **rethink**, review, revise, reassess, think again
reconstruct *verb* **1 = rebuild**, restore, renovate, recreate, regenerate • *The old bridge has been completely reconstructed.*
2 = deduce, piece together • *The police reconstructed the scene of the crime.*
record *noun* **1 = document**, file, account, register, journal, archives, minutes, blotter (*US*) • *medical records*
2 = background, career, curriculum vitae, résumé, track record (*informal*) • *You will be rejected if you have a criminal record.*
3 = evidence, witness, testimony, trace, documentation
4 = disc, single, album, vinyl, LP
▷ **off the record = confidential**, private, unofficial, not for publication
▶ *verb* **5 = document**, enter, register, log, make a note of, write down • *Her diary records her daily life in detail.*
6 = tape, video, tape-record, make a recording of, video-tape
7 = register, say, show, indicate, give evidence of
See also: **entry, list, note, write**
recorder *noun* = **chronicler**, clerk, historian, scribe, archivist, diarist
recording *noun* = **record**, video, tape, disc
recount *verb* = **tell**, report, describe, relate, repeat, depict, narrate, recite
recoup *verb* **1 = regain**, recover, retrieve, win back
2 = compensate, refund, reimburse, repay, remunerate, make up for, requite

r

recourse noun = **option**, choice, resource, alternative, resort, remedy, expedient, way out

recover verb 1 = **get better**, improve, revive, recuperate, convalesce, get well • *He has still not fully recovered.*
2 = **regain**, retrieve, recoup, recapture, get back • *They took legal action to recover the money.*

recovery noun 1 = **improvement**, healing, revival, recuperation • *He made a remarkable recovery after his illness.*
2 = **retrieval**, restoration, recapture, reclamation • *a reward for the recovery of the painting*

recreate See **reconstruct**

recreation noun = **pastime**, play, sport, fun, entertainment, diversion, amusement, hobby, relaxation, enjoyment, leisure activity

recrimination noun = **bickering**, quarrel, counterattack, mutual accusation, squabbling

recruit verb 1 = **enlist**, draft, muster, enrol • *He helped to recruit volunteers.*
2 = **win** or **win over**, obtain, engage, procure
▸ noun 3 = **beginner**, convert, novice, trainee • *the latest batch of recruits*

recruitment See **employment**

rectify verb = **correct**, right, improve, fix, repair, adjust, remedy, redress, emend

rectitude noun = **morality**, principle, integrity, honesty, honor, virtue, decency, goodness, probity

recuperate verb = **recover**, improve, mend, convalesce, get better

recuperation See **recovery**

recur verb = **happen again**, return, repeat, persist, revert, reappear, come again

recurrent adjective = **periodic**, continued, frequent, habitual, recurring

recycle verb = **reprocess**, save, salvage, reclaim, reuse

red adjective 1 = **crimson**, coral, cherry, ruby, scarlet, carmine, vermilion
2 (~ *hair*) = **chestnut**, sandy, carroty, flame-coloured, reddish, titian
3 = **flushed**, embarrassed, blushing, florid, shamefaced
▹ **red tape** See **bureaucracy**
▸ noun
▹ **in the red** (*Informal*) = **in debt**, insolvent, in arrears, overdrawn
▹ **see red** (*Informal*) = **lose one's temper**, blow one's top, crack up (*informal*), fly off the handle (*informal*), go ballistic (*slang*), go mad (*informal*)

SHADES OF RED

burgundy	magenta
cardinal	maroon
carmine	poppy
cerise	raspberry
cherry	ruby
claret	scarlet
crimson	strawberry
flame	vermilion

---

red-blooded adjective (*Informal*) = **vigorous**, strong, robust, lusty, virile

redden verb = **go red**, flush, colour or colour up, crimson, blush

redeem verb 1 = **make up for**, atone for, compensate for, make amends for
2 = **reinstate**, absolve, restore to favour
3 = **save**, free, deliver, ransom, liberate, emancipate
4 = **buy back**, recover, regain, retrieve, reclaim, repurchase

redemption noun
1 = **compensation**, amends, reparation, atonement
2 = **salvation**, release, rescue, liberation, emancipation, deliverance
3 = **trade-in**, recovery, repurchase, reclamation,

retrieval, repossession
red-faced See **embarrassed**
red-handed adjective = **in the act**, flagrante delicto or in flagrante delicto
redolent adjective
1 = **reminiscent**, suggestive, evocative
2 = **scented**, aromatic, fragrant, odorous, perfumed, sweet-smelling
redoubtable adjective
= **formidable**, strong, powerful, mighty, fearful, fearsome
redress verb 1 = **make amends for**, compensate for, make up for
2 = **put right**, balance, regulate, correct, adjust, rectify, even up
▶ noun 3 = **amends**, payment, compensation, reparation, atonement, recompense
reduce verb 1 = **lessen**, cut, lower, decrease, diminish, shorten, curtail, cut down • Gradually reduce the dosage.
OPPOSITE: increase
2 = **degrade**, force, drive, demote, downgrade • The village was reduced to rubble.
See also: **decline, weaken**
reduced See **low**
reduction noun 1 = **decrease**, diminution, minimizing, lowering, lessening
2 = **cut**, cutback, cutting, depletion, trimming, pruning, scaling down
3 = **discount**, slash (informal), concession, markdown, price cut
redundancy noun
1 = **superfluity**, surplus, excess, surfeit, uselessness, superabundance, expendability
2 = **unemployment**, layoff, joblessness, the axe (informal), the sack (informal)
redundant adjective
= **superfluous**, extra, surplus, unnecessary, unwanted, inessential, supernumerary
reek verb 1 = **stink**, smell
▶ noun 2 = **stink**, odor, fetor, smell, stench
reeking See **smelly**
reel verb 1 = **stagger**, rock,

pitch, roll, sway, lurch
2 = **whirl**, spin, swirl, revolve
re-establish See **renew, restore**
refer verb 1 = **mention**, cite, allude, bring up • In his speech, he referred to a recent trip to the Maritimes.
2 = **consult**, look up • I had to refer to the manual.
3 = **relate**, concern, apply, belong, pertain, be relevant to
4 = **direct**, point, send, guide
referee noun 1 = **umpire**, judge, arbitrator, ref (informal), adjudicator, arbiter
▶ verb 2 = **umpire**, judge, mediate, adjudicate, arbitrate
reference noun 1 = **citation**, note, mention, quotation, allusion
2 = **testimonial**, character, recommendation, endorsement, credentials
3 = **relevance**, connection, relation, bearing, applicability
referendum noun = **public vote**, plebiscite, popular vote
refine verb 1 = **purify**, process, clarify, filter, cleanse, distill
2 = **improve**, perfect, polish, hone
refined adjective 1 = **cultured**, polite, civilized, genteel • His speech and manner are very refined.
OPPOSITE: common
2 = **purified**, pure, distilled, filtered • refined oil
3 = **discerning**, fine, sensitive, delicate, precise, discriminating, fastidious
See also: **sophisticated**
refinement noun
1 = **sophistication**, culture, taste, courtesy, discrimination, polish, cultivation, civility, breeding, gentility, good breeding
2 = **subtlety**, nuance, nicety, fine point
3 = **purification**, clarification, distillation, cleansing, filtering, processing
reflect verb 1 = **return**, mirror, echo, reproduce, throw back
2 = **show**, reveal, indicate, display, demonstrate, manifest

r

3 = think, consider, wonder, ponder, muse, meditate, cogitate, ruminate

reflection noun **1 = image**, echo, mirror image
2 = thought, idea, opinion, consideration, observation, meditation, musing, thinking, contemplation, cogitation

reflective adjective = **thoughtful**, meditative, contemplative, pensive

reflex See **automatic**

reform noun **1 = improvement**, amendment, correction, rehabilitation • radical economic reforms
▶ verb **2 = improve**, correct, amend, better, rehabilitate, rectify • their plans to reform the economy
3 = mend one's ways, clean up one's act (informal), go straight (informal), shape up (informal), turn over a new leaf
See also: **change, transform**

refractory adjective
= **unmanageable**, difficult, uncontrollable, unruly, intractable, wilful, disobedient, headstrong, high-maintenance

refrain[1] verb = **stop**, avoid, cease, renounce, abstain, desist, forbear, leave off

refrain[2] noun = **chorus**, tune, melody

refresh verb **1 = revive**, brace, rejuvenate, enliven, stimulate • A glass of juice will refresh you.
2 = stimulate, prompt, renew, jog

refreshing adjective
1 = invigorating, fresh, bracing, stimulating
2 = new, original, novel

refreshment noun
▷ **refreshments = food and drink**, drinks, snacks, tidbits

refrigerate verb = **cool**, freeze, chill, keep cold

refuge noun = **shelter**, harbour, haven, asylum, sanctuary
• During the storm, we took refuge in the abandoned cabin.
See also: **retreat**

refugee noun = **exile**, escapee, displaced person, émigré

refund verb **1 = repay**, return, restore, reimburse, pay back
▶ noun **2 = repayment**, return, reimbursement

refurbish verb = **renovate**, repair, restore, revamp, overhaul, mend, clean up, do up (informal)

refusal noun = **rejection**, denial, rebuff, knock-back (slang)

refuse[1] verb **1 = deny**, decline, withhold, abstain • He refused to divulge the contents of the letter.
2 = decline, reject, spurn, turn down • He offered me a sandwich, which I refused.
OPPOSITE: accept
See also: **resist**

refuse[2] noun = **garbage**, waste, junk (informal), trash, litter, rubbish • a weekly collection of refuse

refute verb = **disprove**, overthrow, discredit, negate, rebut, prove false

regain verb **1 = recover**, retrieve, recoup, recapture, get back, take back, win back
2 = get back to, reach again, return to

regal adjective = **royal**, magnificent, noble, majestic, princely, kingly or queenly

regale verb = **entertain**, delight, divert, amuse

regalia plural noun = **trappings**, paraphernalia, accoutrements, decorations, emblems, finery

regard verb **1 = consider**, see, judge, view, look on, think of • I regard creativity as a gift.
2 = look at, watch, eye, contemplate, scrutinize, gaze • She regarded him curiously for a moment.
▷ **as regards = concerning**, regarding, pertaining to, relating to
▶ noun **3 = respect**, concern, care, thought, consideration, esteem
4 = look, scrutiny, glance, stare, gaze
See also: **admiration, rate**

regarding *preposition*
= **concerning**, about, re, as
regards, in regard to or with
regard to, on the subject of,
respecting, with reference to

regardless *adjective* 1 = **heedless**,
reckless, rash, negligent,
indifferent, inconsiderate,
neglectful, unmindful
▶ *adverb* 2 = **anyway**,
nevertheless, in any case, in
spite of everything
▷ **regardless of** See **despite, in
spite of**

regards *plural noun* = **good wishes**,
best wishes, compliments,
greetings, respects

regenerate *verb* = **renew**, restore,
revive, rejuvenate, invigorate,
reinvigorate, reawaken, breathe
new life into

regime *noun* = **government**,
system, rule, leadership,
management, reign

regimented *adjective*
= **controlled**, organized,
regulated, disciplined, ordered,
systematized

region *noun* = **area**, quarter,
land, sector, zone, territory,
district, tract, locality • *a remote
mountainous region*

regional *adjective* = **local**,
provincial, district, parochial,
zonal

register *noun* 1 = **list**, record, file,
roll, roster, log, chronicle, diary,
archives, catalogue
▶ *verb* 2 = **record**, list, note,
enter, chronicle, enlist, enrol,
catalogue
3 = **show**, mark, reveal, indicate,
express, display, exhibit,
manifest

regress *verb* = **revert**, return,
deteriorate, lapse, degenerate,
relapse, backslide, fall away or
fall off, go back

regret *verb* 1 = **be sorry**, mourn,
grieve, lament, repent • *I gave in
to him, and I have regretted it ever
since.*
▶ *noun* 2 = **sorrow**, grief,
remorse, repentance, penitence,
pang of conscience • *He expressed*
regret that he had caused any offence.
See also: **disappointment**

regretful *adjective* = **sorry**, sad,
remorseful, apologetic, contrite,
penitent, repentant, rueful,
sorrowful

regrettable *adjective*
= **unfortunate**, sad, shameful,
lamentable, disappointing,
distressing

> **CONFUSABLES**
>
> *Regrettable* means *unfortunate* or
> *unwelcome*.
> *Regretful* means *sorry*.

regular *adjective* 1 = **even**, steady,
uniform, consistent, constant,
periodic, rhythmic • *soft music
with a regular beat*
OPPOSITE: irregular
2 = **normal**, usual, routine,
typical, ordinary, everyday,
customary, habitual • *I was filling
in for the regular server.*
3 = **systematic**, set, even, steady,
uniform, consistent, constant,
stated, fixed, ordered
See also: **average, continual,
conventional, formal, orderly,
standard**

regularity See **order**

regulate *verb* 1 = **control**, run,
rule, manage, direct, handle,
guide, govern, supervise
2 = **adjust**, fit, balance,
moderate, tune, modulate

regulation *noun* 1 = **rule**, order,
law, dictate, decree, statute,
edict, precept
2 = **control**, government,
management, direction,
supervision
3 = **adjustment**, modulation,
tuning

regulations See **bureaucracy**

regurgitate *verb* = **vomit**, spew
(*slang*), slang, puke (*slang*),
disgorge, barf (*slang*), throw up
(*informal*), spew out or spew up

rehabilitate *verb*
1 = **reintegrate**, adjust
2 = **restore**, save, clear, reform,
redeem

rehabilitation See **reform**

rehash *verb* 1 = **rework**, rewrite,
reuse, rejig (*informal*), refashion

▶ *noun* **2 = reworking**, rewrite, new version, rearrangement

rehearsal *noun* = **practice**, drill, preparation, rehearsing, run-through

rehearse *verb* = **practise**, prepare, train, repeat, drill, recite, go over, run through

reheat See **heat**

reign *noun* **1 = rule**, power, control, command, monarchy, dominion

▶ *verb* **2 = rule**, influence, govern, command, be in power

3 = be supreme, prevail, hold sway, predominate

reimburse *verb* = **pay back**, return, refund, compensate, repay, remunerate, recompense

rein *verb* **1 = control**, limit, check, halt, restrict, curb, restrain, hold back

▶ *noun* **2 = control**, hold, check, curb, brake, restraint, harness, bridle

reincarnation *noun* = **rebirth**, transmigration of souls

reinforce *verb* = **support**, stress, supplement, strengthen, bolster, emphasize, prop, toughen, fortify

reinforcement *noun*
1 = strengthening, increase, fortification, augmentation
2 = support, stay, brace, prop, buttress
▷ **reinforcements = reserves**, support, additional troops *or* fresh troops, auxiliaries

reinstate *verb* = **restore**, return, recall, replace, re-establish

reintroduce See **restore**

reiterate *verb* = **repeat**, restate, do again, say again

reject *verb* **1 = refuse**, decline
2 = deny, renounce, rebuff, spurn, say no to, turn down • *All my suggestions were rejected.*
OPPOSITE: accept
3 = rebuff, refuse, spurn, jilt, repulse, say no to, turn down
4 = discard, eliminate, scrap, jettison, throw away *or* throw out

▶ *noun* **5 = castoff**, second, discard

See also: **boycott**

rejection *noun* **1 = refusal**, veto, denial, dismissal, exclusion, repudiation, renunciation, thumbs down
2 = rebuff, refusal, brushoff (*slang*), kick in the teeth (*slang*), knock-back (*slang*)

rejig *verb* = **rearrange**, alter, manipulate, tweak, reorganize, juggle

rejoice *verb* = **be overjoyed**, celebrate, delight, glory • *Today we can rejoice in our success.*

rejoicing *noun* = **happiness**, celebration, joy, jubilation, elation, exultation, gladness, merrymaking

rejoin *verb* = **reply**, answer, respond, retort, riposte

rejoinder *noun* = **reply**, response, answer, comeback (*informal*), retort, riposte

rejuvenate *verb* = **revitalize**, restore, renew, refresh, reinvigorate, regenerate, breathe new life into

relapse *verb* **1 = lapse**, fail, revert, degenerate, backslide, regress, slip back
2 = worsen, fail, sink, weaken, sicken, fade, deteriorate
▶ *noun* **3 = lapse**, backsliding, regression, retrogression
4 = worsening, deterioration, turn for the worse, weakening

relate *verb* **1 = connect**, link, join, couple, associate, correlate
2 = concern, apply, refer, pertain, be relevant to, have to do with
3 = tell, report, detail, describe, recount, narrate, recite

related *adjective* **1 = akin**, kindred
2 = associated, joint, akin, connected, affiliated, interconnected, linked

relating to See **about**

relation *noun* **1 = connection**, link, relationship, bond, bearing, correlation • *This theory bears no relation to reality.*
2 = relative, kin • *I was staying with relations in Edmonton.*

r

3 = kinship, affinity, kindred

relations *plural noun* **1 = dealings**, contact, relationship, interaction, intercourse, affairs, connections

2 = family, tribe, clan, kin, kindred, kinsfolk, kinsmen, relatives

relationship *noun*

1 = association, connection, bond, affinity, rapport • *He has a friendly relationship with his customers.*

2 = connection, link, parallel, correlation • *the relationship between humans and their environment*

3 = affair, liaison

See also: **relation, tie**

relative *adjective* **1 = dependent**, related, contingent, comparative, allied, associated, proportionate, corresponding

2 = relevant, appropriate, applicable, pertinent, apposite, apropos, germane

▶ *noun* **3 = relation**, kinsman *or* kinswoman, member of one's family *or* member of the family

relatively *adverb*
= comparatively, rather, somewhat

relax *verb* **1 = take it easy**, rest, unwind, laze, veg out (*slang*) • *I never have any time to relax.*

2 = lessen, reduce, lower, ease, moderate, weaken, relieve, loosen, abate, ebb, slacken, let up

See also: **calm, lift**

relaxation *noun* **= leisure**, rest, fun, pleasure, recreation, enjoyment

relaxed *adjective* **1 = at ease**, easy, cool, calm, comfortable, serene, unflustered • *As soon as I made the decision, I felt more relaxed.*

OPPOSITE: tense

2 = comfortable, calm, peaceful, casual, informal • *The atmosphere at lunch was relaxed.*

OPPOSITE: tense

See also: **cozy, leisurely, secure**

relaxing *See* **comfortable**

relay *noun* **1 = shift**, turn, relief

2 = message, transmission, dispatch

▶ *verb* **3 = pass on**, send, carry, broadcast, spread, communicate, transmit, stream

release *verb* **1 = set free**, free, deliver, discharge, liberate, extricate, let go • *negotiations to release the hostages*

2 = issue, launch, publish, put out • *The DVD will be released next week.*

3 = acquit, exonerate, absolve, let go, let off

▶ *noun* **4 = liberation**, freedom, discharge, liberty, emancipation • *his release from prison*

5 = acquittal, exemption, exoneration, absolution

6 = issue, publication, proclamation

See also: **emit**

relegate *verb* **= demote**, downgrade

relent *verb* **= be merciful**, yield, soften, capitulate, change one's mind, come around, have pity, show mercy

relentless *adjective*

1 = unremitting, persistent, sustained, non-stop, unrelenting, incessant

2 = merciless, fierce, cruel, ruthless, unrelenting, implacable, pitiless, remorseless • *The pressure was relentless.*

See also: **constant**

relevant *adjective* **= pertinent**, appropriate, applicable, apt • *We have passed along all relevant information.*

OPPOSITE: irrelevant

reliable *adjective* **= dependable**, safe, sure, sound, true, faithful, staunch, trustworthy • *You have to demonstrate that you are reliable.*

OPPOSITE: unreliable

See also: **responsible, trusty**

reliance *noun* **= trust**, confidence, faith, belief, dependence

relic *noun* **= remnant**, trace, souvenir, fragment, memento, vestige, keepsake

▷ **relics** *See* **remains**

r

relief noun 1 = **ease**, release, cure, comfort, remedy, solace, mitigation, deliverance
2 = **rest**, break, breather (*informal*), relaxation, respite
3 = **aid**, help, support, assistance, succour

relieve verb 1 = **ease**, console, calm, cure, relax, comfort, soften, alleviate, mitigate, soothe, assuage
2 = **help**, support, assist, aid, sustain, succour
▷ **relieve from** See **spare**

religious adjective 1 = **spiritual**, holy, sacred, theological, doctrinal, devotional • *religious worship*
2 = **devout**, righteous, pious, godly • *They are both very religious.*
3 = **conscientious**, faithful, rigid, meticulous, scrupulous, punctilious

relinquish verb = **give up**, leave, drop, abandon, surrender, renounce, cede, abdicate, forsake, let go

relish verb 1 = **enjoy**, like, fancy, delight in, revel in, savour
▶ noun 2 = **enjoyment**, love, taste, fancy, penchant, fondness, liking, gusto, predilection, partiality
3 = **condiment**, sauce, seasoning
4 = **flavour**, taste, trace, smack, spice, piquancy, tang

relocate See **move**

reluctance noun = **unwillingness**, dislike, distaste, aversion, loathing, disinclination, repugnance

reluctant adjective = **unwilling**, slow, hesitant, loath, averse to, disinclined • *He was reluctant to ask for help.*
OPPOSITE: eager

rely verb = **depend**, bank, trust, count, bet

remain verb 1 = **stay behind**, wait, linger, be left • *You'll have to remain in hospital for the time being.*
2 = **continue**, last, stay, survive, endure, go on • *The men remained silent.*

remainder noun = **rest**, last, balance, others, remnants, remains • *He gulped down the remainder of his milk.*
See also: **difference**

remaining adjective = **left-over**, outstanding, unfinished, lingering, persisting, surviving

remains plural noun
1 = **remnants**, debris, residue, dregs, leftovers, relics, scraps, vestiges • *the remains of an ancient dwelling*
2 = **body**, carcass, corpse, cadaver
See also: **remainder**, **ruin**

remark verb 1 = **comment**, say, state, mention, observe • *She had remarked on the boy's improvement.*
2 = **notice**, see, note, mark, observe, perceive, espy, make out
▶ noun 3 = **comment**, statement, word, observation, utterance • *a funny remark*
See also: **expression**

remarkable adjective = **extraordinary**, rare, unusual, wonderful, notable, outstanding, uncommon, striking, singular, surprising

remarkably See **really**

remedy noun 1 = **cure**, treatment, medicine, nostrum
▶ verb 2 = **put right**, fix, correct,

r

TYPES OF RELIGION

animism	Islam	Sikhism
Baha'ism	Jainism	Taoism
Buddhism	Judaism	Zen
Christianity	Rastafarianism	Zoroastrianism
Confucianism	shamanism	
Hinduism	Shinto	

rectify, set to rights

remember verb 1 = **recall**, recognize, retain, call to mind • *I do not remember the exact words.*
2 = **bear in mind**, keep in mind
OPPOSITE: forget

remembrance noun
1 = **memory**, recall, thought, recollection, reminiscence
2 = **souvenir**, reminder, token, memento, keepsake
3 = **commemoration**, memorial, monument

remind verb = **make someone remember**, bring back to = **jog someone's memory**, put in mind, refresh someone's memory • *He reminds me of myself at that age.*
See also: **prompt**

reminder See **note, souvenir**

reminisce verb = **recall**, remember, hark back, look back, recollect, think back

reminiscence noun
= **recollection**, recall, memory, memoir, remembrance, anecdote

reminiscent adjective
= **suggestive**, similar, evocative

remiss adjective = **careless**, lax, negligent, thoughtless, forgetful, heedless, neglectful

remission noun 1 = **pardon**, release, exemption, discharge, amnesty, reprieve, absolution
2 = **lessening**, lull, relaxation, respite, ebb, abatement, alleviation

remit verb 1 = **send**, forward, mail, dispatch, transmit
2 = **cancel**, stop, halt, rescind, repeal
3 = **postpone**, delay, suspend, shelve, defer, put off
▶ noun 4 = **instructions**, brief, guidelines, orders

remittance noun = **payment**, fee, allowance

remnant noun = **remainder**, end, rest, trace, fragment, residue, vestige, leftovers, remains

remonstrate verb = **argue**, protest, dispute, object, dissent, take issue

remorse noun = **regret**, shame, grief, guilt, sorrow, anguish, contrition, repentance, penitence, compunction

remorseful adjective = **regretful**, guilty, sorry, ashamed, apologetic, contrite, conscience-stricken, penitent, repentant

remorseless adjective
1 = **pitiless**, cruel, inhumane, ruthless, callous, merciless
2 = **relentless**, inexorable

remote adjective 1 = **distant**, isolated, lonely, outlying, inaccessible, far-off • *a remote cabin in the mountains*
2 = **aloof**, cold, distant, reserved, detached, withdrawn • *She appeared remote and not interested in meeting anyone.*
3 = **slight**, small, poor, slim, slender • *The chances of his making the team are pretty remote.*
See also: **far, impersonal**

removal noun 1 = **taking away**, **taking off**, or **taking out**, withdrawal, elimination, eradication, ejection, extraction, dislodgment, uprooting, clear-out (informal)
2 = **dismissal**, expulsion
3 = **move**, departure, transfer, relocation

remove verb 1 = **take away**, eliminate, withdraw, erase, extract, eject, delete, detach, excise, get rid of, take off, take out, clear out (informal), efface, expunge • *I removed the splinter from my finger.*
2 = **dismiss**, oust, expel, depose, discharge, dethrone, throw out
3 = **move**, depart, relocate, flit (Scot & Northern English dialect)
See also: **banish, lift**

remunerate verb = **pay**, reward, compensate, reimburse, repay, recompense, requite

remuneration noun = **payment**, return, pay, income, fee, salary, reward, stipend, earnings, wages

remunerative adjective
= **profitable**, economic, lucrative, worthwhile,

r

rewarding, moneymaking, paying

renaissance, renascence *noun*
= **rebirth**, revival, renewal, restoration, resurgence, reappearance, reawakening

rend *verb* = **tear**, separate, rip, rupture, wrench

render *verb* 1 = **make**, leave, cause to become

2 = **provide**, give, pay, supply, present, submit, tender, furnish, hand out

3 = **represent**, do, play, give, act, perform, portray, depict

rendezvous *noun*
1 = **appointment**, meeting, date, engagement, tryst, assignation
2 = **meeting place**, venue, gathering point
▶ *verb* 3 = **meet**, gather, assemble, come together, join up

rendition *noun* 1 = **performance**, version, reading, arrangement, presentation, portrayal, interpretation, rendering
2 = **translation**, version, reading, interpretation, transcription

renegade *noun* 1 = **deserter**, defector, traitor, apostate, turncoat
▶ *adjective* 2 = **traitorous**, rebellious, apostate, unfaithful, disloyal

renege *verb* = **break one's word**, default, back out, break a promise, go back

renew *verb* 1 = **recommence**, resume, reopen, re-establish, begin again • *The two countries renewed diplomatic relations.*
2 = **restore**, repair, overhaul, mend, renovate, refurbish, modernize, refit
3 = **replace**, refresh, replenish, restock

renounce *verb* (*Formal*) = **give up**, reject, relinquish, disown • *She renounced her claim to the inheritance.*
See also: **deny, surrender**

renovate *verb* = **restore**, repair, revamp, refurbish, modernize, make over, recondition • *They*

spent thousands renovating the house.
See also: **decorate, mend, reconstruct**

renown *noun* = **fame**, note, reputation, distinction, repute, eminence

renowned *adjective* = **famous**, well-known, notable, celebrated, distinguished, eminent, noted, esteemed

rent[1] *verb* 1 = **lease**, hire, charter • *They rented an apartment downtown.*
▶ *noun* 2 = **lease**, fee, payment, hire, rental

rent[2] *noun* = **tear**, opening, hole, split, slash, rip, gash, slit

renunciation *noun* = **giving up**, rejection, denial, abandonment, abdication, repudiation, abjuration, disavowal, forswearing, relinquishment

reopen See **renew**

reorganize *verb* = **rearrange**, restructure, reshuffle

repair *noun* 1 = **mend**, restoration • *She did the house repairs herself.*
▶ *verb* 2 = **mend**, fix, restore, patch, renovate, patch up • *The money will be used to repair faulty equipment.*
See also: **piece together**

reparation *noun*
= **compensation**, satisfaction, restitution, atonement, damages, recompense

repartee *noun* = **wit**, banter, wordplay, badinage, riposte, wittiness

repast *noun* = **meal**, food

repay *verb* 1 = **pay back**, refund, settle up • *It will take me years to repay the loan.*
2 = **get even with** (*informal*), avenge, revenge, retaliate, reciprocate, hit back
See also: **compensate, return**

repeal *verb* 1 = **abolish**, recall, cancel, reverse, revoke, annul, nullify, invalidate
▶ *noun* 2 = **abolition**, cancellation, annulment, invalidation, rescindment

repeat verb 1 = **reiterate**, echo, say again • *Since you didn't listen, I'll repeat that.*
2 = **repetition**, echo, replay, rerun, reiteration, reshowing
See also: **quote, stress**

repeated See **continual, frequent**

repeatedly adverb = **over and over**, often, frequently, many times

repel verb 1 = **disgust**, sicken, offend, revolt • *The thought of spiders repels me.*
OPPOSITE: attract
2 = **drive off**, resist, repulse • *troops along the border ready to repel an enemy attack*

repellent adjective 1 = **disgusting**, offensive, sickening, hateful, abhorrent, noxious, horrid, repulsive, repugnant, revolting, loathsome, nauseating, scuzzy (slang)
2 = **proof**, resistant, impermeable, repelling

repent verb = **regret**, rue, be sorry, feel remorse

repentance noun = **regret**, grief, guilt, remorse, contrition, penitence, compunction

repentant adjective = **regretful**, sorry, remorseful, contrite, penitent, rueful

repercussion noun
▷ **repercussions**
= **consequences**, result, sequel, backlash, side effects

repertoire noun = **range**, list, stock, store, supply, collection, repertory

repetition noun = **repeating**, echo, renewal, recurrence, restatement, reiteration, replication, tautology

repetitious adjective = **long-winded**, tedious, verbose, prolix, tautological, wordy

repetitive adjective
= **monotonous**, mechanical, boring, dull, tedious, recurrent, unchanging, unvaried

rephrase verb = **reword**, paraphrase, put differently

repine verb = **complain**, fret, grumble, moan

replace verb = **take the place of**, succeed, supplant, supersede, take over from • *She replaced the singer at the last minute.*
See also: **change, substitute**

replacement noun = **successor**, relief, substitute, proxy, surrogate, stand-in • *He has nominated his assistant as his replacement.*

replenish verb = **refill**, provide, replace, fill, restore, reload, top up

replete adjective = **full**, crammed, filled, full up, glutted, gorged, stuffed

replica noun = **duplicate**, model, copy, reproduction, imitation, facsimile, carbon copy (informal)

replicate verb = **copy**, mimic, recreate, duplicate, reproduce, reduplicate

reply verb 1 = **answer**, return, respond, counter, retort • *He did not even have the courtesy to reply to my email.*
▶ noun 2 = **answer**, response, retort • *There was a trace of irony in his reply.*

report verb 1 = **communicate**, state, cover, describe, notify, inform of • *He reported the theft to the police.*
2 = **present oneself**, come, appear, arrive, turn up
▶ noun 3 = **account**, statement, description • *reports of a tornado touching down*
4 = **article**, story, piece, write-up
5 = **rumor**, talk, buzz, gossip, hearsay
6 = **bang**, blast, sound, explosion, boom, crack, noise, discharge, detonation
See also: **announcement, feature, item, review**

reporter noun = **journalist**, correspondent, hack (derogatory), writer, pressman

repose noun 1 = **peace**, rest, ease, relaxation, respite, stillness, tranquillity, quietness
2 = **composure**, poise, calmness, self-possession

3 = sleep, slumber
▶ *verb* **4 = rest**, lie, recline, lie down, rest upon

repository *noun* **= store**, vault, treasury, storehouse, depository

reprehensible *adjective* **= blameworthy**, bad, disgraceful, shameful, culpable, unworthy

represent *verb* **1 = stand for**, mean, symbolize • *Locate the icon on the desktop that represents your connection.*
2 = portray, show, picture, describe, depict • *The media tends to represent him as a hero.*
3 = symbolize, embody, exemplify, epitomize, typify, personify

representation *noun* **= portrayal**, picture, account, image, model, portrait, description, depiction, illustration, likeness

representative *noun*
1 = delegate, agent, deputy, spokesperson, proxy • *Employees from each department elect a representative.*
2 = salesman, agent, rep, commercial traveller
▶ *adjective* **3 = typical**, characteristic, illustrative • *fairly representative groups of adults*
See also: **official, substitute**

repress *verb* **1 = inhibit**, control, check, curb, stifle, restrain, suppress, bottle up, hold back
2 = subdue, quell, subjugate

repressed See **pent-up**

repression *noun* **= subjugation**, control, restraint, domination, constraint, tyranny, suppression, despotism

repressive *adjective* **= oppressive**, absolute, authoritarian, despotic, dictatorial, tyrannical

reprieve *verb* **1 = grant a stay of execution to**, pardon, let off the hook (*slang*)
2 = relieve, alleviate, mitigate, allay, abate, palliate
▶ *noun* **3 = stay of execution**, amnesty, pardon, postponement, remission, deferment
4 = relief, respite, mitigation, alleviation, palliation

reprimand *verb* **1 = blame**, censure, rebuke, scold, rap over the knuckles, lower the boom (*slang*)
▶ *noun* **2 = blame**, censure, rebuke, reproach, reproof, talking-to (*informal*)

reprisal *noun* **= retaliation**, revenge, vengeance, retribution

reproach *noun* **1 = blame**, rebuke, condemnation, censure, disapproval, opprobrium
▶ *verb* **2 = blame**, criticize, condemn, censure, lambast *or* lambaste, rebuke, reprimand, scold, upbraid

reproachful *adjective* **= critical**, censorious, condemnatory, disapproving, fault-finding, reproving

reprobate *noun* **1 = scoundrel**, bad egg (*old-fashioned, informal*), degenerate, miscreant, evildoer, rake, villain, rascal, profligate
▶ *adjective* **2 = depraved**, base, bad, corrupt, abandoned, wicked, immoral, degenerate, sinful, dissolute

reproduce *verb* **1 = copy**, match, repeat, mirror, echo, recreate, replicate, duplicate, imitate
2 = breed, spawn, multiply, procreate, propagate

reproduction *noun* **1 = breeding**, increase, generation, multiplication
2 = copy, picture, print, replica, duplicate, imitation, facsimile

reproof *noun* **= rebuke**, blame, criticism, reprimand, condemnation, censure, scolding

reprove *verb* **= rebuke**, blame, condemn, censure, berate, reprimand, scold, tell off (*informal*)

republic See **state**

repudiate *verb* **= reject**, deny, renounce, disavow, disown, disclaim

repugnance *noun* **= distaste**,

hatred, disgust, dislike, aversion, loathing, abhorrence

repugnant *adjective*
= **distasteful**, offensive, repellent, sickening, abhorrent, vile, disgusting, revolting, loathsome, nauseating

repulse *verb* 1 = **drive back**, rebuff, repel, beat off, fight off, ward off

2 = **reject**, refuse, snub, rebuff, spurn, turn down

repulsion *noun* = **distaste**, hatred, disgust, revulsion, aversion, loathing, abhorrence, detestation, repugnance

repulsive *adjective* = **disgusting**, foul, repellent, sickening, abhorrent, vile, revolting, loathsome, nauseating, scuzzy (*slang*)

reputable *adjective* = **respectable**, good, excellent, reliable, worthy, trustworthy, honorable, creditable, well-thought-of

reputation *noun* = **name**, character, standing, stature, renown, repute • *The college has a good reputation.*
See also: **fame**

repute *noun* = **reputation**, name, celebrity, standing, fame, distinction, stature, renown, eminence

reputed *adjective* = **supposed**, alleged, estimated, held, considered, believed, deemed, reckoned, regarded

reputedly *adverb* = **supposedly**, allegedly, apparently, seemingly

request *verb* 1 = **ask for**, seek, beg • *She requested that the door be left open.*
▶ *noun* 2 = **appeal**, call, application, plea • *The principal agreed to our request.*

require *verb* 1 = **need**, want, demand, be in need of, depend on • *A baby requires warmth and security.*

2 = **demand**, order, direct, compel, instruct, oblige • *The rules require employers to provide safety training.*
See also: **expect, involve, take**

required *adjective* = **needed**, necessary, essential, requisite, obligatory, called for

requirement *noun* = **necessity**, need, demand, essential, specification • *The products met all safety requirements.*
See also: **condition, standard**

requisite *adjective* 1 = **necessary**, essential, needed, required, indispensable, obligatory, called for, needful
▶ *noun* 2 = **necessity**, need, must, condition, requirement, essential, prerequisite

requisition *verb* 1 = **demand**, request, call for
▶ *noun* 2 = **demand**, call, request, summons

requital *noun* = **return**, repayment

requite *verb* = **return**, respond, repay, retaliate, reciprocate, get even, give in return, pay (someone) back in his own coin *or* pay (someone) back in her own coin

reschedule *See* **put off**

rescind *verb* = **annul**, cancel, repeal, invalidate, countermand, declare null and void, set aside

rescue *verb* 1 = **save**, release, recover, deliver, salvage, redeem, liberate, get out
▶ *noun* 2 = **saving**, release, recovery, salvage, redemption, liberation, salvation, deliverance, search and rescue

research *noun* 1 = **investigation**, study, analysis, exploration, examination • *funds for AIDS research*
▶ *verb* 2 = **investigate**, study, explore, examine, analyze • *I'm researching the history of the fisheries.*

resemblance *noun* = **similarity**, parallel, correspondence, likeness, analogy • *I can see a resemblance between you.*

resemble *verb* = **be like**, parallel, bear a resemblance to, be similar to, look like, take after • *He resembles his grandfather when he was a young man.*

resent *verb* = **be bitter about**,

dislike, be angry about, be offended by, object to, take offence at • *I resent the slur on my character.*
See also: **envy**

resentful *adjective* = **bitter**, angry, aggrieved, embittered, huffy, indignant, offended • *an unhappy and resentful team*
See also: **jealous, sulky**

resentment *noun* = **bitterness**, anger, grudge, animosity, huff, indignation, rancour • *There is growing resentment against the new owners.*
See also: **envy, hostility**

reservation *noun* 1 = **doubt**, hesitancy, scruple
2 = **condition**, rider, qualification, stipulation, proviso
3 = **reserve**, territory, preserve, sanctuary

reserve *verb* 1 = **keep**, hold, save, store, stockpile, hoard, put away, set aside • *Hotel rooms have been reserved for us.*
2 = **book**, secure, engage, prearrange
▶ *noun* 3 = **store**, fund, stock, supply, stockpile, cache, hoard • *a drain on the cash reserves*
4 = **reservation**, park, preserve, tract, sanctuary
5 = **shyness**, silence, restraint, reservation, constraint, secretiveness, reticence, taciturnity
▶ *adjective* 6 = **substitute**, extra, spare, secondary, auxiliary, fall-back
See also: **bank**

reserved *adjective*
1 = **uncommunicative**, shy, silent, secretive, restrained, reticent, retiring, standoffish, taciturn, undemonstrative
2 = **set aside**, restricted, held, engaged, retained, booked, kept, spoken for, taken

reservoir *noun* 1 = **lake**, tank, pond, basin
2 = **store**, stock, supply, source, pool, reserves

reshuffle *noun* (Politics)

1 = **reorganization**, change, revision, redistribution, restructuring, rearrangement, regrouping
▶ *verb* 2 = **reorganize**, restructure, revise, regroup, redistribute, rearrange, change around

reside *verb* = **live**, stay, abide, lodge, inhabit, dwell

residence *noun* = **home**, place, house, apartment, flat, lodging, dwelling, abode, habitation, domicile, bachelorette (*Canad*)

resident *noun* = **inhabitant**, local, citizen, tenant, occupant, occupier, lodger, landed immigrant (*Canad*), livyer or liveyer (*Canad Nfld*), permanent resident (*Canad*)

residual *adjective* = **remaining**, unused, leftover, unconsumed, vestigial

residue *noun* = **remainder**, rest, extra, surplus, excess, remnant, dregs, leftovers, remains

resign *verb* 1 = **quit**, leave, abdicate, hand in your notice, step down • *I resigned from the company.*
2 = **give up**, abandon, surrender, yield, renounce, relinquish, forgo, forsake
▷ **resign oneself** = **accept**, bow, reconcile oneself • *She had resigned herself to losing her job.*

resignation *noun* 1 = **leaving**, departure, abandonment, abdication
2 = **acceptance**, submission, compliance, patience, endurance, passivity, acquiescence, nonresistance, sufferance

resigned *adjective* = **stoical**, patient, subdued, compliant, long-suffering, unresisting

resilient *adjective* 1 = **tough**, strong, buoyant, hardy, irrepressible
2 = **flexible**, plastic, elastic, rubbery, supple, pliable, springy

resist *verb* 1 = **oppose**, fight, refuse, defy, struggle against • *They resisted our attempts to change*

the yearbook's format.
OPPOSITE: accept
2 = refrain from, avoid, forgo, abstain from, forbear, keep from
3 = withstand, be proof against
See also: **rebel, repel**

resistance noun = **opposition**, fight, battle, struggle, obstruction, fighting, defiance, impediment, hindrance

resistant adjective
1 = impervious, strong, hard, tough, proof against, unaffected by
2 = opposed, hostile, unwilling, intractable, intransigent, antagonistic

resolute adjective = **determined**, set, firm, steadfast, dogged, tenacious, inflexible, strong-willed, unshakable, fixed, immovable, unwavering

resolution noun
1 = determination, resolve, purpose, perseverance, tenacity, willpower, firmness, doggedness, resoluteness, steadfastness
2 = decision, aim, resolve, purpose, intention, declaration, intent, determination

resolve verb **1 = decide**, determine, intend, make up your mind • *She resolved to report the matter.*
2 = work out, solve, overcome, clear up, find a solution to, sort out • *We must find a way to resolve these problems.*
3 = break down, reduce, separate, analyze
▶ noun **4 = determination**, resolution, tenacity • *He didn't weaken in his resolve.*
5 = decision, resolution, purpose, intention, objective
See also: **settle, will**

resolved See **serious**

resonant adjective = **echoing**, ringing, booming, resounding, reverberating, sonorous

resonate See **ring**

resort noun **1 = holiday centre**, spot, retreat, haunt, tourist centre

2 = recourse, reference
▶ verb
▷ **resort to = use**, employ, utilize, fall back on, have recourse to, turn to

resound verb = **echo**, ring, resonate, reverberate, re-echo

resounding adjective
= **echoing**, full, powerful, ringing, booming, resonant, reverberating, sonorous

resource noun **1 = ingenuity**, ability, initiative, capability, inventiveness, cleverness
2 = means, course, device, resort, expedient

resourceful adjective = **ingenious**, able, bright, capable, creative, clever, inventive

resources plural noun = **reserves**, money, capital, wealth, riches, assets, funds, holdings, supplies

respect verb **1 = think highly of**, honour, admire, venerate, have a good opinion of, have a high opinion of, look up to • *I want her to respect me as a dedicated student.*
OPPOSITE: disrespect
2 = show consideration for, follow, observe, heed, honour, obey, abide by, adhere to, comply with
▶ noun **3 = regard**, admiration, esteem, reverence • *We have no respect for him at all.*
OPPOSITE: disrespect
4 = point, way, feature, matter, detail, sense, particular, aspect, characteristic
5 = relation, connection, regard, reference, bearing
See also: **appreciate, approval, approve, consider, consideration, value**

respectable adjective
1 = honourable, good, proper, decent, worthy, upright, reputable • *respectable families*
2 = reasonable, fair, decent, considerable, appreciable • *a respectable rate of economic growth*

respectful adjective = **polite**, civil, courteous, deferential, mannerly, reverent, well-mannered

respective adjective = **specific**, own, individual, particular, relevant

respite noun = **pause**, break, rest, halt, relief, recess, cessation, lull, interval

resplendent adjective = **brilliant**, bright, glorious, splendid, radiant, dazzling, shining

respond verb = **answer**, return, counter, react, reply, rejoin, retort, reciprocate
▷ **respond to** See **identify with**

response noun = **answer**, return, reaction, reply, feedback, counterattack, retort, rejoinder

responsibility noun 1 = **duty**, obligation, onus • *The garden is your responsibility.*
2 = **fault**, blame, liability, guilt • *We must all accept responsibility for our mistakes.*
3 = **authority**, power, importance
4 = **level-headedness**, dependability, conscientiousness, rationality, sensibleness, trustworthiness
See also: **concern, function, job**

responsible adjective 1 = **in charge**, in control • *The music teacher is responsible for the band.*
2 = **to blame**, guilty, at fault • *I hold you responsible for this mess.*
3 = **sensible**, sound, reliable, dependable, trustworthy, level-headed • *He had to show that he would be a responsible pet owner.*
OPPOSITE: irresponsible
4 = **accountable**, liable, answerable

responsive adjective = **sensitive**, open, alive, susceptible, receptive, reactive, impressionable

rest¹ noun 1 = **break**, holiday, vacation, leisure, relaxation, respite, staycation (*informal*) • *I'll start again after a rest.*
2 = **relaxation**, relief, calm, leisure, inactivity, repose, stillness, tranquillity
3 = **support**, base, stand, holder, prop
▷ verb 4 = **relax**, idle, have a

break, laze, put your feet up, sit down, take it easy • *She rested briefly before going on.*
5 = **be supported**, sit, lie, lean, prop, recline, repose
See also: **pause, put, set**

rest² noun = **remainder**, surplus, balance, others • *Take what you want and leave the rest.*

restaurant noun = **bistro**, cafeteria, diner, café, eatery, tearoom

restful adjective = **relaxing**, quiet, calm, peaceful, soothing, tranquil, serene, calming, relaxed

restitution noun = **compensation**, amends, reparation, recompense, requital

restive adjective = **restless**, nervous, impatient, edgy, fidgety, jumpy, on edge, wired (*slang*)

restless adjective 1 = **unsettled**, edgy, fidgety, jumpy, fretful, on edge • *She had been restless and irritable all day*
2 = **moving**, unstable, nomadic, transient, unsettled, roving, wandering
See also: **active, busy, impatient**

restlessness noun
1 = **movement**, activity, unrest, bustle
2 = **restiveness**, nervousness, edginess, jitters (*informal*), jumpiness, unsettledness

restoration noun 1 = **repair**, reconstruction, renovation, revival, renewal, revitalization
2 = **reinstatement**, return, replacement, restitution, re-establishment

restore verb 1 = **reinstate**, return, reintroduce, re-establish • *He was anxious to restore his reputation.*
2 = **repair**, rebuild, mend, renovate, refurbish, reconstruct, fix up • *experts who specialize in restoring old paintings*
3 = **revive**, strengthen, refresh, revitalize, build up
4 = **return**, recover, replace, reinstate, bring back, give back, hand back, send back

See also: **piece together**

restrain *verb* = **hold back**, control, contain, curb, hamper, hinder, inhibit • *He had to be restrained by his friends.*
See also: **check, restrict, suppress**

restrained *adjective* = **controlled**, calm, moderate, mild, self-controlled, undemonstrative

restraint *noun* **1** = **self-control**, control, moderation, inhibition, self-restraint, self-discipline, self-possession
2 = **limitation**, ban, limit, check, curb, rein, embargo, interdict

restrict *verb* = **limit**, contain, hamper, restrain, confine, impede, inhibit, handicap • *laws to restrict foreign imports*

restriction *noun* = **limitation**, control, limit, regulation, curb, restraint, constraint, stipulation • *travel restrictions*

result *noun* **1** = **consequence**, product, effect, outcome, upshot • *the result of many rehearsals*
▶ *verb* **2** = **arise**, follow, happen, develop, stem, ensue, derive • *The crash resulted from a defect in the aircraft.*
▷ **result in** = **cause**, bring about, lead to • *Fifty per cent of road accidents result in head injuries.*
See also: **bring**

resume *verb* = **begin again**, continue, proceed, reopen, restart, carry on, go on

résumé *noun* = **CV** or **curriculum vitae**, summary, rundown (*informal*), synopsis, recapitulation, précis

resumption *noun* = **continuation**, restart, renewal, resurgence, carrying on, re-establishment, reopening

resurgence *noun* = **revival**, return, resumption, renaissance, rebirth, resurrection, re-emergence

resurrect *verb* = **revive**, renew, reintroduce, bring back

resurrection *noun* = **revival**, return, renewal, restoration, resurgence, renaissance, reappearance, rebirth

resuscitate *verb* = **revive**, save, resurrect, revitalize, bring round

retain *verb* **1** = **keep**, hold, save, reserve, maintain, preserve, hold back
2 = **hire**, pay, reserve, commission, engage, employ

retainer *noun* **1** = **fee**, advance, deposit
2 = **servant**, domestic, attendant

retaliate *verb* = **pay someone back**, get back at, get even with, get your own back, hit back, take revenge • *The army will retaliate against any attacks.*
See also: **revenge**

retaliation *noun* = **revenge**, repayment, reprisal, vengeance, an eye for an eye, counterblow, reciprocation, requital

retard *verb* = **slow down**, arrest, delay, check, hinder, impede, handicap, hold back *or* hold up, set back

retch *verb* = **gag**, barf (*slang*), vomit, spew, heave, puke (*slang*), regurgitate, throw up (*informal*)

reticence *noun* = **silence**, reserve, quietness, taciturnity

reticent *adjective* = **uncommunicative**, quiet, silent, tight-lipped, reserved, close-lipped, taciturn, unforthcoming

retinue *noun* = **attendants**, escort, entourage, aides, followers, servants

retire *verb* **1** = **stop working**, give up work
2 = **withdraw**, leave, exit, depart, go away
3 = **go to bed**, hit the hay (*slang*), hit the sack (*slang*), turn in (*informal*)

retirement *noun* = **withdrawal**, privacy, retreat, solitude, seclusion

retiring *adjective* = **shy**, quiet, timid, reserved, unassuming, self-effacing, bashful, unassertive

retort *verb* **1** = **reply**, return, answer, respond, counter, come back with, riposte

r

▶ *noun* **2 = reply**, response, answer, comeback (*informal*), rejoinder, riposte

retract *verb* **1 = withdraw**, deny, renounce, revoke, renege, recant, disavow, disclaim, eat one's words, take back
2 = draw in, pull back, pull in, sheathe

retreat *verb* **1 = withdraw**, back away, back off, draw back, pull back • *The rebels retreated from the town.*
OPPOSITE: advance
▶ *noun* **2 = withdrawal**, flight, evacuation, departure • *the long retreat from the capital*
OPPOSITE: advance
3 = refuge, haven, sanctuary • *He spent the day hidden away in his country retreat.*

retrench *verb* **= economize**, save, cut back, make economies, tighten one's belt

retrenchment *noun* **= cutback**, cut, economy, cost-cutting, tightening one's belt

retribution *noun* **= punishment**, justice, revenge, retaliation, reprisal, vengeance, reckoning, Nemesis

retrieval *See* **recovery**

retrieve *verb* **= get back**, save, recover, restore, regain, recoup, redeem, recapture, win back

retrograde *adjective* **= deteriorating**, downward, backward, degenerative, regressive, declining, retrogressive, worsening

retrogress *verb* **= deteriorate**, decline, worsen, relapse, backslide, regress, go back, go downhill (*informal*)

retrospect *noun* **= hindsight**, review, re-examination

return *verb* **1 = go back**, reappear, come back, turn back • *The plane failed to return at the scheduled time.*
2 = give back, refund, reimburse, repay, pay back, recompense • *You can return the coat if it doesn't fit.*
3 = put back, replace, restore, reinstate, re-establish

4 = reply, answer, respond, retort
5 = elect, choose, vote in
▶ *noun* **6 = restoration**, reinstatement, re-establishment
7 = reappearance, recurrence
8 = retreat, rebound, recoil
9 = profit, interest, gain, income, revenue, yield, proceeds, takings
10 = report, list, statement, form, account, summary
11 = reply, response, answer, comeback (*informal*), retort, rejoinder
See also: **vote**

reunion *See* **meeting**

revamp *verb* **= renovate**, restore, overhaul, refurbish, do up (*informal*), recondition

reveal *verb* **1 = make known**, announce, disclose, divulge, get off your chest (*informal*) • *They were not ready to reveal any of the details.*
2 = uncover, unveil, unearth, bring to light, lay bare • *The carpet was removed to reveal the original pine floor.*
See also: **betray, expose, indicate, show**

revel *verb* **1 = celebrate**, carouse, live it up (*informal*), make merry
▷ **revel in = enjoy**, relish, delight in, indulge in, lap up, luxuriate in, take pleasure in, thrive on
▶ *noun* **2** (*often plural*) **= merrymaking**, party, celebration, festivity, spree, carousal

revelation *noun* **= disclosure**, news, exposure, exhibition, publication, proclamation, unveiling, exposé, uncovering, unearthing

reveller *noun* **= merrymaker**, partygoer, carouser

revelry *noun* **= festivity**, party, fun, celebration, spree, carousal, jollity, merrymaking

revenge *noun* **1 = retaliation**, reprisal, vengeance, retribution • *acts of revenge*
▶ *verb* **2 = avenge**, retaliate, get

even, get your own back, hit
back, pay someone back • *He
vowed to revenge himself on his
enemies.*
revenue *noun* = **income**, gain,
yield, proceeds, profits, receipts,
returns, takings
reverberate *verb* = **echo**, ring,
resound, vibrate, re-echo
revere *verb* = **be in awe of**, respect,
honor, worship, reverence,
venerate, exalt, look up to
reverence *noun* = **awe**, respect,
honor, worship, admiration,
high esteem, veneration
reverent *adjective* = **respectful**,
humble, deferential, awed,
reverential
reverie *noun* = **daydream**,
abstraction, brown study,
woolgathering
reverse *verb* **1** = **change**,
overturn, retract, overrule,
invalidate • *They won't reverse the
decision to increase prices.*
2 = **turn around**, upend, invert,
transpose, turn back, turn over,
turn upside down
3 = **go backwards**, back, retreat,
back up, move backwards
▶ *noun* **4** = **opposite**, contrary,
converse • *The reverse seldom
applies.*
5 = **back**, rear, underside, other
side, wrong side
6 = **misfortune**, blow, failure,
setback, disappointment,
reversal, mishap, hardship,
adversity, misadventure,
affliction
▶ *adjective* **7** = **opposite**, contrary,
converse
revert *verb* = **return**, resume,
come back, go back
review *noun* **1** = **critique**, notice,
criticism, commentary • *The
school play received excellent
reviews.*
2 = **survey**, report, study,
analysis, examination • *a review
of safety procedures*
3 = **magazine**, journal,
periodical
4 (*Military*) = **inspection**, parade,
march past

▶ *verb* **5** = **assess**, study, judge,
criticize, evaluate
6 = **reconsider**, revise, rethink,
reassess, re-examine, re-
evaluate, think over
7 = **look back on**, recall,
remember, recollect, reflect on
8 = **inspect**, examine
See also: **summary**
reviewer *noun* = **critic**, judge,
commentator
revile *verb* = **malign**, abuse, knock
(*informal*), denigrate, reproach,
bad-mouth (*slang*), run down,
vilify
revise *verb* = **change**, update,
correct, edit, revamp, amend
• *The second edition was completely
revised.*
revision *noun* = **change**,
amendment, correction,
emendation, updating
revival *noun* = **renewal**,
resurgence, renaissance, rebirth,
revitalization, resurrection,
reawakening
revive *verb* = **revitalize**, rally,
resuscitate • *an attempt to revive
the stagnant economy*
See also: **recover**, **refresh**
revoke *verb* = **cancel**, withdraw,
reverse, quash, retract, rescind,
repeal, negate, annul, nullify,
invalidate, countermand,
disclaim, obviate, set aside
revolt *noun* **1** = **uprising**,
insurgency, revolution,
rebellion, rising, insurrection,
mutiny
▶ *verb* **2** = **rebel**, rise, resist,
mutiny
3 = **disgust**, sicken, repel,
nauseate, repulse, gross out
(*slang*), make one's flesh creep,
turn one's stomach
revolting *adjective* = **disgusting**,
foul, horrible, repellent,
sickening, horrid, repulsive,
repugnant, nauseating, scuzzy
(*slang*), yucky or yukky (*slang*)
revolution *noun* **1** = **revolt**,
insurgency, coup, rebellion,
uprising, rising, mutiny
2 = **transformation**, shift,
innovation, upheaval,

r

reformation, sea change
3 = rotation, turn, cycle, circle,
spin, orbit, lap, circuit
revolutionary adjective **1 = rebel**,
insurgent, extremist, radical,
subversive
2 = innovative, new, different,
novel, radical, progressive,
drastic, ground-breaking
▶ noun **3 = rebel**, insurgent,
revolutionist
revolutionize verb **= transform**,
reform, modernize
revolve verb **= rotate**, turn, circle,
spin, orbit, twist, wheel, whirl,
go round
revulsion noun **= disgust**,
loathing, abhorrence,
detestation, repugnance,
repulsion
reward noun **1 = payment**, bonus,
bounty, prize • As a reward for good
behaviour, praise your child.
2 = punishment, retribution,
just deserts
▶ verb **3 = pay**, compensate,
repay, remunerate, recompense
rewarding adjective
= worthwhile, valuable,
productive, profitable,
beneficial, fruitful, enriching,
fulfilling, satisfying
rhapsodize verb **= enthuse**, rave
(informal), gush, go into ecstasies
rhetoric noun **1 = oratory**,
eloquence
2 = hyperbole, bombast,
grandiloquence,
magniloquence, verbosity,
wordiness
rhetorical adjective **= oratorical**,
bombastic, verbose,
declamatory, grandiloquent,
high-flown, magniloquent
rhyme noun **1 = poetry**, song,
poem, verse, ode
▶ verb **2 = sound like**, harmonize
rhythm noun **= beat**, time, pulse,
tempo • His body twists and sways
to the rhythm.
rhythmic, rhythmical adjective
= cadenced, musical, periodic,
lilting, metrical, pulsating,
throbbing
ribald adjective **= rude**, blue,

broad, naughty, coarse, bawdy,
earthy, obscene, racy, vulgar,
smutty
rich adjective **1 = wealthy**,
affluent, prosperous, loaded
(slang), opulent, well off • You're
going to be a very rich person.
OPPOSITE: poor
2 = abundant, plentiful, fertile
• Bananas are rich in vitamin A.
3 = well-stocked, full,
productive, well-supplied
4 = full-bodied, sweet, fatty,
tasty, creamy, luscious,
succulent
See also: **colourful**
riches plural noun **= wealth**,
substance, plenty, fortune,
treasure, affluence, assets,
resources
richly adverb **1 = elaborately**,
elegantly, exquisitely, lavishly,
luxuriously, sumptuously,
expensively, gorgeously,
opulently, splendidly
2 = fully, well, properly,
thoroughly, appropriately,
suitably, amply
rickety adjective **= shaky**,
precarious, insecure, unsteady,
wobbly, ramshackle, unsound,
tottering
ricochet See **bounce**
rid verb **= free**, clear, deliver,
relieve, purge, disburden,
disencumber, make free,
unburden
▷ **get rid of = dispose of**, remove,
dump, eject, jettison, weed out
• a coach who wanted to get rid of me
riddle noun **= puzzle**, problem,
mystery, conundrum, enigma,
poser
riddled adjective **= filled**,
damaged, infested, permeated,
pervaded, spoilt
ride verb **1 = control**, manage,
handle
2 = travel, go, move, be carried
▶ noun **3 = trip**, drive, lift,
journey, outing, jaunt
ridge See **top**
ridicule noun **1 = mockery**,
laughter, scorn, jeer, derision,
chaff, gibe, raillery

▶ *verb* **2** = **laugh at**, mock, jeer, deride, sneer, chaff, make fun of, poke fun at

ridiculous *adjective* = **laughable**, absurd, ludicrous, preposterous
• *It is ridiculous to suggest we are having secret meetings.*
See also: **crazy, silly**

rife *adjective* = **widespread**, general, common, frequent, universal, rampant, prevalent, ubiquitous

riffraff *noun* = **rabble**, dregs of society (*slang*), hoi polloi, scum of the earth (*slang*)

rifle *verb* = **ransack**, strip, sack, rob, loot, plunder, pillage, burglarize, go through

rift *noun* **1** = **breach**, division, split, separation, disagreement, quarrel, falling out (*informal*)
2 = **split**, break, opening, crack, gap, flaw, fault, fissure, cleft, crevice

rig *verb* **1** = **fix** (*informal*), engineer, arrange, manipulate, gerrymander, tamper with
2 = **equip**, furnish, fit out, supply, outfit
▷ **rig out** = **dress**, clothe, costume, array, attire; = **equip**, fit, furnish, outfit
▷ **rig up** = **set up**, build, arrange, assemble, construct, erect, improvize, fix up, put together, put up
▶ *noun* **3** = **apparatus**, equipment, tackle, gear, fittings, fixtures

right *adjective* **1** = **correct**, true, strict, accurate, exact, valid, genuine, precise, factual • *That clock never tells the right time.*
OPPOSITE: **wrong**
2 = **proper**, fit, OK (*informal*), appropriate, acceptable, suitable, fitting, desirable, done, seemly • *The time is right for our escape.*
3 = **just**, good, fair, proper, moral, ethical, honest, lawful, equitable
▶ *noun* **4** = **justice**, honour, equity, integrity, fairness, virtue, morality, legality • *At least*

he knew right from wrong.
5 = **prerogative**, business, claim, power, authority, due, freedom, licence, permission, privilege, liberty
▶ *adverb* **6** = **correctly**, exactly, truly, precisely, accurately, genuinely
7 = **properly**, appropriately, suitably, fittingly, aptly
8 = **straight**, quickly, directly, promptly, straightaway
9 = **exactly**, precisely, squarely
▷ **right away** *adverb*
= **immediately**, now, directly, instantly, straightaway, at once, forthwith, pronto (*informal*)
▷ **right now** *See* **now**
▶ *verb* **10** = **rectify**, settle, fix, correct, redress, straighten, put right, sort out
See also: **immediately**

│ INFORMALLY SPEAKING
│ **in the right**: morally correct
│ **right now**: immediately

righteous *adjective* = **virtuous**, good, just, fair, moral, ethical, honest, pure, upright, honorable

righteousness *noun* = **virtue**, justice, integrity, honesty, honour, morality, goodness, purity, probity, rectitude, uprightness

rightful *adjective* = **lawful**, just, real, legal, due, true, proper, legitimate, valid

right-hand man *See* **assistant, helper**

righting *See* **correction**

right-wing *adjective*
= **conservative**, reactionary
• *some right-wing groups*

rigid *adjective* **1** = **strict**, set, stringent, inflexible, fixed
• *Hospital routines for nurses are sometimes very rigid.*
2 = **stiff**, hard, firm, solid • *rigid plastic containers*
OPPOSITE: **flexible**
See also: **tense, tight**

rigmarole *noun* = **procedure**, bother, nonsense, fuss, hassle (*informal*), palaver

rigorous *adjective* = **strict**, hard, tough, severe, harsh, stringent,

r

stern, demanding, exacting, inflexible

rigorously See **well**

rigour noun **1 = strictness**, rigidity, harshness, inflexibility, sternness, stringency
2 = hardship, trial, suffering, ordeal, privation

rig-out noun = **outfit**, dress, gear (informal), costume, garb, get-up (informal), togs

rile verb = **anger**, aggravate (informal), irk, annoy, irritate, get one's back up or put one's back up

rim noun = **edge**, border, margin, brink, lip, verge, brim

rind noun = **skin**, peel, crust, husk, outer layer

ring[1] noun **1 = circle**, round, band, hoop, loop • a ring of blue smoke
2 = gang, cell, band, syndicate • a drug-trafficking ring
3 = arena, rink, circus, enclosure
▶ verb **4 = encircle**, surround, enclose, gird, girdle

ring[2] verb **1 = chime**, toll, resonate, clang, peal • He heard the school bell ring.
▶ noun **2 = chime**, knell, peal
See also: **sound**

ringleader See **leader**

rinse verb = **wash**, clean, dip, splash, cleanse, bathe

riot noun **1 = disturbance**, disorder, strife, anarchy, mob violence • a prison riot
2 = revelry, festivity, frolic, carousal, high jinks, merrymaking
3 = profusion, show, display, splash, extravaganza
▷ **run riot = rampage**, be out of control, go wild; **= grow profusely**, spread like wildfire
▶ verb **4 = rampage**, go on the rampage, run riot, take to the streets • They rioted in protest against the government.

riotous adjective
1 = unrestrained, wild, loud, noisy, boisterous, uproarious
2 = unruly, violent, disorderly, lawless, rowdy, rebellious, anarchic, ungovernable

rip verb **1 = tear**, cut, split, slash, burst, claw, gash, slit, lacerate, rend
▷ **rip off** (Slang) = **swindle**, rob, con (informal), cheat, defraud, fleece
▶ noun **2 = tear**, cut, hole, split, slash, rent, gash, slit, laceration

ripe adjective **1 = mature**, ready, seasoned, mellow, ripened
2 = suitable, right, ideal, timely, opportune, favourable, auspicious

ripen verb = **mature**, season, develop, burgeon, grow ripe

rip-off noun = **swindle**, fraud, theft, scam (slang), con (informal), cheat, con trick (informal)

riposte noun **1 = retort**, response, answer, comeback (informal), reply, rejoinder, sally
▶ verb **2 = retort**, answer, respond, reply, come back

ripple See **wave**

rise verb **1 = go up**, climb, ascend, move up • smoke rising from the volcano
2 = increase, grow, mount, intensify, go up • House prices are expected to rise this year.
OPPOSITE: fall
3 = get up, arise, get to one's feet, stand up
4 = get steeper, ascend, go uphill, slope upwards
5 = rebel, revolt, mutiny
6 = originate, issue, happen, spring, occur
▷ **rise to** See **reach**
▶ noun **7 = increase**, improvement, upsurge • a rise in prices
OPPOSITE: fall
8 = advancement, progress, climb, promotion
9 = upward slope, ascent, incline, elevation
▷ **give rise to = cause**, produce, effect, bring about, result in
See also: **gain, jump, slope**

| CONFUSABLES
Rise means get up or go up.
Raise means lift up.

risk noun **1 = danger**, gamble, peril, pitfall • That's a risk

I'm happy to take.
▶ verb **2 = dare**, chance, gamble, jeopardize, put in jeopardy • *If he doesn't play, he risks losing his place in the team.*
See also: **endanger, possibility, threat**
risky adjective **= dangerous**, chancy (informal), unsafe, uncertain, hazardous, perilous
risqué adjective **= suggestive**, blue, improper, naughty, bawdy, indelicate, racy, ribald
rite noun **= ceremony**, practice, procedure, custom, ritual, observance
ritual noun **1 = ceremony**, rite, observance
2 = custom, practice, procedure, convention, tradition, routine, habit, protocol
▶ adjective **3 = ceremonial**, routine, conventional, customary, habitual
ritzy adjective (Slang) **= luxurious**, grand, luxury, posh (informal, chiefly Brit), plush (informal), deluxe, sumptuous, swanky or swank (informal), high-class
rival noun **1 = opponent**, challenger, adversary, antagonist • *She is well ahead of her nearest rival.*
▶ verb **2 = equal**, match, be a match for • *For beauty, few beaches rival those of Prince Edward Island.*
▶ adjective **3 = competing**, conflicting, opposing
See also: **competitor**
rivalry noun **= competition**, opposition, contest, conflict, contention
river noun **1 = stream**, brook, waterway, creek, tributary

TYPES OF RIVER	
brook	stream
creek	tributary
estuary	watercourse
rivulet	waterway
side channel (Canad)	

2 = flow, flood, rush, spate, torrent
riveting adjective **= enthralling**, hypnotic, absorbing, captivating, engrossing, fascinating, gripping, spellbinding
road noun **= street**, track, route, highway, roadway, grid road (Canad), direction, path, lane, artery, avenue, pathway, course, bypass, alley, freeway, interstate (US), expressway, boulevard, thoroughfare, parkway, turnpike, winter road (Canad), ice road (Canad) • *There was very little traffic on the mining road.*
See also: **way**
roam verb **= wander**, travel, walk, range, stray, rove, ramble, prowl
roar verb **1 = cry**, shout, yell, bay, howl, bellow, bawl
2 = guffaw, hoot, laugh heartily, split one's sides (informal)
▶ noun **3 = cry**, shout, yell, outcry, howl, bellow
4 = guffaw, hoot
roast See **cook**
rob verb **= steal from**, con (informal), loot, defraud, swindle, burgle, burglarize • *He was robbed of all his money.*
robber noun **= thief**, bandit, fraud, cheat, burglar, raider, looter, stealer, con man (informal), mugger (informal), plunderer
robbery noun **= theft**, raid, burglary, larceny, swindle, plunder, pillage, mugging (informal), rip-off (slang), hold-up, stealing, stick-up (slang)
robe noun **1 = gown**, habit, costume
▶ verb **2 = clothe**, dress, garb
robot noun **= machine**, android, automaton, mechanical man
robust adjective **= strong**, tough, healthy, powerful, fit, vigorous, muscular, sturdy, hardy, stout, hale, strapping
rock¹ noun **= stone**, boulder
rock² verb **1 = sway**, pitch, roll, toss, swing, reel, lurch
2 = shock, surprise, shake,

r

stun, astonish, stagger, astound
rocket See **bomb, explode**
rocky[1] adjective = **rough**, rugged, craggy, stony
rocky[2] adjective = **unstable**, shaky, unsteady, wobbly, rickety
rod noun = **stick**, staff, bar, pole, shaft, baton, cane, wand
rogue noun = **scoundrel**, fraud, crook (informal), rascal, villain, scamp
role noun 1 = **job**, post, part, position, duty, capacity, function, task
2 = **part**, character, portrayal, representation
roll verb 1 = **turn**, spin, wheel, revolve, rotate, whirl, twirl, swivel, trundle, go round
2 = **wind**, wrap, bind, envelop, swathe, enfold, furl
3 = **flow**, run, undulate
4 = **flatten**, even, level, press, smooth
5 = **tumble**, rock, toss, reel, sway, lurch
▶ noun 6 = **turn**, cycle, spin, wheel, revolution, reel, rotation, whirl, twirl
7 = **register**, record, list, index, census
8 = **rumble**, boom, roar, thunder, reverberation
rollicking adjective = **boisterous**, lively, hearty, playful, exuberant, carefree, jaunty, devil-may-care
roly-poly adjective = **plump**, fat, rounded, chubby, pudgy, buxom, tubby
romance noun 1 = **love affair**, relationship, affair, attachment, liaison, amour
2 = **excitement**, mystery, charm, glamour, colour, fascination
3 = **story**, legend, tale, fantasy, melodrama, fairy tale, love story
romantic adjective 1 = **loving**, tender, passionate, amorous • a romantic relationship
2 = **idealistic**, unrealistic, impractical, dreamy, starry-eyed
3 = **exciting**, mysterious, glamorous, colourful, fascinating

▶ noun 4 = **idealist**, dreamer, sentimentalist
romp verb 1 = **frolic**, sport, caper, cavort, frisk, gambol, have fun
2 = **win easily**, walk it (informal), win by a mile (informal), win hands down
▶ noun 3 = **frolic**, caper, lark (informal)
room noun 1 = **chamber**, office
• You can stay in my room.
2 = **space**, capacity, elbow room
• There wasn't enough room in the car.
3 = **opportunity**, chance, occasion, scope
▷ **rooms** See **apartment**
roomy adjective = **spacious**, large, wide, broad, extensive, generous, sizable or sizeable, ample, capacious, commodious
root[1] noun 1 = **stem**, rhizome, tuber
2 = **source**, cause, base, heart, seat, bottom, seed, core, foundation, origin, nucleus
▷ **roots** = **sense of belonging**, home, family, heritage, birthplace, cradle, origins
▶ verb 3 = **establish**, set, ground, stick, fix, anchor, implant, moor, fasten
root[2] verb = **dig**, burrow, ferret
▷ **root out** = **get rid of**, remove, eliminate, eradicate, abolish, exterminate, do away with, extirpate, weed out
rooted adjective = **deep-seated**, firm, deep, established, entrenched, ingrained, confirmed, deeply felt, fixed
rope noun = **cord**, line, cable, strand, hawser
▷ **know the ropes** = **be experienced**, be an old hand, be knowledgeable
rope in verb = **persuade**, involve, engage, enlist, inveigle, talk into
ropey, ropy adjective (Informal)
1 = **inferior**, poor, inadequate, lousy (slang), deficient, substandard, of poor quality
2 = **unwell**, lousy (slang), below par, off colour, under the weather (informal)
roster noun = **rota**, list, schedule,

roll, table, register, agenda, catalogue

rostrum noun = **stage**, stand, platform, podium, dais

rosy adjective 1 = **pink**, red
2 = **glowing**, radiant, blooming, healthy-looking, ruddy
3 = **promising**, bright, optimistic, hopeful, cheerful, favorable, auspicious, encouraging

rot verb 1 = **decay**, spoil, decompose, fester • *The grain started rotting in the silos.*
RELATED WORD
adjective: putrid
2 = **deteriorate**, decline, waste away
▶ noun 3 = **decay**, deterioration, mould, putrefaction, putrescence • *The wood was not protected against rot.*
See also: **eat away**

rotary adjective = **revolving**, turning, rotating, spinning

rotate verb 1 = **revolve**, turn, spin, wheel, reel, pivot, swivel, gyrate, go round
2 = **take turns**, switch, alternate

rotation noun 1 = **revolution**, turn, spin, orbit, wheel, reel, turning, spinning
2 = **sequence**, cycle, succession, alternation, switching

rotten adjective 1 = **decayed**, bad, sour, mouldy, decomposed • *The old wooden window frame is rotten.*
2 (informal) = **inferior**, poor, lousy (slang), unsatisfactory • *It's a rotten idea.*
3 = **corrupt**, immoral, crooked (informal), dishonest, dishonourable, perfidious
4 (Informal) = **despicable**, base, mean, dirty, nasty, lousy (slang), contemptible, scuzzy (slang)
See also: **shabby, terrible**

rotund adjective 1 = **round**, rounded, globular, spherical
2 = **plump**, fat, portly, chubby, fleshy, stout, pudgy, corpulent, tubby

rough adjective 1 = **uneven**, rocky, rugged, bumpy, craggy

• *My bicycle bumped along the rough ground.*
OPPOSITE: smooth
2 = **unpleasant**, hard, tough, difficult • *He's been through a rough time.*
3 = **approximate**, estimated, vague, sketchy • *I can give you a rough idea of the time.*
4 = **ungracious**, blunt, rude, coarse, brusque, impolite, unceremonious, uncivil, uncouth, unmannerly
5 = **stormy**, wild, turbulent, choppy, squally
6 = **nasty**, hard, tough, violent, harsh, cruel, unpleasant, unfeeling
7 = **basic**, crude, incomplete, unfinished, sketchy, imperfect, rudimentary, unrefined, unpolished
▶ verb
▷ **rough out** = **outline**, plan, draft, sketch
▶ noun 8 = **outline**, draft, mock-up, preliminary sketch
See also: **broad, jagged, primitive**

> INFORMALLY SPEAKING
> **rough in**: shape or sketch roughly
> **rough it**: do without conveniences

rough-and-ready adjective = **makeshift**, crude, provisional, sketchy, unrefined, stopgap, improvised, unpolished

roughly See **about**

round adjective 1 = **spherical**, circular, rounded, cylindrical • *a round pizza in a square box*
2 = **plump**, full, ample, fleshy, rotund, full-fleshed
▶ noun 3 = **stage**, period, session, lap • *After round three, two contestants shared the lead.*
4 = **sphere**, ball, band, ring, circle, globe, disc, orb
5 = **series**, session, cycle, sequence, succession
6 = **course**, beat, series, schedule, tour, routine, circuit
▶ verb 7 = **go round**, turn, circle, bypass, skirt, flank, encircle

r

▷ **round off** = **complete**, close, conclude, finish off

▷ **round up** = **gather**, group, drive, rally, collect, herd, muster, marshal

roundabout adjective = **indirect**, oblique, evasive, devious, tortuous, circuitous, discursive

rounded See **blunt, round**

roundup noun = **gathering**, rally, collection, assembly, muster, herding, marshalling

rouse verb **1** = **wake up**, call, rise, wake, awaken
2 = **excite**, move, anger, provoke, stir, stimulate, incite, inflame, agitate, animate

rousing adjective = **lively**, exciting, spirited, moving, inspiring, stimulating, stirring

rout noun **1** = **defeat**, beating, overthrow, debacle, drubbing, thrashing
▶ verb **2** = **defeat**, beat, destroy, crush, trounce, overthrow, conquer, drub, thrash, wipe the floor with (informal)

route noun = **way**, road, course, channel, path, itinerary • the direct route to the downtown area
See also: **direction, line, passage**

routine adjective **1** = **usual**, standard, regular, normal, typical, ordinary, everyday • a series of routine medical tests
2 = **boring**, predictable, dull, tedious, tiresome, humdrum
▶ noun **3** = **procedure**, program, system, order, schedule, practice, pattern • The players had to change their daily routine.
See also: **custom, habit, stock, straightforward**

rove verb = **wander**, range, drift, roam, stray, ramble, traipse (informal)

row¹ noun = **line**, bank, rank, column, queue • She was greeted by a row of glum faces.

row² noun **1** = **quarrel**, argument, altercation, squabble • This could provoke a major diplomatic row with neighbouring countries.
2 = **disturbance**, noise, uproar, racket, commotion, tumult, rumpus
▶ verb **3** = **quarrel**, fight, dispute, argue, squabble, wrangle
See also: **disagreement**

rowdy adjective = **disorderly**, wild, noisy, boisterous, unruly • He complained to the police about rowdy neighbours.

royal adjective **1** = **regal**, sovereign, imperial • the royal yacht
2 = **splendid**, grand, impressive, magnificent, majestic, stately

rub verb **1** = **polish**, clean, shine, wipe, scour
2 = **chafe**, scrape, fray, grate, abrade
▷ **rub out** = **erase**, remove, cancel, delete, obliterate, efface, wipe out
▶ noun **3** = **polish**, stroke, shine, wipe
4 = **massage**, caress, kneading

rubbish noun **1** = **waste**, refuse, garbage, trash, litter • tons of rubbish waiting to be dumped
2 = **nonsense**, garbage, drivel, hot air (informal) • Don't talk rubbish!
See also: **junk**

ruckus noun (Informal) = **uproar**, trouble, disturbance, fuss, commotion, fracas, hoopla

ructions plural noun (Informal) = **uproar**, trouble, row, disturbance, fuss, commotion, fracas, hue and cry

ruddy adjective = **rosy**, healthy, red, fresh, glowing, radiant, blooming, reddish, rosy-cheeked

rude adjective **1** = **impolite**, disrespectful, impertinent, impudent, insolent • He is rude to her friends.
OPPOSITE: polite
2 = **unpleasant**, violent, abrupt • a rude awakening
3 = **vulgar**, rough, coarse, boorish, uncivilized, brutish, graceless, loutish, oafish, uncouth, uncultured
4 = **roughly-made**, crude, simple, rough, raw, makeshift,

primitive, artless, inartistic, inelegant
See also: **abusive, common, dirty, indecent**

rudimentary adjective = **basic**, early, initial, fundamental, elementary, primitive, undeveloped

rudiments plural noun = **basics**, foundation, beginnings, elements, essentials, fundamentals

rue verb = **regret**, mourn, lament, repent, be sorry for, kick oneself for

rueful adjective = **regretful**, sorry, mournful, remorseful, contrite, penitent, repentant, sorrowful

ruffian noun = **thug**, bully, brute, hooligan, hoodlum, tough

ruffle verb 1 = **disarrange**, disorder, dishevel, rumple, tousle, mess up
2 = **annoy**, upset, irritate, agitate, fluster, peeve (informal), nettle, tick off

rugged adjective 1 = **rough**, difficult, rocky, irregular, bumpy, uneven, jagged, ragged, craggy, broken
2 = **strong-featured**, rough-hewn, weather-beaten
3 = **tough**, strong, robust, husky (informal), muscular, sturdy, burly, brawny, well-built

ruin verb 1 = **destroy**, break, damage, devastate, spoil, wreck, impair, mar, undo, mess up (informal) • The crops have been ruined.
2 = **bankrupt**, impoverish, pauperize
3 = **spoil**, damage, blow (slang), botch, make a mess of, mess up, screw up (informal)
▶ noun 4 = **destruction**, fall, devastation, downfall, decay, disrepair • The old factory was in a state of ruin.
5 = **wreckage**, shell, wreck, remains • the burned-out ruins of the building
6 = **disrepair**, wreckage, decay, disintegration, ruination

7 = **bankruptcy**, insolvency, destitution
See also: **crash, harm**

ruined See **derelict**

ruinous adjective 1 = **devastating**, disastrous, dire, catastrophic, destructive, calamitous, shattering
2 = **extravagant**, crippling, wasteful, immoderate

rule noun 1 = **regulation**, order, law, guideline, decree • This was against the rules.
2 = **custom**, practice, procedure, convention, tradition, routine, habit
3 = **government**, power, control, authority, regime, command, reign, jurisdiction, mastery, dominion
▷ **as a rule** = **usually**, generally, mainly, normally, on the whole • As a rule, I eat my meals in front of the TV.
▶ verb 4 = **govern**, lead, reign, administer, be in power • He rules the country with a strong hand.
5 = **be prevalent**, prevail, be customary, predominate, preponderate
6 = **decree**, judge, decide, settle, pronounce
See also: **line**
▷ **rule out** = **exclude**, ban, reject, eliminate, dismiss, prohibit, disqualify, preclude, debar, leave out

ruler noun 1 = **governor**, leader, premier, commander, monarch, sovereign, head of state, prime minister
2 = **measure**, rule, yardstick • He was a weak-willed and indecisive ruler.

rules See **standards**

ruling noun 1 = **decision**, verdict, judgment, decree, pronouncement, adjudication
▶ adjective 2 = **governing**, commanding, controlling, reigning
3 = **predominant**, chief, main, principal, dominant, pre-eminent, preponderant, prevailing

ruminate verb = **ponder**, think, consider, reflect, deliberate, contemplate, muse, cogitate, mull over, turn over in one's mind

rummage verb = **search**, hunt, root, forage, delve, ransack

rumour noun = **story**, word, gossip, hearsay, whisper
• *persistent rumours of problems within the team*

rumoured See **supposed**

rump noun = **buttocks**, bottom, backside (*informal*), seat, butt (*informal*), rear, posterior, buns (*slang*), derrière (*euphemistic*), hindquarters, rear end

rumpus noun = **commotion**, row, noise, uproar, disturbance, fuss, furor, hue and cry

run verb 1 = **race**, sprint, bolt, jog, gallop • *I excused myself and ran back to the telephone.*
2 = **manage**, control, direct, administer, be in charge of, look after • *He ran a small hotel.*
3 = **flee**, bolt, beat a retreat, beat it (*slang*), escape, make a run for it, take flight, take off (*informal*), take to one's heels
4 = **move**, go, pass, course, roll, skim, glide
5 = **work**, go, operate, perform, function
6 = **continue**, go, reach, extend, stretch, proceed
7 = **flow**, go, leak, spill, pour, stream, discharge, gush, spout
8 = **melt**, dissolve, liquefy, go soft
9 = **publish**, feature, display, print
10 = **compete**, stand, contend, be a candidate, put oneself up for, take part, re-offer (*Canad*)
11 = **smuggle**, bootleg, traffic in
▷ **run across** See **meet**, encounter, bump into, come across, run into
▷ **run amok** See **rampage**
▷ **run around** See **associate**
▷ **run away** = **flee**, bolt, abscond, escape, fly the coop (*informal*), make a run for it, scram (*informal*), take to one's heels
▷ **run down** = **criticize**, bad-mouth (*slang*), knock (*informal*), decry, disparage, denigrate, belittle; = **reduce**, cut, decrease, trim, curtail, downsize, cut back, downscale; = **knock down**, hit, knock over, run into, run over; = **weaken**, exhaust, debilitate
▷ **run into** = **meet**, encounter, bump into, come across *or* come upon, run across; = **hit**, strike, collide with
▷ **run off** = **flee**, bolt, escape, fly the coop (*informal*), make off, run away, take flight, take to one's heels
▷ **run out** = **be used up**, end, finish, fail, be exhausted, dry up, give out
▷ **run over** = **knock down**, hit, knock over, run down; = **go through**, check, rehearse, go over, run through
▷ **run riot** See **rampage, riot**
▷ **run through** = **rehearse**, read, practise, go over, run over
▶ noun 12 = **race**, rush, sprint, dash, jog, spurt, gallop
13 = **ride**, drive, trip, spin (*informal*), outing, excursion, jaunt
14 = **sequence**, season, period, series, course, stretch, string, spell
15 = **enclosure**, pen, coop
▷ **in the long run** = **eventually**, ultimately, in the end
See also: **conduct, head, range, supervise**

| INFORMALLY SPEAKING
run across (or into): meet by chance
run out on: desert someone
run up against: face a problem or difficulty
run with: go ahead creatively with a plan

runaway noun 1 = **fugitive**, refugee, deserter, escapee, truant
▶ adjective 2 = **escaped**, wild, loose, fugitive, fleeing

rundown See **outline, summary**

run-down adjective
1 = **exhausted**, weak, unhealthy,

weary, worn-out, below par, debilitated, drained, enervated
2 = dilapidated, shabby, seedy, decrepit, worn-out, ramshackle, broken-down
runner noun **1 = athlete**, sprinter, jogger
2 = messenger, courier, dispatch bearer, errand boy
running adjective **1 = continuous**, constant, perpetual, uninterrupted, incessant, unbroken, twenty-four-seven (slang)
2 = flowing, moving, streaming
▶ noun **3 = management**, control, organization, leadership, administration, direction, supervision
4 = working, operation, performance, maintenance, functioning
runny adjective **= flowing**, liquid, fluid, watery, liquefied, melted
run-of-the-mill adjective **= ordinary**, average, mediocre, tolerable, passable, middling, undistinguished, unexceptional
rupture noun **1 = break**, tear, split, crack, breach, rent, burst, fissure
▶ verb **2 = break**, separate, tear, split, crack, burst, sever
rural adjective **= rustic**, country, agricultural, pastoral, sylvan
ruse noun **= trick**, device, hoax, dodge, ploy, manoeuvre, subterfuge, stratagem
rush verb **1 = hurry**, run, shoot, race, fly, dash, hasten, hustle, gush, scurry • Someone rushed out of the building.
2 = push, pressure, press, hurry • Ministers won't be rushed into a response.

3 = attack, charge, storm
▶ noun **4 = hurry**, race, scramble, dash, stampede, bustle, outrush • the rush not to be late for school
5 = attack, charge, assault, onslaught
▶ adjective **6 = hasty**, fast, quick, rapid, urgent, swift, hurried
See also: **bolt, burst, flood, speed, wave**
rust noun **1 = corrosion**, oxidation
2 = mildew, must, rot, blight, mould
▶ verb **3 = corrode**, oxidize
rustic adjective **1 = rural**, country, pastoral, sylvan
2 = uncouth, crude, rough, awkward, coarse
▶ noun **3 = yokel**, peasant, redneck (slang), hick (informal), hillbilly, boor, bumpkin, clod, clodhopper (informal)
rustle verb **1 = crackle**, whisper, crinkle
▶ noun **2 = crackle**, whisper, crinkling, rustling
rusty adjective **1 = corroded**, oxidized, rust-covered, rusted
2 = reddish-brown, chestnut, coppery, reddish, russet, rust-coloured
3 = out of practice, weak, stale, unpractised
rut noun **1 = groove**, track, trough, furrow, indentation, wheel mark
2 = habit, system, pattern, routine, dead end
ruthless adjective **= merciless**, harsh, brutal, cruel, relentless, callous, heartless, pitiless, remorseless
rutted adjective **= grooved**, cut, marked, furrowed, gouged, holed, indented, scored

Ss

sabotage *noun* **1 = damage**, destruction, disruption, subversion, wrecking
▶ *verb* **2 = damage**, destroy, disrupt, wreck, vandalize, disable, incapacitate, subvert

saccharine *adjective* **= oversweet**, sugary, sickly, cloying, honeyed, nauseating, syrupy

sack[1] *noun* **1 = bag**, pocket, pouch, receptacle
▶ *verb (Informal)* **2 = dismiss**, fire, discharge • *sacked for missing work so often*

sack[2] *noun* **1 = plundering**, pillage, looting
▶ *verb* **2 = plunder**, raid, strip, ruin, rob, loot, pillage

sacred *adjective* **1 = holy**, divine, hallowed, blessed, revered, sanctified
2 = religious, holy, ecclesiastical
3 = inviolable, protected, sacrosanct

sacrifice *verb* **1 = give up**, surrender, forgo, forfeit • *He sacrificed his personal life for his career.*
2 = offer, immolate, offer up
▶ *noun* **3 = surrender**, renunciation, self-denial • *He was willing to make any sacrifice for peace.*
4 = offering, oblation

sacrilege *noun* **= desecration**, violation, blasphemy, heresy, irreverence, impiety, profanation

sacrilegious *adjective* **= profane**, irreverent, blasphemous, desecrating, impious, irreligious

sacrosanct *adjective* **= inviolable**, sacred, hallowed, untouchable, inviolate, sanctified, set apart

sad *adjective* **1 = unhappy**, down, low, blue, dismal, depressed, gloomy, mournful, dejected, melancholy, grief-stricken, glum, downcast, wistful • *The loss of our friendship makes me sad.*
OPPOSITE: happy
2 = tragic, dismal, gloomy, pathetic, poignant, mournful, moving, melancholy, depressing, harrowing, heart-rending, upsetting • *a sad song*
3 = deplorable, bad, sorry, lamentable, wretched
See also: **miserable**

sadden *verb* **= upset**, grieve, distress, depress, deject, make sad

saddened See **disappointed**
saddening See **painful**

saddle *verb* **= burden**, load, encumber

sadistic *adjective* **= cruel**, brutal, vicious, ruthless, barbarous

sadness *noun* **= unhappiness**, depression, melancholy, despondency, dejection • *I said goodbye with a mixture of sadness and joy.*
OPPOSITE: happiness
See also: **grief, misery, sorrow**

safe *adjective* **1 = harmless**, innocuous, wholesome • *This is not a safe place after dark.*
OPPOSITE: dangerous
2 = secure, OK *(informal)*, protected, all right, in safe hands, out of danger, out of harm's way, safe and sound • *I feel warm and safe with you.*
3 = unharmed, intact, unhurt, unscathed, undamaged, all right, O.K. or okay *(informal)*
4 = risk-free, certain, sound, secure, impregnable
▶ *noun* **5 = strongbox**, vault, coffer, repository, deposit box, safe-deposit box

See also: **immune, reliable**
safe and sound *See* **safe**
safeguard *verb* 1 = **protect**, save, defend, guard, preserve, shield, look after • *international action to safeguard the ozone layer*
▶ *noun* 2 = **protection**, defence, cover, barrier • *adequate safeguards for civil liberties*
See also: **precaution**
safely *adverb* = **in safety**, in one piece, safe and sound, with impunity, without risk
safety *noun* 1 = **security**, protection, immunity • *I was very anxious about their safety.*
OPPOSITE: danger
2 = **shelter**, cover, refuge, sanctuary
sag *verb* 1 = **sink**, fall, bag, slump, dip, droop, give way, hang loosely
2 = **flag**, weaken, tire, wane, wilt, droop
saga *noun* = **tale**, story, legend, epic, narrative, yarn
sage *noun* 1 = **wise man**, master, elder, guru, philosopher
▶ *adjective* 2 = **wise**, sensible, judicious, sagacious, sapient
sagging *See* **flabby**
sail *verb* 1 = **set sail**, embark
2 = **glide**, fly, sweep, soar, wing, float, drift, skim
3 = **pilot**, steer
sailor *noun* = **mariner**, marine, seaman, seafarer, sea dog
saintly *adjective* = **virtuous**, religious, holy, righteous, pious, godly, saintlike
sake *noun* 1 = **benefit**, good, interest, account, behalf, welfare
2 = **purpose**, end, aim, reason, objective, motive
salacious *adjective* = **lascivious**, erotic, lewd, carnal, lecherous, libidinous, lustful
salary *noun* = **pay**, income, wage, earnings, wages
sale *noun* = **selling**, deal, transaction, marketing, disposal
▷ **for sale** = **available to buy**, obtainable, on the market
salient *adjective* = **prominent**,

important, outstanding, striking, pronounced, noticeable, conspicuous
sallow *adjective* = **wan**, unhealthy, pale, anemic, yellowish, pasty, sickly, pallid
salt *noun* 1 = **seasoning**, taste, relish, flavour, savour
▷ **with a grain of salt, with a pinch of salt** = **skeptically**, suspiciously, cynically, disbelievingly, with reservations
▶ *adjective* 2 = **salty**, saline, brackish, briny
salted *See* **salty**
salty *adjective* = **salt**, brackish, briny, salted • *salty bacon*
salubrious *adjective* = **healthy**, beneficial, wholesome, good for one, health-giving
salutary *adjective* = **beneficial**, valuable, useful, profitable, advantageous, good for one
salute *noun* 1 = **greeting**, address, recognition, salutation
▶ *verb* 2 = **greet**, address, welcome, acknowledge, hail
3 = **honour**, recognize, acknowledge, pay tribute to *or* pay homage to
salvage *verb* = **save**, recover, rescue, retrieve, redeem
salvation *noun* = **saving**, rescue, escape, redemption, preservation, deliverance
salve *noun* = **balm**, cream, lotion, ointment, emollient
same *adjective* 1 = **identical**, equivalent, equal, alike, indistinguishable • *The two words have the same sound but different spellings.*
OPPOSITE: different
2 = **aforementioned**, aforesaid
3 = **unchanged**, consistent, constant, unaltered, changeless, invariable, unvarying
See also: **like**
sameness *See* **similarity**
sample *noun* 1 = **specimen**, model, example, pattern, instance
▶ *verb* 2 = **test**, try, experience, taste, inspect
▶ *adjective* 3 = **test**, trial,

S

representative, specimen

sanctify *verb* = **consecrate**, cleanse, hallow

sanctimonious *adjective* = **holier-than-thou**, hypocritical, smug, pious, self-righteous

sanction *verb* **1** = **permit**, back, support, allow, approve, endorse, authorize • *He is ready to sanction the use of force.*
OPPOSITE: veto
▶ *noun* **2** = **permission**, support, approval, blessing, authorization, backing • *The treaty required the sanction of Parliament.*
See also: **let**

sanctions *noun* = **ban**, boycott, embargo, penalties • *Canada is considering imposing sanctions against the regime.*

sanctity *noun* **1** = **sacredness**, inviolability
2 = **holiness**, grace, goodness, piety, godliness, righteousness

sanctuary *noun* **1** = **shrine**, church, temple, altar
2 = **protection**, retreat, shelter, refuge, haven, asylum
3 = **reserve**, conservation area, national park, nature reserve

sands See **beach**

sane *adjective* **1** = **rational**, normal, lucid • *This was not the act of a sane person.*
OPPOSITE: mad
2 = **sensible**, sound, reasonable, rational, judicious, level-headed • *a sane and practical policy*

sanguine *adjective* = **cheerful**, confident, optimistic, hopeful, buoyant

sanitary *adjective* = **hygienic**, healthy, clean, wholesome, germ-free

sanitation See **hygiene**

sanity *noun* **1** = **mental health**, reason, normality, rationality, saneness
2 = **good sense**, sense, common sense, level-headedness, rationality

sap[1] *noun* **1** = **vital fluid**, essence, lifeblood

2 (*Informal*) = **fool**, idiot, jerk (*slang*), dork (*slang*), ninny, schmuck (*slang*), simpleton

sap[2] *verb* = **weaken**, drain, undermine, exhaust, deplete

sarcasm *noun* = **irony**, satire, bitterness, mockery, cynicism, derision

sarcastic *adjective* = **ironic**, satirical, caustic, sardonic • *A sarcastic remark was on the tip of her tongue.*

sarcophagus See **tomb**

sardonic *adjective* = **mocking**, dry, ironic, cynical, sarcastic, wry, derisive, sneering

Satan *noun* = **The Devil**, Beelzebub, Lord of the Flies, Lucifer, Mephistopheles, Prince of Darkness, The Evil One

satanic *adjective* = **evil**, black, wicked, demonic, devilish, hellish, diabolic, fiendish, infernal

satiate *verb* **1** = **glut**, stuff, gorge, nauseate, cloy, jade, overfill, surfeit
2 = **satisfy**, sate, slake

satire *noun* = **mockery**, caricature, parody, irony, spoof (*informal*), ridicule, lampoon, burlesque, piss-take (*informal*)

satirical, satiric *adjective* = **mocking**, cutting, ironic, caustic, incisive, biting

satirize *verb* = **ridicule**, parody, deride, lampoon, burlesque, pillory

satisfaction *noun*
1 = **contentment**, content, comfort, pride, happiness, pleasure, enjoyment, satiety, repletion
2 = **fulfillment**, achievement, gratification, assuaging

satisfactorily See **well**

satisfactory *adjective* = **adequate**, acceptable, sufficient, passable, all right, good enough • *a satisfactory explanation*
OPPOSITE: unsatisfactory
See also: **decent, suitable**

satisfied *adjective* = **content**,

S

happy, pleased, contented • *We are not satisfied with these results.*
OPPOSITE: disappointed
See also: **certain, confident, sure**

satisfy verb 1 = **gratify**, please, indulge • *a solution that I hope will satisfy everyone*
2 = **convince**, persuade, reassure, put someone's mind at rest • *He had to satisfy the doctors that he was fit to play.*
3 = **fulfill**, meet • *Applicants must satisfy the conditions for admission.*
See also: **suit**

saturate verb = **soak**, steep, drench, imbue, souse, suffuse, waterlog, wet through

saturated adjective = **soaked**, waterlogged, sodden, dripping, drenched, soaking or soaking wet, sopping or sopping wet, wet through

saturnine adjective = **gloomy**, grave, sombre, dour, glum, morose

saucy adjective 1 = **impudent**, forward, rude, cheeky (*informal*), presumptuous, impertinent, insolent, pert
2 = **jaunty**, gay, dashing, perky

saunter verb 1 = **stroll**, wander, roam, ramble, meander, amble, mosey (*informal*)
▶ noun 2 = **stroll**, turn, walk, airing, ramble, amble

savage adjective 1 = **cruel**, violent, brutal, vicious, ferocious, inhuman, barbaric, barbarous • *a savage attack*
2 = **wild**, feral, undomesticated, untamed, animalistic
3 = **uncultivated**, rough, rugged, uncivilized
4 = **primitive**, rude, unspoiled
▶ noun 5 = **lout**, monster, beast, brute, barbarian • *They really are a bunch of savages.*
▶ verb 6 = **attack**, bite, maul • *savaged to death by the animal*

savagery noun = **cruelty**, brutality, ferocity, viciousness, barbarity, ruthlessness

save verb 1 = **rescue**, deliver, salvage, redeem, come to someone's rescue • *He saved my life.*
2 = **protect**, preserve, safeguard, keep safe • *a new surgical technique which could save lives*
3 = **keep**, reserve, hoard, set aside • *I'm saving for a new computer.*
OPPOSITE: waste
▷ **save from** See **spare**
See also: **but, except, stockpile, store**

saving noun 1 = **economy**, reduction, bargain, discount
▷ **savings** = **nest egg**, fund, store, reserves, resources
▶ adjective 2 = **redeeming**, compensatory, extenuating

saviour noun = **rescuer**, defender, preserver, protector, liberator, deliverer, redeemer

Saviour noun = **Christ**, Jesus, Messiah, Redeemer

savoir-faire noun = **social graces**, poise, diplomacy, discretion, finesse, tact, social know-how (*informal*), urbanity, worldliness

savour verb 1 = **enjoy**, appreciate, relish, delight in, luxuriate in, revel in
2 (often with *of*) = **suggest**, smack, be suggestive, show signs
▶ noun 3 = **flavour**, taste, smell, smack, relish, piquancy, tang

savoury adjective = **spicy**, rich, tasty, palatable, luscious, appetizing, full-flavoured, mouthwatering, piquant

say verb 1 = **speak**, announce, state, declare, maintain, voice, remark, mention, pronounce, assert, utter, affirm • *She said they were very impressed.*
2 = **suppose**, estimate, guess, assume, imagine, presume, conjecture, surmise
3 = **express**, communicate, convey, imply
▷ **say again** See **repeat**
▷ **say no to** See **reject**
▷ **say sorry** See **apologize**
▶ noun 4 = **chance to speak**, vote, voice • *voters who want a say in the matter*
5 = **influence**, power, authority,

s

weight, clout (*informal*)
See also: **choice, comment, observe**
saying *noun* = **proverb**, adage, maxim, axiom • *the saying "charity begins at home"*
scalding *See* **hot**
scale[1] *noun* = **flake**, plate, layer, lamina
scale[2] *noun* **1** = **graduation**, series, ranking, sequence, progression, ladder, hierarchy, gradation, steps
2 = **ratio**, proportion
3 = **degree**, reach, range, extent, scope
▶ *verb* **4** = **climb**, mount, ascend, clamber, surmount, escalade
5 = **adjust**, regulate, proportion
scale drawing *See* **plan**
scam *verb* (*Slang*) **1** = **swindle**, fix, cheat, cook the books (*informal*), diddle (*informal*), wangle (*informal*)
▶ *noun* **2** (*Slang*) = **swindle**, fraud, fix, racket (*slang*)
scamp *noun* = **rascal**, monkey, devil, rogue, imp, scallywag (*informal*)
scamper *verb* = **run**, romp, dash, scuttle, hurry, hasten, dart, scurry, scoot
scan *verb* **1** = **glance over**, eye, check, examine, skim, check out (*informal*), look through, run one's eye over, run over
2 = **scrutinize**, search, survey, investigate, sweep, scour
scandal *noun* **1** = **crime**, wrongdoing, disgrace, embarrassment, offence, sin
2 = **shame**, stigma, disgrace, discredit, defamation, infamy, dishonour, ignominy, opprobrium
3 = **gossip**, talk, dirt, slander, aspersion, rumours, tattle
scandalize *verb* = **shock**, outrage, offend, horrify, appall, affront
scandalous *adjective*
1 = **shocking**, infamous, outrageous, disgraceful, shameful, unseemly, disreputable
2 = **slanderous**, untrue,

defamatory, libelous, scurrilous
scant *adjective* = **meagre**, little, minimal, sparse, barely sufficient
scanty *adjective* = **meagre**, short, poor, thin, inadequate, bare, insufficient, lousy (*slang*), sparse, scant, deficient, skimpy
scapegoat *noun* = **whipping boy**, fall guy (*informal*)
scar *noun* **1** = **mark**, injury, wound, blemish
▶ *verb* **2** = **mark**, damage, disfigure
scarce *adjective* = **rare**, few, unusual, uncommon • *Jobs are becoming increasingly scarce.*
OPPOSITE: common
See also: **inadequate**
scarcely *adverb* **1** = **hardly**, barely
2 = **definitely not**, hardly
scarcity *noun* = **shortage**, want, lack, deficiency, dearth, insufficiency, paucity, rareness
scare *verb* **1** = **frighten**, alarm, intimidate, terrify, terrorize, startle, unnerve, give someone a fright • *You're scaring me!*
▶ *noun* **2** = **fright**, start, shock
• *We had a bit of a scare.*
3 = **alert**, panic, hysteria
• *Despite the health scare, there are no plans to withdraw the drug.*
scared *adjective* = **frightened**, fearful, shaken, panicky, panic-stricken, petrified, startled, terrified
scarper *verb* (*Slang*) = **run away**, flee, disappear, abscond, beat it (*slang*), clear off (*informal*), run for it, scram (*informal*), take to one's heels
scary *adjective* (*Informal*)
= **frightening**, eerie, spooky, creepy (*informal*), hair-raising, alarming, chilling, terrifying, unnerving • *Camping can be scary at night.*
scathing *adjective* = **critical**, harsh, cutting, sarcastic, caustic, biting, scornful, trenchant, withering
scatter *verb* **1** = **throw about**, shower, sprinkle, sow • *She scattered the rose petals.*

S

OPPOSITE: gather
2 = disperse, dispel, disband, dissipate
See also: **distribute**

scatterbrain *noun*
= **featherbrain**, butterfly, flibbertigibbet

scenario *noun* = **story line**, outline, summary, synopsis, résumé

scene *noun* **1 = view**, landscape, panorama • *a village scene*
2 = site, place, spot, location, setting • *the scene of the crime*
3 = world, business, environment, arena • *the music scene*
4 = setting, set, location, background, backdrop
5 = show, picture, display, drama, exhibition, sight, spectacle, pageant
6 = act, part, division, episode
7 = fuss, performance, row, exhibition, tantrum, commotion, to-do

scenery *noun* **1 = landscape**, view, terrain, surroundings, panorama • *Drive slowly, and enjoy the scenery.*
2 (*Theatre*) **= set**, setting, backdrop, flats, stage set

scenic *adjective* = **picturesque**, beautiful, spectacular, striking, panoramic

scent *noun* **1 = fragrance**, smell, perfume, aroma, bouquet, odour
2 = trail, track, spoor
▶ *verb* **3 = detect**, sense, smell, sniff, discern, nose out

scented *adjective* = **fragrant**, aromatic, odoriferous, perfumed, sweet-smelling

schedule *noun* **1 = plan**, program, list, inventory, agenda, timetable, calendar, catalogue
▶ *verb* **2 = plan**, program, book, appoint, organize, arrange

scheduled *See* **set**

scheme *noun* **1 = plan**, program, system, project, proposal, strategy, road map, tactics
2 = diagram, draft, outline, pattern, chart, blueprint, layout
3 = plot, conspiracy, intrigue,

ploy, ruse, manoeuvre, subterfuge, stratagem
▶ *verb* **4 = plan**, project, lay plans, work out
5 = plot, intrigue, conspire, collude, manoeuvre, machinate

scheming *adjective* = **calculating**, tricky, wily, sly, cunning, artful, conniving, underhand

schism *noun* = **division**, break, split, breach, separation, rift, rupture

scholar *noun* **1 = intellectual**, academic, savant
2 = student, pupil, schoolboy *or* schoolgirl, learner, disciple

scholarly *adjective* = **learned**, academic, intellectual, bookish, scholastic, erudite, lettered

scholarship *noun* **1 = learning**, education, knowledge, book-learning, erudition
2 = grant, fellowship, bursary

scholastic *adjective* = **learned**, academic, scholarly, lettered

school *noun* **1 = academy**, college, institution, institute, faculty, seminary
2 = group, set, circle, faction, denomination, adherents, devotees, disciples, followers
▶ *verb* **3 = train**, coach, drill, discipline, educate, instruct, tutor

schooling *noun* **1 = teaching**, education, tuition
2 = training, drill, instruction, coaching

science *noun* **1 = discipline**, body of knowledge, branch of knowledge
2 = skill, art, technique

scientific *adjective* = **systematic**, accurate, exact, precise, controlled, mathematical

scientist *noun* = **inventor**, technophile

scintillating *adjective* = **brilliant**, bright, exciting, animated, sparkling, lively, dazzling, glittering, stimulating

scoff[1] *verb* = **scorn**, knock (*informal*), mock, jeer, ridicule, deride, despise, belittle, sneer, pooh-pooh, laugh at

S

scoff² verb = **gobble** or **gobble up**, bolt, wolf, guzzle, devour, gorge oneself on, gulp down

scold verb = **reprimand**, rebuke, lecture, chide, tell off (informal) • She scolded the child for being naughty.
See also: **abuse**

scolding noun = **rebuke**, row, lecture, telling-off (informal)

scoop noun 1 = **ladle**, spoon, dipper
2 = **exclusive**, revelation, sensation, exposé
▶ verb 3 (often with up) = **gather up**, lift, pick up, take up
4 (often with out) = **hollow**, bail, empty, dig, shovel, gouge, excavate

scope noun 1 = **opportunity**, space, room, freedom, liberty, latitude
2 = **range**, area, reach, capacity, outlook, orbit, span, sphere

scorch verb = **burn**, roast, wither, sear, singe, shrivel, parch

scorching adjective = **burning**, red-hot, fiery, flaming, roasting, baking, boiling, searing

score noun 1 = **points**, record, result, mark, total, outcome, grade
2 = **grounds**, cause, reason, ground, basis
3 = **grievance**, injury, wrong, injustice, grudge
▷ **scores** = **lots**, hundreds, masses, millions, multitudes, myriads, swarms
▶ verb 4 = **gain**, make, win, post, net, achieve, nail, chalk up (informal), sports, notch up (informal)
5 = **keep count**, record, count, register, tally
6 = **cut**, mark, slash, scratch, scrape, gouge, graze, deface
7 (with out or through) = **cross out**, cancel, delete, obliterate, strike out
8 (Music) = **arrange**, set, adapt, orchestrate

scorn noun 1 = **contempt**, disdain, mockery, derision • The proposal was greeted with scorn.

▶ verb 2 = **despise**, slight, disdain, look down on • He scorns the work of others.
See also: **belittle**

scornful adjective = **contemptuous**, scathing, disdainful, sneering, supercilious, withering • He is deeply scornful of his rivals.

scoundrel noun = **rogue**, bastard (offensive), heel (slang), miscreant, good-for-nothing, rascal, reprobate, villain, swine, scamp

scour¹ verb = **scrub**, clean, wash, buff, rub, polish, abrade

scour² verb = **search**, beat, hunt, comb, ransack

scourge noun 1 = **affliction**, terror, plague, curse, pest, misfortune, torment, bane, infliction
2 = **whip**, switch, cat, lash, strap, thong
▶ verb 3 = **afflict**, plague, curse, terrorize, torment
4 = **whip**, beat, lash, thrash, cane, flog, horsewhip

scout noun 1 = **vanguard**, lookout, precursor, advance guard, outrider, reconnoitrer
▶ verb 2 = **reconnoitre**, probe, investigate, observe, survey, watch, spy

scowl verb 1 = **glower**, frown, lour or lower
▶ noun 2 = **glower**, frown, black look, dirty look

scrabble verb = **scrape**, scramble, scratch, claw

scraggy adjective = **scrawny**, lean, skinny, bony, angular

scram verb = **go away**, leave, abscond, beat it (slang), clear off (informal), get lost (informal), make oneself scarce (informal), make tracks, vamoose (slang)

scramble verb 1 = **struggle**, climb, swarm, crawl, scrabble
2 = **strive**, run, push, rush, vie, contend, jostle
▶ noun 3 = **climb**, trek
4 = **struggle**, race, competition, rush, confusion, melee or mêlée, commotion, tussle

scrap¹ noun 1 = **piece**, part,

bit, grain, portion, particle, fragment, snippet, crumb, sliver, morsel

2 = waste, junk, off cuts

▷ **scraps = leftovers**, bits, leavings, remains

▶ verb **3 = discard**, drop, abandon, ditch (slang), jettison, throw away or throw out, write off

scrap² (Informal) noun **1 = fight**, battle, dispute, row, argument, disagreement, squabble, wrangle, quarrel

▶ verb **2 = fight**, argue, row, squabble, wrangle

scrape verb **1 = graze**, skin, scratch, scour, scuff • We had to scrape the frost from the windshield.

2 = grate, grind, scratch, rasp • her shoes scraping across the ground

3 = clean, remove, erase, rub, scour

4 = scrimp, save, stint, pinch, skimp

▷ **scrape through = get by** (informal), struggle, just make it

▶ noun **5** (Informal) = **predicament**, fix (informal), difficulty, mess, plight, dilemma, awkward situation, tight spot

scrapheap noun

▷ **on the scrapheap = discarded**, ditched (slang), jettisoned, redundant, put out to pasture (informal)

scrappy adjective = **incomplete**, sketchy, piecemeal, disjointed, bitty, fragmentary, thrown together

scratch verb **1 = mark**, score, cut, damage, claw, scrape, grate, graze, etch, lacerate

2 = withdraw, cancel, eliminate, erase, delete, abolish, call off, pull out

▶ noun **3 = mark**, scrape, graze, blemish, gash, laceration, claw mark

▷ **up to scratch = adequate**, acceptable, sufficient, satisfactory, up to standard

▶ adjective **5 = improvised**, impromptu, rough-and-ready

scrawl verb = **scribble**, writing, doodle, squiggle

scrawny adjective = **thin**, lean, skinny, gaunt, bony, scraggy, skin-and-bones (informal), undernourished

scream verb **1 = cry**, shout, yell, howl, screech, shriek, squeal • lots of people screaming on a roller coaster

▶ noun **2 = cry**, yell, howl, screech, shriek, squeal • The child let out a scream.

screech noun, verb = **cry**, scream, shriek

screen noun **1 = cover**, guard, shelter, shield, cloak, shade, canopy, partition, awning, room divider

2 = mesh, net

▶ verb **3 = cover**, hide, mask, cloak, veil, shade, conceal

4 = protect, defend, guard, shelter, shield

5 = vet, examine, sort, scan, evaluate, filter, gauge, sift

6 = broadcast, show, present, put on

screw verb **1 = turn**, tighten, twist

2 (Informal) (often with out of) = **extort**, extract, wrest, wring

screw up verb **1** (Informal) = **bungle**, botch, spoil, mishandle, make a mess of (slang), mess up

2 = distort, wrinkle, pucker, contort

screwy adjective = **crazy**, odd, eccentric, nutty (slang), loopy (informal), off-the-wall (slang), crackpot (informal), out to lunch (informal), weird

scribble verb = **scrawl**, write, jot, dash off

scribe noun = **copyist**, writer, amanuensis

scrimp verb = **economize**, save, stint, scrape, skimp, be frugal, tighten one's belt

script noun **1 = text**, book, copy, dialogue, libretto, lines, words

2 = handwriting, writing, calligraphy, penmanship

scriptural See **religious**

Scripture noun = **The Bible**, Holy Bible, Holy Scripture, Holy Writ, The Good Book, The Gospels, The Scriptures

scrounge verb = **mooch**, beg, bum, sponge (*informal*) • *He's always scrounging for money.*

scrounger adjective = **cadger**, parasite, freeloader (*slang*), sponger (*informal*)

scrub verb = **scour**, clean, rub, cleanse

scruffy adjective = **shabby**, ragged, seedy, tatty, unkempt • *four scruffy boys*
OPPOSITE: smart

scrumptious adjective (*Informal*) = **delicious**, yummy (*informal*), delectable, luscious, succulent, appetizing, mouthwatering

scruple noun 1 = **misgiving**, doubt, reluctance, hesitation, qualm, uneasiness, compunction, second thoughts
▶ verb 2 = **have misgivings about**, doubt, hesitate, demur, have qualms about, think twice about

scruples plural noun = **conscience**, principle, standards

scrupulous adjective 1 = **moral**, upright, principled, conscientious, honorable
2 = **careful**, strict, exact, precise, rigorous, meticulous, fastidious, punctilious

scrutinize verb = **examine**, study, search, scan, inspect, pore over • *She scrutinized his features.*
See also: **observe, regard**

scrutiny noun = **examination**, study, investigation, search, analysis, inspection, exploration, perusal

scuff See **scrape**

scuffle verb 1 = **fight**, struggle, clash, grapple, jostle, tussle
▶ noun 2 = **fight**, brawl, skirmish, disturbance, fray, scrimmage, commotion, tussle

sculpt See **carve, model**

sculpture verb = **carve**, form, model, fashion, shape, sculpt, mould, chisel, hew

scum noun 1 = **impurities**, film, froth, dross
2 = **rabble**, trash, dregs of society, riffraff

scupper verb = **destroy**, defeat, ruin, wreck, demolish, torpedo, put paid to

scurrilous adjective = **slanderous**, abusive, scandalous, defamatory, insulting, vituperative

scurry verb 1 = **hurry**, race, sprint, dash, scuttle, scamper, dart, scoot
▶ noun 2 = **flurry**, whirl, scampering

scuttle verb = **run**, rush, hurry, bustle, hasten, scamper, scurry, scoot

sea noun 1 = **ocean**, main, the deep, the waves
2 = **mass**, abundance, multitude, expanse, plethora, profusion
▷ **at sea** = **bewildered**, lost, confused, baffled, mystified, puzzled

seafaring adjective = **nautical**, marine, naval, maritime

seal noun 1 = **authentication**, stamp, confirmation, ratification, insignia, imprimatur
▶ verb 2 = **close**, stop, shut, plug, enclose, stopper, fasten, bung, stop up
3 = **authenticate**, confirm, stamp, ratify, validate
4 = **settle**, conclude, clinch, finalize, consummate
▷ **seal off** = **isolate**, quarantine, segregate, put out of bounds

sealed See **shut**

seam noun 1 = **joint**, closure
2 = **layer**, vein, stratum, lode
3 = **ridge**, line, wrinkle, furrow

sear verb = **scorch**, burn, sizzle

search verb 1 = **hunt**, look, seek, comb, scour, forage, sift • *The RCMP is searching for the missing men.*
▷ **search for** See **seek**
▶ noun 2 = **hunt**, quest • *Police will resume the search today.*

searching adjective = **keen**, close, sharp, intent, piercing, penetrating, probing, quizzical

seashore *See* **beach**
seaside *See* **beach, coast**
season *noun* 1 = **period**, time, term, spell
▶ *verb* 2 = **flavour**, salt, spice, enliven, pep up
seasonable *adjective*
= **appropriate**, fit, timely, suitable, convenient, opportune, well-timed, providential
seasoned *adjective*
= **experienced**, veteran, hardened, practised, time-served
seasoning *noun* = **flavouring**, sauce, spice, relish, dressing, condiment, salt and pepper
seat *noun* 1 = **chair**, settle, bench, stall, stool, pew
2 = **centre**, place, site, heart, source, capital, situation, hub
3 = **residence**, house, mansion, abode, ancestral hall
4 = **membership**, place, chair, constituency, incumbency
▶ *verb* 5 = **sit**, set, place, settle, fix, locate, install
6 = **hold**, take, contain, sit, accommodate, cater for
seating *noun* = **accommodation**, room, chairs, places, seats
secede *verb* = **withdraw**, leave, resign, quit, break with, pull out, split from
secluded *adjective* = **private**, isolated, lonely, solitary, sheltered, cloistered, cut off, out-of-the-way
seclusion *noun* = **privacy**, shelter, isolation, solitude
second[1] *adjective* 1 = **next**, subsequent, following, succeeding
2 = **additional**, other, further, extra, alternative
3 = **inferior**, lower, secondary, lesser, subordinate
▷ **second in command** = **deputy**, number two, right-hand man
▶ *noun* 4 = **supporter**, assistant, backer, helper
▶ *verb* 5 = **support**, back, assist, approve, endorse, go along with
second[2] *noun* = **moment**, minute,

flash, instant, sec (*informal*), jiffy (*informal*), trice
secondary *adjective*
1 = **subordinate**, lower, minor, lesser, inferior, unimportant
2 = **resultant**, contingent, indirect, derived
3 = **backup**, reserve, subsidiary, auxiliary, fall-back, supporting
second-class *adjective* = **inferior**, mediocre, indifferent, second-best, second-rate, undistinguished, uninspiring
second-hand *adjective* 1 = **used**, hand-me-down (*informal*), nearly new
▶ *adverb* 2 = **indirectly**
secondly *adverb* = **next**, second, in the second place
second-rate *adjective* = **inferior**, poor, mediocre, shoddy, low-grade, tacky (*informal*), substandard, low-quality, rubbishy, tawdry, two-bit (*slang*)
secrecy *noun* 1 = **mystery**, privacy, silence, confidentiality, concealment
2 = **secretiveness**, stealth, clandestineness, covertness, furtiveness
secret *adjective* 1 = **undisclosed**, underground, confidential, undercover, closet (*informal*), covert, hidden, furtive • *a secret location*
RELATED WORD
adjective: cryptic
2 = **stealthy**, secretive, sly, underhand
3 = **mysterious**, clandestine, cryptic, arcane, occult, abstruse
▶ *noun* 4 = **mystery**, key, code, enigma
▷ **in secret** = **secretly**, surreptitiously, slyly
See also: **private**
secrete[1] *verb* = **give off**, emit, exude, emanate
secrete[2] *verb* = **hide**, conceal, cache, stash (*informal*), stow, harbor
secretive *adjective* = **reticent**, cagey (*informal*), reserved • *He was very secretive about his family affairs.*
See also: **mysterious**

S

secretly adverb = **in secret**, quietly, privately, surreptitiously, covertly, clandestinely, furtively, stealthily

sect noun = **group**, party, division, camp, faction, denomination, schism

sectarian adjective 1 = **narrow-minded**, limited, partisan, factional, fanatical, parochial, dogmatic, bigoted, doctrinaire
▶ noun 2 = **bigot**, extremist, partisan, fanatic, zealot, dogmatist

section noun 1 = **part**, division, piece, portion, segment, instalment • *this section of the Trans-Canada Highway*
2 (*Chiefly US*) = **district**, area, region, sector, zone
See also: **compartment, department, extract, passage**

sector noun = **part**, area, quarter, region, division, zone, district

secular adjective = **worldly**, lay, civil, earthly, temporal, nonspiritual

secure verb 1 (*Formal*) = **obtain**, get, gain, acquire, procure • *His achievements helped him to secure the job.*
2 = **make safe**, strengthen, fortify, make impregnable • *We need to secure the building against attack.*
3 = **fasten**, fix, lock, bind, attach, moor, tie up • *to secure the picture to the wall*
OPPOSITE: release
▶ adjective 4 = **safe**, protected, fortified, impregnable, shielded • *Make sure your home is as secure as possible.*
5 = **fixed**, firm, solid, tight, stable, locked, fastened • *Those bookshelves don't look very secure.*
6 = **confident**, safe, protected, reassured, relaxed • *They felt secure when they were with each other.*
OPPOSITE: insecure
See also: **close, steady, tie, win**

securely See **fast**

security noun 1 = **precautions**, protection, defence, safeguards, safety measures
2 = **safety**, care, custody, refuge, sanctuary, safekeeping
3 = **sureness**, confidence, conviction, assurance, certainty, reliance, positiveness
4 = **pledge**, insurance, hostage, guarantee, collateral, pawn, surety, gage

sedate adjective = **calm**, cool, dignified, tranquil, serene, collected, composed

sedative adjective 1 = **calming**, soothing, anodyne, relaxing, tranquilizing
▶ noun 2 = **tranquilizer**, downer or down (*slang*), anodyne

sedentary adjective = **inactive**, desk, sitting, desk-bound, seated

sediment noun = **dregs**, deposit, residue, grounds, lees

sedition noun = **rabble-rousing**, agitation, subversion, incitement to riot

seditious adjective = **revolutionary**, dissident, subversive, rebellious, mutinous, refractory

seduce verb 1 = **corrupt**, dishonour, debauch, deflower, deprave
2 = **tempt**, lure, mislead, entice, deceive, beguile, inveigle, lead astray

seduction noun 1 = **corruption**
2 = **temptation**, lure, snare, enticement

seductive adjective = **tempting**, attractive, provocative, alluring, bewitching, enticing, inviting

seductress noun = **temptress**, siren, enchantress, *femme fatale* (*French*), succubus, vamp (*informal*)

see verb 1 = **perceive**, look, spot, notice, sight, observe, glimpse, behold, discern, catch sight of, descry, espy • *Did you see what happened?*
2 = **understand**, get, follow, realize, appreciate, grasp, comprehend • *I see what you mean.*
3 = **find out**, discover, determine, ascertain • *I'll see*

what's happening outside.
4 = **make sure**, ensure, guarantee, make certain, see to it
5 = **consider**, decide, reflect, deliberate, think over
6 = **visit**, receive, interview, consult, confer with, speak to
7 = **go out with**, court, date (*informal*), go steady with (*informal*)
8 = **accompany**, lead, show, walk, escort, usher
▷ **see eye to eye** *See* **agree**
▷ **see through** = **be undeceived by**, penetrate, fathom, be wise to (*informal*), not fall for
▷ **see (someone) through** = **help out**, support, stick by
▷ **see (something) through** = **persevere** *or* **persevere with**, persist, keep at, stick out (*informal*)
▷ **see to** *See* **deal, take care of**
See also: **know, note, picture, regard, tell, watch, witness**
seed *noun* **1** = **grain**, egg, embryo, germ, spore, kernel, pip, ovum
2 = **origin**, start, source, beginning, germ, nucleus
3 = **offspring**, issue, progeny, children, descendants
▷ **go to seed, run to seed** = **decline**, deteriorate, decay, degenerate, go downhill (*informal*), go to pot, let oneself go
seedy (*Informal*) *adjective* = **shabby**, dirty, dilapidated, run-down, grubby, mangy, sleazy, squalid, scuzzy (*slang*), tatty
seeing *conjunction* = **since**, as, inasmuch as, in view of the fact that
seek *verb* **1** = **look for**, hunt, be after, search for • *The police were still seeking information.*
2 = **try**, attempt, aim, strive, endeavour, aspire to • *She is seeking re-election as class president.*
See also: **ask, request, search**
seem *verb* = **appear**, look, give the impression, look like • *He seemed such a quiet man.*
▷ **seem to be** *See* **look**
seemly *adjective* = **fitting**, fit,

appropriate, correct, proper, decent, suitable, becoming, decorous
seep *verb* = **ooze**, well, leak, soak, trickle, exude, permeate
seer *noun* = **prophet**, sibyl, soothsayer
seesaw *verb* = **alternate**, swing, fluctuate, oscillate
seethe *verb* **1** = **be furious**, rage, simmer, fume, be livid, go ballistic (*slang*), see red (*informal*)
2 = **bubble**, boil, foam, froth, fizz
segment *noun* = **section**, part, bit, division, piece, portion, slice, wedge
segregate *verb* = **set apart**, separate, isolate, dissociate, discriminate against
segregation *noun* = **separation**, discrimination, isolation, apartheid
seize *verb* **1** = **grab**, snatch, grasp • *He seized the phone.*
2 = **take possession of**, appropriate, confiscate, annex, impound • *Rebels have seized the airport.*
3 = **capture**, arrest, catch, hijack, apprehend, take captive
See also: **kidnap, possess**
seizure *noun* **1** = **attack**, fit, spasm, convulsion, paroxysm
2 = **capture**, arrest, apprehension
3 = **taking**, confiscation, annexation, commandeering, grabbing
seldom *adverb* = **rarely**, infrequently, hardly ever, not often
select *verb* **1** = **choose**, take, pick, decide on, opt for, settle on, single out • *They selected new members for the debating team.*
▷ *adjective* **2** = **choice**, prime, special, superior, first-class, hand-picked, first-rate • *a select group of top-ranked skiers*
3 = **exclusive**, elite, privileged, cliquish
See also: **nominate**
selection *noun* **1** = **choice**, pick, option, preference, choosing
2 = **range**, choice, collection,

s

variety, medley, assortment

selective adjective = **particular**, careful, discerning, discriminating

self-assurance noun = **confidence**, self-confidence, assertiveness, positiveness, self-possession

self-assured See **confident**

self-centred adjective = **selfish**, narcissistic, egotistic, self-seeking

self-confidence noun = **self-assurance**, confidence, poise, nerve, aplomb

self-confident adjective = **self-assured**, confident, assured, poised, sure of oneself

self-conscious adjective = **embarrassed**, nervous, uncomfortable, awkward, insecure, bashful, diffident, ill at ease, wired (slang)

self-consciousness See **embarrassment**

self-control noun = **willpower**, restraint, self-restraint, self-discipline

self-denial See **sacrifice**

self-esteem noun = **self-respect**, confidence, pride, faith in oneself, self-assurance, self-regard

self-evident adjective = **obvious**, clear, undeniable, inescapable, incontrovertible

self-importance See **conceit**

self-important adjective = **conceited**, cocky, pompous, bigheaded, full of oneself, swollen-headed

self-indulgence noun = **intemperance**, excess, extravagance

selfish adjective = **self-centred**, greedy, egoistic or egoistical, egotistic or egotistical • his greedy and selfish behaviour

selfless adjective = **unselfish**, generous, altruistic, self-denying, self-sacrificing

self-possessed adjective = **self-assured**, cool, confident, collected, poised, unruffled

self-possession See **confidence**

self-propelled See **automatic**

self-reliant adjective = **independent**, self-sufficient, self-supporting

self-respect noun = **pride**, dignity, morale, self-esteem

self-restraint noun = **self-control**, willpower, self-command, self-discipline

self-righteous adjective = **sanctimonious**, superior, complacent, smug, holier-than-thou, priggish, self-satisfied

self-sacrifice noun = **selflessness**, generosity, altruism, self-denial

self-satisfied adjective = **smug**, complacent, pleased with oneself, self-congratulatory • a self-satisfied smile

self-seeking adjective = **selfish**, self-serving, careerist, looking out for number one (informal), out for what one can get, self-interested

self-sufficient See **independent**

sell verb **1** = **deal in**, stock, peddle, hawk, trade in • a convenience store that sells stamps
OPPOSITE: buy
2 = **trade**, exchange, barter
▷ **sell at** See **cost**
▷ **sell out** = **run out of**, be out of stock of, dispose of, get rid of; (Informal) = **betray**, double-cross (informal), sell down the river (informal), stab in the back

seller noun = **dealer**, retailer, agent, supplier, merchant, vendor, salesman or saleswoman, purveyor

selling noun = **dealing**, business, traffic, trading

selling price See **value**

semblance noun = **appearance**, show, mask, aspect, resemblance, pretense, veneer, façade

seminal adjective = **influential**, important, original, innovative, ground-breaking, formative

send verb **1** = **dispatch**, forward, remit • She sent a basket of fruit and a card.

2 = transmit, broadcast • *The pilot was trying to send a distress signal.*

3 = propel, fire, shoot, cast, hurl, fling, let fly

▷ **send for = summon**, order, request, call for

▷ **send in** See **submit**

▷ **send out** See **emit**

▷ **send up = parody**, mock, mimic, spoof (*informal*), satirize, imitate, lampoon, burlesque, make fun of, take off (*informal*)

sendoff noun **= farewell**, start, departure, leave-taking, valediction

send-up noun **= parody**, satire, imitation, spoof (*informal*), take-off (*informal*), piss-take (*informal*)

senile adjective **= doddering**, decrepit, doting, in one's dotage

senility noun **= dotage**, decrepitude, infirmity, loss of one's faculties, senile dementia

senior adjective **1 = higher ranking**, superior, better • *senior jobs*

2 = older, elder
OPPOSITE: junior

senior citizen noun **= pensioner**, old fogey (*slang*), old person or elderly person, retired person

seniority noun **= superiority**, rank, priority, precedence

sensation noun **1 = feeling**, sense, perception, awareness, impression, consciousness

2 = excitement, stir, thrill, furor, commotion

sensational adjective

1 = dramatic, amazing, exciting, thrilling, shocking, awesome, astounding, melodramatic, shock-horror (*facetious*)

2 = excellent, cool (*informal*), impressive, awesome (*informal*), fabulous (*informal*), marvellous, mind-blowing (*informal*), out of this world (*informal*), phat (*slang*), superb

sense noun **1 = feeling**, impression, consciousness • *an overwhelming sense of guilt*

2 = intelligence, reason, judgment, wisdom, brains,

common sense • *He had the good sense to call me at once.*

3 = faculty, feeling, sensation

4 = meaning, import, implication, drift, significance, gist

▷ **sense of duty** See **principle**

▷ **sense of right and wrong** See **conscience**

▶ verb **5 = perceive**, feel, realize, be aware of, get the impression, have a hunch • *She sensed he wasn't telling her the whole story.*

senseless adjective **1 = stupid**, mad, crazy, ridiculous, silly, foolish, pointless, irrational, mindless, illogical, idiotic, nonsensical, inane, asinine, bonkers (*informal*), daft (*informal*)

2 = unconscious, out, insensible, out cold, stunned

sensibility noun **1** (*often plural*) **= feelings**, emotions, moral sense, sentiments, susceptibilities

2 = sensitivity, susceptibility, responsiveness, sensitiveness

sensible adjective **1 = wise**, sound, practical, prudent, rational, down-to-earth, judicious • *a sensible, level-headed approach*
OPPOSITE: foolish

2 (usually with *of*) **= aware**, conscious, mindful, sensitive to
See also: **logical**, **realistic**, **reasonable**, **responsible**, **sane**

sensitive adjective **1 = touchy**, easily offended, easily upset, thin-skinned • *He was sensitive about his height.*

2 = delicate, tender, easily hurt

3 = susceptible, responsive, impressionable, easily affected, touchy-feely (*informal*)

4 = responsive, fine, acute, keen, precise
See also: **sore**, **tactful**, **tricky**, **understanding**, **vulnerable**

sensitivity noun **= sensitiveness**, delicacy, susceptibility, responsiveness, receptiveness

sensual adjective **1 = physical**, animal, bodily, luxurious, voluptuous, carnal, fleshly

2 = erotic, sexual, raunchy

s

(slang), lewd, lascivious,
lecherous, lustful
sensuality noun = **eroticism**,
carnality, lasciviousness,
lecherousness, lewdness,
sexiness (informal),
voluptuousness
sensuous adjective
1 = **pleasurable**, gratifying
2 = **pleasure-seeking**,
hedonistic, sybaritic
sentence noun 1 = **punishment**,
decision, order, ruling, verdict,
judgment, condemnation,
decree
▶ verb 2 = **condemn**, penalize,
doom
sententious adjective
= **pompous**, judgmental,
canting, moralistic,
preachifying (informal),
sanctimonious
sentient adjective = **feeling**,
living, sensitive, conscious
sentiment noun 1 = **emotion**,
sensibility, tenderness
2 (often plural) = **feeling**, view,
idea, opinion, judgment, belief,
attitude
3 = **sentimentality**,
emotionalism, mawkishness,
romanticism
sentimental adjective
= **romantic**, sloppy (informal),
nostalgic, mushy (informal),
maudlin • sentimental love stories
See also: **corny**
sentimentality noun
= **romanticism**, nostalgia,
corniness (slang), emotionalism,
mawkishness, schmaltz (slang)
sentinel noun = **guard**, watch,
lookout, sentry, watchman
sentry See **guard**
separable adjective
= **distinguishable**, detachable,
divisible
separate adjective
1 = **unconnected**, isolated,
disconnected, discrete,
detached, divorced • The question
muddles up two separate issues.
2 = **individual**, single, alone,
apart, particular, distinct,
solitary

▶ verb 3 = **divide**, disconnect,
detach • We were separated from our
friends when we changed schools.
OPPOSITE: connect
4 = **split up**, part, divorce, break
up • Her parents separated when she
was very young.
5 = **isolate**, segregate, single out
See also: **different,
independent, sort, split**
separated adjective
= **disconnected**, separate,
apart, divided, disassociated,
disunited, parted, sundered
separately adverb = **individually**,
alone, apart, severally, singly
separation noun 1 = **division**,
break, gap, disconnection,
dissociation, disunion
2 = **split-up**, split, divorce, rift,
break-up, parting
septic adjective = **infected**, putrid,
festering, poisoned, putrefying,
suppurating
sepulchre noun = **tomb**, grave,
vault, mausoleum, burial place
sequel noun 1 = **follow-up**,
development, continuation
2 = **consequence**, end, result,
conclusion, outcome, upshot
sequence noun 1 = **succession**,
series, course, chain, string,
cycle, progression • an unbroken
sequence of victories
2 = **order**, structure, pattern,
arrangement, progression • the
colour sequence: yellow, orange,
purple, blue
serene adjective = **calm**, peaceful,
tranquil, composed, unruffled,
untroubled
serenity noun = **calmness**, peace,
calm, composure, stillness,
tranquillity, peacefulness,
quietness
series noun = **sequence**, run,
chain, string, succession • a series
of loud explosions
See also: **range, set**
serious adjective 1 = **grave**, bad,
dangerous, critical, severe,
intense, extreme, acute, grim,
precarious, grievous, alarming,
worrying • They survived their
serious injuries.

2 = **important**, difficult, significant, deep, crucial, grave, urgent, profound, far-reaching, pressing, momentous, weighty • *I regard this as a serious matter.* OPPOSITE: funny

3 = **sincere**, honest, genuine, earnest, heartfelt, resolute, in earnest, resolved • *I was not quite sure whether he was serious.*

4 = **solemn**, grave, sober, earnest, stern, staid, humourless, pensive • *She's quite a serious person.*
See also: **heavy**

seriously *adverb* **1** = **gravely**, badly, severely, critically, dangerously, acutely

2 = **sincerely**, gravely, in earnest

seriousness *noun*
1 = **importance**, gravity, significance, urgency

2 = **solemnity**, gravity, gravitas, earnestness

sermon *noun* **1** = **homily**, address

2 = **lecture**, harangue, talking-to (*informal*)

serrated *See* **jagged**

servant *noun* = **attendant**, help, domestic, maid, retainer, slave

serve *verb* **1** = **work for**, help, assist, aid, attend to, minister to, wait on

2 = **perform**, do, complete, act, fulfill, discharge

3 = **provide**, supply, present, deliver, dish up, set out

4 = **be adequate**, do, suit, satisfy, suffice, answer the purpose, be acceptable, function as
▷ **serve as** *See* **form**

service *noun* **1** = **help**, use, benefit, assistance, avail, usefulness

2 = **work**, business, office, duty, employment, labour

3 = **overhaul**, check, maintenance

4 = **ceremony**, rite, worship, observance

▶ *verb* **5** = **overhaul**, check, maintain, tune *or* tune up, fine tune, go over

serviceable *adjective* = **useful**, profitable, helpful, practical, beneficial, operative, functional, usable, utilitarian

servile *adjective* = **subservient**, abject, fawning, grovelling, obsequious, sycophantic, toadying

serving *noun* = **portion**, helping

session *noun* = **meeting**, period, conference, hearing, discussion, assembly, congress, sitting

set[1] *verb* **1** = **put**, place, position, rest, lay, stick, locate, deposit • *She set her briefcase down on the floor.*

2 = **prepare**, spread, lay, arrange, make ready

3 = **harden**, cake, solidify, stiffen, thicken, crystallize, congeal

4 = **arrange**, schedule, decide *or* decide upon, determine, settle, fix, establish, appoint, resolve, specify, fix up

5 = **assign**, impose, prescribe, specify, decree, ordain, allot

6 = **go down**, decline, sink, disappear, dip, vanish, subside

▷ **set about** *See* **begin**, **start**

▷ **set against one another** *See* **divide**

▷ **set aside** = **reserve**, save, separate, select, earmark, keep (back), single out, set apart, put aside; = **reject**, cancel, dismiss, reverse, overturn, quash, overrule, discard, annul, nullify, repudiate, abrogate, render null and void

▷ **set back** = **hold up**, delay, slow, hinder, impede, retard

▷ **set down** *See* **lay**

▷ **set free** *See* **discharge**, **release**

▷ **set loose** *See* **free**

▷ **set off** = **leave**, depart, embark, start out, ship out; = **detonate**, explode, ignite

▷ **set out** *See* **lay**

▷ **set up** = **arrange**, establish, organize, install, institute • *setting up a system of communication;* = **build**, raise, assemble, construct, erect, put together, put up
See also: **start**

S

▷ **set upon** See **attack**

▶ *adjective* **7** = **fixed**, firm, scheduled, established, arranged, predetermined • *a set charge*

8 = **inflexible**, stubborn, rigid, hard and fast, immovable

9 = **conventional**, stock, traditional, stereotyped, unspontaneous

▷ **set on** = **determined**, intent, bent, resolute

▶ *noun* **10** = **position**, attitude, posture, carriage, bearing

11 = **scenery**, scene, setting, stage set

See also: **insert, ready, time**

| CONFUSABLES
Set means *put down*, and always takes an object.
Sit means *rest your rear end on something*, and usually does not take an object.

set^2 *noun* **1** = **series**, equipment, kit, outfit, ensemble, batch, compendium, assemblage • *a set of tools*

2 = **group**, company, crowd, band, gang, circle, faction, clique, coterie

See also: **bunch, category, class, lot**

setback *noun* = **hold-up**, defeat, check, blow, reverse, disappointment, hitch, misfortune

setting *noun* = **surroundings**, set, site, scene, location, background, context, backdrop, scenery

settle *verb* **1** = **resolve**, decide, reconcile, clear up, dispose of, put an end to, straighten out • *The dispute has been settled*.

2 = **decide on**, agree, determine, fix, arrange • *Let's settle where we're going tonight*.

3 = **move to**, make your home, put down roots, take up residence • *My grandparents settled in Manitoba.*

4 = **put in order**, order, regulate, adjust, straighten out, work out

5 = **land**, light (*archaic*), descend, alight, come to rest

6 = **colonize**, people, pioneer, populate

7 = **calm**, quiet, relax, relieve, reassure, quell, lull, soothe, pacify, quieten

8 = **pay**, clear, square *or* square up, discharge, pony up (*informal*)

See also: **confirm, lay**

▷ **settle on** See **pick, select**

▷ **settle up** See **repay**

settled See **definite**

settlement *noun* **1** = **agreement**, conclusion, arrangement, confirmation, establishment, working out

2 = **payment**, discharge, clearing

3 = **colony**, community, outpost, encampment

settler *noun* = **colonist**, immigrant, pioneer, colonizer, frontiersman

setup *noun* = **arrangement**, system, organization, regime, structure, conditions

sever *verb* **1** = **cut**, part, separate, split, divide, disconnect, detach, cut in two, disjoin

2 = **break off**, terminate, dissociate, put an end to

several *adjective* = **some**, various, assorted, sundry • *several boxes filled with CDs and DVDs*

See also: **numerous**

severe *adjective* **1** = **serious**, deep, critical, intense, extreme, grave, terrible, acute, dire • *severe financial problems*

OPPOSITE: mild

2 = **strict**, hard, harsh, stern • *a severe sentence appropriate to the crime*

3 = **grim**, serious, grave, stern, tight-lipped, disapproving, forbidding, unsmiling

4 = **plain**, classic, austere, simple, restrained, Spartan, unadorned, unembellished, unfussy

See also: **drastic, violent**

severely *adverb* **1** = **strictly**, sharply, harshly, sternly

2 = **seriously**, extremely, badly, gravely, acutely

severity *noun* = **strictness**, toughness, harshness,

S

hardness, severeness, sternness

sex noun **1 = gender**
2 = intercourse or **sexual intercourse**, lovemaking, coition, coitus, copulation, fornication, sexual relations

sexism See **prejudice**

sexual adjective **1 = carnal**, intimate, sexy, erotic, sensual
2 = reproductive, sex, genital, procreative

sexual intercourse noun
= copulation, union, sex, carnal knowledge, coition, coitus

sexuality noun **= desire**, lust, carnality, eroticism, sensuality, sexiness (informal)

sexy adjective **= erotic**, seductive, sensual, voluptuous, sensuous
• a sexy voice

shabby adjective **1 = tatty**, scruffy, dilapidated, ragged, seedy, run-down, threadbare, worn, raggedy, down at heel, the worse for wear • a shabby overcoat
2 = contemptible, mean, dirty, despicable, rotten (informal)
• shabby treatment

shack noun **= hut**, shed, cabin, shanty

shackle noun **1** (often plural)
= fetter, bond, chain, iron, leg-iron, manacle
▶ verb **2 = fetter**, chain, bind, manacle, put in irons

shade noun **1 = shadow**, dusk, gloom, dimness, gloominess, semidarkness
2 = screen, cover, shield, blind, veil, curtain, canopy, covering
3 = hue, tone, colour, tint, tinge
4 = dash, hint, trace, suggestion
5 (Literary) **= ghost**, spirit, phantom, apparition, spectre
▷ **put into the shade = outshine**, eclipse, overshadow, outclass
▶ verb **6 = cover**, protect, screen, hide, shield, veil, conceal, obscure
7 = darken, cloud, shadow, dim

shadow noun **1 = shade**, cover, darkness, dusk, gloom, dimness
2 = trace, hint, suggestion, suspicion
3 = cloud, sadness, gloom, blight

▶ verb **4 = shade**, screen, shield, darken, overhang
5 = follow, trail, tail (informal), stalk

shadowy adjective **1 = dark**, gloomy, murky, dim, shady, shaded, dusky
2 = vague, faint, dim, phantom, ghostly, nebulous, dreamlike, spectral, unsubstantial

shady adjective **1 = shaded**, cool, dim
2 (Informal) **= crooked**, disreputable, suspect, suspicious, questionable, unethical, dubious, sketchy (informal), shifty

shaft noun **1 = handle**, stem, pole, rod, shank
2 = ray, beam, gleam

shaggy adjective **= unkempt**, rough, hairy, long-haired, hirsute, tousled, unshorn

shake verb **1 = wave**, flourish, agitate, brandish • You have to shake the bottle before use.
2 = vibrate, quake, jolt, shiver, tremble, shudder, quiver • The whole building shook with the force of the blast.
3 = upset, shock, disturb, rattle, distress, unnerve • The news shook me quite a bit.
▶ noun **4 = vibration**, jolt, tremor, jerk, agitation, shiver, convulsion, shudder, quaking, trembling

INFORMALLY SPEAKING
no great shakes: not unusual or important
shake down: cause to settle down or function normally

shake up verb **1 = stir** or **stir up**, mix, churn or churn up, agitate
2 = upset, shock, disturb, unsettle

shaky adjective **1 = unsteady**, unstable, wobbly, rickety, tottering, trembling • threatening an already shaky economy
2 = uncertain, suspect, questionable, dubious, iffy (informal)

shallow adjective **1 = superficial**, surface, empty, slight, trivial

S

2 = **unintelligent**, simple, ignorant, foolish, frivolous, puerile

sham noun **1** = **phony** (informal), fraud, counterfeit, hoax, forgery, impostor, imitation, pretense, humbug

▶ adjective **2** = **false**, counterfeit, artificial, mock, bogus, phony (informal), simulated, imitation, feigned, pretended

▶ verb **3** = **fake**, affect, assume, pretend, simulate, feign, put on

shambles noun = **chaos**, disorder, mess, confusion, havoc, disarray, muddle, madhouse

shame noun **1** = **embarrassment**, humiliation, ignominy • *She felt a deep sense of shame.*

2 = **disgrace**, scandal, discredit, dishonour • *I don't want to bring shame on the family.*

▶ verb **3** = **embarrass**, disgrace, humiliate • *Her son's behaviour had shamed her.*

4 = **dishonour**, smear, stain, degrade, blot, defile, debase
See also: **pity**

shamefaced adjective = **embarrassed**, ashamed, red-faced, sheepish, abashed, humiliated, mortified

shameful adjective

1 = **embarrassing**, humiliating, mortifying

2 = **disgraceful**, low, base, mean, outrageous, wicked, scandalous, dishonourable

shameless adjective = **brazen**, flagrant, unabashed, barefaced, unashamed • *shameless dishonesty*

shampoo See **wash**

shanty noun = **shack**, shed, cabin, hut

shape noun **1** = **form**, figure, outline, contours, lines • *a round shape*

2 = **pattern**, model, frame, mould

3 = **condition**, health, state, trim, fettle

▶ verb **4** = **form**, make, model, fashion, mould • *Shape the dough into a loaf.*

5 = **develop**, plan, frame,

modify, adapt, devise
See also: **body, build, design, determine**

shapeless adjective = **formless**, irregular, amorphous, misshapen, unstructured

shapely adjective = **well-formed**, trim, elegant, neat, graceful, curvaceous, well-proportioned

share verb **1** = **divide**, split • *We shared a pizza.*

▷ **share out** See **distribute**

▶ noun **2** = **portion**, quota, ration, allotment • *a share of the profits*

▷ **shares** See **stock**
See also: **proportion**

shark See **crook**

sharp adjective **1** = **keen**, pointed, jagged, razor-sharp • *a sharp knife*
OPPOSITE: blunt

2 = **quick-witted**, quick, alert, bright, observant, astute, perceptive • *a sharp intellect*

3 = **sudden**, marked, abrupt • *a sharp rise in prices*

4 = **clear**, distinct, crisp, well-defined

5 = **dishonest**, wily, crafty, unscrupulous, sly, cunning, artful

6 = **cutting**, bitter, harsh, barbed, hurtful, caustic, biting

7 = **sour**, hot, acid, tart, pungent, acrid, piquant

8 = **acute**, severe, intense, shooting, painful, piercing, stabbing

▶ adverb **9** = **promptly**, exactly, precisely, on the dot, on time, punctually
See also: **brilliant, intelligent, prompt, shrewd, shrill**

sharpen verb = **whet**, edge, grind, hone

shatter verb **1** = **smash**, break, crack, crush, burst, pulverize

2 = **destroy**, ruin, wreck, demolish, torpedo

shattered adjective (Informal) = **devastated**, crushed, blown away

shave verb = **trim**, crop, pare, shear

shed¹ noun = **hut**, shack,

s

outhouse, woodshed

shed² verb **1 = give out**, give, drop, cast, spill, shower, emit, scatter, radiate

2 = cast off, discard, slough, moult

sheen noun **= shine**, polish, gloss, gleam, brightness, lustre

sheepish adjective

= embarrassed, ashamed, self-conscious, abashed, mortified, shamefaced

sheer adjective **1 = total**, complete, pure, absolute, utter, unqualified • *scenes of sheer beauty*

2 = steep, vertical, perpendicular • *There was a sheer drop just outside my window.*

3 = fine, thin, delicate, lightweight • *sheer curtains*
OPPOSITE: thick
See also: **perfect, rank, transparent**

sheet noun **1 = coat**, film, surface, layer, overlay, veneer, stratum, lamina

2 = piece, panel, plate, slab

3 = expanse, area, sweep, stretch, blanket, covering

shell noun **1 = case**, pod, husk

2 = frame, structure, framework, hull

▶ verb **3 = bomb**, attack, blitz, bombard, strafe

▷ **shell out** verb **= pay out**, give, fork out (*slang*), hand over

shelter noun **1 = refuge**, sanctuary, hostel • *a bus shelter*

2 = protection, safety, cover, harbour, refuge, haven, asylum, sanctuary • *During the flood, we took shelter in the school gym.*

▶ verb **3 = take cover**, hide, huddle • *a man sheltering in a doorway*

4 = protect, hide, shield, harbour • *A neighbour sheltered the boy for seven days.*
See also: **accommodate, defend, guard**

sheltered adjective **= protected**, quiet, isolated, shaded, secluded, cloistered, screened, shielded

shelve verb **= postpone**, suspend, freeze, defer, put aside, put

on ice, put on the back burner (*informal*), take a rain check on (*informal*)

shepherd verb **= guide**, conduct, steer, herd, usher

shield noun **1 = protection**, cover, screen, guard, shelter, safeguard, defence

▶ verb **2 = protect**, defend, cover, screen, guard, shelter, safeguard

shielded See **secure**

shift verb **1 = move**, displace, relocate, budge, reposition, rearrange, move around

▶ noun **2 = move**, displacement, rearrangement, shifting

shiftless adjective **= lazy**, idle, lackadaisical, aimless, good-for-nothing, slothful, unambitious, unenterprising

shifty adjective **= untrustworthy**, slippery, tricky, sly, deceitful, evasive, devious, furtive, underhand

shimmer verb **1 = gleam**, twinkle, glisten, scintillate

▶ noun **2 = gleam**, iridescence

shimmering See **shining**

shine verb **1 = gleam**, beam, glow, sparkle, shimmer, radiate • *The sun is shining.*

2 = polish, brush, buff, burnish

3 = stand out, excel, be conspicuous

▶ noun **4 = brightness**, light, sparkle, shimmer, glare, gleam, radiance

5 = polish, gloss, sheen, lustre
See also: **finish**

shining adjective **= bright**, brilliant, sparkling, luminous, radiant, gleaming, shimmering • *shining stainless steel*

shiny adjective **= bright**, polished, glossy, gleaming, glistening, lustrous

ship noun **= vessel**, boat, craft

shipment See **load, transport**

shipshape adjective **= tidy**, trim, neat, orderly, well-organized, spick-and-span, well-ordered

shirk verb **= dodge**, avoid, evade, get out of, slack

shirker noun **= slacker**, dodger, clock-watcher, idler

S

shiver[1] *verb* **1 = tremble**, shake, quake, shudder, quiver
▶ *noun* **2 = trembling**, tremor, flutter, shudder, quiver

shiver[2] *verb* **= splinter**, break, crack, smash, shatter, fragment, smash to smithereens

shivery *adjective* **= shaking**, cold, shaky, chilly, chilled, quaking, quivery

shock *noun* **1 = upset**, blow, trauma, distress, bombshell • *The extent of the damage came as a shock.*
2 = impact, blow, clash, collision, crash
▶ *verb* **3 = upset**, shake, stun, paralyze, stagger, traumatize, numb • *I was shocked by his appearance.*
4 = offend, outrage, disgust, appal • *She is very easily shocked.*
See also: **amaze, amazement, horrify, scare, surprise**

shocking *adjective* **= dreadful**, outrageous, disgraceful, appalling, scandalous, atrocious, sickening, ghastly, disgusting, revolting, horrifying, nauseating

shoddy *adjective* **= inferior**, poor, second-rate, trashy, rubbishy, slipshod, tawdry

shoot *verb* **1 = hit**, kill, blast (*slang*), plug (*slang*), bring down, open fire
2 = fire, launch, project, propel, discharge, emit, hurl, fling
3 = speed, charge, race, fly, streak, rush, tear, bolt, dash, dart, hurtle
▷ **shoot up** *See* **explode**
▶ *noun* **4 = sprout**, branch, bud, offshoot, sprig

shop *noun* **1 = store**, supermarket, boutique, emporium, hypermarket
2 = factory, plant, shop, mill, works
▶ *verb* **3 = go shopping**, buy, purchase

shoplifter *See* **thief**

shopper *See* **customer**

shore *noun* **= beach**, coast, strand (*poetic*), sands, seashore

▶ *verb*
▷ **shore up = support**, hold, strengthen, brace, prop, reinforce, underpin, buttress

short *adjective* **1 = brief**, short-lived, momentary, fleeting • *a short break*
OPPOSITE: long
2 = small, little, squat, diminutive, petite, dumpy • *a short, elderly man*
OPPOSITE: tall
3 = concise, brief, summary, terse, succinct, compressed, laconic, pithy, abridged • *a short speech*
4 (often with *of*) **= lacking**, low or low on, limited, scarce, scant, deficient, wanting
5 = abrupt, sharp, terse, brusque, curt, discourteous, impolite, uncivil
▶ *adverb* **6 = abruptly**, suddenly, without warning
See also: **inadequate, insufficient**

shortage *noun* **= lack**, want, shortfall, deficiency, scarcity, dearth • *a shortage of funds*
OPPOSITE: abundance

shortcoming *noun* **= failing**, flaw, weakness, defect, fault, imperfection

shorten *verb* **= cut**, trim, abbreviate
OPPOSITE: lengthen
See also: **reduce**

shortfall *See* **shortage**

short-lived *See* **short**

shortly *adverb* **= soon**, presently, before long, in a little while

short-sighted *adjective* **1 = near-sighted**, myopic
2 = imprudent, ill-advised, impractical, ill-considered, impolitic, improvident, injudicious, unthinking

short-tempered *adjective* **= quick-tempered**, impatient, irascible, hot-tempered, testy

shot *noun* **1 = throw**, discharge, lob, pot shot
2 = ammunition, lead, ball, bullet, pellet, slug, projectile
3 = marksman, shooter

s

4 (*Slang*) = **attempt**, go (*informal*), try, turn, effort, stab (*informal*), endeavour

shoulder *verb* **1** = **bear**, carry, accept, assume, be responsible for, take on
2 = **push**, press, elbow, shove, jostle
▶ *noun*
▷ **shoulder to shoulder** *See* **together**

shout *noun* **1** = **cry**, scream, roar, yell, bellow • *I heard a distant shout.*
▶ *verb* **2** = **cry**, call, scream, roar, yell, bellow, bawl • *He shouted something to his brother.*
▷ **shout down** = **drown out**, silence, overwhelm, drown

shove *verb* = **push**, drive, press, propel, elbow, thrust, jostle
▷ **shove off** = **go away**, leave, depart, clear off (*informal*), push off (*informal*), scram (*informal*)

shovel *verb* = **move**, load, toss, scoop, heap, ladle, dredge

show *verb* **1** = **prove**, demonstrate • *Tests show that drinking impairs your ability to drive.*
2 = **demonstrate**, teach, instruct • *I'll show you how to used this digital camera.*
3 = **display**, reveal, indicate, demonstrate, manifest • *Her sketches showed artistic promise.*
4 = **exhibit**, present, display
5 = **guide**, lead, attend, conduct, accompany, escort
▷ **show off** = **exhibit**, display, demonstrate, parade, flaunt, hot dog (*slang*); = **boast**, brag, swagger, blow one's own trumpet
▷ **show signs of** *See* **promise**
▷ **show up** = **stand out**, appear, be conspicuous, be visible; = **reveal**, highlight, expose, lay bare; (*Informal*) = **embarrass**, mortify, let down, put to shame; = **arrive**, come, appear, turn up
▶ *noun* **6** = **exhibition**, display, presentation • *a fashion show*
7 = **pretence**, air, display, pose, semblance • *a show of affection*

8 = **entertainment**, production, presentation
See also: **betray, expose, fair, front, play, program, represent**

| INFORMALLY SPEAKING
| **get the show on the road**: get started
| **run the show**: be in charge

showdown *noun* = **confrontation**, clash, face-off (*slang*)

shower *noun* **1** = **deluge**, stream, barrage, volley, torrent
▷ **showers** *See* **rain**
▶ *verb* **2** = **inundate**, rain, pour, lavish, heap, deluge

showery *See* **wet**

showman *noun* = **performer**, entertainer

show-off *noun* = **exhibitionist**, boaster, braggart, poseur, hot dog (*slang*)

showy *adjective* **1** = **ostentatious**, flash (*informal*), flamboyant, flashy, brash, over the top (*informal*)
2 = **gaudy**, loud, garish

shred *noun* **1** = **strip**, bit, piece, scrap, fragment, tatter, sliver
2 = **particle**, grain, trace, scrap, atom, iota, jot

shrew *noun* = **nag**, scold, spitfire, vixen, harpy, harridan

shrewd *adjective* = **astute**, sharp, smart, crafty, perceptive, canny • *a shrewd manager*
See also: **acute, clever, keen, wise**

shrewdness *noun* = **astuteness**, judgment, discernment, sharpness, canniness, perspicacity, quick wits, smartness

shriek *verb, noun* = **scream**, cry, yell, screech, squeal

shrill *adjective* = **piercing**, sharp, penetrating • *the shrill whistle of the engine*

shrink *verb* **1** = **get smaller**, contract, narrow, diminish, dwindle • *My sweater shrank in the wash.*
OPPOSITE: grow
2 = **recoil**, cringe, quail,

S

flinch, cower, draw back
See also: **decrease, lessen**
shrinkage *See* **decline**
shrivel *verb* = **wither**, shrink,
wilt, dehydrate, desiccate, wizen
shroud *noun* 1 = **winding sheet**,
grave clothes
2 = **covering**, screen, veil, pall,
mantle
▶ *verb* 3 = **conceal**, cover, screen,
hide, blanket, cloak, veil,
envelop
shudder *verb* 1 = **shiver**, shake,
quake, tremble, quiver, convulse
▶ *noun* 2 = **shiver**, tremor,
spasm, quiver
shuffle *verb* 1 = **scuffle**, drag,
scrape, shamble
2 = **rearrange**, disorder, mix,
jumble, disarrange
shun *verb* = **avoid**, keep away
from, steer clear of
shunned *See* **unpopular**
shut *verb* 1 = **close**, slam, fasten
• *Someone had forgotten to shut the
door.*
OPPOSITE: open
▶ *adjective* 2 = **closed**, sealed,
fastened • *An aroma of baking bread
came from behind the shut door.*
OPPOSITE: open
shut down *verb* 1 = **stop**, halt,
switch off
2 = **close**, shut up
shut out *verb* = **exclude**, bar,
debar, keep out, lock out
shuttle *verb* = **go back and forth**,
alternate, commute, go to and
fro
shut up *verb* 1 (*Informal*) = **be
quiet**, silence, gag, hush, fall
silent, hold one's tongue
2 = **confine**, imprison, cage,
incarcerate, coop up, immure
shy *adjective* 1 = **timid**, self-
conscious, self-effacing,
bashful, retiring, diffident • *a
shy, quiet-spoken man*
OPPOSITE: bold
2 = **cautious**, suspicious, wary,
hesitant, chary, distrustful
▶ *verb* 3 (sometimes with *away*)
= **recoil**, start, balk, flinch, draw
back
shyness *noun* = **timidity**,

bashfulness, diffidence, lack of
confidence, self-consciousness,
timidity, timorousness
sick *adjective* 1 = **unwell**, ailing,
under par, under the weather
• *The emergency room was full of very
sick people.*
OPPOSITE: well
2 = **nauseous**, ill, queasy • *The
very thought of food made him sick.*
3 (*Informal*) = **morbid**, black,
sadistic, macabre, ghoulish
▷ **sick of** = **tired**, weary, bored,
fed up • *I'm sick of your
complaints.*
▷ **sick person** *See* **patient**
See also: **unhealthy**
sicken *verb* 1 = **disgust**, revolt,
repel, nauseate, gross out (*slang*),
turn one's stomach
2 = **fall ill**, ail, take sick
sickening *adjective* = **disgusting**,
offensive, foul, gross (*slang*), vile,
distasteful, repulsive, revolting,
loathsome, nauseating,
noisome, scuzzy (*slang*),
stomach-turning (*informal*),
yucky or yukky (*slang*)
sickly *adjective* 1 = **unhealthy**,
weak, ailing, delicate, faint,
feeble, infirm, pallid, wan,
peaky
2 = **nauseating**, cloying,
mawkish
sickness *noun* 1 = **illness**,
disease, complaint, disorder,
bug (*informal*), ailment, malady,
affliction
2 = **nausea**, queasiness,
vomiting
side *noun* 1 = **edge**, shoulder • *Her
legs hung over the side of the bed.*
RELATED WORD
adjective: lateral
2 = **party**, team, camp, faction
• *Both sides began to prepare for the
debate.*
3 = **part**, face, hand, view,
surface, aspect, flank, facet
4 = **point of view**, stand,
position, opinion, viewpoint,
angle, standpoint, slant
▷ **side by side** *See* **together**
▶ *adjective* 5 = **subordinate**,
minor, subsidiary, secondary,

lesser, marginal, ancillary, incidental
See also: **bank, point**
▷ verb
▷ **side with** = **support**, agree with, stand up for, take the part of • *He always sided with his sister.*

sidelong adjective = **sideways**, indirect, covert, oblique

sidestep verb = **avoid**, duck (informal), skirt, circumvent, evade, dodge

sidetrack verb = **distract**, divert, deflect

sideways adverb 1 = **obliquely**, edgeways, laterally, sidelong, to the side
▷ adjective 2 = **oblique**, sidelong

sidle verb = **edge**, steal, inch, creep, sneak, slink

siesta noun = **nap**, sleep, snooze (informal), doze, catnap, forty winks (informal)

sieve noun 1 = **strainer**, colander
▷ verb 2 = **sift**, separate, strain

sift verb 1 = **sieve**, separate, filter
2 = **examine**, research, investigate, analyze, scrutinize, go through, work over

sight noun 1 = **vision**, visibility, eyesight • *The singer lost his sight when he was a child.*
RELATED WORDS
adjectives: optical, visual
2 = **spectacle**, scene, display • *It was a ghastly sight.*
3 = **view**, appearance, perception, visibility, range of vision
4 = **eyesore**, mess, monstrosity
▷ **catch sight of** = **spot**, glimpse, espy
▷ verb 5 = **spot**, see • *He had been sighted in the Maritimes.*

| CONFUSABLES
Sight means *view* or *ability to see.*
Site means *area of ground* or *place for an activity.*

sign noun 1 = **symbol**, mark, character, icon, logo, emblem • *The negative number is preceded by a minus sign.*
2 = **notice**, board, placard • *a sign saying that the highway was closed*
3 = **indication**, evidence,

symptom, hint, trace, clue, token • *the first signs of recovery*
4 = **omen**, warning, auspice, augury, foreboding, portent
▷ verb 5 = **autograph**, endorse, initial, inscribe
6 = **gesture**, indicate, signal, beckon, gesticulate
▷ **sign up** See **hire, join**
See also: **premonition**

signal noun 1 = **sign**, gesture, cue, beacon • *a distress signal*
▷ verb 2 = **gesture**, sign, wave, motion, nod, beckon, gesticulate • *He was frantically signalling me to stop talking.*
▷ **signal to** See **hail**
See also: **indicate, indication**

significance noun
1 = **importance**, weight, moment, consequence, relevance
2 = **meaning**, point, force, message, import, sense, implication or implications, purport

significant adjective
1 = **important**, impressive, considerable, notable, marked, striking, pronounced • *This drug seems to have a significant effect on the disease.*
OPPOSITE: insignificant
2 = **meaningful**, indicative, suggestive, expressive, eloquent
See also: **major, serious, special**

signify verb 1 = **indicate**, suggest, mean, intimate, imply, denote, portend, be a sign of, betoken, connote
2 = **matter**, count, be important, carry weight

silence noun 1 = **quiet**, peace, calm, lull, hush, stillness • *There was a momentary silence.*
OPPOSITE: noise
2 = **reticence**, muteness, speechlessness • *breaking his silence for the first time about the incident*
▷ verb 3 = **quiet**, still, stifle, suppress, gag, muffle, deaden • *The shock silenced her completely.*

silent adjective 1 = **mute**, dumb, speechless, taciturn, wordless

• *The class fell silent as the teacher entered.*

2 = quiet, still, hushed, soundless • *The room was silent except for the ticking of the clock.*
OPPOSITE: noisy

silently adjective **= quietly**, inaudibly, in silence, mutely, noiselessly, soundlessly, without a sound, wordlessly

silhouette noun **1 = outline**, form, shape, profile
▶ verb **2 = outline**, etch, stand out

silky adjective **= smooth**, sleek, velvety, silken

silliness See **stupidity**

silly adjective **= foolish**, stupid, ridiculous, absurd, idiotic, inane • *I know it's silly to get so upset.*
See also: **frivolous, unwise**

silt noun **= sediment**, deposit, sludge, ooze, alluvium
▶ verb
▷ **silt up = clog**, choke, congest

similar adjective **= like**, uniform, comparable, alike, analogous • *a bike similar to mine*
OPPOSITE: different

similarity noun **= resemblance**, likeness, analogy, sameness • *the similarity of our backgrounds*
OPPOSITE: difference

similarly See **alike**

simmer verb **= fume**, rage, smoulder, seethe, be angry
▷ **simmer down** verb **= calm down**, control oneself, cool off or cool down, de-stress

simper verb **= smile coyly**, smirk, smile affectedly

simple adjective **1 = easy**, elementary, straightforward, understandable, uncomplicated • *a simple task*
OPPOSITE: complicated
2 = plain, clean, severe, classic • *a simple but stylish outfit*
OPPOSITE: elaborate
3 = pure, elementary, unalloyed, uncombined, unmixed
4 = artless, natural, innocent, sincere, naive, unaffected, childlike, unsophisticated, guileless, ingenuous

5 = honest, direct, basic, naked, plain, stark, sincere, frank, bald
6 = humble, modest, unpretentious, homey, dumpy (*informal*)
7 = feeble-minded, slow, stupid, foolish, moronic, halfwitted
See also: **crude, primitive**

simple-minded adjective **= feeble-minded**, simple, stupid, idiot, backward, foolish, idiotic, halfwitted, dim-witted

simpleton noun **= halfwit**, fool, idiot, moron, imbecile (*informal*), doofus (*slang*), dork (*slang*), dullard, schmuck (*slang*)

simplicity noun **1 = ease**, clarity, clearness, straightforwardness
2 = plainness, restraint, purity, lack of adornment
3 = artlessness, innocence, openness, candour, directness, naivety

simplify verb **= make simpler**, streamline • *measures intended to simplify the procedure*

simply adverb **1 = plainly**, easily, clearly, directly, naturally, intelligibly, straightforwardly, unpretentiously
2 = just, only, merely, solely, purely
3 = totally, really, completely, absolutely, wholly, utterly

simulate verb **= pretend**, act, affect, sham, feign, put on

simulated See **false**

simultaneous adjective **= coinciding**, concurrent, coincident, at the same time, contemporaneous, synchronous

simultaneously adverb **= at the same time**, together, concurrently

sin noun **1 = crime**, wrong, offence, evil, wickedness, iniquity • *preaching against sin*
▶ verb **2 = do wrong** • *I admit that I have sinned.*

since See **because**

sincere adjective **= honest**, real, genuine, heartfelt, wholehearted • *my sincere apologies*

OPPOSITE: insincere
See also: **serious**

sincerely adverb = **honestly**, seriously, truly, genuinely, wholeheartedly, earnestly, in earnest

sincerity noun = **honesty**, truth, seriousness, candour, frankness, genuineness

sinecure noun = **soft job** (informal), gravy train (slang), money for jam or money for old rope (informal), soft option

sinful adjective = **wicked**, bad, guilty, criminal, corrupt, immoral, erring, iniquitous

sing verb 1 = **warble**, chant, pipe, carol, chirp, croon, yodel, trill
2 = **hum**, buzz, whine, purr

singe verb = **burn**, char, scorch, sear

singer noun = **vocalist**, crooner, diva, soloist, balladeer, cantor, chorister, minstrel, divo

single adjective 1 = **one**, only, lone, sole, solitary • the beauty of a single rose
2 = **unmarried**, bachelor or bachelorette (feminine), unattached • I'm surprised you're still single.
3 = **individual**, separate • a single room
4 = **simple**, unblended, unmixed
▶ verb 5 (usually with out) = **pick**, choose, separate, select, distinguish, fix on, pick on or pick out, set apart
See also: **alone**

single-handed adverb = **unaided**, alone, solo, independently, unassisted, by oneself, on one's own, without help

single-minded adjective = **determined**, dedicated, dogged, fixed, unswerving

singly adverb = **one by one**, separately, individually, one at a time

singular adjective
1 = **remarkable**, rare, unique, exceptional, uncommon • an artist of singular talent
2 = **unusual**, extraordinary • a singular and eccentric character

3 = **single**, individual, separate, sole
See also: **curious, odd, particular, weird**

singularly adverb = **remarkably**, especially, particularly, notably, unusually, exceptionally, uncommonly, outstandingly

sinister adjective = **threatening**, evil, ominous, forbidding, menacing • There was something cold and sinister about him.
See also: **creepy**

sink verb 1 = **descend**, fall, drop, lower, founder, plunge, dip, subside, submerge, go down, go under
2 = **fall**, drop, collapse, slip, lapse, subside, abate
3 = **decline**, fail, flag, worsen, weaken, fade, deteriorate, diminish, dwindle, lessen, decay
4 = **dig**, drive, drill, bore, excavate
5 = **stoop**, be reduced to, lower oneself
▷ **sink in** = **be understood**, register (informal), penetrate, get through to

sinner noun = **wrongdoer**, offender, miscreant, evildoer, malefactor, transgressor

sip verb 1 = **drink**, sample, taste, sup
▶ noun 2 = **swallow**, drop, taste, thimbleful

siren See **alarm**

sissy noun 1 = **wimp** (informal), coward, mama's boy, softie (informal), weakling, pantywaist (informal)
▶ adjective 2 = **wimpish** or **wimpy** (informal), cowardly, feeble, effeminate, weak, soft (informal), unmanly

sit verb 1 = **rest**, settle, perch
2 = **convene**, meet, deliberate, assemble
3 = **officiate**, preside

sit down See **rest**

site noun 1 = **location**, place, position, spot, plot, setting
▶ verb 2 = **locate**, set, place, position, install, situate

sited See **located**

S

situate See **place**

situated See **located**

situation noun 1 = **state of affairs**, case, scenario, plight, circumstances • a serious situation
2 = **location**, place, site, position, spot, setting
3 = **status**, station, rank
4 = **job**, post, place, office, position, employment
See also: **affair, matter, state**

sixth sense See **instinct**

sizable, sizeable adjective = **large**, substantial, decent, considerable, respectable, goodly, largish, supersize

size noun = **dimensions**, extent, bulk, immensity, proportions • the size of the audience
See also: **area, capacity, quantity**
▷ verb
▷ **size up** = **assess**, evaluate, appraise, take stock of

sizzle verb = **hiss**, fry, spit, crackle, frizzle

skedaddle verb (Slang) = **run away**, flee, disappear, abscond, beat it (slang), clear off (informal), run for it, scram (informal), take to one's heels

skeleton noun = **framework**, draft, frame, structure, outline, sketch, bare bones

skeptic noun = **doubter**, cynic, disbeliever, doubting Thomas

skeptical adjective = **doubtful**, dubious, cynical, incredulous, unconvinced, mistrustful, disbelieving

skepticism noun = **doubt**, disbelief, cynicism, incredulity, unbelief

sketch noun 1 = **drawing**, plan, design, draft, outline, delineation
▷ verb 2 = **draw**, represent, draft, outline, depict, delineate, rough out

sketchy adjective = **incomplete**, rough, inadequate, superficial, scrappy, skimpy, cursory, perfunctory

skilful adjective = **expert**, able, skilled, competent, accomplished, adept, proficient, masterly • the NHL's most skilful player
OPPOSITE: incompetent
See also: **capable**

skilfully See **well**

skill noun = **expertise**, facility, ability, knack, competence, proficiency, dexterity • This task requires great skill.
See also: **qualification**

skilled adjective = **expert**, able, professional, experienced, competent, trained, accomplished, proficient, skilful, masterly • skilled workers, such as plumbers
OPPOSITE: incompetent
See also: **perfect, practical**

skim verb 1 = **separate**, cream
2 = **glide**, fly, coast, soar, float, sail
3 (usually with through) = **scan**, glance, run one's eye over

skimp verb = **stint**, scamp, be mean with, be sparing with, cut corners, scrimp

skin noun 1 = **hide**, pelt, fell
2 = **coating**, film, outside, peel, crust, casing, rind, husk
▷ verb 3 = **peel**, scrape, flay
▷ **skin alive** (Informal) = **attack**, assault, assail, let have it (informal), let loose on (informal)

skinflint noun = **miser**, niggard, penny-pincher (informal), Scrooge

skinny adjective = **thin**, lean, bony, scrawny, emaciated, undernourished • a skinny little boy
OPPOSITE: plump
See also: **puny**

skip verb 1 = **hop**, trip, dance, bounce, bob, caper, prance, flit, frisk, gambol
2 = **leave out**, eschew, omit, give (something) a miss, miss out, pass over

skirmish noun 1 = **fight**, battle, conflict, clash, scrap (informal), encounter, brush, fracas
▷ verb 2 = **fight**, clash, collide

skirt verb 1 = **border**, edge, flank
2 (often with around or round)

= **avoid**, circumvent, evade, steer clear of

skit noun 1 = **parody**, sketch, spoof (informal), burlesque
2 = **play**, performance, drama, comedy

skittish adjective = **nervous**, lively, restive, fidgety, jumpy, excitable, highly strung, wired (slang)

skulduggery noun (Informal) = **trickery**, double-dealing, duplicity, machinations, underhandedness

skulk verb = **lurk**, creep, sneak, prowl, slink

sky noun = **heavens**, firmament

slab noun = **piece**, portion, slice, chunk, lump, wedge

slack adjective 1 = **loose**, lax, limp, baggy, relaxed
2 = **negligent**, idle, lax, lazy, inactive, remiss, neglectful, slapdash, slipshod
3 = **slow**, quiet, sluggish, dull, inactive, slow-moving
▶ noun 4 = **room**, give (informal), excess, leeway
▶ verb 5 = **shirk**, idle, dodge

slacken, slack off verb = **lessen**, reduce, decrease, moderate, relax, diminish, abate, drop off

slacker noun = **layabout**, idler, dodger, loafer, couch potato (slang), shirker

slake verb = **satisfy**, assuage, quench, sate

slam verb = **bang**, crash, throw, smash, dash, hurl, fling

slander noun 1 = **defamation**, scandal, smear, libel, slur • He is now suing the company for slander.
▶ verb 2 = **defame**, smear, libel, malign • He has been charged with slandering the mayor.

slanderous adjective = **defamatory**, malicious, damaging, libellous

slant verb 1 = **slope**, list, lean, heel, bend, tilt, incline, cant, bevel
2 = **bias**, twist, angle, colour, distort
▶ noun 3 = **slope**, grade, tilt, incline, camber, gradient
4 = **bias**, emphasis, angle,

prejudice, one-sidedness, point of view

slanted See **biased**

slanting adjective = **sloping**, bent, oblique, diagonal, inclined, tilted, angled, at an angle, tilting

slap noun 1 = **smack**, blow, cuff, spank
▶ verb 2 = **smack**, paddle, cuff, clap, spank

slapdash adjective = **careless**, sloppy (informal), messy, hurried, hasty, clumsy, slipshod

slash verb 1 = **cut**, score, rip, hack, gash, slit, lacerate, rend
2 = **reduce**, cut, drop, lower
▶ noun 3 = **cut**, rent, rip, gash, slit, laceration, incision

slate verb = **schedule**, plan, program, book, appoint, arrange

slaughter verb 1 = **murder**, kill, slay, massacre, butcher
▶ noun 2 = **murder**, killing, massacre, slaying, carnage, bloodshed, butchery

slaughterhouse noun = **abattoir**

slave noun 1 = **servant**, drudge, serf, vassal
▶ verb 2 = **toil**, slog, drudge

slavery noun = **enslavement**, captivity, bondage, servitude, subjugation

slavish adjective 1 = **servile**, base, abject, submissive, cringing, fawning, grovelling, obsequious, sycophantic
2 = **imitative**, second-hand, unimaginative, unoriginal

slay verb = **kill**, murder, slaughter, massacre, butcher, mow down

slaying See **murder**

sleaze noun = **corruption**, fraud, bribery, extortion, dishonesty, unscrupulousness, venality

sleazy adjective = **sordid**, low, squalid, seedy, run-down, disreputable, scuzzy (slang)

sleek adjective = **glossy**, smooth, shiny, lustrous

sleep noun 1 = **slumber**, nap, snooze (informal), hibernation, doze • They were exhausted from lack of sleep.
▶ verb 2 = **slumber**, hibernate,

snooze (*informal*), doze, take a nap
• *The baby slept during the car ride.*

sleepless *adjective* = **wakeful**,
restless, insomniac

sleepy *adjective* **1** = **drowsy**,
sluggish, lethargic • *Do you feel
sleepy during the day?*
2 = **quiet**, dull • *a sleepy little village*
See also: **tired**

slender *adjective* **1** = **slim**, slight,
lean • *a tall, slender woman*
2 = **faint**, small, remote, slight,
slim • *He won, but only by a slender
majority.*
3 = **meagre**, little, small, scant,
scanty
See also: **minute, narrow**

sleuth *noun* = **detective**,
investigator or private
investigator, gumshoe (*slang*),
private eye (*informal*)

slice *noun* **1** = **share**, cut, portion,
segment, wedge, sliver, helping
▶ *verb* **2** = **cut**, divide, carve, sever

slick *adjective* **1** = **glib**, smooth,
polished, plausible, specious
2 = **skilful**, professional,
polished, deft, adroit, dexterous
▶ *verb* **3** = **smooth**, sleek, plaster
down

slide *verb* = **slip**, coast, skim, glide,
slither

slight *adjective* **1** = **small**, minor,
insignificant, paltry, negligible,
trivial, inconsiderable, scanty • *a
slight dent*
OPPOSITE: large
2 = **slim**, small, spare, delicate,
fragile, feeble, lightly-built
▶ *verb* **3** = **snub**, ignore, insult,
scorn, disdain, affront, blow off
(*slang*)
▶ *noun* **4** = **snub**, insult, neglect,
rebuff, affront, slap in the face
(*informal*), cold shoulder or the
cold shoulder
See also: **light, remote, slender,
unimportant**

slightest See **least**

slightly *adverb* = **a little**,
somewhat

slim *adjective* **1** = **slender**, trim,
narrow, thin, slight, lean, svelte
2 = **slight**, poor, remote, faint,
slender

▶ *verb* **3** = **lose weight**, reduce,
diet

slimy *adjective* **1** = **viscous**,
clammy, glutinous, oozy
2 = **obsequious**, oily, creeping,
grovelling, servile, smarmy (*Brit
informal*), unctuous

sling *verb* **1** = **throw**, cast, toss,
shy, hurl, lob (*informal*), fling,
heave, chuck (*informal*)
2 = **hang**, suspend, dangle

slink *verb* = **creep**, steal, slip,
sneak, prowl, skulk

slinky *adjective* = **figure-hugging**,
clinging, close-fitting, skintight

slip *verb* **1** = **sneak**, steal, creep
• *She slipped downstairs and out of
the house.*
2 = **fall**, skid
3 = **slide**, skate, glide, slither
4 (sometimes with *up*) = **make
a mistake**, err, blunder,
miscalculate
▷ **let slip** = **give away**, reveal,
leak, disclose, divulge
▶ *noun* **5** = **mistake**, error,
blunder, slip-up • *a slip of the
tongue*
▷ **give (someone) the slip**
= **escape from**, elude, evade,
dodge, get away from, lose
(someone)

> **INFORMALLY SPEAKING**
> **give someone the slip**: evade
> someone
> **let slip**: tell without meaning
> to
> **slip one over on**: get the
> advantage of, especially by
> trickery
> **slip up**: make a mistake

slippery *adjective* **1** = **smooth**,
unsafe, icy, greasy, glassy, slippy
(*informal, dialect*)
2 = **devious**, tricky, dishonest,
crafty, cunning, evasive,
untrustworthy, shifty

slipshod *adjective* = **careless**,
casual, sloppy (*informal*),
slapdash, slovenly, untidy

slit *noun* **1** = **cut**, opening, tear,
split, rent, gash, incision
▶ *verb* **2** = **cut** or **cut open**, slash,
rip, knife, pierce, gash, lance

slither *verb* = **slide**, slip, snake,

glide, undulate, slink

sliver noun = **shred**, fragment, splinter, shaving, paring

slobber verb = **drool**, dribble, salivate, drivel, slaver

slobbish adjective = **messy**, unclean, slovenly, unkempt, untidy

slog verb 1 = **work**, labour, slave, toil, plod, plow through
2 = **trudge**, trek, tramp
3 = **hit**, strike, punch, thump, wallop (informal), sock (slang), slug
▷ **slog away** See **work**
▶ noun 4 = **work**, effort, struggle, labour, exertion
5 = **trudge**, hike, trek, tramp

slogan noun = **motto**, jingle
• Alberta's slogan is "Canada's Rocky Mountain Playground."

slop verb 1 = **spill**, splash, overflow, slosh (informal)
▶ noun 2 (Informal) = **food**, mess (slang), grub (slang)

slope noun 1 = **incline**, pitch, grade, ramp, inclination, gradient, declination, declivity
• The street is on a slope.
▶ verb 2 = **slant**, fall, rise • The bank sloped sharply down to the river.
See also: **tilt**

sloping adjective = **slanting**, oblique, leaning, inclined

sloppy adjective 1 = **careless**, messy, slipshod, slovenly, untidy
2 = **sentimental**, slushy (informal), gushing, mawkish

slot noun 1 = **opening**, hole, groove, vent, slit, aperture
2 (Informal) = **place**, time, space, position, opening, vacancy
▶ verb 3 = **fit**, insert, fit in

sloth noun = **laziness**, inactivity, sluggishness, inertia, idleness, slackness, torpor

slothful adjective = **lazy**, idle, inactive, indolent, workshy

slouch verb = **slump**, stoop, droop, loll

slovenly adjective = **careless**, sloppy (informal), slack, negligent, disorderly, slapdash, slipshod, untidy

slow adjective 1 = **unhurried**, sluggish, gradual, leisurely, lingering, ponderous • slow, regular breathing
OPPOSITE: fast
2 = **stupid**, thick, dense, dim, obtuse • I must be pretty slow if I didn't get that joke.
3 = **prolonged**, gradual, protracted, lingering, long-drawn-out
4 = **late**, behind, delayed, backward, tardy
See also: **reluctant**
▶ verb
▷ **slow (down)** = **decelerate**, check • The car slowed and then stopped.

slowly adverb = **gradually**, by degrees, unhurriedly • She turned and began to walk away slowly.
OPPOSITE: quickly

sludge noun = **sediment**, mud, mire, residue, ooze, muck, silt, slime

sluggish adjective = **inactive**, slow, heavy, dull, lethargic, indolent, inert, slothful, torpid

slum noun = **hovel**, ghetto

slumber verb = **sleep**, nap, snooze (informal), doze, drowse

slump verb 1 = **fall**, crash, collapse, slip, sink, plunge
2 = **sag**, hunch, slouch, droop, loll
▶ noun 3 = **fall**, drop, crash, decline, collapse, reverse, downturn, trough
4 = **recession**, depression

slur noun = **insult**, smear, stain, affront, innuendo, insinuation, aspersion, calumny

slushy See **sentimental**

slut noun (Offensive) = **tart**, ho (slang), whore, trollop

sly adjective 1 = **cunning**, wily, crafty, devious, scheming, underhand • devious, sly, and manipulative
2 = **roguish**, arch, mischievous, impish, knowing
▶ noun
▷ **on the sly** = **secretly**, privately, surreptitiously, covertly, on the quiet
See also: **sneaky**

S

smack verb **1** = **slap**, hit, paddle, cuff, clap, strike, spank
▷ noun **2** = **slap**, blow
▷ adverb **3** (Informal) = **directly**, right, straight, exactly, slap (informal), precisely, squarely

small adjective **1** = **little**, minute, tiny, mini, miniature, wee, diminutive, petite, pygmy or pigmy, undersized, teeny, teeny-weeny • a small child
OPPOSITE: large
2 = **unimportant**, minor, petty, insignificant, paltry, negligible, trivial, trifling • small changes
3 = **petty**, base, mean, narrow
4 = **modest**, humble, unpretentious
See also: **fine, low, remote, slender, slight**

smallest See **least**

small-minded adjective = **petty**, mean, intolerant, narrow-minded, bigoted, ungenerous

small-time adjective = **minor**, petty, insignificant, unimportant, of no account

smarmy adjective (Brit informal) = **obsequious**, smooth, suave, crawling, ingratiating, servile, sycophantic, toadying, unctuous

smart adjective **1** = **neat**, elegant, stylish, chic, spruce • a smart navy blue outfit
OPPOSITE: scruffy
2 = **clever**, bright, intelligent, shrewd, ingenious, astute, canny • a smart idea
OPPOSITE: stupid
3 = **brisk**, quick, vigorous, lively
▷ verb **4** = **sting**, hurt, burn
▷ noun **5** = **sting**, pain, soreness
See also: **brilliant, posh**

smart aleck noun (Informal) = **know-it-all** (informal), smarty pants (informal), wise guy (informal)

smarten verb = **tidy**, groom, put in order, put to rights, spruce up

smarting See **sore**

smash verb **1** = **break**, crush, shatter, demolish, pulverize
2 = **collide**, crash
3 = **destroy**, ruin, trash (slang), wreck, lay waste

▷ **smash into** See **hit**
▷ noun **4** = **destruction**, collapse, failure, ruin, downfall
5 = **collision**, crash, accident

smashed See **broken**

smattering noun = **modicum**, bit, rudiments

smear verb **1** = **spread over**, cover, coat, bedaub, daub, rub on
2 = **smudge**, soil, dirty, stain, sully
3 = **slander**, blacken, besmirch, malign
▷ noun **4** = **smudge**, streak, blot, splotch, blotch, daub
5 = **slander**, libel, defamation, calumny

smell noun **1** = **odour**, scent, perfume, aroma, fragrance • a smell of damp wood
2 = **stink**, reek, stench • the nasty smell of ashtrays
▷ verb **3** = **stink**, reek • Do my feet smell?
4 = **sniff**, scent • I could smell muffins baking in the oven.

smelly adjective = **stinking**, foul, reeking • smelly socks
OPPOSITE: fragrant

smile verb **1** = **grin**, beam, smirk
▷ noun **2** = **grin**, beam, smirk • She gave me a big smile.

smirk noun = **smug look**, simper

smitten adjective **1** = **afflicted**, laid low, plagued, struck
2 = **infatuated**, beguiled, bewitched, captivated, charmed, enamoured

smoke verb **1** = **smoulder**, fume
2 = **puff**, draw, inhale, vape

smooth adjective **1** = **sleek**, polished, glossy, silky, glassy • a smooth wooden surface
OPPOSITE: rough
2 = **even**, level, plane, flat, flush, horizontal
3 = **easy**, effortless, well-ordered
4 = **flowing**, regular, steady, uniform, rhythmic
5 = **suave**, slick, persuasive, glib, facile, smarmy (Brit informal), unctuous, urbane
6 = **mellow**, mild, pleasant, agreeable
▷ verb **7** = **flatten**, level, plane,

press, iron
8 = calm, ease, soften, mitigate, appease, assuage, mollify

smoothly See **well**

smother verb **1 = suffocate**, choke, stifle, strangle

2 = suppress, hide, stifle, conceal, muffle, repress

smoulder verb = **seethe**, boil, rage, simmer, fume
See also: **glow**

smudge verb **1 = smear**, mark, dirty, daub, smirch
▸ noun **2 = smear**, blemish, blot

smug adjective = **self-satisfied**, superior, complacent, conceited • They looked at each other in smug satisfaction.

smuggle See **sneak**

smuggler noun = **trafficker**, runner, bootlegger

smugness See **pride**

smutty adjective = **obscene**, crude, blue, dirty, indecent, vulgar, coarse, suggestive, bawdy, indelicate

snack noun = **light meal**, bite, refreshment or refreshments

snag noun **1 = difficulty**, problem, catch, disadvantage, drawback • The snag was that he had no transportation.
▸ verb **2 = catch**, tear, rip
See also: **stick**

snap verb **1 = break**, separate, crack

2 = crackle, pop, click

3 = bite at, bite, nip, snatch

4 = speak sharply, bark, jump down (someone's) throat (informal), lash out at

▷ **snap up = seize**, grab, pounce upon, take advantage of
▸ noun **5 = crackle**, pop

6 = bite, grab, nip

▸ adjective **7 = instant**, immediate, sudden, spur-of-the-moment

snappy adjective **1 = irritable**, cross, edgy, testy, touchy

2 = smart, cool (informal), chic, fashionable, dapper, stylish, phat (slang)

snare noun **1 = trap**, net, wire, gin, noose

▸ verb **2 = trap**, net, catch, seize, wire, entrap

snarl verb (often with up) = **tangle**, entangle, muddle, entwine, ravel

snarl-up noun = **tangle**, confusion, muddle, entanglement

snatch verb **1 = seize**, grab, grip, clutch, grasp

▷ **snatch a glimpse** See **peek**
▸ noun **2 = bit**, part, piece, fragment, snippet

sneak verb **1 = slink**, steal, slip, lurk, sidle • Sometimes she would sneak out to see me.

2 = slip, spirit, smuggle • He was caught trying to sneak the book out of the library.

▷ **sneak a look** See **peek**
▸ noun **3 = informer**, telltale

sneaking adjective **1 = nagging**, persistent, uncomfortable, worrying

2 = secret, private, hidden, undivulged, unexpressed, unvoiced

sneaky adjective = **sly**, dishonest, crafty, deceitful, devious, slippery, untrustworthy • He only won by using sneaky tactics.

sneer noun **1 = scorn**, jeer, ridicule, mockery, derision, gibe
▸ verb **2 = scorn**, laugh, mock, jeer, ridicule, deride, disdain

sneering See **scornful**

snide adjective = **nasty**, malicious, cynical, hurtful, sarcastic, disparaging, ill-natured, scornful, sneering, spiteful

sniff verb = **inhale**, breathe, smell

snigger noun, verb = **laugh**, giggle, snicker, titter

snip verb **1 = cut**, clip, crop, trim, dock, shave
▸ noun **2 = bit**, piece, scrap, shred, fragment, clipping

snipe verb = **criticize**, knock (informal), jeer, carp, disparage, denigrate, put down

snippet noun = **piece**, part, scrap, shred, fragment

snitch verb **1** (Informal) = **inform on**, grass on (Brit slang), tattle on, tell on (informal), tell tales

▶ *noun* **2 = informer**, telltale, tattletale

snivel *verb* **= whine**, cry, moan, whimper, sniffle

snob *noun* **= elitist**, highbrow, prig

snobbery *noun* **= arrogance**, pride, pretension, airs, snobbishness

snobbish *adjective* **= superior**, arrogant, pretentious, patronizing, snooty (*informal*), stuck-up (*informal*)

snoop *verb* **= pry**, spy, interfere, poke one's nose in (*informal*)

snooper *noun* **= busybody**, meddler, snoop (*informal*), nosy rosy (*US informal*)

snooze *verb* **1 = doze**, nap, catnap, take forty winks (*informal*)
▶ *noun* **2 = doze**, nap, siesta, catnap, forty winks (*informal*)

snub *verb* **1 = insult**, cut (*informal*), avoid, ignore, slight, humiliate, rebuff, blow off (*slang*), cold-shoulder, put down
▶ *noun* **2 = insult**, affront, put-down, slap in the face

snug *adjective* **= cozy**, warm, comfortable, comfy (*informal*), homey

snuggle *verb* **= nestle**, cuddle, nuzzle

so *See* **therefore**
▷ **so-so** *See* **tolerable**

soak *verb* **1 = wet**, steep, bathe, permeate • *The water had soaked his jacket.*
2 = penetrate, seep, permeate
▷ **soak up = absorb**, assimilate

soaked *See* **wet**

soaking *adjective* **= wet through**, sodden, dripping, drenched, saturated, soaked, sopping, streaming, wringing wet

soar *verb* **1 = ascend**, rise, fly, wing, mount
2 = rise, rocket, climb, escalate, shoot up

soaring *See* **tall**

sob *verb* **= cry**, weep, howl, shed tears

sober *adjective* **1 = abstinent**, moderate, temperate, abstemious

2 = serious, cool, steady, reasonable, grave, solemn, rational, sedate, staid, composed, level-headed
3 = plain, dark, drab, dumpy (*informal*), frowzy, quiet, subdued, sombre

sobriety *noun* **1 = abstinence**, moderation, abstemiousness, nonindulgence, soberness, temperance
2 = seriousness, gravity, level-headedness, solemnity, staidness, steadiness

so-called *adjective* **= alleged**, self-styled, supposed, pretended, professed

sociable *adjective* **= friendly**, outgoing, gregarious • *She's usually outgoing and sociable.*

social *adjective* **1 = communal**, group, public, community, general, common, collective
▶ *noun* **2 = get-together** (*informal*), party, gathering

socialist *See* **left-wing**

socialize *verb* **= mix**, fraternize, get about *or* get around, go out

society *noun* **1 = culture**, civilization • *a major problem in society*
2 = organization, group, union, club, league, association, circle, institute, guild • *the school debating society*
3 = upper classes, elite, beau monde, gentry, high society
4 = companionship, company, friendship, fellowship
See also: **body**, **public**

sodden *adjective* **= soaked**, soggy, waterlogged, drenched, saturated, sopping

sofa *noun* **= couch**, chaise longue, divan, settee

soft *adjective* **1 = flexible**, supple, pliable • *a soft bed*
OPPOSITE: hard
2 = quiet, low, gentle, muted, subdued, mellow • *a soft tapping at my door*
3 = pale, light, faint, dim, subdued, mellow, pastel • *The soft lights made the room seem romantic.*
OPPOSITE: bright

s

4 = yielding, elastic, spongy, gelatinous, pulpy, squashy

5 = velvety, smooth, silky, downy, feathery, fleecy

6 = dim, faint, restful, dimmed

7 = mild, balmy, temperate

8 = lenient, lax, easy-going, indulgent, spineless, permissive, overindulgent

9 = out of condition, weak, limp, effeminate, flabby, flaccid

10 (*Informal*) **= easy**, comfortable, undemanding

11 = kind, sensitive, gentle, sentimental, compassionate, tenderhearted, touchy-feely (*informal*)

soften *verb* **= lessen**, still, ease, moderate, subdue, temper, cushion, mitigate, appease, allay, mollify

softhearted *adjective* **= kind**, tender, charitable, sympathetic, sentimental, compassionate, tenderhearted, warm-hearted

soggy *adjective* **= sodden**, waterlogged, moist, dripping, saturated, soaked, sopping

soil[1] *noun* **1 = earth**, ground, dirt, clay • *The soil is reasonably moist after the rain*.

2 = land, country

soil[2] *verb* **= dirty**, foul, pollute, smear, stain, spatter • *He soiled his new white shirt*.

OPPOSITE: **clean**

soiled *See* **dirty**

solace *noun* **1 = comfort**, relief, consolation

▶ *verb* **2 = comfort**, console

soldier *noun* **= fighter**, serviceman, man-at-arms, warrior, trooper

sole *adjective* **= only**, one, single, individual, alone, exclusive, solitary

solely *adverb* **= only**, alone, completely, entirely, merely, exclusively

solemn *adjective* **1 = serious**, grave, sober, earnest, staid • *a taciturn man with a solemn expression*

2 = formal, grand, grave, ceremonial, dignified, momentous, stately

See also: **grim, heavy**

solemnity *noun* **1 = seriousness**, gravity, earnestness

2 = formality, grandeur, impressiveness, momentousness

solicitor *See* **lawyer**

solicitous *adjective* **= concerned**, careful, anxious, attentive

solicitude *noun* **= concern**, care, regard, consideration, anxiety, attentiveness

solid *adjective* **1 = firm**, hard • *a solid block of ice*

2 = strong, stable, substantial, sturdy • *a solid structure*

3 = sound, good, real, pure, reliable, genuine

4 = reliable, worthy, upright, dependable, trusty, upstanding

See also: **rigid, secure, stiff, stocky, tough**

solidarity *noun* **= unity**, accord, unification, cohesion, unanimity, concordance, like-mindedness, team spirit

solidify *verb* **= harden**, set, cake, jell, coagulate, cohere, congeal

solitary *adjective* **1 = unsociable**, isolated, reclusive, cloistered, unsocial

2 = lone, single, alone, sole

3 = lonely, lonesome, companionless, friendless

4 = isolated, remote, hidden, out-of-the-way, unfrequented

solitude *noun* **= isolation**, privacy, loneliness, seclusion • *She went to the cottage for a few days of solitude*.

solution *noun* **1 = answer**, result, key, explanation

2 (*Chemistry*) **= mixture**, mix, compound, blend, solvent

solve *verb* **= resolve**, crack, decipher, clear up, get to the bottom of, work out • *attempts to solve the mystery*

sombre *adjective* **1 = dark**, gloomy, sober, dull, dim, drab

2 = gloomy, sad, grave, dismal, sober, mournful, lugubrious, joyless, doleful

some *See* **several**

somebody noun = **celebrity**,
name, star, notable, dignitary,
luminary, household name,
megastar (informal), personage

someday adverb = **one day**,
eventually, one of these days or
one of these fine days, sooner
or later

somehow adverb = **one way or
another**, by fair means or foul,
by hook or crook or by hook or
by crook, by some means or
other, come hell or high water
(informal), come what may

sometimes adverb
= **occasionally**, at times, every
now and then, every so often,
from time to time, now and
again, now and then, once in a
while • *People sometimes think I'm
older than I am.*

somewhat See **quite, rather**

song noun = **ballad**, number, air,
tune, chant, chorus, anthem,
hymn, carol, psalm, ditty

soon adverb = **before long**, shortly,
presently, any minute now, in a
minute, in the near future • *You'll
be hearing from us very soon.*
OPPOSITE: later

sooner See **before**

soothe verb 1 = **calm**, still, quiet,
lull, appease, allay, hush, pacify,
mollify, de-stress
2 = **relieve**, ease, alleviate,
assuage

soothing adjective = **calming**,
palliative, restful, emollient,
relaxing

soothsayer noun = **prophet**,
diviner, fortune-teller, seer, sibyl

sophisticated adjective
1 = **cultured**, cosmopolitan,
cultivated, refined, urbane • *a
charming, sophisticated companion*
2 = **complicated**, complex,
advanced, elaborate, refined,
intricate • *a sophisticated piece of
equipment*
OPPOSITE: simple
See also: **polite**

sophistication noun = **savoir-
faire**, poise, finesse, urbanity,
worldliness, worldly wisdom

soporific adjective 1 = **sleep-**

inducing, sedative, somnolent,
tranquilizing
▶ noun 2 = **sedative**, narcotic,
opiate, tranquilizer

soppy adjective (Informal)
= **sentimental**, slushy (informal),
overemotional, schmaltzy
(slang), weepy (informal)

sorcerer noun = **magician**,
wizard, witch, enchanter,
necromancer, warlock

sorcery noun = **black magic**,
magic, witchcraft, wizardry,
black art, enchantment,
necromancy

sordid adjective 1 = **dirty**, foul,
filthy, sleazy, squalid, seedy,
unclean, scuzzy (slang)
2 = **base**, low, vicious, shameful,
degenerate, shabby, vile,
debauched
3 = **mercenary**, selfish,
avaricious, covetous, grasping

sore adjective 1 = **painful**,
sensitive, raw, tender, inflamed,
smarting • *a sore throat*
2 = **annoying**, severe, sharp,
troublesome
3 = **annoyed**, hurt, cross,
upset, angry, irritated, pained,
resentful, aggrieved, irked,
stung
4 = **urgent**, critical, extreme,
desperate, acute, dire, pressing

soreness See **pain**

sorrow noun 1 = **grief**, pain,
regret, woe (formal), misery,
sadness, unhappiness,
heartache, melancholy,
mourning • *a time of great sorrow*
OPPOSITE: joy
2 = **trouble**, worry, woe (formal),
hardship, misfortune,
heartache • *the joys and sorrows
of family life*
OPPOSITE: joy
▶ verb 3 = **grieve**, mourn,
lament, bemoan, agonize, be
sad, bewail
See also: **distress, evil**

sorrowful adjective = **sad**, sorry,
dismal, unhappy, woeful,
miserable, mournful, dejected,
wretched, doleful, grieving,
woebegone

sorry adjective **1 = regretful**, remorseful, apologetic, penitent, repentant • *I'm terribly sorry to bother you.*

2 = sympathetic, moved • *I was sorry to hear about your grandfather's death.*

3 = wretched, poor, sad, pathetic, miserable, deplorable, pitiful • *He was in a pretty sorry state when we found him.*
See also: **ashamed, guilty**

sort noun **1 = kind**, make, group, type, class, brand, style, category, variety, species • *a dozen trees of various sorts*

▷ verb **2 = arrange**, group, separate, divide, grade, classify, categorize • *He sorted the emails into three folders.*
See also: **form**

sort out verb **1 = resolve**, clarify, clear up

2 = organize, tidy up

sought-after See **popular**

soul noun **1 = spirit**, life, essence, vital force

2 = personification, type, essence, epitome, embodiment, quintessence

3 = person, man or woman, body, individual, being, creature

sound¹ noun **1 = noise**, tone, racket, din, hubbub • *the sounds of happy children*
OPPOSITE: silence
RELATED WORDS
adjectives: sonic, acoustic

2 = idea, look, impression, drift

▷ verb **3 = resound**, blow, ring, toll, chime, clang, peal, set off • *A young man sounded the bell.*

4 = seem, look, appear

5 = express, announce, declare, pronounce, utter, articulate

sound² adjective **1 = in good condition**, fine, healthy, fit, robust, intact, all right • *His mind and body were still sound.*

2 = sensible, good, solid, reasonable, reliable, valid, down-to-earth • *a sound financial proposition*

3 = deep, unbroken, undisturbed, untroubled

See also: **logical, responsible, sane, well**

sound³ verb **= fathom**, probe, plumb

▷ **sound out = probe**, question, pump, canvass, see how the land lies

soundless See **silent**

sour adjective **1 = sharp**, bitter, acid, tart, pungent • *That apple is too sour for me.*
OPPOSITE: sweet

2 = rancid, off, curdled • *This cream's gone sour.*

3 = bitter, tart, disagreeable, embittered, jaundiced • *a sour expression*
See also: **rotten, stale**

source noun **1 = origin**, cause, beginning, fountain, originator, derivation, fount, fountainhead, wellspring • *the source of his confidence*

2 = informant, authority
See also: **head**

souvenir noun **= keepsake**, reminder, relic, memento • *a souvenir of our vacation*

sovereign noun **1 = monarch**, chief, king or queen, prince or princess, ruler, emperor or empress, potentate

▷ adjective **2 = supreme**, ruling, principal, royal, absolute, imperial, kingly or queenly

3 = excellent, efficient, effectual, efficacious

sovereignty noun **= supreme power**, domination, supremacy, primacy, kingship

sow verb **= scatter**, plant, seed, implant

space noun **1 = room**, capacity, accommodation • *a car with plenty of interior space*
RELATED WORD
adjective: spatial

2 = gap, blank, distance, interval • *the space between the two tables*

3 = period, time, while, span, interval • *two incidents in the space of a week*
See also: **length, opening, stretch**

S

spacious adjective = **roomy**, large, huge, broad, extensive, vast, ample, expansive • a spacious lobby

spadework noun = **preparation**, labour, groundwork, donkey-work

span noun 1 = **extent**, reach, spread, amount, stretch, distance, length
2 = **period**, term, spell, duration
▶ verb 3 = **extend across**, link, cover, cross, bridge, traverse

spank verb = **smack**, paddle, cuff, slap

spar verb = **argue**, row, scrap (informal), squabble, wrangle, bicker

spare adjective 1 = **extra**, free, surplus, superfluous • Luckily I had a spare pair of glasses.
2 = **thin**, lean, gaunt, meagre, wiry • He was a small, spare man with an abrupt and caustic wit.
▷ **spare time** = **leisure**, free time, odd moments
▶ verb 3 = **afford**, give, let someone have • Can you spare a loonie?
4 = **have mercy on**, pardon, let off (informal), relieve from, save from • I wanted to spare them that suffering.

sparing adjective = **economical**, saving, careful, prudent, thrifty, frugal

spark noun 1 = **flicker**, flash, flare, gleam, glint
2 = **trace**, hint, scrap, atom, vestige, jot
▶ verb 3 (often with off) = **start**, trigger or trigger off, inspire, provoke, stimulate, precipitate, set off

sparkle verb 1 = **glitter**, shimmer, gleam, twinkle, glisten • Stars sparkled like diamonds.
▶ noun 2 = **glitter**, flash, brilliance, gleam, flicker, twinkle, glint
3 = **vivacity**, life, spirit, dash, vitality, élan
See also: **shine**

sparkling adjective
1 = **carbonated**, frothy, bubbly, effervescent, fizzy, foamy, gassy
2 = **vibrant**, bright, brilliant, animated, lively, ebullient, effervescent, vivacious
3 = **glittering**, twinkling, lustrous, flashing, shining, shimmering, scintillating, glistening, glinting, gleaming

sparse adjective = **scattered**, scarce, meagre, few and far between, scanty

spartan adjective = **austere**, severe, strict, plain, rigorous, disciplined, frugal, ascetic, self-denying

spasm noun 1 = **convulsion**, contraction, twitch, paroxysm
2 = **burst**, fit, seizure, outburst, eruption, frenzy

spasmodic adjective = **sporadic**, irregular, jerky, erratic, intermittent, convulsive, fitful

spate noun = **flood**, rush, flow, outpouring, deluge, torrent

spatter See **soil** ²

speak verb = **say**, talk, lecture
▷ **speak out**, **speak up** = **speak one's mind**, have one's say, make one's position plain, voice one's opinions
▷ **speak out against** See **oppose**

speaker noun = **orator**, spokesman or spokeswoman, spokesperson, lecturer, public speaker

spearhead verb = **lead**, head, launch, pioneer, initiate, set in motion, set off

special adjective 1 = **exceptional**, important, significant, unique • You are very special to me.
OPPOSITE: ordinary
2 = **particular**, individual, specific, characteristic, distinctive, peculiar • the special needs of the chronically ill
OPPOSITE: general
See also: **different, personal, private, select**

specialist noun = **expert**, authority, professional, master, buff (informal), virtuoso, connoisseur

specialty noun = **forte**, bag (slang, dated), speciality, métier, pièce de résistance (French)

species noun = **kind**, group, type, class, sort, category, variety, breed

specific adjective 1 = **particular**, special, characteristic, distinguishing

2 = **definite**, express, exact, explicit, stipulate, precise, unequivocal, clear-cut

specification noun = **requirement**, condition, detail, particular, qualification, stipulation

specify verb = **state**, name, indicate, stipulate, be specific about, spell out • Specify the size and colour you want.

specimen noun = **sample**, type, model, example, representative, pattern, instance, exemplification

speck noun 1 = **mark**, spot, stain, dot, blemish, speckle, fleck, mote

2 = **particle**, bit, grain, shred, atom, mite, iota, jot

speckled adjective = **flecked**, spotted, dotted, dappled, mottled, sprinkled

spectacle noun 1 = **sight**, scene, wonder, phenomenon, marvel, curiosity

2 = **show**, event, performance, display, exhibition, extravaganza, pageant

spectacular adjective

1 = **impressive**, cool (informal), dramatic, grand, sensational, magnificent, striking, splendid, dazzling, phat (slang), stunning (informal)

▶ noun 2 = **show**, display, spectacle

spectator noun = **onlooker**, witness, observer, bystander, eyewitness • Spectators lined the route.

spectre noun = **ghost**, vision, spirit, phantom, apparition, wraith

speculate verb 1 = **conjecture**, consider, wonder, suppose, guess, theorize, hypothesize, surmise

2 = **gamble**, risk, venture, hazard

speculation noun

1 = **conjecture**, opinion, theory, hypothesis, surmise, guesswork, supposition

2 = **gamble**, risk, hazard

speculative adjective = **hypothetical**, academic, theoretical, conjectural, notional, suppositional

speech noun 1 = **talk**, address, lecture, discourse • He delivered his speech in French.

2 = **communication**, talk, discussion, conversation, dialogue

3 = **language**, tongue, dialect, jargon, parlance, articulation, diction, enunciation, idiom

speechless adjective 1 = **mute**, silent, dumb, inarticulate, wordless

2 = **astounded**, shocked, aghast, amazed, dazed

speechlessness See **silence**

speed noun 1 = **swiftness**, pace, momentum, hurry, velocity, haste, rapidity • a speed of 120 km/h

▶ verb 2 = **race**, career, rush, tear, flash, gallop • The pair sped off when the police arrived.

3 = **help**, assist, boost, advance, aid, facilitate, expedite

▷ **speed up** = **accelerate**, gather momentum, increase the tempo

See also: **fly, rate**

speedily See **quickly**

speedy adjective = **quick**, fast, prompt, express, immediate, rapid, swift, hurried, precipitate, hasty, headlong

spell¹ verb = **indicate**, mean, imply, signify, augur, portend, point to

▷ **spell out** See **specify**

spell² noun 1 = **incantation**, charm

2 = **enchantment**, magic, allure, glamour, fascination, mojo (slang), bewitchment

spell³ noun = **period**, time, season, term, course, stretch, bout,

S

interval

spellbound *adjective* = **entranced**, bewitched, captivated, charmed, enthralled, fascinated, gripped, mesmerized, rapt

spend *verb* 1 = **pay out**, expend, disburse, fork out (*slang*)
2 = **pass**, fill, occupy, while away
3 = **use up**, waste, consume, empty, drain, exhaust, squander, dissipate, run through

spendthrift *noun*
1 = **squanderer**, spender, big spender, profligate, waster
▶ *adjective* 2 = **wasteful**, extravagant, improvident, prodigal, profligate

spew *verb* = **vomit**, puke (*slang*), disgorge, barf (*slang*), regurgitate, throw up (*informal*)

sphere *noun* 1 = **ball**, circle, globe, orb, globule
2 = **field**, province, department, territory, capacity, function, patch, turf (*slang*), domain, scope, realm

spherical *adjective* = **round**, rotund, globe-shaped, globular

spice *noun* 1 = **seasoning**, relish, savour
2 = **excitement**, colour, pep, zest, zing (*informal*), piquancy

spicy *adjective* 1 = **hot**, seasoned, aromatic, piquant, savoury
2 (*Informal*) = **risqué**, hot (*informal*), scandalous, racy, suggestive, indelicate, ribald, titillating

spike *noun* 1 = **point**, spine, barb, prong
▶ *verb* 2 = **impale**, stick, spit, spear

spill *verb* 1 = **pour**, discharge, overflow, disgorge, slop over
▶ *noun* 2 = **fall**, tumble

spin *verb* 1 = **revolve**, turn, rotate, whirl, pirouette • *as the earth spins on its axis*
2 = **reel**, swim, whirl
▷ **spin out** = **prolong**, delay, extend, lengthen, amplify, drag out, draw out
▶ *noun* 3 = **revolution**, roll, whirl, gyration
4 (*Informal*) = **drive**, ride, joy ride

(*informal*)

spine *noun* 1 = **backbone**, spinal column, vertebrae, vertebral column
2 = **barb**, spur, spike, needle, ray, quill

spine-chilling *adjective* = **frightening**, scary (*informal*), eerie, spooky (*informal*), bloodcurdling, horrifying, terrifying

spineless *adjective* = **weak**, soft, cowardly, feeble, gutless (*informal*), faint-hearted, lily-livered, weak-kneed (*informal*)

spiral *noun* 1 = **coil**, corkscrew, helix, whorl
▶ *adjective* 2 = **coiled**, helical, whorled, winding

spirit *noun* 1 = **soul**, life force
• *They believed his spirit had left his body.*
2 = **ghost**, spectre, phantom, apparition, sprite • *a protection against evil spirits*
3 = **energy**, force, fire, animation, enthusiasm, vigour, mettle, zest, brio • *They played with spirit.*
4 = **feeling**, atmosphere, tone, tenor, gist
5 = **temperament**, character, outlook, attitude, temper, disposition
6 = **courage**, backbone, grit, gameness, guts (*informal*), spunk (*informal*)
7 = **essence**, sense, purpose, substance, intention, meaning, purport
▷ **spirits** = **mood**, humour, morale, feelings, frame of mind
▶ *verb* 8 (with *away* or *off*) = **remove**, carry, steal, seize, abduct, abstract, whisk, purloin
See also: **sneak**

spirited *adjective* = **lively**, active, animated, energetic, feisty (*informal*), vivacious, mettlesome

spirits See **alcohol**

spiritual *adjective* = **sacred**, religious, holy, divine, devotional

spit *verb* 1 = **eject**, expectorate, splutter, throw out

▶ noun **2 = saliva**, dribble, drool, slaver, spittle

spite noun **1 = malice**, venom, ill will, malevolence, spitefulness • He just did it out of spite.

▷ **in spite of = despite**, though, although, notwithstanding, even though, regardless of • In spite of all the rain, we drove to the campgrounds.

▶ verb **2 = hurt**, injure, harm, annoy, vex

spiteful adjective **= malicious**, nasty, cruel, venomous, vindictive, catty (informal), malevolent, snide • a stream of spiteful telephone calls
See also: **unkind**

spitefulness See **spite**

spitting image See **look-alike**

splash verb **1 = scatter**, spray, wet, shower, sprinkle, spatter, slop

2 = publicize, broadcast, trumpet, plaster

▷ **splash out** (Informal) **= spend**, be extravagant, splurge, spare no expense

▶ noun **3 = dash**, touch, burst, patch, spattering

4 (Informal) **= display**, effect, impact, stir, sensation

splendid adjective **1 = excellent**, great (informal), fine, wonderful, fantastic (informal), glorious, marvellous • I've had a splendid time.

2 = magnificent, grand, impressive, gorgeous, superb, imposing • a splendid old mansion
See also: **first-rate**

splendidly See **well**

splendour noun **= magnificence**, show, display, glory, spectacle, brilliance, richness, grandeur, pomp, brightness, sumptuousness

splinter noun **1 = sliver**, chip, fragment, flake

▶ verb **2 = shatter**, split, fracture, disintegrate

split verb **1 = separate**, part, fork, diverge • The ship split in two.

2 = crack, burst, rip, come apart • His trousers split.

3 = share out, distribute, divide, halve, allocate, allot, partition, apportion

▷ **split up = separate**, part, divorce, break up

▶ noun **4 = crack**, tear, rip, fissure • There's a split in my mattress.

5 = division, breach, breakup, rift, divergence • the split between the two sides of the family

▶ adjective **6 = divided**, fractured, ruptured, cleft, broken, cracked
See also: **hole, share**

spoil verb **1 = ruin**, damage, destroy, harm, wreck, impair, mar, mess up • Don't let it spoil your vacation.

2 = indulge, pamper • Grandparents often spoil their grandchildren.

3 = go bad, decay, decompose, addle, curdle, turn, rot

▶ noun

▷ **spoils = booty**, treasure, loot, prey, swag (slang), plunder

spoilsport noun **= killjoy**, damper, misery (informal), grinch (informal), sourpuss, wet blanket (informal), buzzkill (slang)

spoken adjective **= said**, oral, verbal, unwritten, expressed, told, uttered, viva voce, voiced

spokesman See **representative**

spokesperson noun **= speaker**, official, spokesman or spokeswoman, voice, mouthpiece, spin doctor (informal)

spokeswoman See **representative**

sponge See **clean, scrounge**

spongy adjective **= porous**, absorbent

sponsor noun **1 = backer**, patron, promoter

▶ verb **2 = back**, fund, finance, promote, subsidize, patronize

spontaneous adjective **= unplanned**, natural, willing, voluntary, impromptu, impulsive, instinctive, unprompted

spoof noun (Informal) **= parody**, satire, caricature, mockery, burlesque

spooky adjective = **eerie**, scary, supernatural, creepy, haunted, ghostly, uncanny, frightening • *The whole place had a slightly spooky atmosphere.*

sporadic adjective = **intermittent**, occasional, irregular, scattered, spasmodic

sport noun 1 = **game**, play, exercise, diversion, recreation, amusement, pastime
2 = **fun**, jest, banter, badinage, joking, teasing
▶ verb 3 (Old-fashioned, informal) = **wear**, display, exhibit, show off

sporting adjective = **fair**, game (informal), sportsmanlike

sporty adjective = **athletic**, outdoor, energetic

spot noun 1 = **mark**, blemish, blot, speck, smudge, blotch • *a navy blue dress with white spots*
2 = **place**, point, site, position, scene, location • *an out-of-the-way spot*
3 = **pimple**, pustule, zit (slang)
4 (Informal) = **predicament**, trouble, difficulty, mess, plight, hot water (informal), tight spot
▶ verb 5 = **see**, detect, sight, observe, discern, catch sight of • *Her drama teacher spotted her ability.*
6 = **mark**, soil, dirty, stain, spatter, speckle, splotch, fleck, mottle, smirch, splodge
See also: **notice**, **random**, **recognize**

> **INFORMALLY SPEAKING**
> **hit the spot**: be exactly what is required
> **in a spot**: in a difficult situation

spotless adjective = **clean**, pure, flawless, impeccable, immaculate, unblemished, gleaming, shining, unstained, unsullied, untarnished

spotlight noun 1 = **attention**, fame, limelight, public eye
▶ verb 2 = **highlight**, accentuate, draw attention to

spotted adjective = **speckled**, dotted, dappled, flecked, mottled

spouse noun = **partner**, husband or wife, mate, consort, significant other (informal)

spout verb = **stream**, shoot, surge, spray, discharge, spurt, gush

sprain See **twist**

sprawl verb = **loll**, slump, lounge, flop, slouch

spray¹ noun 1 = **droplets**, drizzle, fine mist
2 = **aerosol**, sprinkler, atomizer
▶ verb 3 = **scatter**, shower, sprinkle, diffuse

spray² noun = **sprig**, branch, corsage, floral arrangement

spread verb 1 = **open**, extend, sprawl, unfold, unfurl, unroll, fan out • *He spread his coat over the bed.*
2 = **coat**, cover, apply, smear, smother, overlay, slather • *Spread the bread with the cream cheese.*
3 = **circulate**, increase, grow, travel, expand, proliferate • *The sense of fear is spreading in the neighbourhood.*
4 = **proliferate**, escalate, multiply
▶ noun 5 = **extent** • *The plant grows to 18 inches with a spread of 24 inches.*
6 = **growth**, increase, expansion, progression, proliferation, upsurge, diffusion • *the spread of the disease*
See also: **communicate**, **distribute**, **lay**, **stretch**

spreading See **infectious**

spree noun = **binge** (informal), bacchanalia, revel, fling, orgy, carousal

sprightly adjective = **lively**, active, energetic, brisk, spirited, nimble, agile, spry, vivacious

spring verb 1 = **jump**, bounce, leap, vault, bound
2 (often with from) = **originate**, come, start, issue, stem, proceed, arise, descend, derive
3 (often with up) = **appear**, develop, mushroom, shoot up
▶ noun 4 = **jump**, leap, vault, bound
5 = **elasticity**, bounce, flexibility, resilience, buoyancy

springy *adjective* = **elastic**, flexible, resilient, buoyant, bouncy, rubbery

sprinkle *verb* = **scatter**, spray, pepper, dust, shower, powder, strew, dredge

sprinkling *noun* = **scattering**, few, handful, dash, sprinkle, dusting

sprint *verb* = **run**, dash, dart, shoot, race, tear

sprite *noun* = **spirit**, brownie, fairy, elf, pixie, goblin, imp

sprout *verb* = **grow**, shoot, develop, spring, bud

spruce *adjective* = **smart**, dapper, trim, neat, well-groomed, well turned out
  ▶ *verb*
  ▷ **spruce up** = **smarten up**, tidy, titivate

spry *adjective* = **active**, nimble, agile, supple, sprightly

spur *noun* 1 = **stimulus**, incentive, motive, impulse, incitement, impetus, inducement
  2 = **goad**, prick
  ▷ **on the spur of the moment** = **on impulse**, impromptu, impulsively, on the spot, without planning
  ▶ *verb* 3 = **incite**, drive, urge, prompt, stimulate, prod, animate, goad, prick, impel

spurious *adjective* = **false**, fake, artificial, bogus, phony (*informal*), sham, pretended, specious, unauthentic

spurn *verb* = **reject**, slight, snub, scorn, rebuff, disdain, despise, repulse

spurt *verb* 1 = **gush**, shoot, surge, erupt, burst, squirt
  ▶ *noun* 2 = **burst**, surge, rush, fit, spate

spy *noun* 1 = **undercover agent**, mole
  ▶ *verb* 2 = **catch sight of**, spot, notice, observe, glimpse, espy

squabble *verb* 1 = **quarrel**, fight, argue, feud, wrangle, bicker • *His parents squabble all the time.*
  ▶ *noun* 2 = **quarrel**, fight, dispute, row, argument, disagreement, altercation, tiff • *There have been minor squabbles about phone bills.*
  See also: **clash**

squad *noun* = **team**, company, group, force, troop, crew, band, gang

squalid *adjective* = **dirty**, filthy, sleazy, sordid, seedy, unclean, scuzzy (*slang*), slummy

squalor *noun* = **filth**, foulness, sleaziness, squalidness

squander *verb* = **waste**, spend, blow (*slang*), misuse, misspend, expend, fritter away

squandering *See* **waste**

square *adjective* 1 = **honest**, fair, ethical, genuine, kosher (*informal*), above board, straight
  2 (*Informal*) = **uncool**, nerdy, dorky (*slang*), unhip
  ▶ *verb* 3 = **even up**, level, adjust, align
  4 (sometimes with *up*) = **pay off**, settle
  5 (often with *with*) = **agree**, match, fit, tally, correspond, reconcile

squash *verb* 1 = **crush**, press, smash, pulp, flatten, mash, distort, compress
  2 = **suppress**, silence, crush, quell, humiliate, annihilate

squashy *adjective* = **soft**, mushy, spongy, pulpy, yielding

squat *See* **crouch**, **low**

squawk *verb* = **cry**, screech, hoot

squeak *verb* = **peep**, pipe, squeal

squeal *noun*, *verb* = **scream**, yell, wail, screech, shriek

squeamish *adjective*
  1 = **fastidious**, delicate, prudish, strait-laced
  2 = **sick**, nauseous, queasy

squeeze *verb* 1 = **press**, crush, grip, clutch, pinch, squash, compress, wring
  2 = **cram**, force, crowd, press, pack, stuff, jam, ram
  3 = **hug**, embrace, cuddle, clasp, enfold
  4 = **extort**, milk, wrest, pressurize
  ▶ *noun* 5 = **hug**, embrace, clasp
  6 = **crush**, crowd, press, jam,

S

squash, congestion

squirm verb = **wriggle**, twist, writhe

squirt noun (Informal) = **child**, girl, baby, boy, kid (informal), infant, minor, toddler, youngster, tot, whippersnapper (old-fashioned)

stab verb 1 = **pierce**, wound, stick, knife, thrust, jab, impale, spear, transfix
▶ noun 2 = **wound**, thrust, jab, puncture, gash, incision
3 = **twinge**, ache, prick, pang
▷ **make a stab at, have a stab at** (Informal) = **attempt**, try, endeavour, have a go

stability noun = **firmness**, strength, soundness, solidity, steadiness

stabilize See **balance, steady**

stable adjective 1 = **firm**, strong, sound, fast, secure, permanent, constant, lasting, established, fixed, immovable
2 = **steady**, sure, reliable, staunch, steadfast

stack noun 1 = **pile**, mass, mountain, load, mound, heap
▶ verb 2 = **pile**, load, assemble, accumulate, amass, heap up

staff noun 1 = **workers**, team, personnel, workforce, employees, human resources
• She made little effort to socialize with other staff members.
2 = **stick**, pole, stave, rod, crook, cane, wand, sceptre

stage noun 1 = **step**, point, period, phase, lap • the closing stages of the race
▶ verb 2 = **organize**, engineer, mount, arrange, orchestrate
• Workers have staged a number of one-day strikes.
See also: **level, perform, round**

stagger verb 1 = **totter**, reel, sway, wobble, lurch
2 = **astound**, shock, shake, stun, overwhelm, astonish, amaze, confound, stupefy
3 = **overlap**, step, alternate

staggering See **amazing**

stagnant adjective = **stale**, still, quiet, sluggish

stagnate verb = **vegetate**,

decline, idle, rust, decay, languish, rot

staid adjective = **sedate**, serious, steady, calm, grave, solemn, sober, composed

stain noun 1 = **mark**, spot, blot
• grass stains
2 = **stigma**, shame, disgrace, slur, dishonor
▶ verb 3 = **mark**, spot, soil, dirty
• Some foods can stain the teeth.
See also: **colour**

stake[1] noun = **pole**, post, stick, picket, pale, paling, palisade

stake[2] noun 1 = **bet**, pledge, wager, ante
2 = **interest**, share, concern, investment, involvement
▶ verb 3 = **bet**, risk, chance, gamble, venture, hazard, wager

stale adjective 1 = **old**, flat, sour, stagnant • a slice of stale bread
OPPOSITE: fresh
2 = **unoriginal**, overused, worn-out, banal, trite, hackneyed, stereotyped, threadbare
See also: **corny, stuffy**

stalk verb = **pursue**, follow, track, hunt, shadow, haunt

stall verb = **play for time**, hedge, temporize

stalwart adjective = **strong**, staunch, sturdy, stout, strapping

stamina noun = **staying power**, force, power, energy, strength, endurance, resilience

stammer verb = **stutter**, stumble, falter, pause, hesitate

stamp noun 1 = **imprint**, mark, brand, signature, earmark, hallmark
▶ verb 2 = **trample**, crush
3 = **identify**, mark, reveal, label, brand, categorize, show to be
4 = **imprint**, mark, print, impress
▷ **stamp out** = **eliminate**, destroy, crush, quell, eradicate, suppress, scotch, put down

stampede noun = **rush**, charge, flight, rout

stance noun 1 = **attitude**, stand, position, viewpoint, standpoint

2 = posture, carriage, bearing, deportment

stand verb **1 = be upright**, rise, be erect, be vertical

2 = put, set, place, position, mount

3 = exist, continue, hold, remain, obtain, prevail, be valid

4 = tolerate, take, allow, bear, handle, endure, stomach, abide, brook, countenance, deal with (slang), put up with (informal)

▷ **stand by = be prepared**, wait; **= support**, back, champion, be loyal to, take (someone's) part

▷ **stand for = represent**, mean, indicate, signify, symbolize, denote, betoken; (Informal) **= tolerate**, bear, endure, brook, put up with

▷ **stand in for = be a substitute for**, represent, cover for, deputize for, take the place of

▷ **stand out = be conspicuous**, be distinct, be obvious, be prominent

▷ **stand up for = support**, defend, champion, uphold, stick up for (informal)

▷ **stand up to** See **brave**

▶ noun **5 = stall**, table, booth

6 = position, opinion, attitude, stance, determination

7 = support, base, stage, platform, rack, bracket, tripod, dais

standard noun **1 = level**, quality, guideline, requirement, criterion, norm, calibre • There will be new standards of hospital cleanliness.

2 = flag, banner, ensign

▶ adjective **3 = usual**, regular, normal, correct, customary, orthodox • It was standard practice for them to consult the parents.

4 = accepted, official, definitive, established, authoritative, approved, recognized

See also: **average, common, conventional, ideal, ordinary, routine, stock, typical**

standardize verb **= bring into line**, regiment, institutionalize

standards plural noun

= principles, ethics, ideals, morals, rules, scruple, values • My father has always had high moral standards.

stand-in noun **= substitute**, reserve, deputy, replacement, surrogate, understudy, stopgap, locum

standing adjective

1 = permanent, regular, lasting, fixed

2 = upright, erect, vertical

▶ noun **3 = status**, position, rank, reputation, footing, repute, eminence

4 = duration, existence, continuance

standoffish adjective **= reserved**, cold, remote, distant, aloof, haughty, unapproachable, unsociable

standpoint noun **= point of view**, position, viewpoint, stance, angle

standstill See **halt**

staple adjective **= principal**, chief, key, main, basic, fundamental, predominant

star noun **1 = celebrity**, idol, luminary • a movie star

2 = heavenly body

3 = leading, major, prominent, brilliant, well-known, celebrated

See also: **feature, personality, success**

stare verb **= gaze**, look, ogle • He stared at the floor, lost in meditation.

stark adjective **1 = harsh**, hard, bare, bleak, grim, barren, austere, severe, plain

2 = absolute, pure, utter, blunt, sheer, downright, unmitigated, out-and-out

▶ adverb **3 = absolutely**, quite, completely, entirely, altogether, wholly, utterly

stark naked See **naked**

start verb **1** arise **= begin**, originate, commence, come into being, come into existence, get under way • School starts again next week.

OPPOSITE: finish

2 = set about, begin, proceed,

commence, embark upon • *The child started to cry.*
OPPOSITE: stop

3 = set in motion, open, trigger, initiate, instigate, get going • *Who started the fight?*
OPPOSITE: stop

4 = establish, begin, launch, create, introduce, found, pioneer, institute, inaugurate, set up • *I started the company seven years ago.*

5 = jump, shy, jerk, flinch, recoil
▶ *noun* **6 = beginning**, birth, opening, foundation, dawn, onset, inauguration, outset, inception (*formal*), initiation, commencement • *His career had an auspicious start.*
OPPOSITE: finish

7 = advantage, lead, edge, head start

8 = jump, spasm, convulsion
See also: **head, scare, surprise**

starter *See* **beginner**

startle *verb* = **surprise**, shock, scare, frighten, make (someone) jump

startled *See* **frightened**

startling *See* **amazing**

starving *adjective* = **hungry**, ravenous, famished, starved

stash (*Informal*) *verb* **1 = store**, hide, stockpile, cache, hoard, stow, secrete, save up, save for a rainy day, salt away
▶ *noun* **2 = hoard**, store, supply, collection, stockpile, cache • *Police found a huge stash of arms.*

state *noun* **1 = condition**, position, situation, shape, plight, predicament, circumstances • *the pathetic state of the roads*

2 = country, land, nation, republic, kingdom • *the state of Denmark*

3 = frame of mind, attitude, mood, humour, spirits

4 = ceremony, display, style, glory, majesty, grandeur, pomp, splendour
▷ **state of affairs** *See* **situation**
▷ **state of mind** *See* **mood**
▶ *verb* **5 = say**, declare, express,

assert, specify, affirm, articulate, expound, aver, propound • *Please state your occupation.*
See also: **observe, remark, report, territory**

stately *adjective* = **grand**, royal, lofty, dignified, noble, majestic, regal, august

statement *noun* = **account**, report, announcement, testimony, declaration, explanation, bulletin, proclamation • *He was depressed when he made that statement.*
See also: **bill, comment, remark, word**

state-of-the-art *adjective* = **latest**, up-to-date, up-to-the-minute, newest

static *adjective* = **stationary**, still, motionless, immobile, fixed, unmoving

station *noun* **1 = headquarters**, base, depot

2 = place, post, position, situation, seat, location

3 = position, post, situation, status, rank, standing
▶ *verb* **4 = assign**, set, post, establish, locate, install

stationary *adjective* = **motionless**, standing, static, fixed, parked, stock-still, unmoving

statistic *See* **figure**

statuesque *adjective* = **well-proportioned**, imposing, Junoesque

stature *noun* = **importance**, rank, standing, prominence, prestige, eminence

status *noun* = **position**, rank, standing, prestige • *the status of children in society*
See also: **level**

statute *See* **law**

staunch[1] *adjective* = **loyal**, firm, sound, true, faithful, stalwart, steadfast, trusty

staunch[2] *verb* = **stop**, stay, check, halt, stem, dam

stay *verb* **1 = remain**, wait, linger, loiter, hang around (*informal*), tarry (*formal*) • *She stayed in bed till noon.*

S

2 = visit, stop, holiday, vacation, stopover, sojourn, stop-off
3 = postponement, delay, halt, suspension, stopping, deferment
See also: **live**
▷ **stay afloat** *See* **float**
▷ **stay behind** *See* **remain**
steadfast *adjective* **= firm**, steady, constant, faithful, staunch, resolute, unshakable, immovable • *She remained steadfast in her belief.*
steady *adjective* **1 = continuous**, even, regular, consistent, constant, non-stop, uninterrupted • *a steady rise in profits*
2 = stable, firm, secure • *She held out a steady hand.*
3 = sensible, calm, balanced, reliable, sober, dependable, equable, level-headed
▶ *verb* **4 = stabilize**, support, secure, brace • *Two men were steadying a ladder.*
See also: **balance, gradual, reasonable, steadfast**
steal *verb* **1 = take**, appropriate, swipe (*slang*), pilfer • *He was accused of stealing a bicycle.*
2 = sneak, slip, creep, tiptoe • *They can steal out and join us later.*
▷ **steal from** *See* **rob**
stealing *See* **theft**
stealth *noun* **= secrecy**, furtiveness, slyness, sneakiness, stealthiness, surreptitiousness, unobtrusiveness
stealthy *adjective* **= secret**, secretive, surreptitious, furtive, sneaking
steam *See* **cook**
steamy *See* **humid**
steep¹ *adjective* **1 = sheer**, vertical • *a steep hill*
OPPOSITE: gradual
2 = excessive, high, unreasonable, exorbitant • *steep prices*
steep² *verb* **1 = soak**, immerse, marinate • *tea leaves steeped in hot water*
2 = saturate, fill, infuse, pervade, permeate, imbue, suffuse

steer *verb* **= direct**, control, conduct, pilot, handle, guide
▷ **steer clear of** *See* **avoid**
stem¹ *noun* **= stalk**, shoot, branch, trunk, axis
▶ *verb*
▷ **stem from = originate in**, arise from, be caused by, derive from
stem² *verb* **= stop**, check, curb, dam, staunch, hold back
stench *noun* **= stink**, foul smell, whiff, reek
stencil *See* **pattern**
step *noun* **1 = footstep**, track, pace, print, stride, footprint, footfall
2 = stage, point, move, phase
3 = action, move, act, measure, means, deed, expedient
4 = degree, level, rank
▶ *verb* **5 = walk**, move, pace, tread
▷ **step down** *See* **resign**
▷ **step in = intervene**, become involved, take action
▷ **step up = increase**, raise, intensify
stereotype *noun* **1 = formula**, pattern
▶ *verb* **2 = categorize**, standardize, pigeonhole, typecast
stereotyped *See* **corny, stock**
sterile *adjective* **1 = germ-free**, antiseptic, sterilized • *Protect the cut with a sterile dressing.*
2 = barren, unproductive • *He found out he was sterile.*
OPPOSITE: fertile
sterilize *verb* **= disinfect**, purify, fumigate
sterilized *adjective* **= clean**, pure, sterile
sterling *adjective* **= excellent**, fine, sound, true, genuine, superlative
stern *adjective* **= severe**, hard, serious, strict, harsh, grim, rigid, austere, inflexible, forbidding
stew *See* **cook**
stick¹ *noun* **= cane**, bat, pole, rod, twig, wand, mace, nightstick • *crowds armed with sticks and stones*
See also: **club**

S

stick² *verb* **1 = thrust**, put, push, stuff, dig, insert, poke, shove, ram, jab • *They stuck a needle in my arm.*

2 = attach, fix, bond, paste, cling, adhere, glue, fuse • *Stick down the tiles, following the instructions.*

3 = catch, jam, snag, lodge • *The paper is stuck in the copier.*

4 (with *out*, *up* etc.) **= protrude**, show, project, extend, poke, bulge, jut, obtrude

5 (*Informal*) **= put**, set, place, lay, deposit

6 = stay, remain, linger, persist

7 (*Slang*) **= tolerate**, take, stand, stomach, abide

▷ **stick up for = defend**, support, champion, stand up for

> **INFORMALLY SPEAKING**
> **stick around**: wait nearby
> **stick in your throat**: be hard for you to accept
> **stick it out**: put up with unpleasant circumstances
> **stick it to someone**: treat someone harshly
> **stick up for**: support or defend someone

sticker *See* **label**

stickler *noun* **= perfectionist**, fanatic, purist, fusspot (*informal*)

sticky *adjective* **1 = tacky**, adhesive • *a sticky smear of peanut butter*

2 (*Informal*) **= difficult**, nasty, delicate, tricky, awkward, unpleasant, embarrassing

3 = humid, close, oppressive, sultry, muggy, clammy, sweltering

stiff *adjective* **1 = inflexible**, hard, firm, solid, rigid, taut • *stiff metal wires*

OPPOSITE: limp

2 = unrelaxed, cold, formal, wooden, forced, unnatural, stilted • *the rather stiff and formal surroundings of the official residence*

3 = difficult, hard, tough, rigorous, formidable, arduous, exacting • *a stiff penalty*

4 = awkward, jerky (*informal*), clumsy, ungainly, graceless, inelegant, ungraceful

5 = severe, hard, heavy, strict, extreme, harsh, drastic

stiffen *verb* **1 = brace**, reinforce, tense, tauten

2 = set, solidify, thicken, harden, crystallize, jell, congeal

stifle *verb* **1 = suppress**, stop, check, silence, restrain, smother, hush, repress

2 = suffocate, choke, smother, strangle, asphyxiate

stifling *See* **stuffy**

stigma *noun* **= disgrace**, shame, stain, slur, dishonour, smirch

still *adjective* **1 = motionless**, calm, stationary, tranquil, inert • *The air was still.*

2 = silent, quiet, hushed

▶ *verb* **3 = quieten**, settle, quiet, silence, calm, lull, allay, soothe, hush, pacify

▶ *conjunction* **4 = however**, but, yet, nevertheless, notwithstanding

See also: **peaceful**

stillness *noun* **= calm**, peace, quiet, silence

stilted *adjective* **= stiff**, wooden, forced, unnatural, constrained

stimulant *noun* **= pick-me-up** (*informal*), upper (*slang*), tonic, restorative

stimulate *verb* **= arouse**, fire, prompt, encourage, spur, provoke, incite, rouse, impel

stimulating *adjective* **= exciting**, provocative, rousing, exhilarating, inspiring, stirring

stimulus *noun* **= incentive**, encouragement, spur, incitement, impetus, inducement, goad

sting *verb* **1 = hurt**, wound, burn, pain, smart, tingle

2 (*Informal*) **= cheat**, defraud, swindle, fleece, overcharge, rip off (*slang*)

stingy *adjective* **= mean**, miserly, niggardly, parsimonious, penny-pinching (*informal*), tightfisted, ungenerous

stink *verb* **1 = reek** • *Something in this kitchen stinks.*

S

▶ *noun* **2 = stench** • *the stink of old fish*
See also: **smell**

stinking *See* **smelly**

stint *verb* **1 = be mean**, be frugal, be sparing, hold back, skimp on
▶ *noun* **2 = time**, share, term, turn, period, shift, stretch, spell, quota

stipulate *verb* **= specify**, agree, contract, require, settle, insist upon

stipulation *noun* **= condition**, agreement, requirement, clause, qualification, specification, precondition, proviso

stipulations *See* **terms**

stir *verb* **1 = mix**, beat, shake, agitate
2 = stimulate, spur, provoke, excite, incite, awaken, arouse, rouse
▷ **stir up** *See* **excite**
▶ *noun* **3 = commotion**, activity, disorder, flurry, excitement, disturbance, fuss, bustle

stirring *See* **impressive, moving**

stock *noun* **1 = shares**, bonds, investments • *the buying of stocks*
2 = goods, merchandise (*formal*) • *The shoe store needs to add more stock.*
3 = supply, store, reserve, stockpile, reservoir • *a stock of ammunition*
4 = lineage, origin, descent, extraction, ancestry • *He claims to be of Loyalist stock.*
5 = property, capital, investment, assets, funds
6 = livestock, cattle, beasts, domestic animals
▶ *verb* **7 = sell**, supply, deal in, trade in • *The store stocks a wide range of paint.*
8 = provide with, supply, equip, furnish, fit out
▷ **stock up = store** or **store up**, save, gather, accumulate, amass, hoard, lay in, put away
▶ *adjective* **9 = standard**, usual, routine, typical • *They supply stock sizes.*
10 = hackneyed, overused,

stereotyped • *National security is the stock excuse for government secrecy.*
See also: **bank, fill**

stockpile *verb* **1 = store up**, save, gather, collect, accumulate, amass, stash, hoard • *People are stockpiling food for the winter.*
▶ *noun* **2 = store**, stock, reserve, arsenal, cache, stash (*informal*), hoard • *stockpiles of fuel*
See also: **supply**

stocky *adjective* **= thickset**, solid, sturdy • *a stocky, middle-aged man*

stodgy *adjective* **1 = heavy**, filling, starchy, leaden
2 = dull, boring, tedious, stuffy, staid, heavy going, unexciting

stoical *adjective* **= resigned**, philosophical, long-suffering, stoic, dispassionate, impassive, phlegmatic, stolid

stoicism *noun* **= resignation**, acceptance, patience, long-suffering, fortitude, forbearance, impassivity, stolidity

stolid *adjective* **= apathetic**, wooden, dull, unemotional, lumpish

stomach *noun* **1 = belly**, tummy (*informal*), paunch • *Breathe in and flatten your stomach.*
2 = inclination, taste, desire, appetite, relish
▶ *verb* **3 = bear**, take, endure, swallow, tolerate, abide
See also: **put up with**

stony *adjective* **= cold**, hard, blank, hostile, icy, chilly, expressionless, unresponsive

stoop *verb* **1 = bend**, duck, bow, lean, hunch, crouch
▷ **stoop to = sink to**, descend to, lower oneself by, resort to
▶ *noun* **2 = slouch**, bad posture, round-shoulderedness

stop *verb* **1 = cease**, end, quit, discontinue, desist, cut out (*informal*) • *I stopped writing when the phone rang.*
OPPOSITE: start
2 = end, finish, conclude, halt, cease, come to an end • *They waited for the blizzard to stop.*

S

OPPOSITE: start
3 = prevent, arrest, check
• *measures to stop smuggling*
4 = plug, block, stem, seal, staunch, obstruct
5 = stay, rest, lodge
▷ **stop working** See **fail**
▶ *noun* **6 = halt**, end, finish, standstill, cessation
7 = stay, break, rest
8 = station, depot, terminus
See also: **suppress, visit**

stopgap *noun* = **makeshift**, resort, substitute, improvization

stoppage *noun* = **stopping**, close, arrest, halt, closure, shutdown, standstill, cutoff, hindrance

stopper See **plug**

store *noun* **1 = supply**, fund, stock, reserve, stockpile, reservoir, cache, hoard • *I have a store of food and water here.*
2 = shop, market, supermarket, boutique, emporium, dépanneur (*Canad Queb*), hypermarket, mart • *I had to race around the stores in the mall.*
3 = storeroom, warehouse, depot • *a grain store*
▶ *verb* **4 = put by**, keep, save, reserve, stockpile, stash, hoard • *The information is stored in the computer.*
▷ **store up** See **stockpile**
See also: **bank, collection, wealth**

storeroom See **store**

stores See **supplies**

storm *noun* **1 = tempest**, hurricane, blizzard, squall, gale
2 = outburst, outbreak, row, turmoil, outcry, disturbance, strife, furor, agitation,

commotion, tumult, rumpus
▶ *verb* **3 = attack**, charge, assault, rush, assail
4 = rage, rant, thunder, rave, bluster
5 = rush, fly, stamp, flounce

stormy *adjective* = **wild**, rough, turbulent, windy, raging, blustery, inclement, squally

story *noun* **1 = tale**, account, legend, narrative, anecdote, yarn • *a science-fiction story*
2 = report, news, feature, article, scoop, news item
See also: **plot**

| **CONFUSABLES**
| *Story* means *narrative.*
| *Storey* means *floor of a building.*

storyline See **plot**

stout *adjective* **1 = fat**, big, heavy, overweight, bulky, portly, plump, burly, fleshy, rotund, corpulent, tubby
2 = strong, robust, stalwart, muscular, sturdy, able-bodied, brawny, strapping
3 = brave, bold, courageous, valiant, plucky, fearless, gallant, resolute, intrepid

stow *verb* = **pack**, store, load, bundle, stash (*informal*), put away

straight *adjective* **1 = upright**, erect, vertical, perpendicular
• *Keep your arms straight.*
OPPOSITE: crooked
2 = level, even, horizontal • *a straight line*
3 = frank, honest, plain, outright, blunt, candid, point-blank, forthright • *They wouldn't give me a straight answer.*
4 = direct, near, short
5 = honest, just, fair, accurate, upright, law-abiding, trustworthy, honourable, above board
6 = successive, consecutive, solid, continuous, running, nonstop
7 = undiluted, pure, neat, unadulterated, unmixed
8 = orderly, organized, tidy, neat, arranged, in order, shipshape
9 (*Slang*) = **conventional**,

WORDS FOR STORM

blizzard
hailstorm
snowstorm
squall
tempest
thunderstorm

conservative, bourgeois
▶ adverb **10 = directly**,
immediately, instantly, at once
See also: **straightforward**
▷ **straight away** adverb
= **immediately**, now, directly,
instantly, at once, right away
straighten verb = **neaten**, order,
arrange, tidy or tidy up, put in
order
▷ **straighten out** *See* **settle**
straightforward adjective
1 = easy, simple, basic, routine,
elementary, uncomplicated • *The
question seemed straightforward
enough.*
OPPOSITE: complicated
2 = honest, open, straight,
direct, plain, frank, candid,
upfront, forthright • *I liked her
straightforward, intelligent manner.*
OPPOSITE: devious
See also: **blunt**
strain¹ noun **1 = stress**, pressure,
tension, anxiety • *the stresses and
strains of a busy career*
2 = exertion, force, effort,
struggle
3 = injury, pull, sprain, wrench
▶ verb **4 = overwork**, tax • *You'll
strain your eyes reading in this light.*
5 = stretch, tighten, distend,
draw tight, tauten
6 = strive, struggle, labour,
endeavour, bend over backwards
(*informal*), give it one's best shot
(*informal*), go for it (*informal*),
knock oneself out (*informal*)
7 = sieve, filter, sift, purify
See also: **burden**, **difficulty**
strain² noun **1 = breed**, family,
race, blood, descent, extraction,
ancestry, lineage
2 = trace, streak, suggestion,
tendency
See also: **variety**
strained adjective **1 = forced**,
false, artificial, unnatural, put
on
2 = tense, difficult, stiff,
awkward, uneasy, embarrassed
strains *See* **tune**
strait noun (*often plural*) = **channel**,
sound, narrows
▷ **straits** = **difficulty**,

plight, dilemma, hardship,
predicament, extremity
strait-laced adjective
= **puritanical**, strict, proper,
prim, narrow-minded,
moralistic, prudish
strand noun = **filament**, string,
thread, fibre
stranded adjective **1 = beached**,
ashore, aground, grounded,
marooned, shipwrecked
2 = helpless, abandoned, high
and dry
strange adjective **1 = odd**, funny,
extraordinary, bizarre, weird,
curious, abnormal, uncommon,
peculiar, hinky (*slang*),
unaccountable, outré • *A strange
thing happened.*
2 = unfamiliar, new, foreign,
novel, alien, exotic • *alone in a
strange country*
See also: **eccentric**
stranger noun = **newcomer**,
guest, visitor, foreigner, alien,
incomer, outlander
strangle verb **1 = throttle**, choke,
asphyxiate, strangulate
2 = suppress, stifle, inhibit,
repress
strap noun **1 = tie**, belt, thong
▶ verb **2 = fasten**, tie, secure,
bind, lash, buckle
strapping adjective = **well-built**,
big, powerful, robust, husky
(*informal*), sturdy, brawny
stratagem noun = **trick**, plan,
device, scheme, dodge, ploy,
ruse, manoeuvre, subterfuge
strategic adjective **1 = tactical**,
diplomatic, planned, deliberate,
calculated, politic
2 = crucial, key, important,
critical, decisive, vital, cardinal
strategy noun = **plan**, policy,
approach, procedure, scheme,
gameplan
stratum *See* **layer**
stray verb **1 = wander**, drift, err,
go astray
2 = digress, deviate, diverge, get
off the point
▶ adjective **3 = lost**, homeless,
abandoned, roaming, vagrant
4 = random, chance, accidental

streak noun 1 = **band**, line, stroke, strip, slash, layer, stripe, vein

2 = **trace**, touch, strain, element, dash, vein

▶ verb 3 = **speed**, fly, tear, flash, sprint, zoom, dart, hurtle, whizz (informal)

stream noun 1 = **river**, bayou, brook, beck, tributary, rivulet

2 = **flow**, run, current, course, surge, rush, tide, drift, torrent

▶ verb 3 = **flow**, run, issue, course, flood, spill, pour, cascade, gush, spout

streamline See **simplify**

streamlined adjective = **efficient**, organized, slick, rationalized, smooth-running

street noun = **road**, row, lane, avenue, roadway, terrace, boulevard, parkway

strength noun 1 = **might**, muscle, stamina, brawn • an astonishing display of physical strength

OPPOSITE: weakness

2 = **intensity**, force, power, vigour, potency, vehemence • the strength of his feelings for her

OPPOSITE: weakness

3 = **strong point**, advantage, asset

See also: **character, energy, merit, virtue**

strengthen verb 1 = **fortify**, encourage, consolidate, toughen, stiffen, harden • This move will strengthen his political standing.

OPPOSITE: weaken

2 = **reinforce**, support, brace, bolster, fortify • The builders had to strengthen the joists with timber.

OPPOSITE: weaken

See also: **build, secure**

strenuous adjective = **demanding**, hard, tough, uphill, arduous, laborious, taxing

stress noun 1 = **worry**, pressure, strain, tension, anxiety, hassle (informal) • the stresses and strains of a busy career

2 = **emphasis**, force, weight, significance

3 = **accent**, beat, emphasis, accentuation

▶ verb 4 = **emphasize**, repeat, underline, accentuate • The leaders have stressed their commitment to the talks.

See also: **burden, care**

stressful See **tense**

stretch verb 1 = **extend**, last, continue, reach, cover, spread, hang, go on • an artificial reef stretching the length of the coast

2 = **reach**, extend, straighten • She arched her back and stretched herself.

OPPOSITE: bend

3 = **pull**, expand, strain, tighten, elongate, distend, draw out

▶ noun 4 = **expanse**, area, sweep, extent, tract • It's a very dangerous stretch of road.

5 = **period**, time, run, term, space, spell, stint • She would study for eight-hour stretches.

See also: **lengthen, range, tax**

strict adjective 1 = **stern**, firm, rigorous, stringent, authoritarian, rigid • His parents are very strict.

2 = **exact**, true, particular, accurate, precise, meticulous • He has never been unemployed, in the strict sense of the word.

3 = **absolute**, total, utter

See also: **faithful, right, severe**

stride See **walk**

strident adjective = **harsh**, raucous, shrill, grating, discordant, jarring, screeching

strife noun = **conflict**, battle, clash, friction, quarrel, discord, dissension

strike verb 1 = **walk out**, revolt, mutiny, down tools

2 = **hit**, beat, knock, hammer, punch, slap, thump, smack, wallop (informal), clobber (slang), cuff, clout (informal)

3 = **collide with**, hit, bump into, run into

4 = **attack**, hit, assault, assail

5 = **occur to**, hit, register (informal), come to, dawn on or dawn upon

striking adjective = **impressive**,

cool (*informal*), dramatic, outstanding, noticeable, conspicuous, phat (*slang*)

string *noun* 1 = **cord**, fibre, twine
2 = **series**, file, line, row, chain, sequence, procession, succession

stringent *adjective* = **strict**, tough, severe, tight, rigorous, rigid, inflexible

stringy *adjective* = **fibrous**, tough, gristly, sinewy

strip[1] *verb* 1 = **undress**, disrobe, unclothe
2 = **plunder**, empty, sack, rob, loot, ransack, divest, pillage, despoil

strip[2] *noun* = **piece**, band, belt, shred

stripe *See* **line**

stripped *See* **bare**

strive *verb* = **try**, seek, attempt, endeavour (*formal*), do your best, do your utmost, make an effort • *She strives hard to keep herself fit.*
See also: **aim, struggle**

stroke *verb* 1 = **caress**, pet, rub, fondle
▷ *noun* 2 = **apoplexy**, attack, collapse, fit, seizure
3 = **blow**, hit, knock, rap, thump, pat

stroll *verb* 1 = **walk**, ramble, promenade, amble, saunter
▷ *noun* 2 = **walk**, turn, constitutional, ramble, promenade, breath of air

strong *adjective* 1 = **powerful**, tough, robust, athletic, muscular, sturdy, burly, hardy, brawny, lusty, strapping • *a strong, robust man*
OPPOSITE: weak
2 = **durable**, substantial, sturdy, heavy-duty, hard-wearing, well-built • *a strong material, which won't crack or chip*
OPPOSITE: fragile
3 = **persuasive**, sound, effective, potent, weighty, well-founded, compelling, convincing, telling
4 = **intense**, firm, deep, violent, fierce, acute, keen, zealous, vehement, fervent, fervid
• *Despite strong opposition, she was victorious.*

OPPOSITE: faint
5 = **extreme**, severe, drastic, forceful
6 = **bright**, brilliant, bold, dazzling
See also: **hard, healthy, passionate, solid, well**
▷ **strong point** *See* **merit**

stronghold *noun* = **fortress**, castle, fort, bastion, citadel, bulwark

structure *noun* 1 = **arrangement**, design, organization, construction, makeup • *the structure of this molecule*
2 = **building**, construction, edifice • *The museum is an impressive structure.*
▷ *verb* 3 = **arrange**, design, shape, organize, assemble, build up
See also: **form, sequence, system**

structuring *See* **organization**

struggle *verb* 1 = **strive**, work, strain, toil • *They had to struggle to make ends meet.*
2 = **fight**, battle, compete, contend, wrestle, grapple
▷ **struggle against** *See* **resist**
▷ *noun* 3 = **effort**, work, labour, toil • *Life became a struggle for survival.*
4 = **fight**, battle, contest, conflict, clash, combat, brush, tussle
See also: **competition**

strut *verb* = **swagger**, parade, peacock, prance

stub *noun* 1 = **butt**, end, remainder, tail, remnant, stump, tail end
2 = **counterfoil**, receipt, ticket stub

stubborn *adjective* = **obstinate**, wilful, dogged, tenacious, inflexible • *a stubborn character who is used to getting her own way*

stubby *adjective* = **stocky**, short, squat, chunky, dumpy, thickset

stuck *adjective* 1 = **fastened**, fast, cemented, fixed, glued, joined
2 (*Informal*) = **baffled**, beaten, stumped

stuck-up *adjective* (*informal*)

S

stud *verb* = **ornament**, spot, dot, bejewel, spangle

= **snobbish**, proud, arrogant, conceited, disdainful, haughty • *She was famous, but she wasn't a bit stuck-up.*
See also: **superior, vain**

student *noun* = **pupil**, schoolchild • *There are 30 students in my class.*

studied *adjective* = **planned**, deliberate, conscious, intentional, premeditated

studio *noun* = **workshop**, atelier

studious *adjective* = **scholarly**, academic, intellectual, hard-working, diligent, bookish, assiduous

study *verb* 1 = **learn**, read up • *He is studying history and economics.*
2 = **contemplate**, examine, pore over • *He studied the map in silence.*
3 = **examine**, research, survey, investigate, analyze, scrutinize, look into
▶ *noun* 4 = **learning**, research, schoolwork, lessons • *the serious study of architecture*
5 = **examination**, review, investigation, survey, inquiry, analysis, inspection, consideration, scrutiny, contemplation
See also: **observe, piece, read**

stuff *noun* 1 = **material**, fabric, textile, cloth
2 = **things**, equipment, tackle, gear, apparatus, paraphernalia, belongings, items • *"That's my stuff," he said, pointing to a bag.*
3 = **substance**, material • *The car was covered in some sticky stuff.*
▶ *verb* 4 = **shove**, force, push, jam, squeeze, thrust, ram, cram • *He stuffed all the paper into a recycling box.*
5 = **fill**, pack, load, cram • *He stood there, stuffing his mouth with popcorn.*
See also: **matter, stick**

stuffing *noun* = **filling**, packing, wadding

stuffy *adjective* 1 = **staid**, formal, old-fashioned, dull, straitlaced • *his lack of stuffy formality*
2 = **stifling**, close, heavy, stale,

oppressive, muggy • *It was hot and stuffy in the classroom.*

stumble *verb* 1 = **trip**, fall, slip, reel, falter, stagger, lurch
2 (with *across* or *on* or *upon*) = **discover**, find, chance upon, come across

stump *verb* = **baffle**, puzzle, confuse, mystify, bewilder, perplex, flummox, nonplus

stumpy *adjective* = **stocky**, short, squat, dumpy, stubby, thickset

stun *verb* = **overcome**, shock, confuse, overpower, astonish, stagger, astound, bewilder, confound, stupefy

stunned *See* **dazed, unconscious**

stunner *See* **beauty**

stunning *adjective* = **wonderful**, cool (*informal*), beautiful, impressive, spectacular, sensational (*informal*), lovely, gorgeous, striking, marvelous, dazzling, phat (*slang*)

stunt *noun* = **feat**, act, trick, exploit, deed

stunted *adjective* = **undersized**, little, small, tiny, diminutive

stupefy *verb* = **astound**, shock, stun, amaze, stagger, daze, dumbfound

stupendous *adjective*
1 = **wonderful**, amazing, sensational (*informal*), superb, breathtaking, marvellous, astounding, overwhelming, staggering
2 = **huge**, vast, enormous, gigantic, mega (*slang*), colossal

stupid *adjective* 1 = **unintelligent**, thick, dim, moronic, obtuse, stunned (*Canad informal*), cretinous (*offensive*), imbecilic • *I'm not stupid, you know.*
2 = **foolish**, absurd, crass, idiotic, inane, asinine, fatuous • *a stupid suggestion*
OPPOSITE: smart
3 = **dazed**, groggy, insensate, semiconscious, stunned, stupefied
See also: **mad, silly, slow, unwise**

stupidity *noun* 1 = **lack of**

intelligence, thickness, slowness, brainlessness, denseness, dimness, dullness, imbecility, obtuseness • *I was astonished by his stupidity.*
2 = foolishness, folly, absurdity, silliness, inanity • *the stupidity of their decision*

stupor *noun* = **daze**, coma, unconsciousness, insensibility, stupefaction

sturdy *adjective* **1 = substantial**, strong, solid, durable, stout, well-built • *The camera was mounted on a sturdy tripod.*
OPPOSITE: fragile
2 = robust, powerful, athletic, muscular, hardy, brawny, lusty
See also: **stocky, tough**

stutter *verb* = **stammer**, stumble, falter, hesitate

style *noun* **1 = manner**, way, approach, method, technique, mode • *a dictatorial management style*
2 = elegance, taste, chic, flair, sophistication • *She has not lost her grace and style.*
3 = design, cut, form, manner
4 = type, kind, sort, category, variety, genre
5 = fashion, trend, rage, mode, vogue
6 = luxury, ease, comfort, affluence, elegance, grandeur
▶ *verb* **7 = design**, cut, fashion, shape, arrange, adapt, tailor
8 = call, term, name, label, dub, entitle, designate
See also: **language, polish**

stylish *adjective* = **smart**, cool (*informal*), designer (*informal*), chic, trendy (*informal*), fashionable, dressy (*informal*), modish, phat (*slang*), voguish

suave *adjective* = **smooth**, sophisticated, charming, polite, courteous, debonair, urbane

subconscious *adjective* = **hidden**, inner, subliminal, intuitive, latent, repressed

subdue *verb* **1 = overcome**, defeat, crush, overpower, quell, vanquish • *The government has not been able to subdue the rebels.*

2 = moderate, soften, suppress, mellow, quieten down, tone down

subdued *adjective* **1 = quiet**, serious, sad, dejected, downcast, chastened, crestfallen, down in the mouth
2 = soft, quiet, subtle, muted, dim, hushed, toned down, unobtrusive

subject *noun* **1 = topic**, point, issue, question, matter, object, theme • *They exchanged views on a wide range of subjects.*
2 = citizen, national
3 = subordinate
▶ *adjective* **4 = subordinate**, satellite, dependent, inferior, obedient
▷ **subject to = liable to**, exposed to, in danger of, open to, prone to, susceptible to, vulnerable to;
= **conditional on**, contingent on, dependent on
▶ *verb* **5 = put through**, expose, submit • *She was subjected to constant interruptions.*
See also: **affair, business**

subjective *adjective* = **personal**, biased, nonobjective, prejudiced

subjugate *verb* = **conquer**, overcome, master, overpower, subdue, quell, suppress, vanquish, enslave

sublime *adjective* = **noble**, high, great, grand, elevated, lofty, glorious, exalted

submerge *verb* = **immerse**, duck, flood, sink, plunge, dip, overwhelm, swamp, overflow, engulf, inundate, deluge

submission *noun* **1 = surrender**, assent, capitulation, giving in, yielding
2 = presentation, entry, handing in, tendering
3 = meekness, resignation, compliance, deference, obedience, passivity, docility

submissive *adjective* = **meek**, passive, compliant, amenable, obedient, docile, accommodating, acquiescent, pliant, tractable, unresisting, yielding

S

submit verb 1 = **surrender**, agree, comply, yield, bow, capitulate, give in • *I submitted to their requests.*
OPPOSITE: resist
2 = **present**, propose, table, tender, hand in, put forward, send in • *The teachers submitted their reports to the principal.*
OPPOSITE: withdraw
See also: **nominate, pose, subject**

subordinate adjective 1 = **lesser**, lower, junior, subject, minor, secondary, dependent, inferior
▶ noun 2 = **inferior**, second, junior, assistant, aide, attendant

subordination noun
= **inferiority**, servitude, inferior status or secondary status, subjection

subscribe verb 1 = **donate**, give, contribute
2 = **support**, endorse, advocate

subscription noun
1 = **membership fee**, annual payment, dues
2 = **donation**, gift, contribution

subsequent adjective = **following**, after, later, successive, ensuing, succeeding

subsequently adverb = **later**, afterwards

subservient adjective = **servile**, abject, deferential, submissive, obsequious, slavish, sycophantic

subside verb 1 = **decrease**, ease, diminish, wane, lessen, abate, ebb, slacken, quieten
2 = **sink**, drop, settle, collapse, lower, cave in

subsidence noun 1 = **sinking**, settling
2 = **decrease**, abatement, easing off, lessening, slackening

subsidiary adjective = **lesser**, minor, secondary, subordinate, supplementary, auxiliary, ancillary

subsidize verb = **fund**, support, finance, promote, sponsor

subsidy noun = **aid**, help, support, grant, assistance, allowance

substance noun 1 = **material**, stuff, element, fabric • *Poisonous*

substances should be labelled as such.
2 = **meaning**, import, significance, essence, gist, main point
3 = **reality**, actuality, concreteness
4 = **wealth**, property, estate, means, assets, resources
See also: **matter**

substantial adjective = **big**, large, important, significant, considerable, sizable or sizeable, ample, supersize

substantiate verb = **support**, confirm, prove, establish, verify, authenticate

substitute verb 1 = **replace**, trade, exchange, switch, swap, interchange • *You can substitute honey for the sugar.*
▶ noun 2 = **replacement**, deputy, representative, makeshift, proxy, surrogate, locum, locum tenens • *an artificial substitute for silk*
3 = **replacement**, second, reserve, alternative, proxy, surrogate, fall-back
See also: **change**

substitution noun
= **replacement**, change, trade, exchange, switch, swap

subterfuge noun = **trick**, dodge, ploy, deception, ruse, manoeuvre, stratagem

subtle adjective 1 = **sophisticated**, delicate, refined
2 = **faint**, slight, delicate, implied, understated
3 = **crafty**, wily, shrewd, ingenious, sly, cunning, devious, artful

subtlety noun 1 = **sophistication**, delicacy, refinement
2 = **cunning**, ingenuity, artfulness, cleverness, craftiness, deviousness, slyness, wiliness

subtract verb = **take away**, deduct, take from • *If you subtract 3 from 5 you get 2.*
OPPOSITE: add

subversive adjective
1 = **seditious**, riotous, treasonous

▶ *noun* **2** = **dissident**, terrorist, traitor, saboteur, fifth columnist

subvert *verb* = **overturn**, undermine, sabotage

succeed *verb* **1** = **be successful**, work, triumph, thrive, flourish, prosper, do well, make it (*informal*) • *To succeed, you must learn to overcome obstacles.*
OPPOSITE: fail
2 = **take over from**, replace • *She is almost certain to succeed me as president.*
3 = **follow**, result, ensue, come next
▷ **succeed in** *See* **manage**
See also: **pass, win**

succeeding *See* **next**

success *noun* **1** = **prosperity**, victory, celebrity, fame, triumph, wealth, eminence • *Do you believe that work is the key to success?*
OPPOSITE: failure
2 = **hit**, star, winner, celebrity, triumph, sensation • *Everyone who knows her says she will be a huge success.*
OPPOSITE: failure
See also: **win**

successful *adjective* = **thriving**, top, lucrative, profitable, rewarding, flourishing • *My mom is a highly successful artist.*

successfully *adverb* = **well**, favourably, victoriously, with flying colours

succession *noun* **1** = **series**, run, order, train, course, chain, cycle, sequence, progression
2 = **taking over**, assumption, inheritance, accession

successive *adjective* = **consecutive**, following, in succession

successor *See* **replacement**

succinct *adjective* = **brief**, compact, terse, concise, laconic, pithy

succour *noun* **1** = **help**, aid, assistance
▶ *verb* **2** = **help**, assist, aid

succulent *adjective* = **juicy**, lush, moist, luscious

succumb *verb* **1** = **surrender**,

submit, yield, capitulate, give in
2 = **die**, fall

sucker *noun* (*Slang*) = **fool**, victim, mug (*Brit slang*), dupe, pushover (*slang*), dork (*slang*), schmuck (*slang*)

sudden *adjective* = **abrupt**, quick, unexpected, swift, hasty • *a sudden cry*
OPPOSITE: gradual
See also: **sharp**

suddenly *adverb* = **abruptly**, unexpectedly, all of a sudden

sue *verb* (*Law*) = **take (someone) to court**, charge, prosecute, indict, summon

suffer *verb* **1** = **undergo**, bear, experience, endure, sustain, go through • *I knew he was suffering some discomfort.*
2 = **tolerate**, put up with (*informal*)
See also: **feel, receive**

sufferer *See* **patient**

suffering *noun* = **pain**, ordeal, distress, misery, hardship, discomfort, anguish, agony, torment

suffice *verb* = **be enough**, do, serve, be adequate, be sufficient, meet requirements, pass muster

sufficient *adjective* = **enough**, adequate, ample • *He had sufficient time to prepare his speech.*
OPPOSITE: insufficient
See also: **satisfactory**

suffocate *verb* = **choke**, stifle, smother, asphyxiate

sugary *See* **sweet**

suggest *verb* **1** = **recommend**, propose, advise, advocate • *My cousin suggested going out for dinner.*
2 = **hint**, indicate, intimate, imply, insinuate • *Reports suggested the factory would close.*
3 = **bring to mind**, evoke
See also: **nominate, raise, vote**

suggestion *noun*
1 = **recommendation**, plan, proposal, proposition • *practical suggestions*
2 = **hint**, trace, indication, insinuation, intimation • *a suggestion of dishonesty*
See also: **advice, idea**

S

suggestive adjective = **smutty**, blue, rude, provocative, racy, bawdy, indelicate, ribald, risqué

suit verb **1** = **be acceptable to**, do, please, satisfy • *They will move only if it suits them.*
2 = **match**, agree, correspond, conform to, go with • *The battery can be shaped to suit any device.*
3 = **outfit**, dress, habit, costume, ensemble, clothing
4 = **lawsuit**, case, cause, trial, action, prosecution, proceeding
See also: **blend, flatter**

suitability noun = **appropriateness**, fitness, aptness, rightness

suitable adjective = **appropriate**, right, fit, proper, acceptable, fitting, satisfactory, apt • *Conditions were not suitable for the vegetation to flourish.*
OPPOSITE: unsuitable
See also: **favourable**

suite noun = **rooms**, apartment

suitor noun (Old-fashioned) = **admirer**, beau (old-fashioned), young man

sulk verb = **be sullen**, pout, be in a huff

sulky adjective = **huffy**, moody, sullen, resentful, petulant • *a sulky adolescent*
See also: **grumpy**

sullen adjective = **morose**, cross, sour, moody, surly, dour, glowering, unsociable

sully verb = **defile**, disgrace, stain, tarnish, besmirch, dishonour, smirch

sultry adjective **1** = **humid**, close, hot, sticky, oppressive, muggy, stifling
2 = **seductive**, sexy (informal), provocative, sensual

sum noun = **total**, amount, whole, tally, aggregate
▶ adjective
▷ **sum total** See **whole**
▶ verb
▷ **sum up** = **summarize**, recapitulate • *He summed up his weekend in one word: "Disastrous."*

summarize verb = **sum up**, epitomize, encapsulate, condense, abridge, précis

summary noun = **synopsis**, review, outline, rundown, summation • *a summary of the report*

summit noun = **peak**, top, head, height, pinnacle, apex, zenith, acme

summon verb **1** = **send for**, call, bid, invite
2 (often with *up*) = **gather**, muster, draw on

sumptuous adjective = **luxurious**, grand, lavish, gorgeous, superb, splendid, opulent

sumptuousness See **luxury**

sunburned adjective = **tanned**, red, brown, burnt, peeling, bronzed

sundry adjective = **various**, some, several, different, assorted, miscellaneous

sunken adjective **1** = **hollow**, drawn, haggard
2 = **lowered**, submerged, buried, recessed

sunny adjective **1** = **bright**, clear, fine, radiant, sunlit, summery, unclouded
2 = **cheerful**, happy, buoyant, joyful, light-hearted, cheery

sunrise noun = **dawn**, daybreak, break of day, cockcrow

sunset noun = **nightfall**, dusk, close of day *or* close of the day, eventide

super adjective (Informal) = **excellent**, sensational (informal), outstanding, glorious, magnificent, marvellous, wonderful, terrific (informal), superb

superb adjective = **splendid**, excellent, wonderful, superior, outstanding, magnificent, breathtaking, marvellous, exquisite, unrivalled • *With superb skill, she managed to make a perfect landing.*
See also: **brilliant, first-rate**

supercilious adjective = **scornful**, lofty, arrogant, contemptuous, disdainful, haughty, snooty (informal), stuck-up (informal)

superficial adjective **1** = **hasty**,

casual, hurried, sketchy, desultory, cursory, perfunctory, slapdash
2 = shallow, silly, frivolous, trivial, empty-headed
3 = surface, external, slight, exterior, on the surface

superfluous *adjective* **= excess**, extra, surplus, spare, redundant, left over, remaining, supernumerary

superhuman *adjective* **1 = heroic**, phenomenal, prodigious
2 = supernatural, paranormal

superintendence *noun*
= supervision, government, charge, control, management, direction

superintendent *noun*
= supervisor, director, chief, manager, governor, inspector, controller, overseer

superior *adjective* **1 = better**, choice, exceptional, deluxe, first-rate, unrivalled, surpassing • *a superior brand of ice cream*
OPPOSITE: inferior
2 = supercilious, lofty, condescending, disdainful, haughty, patronizing, snobbish, stuck-up *(informal)* • *He stood there looking superior.*
3 = first-class, choice, excellent, exclusive, exceptional, deluxe, first-rate
▶ *noun* **4 = boss** *(informal)*, senior, manager, supervisor • *his immediate superior*
OPPOSITE: inferior
See also: **prime, select, smug, superb**

superiority *noun* **= supremacy**, lead, advantage, excellence, ascendancy, predominance

superlative *adjective*
= outstanding, excellent, supreme, unparalleled, unsurpassed, unrivalled

supermarket See **store**

supernatural *adjective*
= paranormal, miraculous, hidden, psychic, ghostly, uncanny, occult, mystic, spectral, unearthly

supersede *verb* **= replace**, oust,

displace, supplant, usurp, take the place of

superstar See **celebrity**

supervise *verb* **= oversee**, run, manage, direct, be in charge of, have charge of, keep an eye on • *He supervised more than 400 volunteers.*
See also: **administer, command, guard, handle, lead**

supervision *noun*
= superintendence, charge, control, care, management, direction, guidance

supervisor *noun* **= boss** *(informal)*, chief, manager, inspector, administrator, foreman, overseer

supplant *verb* **= replace**, oust, displace, supersede, take the place of

supple *adjective* **= flexible**, limber, lissom *or* lissome, lithe, pliable, pliant

supplement *verb* **1 = add to**, reinforce, complement, augment, top up • *I suggest supplementing your diet with vitamin A.*
▶ *noun* **2 = addition**, extra, complement, appendix, sidebar • *a supplement to their basic pension*
See also: **add**

supplementary *adjective*
= additional, extra, secondary, add-on, auxiliary, ancillary

supplication *noun* **= plea**, appeal, request, prayer, petition, entreaty

supplies *plural noun* **= provisions**, equipment, rations, stores • *I had only a litre of water in my emergency supplies.*

supply *verb* **1 = provide**, give, equip, furnish • *an agreement not to supply chemical weapons*
▶ *noun* **2 = store**, fund, stock, reserve, stockpile, cache, hoard • *a plentiful supply of vegetables*
See also: **issue**

support *verb* **1 = back**, second, defend, champion, promote, uphold, side with, make a pitch for *(slang)* • *We supported her political campaign.*

S

OPPOSITE: oppose
2 = help, encourage • *Try to support each other when one of you is feeling down.*
3 = hold up, brace, bolster, reinforce, buttress, prop up, shore up • *Thick wooden posts support the deck.*
4 = provide for, keep, fund, finance, maintain, sustain, look after
5 = bear out, confirm, verify, substantiate, corroborate
▶ noun **6 = prop**, post, brace, foundation, pillar, abutment, stanchion • *the metal supports that hold up the canvas*
7 = help, aid, assistance, backing, loyalty, encouragement, endorsation (*Canad*)
8 = supporter, second, prop, backer, mainstay, tower of strength
9 = upkeep, keep, maintenance, sustenance, subsistence
See also: **advocate, bear, blessing, comfort, favour, sanction, steady, strengthen**
supporter noun = **follower**, fan, champion, advocate, ally, sponsor, adherent • *He is a strong supporter of the plan.*
See also: **defender, helper**
supportive adjective = **helpful**, understanding, sympathetic, encouraging
suppose verb **1 = think**, expect, believe, guess, assume, imagine, presume • *Where do you suppose he has gone?*
2 = imagine, consider, pretend, hypothesize, conjecture, postulate
See also: **conclude, figure, reckon, suspect**
supposed adjective **1 = expected**, required, meant, obliged • *You're not supposed to leave the children on their own.*
2 = assumed, alleged, presumed, reputed, believed, meant, rumoured • *What is his son supposed to have said?*
supposedly adverb

= **presumably**, allegedly, theoretically, hypothetically, ostensibly
supposition noun = **guess**, speculation, theory, hypothesis, presumption, conjecture, surmise
suppress verb **1 = stop**, crush, quash, quell, stamp out • *international attempts to suppress drug trafficking*
2 = restrain, contain, curb, stifle, conceal, smother, repress • *She barely suppressed a gasp.*
See also: **silence**
suppressed See **pent-up**
suppression noun = **elimination**, check, crushing, quashing, smothering
supremacy noun = **domination**, sovereignty, sway, mastery, primacy, predominance, supreme power
supreme adjective = **highest**, top, chief, principal, ultimate, foremost, pre-eminent, paramount, greatest, leading • *They conspired to seize supreme power.*
See also: **absolute, ideal, incomparable**
supremo noun = **head**, leader, director, commander, governor, boss (*informal*), master, principal, ruler, alpha male
sure adjective **1 = certain**, clear, positive, convinced, definite, satisfied • *She was no longer sure how she felt about him.*
OPPOSITE: unsure
2 = reliable, definite, dependable, trustworthy, undeniable, foolproof, infallible • *a sure sign that something is wrong*
3 = inevitable, bound, assured, inescapable, guaranteed
See also: **confident, yes**

▎**INFORMALLY SPEAKING**
for sure: without doubt
sure enough: definitely
surely adverb = **undoubtedly**, certainly, definitely, unquestionably, doubtlessly, indubitably, without doubt

surface noun 1 = **outside**, top, face, side, exterior, covering, veneer
▶ verb 2 = **appear**, emerge, arise, materialize, transpire, come to light, come up, crop up (informal)

surfeit noun = **excess**, glut, plethora, superfluity

surge noun 1 = **rush**, flood, flow, outpouring, gush
2 = **wave**, swell, roller, billow
▶ verb 3 = **rush**, rise, roll, gush, heave

surly adjective = **ill-tempered**, cross, sullen, churlish, grouchy (informal), morose, sulky, uncivil, ungracious

surmise verb 1 = **guess**, suppose, imagine, speculate, presume, conjecture
▶ noun 2 = **guess**, speculation, assumption, presumption, conjecture, supposition

surmount See **overcome**

surpass verb = **outdo**, beat, exceed, eclipse, outshine, excel, outstrip, transcend

surpassing adjective = **supreme**, extraordinary, exceptional, outstanding, incomparable, unrivaled, matchless

surplus noun 1 = **excess**, balance, remainder, residue, surfeit
▶ adjective 2 = **excess**, extra, odd, spare, superfluous, remaining

surprise noun 1 = **shock**, start, revelation, jolt, bombshell • The resignation came as a complete surprise.
2 = **amazement**, wonder, astonishment, incredulity • an exclamation of surprise
▶ verb 3 = **amaze**, stun, astonish, stagger, astound, take aback • I was surprised by the vehemence of his criticism.
4 = **catch unawares** or **catch off-guard**, discover, startle, spring upon

surprised adjective = **amazed**, speechless, astonished, taken by surprise, thunderstruck

surprising adjective = **amazing**, unusual, remarkable, extraordinary, unexpected, incredible, astonishing, staggering

surrender verb 1 = **give in**, submit, yield, succumb, capitulate • We'll never surrender to terrorists.
2 = **give up**, yield, renounce, relinquish, cede • We have surrendered our political authority for economic gain.
▶ noun 3 = **submission**, capitulation • unconditional surrender
See also: **sacrifice**

surreptitious adjective = **secret**, covert, sly, stealthy, furtive, underhand

surrogate noun = **substitute**, representative, proxy, stand-in

surround verb = **enclose**, encompass, envelop, encircle, hem in • He was surrounded by bodyguards.

surrounded by See **among**

surroundings plural noun = **environment**, neighbourhood, location, background, setting • He felt a longing for familiar surroundings.
See also: **scenery**

surveillance noun = **observation**, watch, inspection, scrutiny, supervision

survey verb 1 = **look over**, view, examine, scan, observe, inspect, contemplate, scrutinize
2 = **assess**, plan, measure, estimate, plot, appraise, size up
▶ noun 3 = **examination**, inspection, scrutiny
4 = **study**, review, inquiry

survive verb = **endure**, last, live, outlive, pull through • companies that survived after the recession
See also: **continue, remain**

susceptible adjective 1 (usually with to) = **liable**, subject, vulnerable, prone, given, inclined, disposed
2 = **responsive**, sensitive, receptive, impressionable, suggestible

suspect verb 1 = **believe**, feel, suppose, guess • I suspect they are secretly planning to raise taxes.

S

2 = distrust, doubt, mistrust • *He suspected her motives.*
▶ *adjective* **3 = dubious**, questionable, doubtful, fishy (*informal*), shifty • *a rather suspect character*
See also: **imagine, question, suspicious**

suspend *verb* **1 = hang**, attach, dangle
2 = postpone, shelve, cease, interrupt, defer, discontinue, cut short, put off

suspense *noun* **= uncertainty**, doubt, expectation, tension, anxiety, insecurity, apprehension, irresolution

suspension *noun*
= postponement, break, interruption, abeyance, breaking off, deferment, discontinuation

suspicion *noun* **1 = distrust**, doubt, skepticism, mistrust, misgiving • *I was regarded with suspicion.*
2 = idea, impression, hunch • *I have a strong suspicion they are lying.*
3 = trace, streak, touch, hint, suggestion, shade, tinge, *soupçon* (*French*)

suspicious *adjective*
1 = distrustful, skeptical, wary, doubtful, apprehensive • *She was rightly suspicious of their motives.*
2 = suspect, funny, questionable, doubtful, dubious, shady, sketchy (*informal*), fishy (*informal*), shifty, hinky (*slang*) • *suspicious circumstances*

sustain *verb* **1 = maintain**, continue, prolong, keep up, protract
2 = keep alive, help, assist, aid, nourish
3 = suffer, feel, bear, experience, undergo, endure, withstand
4 = support, bear, uphold

sustained *adjective* **= continuous**, steady, constant, prolonged, perpetual, nonstop, twenty-four-seven (*slang*), unremitting

swab See **clean**

swagger *verb* **= show off** (*informal*), parade, boast, brag

swaggering See **boastful**

swallow *verb* **= gulp**, eat, drink, consume, devour, swig (*informal*), chow down (*slang*)

swamp *noun* **1 = bog**, mire, quagmire, marsh, slough, morass, fen
▶ *verb* **2 = flood**, sink, capsize, engulf, inundate, submerge
3 = overwhelm, flood, overload, inundate

swap *verb* **= exchange**, trade, switch, interchange, barter • *I swapped DVDs with my friend.*
See also: **change, substitute**

swarm *noun* **1 = multitude**, host, crowd, army, mass, herd, flock, throng, horde
▶ *verb* **2 = crowd**, mass, stream, flock, throng
3 = teem, abound, crawl, bristle

swarthy *adjective* **= dark-skinned**, black, dark, brown, dark-complexioned, dusky

swashbuckling *adjective*
= dashing, bold, daredevil, flamboyant

swathe *verb* **= wrap**, cloak, drape, shroud, envelop, bundle up

sway *verb* **1 = move from side to side**, rock, roll, swing, lean, bend
2 = influence, affect, guide, persuade, induce
▶ *noun* **3 = power**, control, authority, influence, clout (*informal*)

swear *verb* **1 = curse**, be foul-mouthed, blaspheme
2 = vow, promise
3 = declare, testify, assert, affirm, attest

swearing *noun* **= bad language**, profanity, blasphemy, cursing, foul language

swearword *noun* **= oath**, curse, profanity, obscenity, expletive, four-letter word

sweat *noun* **1 = perspiration**
2 (*Informal*) **= labour**, chore, toil, drudgery
3 (*Informal*) **= worry**, strain, panic, anxiety, distress, agitation
▶ *verb* **4 = perspire**, glow
5 (*Informal*) **= worry**, suffer, fret, agonize, torture oneself

sweaty adjective = **perspiring**, sticky, clammy

sweep verb 1 = **clear**, remove, clean, brush
2 = **sail**, pass, fly, tear, zoom, skim, glide
▷ **sweep away** See **wash**
▶ noun 3 = **arc**, move, stroke, swing, bend, curve
4 = **extent**, range, stretch, scope

sweeping adjective 1 = **wide-ranging**, global, wide, broad, extensive, comprehensive, all-inclusive, all-embracing
2 = **indiscriminate**, blanket, wholesale, exaggerated, unqualified, overstated

sweet adjective 1 = **sugary**, sweetened, cloying • *a cup of sweet tea*
OPPOSITE: sour
2 = **fragrant**, aromatic, perfumed, sweet-smelling • *the sweet smell of roses*
3 = **melodious**, musical, mellow, harmonious, tuneful • *the sweet sounds of children's singing*
4 = **charming**, kind, winning, cute, engaging, appealing, delightful, lovable, likable or likeable, agreeable
▶ noun 5 (usually plural) = **confectionery**, candy, bonbon

sweeten verb 1 = **sugar**
2 = **mollify**, appease, soothe, pacify

sweetened See **sweet**

sweetheart noun = **lover**, love, beloved, boyfriend or girlfriend, dear, darling, main squeeze (slang)

sweet-smelling See **fragrant**, **sweet**

swell verb 1 = **expand**, increase, rise, grow, balloon, bulge, enlarge, bloat, dilate, distend
▶ noun 2 = **wave**, surge, billow

swelling noun = **enlargement**, bump, lump, inflammation, bulge, distension, protuberance

sweltering adjective = **hot**, burning, oppressive, boiling, scorching, stifling

swerve verb = **veer**, turn, swing • *He swerved to avoid a truck.*

See also: **curve, dodge**

swift adjective = **quick**, fast, prompt, express, rapid, speedy, brisk, hurried • *Make a swift decision.*
OPPOSITE: slow
See also: **brief, hasty, sudden**

swiftly adverb = **quickly**, fast, rapidly, promptly, hurriedly, speedily

swiftness noun = **speed**, velocity, quickness, promptness, rapidity, speediness

swig See **drink**

swindle verb 1 = **cheat**, con, defraud, fleece, rip (someone) off (slang), trick, sting (informal)
▶ noun 2 = **fraud**, deception, con trick (informal), scam (slang), racket, rip-off (slang)

swindler noun = **cheat**, fraud, shark, rogue, trickster, con man (informal)

swine See **pig**

swing verb 1 = **sway**, rock, wave, veer, oscillate
2 (usually with round) = **turn**, curve, pivot, rotate, swivel
3 = **hang**, suspend, dangle
▶ noun 4 = **swaying**, oscillation

swipe verb 1 = **hit**, strike, slap, wallop (informal), lash out at
2 (slang) = **steal**, lift (informal), appropriate, filch, pinch (informal), purloin
▶ noun 3 = **blow**, slap, smack, wallop (informal), cuff, clout (informal)

swirl verb = **whirl**, spin, twist, churn, eddy

switch noun 1 = **change**, shift, reversal
2 = **exchange**, swap, substitution
▶ verb 3 = **change**, shift, divert, deflect, deviate
4 = **exchange**, swap, substitute

swivel verb = **turn**, spin, revolve, pivot, rotate

swollen adjective = **enlarged**, bloated, distended, inflamed, puffed up

swoon See **faint**

swoop verb 1 = **pounce**, sweep, rush, dive, descend, stoop
▶ noun 2 = **pounce**, drop, sweep,

S

rush, plunge, descent, lunge,
stoop

sycophant *noun* = **crawler**, suck
(*chiefly Canad*), brown-noser (*slang*),
fawner, flatterer, toady, yes man,
apple polisher (*informal*), groupie
(*slang*), appeaser, flunky, kiss-ass
(*informal*)

sycophantic *adjective*
= **obsequious**, slimy, crawling,
fawning, flattering, grovelling,
ingratiating, servile, smarmy
(*Brit informal*), toadying,
unctuous

syllabus *noun* = **course of study**,
curriculum

symbol *noun* = **sign**, mark, figure,
icon, logo, representation, token,
emblem, badge, emoticon, emoji

symbolic *adjective*
= **representative**, emblematic,
figurative, allegorical

symbolize *verb* = **represent**,
mean, signify, denote, typify,
personify, stand for

symmetrical *adjective*
= **balanced**, regular, in
proportion

symmetry *noun* = **balance**, order,
proportion, regularity, evenness

sympathetic *adjective* 1 = **caring**,
kind, warm, interested,
understanding, concerned,
supportive, compassionate,
pitying
2 = **like-minded**, friendly,

compatible, agreeable,
congenial, companionable

sympathize *verb* 1 = **feel for**,
pity, commiserate, condole
2 = **agree**, understand, side with

sympathizer *noun* = **supporter**,
partisan, well-wisher

sympathy *noun* 1 = **compassion**,
empathy, understanding, pity
• *My heartfelt sympathy goes out to
all the relatives.*
2 = **agreement**, affinity, rapport,
fellow feeling

symptom *noun* = **sign**, mark,
warning, indication, expression,
token

symptomatic *adjective*
= **indicative**, characteristic,
suggestive

syndicate *See* **association,
ring**

synopsis *See* **outline,
summary**

synthetic *adjective* = **artificial**,
fake, man-made

system *noun* 1 = **method**,
procedure, technique, routine
• *the advantages of the new system
over the old one*
2 = **arrangement**, structure
• *the current systems of animal
classification*
See also: **plan, process**

systematic *adjective*
= **methodical**, efficient,
organized, orderly

S

Tt

table *noun* 1 = **counter**, board, stand, bench
2 = **list**, record, schedule, roll, register, chart, catalogue, diagram, tabulation
▶ *verb* 3 = **submit**, move, suggest, propose, enter, put forward

tableau *noun* = **picture**, scene, representation, spectacle

taboo *noun* 1 = **prohibition**, ban, restriction, anathema, interdict, proscription
▶ *adjective* 2 = **forbidden**, unacceptable, outlawed, anathema, banned, prohibited, proscribed, unmentionable

tacit *adjective* = **implied**, undeclared, implicit, unspoken, inferred, understood, unexpressed, unstated

taciturn *adjective* = **uncommunicative**, quiet, silent, tight-lipped, reserved, reticent, unforthcoming, withdrawn

tack¹ *noun* 1 = **pin**, nail, pushpin, thumbtack
▶ *verb* 2 = **fasten**, fix, attach, nail, pin, affix
3 = **stitch**, baste
▷ **tack on** = **append**, add, tag, attach

tack² *noun* = **course**, plan, way, line, approach, direction, procedure, path, method, heading

tackle *verb* 1 = **deal with**, attempt, come to grips with or get to grips with, embark upon, get stuck into (*informal*), undertake, set about
2 = **confront**, challenge
3 = **intercept**, stop, halt, grab, seize, grasp
▶ *noun* 4 = **block**, challenge

5 = **equipment**, gear, apparatus, paraphernalia, accoutrements, tools, trappings

tacky¹ *adjective* = **sticky**, wet, adhesive, gummy, gluey

tacky² *adjective* (*Informal*) = **vulgar**, cheap, shoddy, tasteless, sleazy, shabby, seedy, off-color, scuzzy (*slang*), tatty

tact *noun* = **diplomacy**, sensitivity, discretion, delicacy • *He has handled the incident with great tact.*
See also: **consideration**

tactful *adjective* = **diplomatic**, sensitive, discreet • *Sorry, that wasn't a very tactful question.*
OPPOSITE: tactless

tactic *noun* = **policy**, move, approach, scheme, method, ploy, manoeuvre, stratagem
▷ **tactics** = **strategy**, playbook (*football*), campaigning, generalship, manoeuvres, plans, power play (*sports*)

tactical *adjective* = **strategic**, diplomatic, smart, shrewd, cunning

tactician *noun* = **strategist**, general, mastermind, planner

tactless *adjective* = **insensitive**, thoughtless, impolite, impolitic, inconsiderate, indelicate, indiscreet, undiplomatic, unsubtle

tag *noun* 1 = **label**, note, mark, ticket, slip, marker, identification, tab, flap
▶ *verb* 2 = **label**, mark
3 (with *along* or *on*) = **accompany**, follow, attend, trail, shadow, tail (*informal*), stalk

tail *noun* 1 = **extremity**, end, appendage, rear end, tailpiece
▷ **turn tail** = **run away**, flee, retreat, cut and run, run off,

take to one's heels

▶ *verb* **2** (*Informal*) = **follow**, track, trail, shadow, stalk

tailor *noun* **1** = **outfitter**, seamstress, clothier, costumier, couturier, dressmaker

▶ *verb* **2** = **adapt**, fashion, style, shape, adjust, modify, alter, customize, mould

taint *verb* **1** = **spoil**, damage, contaminate, ruin, corrupt, pollute, stain, tarnish, blemish, defile, sully

▶ *noun* **2** = **stain**, spot, flaw, defect, fault, blemish, blot, black mark, demerit

take *verb* **1** = **require**, demand
• *He takes three hours to get ready.*
2 = **carry**, bring, ferry, transport, fetch, convey • *I'll take these papers home and read them.*
3 = **lead**, bring, conduct, guide, escort, usher • *She took me to a Mexican restaurant.*
4 = **capture**, get, catch, acquire, secure, seize, obtain, grip, grasp
5 = **steal**, appropriate, pocket, pinch (*informal*), misappropriate, purloin
6 = **tolerate**, stand, bear, endure, stomach, withstand, abide, put up with (*informal*)
7 = **have room for**, hold, contain, accept, accommodate
8 = **subtract**, remove, eliminate, deduct
9 = **assume**, believe, consider, understand, regard, perceive, presume

See also: **choose, receive, select**
▷ **take aback** *See* **surprise**
▷ **take advantage of** *See* **impose on, profit**
▷ **take after** *See* **resemble**
▷ **take away** *See* **remove, subtract**
▷ **take care of** = **look after**, watch, protect, mind, nurse, tend, care for • *There was nobody to take care of the children.*
OPPOSITE: neglect; = **deal with**, manage, handle, attend to, cope with, see to • *"Do you need clean sheets?" "No, your husband took care of that."*

See also: **deal, process**
▷ **take down** *See* **lower, write**
▷ **take for** *See* **mistake**
▷ **take from** *See* **subtract**
▷ **take in** = **deceive**, trick, mislead, fool, con (*informal*), dupe
• *He was a real charmer who totally took me in;* = **understand**, get, appreciate, absorb, grasp, digest, comprehend, assimilate • *She seemed to take in all he said.*
See also: **admit, involve, receive**
▷ **take into account** *See* **consider**
▷ **take off** = **remove**, discard, peel off, strip off; = **lift off**, take to the air; (*Informal*) = **depart**, go, leave, disappear, abscond, decamp, slope off
▷ **take on** = **compete against**, face, fight, oppose, vie with, pit oneself against, contend with; = **hire**, engage, retain, employ, enlist, enrol; = **accept**, shoulder, tackle, undertake, step up to the plate (*informal*), agree to do; = **acquire**, assume, come to have
▷ **take out** = **extract**, remove, pull out, yank out, draw (out)
▷ **take over** *See* **possess**
▷ **take over from** *See* **replace, succeed**
▷ **take part** *See* **participate, play**
▷ **take place** = **happen**, occur, transpire (*informal*), go on, come about
▷ **take up** = **occupy**, cover, fill, consume, absorb, extend over, use up; = **start**, adopt, become involved in, engage in

> INFORMALLY SPEAKING
> **on the take**: accepting bribes
> **take five**: take a break
> **take it out of**: tire out
> **take lying down**: accept something undesirable without a protest
> **take out**: remove or get rid of

takeoff *noun* = **departure**, launch, liftoff
takeover *noun* = **merger**, coup, incorporation
taking *adjective* = **charming**,

attractive, engaging, likable or likeable, beguiling, captivating, enchanting, fetching (*informal*), prepossessing
▶ *noun*
▷ **taking on** *See* **employment**
▷ **takings** = **revenue**, take, income, earnings, proceeds, profits, receipts, returns

tale *noun* = **story**, account, legend, saga, narrative, anecdote, yarn (*informal*), fable

talent *noun* = **ability**, gift, capacity, genius, knack, flair, aptitude • *Both children have a talent for music.*

talented *adjective* = **gifted**, able, brilliant

talisman *noun* = **charm**, mascot, fetish, amulet, lucky charm

talk *verb* **1** = **speak**, chat, communicate, gossip, chatter, converse, chew the fat (*slang*), utter • *They were talking about environmental hazards.*
2 = **discuss**, negotiate, confer, confabulate, parley
3 = **inform**, blab, give the game away, let the cat out of the bag, tell all
▶ *noun* **4** = **conversation**, chat, chatter • *We had a long talk about her future.*
5 = **speech**, address, lecture, sermon, discourse • *a talk about career choices*
See also: **discussion, say, word**

> **INFORMALLY SPEAKING**
> **look who's talking**: the person criticizing is equally guilty
> **now you're talking**: now you're saying what I want to hear
> **talk big**: boast
> **you should talk**: you are guilty of the thing you are criticizing
> **talk about** *See* **discuss**
> **talk into** *See* **coax, persuade**

talkative *adjective* = **communicative**, chatty, long-winded • *His eyes grew bright, and he suddenly became very talkative.*

talker *noun* = **speaker**, lecturer, orator, chatterbox, conversationalist

talking-to *noun* = **reprimand**, criticism, rebuke, lecture, scolding, reproach, reproof, telling-off (*informal*)

tall *adjective* **1** = **high**, lofty, towering, lanky, soaring • *tall buildings*
OPPOSITE: short
2 (~ *tale*) = **implausible**, incredible, unbelievable, exaggerated, absurd, far-fetched, preposterous, cock-and-bull (*informal*)
3 (~ *order*) = **difficult**, hard, unreasonable, demanding, well-nigh impossible

tally *verb* **1** = **agree**, accord, match, fit, square, coincide, correspond, conform, harmonize, concur
▶ *noun* **2** = **record**, score, mark, total, count, reckoning, running total

tame *adjective* **1** = **domesticated**, gentle, disciplined, amenable, obedient, docile, broken, tractable
2 = **submissive**, manageable, subdued, compliant, obedient, docile, meek, unresisting
3 = **uninteresting**, boring, dull, bland, humdrum, insipid, unexciting, uninspiring, vapid
▶ *verb* **4** = **domesticate**, train, break in, house-train
5 = **discipline**, master, humble, subdue, suppress, conquer, subjugate, bring to heel

tamper *verb* = **interfere**, alter, fiddle (*informal*), meddle, tinker, fool around (*informal*), mess around

tang *See* **taste**

tangible *adjective* = **definite**, real, positive, material, actual, concrete, palpable, perceptible

tangle *noun* **1** = **knot**, mass, web, mat, muddle, jumble • *a tangle of wires*
2 = **confusion**, fix (*informal*), jam, complication, mess, mix-up, entanglement, imbroglio
▶ *verb* **3** = **twist**, catch, knot, jumble • *Dolphins can get tangled in fishing nets and drown.*

t

4 (often with *with*) = **come into conflict**, dispute, contest, contend, come up against, cross swords, lock horns

tangled *adjective* **1** = **twisted**, messy, entangled, knotted, jumbled, matted, snarled, tousled

2 = **complicated**, complex, messy, involved, confused, convoluted, knotty, mixed-up

tangy *adjective* = **sharp**, spicy, tart, pungent, piquant

tantalize *verb* = **torment**, torture, frustrate, taunt, tease, lead on

tantamount *adjective* = **equivalent**, equal, synonymous, commensurate

tantrum *noun* = **outburst**, fit, temper, flare-up, hysterics

tap[1] *verb* **1** = **knock**, strike, beat, touch, rap, pat, drum
 ▶ *noun* **2** = **knock**, touch, rap, pat

tap[2] *noun* **1** = **valve**, stopcock
 ▷ **on tap** = **on draft**; (*Informal*) = **available**, ready, at hand, in reserve, on hand
 ▶ *verb* **2** = **listen in on**, bug (*informal*), eavesdrop on
 3 = **draw off**, drain, bleed, siphon off

tape *noun* **1** = **strip**, band, ribbon
 ▶ *verb* **2** = **record**, video, tape-record
 3 = **bind**, stick, secure, seal, wrap

taper *verb* = **narrow**, thin, come to a point
 ▷ **taper off** = **lessen**, reduce, decrease, fade, dwindle, wane, subside, die away, wind down

target *noun* **1** = **goal**, end, mark, aim, object, intention, objective, ambition
 2 = **victim**, butt, scapegoat

tariff *noun* = **tax**, duty, toll, levy, excise

tarnish *verb* **1** = **stain**, taint, darken, blacken, blemish, blot, sully, discolour
 ▶ *noun* **2** = **stain**, spot, taint, blemish, blot, discoloration

tarry *See* **stay**

tart[1] *noun* = **pie**, pastry, tartlet

tart[2] *adjective* = **sharp**, bitter, acid, sour, tangy, pungent, piquant, vinegary

tart[3] *noun* = **slut**, prostitute, ho (*slang*), whore, call girl, floozy (*slang*), trollop

task *noun* = **job**, mission, duty, assignment, chore, undertaking
 • *I had the task of breaking the bad news.*
 ▷ **take to task** = **criticize**, blame, reprimand, censure, scold, reproach, upbraid, reprove, tell off (*informal*)
 See also: **work**

taste *noun* **1** = **flavour**, tang • *I like the taste of this juice.*
 2 = **mouthful**, bite, sip • *I'll have a taste of your dessert.*
 3 = **liking**, appetite, penchant (*formal*), fondness • *a taste for adventure*
 4 = **refinement**, style, judgment, discrimination, appreciation, elegance, sophistication, discernment
 ▶ *verb* **5** = **distinguish**, perceive, differentiate, discern
 6 = **sample**, try, test, sip, savour
 7 = **have a flavour of**, savour of, smack of
 8 = **experience**, know, undergo, encounter, meet with, partake of

tasteful *adjective* = **refined**, artistic, elegant, stylish, exquisite, polished, cultured, cultivated, discriminating, in good taste

tasteless *adjective* **1** = **bland**, insipid • *The fish was overcooked and tasteless.*
 OPPOSITE: tasty
 2 = **vulgar**, flashy, tacky (*informal*), gaudy, garish, tawdry • *a house crammed with tasteless ornaments*
 OPPOSITE: tasteful
 See also: **crude**

tasty *adjective* = **delicious**, palatable, luscious, appetizing • *The food was very tasty.*
 OPPOSITE: tasteless

tattered *See* **worn out**

tatters *noun*
 ▷ **in tatters** = **ragged**, down at

t

heel, in rags, in shreds, ripped, tattered, threadbare, torn

tattoo *See* **parade**

tatty *adjective* = **shabby**, dilapidated, ragged, neglected, run-down, bedraggled, down at heel, threadbare, worn

taunt *verb* **1** = **jeer**, insult, provoke, mock, ridicule, tease, deride, torment
▶ *noun* **2** = **jeer**, insult, dig, provocation, ridicule, sarcasm, derision, gibe, teasing

taut *adjective* = **tight**, tense, strained, rigid, stretched, flexed, stressed

tavern *noun* = **bar**, pub, inn, alehouse (*archaic*), hostelry, parlour (*Canad*), brasserie (*Canad Queb*), public house, booze can (*Canad*), beer parlour (*Canad*), beverage room (*Canad*)

tawdry *adjective* = **vulgar**, cheap, flashy, gaudy, gimcrack, tasteless, tacky (*informal*), tatty, tinselly

tax *noun* **1** = **duty**, tariff, levy (*formal*) • *the tax on new cars*
▶ *verb* **2** = **strain**, stretch, drain, exhaust, sap • *Those kids tax my patience.*
3 = **charge**, rate, assess

taxing *adjective* = **demanding**, tough, stressful, onerous, exacting, exhausting, punishing, sapping, tiring, trying

teach *verb* = **instruct**, school, coach, train, drill, educate, tutor • *She taught me to read.*
See also: **lecture, show**

teacher *noun* = **instructor**, coach, professor, guru, lecturer, tutor • *a geography teacher*

team *noun* **1** = **group**, side, crew, band, gang, squad, troupe • *the football team*
▶ *verb* **2** (often with *up*) = **join forces**, unite, co-operate, collaborate, link up, pair up, work together • *A friend suggested that we team up for a working vacation.*
See also: **party, staff**

teammate *See* **partner**

teamwork *noun* = **cooperation**, unity, collaboration, harmony, coordination, fellowship, esprit de corps

tear *noun* **1** = **rip**, hole, split, scratch, rupture • *a tear in the curtains*
▶ *verb* **2** = **rip**, split, scratch, shred, rupture • *She nearly tore my jacket.*
3 = **rush**, charge, shoot, race, fly, speed, dash, zoom, dart • *He tore through busy streets in a high-speed chase.*

tearful *adjective* = **weeping**, blubbering, crying, in tears, lachrymose, sobbing, weepy (*informal*), whimpering

tears *plural noun* = **crying**, blubbering, sobbing, wailing, weeping
▷ **in tears** = **crying**, distressed, blubbering, sobbing, weeping

tease *verb* = **make fun of**, needle (*informal*), mock, taunt, pull someone's chain (*informal*) • *He used to tease me about wanting to act.*
See also: **bully, joke, pick on, provoke**

technical *adjective* = **scientific**, specialist, skilled, specialized, technological, hi-tech *or* high-tech

technique *noun* **1** = **method**, way, system, approach, style, procedure, manner, means, mode
2 = **skill**, performance, touch, execution, craft, proficiency, artistry, craftsmanship

tedious *adjective* = **boring**, dull, dreary, drab, tiresome, monotonous, mind-numbing, humdrum, irksome, laborious, wearisome

tedium *noun* = **boredom**, routine, drabness, dreariness, dullness, monotony, sameness, tediousness

teem *See* **crawl, rain**

teeming[1] *adjective* = **full**, alive, thick, abundant, brimming, bristling, bursting, crawling, overflowing, swarming

t

teeming[2] *adjective* = **pouring**, pelting, raining cats and dogs (*informal*)

teenager *noun* = **youth**, girl, boy, minor, adolescent, juvenile

teeter *verb* = **wobble**, rock, sway, stagger, waver, seesaw, totter

teetotaller, teetotaler *noun* = **nondrinker**, abstainer

telepathy *noun* = **mind-reading**, E.S.P., sixth sense

telephone *noun* 1 = **phone**, line, landline, cell, handset, horn (*informal*), iPhone (*trademark*), blower (*informal*), cell phone, camera phone, smart phone, video phone, carphone, internet phone
▶ *verb* 2 = **call**, phone, dial

telescope *noun* 1 = **spyglass**, glass
▶ *verb* 2 = **shorten**, contract, shrink, compress, abbreviate, condense, abridge

television *noun* = **TV**, small screen (*informal*), the tube (*slang*)

tell *verb* 1 = **inform**, advise, notify, acquaint, apprise • *They told us the dreadful news.*
2 = **order**, direct, command, instruct, call upon, enjoin • *A passerby told the driver to move his car.*
3 = **see**, discern • *I could tell he was scared.*
4 = **describe**, report, relate, portray, depict, recount, chronicle, narrate
5 = **distinguish**, identify, discriminate, differentiate, discern
6 = **have effect** *or* **take effect**, count, register, weigh, carry weight, make its presence felt, take its toll
See also: **announce**
▷ **tell a lie** *See* **lie**
▷ **tell apart** *See* **distinguish**
▷ **tell off** = **reprimand**, censure, berate, chide, lecture, rebuke, scold, reproach
▷ **tell on** *See* **inform on**
▷ **tell the difference** *See* **distinguish**

INFORMALLY SPEAKING
tell it like it is: tell the plain truth
tell me about it: I have experienced exactly what you mean
you're telling me: I agree completely

telling *adjective* = **effective**, significant, powerful, impressive, decisive, influential, considerable, marked, striking, forceful

telling-off *noun* = **reprimand**, criticism, rebuke, lecture, scolding, reproach, reproof, talking-to

temerity *noun* = **audacity**, front, nerve (*informal*), recklessness, chutzpah (*informal*), boldness, effrontery, impudence, rashness

temper *noun* 1 = **rage**, passion, fury, tantrum, bad mood
2 = **irritability**, passion, resentment, hot-headedness, irascibility, petulance, surliness
3 = **self-control**, cool (*slang*), composure, calmness, equanimity
4 = **frame of mind**, mind, nature, constitution, mood, disposition, humor, temperament
▶ *verb* 5 = **moderate**, soften, restrain, lessen, mitigate, soothe, assuage, mollify, tone down
6 = **strengthen**, toughen, harden, anneal

temperament *noun* 1 = **nature**, character, outlook, constitution, personality, temper, bent, disposition, make-up, humour
2 = **moodiness**, anger, volatility, excitability, hot-headedness, petulance

temperamental *adjective*
1 = **moody**, emotional, sensitive, volatile, irritable, touchy, capricious, excitable, highly strung, hypersensitive
2 = **unreliable**, unpredictable, inconsistent, erratic, inconstant

temperance *noun*
1 = **moderation**, restraint,

discretion, self-control, self-restraint, continence, forbearance, self-discipline
2 = **teetotalism**, abstinence, sobriety, abstemiousness

temperate adjective **1** = **mild**, fair, cool, calm, moderate, gentle, pleasant
2 = **self-restrained**, calm, moderate, reasonable, mild, sensible, dispassionate, composed, even-tempered, self-controlled

tempest noun = **storm**, hurricane, tornado, cyclone, typhoon, squall, gale

tempestuous adjective
1 = **stormy**, turbulent, windy, gusty, raging, blustery, inclement, squally
2 = **passionate**, violent, wild, emotional, intense, heated, stormy, furious, turbulent, boisterous

template See **pattern**

temple noun = **shrine**, church, sanctuary, place of worship

tempo See **rate**, **rhythm**

temporarily adverb = **briefly**, momentarily, fleetingly, for the time being, pro tem

temporary adjective = **impermanent**, interim, passing, provisional, momentary, fleeting, transient, ephemeral, transitory • a temporary loss of memory
OPPOSITE: permanent

tempt verb = **entice**, lure, seduce • Don't tempt me to eat anything else. See also: **attract**

temptation noun = **enticement**, pull, lure, inducement, seduction, allurement, tantalization

tempting adjective = **inviting**, attractive, alluring, seductive, appetizing, enticing, mouthwatering, tantalizing

tenable adjective = **sound**, reasonable, viable, rational, plausible, justifiable, believable, arguable, defensible

tenacious adjective **1** = **firm**, strong, tight, iron, forceful, unshakable, clinging, immovable
2 = **stubborn**, persistent, adamant, determined, steadfast, resolute, dogged, unyielding, obdurate, obstinate, unswerving

tenacity noun = **perseverance**, application, resolve, determination, persistence, doggedness, obduracy, steadfastness, stubbornness

tenancy noun = **lease**, possession, residence, occupancy, renting

tenant noun = **leaseholder**, resident, renter, occupant, inhabitant, occupier, lessee

tend[1] verb **1** = **be inclined**, be apt, be liable, be prone, have a tendency • I tend to forget things.
2 = **go**, point, head, bear, aim, lean (toward), make for

tend[2] verb = **take care of**, nurse, care for, look after • the way we tend our cattle

tendency noun = **inclination**, leaning, propensity • a tendency to be critical

tender[1] adjective **1** = **gentle**, kind, warm, sensitive, loving, compassionate, caring, affectionate • tender loving care
OPPOSITE: tough
2 = **sore**, sensitive, raw, painful, aching, bruised, inflamed • My stomach felt very tender.
3 = **vulnerable**, young, sensitive, raw, youthful, inexperienced, immature, impressionable
See also: **romantic**

tender[2] verb **1** = **offer**, hand in • She tendered her resignation from the job.
▶ noun **2** = **estimate**, bid, package, submission • Builders will be asked to submit a tender for the work.
▷ **legal tender** = **currency**, money, cash
See also: **submit**

tenderness noun **1** = **gentleness**, care, love, consideration, sympathy, affection, compassion, warmth, kindness, sentimentality

2 = soreness, pain, sensitivity, inflammation

tenet See **belief**

tense adjective **1 = nervous**, anxious, edgy, jittery, uptight (informal), jumpy • Never had she seen him so tense.
OPPOSITE: calm
2 = stressful, anxious, nerve-racking • the tense atmosphere during the last moments of the game
3 = tight, strained, rigid, taut • jaw muscles tense with anger
OPPOSITE: relaxed
▶ verb **4 = tighten**, strain, stretch, brace, flex

tension noun **1 = strain**, pressure, stress, anxiety, suspense, hostility, apprehension, nervousness, unease
2 = tightness, pressure, stress, stiffness, rigidity, stretching, tautness

tentative adjective
1 = unconfirmed, experimental, indefinite, provisional, speculative, unsettled, conjectural
2 = hesitant, cautious, uncertain, unsure, undecided, doubtful, timid, diffident, faltering

tenuous adjective **= slight**, weak, shaky, doubtful, dubious, sketchy, flimsy, nebulous, insubstantial

tenure See **possession**

tepid adjective **1 = lukewarm**, warmish
2 = half-hearted, cool, indifferent, lukewarm, apathetic, unenthusiastic

term noun **1 = period**, time, session, stretch, spell • Her term as president of the student council was about to end.
2 = word, name, expression, designation • the medical term for a heart attack
▶ verb **3 = call**, name, label, style, dub, entitle, designate
See also: **length**

terminal adjective **1 = fatal**, deadly, killing, lethal, incurable, mortal

2 = final, last, extreme, ultimate, utmost, concluding
▶ noun **3 = terminus**, station, depot, end of the line

terminate verb **= end**, close, stop, finish, complete, conclude, cease, discontinue, abort

termination noun **= ending**, end, finish, abortion, conclusion, completion, cessation, discontinuation
▷ **termination of employment** See **fire**, **sack**

terminology noun **= language**, vocabulary, jargon, nomenclature, phraseology, terms

terminus noun **= end of the line**, station, garage, depot, last stop

terms plural noun **1 = conditions**, provisions, proviso, stipulations • the terms of the agreement
2 = relationship, status, standing, footing, relations
See also: **condition**

terrain noun **= ground**, country, land, landscape, going, topography

terrestrial adjective **= earthly**, global, worldly

terrible adjective **1 = awful**, desperate, horrible, horrendous, appalling, rotten, dreadful, horrid, frightful • a terrible illness
2 = bad, horrible, dire, awful, appalling, rotten, dreadful, abysmal • That is a truly terrible haircut.
OPPOSITE: excellent
See also: **severe**

terribly adverb **= extremely**, very, seriously, desperately, thoroughly, awfully (informal), decidedly, exceedingly

terrific adjective **1 = great**, huge, intense, tremendous, enormous, fearful, gigantic
2 (Informal) **= excellent**, amazing, wonderful, brilliant, fantastic (informal), sensational (informal), outstanding, magnificent, superb, marvellous, stupendous

terrified adjective **= frightened**, scared, alarmed, panic-stricken,

appalled, horrified, horror-
struck, petrified

terrify verb = **frighten**, shock,
scare, alarm, horrify, appall,
terrorize, make one's hair stand
on end

terrifying adjective = **frightening**,
scary (informal), fearful,
daunting, appalling, dreadful,
fearsome, hair-raising,
alarming, intimidating,
unnerving, baleful, menacing

territory noun = **district**, country,
province, state, area, land,
nation, domain, dominion
• disputed territory
See also: **colony, field, habitat,
region**

terror noun 1 = **fear**, shock, alarm,
panic, horror, anxiety, dread,
fright
2 = **scourge**, devil, monster,
bogeyman, fiend, bugbear

terrorism See **violence**

terrorize verb browbeat = **bully**,
threaten, intimidate, menace,
coerce, oppress

terse adjective 1 = **concise**, short,
brief, condensed, succinct,
laconic, monosyllabic, pithy
2 = **curt**, short, abrupt, snappy,
brusque

test verb 1 = **check**, try, assess, try
out, run up the flagpole (informal)
• The company is testing a new
product.
▶ noun 2 = **check**, trial,
assessment • the banning of nuclear
tests
See also: **exam, examine**

testament noun 1 = **proof**,
evidence, witness, tribute,
testimony, demonstration
2 = **will**, last wishes

testify verb = **bear witness**, state,
swear, assert, certify, affirm,
vouch, corroborate, attest

testimonial noun = **tribute**,
recommendation, reference,
endorsement, commendation

testimony noun 1 = **evidence**,
statement, submission,
affidavit, deposition
2 = **proof**, support, evidence,
demonstration, indication,

verification, manifestation,
corroboration

testing adjective = **difficult**,
tough, rigorous, arduous,
strenuous, demanding,
exacting, challenging,
searching, taxing

tether noun 1 = **rope**, lead, chain,
leash, halter, fetter
▷ **at the end of one's tether**
= **exasperated**, at one's wits'
end, exhausted
▶ verb 2 = **tie**, secure, chain,
bind, fasten, fetter

text noun 1 = **contents**, body
2 = **words**, wording

textbook See **book**

textiles See **cloth**

texture noun = **feel**, consistency
• the bumpy texture of an orange
See also: **finish**

thank verb = **say thank you**, show
one's appreciation

thankful adjective = **grateful**,
pleased, appreciative, relieved,
indebted, beholden, obliged

thankless adjective
= **unrewarding**, fruitless,
unprofitable, unappreciated,
unrequited

thanks plural noun = **gratitude**,
credit, recognition,
appreciation, kudos,
acknowledgment, gratefulness
▷ **thanks to = because of**,
through, as a result of, due to,
owing to

thaw verb = **melt**, warm, dissolve,
soften, liquefy, defrost, unfreeze

theatrical adjective 1 = **dramatic**,
Thespian
2 = **exaggerated**, dramatic,
affected, showy, histrionic,
mannered, melodramatic,
ostentatious, stagy

theft noun = **stealing**, robbery
• the theft of classified documents

theme noun 1 = **subject**, idea,
topic, keynote, subject matter
2 = **motif**, leitmotif, through-
line

theological adjective = **religious**,
doctrinal, ecclesiastical

theoretical adjective = **abstract**,
academic, speculative,

t

hypothetical, conjectural, notional

theorize *verb* = **speculate**, project, suppose, guess, formulate, hypothesize, conjecture, propound

theory *noun* = **hypothesis**, conjecture, supposition
• *Darwin's theory of evolution*

therapeutic *adjective* = **beneficial**, good, healing, corrective, remedial, restorative, curative, salutary

therapist *noun* = **healer**, physician

therapy *noun* = **remedy**, treatment, cure, healing

there *See* **present**

therefore *adverb* = **consequently**, so, thus, hence, as a result, for that reason • *Muscles need lots of fuel and therefore burn lots of calories.*

thesis *noun* 1 = **dissertation**, paper, essay, treatise, monograph
2 = **proposition**, view, idea, proposal, opinion, theory, contention, hypothesis

thick *adjective* 1 = **wide**, fat • *a thick stone wall*
OPPOSITE: thin
2 = **condensed**, concentrated, clotted • *thick soup*
OPPOSITE: watery
3 = **dense**, lush, bristling, luxuriant • *thick dark hair*
OPPOSITE: sparse
4 (*Informal*) = **friendly**, close, familiar, intimate, devoted, inseparable, pally (*informal*)
5 = **full**, packed, covered, brimming, bristling, bursting, crawling, swarming, teeming
▷ **a bit thick** = **unfair**, unreasonable, unjust
See also: **broad, dim, slow, stupid**

thicken *verb* = **set**, clot, condense, congeal • *The clouds thickened.*
OPPOSITE: thin

thicket *noun* = **wood**, brake, covert, grove, coppice, copse

thickset *adjective* = **stocky**, strong, heavy, muscular, bulky, sturdy, burly, well-built

thief *noun* = **robber**, burglar, crook, shoplifter, mugger, pickpocket, finger man (*slang*), housebreaker, pilferer • *a car thief*

thieve *verb* = **steal**, filch, rob, pinch (*informal*), swipe (*slang*), pilfer, purloin

thin *adjective* 1 = **narrow**, fine, slim, attenuated • *The material was too thin.*
OPPOSITE: thick
2 = **slim**, slight, lean, spare, skinny, slender, skeletal, bony, scrawny, emaciated, spindly • *a tall, thin man*
3 = **meagre**, scarce, scattered, sparse, deficient, skimpy, scanty, wispy
4 = **watery**, weak, diluted, runny
• *thin soup*
5 = **delicate**, fine, sheer, flimsy, diaphanous, filmy, gossamer, unsubstantial
6 = **unconvincing**, poor, weak, inadequate, lousy (*slang*), lame, superficial, feeble, flimsy

thing *noun* 1 = **article**, object
• *What's that thing doing here?*
2 (*Informal*) = **obsession**, mania, preoccupation, phobia, fixation, fetish, bee in one's bonnet, hang-up (*informal*)
▷ **things** = **possessions**, stuff, gear, belongings, effects • *She told him to take all his things with him.*
See also: **complex, item**

> INFORMALLY SPEAKING
> **know a thing or two**: be experienced
> **make a (big) thing (out) of**: give too much importance to
> **make a good thing of**: profit from

think *verb* 1 = **ponder**, consider, reflect, deliberate, contemplate, muse, meditate, mull over, cogitate, ruminate • *Let's think what we can do next.*
2 = **believe**, hold, consider, judge, imagine, deem, reckon
• *I think you're the best rower on the team.*
See also: **assume, expect, feel, guess, suppose**

t

▷ **think about** See **consider, contemplate**

▷ **think of** See **contemplate, regard**

▷ **think up** = **devise**, create, invent, concoct, visualize, come up with, contrive, dream up

thinker noun = **philosopher**, brain (informal), mastermind, sage, theorist, intellect (informal), wise man

thinking noun 1 = **reasoning**, position, view, idea, opinion, theory, judgment, conjecture
▸ adjective 2 = **thoughtful**, intelligent, rational, reasoning, philosophical, reflective, meditative, contemplative

thin-skinned See **sensitive**

thirst noun 1 = **thirstiness**, drought, dryness
2 = **craving**, desire, passion, appetite, longing, yearning, hankering, keenness

thirsty adjective 1 = **parched**, dry, arid, dehydrated
2 = **eager**, hungry, avid, greedy, craving, desirous, longing, yearning

thorn noun = **prickle**, spike, spine, barb

thorny adjective = **prickly**, sharp, barbed, pointed, spiky, spiny, bristly

thorough adjective = **full**, complete, comprehensive, intensive, exhaustive, painstaking, meticulous, scrupulous • a thorough examination
See also: **absolute, careful, utter**

thoroughbred adjective = **purebred**, pedigree

thoroughfare noun = **road**, way, street, highway, passage, avenue, passageway

thoroughly adverb 1 = **carefully**, fully, efficiently, painstakingly, meticulously, intensively, conscientiously, assiduously, exhaustively, from top to bottom, scrupulously
2 = **completely**, quite, absolutely, totally, perfectly, utterly, downright, to the hilt

though conjunction 1 = **although**, while, notwithstanding, even if, even though
▸ adverb 2 = **nevertheless**, still, however, yet, notwithstanding, nonetheless, for all that

thought noun 1 = **idea**, view, opinion, notion • his thoughts on love
2 = **thinking**, consideration, deliberation, reflection, meditation, contemplation
• After much thought I decided to become a teacher.
3 = **consideration**, study, attention, regard, scrutiny, heed
4 = **intention**, plan, aim, idea, design, object, purpose, notion
5 = **expectation**, hope, prospect, anticipation, aspiration

thoughtful adjective 1 = **pensive**, reflective, contemplative • She was looking very thoughtful.
2 = **considerate**, kind, caring, attentive • a thoughtful and caring man
OPPOSITE: thoughtless
3 = **well-thought-out**, prudent, astute, canny
See also: **humane**

thoughtless adjective
= **inconsiderate**, insensitive, tactless • It was thoughtless of her to mention it.
See also: **irresponsible, unkind**

thrash verb 1 = **beat**, belt (informal), cane, flog, paddle, whip, scourge, spank
2 = **defeat**, beat, crush, slaughter (informal), trounce, run rings around (informal), wipe the floor with (informal)
3 = **thresh**, jerk, flail, writhe, toss and turn
▷ **thrash out** = **settle**, debate, discuss, resolve, solve, argue out, have out, talk over

thrashing noun 1 = **beating**, belting (informal), flogging, punishment, whipping
2 = **defeat**, beating, hammering (informal), trouncing

thread noun 1 = **strand**, line, string, fibre, yarn, filament

2 = theme, plot, direction, drift, story line, train of thought
▶ *verb* **3 = pass**, pick or pick one's way, ease, squeeze through
threadbare *adjective* **1 = shabby**, old, ragged, down at heel, frayed, tattered, tatty, worn
2 = hackneyed, familiar, conventional, tired, stale, commonplace, overused, well-worn, trite, stereotyped
threat *noun* **1 = threatening remark**, menace • *death threats*
2 = danger, risk, hazard, menace • *the threat of tropical storms*
3 = warning, omen, presage, foreboding, foreshadowing, portent, writing on the wall
threaten *verb* **1 = menace**, make threats to • *He threatened to reveal the secret.*
2 = endanger, jeopardize, put at risk, put in jeopardy • *The new department store is threatening the business of the smaller shops.*
3 = foreshadow, impend, presage, forebode, portend
threatening *adjective*
1 = menacing, bullying, intimidatory
2 = ominous, grim, sinister, inauspicious, forbidding
threatening remark *See* **threat**
threshold *noun* **1 = entrance**, door, doorstep, doorway
2 = start, opening, beginning, dawn, brink, verge, outset, inception
3 = lower limit, minimum
thrift *noun* **= economy**, saving, prudence, frugality, carefulness, parsimony, thriftiness
thrifty *adjective* **= economical**, careful, prudent, frugal • *thrifty shoppers*
thrill *noun* **1 = excitement**, high (*informal*), kick (*informal*) • *the thrill of the game*
▶ *verb* **2 = excite**, give a kick (*informal*) • *It thrilled me to see her looking so happy.*
See also: **delight**
thrilled *See* **excited**

thrilling *adjective* **= exciting**, sensational, rousing, electrifying, gripping, riveting, stimulating, stirring
thrive *verb* **= flourish**, prosper, do well • *His company continues to thrive.*
See also: **succeed**
thriving *adjective* **= flourishing**, well, healthy, successful, prosperous, blooming, booming, burgeoning
throb *verb* **1 = pulsate**, beat, pound, thump, pulse, vibrate, palpitate
▶ *noun* **2 = pulse**, beat, thump, vibration, thumping, palpitation, pounding, pulsating
throng *noun* **1 = crowd**, host, mass, pack, crush, mob, swarm, multitude, horde
▶ *verb* **2 = crowd**, pack, flock, converge, congregate, mill around, swarm around
throttle *verb* **= strangle**, choke, garrotte, strangulate
through *preposition* **1 = between**, by, past
2 = because of, via, by means of, by way of, using
3 = during, in, throughout
▶ *adjective* **4 = finished**, completed, done, ended
▶ *adverb*
▷ **through and through = completely**, fully, totally, entirely, altogether, thoroughly, wholly, utterly
throughout *adverb* **= right through**, everywhere, all over, from start to finish
throw *verb* **1 = hurl**, pitch, cast, toss, lob, fling, sling, chuck • *throwing a tennis ball against a wall*
2 (*Informal*) **= confuse**, baffle, astonish, faze, disconcert, confound, dumbfound
▷ **throw away = discard**, reject, dump (*informal*), scrap, ditch (*slang*), jettison, dispense with, dispose of, get rid of, throw out
▷ **throw out** *See* **discard, dump**
▶ *noun* **3 = toss**, pitch, lob (*informal*), fling, sling, heave

INFORMALLY SPEAKING
throw cold water on:
discourage
throw in: add as a bonus
throw off: produce something
in a casual way
throw up: vomit
throw yourself into: do
enthusiastically

throwaway adjective
1 = **disposable**, one-use,
nonreturnable
2 = **casual**, passing, careless,
offhand, understated

thrust verb **1** = **push**, force, drive,
plunge, jam, propel, shove, ram
▶ noun **2** = **push**, drive, stab,
poke, shove, prod, lunge
3 = **momentum**, impetus

thud noun, verb = **thump**, crash,
knock, smack, clunk

thug noun = **ruffian**, tough,
bandit, hooligan, hoodlum • *a
gang of armed thugs*

thump noun **1** = **thud**, crash,
bang, clunk, thwack
2 = **blow**, knock, punch, rap,
smack, wallop (*informal*), whack,
clout (*informal*)
▶ verb **3** = **strike**, hit, beat,
pound, knock, punch, smack,
wallop (*informal*), clobber (*slang*),
whack, clout (*informal*)

thunder noun **1** = **rumble**, crash,
explosion, boom
▶ verb **2** = **rumble**, crash, boom,
roar, resound, reverberate, peal
3 = **shout**, roar, yell, bark, bellow

thunderous adjective = **loud**,
noisy, tumultuous, ear-
splitting, booming, deafening,
resounding, roaring

thunderstruck adjective
= **amazed**, shocked, staggered,
dumbfounded, open-mouthed,
astonished, astounded,
flabbergasted (*informal*),
stunned, taken aback

thus adverb **1** = **therefore**, so,
then, accordingly, hence,
consequently, ergo, for this
reason, on that account
2 = **in this way**, so, as follows,
like this

thwart verb = **frustrate**, prevent,

foil, hinder, stymie, obstruct,
snooker, outwit

tick¹ noun **1** = **mark**, stroke, dash
2 = **clicking**, tapping, ticktock
▶ verb **3** = **mark**, indicate, check
off
4 = **click**, tap, ticktock

tick² noun = **mite**, bug, insect

tick³ noun = **credit**, account

ticket noun **1** = **voucher**, pass,
card, slip, certificate, token,
coupon
2 = **label**, card, slip, tag, marker,
sticker, tab, docket

tidbit noun = **delicacy**, treat,
snack, dainty, morsel

tide noun **1** = **current**, flow,
stream, ebb, undertow, tideway
2 = **trend**, movement, direction,
drift, tendency

tidings See **news**

tidy adjective **1** = **neat**, orderly • *a
tidy desk*
OPPOSITE: untidy
2 (*Informal*) = **considerable**, large,
healthy, substantial, generous,
sizable *or* sizeable, handsome,
ample, goodly
▶ verb **3** = **neaten**, straighten,
spruce up • *He tidied the garage.*
OPPOSITE: mess up

tie verb **1** = **fasten**, secure, bind,
lash, knot, rope, tether, truss
• *They tied the ends of the bag
securely.*
OPPOSITE: untie
2 = **restrict**, limit, bind, hamper,
hinder, restrain, confine
3 = **draw**, match, equal
▷ **tie up** See **secure**
▶ noun
4 = **draw**, deadlock, dead heat,
saw-off (*Canad*) • *The game ended
in a tie.*
5 = **bond**, connection,
relationship, affiliation, affinity
• *I have very close ties with their
family.*
6 = **fastening**, link, bond, cord,
knot, fetter, ligature
See also: **association, attach,
join**

tier noun = **row**, level, line, bank,
story, rank, layer, stratum

tiff See **disagreement, squabble**

t

tight adjective **1** = **close-fitting**, snug, constricted • *The shoes are too tight.*
OPPOSITE: loose
2 = **secure**, firm • *a tight knot*
3 = **taut**, tense, rigid • *Pull the rope tight to make a knot.*
OPPOSITE: slack
4 = **limited**, close, narrow, cramped, constricted
5 (*Informal*) = **miserly**, mean, stingy, grasping, niggardly, parsimonious, tightfisted
6 = **close**, even, evenly-balanced, well-matched
▷ **tight spot** See **hole**, **predicament**

tighten verb = **squeeze**, close, narrow, constrict

tightly See **fast**

till¹ verb = **cultivate**, work, dig, plow

till² noun = **cash register**, cash box

tilt verb **1** = **slant**, list, tip, lean, slope, incline, cant • *He tilted his chair back on two legs.*
▶ noun **2** = **slope**, list, grade, angle, incline, slant, gradient, camber • *the tilt of the earth's axis*
3 (*Medieval history*) = **joust**, fight, tournament, combat, duel, lists
▷ **full tilt**, **at full tilt** = **full speed**, headlong, for dear life

timber noun = **wood**, beams, boards, logs, planks, trees

timbre noun = **tone**, ring, resonance, colour

time noun **1** = **period**, while, stretch, spell, interval • *I enjoyed my time in New Brunswick.*
RELATED WORD
adjective: temporal
2 = **occasion**, point, stage, instance, juncture
3 (*Music*) = **tempo**, beat, measure, rhythm
▷ **time off** = **vacation**, leave, holiday, leisure
▶ verb **4** = **schedule**, set • *We had timed our visit for the school break.*
See also: **chance**, **life**, **moment**, **space**, **term**

timeless adjective = **eternal**, permanent, lasting, enduring, immortal, ageless, everlasting, changeless

timely adjective = **opportune**, appropriate, suitable, convenient, judicious, well-timed, propitious, seasonable

timetable noun = **schedule**, program, list, agenda, calendar, diary, curriculum

timid adjective = **nervous**, shy, cowardly, bashful, diffident • *a timid kitten*
OPPOSITE: bold
See also: **meek**

timorous adjective = **timid**, shy, fearful, apprehensive, coy, bashful, diffident, faint-hearted, shrinking

tinge noun **1** = **tint**, shade, colour
2 = **trace**, drop, bit, touch, suggestion, dash, smattering, sprinkling
▶ verb **3** = **tint**, colour, imbue, suffuse

tingle verb **1** = **prickle**, sting, itch, tickle, have goose pimples
▶ noun **2** = **prickling**, thrill, shiver, itch, quiver, goose pimples, pins and needles (*informal*)

tinker verb = **meddle**, play, fiddle (*informal*), dabble, putter, mess around

tint noun **1** = **shade**, tone, colour, hue
2 = **dye**, wash, rinse, tinge, tincture
▶ verb **3** = **dye**, colour

tiny adjective = **minute**, miniature, diminutive, negligible, microscopic • *The living room is tiny.*
OPPOSITE: huge

tip¹ noun **1** = **end**, point, top, head, summit, peak, pinnacle, extremity
▶ verb **2** = **cap**, top, finish, crown, surmount

tip² noun **1** = **gratuity**, gift
2 = **hint**, warning, suggestion, clue, pointer, heads-up
▶ verb **3** = **reward**, remunerate
4 = **advise**, suggest, warn, caution, forewarn

tip³ *verb* **1 = tilt**, list, lean, incline, slant
2 = dump, empty, unload, pour out
▷ **tip over** See **overturn**
▶ *noun* **3 = dump**, refuse heap, rubbish heap

tipple *verb* **1 = drink**, indulge (*informal*), imbibe, swig, quaff, tope
▶ *noun* **2 = alcohol**, drink, liquor, booze (*informal*)

tipsy *adjective* = **drunk**, happy, fuzzy, mellow, three sheets to the wind

tiptoe See **steal**

tirade *noun* = **outburst**, lecture, diatribe, fulmination, harangue, invective

tire *verb* **1 = exhaust**, drain, fatigue • *Early-morning practice sessions often tire me.*
2 = bore, irk, irritate, weary, exasperate
▷ **tire out** See **exhaust**
See also: **wear out**

tired *adjective* **1 = exhausted**, weary, drowsy, sleepy, drained, fatigued, tuckered out (*informal*), worn out • *I'm too tired to go out tonight.*
2 = bored, sick, weary, fed up
3 = hackneyed, old, stale, well-worn, corny (*slang*), trite, clichéd, outworn, threadbare
See also: **sick of**

tireless *adjective* = **energetic**, vigorous, resolute, industrious, indefatigable, unflagging, untiring

tiresome *adjective* = **boring**, dull, tedious, irksome, irritating, trying, vexatious, wearing, wearisome

tiring *adjective* = **exhausting**, tough, arduous, strenuous, demanding, exacting, laborious, wearing

titillate *verb* = **excite**, interest, thrill, stimulate, tease, arouse, tantalize

titillating *adjective* = **exciting**, provocative, lurid, suggestive, interesting, arousing, stimulating, teasing

title *noun* **1 = name**, term, handle (*slang*), designation, moniker *or* monicker (*slang*)
2 = championship, crown
3 = ownership, right, claim, privilege, entitlement, prerogative
▷ **title holder** See **champion**

titter *verb* = **laugh**, chuckle, giggle, chortle (*informal*), snigger

tizzy *noun* (*Informal*) = **panic**, state (*informal*), sweat (*informal*), agitation, commotion, fluster

toady *noun* **1 = sycophant**, brown-noser (*slang*), creep (*slang*), lackey, minion, flatterer, flunkey, hanger-on, scuzzbucket (*slang*), yes man
▶ *verb* **2 = fawn on**, brown-nose (*slang*), flatter, grovel, kiss ass (*slang*), kowtow to, pander to, suck up to (*informal*)

toast¹ *verb* = **brown**, warm, heat, grill, roast

toast² *noun* **1 = tribute**, health, pledge, salute, compliment, salutation
2 = favourite, hero *or* heroine, darling
▶ *verb* **3 = drink to**, salute, drink the health of *or* drink to the health of

today's See **current**

toddler See **child**

to-do See **fuss**

together *adverb* **1 = collectively**, jointly, en masse, in unison, shoulder to shoulder, side by side • *We went on long bicycle rides together.*
2 = simultaneously, concurrently, as one, at once, with one accord • *Three horses crossed the finish line together.*
▶ *adjective* **3** (*Informal*) = **composed**, well-balanced, well-adjusted

toil *noun* **1 = hard work**, effort, application, exertion, drudgery, elbow grease (*informal*), sweat, slog
▶ *verb* **2 = work**, drudge, struggle, sweat (*informal*), slave, strive, labour, slog, work one's fingers to the bone

toilet noun = **lavatory**, can (slang), bathroom, washroom, restroom, latrine, commode, comfort station, men's room, ladies' room, urinal, privy, water closet, W.C., honey-bucket (slang)

token noun 1 = **symbol**, sign, note, mark, indication, expression, representation, badge
▶ adjective 2 = **nominal**, symbolic, minimal, hollow, superficial, perfunctory

tolerable adjective 1 = **bearable**, acceptable • The pain was tolerable. OPPOSITE: unbearable
2 = **acceptable**, OK (informal), reasonable, adequate, so-so, passable • a tolerable salary
See also: **decent**

tolerance noun 1 = **broad-mindedness**, indulgence, forbearance, open-mindedness, permissiveness
2 = **endurance**, resistance, toughness, resilience, stamina, fortitude, hardiness, staying power

tolerant adjective = **broad-minded**, liberal, understanding, open-minded • a tolerant society OPPOSITE: narrow-minded

tolerate verb 1 = **put up with**, accept • We will not tolerate such behaviour in our classroom.
2 = **endure**, stand, bear • She can no longer tolerate the position that she's in.
See also: **allow**

toleration noun = **acceptance**, sanction, allowance, endurance, indulgence, permissiveness

toll[1] verb 1 = **ring**, strike, sound, chime, knell, clang, peal
▶ noun 2 = **ringing**, chime, knell, clang, peal

toll[2] noun 1 = **charge**, tax, fee, payment, duty, tariff, levy
2 = **damage**, cost, loss, penalty

tomb noun = **grave**, vault, sarcophagus, mausoleum, sepulchre • Howard Carter discovered King Tut's tomb.

tombstone noun = **gravestone**, memorial, marker, monument, headstone

tome See **book**

tomfoolery noun = **foolishness**, stupidity, silliness, buffoonery, clowning, fooling around (informal), horseplay, shenanigans (informal), skylarking (informal)

ton noun (Informal, often plural) = **a lot**, ocean, quantity, great deal, stacks

tone noun 1 = **pitch**, inflection, timbre, intonation, modulation
2 = **manner**, feel, air, character, style, spirit, attitude, mood, temper
3 = **colour**, shade, hue, tint, tinge
▶ verb 4 = **harmonize**, match, suit, blend, go well with
▷ **tone down** = **moderate**, reduce, soften, subdue, temper, restrain, play down

tongue noun = **language**, speech, dialect, parlance

tonic noun = **stimulant**, boost, restorative, pick-me-up (informal), shot in the arm (informal)

too adverb 1 = **as well**, besides, moreover, likewise, in addition, into the bargain • You were there too.
2 = **excessively**, overly, unduly, unreasonably, over- • You've had too many late nights.
See also: **also**

tool noun 1 = **implement**, instrument, utensil • The best tool for the purpose is a pair of shears.
2 = **puppet**, creature, pawn, lackey, minion, stooge (slang), cat's-paw, flunkey, hireling
See also: **gadget**

top noun 1 = **peak**, head, summit, crown, height, crest, ridge, culmination, brow, pinnacle, apex, apex, zenith, high point, acme, apogee • I waited at the top of the stairs.
OPPOSITE: bottom
2 = **first place**, lead, head
3 = **lid**, cap, stopper • a bottle top
▶ adjective 4 = **leading**, lead,

head, chief, prime, premier, principal, elite, best, foremost, pre-eminent, highest • *She was the top student in physics.*

▶ *verb* **5 = exceed**, cap, surpass, outstrip, go beyond • *The temperature topped 23°C.*

6 = surpass, beat, eclipse, better, outdo, improve on • *You'll never manage to top that story.*

7 = cover, finish, cap, crown, garnish

8 = lead, head, be first

See also: **maximum, prize, successful, supreme**

> **INFORMALLY SPEAKING**
> **from top to bottom:** completely
> **off the top of your head:** without preparation
> **over the top:** to an exaggerated degree

▷ **top up** See **augment, supplement**

topic *noun* = **subject**, point, issue, question, matter, theme, subject matter

topical *adjective* = **current**, popular, contemporary, up-to-date, newsworthy, up-to-the-minute

topmost *adjective* = **highest**, top, principal, dominant, foremost, supreme, paramount, uppermost, leading

topple *verb* **1 = fall over**, fall, collapse, tumble, overturn, keel over, overbalance, totter

2 = overthrow, oust, overturn, unseat, bring down, bring low

topsy-turvy *adjective* = **confused**, messy, chaotic, disorderly, upside-down, inside-out, disorganized, jumbled, mixed-up

torment *verb* **1 = torture**, rack, distress, crucify

2 = tease, bother, harass, annoy, irritate, nag, hassle (*informal*), vex, pester

▶ *noun* **3 = suffering**, pain, torture, hell, distress, misery, anguish, agony

torn *adjective* **1 = cut**, split, rent, slit, ragged, lacerated, ripped

2 = undecided, uncertain, unsure, in two minds (*informal*), irresolute, vacillating, wavering

tornado *noun* = **whirlwind**, storm, hurricane, cyclone, typhoon, squall, tempest, gale

torpedo *noun* See **bomb**

torpor *noun* = **inactivity**, sluggishness, apathy, drowsiness, laziness, sloth, lethargy, indolence, listlessness

torrent *noun* = **stream**, flood, rush, flow, tide, spate, cascade, deluge, downpour

torrid *adjective* **1 = arid**, parched, dried, scorched

2 = passionate, intense, steamy (*informal*), ardent, fervent

tortuous *adjective* **1 = winding**, indirect, twisty, convoluted, mazy, serpentine, circuitous, meandering, sinuous, twisting

2 = complicated, tricky, indirect, involved, ambiguous, roundabout, devious, convoluted

torture *verb* **1 = torment**, rack, distress, afflict, persecute, crucify, put on the rack

▶ *noun* **2 = torment**, pain, suffering, distress, persecution, anguish, agony

toss *verb* **1 = throw**, launch, pitch, cast, flip, hurl, lob (*informal*), fling, sling

2 = thrash, rock, roll, shake, wriggle, writhe

▶ *noun* **3 = throw**, pitch, lob (*informal*)

tot¹ *noun* = **infant**, child, baby, toddler, mite

tot² *verb* = **add up**, total, tally, calculate, reckon, count up

total *noun* **1 = sum**, whole, aggregate, the whole schmear (*informal*), the whole enchilada (*slang*) • *The companies have a total of 550 employees.*

▶ *adjective* **2 = complete**, absolute, outright, utter, unconditional, unqualified, undivided, unmitigated, out-and-out • *a total failure*

▶ *verb* **3 = amount to**, add up to, come to • *Their debts totalled over a thousand dollars.*

t

4 = add up, reckon, tot up
See also: **add, figure, sheer**

totalitarian *adjective*
= **dictatorial**, authoritarian, oppressive, undemocratic, despotic, tyrannous

totality *noun* = **whole**, total, aggregate, sum, entirety

totally *adverb* = **completely**, fully, absolutely, entirely, thoroughly, wholly, utterly, comprehensively, one hundred per cent

totter *verb* = **stagger**, stumble, reel, falter, sway, lurch

tottering See **shaky, unsteady**

touch *verb* **1 = handle**, feel, finger • *Don't touch the screen.*
RELATED WORD
adjective: tactile
2 = meet, brush, graze • *I lowered my legs until my feet touched the floor.*
3 = affect, move, stir • *I was touched by his kindness.*
4 = consume, eat, drink, chow down (*slang*), partake of
5 = match, rival, equal, parallel, compare with, hold a candle to (*informal*)
▷ **touch and go = risky**, close, near, critical, precarious, nerve-racking
▷ **touch down** See **land**
▷ **touch on = refer to**, cover, mention, allude to, bring in, deal with, speak of
▷ **touch upon** See **mention**
▶ *noun* **6 = feeling**, handling, physical contact
7 = contact, stroke, tap, brush, pat
8 = bit, drop, spot, trace, dash, smattering, jot, small amount, soupçon (*French*)
9 = style, way, method, technique, manner, trademark
See also: **note, reach**

touching *adjective* = **moving**, poignant, affecting • *a touching tale*

touchstone *noun* = **standard**, measure, par, criterion, gauge, norm, yardstick

touchy *adjective* = **oversensitive**, sensitive, easily offended

• *He's very touchy about that.*

tough *adjective* **1 = strong**, robust, rugged, resilient, hardened, hardy • *She is tough and ambitious.*
2 = resilient, strong, solid, robust, rugged, durable, sturdy, hard-wearing, leathery • *an apple with a rather tough skin*
OPPOSITE: fragile
3 = difficult, hard, arduous, exacting • *a tough childhood*
OPPOSITE: easy
4 = rough, violent, ruthless, pugnacious, hard-boiled
5 = strict, hard, firm, severe, stern, resolute, merciless, unbending
6 (*Informal*) **= unlucky**, unfortunate, regrettable, lamentable
▶ *noun* **7 = ruffian**, bully, thug, roughneck (*slang*), hooligan, bruiser (*informal*)
See also: **stiff**

toughen See **strengthen**

tour *noun* **1 = journey**, trip, outing, expedition, excursion, jaunt
▶ *verb* **2 = visit**, explore, journey, sightsee, go around, travel through

tourist *noun* = **traveller**, globetrotter, tripper, excursionist, holiday-maker, sightseer, voyager

tournament *noun*
= **competition**, series, event, meeting, contest

tow *verb* = **pull**, draw, drag, haul, tug, lug

towards *preposition* **1 = in the direction of**, to, for, en route for, on the way to
2 = regarding, for, about, concerning, with regard to, with respect to

tower *noun* = **column**, pillar, skyscraper, turret, obelisk, steeple, belfry

towering *adjective* = **tall**, high, impressive, elevated, lofty, magnificent, colossal, imposing, soaring

town See **city**

toxic *adjective* = **poisonous**,

deadly, harmful, lethal, septic, noxious, pernicious, pestilential

toxin See **poison**

toy noun 1 = **plaything**, game, doll
▶ verb 2 = **play**, fool, fiddle (informal), amuse oneself, dally or fool around, trifle

trace verb 1 = **find**, locate, track down • Police are trying to trace the owner.
2 = **copy**, draw, outline, sketch
▶ noun 3 = **indication**, record, sign, evidence, remnant, vestige • No trace of him had been found.
4 = **bit**, drop, touch, hint, suggestion, suspicion, dash, whiff, tinge • to write without a trace of sensationalism
5 = **track**, trail, path, footprint, footstep, footmark, spoor
See also: **lead, note**

track noun 1 = **path**, way, line, road, course, orbit, pathway, trajectory
2 = **trail**, mark, wake, path, trace, footprint, footstep, footmark, spoor
3 = **line**, permanent way, rails
▶ verb 4 = **follow**, trail, pursue, chase, trace, shadow, tail (informal), stalk, hunt down
▷ **track down** = **find**, discover, trace, unearth, dig up, hunt down, run to earth or run to ground, sniff out

track record See **record**

tract¹ noun = **area**, region, plot, territory, stretch, district, extent, expanse, townsite (chiefly Canad)

tract² noun = **treatise**, essay, pamphlet, booklet, homily, dissertation, monograph

tractable adjective = **manageable**, willing, tame, compliant, amenable, obedient, docile, submissive, biddable, yielding

traction noun = **grip**, pull, purchase, resistance, friction

trade noun 1 = **commerce**, business • foreign trade
RELATED WORD
adjective: mercantile
2 = **occupation**, business, line, profession, line of work • He

learned his trade as an apprentice in the plumbing company.
▶ verb 3 = **deal**, traffic, do business • They had years of experience of trading with China.
4 = **exchange**, switch, swap, barter
See also: **change, job**
▷ **trade in** See **sell, stock**

trader noun = **dealer**, broker, merchant • a timber trader

tradesman noun 1 = **craftsman**, artisan, journeyman, workman
2 = **shopkeeper**, retailer, dealer, supplier, seller, merchant, vendor, purveyor

trading See **business**

tradition noun = **custom**, convention • the rich traditions of Afro-Cuban music
See also: **habit**

traditional adjective = **conventional**, established • traditional styles of dress
OPPOSITE: unconventional
See also: **conservative**

traffic noun 1 = **transportation**, transportation, freight, vehicles
2 = **trade**, business, truck, exchange, commerce, dealings, peddling
▶ verb 3 = **trade**, deal, exchange, bargain, peddle, do business, have dealings

tragedy noun = **disaster**, catastrophe, adversity, calamity, misfortune

tragic adjective = **distressing**, heartbreaking, heart-rending • a tragic accident
See also: **sad**

trail noun 1 = **path**, way, road, track, route, footpath
2 = **tracks**, wake, path, trace, scent, footprints, marks, spoor
▶ verb 3 = **drag**, pull, draw, haul, tow, dangle
4 = **lag**, follow, linger, dawdle, loiter, hang back, straggle, traipse (informal)
5 = **follow**, track, hunt, pursue, chase, trace, shadow, tail (informal), stalk

train verb 1 = **instruct**, school, coach, teach, drill, educate, tutor

• *We train them in bricklaying.*
2 = **exercise**, prepare, work out
3 = **aim**, point, level, focus, direct
▶ *noun* **4** = **sequence**, set, series, chain, string, progression, succession
See also: **practise**

trained *See* **skilled**

trainee *See* **beginner, recruit**

trainer *noun* = **coach**, handler

training *noun* **1** = **instruction**, education, tuition, discipline, teaching, schooling, grounding, coaching
2 = **practice**, exercise, preparation, working out

traipse *verb* = **trudge**, trail, slouch, drag oneself, footslog, tramp

trait *noun* = **characteristic**, feature, quality, attribute, quirk, mannerism, idiosyncrasy, peculiarity

traitor *noun* = **betrayer**, rebel, deserter, renegade, defector, Judas, apostate, turncoat, back-stabber, quisling

trajectory *noun* = **path**, line, track, course, route, flight path

tramp *verb* **1** = **hike**, walk, march, roam, trek, rove, ramble, slog, footslog
2 = **trudge**, stump, toil, plod, traipse (*informal*)
▶ *noun* **3** = **vagrant**, derelict, down-and-out, drifter
4 = **hike**, march, trek, ramble, slog
5 = **tread**, stamp, footstep, footfall

trample *verb* = **crush**, stamp, squash, flatten, tread, run over, walk over

trance *noun* = **daze**, dream, unconsciousness, abstraction, rapture, reverie, stupor

tranquil *adjective* = **calm**, still, quiet, peaceful, sedate, serene, undisturbed, restful, placid

tranquility *noun* = **calm**, rest, peace, quiet, hush, serenity, repose, stillness, placidity
See also: **peace, quiet**

tranquilize *verb* = **calm**, quiet, relax, quell, lull, sedate, soothe, pacify, settle one's nerves

tranquilizer *noun* = **sedative**, downer (*slang*), opiate, bromide, barbiturate

transaction *noun* = **deal**, business, negotiation, bargain, enterprise, undertaking

transcend *verb* = **surpass**, exceed, eclipse, excel, outstrip, outdo, go beyond, rise above

transcendent *adjective* = **unparalleled**, pre-eminent, sublime, consummate, incomparable, unrivalled, matchless, unequalled

transcribe *verb* = **write out**, transfer, reproduce, copy out, take down

transcript *noun* = **copy**, record, manuscript, reproduction, duplicate, transcription

transfer *verb* **1** = **move**, change, shift, transplant, transport, relocate, convey, hand over, pass on, transpose
▶ *noun* **2** = **move**, change, shift, transmission, translation, handover, relocation, transference, transposition

transfix *verb* **1** = **stun**, hold, paralyze, fascinate, mesmerize, engross, hypnotize
2 = **pierce**, impale, puncture, spear, skewer, run through

transform *verb* = **change**, reform, convert, alter, revolutionize, make over • *This technology has transformed our society.*
See also: **turn**

transformation *noun* = **change**, conversion, revolution, alteration, metamorphosis, sea change, transmutation

transgress *verb* = **break the law**, violate, offend, infringe, sin, contravene, trespass, disobey, encroach

transgression *noun* = **crime**, violation, infringement, wrongdoing, offence, sin, infraction, trespass, misdemeanour, misdeed, encroachment, contravention

transgressor *noun* = **criminal**, offender, culprit, villain, wrongdoer, lawbreaker, miscreant, sinner, perp (*informal*), trespasser

transient *adjective* = **temporary**, brief, passing, short-lived, momentary, fleeting, ephemeral, transitory, impermanent

transit *noun* = **movement**, transfer, transport, transportation, passage, crossing, carriage, conveyance

transition *noun* = **change**, development, shift, conversion, passing, progression, alteration, metamorphosis, transmutation

transitional *adjective*
1 = **changing**, fluid, passing, developmental, intermediate, unsettled
2 = **temporary**, provisional

transitory *adjective* = **short-lived**, short, brief, temporary, passing, momentary, fleeting, transient, ephemeral, impermanent

translate *verb* = **interpret**, convert, render, decode, decipher, construe, paraphrase

translation *noun*
= **interpretation**, version, rendition, rendering, paraphrase, decoding

translucent *See* **clear**, **transparent**

transmission *noun*
1 = **transfer**, spread, shipment, dissemination, conveyance, sending, transference
2 = **broadcasting**, showing, dissemination, putting out, relaying, sending
3 = **program**, show, broadcast

transmit *verb* 1 = **pass on**, send, carry, bear, spread, transfer, convey, disseminate, impart, hand on
2 = **broadcast**, stream, radio, relay, disseminate, send out

transparency *noun* 1 = **clarity**, clearness, limpidity, pellucidness, translucence
2 = **photograph**, slide

transparent *adjective* 1 = **clear**, sheer, translucent, crystalline
• *a sheet of transparent plastic*

2 = **obvious**, patent, plain, explicit, evident, recognizable, manifest, unambiguous, undisguised

transpire *verb* 1 = **become known**, emerge, come out, come to light
2 (*Informal*) = **happen**, chance, occur, arise, befall, come about, take place

transplant *verb* = **transfer**, remove, shift, displace, relocate, uproot, resettle

transport *verb* 1 = **convey**, carry, ship, transfer • *They use tankers to transport the oil.*
2 = **exile**, deport, banish
See also: **bring, take**

transportation *noun*
1 = **vehicle**, transportation, conveyance
2 = **transportation**, transit, shipment • *The prices quoted include transport.*

transpose *verb* = **interchange**, change, move, exchange, transfer, shift, switch, alter, swap, substitute, reorder

trap *noun* 1 = **snare**, net • *a bear trap*
2 = **trick**, ambush, deception, ruse, subterfuge, stratagem, wile
▶ *verb* 3 = **catch**, corner, snare
• *a more humane way to trap the creatures*
4 = **trick**, dupe • *Were you trying to trap her into making a confession?*

trapping *See* **capture**

trappings *plural noun*
= **accessories**, equipment, gear, paraphernalia, accoutrements, finery, furnishings, panoply, things, trimmings

trash *noun* 1 = **garbage**, refuse, waste, rubbish • *They pick up the trash on Mondays.*
2 = **nonsense**, garbage (*informal*), rubbish • *Don't read that awful trash.*
▶ *verb* 3 = **destroy**, defeat, ruin, wreck, trounce, demolish, torpedo, put paid to
See also: **junk**

trashy *adjective* = **worthless**,

cheap, shoddy, inferior, shabby, rubbishy, tawdry

trauma noun = **shock**, hurt, pain, torture, suffering, ordeal, anguish, agony

traumatic adjective = **shocking**, painful, hurtful, injurious, agonizing, damaging, disturbing, scarring, upsetting, wounding

traumatize See **shock**

travel verb 1 = **go**, journey, make your way, take a trip • *You had better travel to Ottawa tomorrow.*
▶ noun 2 (*usually plural*) = **journey**, trip, tour, expedition, voyage, excursion, globetrotting, wandering
See also: **proceed, spread**

traveller noun = **voyager**, tourist, explorer, gypsy, globetrotter, wanderer, holiday-maker, wayfarer

travelling adjective = **itinerant**, mobile, migrant, nomadic, peripatetic, roaming, roving, touring, wandering, wayfaring

traverse verb = **cross**, span, go over, travel over

travesty noun 1 = **mockery**, caricature, distortion, parody, lampoon, perversion, burlesque
▶ verb 2 = **mock**, caricature, parody, ridicule, distort, lampoon, burlesque, make a mockery of

treacherous adjective
1 = **disloyal**, untrustworthy, unfaithful • *He denounced the party's treacherous leaders.*
OPPOSITE: loyal
2 = **dangerous**, hazardous, perilous • *treacherous mountain roads*
See also: **two-faced**

treachery noun = **betrayal**, treason, infidelity, back-stabbing (*informal*), disloyalty, double-dealing, duplicity, faithlessness, perfidy

tread verb 1 = **step**, walk, pace, hike, march, stamp, stride
2 = **trample**, squash, crush underfoot
▶ noun 3 = **step**, walk, pace, stride, footstep, gait, footfall

treason noun = **disloyalty**, treachery, mutiny, back-stabbing (*informal*), duplicity, lese-majesty, perfidy, sedition, traitorousness

treasonable adjective = **disloyal**, treacherous, subversive, mutinous, perfidious, seditious, traitorous

treasure verb 1 = **prize**, value, cherish, hold dear • *We treasure our friendship.*
2 = **riches**, money, gold, cash, wealth, fortune, jewels, valuables
3 = **darling**, jewel, gem, apple of one's eye, nonpareil, paragon, pride and joy
See also: **appreciate, dear**

treasured See **beloved, dear**

treasures See **valuables**

treasury noun = **storehouse**, store, bank, vault, cache, hoard, repository

treat verb 1 = **behave toward**, act toward, deal with • *She treated most of us with indifference.*
2 = **attend to**, nurse, care for • *the doctor who treated me*
3 = **entertain**, provide, stand (*informal*), regale, lay on
▶ noun 4 = **entertainment**, party, gift, celebration, feast, banquet, refreshment
5 = **pleasure**, surprise, fun, thrill, delight, joy, satisfaction, enjoyment
See also: **luxury**

treatise noun = **essay**, study, work, paper, tract, pamphlet, thesis, dissertation, monograph

treatment noun 1 = **care**, surgery, medication, therapy, medicine, cure, healing, remedy
2 = **handling**, action, conduct, management, dealing, behaviour, manipulation

treaty noun = **agreement**, contract, alliance, convention, pact, compact, covenant, concordat, entente

trek noun 1 = **journey**, hike, march, expedition, odyssey, safari

t

2 = slog, tramp
▶ *verb* **3 = journey**, hike, march, rove
4 = slog, trudge, footslog, traipse (*informal*), tramp

tremble *verb* **1 = shake**, quake, wobble, shiver, vibrate, shudder, quiver, totter
▶ *noun* **2 = shake**, quake, vibration, tremor, wobble, shiver, shudder, quiver

trembling *See* **shaky**

tremendous *adjective* **1 = huge**, great, enormous, terrific, immense, formidable, gigantic, colossal, stupendous
2 (*Informal*) **= excellent**, great, amazing, wonderful, brilliant, extraordinary, fantastic (*informal*), exceptional, sensational (*informal*), marvelous

tremor *noun* **1 = shake**, wobble, shiver, quiver, quaking, quaver, trembling
2 = earthquake, shock, quake (*informal*)

trench *noun* **= ditch**, channel, drain, excavation, gutter, trough, furrow

trenchant *adjective* **1 = scathing**, cutting, pointed, caustic, acerbic, pungent, incisive, penetrating
2 = effective, strong, powerful, potent, energetic, vigorous, forceful

trend *noun* **1 = tendency**, current, direction, flow, bias, drift, inclination, leaning
2 = fashion, thing, style, rage, mode, vogue, fad (*informal*), craze

trendy *adjective* **= fashionable**, in, latest, stylish, chic, in fashion, in vogue • *a trendy night club*

trepidation *noun* **= anxiety**, fear, worry, alarm, dread, apprehension, nervousness, consternation, uneasiness, disquiet

trespass *verb* **1 = intrude**, invade, infringe, encroach, obtrude
▶ *noun* **2 = intrusion**, invasion, infringement, encroachment, unlawful entry

trespasser *noun* **= intruder**, invader, poacher, interloper

trial *noun* **1 = hearing**, tribunal, litigation
2 = test, experiment, probation, audition, dry run (*informal*), test-run
3 = hardship, trouble, suffering, ordeal, distress, adversity, affliction, tribulation

tribe *noun* **= race**, people, family, clan

tribulation *See* **difficulty**, **ordeal**

tribunal *noun* **= hearing**, court, trial

tribute *noun* **1 = accolade**, honour, testimony, praise, compliment • *Police paid tribute to her courage.*
2 = payment, charge, tax, ransom, homage

trice *See* **instant**, **minute**

trick *noun* **1 = deception**, con (*informal*), hoax, ploy, ruse • *We are playing a trick on my little brother.*
2 = joke, antic, jape, stunt, prank, practical joke
3 = secret, hang (*informal*), skill, technique, knack, know-how (*informal*)
4 = mannerism, practice, habit, characteristic, trait, quirk, foible, idiosyncrasy, peculiarity
▶ *verb* **5 = deceive**, fool, con (*informal*), dupe, take in • *They tricked me into giving them all my money.*
See also: **trap**

| **INFORMALLY SPEAKING**
How's tricks?: How are you?
not miss a trick: be very alert

trickery *noun* **= deception**, deceit, dishonesty, cheating, chicanery, guile, monkey business (*informal*)

trickle *verb* **1 = dribble**, run, drop, stream, drip, seep, ooze, exude
▶ *noun* **2 = dribble**, drip, seepage

tricky *adjective* **1 = difficult**, hard, complex, sensitive, complicated, delicate, problematic, puzzling • *This could be a very tricky problem.*
2 = crafty, slippery, wily, sly, cunning, deceitful, devious, artful, scheming

trifle *noun* **1 = knick-knack**, toy,

t

plaything, bauble, bagatelle
▶ verb 2 = **toy**, play, dally, mess around

trifling adjective = **insignificant**, paltry, worthless, negligible, trivial, unimportant, measly

trigger verb = **set off**, start, cause, produce, prompt, generate, provoke, activate, set in motion, spark off

trim adjective 1 = **neat**, dapper, smart, tidy, spruce, shipshape, well-groomed
2 = **slender**, fit, slim, sleek, streamlined, shapely, svelte, willowy
▶ verb 3 = **cut**, clip, crop, shave, tidy, pare, prune, even up
4 = **decorate**, dress, array, adorn, ornament, embellish, beautify, deck out
▶ noun 5 = **decoration**, border, trimming, embellishment, frill, piping, adornment, edging, ornamentation
6 = **condition**, health, state, shape (informal), fitness, fettle
7 = **cut**, crop, shave, clipping, pruning, shearing, tidying up

trimming noun = **decoration**, border, embellishment, frill, piping, adornment, edging, ornamentation
▷ **trimmings** = **extras**, paraphernalia, accessories, accompaniments, frills, ornaments, trappings

trinity noun = **threesome**, trio, triumvirate, triad

trinket noun = **ornament**, toy, trifle, bauble, bagatelle, knick-knack

trio noun = **threesome**, trilogy, triumvirate, triad, trinity

trip noun 1 = **journey**, outing, voyage, excursion, jaunt • a business trip
2 = **stumble**, fall, slip, misstep
▶ verb 3 = **stumble**, fall over, lose your footing • I tripped on the stairs.
4 = **catch out**, trap
5 = **skip**, dance, hop, gambol
See also: **drive**

triple adjective 1 = **threefold**, three-way, tripartite
▶ verb 2 = **treble**, increase threefold

trite adjective = **unoriginal**, tired, stale, commonplace, banal, clichéd, hackneyed, stereotyped, threadbare

triumph noun 1 = **success**, victory • The championships proved to be a personal triumph for the coach.
OPPOSITE: failure
2 = **joy**, pride, happiness, jubilation, elation, exultation, rejoicing
▶ verb 3 (often with over) = **succeed**, win, prevail, come out on top (informal) • a symbol of good triumphing over evil
OPPOSITE: fail
4 = **rejoice**, celebrate, glory, revel, crow, exult, gloat

triumphant adjective 1 = **victorious**, successful, winning, conquering
2 = **celebratory**, proud, jubilant, elated, exultant

trivia plural noun = **minutiae**, details, trifles, trivialities

trivial adjective = **unimportant**, minor, slight, petty, insignificant, paltry, negligible, trifling • She doesn't concern herself with such trivial details.
OPPOSITE: important
See also: **worthless**

triviality noun = **insignificance**, meaninglessness, pettiness, unimportance, worthlessness

trivialize verb = **undervalue**, minimize, underestimate, belittle, laugh off, make light of, play down, scoff at, underplay

troop noun 1 = **group**, company, team, body, unit, crowd, band, squad, multitude, horde
▷ **troops** = **soldiers**, army, men, armed forces, servicemen, soldiery
▶ verb 2 = **flock**, march, stream, swarm, throng, traipse (informal)

trophy noun = **prize**, award, cup, souvenir, memento, booty, laurels, spoils

tropical adjective = **hot**, torrid,

steamy, sultry, stifling, sweltering

trot verb **1 = run**, jog, scamper, canter, lope
▶ noun **2 = run**, jog, canter, lope

trouble noun **1 = problem**, difficulty, bother, hassle (informal) • financial troubles
2 = distress, worry, pain, woe, anxiety, grief, sorrow, misfortune, torment, disquiet
3 = ailment, disease, complaint, failure, illness, disorder, defect, malfunction
4 = disorder, bother (informal), unrest, disturbance, strife, agitation, commotion, discord, tumult
5 = effort, work, care, thought, inconvenience, labour, exertion, pains
▶ verb **6 = worry**, disturb, bother, agitate • He was troubled by his brother's decision.
7 = inconvenience, disturb, bother, impose upon, put out • May I trouble you for some milk?
8 = take pains, exert oneself, make an effort, take the time
See also: **burden, concern, drawback, jam**

troubled adjective **1 = anxious**, upset, concerned, distressed, worried, uneasy, disturbed, apprehensive, unsettled, dismayed, disconcerted, perturbed, ill at ease, discomposed, bothered, agitated
2 = difficult, hard, tough, dark, stressful, problematic, unsettled

troublesome adjective
1 = worrying, difficult, tricky, inconvenient, demanding, annoying, irksome, high-maintenance, taxing, trying, vexatious
2 = disorderly, violent, turbulent, undisciplined, unruly, rowdy, rebellious, uncooperative

trough noun **1 = manger**, water trough
2 = channel, depression, ditch, canal, trench, duct, gutter, gully, furrow

trounce verb **= thrash**, beat, crush, drub, hammer (informal), rout, slaughter (informal), wipe the floor with (informal)

trouncing See **defeat**

troupe noun **= company**, band, cast

truancy noun **= absence**, absence without leave, malingering, shirking

truant noun **= absentee**, runaway, malingerer, shirker

truce noun **= ceasefire**, peace, moratorium, cessation, lull, respite, let-up (informal), armistice

truculent adjective **= hostile**, aggressive, defiant, belligerent, pugnacious, bellicose, ill-tempered, obstreperous

trudge verb **1 = plod**, lumber, trek, stump, slog, footslog, traipse (informal), tramp
▶ noun **2 = tramp**, hike, march, trek, slog, footslog, traipse (informal)

true adjective **1 = correct**, accurate, factual • The movie is based on a true story.
OPPOSITE: inaccurate
2 = genuine, real, authentic, bona fide • He disguised his true feelings.
3 = faithful, steady, reliable, loyal, dedicated, staunch, devoted, trustworthy, dutiful
4 = exact, perfect, accurate, precise, on target, unerring
OPPOSITE: false
See also: **actual, realistic, right, strict, trusty**

truism noun **= cliché**, commonplace, bromide, axiom, platitude

truly adverb **1 = correctly**, exactly, precisely, genuinely, rightly, legitimately, truthfully, factually, authenticly
2 = faithfully, steadily, sincerely, staunchly, dutifully, devotedly, loyally
3 = really, very, extremely, indeed, greatly

trumpet noun **1 = horn**, bugle, clarion

t

▶ verb **2 = proclaim**, announce, broadcast, advertise, tout (*informal*), shout from the rooftops

trump up verb **= invent**, create, fake, fabricate, concoct, contrive, cook up (*informal*), make up

truncate verb **= shorten**, trim, dock, curtail, pare, prune, abbreviate, lop, cut short

truncheon noun **= club**, staff, baton, blackjack, cudgel, nightstick, billy club

trunk noun **1 = stem**, stalk, bole
2 = chest, case, box, casket, coffer, crate
3 = body, torso
4 = snout, proboscis

truss verb **1 = tie**, secure, bind, strap, tether, fasten, make fast
▶ noun **2** (*Medical*) **= support**, bandage
3 = joist, support, stay, brace, prop, beam, buttress, strut, stanchion

trust verb **1 = believe in**, count on, depend on, have confidence in, have faith in, place your trust in, rely upon • *He can be trusted to honour his promise.*
2 = entrust, give, commit, delegate, assign, confide, consign
3 = expect, hope, suppose, assume, presume, surmise
▶ noun **4 = confidence**, credit, expectation, conviction, faith, belief, assurance, certainty, reliance, credence
See also: **believe, depend, gullible**

trustful, trusting adjective **= unsuspecting**, naive, gullible, unwary, credulous, unsuspicious
See also: **gullible**

trustworthy adjective **= dependable**, responsible, honest, reliable, staunch, principled, steadfast, reputable, honourable, trusty

trusty adjective **= reliable**, firm, true, solid, faithful, staunch, dependable, trustworthy • *a trusty member of the crew*
See also: **loyal**

truth noun **= fact**, reality • *I'm keen to get to the truth of what happened.*
RELATED WORDS
adjectives: veritable, veracious

truthful adjective **= honest**, straight, true, precise, sincere, frank, candid, trustworthy

try verb **1 = attempt**, seek, strive, endeavour (*formal*), make an attempt, make an effort • *I tried hard to persuade him to stay.*
2 = test, sample, check out (*informal*), try out • *He wanted me to try the cake.*
▷ **try out** *See* **test, try**
▷ **try your hand at** *See* **attempt**
▶ noun **3 = attempt**, go (*informal*), shot, effort, endeavour • *After a few tries he pressed the right button.*

trying adjective **= annoying**, hard, tough, difficult, stressful, tiresome, bothersome, exasperating, high-maintenance, taxing, wearisome

tryst *See* **meeting**

tubby adjective **= fat**, overweight, obese, portly, plump, chubby, stout, corpulent

tuck verb **1 = push**, gather, fold, insert
▶ noun **2 = fold**, gather, pinch, pleat

tuckered out *See* **tired, weary**

tuft noun **= clump**, collection, bunch, cluster, knot, tussock

tug verb **1 = pull**, draw, drag, haul, yank, pluck, jerk, wrench, heave • *The puppy tugged at its leash.*
▶ noun **2 = pull**, yank, jerk, wrench, heave • *He felt a tug at his arm.*

tuition noun **1 = fees**, price, cost, bill, charges, enrolment fees, maintenance fees
2 = training, education, instruction, teaching, schooling, tutelage, lessons, tutoring

tumble verb **1 = fall**, drop, topple, stumble, plummet, flop
▶ noun **2 = fall**, drop, trip, spill, plunge, stumble

tumbledown adjective **= dilapidated**, rickety, decrepit, ramshackle, crumbling, ruined

tummy See **stomach**

tumour noun = **growth**, cancer, lump, sarcoma (*medical*), carcinoma (*pathology*), swelling See also: **boil**

tumult noun = **commotion**, row, riot, turmoil, uproar, upheaval, clamor, pandemonium, din, hubbub

tumultuous adjective = **wild**, excited, turbulent, noisy, boisterous, unruly, rowdy, riotous, uproarious, wired (*slang*)

tune noun 1 = **melody**, strains
• She was humming a merry little tune.
2 = **harmony**, pitch, concord, consonance, euphony
▶ verb 3 = **adjust**, pitch, regulate, adapt, harmonize, attune

tuneful adjective = **melodious**, musical, pleasant, catchy, melodic, harmonious, euphonious, mellifluous

tuneless adjective = **discordant**, harsh, atonal, cacophonous, dissonant, unmusical

tunnel noun 1 = **passage**, hole, channel, subway, shaft, burrow, underpass, passageway
▶ verb 2 = **dig**, mine, burrow, excavate, scoop out

turbulence noun = **confusion**, disorder, turmoil, unrest, instability, upheaval, agitation, commotion, tumult

turbulent adjective = **stormy**, rough, furious, tumultuous, raging, choppy, blustery, tempestuous, agitated, foaming

turf noun = **grass**, sod, sward
▷ **the turf** = **horse-racing**, racing, the flat

turmoil noun = **confusion**, disorder, chaos, uproar, upheaval, disarray, agitation, commotion, tumult

turn verb 1 = **rotate**, spin, twist, pivot, rotate, whirl, twirl, swivel
• She had turned the chair to face the door.
2 = **change**, convert, transform, mutate, metamorphose, transfigure, transmute • A hobby

can be turned into a career.
3 = **change course**, move, shift, switch, wheel, veer, swerve
4 = **shape**, make, fashion, frame, mould
5 = **go bad**, curdle, spoil, taint, sour
▷ **turn back** See **return**
▷ **turn down** = **lower**, soften, lessen, mute, muffle, quieten; = **refuse**, decline, reject, rebuff, spurn, repudiate
▷ **turn in** = **be disloyal to**, double-cross (*informal*), stab in the back, be unfaithful to, sell down the river (*informal*), inform on, sell out (*informal*), be treacherous to; = **go to bed**, go to sleep, hit the sack (*slang*); = **hand in**, return, deliver, submit, surrender, tender, give up, hand over
▷ **turn off** = **switch off**, stop, unplug, cut out, put out, shut down, turn out
▷ **turn on** = **switch on**, start, activate, ignite, kick-start, start up; = **attack**, assault, assail, fall on, round on; (*Informal*) = **arouse**, attract, please, excite, thrill, stimulate, titillate
▷ **turn out** See **work out**
▷ **turn red** See **blush**
▷ **turn under** See **fold**
▷ **turn up** = **arrive**, come, appear, attend, put in an appearance, show one's face, show up (*informal*); = **find**, reveal, discover, expose, disclose, unearth, dig up; = **come to light**, crop up (*informal*), pop up; = **increase**, raise, boost, intensify, enhance, amplify
▶ noun 6 = **chance**, go (*informal*), opportunity • Tonight it's my turn to cook.
7 = **rotation**, cycle, circle, spin, twist, revolution, whirl, gyration
8 = **change of direction**, shift, departure, deviation
9 = **direction**, trend, drift, tendency, heading
10 = **deed**, service, action, act, gesture, favour

See also: **bend, curve, get, grow**

turncoat noun = **traitor**, deserter, renegade, defector, apostate, backslider

turning noun = **junction**, turn, bend, curve, turn-off, crossroads, side road
▷ **turning point** = **crossroads**, change, crisis, crux, moment of truth

turnout noun = **attendance**, number, crowd, audience, assembly, gate, congregation, throng

turnover noun 1 = **output**, business, productivity
2 = **movement**, change, coming and going

tussle noun 1 = **fight**, battle, struggle, contest, conflict, scrap (informal), brawl, scuffle
▶ verb 2 = **fight**, battle, struggle, scrap (informal), vie, wrestle, grapple, scuffle

tutor noun 1 = **teacher**, coach, guide, instructor, guru, mentor, lecturer, educator, guardian
▶ verb 2 = **teach**, school, coach, train, guide, drill, educate, instruct

tutoring See **lesson**

twaddle noun = **nonsense**, garbage (informal), rubbish, drivel, claptrap (informal), gobbledegook (informal), poppycock (informal)

tweak verb, noun = **twist**, pull, squeeze, pinch, jerk

twice See **double**

twig noun = **branch**, shoot, stick, spray, sprig

twilight noun = **dusk**, evening, sunset, gloom, sundown, dimness, gloaming (poetic), half-light

twin noun 1 = **double**, match, fellow, counterpart, mate, clone, duplicate, likeness, look-alike
▶ verb 2 = **pair**, link, join, couple, match, yoke

twine noun 1 = **string**, cord, yarn
▶ verb 2 = **coil**, wind, curl, twist, spiral, bend, loop, encircle

twinge noun = **pain**, stab, stitch, spasm, prick, pang

twinkle verb 1 = **sparkle**, shine, flash, shimmer, glitter, blink, gleam, flicker, glisten, glint
▶ noun 2 = **sparkle**, spark, flash, shimmer, gleam, flicker, glimmer

twirl verb 1 = **turn**, wind, spin, twist, wheel, revolve, pivot, rotate, whirl, pirouette
▶ noun 2 = **turn**, spin, twist, wheel, revolution, rotation, whirl, pirouette

twist verb 1 = **turn around**, curl • I twisted the light bulb into the socket.
2 = **wind**, twine • The fibres are twisted together during spinning.
3 = **distort**, bend, mangle, screw up • The truck sat in the intersection with a broken headlight and a twisted fender.
4 = **sprain**, wrench • I've twisted my ankle.
▶ noun 5 = **wind**, curl, spin, coil, swivel
6 = **development**, change, turn, surprise, revelation, variation, slant
7 = **curve**, turn, bend, arc, meander, undulation, zigzag
8 = **distortion**, flaw, defect, warp, kink, deformation, imperfection
See also: **misrepresent, tangle**

twisted See **crooked**

twitch verb 1 = **jerk**, jump, flutter, squirm
▶ noun 2 = **jerk**, jump, flutter, spasm, tic

two-faced adjective = **hypocritical**, false, treacherous, dishonest, deceitful, disloyal, insincere • a two-faced, manipulative person

twofold See **double**

two-timing See **unfaithful**

tycoon noun = **magnate**, mogul, baron, financier, capitalist, industrialist, fat cat (slang), plutocrat

type noun = **kind**, make, group, class, brand, style, sort, variety, species, breed • There are various types of dogs suitable as pets.
See also: **category, form**

typhoon *noun* = **storm**, tornado, cyclone, squall, tempest

typical *adjective* = **characteristic**, stock, average, standard, regular, normal, representative, usual • *a typical Winnipeg winter* OPPOSITE: uncharacteristic
See also: **natural, routine**

typically *See* **on average**

typify *verb* = **symbolize**, represent, characterize, illustrate, embody, exemplify, epitomize, personify, sum up

tyrannical *adjective* = **oppressive**, cruel, authoritarian, autocratic, despotic, dictatorial, imperious, high-handed, domineering, overbearing, tyrannous

tyranny *noun* = **oppression**, dictatorship, cruelty, absolutism, authoritarianism, autocracy, despotism, high-handedness, imperiousness

tyrant *noun* = **dictator**, bully, authoritarian, despot, absolutist, autocrat, martinet, oppressor, slave-driver

t

Uu

ubiquitous *adjective* = **ever-present**, everywhere, universal, pervasive, omnipresent

ugly *adjective* **1** = **unattractive**, unsightly • *an ugly expression on his face*
2 = **unpleasant**, terrible, shocking, objectionable, horrid, distasteful, disagreeable
3 = **ominous**, dangerous, sinister, baleful, menacing
OPPOSITE: beautiful

ulcer *noun* = **sore**, boil, abscess, gumboil, peptic ulcer, pustule

ulterior *adjective* = **hidden**, secret, undisclosed, covert, concealed

ultimate *adjective* **1** = **final**, last, eventual • *It is not possible to predict the ultimate results.*
2 = **supreme**, utmost, paramount, greatest • *the ultimate goal of any player*
▶ *noun* **3** = **epitome**, peak, extreme, height • *This hotel is the ultimate in luxury.*
See also: **limit**

ultimately *adverb* = **finally**, eventually, after all, at last, in due time, in the end, sooner or later

umpire *noun* **1** = **referee**, judge, arbitrator, arbiter, ump (*informal*)
▶ *verb* **2** = **referee**, judge, adjudicate, arbitrate

umpteen See **many**

unabashed *adjective* = **unembarrassed**, bold, brazen, blatant

unable *adjective* = **incapable**, unfit, powerless, impotent, unqualified, ineffectual

unabridged *adjective* = **uncut**, complete, whole, full-length, unexpurgated

unacceptable *adjective* = **unsatisfactory**, objectionable, displeasing

unaccompanied *adjective*
1 = **alone**, solo, lone, unescorted, by oneself, on one's own
2 (*Music*) = **a cappella**

unaccountable *adjective*
1 = **inexplicable**, odd, mysterious, unfathomable, baffling, puzzling, unexplainable
2 = **not answerable**, exempt, not responsible

unaccustomed *adjective* = **unfamiliar**, new, strange, unwonted
▷ **unaccustomed to** = **not used to**, inexperienced at, unfamiliar with, unused to

unadventurous See **conventional**

unaffected[1] *adjective* = **natural**, simple, plain, genuine, sincere, unpretentious, artless

unaffected[2] *adjective* = **impervious**, proof, untouched, unmoved, unresponsive

unafraid *adjective* = **fearless**, daring, intrepid, dauntless

unaided See **independent, on one's own**

unalterable *adjective* = **unchangeable**, permanent, fixed, immutable

unanimity *noun* = **agreement**, accord, consensus, harmony, assent, unison, concord, concurrence, like-mindedness

unanimous *adjective* = **agreed**, common, concerted, like-minded, harmonious, in agreement, united

unanimously *adverb* = **without exception**, as one, in concert, of one mind, with one accord

u

unanswerable *adjective*
= **indisputable**, absolute,
conclusive, incontrovertible,
incontestable

unanswered *adjective*
= **unresolved**, open, disputed,
undecided

unappetizing *adjective*
= **unpleasant**, distasteful,
unattractive, repulsive,
unpalatable, unappealing,
scuzzy (*slang*)

unappreciative See **ungrateful**

unapproachable *adjective*
1 = **unfriendly**, cool, remote,
distant, chilly, reserved, aloof,
standoffish
2 = **inaccessible**, remote, out of
reach

unarmed *adjective* = **defenceless**,
open, weak, unprotected,
helpless, exposed

unashamed See **shameless**

unassailable *adjective*
= **impregnable**, secure,
invincible, invulnerable

unassuming *adjective* = **modest**,
quiet, humble, reserved,
unpretentious, self-effacing,
retiring, unassertive,
unobtrusive

unattached *adjective* 1 = **free**,
independent
2 = **single**, available, unmarried,
not spoken for, unengaged

unattended *adjective*
1 = **abandoned**, unguarded,
unwatched
2 = **alone**, unaccompanied, on
one's own

unattractive See **ugly**

unauthorized *adjective*
= **illegal**, unofficial, unlawful,
unsanctioned

unavoidable *adjective*
= **inevitable**, certain,
inescapable, fated

unaware *adjective* = **ignorant**,
unconscious, unsuspecting,
oblivious • *Many people are
unaware of how much they eat.*
OPPOSITE: aware

unawares *adverb* 1 = **by surprise**,
suddenly, unexpectedly, off
guard

2 = **unknowingly**, accidentally,
inadvertently, unwittingly, by
accident

unbalanced *adjective* 1 = **biased**,
unfair, partial, partisan, one-
sided, prejudiced
2 = **shaky**, unstable, lopsided,
uneven, wobbly
3 = **deranged**, mad, crazy,
unstable, eccentric, insane,
irrational, disturbed, demented,
non compos mentis (*Latin*), not all
there, unhinged

unbearable *adjective*
= **intolerable**, unacceptable,
oppressive • *Life was unbearable for
the victims of the earthquake.*
OPPOSITE: tolerable

unbeatable *adjective*
= **invincible**, indomitable

unbeaten *adjective* = **undefeated**,
victorious, triumphant

unbecoming *adjective*
1 = **unattractive**, unflattering,
unsuitable, unsightly,
unbefitting
2 = **unseemly**, offensive,
improper, discreditable

unbelievable *adjective*
1 = **wonderful**, incredible,
colossal, stupendous • *He showed
unbelievable courage.*
2 = **incredible**, improbable,
inconceivable, preposterous,
implausible, unconvincing • *He
came up with some unbelievable story.*
OPPOSITE: believable
See also: **unlikely**

unbending *adjective* = **inflexible**,
firm, tough, severe, strict,
stubborn, rigid, resolute,
uncompromising, intractable

unbiased *adjective* = **fair**, just,
objective, neutral, impartial,
equitable, disinterested,
unprejudiced

unblemished *adjective* = **spotless**,
perfect, pure, flawless,
impeccable, immaculate,
untarnished

unborn *adjective* = **expected**,
embryonic, fetal, awaited

unbreakable *adjective*
= **indestructible**, strong,
lasting, rugged, durable

unbridled *adjective*
= **unrestrained**, excessive, unchecked, unruly, wanton, intemperate, licentious, riotous

unbroken *adjective* **1** = **intact**, complete, whole, entire **2** = **continuous**, constant, uninterrupted, incessant, twenty-four-seven (*slang*)

unburden *verb* = **confess**, reveal, disclose, confide, get (something) off one's chest (*informal*)

uncalled-for *adjective*
= **unnecessary**, unwarranted, unjustified, needless, gratuitous, undeserved

uncanny *adjective* **1** = **weird**, mysterious, strange, supernatural, unnatural, unearthly **2** = **extraordinary**, unusual, remarkable, incredible, exceptional, miraculous, astounding

unceasing *adjective* = **continual**, constant, continuous, endless, perpetual, nonstop, incessant, twenty-four-seven (*slang*)

uncertain *adjective* **1** = **unsure**, unclear, undecided, doubtful, dubious • *For a moment he looked uncertain as to how to respond.* OPPOSITE: certain **2** = **doubtful**, indefinite, ambiguous, indeterminate • *facing an uncertain future* OPPOSITE: certain *See also:* **vague**

uncertainty *noun* = **doubt**, confusion, ambiguity, indecision, unpredictability, hesitancy, dubiety, reasonable doubt (*law*)

unchangeable *adjective*
= **unalterable**, permanent, stable, constant, irreversible, fixed, immutable, invariable

unchanging *adjective* = **constant**, permanent, lasting, enduring, eternal, perpetual, continuing, immutable, twenty-four-seven (*slang*), unvarying

uncharitable *adjective* = **unkind**, cruel, hardhearted, unfeeling, ungenerous

uncharted *adjective*
= **unexplored**, unknown, strange, unfamiliar, undiscovered

uncivil *adjective* = **impolite**, rude, bad-mannered, discourteous, ill-mannered, unmannerly

uncivilized *adjective*
1 = **primitive**, wild, savage, barbarian **2** = **uncouth**, coarse, boorish, uneducated, philistine, uncultivated

unclean *adjective* = **dirty**, foul, evil, corrupt, polluted, filthy, defiled, impure, scuzzy (*slang*), soiled, stained

unclear *adjective* **1** = **uncertain**, confused, ambiguous, vague • *It is unclear how much support they have.* OPPOSITE: clear **2** = **indistinct**, vague, faint, obscure, dim, fuzzy, hazy, shadowy, undefined, blurred

unclothed See **naked**

uncomfortable *adjective*
1 = **painful**, awkward, cramped, ill-fitting, disagreeable • *an uncomfortable bed* OPPOSITE: comfortable **2** = **uneasy**, awkward, embarrassed, self-conscious, ill at ease • *Talking about money made her uncomfortable.* OPPOSITE: comfortable

uncommitted *adjective*
= **uninvolved**, free, neutral, floating, nonaligned, not involved, unattached

uncommon *adjective* **1** = **rare**, few, unusual, extraordinary, exceptional, scarce, sparse, infrequent, out of the ordinary • *This type of weather is uncommon.* OPPOSITE: common **2** = **extraordinary**, great, intense, extreme, remarkable, acute, exceptional • *She had read his last email with uncommon interest.* *See also:* **particular, singular, strange**

uncommonly *adverb* **1** = **rarely**, occasionally, seldom, infrequently, hardly ever
2 = **exceptionally**, very, particularly

uncommunicative *adjective* = **reticent**, close, silent, secretive, tight-lipped, reserved, taciturn, unforthcoming

uncomplicated See **simple**, **straightforward**

uncompromising *adjective* = **inflexible**, firm, tough, strict, rigid, intransigent, inexorable, unbending

unconcern *noun* = **indifference**, detachment, apathy, aloofness, lack of interest, nonchalance

unconcerned *adjective* = **indifferent**, cool, distant, unmoved, apathetic, aloof, dispassionate, uninterested, detached

unconditional *adjective* = **absolute**, complete, full, total, positive, entire, outright, unlimited, unqualified, unreserved

unconnected *adjective*
1 = **separate**, divided, detached
2 = **incoherent**, irrelevant, meaningless, illogical, disjointed

unconscious *adjective*
1 = **senseless**, asleep, stunned
• *By the time the ambulance arrived, he was unconscious.*
OPPOSITE: conscious
2 = **unaware**, unsuspecting, oblivious, unknowing • *quite unconscious of their presence*
OPPOSITE: aware
3 = **unintentional**, accidental, inadvertent, unwitting
See also: **ignorant**

uncontaminated See **clean**

uncontrollable *adjective* = **wild**, strong, violent, mad, furious, frantic, unruly

uncontrolled *adjective* = **unrestrained**, rampant, undisciplined, unchecked, unbridled, riotous

unconventional *adjective* = **unusual**, individual, original, odd, irregular, eccentric, left-field (*informal*), unorthodox, offbeat, nonconformist, outré

unconvinced See **dubious**

unconvincing *adjective* = **implausible**, suspect, weak, unlikely, thin, questionable, improbable, dubious, lame, feeble, flimsy

uncooperative *adjective* = **unhelpful**, difficult, obstructive, awkward, disobliging, high-maintenance

uncoordinated *adjective* = **clumsy**, awkward, lumbering, ungainly, bungling, graceless, maladroit, ungraceful
See also: **clumsy**

uncouth *adjective* = **coarse**, crude, rough, rude, vulgar, boorish, graceless, ill-mannered, loutish, oafish

uncover *verb* **1** = **reveal**, expose, unearth, bring to light, show up
• *Teachers had uncovered evidence of cheating.*
2 = **open**, reveal, unveil, expose, unearth, unwrap, lay bare
• *Uncover the pot and drain the vegetables.*

uncovered See **bare**, **open**

uncritical *adjective* = **undiscriminating**, indiscriminate, undiscerning

uncultivated See **wild**

uncut See **whole**

undecided *adjective* **1** = **unsure**, uncertain, hesitant, dithering, in two minds, irresolute, torn
2 = **unsettled**, open, indefinite, moot, undetermined, iffy (*informal*), debatable, unconcluded

undefined *adjective*
1 = **unspecified**, unclear, inexact, imprecise
2 = **indistinct**, vague, indefinite, formless

undeniable *adjective* = **certain**, clear, sure, obvious, indisputable, incontrovertible, unquestionable

undeniably See **certainly**

under *preposition* **1** = **below**, beneath, underneath • *a labyrinth*

of tunnels under the ground
OPPOSITE: above
2 = subject to, governed by,
secondary to, subordinate to
▷ **under the weather** See **sick**
▷ **under way = in progress**,
begun, going on, started
▶ *adverb* **3 = below**, down, lower,
beneath
underclothes *plural noun*
= underwear, lingerie, undies
(*informal*), undergarments
undercover *adjective* **= secret**,
private, covert, hidden,
concealed
undercurrent *noun*
1 = undertow, riptide
2 = undertone, sense, feeling,
hint, suggestion, atmosphere,
tendency, overtone, vibes (*slang*),
tinge
underdog *noun* **= weaker party**,
outsider, little fellow (*informal*)
underestimate *verb*
= underrate, minimize,
undervalue, belittle,
miscalculate
underfed See **skinny**
undergo *verb* **= experience**,
suffer, endure, be subjected to,
go through • *He had to undergo
major surgery.*
See also: **feel, have, receive**
underground *adjective*
1 = subterranean, covered,
buried
2 = secret, clandestine, covert,
hidden
▶ *noun*
▷ **the underground = the
Resistance**, partisans
undergrowth *noun* **= scrub**,
brush, bracken, briars,
underbrush
underhand, underhanded
adjective **= sly**, secret, dishonest,
crafty, sneaky, deceitful, devious,
stealthy, down and dirty
(*informal*), furtive
underline *verb* **1 = underscore**,
mark
2 = emphasize, stress, highlight,
accentuate
underling See **inferior**
underlying *adjective*

= fundamental, prime, primary,
basic, elementary, intrinsic
undermine *verb* **= weaken**,
impair, sap, subvert • *You're trying
to undermine my confidence again.*
OPPOSITE: strengthen
underneath See **below, under**
undernourished See **skinny**
underprivileged *adjective*
= disadvantaged, poor,
impoverished, needy, destitute,
deprived
underrate *verb* **= underestimate**,
discount, undervalue, belittle
undersized *adjective* **= stunted**,
small, miniature, pygmy or
pigmy, dwarfish
understand *verb*
1 = comprehend, get, see, follow,
grasp, catch on, take in • *Do you
understand what I'm saying?*
2 = realize, appreciate, grasp,
comprehend, fathom • *too young
to understand what was going on*
3 = hear, believe, learn, gather • *I
understand she hasn't been well.*
See also: **know**
understandable *adjective*
= reasonable, natural,
legitimate, justifiable, to be
expected
understanding *noun*
1 = perception, knowledge,
appreciation, grasp,
comprehension • *a basic
understanding of computers*
2 = agreement, accord, pact
• *There was an understanding among
the players.*
3 = interpretation, view, idea,
opinion, judgment, belief,
perception, notion
▶ *adjective* **4 = sympathetic**,
sensitive, compassionate,
considerate • *Fortunately, he had an
understanding family.*
See also: **experience,
intelligence, pity, sympathy,
tolerant**
understood *adjective*
1 = implied, implicit, tacit,
unspoken, inferred, unstated
2 = assumed, accepted, taken for
granted
understudy *noun* **= stand-in**,

u

reserve, replacement, substitute
undertake verb = **agree**, contract,
promise, pledge, guarantee,
engage, bargain
undertaking noun 1 = **task**, job,
business, project, operation,
affair, venture, enterprise,
endeavour • *Organizing the talent
show has been a massive undertaking.*
2 = **promise**, word, pledge, vow,
commitment, assurance
See also: **act, guarantee**
undertone noun 1 = **murmur**,
whisper
2 = **undercurrent**, touch, hint,
trace, suggestion, tinge
undertow *See* **current**
undervalue verb = **underrate**,
minimize, underestimate,
misjudge, depreciate, hold
cheap
underwater adjective
= **submerged**, submarine,
sunken
underwear noun = **underclothes**,
lingerie, undies (*informal*),
undergarments, underthings
underweight adjective = **skinny**,
undersized, puny, emaciated,
half-starved, skin and bone
(*informal*), undernourished
underworld noun 1 = **criminals**,
gangland (*informal*), gangsters,
organized crime
2 = **nether world**, Hades, nether
regions
underwrite verb 1 = **finance**,
back, fund, guarantee, sponsor,
subsidize, insure
2 = **sign**, endorse, initial
undesirable adjective
= **unwanted**, unacceptable,
unwelcome, unattractive,
unsuitable, objectionable,
distasteful, disagreeable
undeveloped adjective
= **potential**, immature, latent
undignified adjective = **unseemly**,
improper, unsuitable,
unbecoming, indecorous,
inelegant
undisciplined adjective
= **uncontrolled**, wild, unruly,
wayward, wilful, unrestrained,
obstreperous

undisguised adjective = **obvious**,
open, patent, explicit, evident,
blatant, overt, unconcealed
undisputed adjective
= **acknowledged**, certain,
unchallenged, accepted,
undeniable, indisputable,
recognized, undoubted
undistinguished adjective
= **ordinary**, everyday, mediocre,
unremarkable, unimpressive,
unexceptional
undisturbed adjective 1 = **quiet**,
tranquil
2 = **calm**, unfazed (*informal*),
sedate, tranquil, serene,
collected, composed, placid,
unperturbed, untroubled
undivided adjective = **complete**,
full, whole, entire, solid,
exclusive, thorough,
undistracted, united
undo verb 1 = **open**, loose, untie,
disentangle, unbutton, unfasten
2 = **reverse**, cancel, offset,
neutralize, annul, invalidate
3 = **ruin**, defeat, destroy, upset,
overturn, undermine, quash,
shatter, wreck, subvert
undoing noun = **downfall**, defeat,
collapse, ruin, shame, disgrace,
overthrow, reversal
undomesticated *See* **wild**
undone adjective = **unfinished**,
left, unfulfilled, neglected,
omitted, unperformed
undoubted adjective = **certain**,
sure, definite, undisputed,
acknowledged, indisputable,
unquestioned, indubitable
undoubtedly adverb = **certainly**,
definitely, surely, doubtless,
assuredly, without doubt
undress verb 1 = **strip**, shed,
disrobe, take off one's clothes
▶ noun 2 = **nakedness**, nudity
undressed *See* **bare, naked**
undue adjective = **excessive**,
extreme, unnecessary, improper,
unwarranted, needless,
uncalled-for
unduly adverb = **excessively**,
unnecessarily, overly,
unreasonably
undying adjective = **eternal**,

permanent, constant, infinite, perpetual, unending, everlasting, deathless, twenty-four-seven (*slang*)

unearth *verb* **1 = discover**, find, reveal, expose, uncover
2 = dig up, exhume, excavate, dredge up

unearthly *adjective* **= eerie**, strange, weird, spooky (*informal*), supernatural, phantom, ghostly, uncanny, spectral

unease *See* **anxiety, worry**

uneasiness *noun* **= anxiety**, worry, doubt, trepidation, misgiving, disquiet, qualms

uneasy *adjective* **1 = anxious**, nervous, worried, agitated, perturbed • *I was very uneasy about these developments.*
OPPOSITE: comfortable
2 = awkward, shaky, tense, strained, uncomfortable, precarious, insecure

uneconomic *adjective* **= unprofitable**, loss-making, nonpaying

uneconomical *See* **wasteful**

uneducated *adjective*
1 = ignorant, illiterate, unlettered, unschooled, untaught
2 = uncultured, lowbrow, uncultivated

unemotional *adjective* **= impassive**, cold, cool, reserved, apathetic, phlegmatic, undemonstrative, unexcitable

unemployed *adjective* **= out of work**, jobless, idle, laid off • *an unemployed mechanic*
OPPOSITE: employed

unending *adjective* **= perpetual**, endless, eternal, continual, interminable, everlasting, unceasing

unendurable *adjective* **= unbearable**, intolerable, insufferable, insupportable

unenthusiastic *adjective* **= indifferent**, apathetic, half-hearted, nonchalant

unenviable *adjective* **= unpleasant**, uncomfortable, undesirable, disagreeable

unequal *adjective* **1 = different**, unlike, disparate, unmatched, dissimilar, differing, varying
2 = disproportionate, irregular, uneven, unbalanced, asymmetrical, ill-matched

unequalled *adjective* **= incomparable**, supreme, paramount, unparalleled, unrivalled, matchless, peerless

unequivocal *adjective* **= clear**, certain, absolute, plain, explicit, definite, manifest, unambiguous, incontrovertible, indubitable

unerring *adjective* **= accurate**, sure, perfect, exact, infallible, unfailing

unethical *adjective* **= immoral**, wrong, illegal, improper, shady (*informal*), dishonest, unscrupulous, disreputable, unprincipled

uneven *adjective* **1 = rough**, bumpy, not level, not smooth • *I tripped and fell on the uneven pavement.*
OPPOSITE: level
2 = irregular, inconsistent, variable, patchy, fluctuating • *six posts of uneven height*
OPPOSITE: even
3 = lopsided, odd, unbalanced
4 = unequal, unfair, ill-matched

uneventful *adjective* **= humdrum**, routine, boring, dull, ho-hum (*informal*), tedious, monotonous, unexciting

unexceptional *adjective* **= ordinary**, normal, conventional, pedestrian, mediocre, commonplace, unremarkable, undistinguished

unexpected *adjective* **= unforeseen**, chance, astonishing, surprising • *Their move was completely unexpected.*
See also: **abrupt, sudden**

unfailing *adjective*
1 = continuous, persistent, endless, boundless, unflagging
2 = reliable, sure, certain, true, loyal, faithful, staunch, dependable

unfair *adjective* **1 = unjust**, wrong,

wrongful • *It's unfair that she had to miss the final game.*
2 = biased, partial, partisan, unjust, one-sided, bigoted, prejudiced
3 = unscrupulous, wrongful, unethical, dishonest, unsporting
OPPOSITE: fair

unfairness *See* **injustice**

unfaithful *adjective*
1 = adulterous, two-timing (*informal*) • *an unfaithful husband*
OPPOSITE: faithful
2 = disloyal, false, treacherous, deceitful, untrustworthy, faithless, traitorous

unfamiliar *adjective* = **strange**, new, foreign, novel, unknown, alien, exotic • *She grew many plants that were unfamiliar to me.*

unfashionable *adjective* = **passé**, old-fashioned, obsolete, antiquated, dated, dumpy (*informal*), frowzy, homely (US), old hat

unfasten *verb* = **undo**, open, separate, detach, loosen, untie, let go, unlace

unfathomable *adjective*
1 = baffling, deep, profound, incomprehensible, inexplicable, impenetrable, indecipherable
2 = immeasurable, bottomless, unmeasured

unfavourable *adjective*
1 = adverse, unfortunate, contrary, unlucky, inauspicious, unpropitious
2 = hostile, negative, unfriendly, inimical

unfeeling *adjective*
1 = hardhearted, cold, cruel, insensitive, callous, apathetic, heartless, pitiless, uncaring
2 = numb, insensate, insensible

unfinished *adjective*
1 = incomplete, half-done, uncompleted, undone
2 = rough, natural, crude, raw, bare, unrefined

unfit *adjective* **1 = incapable**, inadequate, useless, lousy (*slang*), incompetent, unqualified, no good
2 = unsuitable, inadequate, ineffective, useless, unsuited
3 = out of shape, unhealthy, feeble, flabby, in poor condition

unflappable *adjective*
= **imperturbable**, cool, calm, collected, composed, impassive, level-headed, self-possessed

unflattering *adjective* **1 = blunt**, critical, honest, candid
2 = unattractive, plain, unbecoming, dumpy (*informal*), frowzy, homely (US)

unflinching *adjective*
= **determined**, firm, steady, staunch, steadfast, resolute, immovable, unfaltering

unflustered *See* **relaxed**

unfold *verb* **1 = open**, expand, unravel, undo, unfurl, unwrap, unroll, spread out
2 = reveal, show, present, disclose, uncover, divulge, make known

unforeseeable *See* **unpredictable**

unforeseen *adjective*
= **unexpected**, sudden, accidental, unanticipated, surprising, unpredicted

unforgettable *adjective*
= **memorable**, impressive, notable, exceptional

unforgivable *adjective*
= **inexcusable**, disgraceful, shameful, deplorable, unpardonable

unfortunate *adjective*
1 = disastrous, adverse, ill-fated, calamitous
2 = unlucky, hapless, unhappy, unsuccessful, doomed, wretched, cursed
3 = regrettable, deplorable, unsuitable, lamentable

unfounded *adjective*
= **groundless**, false, idle, baseless, unjustified, spurious

unfriendly *adjective* **1 = hostile**, cold, aloof, antagonistic, unkind, disagreeable • *He can expect an unfriendly welcome.*
OPPOSITE: friendly
2 = unfavourable, hostile, alien, inhospitable

See also: **unpleasant**
unfurl See **spread**
unfurnished See **empty**
ungainliness See **clumsiness**
ungainly adjective = **awkward**, clumsy, lumbering, inelegant, ungraceful
ungodly adjective
1 = **unreasonable**, outrageous, dreadful, intolerable, unearthly
2 = **wicked**, corrupt, immoral, profane, sinful, depraved, godless, impious, irreligious
ungracious adjective = **bad-mannered**, rude, churlish, discourteous, impolite, uncivil, unmannerly
ungrateful adjective
= **unappreciative**, unthankful
• the most miserable and ungrateful people on earth
OPPOSITE: grateful
unguarded adjective
1 = **unprotected**, vulnerable, defenceless, undefended
2 = **careless**, rash, imprudent, thoughtless, unwary, heedless, ill-considered, incautious, unthinking
unhappiness noun = **sadness**, depression, misery, sorrow, gloom, heartache, melancholy, despondency, blues, dejection, low spirits, wretchedness
unhappy adjective 1 = **sad**, down, depressed, miserable, despondent • He was a shy, sometimes unhappy man.
OPPOSITE: happy
2 = **unlucky**, unfortunate, hapless, ill-fated, wretched, cursed
See also: **upset**
unharmed adjective = **unhurt**, safe, sound, whole, intact, unscathed, undamaged
unhealthy adjective 1 = **harmful**, unsanitary, noxious, bad for you, unwholesome • an unhealthy lifestyle
OPPOSITE: healthy
2 = **sick**, ill, ailing, not well, unwell • an unhealthy-looking man
OPPOSITE: healthy
See also: **perverted**

unheard-of adjective
1 = **unprecedented**, new, novel, unique, singular, inconceivable
2 = **shocking**, outrageous, disgraceful, preposterous
3 = **obscure**, unknown, unfamiliar
unhesitating adjective
1 = **instant**, ready, prompt, immediate
2 = **wholehearted**, resolute, unfaltering, unquestioning, unreserved
unholy adjective = **evil**, corrupt, wicked, profane, sinful, ungodly
unhurried adjective = **leisurely**, slow, easy, sedate
unhurriedly See **slowly**
unidentified adjective
= **unnamed**, anonymous, unfamiliar, unrecognized, nameless
unification noun = **union**, coalition, alliance, federation, amalgamation, confederation, coalescence, uniting
uniform noun 1 = **outfit**, suit, dress, habit, costume, garb, regalia, livery
▶ adjective 2 = **unvarying**, even, regular, consistent, constant, smooth, unchanging
3 = **alike**, like, same, similar, equal, on a level playing field (informal)
uniformity noun 1 = **regularity**, similarity, constancy, evenness, invariability, sameness
2 = **monotony**, dullness, flatness, sameness, tedium
uniformly See **alike**
unify verb = **unite**, join, combine, merge, consolidate, amalgamate, confederate
unimaginable adjective
= **inconceivable**, impossible, incredible, fantastic, unbelievable
unimaginative adjective
= **unoriginal**, ordinary, hack, pedestrian, predictable, derivative, dull, uninspired, banal, hackneyed, prosaic, uncreative
unimportant adjective

= **insignificant**, minor, slight, paltry, trivial • *The difference in their ages seemed unimportant at the time.*
OPPOSITE: important
See also: **petty**

uninhabited *adjective* = **deserted**, empty, vacant, barren, desolate, unpopulated

uninhibited *adjective*
1 = **unselfconscious**, open, free, natural, spontaneous, liberated, relaxed, unrepressed, unreserved
2 = **unrestrained**, free, unrestricted, unchecked, uncontrolled, unbridled, unconstrained

uninspired *adjective*
= **unimaginative**, ordinary, dull, banal, humdrum, prosaic, unexciting, unoriginal

unintelligent *adjective* = **stupid**, dense, dull, foolish, braindead (*informal*), brainless, slow, thick, obtuse

unintelligible *adjective*
= **incomprehensible**, meaningless, incoherent, inarticulate, indistinct, jumbled, muddled

unintentional *adjective*
= **accidental**, casual, unconscious, unintended, inadvertent, involuntary

uninterested *adjective*
= **indifferent**, passive, bored, apathetic, unconcerned, nonchalant, impassive • *I'm completely uninterested in anything you have to say.*
OPPOSITE: interested

| CONFUSABLES
Uninterested means *having no interest in someone or something. Disinterested* means *impartial.*

uninteresting *adjective*
= **boring**, dry, flat, dull, dreary, drab, tedious, monotonous, humdrum, unexciting

uninterrupted *adjective*
= **continuous**, steady, constant, sustained, nonstop, unbroken

union *noun* **1** = **alliance**, league, coalition, association, federation, confederation • *the Canadian Union of Public Employees*
2 = **amalgamation**, combination, blend, mixture, conjunction, fusion, unification, amalgam, synthesis • *The majority voted for union with the larger organization.*
3 = **agreement**, accord, unity, harmony, unison, unanimity, concord
See also: **bond, club, society**

unique *adjective* **1** = **distinct**, only, single, lone, solitary
2 = **unparalleled**, unmatched, incomparable, unrivalled, inimitable, matchless, unequalled

unison *noun* = **agreement**, accord, concert, unity, accordance, harmony, concord

unit *noun* **1** = **item**, whole, entity
2 = **part**, member, section, element, component, segment, constituent
3 = **section**, group, detachment, platoon
4 = **measure**, quantity, measurement

unite *verb* **1** = **cooperate**, join, combine, merge, collaborate, join forces, link up, pull together, work together • *We must unite to fight our common enemy.*
OPPOSITE: divide
2 = **join**, link, couple, combine, merge, blend, unify, fuse, amalgamate
See also: **team**

united *adjective* **1** = **combined**, collective, unified, concerted, allied, affiliated, pooled, banded together
2 = **in agreement**, unanimous, agreed, of one mind, of the same opinion

unity *noun* **1** = **wholeness**, union, integrity, entity, oneness, singleness
2 = **agreement**, accord, consensus, solidarity, harmony, assent, unison, concord

universal *adjective* = **widespread**, general, common, worldwide,

u

unlimited, multicultural or muliticulti, catholic, overarching • These programs have a universal appeal.
See also: **broad, mass, popular, public**

universally adverb = **everywhere**, always, invariably, without exception

universe noun = **cosmos**, nature, creation, macrocosm

unjust adjective = **unfair**, wrong, partial, partisan, wrongful, one-sided, biased, prejudiced

unjustifiable adjective = **inexcusable**, wrong, unacceptable, outrageous, indefensible, unforgivable, unpardonable

unkempt adjective **1** = **uncombed**, shaggy, tousled **2** = **untidy**, messy, dishevelled, disordered, slovenly, ungroomed

unkind adjective = **cruel**, mean, nasty, malicious, thoughtless, spiteful • It's very unkind to describe her in those terms.
OPPOSITE: kind
See also: **hostile, unfriendly**

unknowing See **unconscious**

unknown adjective **1** = **obscure**, humble, unfamiliar, unsung • She was an unknown at that time.
OPPOSITE: famous
2 = **unrevealed**, secret, dark, mysterious, hidden, concealed
3 = **strange**, new, alien
4 = **unidentified**, anonymous, unnamed, uncharted, undiscovered, nameless, unexplored

unlawful adjective = **illegal**, criminal, illicit, outlawed, banned, forbidden, prohibited

unleash verb = **release**, free, let go, let loose

unlike adjective = **different from**, dissimilar to, distinct from, divergent from, far from • She was unlike her sister.
OPPOSITE: like
See also: **different**

unlikely adjective
1 = **unbelievable**, incredible, implausible, unconvincing

• an unlikely story
OPPOSITE: likely
2 = **improbable**, remote, slight, faint, doubtful • It seems unlikely that there will be a sequel to the film.

unlimited adjective **1** = **infinite**, great, extensive, vast, countless, endless, immense, limitless, boundless, unbounded
2 = **total**, complete, full, absolute, unrestricted, unqualified

unload verb = **empty**, dump, relieve, discharge, unpack, lighten

unlock verb = **open**, release, undo, unfasten, unlatch

unlocked See **open**

unlooked-for adjective = **unexpected**, chance, unforeseen, fortuitous, unanticipated, surprising, unpredicted

unloved adjective = **neglected**, unwanted, unpopular, forsaken, loveless, rejected, spurned

unlucky adjective
1 = **unfortunate**, hapless, wretched, cursed, luckless • He was unlucky not to score during the first period.
OPPOSITE: lucky
2 = **ill-fated**, doomed, ominous, inauspicious, unfavourable

unmarked See **blank**

unmarried adjective = **single**, bachelor, maiden, unattached, unwed

unmask verb = **reveal**, discover, expose, disclose, uncover, lay bare

unmentionable adjective = **taboo**, shocking, obscene, shameful, indecent, scandalous, unspeakable, forbidden, unsayable

unmerciful adjective = **merciless**, hard, brutal, cruel, ruthless, implacable, pitiless, remorseless

unmistakable adjective = **clear**, sure, certain, obvious, plain, evident, distinct, manifest, unambiguous

unmitigated adjective
1 = **unrelieved**, intense,

persistent, unbroken,
unalleviated, undiminished
2 = complete, absolute,
outright, utter, thorough, sheer,
downright, arrant
unmoved adjective = **unaffected**,
cold, untouched, indifferent,
unimpressed, unresponsive,
impassive
unnatural adjective **1 = strange**,
extraordinary, outlandish,
queer, freakish
2 = abnormal, odd, unusual,
irregular, perverse, perverted,
anomalous
3 = false, artificial, stiff,
affected, phony (informal), forced,
stilted, feigned, insincere
unnecessary adjective
= **needless**, pointless, uncalled-
for • He frowns upon unnecessary
expense.
OPPOSITE: necessary
unnerve verb = **shake**, upset,
discourage, rattle (informal),
intimidate, frighten, dismay,
dishearten, demoralize, faze,
fluster, psych out (informal)
unnerving See **scary**
unnoticed adjective
= **unobserved**, unheeded,
unseen, unrecognized,
neglected, disregarded, ignored,
overlooked, unperceived
unobtrusive adjective
= **inconspicuous**, quiet,
modest, low-key, restrained,
unassuming, self-effacing,
retiring
unoccupied adjective = **empty**,
vacant, uninhabited
unofficial adjective
= **unauthorized**, private,
informal, unconfirmed
unorthodox adjective
= **unconventional**, unusual,
abnormal, irregular, off-the-
wall (slang)
unpaid adjective **1 = voluntary**,
honorary, unsalaried
2 = owing, due, overdue,
outstanding, payable, unsettled
unpalatable adjective
= **unpleasant**, offensive,
horrid, distasteful, repugnant,

disagreeable, unappetizing,
unsavoury
unparalleled adjective
= **unequalled**, unique,
unprecedented, unmatched,
superlative, incomparable,
unsurpassed, matchless
unpardonable adjective
= **unforgivable**, disgraceful,
inexcusable, deplorable,
indefensible
unperturbed adjective = **calm**,
cool, unfazed (informal), as cool
as a cucumber, composed,
placid, unruffled, untroubled,
unworried
unpleasant adjective **1 = nasty**,
bad, distasteful, repulsive,
unpalatable, disagreeable • It has
a very unpleasant smell.
OPPOSITE: pleasant
2 = obnoxious, rude,
objectionable, unfriendly,
horrid, disagreeable • a thoroughly
unpleasant person
OPPOSITE: pleasant
See also: **horrible, painful,
rough**
unpolluted See **clean**
unpopular adjective = **disliked**,
undesirable, detested, shunned
• an unpopular idea
OPPOSITE: popular
unprecedented adjective
= **extraordinary**, new, original,
novel, remarkable, abnormal,
singular, unheard-of
unpredictable adjective
= **inconstant**, chance, doubtful,
unforeseeable, hit or miss
(informal) • England's notoriously
unpredictable weather
OPPOSITE: predictable
See also: **changeable**
unprejudiced adjective
= **impartial**, just, fair, objective,
balanced, unbiased, open-
minded
unprepared adjective **1 = taken
off guard**, unaware, surprised,
unready
2 = improvised, spontaneous,
ad-lib, off the cuff (informal)
unpretentious adjective
= **modest**, simple, humble,

u

plain, straightforward, unaffected, unassuming, homey, dumpy (*informal*), unostentatious

unprincipled *adjective*
= **dishonest**, unethical, immoral, crooked, unscrupulous, devious, amoral, underhand

unproductive *adjective*
1 = **useless**, ineffective, idle, vain, futile, fruitless, unprofitable, unrewarding
2 = **barren**, sterile, fruitless

unprofessional *adjective*
1 = **unethical**, lax, improper, negligent, unprincipled
2 = **amateurish**, incompetent, inefficient, inexpert

unprotected *adjective*
= **vulnerable**, open, helpless, defenceless, undefended

unqualified *adjective* 1 = **unfit**, unprepared, incompetent, incapable, ineligible, ill-equipped
2 = **total**, complete, absolute, outright, utter, thorough, downright

unquestionable *adjective*
= **certain**, clear, sure, absolute, definite, conclusive, unmistakable, unequivocal, undeniable, indisputable, incontrovertible

unquestionably See **certainly**

unravel *verb* 1 = **undo**, free, separate, unwind, untangle, disentangle
2 = **solve**, explain, resolve, figure out (*informal*), work out

unreal *adjective* 1 = **imaginary**, fabulous, visionary, fanciful, make-believe, illusory, dreamlike
2 = **insubstantial**, intangible, immaterial, nebulous
3 = **fake**, false, artificial, mock, sham, insincere, pretended

unrealistic *adjective*
= **impractical**, romantic, improbable, unworkable, impracticable

unreasonable *adjective*
1 = **excessive**, unfair,

unwarranted, unjust, undue, extortionate, immoderate
2 = **biased**, opinionated, blinkered

unreasonably See **too**

unrelated *adjective*
1 = **unconnected**, different, unlike
2 = **irrelevant**, inappropriate, unconnected, extraneous, inapplicable

unrelenting See **relentless**

unreliable *adjective*
1 = **undependable**, irresponsible, treacherous, untrustworthy
2 = **inaccurate**, false, uncertain, deceptive, implausible, unsound, fallible

unremitting See **relentless**

unrepentant *adjective*
= **impenitent**, abandoned, shameless, callous, hardened, incorrigible, unremorseful

unreserved *adjective* 1 = **total**, complete, full, entire, absolute, unlimited, wholehearted
2 = **open**, free, outgoing, unrestrained, demonstrative, extroverted, uninhibited

unresolved *adjective*
= **undecided**, unanswered, vague, doubtful, moot, unsolved, undetermined, unsettled

unrest *noun* = **discontent**, protest, rebellion, strife, agitation, discord, dissension, sedition

unrestrained *adjective*
= **uncontrolled**, free, abandoned, unchecked, unbridled, immoderate, intemperate, unbounded, uninhibited

unrestricted *adjective*
1 = **unlimited**, open, free, absolute, unregulated, unbounded
2 = **open**, public

unrivalled *adjective*
= **unparalleled**, superior, supreme, superb, unmatched, incomparable, unsurpassed, matchless, unequalled, beyond compare

unroll *See* **spread**

unruly *adjective* = **uncontrollable**, wild, wayward, rebellious, wilful, disobedient, mutinous

unsafe *adjective* = **dangerous**, risky, hazardous, unreliable, perilous, sketchy (*informal*), insecure

unsatisfactory *adjective*
= **unacceptable**, poor, inadequate, mediocre, disappointing • *His work was judged unsatisfactory.*
OPPOSITE: satisfactory
See also: **rotten**

unsavoury *adjective*
1 = **unpleasant**, offensive, nasty, repellent, distasteful, obnoxious, repulsive, revolting, scuzzy (*slang*)
2 = **unappetizing**, sickening, unpalatable, nauseating

unscathed *adjective* = **unharmed**, safe, whole, unhurt, unmarked, uninjured

unscrupulous *adjective*
= **unprincipled**, corrupt, improper, unethical, immoral, dishonest, dishonourable

unseat *verb* 1 = **throw**, unhorse, unsaddle
2 = **depose**, remove, oust, displace, overthrow, dethrone

unsecured *See* **loose**

unseemly *adjective* = **improper**, inappropriate, unsuitable, unbecoming, undignified, indecorous

unseen *adjective* 1 = **unobserved**, unnoticed, undetected
2 = **hidden**, invisible, obscure, concealed

unselfish *adjective* = **generous**, kind, noble, selfless, altruistic, magnanimous, self-sacrificing

unsettle *verb* = **disturb**, trouble, upset, confuse, bother, agitate, ruffle, faze, disconcert, fluster, perturb

unsettled *adjective* 1 = **unstable**, shaky, disorderly, insecure, unsteady
2 = **restless**, anxious, tense, confused, restive, shaken,

disturbed, agitated, flustered, wired (*slang*)
3 = **changing**, uncertain, variable, inconstant

unshakable *adjective* = **firm**, sure, absolute, staunch, steadfast, fixed, immovable, unswerving, unwavering

unsharpened *See* **blunt**

unsightly *adjective* = **ugly**, unattractive, horrid, hideous, repulsive, disagreeable, dumpy (*informal*), homely (*US*), scuzzy (*slang*)

unskilled *adjective*
= **unprofessional**, amateurish, inexperienced, unqualified, untrained

unsociable *adjective*
= **unfriendly**, cold, distant, hostile, chilly, retiring, unforthcoming, withdrawn

unsolicited *adjective*
= **unrequested**, gratuitous, uninvited, unasked for, uncalled-for, unsought

unsophisticated *adjective*
1 = **natural**, unaffected, childlike, artless, guileless, ingenuous
2 = **simple**, plain, unrefined, homey, uncomplicated, dumpy (*informal*), frowzy, unspecialized

unsound *adjective* 1 = **unhealthy**, weak, ill, ailing, unstable, defective, diseased, unbalanced, unwell
2 = **unreliable**, weak, false, shaky, flawed, defective, illogical, fallacious, specious

unspeakable *adjective*
1 = **indescribable**, unbelievable, unimaginable, inconceivable
2 = **dreadful**, horrible, shocking, awful, appalling, heinous, monstrous, abominable

unspoiled *adjective*
1 = **unchanged**, intact, perfect, untouched, undamaged, preserved
2 = **natural**, innocent, unaffected, artless

unspoken *adjective* = **tacit**, implicit, implied, understood, unexpressed, unstated

u

unstable adjective 1 = **insecure**, shaky, precarious, unsteady, wobbly, unsettled, tottering
2 = **changeable**, volatile, unpredictable, variable, fitful, fluctuating, inconstant
3 = **unpredictable**, inconsistent, erratic, irrational, temperamental, capricious, changeable

unsteady adjective 1 = **unstable**, unsafe, shaky, precarious, wobbly, rickety, tottering • *a slightly unsteady item of furniture*
OPPOSITE: steady
2 = **changeable**, volatile, erratic, temperamental, unsettled, inconstant

unsuccessful adjective
1 = **useless**, failed, vain, futile, fruitless, unproductive, unavailing
2 = **unlucky**, unfortunate, hapless, luckless

unsuitable adjective
= **inappropriate**, unacceptable, unfit, improper • *Her shoes were unsuitable for walking any distance.*
OPPOSITE: suitable
See also: **useless**

unsung See **unknown**

unsure adjective 1 = **unconfident**, insecure, unassured
2 = **doubtful**, suspicious, skeptical, dubious, hesitant, unconvinced, distrustful, mistrustful

unsuspecting adjective
= **trusting**, gullible, unwary, credulous, trustful

unswerving adjective = **constant**, firm, true, steady, staunch, steadfast, resolute, single-minded, unwavering

unsympathetic adjective
= **insensitive**, hard, cold, harsh, cruel, callous, unmoved, heartless, unkind, unfeeling

untamed See **wild**

untangle verb = **disentangle**, unravel, extricate, unsnarl

untenable adjective
= **unsustainable**, weak, shaky, groundless, illogical, indefensible, unsound, insupportable

unthankful See **ungrateful**

unthinkable adjective
1 = **impossible**, unreasonable, absurd, out of the question
2 = **inconceivable**, incredible, unimaginable, implausible

untidy adjective = **messy**, chaotic, cluttered, bedraggled, jumbled, unkempt • *The place quickly became untidy.*
OPPOSITE: tidy
See also: **confused**

untie verb = **undo**, release, free, loosen, unbind, unfasten, unknot, unlace

untimely adjective 1 = **early**, premature
2 = **ill-timed**, inappropriate, inconvenient, awkward, inopportune, mistimed

untiring adjective = **tireless**, steady, constant, determined, dogged, persevering, unflagging, unremitting

untold adjective
1 = **indescribable**, unthinkable, unimaginable, inexpressible, undreamed of, unutterable
2 = **countless**, myriad, innumerable, incalculable, numberless, uncountable

untouched adjective
= **unharmed**, intact, unhurt, unscathed, uninjured, undamaged

untoward adjective
1 = **troublesome**, unfortunate, inconvenient, awkward, annoying, irritating
2 = **unfavourable**, adverse, unlucky, inauspicious, inopportune

untrained adjective = **amateur**, green, raw, inexperienced, unqualified, uneducated, unskilled, unschooled, untaught

untroubled adjective
= **undisturbed**, cool, calm, peaceful, unfazed (*informal*), tranquil, placid, unperturbed, unworried

untrue adjective 1 = **false**,

incorrect, inaccurate, mistaken, erroneous, fictitious, misleading • *The allegations were completely untrue.*
OPPOSITE: true
2 = unfaithful, false, treacherous, deceitful, untrustworthy, disloyal, faithless, inconstant
See also: **wrong**

untrustworthy *adjective*
= **unreliable**, false, slippery, tricky, treacherous, dishonest, deceitful, devious, disloyal

untruth *noun* = **lie**, deceit, fib, falsehood, story, white lie

untruthful *adjective* = **dishonest**, false, deceptive, deceitful, lying, mendacious

unused *See* **waste**

unusual *adjective* **1 = rare**, uncommon • *many rare and unusual plants*
OPPOSITE: common
2 = extraordinary, curious, exceptional, unconventional
See also: **funny, scarce, singular**

unveil *verb* = **reveal**, expose, disclose, uncover, divulge, make known

unwanted *adjective* = **undesired**, unsolicited, unwelcome, outcast, unneeded, uninvited, rejected

unwarranted *adjective*
= **unnecessary**, unjustified, inexcusable, groundless, unprovoked, gratuitous, indefensible, uncalled-for

unwavering *adjective*
= **steady**, consistent, staunch, determined, steadfast, resolute, unshakable, immovable, unswerving

unwelcome *adjective*
1 = unwanted, unacceptable, undesirable, excluded, rejected
2 = disagreeable, unpleasant, undesirable, distasteful, displeasing

unwell *adjective* = **ill**, sick, ailing, queasy • *He felt unwell and had to go home early.*
OPPOSITE: well
See also: **unhealthy**

unwholesome *adjective*
1 = harmful, unhealthy, poisonous, noxious, deleterious
2 = wicked, bad, evil, immoral, degrading, corrupting, demoralizing

unwieldy *adjective* **1 = awkward**, inconvenient, cumbersome, unmanageable
2 = bulky, massive, hefty, clumsy, ponderous

unwilling *adjective* = **reluctant**, loath, averse to, grudging • *an unwilling participant in school sports*
OPPOSITE: willing

unwind *verb* **1 = unravel**, undo, slacken, unroll, uncoil, untwine, untwist
2 = relax, de-stress, loosen up, take it easy, wind down

unwise *adjective* = **foolish**, stupid, silly, irresponsible, rash, senseless, idiotic • *It would be unwise to expect too much of him.*
OPPOSITE: wise

unwitting *adjective*
1 = unintentional, chance, accidental, unplanned, inadvertent, involuntary
2 = unknowing, innocent, unaware, unconscious, unsuspecting, ignorant

unworldly *adjective* **1 = spiritual**, metaphysical, nonmaterialistic
2 = naive, innocent, idealistic, unsophisticated

unworthy *adjective*
1 = undeserving, not fit for, not good enough
2 = dishonourable, base, disgraceful, shameful, degrading, lousy (*slang*), contemptible, discreditable, disreputable, ignoble
▷ **unworthy of = unbefitting**, inappropriate, beneath, unsuitable, unbecoming, unseemly, unfitting

unwrap *See* **uncover**

unwritten *adjective* **1 = oral**, vocal
2 = customary, accepted, tacit, understood

unyielding *adjective* = **firm**, tough, stubborn, adamant, rigid, resolute, uncompromising,

u

inflexible, immovable, obdurate, obstinate, stiff-necked

up *See* **over**

up-and-coming *See* **in the making**

upbeat *adjective* = **cheerful**, positive, optimistic, hopeful, cheery, encouraging

upbraid *verb* = **scold**, rebuke, reprimand, berate, admonish, reproach, reprove

upbringing *noun* = **education**, training, raising, breeding, rearing

upcoming *See* **near**

update *verb* = **bring up to date**, upgrade, renew, amend, modernize

upgrade *verb* 1 = **improve**, enhance, better
2 = **promote**, raise, advance, elevate

upheaval *noun* = **disturbance**, disorder, revolution, disruption, turmoil

uphill *adjective* 1 = **ascending**, rising, mounting, climbing
2 = **arduous**, hard, tough, difficult, strenuous, gruelling, exhausting, laborious, taxing

uphold *verb* = **support**, back, defend, aid, endorse, champion, maintain, promote, advocate, sustain

upkeep *noun* 1 = **maintenance**, keep, preservation, running, overheads • *The money will be used for the upkeep of the grounds.*
2 = **overheads**, expenditure, expenses, running costs

uplift *verb* 1 = **raise**, hoist, elevate, lift up
2 = **improve**, raise, advance, inspire, refine, better, edify
▶ *noun* 3 = **improvement**, enrichment, advancement, enhancement, refinement, enlightenment, edification

upmarket *adjective* (*Informal*) = **high-class**, grand, luxurious, classy (*informal*), smart, stylish, swanky *or* swank (*informal*), upscale, upper-class

upper *adjective* 1 = **higher**, high, top, loftier, topmost

2 = **superior**, important, eminent, greater
▷ **upper hand** = **control**, edge, advantage, mastery, supremacy, ascendancy
▷ **upper limit** *See* **maximum**

upper-class *adjective* = **aristocratic**, noble, blue-blooded, highborn, high-class, patrician

uppermost *adjective* 1 = **top**, highest, loftiest, topmost
2 = **supreme**, chief, main, principal, dominant, foremost, greatest, leading

uppity *adjective* (*Informal*) = **conceited**, cocky, bumptious, full of oneself, impertinent, self-important

upright *adjective* 1 = **vertical**, straight, erect, perpendicular
2 = **honest**, good, just, ethical, principled, conscientious, honourable, righteous, virtuous

uprising *noun* = **rebellion**, revolution, disturbance, revolt, rising, insurrection, mutiny, insurgence

uproar *noun* = **commotion**, riot, turmoil, noise, outcry, furor, mayhem, racket, pandemonium, din

uproarious *adjective*
1 = **hilarious**, hysterical, rib-tickling, rip-roaring (*informal*), side-splitting, very funny
2 = **boisterous**, loud, unrestrained, rollicking

uproot *verb* 1 = **pull up**, dig up, rip up, root out, weed out
2 = **displace**, exile

upscale *See* **exclusive, posh**

upset *adjective* 1 = **distressed**, hurt, troubled, unhappy, frantic, agitated • *She was very upset when she heard the news.*
2 = **sick**, ill, queasy
3 = **disordered**, chaotic, confused, disarrayed, in disarray, muddled
4 = **overturned**, capsized, spilled, upside down
▶ *verb* 5 = **distress**, disturb, bother, grieve, agitate, ruffle
• *The whole incident upset me terribly.*

u

6 = overturn, spill, capsize, knock over • *Don't upset that pile of papers.*
7 = mess up, change, disorder, disturb, spoil, disorganize
8 = distress, trouble, disturb, bother, grieve, agitate, ruffle, faze, disconcert, fluster, perturb
▶ *verb* **9 = reversal**, defeat, shake-up (*informal*)
10 = illness, complaint, disorder, bug (*informal*), sickness, malady
11 = distress, worry, trouble, shock, bother, disturbance, agitation
See also: **blow, shake**

upsetting *See* **sad**

upshot *noun* **= result**, end, outcome, finale, sequel, culmination, end result

upside down *adjective*
1 = inverted, backward, overturned, upturned
2 = confused, chaotic, disordered, topsy-turvy, muddled

upstanding *adjective* **= honest**, good, moral, ethical, upright, principled, honourable, incorruptible

upstart *noun* **= social climber**, arriviste, *nouveau riche* (*French*), parvenu

upsurge *noun* **= increase**, rise, growth, boost, escalation, upturn

uptight *adjective* (*Informal*)
= tense, anxious, uneasy, edgy, on edge, wired (*slang*)

up to *See* **equal to**

up-to-date *adjective* **= modern**, current, cool (*informal*), stylish, trendy (*informal*), fashionable, up-to-the-minute, in vogue, phat (*slang*)

up-to-the-minute *See* **current, modern**

upturn *noun* **= rise**, increase, improvement, recovery, revival, advancement, upswing, upsurge

urban *adjective* **= civic**, city, town, municipal, metropolitan

urbane *adjective* **= sophisticated**, smooth, refined, polished, courteous, suave, cultured, cultivated, debonair, well-bred

urchin *noun* **= ragamuffin**, brat, gamin, waif

urge *noun* **1 = impulse**, drive, wish, desire, longing, compulsion • *stifling the urge to scream*
▶ *verb* **2 = beg**, plead, press, implore, beseech (*formal*) • *He urged the referee to change her ruling.*
3 = advocate, support, recommend, advise, counsel
4 = drive, force, push, press, spur, compel, induce, incite, goad, impel
See also: **insist, instinct, whim**

urgency *noun* **= importance**, need, pressure, gravity, hurry, necessity, seriousness, extremity

urgent *adjective* **= crucial**, immediate, pressing, imperative, compelling • *an urgent need for food and water*
See also: **serious**

usable *adjective* **= serviceable**, current, available, working, practical, valid, functional, utilizable

usage *noun* **1 = use**, control, operation, management, employment, handling, running
2 = practice, procedure, regime, convention, method, routine, habit, custom, mode

use *verb* **1 = employ**, operate, apply, utilize, ply, call into play, avail oneself of • *Use a sharp knife to trim the edges.*
2 = take advantage of, exploit, manipulate
3 = consume, spend, exhaust, expend, run through
▷ **use up = consume**, finish, drain, absorb, exhaust, run through
▶ *noun* **4 = usage**, operation, application, employment • *the use of force*
5 = purpose, point, end, object • *of no practical use whatsoever*
6 = good, help, point, service, profit, benefit, value, advantage, avail, usefulness
See also: **impose on, wear**

u

used *adjective* = **second-hand**, cast-off, nearly new, shopworn
▷ **used to** = **accustomed to**, familiar with

useful *adjective* = **helpful**, effective, valuable, practical, beneficial, worthwhile • *a great deal of useful information*
OPPOSITE: useless
See also: **convenient, handy, productive**

usefulness *noun* = **helpfulness**, use, benefit, value, worth, utility, effectiveness, convenience, efficacy, practicality

useless *adjective* 1 = **worthless**, futile, unproductive, impractical, unsuitable • *We realized that our money was useless here.*
OPPOSITE: useful
2 (*Informal*) = **inept**, incompetent, hopeless, ineffectual, no good
See also: **inadequate, vain**

usher *noun* 1 = **attendant**, guide, escort, doorkeeper, doorman
▶ *verb* 2 = **escort**, lead, conduct, direct, guide

usual *adjective* = **normal**, common, standard, regular, customary, habitual, accustomed • *sitting at his usual table*
See also: **average, natural, ordinary, routine, stock, typical**

usually *adverb* = **normally**, mostly, generally, mainly, commonly, as a rule, habitually, on the whole

usurp *verb* = **seize**, take, assume, appropriate, wrest, commandeer, take over

utensil See **tool**

utility *noun* = **usefulness**, benefit, convenience, efficacy, practicality, serviceableness

utilize *verb* = **use**, employ, avail oneself of, make use of, put to use, take advantage of, turn to account, call into play

utmost *adjective* 1 = **greatest**, chief, maximum, supreme, pre-eminent, paramount, highest
2 = **farthest**, last, final, extreme
▶ *noun* 3 = **best**, greatest, hardest, highest

Utopia *noun* = **paradise**, heaven, Eden, bliss, Garden of Eden, Shangri-la

Utopian *adjective* = **perfect**, dream, ideal, romantic, fantasy, visionary, imaginary, idealistic

utter[1] *verb* = **say**, speak, express, voice, pronounce, articulate
See also: **emit**

utter[2] *adjective* = **absolute**, complete, total, perfect, pure, outright, thorough, sheer, consummate, out-and-out
• *scenes of utter chaos*
See also: **rank**

utterance *noun* = **speech**, statement, announcement, remark, expression, declaration, words

utterly *adverb* = **totally**, completely, fully, extremely, absolutely, entirely, perfectly, thoroughly

u

Vv

vacancy *noun* = **job**, post, position, situation, opportunity, opening

vacant *adjective* **1** = **unoccupied**, free, available, empty, void, idle, unfilled, untenanted

2 = **vague**, blank, idle, dreamy, inane, absent-minded, abstracted, vacuous

vacate *verb* = **leave**, quit, evacuate

vacation *noun* = **holiday**, leave, break, trip, rest, tour, recess, furlough, time off, staycation (*informal*), leave of absence, minibreak, awayday • *I'm exhausted! I really need a vacation.*

vacuous *adjective* = **unintelligent**, blank, stupid, vacant, inane, uncomprehending

vacuum *noun* = **emptiness**, space, gap, void, nothingness, vacuity

vagabond *noun* = **tramp**, rover, panhandler, beggar, itinerant, vagrant, down-and-out

vagrant *noun* **1** = **tramp**, hobo, drifter, itinerant, wanderer, rolling stone

▶ *adjective* **2** = **vagabond**, nomadic, unsettled, itinerant, roaming, rootless, roving

vague *adjective* = **unclear**, loose, uncertain, indefinite, hazy, indistinct • *vague promises about a raise*

OPPOSITE: clear

See also: **broad, dim, faint, rough**

vain *adjective* **1** = **conceited**, proud, egotistical, ostentatious, stuck-up (*informal*) • *I think he is shallow and vain.*

2 = **futile**, useless, fruitless, unproductive, abortive • *He made a vain effort to cheer her up.*

OPPOSITE: successful

▶ *noun*

▷ **in vain** = **unsuccessful**, fruitless, to no avail, wasted • *Her complaints were in vain.*

See also: **fond, hopeless**

valiant *adjective* = **brave**, bold, heroic, courageous, fearless, gallant, intrepid, lion-hearted

valid *adjective* **1** = **sound**, good, logical, well-founded, cogent, convincing, telling, well-grounded

2 = **legal**, official, legitimate, genuine, authentic, lawful, bona fide

validate *verb* = **confirm**, endorse, authorize, ratify, certify, authenticate, substantiate, corroborate

validity *noun* **1** = **soundness**, force, power, weight, strength, cogency

2 = **legality**, right, authority, legitimacy, lawfulness

valley *noun* = **hollow**, depression, glen, dell, dale, vale

---

TYPES OF VALLEY

canyon	glen
chasm	gorge
coulee	gulch
dale	gully
defile	hollow
dell	ravine
depression	vale

---

valour *noun* = **bravery**, spirit, courage, heroism, boldness, fearlessness, gallantry, intrepidity

valuable *adjective* **1** = **useful**,

important, helpful, beneficial, worthwhile, prized • *The experience was very valuable.*
OPPOSITE: useless
2 = **precious**, expensive, costly • *valuable old baseball cards*
OPPOSITE: worthless
See also: **productive**
▶ noun
▷ **valuables** = **treasures**, heirlooms • *Leave your valuables at home.*

valuation See **estimate**

value noun 1 = **importance**, use, benefit, worth, advantage, merit, effectiveness, virtue, usefulness • *the value of a balanced diet*
2 = **cost**, price, worth, market price, selling price • *The value of their house has doubled.*
▷ **values** = **principles**, ethics, standards *or* moral standards
▶ verb 3 = **appreciate**, respect, treasure, cherish, prize, have a high opinion of, rate highly • *Do you value your friends?*
4 = **evaluate**, price, cost, estimate, assess, appraise • *I have had my jewellery valued for insurance purposes.*
See also: **admire, ideal, quality**

valueless See **worthless**

vandal noun = **hooligan**, rowdy, delinquent

vanguard noun = **forefront**, van, spearhead, cutting edge, forerunners, front line, leaders, trailblazers, trendsetters, point-man

vanish verb 1 = **disappear**, fade, recede, become invisible, be lost to view • *The moon vanished behind a cloud.*
OPPOSITE: appear
2 = **die out**, pass, cease, dissolve, evaporate, become extinct, cease to exist, fade away, go away, melt away • *Dinosaurs vanished from the earth millions of years ago.*
See also: **melt**

vanished See **lost**

vanity noun = **pride**, arrogance, narcissism, conceit, conceitedness, egotism

vanquish verb = **defeat**, beat, overcome, crush, rout, trounce, conquer • *a happy ending in which the hero vanquishes the villains*
See also: **subdue**

vapid adjective = **dull**, weak, flat, tame, boring, bland, insipid, uninspiring, uninteresting, wishy-washy (*informal*)

vapour noun = **mist**, steam, fog, haze, exhalation
See also: **cloud**

variable adjective = **changeable**, flexible, unstable, uneven, unsteady, temperamental, fluctuating, inconstant, mutable, shifting

variance noun
▷ **at variance** = **in disagreement**, at loggerheads, at odds, conflicting, out of line

variant adjective 1 = **different**, alternative, modified, divergent
▶ noun 2 = **variation**, development, alternative, modification

variation noun = **change**, difference, departure, diversification, alteration, deviation • *a variation of the usual route*

varied adjective = **different**, various, mixed, diverse, assorted, miscellaneous, heterogeneous, motley, sundry

variety noun 1 = **range**, collection, array, mixture, medley, assortment • *a wide variety of readers*
2 = **type**, kind, class, strain, sort, category • *a new variety of celery*
3 = **diversity**, change, difference, variation, discrepancy, diversification, multifariousness
See also: **breed, choice, form**

various adjective = **different**, diverse, disparate, assorted, miscellaneous, sundry • *trees of various sorts*
See also: **several**

varnish noun, verb = **lacquer**, polish, gloss, glaze

vary verb 1 = **change**, alter, alternate, fluctuate • *weather*

patterns vary greatly
2 = alternate, modify, diversify
• Vary your routes as much as possible.
See also: **range**
vast adjective = **huge**, great, giant, massive, enormous, immense, gigantic, colossal • vast stretches of farmland
OPPOSITE: tiny
See also: **broad, extensive, large, spacious**
vault[1] noun **1 = strongroom**, repository, depository
2 = crypt, tomb, cellar, mausoleum, catacomb, charnel house, undercroft
vault[2] verb = **jump**, clear, spring, hurdle, leap, bound
vaulted adjective = **arched**, cavernous, domed
veer verb = **change course**, turn, shift, sheer, swerve, change direction
vegetate verb = **stagnate**, deteriorate, idle, languish, loaf, go to seed
vehemence noun = **forcefulness**, force, energy, passion, intensity, emphasis, vigour, ardour, fervour
vehement adjective = **strong**, powerful, intense, fierce, passionate, forceful, impassioned, emphatic, ardent, fervent
vehicle noun **1 = conveyance**, transport, transportation
2 = medium, channel, organ, means, mechanism, apparatus
veil noun **1 = cover**, film, screen, mask, blind, cloak, curtain, disguise, shroud
▶ verb **2 = cover**, screen, hide, mask, shield, cloak, conceal, obscure, disguise
veiled adjective = **disguised**, covert, implied, masked, concealed, hinted at, suppressed
vein noun **1 = blood vessel**
2 = seam, current, course, streak, stripe, stratum, lode
3 = mood, note, style, tone, tenor, mode, temper
velocity noun = **speed**, pace,

quickness, rapidity, swiftness
velvety adjective = **soft**, smooth, delicate, downy
vendetta noun = **feud**, quarrel, bad blood
veneer noun = **mask**, show, front, appearance, guise, pretense, semblance, façade
venerable adjective = **respected**, wise, sage, august, esteemed, honoured, revered, worshipped
venerate verb = **respect**, honour, revere, worship, adore, esteem, reverence, look up to
venerated See **holy**
vengeance noun = **revenge**, reprisal, retaliation, retribution
venom noun **1 = malice**, hate, spite, bitterness, virulence, spleen, acrimony, rancour
2 = poison, toxin, bane
venomous adjective
1 = malicious, hostile, vicious, savage, malignant, vindictive, rancorous, spiteful
2 = poisonous, toxic, virulent, noxious, mephitic
vent noun **1 = outlet**, opening, duct, aperture, orifice
▶ verb **2 = express**, release, air, voice, discharge, emit, utter, give vent to, pour out
venture noun **1 = undertaking**, risk, project, gamble, hazard, adventure, enterprise, endeavour
▶ verb **2 = risk**, chance, stake, speculate, hazard, wager
3 = dare, volunteer, hazard, presume, make bold, take the liberty
4 = go, embark on, plunge into, set out
verbal adjective = **spoken**, oral, word-of-mouth, unwritten
verbatim adverb = **exactly**, precisely, to the letter, word for word
verbose adjective = **long-winded**, windy, diffuse, circumlocutory, periphrastic, prolix, tautological, wordy
verbosity noun = **long-windedness**, loquaciousness, prolixity, verboseness, wordiness

V

verdant *adjective* = **green**, fresh, leafy, lush, grassy, flourishing

verdict *noun* = **decision**, finding, opinion, conclusion, judgment
• *The doctor's verdict is that I am fine.*

verge *noun* = **border**, limit, edge, margin, brink, boundary, threshold, brim
▶ *verb*
▷ **verge on** = **come close to**, border, approach

verification *noun* = **proof**, confirmation, validation, authentication, corroboration, substantiation

verified *See* **actual**

verify *verb* = **confirm**, support, check, prove, authenticate, validate, substantiate, corroborate, bear out

vernacular *noun* = **speech**, dialect, parlance, idiom, patois

versatile *adjective* = **adaptable**, flexible, all-purpose, all-around, variable, adjustable, multifaceted, resourceful

versed *adjective* = **knowledgeable**, familiar, experienced, seasoned, proficient, acquainted, conversant, practised, well informed

version *noun* **1** = **form**, design, model, style, variant
2 = **account**, portrayal, adaptation, interpretation, rendering

versus *See* **against**

vertical *adjective* = **upright**, erect, on end, perpendicular

vertigo *noun* = **dizziness**, giddiness, light-headedness

verve *noun* = **enthusiasm**, energy, spirit, animation, sparkle, vitality, gusto, liveliness

very *adverb* **1** = **extremely**, really, highly, deeply, greatly, terribly
• *very bad dreams*
▷ **very much** *See* **far**
▶ *adjective* **2** = **exact**, precise, selfsame

vessel *noun* **1** = **ship**, boat, craft
2 = **container**, pot, utensil, receptacle

vest *verb* (with *in* or *with*) = **place**, settle, invest, bestow, confer, entrust, endow, consign

vestibule *noun* = **hall**, lobby, porch, foyer, anteroom, portico

vestige *noun* = **trace**, suspicion, scrap, indication, remnant, glimmer

vestiges *See* **remains**

vet *verb* = **check**, review, investigate, examine, scrutinize, appraise

veteran *noun* **1** = **old hand**, old stager, past master, warhorse (*informal*)
▶ *adjective* **2** = **long-serving**, old, seasoned, battle-scarred

veto *verb* **1** = **ban**, prohibit, forbid
• *They vetoed our plans for a party.*
▶ *noun* **2** = **ban**, prohibition • *The five permanent members of the UN Security Council have the power of veto.*

vex *verb* = **annoy**, worry, trouble, upset, plague, bother, distress, irritate, exasperate

vexation *noun* **1** = **annoyance**, frustration, pique, displeasure, dissatisfaction, irritation, chagrin, exasperation
2 = **problem**, worry, trouble, difficulty, bother, headache (*informal*), hassle (*informal*), nuisance

viable *adjective* = **workable**, feasible, applicable, usable, operable, practicable

vibrant *adjective* = **energetic**, alive, animated, dynamic, sparkling, vigorous, spirited, vivid, vivacious

vibrate *verb* = **shake**, fluctuate, sway, reverberate, tremble, shudder, throb, quiver, pulsate, oscillate

vibration *noun* = **shaking**, shake, tremor, shudder, quiver, oscillation, pulsation, reverberation, throbbing, trembling

vicarious *adjective* = **indirect**, surrogate, delegated, substituted

vice *noun* **1** = **wickedness**, corruption, evil, sin, immorality, depravity, iniquity, turpitude
2 = **fault**, weakness, defect,

shortcoming, blemish, failing, imperfection

vice versa *adverb* = **the other way round**, conversely, contrariwise, in reverse

vicinity *noun* = **neighbourhood**, area, district, proximity, locality, environs, neck of the woods (*informal*)

vicious *adjective* 1 = **savage**, violent, cruel, ferocious, wicked, barbarous
2 = **malicious**, mean, cruel, venomous, vindictive, spiteful

viciousness See **cruelty**

victim *noun* = **casualty**, sacrifice, fatality, sufferer, martyr, scapegoat

victimize *verb* = **persecute**, discriminate against, pick on

victor *noun* = **winner**, champion, conqueror, prizewinner, vanquisher

victorious *adjective* = **winning**, first, champion, successful, triumphant, conquering, prizewinning, vanquishing

victory *noun* = **win**, success, triumph, superiority, laurels
• *the Canadiens' fourth consecutive victory*
OPPOSITE: defeat

vie *verb* = **compete**, struggle, contend, strive

view *noun* 1 = **opinion**, conviction, feeling, belief, attitude, point of view • *his political views*
2 = **scene**, perspective, aspect, landscape, spectacle, panorama • *There was a beautiful view from the window.*
3 = **vision**, sight
▶ *verb* 4 = **regard**, consider, judge, deem • *They viewed me with contempt.*
See also: **idea, judgment, observe, outlook, scenery, thought, watch**

viewer *noun* = **watcher**, observer, spectator, onlooker

viewpoint *noun* = **point of view**, opinion, conviction, feeling, belief, attitude • *We all have our own personal viewpoints.*

vigilance *noun* = **watchfulness**, caution, observance, alertness, attentiveness, carefulness, circumspection

vigilant *adjective* = **watchful**, alert, careful, cautious, attentive, circumspect, on one's guard, on the lookout, wakeful

vigorous *adjective* = **energetic**, strong, powerful, active, dynamic, spirited, lively, forceful, strenuous, lusty

vigorously *adverb*
= **energetically**, hard, strongly, forcefully, strenuously, lustily

vigour *noun* = **energy**, power, strength, spirit, animation, vitality, dynamism, gusto, verve, liveliness, forcefulness
See also: **drive**

vile *adjective* 1 = **wicked**, evil, corrupt, degenerate, nefarious, perverted, depraved
2 = **disgusting**, offensive, foul, nasty, sickening, horrid, repulsive, repugnant, revolting, nauseating, scuzzy (*slang*)

vilify *verb* = **malign**, abuse, smear, berate, disparage, slander, denigrate, revile

villain *noun* 1 = **evildoer**, criminal, rogue, miscreant, reprobate, scoundrel, wretch
2 = **bad guy** (*informal*), antihero

villainous *adjective* = **wicked**, bad, evil, vicious, cruel, degenerate, vile, nefarious, depraved, fiendish

villainy *noun* = **wickedness**, vice, delinquency, depravity, devilry, iniquity, turpitude

vindicate *verb* 1 = **clear**, acquit, exonerate, rehabilitate, absolve, exculpate
2 = **justify**, defend, excuse

vindication *noun*
1 = **exoneration**, rehabilitation, exculpation
2 = **justification**, excuse, defence

vindictive *adjective* = **vengeful**, malicious, unrelenting, resentful, implacable, revengeful, spiteful, unforgiving

vintage *adjective* = **high-quality**,

V

prime, choice, select, classic, superior, best

violate verb **1 = break**, infringe, disregard, contravene, disobey, encroach upon, transgress
2 = desecrate, abuse, pollute, profane, defile, dishonour, befoul
3 = rape, abuse, assault, debauch, ravish

violated See **broken**

violation noun **1 = breach**, abuse, infringement, infraction, trespass, transgression, encroachment, contravention
2 = desecration, defilement, profanation, sacrilege, spoliation

violence noun **1 = brutality**, force, terrorism, bloodshed, cruelty, savagery • *Twenty people were injured in the violence.*
2 = intensity, force, severity, fervour, harshness, vehemence • *She gestured with sudden violence.*

violent adjective **1 = brutal**, vicious, cruel, murderous, savage, bloodthirsty • *violent criminals*
OPPOSITE: gentle
2 = powerful, strong, wild, rough, turbulent, raging • *violent storms*
3 = intense, strong, powerful, severe, acute, furious • *the violent reaction to his plans*
See also: **rude**

V.I.P. noun **= celebrity**, star, somebody, luminary, big name, muckymuck

virgin noun **1 = maiden**, girl
▷ adjective **2 = pure**, immaculate, chaste, uncorrupted, undefiled, vestal, virginal

virginal See **innocent**

virginity noun **= chastity**, maidenhood

virile adjective **= manly**, strong, vigorous, macho, masculine, lusty, manlike, red-blooded

virility noun **= masculinity**, manhood, vigour, machismo

virtual adjective **= practical**, essential, in all but name

virtually adverb **= practically**, nearly, almost, as good as, in all but name, in effect, in essence

virtue noun **1 = goodness**, integrity, morality • *a paragon of virtue*
2 = merit, advantage, asset, strength, plus, attribute • *the virtue of neatness*
▷ **by virtue of = because of**, as a result of, by dint of, on account of, thanks to • *The article stuck in my mind by virtue of one detail.*
See also: **right**, **value**

virtuosity noun **= mastery**, skill, craft, expertise, polish, flair, brilliance, panache

virtuoso noun **= master**, artist, genius, maestro, magician

virtuous adjective **= good**, moral, ethical, worthy, upright, honourable, righteous, incorruptible, praiseworthy

virulent adjective **= deadly**, toxic, lethal, poisonous, venomous, pernicious

viscous adjective **= thick**, sticky, gelatinous, syrupy

visibility See **sight**

visible adjective **1 = perceptible**, clear, conspicuous, distinguishable, in sight, observable • *The warning lights were clearly visible.*
OPPOSITE: invisible
2 = obvious, apparent, plain, evident, noticeable, manifest • *There was little visible excitement.*

vision noun **1 = image**, dream, ideal, fantasy, conception, daydream • *my vision of the future*
2 = foresight, insight, imagination, intuition • *a total lack of vision and imagination*
3 = hallucination, illusion, spectre, phantom, mirage, apparition • *She was convinced her visions were real.*
4 = sight, view, perception, eyesight, seeing

visionary adjective **1 = prophetic**, mystical
2 = idealistic, romantic, speculative, unrealistic, impractical, unworkable, utopian, quixotic, starry-eyed

▶ *noun* **3** = **prophet**, mystic, seer

visit *verb* **1** = **call on**, go to see, look up, swing by (*informal*)
• *He wanted to visit his brother in California.*
▶ *noun* **2** = **call**, stop, stay • *They had recently paid him a visit.*
See also: **frequent**

visitation *noun* **1** = **inspection**, visit, examination
2 = **catastrophe**, disaster, punishment, ordeal, scourge, calamity, blight, cataclysm

visitor *noun* = **guest**, company, caller

vista *noun* = **view**, prospect, perspective, panorama

visual *adjective* **1** = **optical**, optic, ocular
2 = **observable**, visible, discernible, perceptible

visualize *verb* = **picture**, imagine, envisage, conceive of

vital *adjective* **1** = **important**, central, critical, necessary, crucial, essential, pivotal, indispensable • *a blockade that cut off vital fuel supplies*
2 = **lively**, active, energetic, dynamic, spirited, vivacious, sprightly • *My grandparents remained active and vital.*
3 = **essential**, necessary, basic, fundamental, imperative, indispensable, requisite

vitality *noun* = **energy**, life, strength, animation, exuberance, vigour, liveliness, vivacity

vitriolic *adjective* = **bitter**, scathing, virulent, venomous, caustic, acerbic, sardonic, envenomed, withering

vivacious *adjective* = **lively**, vital, upbeat (*informal*), sparkling, spirited, ebullient, bubbling, high-spirited, sprightly

vivacity *noun* = **liveliness**, energy, spirit, animation, sparkle, ebullience, gaiety, high spirits, sprightliness

vivid *adjective* **1** = **bright**, clear, rich, intense, brilliant, colourful, glowing
2 = **lifelike**, powerful, dramatic, realistic, graphic, memorable, stirring, telling, true to life

vocabulary *noun* **1** = **language**, words
2 = **wordbook**, dictionary, glossary, lexicon

vocal *adjective* **1** = **spoken**, oral, said, uttered, voiced
2 = **outspoken**, frank, articulate, strident, expressive, eloquent, vociferous, forthright, plain-spoken

vocation *noun* = **profession**, trade, job, career, mission, pursuit, calling

vociferous *adjective* = **outspoken**, vocal, loud, noisy, strident, vehement, clamorous, uproarious

vogue *noun* = **fashion**, way, trend, style, custom, mode, craze
▷ **in vogue** = **popular**, current, prevalent, chic, trendy, accepted, in favor, in use

voice *noun* **1** = **sound**, tone, utterance, articulation
2 = **say**, will, vote, view, wish
▶ *verb* **3** = **express**, air, declare, utter, articulate, enunciate

void *noun* **1** = **emptiness**, space, lack, gap, vacuum, blankness, vacuity
▶ *adjective* **2** = **invalid**, ineffective, useless, vain, worthless, inoperative, null and void
3 = **empty**, free, bare, vacant, unfilled, unoccupied, tenantless
▶ *verb* **4** = **invalidate**, cancel, rescind, nullify
5 = **empty**, evacuate, drain

volatile *adjective* **1** = **changeable**, explosive, unstable, variable, unsteady, unsettled, inconstant
2 = **temperamental**, erratic, fickle, mercurial, up and down (*informal*)

volition *noun* = **free will**, will, choice, preference, discretion, choosing

volley *noun* = **barrage**, blast, hail, burst, shower, salvo, bombardment, cannonade, fusillade

voluble *adjective* = **talkative**,

forthcoming, articulate, fluent, glib, loquacious

volume noun 1 = **capacity**, compass, dimensions
2 = **amount**, body, total, mass, aggregate, bulk, quantity
3 = **book**, title, publication, tome, treatise

voluminous adjective = **large**, vast, ample, cavernous, roomy, capacious

voluntarily adverb = **willingly**, freely, by choice, off one's own bat, of one's own accord

voluntary adjective = **unforced**, free, willing, optional, spontaneous, discretionary

volunteer verb = **offer**, step forward

voluptuous adjective 1 = **buxom**, ample, seductive, curvaceous (informal), enticing, shapely
2 = **sensual**, luxurious, hedonistic, self-indulgent, epicurean, licentious, sybaritic

vomit verb = **be sick**, heave, puke (informal), bring up, regurgitate • Any product made from milk made him vomit.

voracious adjective
1 = **gluttonous**, hungry, greedy, insatiable, ravenous, omnivorous
2 = **avid**, hungry, insatiable, uncontrolled, rapacious, unquenchable

vortex noun = **whirlpool**, maelstrom, eddy

vote noun 1 = **poll**, ballot, referendum, plebiscite • Do you think we should have a vote on that?
▷ verb 2 = **cast a vote**, return,

opt, go to the polls • Many people will vote for the opposition.
3 = **suggest**, propose, recommend • I vote that we all go to the mall.
See also: **say**

vouch verb
▷ **vouch for** = **guarantee**, certify, answer for, give assurance of, stand witness, swear to;
= **confirm**, support, uphold, assert, affirm, attest to

voucher noun = **ticket**, token, coupon

vow noun 1 = **promise**, pledge, oath
▷ verb 2 = **promise**, pledge, swear, affirm

voyage noun = **journey**, trip, cruise, passage, crossing

vulgar adjective 1 = **crude**, dirty, rude, indecent, coarse, uncouth • vulgar language
OPPOSITE: refined
2 = **tasteless**, common, flashy, gaudy, garish, tawdry • I think it's a very vulgar building.
OPPOSITE: sophisticated
See also: **low, naughty**

vulgarity noun 1 = **crudeness**, coarseness, indelicacy, ribaldry, rudeness
2 = **tastelessness**, bad taste

vulnerability See **weakness**

vulnerable adjective 1 = **weak**, sensitive, susceptible, exposed • vulnerable old people
2 = **exposed**, accessible, unprotected, assailable, defenceless, wide open
See also: **helpless, impressionable**

v

Ww

wacky adjective (Informal) = **crazy**, stupid, silly, absurd, foolish, idiotic, asinine, crackpot (informal), witless

wad noun = **mass**, roll, bundle, hunk

waddle verb = **shuffle**, sway, wobble, toddle, totter

wade verb = **walk through**, splash, paddle, ford
▷ **wade through = work one's way through**, drudge at, labour at, peg away at, plow through, toil at

waffle verb 1 = **waver**, falter, sway, hesitate, seesaw, teeter, fluctuate, be doubtful, be uncertain, be unsure, oscillate, be undecided, blow hot and cold (informal), temporize, be unable to decide, keep changing your mind, swither, be unable to make up your mind, dillydally
2 = **prattle**, blather, jabber, prate
▶ noun 3 = **verbosity**, padding, prolixity, verbiage, wordiness, yadda yadda yadda (slang)

waft verb = **carry**, bear, transport, float, drift, convey

wag verb 1 = **wave**, shake, stir, nod, bob, vibrate, quiver, wiggle
▶ noun 2 = **wave**, shake, nod, vibration, bob, quiver, wiggle

wage noun 1 Also **wages** = **payment**, pay, income, fee, salary, reward, allowance, stipend, remuneration, recompense, emolument
▶ verb 2 = **engage in**, conduct, pursue, practise, prosecute, undertake, proceed with, carry on

wager noun 1 = **bet**, gamble
▶ verb 2 = **bet**, risk, chance, lay, pledge, stake, gamble, venture, speculate

waggle verb = **wag**, wave, shake, wobble, flutter, wiggle, oscillate

waif noun = **stray**, orphan, foundling

wail verb 1 = **cry**, grieve, lament, weep, howl, bawl, yowl
▶ noun 2 = **cry**, complaint, lament, howl, moan, weeping, yowl

wait verb 1 = **stay**, remain, linger, pause, stand by • *Wait until we get there.*
▷ **wait on, wait upon = serve**, attend, tend, minister to
▶ noun 2 = **delay**, pause, interval • *They faced a long wait for the ferry to Victoria.*

waiter, waitress noun = **attendant**, server, steward or stewardess

waive verb = **give up**, abandon, renounce, relinquish, forgo, remit, dispense with, set aside

wake¹ verb 1 = **awake**, stir, awaken, rouse, come to, waken • *It was still dark when he woke.*
2 = **activate**, fire, provoke, excite, stimulate, arouse, animate, galvanize, kindle, stir up
▶ noun 3 = **vigil**, watch, funeral, deathwatch

wake² noun = **slipstream**, track, train, trail, path, wash, aftermath, backwash, waves

wakeful adjective 1 = **sleepless**, restless, insomniac
2 = **watchful**, alive, alert, wary, vigilant, attentive, observant, on guard

waken verb = **awaken**, stir, activate, awake, arouse, rouse

walk verb 1 = **go**, move, step, pace, hike, march, stride, stroll, amble • *I walked slowly along the road.*
2 = **escort**, take, convoy, accompany

W

▶ *noun* **3** = **stroll**, hike, march, constitutional, trek, ramble, promenade, saunter, perambulation • *We'll have a quick walk before it gets dark.*
4 = **gait**, step, pace, stride, carriage • *Despite his gangling walk, he is a good dancer.*
5 = **path**, trail, lane, alley, avenue, promenade, esplanade, footpath
▷ **walk of life** = **profession**, trade, line, career, field, calling, vocation
walker *noun* = **pedestrian**, hiker, rambler, wayfarer
walkout *noun* = **strike**, protest, stoppage, industrial action
walkover *noun* = **pushover** (*slang*), breeze (*informal*), cakewalk (*informal*), child's play (*informal*), picnic (*informal*), laugher (*informal*), no-brainer (*slang*), cinch (*slang*), piece of cake (*informal*), slam dunk (*informal*)
wall *noun* **1** = **partition**, screen, enclosure
2 = **barrier**, fence, hedge, obstacle, obstruction, impediment
wallet *noun* = **holder**, case, purse, pocketbook, pouch
wallop *verb* **1** = **hit**, strike, beat, pound, batter, thump, pummel, clobber (*slang*), whack, thrash
▶ *noun* **2** = **blow**, punch, thump, bash, smack, whack, slug, thwack
wallow *verb* **1** = **revel**, delight, glory, bask, relish, luxuriate, take pleasure
2 = **roll about**, splash around
wan *adjective* = **pale**, white, anemic, pasty, sickly, pallid, ashen, washed out
wand *noun* = **stick**, baton, rod
wander *verb* **1** = **roam**, range, cruise, drift, stroll, ramble • *They wandered aimlessly around the village.*
2 = **stray**, depart, veer, err, swerve, deviate, diverge, digress, go astray
▶ *noun* **3** = **excursion**, cruise, ramble, meander
wanderer *noun* = **traveller**, rover, gypsy, nomad, drifter, rambler, vagabond, voyager
wandering *adjective* = **nomadic**, migratory, itinerant, peripatetic, rootless, roving, travelling, vagrant, wayfaring
wane *verb* = **decline**, fail, decrease, weaken, fade, diminish, dwindle, lessen, subside, ebb, taper off
▶ *noun*
▷ **on the wane** = **declining**, fading, dwindling, ebbing, obsolescent, on the decline, tapering off, weakening
wangle *verb* = **contrive**, engineer, arrange, fix (*informal*), manipulate, manoeuvre, pull off
want *verb* **1** = **desire**, wish, covet, crave • *I want black running shoes for a change.*
2 = **need**, demand, require, lack, be deficient in • *My hair wants cutting.*
▶ *noun* **3** = **lack**, shortage, absence, deficiency, scarcity • *becoming weak from want of rest*
OPPOSITE: abundance
4 = **wish**, need, requirement, desire, appetite, longing, craving, yearning
5 = **poverty**, destitution, neediness, penury, privation
See also: **hardship**
wanting *adjective* **1** = **lacking**, short, missing, shy, incomplete, absent
2 = **inadequate**, poor, faulty, defective, lousy (*slang*), deficient, substandard, imperfect, unsound
wanton *adjective* **1** = **gratuitous**, senseless, arbitrary, needless, groundless, unprovoked, unjustifiable, wilful, motiveless, uncalled-for
2 = **promiscuous**, loose, immoral, shameless, dissipated, dissolute, lecherous, libidinous, lustful, unchaste
war *noun* **1** = **fighting**, conflict, combat, warfare, strife, hostilities • *The war dragged on for five years.*
OPPOSITE: peace

RELATED WORDS
adjectives: belligerent, martial
▶ *verb* **2 = fight**, battle, clash,
combat • *The two countries had been
warring with each other for years.*

warble *verb* = **sing**, chirp, twitter,
trill

ward *noun* **1 = room**, area,
department, wing
2 = district, area, quarter,
division, zone, precinct
3 = dependant, charge, minor,
pupil, protégé
▶ *verb*
▷ **ward off = avert**, avoid,
deflect, repel, parry, fend off,
stave off

warden *noun* **1 = jailer**, guard,
custodian, prison officer
2 = keeper, curator, ranger,
administrator, superintendent,
caretaker, guardian, custodian

wardrobe *noun* **1 = clothes
cupboard**, closet
2 = clothes, apparel, attire

warehouse *noun* = **store**,
depot, storehouse, depository,
stockroom

wares *plural noun* = **goods**, stock,
produce, stuff, merchandise,
commodities, products

warfare *noun* = **war**, battle,
conflict, combat, fighting, arms,
hostilities

warily *adverb* = **cautiously**,
carefully, gingerly, suspiciously,
charily, circumspectly,
distrustfully, vigilantly,
watchfully, with care

warlike *adjective* = **belligerent**,
aggressive, hostile, martial,
hawkish, bloodthirsty, bellicose,
warmongering

warlock *noun* = **magician**,
wizard, sorcerer, conjurer,
enchanter

warm *adjective* **1 = heated**,
pleasant, balmy, lukewarm,
tepid • *a warm spring day*
OPPOSITE: cold
2 = friendly, loving, cordial,
affectionate, amiable, genial • *a
warm and likable personality*
OPPOSITE: unfriendly
▶ *verb* **3 = heat**, melt, thaw, heat

up, warm up • *The sun came out
and warmed the garden.*
OPPOSITE: cool
▷ **warm up** See **heat, warm**
See also: **cozy, hot, tender**

warmonger *noun* = **belligerent**,
hawk, militarist, sabre-rattler

warmth *noun* **1 = heat**, hotness,
warmness
2 = affection, love, tenderness,
amorousness, cordiality,
heartiness, kindliness

warn *verb* = **caution**, alert, notify,
forewarn • *I warned her about the
tires on her bike.*

warning *noun* = **caution**, alert,
notice, alarm, premonition
• *advance warning of the attack*
See also: **indication, lecture,
omen**

warp *verb* **1 = twist**, bend, distort,
deform, contort
▶ *noun* **2 = twist**, bend,
distortion, kink, contortion

warped See **crooked**

warrant *noun* **1 = authorization**,
authority, sanction, permit,
licence, permission
▶ *verb* **2 = call for**, demand,
require, sanction, permit,
deserve, license, excuse, justify,
necessitate
3 = guarantee, declare, pledge,
certify, affirm, attest, vouch for

warranty *noun* = **guarantee**,
contract, pledge, bond,
certificate, assurance, covenant

warrior *noun* = **soldier**, fighter,
combatant, gladiator, man-at-
arms

wary *adjective* = **cautious**,
suspicious, vigilant, guarded,
distrustful • *She was wary of
making a commitment.*
See also: **alert**

wash *verb* **1 = clean**, launder,
scrub, cleanse, shampoo, rinse,
bathe • *He got a job washing dishes.*
2 = sweep away, erode, carry off
• *washed ashore by the waves*
3 (*Informal*) = **be plausible**, stick,
bear scrutiny, be convincing,
carry weight, hold up, hold
water, stand up
▷ **wash out** See **fade**

W

▶ noun **4 = cleaning**, scrub, rinse, cleansing, laundering
5 = coat, film, layer, coating, overlay
6 = surge, wave, swell
washed See **clean**
washout noun **= failure**, disaster, disappointment, flop (*informal*), fiasco, dud (*informal*)
washroom noun **= lavatory**, privy, loo, latrine, toilet, bathroom, convenience or public convenience, restroom, outhouse, powder room, water closet, W.C.
waste verb **1 = squander**, fritter away, throw away • *I wouldn't waste my money on something like that.*
OPPOSITE: save
▷ **waste away = decline**, fade, crumble, dwindle, wane, decay, wither, atrophy, wear out
▶ noun **2 = squandering**, misuse, extravagance, dissipation, misapplication, prodigality • *What a complete waste of money!*
3 = garbage, refuse, scrap, debris, trash, litter, rubbish, dross, leftovers
▷ **wastes = desert**, wilderness, wasteland
▶ adjective **4 = unwanted**, unused, leftover, superfluous • *waste paper*
5 = uncultivated, wild, empty, bare, barren, unproductive, uninhabited, desolate
wasted See **in vain, weak**
wasteful adjective **= extravagant**, uneconomical • *wasteful duplication of effort*
OPPOSITE: thrifty
waster noun **= layabout**, idler, loafer, couch potato (*slang*), good-for-nothing, shirker, wastrel
watch noun **1 = guard**, surveillance, observation, supervision • *Keep a close watch on the swimmers.*
2 = wristwatch, chronometer, timepiece
▶ verb **3 = look at**, see, view, observe, gaze at, pay attention • *I don't watch television very often.*

4 = guard, mind, look after, take care of • *Please watch the baby carefully.*
See also: **regard, witness**
▷ **watch out = be careful**, be alert, be watchful, keep your eyes open, look out • *You have to watch out for snakes in the swamp.*
See also: **beware**
▷ **watch over** See **guard**
watchdog noun **1 = guard dog**
2 = guardian, monitor, protector, custodian, scrutineer
watchful adjective **= alert**, suspicious, wary, vigilant, attentive, observant, on the lookout, wide awake
watchman noun **= guard**, warden, custodian, sentry, sentinel, security guard
watchword noun **= motto**, slogan, maxim, catchword, battle cry, byword, catch phrase, rallying cry
water noun **1 = liquid**, H_2O
▶ verb **2 = moisten**, spray, soak, douse, dampen, drench, hose, irrigate
▷ **water down = dilute**, water, weaken, thin
waterfall noun **= cascade**, fall, cataract

TYPES OF WATERFALL

cascade	linn (*Scottish*)
cataract	rapids
chute	torrent
falls	whitewater

---

waterlogged See **wet**
watertight adjective
1 = waterproof
2 = foolproof, sound, flawless, airtight, unassailable, impregnable, hermetic
watery adjective **1 = wet**, liquid, fluid, soggy, damp, moist, aqueous
2 = diluted, weak, thin, runny, watered-down, washy
wave verb **1 = flap**, shake,

flourish, flutter, brandish, undulate, oscillate • *The doctor waved a piece of paper at me.*
2 = signal, sign, direct, indicate, gesture, beckon, gesticulate
▷ **wave down** See **hail**
▶ *noun* **3 = ripple**, surge, swell, roller, bore, breaker, tidal bore • *the sound of the waves breaking on the shore*
4 = outbreak, surge, flood, rush, movement, trend, upsurge • *the heat wave*
See also: **rash**
waver *verb* **1 = hesitate**, falter, seesaw, fluctuate, dither, vacillate, hum and haw
2 = tremble, shake, wobble, flicker, quiver, totter
wavering See **hesitant**
wax *verb* **= increase**, grow, develop, expand, swell, magnify, enlarge
way *noun* **1 = method**, approach, procedure, technique, manner, means • *an excellent way of cooking meat*
2 = custom, conduct, practice, style, manner • *Our neighbours' ways are certainly different from our own.*
3 = route, road, course, path, lane • *I can't remember the way.*
4 = journey, approach, march, passage
5 = distance, stretch, length
See also: **direction, fashion**

| INFORMALLY SPEAKING
go out of your way: make a special effort
no way: absolutely not
under way: going on or in progress
▷ **way in** See **entrance, entry**
wayfarer *noun* **= traveller**, rover, gypsy, nomad, itinerant, wanderer, voyager
ways See **conduct**
wayward *adjective* **= erratic**, unpredictable, unruly, unmanageable, capricious, inconstant, ungovernable
weak *adjective* **1 = feeble**, delicate, faint, frail, sickly, puny, wasted • *a weak heart*

OPPOSITE: strong
2 = deficient, faulty, inadequate • *a weak economy*
3 = spineless, powerless • *He was a weak man who wouldn't stand up for himself.*
OPPOSITE: resolute
4 = unsafe, vulnerable, unprotected, helpless, exposed, unguarded, defenceless
5 = unconvincing, pathetic, lame, hollow, unsatisfactory, feeble, flimsy
6 = tasteless, thin, diluted, runny, watery, insipid
See also: **flat, mild**
weaken *verb* **1 = lessen**, fail, reduce, flag, undermine, diminish, wane, sap • *Her authority was weakened by their actions.*
OPPOSITE: strengthen
2 = dilute, thin out, water down
weakling *noun* **= sissy**, baby (*informal*), drip (*informal*), wimp (*informal*), pantywaist (*informal*)
weakness *noun* **1 = frailty**, vulnerability, fragility • *Extreme weakness caused him to collapse.*
OPPOSITE: strength
2 = liking, passion, penchant, fondness • *a weakness for chocolate*
OPPOSITE: dislike
3 = failing, lack, flaw, defect, fault, deficiency, shortcoming, blemish, imperfection
See also: **disadvantage, love**
wealth *noun* **1 = riches**, money, substance, fortune, means, prosperity, affluence • *Wealth cannot buy happiness.*
2 = abundance, store, plenty, bounty • *a wealth of information*
OPPOSITE: shortage
See also: **success**
wealthy *adjective* **= rich**, comfortable, affluent, prosperous, opulent, well-to-do • *She came from a very wealthy background.*
OPPOSITE: poor
wear *verb* **1 = be dressed in**, sport, don, be clothed in, have on, put on • *He was wearing a brown suit.*
2 = deteriorate, erode, rub, fray,

w

corrode, wash away • *The carpet is badly worn.*

3 = show, display, exhibit

▷ **wear away** See **eat away**, **erode**

▷ **wear down** See **erode**

▷ **wear off = subside**, disappear, decrease, fade, diminish, dwindle, wane, peter out

▷ **wear out = exhaust**, tire, weary • *The past few days have really worn me out.*

▶ *noun* **4 = damage**, use, erosion, deterioration, corrosion • *The tires showed signs of wear.*

5 = clothes, dress, gear (*informal*), costume, apparel, attire, garb, garments, things

wearied See **bored**

weariness *noun* = **tiredness**, fatigue, exhaustion, drowsiness, lethargy, languor, lassitude, listlessness

wearing *adjective* = **tiresome**, oppressive, exasperating, fatiguing, irksome, trying, wearisome

wearisome *adjective* = **tedious**, boring, troublesome, oppressive, tiresome, annoying, exhausting, fatiguing, irksome, trying, wearing

weary *adjective* **1 = tired**, drained, exhausted, fatigued, tuckered out (*informal*), worn out • *I'm just too weary to walk another step.*

2 = tiring, arduous, tiresome, laborious, wearisome

▶ *verb* **3 = tire**, tax, drain, fatigue, sap, enervate, take it out

of (*informal*), tire out, wear out

See also: **sick of**

weather *noun* **1 = climate**, conditions

▶ *verb* **2 = withstand**, stand, survive, overcome, endure, resist, brave, come through, ride out

weave *verb* **1 = knit**, intertwine, braid, entwine, interlace, plait

2 = create, build, spin, construct, fabricate, contrive, make up, put together

3 = zigzag, wind, crisscross

web *noun* **1 = spider's web**, cobweb

2 = network, tangle, lattice

wed *verb* **1 = marry**, get married, take the plunge (*informal*), tie the knot (*informal*)

2 = unite, link, join, combine, ally, merge, blend, interweave

wedding *noun* = **marriage**, nuptials, wedlock

wedge *noun* **1 = block**, chunk, lump

▶ *verb* **2 = squeeze**, force, crowd, pack, stuff, jam, lodge, thrust, ram, cram

wedlock *noun* = **marriage**, matrimony

wee See **tiny**

weed out *verb* = **eliminate**, remove, eradicate, uproot, dispense with, get rid of, root out

weedy *adjective* = **weak**, frail, feeble, ineffectual, thin, skinny, puny

weep *verb* = **cry**, mourn, lament, sob, whimper,

WORDS USED TO DESCRIBE THE WEATHER

balmy	dull	rainy
blustery	fine	showery
breezy	foggy	snowy
clammy	hot	stormy
clear	humid	sultry
close	icy	sunny
cloudy	mild	thundery
cold	misty	wet
drizzly	muggy	windy
dry	overcast	

w

blubber, shed tears, snivel
weepy adjective (Informal)
= **sentimental**, slushy (informal),
overemotional, schmaltzy (slang)
weigh verb 1 = **have a weight of**,
tip the scales at (informal)
2 = **consider**, examine, evaluate,
ponder, contemplate, deliberate
upon, meditate upon, reflect
upon, think over
3 = **matter**, count, carry weight
weight noun 1 = **heaviness**, mass,
load, tonnage, poundage
2 = **importance**, power,
authority, value, impact, import,
influence, consequence
▶ verb 3 = **load**, freight
4 = **bias**, load, slant, unbalance
weighted See **biased**
weighty adjective 1 = **important**,
serious, significant, crucial,
grave, solemn, momentous,
consequential, portentous
2 = **heavy**, massive, hefty
(informal), cumbersome,
burdensome, ponderous
weird adjective = **strange**, odd,
funny, extraordinary, bizarre,
curious, singular (formal),
peculiar • I had such a weird dream
last night.
OPPOSITE: ordinary
See also: **eccentric**
welcome verb 1 = **greet**, meet,
receive, hail, embrace
▶ noun 2 = **greeting**, reception,
acceptance, hospitality,
salutation
▶ adjective 3 = **pleasing**,
acceptable, pleasant, desirable,
delightful, agreeable,
appreciated, gratifying,
refreshing
4 = **free**, under no obligation
welcoming See **favourable**,
friendly
weld verb = **join**, link, bond,
connect, bind, unite, fuse, solder
welfare noun 1 = **wellbeing**,
good, health, interest, benefit,
advantage, happiness,
prosperity
2 = **benefit**, grant, gift,
assistance, handout
well[1] adverb 1 = **satisfactorily**,

successfully, smoothly,
splendidly • The interview went
well.
2 = **skilfully**, effectively,
adequately, efficiently,
professionally, expertly,
admirably, ably, competently
• He draws well.
OPPOSITE: badly
3 = **thoroughly**, completely,
highly, fully, closely, rigorously,
meticulously, amply • The dishes
should be well washed and well dried.
4 = **kindly**, favourably,
humanely, compassionately,
considerately, with
consideration • She treats her
employees well.
5 = **prosperously**, comfortably
6 = **intimately**, fully, deeply,
thoroughly, profoundly
7 = **suitably**, properly, fairly,
rightly, fittingly, justly
8 = **considerably**, highly,
fully, greatly, substantially,
thoroughly, heartily,
abundantly, amply, very much
▶ **well off** See **rich**
▶ adjective 9 = **healthy**, strong,
sound, fit, robust, in good
condition, in good health • I'm
not very well today.
OPPOSITE: sick
10 = **satisfactory**, right, fine,
proper, pleasing, agreeable,
thriving
well[2] noun 1 = **hole**, oiler, pit,
shaft, bore
▶ verb 2 = **flow**, spring, surge, jet,
pour, spurt, gush, spout
well-behaved See **polite**
well-being See **comfort**, **health**
well-built See **sturdy**
well-known adjective = **famous**,
popular, familiar, renowned,
celebrated, noted
well-liked See **popular**
well-mannered See **polite**
well-off adjective = **rich**,
comfortable (informal), wealthy,
affluent, prosperous, well-
heeled (informal), well-to-do,
moneyed
well-to-do adjective = **rich**,
comfortable (informal), wealthy,

affluent, prosperous, well-heeled (*informal*), well-off, moneyed

well-versed See **experienced**

well-worn adjective = **hackneyed**, stale, commonplace, overused, banal, trite, stereotyped

welt noun = **mark**, streak, stripe, contusion, wale, weal

welter noun = **jumble**, confusion, web, mess, tangle, muddle

wet adjective 1 = **damp**, waterlogged, moist, sodden, drenched, saturated, soaked
• *Don't get your feet wet.*
OPPOSITE: dry
2 = **rainy**, misty, humid, showery
• *It was a miserable, wet day.*
OPPOSITE: dry
▶ noun 3 = **rain**, drizzle
4 = **moisture**, water, liquid, humidity, damp, condensation, dampness, wetness
▶ verb 5 = **moisten**, water, spray, soak, dampen, irrigate • *Wet the edges and stick them together.*
OPPOSITE: dry

whack verb 1 = **strike**, hit, belt (*informal*), bang, thump, smack, wallop (*informal*), clobber (*slang*), thrash, thwack
▶ noun 2 = **blow**, hit, stroke, belt (*informal*), bang, thump, smack, wallop (*informal*), thwack
3 (*Informal*) = **share**, part, cut (*informal*), bit, portion, quota
4 (*Informal*) = **attempt**, go (*informal*), try, turn, shot (*informal*), crack (*informal*), stab (*informal*), bash (*informal*)

wharf noun = **dock**, pier, jetty, landing stage, quay

wheedle verb = **coax**, persuade, entice, cajole, inveigle

wheel noun 1 = **circle**, turn, spin, revolution, rotation, pivot, gyration
▶ verb 2 = **turn**, swing, spin, revolve, rotate, whirl, twirl, swivel, gyrate, pirouette

wheeze verb 1 = **gasp**, cough, whistle, hiss, rasp
▶ noun 2 = **gasp**, cough, whistle, hiss, rasp
3 (*Brit slang*) = **trick**, plan, idea,

scheme, stunt, ploy, ruse

whereabouts noun = **position**, site, situation, location

wherewithal noun = **resources**, money, capital, means, funds, supplies

whet verb 1 (~ *someone's appetite*) = **stimulate**, excite, stir, enhance, awaken, arouse, rouse, quicken, kindle
2 = **sharpen**, hone

whiff noun = **smell**, hint, scent, sniff, aroma, odour

while conjunction 1 = **at the same time as**, during the time that, for the period that
▶ noun 2 = **time**, period *or* period of time, space, stretch, patch, spell, interval (*informal*), stint

whim noun = **impulse**, urge, fancy, fad, craze • *We decided to go there more or less on a whim.*

whimper verb 1 = **cry**, weep, whine, sob, moan, snivel
▶ noun 2 = **sob**, whine, moan, snivel

whimsical adjective = **fanciful**, odd, unusual, funny, curious, eccentric, playful, quaint, freakish

whine noun 1 = **cry**, sob, wail, moan, whimper
2 = **complaint**, grumble, moan, gripe (*informal*), grouse, grouch (*informal*)

whip noun 1 = **lash**, crop, scourge, cane, birch, cat-o'-nine-tails
▶ verb 2 = **lash**, beat, paddle, cane, flog, birch, flagellate, strap, scourge, thrash, spank
3 (*Informal*) = **dash**, shoot, fly, rush, tear, dive, whisk, dart
4 = **whisk**, beat
5 = **incite**, drive, spur, stir, agitate, foment, goad, work up
▷ **whip up** See **incite**

whirl verb 1 = **spin**, turn, roll, twist, swirl, revolve, rotate, twirl, pirouette
2 = **feel dizzy**, spin, reel
▶ noun 3 = **revolution**, turn, roll, spin, twist, swirl, rotation, twirl, pirouette
4 = **bustle**, series, round, flurry, succession, merry-go-round

5 = confusion, spin, daze, dither, giddiness

whirlwind noun **1 = tornado**, waterspout
▶ adjective **2 = rapid**, short, quick, speedy, swift, hasty

whisk verb **1 = flick**, sweep, brush, whip
2 = beat, whip, fluff up
▶ noun **3 = flick**, sweep, brush, whip
4 = beater

whisper verb **1 = murmur**, breathe
2 = rustle, sigh, swish, hiss
▶ noun **3 = murmur**, undertone
4 = rustle, sigh, swish, hiss

white adjective **= pale**, pasty, pallid, wan, ashen

SHADES OF WHITE

cream	off-white
ivory	pearl
magnolia	snow-white

---

white-collar adjective **= clerical**, professional, salaried, nonmanual
whiten verb **1 = pale**, fade, blanch
2 = bleach
whitewash noun **1 = cover-up**, camouflage, deception, concealment
▶ verb **2 = cover up**, suppress, conceal, camouflage, gloss over
whittle verb **= carve**, cut, shape, trim, shave, pare, hew
▷ **whittle down, whittle away = reduce**, consume, erode, eat away, wear away
whole adjective **1 = complete**, full, total, entire, uncut, undivided • We spent the whole summer away.
2 = undamaged, intact, unharmed, untouched, unscathed, unbroken, in one piece
▶ noun **3 = total**, all, lot, everything, aggregate, sum total, the whole schmear (informal), the whole enchilada

(slang) • the whole of Asia
4 = unit, ensemble, entirety, totality
▷ **on the whole = all in all**, all things considered, by and large; **= generally**, mostly, predominantly, as a rule, in general, in the main
wholehearted adjective **= sincere**, enthusiastic, committed, dedicated, devoted, determined, zealous, unstinting
wholesale adjective **1 = extensive**, mass, broad, comprehensive, wide-ranging, far-reaching, indiscriminate, sweeping
▶ adverb **2 = extensively**, indiscriminately, comprehensively
wholesome adjective **1 = beneficial**, good, healthy, nutritious, nourishing, salubrious
2 = moral, decent, respectable, edifying, improving
wholly adverb **= completely**, fully, totally, entirely, perfectly, altogether, thoroughly, utterly, in every respect
whopper noun **1 = giant**, monster, mammoth, colossus, jumbo (informal), crackerjack (informal), leviathan
2 = big lie, fabrication, falsehood, tall tale (informal), untruth
whopping adjective **= gigantic**, big, great, huge, giant, massive, enormous, mammoth
whore noun **= prostitute**, ho (slang), tart (informal), call girl, streetwalker
wicked adjective **1 = evil**, bad, vicious, atrocious, sinful, depraved • That was a wicked thing to do.
2 = mischievous, naughty, impish • She always felt wicked when eating chocolate.
wickedness See evil, sin
wide adjective **1 = broad**, large, extensive, vast, immense, far-reaching, expansive, sweeping • It should be wide enough to give

plenty of working space.
OPPOSITE: narrow
2 = expanded, dilated,
distended, outspread,
outstretched • *His eyes were wide
with disbelief.*
3 = spacious, full, loose, baggy,
roomy, capacious, commodious
4 = distant, remote, off course,
off target
OPPOSITE: narrow
▶ *adverb* **5 = fully**, completely
• *Open wide!*
6 = off target, out, astray, off
course, off the mark
See also: **thick**

widen *verb* = **broaden**, extend,
spread, expand, stretch, enlarge,
dilate

wide-ranging *See* **broad**

widespread *adjective* = **extensive**,
common, broad, prevalent, rife,
pervasive • *Food shortages are
widespread.*
See also: **general, mass,
universal**

width *noun* = **breadth**, span,
extent, scope, compass,
thickness, diameter, girth

wield *verb.* **1 = brandish**, use,
manage, handle, swing, employ,
flourish, manipulate, ply
2 (~ *power*) = **exert**, have, exercise,
maintain, possess

wife *noun* = **spouse**, partner, mate,
bride, better half (*humorous*)

wiggle *verb, noun* = **jerk**, shake,
flutter, wag, squirm, twitch,
shimmy, jiggle, oscillate, wave,
writhe

wild *adjective* **1 = natural**,
free, fierce, uncultivated,
undomesticated, untamed • *a
meadow of wild flowers*
2 = stormy, violent, rough,
raging, howling • *They were not
deterred by the wild weather.*
3 = uncontrolled, turbulent,
boisterous, wayward, rowdy
• *wild with excitement*
4 = uncivilized, fierce, ferocious,
savage, primitive, barbaric,
barbarous, brutish
5 = excited, crazy (*informal*),
enthusiastic, hysterical,

raving, wired (*slang*)
▶ *noun*
▷ **wilds** = **wilderness**, desert,
wasteland, back of beyond
(*informal*), middle of nowhere
(*informal*)
See also: **fanatical,
irresponsible, rampage**

wilderness *noun* = **desert**, jungle,
wasteland, wilds

wildness *See* **abandon**

wiles *plural noun* = **trickery**,
cunning, artfulness, chicanery,
craftiness, guile, slyness

wilful *adjective* **1 = obstinate**,
stubborn, determined, perverse,
uncompromising, inflexible,
intransigent, headstrong,
obdurate, pig-headed
2 = intentional, deliberate,
conscious, voluntary, intended,
purposeful
See also: **obstinate, stubborn**

will *verb* **1 = bequeath**, leave, pass
on • *He had willed his fortune to his
children.*
2 = wish, want, prefer, desire,
see fit
▶ *noun* **3 = determination**,
resolution, resolve, purpose,
willpower • *the will to win*
4 = wish, choice, mind,
inclination, volition • *the will of
the people*
5 = testament, last wishes
RELATED WORD
adjective: voluntary

willing *adjective* = **ready**, game,
happy, eager, prepared,
agreeable • *a willing helper*
OPPOSITE: unwilling

willingly *adverb* = **readily**,
voluntarily, freely, happily,
eagerly, gladly, cheerfully, by
choice, of one's own accord

willingness *noun* = **inclination**,
will, agreement, wish, consent,
volition

willowy *adjective* = **slender**, slim,
graceful, supple, lithe, svelte,
sylphlike

willpower *noun* = **self-control**,
drive, resolution, resolve,
determination, grit, self-
discipline, single-mindedness

W

wilt verb 1 = **droop**, sag, wither, shrivel

2 = **weaken**, flag, fade, wane, languish

wily adjective = **cunning**, sharp, tricky, crafty, shrewd, sly, astute, artful, guileful

wimp noun (Informal) = **weakling**, mouse, loser (slang), drip (informal), coward, sissy, softy or softie

wimpy adjective (Informal) = **feeble**, ineffectual, effete, weak, soft, spineless, weedy (informal), timorous

win verb 1 = **be victorious**, succeed, prevail, triumph, come first • The top four teams all won.
OPPOSITE: lose

2 = **gain**, get, secure, achieve, attain • trying to win the support of the community

▷ **win over** = **convince**, convert, influence, persuade, sway, bring round or talk round, prevail upon

▶ noun 3 = **victory**, success, triumph • Last night's win was an important one.
OPPOSITE: defeat
See also: **earn**

wince verb 1 = **flinch**, start, shrink, cringe, quail, recoil, cower, blench, draw back

▶ noun 2 = **flinch**, start, cringe

wind¹ noun 1 = **air**, blast, draft, breeze, gust, zephyr

2 = **breath**, puff, respiration

WORDS FOR WIND

Alberta clipper (Canad)
breeze
Chinook (Canad)
cyclone
gale
gust
hurricane
squall
tornado
typhoon
whirlwind

---

3 = **flatulence**, gas

4 = **talk**, bluster, babble, blather, boasting, hot air, humbug

▷ **get wind of** = **hear about**, notice, get an inkling of, hear tell of, learn of, find out about

wind² verb 1 = **coil**, roll, curl, twist, reel, spiral, loop, encircle

2 = **meander**, turn, snake, twist, bend, curve, ramble, zigzag

▷ **wind up** = **end**, close, finish, settle, conclude, finalize, terminate, wrap up; = **end up**, be left, finish up

windfall noun = **godsend**, find, jackpot, bonanza, manna from heaven

windy adjective = **breezy**, wild, stormy, gusty, blustery, windswept, blowy, squally

wing noun 1 = **faction**, group, arm, section, branch

▶ verb 2 = **fly**, soar, glide

3 = **wound**, hit, clip

wink verb 1 = **blink**, bat, flutter

2 = **twinkle**, flash, sparkle, gleam, glimmer

▶ noun 3 = **blink**, flutter

winkle out verb = **extract**, dislodge, extricate, dig out, draw out, force out, prise out

winner noun = **victor**, champion, conqueror • The winners will be notified by mail.
OPPOSITE: loser
See also: **success**

winning adjective 1 = **victorious**, successful, triumphant, conquering

2 = **charming**, attractive, cute, engaging, pleasing, alluring, likable or likeable, disarming, enchanting, endearing

winnings plural noun = **spoils**, prize, gains, proceeds, profits, takings

winnow verb = **separate**, select, divide, sift, sort out

wintry adjective = **cold**, icy, snowy, chilly, frosty, freezing, frozen

wipe verb 1 = **clean**, brush, rub, mop, swab, sponge

2 = **erase**, remove

▷ **wipe out** = **destroy**, erase, massacre, eradicate, annihilate,

w

obliterate, exterminate,
expunge
▶ *noun* **3** = **rub**, brush
wiry *adjective* = **lean**, strong,
tough, sinewy
wisdom *noun* = **insight**, reason,
knowledge, judgment,
discernment • *the wisdom that
comes from experience*
OPPOSITE: foolishness
RELATED WORD
adjective: sagacious
See also: **sense**
wise *adjective* = **sensible**, rational,
informed, judicious, perceptive,
shrewd • *a wise person*
OPPOSITE: foolish
See also: **logical, reasonable**
wisecrack *noun* (*Informal*)
1 = **joke**, quip, jest, jibe,
witticism
▶ *verb* **2** = **joke**, quip, jest, jibe
wish *noun* **1** = **desire**, want, urge,
hunger, longing, hankering • *She
was sincere in her wish to make up
with me.*
▶ *verb* **2** = **want**, long, desire,
hunger, thirst, yearn • *We wished
to return.*
See also: **will**
wispy *adjective* = **thin**, fine,
delicate, fragile, frail, flimsy,
attenuated
wistful *adjective* = **melancholy**,
thoughtful, longing,
reflective, dreamy, meditative,
contemplative, pensive
wit *noun* **1** = **humor**, banter,
wordplay, badinage, drollery,
jocularity, raillery, repartee
2 = **humorist**, card (*informal*),
comedian, wag, joker
3 = **cleverness**, sense, wisdom,
intellect, ingenuity, acumen,
brains, common sense
witch *noun* = **enchantress**,
magician, crone, hag, sorceress
witchcraft *noun* = **magic**,
sorcery, wizardry, enchantment,
necromancy, occultism, the
black art, voodoo
withdraw *verb* **1** = **remove**,
extract, draw out, take out • *I
withdrew some money from the bank.*
2 = **back out**, leave, retire,

retreat, pull out • *They withdrew
from the conference.*
withdrawal *noun* = **removal**,
extraction
withdrawn *adjective*
= **uncommunicative**,
distant, shy, reserved,
introverted, retiring, taciturn,
unforthcoming
wither *verb* = **decline**, fade, wilt,
droop, shrivel • *Will the company
flourish or wither?*
withering *adjective* = **scornful**,
hurtful, devastating,
humiliating, mortifying,
snubbing
withhold *verb* = **keep back**,
reserve, refuse, hide, retain,
suppress, conceal, hold back
without charge See **free**
without delay See **now**
without doubt See **certainly**
withstand *verb* = **resist**, bear,
suffer, oppose, endure, tolerate,
cope with, hold off, stand up to
witless *adjective* = **foolish**, stupid,
silly, senseless, idiotic, inane,
moronic, halfwitted
witness *noun* **1** = **observer**,
spectator, bystander, eyewitness,
onlooker • *The police appealed for
witnesses to come forward.*
2 = **testifier**, corroborator
▶ *verb* **3** = **see**, watch, observe, be
present at • *Anyone who witnessed
the attack should call the police.*
4 = **sign**, endorse, countersign
wits *plural noun* = **intelligence**,
reason, sense, understanding,
comprehension, ingenuity,
acumen, brains (*informal*),
cleverness, faculties
witticism *noun* = **quip**, pun, one-
liner (*slang*), bon mot, riposte
witty *adjective* = **humorous**,
funny, brilliant, sparkling,
clever, amusing • *He's so witty I
could listen to him for hours.*
wizard *noun* = **magician**, witch,
shaman, sorcerer, conjurer,
magus, necromancer, occultist,
warlock
wizardry *noun* = **magic**, sorcery,
witchcraft, voodoo
wizened *adjective* = **wrinkled**,

dried up, gnarled, lined, shrivelled, shrunken, withered

wobble verb 1 = **shake**, rock, sway, teeter, tremble, totter
▶ noun 2 = **unsteadiness**, shake, tremor, tremble

wobbly adjective = **unsteady**, shaky, uneven, rickety, teetering, tottering

woe noun = **misery**, grief, distress, sadness, sorrow, anguish, gloom, agony, unhappiness, wretchedness

woeful adjective 1 = **sad**, tragic, dismal, pathetic, miserable, deplorable, grievous, lamentable, wretched, distressing
2 = **pitiful**, bad, poor, sorry, pathetic, appalling, dreadful, deplorable, feeble, abysmal

wolf See **gobble**

woman noun = **lady**, female • The woman over there is my aunt.
See also: **adult**

womanizer noun = **philanderer**, Casanova, Don Juan, lecher, seducer

womanly adjective = **feminine**, warm, female, tender, ladylike, motherly, matronly

wonder verb 1 = **ask oneself**, speculate, puzzle, ponder • I wondered what that noise was.
2 = **be amazed**, marvel, boggle, be astonished • He wondered at their sudden change of plans.
▶ noun 3 = **phenomenon**, miracle, spectacle, marvel • one of the wonders of nature
4 = **amazement**, surprise, awe, admiration, fascination, astonishment, bewilderment, wonderment

wonderful adjective 1 = **excellent**, great (informal), tremendous, superb, marvellous • It's wonderful to see you.
2 = **remarkable**, amazing, incredible, magnificent, astounding • The sunset was a truly wonderful sight.
See also: **brilliant, grand, splendid**

wonky adjective 1 = **askew**, crooked, awry, out of alignment
2 = **shaky**, unsteady, wobbly

wont See **custom**

woo verb = **court**, pursue, cultivate, make a pitch for (slang)

wood noun 1 = **timber**
2 = **woodland**, forest, grove, thicket, coppice, copse

wooded adjective = **tree-covered**, forested, sylvan (poetic), timbered, tree-clad

wooden adjective 1 = **woody**, timber, ligneous
2 = **expressionless**, lifeless, unresponsive, deadpan

wool noun = **fleece**, hair, yarn

woolly adjective 1 = **fleecy**, hairy, shaggy, woollen
2 = **vague**, unclear, indefinite, confused, hazy, ill-defined, indistinct, muddled

word noun 1 = **remark**, statement, comment, utterance • I'd like to say a word of thanks to everyone who helped me.
2 = **chat**, talk, discussion, conversation • May I please have a quick word with you?
3 = **message**, announcement, news, information, communication, intelligence, bulletin • Since then we've had no word from them.
4 = **promise**, pledge, assurance, oath, word of honour • He gave me his word that he would be there.
5 = **term**, name, expression
6 = **command**, order, mandate, decree, bidding
▶ verb 7 = **express**, say, put, state, phrase, utter, couch
See also: **bond, guarantee, rumour**

> **INFORMALLY SPEAKING**
> **eat your words**: take back what you have said
> **have the last word**: make the final, decisive statement in an argument
> **take the words out of someone's mouth**: say exactly what someone else was about to say
> **word for word**: in the exact words

W

wording noun = **phraseology**, language, terminology, phrasing, words

wordless See **silent**

word of honour See **word**

wordy adjective = **long-winded**, windy, diffuse, rambling, verbose, prolix

work verb 1 = **labour**, slave, toil, slog away • *I had to work ten hours a day.*
OPPOSITE: laze
2 = **be employed**, be in work
3 = **operate**, use, move, drive, control, manage, handle, manipulate
4 = **function**, go, run, operate
5 = **cultivate**, farm, dig, till
6 = **manipulate**, form, fashion, shape, mould, knead
▷ **work out** = **solve**, resolve, calculate, figure out • *It took us some time to work out what was happening;* = **happen**, go, develop, turn out • *Things didn't work out that way after all.*
See also: **comprehend, crack, reckon**
▷ **work together** = **co-operate**, unite, team up
▶ noun 7 = **employment**, job, business, occupation, craft, profession, livelihood • *She's trying to find work.*
8 = **task**, job, duty, assignment, chore • *Sometimes he had to take work home.*
9 = **effort**, industry, sweat, labour, toil, exertion, drudgery, elbow grease (*facetious*)
10 = **handiwork**, production, piece, creation, achievement, composition, opus
See also: **act, behave, book, exercise, struggle, succeed**

| INFORMALLY SPEAKING
| **make short work of**: do or get rid of quickly
| **work on**: try to persuade
| **work up**: bring something to a more complete condition

workable adjective = **viable**, possible, practical, feasible, doable, practicable

worker noun = **employee**, labourer, craftsperson • *seeking a reliable research worker*
▷ **workers** See **labour, staff**

workforce See **labour, staff**

working adjective 1 = **employed**, active, in work
2 = **functioning**, operative, going, running

workman noun = **labourer**, worker, hand, employee, mechanic, operative, artisan, journeyman, craftsman, tradesman

workmanship noun = **skill**, technique, expertise, artistry, craftsmanship, handiwork

workmate See **associate, colleague**

works plural noun 1 = **factory**, plant, mill, workshop
2 = **writings**, output, canon, *oeuvre* (French)
3 = **mechanism**, action, movement, machinery, parts, workings

workshop noun = **workroom**, plant, factory, studio, mill

world noun 1 = **earth**, globe
2 = **mankind**, man, everyone, everybody, humanity, humankind, the public
3 = **sphere**, area, field, environment, domain, realm

worldly adjective 1 = **earthly**, physical, secular, profane, terrestrial, temporal
2 = **materialistic**, selfish, greedy, grasping
3 = **worldly-wise**, sophisticated, experienced, cosmopolitan, blasé, knowing, urbane

worldwide adjective = **global**, international, general, pandemic, universal, ubiquitous, omnipresent

worn adjective = **ragged**, shabby, frayed, tattered, tatty, the worse for wear, threadbare

worn out adjective 1 = **worn**, broken-down, tattered, threadbare • *These shoes are worn out.*
2 = **exhausted**, tired, weary, fatigued, prostrate • *You must be worn out after the trip.*

w

worried *adjective* = **anxious**, troubled, nervous, concerned, uneasy, bothered • *I'm worried about our lost dog.*
OPPOSITE: unconcerned

worry *verb* **1** = **be anxious**, fret, brood, feel uneasy • *Don't worry, it's bound to arrive soon.*
2 = **trouble**, plague, bother, hassle (*informal*), pester • *I didn't want to worry the kids with this.*
▶ *noun* **3** = **anxiety**, concern, fear, apprehension, unease, misgiving • *a major source of worry*
4 = **problem**, care, trouble, bother, hassle (*informal*)
See also: **agitate, burden, distress, disturb, sorrow, stress**

worrying See **serious**

worsen *verb* **1** = **deteriorate**, decline, degenerate, go downhill • *Their relationship worsened.*
OPPOSITE: improve
2 = **aggravate**, damage, exacerbate

worship *verb* **1** = **revere**, honour, venerate • *a place where people can worship*
2 = **love**, adore, idolize • *She had worshipped him from afar for years.*
OPPOSITE: despise
▶ *noun* **3** = **adoration**, praise, homage, devotion, admiration, adulation • *Fans treated the home team with a respect close to worship.*

PLACES OF WORSHIP

cathedral
chapel
church
gurdwara
meeting house
mosque
pagoda
shrine
sweat lodge (*Canad*)
synagogue
tabernacle
temple

---

worth *noun* **1** = **value**, price, rate, cost, valuation
2 = **merit**, value, quality, importance, excellence, goodness, usefulness, worthiness

worthless *adjective* **1** = **valueless**, poor, useless, meaningless, paltry, trivial, trifling • *a worthless piece of junk*
OPPOSITE: valuable
2 = **good-for-nothing**, despicable, lousy (*slang*), vile, contemptible, scuzzy (*slang*)
See also: **empty**

worthwhile *adjective* = **useful**, valuable, productive, profitable, helpful, beneficial, constructive, expedient

worthy *adjective* = **praiseworthy**, valuable, worthwhile, deserving, admirable, laudable, meritorious, virtuous, creditable

would-be *adjective* = **budding**, unfulfilled, self-appointed, self-styled, wannabe (*informal*)

would like See **fancy**

wound *noun* **1** = **injury**, cut, hurt, trauma (*pathology*), lesion, gash, laceration
2 = **insult**, slight, offence
▶ *verb* **3** = **injure**, cut, hurt, wing, pierce, gash, lacerate
4 = **offend**, hurt, sting, annoy, mortify, cut (someone) to the quick

wounded See **hurt**

wrangle *verb* **1** = **argue**, fight, dispute, row, contend, disagree, squabble, quarrel, bicker
▶ *noun* **2** = **argument**, dispute, row, altercation, squabble, quarrel, bickering, tiff

wrap *verb* **1** = **cover**, package, pack, bind, shroud, enclose, swathe, encase, bundle up, enfold
▶ *noun* **2** = **cloak**, cape, mantle, shawl, stole

wrapper *noun* = **cover**, case, jacket, packaging, envelope, wrapping

wrap up *verb* **1** = **giftwrap**, package, pack, bundle up
2 (*Informal*) = **end**, conclude,

W

terminate, finish off, polish off, round off, wind up
▷ **wrapped up** See **preoccupied**
wrath noun = **anger**, rage, temper, ire, displeasure, resentment, fury, indignation
wreak See **bring**
wreath noun = **garland**, band, ring, crown, festoon, chaplet
wreck verb 1 = **destroy**, break, devastate, smash, ruin, spoil, shatter, demolish
▶ noun 2 = **shipwreck**, hulk, sinking
3 Also **wreckage** = **remains**, debris, ruin, rubble, heap, fragments, pieces, rust bucket, remnants
4 = **collision**, crash, accident, pile-up smash car crash, car accident
wrench verb 1 = **twist**, force, pull, tear, rip, yank, jerk, tug
2 = **sprain**, strain, rick
▶ noun 3 = **twist**, pull, rip, yank, jerk, tug
4 = **sprain**, strain, twist
5 = **blow**, shock, upheaval, pang
6 = **spanner**, adjustable spanner
wrest verb = **seize**, take, win, force, extract, wrench
wrestle verb = **fight**, battle, struggle, combat, grapple, scuffle, tussle
wretch noun = **scoundrel**, worm, rogue, swine, rascal, miscreant, good-for-nothing
wretched adjective 1 = **unhappy**, hapless, depressed, miserable, dejected, downcast, disconsolate, forlorn, woebegone
2 = **worthless**, poor, sorry, pathetic, miserable, paltry, inferior
wriggle verb 1 = **twist**, turn, jerk, squirm, jiggle, wiggle, writhe
2 = **crawl**, snake, worm, slink, zigzag
▷ **wriggle out of** = **avoid**, dodge, manoeuvre, extricate oneself, worm out of
▶ noun 3 = **twist**, turn, jerk, squirm, jiggle, wiggle
wring verb = **twist**, force, squeeze, extract, screw

wrinkle noun 1 = **crease**, line, fold, crumple, furrow, corrugation, crinkle, crow's-foot
▶ verb 2 = **crease**, gather, fold, crumple, corrugate, pucker, rumple, furrow
writ noun = **summons**, document, decree, court order

FEATURES OF WRITING

character	plot
dialogue	setting
imagery	subplot
motif	theme

---

write verb = **record**, compose, correspond, inscribe, take down
• Write your name and address on a piece of paper.
▷ **write down** See **record**

STYLES USED IN WRITING

alliteration	parody
cliché	pun
idiom	satire
metaphor	simile
narrative	

---

writer noun = **author**, novelist, hack, scribe, penpusher, scribbler, wordsmith
writhe verb = **squirm**, struggle, toss, twist, thrash, jerk, wiggle, wriggle, thresh
writing noun 1 = **script**, hand, scrawl, handwriting, scribble, calligraphy, penmanship
2 = **document**, work, book, publication, composition, opus
wrong adjective 1 = **incorrect**, false, faulty, mistaken, untrue, unsound • That was the wrong answer.
OPPOSITE: right
2 = **bad**, illegal, unfair, evil, immoral, unjust, crooked • It's wrong to hurt people.

OPPOSITE: right
3 = inappropriate,
unacceptable, incorrect,
undesirable, unsuitable,
unbecoming, unseemly,
incongruous
4 = defective, faulty, awry,
amiss, askew
▶ noun **5 = crime**, abuse,
grievance, sin, injustice • *the
wrongs of our society*
▶ adverb **6 = incorrectly**,
badly, mistakenly, wrongly,
erroneously, inaccurately
7 = amiss, awry, astray, askew
▶ verb **8 = mistreat**, abuse, hurt,

harm, cheat, oppress, malign,
dishonour, take advantage of
wrongdoer noun = **offender**,
criminal, culprit, villain,
delinquent, lawbreaker,
miscreant, sinner, evildoer, perp
(*informal*)
wrongful adjective = **improper**,
criminal, illegal, evil, unethical,
unlawful, wicked, immoral,
unjust, illegitimate
wry adjective **1 = ironic**, dry,
sarcastic, sardonic, droll,
mocking
2 = contorted, twisted, uneven,
crooked

TYPES OF WRITING

autobiography	legend	poem
ballad	letter	report
biography	lyric	review
column	memoir	rhyme
dissertation	myth	riddle
editorial	narrative	script
epitaph	nonfiction	story
essay	novel	thesis
fable	obituary	verse
feature	parable	
fiction	play	

W

Xx

Xmas *noun* = **Christmas**, Noel, Yule, festive season, Yuletide

X-rated *adjective* = **pornographic**, adult, dirty, graphic, obscene, hardcore (*slang*), scuzzy (*slang*)

X-rays *plural noun* = **Röntgen rays** (*old-fashioned*)

Yy

yank *verb, noun* = **pull**, snatch, hitch, jerk, tug, wrench

yardstick *noun* = **standard**, measure, par, benchmark, criterion, gauge, touchstone

yarn *noun* **1** = **thread**, fibre **2** (*Old-fashioned, informal*) = **story**, tale, anecdote, fable, cock-and-bull story (*informal*), tall tale (*informal*)

yawning *adjective* = **gaping**, wide, vast, cavernous

yearly *adjective* **1** = **annual** ▶ *adverb* **2** = **annually**, every year, once a year, per annum

yearn *verb* = **long**, desire, hunger, ache, covet, crave, itch, hanker

yearning See **desire, longing**

yell *verb* **1** = **scream**, shout, howl, screech, shriek, holler (*informal*), squeal, bawl ▶ *noun* **2** = **scream**, cry, howl, whoop, screech, shriek

yell at *verb* (*Informal*) = **criticize**, rebuke, censure, scold, tear into (*informal*)

yellow *adjective, noun*

SHADES OF YELLOW

amber	mustard
canary	primrose
champagne	saffron
citrus	sand
daffodil	straw
gold	topaz
lemon	

---

yelp *verb* = **cry**, yap, yowl

yen *noun* = **longing**, desire, passion, hunger, ache, craving, thirst, itch, yearning, hankering

yes *interjection* = **sure**, okay • *"Are you a friend of his?" "Yes."* OPPOSITE: no

yes man *noun* = **sycophant**, brown-noser (*slang*), minion, timeserver, toady

yet *conjunction* **1** = **nevertheless**, still, however, notwithstanding ▶ *adverb* **2** = **so far**, as yet, thus far, until now, up to now **3** = **still**, besides, in addition, into the bargain, to boot **4** = **now**, just now, right now, so soon

yield *verb* **1** = **produce**, give, return, provide, earn, net, bear, supply, generate, bring forth **2** = **surrender**, resign, submit, bow, relinquish, succumb, capitulate, give in ▶ *noun* **3** = **profit**, return, income, revenue, output, earnings, takings **4** = **produce**, crop, harvest

yielding *adjective* **1** = **submissive**, flexible, compliant, obedient, docile, accommodating, acquiescent, biddable, pliant **2** = **soft**, elastic, spongy, supple, pliable, springy, unresisting

yoke *verb* = **burden**, land, load, saddle, encumber

yokel *noun* = **peasant**, countryman, rustic, redneck (*slang*), hick (*informal, chiefly US & Canad*), hillbilly, bumpkin or country bumpkin

young *adjective* **1** = **immature**, little, junior, infant, adolescent, youthful, juvenile • *young people* OPPOSITE: old **2** = **new**, early, recent, fledgling, undeveloped ▶ *plural noun* **3** = **offspring**, family, litter, brood, babies, little ones • *The hen may not be able to feed its young.*

y

youngster *noun* = **youth**, girl, boy, kid (*informal*), teenager, juvenile, lad, lass

youth *noun* **1** = **immaturity**, adolescence, boyhood, girlhood, salad days

2 = **boy**, kid (*informal*), teenager, youngster, adolescent, lad, stripling, young man

youthful *adjective* = **young**, juvenile, inexperienced, childish, immature, boyish, fresh-faced, girlish, rosy-cheeked

yummy *adjective* (*Informal*) = **delicious**, good, edible, delectable, mouth-watering, tasty

y

Zz

zany *adjective* = **comical**, crazy, eccentric, goofy (*informal*), clownish, wacky (*slang*)

zeal *noun* = **enthusiasm**, spirit, passion, zest, eagerness, gusto, verve, fanaticism, ardour, fervour, keenness

zealot *noun* = **fanatic**, militant, extremist, enthusiast, bigot

zealous *adjective* = **enthusiastic**, eager, keen, passionate, devoted, impassioned, ardent, fervent, fanatical

zenith *noun* = **height**, top, summit, peak, crest, climax, pinnacle, apex, acme, apogee, high point

zero *noun* **1** = **nothing**, zip (*informal*), nil, naught (*archaic or literary*), nada (*Informal*), zilch (*informal*) • *I will now count from zero to ten.*
2 = **bottom**, nadir, rock bottom

zest *noun* **1** = **enjoyment**, appetite, relish, zeal, gusto, keenness
2 = **flavor**, interest, taste, charm, spice, relish, piquancy, pungency, tang

zip *noun* **1** (*Informal*) = **energy**, drive, zest, vigor, gusto, verve, liveliness
▶ *verb* **2** = **speed**, shoot, fly, flash, zoom, whizz (*informal*)

zone *noun* = **area**, region, sector, district, section, belt, sphere

zoom *verb* = **speed**, shoot, fly, rush, flash, dash, pelt, hurtle, whizz (*informal*)